CLYMER® MANUALS

HONDA
VT750 SHADOW SHAFT DRIVE • 2004-2013

WHAT'S IN YOUR TOOLBOX?

CLYMER

CLYMER PROSERIES

I&T SHOP MANUALS

More information available at Clymer.com
Phone: 805-498-6703

Haynes Publishing Group
Sparkford Nr Yeovil
Somerset BA22 7JJ England

Haynes North America, Inc
861 Lawrence Drive
Newbury Park
California 91320 USA

ISBN 10: 1-62092-150-2
ISBN-13: 978-1-62092-150-0
Library of Congress: 2015931495

Author: Ron Wright

© Haynes North America, Inc. 2015
With permission from J.H. Haynes & Co. Ltd.

Clymer is a registered trademark of Haynes North America, Inc.

Printed in the U.S.A.

All rights reserved. No part of this book may be reproduced or transmitted in any form or by any means, electronic or mechanical, including photocopying, recording or by any information storage or retrieval system, without permission in writing from the copyright holder.

While every attempt is made to ensure that the information in this manual is correct, no liability can be accepted by the authors or publishers for loss, damage or injury caused by any errors in, or omissions from, the information given.

M232, 14-592   ABCDEFGHIJKLMNOPQRST

Chapter One General Information	**1**
Chapter Two Troubleshooting	**2**
Chapter Three Lubrication, Maintenance and Tune-up	**3**
Chapter Four Engine Top End	**4**
Chapter Five Engine Lower End	**5**
Chapter Six Clutch and External Shift Mechanism	**6**
Chapter Seven Transmission and Internal Gearshift Mechanism	**7**
Chapter Eight Carburetor and Emission Control Systems	**8**
Chapter Nine Fuel and Injection and Emission Control Systems	**9**
Chapter Ten Electrical System	**10**
Chapter Eleven Cooling System	**11**
Chapter Twelve Wheels and Tires	**12**
Chapter Thirteen Front Suspension and Steering	**13**
Chapter Fourteen Rear Suspension and Final Drive	**14**
Chapter Fifteen Brakes	**15**
Chapter Sixteen Anti-Lock Brake System	**16**
Chapter Seventeen Body and Exhaust Sytem	**17**
Index	**I**
Wiring Diagrams	**W**

Common spark plug conditions

NORMAL
Symptoms: Brown to grayish-tan color and slight electrode wear. Correct heat range for engine and operating conditions.
Recommendation: When new spark plugs are installed, replace with plugs of the same heat range.

WORN
Symptoms: Rounded electrodes with a small amount of deposits on the firing end. Normal color. Causes hard starting in damp or cold weather and poor fuel economy.
Recommendation: Plugs have been left in the engine too long. Replace with new plugs of the same heat range. Follow the recommended maintenance schedule.

CARBON DEPOSITS
Symptoms: Dry sooty deposits indicate a rich mixture or weak ignition. Causes misfiring, hard starting and hesitation.
Recommendation: Make sure the plug has the correct heat range. Check for a clogged air filter or problem in the fuel system or engine management system. Also check for ignition system problems.

ASH DEPOSITS
Symptoms: Light brown deposits encrusted on the side or center electrodes or both. Derived from oil and/or fuel additives. Excessive amounts may mask the spark, causing misfiring and hesitation during acceleration.
Recommendation: If excessive deposits accumulate over a short time or low mileage, install new valve guide seals to prevent seepage of oil into the combustion chambers. Also try changing gasoline brands.

OIL DEPOSITS
Symptoms: Oily coating caused by poor oil control. Oil is leaking past worn valve guides or piston rings into the combustion chamber. Causes hard starting, misfiring and hesitation.
Recommendation: Correct the mechanical condition with necessary repairs and install new plugs.

GAP BRIDGING
Symptoms: Combustion deposits lodge between the electrodes. Heavy deposits accumulate and bridge the electrode gap. The plug ceases to fire, resulting in a dead cylinder.
Recommendation: Locate the faulty plug and remove the deposits from between the electrodes.

TOO HOT
Symptoms: Blistered, white insulator, eroded electrode and absence of deposits. Results in shortened plug life.
Recommendation: Check for the correct plug heat range, over-advanced ignition timing, lean fuel mixture, intake manifold vacuum leaks, sticking valves and insufficient engine cooling.

PREIGNITION
Symptoms: Melted electrodes. Insulators are white, but may be dirty due to misfiring or flying debris in the combustion chamber. Can lead to engine damage.
Recommendation: Check for the correct plug heat range, over-advanced ignition timing, lean fuel mixture, insufficient engine cooling and lack of lubrication.

HIGH SPEED GLAZING
Symptoms: Insulator has yellowish, glazed appearance. Indicates that combustion chamber temperatures have risen suddenly during hard acceleration. Normal deposits melt to form a conductive coating. Causes misfiring at high speeds.
Recommendation: Install new plugs. Consider using a colder plug if driving habits warrant.

DETONATION
Symptoms: Insulators may be cracked or chipped. Improper gap setting techniques can also result in a fractured insulator tip. Can lead to piston damage.
Recommendation: Make sure the fuel anti-knock values meet engine requirements. Use care when setting the gaps on new plugs. Avoid lugging the engine.

MECHANICAL DAMAGE
Symptoms: May be caused by a foreign object in the combustion chamber or the piston striking an incorrect reach (too long) plug. Causes a dead cylinder and could result in piston damage.
Recommendation: Repair the mechanical damage. Remove the foreign object from the engine and/or install the correct reach plug.

CONTENTS

QUICK REFERENCE DATA IX

CHAPTER ONE
GENERAL INFORMATION 1
    Manual organization
    Warnings, cautions and notes
    Safety
    Serial numbers and information labels
    Fasteners
    Tools
    Measuring tools
    Electrical system fundamentals
    Service methods
    Shop supplies
    Storage

CHAPTER TWO
TROUBLESHOOTING 31
    Starting the engine
    Engine will not start
    Poor engine performance
    Fuel system, carbureted models
    Fuel system, fuel injected models
    Engine
    Engine lubrication
    Cylinder leakdown test
    Clutch
    Gearshift linkage
    Transmission
    Electrical testing
    Output gearcase
    Final drive
    Front suspension and steering
    Brake system

CHAPTER THREE
LUBRICATION, MAINTENANCE AND TUNE-UP 57

    Tune-up
    Engine rotation
    Fuel
    Air filter
    Sub-air filters (carbureted models)
    Crankcase breather inspection
    Engine compression test
    Spark plugs
    Ignition timing
    Valve clearance
    Idle speed
    Fuel system hose inspection
    Fuel filter replacement (fuel injected models)
    Throttle cables
    Clutch cable and clutch lever
    Choke cable inspection and adjustment
     (carbureted models)
    Engine oil and filter
    Engine oil pressure check
    Cooling system
    Evaporative emission control system
     (California models)
    Battery
    Final drive oil
    Tires and wheels
    Pulse secondary air supply system
    Steering bearings
    Front suspension check
    Rear suspension check
    Brake system
    Headlight aim
    Sidestand and ignition cut-off switch test
    Front fork oil change
    Fastener inspection
    Maintenance and lubrication schedule
    Specifications

CHAPTER FOUR
ENGINE TOP END 93

    Servicing the engine in the frame
    Outer cylinder covers
    Cylinder head covers
    Camshafts
    Cam chain tensioner and cam chain
    Cylinder head
    Valves and valve components
    Cylinder
    Piston and piston rings
    Cylinder studs
    Specifications

CHAPTER FIVE
ENGINE LOWER END 133

    Servicing the engine in the frame
    Engine
    Engine break-in
    Restarting the engine
    Crankcase
    Transmission and output drive gear bearings
    Main journal bearings and crankshaft main
journal oil clearance
    Crankshaft
    Connecting rods
    Oil pump
    Output gearcase
    Output gearcase seal replacement
    Output gearcase overhaul
    Output drive and driven gear measurements
    Specifications

CHAPTER SIX
CLUTCH AND EXTERNAL SHIFT MECHANISM 185

- Clutch and external shift mechanism
- Clutch cable replacement
- Right crankcase cover
- Clutch release lever
- Clutch
- Primary drive gear
- External shift mechanism
- Specifications

CHAPTER SEVEN
TRANSMISSION AND INTERNAL SHIFT MECHANISM 207

- Transmission
- Transmission inspection
- Internal shift mechanism
- Specifications,

CHAPTER EIGHT
CARBURETOR AND EMISSION CONTROL SYSTEMS. 221

- Fuel hose identification
- Fuel tank
- Fuel valve
- Air filter housing
- Carburetor
- Intake manifold
- Pilot screw adjustment
- High altitude adjustment
- Throttle cable replacement
- Choke cable replacement
- Crankcase breather system
- Pulse secondary air supply system
- Evaporative emission control system (California models)
- Specifications

CHAPTER NINE
FUEL INJECTION AND EMISSION CONTROL SYSTEMS 253

- Fuel system precautions
- Depressurizing the fuel system
- Fuel pressure test
- Fuel pump/sub fuel tank assembly
- Air filter housing
- Throttle body
- Intake manifold
- Fuel injectors, injector cap and fuel feed hose
- Sensor unit
- Bank angle sensor
- Engine stop relay
- Engine Control Module (ECM)
- Fuel cut-off relay
- Throttle cable replacement
- Emission control system labels
- Pulse secondary air supply system
- Evaporative emission control system (California models)
- Malfunction indicator lamp (MIL)
- DTC troubleshooting
- Specifications
- Diagnostic trouble codes

CHAPTER TEN
ELECTRICAL SYSTEM 291

Electrical component replacement
Electrical connectors
Battery
Charging system
Left crankcase cover and stator coil
Flywheel, starter clutch and starter drive gears
Ignition system testing
Ignition coils
Crankshaft Position (CKP) sensor
Ignition Control Module (ICM)
  (carbureted models)
Throttle Position (TP) sensor
  (carbureted models)
Starter system troubleshooting
Starter: 2004-2007 Aero models
Starter: 2008-2009 and 2011-2013 Aero
  models, 2010-2013 Spirit models and all
  Phantom models
Starter relay switch
Clutch diode
Lighting system
Upper fork bridge indicator lights
  (2008-2009 and 2011-2013 Aero models,
  2012-2013 Spirit and Phantom models)
Vehicle Speed (VS) sensor
Coolant temperature indicator and Engine
  Coolant Temperature (ECT) sensor
Fan control relay (fuel injected models)
Oil pressure switch and oil pressure indicator
Neutral switch
Fuel reserve indicator and fuel reserve sensor
  (fuel injected models)
Sidestand switch
Clutch switch
Front brake light switch
Rear brake light switch
Ignition switch
Handlebar switch
Switch continuity test
Turn signal relay
Horn
Fuse box
Fuses
Fuse box relays (ABS models
Maintenance free battery charging times
Specifications

CHAPTER ELEVEN
COOLING SYSTEM 367

Cooling system inspection
Radiator
Cooling fan
Coolant reserve tank
Thermostat
Thermostat housing
Water pump
Specifications

CHAPTER TWELVE
WHEELS AND TIRES 379

Motorcycle lift
Front wheel
Rear wheel and driven flange
Driven flange dampers
Front and rear hubs
Wheel service
Tire changing
Wheel balance
Specifications

CHAPTER THIRTEEN
FRONT SUSPENSION AND STEERING **403**

Handlebar
Handlebar grips and weights
Front fork
Steering head and stem

Steering bearing preload inspection
Steering head bearing race replacement
Steering stem bearing race replacement
Specifications

CHAPTER FOURTEEN
REAR SUSPENSION AND FINAL DRIVE **431**

Shock absorber
Rear swing arm
Final drive unit and drive shaft
Final drive unit overhaul

Final drive housing bearing replacement
Ring and pinion gear measurements
Specifications

CHAPTER FIFTEEN
BRAKES **461**

Brake service
Brake bleeding
Brake fluid draining
Brake fluid flushing
Front brake pads
Front brake caliper
Front master cylinder
Rear brake pads (ABS models)

Rear brake caliper (ABS models)
Rear master cylinder (ABS models)
Brake hose and brake pipe replacement
Brake discs and pulser rings
Rear drum brake
Rear brake pedal: drum brake models
Rear brake pedal: ABS models
Specifications

CHAPTER SIXTEEN
ANTI_LOCK BRAKE SYSTEM **503**

ABS service precautions
ABS indicator operation
DTC troubleshooting
ABS indicator circuit troubleshooting
Wheel speed sensors
Pulser rings

Proportional Control Valve (PCV)
ABS modulator/ECU
ABS wheel speed sensor air gap
ABS diagnostic trouble codes
Specifications

CHAPTER SEVENTEEN
BODY AND EXHAUST SYSTEM 523
- Seat
- Side covers
- Left crankcase rear cover
- Steering covers
- Front fender
- Rear fender
- Sidestand
- Footpegs
- Exhaust system
- Specifications

INDEX 536

WIRING DIAGRAMS 543

QUICK REFERENCE DATA

MODEL: _____   YEAR: _____

VIN NUMBER: _____

ENGINE SERIAL NUMBER: _____

THROTTLE BODY SERIAL NUMBER OR I.D. MARK: _____

TIRE INFLATION PRESSURE AND TREAD DEPTH*

	Front	Rear
Tire inflation pressure		
Rider (90 kg [200 lbs])	200 kPa (29 psi)	200 kPa (29 psi)
Maximum weight capacity	200 kPa (29 psi)	250 kPa (36 psi)
Tread depth (minimum)	1.5 mm (0.06 in.)	2.0 mm (0.08 in.)

* The tire inflation pressures listed here are for factory equipped tires. Aftermarket tires may require different inflation pressure. Refer to tire manufacturer's specifications.

RECOMMENDED LUBRICANTS AND FUEL

Air filter	Foam air filter oil
Brake fluid	DOT 4
Engine oil	
Grade	API SG or higher/JASO MA*
Viscosity	SAE10W-30*
Fork oil	Pro Honda Suspension Fluid SS-8
Fuel	
CRF230F models	Octane rating of 91 or higher
CRF230L and CRF230M models	Octane rating of 86 or higher
Steering and suspension lubricant	Multipurpose grease

*See text for additional information.

RECOMMENDED LUBRICANTS AND FUEL

Brake fluid	DOT 4 brake fluid
Control cables	Cable lubricant
Coolant	
Standard concentration	50% mixture coolant and purified water
Type	Honda HP coolant or an equivalent (1)
Engine oil	
Classification	
JASCO T 903 standard rating	MA
API rating	SG or higher (2)
Viscosity rating	SAE 10W-30
Final drive oil	Hypoid gear oil, SAE 80 weight
Fork oil	Pro Honda Suspension Fluid SS-8 or equivalent 10 wt
fork oil	
Fuel	Unleaded gasoline with a pump octane number of 86 or higher

1. Coolant must not contain silicate inhibitors as they can cause premature wear to the water pump seals. Refer to text for further information.
2. API "SG" or higher classified oils not specified as "ENERGY CONSERVING" can be used. Refer to text for additional information.

ENGINE OIL CAPACITY

	L	U.S. qt.
Engine oil change only	2.5	2.64
Engine oil and filter change	2.6	2.75
Engine disassembly	3.2	3.38

COOLANT CAPACITY

	L	U.S. qt.
Radiator and engine	1.58	1.67
Reserve tank	0.38	0.40

FINAL DRIVE OIL CAPACITY

	cc	U.S. oz.
After overhaul	170	5.7
Oil change	160	5.4

TUNE-UP SPECIFICATIONS

Clutch lever free play	10-20 mm (3/8-3/4 in.)
Cylinder number	No. 1 (rear)
	No. 2 (front)
Engine compression (standard pressure)	1275-1471 kPa (185-213 psi) @ 400 rpm
Engine idle speed	1100-1300 rpm
Firing order	Front (308 degrees)— rear (412 degrees)—front
Ignition timing	
Carbureted models	F mark (13° BTDC @ idle)
Fuel injected models	F mark (8° BTDC @ idle)
Oil pressure @ 5000 rpm	530 kPa (77 psi) @ 80° C (176° F)
Rear brake pedal free play	
Non-ABS models	20-30 mm (13/16-1 3/16 in.)
Rear brake pedal height	
Non-ABS models	75 mm (3.0 in.) above top of foot peg
Rear master cylinder pushrod adjustment length	
Aero models equipped with ABS	82.0-84.0 mm (3.23-3.31 in.)
Spirit models equipped with ABS	83.0 mm (3.27 in.)
Spark plug gap	0.8-0.9 mm (0.031-0.035 in.)
Spark plug type	
Carbureted models	
NGK	
Standard	DPR6EA-9
Extended high speed use	DPR7EA-9
Denso	
Standard	X20EPR-U9
Extended high speed use	X22EPR-U9
Fuel injected models	
NGK	
Standard	DPR7EA-9
Extended high speed use	DPR8EA-9
Denso	
Standard	X22EPR-U9
Extended high speed use	X24EPR-U9
Valve clearance*	
Intake	0.13-0.17 mm (0.005-0.007 in.)
Exhaust	0.18-0.22 mm (0.007-0.009 in.)
Throttle grip free play	2-6 mm (1/16-1/4 in.)

*Engine and air temperature below 35°C (95°F)

MAINTENANCE TORQUE SPECIFICATIONS

	N.m	in.-lb.	ft.-lb.
Alternator cover socket bolts			
2004-2009 Aero models	9.8	87	--
All other models	10	89	--
Brake lever pivot bolt	1.0	8.9	--
Brake lever pivot nut			
2004-2009 Aero models	5.9	52	--
All other models	6.0	53	--
Brake pedal adjuster locknut			
2004-2009 Aero models without ABS	9.8	87	--
Clutch lever pivot bolt	1.0	8.9	--
Clutch lever pivot nut			
2004-2009 Aero models	5.9	52	--
All other models	6.0	53	--
Coolant drain bolt	13	115	--
Crankshaft hole cap (1, 2)	15	--	11
Engine oil drain bolt	29	--	21
Final drive oil drain bolt	12	106	--
Final drive oil fill cap	12	106	--
Oil filter (2)	26	--	19
Rear master cylinder pushrod locknut (ABS models)	18	--	13
Spark plug			
Aero			
2004-2009	16	--	12
2011-2013	18	--	13
Shadow Spirit and Phantom	18	--	13
Timing hole cap (1, 2)	10	89	--
Valve adjust screw locknut (3)	23	--	17

1. Lubricate threads with grease.
2. Lubricate O-ring with engine oil.
3. Lubricate threads and flange surface with engine oil.

NOTES

CLYMER® MANUALS

HONDA
VT750 SHADOW SHAFT DRIVE • 2004-2013

CHAPTER ONE

GENERAL INFORMATION

This detailed and comprehensive manual covers the Honda VT750 shaft drive models from 2004-2013. The text provides complete information on maintenance, tune-up, repair and overhaul. Hundreds of photos and drawings guide the reader through every job. All procedures are in step-by-step format and designed for the reader who may be working on the motorcycle for the first time.

MANUAL ORGANIZATION

A shop manual is a reference tool and, as in all Clymer manuals, the chapters are thumb-tabbed for easy reference. Important items are indexed at the end of the manual. Frequently used specifications and capacities from individual chapters are summarized in the *Quick Reference Data* at the front of the manual.

During some of the procedures there will be references to headings in other chapters or sections of the manual. When a specific heading is called out in a step it is *italicized* as it appears in the manual. If a sub-heading is indicated as being "in this section" it is located within the same main heading. For example, the sub-heading *Handling Gasoline Safely* is located within the main heading SAFETY.

This chapter provides general information on shop safety, tool use, service fundamentals and shop supplies. **Tables 1-7** at the end of the chapter provide general motorcycle, mechanical and shop information.

Chapter Two provides methods for quick and accurate diagnoses of problems. Troubleshooting procedures present typical symptoms and logical methods to pinpoint and repair a problem.

Chapter Three explains all routine maintenance.

Subsequent chapters describe specific systems, such as engine, output gearcase, clutch, transmission shafts, fuel system, exhaust system, drive system, suspension, brakes and body components.

Specification tables, when applicable, are located at the end of each chapter.

WARNINGS, CAUTIONS AND NOTES

The terms WARNING, CAUTION and NOTE have specific meanings in this manual.

A WARNING emphasizes areas where injury or even death could result from negligence. Mechanical damage may also occur. WARNINGS are to be taken seriously.

A CAUTION emphasizes areas where equipment damage could result. Disregarding a CAUTION could cause permanent mechanical damage, though injury is unlikely.

A NOTE provides additional information to make a step or procedure easier or clearer. Disregarding a NOTE could cause inconvenience, but would not cause equipment damage or injury.

SAFETY

Professional mechanics can work for years and never sustain a serious injury or mishap. Follow these guidelines and practice common sense to safely service the motorcycle:

1. Do not operate the motorcycle in an enclosed area. The exhaust gasses contain carbon monoxide, an odorless, colorless and tasteless poisonous gas. Carbon monoxide levels build quickly in small enclosed areas and can cause unconsciousness and death in a short time. Make sure the work area is properly ventilated, or operate the motorcycle outside.

2. *Never* use gasoline or any flammable liquid to clean parts. Refer to *Handling Gasoline Safely* and *Cleaning Parts* in this section.
3. *Never* smoke or use a torch in the vicinity of flammable liquids, such as gasoline or cleaning solvent.
4. Do not remove the radiator cap or cooling system hose while the engine is hot. The cooling system is pressurized and the high temperature coolant may cause injury.
5. Dispose of and store coolant in a safe manner. Do not allow children or pets access to open containers of coolant. Animals are attracted to antifreeze.
6. Avoid contact with engine oil and other chemicals. Most are known carcinogens. Wash your hands thoroughly after coming in contact with engine oil. If possible, wear a pair of disposable gloves.
7. If welding or brazing on the motorcycle, remove the fuel tank and shocks to a safe distance at least 50 ft. (15 m) away.
8. Use the correct types and sizes of tools to avoid damaging fasteners.
9. Keep tools clean and in good condition. Replace or repair worn or damaged equipment.
10. When loosening a tight fastener, be guided by what would happen if the tool slips.
11. When replacing fasteners, make sure the new fasteners are the same size and strength as the originals.
12. Keep the work area clean and organized.
13. Wear eye protection *any time* the safety of your eyes is in question. This includes procedures involving drilling, grinding, hammering, compressed air and chemicals.
14. Wear the correct clothing for the job. Tie up or cover long hair so it can not catch in moving equipment.
15. Do not carry sharp tools in clothing pockets.
16. Always have an approved fire extinguisher available. Make sure it is rated for gasoline (Class B) and electrical (Class C) fires.
17. Do not use compressed air to clean clothes, the motorcycle or the work area. Debris may be blown into the eyes or skin. *Never* direct compressed air at anyone. Do not allow children to use or play with any compressed air equipment.
18. When using compressed air to dry rotating parts, hold the part so it cannot rotate. Do not allow the force of the air to spin the part. The air jet is capable of rotating parts at extreme speeds. The part may be damaged or disintegrate, causing serious injury.
19. Do not inhale the dust created by brake pad and clutch wear. These particles may contain asbestos. In addition, some types of insulating materials and gaskets may contain asbestos. Inhaling asbestos particles is hazardous to health.
20. Never work on the motorcycle while someone is working under it.
21. When placing the motorcycle on a stand or overhead lift, make sure it is secure before walking away.

Handling Gasoline Safely

Gasoline is a volatile flammable liquid and is one of the most dangerous items in the shop. Because gasoline is used so often, many people forget that it is hazardous. Only use gasoline as fuel for gasoline internal combustion engines. Keep in mind when working on a motorcycle, gasoline is always present in the fuel tank and all of the fuel system components. To avoid an accident when working around the fuel system, carefully observe the following precautions:

1. *Never* use gasoline to clean parts. Refer to *Cleaning Parts* in this section.
2. When working on the fuel system, work outside or in a well-ventilated area.
3. Do not add fuel to the fuel tank or service the fuel system while the motorcycle is near open flames, sparks or where someone is smoking. Gasoline vapor is heavier than air, collects in low areas and is more easily ignited than liquid gasoline.

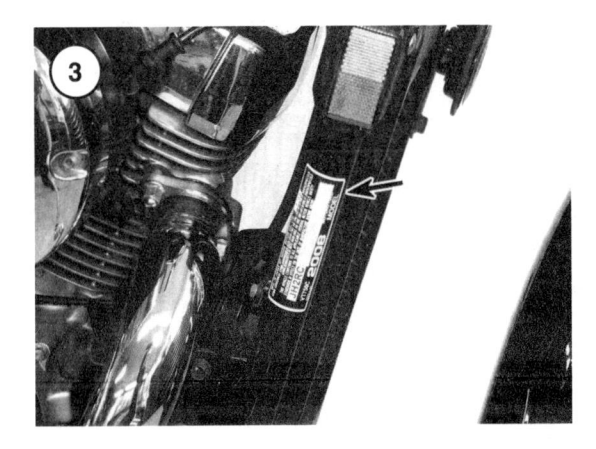

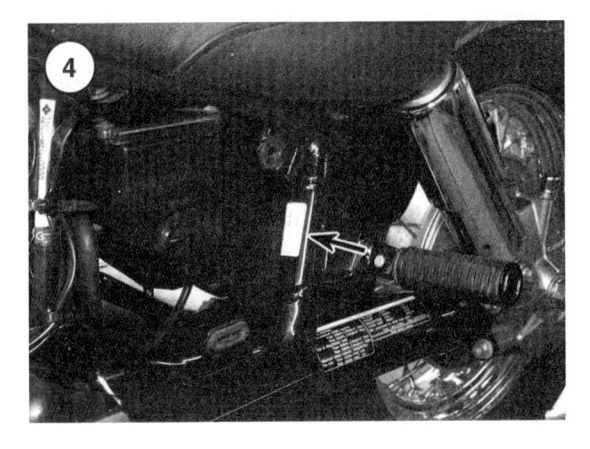

GENERAL INFORMATION

1. Read and observe the entire product label before using any chemical. Always know what type of chemical is being used and whether it is poisonous and/or flammable.
2. Do not use more than one type of cleaning solvent at a time. If mixing chemicals is required, measure the proper amounts according to the manufacturer.
3. Work in a well-ventilated area.
4. Wear chemical-resistant gloves.
5. Wear safety glasses.
6. Wear a vapor respirator if the instructions call for it.
7. Wash hands and arms thoroughly after cleaning parts.
8. Keep chemicals away from children and pets, especially coolant. Animals are attracted to antifreeze.
9. Thoroughly clean all oil, grease and cleaner residue from any part that must be heated.
10. Use a nylon brush when cleaning parts. Metal brushes may cause a spark.
11. When using a parts washer, only use the solvent recommended by the manufacturer. Make sure the parts washer is equipped with a metal lid that will lower in case of fire.

Warning Labels

Most manufacturers attach information and warning labels to the motorcycle. These labels contain instructions that are important to safety when operating, servicing, transporting and storing the motorcycle. Refer to the owner's manual for the description and location of labels. Order replacement labels from the manufacturer if they are missing or damaged.

SERIAL NUMBERS AND INFORMATION LABELS

Serial numbers are located on several parts of the motorcycle. Record these numbers in the *Quick Reference Data* section in the front of the manual. Have these numbers available when ordering parts.

The vehicle identification label (VIN) is located on the right side of the steering head **(Figure 1)**.

The engine serial number is stamped on the left side of the crankcase **(Figure 2)**.

The safety certification label is attached on the front, right side frame tube **(Figure 3)**.

A color label is attached to the frame, behind the left side cover **(Figure 4)**. Always refer to this number when ordering painted parts.

An identification number is also stamped on the carburetor (VT750C and VT750C2) and throttle body (VT750C2B).

4. Allow the engine to cool completely before working on any fuel system component.
5. Do not store gasoline in glass containers. If the glass breaks, an explosion or fire may occur.
6. Immediately wipe up spilled gasoline with rags. Store the rags in a metal container with a lid until they can be properly disposed, or place them outside in a safe place for the fuel to evaporate.
7. Do not pour water onto a gasoline fire. Water spreads the fire and makes it more difficult to put out. Use a class B, BC or ABC fire extinguisher to extinguish the fire.
8. Always turn off the engine before refueling. Do not spill fuel onto the engine or exhaust system. Do not overfill the fuel tank. Leave an air space at the top of the tank to allow room for the fuel to expand due to temperature fluctuations.

Cleaning Parts

Cleaning parts is one of the more tedious and difficult service jobs performed in the home garage. Many types of chemical cleaners and solvents are available for shop use. Most are poisonous and extremely flammable. To prevent chemical exposure, vapor buildup, fire and injury, observe each product's warning label and note the following:

Labels for tire pressure, emission control, dealership service and other miscellaneous data are located under the seat on the rear fender and on various other places on the motorcycle.

FASTENERS

WARNING
Do not install fasteners with a strength classification lower than what was originally installed by the manufacturer. Doing so may cause equipment failure and/or damage.

Proper fastener selection and installation is important to ensure the motorcycle operates as designed and can be serviced efficiently. The choice of original equipment fasteners is not arrived at by chance. Make sure replacement fasteners meet the requirements.

Threaded Fasteners

Threaded fasteners secure most of the components on the motorcycle. Most are tightened by turning them clockwise (right-hand threads). If the normal rotation of the component being tightened would loosen the fastener, it may have left-hand threads. If a left-hand threaded fastener is used, it is noted in the text.

Two dimensions are required to match the thread size of the fastener: the number of threads in a given distance and the outside diameter of the threads.

Two systems are currently used to specify threaded fastener dimensions: the U.S. Standard system and the metric system. Pay particular attention when working with unidentified fasteners; mismatching thread types can damage threads.

To ensure the fastener threads are not mismatched or cross-threaded, start all fasteners by hand. If a fastener is difficult to start or turn, determine the cause before tightening with a wrench.

Match fasteners by their length (L, **Figure 5**), diameter (D) and pitch (T), or distance between thread crests. A typical metric bolt may be identified by the numbers, 8—1.25 × 130. This indicates the bolt has a diameter of 8 mm, the distance between thread crests is 1.25 mm and the length is 130 mm. Always measure bolt length (L) as shown in **Figure 5** to avoid installing replacements of the wrong lengths.

If a number is located on the top of a metric fastener **(Figure 5)**, this indicates the strength. The higher the number, the stronger the fastener. Typically, unnumbered fasteners are the weakest.

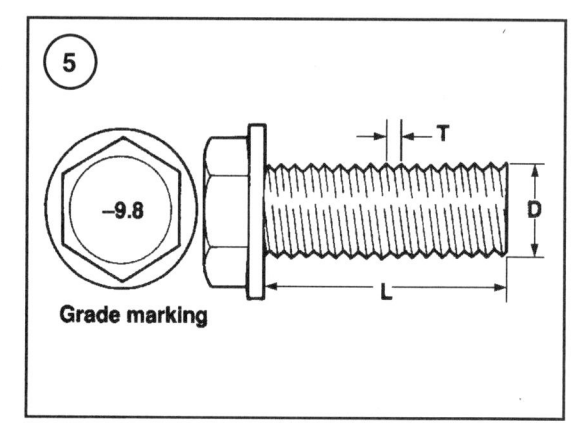

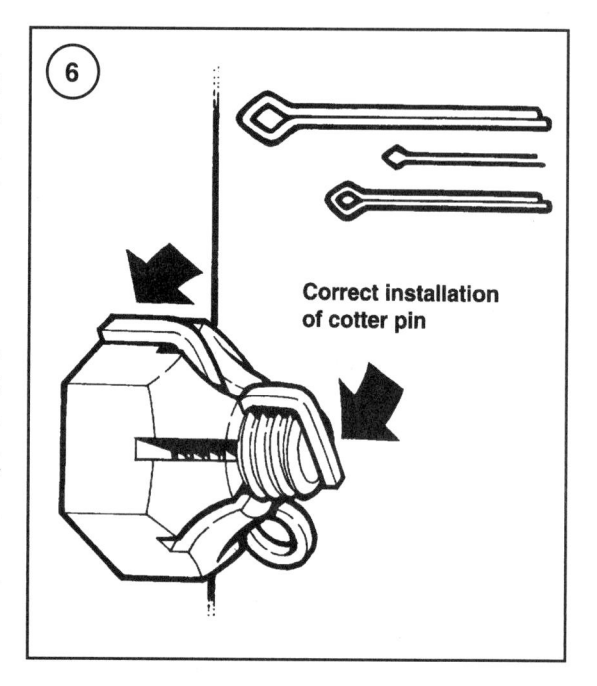

Many screws, bolts and studs are combined with nuts to secure particular components. To indicate the size of a nut, manufacturers specify the internal diameter and thread pitch.

The measurement across two flats on a nut or bolt indicates the wrench size.

Torque Specifications

The materials used in the manufacture of the motorcycle may be subjected to uneven stresses if fasteners are not installed and tightened correctly. Improperly installed fasteners or ones that worked loose can cause extensive damage. It is critical to use an accurate torque wrench, as described in this chapter, with the torque specifications in this manual.

Specifications for torque are provided in Newton-meters (N•m), foot-pounds (ft.-lb.) and inch-pounds (in.-lb.). Refer to **Table 7** for general torque recom-

GENERAL INFORMATION

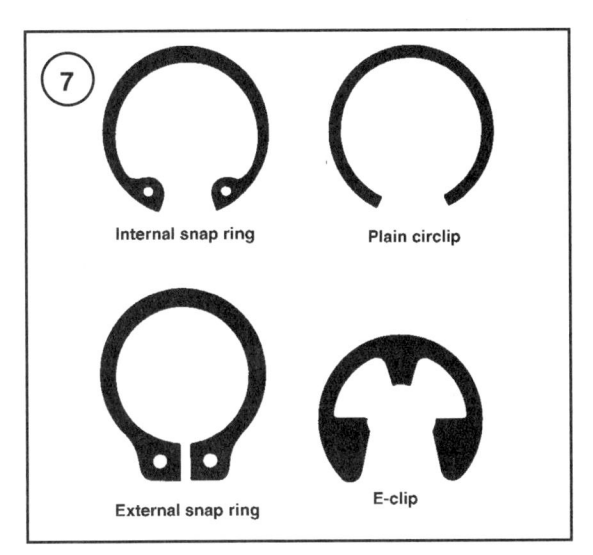

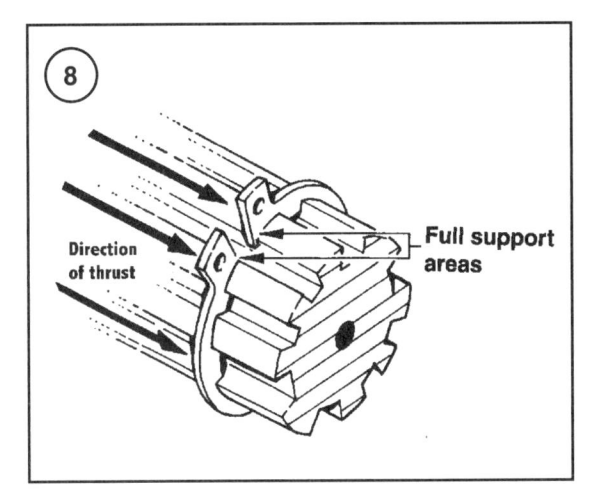

mendations. To use **Table 7**, first determine the size of the fastener as described in *Threaded Fasteners* in this section. Torque specifications for specific components are at the end of the appropriate chapters. Torque wrenches are covered in the *Tools* section of this chapter.

Self-Locking Fasteners

Several types of bolts, screws and nuts incorporate a system that creates interference between the two fasteners. Interference is achieved in various ways. The most common types used are those with a nylon insert nut and those with a dry adhesive coating on the threads of a bolt.

Self-locking fasteners offer greater holding strength than standard fasteners, which improves their resistance to vibration. Self-locking fasteners cannot be reused. The materials used to form the lock become distorted after the initial installation and removal. Do not replace self-locking fasteners with standard fasteners.

Some Honda replacement fasteners are equipped with a threadlock preapplied to the fastener threads. When replacing these fasteners, do not apply a separate threadlock. When it is necessary to reuse one of these fasteners, completely remove all threadlock residue from the threads. Then apply the threadlock specified in the text.

Washers

The two basic types of washers are flat washers and lockwashers. Flat washers are simple discs with a hole to fit a screw or bolt. Lockwashers are used to prevent a fastener from working loose. Washers can be used as spacers and seals or to help distribute fastener load and prevent the fastener from damaging the component.

As with fasteners, when replacing washers make sure the replacements meet the original specifications.

Cotter Pins

A cotter pin is a split metal pin inserted into a hole or slot to prevent a fastener from loosening. In certain applications, such as the rear axle, the fastener must be secured in this way. For these applications, a cotter pin and castellated (slotted) nut is used.

To use a cotter pin, first make sure the diameter is correct for the hole in the fastener. After correctly tightening the fastener and aligning the holes, insert the cotter pin through the hole and bend the ends over the fastener **(Figure 6)**. Unless instructed to do so, never loosen a tightened fastener to align the holes. If the holes do not align, tighten the fastener just enough to achieve alignment.

Cotter pins are available in various diameters and lengths. Measure length from the bottom of the head to the tip of the shortest pin.

Snap Rings and E-clips

Snap rings **(Figure 7)** are circular-shaped metal retaining clips. They are required to secure parts and gears in place on parts such as shafts, pins or rods. External type snap rings are used to retain items on shafts. Internal type snap rings secure parts within housing bores. In some applications, in addition to securing the component(s), snap rings of varying thicknesses also determine endplay. These are usually called selective snap rings.

The two basic types of snap rings are machined and stamped snap rings. Machined snap rings **(Figure 8)** can be installed in either direction because both faces have sharp edges. Stamped snap rings **(Figure 9)** are manufactured with a sharp edge and round edge. When installing a stamped snap ring in a thrust application, install the sharp edge facing away from the part producing the thrust.

E-clips are used when it is not practical to use a snap ring. Remove E-clips with a flat blade screwdriver by prying between the shaft and E-clip. To install an E-clip, center it over the shaft groove and push or tap it into place.

Observe the following when installing snap rings:
1. Remove and install snap rings with snap ring pliers. Refer to *Tools* in this chapter.
2. In some applications, it may be necessary to replace snap rings after removing them.
3. Compress or expand snap rings just far enough to install them. If overly compressed or expanded, they lose their retaining ability.
4. After installing a snap ring, make sure it seats completely.
5. Wear eye protection when removing and installing snap rings.

SHOP SUPPLIES

The following section describes the types of shop supplies most often required. Read the product label and follow the manufacturer's recommendations.

Lubricants and Fluids

Engine oils

Engine oil for use in a four-stroke motorcycle engine use is classified by three standards: the Japanese Automobile Standards Organization (JASO) T 903 certification standard, the American Petroleum Institute (API) service classification, and the Society of Automotive Engineers (SAE) viscosity index.

The JASO certification specifies the oil has passed requirements specified by Japanese motorcycle manufacturers. The JASO certification label **(Figure 10)** identifies which of the two separate classifications the oil meets. It also includes a registration number to indicate that the oil has passed all JASO certification standards for use in four-stroke motorcycle engines.

Two letters **(Figure 11)** are used to indicate the API service classification. A number, or a sequence of numbers and a letter (10W-40, **Figure 12**) identify the oil's SAE viscosity rating. The API service classification and the SAE viscosity index are not indications of oil quality.

Viscosity is an indication of the oil's thickness. Thin oils have a lower number while thick oils have a higher number. Engine oils fall into the 5- to 50-weight range for single-grade oils.

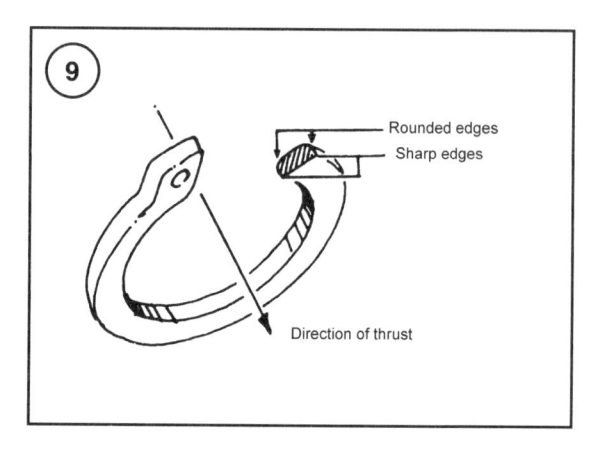

Most manufacturers recommend multi-grade oil. These oils perform efficiently across a wide range of operating conditions. A W after the first number indicates that the oil is a multi-grade type and it shows the low-temperature viscosity.

Always use oil with a classification recommended by the manufacturer. Using oil with a different classification can cause engine damage. Do not use oil with oil additives or oil with graphite or molybdenum additives. Do not use vegetable, non-detergent or castor-based racing oils.

Use a high-quality motorcycle oil with a JASO rating of MA or an API oil with an SG or higher classification that does not specify it as ENERGY CONSERVING **(Figure 12)**. Use SAE 10-30 oil for

GENERAL INFORMATION

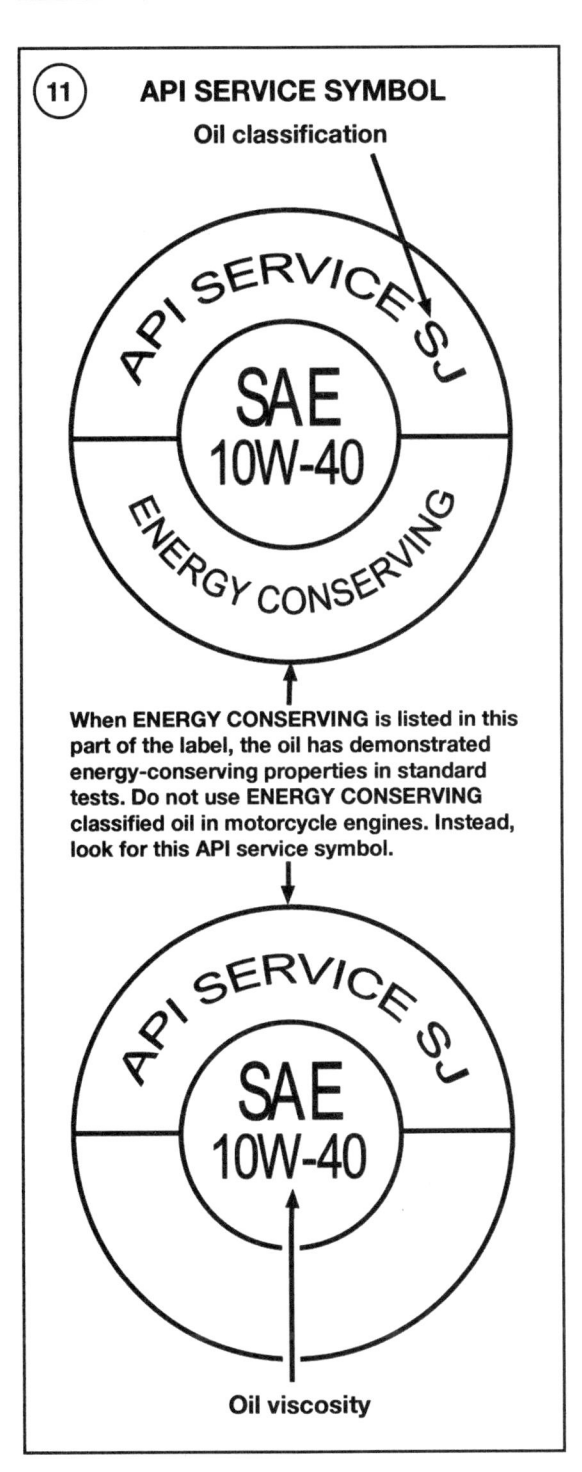

(11) API SERVICE SYMBOL
Oil classification

When ENERGY CONSERVING is listed in this part of the label, the oil has demonstrated energy-conserving properties in standard tests. Do not use ENERGY CONSERVING classified oil in motorcycle engines. Instead, look for this API service symbol.

Oil viscosity

cool and warm climates and a heavier viscosity oil in hot climates.

Greases

Grease is lubricating oil with thickening agents added to it. The National Lubricating Grease Institute (NLGI) grades grease. Grades range from No. 000 to No. 6, with No. 6 being the thickest. Typical multipurpose grease is NLGI No. 2. For specific applications, manufacturers may recommend a water-resistant type grease or one with an additive, such as molybdenum disulfide (MoS2).

Brake fluid

> **WARNING**
> *Never put a mineral-based (petroleum) oil into the brake system. Mineral oil causes rubber parts in the system to swell and break apart, causing complete brake failure.*

Brake fluid is the hydraulic fluid used to transmit hydraulic pressure (force) to the wheel brakes. The Department of Transportation (DOT) brake fluid classification is displayed on the fluid container. The models covered in this manual require DOT 4 brake fluid.

Each type of brake fluid has its own definite properties. Do not intermix different types of brake fluid; this may cause brake system failure. DOT 5 silicone brake fluid is not compatible with other brake fluids or in systems for which it was not designed. Mixing DOT 5 fluid with other fluids may cause brake system failure. When adding brake fluid, *only* use fresh DOT 4 brake fluid from a sealed container.

Brake fluid damages any plastic, painted or plated surface it contacts. Use extreme care when working with brake fluid, and remove any spills immediately with soap and water.

Hydraulic brake systems require clean and moisture free brake fluid. Never reuse brake fluid. Keep containers and reservoirs properly sealed.

Coolant

Coolant is a mixture of water and antifreeze used to dissipate engine heat. Ethylene glycol is the most common form of antifreeze used. Check the motorcycle manufacturer's recommendations (Chapter Three) when selecting antifreeze. Most require one specifically designed for use in aluminum engines. These types of antifreeze have additives that inhibit corrosion.

Only mix distilled water with antifreeze. Impurities in tap water may damage internal cooling system passages.

Final drive gear oil

Gear oil is a thick oil specially formulated for final drive units. Always use gear oil with a classification and viscosity recommended by the manufacturer (Chapter

Three). Do not use engine oil or transmission oil recommended for two-stroke engines or automobiles

Cleaners, Degreasers and Solvents

Many chemicals are available to remove oil, grease and other residue from the motorcycle. Before using cleaning solvents, consider their uses and disposal methods, particularly if they are not water-soluble. Local ordinances may require special procedures for the disposal of many types of cleaning chemicals. Refer to *Safety* and *Cleaning Parts* in this chapter for more information on their uses.

Use brake parts cleaner to clean brake system components when contact with petroleum-based products will damage seals. Brake parts cleaner leaves no residue. Use electrical contact cleaner to clean electrical connections and components without leaving any residue. Carburetor cleaner is a powerful solvent used to remove fuel deposits and varnish from fuel system components. Use this cleaner carefully; it may damage finishes.

Generally, degreasers are strong cleaners used to remove heavy accumulations of grease from engine and frame components.

Most solvents are designed to be used with a parts washing cabinet for individual component cleaning. For safety, use only nonflammable solvents or those with a high flash point.

Gasket Sealant

Sealants are typically used in combination with a gasket or seal. Occasionally they are used alone. Follow the manufacturer's recommendation when using sealants. Use extreme care when choosing a sealant different from the type originally recommended. Choose sealants based on their resistance to heat, various fluids and their sealing capabilities.

One of the most common sealants is RTV, or room temperature vulcanizing, sealant. This sealant cures at room temperature over a specific time period. This allows the repositioning of components without damaging gaskets.

Moisture in the air causes the RTV sealant to cure. Always install the tube cap as soon as possible after applying RTV sealant. RTV sealant has a limited shelf life and will not cure properly if it has expired. Keep partial tubes sealed and discard them if they have surpassed the expiration date. If there is no expiration date on a sealant tube, use a permanent marker and write the date on the tube when it is first opened. Manufacturers usually specify a shelf life of one year after a container is opened, though it is recommended to contact the sealant manufacturer to confirm shelf life.

Removing sealant

Sealant is used on many engine gasket surfaces. When cleaning parts after disassembly, a razor blade or gasket scraper is required to remove the sealer residue that cannot be pulled off by hand from the gasket surfaces.

Applying RTV sealant

Clean all old sealer residue from the mating surfaces. Then inspect the mating surfaces for damage. Remove all sealer material from blind threaded holes; it can cause inaccurate bolt torque. Spray the mating surfaces with aerosol parts cleaner, and then wipe with a lint-free cloth. Because gasket surfaces must be dry and oil-free for the sealant to adhere, be thorough when cleaning and drying the parts.

Apply sealant in a continuous bead along the gasket surface. Circle all the fastener holes unless otherwise specified. Do not allow any sealant to enter these holes. Assemble and tighten the fasteners to the specified torque within the time frame recommended by the sealant manufacturer.

Gasket Remover

Aerosol gasket remover can help remove stubborn gaskets. This product can speed up the removal process and prevent damage to the mating surface that may be caused by using a scraping tool. Most of these types of products are very caustic. Follow the gasket remover manufacturer's instructions for use.

Threadlock

CAUTION
Threadlock is anaerobic and will damage most plastic parts and surfaces. Use caution when using these products in areas where plastic components are located.

Threadlock is available in various strengths, temperatures and repair applications. Threadlock, when applied to fastener threads and allowed to dry, becomes solid filler between the threads. This makes it difficult for the fastener to work loose from vibration or heat expansion and contraction. Some threadlock formulas also provide a seal against fluid leaks.

GENERAL INFORMATION

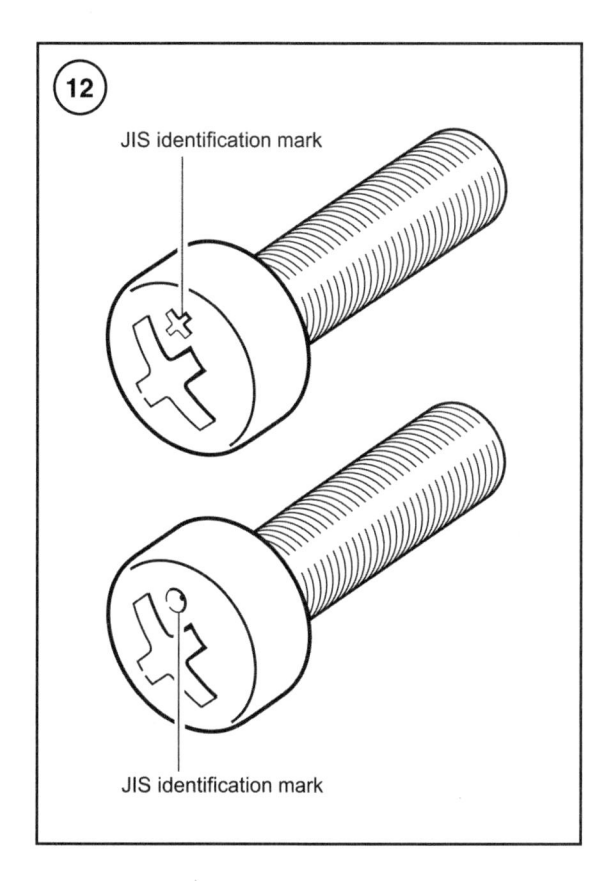

12

JIS identification mark

JIS identification mark

Before applying threadlock, remove any old threadlock residue from all thread areas and clean them with aerosol parts cleaner. Use the threadlock sparingly. Excess fluid can run into adjoining parts.

TOOLS

Most of the procedures in this manual can be carried out with hand tools and test equipment familiar to the home mechanic. Always use the correct tools for the job. Keep tools organized and clean and store them in a tool chest with related tools organized together.

Quality tools are essential. The best are constructed of high-strength alloy steel. These tools are light, easy-to-use and resistant to wear. Their working surfaces are devoid of sharp edges and the tools are carefully polished. They have an easy-to-clean finish and are comfortable to use. Quality tools are a good investment.

When purchasing tools to perform the procedures covered in this manual, consider the tool's potential frequency of use. If a tool kit is just now being started, consider purchasing a tool set from a quality tool supplier. These sets are available in many tool combinations and offer substantial savings when compared to individually purchased tools. As work experience grows and tasks become more complicated, specialized tools can be added.

Some of the procedures in this manual specify special tools. In most cases, the tool is illustrated in use. Well-equipped mechanics may be able to substitute similar tools or fabricate a suitable replacement. However, in some cases, the specialized equipment or expertise may make it impractical for the home mechanic to attempt the procedure. When necessary, such operations are identified in the text with the recommendation to have a dealership or specialist perform the task. It may be less expensive to have a professional perform these jobs, especially when considering the cost of the equipment.

The manufacturer's part number is provided for many of the tools mentioned in this manual. These part numbers are correct at the time of original publication. The publisher cannot guarantee the part number will be correct to the tool's availability in the future.

Screwdrivers

The two basic types of screwdrivers are the slotted tip (flat blade) and the Phillips tip. These are available in sets that often include an assortment of tip sizes and shaft lengths.

As with all tools, use the correct screwdriver. Make sure the size of the tip conforms to the size and shape of the fastener. Use them only for driving screws. Never use a screwdriver for prying or chiseling. Repair or replace worn or damaged screwdrivers. A worn tip may damage the fastener, making it difficult to remove.

Phillips-head screws are often damaged by incorrectly fitting screwdrivers. Quality Phillips screwdrivers are manufactured with their crosshead tip machined to Phillips Screw Company specifications. Poor quality or damaged Phillips screwdrivers can back out and round over the screw head (camout). Compounding the problem of using poor quality screwdrivers are Phillips-head screws made from weak or soft materials and screws initially installed with air tools.

JIS screwdrivers are made to Japanese Industry Standards with tips designed to fit JIS screws without damaging the screw head (camout). JIS screws are often damaged by non JIS screwdrivers because the typical Phillips screwdriver will camout and damage the screw head, especially when the screw is tight. JIS screws can be identified by a single punch mark or X mark on the screw head **(Figure 12)**. JIS screwdrivers and tips work very well on non-JIS screws.

When a JIS screwdriver is not available, an effective screwdriver for Phillips screws is the ACR Phillips II screwdriver. Horizontal anti-camout ribs

(ACR) on the driving faces or flutes of the screwdriver tip **(Figure 13)** improve the tool's grip. While designed for ACR Phillips II screws, ACR Philips II screwdrivers also work well on all common Phillips screws. ACR screwdrivers in different tip sizes and interchangeable bits to fit screwdriver bit holders are available.

Another way to prevent camout and increase the grip of a Phillips screwdriver is to apply valve grinding compound onto the screwdriver tip. After loosening/tightening the screw, clean the screw recess.

Wrenches

Box-end, open-end and combination wrenches **(Figure 14)** are available in a variety of types and sizes.

The number stamped on the wrench refers to the distance between the work areas. This size must match the size of the fastener(s).

The box-end wrench is an excellent tool because it grips the fastener on all sides. This reduces the chance of the tool slipping. The box-end wrench is designed with either a 6- or 12-point opening. For stubborn or damaged fasteners, the 6-point provides superior holding ability by contacting the fastener across a wider area at all six edges. For general use, the 12-point works well. It allows the wrench to be removed and reinstalled without moving the handle over such a wide arc.

An open-end wrench is fast and works best in areas with limited overhead access. It contacts the fastener at only two points, and is subject to slipping under heavy force or if the tool or fastener is worn. A box-end wrench is preferred in most instances, especially when breaking loose a fastener and applying the final torque to it.

The combination wrench has a box-end on one end, and an open-end on the other. This combination makes it a convenient tool.

Adjustable Wrenches

An adjustable wrench **(Figure 15)** can fit nearly any nut or bolt head that has clear access around its entire perimeter.

However, adjustable wrenches contact the fastener at only two points, which makes them more subject to slipping off the fastener. One jaw is adjustable and may loosen, which increases this possibility. Make certain the solid jaw is the one transmitting the force.

Adjustable wrenches are typically used to prevent a large nut or bolt from turning while the other end is

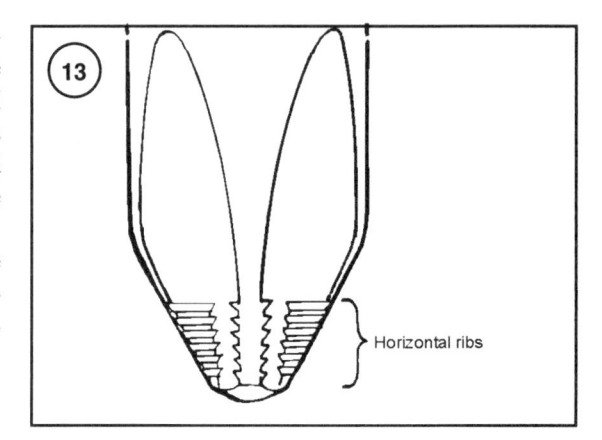

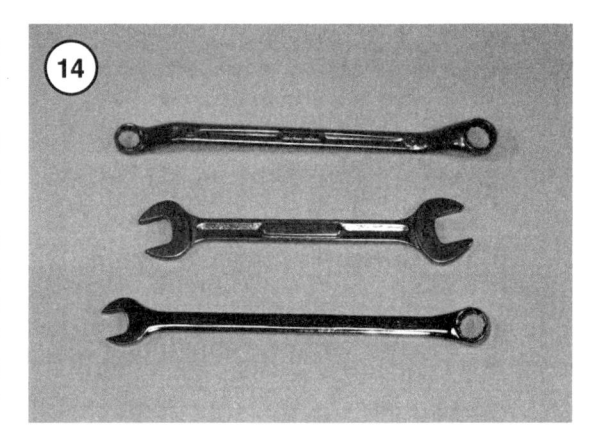

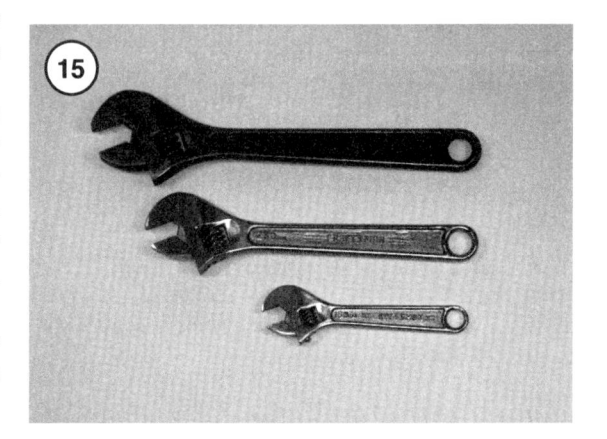

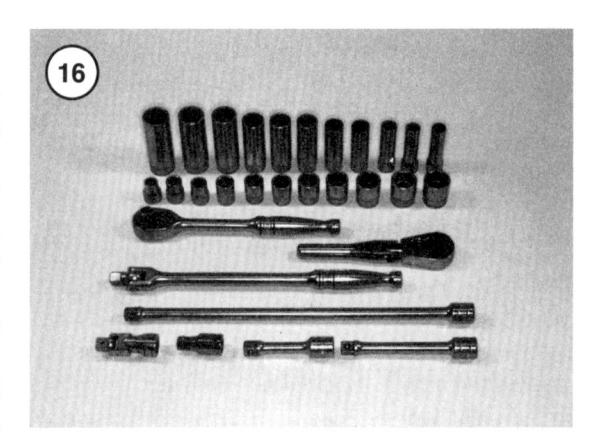

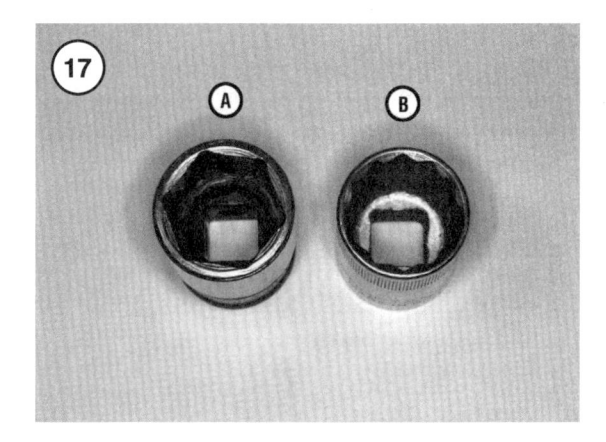

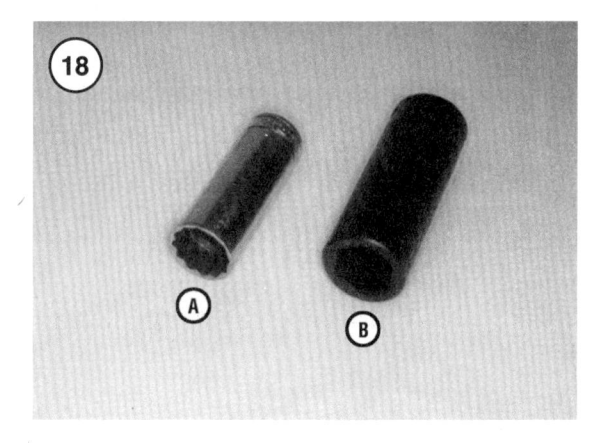

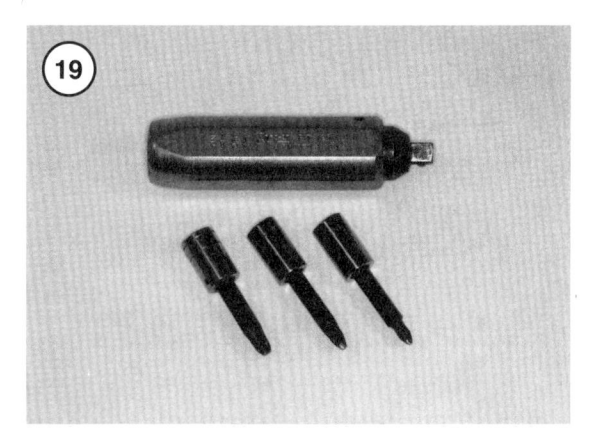

GENERAL INFORMATION

Sockets that attach to a ratchet handle (**Figure 16**) are available with 6-point (A, **Figure 17**) or 12-point (B) openings and different drive sizes. The drive size indicates the size of the square hole that accepts the ratchet handle. The number stamped on the socket is the size of the work area and must match the fastener head.

As with wrenches, a 6-point socket provides superior-holding ability, while a 12-point socket needs to be moved only half as far to reposition it on the fastener.

Sockets are designated for either hand or impact use. Impact sockets are made of a thicker material for more durability. Compare the size and wall thickness of a 19-mm hand socket (A, **Figure 18**) and the 19-mm impact socket (B). Use impact sockets when using an impact driver or air tool. Use hand sockets with hand-driven attachments.

Various attachments (**Figure 16**) are available for sockets. The ratchet is the most versatile. It allows the user to install or remove the nut without removing the socket. Flexible ratchet heads in varying lengths allow the socket to be turned with varying force and at odd angles. The speed handle is used for fast operation. Extension bars allow the socket setup to reach difficult areas.

Sockets combined with any number of drivers make them undoubtedly the fastest, safest and most convenient tool for fastener removal and installation.

Impact Driver

WARNING
Do not use hand sockets with air or impact tools because they may shatter and cause injury. Always wear eye protection when using impact or air tools.

An impact driver provides extra force for removing fasteners by converting the impact of a hammer into a turning motion. This makes it possible to remove stubborn fasteners without damaging them. Impact drivers and interchangeable bits (**Figure 19**) are available from most tool suppliers. When using a socket with an impact driver, make sure the socket is designed for impact use. Refer to *Socket Wrenches, Ratchets and Handles* in this section.

Allen Wrenches

Allen, or setscrew wrenches (**Figure 20**), are used on fasteners with hexagonal recesses in the fastener head. These wrenches are available in a L-shaped

being loosened or tightened with a box-end or socket wrench.

Socket Wrenches, Ratchets and Handles

WARNING
Do not use hand sockets with air or impact tools; they may shatter and cause injury. Always wear eye protection when using impact or air tools.

bar, socket and T-handle types. Allen bolts are sometimes called socket bolts.

Torx Fasteners

A Torx fastener head is a 6-point star-shaped pattern. Torx fasteners are identified with a T and a number indicating their drive size. For example, T25 Torx drivers are available in L-shaped bars, sockets (A, **Figure 21**) and T-handles. Tamper-resistant Torx fasteners are also used and have a round shaft in the center of the fastener head. Tamper-resistance Torx fasteners require a Torx bit with a hole in the center of the bit (B, **Figure 21**) to accommodate the fastener shaft.

Torque Wrenches

A torque wrench (**Figure 22**) is used with a socket, torque adapter or similar extension to tighten a fastener to a measured torque. Torque wrenches come in several drive sizes (1/4, 3/8, 1/2 and 3/4 inch) and utilize various methods of displaying the torque value. The drive size indicates the size of the square drive that accepts the socket, adapter or extension. Common methods of displaying the torque value are the reflecting beam, the dial indicator and the audible click. When choosing a torque wrench, consider the torque range, drive size and accuracy. The torque specifications in this manual provide an indication of the range required. A torque wrench is a precision tool that must be properly cared for in order to remain accurate. Store torque wrenches in cases or separate padded drawers within a toolbox. Follow the tool manufacturer's instructions for their care and calibration.

Torque Adapters

Torque adapters (**Figure 23**, typical), or extensions, extend or reduce the reach of a torque wrench. Specific adapters are required to perform some of the procedures in this manual. These are available from the motorcycle manufacturer or they may be fabricated to suit a specific purpose.

If a torque adapter changes the effective lever length, the torque reading on the wrench will not equal the actual torque applied to the fastener. It is necessary to recalibrate the torque setting on the wrench to compensate for the change of lever length. When a torque adapter is used at a right angle to the drive head, calibration is not required because the lever length has not changed.

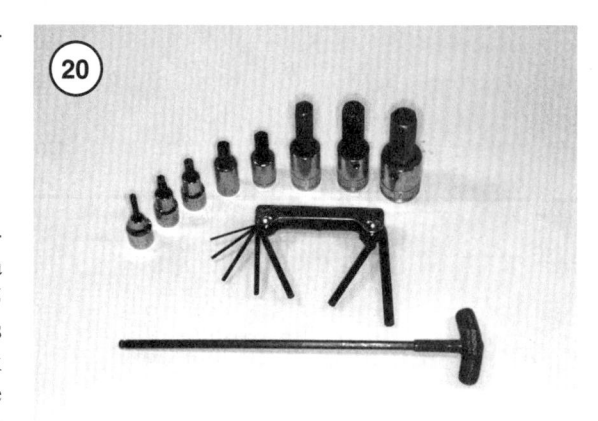

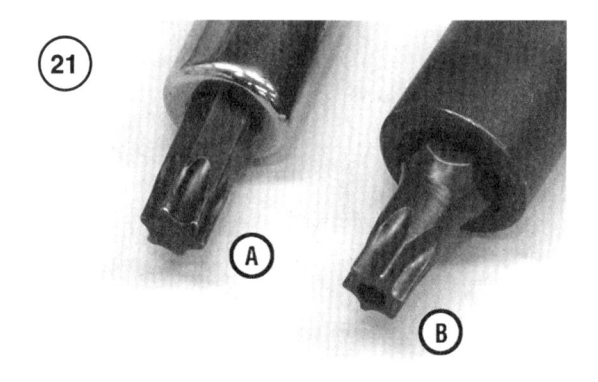

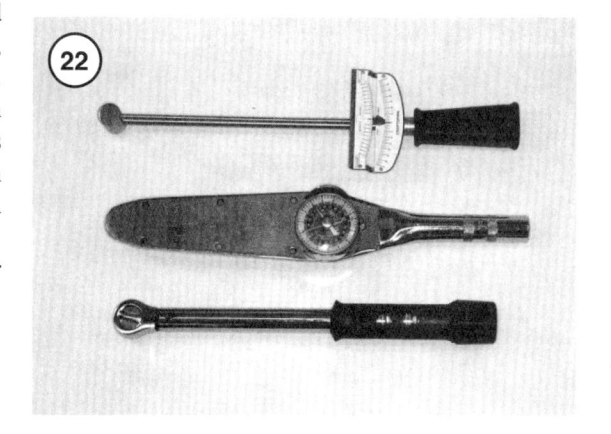

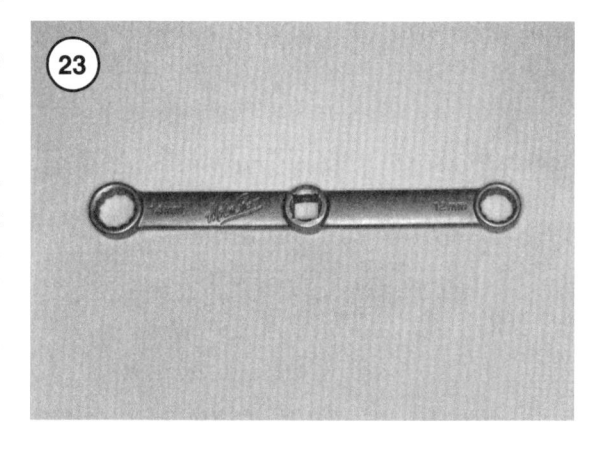

GENERAL INFORMATION

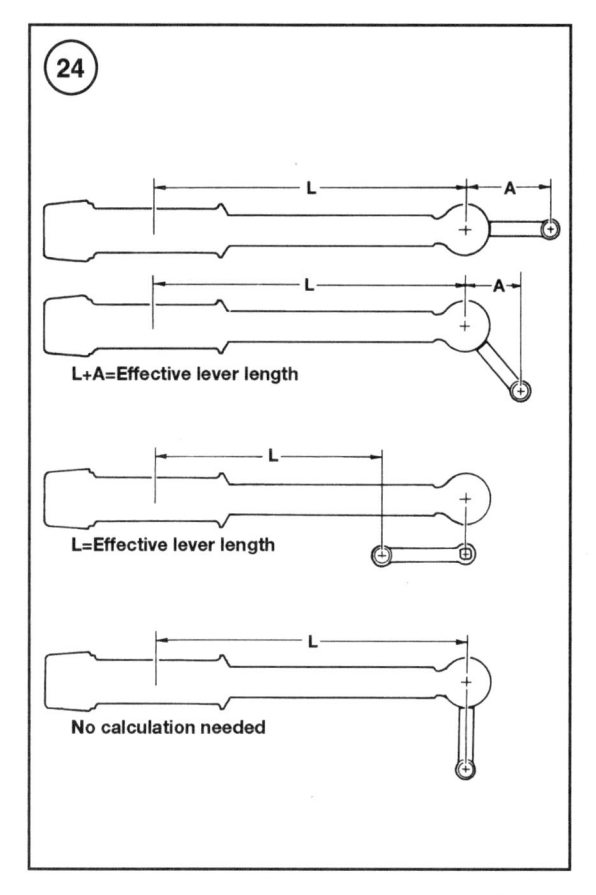

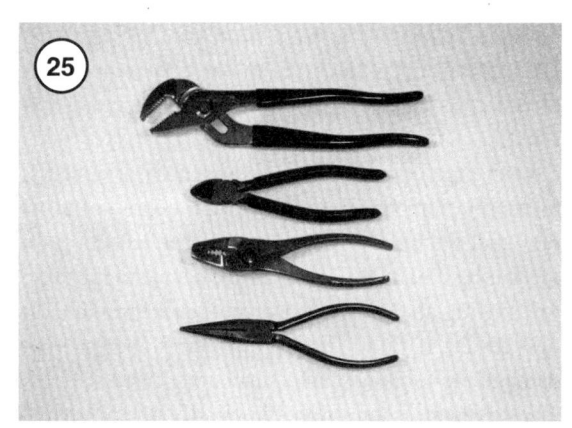

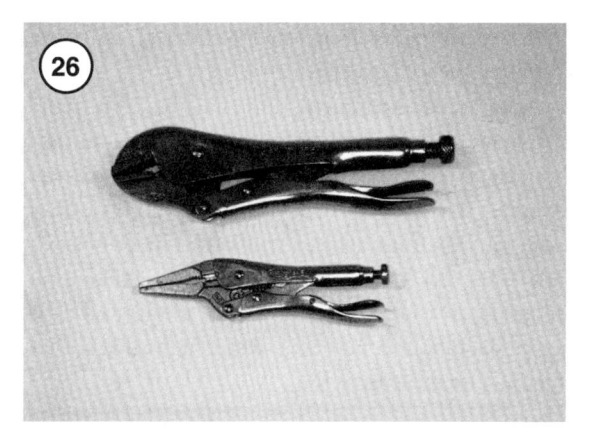

To recalculate a torque reading when using a torque adapter, use the following formula, and refer to Figure 24.

$$TW = \frac{TA \times L}{L + A}$$

TW is the torque setting or dial reading on the wrench.

TA is the torque specification and the actual amount of torque that will be applied to the fastener.

A is the amount the adapter increases (or in some cases reduces) the effective lever length as measured along the centerline of the torque wrench.

L is the lever length of the wrench as measured from the center of the drive to the center of the grip.

The effective lever length is the sum of L and A.

Example:
TA = 20 ft.-lb.
A = 3 in.
L = 14 in.

$$TW = \frac{20 \times 14}{14 + 3} = \frac{280}{17} = 16.5 \text{ ft.-lb.}$$

In this example, the torque wrench would be set to the recalculated torque value (TW = 16.5 ft.-lb.). When using a beam-type wrench, tighten the fastener until the pointer aligns with 16.5 ft.-lb. In this example, although the torque wrench is pre set to 16.5 ft.-lb., the actual torque is 20 ft.-lb.

Pliers

Pliers come in a wide range of types and sizes. Pliers are useful for holding, cutting, bending, and crimping. Do not use them to turn fasteners unless they are designed to do so. **Figure 25** and **Figure 26** show several types of pliers. Each design has a specialized function. Slip-joint pliers are general-purpose pliers used for gripping and bending. Diagonal cutting pliers are needed to cut wire and can be used to remove cotter pins. Needlenose pliers are used to hold or bend small objects. Locking pliers **(Figure 26)** hold objects tightly. They have many uses ranging from holding two parts together, to gripping the end of a broken stud. Use caution when using locking pliers; the sharp jaws will damage the objects they hold.

Snap Ring Pliers

WARNING
Snap rings can slip and fly off when removing and installing them. In addition, the snap ring pliers tips may break. Always wear eye protection when using snap ring pliers.

Snap ring pliers are specialized pliers with tips that fit into the ends of snap rings to remove and install them.

Snap ring pliers **(Figure 27)** are available with a fixed action (either internal or external) or are convertible (one tool works on both internal and external snap rings). They may have fixed tips or interchangeable ones of various sizes and angles. For general use, select convertible type pliers with interchangeable tips.

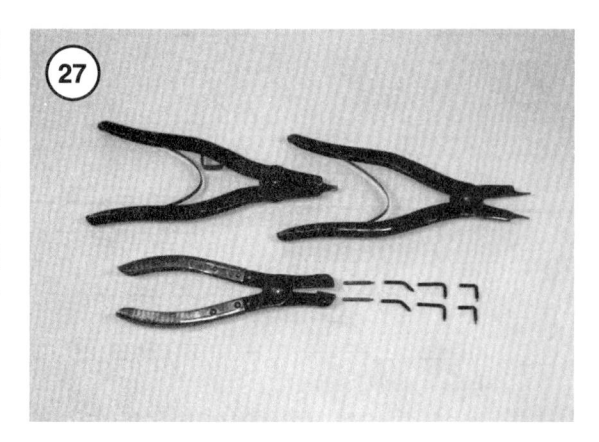

Hammers

WARNING
Always wear eye protection when using hammers. Make sure the hammer face is in good condition and the handle is not cracked. Select the correct hammer for the job and make sure to strike the object squarely. Do not use the handle or the side of the hammer to strike an object.

Various types of hammers are available to fit a number of applications. A ball-peen hammer is used to strike another tool, such as a punch or chisel. Soft-faced hammers are required when a metal object must be struck without damaging it. Never use a metal-faced hammer on engine and suspension components; damage will occur in most cases.

Ignition Grounding Tool

Some test procedures in this manual require turning the engine over without starting it. Do not remove the spark plug cap(s) and crank the engine without grounding the plug cap(s). Doing so will damage the ignition system.

An effective way to ground the system is to fabricate the tool shown in **Figure 28** from a No. 6 screw, two washers and a length of wire with an alligator clip soldered on one end. To use the tool, insert it into the spark plug cap and attach the alligator clip to a known engine ground. A separate grounding tool is required for each spark plug cap.

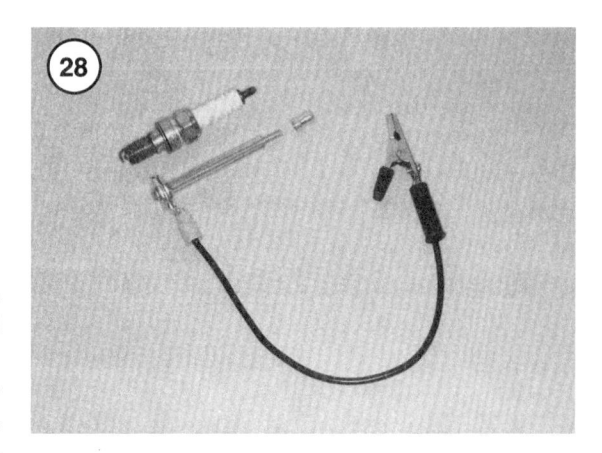

This tool is safer than a spark plug or spark tester because there is no spark firing across the end of the plug/tester to potentially ignite fuel vapor spraying from an open spark plug hole or leaking fuel component.

MEASURING TOOLS

The ability to accurately measure components is essential to successfully service many components. Equipment is manufactured to close tolerances, and obtaining consistently accurate measurements is essential.

Each type of measuring instrument is designed to measure a dimension with a certain degree of accuracy and within a certain range. When selecting the measuring tool, make sure it is applicable to the task.

As with all tools, measuring tools provide the best results if cared for properly. Improper use can damage the tool and cause inaccurate results. If any measurement is questionable, verify the measurement using another tool. A standard gauge is usually provided with measuring tools to check accuracy and calibrate the tool if necessary.

Accurate measurements are only possible if the mechanic possesses a feel for using the tool. Heavy-handed use of measuring tools produces less accurate results. Hold the tool gently by the fingertips so the point at which the tool contacts the object is easily felt. This feel for the equipment will produce more accurate measurements and reduce the risk of damaging the tool or component. Refer to the this section for specific measuring tools.

GENERAL INFORMATION

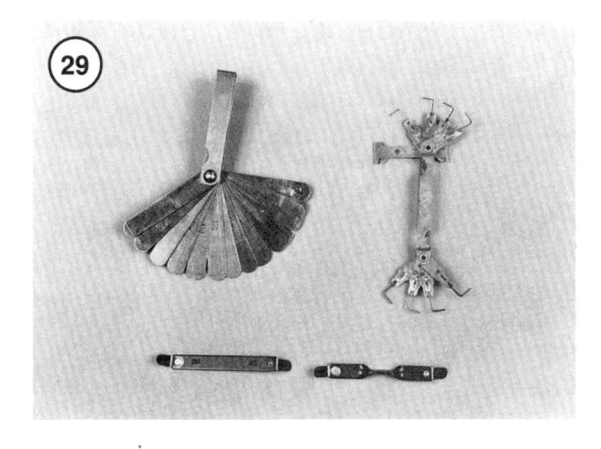

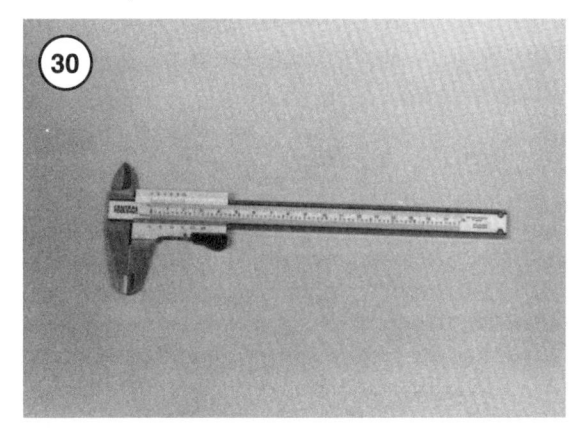

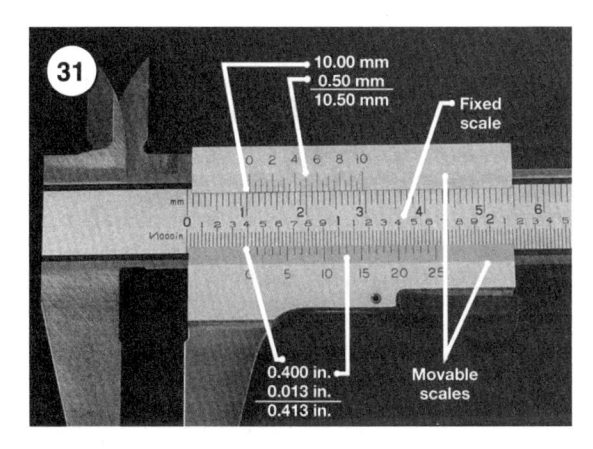

Feeler Gauge

The feeler, or thickness gauge (**Figure 29**), is used for measuring the distance between two surfaces.

A feeler gauge set consists of an assortment of steel strips of graduated thicknesses. Each blade is marked with its thickness. Blades can be of various lengths and angles for different procedures.

A common use for a feeler gauge is to measure valve clearance. Wire (round) type gauges are used to measure spark plug gap.

Calipers

Calipers (**Figure 30**) are excellent tools for obtaining inside, outside and depth measurements. Although not as precise as a micrometer, they allow reasonable precision, typically to within 0.05 mm (0.001 in.). Most calipers have a range up to 150 mm (6 in.).

Calipers are available in dial, vernier or digital versions. Dial calipers have a dial readout that provides convenient reading. Vernier calipers have marked scales that must be compared to determine the measurement. The digital caliper uses an LCD to show the measurement.

Properly maintain the measuring surfaces of the caliper. There must not be any dirt or burrs between the tool and the object being measured. Never force the caliper closed around an object; close the caliper around the highest point so it can be removed with a slight drag. Some calipers require calibration. Always refer to the tool manufacturer's instructions when using a new or unfamiliar caliper.

To read a vernier caliper, refer to **Figure 31**. The fixed scale is marked in 1 mm increments. Ten individual lines on the fixed scale equal 1 cm. The movable scale is marked in 0.05 mm (hundredth) increments. To obtain a reading, establish the first number by the location of the 0 line on the movable scale in relation to the first line to the left on the fixed scale. In this example, the number is 10 mm. To determine the next number, note which of the lines on the movable scale align with a mark on the fixed scale. A number of lines will seem close, but only one will align exactly. In this case, 0.50 mm is the reading to add to the first number. The result of adding 10 mm and 0.50 mm is a measurement of 10.50 mm.

Micrometers

A micrometer (**Figure 32**) is an instrument designed for linear measurement using the decimal divisions of the inch or meter. While there are many types and styles of micrometers, most of the procedures in this manual call for an outside micrometer. The outside micrometer is used to measure the outside diameter of cylindrical forms and the thicknesses of materials.

A micrometer's size indicates the minimum and maximum size of a part that it can measure. The usual sizes are 0-25 mm (0-1 in.), 25-50 mm (1-2 in.), 50-75 mm (2-3 in.) and 75-100 mm (3-4 in.).

Micrometers that cover a wider range of measurements are available. These use a large frame with interchangeable anvils of various lengths. This type of micrometer offers a cost savings; however, its overall size may make it less convenient.

Adjustment

Before using a micrometer, check its adjustment as follows.
1. Clean the anvil and spindle faces.
2A To check a 0-1 in. or 0-25 mm micrometer:
   a. Turn the thimble until the spindle contacts the anvil. If the micrometer has a ratchet stop, use it to ensure the proper amount of pressure is applied.
   b. If the adjustment is correct, the 0 mark on the thimble will align exactly with the 0 mark on the sleeve line. If the marks do not align, the micrometer is out of adjustment.
   c. Follow the tool manufacturer's instructions to adjust the micrometer.
2B. To check a micrometer larger than 1 in. or 25 mm, use the standard gauge supplied by the manufacturer. A standard gauge is a steel block, disc or rod that is machined to an exact size.
   a. Place the standard gauge between the spindle and anvil and measure its outside diameter or length. If the micrometer has a ratchet stop, use it to ensure the proper amount of pressure is applied.
   b. If the adjustment is correct, the 0 mark on the thimble will align exactly with the 0 mark on the sleeve line. If the marks do not align, the micrometer is out of adjustment.
   c. Follow the tool manufacturer's instructions to adjust the micrometer.

Care

Micrometers are precision instruments. They must be used and maintained with great care. Note the following:
1. Store micrometers in protective cases or separate padded drawers in a toolbox.
2. When in storage, make sure the spindle and anvil faces do not contact each other or another object. If they do, temperature changes and corrosion may damage the contact faces.

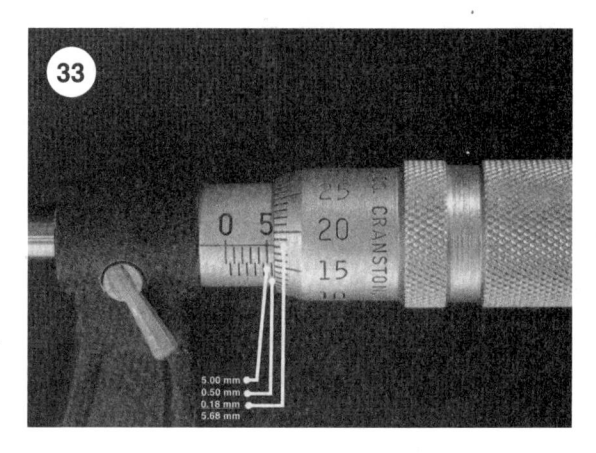

3. Do not clean a micrometer with compressed air. Dirt forced into the tool causes wear.
4. Lubricate micrometers to prevent corrosion.

Reading

When reading a micrometer, numbers are taken from different scales and added together.

For accurate results, properly maintain the measuring surfaces of the micrometer. There cannot be any dirt or burrs between the tool and the measured object. Never force the micrometer closed around an object. Close the micrometer around the highest point so it can be removed with a slight drag.

The standard metric micrometer is accurate to one one-hundredth of a millimeter (0.01 mm). The sleeve line is graduated in millimeter and half millimeter increments. The marks on the upper half of the sleeve line equal 1.00 mm. Each fifth mark above the sleeve line is identified with a number. The number sequence depends on the size of the micrometer. A 0-25 mm micrometer, for example, will have sleeve marks numbered 0 through 25 in 5 mm increments. This numbering sequence continues with larger micrometers. On all metric micrometers, each mark on the lower half of the sleeve equals 0.50 mm.

The tapered end of the thimble has 50 lines marked around it. Each mark equals 0.01 mm. One complete turn of the thimble aligns its 0 mark with the first line on the lower half of the sleeve line, or 0.50 mm.

When reading a metric micrometer, add the number of millimeters and half-millimeters on the sleeve line to the number of one one-hundredth millimeters on the thimble. Perform the following steps while referring to **Figure 33**.
1. Read the upper half of the sleeve line and count the number of lines visible. Each upper line equals 1 mm.
2. See if the half-millimeter line is visible on the lower sleeve line. If so, add 0.50 mm to the reading.

GENERAL INFORMATION

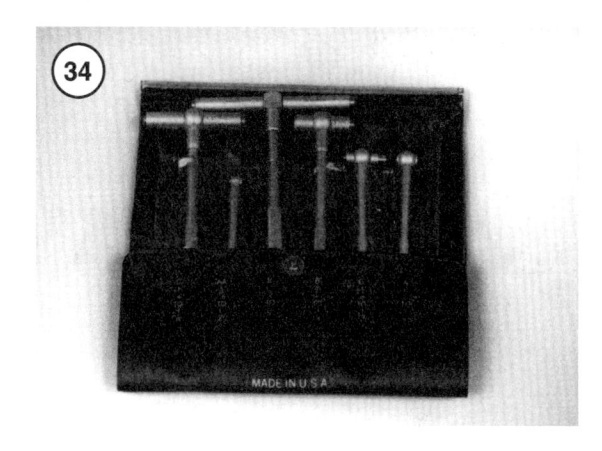

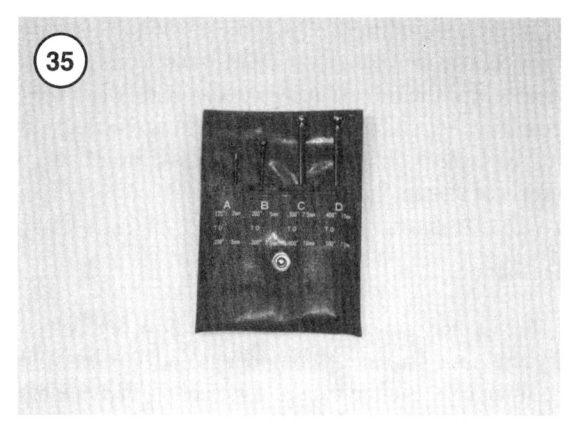

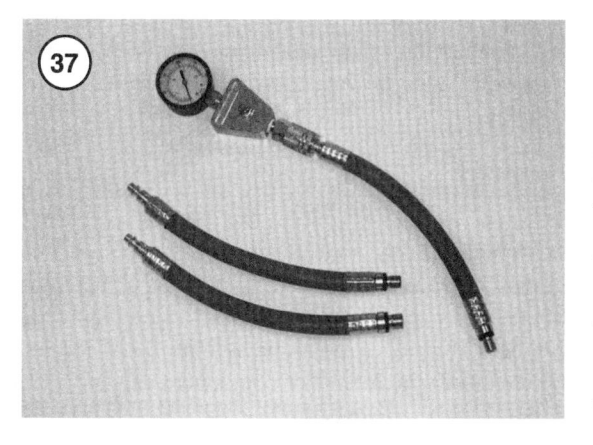

3. Read the thimble mark that aligns with the sleeve line. Each thimble mark equals 0.01 mm.
4. If a thimble mark does not align exactly with the sleeve line, estimate the amount between the lines. For accurate readings in two-thousandths of a millimeter (0.002 mm), use a metric vernier micrometer.
5. Add the readings from all the steps together.

Telescoping and Small Hole Gauges

Use telescoping gauges (**Figure 34**) and small hole gauges (**Figure 35**) to measure bores. Neither gauge has a scale for direct readings. An outside micrometer must be used to determine the reading.

To use a telescoping gauge, select the correct size gauge for the bore. Compress the movable post and carefully insert the gauge into the bore. Carefully move the gauge in the bore to make sure it is centered. Tighten the knurled end of the gauge to hold the moveable post in position. Remove the gauge and measure the length of the posts. Telescoping gauges are typically used to measure cylinder bores.

To use a small hole gauge, select the correct size gauge for the bore. Carefully insert the gauge into the bore. Tighten the knurled end of the gauge to carefully expand the gauge fingers to the limit within the bore. Do not overtighten the gauge; there is no built-in release. Excessive tightening can damage the bore surface and tool. Remove the gauge and measure the outside dimension with a micrometer (**Figure 32**). Small hole gauges are typically used to measure valve guides.

Dial Indicator

A dial indicator (**Figure 36**) is a gauge with a dial face and needle used to measure variations in dimensions and movements. Measuring brake rotor runout is a typical use for a dial indicator.

Dial indicators are available in various ranges and graduations and with three types of mounting bases: magnetic, clamp or screw-in stud.

Cylinder Bore Gauge

A cylinder bore gauge is similar to a dial indicator. These typically consist of a dial indicator, handle and different length adapters (anvils) to fit the gauge to various bore sizes. The bore gauge is used to measure bore size, taper and out-of-round. When using a bore gauge, follow the tool manufacturer's instructions.

Compression Gauge

A compression gauge (**Figure 37**) measures combustion chamber (cylinder) pressure, usually in psi or kPa. The gauge adapter is either inserted and held in place or screwed into the spark plug hole to obtain the reading. Disable the engine so it will not start and hold the throttle in the wide-open position when performing a compression test. An engine that does not have adequate compression cannot be properly tuned. Refer to Chapter Three.

Multimeter

A multimeter **(Figure 38)** is an essential tool for electrical system diagnosis. The voltage function indicates the voltage applied or available to various electrical components. The ohmmeter function tests circuits for continuity, or lack of continuity, and measures the resistance of a circuit.

Some manufacturers' specifications for electrical components are based on results using a specific test meter. Results may vary if using a meter not recommend by the manufacturer. Such requirements are noted when applicable.

Ohmmeter (analog) calibration

Each time an analog ohmmeter is used or the scale is changed, the ohmmeter must be calibrated.

Digital ohmmeters do not require calibration.
1. Make sure the meter battery is in good condition.
2. Make sure the meter probes are in good condition.
3. Touch the two probes together and observe the needle location on the ohms scale. The needle must align with the 0 mark to obtain accurate measurements.
4. If necessary, rotate the meter ohms adjust knob until the needle and 0 mark align.

ELECTRICAL SYSTEM FUNDAMENTALS

A thorough study of the many types of electrical systems used in today's motorcycles is beyond the scope of this manual. However, a basic understanding of voltage, resistance and amperage is necessary to perform diagnostic tests.

Refer to Chapter Two for troubleshooting.

Voltage

Voltage is the electrical potential or pressure in an electrical circuit and is expressed in volts. The more pressure (voltage) in a circuit, the more work can be performed.

Direct current (DC) voltage means the electricity flows in one direction. All circuits powered by a battery are DC circuits.

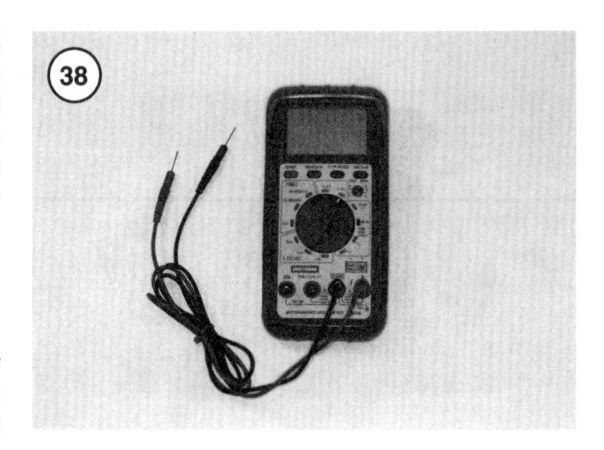

Alternating current (AC) means the electricity flows in one direction momentarily and then switches to the opposite direction. Alternator output is an example of AC voltage. This voltage must be changed or rectified to direct current to operate in a battery powered system.

Resistance

Resistance is the opposition to the flow of electricity within a circuit or component and is measured in ohms. Resistance causes a reduction in available current and voltage.

Resistance is measured in an inactive circuit with an ohmmeter. The ohmmeter sends a small amount of current into the circuit and measures how difficult it is to push the current through the circuit.

An ohmmeter, although useful, is not always a good indicator of a circuit's actual ability under operating conditions. This is due to the low voltage (6-9 volts) that the meter uses to test the circuit. The voltage in an ignition coil secondary winding can be several thousand volts. Such high voltage can cause the coil to malfunction, even though it tests acceptable during a resistance test.

Resistance generally increases with temperature. Perform all testing with the component or circuit at room temperature. Resistance tests performed at high temperatures may indicate false resistance readings and cause the unnecessary replacement of a component.

Amperage

Amperage is the unit of measure for the amount of current within a circuit. Current is the actual flow of electricity. The higher the current, the more work can be performed up to a given point. If the current flow exceeds the circuit or component capacity, the system will be damaged.

GENERAL INFORMATION

SERVICE METHODS

Many of the procedures in this manual are straightforward and can be performed by anyone reasonably competent with tools. However, consider previous experience carefully before performing any operation involving complicated procedures.

1. Front, in this manual, refers to the front of the motorcycle. The front of any component is the end closest to the front of the motorcycle. The left and right sides refer to the position of the parts as viewed by the rider sitting on the seat facing forward.
2. When servicing the motorcycle, secure it in a safe manner.
3. Label all similar parts for location and mark all mating parts for position. If possible, photograph or draw the number and thickness of any shim as it is removed. Identify parts by placing them in sealed and labeled plastic bags. It is possible for carefully laid out parts to become disturbed, making it difficult to reassemble the components correctly without a diagram.
4. Label disconnected hoses, wires and connectors with masking tape and a marking pen. Do not rely on memory alone.
5. Protect finished surfaces from physical damage or corrosion. Keep gasoline and other chemicals off painted surfaces.
6. Use penetrating oil on frozen or tight bolts. Avoid using heat where possible. Heat can warp, melt or affect the temper of parts. Heat also damages the finish of paint and plastics. Refer to *Heating Components* in this section.
7. When a part is a press fit or requires a special tool for removal, the information or type of tool is identified in the text. Otherwise, if a part is difficult to remove or install, determine the cause before proceeding.
8. To prevent objects or debris from falling into the engine, cover all openings.
9. Read each procedure thoroughly and compare the figures to the actual components before starting the procedure. Perform the procedure in sequence.
10. Recommendations are occasionally made to refer service to a dealership or specialist. In these cases, the work can be performed more economically by the specialist than by the home mechanic.
11. The term *replace* means to discard a defective part and replace it with a new part. *Overhaul* means to remove, disassemble, inspect, measure, repair and/or replace parts as required to recondition an assembly.
12. Some operations require the use of a hydraulic press. If a press is not available, have these operations performed by a shop equipped with the necessary equipment. Do not use makeshift equipment that may damage the motorcycle. Do not direct high-pressure water at steering bearings, fuel system hoses, wheel bearings, suspension or electrical components. The water forces the grease out of the bearings and could damage the seals.
13. Repairs are much faster and easier if the motorcycle is clean before starting work. Degrease the motorcycle with a commercial degreaser; follow the directions on the container for the best results. Clean all parts with cleaning solvent.
14. If special tools are required, have them available before starting the procedure. When special tools are required, they will be described at the beginning of the procedure.
15. Make sure all shims and washers are reinstalled in the same location and position.
16. Whenever rotating parts contact a stationary part, look for a shim or washer.
17. Use new gaskets if there is any doubt about the condition of old ones.
18. If self-locking fasteners are used, replace them. Do not install standard fasteners in place of self-locking ones.
19. Use grease to hold small parts in place if they tend to fall out during assembly. Do not apply grease to electrical or brake components.
20. Dowel pins may remove easily or remain stuck in place. If stuck, it is best to leave them in place unless they are damaged and require replacement.

Heating Components

WARNING
Wear protective gloves to prevent burns and injury when heating parts.

CAUTION
Do not use a welding torch when heating parts. A welding torch applies excessive heat to a small area very quickly, which can damage parts.

A heat gun or propane torch may be required during some of the service procedures in this manual. Read the safety and operating information supplied by the manufacturer of the heat gun or propane torch while also noting the following:

1. The work area should be clean and dry. Remove all combustible components and materials from the work area. Wipe up all grease, oil and other fluids from parts. Check for leaking or damaged fuel system components. Repair or remove these parts before beginning work.
2. Never use a flame near the battery, fuel tank, fuel lines or other flammable materials.

3. When using a heat gun, remember that the temperature can be in excess of 540° C (1000° F).
4. Have a fire extinguisher near the job.
5. Always wear protective goggles and gloves when heating parts.
6. Before heating a part installed on the motorcycle, check areas around the part and those *hidden* that could be damaged or possibly ignite. Do not heat surfaces than can be damaged by heat. Shield materials near the part or area to be heated. For example, cables and wiring harnesses.
7. Before heating a part, read the entire procedure to make sure the required tools are available. This allows quick work while the part is at its optimum temperature.
8. The amount of heat recommended to remove or install a part is typically listed in the procedure. However, before heating parts without a specific recommendation, consider the possible effects. To avoid damaging a part, monitor the temperature with heat sticks or an infrared thermometer, if possible. Another way, though not as accurate, is to place tiny drops of water on the part. When the water starts to sizzle, the part is hot enough. Keep the heat source in motion to prevent overheating.

Removing Frozen Fasteners

If a fastener cannot be removed, several methods may be used to loosen it. First, liberally apply penetrating oil, and let it penetrate for 10-15 minutes. Rap the fastener several times with a small hammer. Do not hit it hard enough to cause damage. Reapply the penetrating oil if necessary.

For frozen screws, apply penetrating oil as described, and then insert a screwdriver in the slot and rap the top of the screwdriver with a hammer. This loosens the rust so the screw can be removed in the normal way. If the screw head is too damaged to use this method, grip the head with locking pliers and twist it out.

If heat is required, refer to *Heating Components* in this section.

Removing Broken Fasteners

If the head breaks off a screw or bolt, several methods are available for removing the remaining portion. If a large portion of the remainder projects out, try gripping it with locking pliers. If the projecting portion is too small, file it to fit a wrench or cut a slot in it to fit a screwdriver **(Figure 39)**.

If the head breaks off flush, use a screw extractor. To do this, center punch the exact center of the screw or bolt (A, **Figure 40**), and then drill a small hole in the screw (B) and tap the extractor into the hole (C). Back the screw out with a wrench on the extractor (D, **Figure 40**).

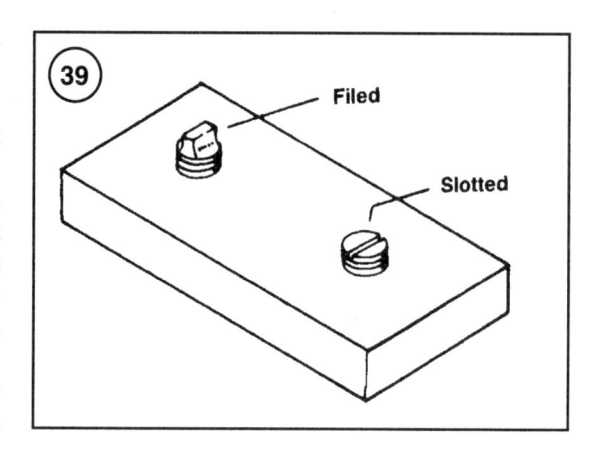

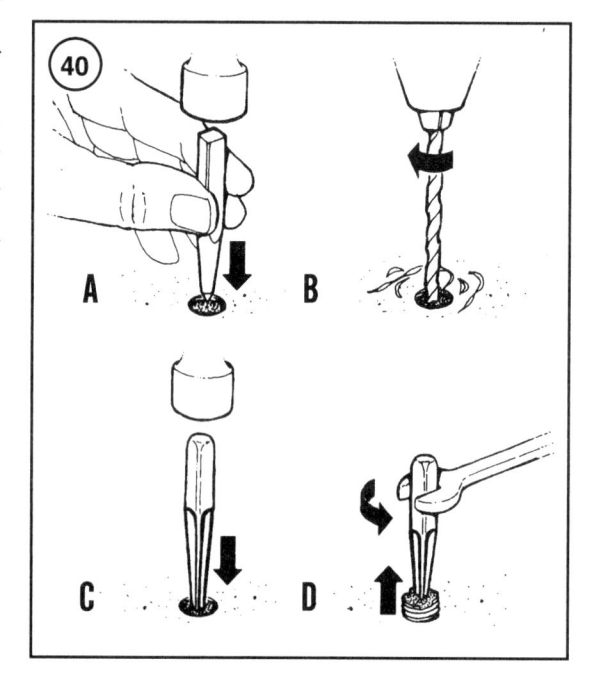

Repairing Damaged Threads

NOTE
Rethreading taps and dies are available for repairing threads. The advantage of a rethreading tap and die compared to a conventional thread cutting tap and die is that the rethreading tools are designed to clean or chase the threads only. They will not cut threads like a conventional thread cutting tap and die.

Occasionally, threads are stripped through carelessness or impact damage. Often the threads can

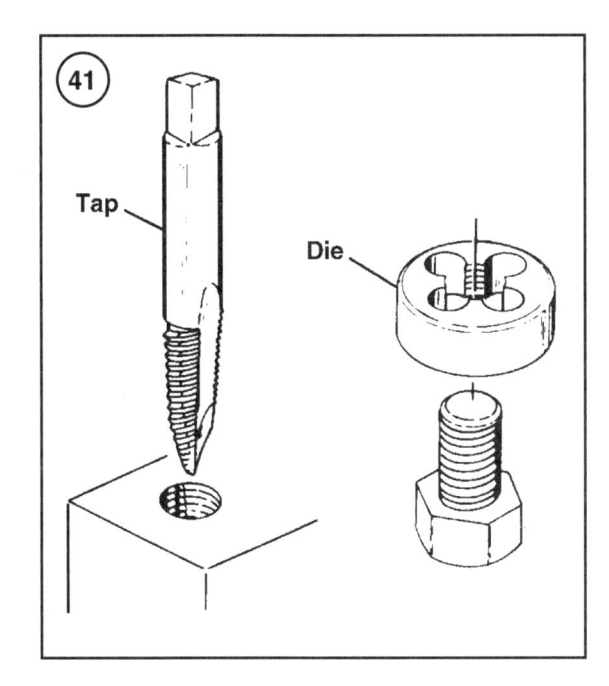

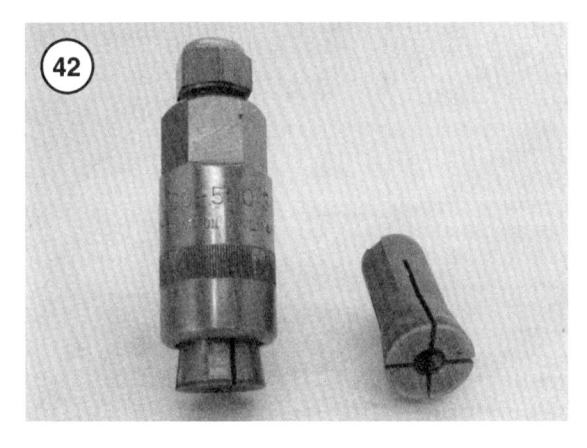

GENERAL INFORMATION

1. Measure and record the height of the stud above the surface.
2. Thread the stud removal tool onto the stud and tighten it, or thread two nuts onto the stud.
3. Remove the stud by turning the stud remover or the lower nut.
4. Remove any threadlock residue from the threaded hole. Clean the threads with an aerosol parts cleaner.
5. Install the stud removal tool onto the new stud, or thread two nuts onto the stud.
6. Apply threadlock to the threads of the stud.
7. Install the stud and tighten with the stud removal tool or the top nut.
8. Install the stud to the height recorded previously or tighten to its torque specification.
9. Remove the stud removal tool or the two nuts.

Removing Hoses

When removing stubborn hoses, do not exert excessive force on the hose or fitting. Remove the hose clamp and carefully insert a small screwdriver or similar blunt nose tool between the fitting and hose. Apply a spray lubricant under the hose and carefully twist the hose off the fitting. Clean the fitting of any corrosion or rubber hose material with a wire brush. Clean the inside of the hose thoroughly. Do not use any lubricant when installing the hose (new or old). The lubricant may allow the hose to come off the fitting, even when the clamp is tightened securely.

Bearings

Bearings are precision parts. They must be maintained with proper lubrication and maintenance. If a bearing is damaged, replace it immediately. When installing a new bearing, make sure to prevent damaging it. Bearing replacement procedures are included in the individual chapters where applicable; however, refer to this section as a guideline.

Unless otherwise specified, install bearings with the manufacturer's mark or number facing outward.

Removal

While bearings are normally removed only when damaged, there may be times when it is necessary to remove a bearing that is in good condition. However, improper bearing removal will damage the bearing and may possibly damage the shaft or case half.

1. Before removing the bearings, note the following:
   a. Refer to the bearing replacement procedure in the appropriate chapter for any special instructions.
   b. Remove any seals that interfere with bearing

be repaired by running a tap (for internal threads on nuts) or die (for external threads on bolts) through the threads **(Figure 41)**. To clean or repair spark plug threads, use a spark plug tap.

If an internal thread is damaged, it may be necessary to install a Helicoil or some other type of thread insert. Follow the manufacturer's instructions when installing it.

If it is necessary to drill and tap a hole, refer to **Table 5** for metric tap and drill sizes.

Stud Removal/Installation

A stud removal tool **(Figure 42)** is available from most tool suppliers. This tool makes the removal and installation of studs easier. If one is not available and the threads on the stud are not damaged, thread two nuts onto the stud and tighten them against each other. Remove the stud by turning the lower nut.

removal. Refer to *Seal Replacement* in this section.

c. When removing more than one bearing, identify the bearings before removing them. Refer to the bearing manufacturer's numbers on the bearing.

d. Note and record the direction in which the bearing numbers face for proper installation.

e. Remove any set plates or bearing retainers before removing the bearings.

2. When using a puller to remove a bearing from a shaft, make sure the shaft is not damaged. Always place a piece of metal between the end of the shaft and the puller screw. In addition, place the puller arms next to the inner bearing race. Refer to **Figure 43**.

3. When using a hammer to remove a bearing from a shaft, do not strike the hammer directly against the shaft. Instead, use a brass or aluminum rod between the hammer and shaft **(Figure 44)** and make sure to support both bearing races with wooden blocks as shown.

4. The ideal method of bearing removal is with a hydraulic press. Note the following when using a press:

a. Always support the inner and outer bearing races with a suitable size wooden or aluminum spacer **(Figure 45)**. If only the outer race is supported, pressure applied against the balls and/or the inner race will damage them.

b. Always make sure the press arm **(Figure 45)** aligns with the center of the shaft. If the arm is not centered, it may damage the bearing and/or shaft.

c. The moment the shaft is free of the bearing, it will drop to the floor. Secure or hold the shaft to prevent it from falling.

d. When removing bearings from a housing, support the housing with 4 × 4 in. wooden blocks to prevent damage to gasket surfaces.

5. Use a blind bearing puller to remove bearings installed in blind holes **(Figure 46)**.

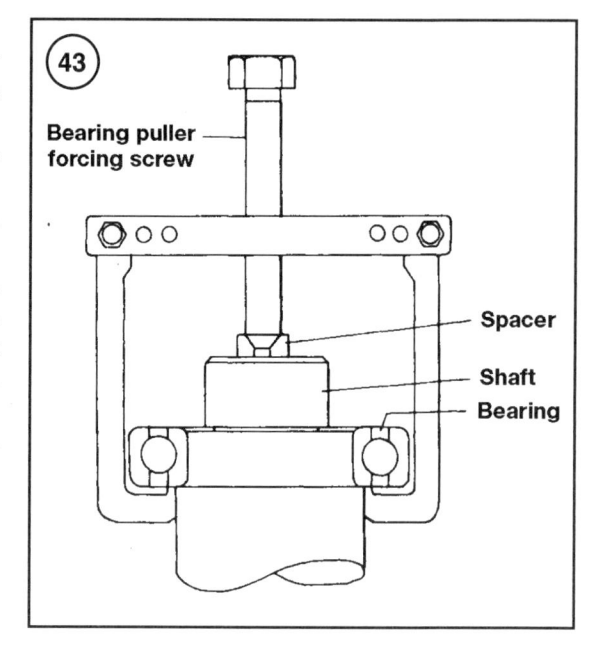

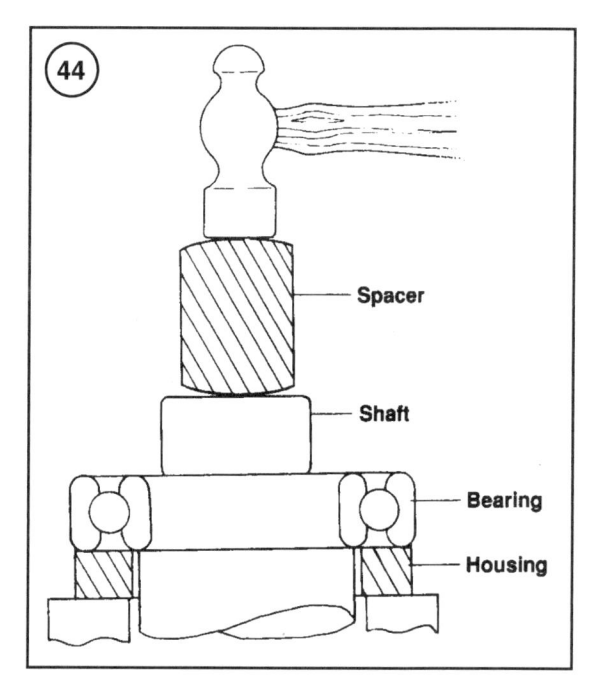

Installation

1. When installing a bearing in a housing, apply pressure to the *outer* bearing race **(Figure 47)**. When installing a bearing on a shaft, apply pressure to the *inner* bearing race **(Figure 48)**.

2. When installing a bearing as described in Step 1, a driver is required. Never strike the bearing directly with a hammer or the bearing will be damaged. When installing a bearing, use a piece of pipe or a driver with a diameter that matches the bearing race. **Figure 49** shows the correct way to use a driver and hammer to install a bearing on a shaft.

3. Step 1 describes how to install a bearing in a housing or over a shaft. However, when installing a bearing over a shaft and into the housing at the same time, a tight fit will be required for both outer and inner bearing races. In this situation, install a spacer underneath the driver tool so pressure is applied evenly across both races. Refer to **Figure 50**. If the outer race is not supported, the balls push against the outer bearing race and damage it.

Interference fit

1. Follow this procedure when installing a bearing over a shaft. When a tight fit is required, the bearing inside diameter will be smaller than the shaft. In this

GENERAL INFORMATION

45 Press ram / Shaft / Bearing / Spacer

46 BLIND BEARING REMOVAL

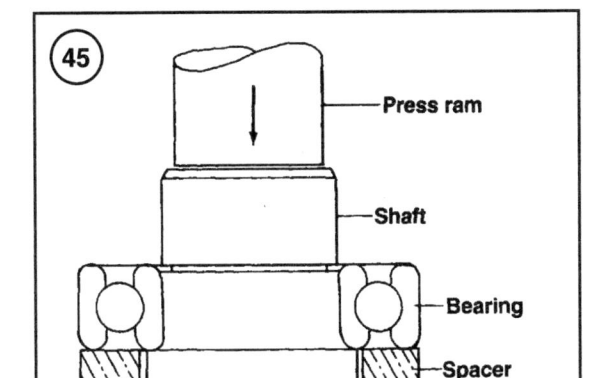

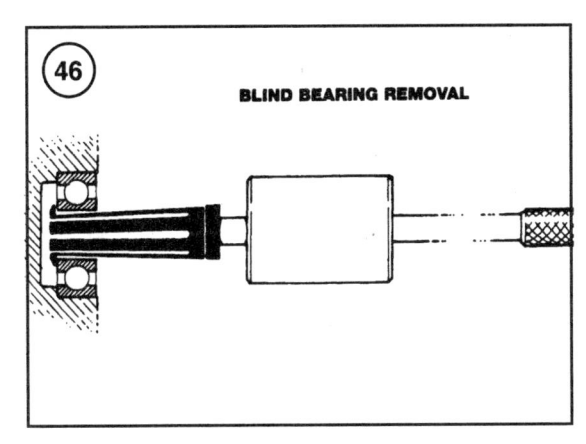

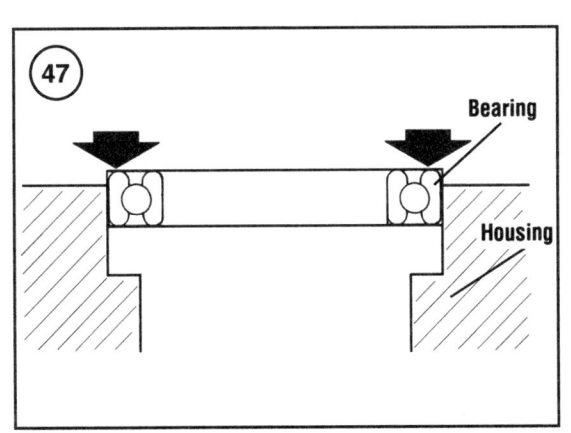

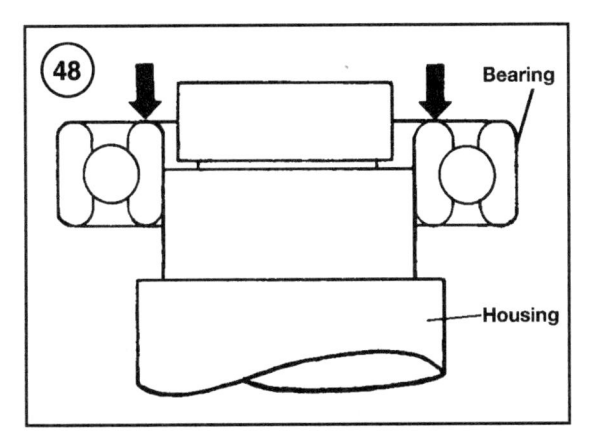

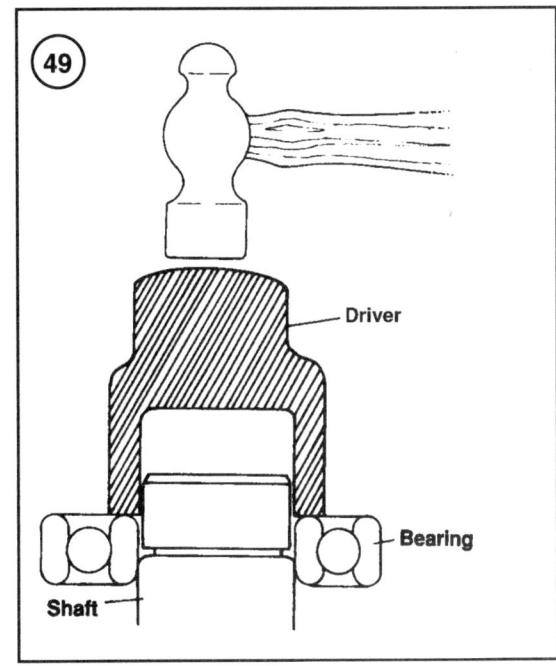

47 Bearing / Housing

48 Bearing / Housing

49 Driver / Bearing / Shaft

case, driving the bearing on the shaft using normal methods may cause bearing damage. Instead, heat the bearing before installation. Note the following:

a. Secure the shaft so it is ready for bearing installation.

b. Clean all residues from the bearing surface of the shaft. Remove burrs with a file.

c. Fill a suitable pot or beaker with clean mineral oil. Place a thermometer rated above 120° C (248° F) in the oil. Support the thermometer so it does not rest on the bottom or side of the pot.

d. Remove the bearing from its wrapper and secure it with a piece of heavy wire bent to hold it in the pot. Hang the bearing in the pot so it does not touch the bottom or sides of the pot.

e. Turn the heat on and monitor the thermometer. When the oil temperature rises to approximately 120° C (248° F), remove the bearing from the pot and quickly install it. If necessary, place a socket on the inner bearing race and tap the bearing into place. As the bearing chills, it tightens on the shaft, so installation must be done quickly. Make sure the bearing is installed completely.

2. Follow this step when removing and installing a bearing in a housing. Bearings are generally installed in a housing with a slight interference fit. Driving the bearing into the housing using normal methods may damage the housing or cause bearing damage. Instead, heat the housing before removing and installing the bearing. Note the following:

a. Before heating the housing in this procedure, wash the housing thoroughly with detergent and water. Rinse and rewash the housing as required to remove all oil and chemicals.

b. Heat the housing to approximately 100° C (212° F) with a heat gun or on a hot plate. Monitor temperature with an infrared thermometer, heat sticks or place tiny drops of water on the housing; if they sizzle and evaporate immediately, the temperature is correct. Heat only one housing at a time.

c. If a hot plate is used, remove the housing and place it on wooden blocks.

d. Hold the housing with the bearing side down and tap the bearing out with a suitable size socket and extension. Repeat for all bearings in the housing. If there is no access behind the bearing, use a blind bearing puller to remove the bearing(s) (**Figure 46**).

e. Before heating the bearing housing, place the new bearing in a freezer, if possible. Chilling a bearing slightly reduces its outside diameter while the heated bearing housing assembly is slightly larger due to heat expansion. This makes bearing installation easier.

f. Reheat the housing and install the new bearing(s). Install the bearings by hand, if possible. If necessary, lightly tap the bearing(s) into the housing with a socket placed on the outer bearing race (**Figure 47**). Do not install bearings by driving on the inner-bearing race. Install the bearing(s) until it seats completely.

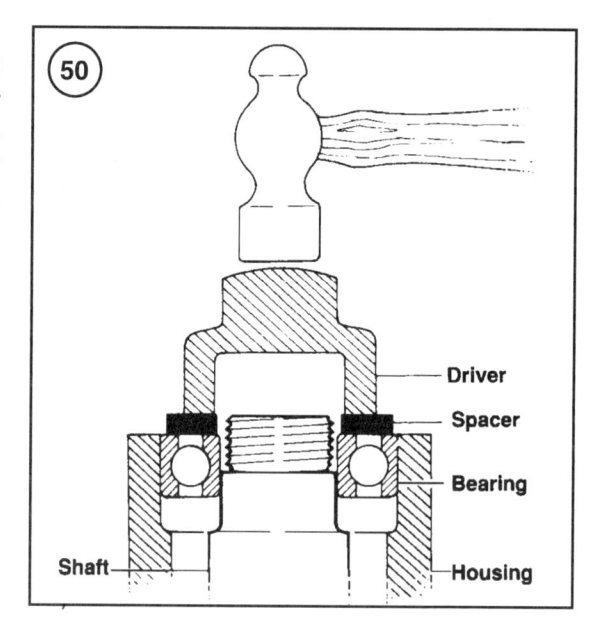

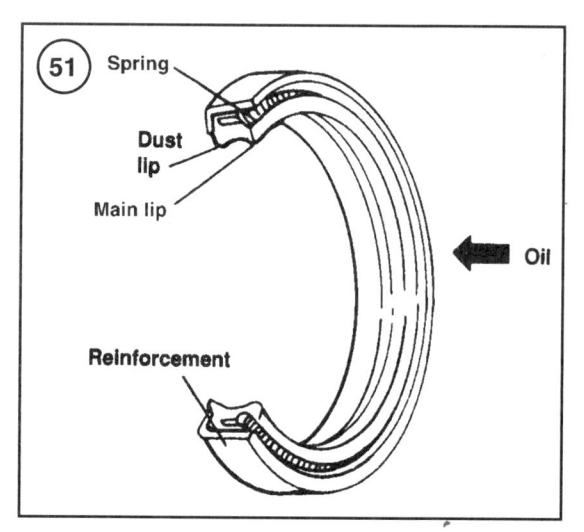

Seal Replacement

Seals (**Figure 51**) are used to contain oil, water, grease or combustion gases in a housing or shaft. Improper removal of a seal can damage the housing or shaft. Improper installation of the seal can damage the seal.

1. Prying is generally the easiest and most effective method of removing a seal from the housing. However, always place a rag under the pry tool (**Figure 52**) to prevent damage to the housing.
2. Before installing a typical rubber seal, pack waterproof grease in the seal lips.
3. In most cases, install seals with the manufacturer's numbers or marks face out.
4. Install seals either by hand or with tools. Center the seal in its bore and attempt to install it by hand. If necessary, install the seal with a socket or bearing driver placed on the outside of the seal as shown in **Figure 53**. Drive the seal squarely into the housing until it is flush with its mounting bore. Never install a seal by hitting against the top of the seal with a hammer.

STORAGE

Several months of non-use can cause a general deterioration of the motorcycle. This is especially true in areas of extreme temperature variations. This deterioration can be minimized with careful preparation for storage. A properly stored motorcycle is much easier to return to service.

Storage Area Selection

When selecting a storage area, consider the following:

1. The storage area must be dry. A heated area is best, but not necessary. It should be insulated to minimize extreme temperature variations.
2. If the building has large window areas, mask them to keep sunlight off the motorcycle.
3. Avoid storage areas close to saltwater.
4. Consider the area's risk of fire, theft or vandalism. Check with your insurer regarding motorcycle coverage while in storage.

GENERAL INFORMATION

riding time since the last service. Fill the engine with the recommended type and quantity of oil.

3. Fill the fuel tank completely.

4. Remove one spark plug from each cylinder head. Ground the spark plug caps to the engine. Refer to *Ignition Ground Tool* in this chapter. Pour a teaspoon (5 ml) of engine oil into each cylinder. Place a rag over the openings and crank the engine to distribute the oil. Reinstall the spark plugs.

5. Remove the battery. Store it in a cool, dry location. Charge the battery once a month. Refer to *Battery* in Chapter Ten for service.

6. Cover the exhaust and intake openings.

7. Apply a protective substance to the plastic and rubber components, including the tires. Make sure to follow the manufacturer's instructions for each type of product being used.

8. Rotate the tires periodically to prevent a flat spot from developing and damaging the tire.

9. Cover the motorcycle with old bed sheets or something similar. Do not cover it with any plastic material that will trap moisture.

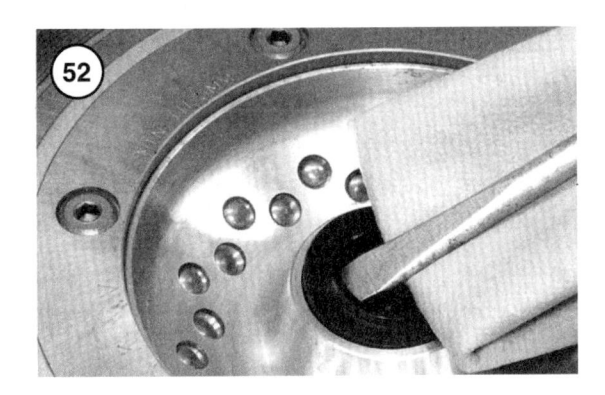

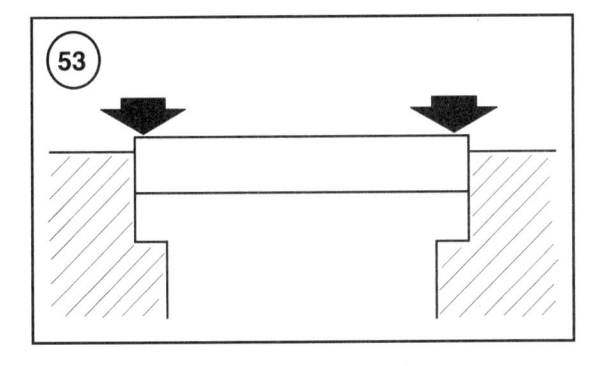

Preparing the Motorcycle for Storage

The amount of preparation a motorcycle should undergo before storage depends on the expected length of non-use, storage area conditions and personal preference. Consider the following list the minimum requirement:

1. Wash the motorcycle thoroughly. Make sure all dirt, mud and road debris are removed.
2. Start the engine and allow it to reach operating temperature. Drain the engine oil regardless of the

Returning the Motorcycle to Service

The amount of service required when returning a motorcycle to service after storage depends on the length of non-use and storage conditions. In addition to performing the reverse of the above procedure, make sure the brakes, clutch, throttle and engine stop switch all work properly before operating the motorcycle. Refer to Chapter Three and evaluate the service intervals to determine which areas require additional service.

Table 1 GENERAL MOTORCYCLE DIMENSIONS

	mm	in.
Footpeg height		
Aero	277	10.9
Spirit		
2007-2009	283	11.1
2010-2013	277	10.9
Phantom	277	10.9
Ground clearance	130	5.1
Overall height		
Aero	1125	44.3
Spirit		
2007-2009	1130	44.5
2010-2013	1125	44.3
Phantom	1090	42.9
Overall length		
Aero	2510	98.8
Spirit	2430	95.7
Phantom	2395	94.3
Overall width		
Aero	920	36.2
Spirit	835	32.9

Table 1 GENERAL MOTORCYCLE DIMENSIONS (continued)

Phantom	825	32.5
Seat height		
Aero	660	26.0
Spirit	655	25.8
Phantom	655	25.8
Wheelbase		
Aero	1640	64.6
Spirit	1655	65.2
Phantom	1640	64.6

Table 2 MOTOTRCYCLE WEIGHT SPECIFICATIONS

	kg	lb.
Curb weight		
Aero		
2004-2007		
49-state and Canada	252	556
California	253	558
2008-2009		
49-state and Canada	251	553
California	254	560
2011-2013		
Non-ABS	257	567
ABS	262	578
Spirit		
2007-2009		
49-state and Canada	243	536
California	246	542
2010-2013		
Non-ABS	246	542
ABS	251	553
Phantom		
U.S. models	250	551
Canada	249	549
Maximum weight capacity		
Aero		
2004-2009		
U.S. models	182	401
Canada	186	410
2011-2013	194	428
Spirit		
2007-2009		
U.S. models	180	397
Canada	184	406
2010-2013	184	406
Phantom		
U.S. models	182	401
Canada	186	410

Table 3 CONVERSION FORMULAS

Multiply:	By:	To get the equivalent of:
Length		
Inches	25.4	Millimeter
Inches	2.54	Centimeter
Miles	1.609	Kilometer
Feet	0.3048	Meter
Millimeter	0.03937	Inches
Centimeter	0.3937	Inches
Kilometer	0.6214	Mile
Meter	3.281	Feet

GENERAL INFORMATION

Table 3 CONVERSION FORMULAS (continued)

Multiply:	By:	To get the equivalent of:
Fluid volume		
U.S. quarts	0.9463	Liters
U.S. gallons	3.785	Liters
U.S. ounces	29.573529	Milliliters
Liters	0.2641721	U.S. gallons
Liters	1.0566882	U.S. quarts
Liters	33.814023	U.S. ounces
Milliliters	0.033814	U.S. ounces
Milliliters	1.0	Cubic centimeters
Milliliters	0.001	Liters
Pressure		
Pounds per square inch	0.070307	Kilograms per square centimeter
Kilograms per square centimeter	14.223343	Pounds per square inch
Kilopascals	0.1450	Pounds per square inch
Pounds per square inch	6.895	Kilopascals
Speed		
Miles per hour	1.609344	Kilometers per hour
Kilometers per hour	0.6213712	Miles per hour
Temperature		
Fahrenheit	(°F − 32) × 0.556	Centigrade
Centigrade	(°C × 1.8) + 32	Fahrenheit
Torque		
Foot-pounds	1.3558	Newton-meters
Foot-pounds	0.138255	Meters-kilograms
Inch-pounds	0.11299	Newton-meters
Newton-meters	0.7375622	Foot-pounds
Newton-meters	8.8507	Inch-pounds
Meters-kilograms	7.2330139	Foot-pounds
Volume		
Cubic inches	16.387064	Cubic centimeters
Cubic centimeters	0.0610237	Cubic inches
Weight		
Ounces	28.3495	Grams
Pounds	0.4535924	Kilograms
Grams	0.035274	Ounces
Kilograms	2.2046224	Pounds

Table 9 TECHNICAL ABBREVIATIONS

ABDC	After bottom dead center
ABS	Anti-lock brake system
API	American Petroleum Institute
ATDC	After top dead center
BBDC	Before bottom dead center
BDC	Bottom dead center
BTDC	Before top dead center
BARO	Barometric pressure sensor
C	Celsius (centigrade)
cc	Cubic centimeters
CDI	Capacitor discharge ignition
cid	Cubic inch displacement
CKP sensor	Crankshaft position sensor
cu. in.	Cubic inches
DLC	Data link connector
DTC	Diagnostic trouble code
ECM	Engine control module
ECT sensor	Engine coolant temperature sensor
EVAP	Evaporative emission
F	Fahrenheit
ft.	Feet
ft.-lb.	Foot-pounds

Table 9 TECHNICAL ABBREVIATIONS (continued)

gal.	Gallons
H/A	High altitude
Hp	Horsepower
ICM	Ignition control module
IACV	Idle air control valve
IAT sensor	Intake air temperature sensor
in.	Inches
in.-lb.	inch-pounds
I.D.	Inside diameter
JIS	Japanese Industrial Standard
k	x 1000
kg	Kilograms
kgm	Kilogram meters
km	kilometer
kPa	Kilopascals
L	Liter
LBS	Linked braking system
m	meter
MAP sensor	Manifold absolute pressure sensor
MAG	Magneto
MIL	Malfunction indicator lamp
ml	Milliliter
mm	millimeter
N.m	Newton-meters
O.D.	Outside diameter
O.S.	Oversize
oz.	Ounces
PAIR	Pulse secondary air injection system
PCV	Proportional control valve
PON	Pump octane number
PGM-FI	Programmed fuel injection
psi	Pounds per square inch
pt.	Pint
qt.	Quart
RON	Research octane number
RPM	Revolutions per minute
RTV	Room temperature vulcanization
SCS connector	Service check short connector
TP sensor	Throttle position sensor
VS sensor	Vehicle speed sensor
wt.	Weight

Table 5 METRIC TAP AND DRILL SIZES

Metric size	Drill equivalent	Decimal fraction	Nearest fraction
3 × 0.50	No. 39	0.0995	3/32
3 × 0.60	3/32	0.0937	3/32
4 × 0.70	No. 30	0.1285	1/8
4 × 0.75	1/8	0.125	1/8
5 × 0.80	No. 19	0.166	11/64
5 × 0.90	No. 20	0.161	5/32
6 × 1.00	No. 9	0.196	13/64
7 × 1.00	16/64	0.234	15/64
8 × 1.00	J	0.277	9/32
8 × 1.25	17/64	0.265	17/64
9 × 1.00	5/16	0.3125	5/16
9 × 1.25	5/16	0.3125	5/16
10 × 1.25	11/32	0.3437	11/32
10 × 1.50	R	0.339	11/32
11 × 1.50	3/8	0.375	3/8
12 × 1.50	13/32	0.406	13/32
12 × 1.75	13/32	0.406	13/32

GENERAL INFORMATION

Table 6 METRIC, INCH AND FRACTIONAL EQUIVALENTS

mm	in.	Nearest fraction	mm	in.	Nearest fraction
1	0.0394	1/32	26	1.0236	1 1/32
2	0.0787	3/32	27	1.0630	1 1/16
3	0.1181	1/8	28	1.1024	1 3/32
4	0.1575	5/32	29	1.1417	1 5/32
5	0.1969	3/16	30	1.1811	1 3/16
6	0.2362	1/4	31	1.2205	1 7/32
7	0.2756	9/32	32	1.2598	1 1/4
8	0.3150	5/16	33	1.2992	1 5/16
9	0.3543	11/32	34	1.3386	1 11/32
10	0.3937	13/32	35	1.3780	1 3/8
11	0.4331	7/16	36	1.4173	1 13/32
12	0.4724	15/32	37	1.4567	1 15/32
13	0.5118	1/2	38	1.4961	1 1/2
14	0.5512	9/16	39	1.5354	1 17/32
15	0.5906	19/32	40	1.5748	1 9/16
16	0.6299	5/8	41	1.6142	1 5/8
17	0.6693	21/32	42	1.6535	1 21/32
18	0.7087	23/32	43	1.6929	1 11/16
19	0.7480	3/4	44	1.7323	1 23/32
20	0.7874	25/32	45	1.7717	1 25/32
21	0.8268	13/16	46	1.8110	1 13/16
22	0.8661	7/8	47	1.8504	1 27/32
23	0.9055	29/32	48	1.8898	1 7/8
24	0.9449	15/16	49	1.9291	1 15/16
25	0.9843	31/32	50	1.9685	1 31/32

Table 7 GENERAL TORQUE RECOMMENDATIONS*

Fastener size or type	N•m	in.-lb.	ft.-lb.
5 mm screw	4	35	–
5 mm bolt and nut	5	44	–
6 mm screw	9	80	–
6 mm bolt and nut	10	89	–
6 mm flange bolt (8 mm head, small flange)	9	80	–
6 mm flange bolt (10 mm head) and nut	12	106	–
8 mm bolt and nut	22	–	16
8 mm flange bolt and nut	27	–	20
10 mm bolt and nut	35	–	26
10 mm flange bolt and nut	40	–	30
12 mm bolt and nut	55	–	40

*General torque recommendations are for fasteners without a specification. Refer to the torque specification table(s) at the end of respective chapter(s) for specific applications.

NOTES

CHAPTER TWO

TROUBLESHOOTING

TROUBLESHOOTING

The troubleshooting procedures described in this chapter provide typical symptoms and logical methods for isolating the cause(s). There may be several ways to solve a problem, but only a systematic approach will be successful in avoiding wasted time and possibly unnecessary parts replacement. Gather as much information as possible to aid in diagnosis. Never assume anything and do not overlook the obvious. Make sure the engine stop switch is in the run position and there is fuel in the tank.

An engine needs three basics to run properly: correct air/fuel mixture, compression and a spark at the correct time. If one of these is missing, the engine will not run.

Learning to recognize symptoms makes troubleshooting easier. In most cases, expensive and complicated test equipment is not needed to determine whether repairs can be performed at home. On the other hand, be realistic and do not start procedures that are beyond your experience and the equipment available. If the motorcycle requires the attention of a professional, describe symptoms and conditions accurately and fully. The more information a technician has available, the easier it is to diagnose the problem.

STARTING THE ENGINE

The following sections describe the recommended starting procedures.

Starting System Operation

1. A sidestand ignition cut-off system is used on all models. The position of the sidestand can affect engine starting. Note the following:
   a. The engine cannot start when the sidestand is down, the transmission is in gear and the clutch lever is released.
   b. The engine can start when the sidestand is down and the transmission is in neutral.
   c. The engine can start when the sidestand is down, the transmission is in gear with the clutch lever pulled in.
   d. If the engine is started with the transmission in neutral and the sidestand down, it will turn off if the transmission is shifted into gear and the clutch is released before the sidestand is raised.
2. On fuel injected models, a bank angle sensor ignition cut-off system is used. This system turns the engine and fuel pump off if the motorcycle is dropped on its side. If this happens, the ignition switch must

be turned to its off position and then turned back to its on position. The engine will not start until these steps are performed.

3. Before starting the engine, shift the transmission into neutral and confirm that the engine stop switch is in its run position (A, **Figure 1**).

> *NOTE*
> *The indicators described here are part of a lamp check system that turns on when the ignition switch is turned on to test indicator operation. If an indicator does not turn on as described. Test the appropriate indicator circuit (Chapter Ten).*

> *NOTE*
> *When the ignition switch is turned on, the coolant temperature indicator should not turn on. If it does, the engine is overheating. Refer to **Engine Overheating** (this chapter).*

4A. On carbureted models, turn the ignition switch on and confirm the following:
  a. The neutral indicator light is on (when transmission is in neutral).
  b. The low oil pressure warning light is on. The warning light should go off a few seconds after the engine starts. If the light stays on, turn the engine off and check the oil level (Chapter Three).

4B. On fuel injected models, turn the ignition switch on and confirm the following:
  a. The neutral indicator light is on (when transmission is in neutral).
  b. The low oil pressure warning light is on. The warning light should go off a few seconds after the engine starts. If the light stays on, turn the engine off and check the oil level (Chapter Three).
  c. The malfunction indicator lamp (MIL) illuminates for a few seconds and then turns off (**Figure 2**). If the indicator stays on, or comes on when the motorcycle is being operated, there is a problem in the programmed fuel injection (PGM-FI) system. Refer to Chapter Nine to retrieve diagnostic trouble codes (DTC) and troubleshoot the system.
  d. The fuel reserve indicator should light for a few seconds and then turn off. If the light remains on, there is approximately 3.3 L (0.87 gal.) or less of fuel remaining in the tank.

5. On models with ABS, the ABS indicator turns on when the ignition switch is turned on and remains on until the motorcycle speed reaches 10 kilometers per hour (6 mph). Refer to *ABS Indicator Light* in *Brake System* in this chapter for additional information.

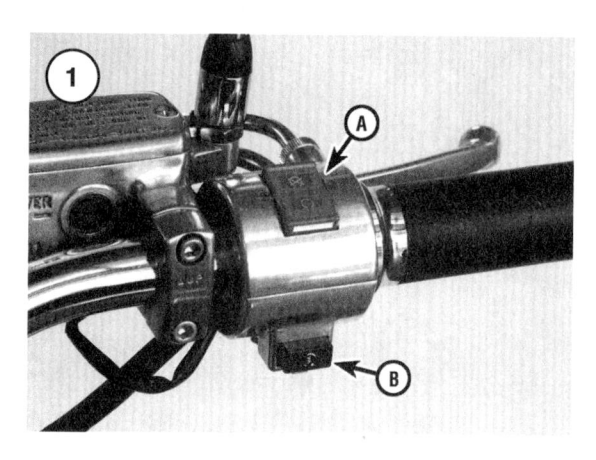

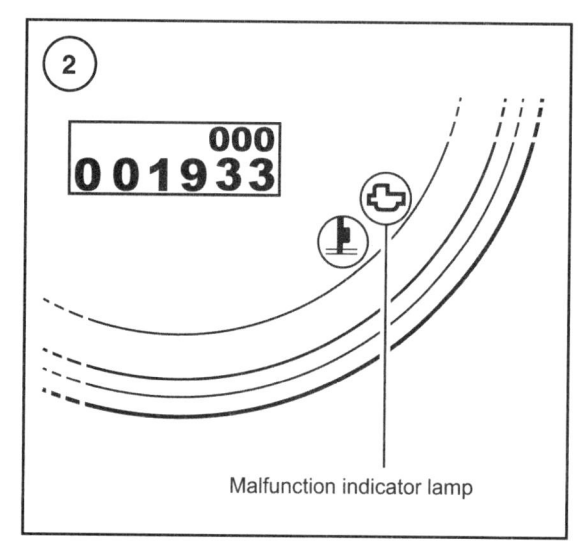

6. The engine is now ready to start. Refer to *Starting Procedure* in this section.

Starting Procedure
(Carbureted Models)

> *NOTE*
> *Do not operate the starter for more than five seconds at a time. Wait approximately 10 seconds between starting attempts.*

Engine cold with air temperature between 10-35° C (50-95° F)

1. Review *Starting System Operation* in this section.
2. Place the engine stop switch (A, **Figure 1**) in the run position.
3. Turn the fuel valve on (A, **Figure 3**, typical).
4. Turn the ignition switch on.

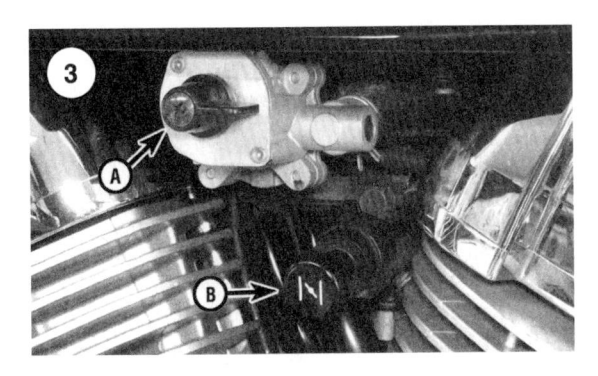

TROUBLESHOOTING

5. Pull the choke lever (B, **Figure 3**) to the fully on position.

> *NOTE*
> *When the engine is started with the throttle open and the choke on, a lean mixture results and causes hard starting.*

6. Operate the starter button (B, **Figure 1**) and start the engine. Do not open the throttle when pressing the starting button.
7. With the engine running, operate the choke lever as required to keep the engine idling.
8. After approximately 15 seconds, push the choke lever (B, **Figure 3**) to the fully off position. If the idle is rough, open the throttle lightly until the engine warms up.

Cold engine with air temperature of 10° C (50°F) or lower

1. Review *Starting System Operation* (this section).
2. Place the engine stop switch (A, **Figure 1**) in the run position.
3. Turn the fuel valve on (A, **Figure 3**).
4. Turn the ignition switch on.
5. Pull the choke lever (B, **Figure 3**) to the fully on position.
6. Operate the starter button (B, **Figure 1**) and start the engine. Do not open the throttle when pressing the starting button.
7. Once the engine is running, open the throttle slightly to help warm the engine. Continue warming the engine until the choke can be turned off and the engine responds to the throttle cleanly.

Warm engine and/or high air temperature 35°C (95° F) or higher

1. Review *Starting System Operation* in this section.
2. Place the engine stop switch (A, **Figure 1**) in the run position.
3. Turn the fuel valve on (A, **Figure 3**).
4. Turn the ignition switch on.

5. Open the throttle slightly (1/8-1/4 turn) and depress the starter button (B, **Figure 1**). Do not use the choke.

Engine flooded

If the engine does not start after a few attempts, it may be flooded. If a gasoline smell is present after attempting to start the engine, and the engine did not start, the engine is probably flooded. To start a flooded engine, perform the following:
1. Review *Starting System Operation* in this section.
2. Place the engine stop switch (A, **Figure 1**) in the run position.
3. Turn the fuel valve on (A, **Figure 3**).
4. Turn the ignition switch on.
5. Push the choke (B, **Figure 3**) off.

> *NOTE*
> *Do not operate the starter motor for more than five seconds at a time. Wait approximately 10 seconds between starting attempts.*

6. Open the throttle completely and depress the starter button (B, **Figure 1**) for five seconds. Note the following:
   a. If the engine starts but idles roughly, vary the throttle position as required until the engine idles and responds smoothly.
   b. If the engine does not start, turn the ignition switch off and wait approximately 10 seconds. Then repeat the procedure for starting a warm engine (this section). If the engine still does not start, refer to *Engine Will Not Start* (this chapter).

> *NOTE*
> *Do not operate the starter motor for more than five seconds at a time. Wait approximately 10 seconds between starting attempts.*

Starting Procedure (Fuel Injected Models)

These models are equipped with an automatic choke. No choke lever is used.

Any air temperature

1. Review *Starting System Operation* in this section.
2. Place the engine stop switch (A, **Figure 1**) in the run position.
3. Turn the ignition switch on. If the fuel reserve indicator stays on, there may not be enough fuel in the tank. Refill the tank with fresh fuel.

4. Depress the starter button (B, **Figure 1**) and start the engine. Do *not* open the throttle when pressing the starter button.

NOTE
*To prevent the engine from starting with the throttle in the wide-open position, the electronic control module (ECM) interrupts the fuel supply if the throttle is in this position while the engine is cranking. The only time it would be necessary to open the throttle all the way is when attempting to start a flooded engine. See **Flooded Engine** in this section.*

Flooded engine

If the engine will not start after a few attempts, and there is a strong gasoline smell, it may be flooded. To start the engine when flooded:
1. Turn the engine stop switch to the run position (A, **Figure 1**).
2. Open the throttle fully.
3. Turn the ignition switch on and operate the starter button (B, **Figure 1**) for five seconds. Release the starter button and close the throttle.
4. Follow the normal starting procedure listed under *Any Air Temperature* in this section. Note the following:
   a. If the engine starts but idles roughly, vary the throttle position slightly until the engine idles and responds smoothly.
   b. If the engine does not start, turn the ignition switch off and wait approximately 10 seconds. Then repeat Steps 1-4 again. If the engine still will not start, refer to *Engine Will Not Start* in this chapter.

ENGINE WILL NOT START

Malfunction Indicator Lamp (MIL) (Fuel Injected Models)

If the malfunction indicator lamp (MIL) stays on when the engine is running, there is a problem in the PGM-FI system. Refer to Chapter Ten to retrieve diagnostic trouble codes (DTC) and troubleshoot the system. If the MIL indicator is not on, refer to *Identifying the Problem* (this section) to isolate a problem in the fuel or ignition system, or low engine compression.

Identifying the Problem

NOTE
An accidentally triggered anti-theft device can cut off power to the ignition system or starter, depending on how it is wired. If such a device is installed, check its operation for a short circuit.

If the engine does not start, perform the following steps in order. Because there are so many things that can cause a starting problem, it is important to narrow the possibilities by following a specific troubleshooting procedure. If the engine fails to start after performing these checks, refer to the troubleshooting procedures indicated in the steps. If the engine starts, but idles or runs roughly, refer to *Poor Engine Performance* in this chapter.

Carbureted Models

1. Refer to *Starting the Engine* in this chapter to make sure the starting procedures are correct.
2A. If the starter does not turn over, perform these quick tests to isolate the starter problem:
   a. Check for a blown ignition/starter fuse as described under *Fuses* in Chapter Ten.
   b. Remove the seat (Chapter Seventeen) and check for loose or corroded battery terminals. Clean and/or tighten the cables as required.
   c. Connect a voltmeter across the battery leads as described in Chapter Ten. Turn the ignition switch on and depress the starter button while reading the voltmeter. If the reading drops below 9.5 volts, the battery may have a weak or damaged cell. Recharge the battery (Chapter Ten) and repeat. If the reading is still below 9.5 volts, perform a battery load test as described in Chapter Ten.
2B. If the starter is turning over correctly, continue the procedure.
3. Check that there is a sufficient amount of fuel in the tank to start the engine. Make sure the fuel valve is positioned correctly for the amount of fuel in the tank.
4. If there is sufficient fuel in the fuel tank, remove one of the spark plugs immediately after attempting to start the engine. The plug's insulator should be wet, indicating that fuel is reaching the engine. Note the following:
   a. If the plug tip is dry, fuel is not reaching the engine. Confirm this condition by checking a spark plug from the other cylinder. A faulty fuel flow problem causes this condition. Refer to *Fuel System (Carbureted Models)* in this chapter.
   b. If there is fuel on each spark plug and the engine will not start, the engine may not have adequate

TROUBLESHOOTING

spark. Continue the procedure.

NOTE
Remove the spark plug caps and examine them for the presence of water.

NOTE
Cracked or damaged spark plug caps and cables can cause intermittent problems that are difficult to diagnose. If the engine occasionally misfires or cuts out, use a spray bottle to wet the spark plug cables and caps while the engine is running. Water that enters a damaged cap or cable causes an arc through the insulating material, resulting in an engine misfire.

5. Inspect the spark plug caps and cables for visible signs of arcing or other damage.
6. Make sure each spark plug cable is secure inside the cap. Push the cap back onto the plug and slightly rotate it to clean the electrical connection between the plug and the connector. Repeat for each cap. If the engine does not start, continue the procedure.
7. Perform the *Spark Test* (this section). If there is a strong spark at each plug, continue the procedure. If there is no spark or if the spark is weak, refer to *Ignition System Testing* (Chapter Ten).
8. If the fuel and ignition systems are working correctly, perform a leakdown test (this chapter) and an engine compression test (Chapter Three). If the leakdown test indicates a problem with a cylinder(s) or the compression is low, refer to *Engine, Low Compression* in this chapter.

Fuel injected models

NOTE
*Review the information on the bank angle sensor function in **Starting the Engine** (this chapter).*

1. Refer to *Starting the Engine* in this chapter to make sure the starting procedures are correct.
2A. If the starter does not turn over, perform these quick tests to isolate the starter problem:
   a. Check for a blown starter relay switch/bank angle sensor fuse as described under *Fuses* in Chapter Ten.
   b. Remove the seat (Chapter Seventeen) and check for loose or corroded battery terminals. Clean and/or tighten the cables as required.
   c. Connect a voltmeter across the battery leads as described in Chapter Ten. Turn the ignition switch on and depress the starter button while reading the voltmeter. If the reading drops below 9.5 volts, the battery may have a weak or damaged cell. Recharge the battery (Chapter Ten) and repeat. If the reading is still below 9.5 volts, perform a battery load test as described in Chapter Ten.

2B. If the starter is turning over correctly, continue the procedure.
3. Check that there is a sufficient amount of fuel in the tank to start the engine.
4. If there is sufficient fuel in the fuel tank and the fuel pump runs for a few seconds when the ignition switch is turned on, remove one of the spark plugs immediately after attempting to start the engine. The plug's insulator should be wet, indicating that fuel is reaching the engine. If the plug tip is dry, fuel is not reaching the engine. Confirm this condition by checking a spark plug from the other cylinder. A faulty fuel flow problem causes this condition. Refer to *Fuel Flow Check* (Chapter Nine), while considering the following possible causes:
   a. Clogged fuel filter (installed in the fuel pump).
   b. Clogged fuel tank breather hose.
   c. Clogged fuel feed hose.
   d. Damaged fuel pump or circuit.
   e. Damaged fuel injector(s).
   f. IACV is stuck closed.
5. If the fuel pump does not operate when the ignition switch is turned on, check for the following:
   a. Blown FI fuse.
   b. Damaged bank angle sensor or circuit.
   c. Damaged ECM power/ground circuit.
   d. Damaged engine stop relay or circuit.
   e. Damaged engine stop switch.

NOTE
Remove the spark plug caps and examine them for the presence of water.

NOTE
Cracked or damaged spark plug caps and cables can cause intermittent problems that are difficult to diagnose. If the engine occasionally misfires or cuts out, use a spray bottle to wet the spark plug cables and caps while the engine is running. Water that enters a damaged cap or cable causes an arc through the insulating material, resulting in an engine misfire.

6. Inspect the spark plug caps and cables for visible signs of arcing or other damage.
7. Make sure each spark plug cable is secure inside the cap. Push the cap back onto the plug and slightly rotate it to clean the electrical connection between the plug and the connector. Repeat for each cap. If the engine does not start, continue the procedure.

8. Perform the *Spark Test* (this section). If there is a strong spark at each plug, continue the procedure. If there is no spark or if the spark is weak, refer to *Ignition System Testing* (Chapter Ten).

9. If the fuel and ignition systems are working correctly, perform a leakdown test (this chapter) and an engine compression test (Chapter Three). If the leakdown test indicates a problem with the cylinder(s) or if the compression is low, refer to *Engine, Low Compression* (this chapter).

Spark Test

Perform a spark test to determine if the ignition system is producing adequate spark. This test can be performed by using a second set of spark plugs and grounding them against the engine. If available, a spark tester can also be used. Because the voltage required to jump the spark tester's gap is sufficiently larger than that of a normally gapped spark plug, the test results are more accurate than with a spark plug.

This test should be performed on both a cold and hot engine. If the test results are positive for each test, the ignition system is working correctly.

> **WARNING**
> *Do not perform this test if there are any fuel leaks on the motorcycle.*

1. Support the motorcycle on its sidestand.
2. Disconnect a spark plug cap from each cylinder. Leave the original spark plugs in the cylinder heads. Check for the presence of water in the plug caps.
3. On fuel injected models, disconnect the fuel pump connector as described in *Engine Compression Test* in Chapter Three.

> **WARNING**
> *Do not hold the spark plug or spark tester; a serious electrical shock may result.*

> **WARNING**
> *If the original spark plugs were removed and are being used to perform the spark test, ground them away from the open spark plug holes. Otherwise, the spark firing across the spark plug could ignite the fuel spraying out of the spark plug holes.*

4. Connect a separate spark plug to each of the spark plugs caps and ground them against the engine (**Figure 4**). If a spark tester (Motion Pro part No. 08-122) is being used, ground it the same way (**Figure 5**). Position the spark plugs and spark tester so the electrodes are visible.

5. Turn the ignition switch on and the engine stop switch to run and push the starter button to turn the engine over. A fat blue spark must be evident between the spark plug or spark tester terminals. Repeat the test at all four spark plug caps.

6. If there is a spark at each plug wire, the ignition system is functioning properly. Check for one or more of the following possible malfunctions:
   a. Faulty fuel system component.
   b. Flooded engine.
   c. Engine damage (low compression).

7. If the spark was weak or if there was no spark at one or more plugs, note the following:
   a. If there is no spark at all of the plugs, perform the peak voltage checks as described in *Ignition System Testing* (Chapter Ten).
   b. If there is no spark at one spark plug only, and the plug is okay, there is a problem with the spark plug wire or plug cap. Remove the spark plug cap and reinstall it. Then, repeat the test.
   c. If there is no spark with one ignition group (two spark plugs, same ignition coil), switch the ignition coils and retest. If there is now spark (both spark plugs), the ignition coil is faulty.
   d. If the problem cannot be found, refer to *Ignition System Testing* in Chapter Ten.

TROUBLESHOOTING

Starter Does Not Turn Over

If the engine will not turn over, the battery or starting system is usually at fault. Perform the following steps in order:

1. Refer to *Starting the Engine* in this chapter for proper switch and sidestand operation.
2A. On carbureted models, check the ignition/starter fuse (Chapter Ten).
2B. On fuel injected models, check the fuel injection and the starter /bank angle sensor fuses (Chapter Ten).
3. Check the battery and battery cables (Chapter Ten).
4. Perform the tests in *Starting System Troubleshooting* in Chapter Ten.
5. Check for ignition system failure. Perform the peak voltage tests in *Ignition System Testing* in Chapter Ten.
6. Check for engine damage.

Starter Turns Over Slowly

For the starter to work correctly, the battery must be 75 percent charged and the battery cables must be clean and in good condition. Inspect and test the battery as described in Chapter Ten. If the battery and battery cables are okay, test the starter as described in Chapter Ten.

Starter Turns Over Correctly, but Engine Will Not Start

Perform the *Spark Test* in this chapter to isolate the problem to the fuel or ignition system. If the ignition and fuel systems are working correctly, the engine has low compression. Refer to *Engine, Low Compression* in this chapter.

Starter Turns over Correctly, but Engine Will Not Turn Over

Check for a damaged starter clutch as described in Chapter Ten.

Starter Relay Switch Clicks, But Engine Will Not Turn Over

1. Check for a damaged idle gear or reduction gear assembly (Chapter Ten).
2. Check for engine damage.

POOR ENGINE PERFORMANCE

If the engine runs, but performance is unsatisfactory, refer to the following section(s) that best describes the symptom(s).

Engine Starts But Stalls and is Hard to Restart

Carbureted models

1. Check for proper fuel flow as described in *Fuel System* (Carbureted Models) in this chapter. If the fuel flow is okay, continue with Step 2.

NOTE
If a cold engine starts okay with the choke but cuts out when the choke is closed or if a warm engine will only start when the choke is on, check for a plugged pilot jet as described under **Carburetor** *in Chapter Eight.*

2. Remove a spark plug from each cylinder and inspect them as described in *Spark Plugs* (Chapter Three).
3A. If the spark plugs are okay, continue the procedure.
3B. If there is an excessive amount of fuel on the spark plugs, note the following:
   a. Check for a dirty or contaminated air filter (Chapter Three).
   b. Check the choke operation and adjustment as described in *Choke Cable Inspection and Adjustment* (Chapter Three).
   c. Check the throttle cables to see if the throttle shaft is partially stuck open. Make sure there is some throttle cable free play as described in *Throttle Cables* (Chapter Three).
   d. Remove the air filter housing (Chapter Eight) and check for fuel leaks at the carburetor.
   e. If there is evidence of fuel overflowing from the carburetor or the carburetor was flooded, remove the carburetor and check the float and float valve as described in Chapter Eight.
4. If the spark plugs are okay, the fuel system could still be the problem, check the following:
   a. Incorrect carburetor adjustment.
   b. Leaking or damaged intake boot or intake manifold.
   c. Contaminated or stale fuel.
5. Check the ignition timing as described in Chapter Three and note the following:
   a. If the ignition timing is correct, continue the procedure.
   b. If the ignition timing is incorrect, the ICM

or CKP sensor may be faulty. Perform the *Ignition System Testing* procedure in Chapter Ten.

6. Perform the *Engine Compression Test* in Chapter Three. If the compression reading for both cylinders is okay, repeat the checks in this section. If the compression reading is low for one or both cylinders, check for the following:
 a. Worn piston rings.
 b. Worn piston(s) and cylinder(s).
 c. Stuck or seized valve.
 d. Leaking cylinder head gasket.
 e. Incorrect valve timing.

Fuel injected models

1. Check for proper fuel flow as described in *Fuel Flow Check* in Chapter Nine. If the fuel flow is okay, continue with Step 2.

2. Remove a spark plug from each cylinder and inspect them as described under *Spark Plugs* in Chapter Three. If the spark plugs are okay, continue with Step 3. If there is an excessive amount of fuel on the spark plugs, note the following:
 a. Check for a dirty or contaminated air filter (Chapter Three).
 b. Inspect the IACV as described in *Idle Air Control Valve* (IACV) in Chapter Nine.
 c. Check the throttle cables to see if the throttle shaft is partially stuck open. Make sure there is some throttle cable free play as described under *Throttle Cables* in Chapter Three.
 d. Remove the air filter housing and check for fuel leaks at the throttle body.

3. If the spark plugs are okay, the fuel system could still be the problem. Check the following:
 a. Leaking or damaged intake boot or intake manifold.
 b. Contaminated or stale fuel.
 c. Perform the *Fuel Pressure Test* in Chapter Nine.

4. Check the ignition timing as described in Chapter Three and note the following:
 a. If the ignition timing is correct, continue with Step 5.
 b. If the ignition timing is incorrect, the ECM or CKP sensor may be faulty. Perform the *Ignition System Testing* procedure in Chapter Ten.

5. Perform the *Engine Compression Test* in Chapter Three. If the compression reading for both cylinders is okay, repeat the checks in this section. If the compression reading is low for one or both cylinders, check for the following:
 a. Worn piston rings.
 b. Worn piston(s) and cylinder(s).
 c. Stuck or seized valve.
 d. Leaking cylinder head gasket.
 e. Incorrect valve timing.

6. Damaged MAP sensor or circuit. Perform the tests in *DTC 1-1* and *DTC 1-2* in *DTC Troubleshooting* in Chapter Nine.

Engine Backfires, Cuts Out or Misfires During Acceleration

A backfire occurs when fuel is burned or ignited in the exhaust system.

1. Lean air/fuel mixture.
2. Loose or damaged exhaust pipe-to-cylinder head connection.
3. Leaks in the intake system.
4. Incorrect ignition timing or a damaged ignition system can cause these conditions. Note the following:
 a. Check for a sheared flywheel Woodruff key (Chapter Ten).
 b. Check the ignition timing (Chapter Three).
 c. Perform the *Ignition System Testing* procedure in Chapter Ten to isolate the damaged ignition system component.
5. Check the following engine components:
 a. Broken valve springs.
 b. Stuck or leaking valves.
 c. Worn or damaged camshaft lobes.
 d. Incorrect valve timing due to incorrect camshaft installation or a mechanical failure.

Engine Backfires on Deceleration

If the engine backfires when the throttle is released, check the following:

1. Lean pilot circuit (carbureted models).
2. Damaged air cutoff valve (carbureted models). This valve is mounted on the carburetor.

NOTE
The PAIR system injects fresh air into the exhaust port.

3. Damaged pulse secondary air injection (PAIR) system:
 a. Clogged, damaged or disconnected PAIR system hoses.
 b. Damaged PAIR check valve(s).
 c. Damaged PAIR control solenoid valve.
4. Incorrect ignition timing or a damaged ignition system can cause these conditions. Note the following:
 a. Check for a sheared flywheel Woodruff key (Chapter Ten).
 b. Check the ignition timing (Chapter Three).

TROUBLESHOOTING

c. Perform the *Ignition System Testing* procedure in Chapter Ten to isolate the damaged ignition system component.
5. Check the following engine components:
   a. Broken valve springs.
   b. Stuck or leaking valves.
   c. Worn or damaged camshaft lobes.
   d. Incorrect valve timing due to incorrect camshaft installation or a mechanical failure.

Poor Fuel Mileage

1. Dirty or clogged air filter.
2. Incorrect ignition timing.
3A. On carbureted models, check the following:
   a. Clogged fuel system.
   b. Damaged EVAP control system (California models).
3B. On fuel injected models, check the following:
   a. Clogged fuel feed hose.
   b. Damaged fuel injector.
   c. Damaged EVAP control system (California models).

Engine Will Not Idle or Idles Roughly (Carbureted Models)

1. Clogged air filter element.
2. Incorrect choke adjustment or plugged choke circuit.
3. Partially blocked fuel tank breather hose.
4. Contaminated or stale fuel.
5. Clogged fuel hose.
6. Poor fuel flow.
7. Incorrect idle speed.
8. Incorrect pilot screw adjustment.
9. Incorrect float level.
10. Plugged carburetor pilot circuit.
11. Inoperative or damaged EVAP control system (California models only).
12. Leaking head gasket(s) or vacuum leak.
13. Intake air leak.
14. Incorrect ignition timing due to an ignition component failure.
15. Low engine compression.

Incorrect Engine Idle Speed (Fuel Injected Models)

Idle speed is too low

1. Faulty fuel supply system.
2. IACV stuck closed.
3. Damaged MAP sensor.

4. Damaged ignition system.
5. Restricted air filter.

Idle speed is too high

1. IACV stuck open.
2. Damaged air filter.
3. Intake air leak.
4. Incorrect ignition timing due to an ignition component failure.
5. Engine top end problem.

Low Engine Power

1. Turn the engine off.
2. Support the motorcycle on a workstand with the rear wheel off the ground, and then spin the rear wheel by hand. If the wheel spins freely, continue the procedure. If the wheel does not spin freely, check for the following conditions:
   a. Dragging brakes.

NOTE
After riding the motorcycle, come to a stop on a level surface (in a safe area away from all traffic). Turn the engine off and shift the transmission into neutral. Walk or push the motorcycle forward. If the motorcycle is harder to push than normal, check for dragging brakes.

   b. Damaged final drive gear assembly. Excessive noise from the final gear housing may indicate bearing or gear damage.
3. Test ride the motorcycle and accelerate quickly from first to second gear.
4A. If the engine speed increased according to throttle position, continue the procedure.
4B. If the engine speed did not increase, check for one or more of the following problems:
   a. Slipping clutch.
   b. Warped clutch plates/discs.
   c. Worn clutch plates/discs.
   d. Weak or damaged clutch springs.
5. Test ride the motorcycle and accelerate lightly.
6A. If the engine speed increased according to throttle position, continue the procedure.
6B. If the engine speed did not increase, check for one or more of the following problems:
   a. Clogged air filter.
   b. Restricted fuel flow.
   c. Pinched fuel tank breather hose.

NOTE
A clogged muffler or exhaust system will prevent some of the burned

exhaust gases from exiting the exhaust port at the end of the exhaust stroke. This condition affects the incoming air/fuel mixture on the intake stroke and reduces engine power.

    d. Clogged or damaged muffler(s). Tap the muffler(s) with a rubber mallet and check for loose or broken baffles.

7. Check for retarded ignition timing (Chapter Three). A decrease in power results when the spark plugs fire later than normal.
8. Check for one or more of the following problems:
    a. Low engine compression.
    b. Worn spark plugs.
    c. Fouled spark plug(s).
    d. Incorrect spark plug heat range.
    e. Weak ignition coil(s).
    f. Incorrect ignition timing (defective ICM or ECM).
    g. Incorrect oil level (too high or too low).
    h. Contaminated oil.
    i. Worn or damaged valve train assembly.
    j. Engine overheating. See *Engine Overheating* in this section.
9. If the engine knocks when it is accelerated or when running at high speed, check for one or more of the following possible malfunctions:
    a. Incorrect fuel type.
    b. Lean fuel mixture.

NOTE
Other signs of advanced ignition timing are engine overheating and hard or uneven engine starting.

    c. Advanced ignition timing (defective ICM or ECM).
    d. Excessive carbon buildup in combustion chamber.
    e. Worn pistons and/or cylinder bores.

Poor Low Speed Performance

1. Check for a leaking or damaged intake boot or intake manifold and loose or damaged air filter housing hose clamps. These conditions will cause an air leak.
2. Perform a spark test (this chapter). Note the following:
    a. If the spark is good, continue the procedure.
    b. If the spark is weak, refer to *Ignition System Testing* (Chapter Ten).
3. Check the ignition timing (Chapter Three).

4A. If ignition timing is correct, continue the procedure.
4B. If the timing is incorrect, refer to *Ignition System Testing* (Chapter Ten).
5. Check the fuel system (this chapter).

Poor High Speed Performance

1. Check ignition timing (Chapter Three).
2A. If ignition timing is correct, continue the procedure.
2B. If the timing is incorrect, refer to *Ignition System Testing* (Chapter Ten).
3. Check the fuel system as described in this chapter.
4. Check the valve clearance (Chapter Three). Note the following:
    a. If the valve clearance is correct, continue the procedure.
    b. If the clearance is incorrect, readjust the valves.
5. Incorrect valve timing and worn or damaged valve springs can cause poor high-speed performance.
    a. If the camshafts were timed just prior to the motorcycle experiencing this type of problem, the cam timing may be incorrect.
    b. If the cam timing was not set or changed, and all of the other inspection procedures in this section failed to locate the problem, inspect the camshafts and valve assembly.
6. Check for a plugged or damaged exhaust system.

FUEL SYSTEM (CARBURETED MODELS)

If the starter turns over and there is spark at each spark plug, poor fuel flow may be preventing the correct amount of fuel from being supplied to the carburetor. The following section determines if fuel is flowing from the fuel tank to the carburetor.

NOTE
A vacuum type fuel valve is used. Fuel is supplied to the engine only when the engine is being started or when running. A diaphragm in the fuel valve shuts off fuel flow when the engine is not running.

NOTE
*Refer to **Fuel Tank** (Chapter Eight) to identify and service the fuel tank and fuel valve hoses described in this section.*

NOTE
All models were originally equipped with a filter screen mounted inside the carburetor and a filter screen mounted inside the fuel tank. When working on an unfamiliar motorcycle, check for an external fuel filter installed by a previous owner that may be plugged or damaged.

NOTE
Carbureted engines with low compression will run lean because there is less intake port vacuum to draw fuel into the engine. Check engine compression as described in Chapter Three.

1. Open the fuel fill cap and make sure there is an adequate amount of fuel in the tank. If a large amount of air is sucked into the tank, the fuel tank breather system is plugged. Refer to *Fuel Tank* in Chapter Eight and check the breather hose (49-state models) or No. 1 (California models) hose at the tank fitting for clogging or damage. On California models, if the No. 1 hose is okay, perform the tests under *Evaporative Emission Control System (California Models)* in Chapter Eight.
2. After attempting to start the engine, remove one of the spark plugs (Chapter Three) and check for the presence of fuel on the plug tip. Note the following:

NOTE
If the motorcycle was not used for some time, and was not properly stored, the fuel may have gone stale, where lighter parts of the fuel have evaporated. Depending on the condition of the fuel, a no-start condition can result.

   a. If there is no fuel visible on the plug, or if you are unsure, check for fuel in the carburetor as described in this section.
   b. If fuel is present on the plug tip, and the engine has spark at all of the spark plugs, check for an excessive intake air leak or the possibility of contaminated or stale fuel.
   c. If there is an excessive amount of fuel on the plug, check for a clogged or plugged air filter. Also check for a flooded carburetor, carburetor throttle valves partially stuck open and a stuck or inoperative choke mechanism.
3. To check for fuel in the carburetor float bowl, perform the following:
   a. Try to start the engine, and if it will not start, turn the ignition switch off.
   b. Remove the air filter housing (Chapter Eight).
   c. Drain the carburetor float bowl as described in *Removal* in *Carburetor* in Chapter Eight.
   d. If fuel drained from the float bowl, examine the fuel for water and other contaminants. If there is water in the fuel, drain and flush the fuel tank, then refill with fresh gasoline. If there are contaminants (rust and dirt) in the fuel, the fuel system including the fuel tank and carburetor should be removed and thoroughly cleaned.
   e. If no fuel drained from the carburetor, continue the procedure.
4. Check fuel flow as follows:
   a. Perform *Troubleshooting* in *Fuel Valve* in Chapter Eight.
   b. If the fuel valve is working correctly but fuel is not flowing from the fuel valve, remove the fuel valve and check it and the fuel screen mounted inside the fuel tank for plugging or damage. Refer to Chapter Eight.
   c. Check the fuel hose connected between the fuel tank and carburetor for clogging or other damage.
   d. If there is fuel flow but the engine still will not start, the carburetor may be contaminated and requires cleaning.
5. On California models, if the problem has not been located, perform the tests under *Evaporative Emission Control System (California Models)* in Chapter Eight.
6. Reroute all hoses as required and check for fuel leaks.

FUEL SYSTEM (FUEL INJECTED MODELS)

The following section isolates common fuel system problems under specific complaints. If the MIL is blinking, check the DTC stored in memory as described in Chapter Nine, then perform the troubleshooting procedure described in Chapter Nine or Chapter Ten. If there is no DTC or the MIL is not blinking, perform the diagnostic procedures as described in this section.

1. If the engine cranks but will not start and the fuel pump can be heard when the ignition switch is turned on, perform the *Fuel Flow Check* in Chapter Nine while considering the following problems:
   a. Clogged fuel filter (mounted on fuel pump).
   b. Plugged fuel tank breather hose.
   c. Plugged fuel feed hose.
   d. Damaged fuel pump.
   e. Damaged fuel injector.
   f. IACV stuck closed. Test the IACV and circuit as described under *DTC 29-1: IACV* in *DTC Troubleshooting* in Chapter Nine.
   g. Intake air leak.
   h. Contaminated fuel.
   i. Damaged ignition system.

2. If the engine cranks but will not start and the fuel pump cannot be heard when the ignition switch is turned on, perform the *ECM Circuit Test* under *Engine Control Module (ECM)* in Chapter Nine. If all tests are normal, consider the following:
   a. Blown FI fuse.
   b. Damaged bank angle sensor or circuit.
   c. Damaged ignition switch or circuit.
   d. Damaged engine stop relay.
3. If the engine is hard to start, but starts and stalls or idles roughly, check the following:
   a. Engine idle speed (Chapter Three).
   b. Test the IACV and circuit as described under *DTC 29-1: IACV* in *DTC Troubleshooting* in Chapter Nine.
   c. Perform the *Fuel Pressure Test* and the *Fuel Flow Check* as described in Chapter Nine.
4. If there is noticeable overall poor performance and fuel economy, perform the *Fuel Pressure Test* and the *Fuel Flow Check* as described in Chapter Eight. Also check for the following:
   a. Damaged or leaking fuel injector.
   b. Plugged fuel feed hose.
   c. Damaged ignition system.
   d. Clogged or blocked air filter.
   e. Faulty TPS.
   f. Faulty ECT sensor

ENGINE

Exhaust Smoke

The color of the exhaust can help diagnose engine problems or operating conditions.

Black

Black smoke is an indication of a rich air/fuel mixture where an excessive amount of fuel is being burned in the combustion chamber. Check for a clogged air filter. On carbureted models, also check for a partially flooded or flooded carburetor (Chapter Eight). On fuel injected models, also check for a stuck fuel injector(s).

Blue

Blue smoke indicates the engine is burning oil in the combustion chamber as it leaks past worn valve stem seals and piston rings. Excessive oil consumption is another indicator of an engine that is burning oil. Perform an engine compression test (Chapter Three) to isolate the problem.

White or steam

It is normal to see white smoke or steam from the exhaust after first starting the engine in cold weather. This is actually condensation formed by the engine during combustion. Once the engine heats up to normal operating temperature, the water evaporates and exits the engine through the crankcase vent system. However, if the motorcycle is ridden for short trips or repeatedly started and stopped without reaching operating temperature, water will start to collect in the crankcase. As this water mixes with the oil in the crankcase, sludge is produced. Sludge can eventually cause engine damage as it circulates through the lubrication system and blocks off oil passages.

Large amounts of steam that continue to exit the exhaust after the engine is running at operating temperature may indicate a cracked cylinder head or cylinder block surface. Pressure test the cooling system as described in Chapter Eleven.

Low Compression

Problems with the engine top end will affect engine performance and drivability. When the engine is suspect, perform a leakdown test (this chapter) and take a compression test (Chapter Three). Interpret the results as described in each procedure to troubleshoot the suspect area. A loss of engine compression can occur through the following areas:
1. Valves:
   a. Incorrect valve adjustment.
   b. Incorrect valve timing.
   c. Worn or damaged valve seats (valve and/or cylinder head).
   d. Bent valves.
   e. Weak or broken valve springs.
   f. Valve stuck open.
2. Cylinder head:
   a. Loose spark plug or damaged spark plug hole.
   b. Damaged cylinder head gasket.
   c. Warped or cracked cylinder head.

Overheating (Cooling System)

WARNING
Do not remove the radiator cap or disconnect any coolant hose immediately after or during engine operation. Scalding fluid and steam may be blown out under pressure and cause serious injury.

TROUBLESHOOTING

A coolant temperature indicator is located on the face of the speedometer. If the coolant temperature is above a preset level when the ignition switch is on, the indicator light on the speedometer face illuminates.

During normal operation the radiator fan does not operate constantly. It turns on when the temperature increases to a specified temperature. Problems in the cooling system can cause the engine to overheat. Because the system is not equipped with a temperature gauge, the actual engine temperature cannot be monitored. The coolant temperature indicator coming on may be the first indicator that the engine is overheating. If this happens, park in a safe spot and turn the engine off. Steam coming from the engine or a part in the cooling system indicates a leak. Do not touch the engine or parts of the cooling system until the engine cools down.

NOTE
To check the electrical part of the cooling system, perform the cooling system electrical tests in Chapter Ten.

Determine the cause of the overheating before operating the motorcycle. Consider the following:
1. Low coolant level.
2. Air in cooling system.
3. Clogged radiator, hose or engine coolant passages.
4. Thermostat stuck closed.
5. Worn or damaged radiator cap.
6. Open or short circuit in the cooling system wiring harness.
7. Damaged water pump.
8. Defective ECT sensor.
9. Defective fan motor switch.
10. Damaged temperature indicator circuit.
11. Damaged fan motor.
12. Damaged radiator fan.

Overheating (Engine)

1. Improper spark plug heat range.
2. Low oil level.
3. Oil not circulating properly. Perform the *Engine Oil Pressure Check* (Chapter Three).
4. Valves leaking.
5. Heavy engine carbon deposits in the combustion chamber.
6. Dragging brake(s).
7. Clutch slipping.

Low Engine Temperature

NOTE
To check the electrical part of the cooling system, perform the cooling system electrical tests in Chapter Ten.

1. Thermostat stuck open.
2. Defective ECT sensor.
3. Damaged temperature indicator circuit.
4. Defective fan motor switch.

Preignition

Preignition is the premature burning of fuel and is caused by hot spots in the combustion chambers. Glowing deposits in the combustion chambers, inadequate cooling or an overheated spark plug(s) can all cause preignition. This is first noticed as a power loss but eventually causes damage to the internal parts of the engine because of higher combustion chamber temperatures.

Detonation

Commonly called spark knock or fuel knock, detonation is the violent explosion of fuel in the combustion chamber before the proper time of ignition. Engine damage can result. Use of low octane gasoline is a common cause of detonation.

Even when using a high octane gasoline, detonation can occur. Other causes are over-advanced ignition timing, lean air/fuel mixture at or near full throttle, inadequate engine cooling or the excessive accumulation of carbon deposits in the combustion chamber (cylinder head and piston crowns).

Power Loss

Refer to *Poor Engine Performance* (this chapter).

Noises

Unusual noises are often the first indication of a developing problem. Investigate any new noises as soon as possible. Something that may be a minor problem, if corrected, could prevent the possibility of more extensive damage.

Use a mechanic's stethoscope or a small section of hose held near your ear (not directly on your ear) with the other end close to the source of the noise to isolate the location. Determining the exact cause of a noise can be difficult. If this is the case, consult with a professional mechanic to determine the cause.

Do not disassemble major components until all other possibilities have been eliminated.

Consider the following when troubleshooting engine noises:

1. Knocking or pinging during acceleration is caused by using a lower octane fuel than recommended. It may also be caused by poor fuel. Pinging can also be caused by an incorrect spark plug heat range or carbon buildup in the combustion chamber.
2. Slapping or rattling noises at low speed or during acceleration may be caused by excessive piston-to-cylinder wall clearance (piston slap). Piston slap is easier to detect when the engine is cold and before the pistons have expanded. Once the engine has warmed up, piston expansion reduces piston-to-cylinder clearance and the noise quiets or dissappears.
3. Knocking or rapping while decelerating is usually caused by excessive rod bearing clearance.
4. Persistent knocking and vibration occurring every crankshaft rotation is usually caused by worn rod or main bearing(s). It can also be caused by broken piston rings or damaged piston pins.
5. A rapid on-off squeal may be a compression leak around the cylinder head gasket or spark plug(s).
6. For a valve train noise, check the following:
   a. Excessive valve clearance.
   b. Worn or damaged camshaft.
   c. Worn or damaged valve train components.
   d. Valve sticking in guide.
   e. Broken valve spring.
   f. Low oil pressure.
   g. Clogged cylinder oil hole or oil passage.
7. For rattles, start checking where the sound is coming from. If a rattle is coming from the right side of the engine, check for a broken exhaust pipe flange assembly.

ENGINE LUBRICATION

An improperly operating engine lubrication system will quickly lead to engine seizure. Check the engine oil level and engine oil pressure as described in Chapter Three. Oil pump service is described in Chapter Five.

High Oil Consumption or Excessive Exhaust Smoke

1. Worn valve guides.
2. Worn or damaged piston rings.

Low Oil Pressure

1. Low oil level.
2. Worn or damaged oil pump.
3. Clogged oil filter.
4. Clogged oil strainer (mounted on oil pump [Chapter Five]).
5. Internal oil leak.
6. Incorrect oil type being used.

High Oil Pressure

1. Oil pressure relief valve stuck closed (mounted on oil pump [Chapter Five]).
2. Clogged oil filter.
3. Clogged oil gallery or oil jet. The oil jet is serviced in *Output Gearcase* in Chapter Five.

No Oil Pressure

1. Low oil level.
2. Damaged oil pump.
3. Clogged oil filter.
4. Clogged oil strainer (mounted on oil pump [Chapter Five]).
5. Internal oil leak.
6. Broken oil pump drive chain or sprockets (Figure 6).

Engine Oil Pressure Warning Light Stays On

1. Low oil pressure.
2. No oil pressure.
3. Damaged oil pressure switch.
4. Short circuit in engine oil pressure switch circuit.

Oil Level Too Low

1. Oil level not maintained at the correct level.
2. Worn piston rings.

TROUBLESHOOTING

3. Worn cylinder.
4. Worn valve guides.
5. Worn valve stem seals.
6. Piston rings incorrectly installed during engine overhaul.
7. External oil leaks.

Oil Contamination

1. Worn or damaged piston ring.
2. Oil and filter not changed at specified intervals or when operating conditions demand more frequent changes.
3. Engine contaminated with flooded water.

CYLINDER LEAKDOWN TEST

A cylinder leakdown test can locate engine problems from leaking valves, a blown head gasket or broken, worn or stuck piston rings. This test is performed by applying compressed air to the cylinder and then measuring the leak percentage or pressure loss.

Follow the manufacturer's directions along with the following information.

1. Start and run the engine until it is warm. Turn it off.
2. Remove a spark plug from the front cylinder as described in Chapter Three.
3. Set the No. 1 piston to top dead center (TDC) on its compression stroke as described under *Valve Clearance* in Chapter Three.
4. Thread the 12-mm test adapter with into the spark plug hole. Connect the air compressor hose to the tester (**Figure 7**).

WARNING
The crankshaft may rotate when compressed air is applied to the cylinder. Remove any tools attached to the end of the crankshaft. To prevent the engine from turning over, shift the transmission into top gear and have an assistant apply the rear brake.

5. Apply compressed air to the leakdown tester. Read the leak rate on the gauge. Note the following:

NOTE
If the engine is showing a 100 percent loss, the piston is probably not at TDC its compression stroke. If the timing marks are aligned, turn the crankshaft 360° and realign the timing marks.

  a. For a new or rebuilt engine, a pressure loss of 0 to 5 percent per cylinder is desired. A loss of 6 to 14 percent is acceptable.
  b. Note the difference between the cylinders. On a used engine, a pressure loss of 10 percent or less between cylinders is satisfactory. A pressure loss exceeding 10 percent between cylinders points to an engine in poor condition.

6. With air pressure still applied to the cylinder, listen for air escaping from various areas. If necessary, use a mechanic's stethoscope to pinpoint the source. Check for the following:
  a. Air leaking through the exhaust pipe indicates a leaking exhaust valve.
  b. Air leaking through the carburetor or throttle body indicates a leaking intake valve.
  c. Air leaking through the crankcase breather tube suggests worn piston rings or a worn cylinder bore.
  d. Air leaking into the cooling system. Start by removing the radiator cap during the test. If air is leaking into the radiator, it can usually be heard escaping when the radiator cap is removed. If the radiator cap is left off, the coolant will bubble during the test. When this condition is indicated, check for a damaged cylinder head gasket or cylinder head and cylinder block surfaces.

7. Remove the leakdown tester and repeat the procedure for the rear cylinder.

CLUTCH

Clutch service is covered in Chapter Six.

No Pressure at Clutch Lever

1. Incorrect clutch adjustment.
2. Broken clutch cable.
3. Damaged clutch release mechanism (**Figure 8**).

Clutch Lever Difficult to Pull In

1. Dry or damaged clutch cable.
2. Kinked or stuck clutch cable.
3. Incorrect clutch cable routing.
4. Damaged clutch release mechanism (**Figure 8**).
5. Damaged clutch release plate bearing (installed in the release plate).

Rough Clutch Operation

Worn, grooved or damaged clutch hub and clutch housing slots.

Clutch Slip

If the engine speed increases without an increase in motorcycle speed, the clutch is probably slipping. The main causes of clutch slippage are:
1. No clutch lever free play.
2. Worn clutch springs.
3. Worn clutch plates.
4. Sticking or damaged clutch release mechanism (**Figure 8**).
5. Clutch plates contaminated by engine oil additive.
6. Low engine oil level.

Clutch Drag

If the clutch will not disengage or if the motorcycle creeps with the transmission in gear and the clutch disengaged, the clutch is dragging. Some main causes of clutch drag are:
1. Excessive clutch lever free play.
2. Warped clutch plates.
3. Loose clutch housing locknut.
4. Damaged clutch release mechanism (**Figure 8**).
5. Clutch plates grabbing (not sliding) on clutch hub or clutch housing.
6. High oil level.
7. Incorrect oil viscosity.
8. Engine oil additive being used.

Difficult Shifting

Shifting problems caused by the clutch are:
1. Incorrect clutch adjustment.
2. Worn or damaged clutch components.
3. Incorrect clutch operation.

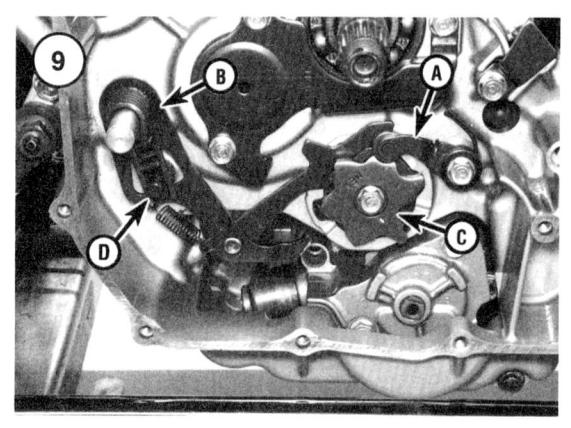

GEARSHIFT LINKAGE

The gearshift linkage assembly connects the shift pedal (external shift mechanism) to the shift drum (internal shift mechanism). Refer to Chapter Six and Chapter Seven to identify the components described in this section.

Transmission Jumps Out of Gear

1. Shift linkage out of adjustment.
2. Damaged stopper arm (A, **Figure 9**).
3. Damaged stopper arm spring.
4. Damaged shift shaft, guide plate or spring assembly (B, **Figure 9**).
5. Worn or damaged shift drum cam (C, **Figure 9**) or shift drum.
6. Bent shift fork shaft(s).
7. Bent or damaged shift fork(s).
8. Worn gear dogs or slots.

Difficult Shifting

1. Incorrect clutch operation.
2. Incorrect oil viscosity.

TROUBLESHOOTING

3. Loose or damaged stopper arm assembly (A, **Figure 9**).
4. Bent shift fork shaft(s).
5. Bent or damaged shift fork(s).
6. Worn gear dogs or slots.
7. Damaged shift drum grooves.
8. Damaged or incorrectly assembled shift shaft assembly (B, **Figure 9**).

Shift Pedal Does Not Return

Shift shaft return spring not centered on pin (D, **Figure 9**), due to broken spring or incorrect assembly.

TRANSMISSION

Transmission symptoms are sometimes difficult to distinguish from clutch symptoms. Before working on the transmission, make sure the clutch and gearshift linkage assembly are not causing the problem. Refer to Chapter Seven for transmission service procedures.

Difficult Shifting

1. Incorrect clutch operation.
2. Bent shift fork(s).
3. Damaged shift fork guide pin(s).
4. Bent shift fork shaft(s).
5. Bent shift shaft.
6. Damaged shift drum grooves.

Jumps Out of Gear

1. Loose or damaged shift shaft stopper arm.
2. Bent or damaged shift fork(s).
3. Bent shift fork shaft(s).
4. Damaged shift drum grooves.
5. Worn gear dogs or slots.
6. Weak or damaged shift shaft return spring.

Incorrect Shift Lever Operation

1. Bent shift pedal or linkage.
2. Stripped shift pedal splines.
3. Damaged shift shaft assembly.

Excessive Gear Noise

1. Worn or damaged transmission bearings.
2. Worn or damaged gears.
3. Excessive gear backlash.

ELECTRICAL TESTING

This section describes electrical troubleshooting and the use of common test equipment.

Never assume anything and do not overlook the obvious, such as a blown fuse or an electrical connector that has separated. Test the simplest and most obvious items first and try to make tests at easily accessible points on the motorcycle. Make sure to troubleshoot systematically and never rule out the possibility of multiple problems.

Refer to the color wiring diagrams at the end of the manual for component and connector identification. Use the wiring diagrams to determine how the circuit should work by tracing the current paths from the power source through the circuit components to ground. Also check any circuits that share the same fuse, ground or switch. If the other circuits work properly and the shared wiring is good, the cause must be in the wiring used only by the suspect circuit. If all related circuits are faulty at the same time, the probable cause is a poor ground connection or a blown fuse(s).

Preliminary Checks and Precautions

Before starting any electrical troubleshooting, perform the following:

1. Inspect the fuse for the suspected circuit, and replace it if blown. Refer to *Fuses* in Chapter Ten.
2. Inspect the battery (Chapter Ten). Make sure it is fully charged and the battery leads are clean and securely attached to the battery terminals.
3. Electrical connectors are often the cause of electrical system problems. Inspect the connectors as follows:
   a. Disconnect each electrical connector in the suspect circuit and make sure there are no bent terminals in the electrical connector. A bent terminal will not connect to its mate, causing an open circuit.
   b. Make sure the terminals are pushed all the way into the connector. If not, carefully push them in with a narrow blade screwdriver or a terminal tool.
   c. Check the wires where they attach to the terminals for damage.
   d. Make sure each terminal is clean and free of corrosion. Clean them, if necessary, and pack the connectors with dielectric grease.

e. Push the connector halves together. Make sure the connectors are fully engaged and locked together.

f. Never pull the wires when disconnecting a connector. Pull only on the connector housing.

4. Never use a self-powered test light on circuits that contain solid-state devices. Sensitive components may be damaged.

Intermittent Problems

Problems that do not occur all the time can be difficult to isolate during testing, for example, a specific problem only occurs when the motorcycle is ridden over rough roads (vibration) or in wet conditions (water penetration). Note the following:

1. Vibration. This is a common problem with loose or damaged electrical connectors.

NOTE
An analog ohmmeter is useful when making this type of test. Slight needle movements are visibly apparent, which indicate a loose connection.

a. Perform a continuity test as described in the appropriate service procedure or under *Continuity Test* in this section.

b. Lightly pull or wiggle the connectors while repeating the test. Do the same when checking the wiring harness and individual components, especially where the wires enter a housing or connector.

c. A change in meter readings indicates a poor connection. Find and repair the problem or replace the part. Check for wires with cracked or broken insulation.

2. Heat. This is a common problem with connectors or joints that have loose or poor connections. As these connections heat up, the connection or joint expands and separates, causing an open circuit. Other heat-related problems occur when a component starts to fail as it heats up.

a. Troubleshoot the problem to isolate the circuit.

CAUTION
A heat gun will quickly raise the temperature of the component being tested. Do not apply heat directly to the solid state devices or use heat in excess of 60° C (140° F) on any electrical component.

b. To check a connector, perform a continuity test as described in the appropriate service procedure or under *Continuity Test* in this section. Then repeat the test while heating the connector with a heat gun. If the meter reading was normal (continuity) when the connector was cold, and then fluctuated or read infinity when heat was applied, the connection is bad.

c. To check a component, allow the engine to cool, and then start and run the engine. Note operational differences when the engine is cold and hot.

d. If the engine will not start, isolate and remove the suspect component. Test it at room temperature and again after heating it with a heat gun. A change in meter readings indicates a temperature problem.

3. Water. When the problem occurs when riding in wet conditions or in areas with high humidity, start and run the engine in a dry area. Then, with the engine running, spray water onto the suspected component/circuit. Water-related problems often stop after the component heats up and dries.

Test Light or Voltmeter

Use a test light to check for voltage in a circuit. Attach one lead to ground and the other lead to various points along the circuit. It does not make a difference which test lead is attached to ground. The bulb lights when voltage is present.

Use a voltmeter in the same manner as the test light to find out if voltage is present in any given circuit. The voltmeter, unlike the test light, also indicates how much voltage is present at each test point.

Voltage test

Unless otherwise specified, make all voltage tests with the electrical connectors still connected. Insert the test leads into the backside of the connector and make sure the test lead touches the electrical terminal within the connector housing. If the test lead only touches the wire insulation, it will cause a false reading.

Always check both sides of the connector because one side may be loose or corroded, thus preventing electrical flow through the connector. This type of test can be performed with a test light or a voltmeter.

1. Attach the voltmeter negative test lead to a confirmed ground location. If possible, use the battery ground connection. Make sure the ground is not insulated.

2. Attach the voltmeter positive test lead to the point to be tested (**Figure 10**).

3. Turn the ignition switch on. If using a test light, the test light will come on if voltage is present. If

TROUBLESHOOTING

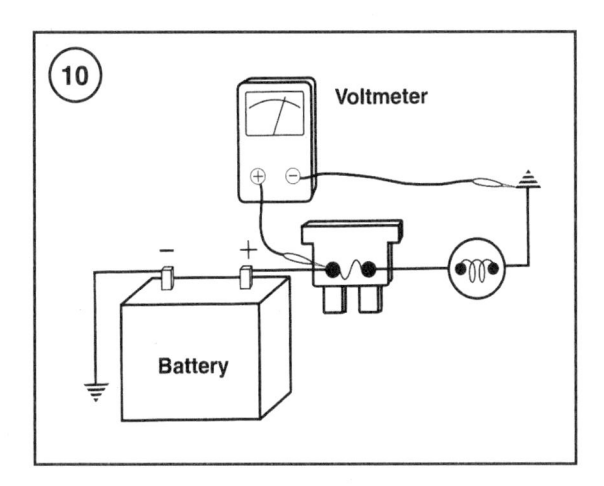

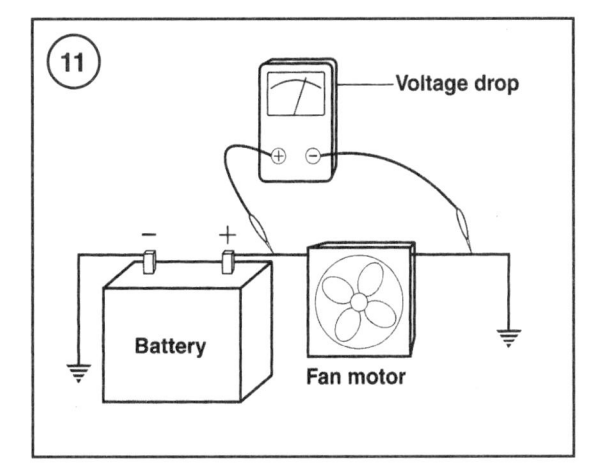

10 Voltmeter / Battery

11 Voltage drop / Battery / Fan motor

using a voltmeter, note the voltage reading. The reading should be within 1 volt of battery voltage. If the voltage is less there is a problem in the circuit.

Voltage drop test

The wires, cables, connectors and switches in the electrical circuit are designed to carry current with low resistance. This ensures current can flow through the circuit with a minimum loss of voltage. Voltage drop indicates where there is resistance in a circuit. A higher-than-normal amount of resistance in a circuit decreases the flow of current and causes the voltage to drop between the source and destination in the circuit.

Since resistance causes voltage to drop, resistance can be measured on an active circuit with a voltmeter. This is a voltage drop test. Basically a voltage drop test determines the voltage at the beginning of a circuit from the voltage at the end of the circuit. If the circuit has no resistance, there will be no voltage drop (the meter will read zero volts). The more resistance the circuit has, the higher the voltmeter reading will be. The chief advantage of the voltmeter drop test over an ohmmeter resistance test is that the circuit is tested while under operation. It is important to remember that a zero reading on a voltage drop test is good, while a reading of battery voltage indicates an open circuit.

To perform a voltage drop:
1. Make sure the battery is fully charged (Chapter Ten).
2. Connect the positive meter test lead to the electrical source (where electricity is coming from). Connect the voltmeter negative test lead to the electrical load (where the electricity is going). Refer to **Figure 11**.
3. Turn the ignition switch on and activate the component(s) in the circuit. When the engine must be turned over (checking the starter circuit for example), disconnect all of the spark plugs caps and ground each one with a grounding tool as described in *Ignition Grounding Tool* in Chapter One. Then operate the starter button to turn the engine over without starting the engine. Limit cranking time to 10 seconds or less.
4. Read the voltage drop (difference in voltage between the source and destination) on the voltmeter. Note the following:
    a. The voltmeter should indicate a voltage drop of less than 0.4 volts. The actual number depends on the amount of current running through the system. If there is a drop of 1 volt or more, there is a problem within the circuit. A voltage drop reading of 12 volts indicates a break in the circuit.
    b. A voltage drop of 1 or more volts indicates that a circuit has excessive resistance.
    c. For example, consider a starting problem where the battery is fully charged but the starter turns over slowly. Voltage drop would be the difference in the voltage at the battery (source) and the voltage at the starter (destination) as the engine is being started (current is flowing through the battery cables). A corroded battery cable would cause a high voltage drop (high resistance) and slow engine cranking.
    d. Common sources of voltage drop are dirty or contaminated connectors, loose connectors and poor ground connections.

Peak voltage testing

Peak voltage tests check the voltage output of the ignition coil and crankshaft position sensor (CKP) at normal cranking speed. These tests make it possible to identify ignition system problems quickly and accurately.

Peak voltage tests require a peak voltage adapter or tester. Refer to *Ignition System Testing* in Chapter Ten.

Testing For a Short with a Voltmeter

A test light may also be used.
1. Remove the blown fuse from the fuse panel.
2. Connect the voltmeter across the fuse terminals in the fuse panel. Turn the ignition switch on and check for battery voltage.
3. With the voltmeter attached to the fuse terminals, wiggle the wiring harness relating to the suspect circuit at approximately 15.2 cm (6 in.) intervals. Start next to the fuse panel and work systematically away from the panel. Note the voltmeter reading while progressing along the harness.
4. If the voltmeter reading changes (test light blinks), there is a short-to-ground at that point in the harness.

Ammeter

Use an ammeter to measure the flow of current (amps) in a circuit **(Figure 12)**. When *connected in series* in a circuit, the ammeter determines if current is flowing through the circuit and if that current flow is excessive because of a short in the circuit. Current flow is often referred to as current draw. Comparing actual current draw in the circuit or component to current draw specification (if specified by the manufacturer) provides useful diagnostic information.

Self-powered Test Light

A self-powered test light can be constructed from a 12-volt light bulb, a pair of test leads and a 12-volt battery. When the test leads are touched together the light bulb should go on.
Use a self-powered test light as follows:
1. Touch the test leads together to make sure the light bulb goes on. If not, correct the problem.
2. Disconnect the motorcycle's battery or remove the fuse(s) that protects the circuit to be tested. Do not connect a self-powered test light to a circuit that has power applied to it.
3. Select two points within the circuit where there should be continuity.
4. Attach one lead of the test light to each point.
5. If there is continuity, the test light bulb will come on.
6. If there is no continuity, the test light bulb will not come on, indicating an open circuit.

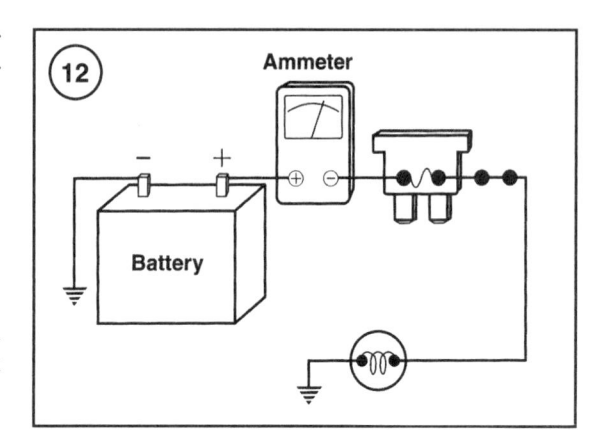

Ohmmeter

CAUTION
To prevent damage to the ohmmeter, never connect it to a circuit that has power applied to it. Always disconnect the battery negative lead before using an ohmmeter.

Use an ohmmeter to measure the resistance (in ohms) to current flow in a circuit or component.

Ohmmeters may be analog type (needle scale) or digital type (LCD or LED readout). Both types of ohmmeters have a switch that allows the user to select different ranges of resistance for accurate readings. The analog ohmmeter also has a set-adjust control which is used to zero or calibrate the meter (digital ohmmeters do not require calibration). Refer to the ohmmeter's instructions to determine the correct scale setting.

Use an ohmmeter by connecting its test leads to the circuit or component to be tested. If an analog meter is used, it must be calibrated by touching the test leads together and turning the set-adjust knob until the meter needle reads zero. When the leads are uncrossed, the needle should move to the other end of the scale, indicating infinite resistance.

During a continuity test, a reading of infinite resistance indicates there is a break in the circuit or component. A reading of zero indicates continuity, that is, there is no measurable resistance in the circuit or component. A measured reading indicates the actual resistance to current flow that is present in that circuit. Even though resistance is present, the circuit has continuity.

Continuity test

Perform a continuity test to determine the integrity of a circuit, wire or component. A circuit has conti-

TROUBLESHOOTING

nuity if it forms a complete circuit; that is if there are no breaks in either the electrical wires or components within the circuit. A circuit with a break in it, on the other hand, has no continuity.

This type of test can be performed with a self-powered test light or an ohmmeter. An ohmmeter gives the best results.
1. Disconnect the negative battery cable or disconnect the test circuit/component from its power source.
2. Attach one test lead (test light or ohmmeter) to one end of the part of the circuit to be tested.
3. Attach the other test lead to the other end of the part or the circuit to be tested.
4. The self-powered test light comes on if there is continuity. An ohmmeter reads 0 or low resistance if there is continuity. A reading of infinite resistance indicates no continuity; the circuit is open.
5. If testing a component, note the resistance and compare this to the specification if available.

Testing for short with an ohmmeter

An analog ohmmeter or one with an audible continuity indicator works best for short testing. A self-powered test light may also be used.
1. Disconnect the negative battery cable.
2. If necessary, remove the blown fuse from the fuse panel.
3. Connect one test lead of the ohmmeter to the load side (battery side) of the fuse terminal in the fuse panel.
4. Connect the other test lead to a confirmed ground location. Make sure the ground is not insulated. If possible, use the battery ground connection.
5. Wiggle the wiring harness relating to the suspect circuit at approximately 15.2 cm (6 in.) intervals. Watch the ohmmeter while progressing along the harness.
6. If the ohmmeter needle moves or the ohmmeter beeps, there is a short-to-ground at that point in the harness.

Jumper Wire

Use a jumper wire to bypass a potential problem and isolate it to a particular point in a circuit. If a faulty circuit works properly with a jumper wire installed, a break exists between the two jumped points in the circuit.

To troubleshoot with a jumper wire, first use the wire to determine if the problem is on the ground side or the load side of a device. Test the ground by connecting the wire between the device and a good ground. If the device comes on, the problem is the connection between the device and ground. If the device does not come on with the jumper wire installed, the device's connection to ground is good, so the problem is between the device and the power source.

To isolate the problem, connect the wire between the battery and the device. If it comes on, the problem is between these two points. Next, connect the wire between the battery and the fuse side of the switch. If the device comes on, the switch is good. By successively moving the wire from one point to another, the problem can be isolated to a particular place in the circuit.

Note the following when using a jumper wire:
1. Make sure the wire gauge (thickness) is the same as that used in the circuit being tested. Smaller gauge wire rapidly overheats and could melt.
2. Make sure the jumper wire has insulated alligator clips. This prevents accidental grounding (sparks) or possible shock. Install an inline fuse/fuse holder in the jumper wire.
3. A jumper wire is a temporary test measure. Do not leave a jumper wire installed as a permanent solution. This creates a fire hazard.
4. Never use a jumper wire across any load (a component or device that is connected and turned on). This would cause a direct short and blow the fuse(s).

OUTPUT GEARCASE

Oil Leaks

1. Damaged oil seal.
2. Loose assembly bolts
3. Damaged housing.

Excessive Output Gearcase Noise

1. Worn or damaged bearings.
2. Worn or damaged gears.
3. Excessive output drive and driven gear backlash.
4. Incorrect shim adjustment.

FINAL DRIVE

Oil Leaks

1. Clogged breather.
2. Oil level too high.
3. Loose or missing case cover mounting bolts.
4. Damaged oil seal(s).

Noise

The final drive operates quietly. Any noise should be investigated and the problem repaired.
1. Low oil level due to a leak.
2. Worn or damaged ring gear and driven flange **(Figure 13)** splines.
3. Worn or damaged driven flange pins.
4. Work or damaged driven flange rubber dampers.
5. Worn or damaged pinion and ring gears.
6. Worn or scored pinion and splines.
7. Excessive backlash between ring and pinion gears.

Excessive Rear Wheel Backlash

With the rear wheel off the ground, apply the rear brake and then try to move the rear wheel back and forth. There should be very little rear wheel backlash. If there is detectable backlash, consider the following possible causes:
1. Worn or damaged ring gear and driven flange **(Figure 13)** splines.
2. Worn or damaged universal joint bearings **(A, Figure 14)**.
3. Worn or damaged drive shaft, universal joint **(B, Figure 14)** or pinion shaft splines.
4. Excessive ring and pinion gear backlash.
5. Excessive play in ring gear bearings.

Rear Wheel Does Not Rotate Freely

1. Damaged drive shaft.
2. Damaged ring and pinion gears.
3. Worn or damaged ring gear and driven flange **(Figure 13)** splines.
4. Worn or damaged universal joint **(Figure 14)**.
5. Brake drag. Refer to *Brake System* in this chapter.

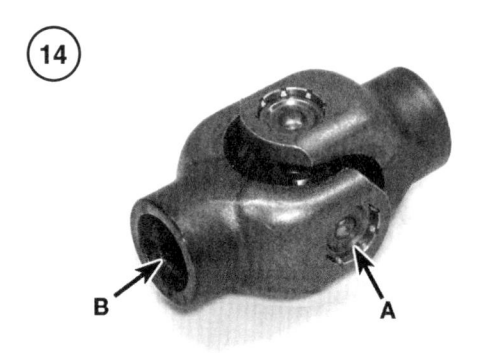

FRONT SUSPENSION AND STEERING

Steering is Sluggish

1. Low tire pressure.
2. Incorrect brake cable, cable or wiring harness routing.
3. Damaged steering bearings.
4. Incorrect steering adjustment (too tight).
5. Dragging brakes.
6. Weak fork springs.

Steers to One Side

1. Bent axle.
2. Bent frame.
3. Worn or damaged wheel bearings.
4. Loose or damaged front fork components.
5. Loose or damaged swing arm pivot bolts and/or bearings.
6. Bent swing arm.
7. Front and rear wheels are not aligned.
8. Front fork legs positioned unevenly in the steering stem.
9. Damaged tire.
10. Unequal fork oil level.

TROUBLESHOOTING

Front Suspension Noise

1. Loose mounting fasteners.
2. Loose or damaged suspension components.
3. Damaged fork spring(s).
4. Worn or damaged fork tube and slider bushings.
5. Low fork oil capacity.
6. Loose or damaged front fender.

Front Wheel Wobble/Vibration

1. Loose front wheel axle.
2. Loose or damaged wheel bearings.
3. Damaged wheel rim.
4. Damaged tire.
5. Flat spot on tire. A flat spot may develop during prolonged storage.
6. Unbalanced tire and wheel assembly.

Hard Suspension
(Front Fork)

1. Excessive tire pressure.
2. Bent fork tube(s).
3. Fork oil level too high.
4. Incorrect fork oil weight.
5. Clogged front fork oil passages.

Hard Suspension
(Rear Shock Absorber)

1. Excessive rear tire pressure.
2. Bent damper rod.
3. Incorrect shock adjustment.
4. Damaged shock absorber bushing(s).
5. Damaged swing arm components.

Soft Suspension
(Front Fork)

1. Low tire pressure.
2. Deteriorated fork oil.
3. Oil level too low.
4. Weak fork springs.
5. Incorrect fork oil weight.

Soft Suspension
(Rear Shock Absorber)

1. Low tire pressure.
2. Incorrect shock adjustment.
3. Weak or damaged shock spring.
4. Shock damper damaged (oil leakage).

BRAKE SYSTEM

WARNING
The brake system is critical to riding performance and safety. Always check the brake operation before riding the motorcycle. Inspect the front and rear brakes frequently and repair any problem immediately.

Disc Brakes

When replacing or refilling the brake fluid, use only DOT 4 brake fluid from a closed container. Refer to Chapter Three and Chapter Fifteen for brake inspection and service.

WARNING
If the brake level in the reservoir drops too low, air can enter the hydraulic system through the master cylinder. Air can also enter the system from loose or damaged hose fittings. Air in the hydraulic system causes a soft or spongy brake lever or pedal action. When it is suspected that air has entered the hydraulic system, flush the brake system and bleed the brakes as described in Chapter Fifteen.

Soft or spongy brake lever or pedal

Quickly operate the front brake lever or rear brake pedal and check to see if the lever/pedal travel distance increases. If the lever/pedal travel does increase while being operated, or feels soft or spongy, there may be air in the brake lines. In this condition, the brake system is not capable of producing sufficient brake force. When an increase in lever/pedal travel is noticed or when the brake feels soft or spongy, check the following possible causes:

1. Air in system.

NOTE
If different handlebars were installed, an extreme bar angle may affect the brake fluid level in the reservoir. Check the fluid level with the handlebar in both left and right lock positions.

2. Low brake fluid level.
3. Worn or damaged brake disc.
4. Contaminated brake fluid.
5. Plugged brake fluid passages.
6. Damaged brake lever or pedal assembly.

NOTE
As the brake pads wear, the brake fluid level in the master cylinder reservoir drops. Whenever adding brake fluid to the reservoirs, visually check the brake pads for wear. If it does not appear that there is an increase in pad wear, check the brake hoses, lines and banjo bolts for leaks.

7. Worn or damaged brake pads.
8. Leak in the brake system.
9. Warped brake disc.

NOTE
A leaking fork seal can allow oil to contaminate the brake pads and disc.

10. Contaminated brake pads and disc.
11. Worn or damaged master cylinder cups and/or cylinder bore.
12. Worn or damaged brake caliper piston seals.
13. Contaminated master cylinder assembly.
14. Contaminated brake caliper assembly.
15. Brake caliper not sliding correctly on fixed shafts.
16. Sticking master cylinder piston assembly.
17. Sticking brake caliper pistons.

Brake drag

When the brakes drag, the brake pads are not capable of moving away from the brake disc when the brake lever or pedal is released. Any of the following causes, if they occur, would prevent correct brake pad movement and cause brake drag.
1. Warped or damaged brake disc.
2. Brake caliper not sliding correctly on fixed shafts (front brake only).
3. Sticking or damaged brake caliper pistons.
4. Contaminated brake pads and disc.
5. Plugged master cylinder port.
6. Contaminated brake fluid and hydraulic passages.
7. Restricted brake hose joint.
8. Loose brake disc mounting bolts.
9. Damaged or misaligned wheel.
10. Incorrect wheel alignment.
11. Incorrectly installed brake caliper.
12. Damaged front wheel.
13. Damaged brake hose or brake line.

Hard brake lever or pedal operation

When the brakes are applied and there is sufficient brake performance but the brake lever or brake pedal operation feels excessively hard, check for the following possible causes:

1. Clogged brake hydraulic system.
2. Sticking caliper piston.
3. Sticking master cylinder piston.
4. Glazed or worn brake pads.
5. Mismatched brake pads.
6. Damaged front brake lever.
7. Damaged rear brake pedal.
8. Brake caliper not sliding correctly on fixed shafts (front brake only)
9. Worn or damaged brake caliper seals.

Brakes grab or lock

1. Damaged brake pad pin bolt. Look for steps or cracks along the pad pin bolt surface.
2. Contaminated brake pads and disc.
3. Contaminated or damaged brake hose(s).
4. Incorrect wheel alignment.
5. Warped brake disc.
6. Loose brake disc mounting bolts.
7. Brake caliper not sliding correctly on fixed shafts (front brake only)
8. Mismatched brake pads.
9. Damaged wheel bearings.

Brake squeal or chatter

1. Contaminated brake pads and disc.
2. Incorrectly installed brake caliper.
3. Warped brake disc.
4. Incorrect wheel alignment.
5. Mismatched brake pads.
6. Incorrectly installed brake pads.

Leaking brake caliper

1. Damaged dust and piston seals.
2. Damaged cylinder bore.
3. Loose caliper body bolts.
4. Loose banjo bolt.
5. Damaged banjo bolt washers.
6. Damaged banjo bolt threads in caliper body.

Leaking master cylinder

1. Damaged master cylinder piston primary or secondary seal.
2. Damaged piston circlip/circlip groove.
3. Worn or damaged master cylinder bore.
4. Loose banjo bolt.
5. Damaged banjo bolt washers.
6. Damaged banjo bolt threads in master cylinder body.

TROUBLESHOOTING

7. Loose or damaged reservoir cap and/or diaphragm.

Drum Brake

Brake Drag and Poor Brake Operation

If the drum brake does not operate at full performance, check for the following conditions:
1. Worn brake shoes.
2. Glazed brake shoe surface.
3. Damaged brake shoes.
4. Worn brake drum inside diameter.
5. Damaged brake drum surface.
6. Brake shoes contaminated with oil or grease.
7. Incorrect brake adjustment.
8. Worn or damaged brake cam.
9. Brake arm incorrectly indexed with the brake cam. Check for improper assembly or damaged splines.
10. Bent or damaged brake rod assembly.
11. Damaged or seized brake pedal assembly.
12. Weak brake shoe return springs.

Brake squeal

1. Worn brake shoes.
2. Contaminated brake shoes.
3. Worn or damaged brake drum.
4. Contaminated brake drum.
5. Weak brake shoe return springs.
6. Incorrect brake adjustment.

Brake pedal slow to return

1. Brake pedal pivot surfaces contaminated or partially seized from corrosion.
2. Bent or damaged brake rod.
3. Incorrect brake adjustment.
4. Worn, damaged or disconnected brake shoe return spring(s).
5. Contaminated brake shoe and brake drum contact surfaces. Check for debris buildup inside brake drum.
6. Worn or damaged brake cam. Also check the brake panel bore for contamination and damage.
7. Incorrect brake shoe installation.
8. Damaged or broken return spring.

ABS Brake System

An optional anti-lock brake system (ABS) and a linked brake system (LBS) are available on some models. The ABS system is an electronically controlled hydraulic system designed to prevent wheel lockup during hard braking and when braking on slippery and loose road surfaces. The front and rear brake systems are also linked on models equipped with ABS. The LBS system links the rear brake system to the front brake. Applying the rear brake pedal applies the rear brake and part of the front brake. Operating the front brake lever applies only the front brake.

During normal braking operations, the LBS system provides the braking for the motorcycle. When the wheel is about to lock, the ABS function modulates the hydraulic pressure in the system by reducing pressure at the brake calipers. When the system senses that the wheel lock condition is reduced, full hydraulic pressure to the calipers is restored. Hydraulic pressure is regulated continuously.

The LBS and ABS are integrated systems. That is, the same hydraulic system components (master cylinders, brake calipers and ABS hydraulic brake lines) are used for both systems. A number of anti-lock components are installed in the brake system to provide anti-lock braking. See Chapter Sixteen for information on troubleshooting and servicing the ABS.

ABS Indicator Light

NOTE

*If the ABS indicator does not turn on when the ignition switch is turned on or stays on when there is no DTC set in memory, refer to **ABS Indicator Circuit Troubleshooting** (Chapter Sixteen).*

The ABS system is programmed with a self-diagnostic capability. Self-diagnosis starts when the motorcycle switch is turned on, indicated when the red ABS indicator on the speedometer panel comes on, and ends when the motorcycle speed reaches 10 kilometers per hour (6 mph), indicated by the ABS indicator turning off.

When the ABS electronic control unit (ECU) detects a fault in the ABS system, the ABS indicator **(Figure 15)** will flash or stay on to alert the rider. A diagnostic trouble code (DTC) is also set in the ECU memory. When the ABS indicator is flashing or stays on, the ABS function is disabled. However, even when the ABS is disabled, the LBS system still operates normally.

The ABS indicator may flash or stay on when the motorcycle is used or ridden under the following conditions:

1. The ABS indicator may blink if the rear wheel is turned when the motorcycle is supported on its centerstand (rear wheel off the ground with ignition switch ON).
2. The motorcycle is ridden continuously on a stretch of rough or bumpy roads.
3. When the motorcycle is ridden through an area with a strong electromagnetic interference, the ECU may set a DTC and disable the ABS. When the ABS is disabled in this manner, erase the DTC and perform the self-diagnosis (Chapter Sixteen). If the ABS indicator goes out during the self-diagnosis, the ABS function has returned and the system is operating correctly.

If the ABS indicator **(Figure 15)** comes on when riding, perform the following:
1. Ride the motorcycle to a safe area away from all traffic and turn the ignition switch OFF.
2. Restart the engine. The ABS indicator should light and stay on until the motorcycle is ridden. If the ABS indicator flashes or stays on, there is a problem with the ABS and the system has been disabled. Retrieve the DTC and service the ABS system (Chapter Sixteen).

CHAPTER THREE

LUBRICATION, MAINTENANCE AND TUNE-UP

Tables 1-8 are at the end of the chapter. **Table 1** notes the maintenance and lubrication schedule.

Before starting any work, review the information in Chapter One.

TUNE-UP

Refer to **Table 2** for tune-up specifications.

To perform a tune-up, service the following items as described in this chapter:
1. Air filter.
2. Engine compression.
3. Spark plugs.
4. Ignition timing.
5. Valve clearance.
6. Engine oil and filter.
7. Cooling system.
8. Final drive oil.
9. Wheels and tires.
10. Suspension components.
11. Brake system.
12. Fasteners.

ENGINE ROTATION

Normal engine rotation is counterclockwise when viewed from the left side (flywheel side) of the engine. Use the flywheel mounting bolt to rotate the crankshaft, and always turn the crankshaft counterclockwise.

FUEL

All models require gasoline with a pump octane number (PON) of 86 or higher or a research octane number (RON) of 91 or higher. Using a gasoline with a lower octane number can cause pinging or spark knock, and lead to engine damage.

When choosing gasoline and filling the fuel tank, note the following:
1. When filling the tank, do not overfill it. There should be no fuel in the filler neck (tube located between the fuel cap and tank).
2. Leaded gasoline will damage the catalytic converters.
3. In some areas of the United States and Canada, oxygenated fuels are being used to reduce exhaust emissions. If using oxygenated fuel, make sure it meets the minimum octane requirements.
4. Because oxygenated fuels can damage plastic and paint, make sure not to spill fuel onto the fuel tank during filling. Wipe up spills promptly with a soft cloth.
5. An ethanol (ethyl or grain alcohol) gasoline blend that contains more than 10 percent ethanol by volume may cause engine starting and performance related problems.
6. A methanol (methyl or wood alcohol) gasoline blend that contains more than 5 percent methanol by volume may cause engine starting and performance related problems. Gasoline that contains methanol must have corrosion inhibitors to protect the metal, plastic and rubber parts in the fuel system from damage.

AIR FILTER

The air filter removes dust and abrasive particles from the air before the air enters the engine. A clogged air filter will decrease the efficiency and life of the engine. With a damaged air filter, very fine particles could enter the engine and cause rapid wear of the piston rings, cylinder and bearings. Never run the motorcycle without the air filter element installed.

Replace the air filter element at the service intervals specified in **Table 1** or when excessively contaminated or damaged. The service intervals in **Table 1** are for general use. However, replace the air filter more often if dusty areas are frequently encountered.

Inspection/Replacement

1. Remove the bolts (**A, Figure 1**) and the air filter cover (**B**).
2. Remove the air filter (**Figure 2**).

NOTE
A dust adhesive has been applied to the OEM stock air filter element. Do not clean the air filter element (Figure 3) with air or any type of chemical cleaner or water.

3. Inspect the air filter element for excessive dirt buildup and/or damage. Check for holes or shredded filter seams. Check the foam seal (**Figure 3**) for cuts, crushed or contaminated areas that could prevent the foam seal from sealing tightly. Do not run the motorcycle with a damaged air filter element or attempt to clean it as it may allow dirt to enter the engine. If the air filter element is in good condition, use it until the indicated time for replacement (**Table 1**).
4. Inspect the air filter housing for dirt and debris that may have passed through the element. Wipe the inside of the air filter housing and the air filter cover with a clean cloth.

CAUTION
Overtightening the air filter cover bolts will crack the plastic cover.

5. Install the air filter element (**Figure 2**), making sure it is aligned with the air box opening and hold it in place. Then, install the air filter cover (**B, Figure 1**) and tighten the bolts (**A**) securely.

SUB-AIR FILTERS (CARBURETED MODELS)

Replace the sub-air filters at the intervals specified in **Table 1**.

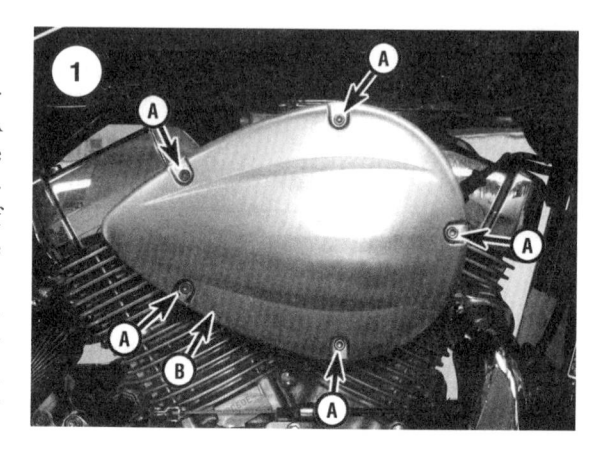

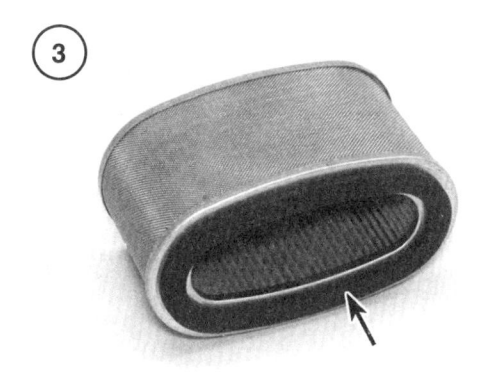

Removal/Installation

The sub-air filters are mounted in front of the battery box and can be difficult to access, especially when attempting to disconnect hoses that have hardened from age.

1. Remove the seat and both side covers (Chapter Seventeen).
2. Remove the battery (Chapter Ten).
3. Remove the fuse box from its mounting position on the battery box (Chapter Ten).
4. Disconnect the voltage regulator connector (Chapter Ten).

LUBRICATION, MAINTENANCE AND TUNE-UP

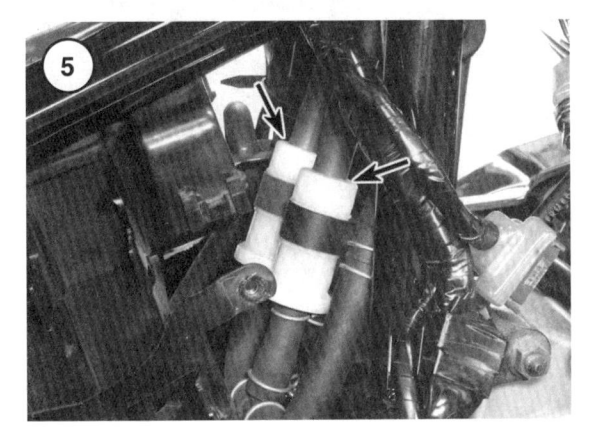

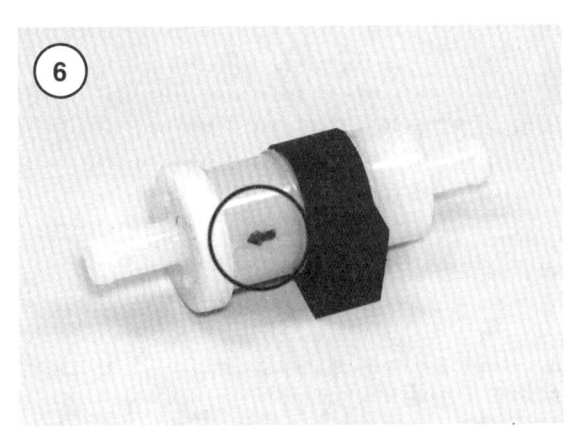

5. Remove the rear ignition coil (Chapter Ten).
6. Disconnect the electrical connector from the top of the starter relay switch. Then, pull the starter relay switch off of its mounting bracket and set aside (Chapter Ten).
7. Remove the voltage regulator (Chapter Ten).
8. From inside the battery box, remove the bolts securing the battery box to the metal mounting bracket.
9. Remove the two mounting bolts (**Figure 4**) securing the metal mounting bracket to the frame. Note the flexible clamp installed on the right mounting bolt.
10. Lift the battery box to free its pin from the grommet, then reposition both the battery box and the metal mounting bracket rearward to provide access around the sub-air filters.
11. Identify and mark the hoses attached to the sub-air filters so they can be reconnected in their original positions.
12. Remove the sub-air filters (**Figure 5**) as follows:
    a. Remove the upper hose from the right side sub-air filter. Then lift the filter to remove its rubber damper from the mounting bracket.
    b. Slide the lower hose clamp down the hose and disconnect the lower hose and remove the sub-air filter.
    c. Repeat the process to remove the left side filter.
13. Check the hoses for cracks, splitting and other damage. Replace if necessary.
14. Install the sub-air filters as follows:
    a. Transfer the rubber dampers from the old to new filters.
    b. Install both sub-air filters with their arrow marks (**Figure 6**) facing down.
    c. Reconnect the lower hoses and clamps, then the upper hose.
    d. Slide the rubber dampers over the mounting brackets.
15. Reverse the removal steps to complete installation.

CRANKCASE BREATHER INSPECTION

The engine is equipped with a crankcase emission control system to prevent fumes and gases from being vented into the atmosphere. However, under various operating conditions, contaminants (water and blow-by gas) that are not burned in the combustion chamber collect in the air filter housing. To remove these contaminants, a transparent drain tube (**Figure 7**) is mounted on the bottom of the air filter housing. At the intervals in **Table 1**, inspect the drain tube for fluid. If necessary, remove the plug at the bottom of the drain tube and drain the contaminants into a container. Reinstall the plug securely onto the drain tube.

Check the drain tube more frequently after riding the motorcycle in rain, after riding long distances under full-throttle, if the motorcycle is washed frequently, or after the motorcycle was dropped on its side.

ENGINE COMPRESSION TEST

A compression test can check the internal condition of the engine (piston rings, pistons, head gasket, valves and cylinders). By checking the compression at each tune-up, a running record may reveal developing problems.

Use the spark plug tool included in the motorcycle's tool kit and a screw-in type compression gauge with a flexible adapter; refer to *Compression Gauge* (Chapter One). Before using the gauge, make sure the rubber gasket on the end of the adapter is not cracked or damaged. This gasket seals the cylinder to ensure accurate compression readings.

1. Make sure the battery is fully charged to ensure proper engine cranking speed.
2. Run the engine until it reaches normal operating temperature, then turn it off.
3. On fuel injected models, perform the following:
    a. Remove the seat (Chapter Seventeen).
    b. Turn the ignition switch off.
    c. Disconnect the fuel pump connector (**Figure 8**).
4. Grasp a spark plug cap and twist it slightly to break it loose, then pull it from the spark plug. Disconnect all of the spark plug caps.
5. Remove one spark plug from one cylinder as described in this chapter.
6. Lubricate the threads of the compression gauge adapter with a *small* amount of antiseize compound and carefully thread the gauge into one of the spark plug holes (**Figure 9**). Tighten the hose by hand to form a good seal.

CAUTION
*When the spark plug leads are disconnected, the electronic ignition will produce the highest voltage possible. This can damage the ICM or other ignition components. To protect the ignition system, install a grounding tool in each spark plug cap. Refer to **Ignition Grounding Tool** in Chapter One. Do not crank the engine more than necessary.*

7. Set the engine stop switch to RUN, and then turn the ignition switch on. Open the throttle completely and using the starter, crank the engine over while reading the compression gauge until there is no further rise in pressure. The compression reading should increase on each stroke. Maximum pressure is usually reached within 4-7 seconds of engine cranking. Record the maximum reading.

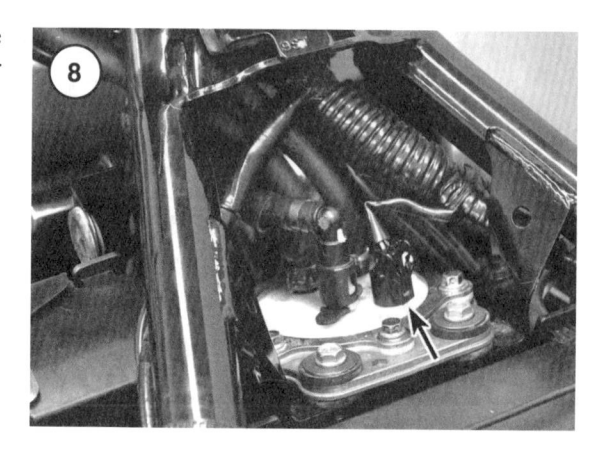

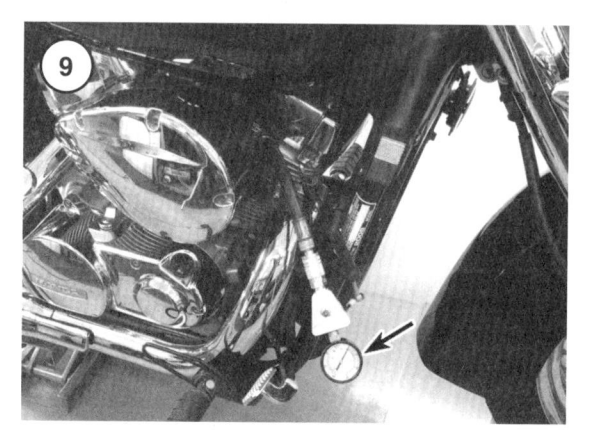

NOTE
If a cylinder requires a longer cranking time to reach its maximum compression reading, there is a problem with that cylinder.

8. Install the spark plug.
9. Repeat the process for the other cylinder and record the result.
10. When interpreting the results, actual readings are not as important as the difference between the readings. **Table 2** lists the standard compression pressure reading. Note the following:
    a. Low compression indicates worn or broken rings, leaking or sticky valves, blown head gasket or a combination of all three. Readings that are lower than normal, but are relatively even among both cylinders indicates piston, ring and cylinder wear.
    b. High compression readings indicate excessive carbon deposits in the combustion chamber and on the piston crowns.
    c. If the compression readings do not differ between cylinders by more than 10 percent, the rings and valves are in good condition.
    d. If a low reading (10 percent difference or more) is obtained on one cylinder, it indicates valve or ring trouble. To determine which, perform

LUBRICATION, MAINTENANCE AND TUNE-UP

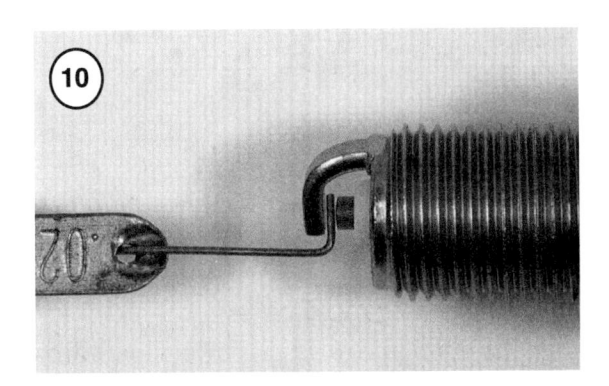

a wet compression test. Pour about a teaspoon (5ml) of engine oil into the spark plug hole. Repeat the compression test and record the reading. If the compression increases significantly, the valves are good but the rings are defective on the low cylinder. If compression does not increase, the valves require servicing.

e. If further troubleshooting is necessary, perform the *Cylinder Leakdown Test* described in Chapter Two.

11. Reverse Steps 1-5 to complete installation.

SPARK PLUGS

Inspect and replace the spark plugs at the service intervals specified in **Table 1**.

Removal

Careful removal of a spark plug is important in preventing grit from entering the combustion chamber. It is also important to know how to remove a plug that is seized, or is resistant to removal. Forcing a seized plug can destroy the threads in the cylinder head.

During removal, label each spark plug with its cylinder number and position in the cylinder head.

1. Grasp a plug cap and twist it slightly to break it loose, then pull it from the spark plug.
2. Blow any dirt that has accumulated around the spark plug.

CAUTION
Dirt that falls through the spark plug hole causes engine wear.

NOTE
The ceramic cover, found on the top of the spark plug, actually extends into the plug to prevent the spark from grounding through the plug metal body and threads. The ceramic cover can be easily damaged from mishandling. Make sure the spark plug socket fits the plug fully before turning the plug.

3. Fit an 18-mm spark plug wrench onto the spark plug, then remove it by turning the wrench counterclockwise. If the plug is seized or drags excessively during removal, stop and perform the following:
   a. Apply penetrating lubricant and allow it to stand for about 15 minutes.
   b. If the plug is completely seized, apply moderate pressure in both directions with the wrench. Only attempt to break the seal so lubricant can penetrate under the spark plug and into the threads. If this does not work, and the engine can still be started, install all of the spark plug caps and start the engine. Allow to completely warm up. The heat of the engine may be enough to expand the parts and allow the plug to be removed.
   c. When a spark plug is loose, but drags excessively during removal, apply penetrating lubricant around the spark plug threads. Turn the plug in (clockwise) to help distribute the lubricant onto the threads. Slowly remove the plug, working it in and out of the cylinder head while continuing to add lubricant. Do not reuse the spark plug.

NOTE
Damaged spark plug threads will require removal of the cylinder head (Chapter Four) for repair.

   d. Inspect the threads in the cylinder head for damage. Clean and true the threads with a spark plug thread-chaser. Apply thick grease onto the thread-chaser threads before using it. The grease will help trap some of the debris cut from the threads to prevent it from falling into the engine.

4. Inspect the spark plug carefully as described in this section.

Gap Measurement

Use *only* a wire feeler gauge when measuring spark plug gap.

1. If installing a new spark plug, remove it from the box and tighten the small terminal adapter installed on the end of the plug.
2. Refer to the spark plug gap listed in **Table 2**. Select the correct size wire feeler gauge and try to slide it past the gap between both electrodes (**Figure 10**). If there is a slight drag as the wire gauge passes through the gap, the setting is correct. If the gap is incorrect, adjust it with a spark plug gauge tool (**Figure 11**).

Installation

1. Wipe a *small* amount of antiseize compound to the plug threads before installing the spark plug. Do not allow the compound to contact the electrodes.

NOTE
Do not overtighten the spark plug. This may crush the gasket and cause a compression leak or damage the cylinder head threads.

2. Screw the spark plug in by hand until it seats. Very little effort should be required; if excessive force is necessary, the plug may be cross-threaded. Unscrew it and try again. When the spark plug is properly seated, tighten it to 16 N.m (12 ft.-lb.) on 2004-2009 Aero models or 18 N.m (13 ft.-lb.) on all other models.
3. Align and press the spark plug cap firmly onto the spark plug.

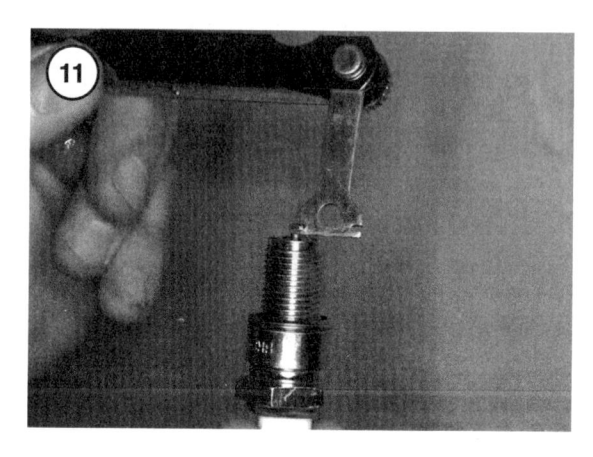

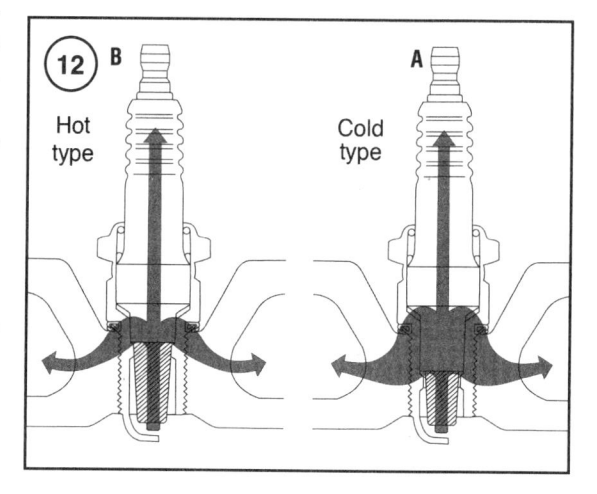

Selection

The proper spark plug **(Table 2)** is very important in obtaining maximum performance and reliability. If the engine is run in hot climates, at high speed or under heavy loads for prolonged periods, a spark plug with a colder heat range may be required. A colder plug **(A, Figure 12)** quickly transfers heat away from its firing tip and to the cylinder head. This is accomplished by a short path up the ceramic insulator and into the body of the spark plug. By transferring heat quickly, the plug remains cool enough to avoid overheating and preignition problems. If the engine is run slowly for prolonged periods, this type of plug will foul and result in poor performance. A colder plug will not cool down a hot engine.

If the engine is run in cold climates or at a slow speed for prolonged periods, a spark plug with a hotter heat range may be required. A hotter plug **(B, Figure 12)** slowly transfers heat away from its firing tip and to the cylinder head. This is accomplished by a long path up the ceramic insulator and into the body of the plug. By transferring heat slowly, the plug remains hot enough to avoid fouling and buildup. If the engine is run in hot climates for fast or prolonged periods, this type of plug will overheat, cause preignition problems and possible melt the electrode. Damage to the piston and cylinder assembly is possible.

When running a stock engine, changing to a different heat range plug is normally not required. Changing to a different heat range plug may be necessary when operating a motorcycle with a modified engine. This type of change is usually based on a recommendation made by the engine builder. Experience in reading spark plugs is also required when trying to determine if a different heat range plug is required. When installing a different heat range plug, go one step hotter or colder from the *recommended* plug. Do not try to correct fuel injection or ignition problems by using different spark plugs. This will only compound the existing problem(s) and possibly lead to severe engine damage.

The reach (length) of a plug is also important **(Figure 13)**. A shorter than normal plug causes hard starting, reduce engine performance and carbon buildup on the exposed cylinder head threads. These same conditions can occur if the correct length plug is used without a gasket. Trying to thread a spark plug into threads with carbon buildup may damage the threads in the cylinder head.

Reading/Inspection

The spark plug is an excellent indicator of how the engine is operating. The condition of a used spark plug can tell a trained mechanic or experienced rider a lot about engine condition and carburetion.

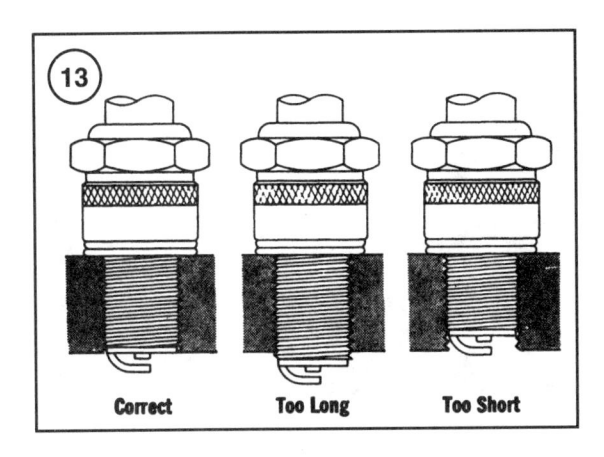

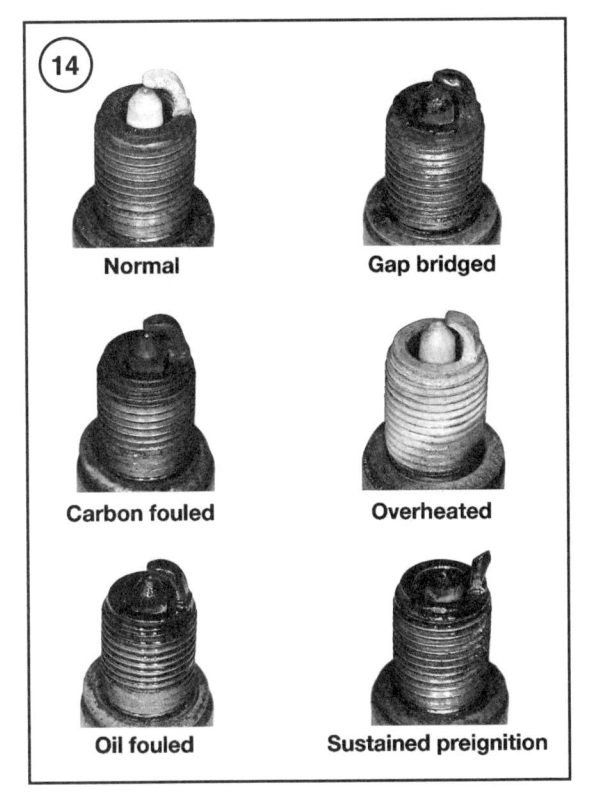

LUBRICATION, MAINTENANCE AND TUNE-UP

or spark plug reader.

b. Refer to **Figure 14** and the following paragraphs provide a description, as well as common causes for each of the conditions.

CAUTION
In all cases, when a spark plug is abnormal, find the cause of the problem before continuing engine operation. Severe engine damage is possible when abnormal plug readings are ignored.

Normal condition

The ceramic insulator around the center electrode is clean and colorless. There should be a gray ring around the center electrode where it separates from the ceramic. No erosion or rounding of the electrodes or abnormal gap is evident. This indicates an engine that has proper fuel mixture and ignition timing. This heat range of plug is appropriate for the conditions in which the engine has been operated. The plug can be reused.

Oil fouled

The plug is wet with black, oily deposits on the electrodes and insulator. The electrodes do not show wear. Replace the spark plug. Check for the following:
1. Clogged air filter.
2. Faulty fuel system.
3. Faulty ignition component.
4. Spark plug heat range too cold.
5. Low engine compression.
6. Engine not properly broken in.

Carbon fouled

The plug is black with a dry, sooty deposit on the entire plug surface. This dry sooty deposit is conductive and can create electrical paths that bypass the electrode gap. This often results in misfiring of the plug. Replace the spark plug. Check for the following:
1. Rich fuel mixture.
2. Faulty fuel system.
3. Spark plug heat range too cold.
4. Clogged air filter.
5. Incorrect choke adjustment or choke valve does not close fully on carbureted models.
6. Faulty ignition component.
7. Low engine compression.

By correctly evaluating the condition of the plug, engine problems can be diagnosed. To correctly read a spark plug, perform the following:
1. Refer to *Installation* in this section when removing and installing the spark plug during this procedure.
2. If a new plug was installed, ride the motorcycle for approximately 15 to 20 minutes so it will begin to color.
3. Accelerate on a straight road at full throttle. Then push the engine stop button, pull the clutch lever in and coast to a stop. Do not stop by downshifting the transmission.
4. Remove the spark plug and examine its firing tip while noting the following:
    a. Inspect the spark plug with a magnifying glass

Overheating

The plug is dry and the insulator has a white or light gray cast. The insulator may also appear blistered. The electrodes may have a burnt appearance and there may be metallic specks on the center electrode and ceramic. This material is being removed from the piston crown. Replace the spark plug. Check for the following:
1. Lean fuel mixture.
2. Faulty fuel system.
3. Spark plug heat range too hot.
4. Faulty ignition component.
5. Air leak at the exhaust pipe or intake manifold.
6. Overtightened spark plug.
7. No crush washer on spark plug.
8. Spark plug heat range too hot.

Gap bridging

The plug is clogged with deposits between the electrodes. The engine may run with a gap-bridged spark plug, but it will misfire. Replace the spark plug. Check for the following:
1. Incorrect oil type.
2. Incorrect fuel or fuel contamination.
3. Excessive carbon deposits in combustion chamber.

Preignition

The plug electrodes are severely eroded or melted. This condition can lead to severe engine damage. Replace the spark plug. Check for the following:
1. Faulty ignition system component.
2. Spark plug heat range too hot.
3. Air leak.
4. Excessive carbon deposits in combustion chamber.

Worn out

The center electrode is rounded from normal combustion. There is no indication of abnormal combustion or engine conditions.

IGNITION TIMING

The ignition control module (ICM [carbureted models]) or engine control module (ECM [fuel injected models]) control ignition timing and are not adjustable. However, checking the ignition timing can provide diagnostic information. If an ignition related problem is suspected, check the ignition timing to confirm proper ignition system operation. Also check the ignition timing after installing a new ignition system component to make sure it is working correctly.

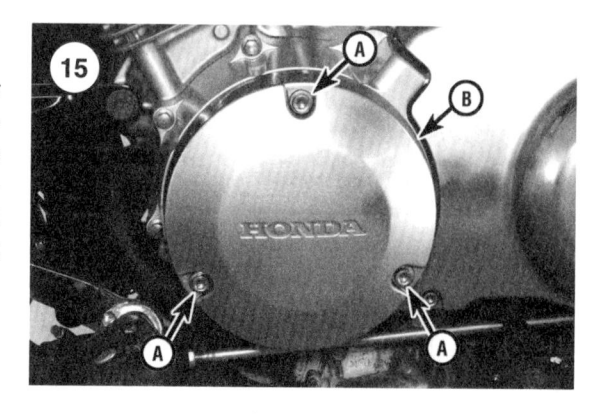

1. Start the engine and warm to normal operating temperature, then turn the engine off.
2. Remove the bolts (A, **Figure 15**) and the alternator cover (B).
3. Remove the timing hole cap (A, **Figure 16**) and its O-ring from the left crankcase cover.
4. Connect a timing light onto one of the front cylinder spark plug wires following the tool manufacturer's instructions.
5. Start the engine and check the idle speed (**Table 2**).
6A. Start the engine and check the idle speed (**Table 2**). On carbureted models, set the idle speed as described in this chapter (if necessary).
6B. On fuel injected models, the idle speed is not adjustable.
7. Check the ignition timing as follows:
   a. Aim the timing light at the timing hole and pull the trigger. The ignition timing is correct if the F mark on the flywheel aligns with the index mark on the left crankcase cover (**Figure 17**) while the engine is running at idle speed. Turn the engine off, and disconnect the timing light.
   b. Connect the timing light to one of the rear cylinder spark plug wires. Start the engine and recheck the ignition timing. The ignition timing is correct if the F mark on the flywheel aligns with the index mark on the left crankcase cover (**Figure 17**) while the engine is running at idle speed.

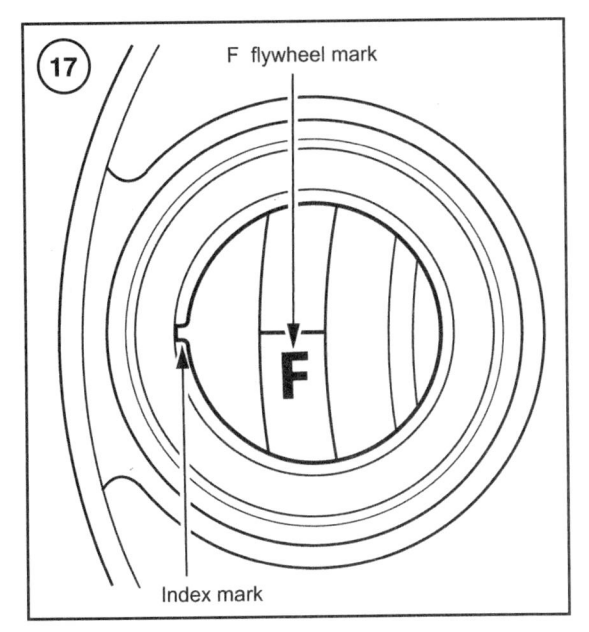

LUBRICATION, MAINTENANCE AND TUNE-UP

17

F flywheel mark

F

Index mark

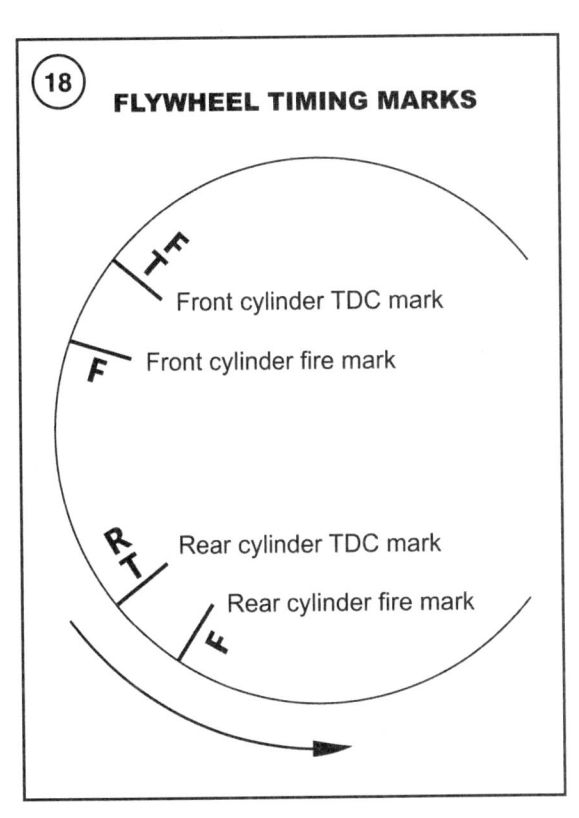

18 FLYWHEEL TIMING MARKS

- F/T Front cylinder TDC mark
- F Front cylinder fire mark
- R/T Rear cylinder TDC mark
- F Rear cylinder fire mark

19

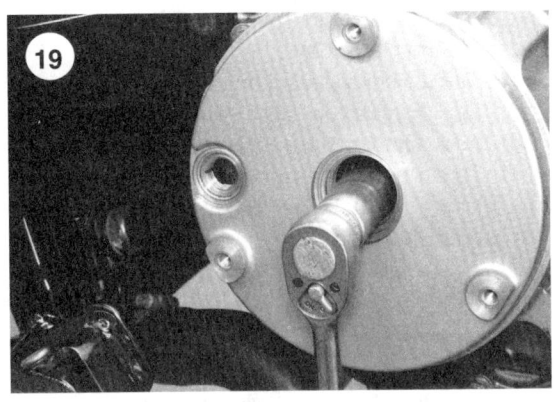

11. Lubricate the timing hole cap (A, **Figure 16**) threads with grease and the O-ring with oil. Tighten the timing hole cap to 10 N.m (89 in.-lb.).
12. Install the alternator cover (**Figure 15**) and tighten the mounting bolts to 10 N.m (89 in.-lb.).

VALVE CLEARANCE

Check the valve clearance at the intervals specified in **Table 1** and adjust if necessary.

Inspection

Refer to **Table 2** for valve clearance specifications.

NOTE
Do not check or adjust the valve clearance when the air or engine temperature is above 35 degrees C (95 degrees F).

1. Support the motorcycle with a jackstand to position it upright. This will make it easier to view the flywheel marks when turning the engine over.
2. Remove both cylinder head covers (Chapter Four).
3. Remove the bolts (A, **Figure 15**) and the alternator cover (B).
4. Remove the timing (A, **Figure 16**) and crankshaft (B) hole caps and their O-rings from the left crankcase cover.
5. Remove one spark plug from each cylinder to make it easier to turn the engine by hand. Cover the spark plug openings.

NOTE
*Always turn the crankshaft counterclockwise, as viewed from the left side of the motorcycle. When doing so, the timing marks will appear in the order shown in **Figure 18**. Use a socket through the left crankcase cover to engage the flywheel bolt (**Figure 19**).*

8. Turn the engine off and disconnect the timing light.
9. If the ignition timing is correct for both cylinders, the ignition system is working correctly. If the ignition timing is incorrect, there is a problem with one or more ignition system components. Refer to *Ignition System Testing* in Chapter Ten.
10. Replace the O-ring on the timing hole cap if leaking or damaged.

6. Set the front cylinder piston at TDC on its compression stroke as follows:
   a. Turn the crankshaft counterclockwise and align the FT mark on the flywheel with the index mark on the left crankcase cover (**Figure 20**).
   b. Try to move each front cylinder head rocker arms by hand. The exhaust rocker arm and both intake rocker arms should have some free play, indicating the front cylinder is at TDC on its compression stroke. If all three rocker arms are tight (no free play), turn the crankshaft 360° (1 turn) counterclockwise and realign the FT mark. The front piston should now be at its TDC position.
7. Measure the clearance of the exhaust valve and both intake valves as follows:
   a. Refer to **Table 2** for the intake and exhaust valve clearances.
   b. Insert a feeler gauge between the valve adjusting screw and the end of the valve stem (**Figure 21**). When the clearance is correct, there is a slight drag on the feeler gauge when it is inserted and withdrawn.
   c. If there is too much or too little drag, adjust the valve clearance as described in this section.
   d. When the front cylinder head valve clearances are correct, continue with Step 8 to check the rear cylinder head valve clearances.
8. Set the rear cylinder piston at TDC on its compression stroke as follows:
   a. Turn the crankshaft counterclockwise and align the RT mark on the flywheel with the index mark on the left crankcase cover (**Figure 22**).
   b. Try to move each rear cylinder head rocker arm (**Figure 21**) by hand. The exhaust rocker arm and both intake rocker arms should have some free play, indicating the rear cylinder is at TDC on its compression stroke. If all three rocker arms are tight (no free play) turn the crankshaft 360° (1 turn) counterclockwise and realign the RT mark. The rear piston should now be at its TDC position.
9. When the clearance of each valve is within specification, reverse Steps 1-5 while noting the following:
   a. Reinstall the spark plugs as described in this chapter.
   b. Replace the O-rings on the timing and crankshaft hole caps if leaking or damaged.
   c. Lubricate the timing hole cap (A, *Figure 16*) threads with grease and the O-ring with oil and tighten to 10 N.m (88 in.-lb.).
   d. Lubricate the crankshaft hole cap (B, *Figure 16*) threads with grease and the O-ring with oil and tighten to 15 N.m (11 ft.-lb.).
   e. Install the alternator cover (B, **Figure 15**) and tighten the mounting bolts (A) to 10 N.m (89 in.-lb.).

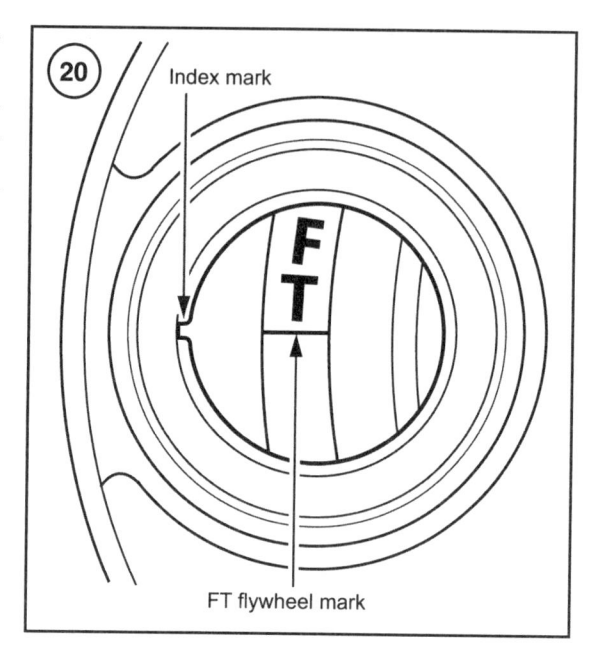

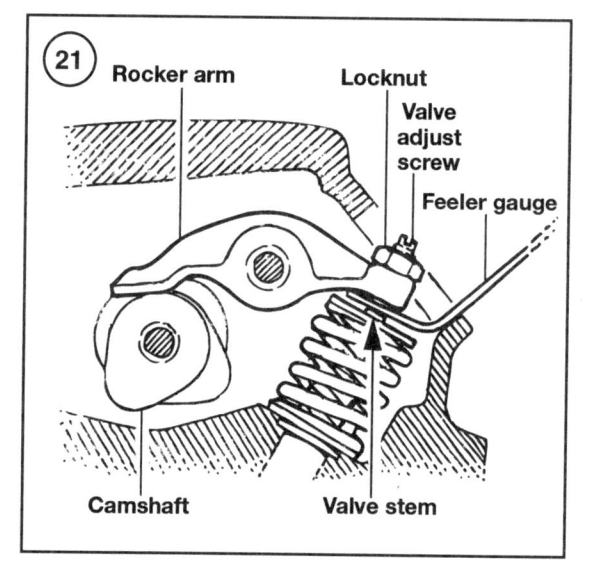

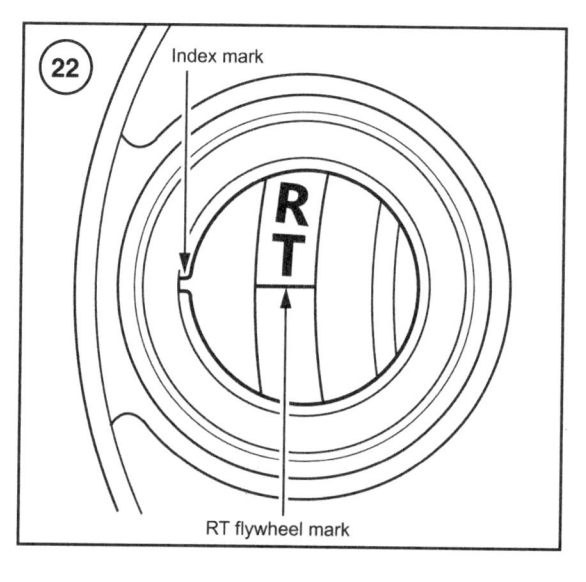

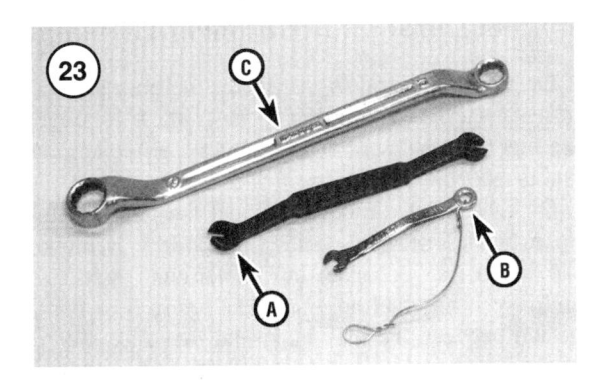

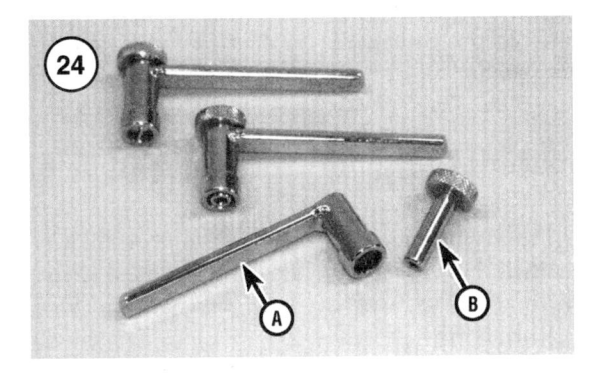

LUBRICATION, MAINTENANCE AND TUNE-UP

ing and tighten the locknut to 23 N.m (17 ft.-lb.).
5. Recheck the valve clearance. If the clearance changed when the locknut was tightened, loosen the locknut and readjust the valve clearance. Repeat until the valve clearance is correct after the locknut is tightened.
6. Check the idle speed as described in this chapter.

IDLE SPEED

WARNING
With the engine idling, move the handlebar from side to side. If the idle speed increases during this movement, the throttle cables need adjusting or may be incorrectly routed through the frame. Correct this problem immediately. Do not ride the motorcycle in this unsafe condition.

Inspection and Adjustment (Carbureted Models)

The engine idle speed is adjusted by turning the idle speed screw **(Figure 25)** on the right side of the engine. **Table 2** lists the correct idle speed.
1. Start the engine and let it warm up approximately 2-3 minutes.
2. Support the motorcycle on its sidestand. Turn the engine off.
3. Connect a portable tachometer following the manufacturer's instructions.
4. Restart the engine and if necessary, adjust the idle speed by turning the idle speed screw **(Figure 25)**.
5. Open and close the throttle a couple of times; check for variation in idle speed. Readjust if necessary.

NOTE
If the engine runs roughly at idle, check for a dirty or contaminated air filter element. If the air filter is okay, the choke valve may be partially stuck open.

Adjustment

Tools

1. An offset 4-mm wrench is required to turn the valve adjust screws. Use a tappet wrench (Honda part No. 07908-KE90100 [A, **Figure 23**]) or a modified 4-mm open end wrench (B, **Figure 23**). An offset 10-mm wrench (C, **Figure 23**) is required to turn the locknuts.
2. A Tappet Tool Set (Motion Pro part No. 08-0073) can also be used by combining the 10-mm wrench (A, **Figure 24**) with the 4-mm hex adjuster (B). These tools can also be used separately.

Procedure

Refer to **Figure 21**.
1. Set the cylinder to TDC on its compression stroke as described in the previous section.
2. Loosen the locknut **(Figure 21)** on the valve adjust screw.
3. Turn the valve adjust screw **(Figure 21)** until the valve clearance (slight drag on feeler gauge) is correct.

NOTE
After loosening a valve adjust screw locknut, lubricate the locknut threads and its seating surface with engine oil.

4. Hold the valve adjust screw to prevent it from turn-

6. Turn the engine off and disconnect the portable tachometer.

Inspection (Fuel Injected Models)

The idle speed is not adjustable. Routinely check the idle speed to make sure the idle air speed system is working correctly.

1. Turn the ignition switch on. If the Malfunction Indicator Lamp (MIL) is blinking, refer to Chapter Nine to read the diagnostic trouble code(s) (DTCs). If the MIL is not blinking, continue the procedure. Turn the ignition switch off.
2. Make sure the air filter is clean as described in this chapter.
3. Make sure the spark plugs are in good condition as described in this chapter.
4. Start the engine and ride the motorcycle until it reaches normal operating temperature (coolant temperatures is 80° [176° F]).
5. Support the motorcycle on its sidestand. Turn the engine off.
6. Connect a portable tachometer following the manufacturer's instructions.
7. Restart the engine and check the idle speed reading on the tachometer. Compare the result to the idle speed specification in **Table 2**.
   a. If the idle speed is correct, turn the engine off and disconnect the portable tachometer.
   b. If the idle speed is incorrect, continue with Step 8.
8. Check the throttle operation and free play as described in this chapter. Note the following:
   a. If the throttle operation and adjustment is incorrect, adjust as described in this chapter.
   b. If the throttle operation and free play are correct, continue with Step 9.
9. Check the engine compression as described in this chapter. Note the following:
   a. If the engine compression is correct and there is no excessive engine noise, continue with Step 10.
   b. If the engine compression is low and/or there is excessive engine noise, refer to *Engine* in Chapter Two. Low compression can cause a rough idle speed and overall poor performance.
10. Check the IACV operation as in *Idle Air Control Valve (IACV)* in Chapter Nine.
11. Turn the engine off and disconnect the portable tachometer.

FUEL SYSTEM HOSE INSPECTION

On carbureted models, inspect the fuel and vacuum hoses at the intervals specified in **Table 1**. Remove the fuel tank as described in Chapter Eight to access and inspect the hoses.

On fuel injected models, inspect the fuel system hoses at the intervals specified in **Table 1**. Remove the fuel tank as described in Chapter Nine to access and inspect the fuel hose and fuel return hose connected between the fuel pump and fuel tank. Refer to *Fuel Injectors, Injector Cap and Fuel Feed Hose* in *Chapter Nine* to access and inspect the fuel feed hose connected between the fuel feed pipe and the fuel pump.

FUEL FILTER REPLACEMENT (FUEL INJECTED MODELS)

The manufacturer does not list a time or mileage interval for replacing the fuel filter installed inside the sub fuel tank. Refer to *Fuel Pump/Sub Fuel Tank* in Chapter Nine.

THROTTLE CABLES

WARNING
An improperly adjusted, assembled or installed throttle grip assembly may cause the throttle to stick open and cause the rider to lose control of the motorcycle. Do not start or ride the motorcycle until the throttle grip is correctly installed, adjusted and snaps back when released.

Throttle Operation

Check the throttle operation at the intervals specified in **Table 1** or whenever the throttle operation feels too tight or loose.

Check for smooth throttle operation from the fully closed to fully open positions. Check at various steering positions. The throttle grip must return to the fully closed position without any hesitation.

Check the throttle cables for damage, wear or deterioration. Make sure the throttle cables are not kinked at any place.

If the throttle does not return to the fully closed position smoothly and the cables do not appear to be damaged, lubricate the throttle cables as described in this chapter. If the throttle still does not return properly, the cables are probably kinked or routed incorrectly. Replace damaged throttle cables.

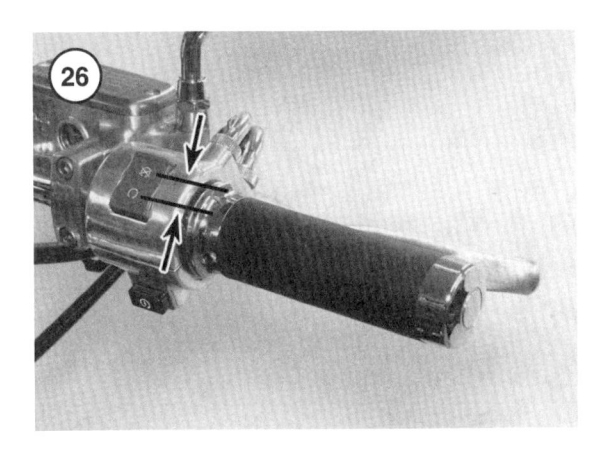

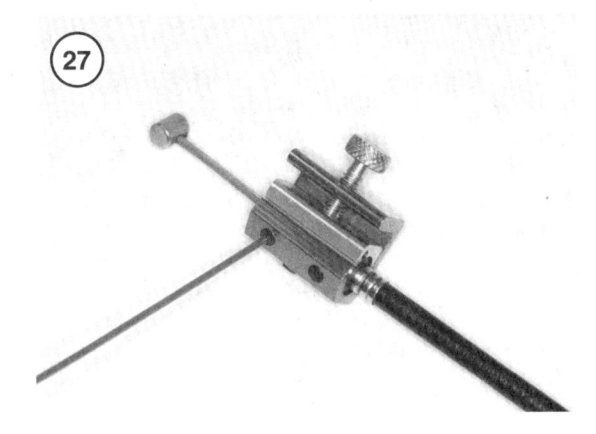

LUBRICATION, MAINTENANCE AND TUNE-UP

CAUTION
When servicing aftermarket cables, follow the cable manufacturer's lubrication requirements.

1A. On carbureted models, disconnect the lower throttle cable ends as described in *Carburetor* in Chapter Eight.
1B. On fuel injected models, disconnect the lower throttle cable ends as described in *Throttle Body* in Chapter Nine.
2. Remove the throttle housing and disconnect the upper throttle cable ends as described in *Handlebar* in Chapter Thirteen.

CAUTION
Do not use chain lube to lubricate control cables unless it is also advertised as a cable lubricant.

NOTE
When using an aerosol type lubricant, cover the area around the nozzle and tube with a plastic bag.

3. Lubricate the cables. **Figure 27** shows a cable lube tool and a cable lubricant. Lubricate each cable until fluid exits through the opposite end of the cable. Wipe up all excess lube from the end of the cables.
4. Lightly lubricate the upper cable ends with grease.
5. Installation is the reverse of removal. Adjust the throttle cables by following the adjustment procedure described below.

Check free play at the throttle grip flange (**Figure 26**) and compare the results to the throttle grip free play specifications (**Table 2**). If necessary, perform the adjustment procedure in this section.

Lubrication

Inspect the throttle operation at the intervals specified in **Table 1**. Lubricate the throttle cables whenever the throttle becomes stiff and sluggish and fails to snap shut after releasing it.

The main cause of cable breakage or stiffness is improper lubrication. Periodic lubrication assures long service life. Inspect the cables for fraying, and check the sheath for chafing. Always replace both throttle cables at the same time.

Because of their design, a cable lubricant tool cannot be mounted on the upper end of both throttle cables. To lubricate the cables at their upper ends, use a can of graphite with a thin hollow tube. After disconnecting the cables at the carburetor, a cable lubricant tool can be mounted on the lower end of both throttle cables.

Adjustment

Cable adjusters are provided at both ends of the pull cable. Minor cable adjustment is made at the upper adjuster at the handlebar. If this does not provide enough adjustment, continue by adjusting the lower adjuster at the carburetor (carbureted models) or throttle body (fuel injected models).

WARNING
If the idle speed increases when the handlebar is turned, check the throttle cable routing. If the routing is correct, check for a damaged cable(s). Correct this problem immediately. Do not ride the motorcycle in this unsafe condition.

1. If minor adjustment is required, perform the following at the throttle grip:
   a. Loosen the locknut (A, **Figure 28**) and turn the upper adjuster (B) in or out to achieve 2-6 mm

(1/16-1/4 in.) free play rotation.

   b. Tighten the locknut and recheck the adjustment. If there is not enough cable adjustment, continue with Step 2.

2A. On carbureted models, if major adjustment is necessary, perform the following:

   a. Remove the air filter housing (Chapter Eight).

   b. Loosen the upper cable locknut (A, **Figure 29**) and turn the adjuster (B) to achieve proper free play rotation at the throttle grip (**Figure 26**). Tighten the locknut (A, **Figure 29**) securely.

   c. Make sure the lower locknut (C, **Figure 29**) is positioned against the bottom of the cable holder.

   d. Recheck free play. If necessary, readjust the upper adjuster as described in this section.

2B. On fuel injected models, if major adjustment is necessary, perform the following:

   a. Remove the air filter housing (Chapter Nine).

   b. Loosen the upper cable locknut (A, **Figure 30**) on the pull cable and turn the adjuster (B) to achieve proper free play rotation at the throttle grip (**Figure 26**). Tighten the locknut (A, **Figure 30**).

   c. Make sure the lower locknut is positioned against the bottom of the cable holder.

   d. Recheck free play. If necessary, readjust the upper adjuster as described in this section.

3. Operate the throttle a few times. The throttle grip should now be adjusted correctly. If not, the throttle cables may be stretched. Replace cables in this condition.

4. Reinstall all parts previously removed.

5. Open and release the throttle grip. Make sure it opens and closes (snaps back) without any binding or roughness. Then support the motorcycle and turn the handlebar from side to side, checking throttle operation at both steering lock positions.

6. Sit on the motorcycle and start the engine with the transmission in neutral. Turn the handlebar from lock-to-lock to check for idle speed variances due to improper cable adjustment, routing or damage.

7. Test ride the motorcycle, slowly at first, to make sure the throttle cables are operating correctly. Readjust if necessary.

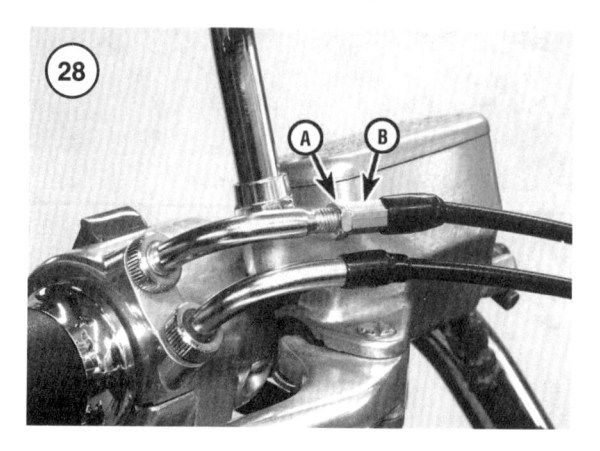

CLUTCH CABLE AND CLUTCH LEVER

Lubrication

Lubricate the clutch cable whenever the clutch lever feels tight or the cable dry.

The main cause of cable breakage or stiffness is improper lubrication. Periodic lubrication assures long service life. Inspect the cable for fraying, and check the sheath for chafing.

A cable lubricant tool can be mounted on the upper end of the cable.

CAUTION
When servicing an aftermarket cable, follow the cable manufacturer's lubrication requirements.

1. Loosen the clutch cable locknut at the clutch lever (A, **Figure 31**) and turn the adjuster (B) to provide as much cable slack as possible. Align the open slots

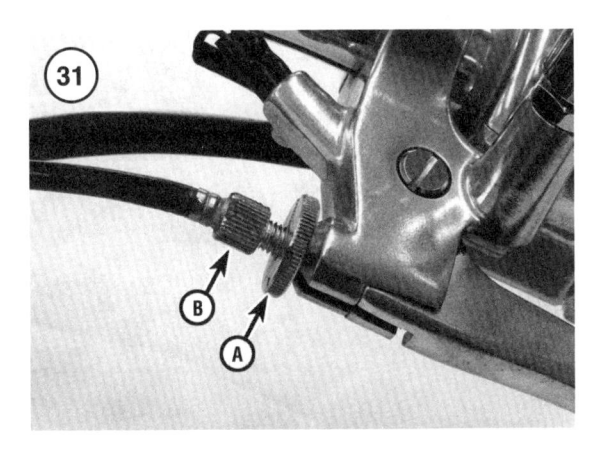

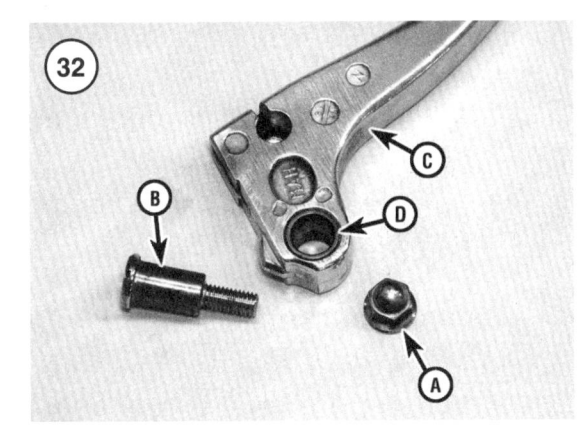

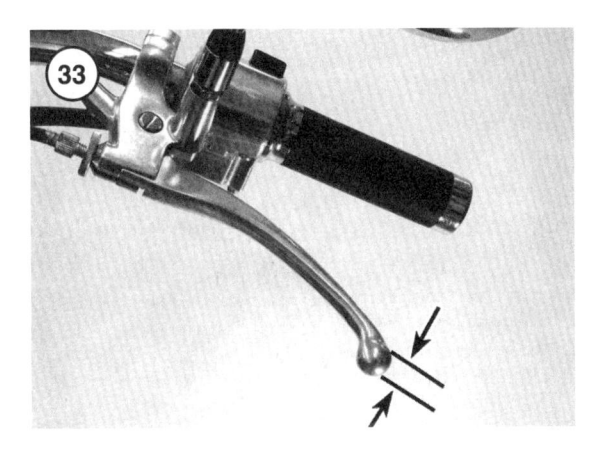

LUBRICATION, MAINTENANCE AND TUNE-UP

NOTE
Cover the area around the nozzle and tube with a plastic bag.

2. Mount a cable lube tool onto the upper end of the cable (**Figure 27**) and lubricate the cable until fluid exits through the opposite end of the cable. Wipe up all excess lube from the end of the cable.
3. Lightly lubricate the upper cable end with grease.
4. Operate the clutch lever. If the clutch lever feels tight or dry, perform the following:
    a. Remove the locknut (A, **Figure 32**), pivot bolt (B) and clutch lever (C).
    b. Clean and dry all parts, including the threads in the clutch lever housing. Check the bushing (D, **Figure 32**) inside the clutch lever for irregular wear or damage. If necessary, replace the clutch lever assembly. The bushing is pressed in place and not available separately. Lubricate the pivot bolt shoulder with grease. Do not lubricate the threads on the pivot bolt, locknut or inside the clutch lever housing.
    c. Install the clutch lever and pivot bolt. Tighten the pivot bolt to 1 N.m (8.9 in.-lb.). Operate the clutch lever to make sure it moves freely.
    d. Hold the pivot bolt and tighten the locknut to 6 N.m (53 in.-lb.). Recheck the clutch lever operation to make sure it moves freely.
5. Reconnect the clutch cable at the clutch lever.
6. Adjust the clutch cable as described in this section.

Adjustment

Check clutch lever free play frequently and adjust when necessary to compensate for clutch cable stretch and drive plate wear. Excessive clutch lever free play prevents the clutch from disengaging and causes clutch drag. Too little or no clutch lever free play does not allow the clutch to fully engage, resulting in clutch slippage. Both conditions cause clutch plate wear. Transmission wear can also result from incorrect clutch adjustment.
1. Operate the clutch lever a few times. If the cable feels tight or dry, lubricate it as described in this section. If clutch cable operation does not improve after lubricating it, replace it (Chapter Six).
2. With the engine turned off, pull the clutch lever until resistance is felt, then stop and measure the free play distance at the end of the clutch lever (**Figure 33**). The clutch lever should have 10-20 mm (3/8-3/4 in.) free play.
3. Make minor adjustments at the clutch cable adjuster mounted at the clutch lever. Loosen the locknut (A, **Figure 31**) and turn the adjuster (B) as required to obtain the correct free play. Tighten the locknut and recheck the adjustment.

in the cable locknut, adjuster and lever housing. Pull the clutch cable's outer sheath out of the adjuster, then slide the inner cable out through the open slots and disconnect it at the lever. If the cable is too tight to disconnect at the adjuster, loosen the cable at the lower adjuster.

CAUTION
Do not use chain lube to lubricate control cables unless it is also advertised as a cable lubricant.

CHAPTER THREE

NOTE
If sufficient free play cannot be obtained at the hand lever, or there is too little thread engagement, use the adjuster at the bottom end of the clutch cable.

4. If sufficient freeplay cannot be achieved, loosen the lower clutch cable adjuster locknut (A, **Figure 34**).
5. At the hand lever, loosen the locknut (A, **Figure 31**) and turn the adjuster screw (B) in to loosen the clutch cable all the way, then turn it out 2-3 turns.
6. At the lower clutch cable adjuster, turn the adjust nut (B, **Figure 34**) until the adjustment is correct or almost correct. Tighten the locknut (A, **Figure 34**).
7. Turn the handlebar adjuster (B, **Figure 31**) as described in Step 3 and adjust the clutch cable. Tighten the locknut (A, **Figure 31**).
8. Check that all locknuts are tight and that both cable ends are properly seated.
9. Start the engine, then pull the clutch lever in and shift the transmission into first gear. Check that the clutch does not drag and that the motorcycle does not stall. Then slowly release the clutch lever while opening the throttle. The motorcycle should begin to move smoothly. If the clutch does not work correctly, turn the engine off and check the clutch adjustment. If the clutch does not work correctly and the adjustment is correct, the clutch cable may be stretched or the drive plates are worn excessively. Service the clutch as described in Chapter Six.

CHOKE CABLE INSPECTION AND ADJUSTMENT (CARBURETED MODELS)

These models use a manually operated choke valve to control the carburetor choke circuit. The choke valve is installed on one end of the choke cable and operates inside the carburetor. The choke knob, mounted on the opposite cable end, open and closes the choke valve. Pulling the choke knob outwards raises the choke valve and opens the choke circuit.

The choke cable is equipped with a friction adjuster that holds the choke cable in position so the choke valve cannot open or close except when the choke knob is operated by hand. Otherwise, the choke cable is free to move, which can cause difficult engine starting (choke valve not opening completely) and an erratic engine idle speed (choke valve not closing completely).

Inspect the choke operation at the intervals specified in **Table 1**.

1. Pull the choke knob (A, **Figure 35**) outward and then push it inward. The cable should move smoothly, but under tension. If there is any binding or roughness, pull the choke knob outward and lightly lubricate the exposed part of the cable with a cable lubricant or light-weight machine oil.
2. To adjust the choke cable, pull the rubber cover (B, **Figure 35**) off of the adjuster. Then turn the adjuster **(Figure 36)** as required so there is no cable movement other than when the choke knob is moved by hand. Slide the rubber cover back into place when the cable is properly adjusted.
3. If the choke cable cannot be properly adjusted or is damaged, replace it as described in Chapter Eight. At the same time, inspect the choke valve for damage and replace if necessary.

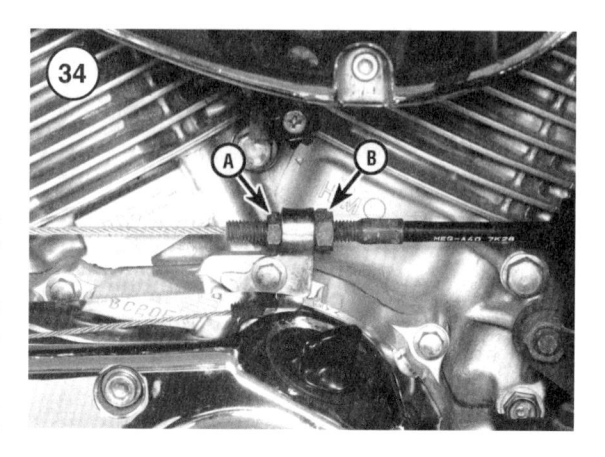

LUBRICATION, MAINTENANCE AND TUNE-UP

WARNING
Prolonged contact with oil may cause skin cancer. Wear rubber gloves and wash hands thoroughly with soap and water after contacting engine oil.

Engine Oil Level Check

Check the engine oil level with the dipstick (**Figure 37**) mounted on the right crankcase cover.

1. Support the motorcycle on its sidestand on a level surface.

CAUTION
To prevent an inaccurate oil level reading, do not apply the throttle when idling the engine.

2. Start the engine and let idle for 3-5 minutes. Make sure the low oil pressure indicator turns off. If the indicator remains on, turn the engine off.
3. Turn the engine off and let the oil settle for 2-3 minutes.

CAUTION
Do not check the oil level with the motorcycle on its sidestand; the oil will flow toward the dipstick, and result in a false reading.

4. Raise and position the motorcycle so the seat is level.
5. Remove the oil filler cap/dipstick (**Figure 37**) and wipe it clean.
6. Reinsert the oil filler cap/dipstick until it seats against the cover opening. Do not screw it in (**Figure 38**).
7. Remove the oil filler cap/dipstick. The oil level should be between the full and low level marks (**Figure 39**).
8. If the oil level is near or below the low level mark (**Figure 39**), add the recommended oil (**Table 3**) to correct the level. Add oil while checking the level to avoid overfilling.
9. Replace the O-ring on the oil filler cap/dipstick if it is starting to deteriorate or harden.
10. Install the oil filler cap/dipstick (**Figure 37**) and tighten securely.
11. If the oil level is too high, do the following:

NOTE
A spray head attachment and its attached hose removed from a typical household cleaning container or spray bottle works well for removing excess oil from the crankcase. Flush the spray

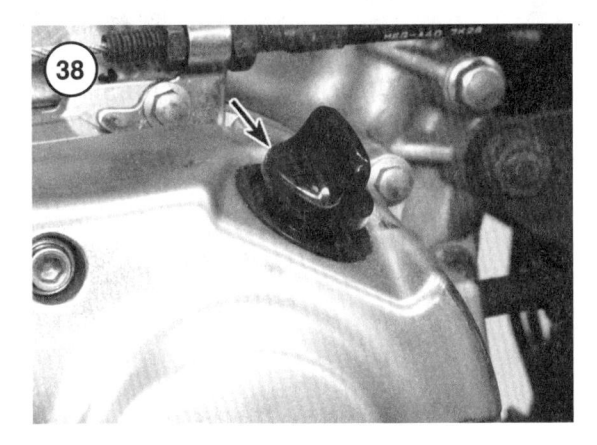

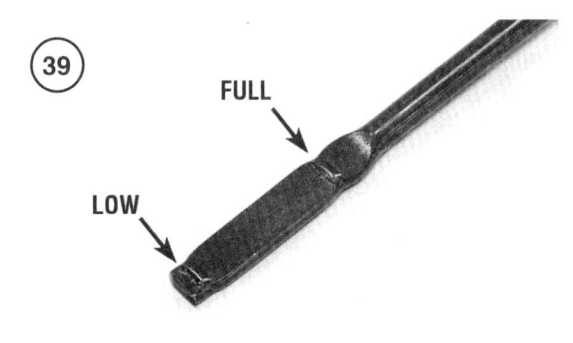

ENGINE OIL AND FILTER

Refer to **Table 1** for the recommended oil and filter change intervals. These intervals assume that the motorcycle is operated in moderate climates. If the motorcycle is operated infrequently, consider a time-based interval. If the motorcycle is operated under dusty conditions, the oil gets dirty quicker and should be changed more frequently than recommended.

Refer to *Engine Oils* under *Shop Supplies* in Chapter One for additional information on engine oil selection. Refer to **Table 3** for engine oil requirements and to **Table 4** for oil capacities.

head attachment and its hose with clean engine oil before using it.

a. Remove the oil filler cap/dipstick **(Figure 37)** and draw out the excess oil using a suitable tool.
b. Recheck the oil level and adjust if necessary.
c. Install the oil filler cap/dipstick and tighten securely.

Engine Oil and Filter Change

NOTE
Warming the engine heats the oil so it flows freely and carries out contamination and sludge.

1. Support the motorcycle on its *sidestand* when draining the engine oil. This ensures complete draining.

WARNING
The engine, exhaust pipes and oil are hot! Work carefully when removing the oil drain bolt and oil filter to avoid contacting the oil or hot engine parts.

2. Clean the area around the oil drain bolt and oil filter.
3. Place a clean drip pan under the crankcase and remove the oil drain bolt **(Figure 40)**.
4. Loosen the oil filler cap/dipstick **(Figure 37)** to help speed up the flow of oil. Allow the oil to drain completely. Discard the crush washer installed on the drain bolt.
5. To replace the oil filter, perform the following:
   a. Install a socket type oil filter wrench squarely onto the oil filter **(Figure 41)** and turn the filter counterclockwise until oil begins to run out, then remove the oil filter. Remove the filter's O-ring if it remained on the crankcase surface and discard it.
   b. Hold the filter over the drain pan and pour out any remaining oil, then place the old filter in a plastic bag and dispose of it properly.
   c. Carefully clean the oil filter sealing surface on the crankcase. Do not allow any dirt or other debris to enter the engine.
   d. Lubricate the rubber seal and threads on the new oil filter with clean engine oil.
   e. Install the new oil filter onto the threaded fitting on the crankcase. Tighten the filter by hand until it contacts the crankcase. Then tighten an additional 3/4 turn. If using the oil filter socket, tighten the oil filter to 26 N.m (19 ft.-lb.).
6. Install the oil drain bolt **(Figure 40)** with a new crush washer and tighten to 29 N.m (21 ft.-lb.).
7. Support the motorcycle on a stand with the seat in a level position.
8. Insert a funnel into the oil filler hole and fill the engine with the correct type **(Table 3)** and quantity of oil **(Table 4)**.
9. Remove the funnel and screw in the oil filler cap/dipstick and its O-ring **(Figure 37)**.

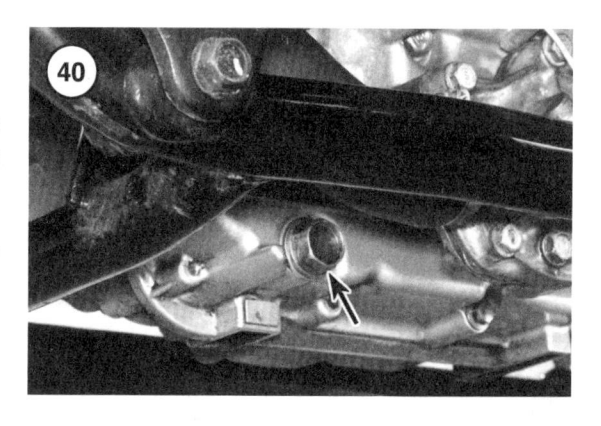

CAUTION
When starting a rebuilt engine for the first time, make sure the motorcycle is positioned with the seat in a level position to make sure oil is picked up by the oil pump and delivered under pressure to engine and transmission components.

10. Start the engine and let it idle.

NOTE
The oil pressure indicator should go out within 1-2 seconds. If it stays on, shut off the engine immediately and locate the problem. Do not run the engine with the oil pressure indicator on.

11. Check the oil filter and drain bolt for leaks.
12. Turn the engine off after 3-5 minutes and check the oil level as described in this chapter. Adjust the oil level if necessary.

LUBRICATION, MAINTENANCE AND TUNE-UP

ENGINE OIL PRESSURE CHECK

WARNING
The engine, exhaust pipes and oil are hot during this procedure! Work carefully to avoid contacting the oil or hot engine parts.

NOTE
Check the engine oil pressure after reassembling the engine or when troubleshooting the lubrication system.

Tools

The following tools, or their equivalents are required to check the oil pressure:
   a. Oil pressure gauge: (Honda part No. 07506-3000001).
   b. Oil pressure adapter: (Honda part No. 07510-4220100).

Procedure

1. Connect a tachometer to the engine following the gauge manufacturer's instructions.
2. Start the engine and allow it to reach normal operating temperature. Turn the engine off.
3. Support the motorcycle on a stand so the seat is level.
4. Remove the oil pressure switch (Chapter Ten).

WARNING
Keep the gauge hose away from the exhaust pipe during this test. If the hose contacts the hot exhaust pipe, it may melt and spray hot oil.

5. Assemble the oil pressure adapter and gauge. Thread the oil pressure gauge adapter into the engine in place of the oil pressure switch. Make sure the fitting is tight to prevent leakage.
6. Check the engine oil level as described in this section. Add oil if necessary.

CAUTION
The oil pressure indicator should go out within 1-2 seconds. If it stays on, shut off the engine immediately and locate the problem. Do not run the engine with the oil pressure indicator on.

7. Start the engine and let it idle until the operating temperature is 80° C (176° F). Check engine temperature with an infrared thermometer if available.
8. Increase engine speed to 5000 rpm and read the oil pressure on the gauge. Refer to the engine oil pressure specification in **Table 2**.
9. Allow the engine to return to idle, then shut it off and remove the test equipment.
10. If the oil pressure is lower or higher than specified, refer to *Engine Lubrication* in Chapter Two.
11. Install the oil pressure switch (Chapter Ten).
12. Check the engine oil level as described in this section. Add oil if necessary.
13. Disconnect and remove the tachometer.

COOLING SYSTEM

WARNING
When performing any service work on the engine or cooling system, never remove the radiator cap, coolant drain bolt or disconnect any coolant hose while the engine and radiator are hot. Scalding fluid and steam may be blown out under pressure and cause serious injury.

Check, inspect and service the cooling system at the intervals in **Table 1**.

Coolant Selection

CAUTION
Many antifreeze solutions contain silicate inhibitors to protect aluminum parts from corrosion damage. However, these silicate inhibitors can cause premature wear to water pump seals. When selecting antifreeze, make sure it does not contain silicate inhibitors.

When adding coolant to the cooling system, use only Pro Honda HP Coolant, or an equivalent ready-to-use, water/coolant blend pre-mixed 50:50 with silicate-free ethylene glycol antifreeze and purified, de-ionized water. If mixing antifreeze and water, use a 50:50 mixture of distilled water and antifreeze that does not contain silicate inhibitors. Use only soft or distilled water. Never use tap or saltwater, as these will damage engine parts.

Radiator Inspection

1. Inspect the front of the radiator for a buildup of insects, mud and other debris. Carefully clean the radiator with compressed air or water from a garden hose. A stiff, small brush can also be used to loosen debris hardened on the radiator. Do not use air or water at a high pressure as this may damage the radiator fins.
2. Straighten bent radiator fins with a small screw-

driver, making sure not to puncture the radiator.
3. Check that the cooling fan blade is tight. If the blade is loose (has noticeable end play), remove the radiator and inspect the blade and tighten the nut (Chapter Eleven).
4. Inspect the radiator for leaks and damage (Chapter Eleven).
5. Inspect the radiator mounting bolt for tightness.

Water Pump Weep Hole

Refer to *Water Pump Weep Hole Check* (Chapter Eleven).

Coolant Test and Inspection

WARNING
Do not remove the radiator cap when the engine is hot.

1. Remove the fuel tank (Chapter Eight or Chapter Nine).
2. Remove the radiator cap **(Figure 42)**.
3. Test the specific gravity of the coolant with an antifreeze tester to ensure adequate temperature and corrosion protection. A 50:50 mixture is recommended. Never allow the mixture become less than 40 percent antifreeze.
4. While the radiator cap is off, inspect the coolant for contamination and debris. Flush the cooling system and replace the coolant if necessary as described in this section.
5. Reinstall the radiator cap **(Figure 42)**.
6. Reinstall the fuel tank (Chapter Eight or Chapter Nine).

Coolant Level

1. Start the engine and allow it to idle until it reaches normal operating temperature.

NOTE
*If the coolant reserve tank is empty, air may have entered the cooling system. Refill and bleed the cooling system as described in **Coolant Change** in this section.*

2. With the engine running at idle speed and the motorcycle positioned upright, the coolant level should between the UPPER and LOWER level marks on the coolant reserve tank **(Figure 43)**.
3. If necessary, add coolant as follows:
   a. Turn the engine off.
   b. Position the motorcycle so that it is upright.

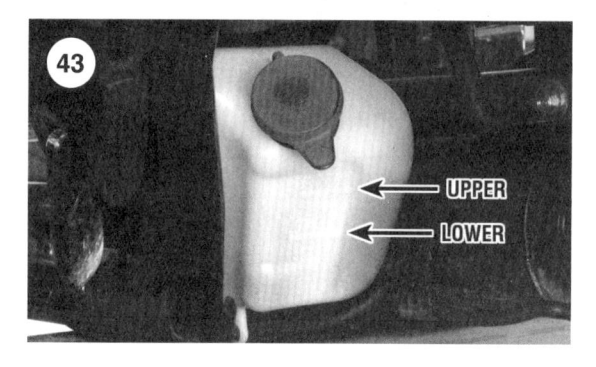

NOTE
*If the coolant level continues to fall and there are no coolant leaks, one or both head gaskets may be leaking. Perform the **Cylinder Leakdown Test** in Chapter Two to troubleshoot the problem.*

   c. Remove the coolant reserve tank cap **(Figure 43)** and add coolant into the reserve tank (not the radiator) to bring the level to the upper mark. Install the cap, making sure it seats firmly around the top of the tank.
   d. Inspect the cooling system for leaks as described in Chapter Eleven.

Coolant Change

WARNING
Antifreeze is toxic waste and should not be disposed of by flushing down a drain or poured onto the ground. Place old antifreeze into a suitable container and dispose of it properly. Do not store coolant where it is accessible to children or pets.

WARNING
*Do not remove the radiator cap **(Figure 42)** if the engine is hot. The coolant is very hot and is under pressure. Severe scalding will result if hot coolant contacts skin.*

LUBRICATION, MAINTENANCE AND TUNE-UP

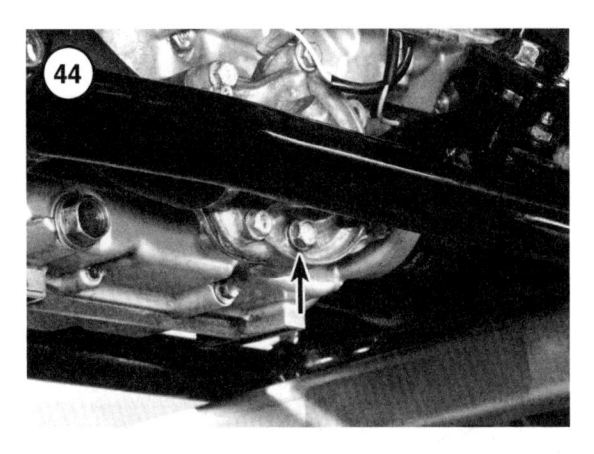

CAUTION
Be careful not to spill antifreeze on painted surfaces as it will damage some surfaces. Wash immediately with soapy water and rinse thoroughly.

Drain, refill and bleed the cooling system at the intervals listed in **Table 1**.

It is sometimes necessary to drain the cooling system when servicing the engine. If the coolant is still in good condition, the coolant can be reused if not contaminated. Drain the coolant into a clean pan and then pour into a container for storage.

Perform the following procedure when the engine is *cold*.

1. Place the motorcycle on a stand so the seat is level.
2. Remove the left crankcase rear cover (Chapter Seventeen).
3. Remove the fuel tank (Chapter Eight or Chapter Nine).

NOTE
If reusing the coolant, clean the water pump, crankcase and lower frame rail to prevent road debris from contaminating the coolant as it passes over it.

NOTE
Coolant will drain under pressure once the radiator cap is removed. It is best to remove the drain bolt first, then the radiator cap.

4. Place a drain pan under the coolant drain bolt. Remove the drain bolt **(Figure 44)** and washer, then hold the drain pan at an angle in front of the drain bolt and have an assistant remove the radiator cap **(Figure 42)**. Allow the coolant to drain completely.
5. Using a garden hose directed through the radiator cap opening, flush the cooling system with water until the water flowing through the drain hole is clear.
6. Install the drain bolt **(Figure 44)** with a new washer and tighten to 13 N.m (115 in.-lb.).
7. Disconnect the siphon hose (lower hose) from the coolant reserve tank **(Figure 43)** and drain the coolant in the tank. Flush the tank with water. Check the end of the siphon hose for cracks, hardness, and other damage. If in good condition reinstall the siphon hose and secure it with the clamp.

CAUTION
*Do not use a higher percentage of antifreeze-to-water solution than is recommended under **Coolant Selection** in this section. A higher concentration of coolant will actually decrease the performance of the cooling system.*

8. Place a funnel in the radiator filler neck and slowly refill the radiator and engine with a mixture of 50 percent antifreeze and 50 percent distilled water. Add coolant to bring the level to the bottom of the filler neck. Add the mixture slowly so it will expel as much air as possible from the cooling system. See *Coolant Selection* in this section before purchasing and mixing coolant. **Table 5** lists engine coolant capacity.
9. Fill the coolant reserve tank to its upper level line **(Figure 43)**.
10. After filling the radiator, bleed the cooling system as follows:
    a. Wrap a towel around the radiator cap opening to help catch some of the coolant that will bubble out of the opening when the engine is running.
    b. Start the engine and allow it to idle for two to three minutes.
    c. Snap the throttle several times to bleed air from the cooling system. When the coolant level drops in the radiator, add coolant to bring the level to the bottom of the filler neck.
    d. When the radiator coolant level has stabilized, install the radiator cap **(Figure 42)**.
11. Start the engine and let it run at idle speed until the engine reaches normal operating temperature. Make sure the coolant level in the coolant reserve tank stabilizes at the correct level. Add coolant to the coolant reserve tank as necessary.
12. Check the coolant drain bolt and coolant reserve tank for leaks.
13. Check the area underneath the motorcycle for any spilt antifreeze and wipe up before moving the motorcycle.
14. Test ride the motorcycle and readjust the coolant level in the reserve tank as described in *Coolant Level* in this section.

PULSE SECONDARY AIR SUPPLY SYSTEM

All models are equipped with a pulse secondary air supply system. At the intervals specified in **Table 1**, check the system hoses and reed valves for damage. Refer to Chapter Eight and Chapter Nine.

EVAPORATIVE EMISSION CONTROL SYSTEM (CALIFORNIA MODELS)

All California models are equipped with an evaporative emission control system. At the intervals specified in **Table 1**, check the system hoses and EVAP canister for damage. Refer to Chapter Eight and Chapter Nine.

BATTERY

The original equipment battery is a maintenance-free type. Maintenance-free batteries do not require periodic electrolyte inspection and water cannot be added. Refer to Chapter Ten for battery service, testing and replacement procedures.

FINAL DRIVE OIL

Inspection

Periodically inspect the final drive unit for oil leaks. Check the area where the rear wheel mounts onto the final drive unit. An oil leak in this area may indicate a leaking ring gear seal. A damaged ring gear seal will also allow oil to drip onto the rear wheel. Then inspect the final drive unit where it bolts onto the swing arm. If oil is found on the bottom of the unit and along the bottom of the swing arm, check for a damaged drive shaft seal or pinion gear seal. Refer to Chapter Fourteen to inspect the final drive assembly.

Oil Level Check

The final drive unit does not burn oil. If the oil level is low, perform the *Inspection* in this section to locate a possible oil leak.

1. Support the motorcycle on its sidestand on level ground.
2. Clean the area around the final drive oil fill cap and remove it (A, **Figure 45**).
3. The oil level must be even with the lower edge of the oil filler hole. If the oil level is low, add the recommended type gear oil **(Table 3)** to correct the level.
4. Inspect the oil fill cap O-ring and replace if leaking or damaged. Lubricate a new O-ring with grease.
5. Install and tighten the oil fill cap to 12 N.m (106 in.-lb.).

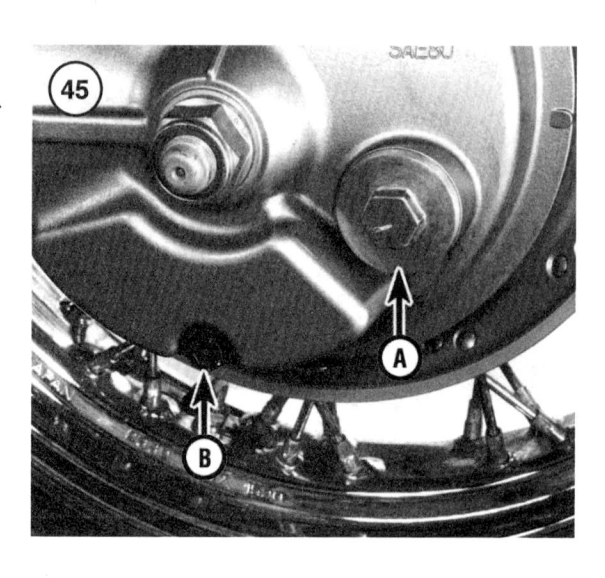

Final Drive Oil Change

The recommended oil change interval is listed in **Table 1**.

1. Ride the motorcycle until the oil in the final drive unit becomes hot.
2. Place the motorcycle on its sidestand on level ground.
3. Place a drain pan under the final drive unit.
4. Remove the oil fill cap (A, **Figure 45**) and the drain bolt (B), and then drain the oil. When the oil stops draining, turn the rear wheel and then allow it rest in different spots to allow oil to drain off the ring gear.
5. Remove and discard the crush washer used on the drain bolt.
6. Install a new crush washer on the drain bolt (B, **Figure 45**) and tighten to 12 N.m (106 in.-lb.).
7. Add the recommended type gear oil **(Table 3)** to bring the oil level even with the lower edge of the oil filler hole. **Table 6** lists final drive oil capacity.
8. Inspect the oil fill cap O-ring and replace if leaking or damaged. Lubricate a new O-ring with grease.
9. Install and tighten the oil fill cap (A, **Figure 45**) to 12 N.m (106 in.-lb.).
10. Wipe off any oil from the bottom of the final drive unit, rear wheel and rear tire.

TIRES AND WHEELS

Tire Pressure

Check and adjust the tire pressure to maintain the tire profile, good traction and handling and to get

LUBRICATION, MAINTENANCE AND TUNE-UP

TIRE PRESSURE

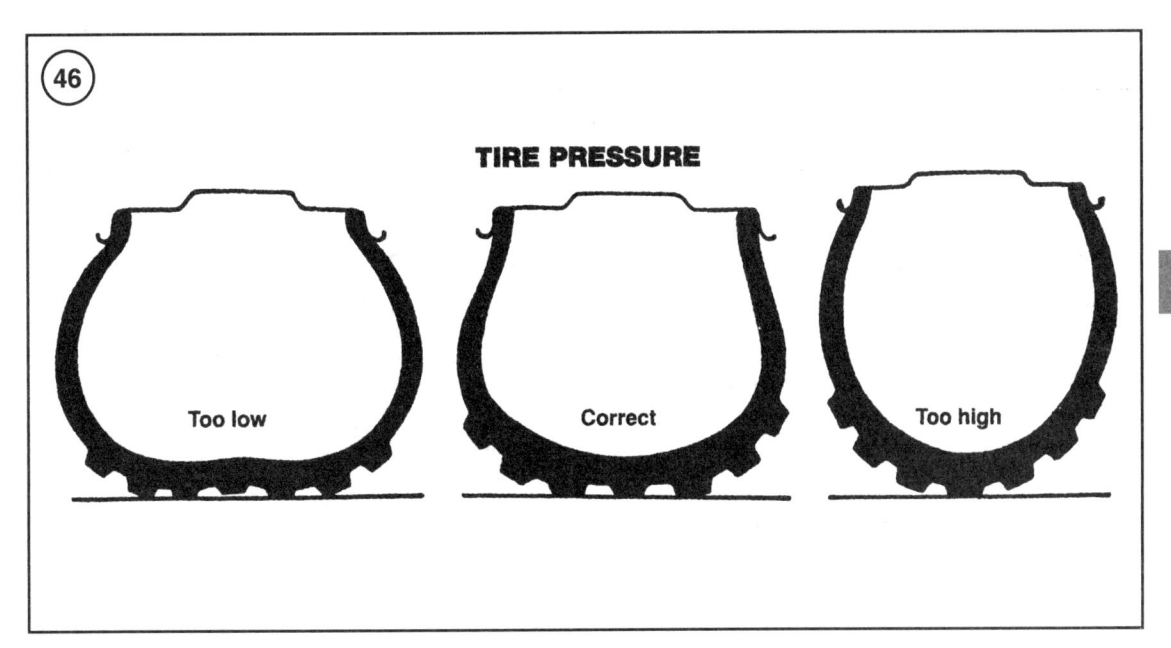

Too low — Correct — Too high

the maximum life out of the tire. Check tire pressure when the tires are *cold*. When the motorcycle is ridden, the tire temperature rises. Never release air pressure from a warm or hot tire to match the recommended tire pressure listed in **Table 7**; doing so may cause the tire to be underinflated. Use an accurate tire pressure gauge.

Tire Inspection

Inspect the tires periodically for excessive wear and damage. Inspect the tires for the following:
1. Deep cuts and imbedded objects, such as nails and stones. If a nail or other object is in a tire, mark its location with a light crayon prior to removing it. This helps to locate the hole in the tube for repair. Refer to Chapter Twelve for tire changing and repair information.
2. Flat spots. Storing the motorcycle for long periods of time with one or both wheels on the ground can cause flat spots.
3. Sidewall cracks and other visual damage.
4. Separating plies.
5. Bulges.
6. Improper tire centering on rim.
7. Damaged tire or tube stem.

Tire Wear Analysis

Analyze abnormal tire wear to determine the cause. Common causes are:
1. Incorrect tire pressure. This is the biggest cause of abnormal tire wear. Compare the wear in the center of the contact patch with the wear at the edges of the contact patch (**Figure 46**). Check tire pressure and examine the tire tread. Note the following:
   a. If a tire shows excessive wear at the edges of the contact patch, but the wear at the center of the contact patch is normal, the tire has been underinflated. Underinflated tires will cause the sidewalls to flex excessively. This results in higher tire temperatures, hard or imprecise steering and abnormal tire wear on the tire edges.

   NOTE
   Large amounts of high-speed riding on straight roads will cause the tires to exhibit a similar wear pattern as described in here.

   b. If a tire shows excessive wear in the center of the contact patch, but wear at the edges of the contact patch is normal, the tire has been overinflated. Overinflated tires will cause the tire to bulge in the center of the tread. This results in a hard ride and abnormal tire wear in the center of the tread. When a properly inflated tire hits a large bump in the road, it has a normal flex or give and is capable of absorbing much of the shock. However, an overinflated tire cannot flex or give and the tire casing (cord material) takes the shock. This weakens and breaks the tire cords and eventually causes tire failure.
2. Overloading.
3. Incorrect wheel alignment.
4. Incorrect wheel balance: The tire and wheel assembly should be balanced when installing a new tire.
5. Worn or damaged wheel bearings.

Tread Depth

Measure the tread depth **(Figure 47)** in the center of the tire using a small ruler or a tread depth gauge. The manufacturer recommends replacing the original equipment tires before the center tread depth has worn to the minimum tread depth specified in **Table 7**.

Tires are also designed with tread wear indicators **(Figure 48)** that begin to appear as the tread depth nears its minimum limit and will align with the tire tread when the tire is worn out. At this point the tire is no longer safe and must be replaced.

Wheel Bearing Inspection

Inspect the wheel bearings once a year, whenever the wheels are removed or when troubleshooting a tire or handling problem. Refer to *Front and Rear Hubs* in Chapter Twelve.

Spokes Tension

On models with laced wheels, check for loose or damaged spokes. Refer to Chapter Twelve.

Wheel Inspection

Check the wheel rims for excessive runout, cracks and other damage. Refer to Chapter Twelve.

STEERING BEARINGS

Inspect the steering bearing adjustment at the intervals specified in **Table 1**.

1. Support the motorcycle on a stand with the front wheel off the ground.
2. Hold onto the handlebars and move them from side to side. Note any binding or roughness.
3. Support the motorcycle so both wheels are on the ground.
4. Sit on the motorcycle and hold onto the handlebar. Apply the front brake lever and try to push the front fork forward. Try to detect any movement in the steering head area. If there is movement, the bearing adjustment is loose and requires adjustment.
5. If any roughness, binding or looseness was detected when performing Step 2 or Step 4, perform the *Steering Bearing Preload Check* in Chapter Thirteen. Service the steering bearings if necessary.

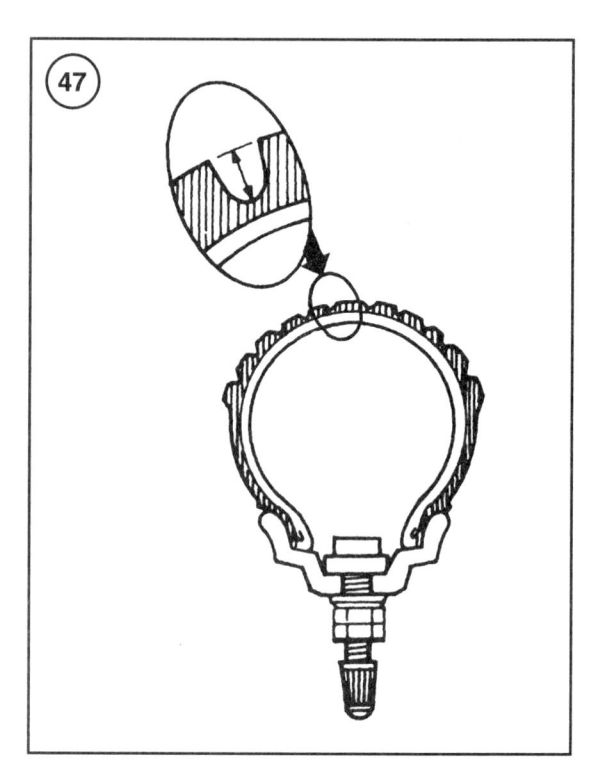

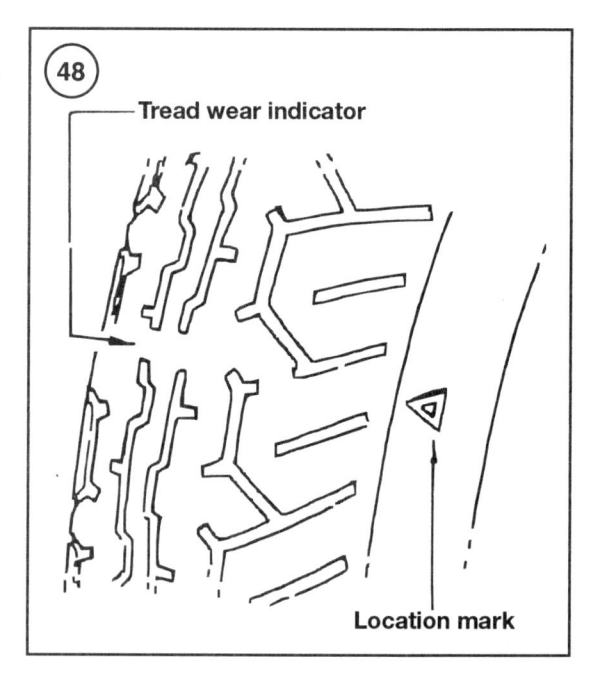

FRONT SUSPENSION CHECK

CAUTION
If any of the suspension fasteners are loose, refer to Chapter Thirteen for service procedures and torque specifications.

Inspect the front suspension at the intervals specified in **Table 1**.

LUBRICATION, MAINTENANCE AND TUNE-UP

Table 1. Immediately inspect the brake components when their operating condition has changed.

Bleeding the front brake, servicing the brake components and replacing the brake pads and brake shoes are covered in Chapter Fifteen.

Inspection

Inspect the front and rear brake operation at the intervals specified in **Table 1** or whenever the braking condition has changed.

Front

1. Support the motorcycle on its sidestand on level ground and shift the transmission into neutral.
2. Apply the front brake lever. Make sure it feels firm. If the lever feels soft or spongy, air has probably entered the system. Bleed the brake as described in Chapter Fifteen.
3. Apply and hold the front brake and check the brake hose and all brake components for leakage.
4. Check the brake hose between the master cylinder and brake caliper. If there are any leaks, tighten the banjo bolt(s) and then bleed the brake system as described in Chapter Fifteen. If this does not stop the leak or if a brake line is obviously damaged, cracked or chafed, replace the brake hose and bleed the system. Refer to Chapter Fifteen for brake system torque specifications.
5. Check the front brake hose routing and for loose or missing fasteners and clamps.
6. Operate the front brake lever. If the brake lever feels tight or dry, perform the following:
   a. Remove the locknut (A, **Figure 49**), pivot bolt (B) and brake lever (C).
   b. Clean and dry all parts, including the threads in the master cylinder. Check the bushing (D, **Figure 49**) inside the brake lever (C) for irregular wear or damage. If necessary, replace the brake lever assembly. The bushing is pressed in place and not available separately. Lubricate the pivot bolt shoulder (B, **Figure 49**) with silicone brake grease. Do not lubricate the threads on the pivot bolt, locknut or inside the master cylinder.
   c. Install the brake lever and pivot bolt. Tighten the pivot bolt to 1 N.m (8.8 in.-lb.). Operate the brake lever to make sure it moves freely.
   d. Hold the pivot bolt and tighten the locknut to 6 N.m (53 in.-lb.). Recheck the brake lever operation to make sure it moves freely.
7. Inspect the boot (**Figure 50**) installed on the end of the master cylinder piston for cracks, deterioration and other damage. If the boot is damaged, replace it as follows:

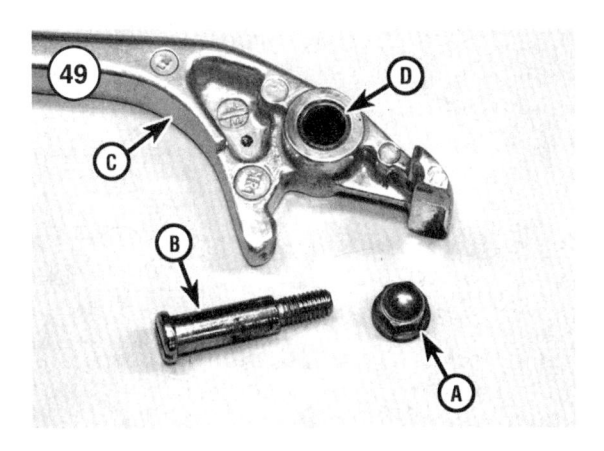

1. Use a soft wet cloth to wipe the front fork tubes to remove any dirt, road tar and other debris on them. As this debris passes by the fork seals, it will eventually damage the seals and cause them to leak oil.
2. Check the front fork for any oil seal leaks or damage.
3. Apply the front brake and pump the fork up and down as vigorously as possible. Check for smooth operation.
4. Make sure the upper and lower fork tube pinch bolts are tight.
5. Check that the handlebar mounting bolts are tight.
6. Make sure the front axle is tight.

REAR SUSPENSION CHECK

CAUTION
If any of the suspension fasteners are loose, refer to Chapter Fourteen for procedures and torque specifications.

Inspect the rear suspension at the intervals specified in **Table 1**.
1. With both wheels on the ground, check the shock absorbers by bouncing on the seat several times.
2. Check the shock absorbers for signs of oil leakage, loose mounting fasteners or other damage.
3. Check the swing arm bearings as described in Chapter Fourteen.
4. Check for loose or missing suspension fasteners.
5. Make sure the rear axle nut is tight.
6. To adjust the rear shock absorbers, refer to Chapter Fourteen.

BRAKE SYSTEM

All models are equipped with a front disc brake and either a rear drum brake or equipped with an ABS system that includes a rear disc brake. Check both brake assemblies at the intervals specified in

a. Remove the brake lever as described in Step 6.
b. Remove the boot **(Figure 50)** from the groove in the end of the master cylinder piston.
c. Check the master cylinder for any fluid leakage, indicating the piston seals are damaged and leaking. If necessary, replace the master cylinder piston assembly (Chapter Fifteen).
d. Slide the new boot over the piston. Seat the large end against the snap ring and the outer lip into the groove in the end of the piston **(Figure 50)**.
e. Lightly lubricate the end of the piston with silicone brake grease.
f. Install the brake lever as described in this section.

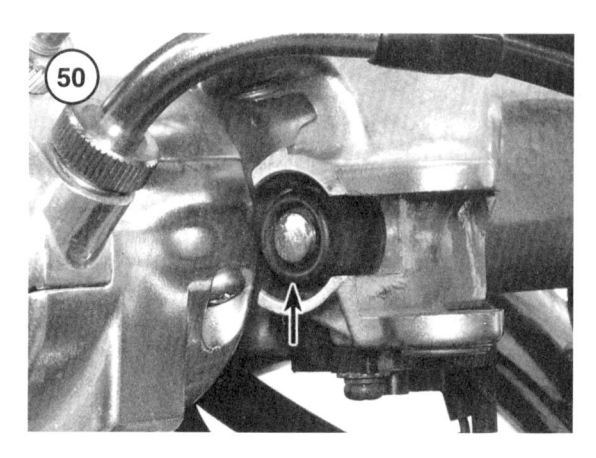

Rear drum brake

1. Support the motorcycle with the rear wheel off the ground. Spin the rear wheel and check for brake drag. Then, apply the rear brake pedal. Make sure it feels firm. If necessary, check and adjust the rear brake as described in this section.
2. If the brake pedal moves roughly, remove the brake pedal assembly and lubricate the brake pedal and its pivot shaft surfaces with grease as described in *Rear Brake Pedal* in Chapter Fifteen.
3. Make sure the rear brake stopper arm (A, **Figure 51**) fasteners are tight and the cotter pins are locked in place.
4. Refer to *Rear Brake Pedal* in Chapter Fifteen and note the following:
   a. Make sure the middle brake rod cotter pins are locked in place.
   b. Make sure the joint arm pinch bolt is tight.
   c. Make sure the rear brake pedal snap ring is seated fully in the pivot shaft groove.

Rear disc brake

1. Support the motorcycle on its sidestand on level ground and shift the transmission into neutral.
2. Apply the front brake lever. Make sure it feels firm. If the lever feels soft or spongy, air has probably entered the system. Bleed the front and rear brake lines (Chapter Fifteen).
3. Apply and hold the rear brake pedal and check the brake hose and all brake components for leakage.
4. Check the brake hose between the master cylinder and brake caliper. If there are any leaks, tighten the banjo bolt(s) and then bleed the brake system as described in Chapter Fifteen. If this does not stop the leak or if a brake line is obviously damaged, cracked or chafed, replace the brake hose and bleed the system. Refer to Chapter Fifteen for brake system torque specifications.
5. Check the front brake hose routing and inspect it for loose or missing fasteners and clamps.
6. Operate the rear brake pedal. If the brake pedal feels tight or dry, remove and lubricate the rear brake pedal assembly (Chapter Fifteen).
7. Inspect the boot installed in the end of the master cylinder for cracks, deterioration and other damage. If the boot is damaged, replace it as described in *Rear Master Cylinder (ABS Models)* in Chapter Fifteen. The boot can be replaced without having to disconnect the brake hose from the master cylinder.

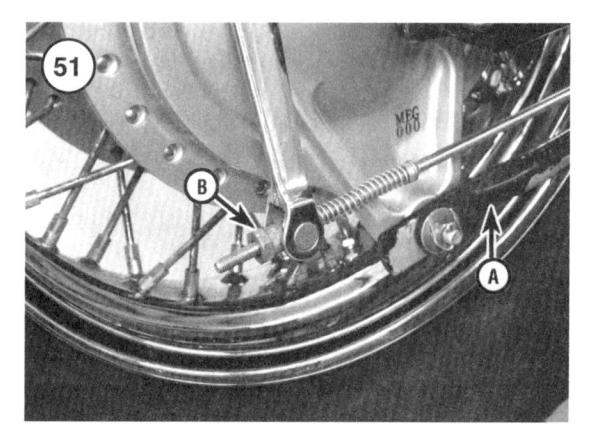

Brake Fluid Selection

> *WARNING*
> *Use DOT 4 brake fluid. Others may cause brake failure. Do not intermix different brands or types of brake fluid as they may not be compatible. Do not intermix silicone based (DOT 5) brake fluid as it can cause brake component damage leading to brake system failure.*

LUBRICATION, MAINTENANCE AND TUNE-UP

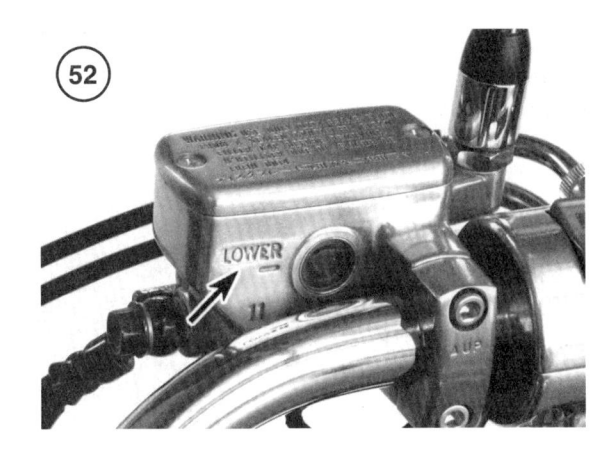

is level.

> **NOTE**
> *If the reservoir is low, check for fluid leaks. If the reservoir is empty, air has probably entered the brake system. Bleed the brake as described in Chapter Fifteen.*

2. The brake fluid level must be above the lower level line in the master cylinder window (**Figure 52**). If the brake fluid level is at or below the lower level line, continue with the procedure.

3. Wipe off the master cylinder cover and remove the cover screws. Then remove the cover, diaphragm plate and diaphragm.

4. Replace the cover screws if the hex portion is starting to round out. Replace the diaphragm if damaged.

5. Add fresh DOT 4 brake fluid and fill the reservoir to the level mark inside the reservoir (**Figure 53**).

6. Wipe off any brake fluid from the edge of the reservoir.

7. Install the diaphragm, diaphragm plate and cover. Install and tighten the cover screws. Then wipe the cover edge with a rag to remove any brake fluid that may have seeped past the diaphragm when the screws were tightened. When the cover screws are tight, turn the handlebar from side to side and check for any leakage around the cover.

8. If the brake fluid level was low, check the brake pads for excessive wear as described in this section.

Rear Brake Fluid Level Check

> **WARNING**
> *Do not check the rear brake fluid level with the motorcycle resting on its sidestand. A false reading will result.*

> **NOTE**
> *A low brake fluid level usually indicates brake pad wear. As the pads wear (become thinner), the brake caliper piston automatically extends farther out of its bore. As the caliper piston moves outward, the brake fluid level lowers in the reservoir to compensate for piston repositioning. However, if the brake fluid level is low and the brake pads are not worn excessively, check for a leak in the brake system.*

1. Support the motorcycle so the seat is level.
2. The brake fluid level must be between the upper and lower level marks on the reservoir housing

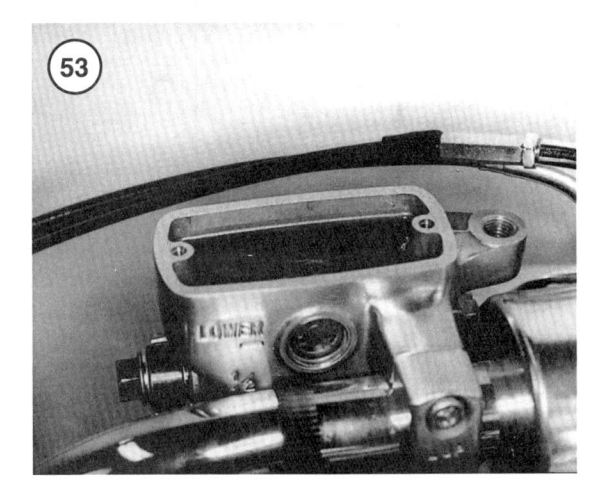

> **CAUTION**
> *Handle brake fluid carefully. Do not spill it on painted or plastic surfaces, as it will damage the surface. Wash the area immediately with soap and water and thoroughly rinse it off.*

Front Brake Fluid Level Check

> **NOTE**
> *A low brake fluid level usually indicates brake pad wear. As the pads wear (become thinner), the brake caliper pistons automatically extend farther out of their bores. As the caliper pistons move outward, the brake fluid level lowers in the reservoir to compensate for piston repositioning. However, if the brake fluid level is low and the brake pads are not worn excessively, check for a leak in the brake system.*

1. Turn the handlebar so the brake master cylinder

(**Figure 54**). If the brake fluid level is at or below the lower level line, continue with Step 3.

> *NOTE*
> *If the reservoir is empty, air has probably entered the brake system. Bleed the brake as described in Chapter Fifteen.*

3. Remove the bolt and outer cover (**Figure 54**).
4. Wipe off the master cylinder cover and unscrew the cover. Then remove the cover, diaphragm plate and diaphragm. Place a paper towel underneath the reservoir.
5. Add fresh DOT 4 brake fluid to fill the reservoir to the upper level mark on the reservoir (**Figure 54**).
6. Install the diaphragm, diaphragm plate and cover and tighten securely. Remove the paper towel.
7. Install the outer cover and tighten its mounting bolt securely. The mounting bolt also secures the reservoir in place.
8. If the brake fluid level was low, check the brake pads for excessive wear as described in this section.

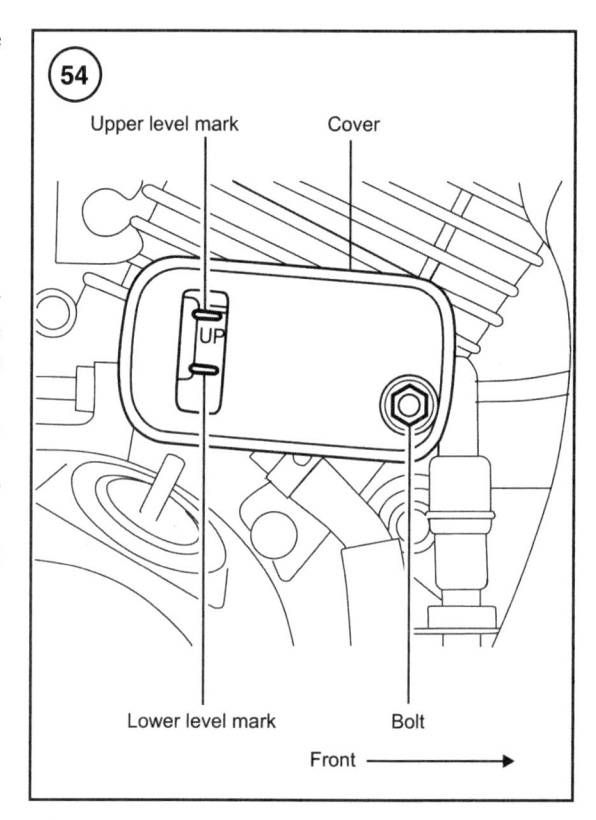

Disc Brake Fluid Change

To maintain peak performance, change the brake fluid as specified in **Table 1** or whenever the caliper or master cylinder is overhauled. To change brake fluid, refer to *Brake Fluid Flushing* in Chapter Fifteen.

Brake Pad Wear

Inspect the brake pads for wear at the intervals specified in **Table 1**.
1. Inspect the brake pads for uneven wear, oil contamination or other damage. Note the following:
   a. Binding or sticking caliper pistons or improper caliper bracket operation can cause uneven pad wear. If the front pads are worn unevenly, remove and service the caliper bracket. If the rear pads are worn unevenly, one of the caliper pistons may be sticking in its bore. Remove and service the rear brake caliper. Refer to Chapter Fifteen.
   b. A damaged fork oil seal will allow oil to run down the fork tube and contaminate the front brake pads and caliper housing. Always check the pads for contamination when a leaking fork seal is detected and replace the fork seal immediately. If fork oil has contaminated the brake caliper, replace the brake pads and overhaul the brake caliper (Chapter Fifteen).
   c. If there is no visible brake pad damage or contamination, perform Step 2.
2. Replace the front or rear brake pads in sets when a pad is worn to the bottom of the wear limit groove. See **Figure 55** (front) or **Figure 56** (rear). Refer to Chapter Fifteen for replacement procedures.

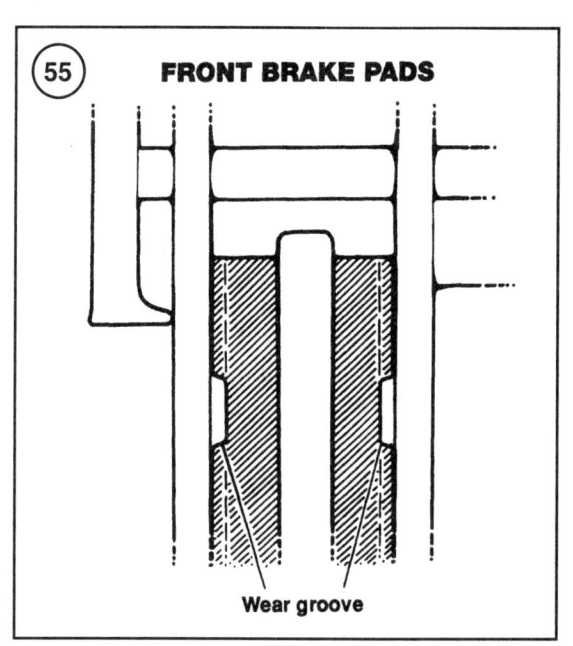

> *NOTE*
> *If it appears the brake pads in a caliper are wearing rapidly, the compensating port in the front master cylinder reservoir or the compensating port in*

LUBRICATION, MAINTENANCE AND TUNE-UP

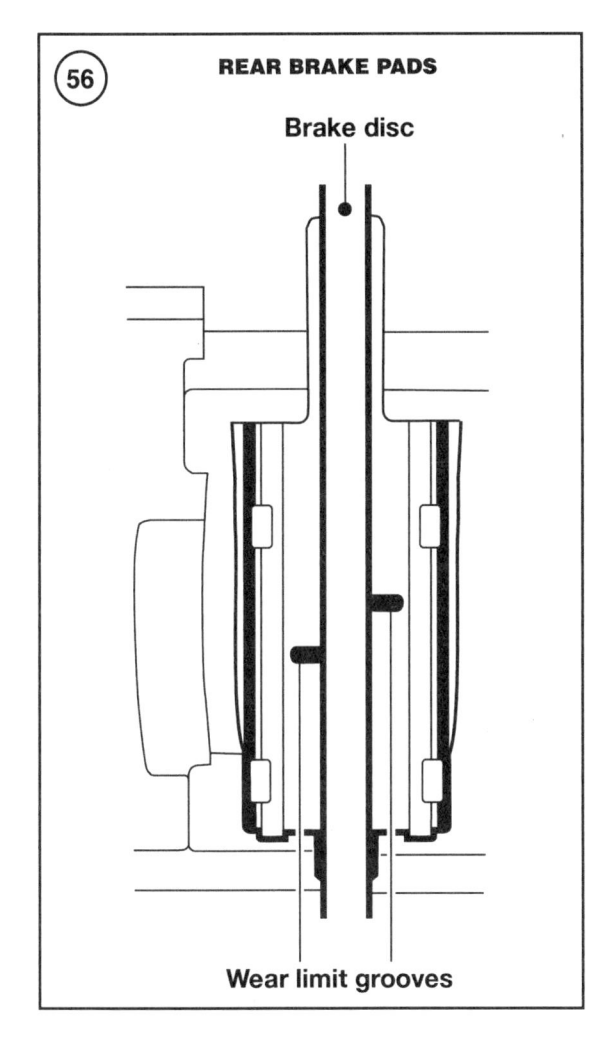

56 REAR BRAKE PADS
Brake disc
Wear limit grooves

57

58

the rear brake master cylinder may be partially plugged. This will prevent the caliper pistons from returning to their rest position when the brake lever or brake pedal is released, causing brake drag. Check the condition of the brake fluid and if it is found to be dirty or contaminated, flush the brake system. In severe cases, both the master cylinder and caliper should be overhauled so all fluid passages can be thoroughly cleaned.

Front Brake Lever Adjustment

There is no adjustment for the front brake lever.

Front Brake Light Switch Inspection

There is no adjustment for the front brake light switch. Check the front brake light switch operation at the intervals specified in **Table 1** or as part of a pre-ride safety check.
1. Turn the ignition switch on.

2. Operate the front brake lever. The brake light should come on just before the brake begins to work. If the brake light does not come on or stays on, test the front brake light switch as described in Chapter Ten. If the front brake light switch is okay, check for a blown bulb if the brake light did not come on.
3. Turn the ignition switch off.

Rear Brake Shoe Wear Inspection

1. Support the motorcycle on its sidestand.
2. Apply the rear brake pedal and hold it in place.
3. If the arrow mark on the brake wear indicator (A, **Figure 57**) aligns with the fixed index mark on the brake panel (B) when the rear brake is applied, the rear brake shoes are excessively worn and require replacement. Replace the rear brake shoes as described in Chapter Fifteen.

Rear Brake Pedal Height

Drum brake models

1. Measure the pedal height from the top of the footpeg rubber to the top of the brake pedal rubber (**Figure 58**). The standard height is 75 mm (3.0 in.).

If the height adjustment is incorrect, continue the procedure.

2. Loosen the adjuster bolt locknut (A, **Figure 59**) and turn the adjuster bolt (B) in or out until the standard pedal height is reached. On 2004-2009 Aero models, hold the adjuster bolt and tighten the locknut to 10 N.m (89 in.-lb.). On all other models, hold the adjuster bolt and tighten the locknut securely.

3. Recheck the pedal height.

4. If the pedal height adjustment was changed, check the rear brake pedal free play and the rear brake light switch adjustment as described in this section. Adjust if necessary.

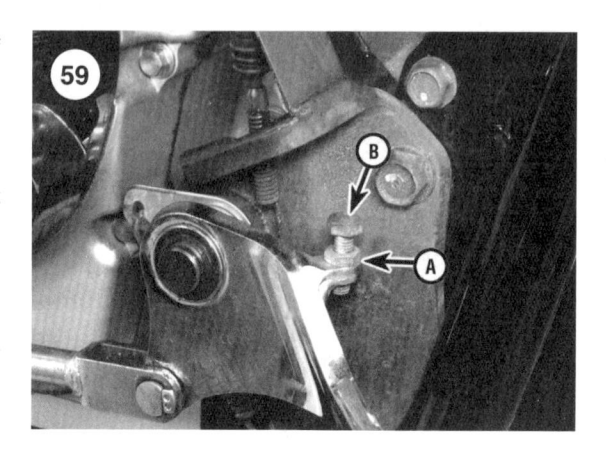

ABS models

On these models, the rear master cylinder pushrod is set to a specified length, measured between the center of the master cylinder's front mounting bolt hole to the center of the clevis hole as shown in **Figure 60**. Refer to **Table 2** for the correct distance. To adjust, loosen the locknut and turn the pushrod as required. Hold the pushrod and tighten the locknut to 18 N.m (13 ft.-lb.) and then remeasure pushrod length.

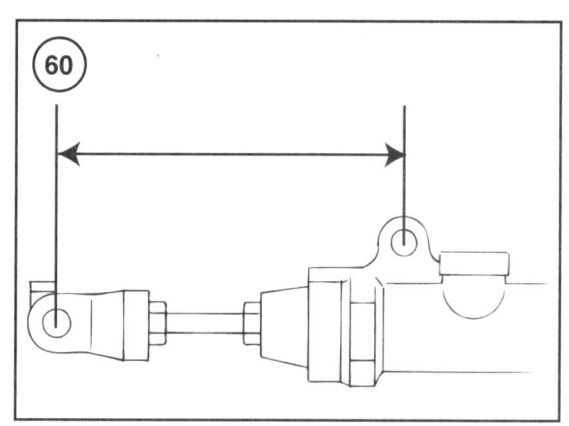

Rear Brake Pedal Free Play

Rear brake drum

1. Support the motorcycle on its sidestand.
2. Before checking and adjusting the free play, check the brake rod and brake arm assemblies for missing parts or damage.
3. Depress the rear brake pedal until resistance is felt at the pedal. The distance the brake pedal moved is rear brake free play **(Figure 61)**. The correct free play measurement is 20-30 mm (13/16-1 3/16 in.). If out of specification, continue with Step 4.
4. Turn the rear brake rod adjusting nut (B, **Figure 51**) to adjust the rear brake free play. After turning the adjusting nut, make sure the notch in the nut seats against the collar.

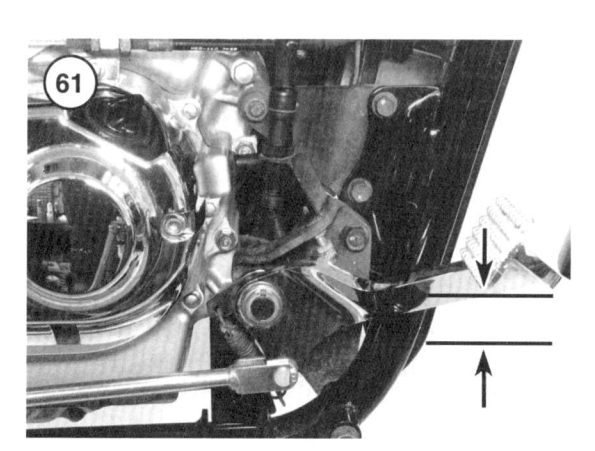

NOTE
If the rear brake pedal free play cannot be adjusted so there is no brake drag, the brake drum and brake shoe linings may be contaminated. Check and service the rear brake as described in Chapter Fifteen.

5. Apply the rear brake a few times, and recheck the free play. Then support the motorcycle with its rear wheel off the ground and spin the wheel, making sure it rotates freely. If there is any noticeable brake drag, the rear brake is adjusted too tightly. Readjust the brake pedal free play to the specification in **Table 2**.

6. Check the rear brake light switch adjustment (this section).

ABS models

There is no free play adjustment for these models.

Rear Brake Light Switch Adjustment

Check the rear brake light switch adjustment at the intervals specified in **Table 1**.

LUBRICATION, MAINTENANCE AND TUNE-UP

HEADLIGHT AIM

Check the headlight aim at the intervals specified in **Table 1**. Refer to *Headlight Adjustment* in Chapter Ten for adjustment procedure.

SIDESTAND AND IGNITION CUT-OFF SWITCH TEST

WARNING
Do not ride the motorcycle until the sidestand switch operates correctly. Riding the motorcycle with the sidestand down will cause the rider to loose control when the sidestand contacts the ground.

NOTE
If the sidestand requires service as described in this section, refer to **Sidestand** *in Chapter Seventeen.*

Check the sidestand and the ignition cut-off system operation at the intervals specified in **Table 1**.
1. Operate the sidestand to check its movement and spring tension. Replace the spring if weak or damaged.
2. Check the sidestand for loose or missing fasteners.
3. Lubricate the sidestand pivot bolt if necessary.
4. Check the sidestand ignition cut-off system as follows:
   a. Park the motorcycle so both wheels are on the ground.
   b. Sit on the motorcycle and raise the sidestand.
   c. Shift the transmission into neutral.
   d. Start the engine, then squeeze the clutch lever and shift the transmission into gear.
   e. Move the sidestand **(Figure 63)** down. When doing so, the engine should stop.
   f. If the engine did not stop as the sidestand was lowered, test the sidestand switch as described in Chapter Ten.

FRONT FORK OIL CHANGE

The manufacturer does not provide a service interval for changing the front fork oil. However, it is good practice to change the fork oil once a year. Because the forks are not equipped with drain screws, they must be removed and partially disassembled for fork oil replacement and oil level adjustment. Refer to Chapter Thirteen.

NOTE
Perform the **Rear Brake Pedal Height** *and* **Rear Brake Pedal Free Play** *adjustments (this chapter) before checking and adjusting the rear brake light switch in this section.*

1. Turn the ignition switch on.
2. Depress the brake pedal. The brake light should come on just before the brake begins to work.
3. If the brake light comes on too late, continue the procedure to adjust the switch.

CAUTION
Do not turn the switch body when adjusting the rear brake light switch. This will damage the wires at the top of the switch. Hold the switch body and turn the adjusting nut.

4. Hold the brake light switch body (A, **Figure 62**) and turn the adjusting nut (B) as required to make the brake light come on earlier.
5. Recheck the rear brake light switch adjustment.
6. Turn the ignition switch off.

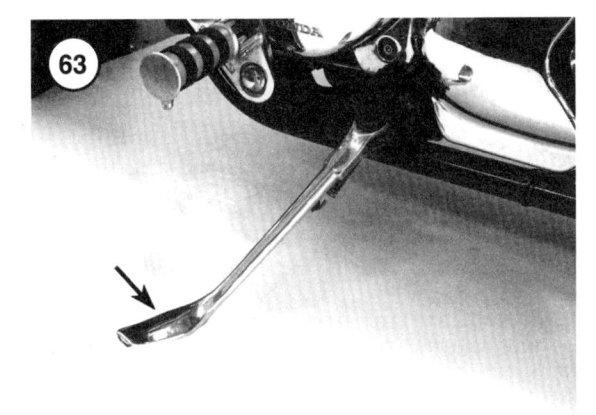

FASTENER INSPECTION

Constant vibration can loosen many fasteners on a motorcycle. Check fastener tightness at the intervals specified in **Table 1**.

1. Check the tightness of all exposed fasteners. Refer to the appropriate chapter for torque specifications.
2. Check that all hose clamps, cable stays and safety clips are properly installed. Replace missing or damaged items.

Table 1 MAINTENANCE AND LUBRICATION SCHEDULE (1)

Weekly/gas stop	Check tire pressure cold; adjust to suit load and speed
	Check condition of tires
	Check brake fluid level; if low, check brakes for excessive wear
	Check brake operation
	Check throttle grip for smooth operation and return
	Check steering play
	Check axle, suspension, controls and linkage fasteners; tighten if necessary
	Check engine oil level; add oil if necessary
	Check lights and horn operation, especially brake light
	Check stop switch operation
	Check coolant level
	Check for any abnormal engine noise and leaks
At 600 miles (1000 km)	
	Replace engine oil and filter
	Check valve clearance; adjust if necessary
	Check engine idle speed on carbureted models; adjust if necessary
	Check front brake system for air in brake line and any loose or damaged fittings
	Check rear brake system for any loose or damage fittings or components
	Check clutch adjustment; adjust if necessary
	Check steering adjustment
	Check tightness of exposed chassis and engine fasteners
	Check tires for wear and damage
	Check wheels for damage and loose or damaged spokes; check for damaged wheel bearings
At 4000 miles (6400 km); thereafter every 4000 miles (6400 km)	
	Check crankcase breather hose and drain water from hose if present (2)
	Check spark plugs for wear and fouling; replace if necessary
	Check engine idle speed on carbureted models; adjust if necessary
	Check clutch adjustment; adjust if necessary
	Check brake fluid level; also check for brake fluid contamination and damaged diaphragms
	Check brake pads for wear; replace if necessary
	Check rear brake linings for wear; replace if necessary
	Check tires for wear and damage
	Check wheels for damage and loose or damaged spokes; check for damaged wheel bearings
At 8000 miles (12900 km); thereafter every 8000 miles (12900 km)	
	Check throttle operation; readjust cables if necessary or replace cables if damaged
	Check fuel line; replace if leaking or damaged
	Check choke operation; readjust cable if necessary or replace cable if damaged
	Replace spark plugs
	Inspect valve clearance; adjust if necessary
	Replace engine oil and filter
	Check final drive oil level, then check oil for water and other contamination

LUBRICATION, MAINTENANCE AND TUNE-UP

Table 1 MAINTENANCE AND LUBRICATION SCHEDULE (continued)

At 8000 miles (12900 km); thereafter every 8000 miles (12900 km) (continued)	Check final drive housing for oil leaks and loose mounting nuts Check engine idle speed on carbureted models; adjust if necessary Check coolant for contamination Check radiator and all coolant hoses for leaks. Check weep hole in bottom of water pump for coolant leakage; replace water pump if necessary Check secondary air supply system for kinked, pinched, disconnected or damaged hoses Check rubber brake hoses and metal brake lines for damage Check disc brake system(s) for air in brake line and any loose or damaged fittings Check rear drum brake system for any loose or damage fittings or components Check brake light switch operation Check headlight aim; adjust if necessary Check side stand operation and fastener tightness Check side stand ignition cut-off system operation; replace the side stand switch, if necessary Check front and rear suspension operation and for loose or missing fasteners; check for oil leaks Check the steering adjustment; adjust as necessary Check the wheels and tires for damage; check for damaged wheel bearings and loose or damaged spokes Check tightness of exposed chassis and engine fasteners Inspect steering head bearings and lubricate as needed.
Every 12,000 miles (19400 km)	Replace the air filter (3) Replace the sub-air filter Inspect the evaporative emission control system (California models)
Every 12,000 miles (19400 km) or every two years, whichever comes first:	Replace brake fluid Replace coolant
Every 24,000 miles (38700 km)	Replace final drive oil

1. Consider this schedule a guide to general maintenance and lubrication intervals. Harder than normal use and exposure to mud, water, and high humidity will require more frequent attention to most maintenance items.
2. Increase service intervals when riding at full throttle or in rain.
3. Service more often when riding in wet or dusty conditions.

Table 2 TUNE-UP SPECIFICATIONS

Clutch lever free play	10-20 mm (3/8-3/4 in.)
Cylinder number	No. 1 (rear) No. 2 (front)
Engine compression (standard pressure)	1275-1471 kPa (185-213 psi) @ 400 rpm
Engine idle speed	1100-1300 rpm
Firing order	Front (308 degrees) — rear (412 degrees) — front
Ignition timing	
Carbureted models	F mark (13° BTDC @ idle)
Fuel injected models	F mark (8° BTDC @ idle)
Oil pressure @ 5000 rpm	530 kPa (77 psi) @ 80° C (176° F)
Rear brake pedal free play	
Non-ABS models	20-30 mm (13/16-1 3/16 in.)
Rear brake pedal height	
Non-ABS models	75 mm (3.0 in.) above top of foot peg
Rear master cylinder pushrod adjustment length	
Aero models equipped with ABS	82.0-84.0 mm (3.23-3.31 in.)
Spirit models equipped with ABS	83.0 mm (3.27 in.)

Table 2 TUNE-UP SPECIFICATIONS (continued)

Spark plug gap	0.8-0.9 mm (0.031-0.035 in.)
Spark plug type	
Carbureted models	
NGK	
Standard	DPR6EA-9
Extended high speed use	DPR7EA-9
Denso	
Standard	X20EPR-U9
Extended high speed use	X22EPR-U9
Fuel injected models	
NGK	
Standard	DPR7EA-9
Extended high speed use	DPR8EA-9
Denso	
Standard	X22EPR-U9
Extended high speed use	X24EPR-U9
Valve clearance*	
Intake	0.13-0.17 mm (0.005-0.007 in.)
Exhaust	0.18-0.22 mm (0.007-0.009 in.)
Throttle grip free play	2-6 mm (1/16-1/4 in.)

*Engine and air temperature below 35°C (95°F)

Table 3 RECOMMENDED LUBRICANTS AND FUEL

Brake fluid	DOT 4 brake fluid
Control cables	Cable lubricant
Coolant	
Standard concentration	50% mixture coolant and purified water
Type	Honda HP coolant or an equivalent (1)
Engine oil	
Classification	
JASCO T 903 standard rating	MA
API rating	SG or higher (2)
Viscosity rating	SAE 10W-30
Final drive oil	Hypoid gear oil, SAE 80 weight
Fork oil	Pro Honda Suspension Fluid SS-8 or equivalent 10 wt
fork oil	
Fuel	Unleaded gasoline with a pump octane number of 86 or higher

1. Coolant must not contain silicate inhibitors as they can cause premature wear to the water pump seals. Refer to text for further information.
2. API "SG" or higher classified oils not specified as "ENERGY CONSERVING" can be used. Refer to text for additional information.

Table 4 ENGINE OIL CAPACITY

	L	U.S. qt.
Engine oil change only	2.5	2.64
Engine oil and filter change	2.6	2.75
Engine disassembly	3.2	3.38

Table 5 COOLANT CAPACITY

	L	U.S. qt.
Radiator and engine	1.58	1.67
Reserve tank	0.38	0.40

Table 6 FINAL DRIVE OIL CAPACITY

	cc	U.S. oz.
After overhaul	170	5.7
Oil change	160	5.4

LUBRICATION, MAINTENANCE AND TUNE-UP

Table 7 TIRE INFLATION PRESSURE AND TREAD DEPTH*

	Front	Rear
Tire inflation pressure		
Rider (90 kg [200 lbs])	200 kPa (29 psi)	200 kPa (29 psi)
Maximum weight capacity	200 kPa (29 psi)	250 kPa (36 psi)
Tread depth (minimum)	1.5 mm (0.06 in.)	2.0 mm (0.08 in.)

*The tire inflation pressures listed here are for factory equipped tires. Aftermarket tires may require different inflation pressure. Refer to tire manufacturer's specifications.

Table 8 MAINTENANCE TORQUE SPECIFICATIONS

	N.m	in.-lb.	ft.-lb.
Alternator cover socket bolts			
2004-2009 Aero models	9.8	87	--
All other models	10	89	--
Brake lever pivot bolt	1.0	8.9	--
Brake lever pivot nut			
2004-2009 Aero models	5.9	52	--
All other models	6.0	53	--
Brake pedal adjuster locknut			
2004-2009 Aero models without ABS	9.8	87	--
Clutch lever pivot bolt	1.0	8.9	--
Clutch lever pivot nut			
2004-2009 Aero models	5.9	52	--
All other models	6.0	53	--
Coolant drain bolt	13	115	--
Crankshaft hole cap (1, 2)	15	--	11
Engine oil drain bolt	29	--	21
Final drive oil drain bolt	12	106	--
Final drive oil fill cap	12	106	--
Oil filter (2)	26	--	19
Rear master cylinder pushrod locknut (ABS models)	18	--	13
Spark plug			
Aero			
2004-2009	16	--	12
2011-2013	18	--	13
Shadow Spirit and Phantom	18	--	13
Timing hole cap (1, 2)	10	89	--
Valve adjust screw locknut (3)	23	--	17

1. Lubricate threads with grease.
2. Lubricate O-ring with engine oil.
3. Lubricate threads and flange surface with engine oil.

CHAPTER FOUR

ENGINE TOP END

Tables 1-4 are at the end of the chapter.
Refer to Chapter Three for valve adjustment
Before starting any work, review the information in Chapter One.

SERVICING THE ENGINE IN THE FRAME

The following components can be serviced with the engine installed in the frame:
  a. Cylinder head covers.
  b. Camshaft removal and installation.
  c. Cam chain tensioner and cam chains.

OUTER CYLINDER COVERS

Removal/installation

Front left side

1. Remove the fuel tank (Chapter Eight or Chapter Nine).
2. Disconnect the spark plug cap.
3. Remove the two mounting bolts and the cover **(Figure 1)**.
4. Installation is the reverse of removal. Tighten the cover mounting bolts to 10 N.m (89 in.-lb.).

Front right side

1. Remove the fuel tank (Chapter Eight or Chapter Nine).
2. Disconnect the spark plug cap.
3. On fuel injected models, remove the air filter housing (Chapter Nine).
4. Remove the front mounting bolt.

5A. On carbureted models, remove the rear cover mounting bolt as follows:
  a. Remove the thermostat housing mounting bolt.
  b. Insert a long 5-mm Allen wrench (Motion Pro part No. 08-0184, or an equivalent) between the two thermostat housing cooling hoses as shown in **Figure 2**. Pull the thermostat housing forward so the tool can be inserted through the narrow gap between the hoses.

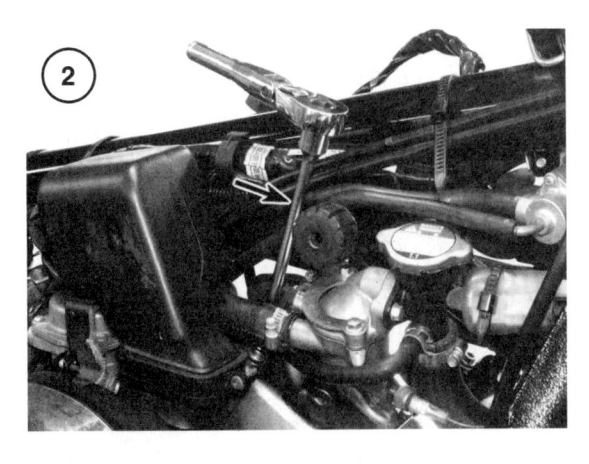

c. Loosen and remove the rear cover mounting bolt.
d. Reposition the thermostat housing and reinstall its mounting bolt to raise the assembly and provide room for cover removal.

5B. On fuel injected models, remove the rear cover mounting bolt.

6. Remove the cover. On carbureted models, move the cover forward, then turn and remove it by pulling its rear end out first **(Figure 3)**.

7. Installation is the reverse of removal. Tighten the cover mounting bolts to 10 N.m (89 in.-lb.).

Rear covers

1. Remove the fuel tank (Chapter Eight or Nine).
2. Disconnect the spark plug cap.
3. Remove the two mounting bolts and the cover. See **Figure 4** (left side) or **Figure 5** (right side).
4. Installation is the reverse of these steps. Tighten the cover mounting bolts to 10 N.m (89 in.-lb.).

CYLINDER HEAD COVERS

Removal

Before removing the cylinder head covers, check for oil leaks around the covers and the mounting bolt rubber seals. If leaks are detected, replace the cover gasket(s) and rubber seal(s) as required. Then clean the area above the covers to prevent dirt and other debris from falling into the engine.

Front

1. Remove the front outer covers as described in this chapter.
2. Disconnect the air supply hose (A, **Figure 6**). Then pull the hose and wedge it on the left side of the frame so it cannot interfere with cover removal. Slide the clamp down the hose so it does not fall into the engine.
3. On carbureted models, disconnect the ECT sensor connector (B, **Figure 6**).
4. On fuel injected models, perform the following:
    a. Remove the front ignition coil (Chapter Ten).
    b. Remove the PAIR check valve (Chapter Eight).
5. Remove the two cover bolts, washers and rubber seals.
6. Remove the thermostat housing mounting bolt. On carbureted models, raise the housing **(Figure 7)** and hook the end of its mounting bracket onto the frame bracket. This step provides clearance above the cover. It is not necessary to drain the cooling system when repositioning the thermostat housing.

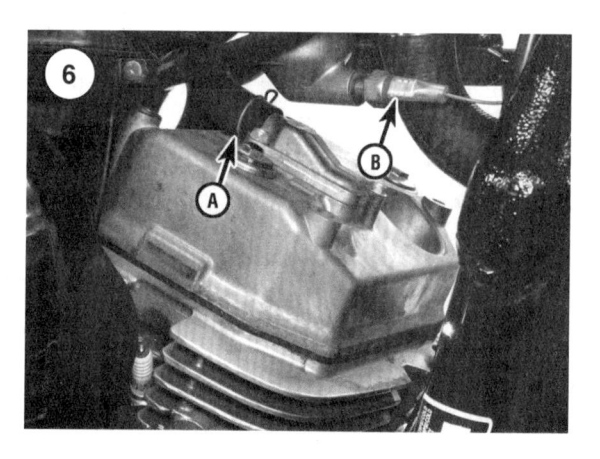

ENGINE TOP END

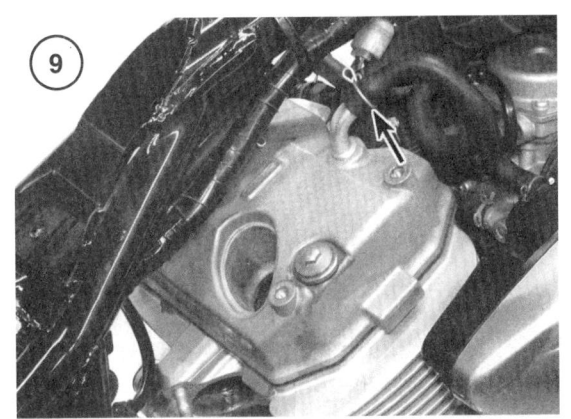

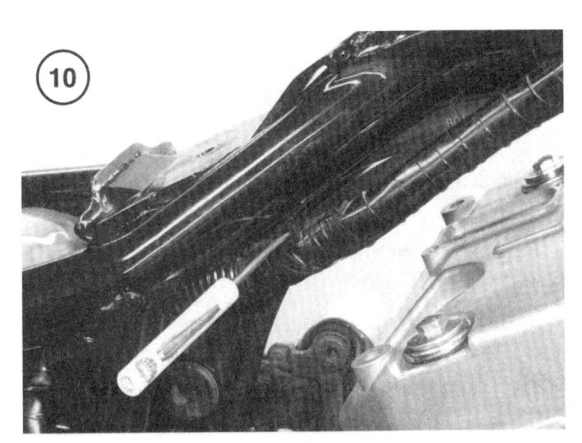

7A. On carbureted models, lift the cylinder head cover, then tilt the front part of the cover down (toward radiator) and then remove it from the right side of the engine **(Figure 8)**.

7B. On fuel injected models, lift the cylinder head cover, then remove it from the left side of the engine.

Rear

1. Remove the rear outer covers as described in this chapter.
2. Disconnect the breather hose **(Figure 9)**.
3. Remove the PAIR check valve (Chapter Eight or Chapter Nine).
4. On ABS models, remove the ignition switch (Chapter Ten).
5. Perform the following to help reposition the wiring harness and hoses when removing the cylinder head cover:
    a. Use a small flat-tipped screwdriver to unlock the wiring harness clamp on the right side of the frame **(Figure 10)**. This allows the wiring harness to be repositioned when removing the cylinder head cover.
    b. Remove the plastic clamp securing the wiring harness and hoses to the frame.
6. Remove the two cover bolts, washers and rubber seals.

NOTE
If the exhaust valve adjuster contacts the cover, turn the engine over until the adjuster moves down and provides clearance.

7. Remove the cylinder head cover **(Figure 11)** from the right side, by carefully moving it past the wiring harness and the valve adjusters. Position yourself on the left side of the motorcycle so you can visually see the inside of the cover as it passes up and over the valve adjusters. Raise the wiring harness as required to provide access when removing the cover.

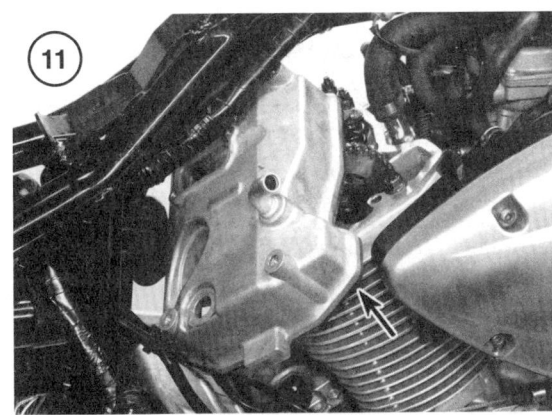

Installation

1. Remove all sealer residue from the cylinder head gasket surface.
2. Fill the cylinder head oil pocket with engine oil **(Figure 12)**.
3. Replace the cylinder head cover rubber washers **(Figure 13)** if damaged.
4. Lubricate the rubber washers with engine oil. Then install a steel and rubber washer on each bolt **(Figure 13)**.
5. Inspect the rubber gasket **(Figure 14)** around the perimeter of the cylinder head cover. Replace the gasket if it is starting to deteriorate or harden.
6. If necessary, replace the rubber gasket or reseal the original gasket as follows:
   a. Remove the old gasket **(Figure 14)** and clean the gasket groove around the perimeter of the cover and around the spark plug hole.

   NOTE
   Apply gasket sealer onto the side of the gasket that seats against the cylinder head cover. Do not apply gasket sealer to the side of the rubber gasket that seats against the cylinder head.

   b. Apply Gasgacinch, or a similar rubber adhesive, to the cylinder head cover grooves and upper side of the new gasket, following the sealant manufacturer's instructions.
   c. Install the gasket into the groove in the cylinder head cover **(Figure 14)**. Make sure the gasket is seated in the cover groove with no gap.
7. Install the cylinder head cover onto the cylinder head. Confirm that the gasket seats squarely onto the cylinder head.
8. Install the cylinder head cover bolts and washers and tighten to 10 N.m (89 in.-lb.).
9. Reverse the steps under *Removal* to complete installation. After starting the engine, check for oil leaks.

CAMSHAFTS

The camshafts can be serviced with the engine installed in the frame.

Camshaft Removal

This section describes removal of both camshafts. If it is only necessary to remove one camshaft, it is still necessary to remove both cylinder head covers to view the camshaft timing marks.

1. Disconnect the battery negative cable (Chapter Ten).
2. Support the motorcycle with a jackstand to position it upright. This will make it easier to view the flywheel and camshaft timing marks when turning the engine over.
3. Remove both cylinder head covers as described in this chapter.
4. Remove the bolts (A, **Figure 15**) and the alternator cover (B).
5. Remove the crankshaft (A, **Figure 16**) and timing hole (B) caps from the left crankcase cover.

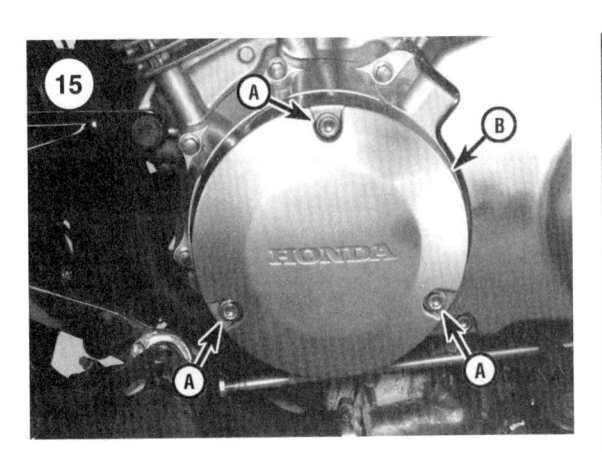

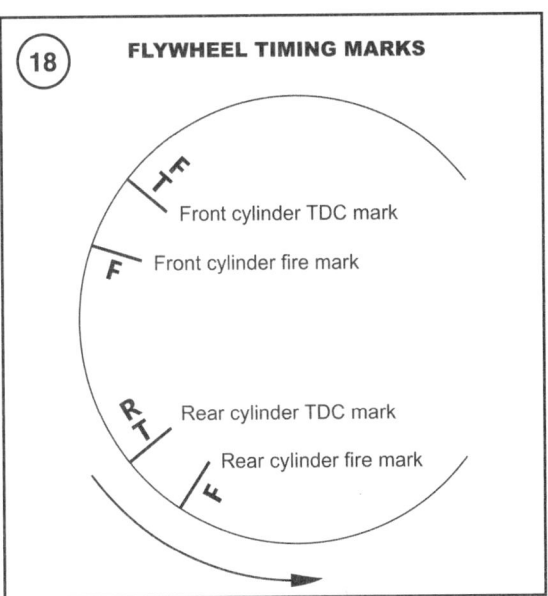

ENGINE TOP END

FLYWHEEL TIMING MARKS

- Front cylinder TDC mark
- Front cylinder fire mark
- Rear cylinder TDC mark
- Rear cylinder fire mark

NOTE
Always turn the crankshaft counterclockwise, as viewed from the left side of the motorcycle, in the following steps. When doing so, the timing marks will appear in the order shown in **Figure 18**. *Use a socket through the left crankcase cover to engage the flywheel bolt* **(Figure 19)**.

NOTE
Before removing the camshafts, rotate the engine as described in Step 8 and check the front and rear camshaft and flywheel timing marks a few times. Confirm that the timing marks and camshaft positions are correct while noting how the camshaft lobes are positioned when the engine is at TDC on its compression stroke. Refer to **Valve Adjustment** *in Chapter Three.*

6. Remove one spark plug from each cylinder to make it easier to turn the engine by hand. Cover the spark plug openings.
7. Before removing the camshaft, inspect the cam chain for excessive wear as follows:
   a. Measure the exposed length of cam chain tensioner wedge B as shown in **Figure 17**.
   b. If the measurement is less than 6 mm, the cam chain is excessively worn and must be replaced as described in this chapter.
   c. Repeat for the opposite cam chain tensioner.

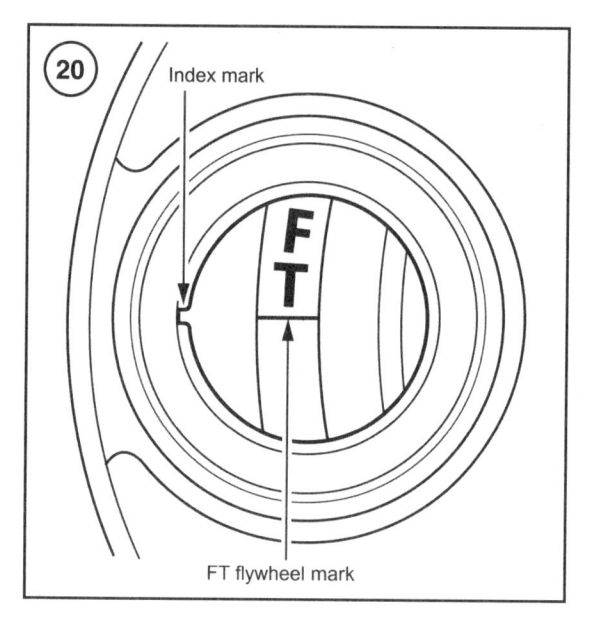

98 CHAPTER FOUR

20 Index mark

FT flywheel mark

NOTE
When removing both camshafts, remove the front camshaft first.

8A. When removing both camshafts or only the front cylinder camshaft, position the front camshaft as follows:
   a. Turn the crankshaft counterclockwise and align the FT mark on the flywheel with the index mark on the left crankcase cover (**Figure 20**).
   b. Check that the index marks on the cam sprocket are aligned with the cylinder head surface (**Figure 21**) and the F mark on the camshaft (**Figure 22**) is facing up. The valve adjusters should have free play, indicating the cam lobes are facing down.
   c. These conditions indicate the front piston is at TDC on its compression stroke. If not, turn the crankshaft one full revolution (360°) counterclockwise and realign the FT mark. The piston should now be at its TDC position.

8B. When removing the rear cylinder camshaft, position the rear camshaft as follows:
   a. Turn the crankshaft counterclockwise and align the RT mark on the flywheel with the index mark on the left crankcase cover (**Figure 23**).
   b. Check that the index marks on the cam sprocket are aligned with the cylinder head surface (**Figure 24**) and the R mark on the camshaft (**Figure 25**) is facing up. The valve adjusters should have free play, indicating the cam lobes are facing down.
   c. These conditions indicate the rear piston is at TDC on its compression stroke. If not, turn the crankshaft one full revolution (360°) counterclockwise and realign the RT mark. The piston should now be at its TDC position.

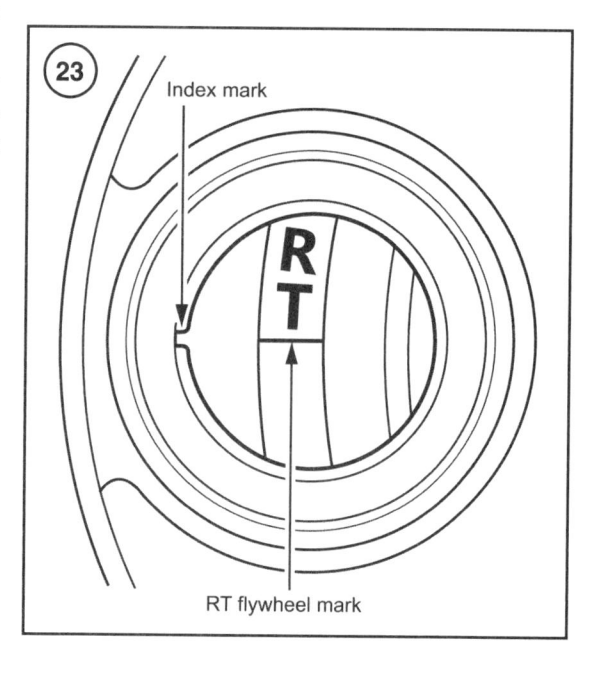

9. Release the cam chain tensioner spring tension against the cam chain as follows:
   a. Refer to **Figure 26** to identify the A and B cam chain tensioner wedges.

21

22

23 Index mark

RT flywheel mark

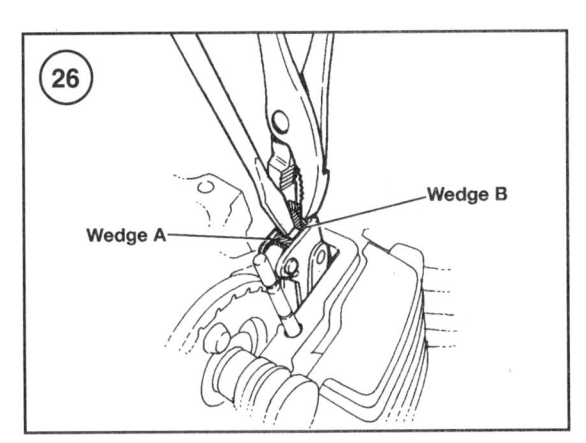

ENGINE TOP END

b. Cover the area around the cam chain tensioner to avoid dropping parts into the engine.
c. Grab wedge B with a pair of pliers and pull it up, then push wedge A down with a screwdriver **(Figure 26)**.
d. Install a 2 mm pin through the hole in wedge B **(Figure 27)** to hold it in position and release spring tension against the cam chain.

10. Turn the crankshaft counterclockwise until the F **(Figure 22)** or R **(Figure 25)** mark on the camshaft is facing down (cam lobes are facing up). Remove the exposed cam sprocket bolt. If necessary, hold the flywheel bolt to prevent the camshaft from turning.

11. Bring the cylinder to TDC on its compression stroke. Remove the other cam sprocket bolt (A, **Figure 28**).

NOTE
The piston must be at TDC on its compression stroke when removing the camshaft holder.

12. Slide the cam sprocket (B, **Figure 28**) off the camshaft flange and secure the cam chain with a length of stiff wire. Remove the cam sprocket.

13. Using a crossing pattern, loosen and then remove the camshaft holder nuts and bolts (A, **Figure 29**).

14. Pull the camshaft holder (B, **Figure 29**) straight up to remove it from the cylinder head. Do not allow the dowel pins to fall into the engine.
15. Remove the camshaft **(Figure 30)**.

NOTE
If both camshafts are to be removed, continue the procedure to remove the rear camshaft.

16. Hold the front cam chain to prevent it from binding on the drive sprocket and position the rear piston at TDC on its compression stroke.

CAUTION
If the crankshaft must be rotated while one or both camshafts are removed, pull up on the cam chain(s) so it properly engages the crankshaft drive sprocket(s). Hold the chain taut on the drive sprocket while rotating the crankshaft. If this is not done, the cam chain could become kinked, which could cause damage to the chain and drive sprocket.

17. Repeat the process to remove the rear camshaft.
18. Inspect the camshaft holders, rocker arms and camshafts as described in this section.

Camshaft Installation

1. Before installing the camshaft(s), note the following:
   a. Rotate the engine counterclockwise with a socket on the flywheel mounting bolt **(Figure 19)**.
   b. Rotating the crankshaft 360° (1 turn) rotates the camshafts 180° (1/2 turn).
   c. Identify the camshafts by the F (front) and R (rear) flange marks identified in **Figure 31**.
   d. When the camshaft timing marks are facing up, the cam lobes will be facing down.
   e. If both camshafts were removed, install the front camshaft first, then the rear camshaft.
   f. If only one camshaft was removed, remove the opposite cylinder head cover (this chapter) so the installed camshaft timing marks can be viewed.
   g. Clean the cam sprocket bolts and camshaft threaded holes of all threadlock residue and oil. These threads must be clean and dry when threadlock is applied to the bolts during assembly.
   h. When working alone, assemble an eye-bolt, 6-mm threaded rod, coupling nuts and washers as shown in **Figure 32**, then place the rear cam chain over the eye bolt. This setup can be used to keep the rear cam chain tight while holding the front cam chain and turning the crankshaft.

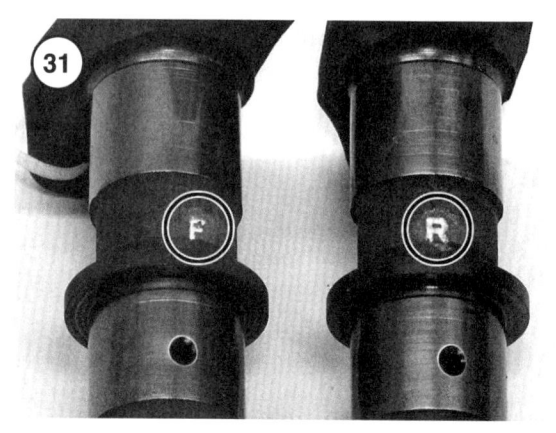

CAUTION
When rotating the crankshaft, pull both cam chains outward to prevent them from jamming against the crankshaft drive sprockets. Doing so could damage the chains and sprockets.

NOTE
After positioning the engine, continue the procedure to install the front and rear camshafts.

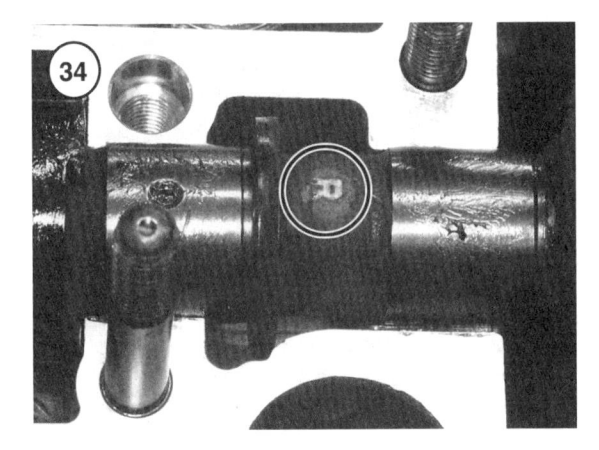

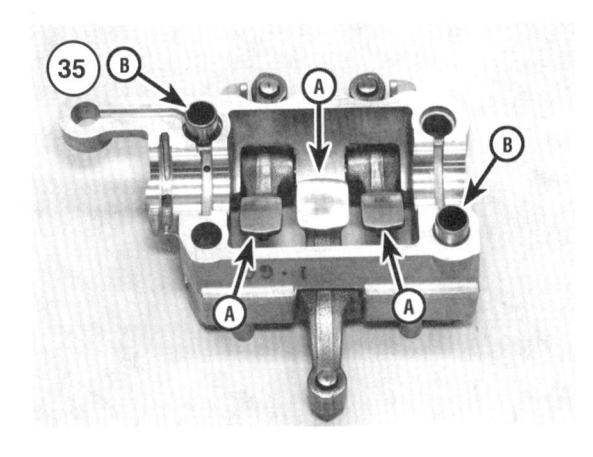

ENGINE TOP END

a. Turn the crankshaft counterclockwise and align the RT mark on the flywheel with the index mark on the left crankcase cover **(Figure 23)**. Then check the position of the R identification mark on the rear camshaft **(Figure 25)**.

b. If the R mark is facing down (cannot be seen), turn the crankshaft counterclockwise 52 degrees and align the FT mark on the flywheel with the index mark on the left crankcase cover **(Figure 20)**. Go to Step 3 and install the front camshaft.

c. If the TDC index mark is facing up, turn the crankshaft counterclockwise 412° (360° + 52°) and align the FT mark on the flywheel with the index mark on the left crankcase cover **(Figure 20)**. Go to Step 4 and install the front camshaft.

2C. If only the rear camshaft was removed, perform the following:

a. Turn the crankshaft counterclockwise and align the FT mark on the flywheel with the index mark on the left crankcase cover **(Figure 20)**. Check the position of the F identification mark on the front camshaft **(Figure 22)**.

b. If the F mark is facing down (cannot be seen), turn the crankshaft counterclockwise 668° (360° + 308°) and align the RT mark on the flywheel with the index mark on the left crankcase cover **(Figure 23)**. Go to Step 3 and install the rear camshaft.

c. If the F mark is facing up, turn the crankshaft counterclockwise 308° and align the RT mark on the flywheel with the index mark on the left crankcase cover **(Figure 23)**. Go to Step 3 and install the rear camshaft.

3. Apply engine assembly lube to the cylinder head camshaft journals, thrust surfaces and cam lobes.

NOTE
*When the camshaft TDC mark is facing up, the camshaft lobes will be facing down. See **Figure 30**, typical.*

2A. If both camshafts were removed, perform the following:

a. Turn the crankshaft counterclockwise and align the FT mark on the flywheel with the index mark on the left crankcase cover **(Figure 20)**. Check that the piston is at TDC. If not, make sure the flywheel is properly installed and indexed with the crankshaft.

b. Go to Step 3 and install the front camshaft.

2B. If only the front camshaft was removed, perform the following:

4. Install the camshaft through the cam chain with its F or R identification mark facing *up*. See **Figure 33** (front) or **Figure 34** (rear).

5. Loosen the valve adjusting screw locknuts and loosen the adjusting screws fully.

6. Lubricate the valve adjuster contact pads (A, **Figure 35**) with engine assembly lube.

7. Make sure the two dowel pins are installed in the camshaft holder (B, **Figure 35**).

8. Install the camshaft holder (B, **Figure 29**) over the camshaft while seating the dowel pins into the cylinder head.

9. Install the camshaft holder bolts and nuts (A, **Figure 29**). Tighten the bolts and nuts in two steps and in a crossing pattern to 23 N.m (17 ft.-lb.).

10. Mesh the camshaft sprocket with the cam chain. The IN mark (**Figure 36**) on the sprocket must face toward the *inside* of the engine.

11. Slip the cam sprocket onto the camshaft flange. Check that the sprocket timing marks align with the cylinder head gasket surface and the camshaft identification mark faces up. The exposed sprocket and camshaft bolt holes must also align. The alignment of these marks is critical as it establishes the cylinder's valve timing. See **Figure 37** (front) or Figure 38 (rear).

NOTE
The camshaft and sprocket mounting bolt threads must be clean and dry.

12. Apply a medium strength threadlock onto the cam sprocket bolt threads.

13. Align the camshaft bolt holes with the holes in the cam sprocket. Install the first cam sprocket bolt and hand-tighten.

14. Turn the crankshaft counterclockwise 360°. Install the second cam sprocket bolt and tighten to 23 N.m (17 ft.-lb.).

15. Turn the crankshaft counterclockwise 360° degrees and tighten the first cam sprocket bolt to 23 N.m (17 ft.-lb.).

16. Remove the 2 mm pin from the cam chain tensioner (**Figure 27**).

17. If both camshafts were removed and the front camshaft was just installed, turn the crankshaft counterclockwise 308° and align the RT mark on the flywheel with the index mark on the left crankcase cover (**Figure 23**). Repeat the procedure to install the rear camshaft.

18. Recheck the camshaft timing as follows:

CAUTION
The timing marks must all align correctly at this time; otherwise, camshaft timing will be incorrect. Do not proceed if the camshaft sprocket timing marks are positioned incorrectly.

a. Turn the crankshaft counterclockwise and align the FT mark on the flywheel with the index mark on the left crankcase cover (**Figure 20**). Check that the front camshaft F identification mark is facing up (**Figure 22**). If the F mark is facing down, turn the crankshaft counterclockwise one turn (360°) and realign the FT mark (**Figure 20**). The timing marks (**Figure 37**) on the front camshaft sprocket must align with the cylinder head surface.

b. Turn the crankshaft counterclockwise 308° and align the RT mark on the flywheel with the index mark on the left crankcase cover (**Figure 23**). The rear camshaft's R identification mark must be facing up (**Figure 25**) and the timing marks on the rear camshaft sprocket must align with the cylinder head surface (**Figure 38**).

19. Adjust the valve clearance as described in Chapter Three.

20. Install the cylinder head covers as described in this chapter.

ENGINE TOP END

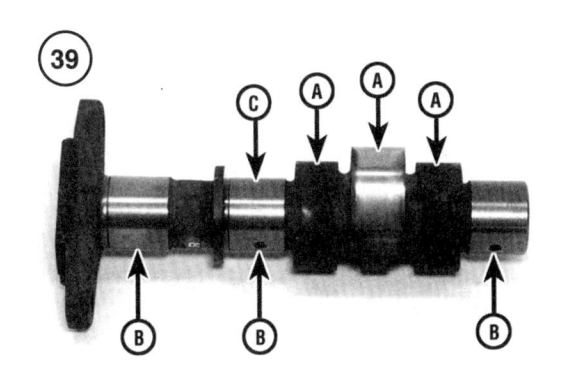

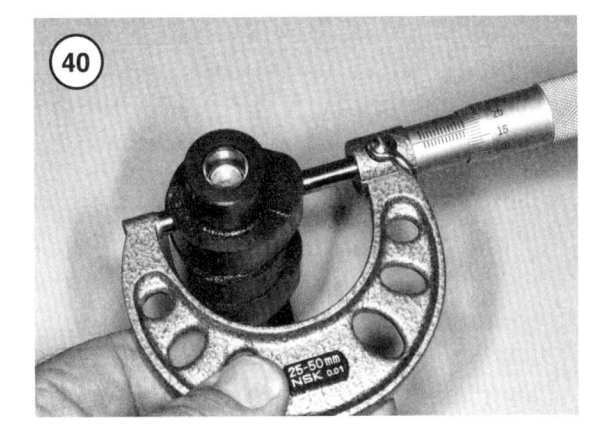

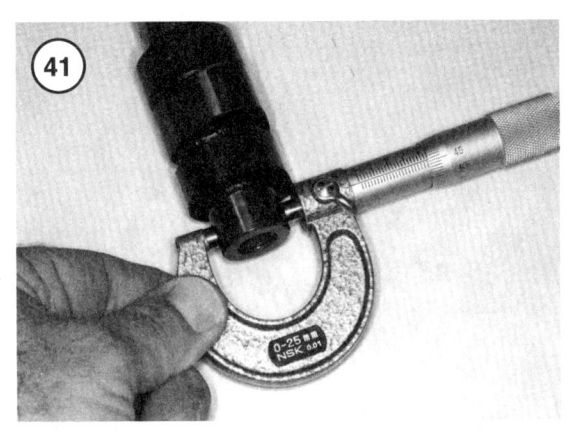

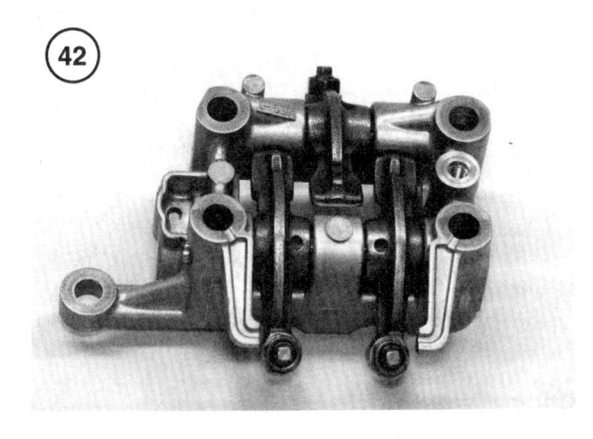

21. Install the alternator cover (B, **Figure 15**) and tighten the mounting bolts (A) to 10 N.m (89 in.-lb.).

Camshaft Inspection

When measuring the camshafts, compare the actual measurements to the specifications in **Table 2**. Replace worn or damaged parts as described in this section.

1. Clean the camshafts in solvent and dry thoroughly. Flush the camshaft oil passages with solvent and compressed air.
2. Clean the camshaft and cam sprocket threads of all threadlock residue.
3. Check the cam lobes (A, **Figure 39**) for wear. The lobes should not be scored and the edges should be square. Replace the camshaft if the lobes are scored, worn or damaged.
4. Check the camshaft bearing journals (B, **Figure 39**) for wear or scoring. Replace the camshaft if the journals are scored, worn or damaged.
5. If the camshaft lobes or journals are excessively worn or damaged, check the journal surfaces in the cylinder head and in the camshaft holder. See *Camshaft Holder Inspection* in this chapter.
6. Measure each cam lobe height **(Figure 40)** with a micrometer.
7. Measure each cam journal outside diameter **(Figure 41)** with a micrometer.
8. Support the camshaft journals on a set of V-blocks or crankshaft truing stand and measure runout with a dial indicator at the point indicated in C, **Figure 39**. Note the following:
    a. If the runout is out of specification, replace the camshaft and measure the camshaft oil clearance as described in this section. If the clearance is out of specification, the camshaft holder and camshaft journals were damaged from the bent camshaft.
    b. If the camshaft was replaced, remeasure the camshaft oil clearance with the new camshaft.
9. Inspect the camshaft sprockets for broken or chipped teeth. Also, inspect the cam chains and drive sprockets mounted on the crankshaft. See *Cam Chain Tensioner and Cam Chain* (this chapter).

Camshaft Holders, Rocker Arms and Shafts

This section covers the camshaft holders, rocker arms and shafts **(Figure 42)**. Procedures for the front and rear assemblies are identical.

Disassembly

> **NOTE**
> Infrequent oil and filter changes may be indicated if the camshaft holder passages are dirty. Contaminated oil passages can cause camshaft and journal failure.

1. Before cleaning and disassembling the camshaft holder **(Figure 42)**, inspect the oil lubrication holes for contamination. Small passages and holes in the camshaft holders provide lubrication for the holder, camshaft and cylinder journals. Make sure these passages and holes are clean and open.
2. Clean the assembled camshaft holder assembly. Then dry with compressed air.

> **NOTE**
> Identify the individual rocker arms so that they can be reinstalled in their original operating positions.

3. Refer to **Figure 43** and remove the rocker arm shafts and rocker arms. The shafts are a slip fit and should slide out of the holder without force.

Camshaft holder inspection

1. Clean and dry the camshaft holder. The dowel pins (A, **Figure 44**) are an interference fit and should not be removed unless they require replacement.
2. Check the camshaft holder (B, **Figure 44**) for stress cracks and other damage.
3. Check the camshaft bearing journals in the camshaft holders (C, **Figure 44**) and cylinder head (A, **Figure 45**) for scoring and seizure marks. If visible damage is present, replace the cylinder head and camshaft holder as a set. To determine operational clearance, perform the *Camshaft Oil Clearance Measurement* procedure in this section.
4. Check the two studs (B, **Figure 45**) for looseness or damage. Retighten loose studs or replace damaged studs as described under *Stud Removal/Installation* in Chapter One.
5. Check the camshaft holder mounting fasteners for damage.

Rocker arms and shafts inspection

When measuring the rocker arm components in this section, compare the actual measurements to the specifications in **Table 2**. Replace parts that are out of specification or show damage as described in this section.

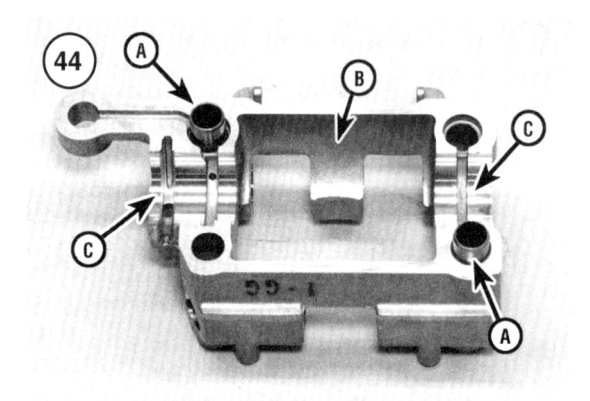

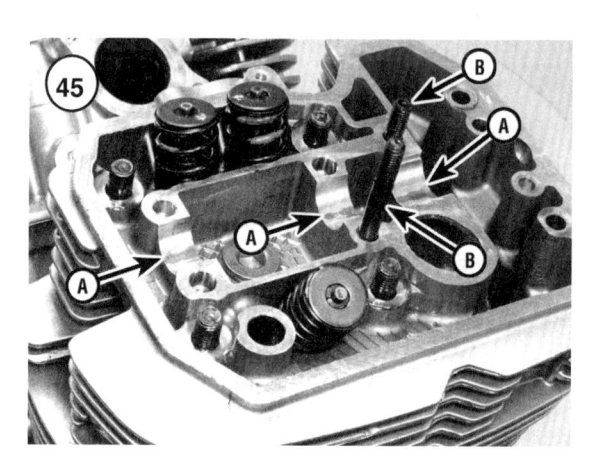

> **NOTE**
> Maintain the alignment of the rocker arm components when cleaning and inspecting the parts. All three rocker arms have different part numbers.

1. Clean and dry the parts.
2. Inspect the rocker arm pad where it rides on the cam lobe (A, **Figure 46**) and where the adjuster rides on the valve stem (B). Check the contact surfaces for flat spots, uneven wear and scoring.

ENGINE TOP END

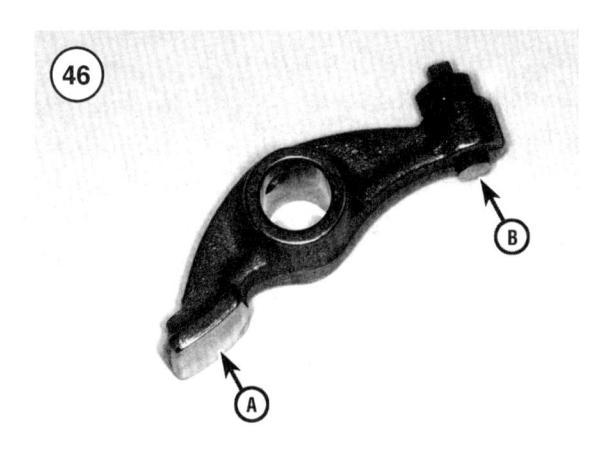

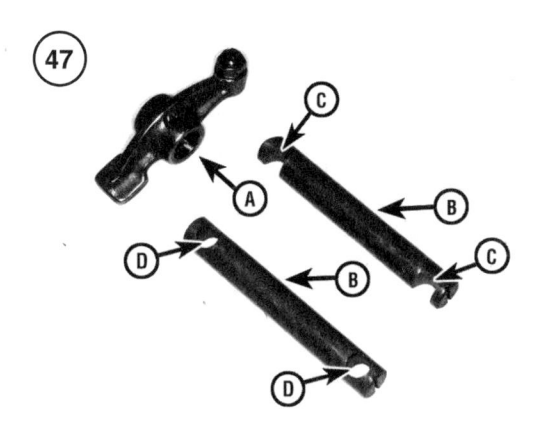

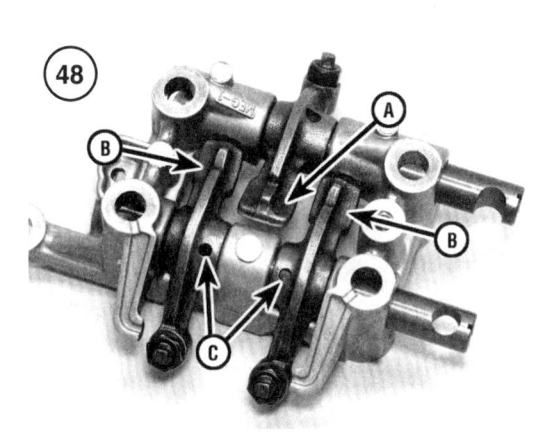

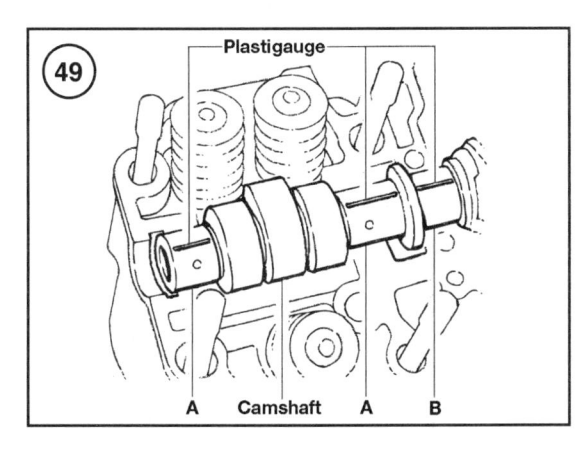

3. Inspect the valve adjuster locknuts for rounding and other damage.
4. Inspect the rocker arm shafts for scoring, cracks or other damage.
5. Measure the rocker arm bore inside diameter (A, **Figure 47**).
6. Measure the rocker arm shaft outside diameter (B, **Figure 47**).
7. Calculate the rocker arm-to-rocker arm shaft clearance as follows:
   a. Subtract the rocker arm shaft outside diameter from the rocker arm bore inside diameter.
   b. Replace the rocker arm and/or the rocker arm shaft if the clearance is out of specification.

Reassembly

1. Make sure the oil passages through the camshaft holder are clear.
2. Lubricate the valve adjuster threads and seating surfaces with engine oil.
3. Lubricate the rocker arm shafts with assembly oil.
4. Install the rocker arms and shafts as shown in **Figure 48**. Note the following:
   a. The exhaust rocker arm pad (A, **Figure 48**) is larger than the pad on the intake rocker arms (B).
   b. Install the exhaust rocker arm shaft and align its notches (C, **Figure 47**) with the stud holes in the camshaft holder.
   c. Install the intake rocker arms with their oil holes facing toward the inside (C, **Figure 48**).
   d. Install the intake rocker arm shaft and align its holes (D, **Figure 47**) with the stud holes in the camshaft holder.

Camshaft Oil Clearance Measurement

Use Plastigage to measure the clearance between the journals on the camshaft cover, camshaft and cylinder head. The camshaft and camshaft holder must be installed on the cylinder head when performing this procedure.

1. Wipe all oil residue from each cam bearing journal (camshaft, camshaft holder and cylinder head). These surfaces must be clean and dry.
2. The original equipment camshafts are identified by the F (front) and R (rear) cast marks indicated in **Figure 31**.
3. Install the camshaft into the cylinder head with its F or R mark facing up. This will position the cam lobes so the valves will not be pressed open when the cam is installed. See *Camshaft Installation* in this chapter.
4. Place a strip of Plastigage material on the top of each camshaft bearing journal **(Figure 49)**, parallel to the camshaft.

5. Install and tighten the camshaft holder as described under in *Camshaft Removal* (this section).

CAUTION
Do not rotate the camshaft with the Plastigage in place.

CAUTION
Loosen the camshaft holder bolts as described or the camshaft holder may be damaged.

6. Loosen and remove the camshaft holder mounting bolts as described in *Camshaft Removal* (this section).
7. Remove the camshaft holder carefully, making sure the camshaft does not rotate. Do not drop the dowel pins into the engine.
8. Measure the widest portion of the flattened Plastigage according to the manufacturer's instructions **(Figure 50)** and compare to the camshaft oil clearance specification in **Table 2**. Note the following:
   a. If all the measurements are within specification, the cylinder head, camshaft and camshaft holder can be reused.
   b. If any measurement exceeds the service limit, replace the camshaft and recheck the oil clearance.
   c. If the new measurement exceeds the service limit with the new camshaft, replace the camshaft holder and cylinder head as a set.
9. Remove all Plastigage material from the camshafts, camshaft holders and cylinder head.

CAM CHAIN TENSIONER AND CAM CHAIN

The engine is equipped with a cam chain tensioner, chain guide and cam chain for each cylinder. The chain tensioner and cam chains can be removed with the engine mounted in the frame. Refer to *Cylinder Head* in this chapter to replace the chain guide.

Cam Chain Tensioner Removal/Inspection/Installation

Procedures required to remove the cam chain tensioner are the same for the front and rear cylinders.
1. Remove the camshaft as described in this chapter.

NOTE
Do not remove the pin (installed during camshaft removal) from the wedge B cam chain tensioner when inspecting the tensioner. This would release the tension spring.

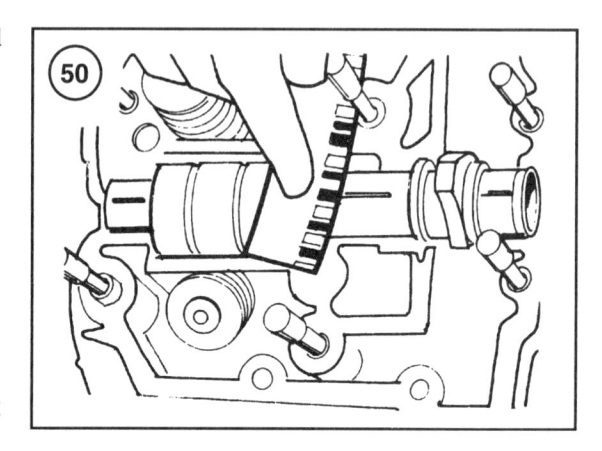

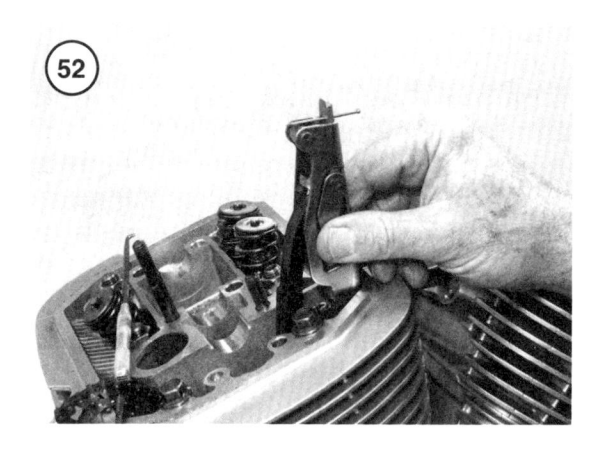

2. Remove the cam chain tensioner mounting bolts **(Figure 51)**, washers and tensioner **(Figure 52)**. Discard the washers.
3. Inspect the chain tensioner for the following:
   a. Cracked or damaged tension spring (A, **Figure 53**).
   b. Worn or damaged tensioner guide (B, **Figure 53**).
4. Pull the cam chain up to make sure the cam chain is properly meshed with the drive sprocket on the crankshaft. Then install the cam chain tensioner **(Figure 52)** into position. Make sure the bottom of

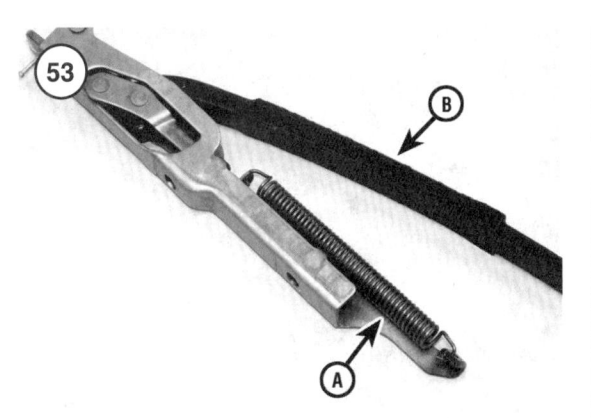

ENGINE TOP END

the tensioner seats into the lower pocket in the crankcase. See **Figure 54** (front) and **Figure 55** (rear).

5. Install a new sealing washer onto each chain tensioner mounting bolt and install them finger-tight. Tighten the upper bolt first, then the lower bolt (**Figure 51**). Tighten both bolts to 10 N.m (89 in.-lb.).

6. Install the camshaft as described in this chapter.

Cam Chain Replacement

Continuous cam chains are used on all models. Do not cut the chains; replacement link components are not available.

NOTE
*Before removing the camshaft, make sure to measure the cam chain tensioner wedge as described under **Camshaft Removal** in this chapter. Replace the cam chain if the measurement indicates a worn chain.*

1. Remove the camshaft as described in this chapter.
2. Drain the engine oil (Chapter Three).
3. To replace the front cam chain, remove the flywheel (Chapter Ten). 
4. To replace the rear cam chain, remove the primary drive gear (Chapter Six).

NOTE
If there is not enough clearance to remove the chain from the sprocket, remove the cam chain tensioner as described in this section. If there is still not enough clearance, it will be necessary to remove the cylinder head and the chain guide as described in this chapter.

5. Pry the guides away from the drive sprocket and remove the cam chain from the sprocket. See **Figure 54** (front) or **Figure 55** (rear). Pull the cam chain up through the chain tunnel and remove the chain.
6. Install the cam chain by reversing these steps. Refill the engine with oil as described in Chapter Three.

Inspection

If the cam chain or chain guides are excessively worn, the cam chain tensioner may not be working properly. Inspect the cam chain tensioner as described in this section.
1. Clean and dry the chain.
2. Inspect the cam chain for:
   a. Worn or damaged pins and rollers.
   b. Cracked or damaged side plates.
3. If the cam chain is excessively worn or damaged, inspect the drive (crankshaft) and driven (camshaft) sprockets for the same wear conditions. The driven sprocket can be replaced separately. An excessively worn or damaged drive sprocket will require crankshaft replacement.

CYLINDER HEAD

The engine must be removed from the frame to service both cylinder heads.

Removal

1. Remove the engine from the frame (Chapter Five).
2. Remove the intake manifold (Chapter Eight or Chapter Nine).
3. Remove the cylinder head cover as described in this chapter.
4. Remove the bolt (A, **Figure 56**) and the water pipe and its O-ring (B) from the cylinder head.
5. Remove the camshaft as described in this chapter.
6. Remove the cam chain tensioner as described in this chapter.
7. Remove the 6-mm bolt (A, **Figure 57**).
8. In a crossing pattern and in several steps, loosen and remove the 8-mm bolts (B, **Figure 57**) and the 10-mm bolts and washers (C)
9. Lift the cylinder head off the engine. If the cylinder head is tight, tap it with a plastic hammer to break its seal. Do not use a metal hammer or pry the head off.
10. Place the cylinder head on wooden blocks to avoid damaging the gasket surfaces.

NOTE
If the dowel pins are tight, do not remove them unless necessary. Stuck or rusted dowel pins are easily damaged during removal.

NOTE
After removing the cylinder head, check the top and bottom gasket surfaces for any indications of leakage. Also, check the head and base gaskets for signs of leakage. A blown gasket could indicate possible cylinder head or cylinder block warpage or other damage.

11. Remove the cylinder head gasket (A, **Figure 58**) and the two dowel pins (B).
12. Remove the chain guide **(Figure 59)**.
13. Cover the cylinder block and chain tunnel with a clean shop cloth.
14. Inspect the cylinder head as described in this section.
15. Refer to *Valves and Valve Components* in this chapter to service the valve assembly.

Installation

1. Clean the cylinder head and cylinder block gasket surfaces.
2. Position the cam chain inside the chain tunnel so it does not interfere with the cylinder head.
3. Install the chain guide by aligning its tabs with the slots in the cylinder **(Figure 59)**. Make sure that the

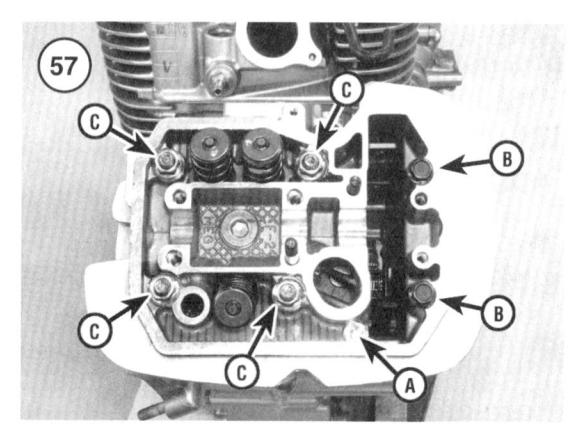

ENGINE TOP END

60

61

62

end of the guide seats into the pocket in the crankcase. See **Figure 54** (front) or **Figure 55** (rear).

4. Install the two dowel pins (B, **Figure 58**).

5. Install a *new* cylinder head gasket (A, **Figure 58**) over the dowel pins and against the cylinder block. Make sure all holes align.

NOTE
*The cylinder heads are not identical. Each cylinder head contains either an F or R identification mark (**Figure 60**).*

6. Install the cylinder head over the dowel pins and against the head gasket. Check that the cylinder head is sitting flush against the head gasket.

7. Pull on the cam chain and make sure it is properly engaged with the drive sprocket on the crankshaft.

8. Clean and dry the cylinder head fasteners. These fasteners must be free of debris. Dirt on the fastener threads or washers may affect bolt torque.

9A. On all models except 2011 and later Aero, lubricate the seating surfaces and threads of the 6-mm bolt, 8-mm bolts and 10-mm nuts and washer with engine oil (**Figure 61**).

9B. On 2011-on Aero models, lubricate the seating surfaces and threads of the 8-mm and 10-mm nuts and washers with engine oil.

10. Install the fasteners and tighten finger-tight in the following order:
  a. 10-mm nuts and washers (C, **Figure 57**).
  b. 8-mm bolts and washers (B, **Figure 57**).
  c. 6-mm bolt (A, **Figure 57**).

11. Tighten the 10-mm nuts in a crossing pattern and in several steps to 47 N.m (35 ft.-lb.).

CAUTION
*If a click-type torque wrench does not break or it feels like the nut is not being tightened properly or the stud is turning, either the stud is damaged or the stud threads in the crankcase are starting to pull or strip. The nut itself could also be damaged. This will require disassembly of the top end and either stud replacement and/or the installation of an insert in the crankcase. See **Cylinder Stud Replacement** in this chapter.*

12. Tighten the 8-mm bolts in several steps to 23 N.m (17 ft.-lb.).

13A. On 2004-2009 Aero models, tighten the 6-mm bolt to 12 N.m (106 in.-lb.).

13B. On all other models, tighten the 6-mm bolts securely.

14. Install the cam chain tensioner as described in this chapter.

15. Lubricate a new O-ring with coolant and install on the water pipe in the direction shown in **Figure 62**. Install the water pipe (B, **Figure 56**) secure with its mounting bolt (A).

16. Reverse Steps 1-3 under *Removal* to complete installation.

17. Start the engine and check for leaks. While doing so, bleed the cooling system as described in Chapter Three.

Inspection

1. Before removing the valves from the cylinder head, perform a solvent test to check the valve face-to-valve seat seal.
   a. Support the cylinder head with the exhaust port facing up (**Figure 63**) and pour solvent or kerosene into the port. Check the combustion chamber for fluid leaking past the exhaust valve. There should be no leakage past the seat in the combustion chamber.
   b. Repeat for the intake valves.
   c. If fluid leaks into the combustion chamber it will be wet. This indicates the valve is not seating correctly.
   d. Check for a damaged valve stem, seat and/or face, or possibly a cracked combustion chamber as described in this section and under *Valves and Valve Components* in this chapter.
2. Remove the spark plugs.
3. Remove all traces of gasket residue from the cylinder head (**Figure 64**) and cylinder block gasket surfaces. Do not scratch the gasket surface. If the gasket residue is hard to remove, place a solvent soaked rag across the cylinder head gasket surface to soften the deposits.

CAUTION
Cleaning the combustion chambers with the valves removed can damage the valve seat surfaces. A damaged or even slightly scratched valve seat causes poor valve seating.

4. Before removing the valves, remove all carbon deposits from the combustion chambers (**Figure 64**) with a wire brush. Take care not to damage the head, valves or spark plug threads.

NOTE
When using a tap to clean spark plug threads, lubricate the tap with an aluminum tap cutting fluid or kerosene.

5. Examine the spark plug threads in the cylinder head for damage. If damage is minor or if the threads are contaminated with carbon, use a spark plug thread tap to clean the threads following the tool manufacturer's instructions. If thread damage is severe, repair the head by installing a steel thread insert (available at many parts retailers). Follow the insert manufacturer's instructions.

NOTE
If the cylinder head was previously bead blasted, cleaning grit must be removed from all head areas.

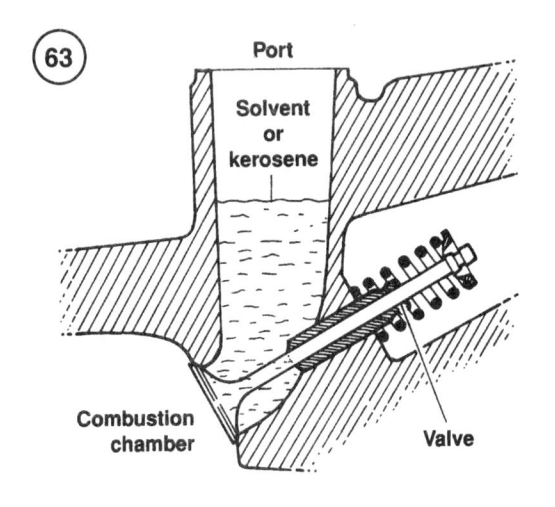

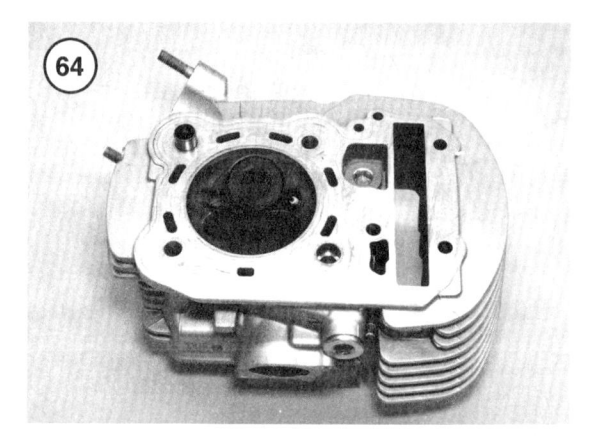

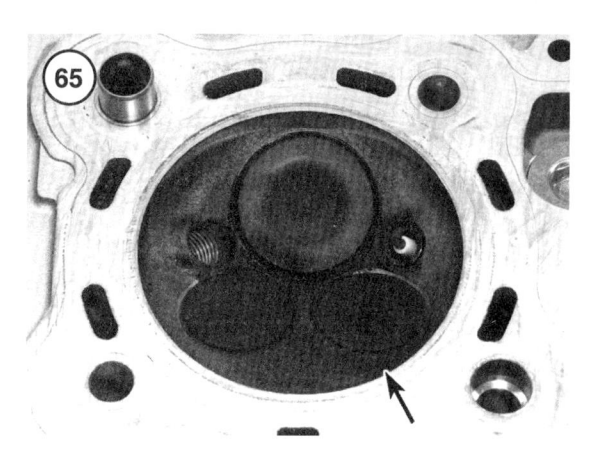

6. Clean the entire head in solvent. Make sure the coolant passageways are clear.
7. Check for cracks in the combustion chamber (**Figure 65**) and exhaust port. A cracked head must be replaced.

CAUTION
Do not clean the piston crown while the piston is installed in the cylinder. Carbon scraped from the top of the pis-

ENGINE TOP END

plug, valves and combustion chamber for aluminum deposits. If these deposits are found, the cylinder is overheating.

9. Place a straightedge across the gasket surface at several points (**Figure 66**). Measure warp by inserting a feeler gauge between the straightedge and cylinder head at each location. Maximum allowable warpage is listed in **Table 2**. If the warpage exceeds this limit, the cylinder head must be resurfaced or replaced. Distortion or nicks in the cylinder head surface could cause an air leak and result in overheating.

10. Check the exhaust pipe studs for looseness or thread damage. Slight thread damage can be repaired with a thread file or die. If thread damage is severe, replace the damaged stud(s) as described in *Stud Removal/Installation* in Chapter One.

11. Check the valves and valve guides as described under *Valves and Valve Components* in this chapter.

Cylinder Head Fasteners Inspection

1. Clean and dry the cylinder head nuts, washers and bolts.
2. Check the nuts for rounding of their hex corners, cracks and other damage. Replace any damaged or questionable nuts as their condition may affect cylinder head torque. Always install new nuts when installing new studs.
3. Check the washers for cracks, uneven surfaces or other damage. Install new washes if necessary.
4. Check the bolts for thread or hex damage. Replace the bolts if necessary.

VALVES AND VALVE COMPONENTS

Due to the number of special tools and the skills required to use them, it is recommended that valve service be referred to a dealership.

Identify all valve components and reinstall in their original position.

Valve Removal

1. Remove the cylinder head as described in this chapter.
2. Mark the parts (**Figure 67**) as they are removed so that they can be reinstalled in their original position.
3. Install a valve spring compressor squarely over the upper retainer with the other end of the tool placed against the valve head. Handle the tool carefully to prevent from damaging the cylinder head gasket surface.
4. Tighten the valve spring compressor until the valve keepers separate and remove them (**Figure 68**).

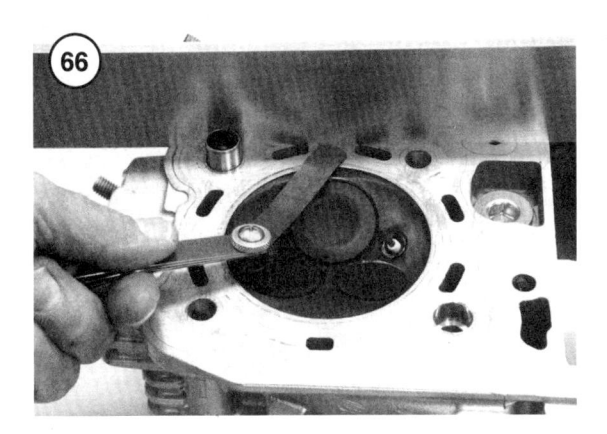

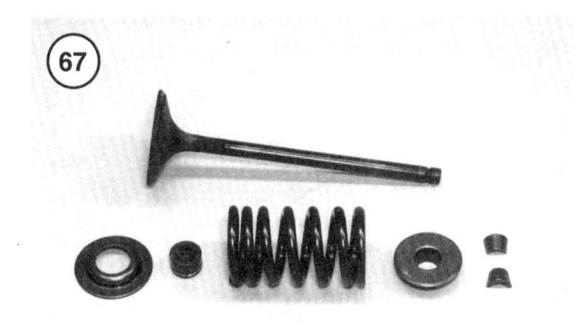

ton may fall between the cylinder wall and piston and onto the piston rings. Because carbon grit is very abrasive, premature cylinder, piston and ring wear will occur. If the piston crowns have heavy deposits of carbon, remove them as described in this chapter to clean them properly. Excessive carbon buildup on the piston crowns reduces piston cooling, raises engine compression and causes overheating.

8. Examine the piston crowns. The crowns should show no signs of wear or damage. If the crown appears pecked or spongy-looking, check the spark

NOTE
After removing the upper retainer and before removing the valve spring, place a zip-tie over the top of the valve spring to help identify its upper and lower ends.

5. Gradually loosen the valve spring compressor and remove it from the head. Remove the upper retainer (A, **Figure 69**) and valve spring (B).

CAUTION
*Remove any burrs from the valve stem groove (**Figure 70**) before removing the valve; otherwise, the valve guide may be damaged as the valve stem passes through it.*

NOTE
If a valve is difficult to remove, it may be bent, causing it to stick in its valve guide. This condition will require valve and valve guide replacement.

6. Remove the valve from its guide while rotating it slightly.
7. Use a pair of pliers to pull the oil seal (**Figure 71**) off the valve guide and discard it.
8. Remove the spring seat (**Figure 72**).
9. Repeat for the remaining intake and exhaust valves.

Valve Installation

Install the valves and their components in their original locations as recorded during removal.
1. Install the spring seat with its shoulder facing up (**Figure 72**).

NOTE
The intake and exhaust valve stem oil seals are different. The exhaust seal is equipped with a wire ring.

2. Lubricate the inside of a *new* oil seal with engine oil. Then push the seal straight down the valve guide until it snaps into the groove in the top of the guide (**Figure 73**). Check that the oil seal is centered and seats squarely on top of the guide. If the seal is cocked to one side, oil will leak past the seal during engine operation. If it is necessary to remove a new seal, do not reuse it.
3. Install the valve as follows:
   a. Coat the valve stem with engine assembly lube.
   b. Install the valve partway into its guide and then slowly turn the valve as it enters the valve stem

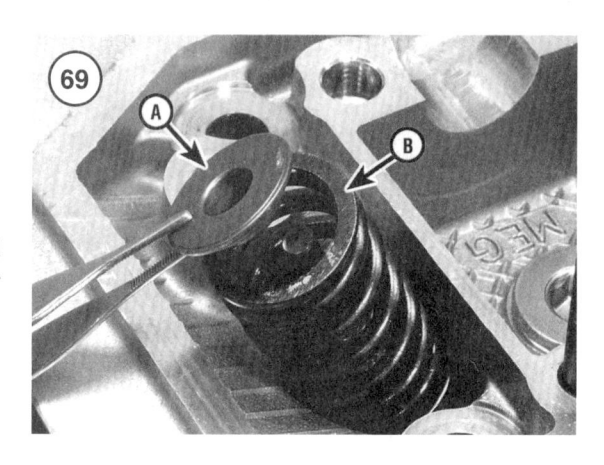

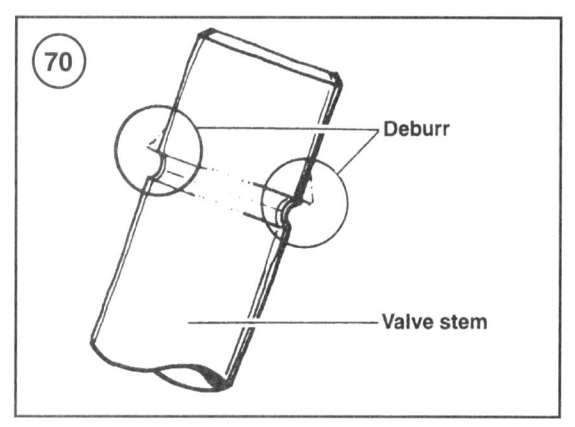

ENGINE TOP END

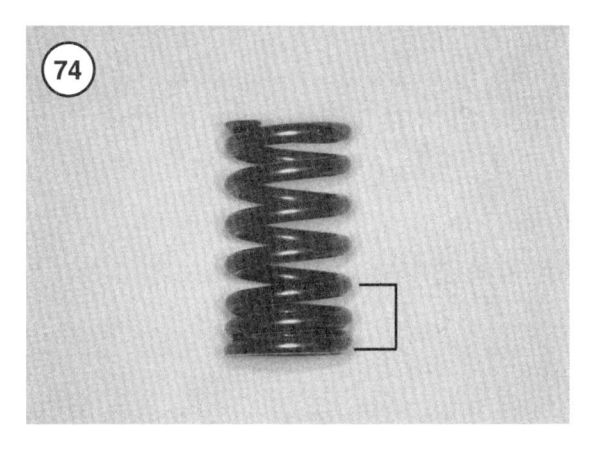

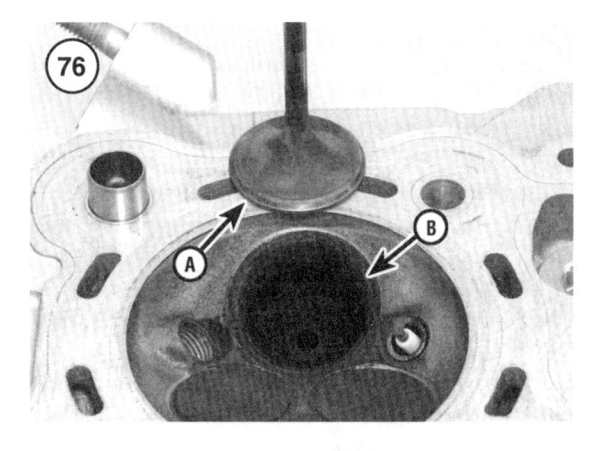

seal and continue turning it until the valve is installed all the way.

c. Make sure the valve moves up and down smoothly.

4. Install exhaust valve springs with their tightly wound coils facing down **(Figure 74)**. See B, **Figure 69**.

5. Install the retainer (A, **Figure 69**) with its shoulder side facing toward the valve spring (B).

CAUTION
To avoid loss of spring tension, do not compress the spring any more than necessary when installing the valve keepers.

6. Compress the valve spring with a valve spring compressor tool and install the valve keepers **(Figure 68)** around the valve stem and into the hole in the top of the retainer. Then slowly release tension on the valve spring while watching the movement of the retainer and keepers. Make sure the keepers fit into the rounded groove in the valve stem **(Figure 75)**. Gently tap the upper retainer with a plastic hammer to seat the keepers.

7. Repeat for the remaining valves.

8. After installing the cylinder head, camshaft and camshaft holders, check and adjust the valve clearance as described in Chapter Three.

Inspection

Valve components

Refer to the specifications in **Table 2**. Replace parts that are damaged or out of specification as described in this section.

1. Clean the valve components in solvent. Do not damage the valve seating surface.

2. Inspect the valve face (A, **Figure 76**) for burning, pitting or other signs of wear. Unevenness of the valve face is an indication that the valve is not serviceable. If the wear on a valve is too extensive to be corrected by hand-lapping the valve into its seat, replace the valve. The face on the valve cannot be ground. Replace the valve if defective.

3. Inspect the valve stems for wear and roughness. Check the valve keeper grooves for damage.

4. Measure each valve stem outside diameter with a micrometer **(Figure 77)** along the surface that operates in the valve guide. Note the following:

   a. If a valve stem is out of specification, discard the valve.

   b. If a valve stem is within specification, record the measurement so it can be used to determine the valve stem-to-guide clearance.

NOTE
The manufacturer recommends reaming the valve guides to remove any carbon buildup before checking and measuring the guides. For the home mechanic it is more practical to remove carbon and varnish from the valve guides with a stiff spiral wire brush. Then clean the valve guides with solvent to wash out all particles and dry with compressed air.

5. Insert each valve into its respective valve guide and move it up and down by hand. The valve should move smoothly.

NOTE
Because valve guides wear unevenly (oval shape), measure each guide at different positions. Use the largest bore diameter measurement when determining its size.

6. Measure each valve guide inside diameter with a small hole gauge and record the measurements. Note the following:
   a. If a valve guide is out of specification, replace it as described in this section.
   b. If a valve guide is within specification, record the measurement so it can be used to determine the valve stem-to-guide clearance.
7. Subtract the valve stem outside diameter measurement from the valve guide inside diameter measurement to determine the valve stem-to-guide clearance. Note the following:
   a. If the clearance is out of specification, determine if a new guide would bring the clearance within specification.
   b. If the clearance would be out of specification with a new guide, replace the valve and guide as a set.
8. Inspect the valve springs as follows:
   a. Inspect each spring for any cracks or other visible damage.
   b. Measure the free length of each valve spring with a caliper **(Figure 78)**.
   c. Replace defective or worn springs.
9. Check the valve keepers for cracks and any surface spots. Replace in pairs.
10. Inspect the spring retainer and spring seat for cracks and other damage.
11. Inspect the valve seats as described in this section.

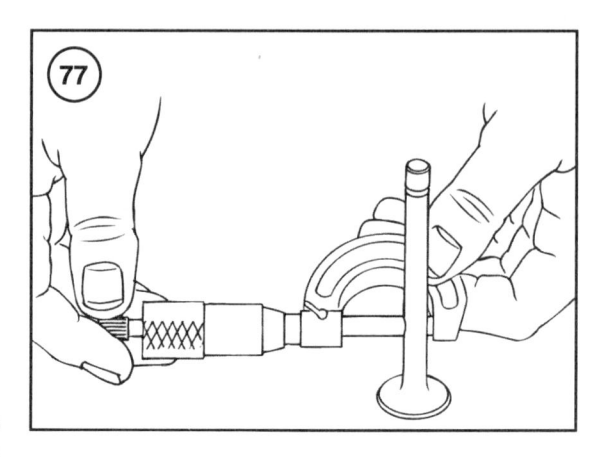

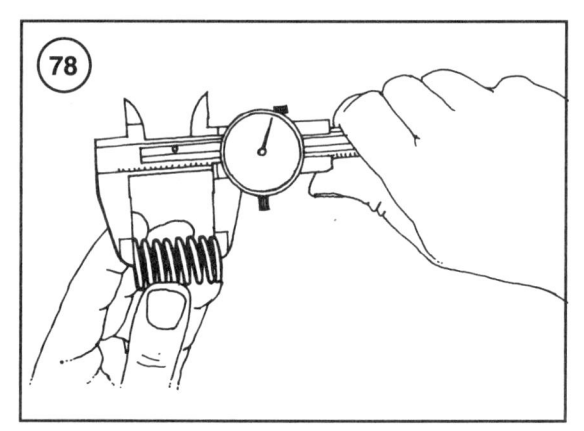

Valve seat

The most accurate method for checking the valve seal is to use a marking compound (machinist's dye), available from auto parts and tool stores. Marking compound is used to locate high or irregular spots when checking or making close fits. Follow the manufacturer's directions.

NOTE
Because of the close operating tolerances within the valve assembly, the valve stem and guide must be within tolerance; otherwise the inspection results will be inaccurate.

1. Remove the valves as described in this chapter.
2. Clean the valve (A, **Figure 76**) and valve seat (B), mating areas with contact cleaner.
3. Thoroughly clean all carbon deposits from the valve face with solvent and dry thoroughly.
4. Spread a thin layer of marking compound evenly on the valve face.
5. Slowly insert the valve into its guide and tap the valve against its seat several times **(Figure 79)** without spinning it.
6. Remove the valve and examine the impression left by the marking compound. If the impression (on

ENGINE TOP END

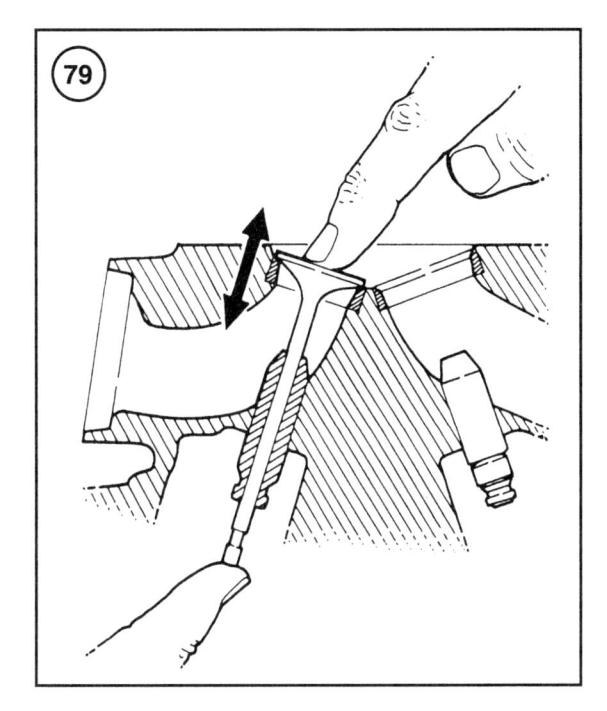

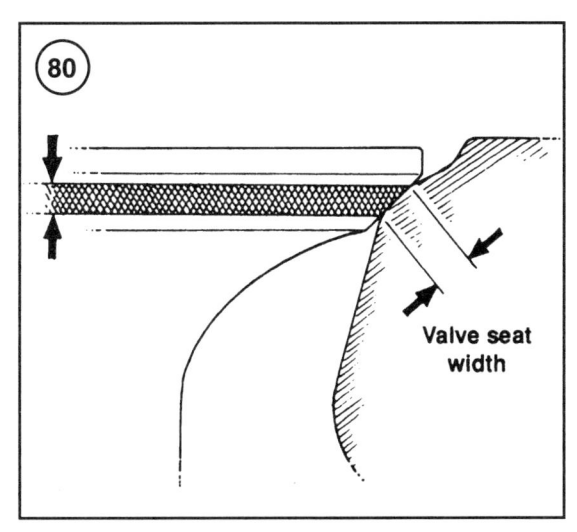

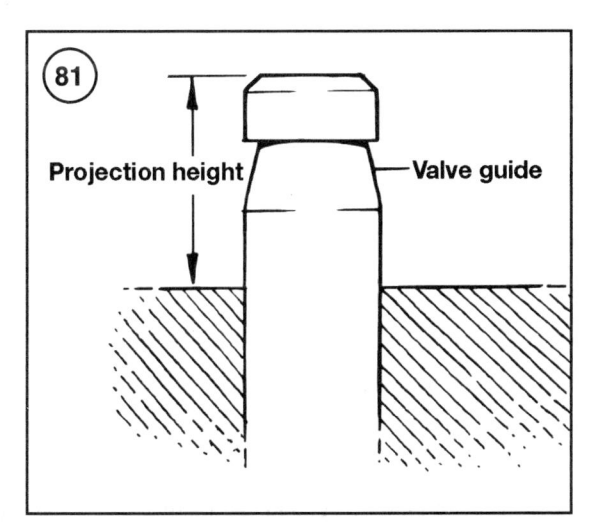

the valve or in the cylinder head) is not even and continuous, and the valve seat width **(Figure 80)** is not within the specified tolerance listed in **Table 2**, the valve seat in the cylinder head must be reconditioned.

7. Closely examine the valve seat in the cylinder head (B, **Figure 76**). It should be smooth and even with a polished seating surface.

8. If the valve seat is not in good condition, recondition the valve seat as described in this chapter.

NOTE
The valve guides must be in good condition and serviced, if necessary, before regrinding the valve seats.

9. Repeat the inspection procedure for the other valves and valve seats.

Valve Guide Replacement

Tools

The following special tools (or their equivalents) are required to remove and install the valve guides. Confirm part numbers with a dealership before ordering them.

1. 5.5 mm valve guide removal driver (Honda part No. 07742-0010100).
2. Valve guide installation driver (Honda part No. 07743-0020000 [not available in the US]).
   a. This is an adjustable valve guide driver for installing the valve guides. Follow the tool manufacturer's instructions for adjusting the driver to the valve guide height.
   b. If this driver is not available for US models, use the 5.5 mm valve guide removal driver (Honda part No. 07742-0010100) to install the valve guides. When using the driver, install the guides to the specified height **(Table 2)** by measuring their projection height with a caliper as described in this section.
3. 5.5 mm valve guide reamer (Honda part No. 07984-200000D [US only] or Honda part No. 07984-2000001).

Procedure

1. Remove all of the valves and valve guide seals from the cylinder head.
2. Place the new valve guides in the freezer for approximately one hour prior to heating the cylinder head. Chilling them will slightly reduce the outside diameter, while the cylinder head is lightly larger due to heat expansion. This makes valve guide removal

and installation much easier. Remove the guides from the freezer one at a time as needed.

3. Measure the valve guide projection height above the cylinder head surface with a caliper **(Figure 81)**. Record the projection height for each valve guide and compare to the specification in **Table 2**.

WARNING
Wear welding gloves to prevent burns.

CAUTION
Do not heat the cylinder head with a torch. The direct heat can destroy the case hardening of the valve guide and may warp the cylinder head.

4. Place the cylinder head on a hot plate and heat to a temperature of 130-140° C (266-284° F). Do not exceed 150° C (300° F). Monitor the temperature with heat sticks, available at welding supply stores, or an infrared thermometer.

5. Remove the head from the hot plate. Place the head on wooden blocks with the combustion chamber facing *up*.

CAUTION
Do not attempt to remove the valve guides if the head is not hot enough. Doing so may damage the valve guide bore in the cylinder head and require replacement of the head.

6. From the combustion chamber side of the head, drive out the valve guide with the valve guide remover **(Figure 82)**. Quickly repeat this step for each valve guide to be replaced. Reheat the head as required. Discard the valve guides after removing them.

7. Allow the head to cool.

8. Inspect and clean the valve guide bores. Check for cracks or any scoring along the bore wall.

9. Reheat the cylinder head as described in Step 4. Then remove it from the hot plate and install it onto the wooden blocks with the camshaft side facing *up*. The valve guide is installed from this side.

10. Remove one new valve guide, either intake or exhaust, from the freezer.

NOTE
*Refer to **Tools** in this section on the use of the valve guide drivers used to install the valve guides.*

11. Align the valve guide in the bore. Use the valve guide installation driver and a hammer to drive in the valve guide until the projection height of the valve guide is within the specification in **Table 2 (Figure 81)**.

12. Repeat to install the remaining valve guides.

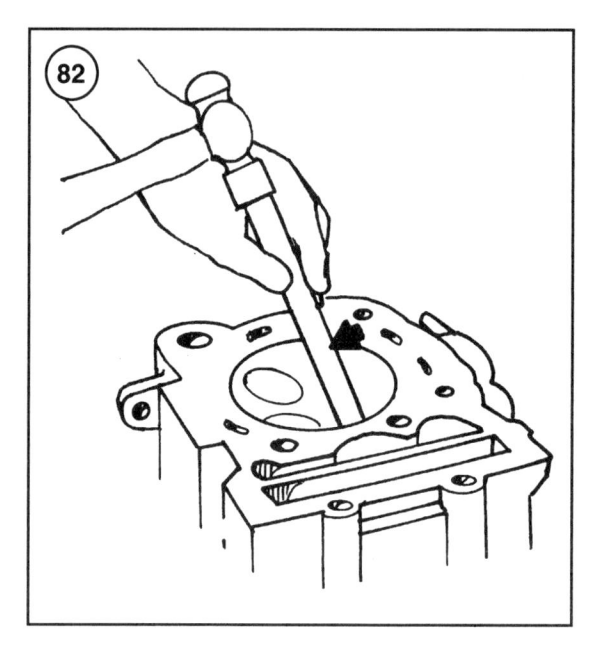

CAUTION
The cylinder head must be cooled to room temperature before reaming the valve guides.

13. Allow the head to cool to room temperature.

14. Ream each valve guide as follows:
   a. Place the head on wooden blocks with the combustion chamber facing up. The guides are reamed from this side.
   b. Thoroughly coat the valve guide and valve guide reamer with cutting oil.

CAUTION
*Always rotate the reamer **clockwise** through the entire length of the guide, both when reaming the guide and when removing the reamer. Rotating the reamer counterclockwise will reverse cut and damage (enlarge) the valve guide.*

CAUTION
Do not allow the reamer to tilt. Keep the tool square to the hole and apply even pressure and twisting motion during the entire operation.

   c. Rotate the reamer clockwise into the valve guide **(Figure 83)**.
   d. Slowly rotate the reamer through the guide, while periodically adding cutting oil.
   e. As the end of the reamer passes through the valve guide, maintain the clockwise motion and work the reamer back out of the guide while continuing to add cutting oil.

ENGINE TOP END

Figure 83 Valve guide reamer, Combustion chamber

Figure 84

Figure 85 Old seat width, 32°

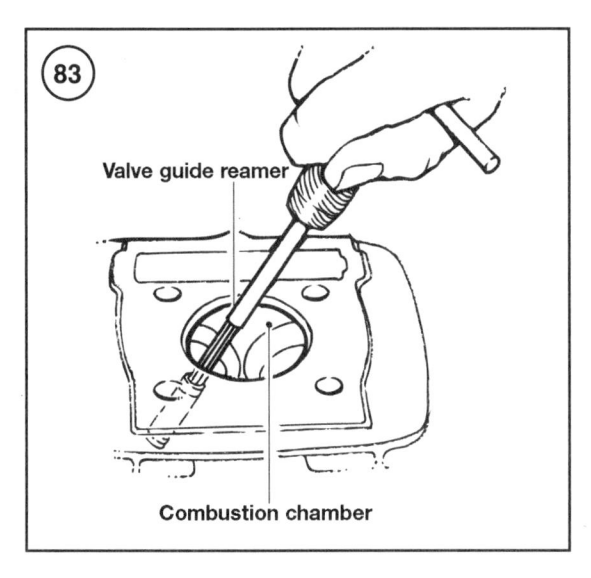

f. Clean the reamer of all chips and relubricate with cutting oil before starting on the next guide. Repeat for each guide as required.

15. Thoroughly clean the cylinder head and all valve components in solvent, then with detergent and hot water to remove all cutting residue. Rinse in cold water. Dry with compressed air.

16. Measure the valve guide inside diameter with a small hole gauge. The measurement must be within the specification listed in **Table 2**.

17. Lubricate the valve guides with engine oil to prevent rust.

18. Lubricate a valve stem with engine oil and pass it through its valve guide, verifying that it moves without any roughness or binding.

19. Reface the valve seats as described under *Valve Seat Reconditioning* in this chapter.

Valve Seat Reconditioning

Tools

Before reconditioning the valve seats, inspect and measure them (this chapter).
The following tools are required:
1. Various angles of valve seat cutters **(Figure 84)**. Follow the tool manufacturer's instructions.
2. Caliper.
3. Gear-marking compound.
4. Valve lapping tool.

Procedure

1. Carefully rotate and insert the solid pilot into the valve guide. Be sure the pilot is correctly seated.
2. Install the 45° cutter and cutter holder onto the solid pilot.

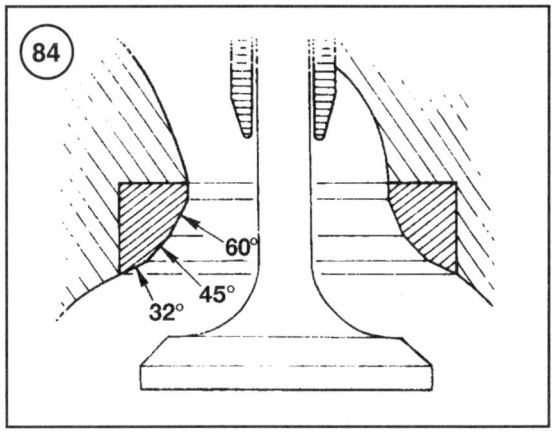

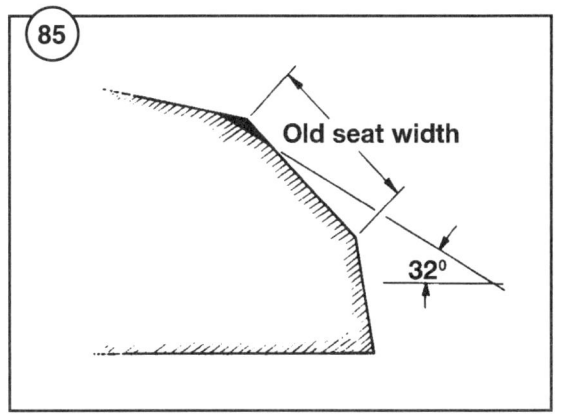

CAUTION
Work slowly and make light cuts. Overcutting the valve seats will recede the valves into the cylinder head, reducing the valve adjustment range. If cutting is excessive, the ability to set the valve adjustment may be lost. This condition requires cylinder head replacement.

3. Using the 45° cutter, de-scale and clean the valve seat with one or two turns.
4. If the seat is still pitted or burned, turn the 45° cutter additional turns until the surface is clean.
5. Measure the valve seat width with a caliper **(Figure 80)**. Record the measurement to use as a reference point when cutting remaining valve seat angles.

CAUTION
The 32° cutter removes material quickly. Work carefully and check the progress often.

6. Install the 32° cutter onto the solid pilot and lightly cut the seat to remove 1/4 of the existing valve seat **(Figure 85)**.

7. Install the 60° cutter onto the solid pilot and lightly cut the seat to remove 1/4 of the existing valve seat (**Figure 86**).

8. Measure the valve seat width with a caliper (**Figure 80**). Then fit the 45° cutter onto the solid pilot and cut the valve seat to the specified width (**Figure 87**) listed in **Table 2**.

9. When the valve seat width is correct, check valve seating as follows:
    a. Clean the valve seat with contact cleaner.
    b. Spread a thin layer of marking compound evenly on the valve face.
    c. Slowly insert the valve into its guide.
    d. Support the valve with two fingers (**Figure 79**) and tap the valve up and down in the cylinder head several times. Do not rotate the valve or a false reading will result.
    e. Remove the valve and examine the impression left by the marking compound.
    f. Measure the valve seat width **Figure 80** and compare to the specified valve seat width (**Table 2**).
    g. The valve contact should be approximately in the center of the valve seat area.

10. If the contact area is too high on the valve, or if it is too wide, use the 32° cutter and carefully remove a portion of the top area of the valve seat material to lower and narrow the contact area on the valve (**Figure 88**).

11. If the contact area is too low on the valve, or too wide, use the 60° cutter and carefully remove a portion of the lower area of the valve seat material to raise and narrow the contact area on the valve (**Figure 88**).

12. After the desired valve seat position and width is obtained, use the 45° cutter to lightly clean off any burrs that may have been caused by previous cuts.

13. When the contact area is correct, lap the valve as described in this chapter.

14. Repeat the reconditioning procedure for all remaining valve seats.

15. Thoroughly clean the cylinder head and all valve components in solvent, then with detergent and hot water. Rinse in cold water and dry with compressed air. Lubricate the valve guides and seats with engine oil to prevent rust.

Valve Lapping

Valve lapping can restore the valve seat without machining if the amount of wear or distortion is not too great.

Perform this procedure if the valve seat width and outside diameter are within specification. A valve lapping tool and compound are required.

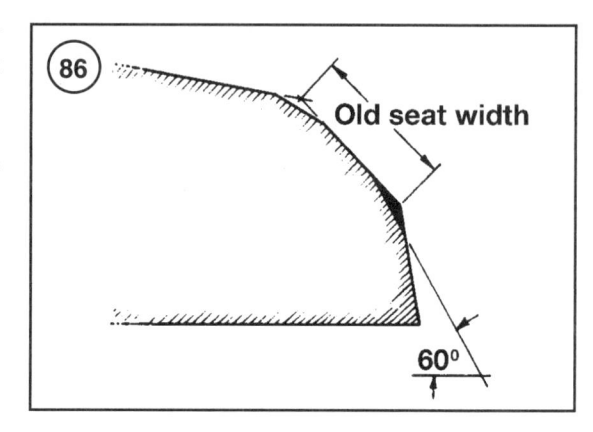

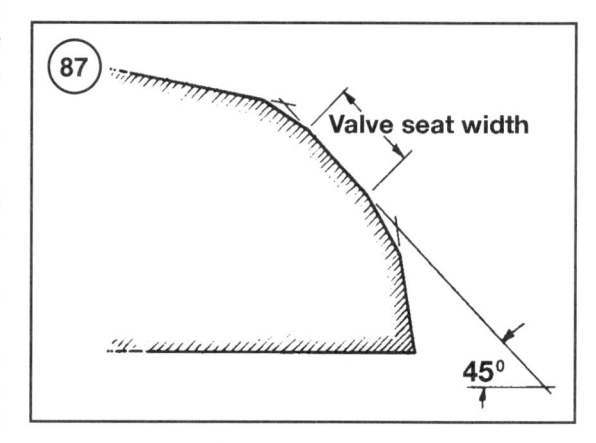

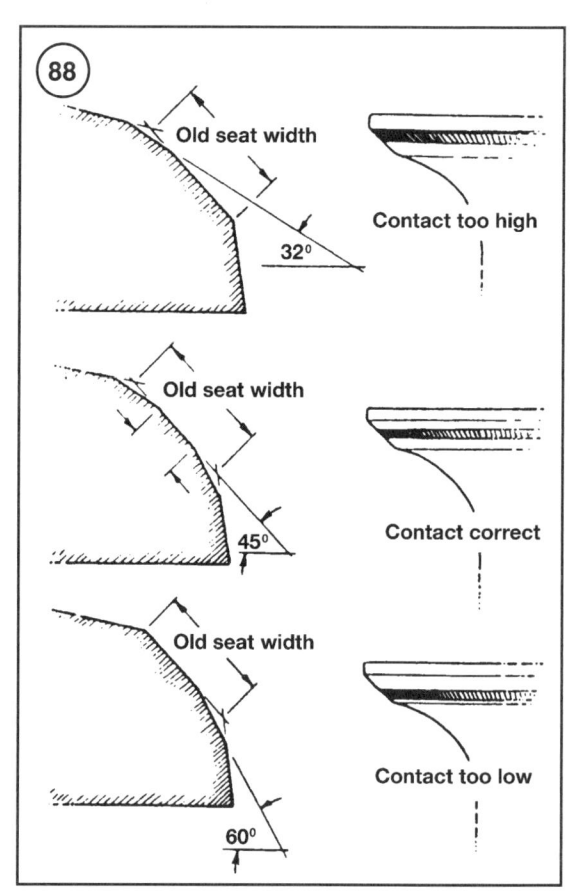

ENGINE TOP END

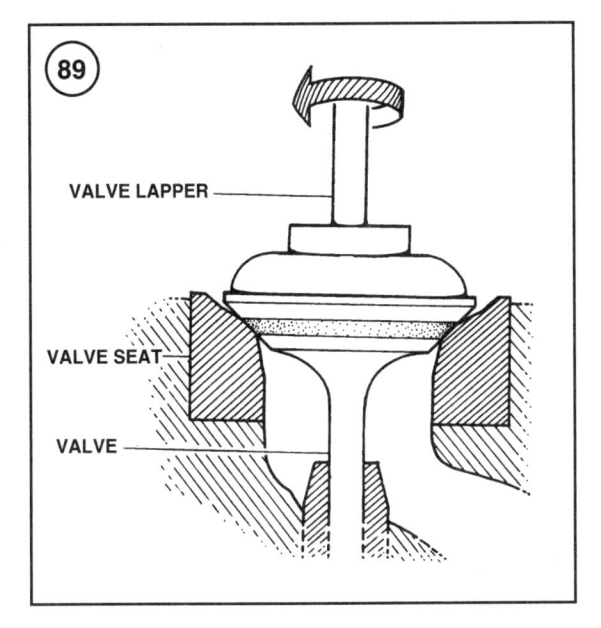

Figure 89 (VALVE LAPPER, VALVE SEAT, VALVE)

CAUTION
Do not allow the valve lapping compound to contact the valve stem or enter the valve guide.

1. Smear a light coating of fine grade valve lapping compound on the valve face seating surface.
2. Insert the valve into the head.
3. Wet the suction cup of the lapping stick and stick it onto the head of the valve. Spin the tool in your hands in both directions, while pressing it against the valve seat and lap the valve to the seat **(Figure 89)**. Every 5 to 10 seconds, lift and rotate the valve 180° in the valve seat. Continue until the gasket surfaces on the valve and seat are smooth and equal in size.
4. Closely examine the valve seat in the cylinder head (B, **Figure 76**). It should be smooth and even with a smooth, polished seating ring.
5. Repeat the lapping procedure for the other valves.

CAUTION
Any compound left on the valves or in the cylinder head causes excessive wear to the engine components.

6. Thoroughly clean the cylinder head and all valve components in solvent, then with detergent and hot water. Rinse in cold water and dry with compressed air. Lubricate the valve guides to prevent rust.
7. Install the valve assemblies as described in this chapter.
8. Perform a solvent test as described in *Inspection* in *Cylinder Head* in this chapter. There should be no leaks past the seat. If fluid leaks past any of the seats, disassemble that valve assembly and repeat the lapping procedure until there is no leakage.
9. After cleaning the cylinder head and valve components in detergent and hot water, apply a light coat of engine oil to all bare metal surfaces to prevent rust formation.

CYLINDER

Service procedures for the front and rear cylinders are the same.

Removal

CAUTION
When it is necessary to rotate the crankshaft, pull up the cam chains so they cannot bind internally.

1. Remove the engine from the frame (Chapter Five).
2. Remove the cylinder head as described in this chapter.
3. If necessary, remove the bolts and hose joint **(Figure 90)** from the front cylinder. Discard the O-ring.
4. Remove the clips **(Figure 91)** from the water pipe.

5. Slide the water pipe into either the front or rear cylinder **(Figure 92)**.
6. Loosen the cylinder by tapping around the perimeter with a rubber or plastic mallet.
7. Pull the cylinder straight up and off the piston and slide it over the studs.
8. If necessary, remove the piston as described in this chapter.
9. Remove and discard the base gasket (A, **Figure 93**).
10. Remove the dowel pins (B, **Figure 93**).
11. If the piston was not removed, slide a length of plastic hose down two of the cylinder studs and rest the piston and rings against them.
12. Cover the crankcase opening.
13. Remove the water pipe **(Figure 94)** and discard both O-rings **(Figure 95)**.
14. Clean and inspect the cylinder as described in this section.

Installation

1. Clean the cylinder and crankcase gasket surfaces.
2. Measure the height of each cylinder stud to check for loose studs and reposition studs if necessary. Refer to *Cylinder Stud* in this chapter.
3. Install the dowel pins (B, **Figure 93**) and a new base gasket (A).
4. If removed, install the piston and rings as described in this chapter.

CAUTION
Make sure the piston pin circlips have been properly installed.

5. Lubricate new O-rings with coolant and install them into the water pipe grooves **(Figure 95)**.

NOTE
The water pipe cannot be installed when both cylinders are installed on the engine.

6. Install the water pipe into one of the cylinders **(Figure 94)**.
7. Install a piston holding fixture (A, **Figure 97**) under the piston. If necessary, fabricate a fixture from a piece of wood **(Figure 98)**.
8. Lubricate the cylinder wall, piston and rings with engine oil. Liberally lubricate the oil control rings and spacer with oil.
9. Stagger the piston ring end gaps around the piston as shown in **Figure 99**.

NOTE
The front and rear cylinders are not identical. The front cylinder is equipped

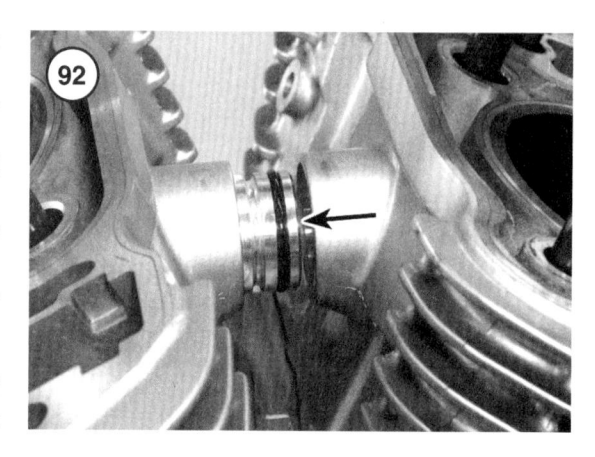

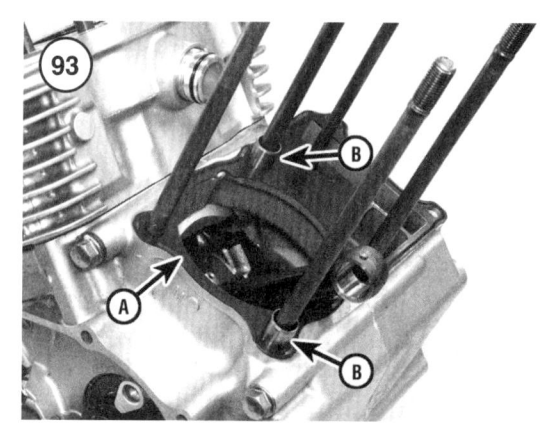

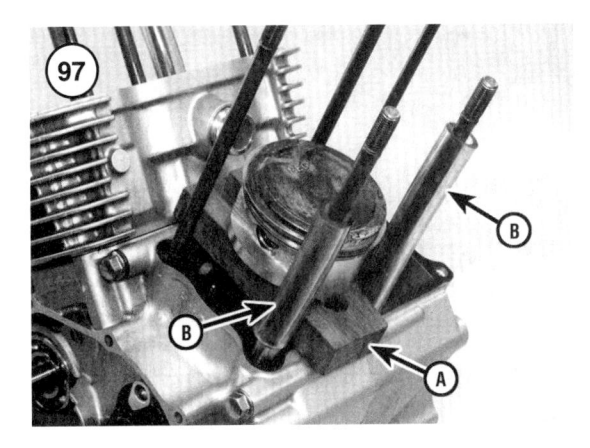

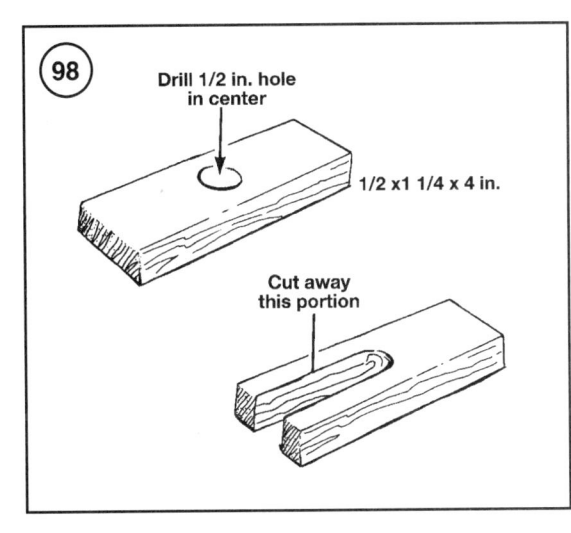

ENGINE TOP END

96

97

98 Drill 1/2 in. hole in center
1/2 x 1 1/4 x 4 in.
Cut away this portion

99 Second ring gap — Top ring gap — 120° — Oil ring lower rail gap — Oil ring upper rail gap

100

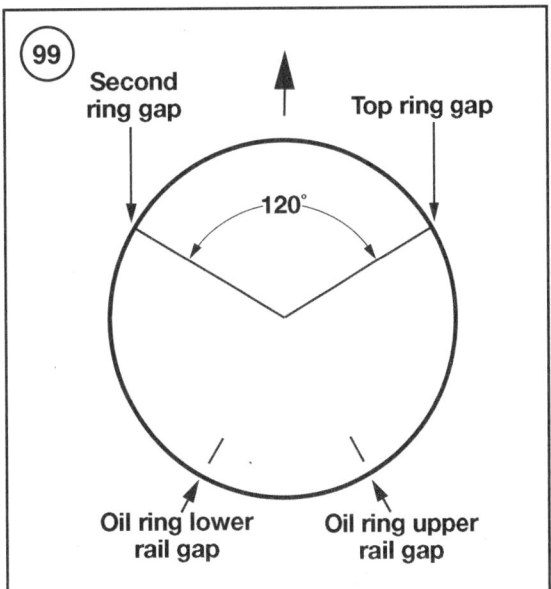

it bottoms on the piston holding fixture (B, **Figure 100**).

11. Remove the piston holding fixture and push the cylinder down into place over the dowel pins and against the base gasket.

12. Install a length of hose (A, **Figure 101**) over one of the cylinder studs and secure it with a nut (B) to hold the cylinder in place when turning the crankshaft.

with a hose joint (Figure 96). The water passage opening on the rear cylinder is blocked off.

10. Align the cylinder (A, **Figure 100**) with the cylinder studs and chain tunnel and lower it onto the piston. Compress each piston ring by hand, one at a time, as it enters the cylinder. Do not force the cylinder past the rings. Push the cylinder down until

CAUTION
When rotating the crankshaft, pull up the cam chains so they do not bind.

13. Pull up on both cam chains and rotate the crankshaft counterclockwise. The piston must move up and down in the bore with no binding or roughness. If there is any interference, a piston ring may have broken during cylinder installation.

14. Repeat these steps to install the other cylinder.

15. Slide the water pipe (**Figure 92**) into the opposite cylinder and secure with the two clips (**Figure 91**). Make sure the clips seat in the grooves completely.
16. Install a new O-ring onto the hose joint and install it onto the front cylinder (**Figure 90**). Tighten the bolt securely.
17. Install the cylinder heads as described in this chapter.

Inspection

When measuring the cylinder in this section, compare the actual measurements to the specifications in **Table 3**. Service the cylinder if it is out of specification or shows damage as described in this section.
1. Soak the cylinder block surfaces in solvent, then carefully remove gasket material from the top and bottom mating surfaces with a scraper. Do not nick or gouge the gasket surfaces or leakage may result.
2. Wash the cylinder block in solvent. Dry with compressed air.
3. Check the cylinder bore surface for scoring, seizure marks, aluminum deposits (from the piston skirt) and other damage. If damage is noted, refer further inspection to a dealership. If the bore surface looks good, continue with step 4.
4. Check the dowel pin holes for cracks or other damage.
5. Place a straight edge across the upper cylinder block surface at the stud holes. Insert a flat feeler gauge between the straight edge and the cylinder block at different locations and check for warping (**Figure 102**).
6. Measure the cylinder bore with a bore gauge or inside micrometer at the points shown in **Figure 103**. Measure in line with the piston pin and again at 90 degrees to the pin. Use the largest measurement to determine cylinder bore. If the taper or out-of-round is greater than specifications, bore the cylinder oversize and install a new piston and rings.
7. Determine piston-to-cylinder clearance as described in *Piston Clearance* in this chapter.
8. If the cylinder is within all service limits, and the current piston is reusable (refer to *Piston and Piston Rings* in this chapter), the cylinder must be deglazed to accommodate new piston rings.
9. Cylinder glaze appears as a hard, shiny surface and is removed by a cylinder hone. As the hone deglazes the cylinder, a crosshatch pattern is left on the cylinder bore. The pattern provides a uniform surface, capable of spreading oil and allowing the rings to seat and seal against the cylinder.
   a. When deglazing the cylinder, apply plenty of honing lubricant to the hone and cylinder surface.  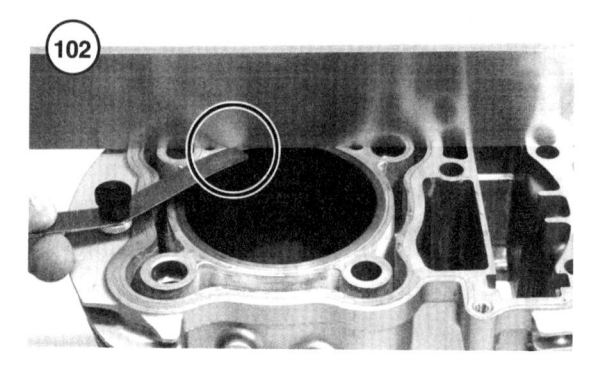 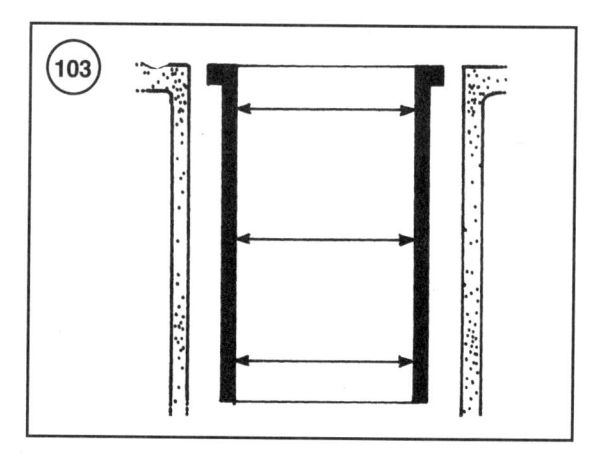
   b. Do not run the hone at high speed, or the crosshatch pattern will not develop.
   c. Move the hone at a moderate and consistent rate in an up and down motion for a time period specified by the manufacturer.
   d. Proper movement speed of the hone is achieved when a 45° crosshatch pattern is visible on the cylinder wall.

CAUTION
Hot soapy water is required to completely clean the cylinder walls. Solvent and kerosene cannot wash fine grit out of cylinder crevices. Any grit left in the cylinder will cause the piston rings and other engine parts to wear unnecessarily.

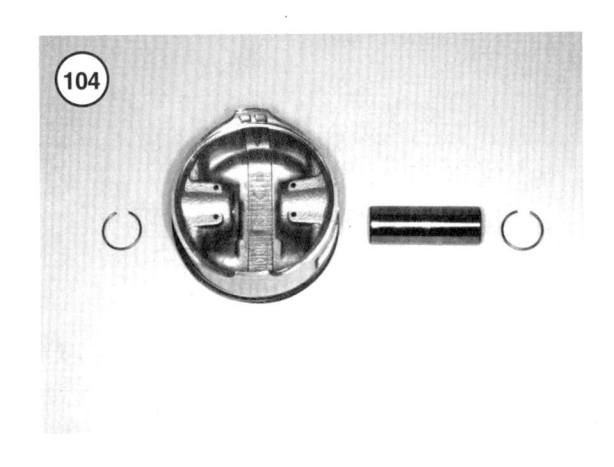

ENGINE TOP END

If the rag is the slightest bit dirty, the wall is not thoroughly cleaned and must be washed again.
  d. When the cylinder wall is clean, lubricate the wall with clean engine oil to prevent rust.
  e. Wrap the cylinder with plastic until engine reassembly.

PISTON AND PISTON RINGS

Refer to **Figure 104** when servicing the piston and rings. Procedures for the front and rear piston and rings are the same.

Piston Removal

CAUTION
When it is necessary to rotate the crankshaft, pull up the cam chains so they do not bind.

CAUTION
Guide the pistons so they are not damaged while entering the crankcase.

1. Remove the cylinder as described in this chapter.
2. Mark the top of the piston with an identification letter (F or R) and a directional arrow pointing toward the front of the engine.
3. Block off the crankcase below the piston with a clean shop cloth to prevent the piston pin circlips from falling into the crankcase.
4. Before removing the piston, hold the rod and rock the piston (**Figure 105**). Any rocking motion (do not confuse with the normal sliding motion) indicates wear on the piston pin, rod bushing, pin bore, or a combination of all three.
5. Support the piston with a piston holding fixture (A, **Figure 97**), and install plastic hoses (B) over the cylinder studs to protect the piston rings when removing the circlips and piston pin.
6. Remove the piston circlip on the side opposite the cam chain (**Figure 106**).

NOTE
The operating clearance between the piston pin and pin bore is such that the piston pin can be removed and installed by hand. However, problems such as varnish on the piston pin, a burred pin bore or circlip groove, or a damaged piston can make it difficult to remove the piston pin.

7. Push the piston pin out of the piston by hand. If the pin is tight, remove the opposite piston circlip

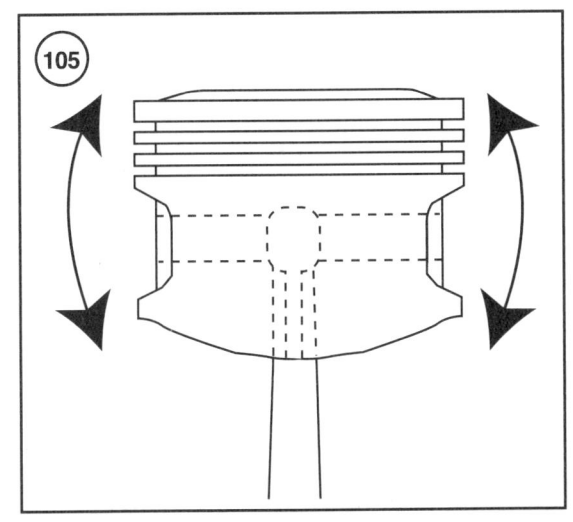

10. After the cylinder has been serviced, clean the cylinder wall as follows:
  a. Wash the outside of the cylinder and the cylinder wall in hot soapy water.
  b. Also wash out any fine grit material from the cooling passages surrounding the cylinder.
  c. After washing the cylinder, wipe the cylinder wall with a clean, lint-free white cloth. It should *not* show any traces of grit or debris.

and use a homemade tool **(Figure 107)** to remove the pin. Do not drive the piston pin out as this action may damage the piston pin, connecting rod or piston. Heat can also be used to ease removal. Heat the piston crown (and not the side of the piston) with a heat gun.

8. Lift the piston off the connecting rod.
9. Repeat for the other piston.
10. Inspect the pistons, piston pins and piston rings as described in this section.

Piston Installation

CAUTION
When it is necessary to rotate the crankshaft, pull up the cam chains so they do not bind.

CAUTION
Guide the pistons so they are not damaged while entering the crankcase.

1. Make sure the crankcase gasket surface is clean.

CAUTION
DO NOT align the piston pin circlip end gap with the cut out in the piston.

2. Before installing the piston, install a *new* piston pin circlip **(Figure 108)** into the piston on the cam chain side of the engine. Make sure the circlip seats in the groove completely.
3. Install the piston rings onto the piston as described in *Cylinder Installation* (this chapter). Make sure the ring end gaps are staggered correctly **(Figure 99)**.
4. Coat the connecting rod small end and piston pin with engine oil.
5. Use the plastic hoses and piston holding fixture to support the piston and protect the piston rings as described under *Piston Removal* in this section.
6. Slide the piston pin into the piston until its end is flush with the piston pin boss.
7. Place the piston over the connecting rod with the marks made on the piston crown facing in their original direction. If installing a new piston, install it with its MEG mark facing toward the center of the engine **(Figure 109)**.
8. Line up the piston pin with the hole in the connecting rod. Push the piston pin through the connecting rod and into the other side of the piston. Center the piston pin in the piston.
9. Block off the crankcase below the piston with a clean shop cloth to prevent the piston pin circlips from falling into the crankcase.

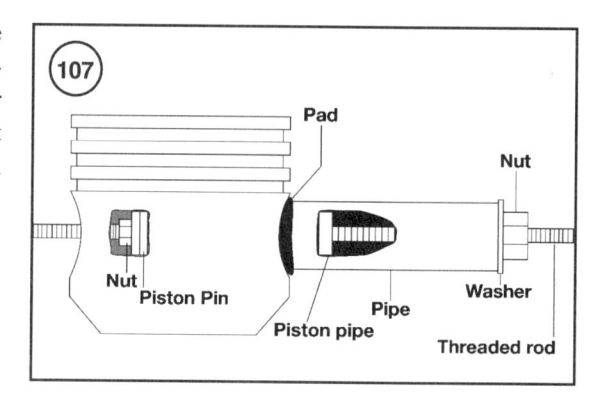

CAUTION
DO NOT align the piston pin circlip end gap with the cut out in the piston.

10. Install a *new* piston pin circlip **(Figure 106)** into the piston. The opposite circlip was already installed. Make sure the circlips seat in the piston grooves completely.
11. Install the cylinder as described in this chapter.

Piston Inspection

1. Remove the piston rings as described in this chapter.
2. Soak the piston in solvent to soften the carbon deposits.

CAUTION
Do not use a wire brush on the piston skirt.

ENGINE TOP END

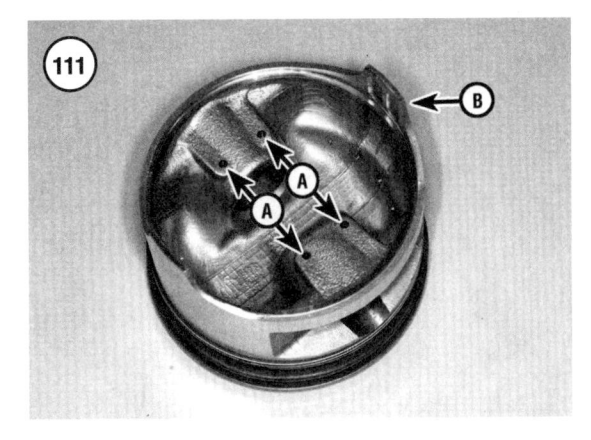

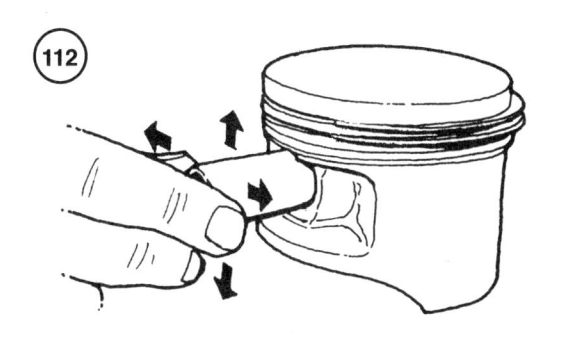

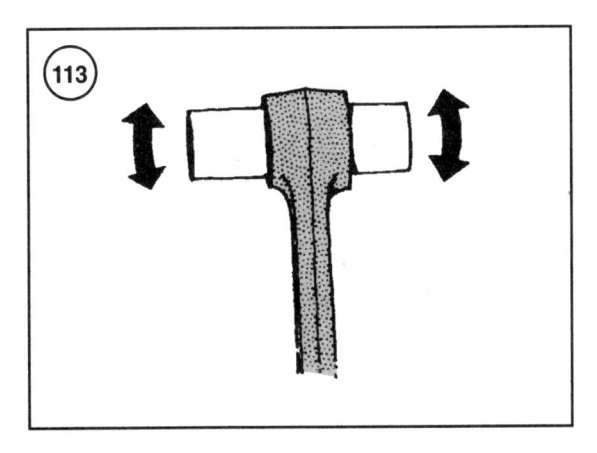

3. Clean the carbon from the piston crown with a soft scraper or wire wheel mounted in a drill. A thick carbon buildup reduces piston cooling and results in detonation and piston damage. Relabel the piston crown alignment marks as soon as it is cleaned.

4. After cleaning the piston, examine the crown. The crown must show no signs of wear or damage. If the crown appears pecked or spongy-looking, also check the spark plug, valves and combustion chamber for aluminum deposits. If these deposits are found, the engine is overheating.

5. Examine each ring groove (A, **Figure 110**) for burrs, dented edges or other damage. Pay particular attention to the top compression ring groove as it usually wears more than the others. Because the oil rings are bathed in oil, these rings and grooves wear little compared to compression rings and their grooves. If there is evidence of oil ring groove wear or if the oil ring is tight and difficult to remove, the piston skirt may have collapsed due to excessive heat. Replace the piston.

6. Clean the oil control holes (A, **Figure 111**) in the piston.

NOTE
If the piston skirt is worn or scuffed unevenly from side-to-side, the connecting rod may be bent or twisted.

7. Check the piston skirt (B, **Figure 111**) for cracks or other damage. If the piston shows signs of partial seizure (bits of aluminum built up on the piston skirt), replace the piston.

8. Check the piston circlip grooves (B, **Figure 110**) for wear, cracks or other damage.

9. Measure piston-to-cylinder clearance as described in *Piston Clearance* (this chapter). Compare the results to specifications listed in **Table 3**.

Piston Pin
Inspection

When measuring the piston pin in this section, compare the actual measurements to the specifications in **Table 3**. Replace the piston pin if out of specification or if it shows damage as described in this section.

1. Clean and dry the piston pin.
2. Inspect the piston pin for chrome flaking or cracks.
3. Oil the piston pin and install it in the piston. Slowly rotate the piston pin and check for tightness or excessive play **(Figure 112)**.
4. Lubricate the piston pin and install it in the connecting rod. Slowly rotate the piston pin and check for radial play **(Figure 113)**.

5. Measure the piston pin bore inside diameter (A, **Figure 114**).
6. Measure the piston pin outside diameter (B, **Figure 114**).
7. Subtract the piston pin outside diameter from the piston pin bore inside diameter. The difference is the piston-to-piston pin clearance.

Connecting Rod Small End Inspection

1. Inspect the connecting rod small end (**Figure 115**) for cracks, scoring or other damage.
2. Measure the connecting rod small end inside diameter.
3. Measure the piston pin outside diameter (B, **Figure 114**).
4. Subtract the piston pin outside diameter from the connecting rod small end inside diameter. The difference is the connecting rod-to-piston pin clearance.
5. Compare the results against the dimension listed in **Table 3**. If out of specification, replace the connecting rod (Chapter Five).

Piston Clearance

1. Make sure the piston skirt and cylinder walls are clean and dry.
2. Measure the cylinder bore with a bore gauge as described in *Cylinder Inspection* in this chapter.
3. Measure the piston diameter with a micrometer at a right angle to the piston pin bore. Measure up 17 mm (0.7 in.) from the bottom edge of the piston skirt (**Figure 116**).
4. Subtract the piston diameter from the largest bore diameter. The difference is piston-to-cylinder clearance. If clearance exceeds the service limit in **Table 3**, determine if the piston, cylinder or both are worn. If necessary, take the cylinder to a dealership that can rebore the cylinder to accept an oversize piston.

Piston Ring Inspection and Removal

A 3-ring type piston and ring assembly is used (**Figure 117**). The top and second rings are compression rings. The lower ring is an oil control ring assembly (consisting of two ring rails and a spacer). Refer to the ring specifications in **Table 3**. Replace the piston rings as a set if out of specification or if they show damage as described in this section.

1. Measure the top and second ring-to-ring groove side clearance with a flat feeler gauge (**Figure 118**). Measure at several places around the ring groove and note the following:

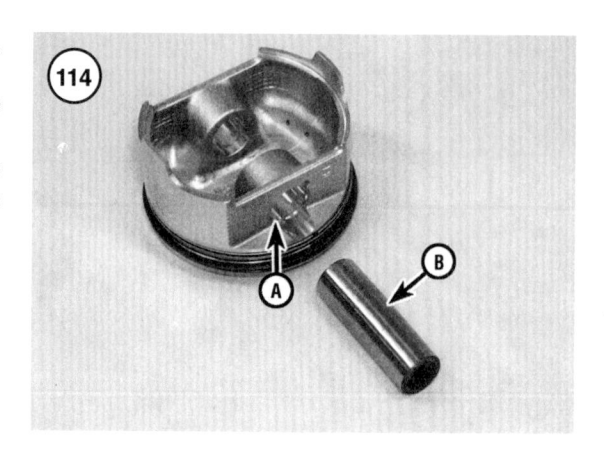

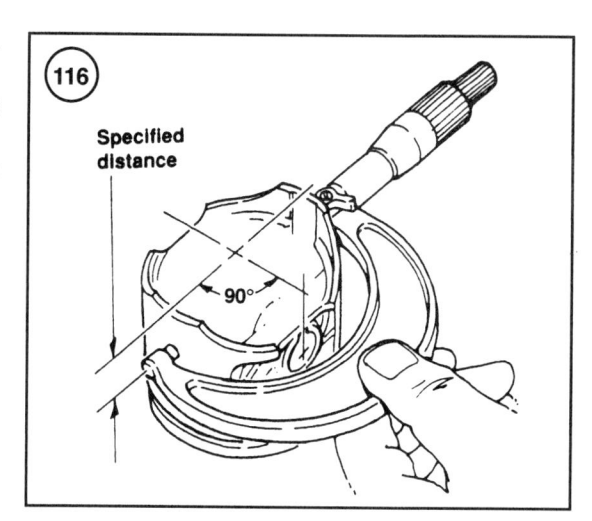

  a. If the clearance is greater than specified, replace the rings. If the clearance is still excessive with new rings, replace the piston.
  b. If the clearance is too small, check the ring and ring groove for carbon and oil residue. Carefully clean the ring without removing any metal from its surface. Clean the piston ring groove as described in this section.

ENGINE TOP END

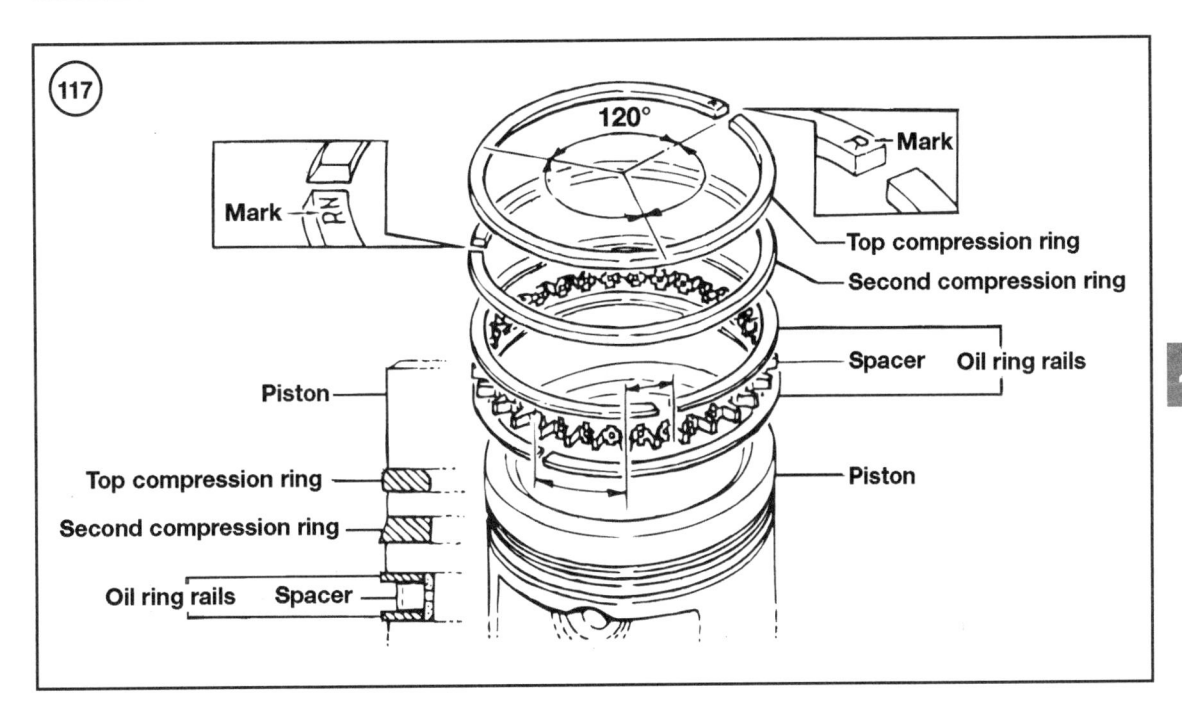

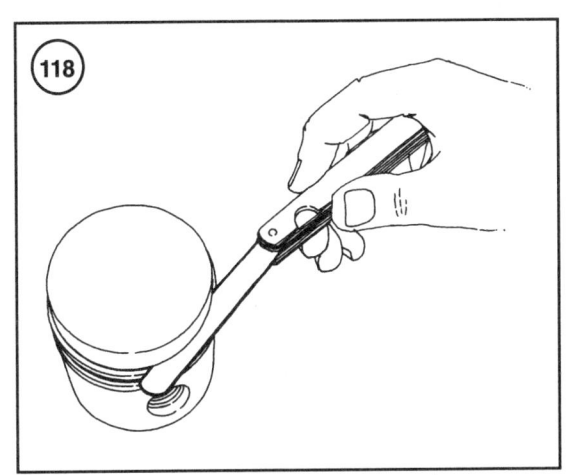

NOTE
*The compression rings are marked with identifying letters (**Figure 117**). However, these letters usually wear off or become difficult to read. When removing the rings, identify and mark the ring position (first or second groove) and which side faces up.*

2. Remove the compression rings by spreading the ring ends by hand (**Figure 119**). Try not to allow the rings to twist during removal. Store the rings in order of removal.

3. Remove the oil ring assembly by first removing the upper (**Figure 117**) and then the lower ring rails. Remove the spacer.

4. Remove carbon and oil residues from the piston ring grooves by carefully cleaning the grooves with

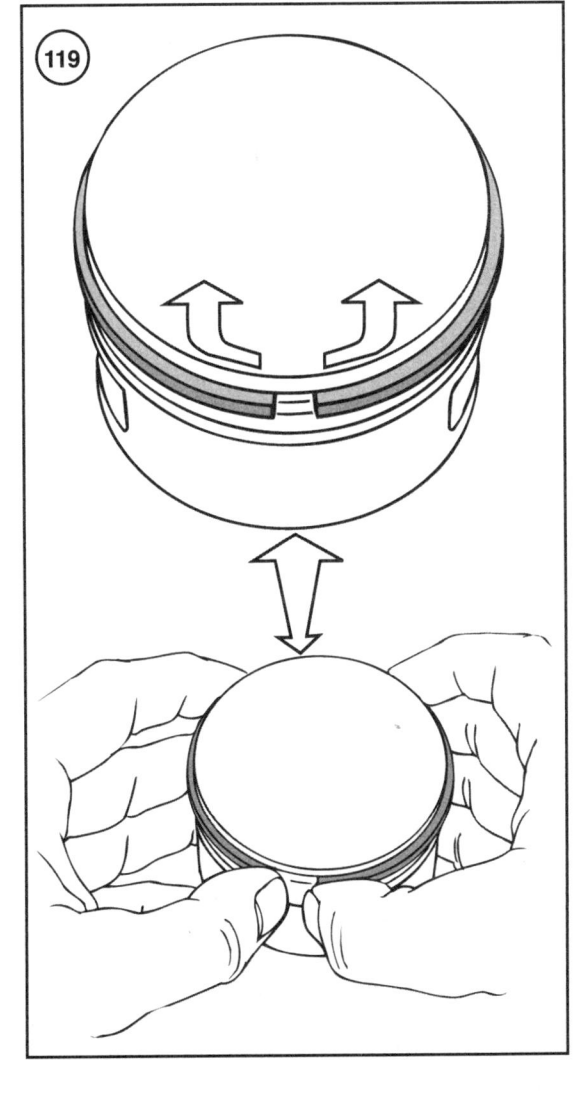

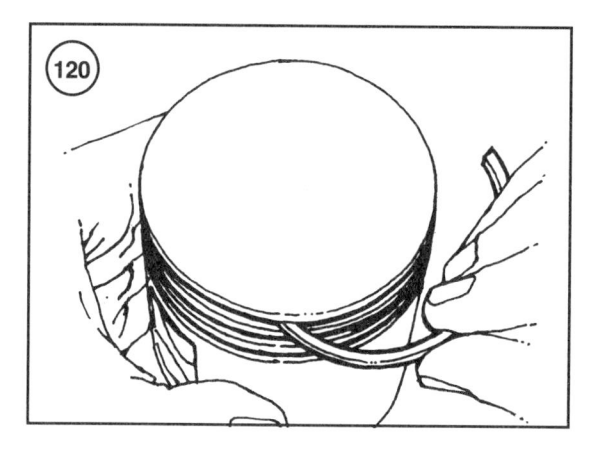

a broken piston ring **(Figure 120)**. Do not remove aluminum material from the ring grooves as this will increase the side clearance.

5. Inspect the ring grooves for burrs, nicks or broken or cracked lands. Replace the piston if necessary.
6. Check the end gap of each ring. Insert the ring into the bottom of the cylinder bore and square it with the cylinder wall by tapping it with the piston **(Figure 121)**. Measure the end gap with a feeler gauge **(Figure 121)**. Replace the rings if the gap is too large. If the gap on the new ring is smaller than specified, hold a small file in a vise. Then grip the ends of the ring with your fingers and slowly enlarge the gap.

NOTE
*When measuring the oil control ring end gap, measure the upper and lower ring rail end gaps only. Do not measure the spacer **(Figure 117)**.*

7. Roll each compression ring around its piston groove **(Figure 122)** to check for binding. Repair minor binding with a fine-cut file.

Piston Ring Installation

1. When installing new piston rings, hone or deglaze the cylinder wall to help the new rings to seat in the cylinder. Refer to *Cylinder Inspection* (this chapter) for further information or refer this service to a dealership. After honing and cleaning the cylinder bore, measure the end gap of each ring and compare to the dimensions in **Table 3**.
2. Clean the cylinder as described in this chapter.
3. Clean and dry the piston and rings.
4. Install the piston rings as follows:
   a. Install the oil ring assembly into the bottom ring groove. Install the spacer first, and then the bottom and top ring rails **(Figure 117)**. Make sure the ends of the spacer butt together **(Figure 123)**. They should not overlap. If re-

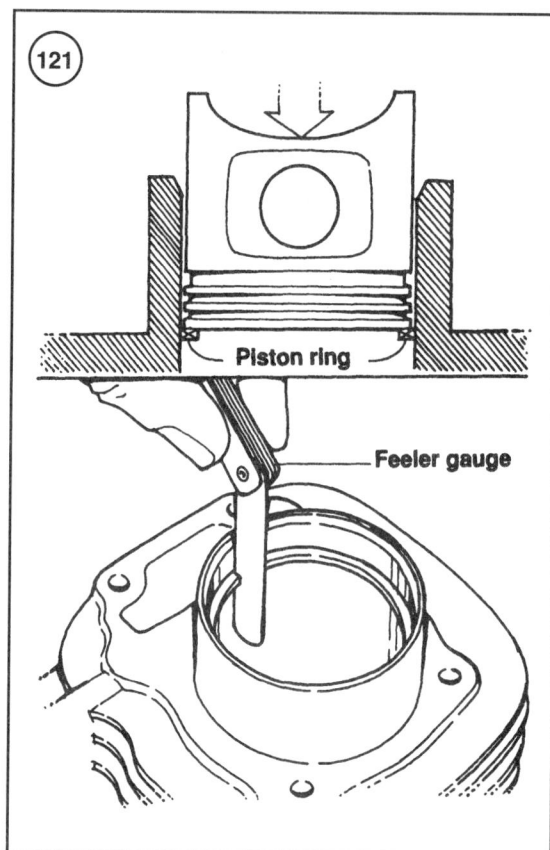

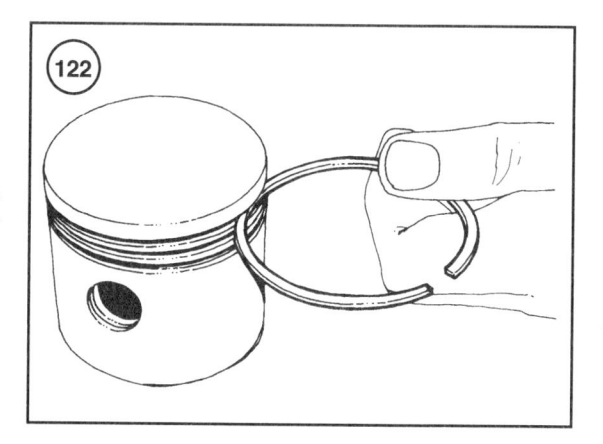

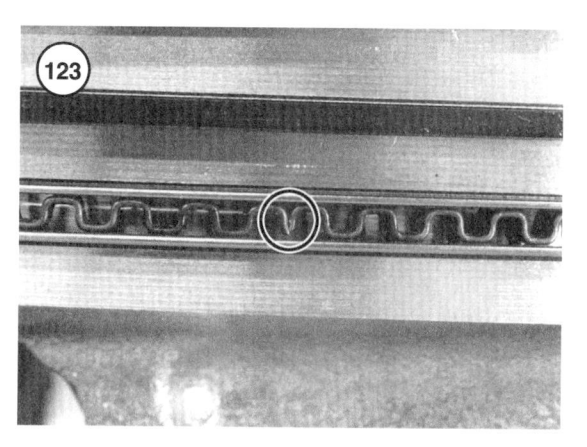

ENGINE TOP END

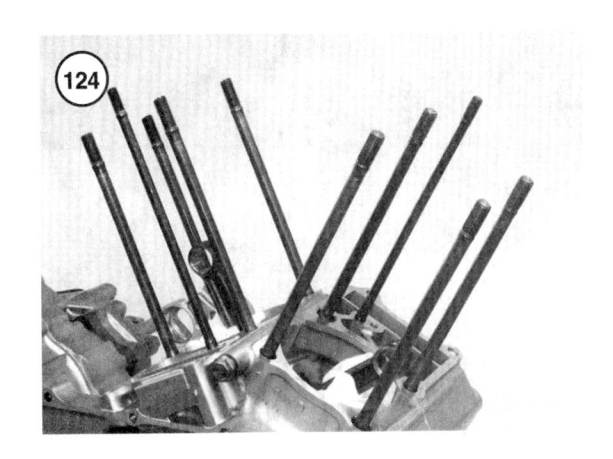

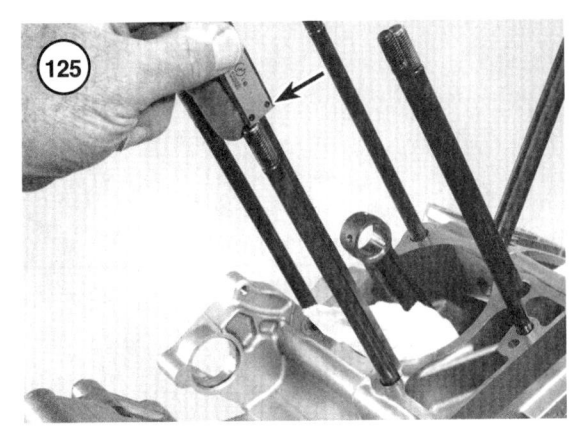

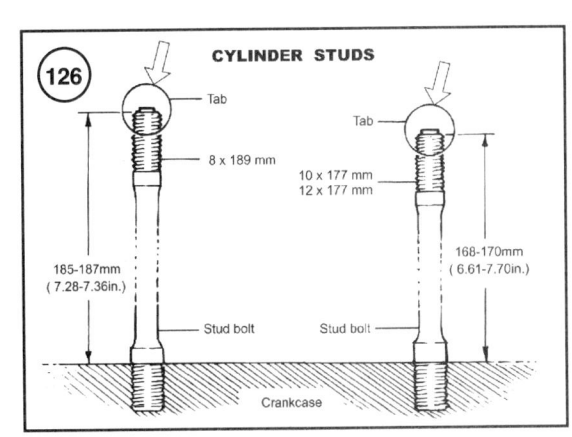

assembling used parts, install the ring rails in their original positions.

b. Install the compression rings by spreading the ring ends by hand **(Figure 119)**.

c. Install the compression rings with their marks **(Figure 117)** facing up or refer to the marks made during removal.

d. Install the second compression ring. This ring has a slight taper and its top side is marked with the letters RN **(Figure 117)**.

e. The top compression ring has a flat contact surface and its top is marked with the letter R **(Figure 117)**.

5. Make sure the rings are seated completely in their grooves all the way around the piston.

NOTE
*Stagger the ring end gaps as described in **Cylinder Installation** in this chapter.*

6. If new parts were installed, follow the *Engine Break-In* procedure in Chapter Five.

CYLINDER STUDS

The studs **(Figure 124)** can be serviced without splitting the crankcase.

1. Measure each stud height from the top of the stud to the crankcase gasket surface as shown in **Figure 125**. Compare the results to the specifications in **Figure 126**. Note the following:

   a. If the cylinder stud height is correct, inspect them as described in this section.

   b. If the cylinder stud height is incorrect, inspect and service the studs as described in this section.

2. Check for loose, bent or damaged studs. Retighten or replace damaged studs as described in this section.

3. Different size and length studs are used **(Figure 126)**. Identify and mark each stud before its removal while also noting the top of the stud.

4. Slip a box-end wrench (same size as nut) over the stud. Thread two nuts onto the stud and tighten securely against each other. Then mount the wrench on the lower nut and turn it to remove the stud **(Figure 127)**. Refer to *Service Methods* (Chapter One) for additional information.

5. Check each stud for bending by rolling it on a flat surface. Inspect the stud threads for damage.

6. After removing a stud, clean the threaded hole in the crankcase. Check for any debris or damaged threads.

7. If the crankcase threads are damaged, install a threaded insert into the hole following the insert manufacturer's instructions.

NOTE
*Make sure to install the stud with its correct side facing up. Refer to the marks made during removal or refer to the stud ends. The top end of the stud can be identified by either a raised tab or a punch mark in the center of the stud (**Figure 126**).*

8. Lubricate the stud's lower end threads with engine oil and install to the dimensions in **Figure 126** using a stud installation tool (**Figure 128** [Motion Pro part No. 08-0152]) or reverse the tool setup used during removal by turning the top nut to tighten the stud.

9. Remeasure the installed height of each stud and compare to the specifications in **Figure 126**.

Table 1 GENERAL ENGINE SPECIFICATIONS

Bore and stroke	79.0 x 76.0 mm (3.11 x 2.99 in.)
Compression ratio	9.6:1
Cylinder alignment	52° V-Twin
Cylinder number	No. 1 (rear)
	No. 2 (front)
Displacement	745 cc (45.5 cu.-in.)
Engine firing order	Front (308 degrees)—rear (412 degrees)—front
Valve timing	
Intake valve	
Opens	
Front	0° BTDC @ 1 mm (0.04 in.) lift
Rear	5° ATDC @ 1 mm (0.04 in.) lift
Closes	25° ABDC @ 1 mm (0.04 in.) lift
Exhaust valve	
Opens	35° BBDC @ 1 mm (0.04 in.) lift
Closes	
Front	0° ATDC @ 1 mm (0.04 in.) lift
Rear	5° BTDC @ 1 mm (0.04 in.) lift

Table 2 CYLINDER HEAD AND VALVE SERVICE SPECIFICATIONS

	New mm (in.)	Service limit mm (in.)
Cylinder head warpage limit	--	0.10 (0.004)
Cam chain tensioner wedge B length	--	6.0 (0.23)
Camshaft		
Lobe height		
Intake	37.188-37.348 (1.4641-1.4704)	37.16 (1.463)
Exhaust	37.605-37.765 (1.4805-1.4868)	37.58 (1.480)
Journal outside diameter	21.959-21.980 (0.8645-0.8654)	21.90 (0.862)
Oil clearance	0.020-0.141 (0.0008-0.0056)	0.16 (0.006)
Runout	--	0.05 (0.002)

ENGINE TOP END

Table 2 CYLINDER HEAD AND VALVE SERVICE SPECIFICATIONS (continued)

	New mm (in.)	Service limit mm (in.)
Rocker arm and shaft		
Rocker arm bore inside diameter	12.000-12.018 (0.4724-0.4731)	12.05 (0.474)
Rocker arm shaft outside diameter	11.966-11.984 (0.4711-0.4718)	11.83 (0.466)
Rocker arm-to-rocker arm shaft clearance	0.016-0.052 (0.0006-0.0020)	0.07 (0.003)
Valve		
Valve stem outside diameter		
Intake	5.475-5.490 (0.2156-0.2161)	5.45 (0.215)
Exhaust	5.455-5.470 (0.2148-0.2154)	5.41 (0.213)
Valve guide inside diameter		
Intake	5.500-5.510 (0.2165-0.2169)	5.56 (0.219)
Exhaust	5.500-5.512 (0.2165-0.2170)	5.56 (0.219)
Valve stem-to-guide clearance		
Intake	0.010-0.035 (0.0004-0.0014)	0.10 (0.004)
Exhaust	0.030-0.057 (0.0012-0.0022)	0.11 (0.004)
Valve guide projection height above cylinder head		
Intake	18.7-18.9 (0.736-0.744)	--
Exhaust	17.2-17.4 (0.677-0.685)	--
Valve seat width	0.90-1.10 (0.035-0.043)	1.5 (0.06)
Valve spring free length		
Intake	42.14 (1.659)	40.58 (1.598)
Exhaust	46.11 (1.815)	44.72 (1.761)

Table 3 PISTON, RINGS AND BORE SPECIFICATIONS

	New mm (in.)	Service limit mm (in.)
Connecting rod small end inside diameter	18.016-18.034 (0.7093-0.7100)	18.07 (0.711)
Connecting rod-to-piston pin clearance	0.016-0.040 (0.0006-0.0016)	0.06 (0.002)
Cylinder		
Bore inside diameter	79.000-79.015 (3.1102-3.1108)	79.10 (3.114)
Out-of-round	--	0.006 (0.002)
Taper	--	0.006 (0.002)
Block warpage limit	--	0.10 (0.004)
Piston-to-cylinder clearance	0.010-0.045 (0.0004-0.0018)	0.10 (0.004)
Piston		
Outside diameter*	78.97-78.99 (3.109-3.110)	78.90 (3.106)
Piston pin bore inside diameter	18.002-18.008 (0.7087-0.7090)	18.05 (0.711)
Piston pin outside diameter	17.994-18.000 (0.7084-0.7087)	17.98 (0.708)

Table 3 PISTON, RINGS AND BORE SPECIFICATIONS (continued)

	New mm (in.)	Service limit mm (in.)
Piston-to-piston pin clearance	0.002-0.014 (0.0001-0.0006)	0.04 (0.002)
Piston rings		
Ring-to-ring groove clearance		
Top ring	0.025-0.055 (0.0010-.0022)	0.08 (0.003)
Second ring	0.015-0.045 (0.0006-0.0018)	0.07 (0.003)
Piston ring end gap		
Top ring	0.15-0.25 (0.006-0.010)	0.4 (0.016)
Second ring	0.25-0.40 (0.010-0.016)	0.6 (0.023)
Oil ring (side rails)	0.20-0.80 (0.008-0.031)	1.0 (0.039)
Piston ring marks		
Top ring	R	
Second ring	RN	

*Refer to text for piston measuring point.

Table 4 ENGINE TOP END TORQUE SPECIFICATIONS

	N.m	in.-lb.	ft.-lb.
Alternator cover socket bolts			
2004-2009 Aero models	9.8	87	--
All other models	10	89	--
Cam chain tensioner bolt (1)			
2004-2009 Areo models	9.8	87	--
All other models	10	89	--
Cam sprocket mounting bolt (2)	23	--	17
Camshaft holder			
Bolt	23	--	17
Nut	23	--	17
Cylinder head cover mounting bolt			
2004-2009 Aero models	9.8	87	--
All other models	10	89	--
Cylinder head fasteners (3)			
6-mm bolt			
Aero models			
2004-2009	12	106	--
2011-2013	Refer to text		
Spirit and Phantom models	Refer to text		
8-mm bolt	23	--	17
10-mm nuts	47	--	35
Outer cylinder cover socket bolts			
2004-2009 Aero models	9.8	87	--
All other models	10	89	--

1. Refer to text for tightening sequence.
2. Apply a medium strength threadlock to bolt threads.
3. Lubricate fastener threads and flange surfaces with engine oil.

CHAPTER FIVE

ENGINE LOWER END

This chapter provides service procedures for lower end components. These include the crankcase, crankshaft, connecting rods, oil pump and output gearcase. This chapter also includes removal and installation procedures for the transmission and internal shift mechanism assemblies. Service procedures for the transmission and internal shift components are described in Chapter Seven.

Refer to **Tables 1-14** at the end of this chapter for specifications.

SERVICING ENGINE IN FRAME

1. The following components can be serviced with the engine mounted in the frame:
   a. Carburetor.
   b. Throttle body.
   c. Camshafts.
   d. Alternator and starter clutch.
   e. Clutch, primary drive and external shift linkage.
   f. Starter motor.
   g. Water pump.
2. The following components require engine removal for service:
   a. Cylinder head, cylinders and pistons.
   b. Crankshaft.
   c. Transmission and internal shift mechanism.
   d. Oil pump.
   e. Output gearcase.

ENGINE

Service Preparations

Before servicing the engine, note the following:
1. Review *Service Methods* and *Measuring Tools* in Chapter One. Accurate measurements are critical to a successful engine rebuild.
2. Prior to removing and disassembling the engine, clean the engine and frame. Keep the work environment as clean as possible.
3. Viewed from the engine's right side, crankshaft rotation is clockwise.
4. Throughout the text there are references to the left and right side of the engine. This refers to the engine as it is mounted in the frame, not how it may sit on the workbench.
5. Always replace worn or damaged fasteners with those of the same size, type and torque requirements. If a specific torque value is not listed in **Table 14**, refer to the general torque recommendations table at the end of Chapter One.
6. Use special tools where noted. Obtain special tools before starting procedure.
7. Store parts and assemblies in well-marked plastic bags and containers. Use masking tape and a permanent, waterproof marking pen to label parts.
8. Use a box of assorted size and color vacuum hose identifiers, such as those shown in **Figure 1** (Lisle part No. 74600), to identify hoses and fittings during

engine removal and disassembly. Automotive and aftermarket parts suppliers carry this kit, or similar equivalents.

9. Use a vise with protective jaws to hold parts.
10. Use a press or special tools when force is required to remove and install parts. Do not try to pry, hammer or otherwise force them on or off.
11. Replace all O-rings and seals during reassembly. Apply a small amount of grease to the inner lips of each new seal to prevent damage when the engine is first started.
12. Top and lower end engine gasket kits can be purchased from the manufacturer. However, the gaskets, washers and O-rings in these kits are not identified. During disassembly, do not discard washers and O-rings after removing them. Label these parts so they can be used to identify the replacement parts.
13. If possible, take photographs of the hose and wire routing before engine removal.
14. When removing the thermostat and the emission control assemblies, disconnect the hoses as close to the engine assembly as possible. This will allow most of the hoses to remain attached to the part being removed and help with routing and reassembly.
15. The dry weight for an assembled engine is listed in **Table 1**. At least three people will be required to remove and install the engine.
16. Two jacks will be required during engine removal. Use a scissor jack, such as the K&L MC450 Center Jack (part No. 37-9841) shown in A, **Figure 2**, to level and support the motorcycle. Use a floor jack (B, **Figure 2**, typical) to secure and position the engine when removing and installing it.

Removal

The engine is difficult to remove and install as a complete assembly. If possible, lighten the engine by removing its subassemblies while it is mounted in the frame.

1. Support the motorcycle securely on a scissor jack.
2. Remove the seat and both side covers (Chapter Seventeen).
3. Remove the speedometer (Chapter Ten).
4. Remove the fuel tank (Chapter Eight or Chapter Nine).
5. If disassembling the engine, perform a compression test (Chapter Three) and a leakdown test (Chapter Two).
6. Disconnect the spark plug caps at the spark plugs.
7. Disconnect the negative battery cable from the battery (Chapter Ten). Place an insulator over the cable end so it cannot fall back across the battery and reconnect itself.
8. Drain the engine oil (Chapter Three).

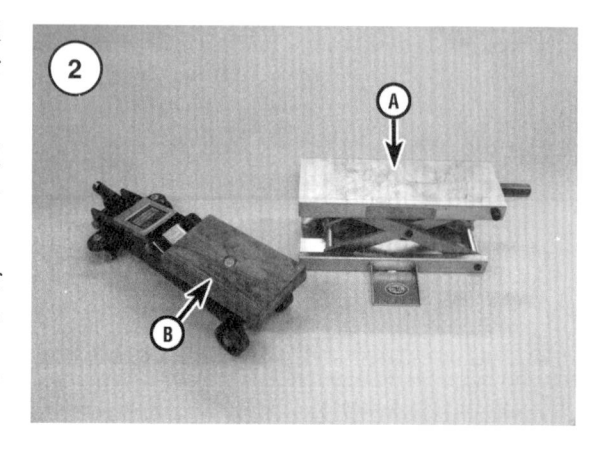

9. Drain the engine coolant (Chapter Three).
10. Remove the exhaust system (Chapter Seventeen).
11. Remove the rear brake pedal (Chapter Fifteen).
12. Remove the left crankcase rear cover and its two mounting brackets (Chapter Seventeen).
13. Remove the thermostat housing (Chapter Eleven).
14. Remove the radiator (Chapter Eleven).
15A. On carbureted models (Chapter Eight) remove the following:
    a. Air filter housing.
    b. Carburetor.
15B. On fuel injected models (Chapter Nine), remove the following:
    a. Air filter housing.
    b. Throttle body.
16. Remove the front and rear outer covers (Chapter Four).
17. Remove the left crankcase cover (Chapter Ten).
18. Remove the clutch cover as described under *Right Crankcase Cover* in Chapter Six.
19. Remove the clutch cable holder bolt (A, **Figure 3**) and holder. Then, disconnect the clutch cable (B) **Figure 3**) from its release lever.

ENGINE LOWER END

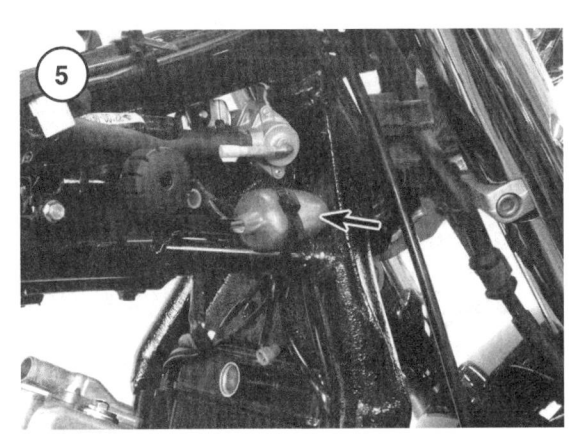

NOTE
Note the routing of the wiring harnesses before disconnecting and removing them in the following steps.

NOTE
Refer to the wiring diagrams at the end of this manual to identify the electrical connectors in Step 19. After disconnecting the connectors, carefully remove the wiring harnesses so they can be removed with the engine (if required) or repositioned to prevent their damage when removing the engine.

20A. On carbureted models, perform the following:
   a. Disconnect the alternator, ignition switch and vehicle speed sensor electrical connectors located in the connector pouch **(Figure 4)** in front of the battery:
   b. Disconnect the crankshaft position sensor 2-pin connector located inside the connector pouch **(Figure 5**, typical) located above the front cylinder head on the right side of the engine.
   c. Open or remove the plastic clamps securing the wiring harnesses to the left side of the engine **(Figure 6**, typical).
   d. Disconnect the neutral switch electrical connector **(Figure 7)**.
   e. Remove the screw and disconnect the oil pressure switch wire terminal at the switch **(Figure 8)**.

20B. On fuel injected models, perform the following:
   a. Disconnect the crankshaft position sensor 2-pin connector located inside the connector pouch **(Figure 5**, typical) located above the front cylinder head on the right side of the engine.
   b. Disconnect the ignition switch connector **(Figure 9)** from the left side of the vehicle, near the tool box compartment.

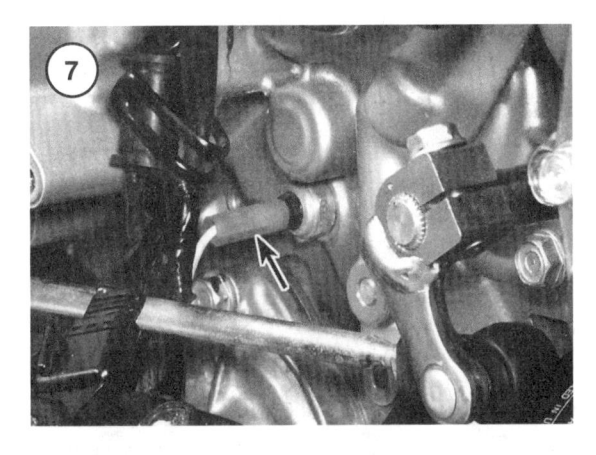

c. Disconnect the alternator, vehicle speed connector, neutral switch and oil pressure switch connectors located on the left side of the vehicle, underneath the ignition switch (**Figure 10**).

d. Open or remove the plastic clamps securing the wiring harnesses to the left side of the engine (**Figure 11**).

21. Remove the pinch bolt and slide the shift arm (A, **Figure 12**) off the shift shaft.

22. Remove the pulse secondary air injection (PAIR) control valve assembly (Chapter Eight or Chapter Nine).

CAUTION
Failure to hold the inner starter motor cable nut may allow the terminal bolt to turn and damage the insulator inside the starter motor. The insulator is not available separately.

23A. On 2004-2007 Aero models, hold the inner nut with a wrench (A, **Figure 13**) and remove the outer nut (B).

23B. On all other models, open the cover, remove the nut and disconnect the starter cable (A, **Figure 14**).

24. Remove the starter motor mounting bolt and disconnect the ground cable (B, **Figure 14**) at the starter motor.

25. Remove the bolts (A, **Figure 15**), nut, and the right footpeg mounting bracket (B).

NOTE
The engine can be removed with the oil filter mounted on the engine. However, removing it allows more room to maneuver the engine during removal and installation.

26. Remove the oil filter (Chapter Three).

27. If the engine will be disassembled or to lighten the engine for removal, remove the following subassemblies:
   a. Starter motor (Chapter Ten).
   b. Left crankcase cover, flywheel and starter clutch (Chapter Ten).
   c. Water pump (Chapter Eleven).
   d. Right crankcase cover and clutch (Chapter Six).
   e. Primary drive gear (Chapter Six).
   f. External shift mechanism (Chapter Six).

28. On ABS models, perform the following:
   a. Remove the two ABS modulator mounting bolts. Refer to *ABS Modulator* in (Chapter Sixteen) to identify the mounting bolts. Do not loosen the brake hoses at the ABS modulator.
   b. Locate the hose joint located between the right, rear side of the engine and the right side of the

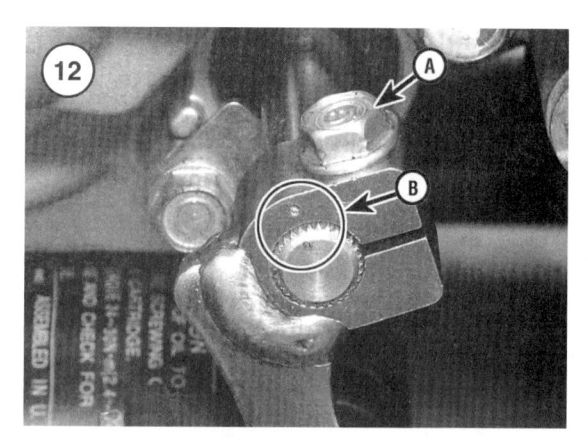

ENGINE LOWER END

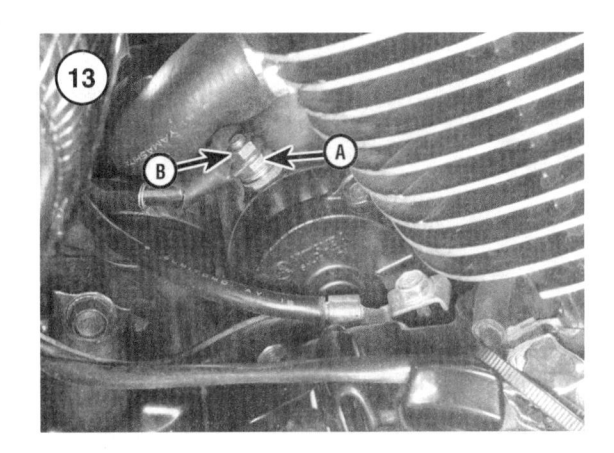

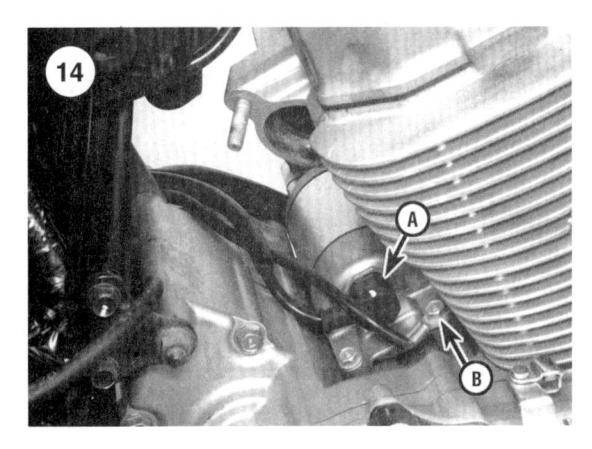

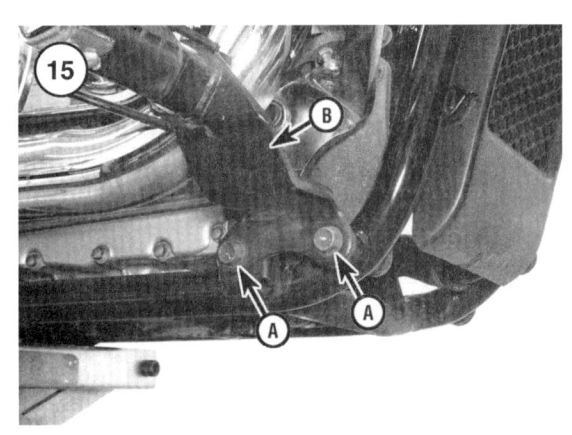

frame. Remove the brake hose mounting bolt and the clamp securing the brake hoses to the frame.

NOTE
If the rear swing arm will be removed for additional service, remove it now as it will be easier to remove and install the engine with the swing arm, universal joint and drive shaft removed from the frame.

29. Check the engine for any remaining hoses or electrical connectors that were not disconnected and disconnect them now. If desired, remove any additional components that will make engine removal and handling easier.

30. Secure a thick wooden block onto a floor jack to protect the engine and position the jack (A, **Figure 16**) underneath the engine. Adjust this jack as required to relieve pressure on the engine when removing the engine mounting bolts in the following steps. The engine must remain balanced on the jack when all mounting hardware is removed.

31. To protect the frame, wrap the right side of the frame with pieces of rubber cut from old inner tubes (B, **Figure 16**) and secure them in place with plastic tie wraps. For areas difficult to cover with rubber inner tubes, use Scotch Blue Tape (part No. 2080) and overlap areas as required to provide adequate protection.

32. Remove the engine mounting nuts, bolts and brackets as follows:

   a. Note and photograph the position of all remaining cables and hoses on how they are routed around the frame, engine and engine mounts after having been disconnected and/or rerouted during the previous steps. While some of the routing positions may differ from original mounting positions, this is how they must be positioned when reinstalling the engine. In some cases, it may be impossible to reroute some the cables and hoses once the engine is reinstalled in the frame.

NOTE
Identify and mark the engine hanger plates and fasteners when removing them.

   b. Note the position and orientation of all brackets, bolts, nuts and washers.

WARNING
When removing the bolts, be aware that the engine may shift in the frame. Keep hands protected and check the stability of the motorcycle and engine after removing each set of bolts.

c. Remove the bolts (A, **Figure 17**), nut, and the rear brake pedal mounting bracket (B, **Figure 17**).

NOTE
Loosen all of the following fasteners in order, then remove them.

d. Rear engine mounting nuts (A and B, **Figure 18**).

NOTE
*If the right crankcase cover is mounted on the engine, remove the lower mounting bolt nut through the access hole in the cover (**Figure 19**).*

e. The upper right rear engine hanger plate bolts and hanger plate (C, **Figure 18**).
f. The lower right rear engine hanger plate bolts and hanger plate (D, **Figure 18**). On California models, the carbon canister is mounted on this plate and can be removed with the plate **(Figure 20)**.
g. Remove the rear engine mounting bolts from the left side. A, **Figure 21** shows the upper bolt.
h. Remove the left rear engine hanger plate bolts and hanger plate (B, **Figure 21**).
i. Remove the front engine mounting nuts from the right side (C, **Figure 17** and A, **Figure 22**).
j. Remove the front engine hanger plate bolts and hanger plate (D, **Figure 17**).
k. Remove the front engine mounting bolts from the left side **(Figure 23)**. Also remove the collar installed between the frame and the right side of the engine (B, **Figure 22**). The engine is now free of the frame.

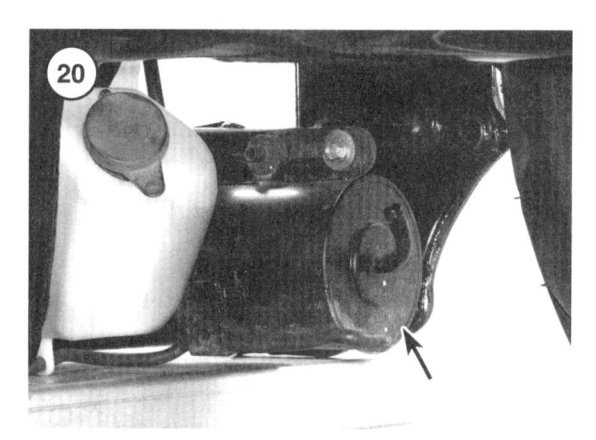

ENGINE LOWER END

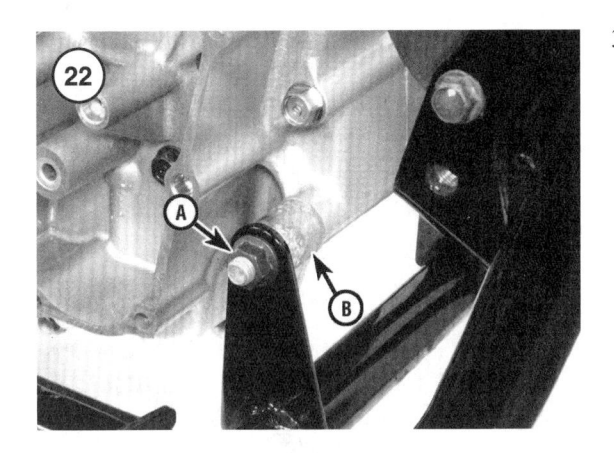

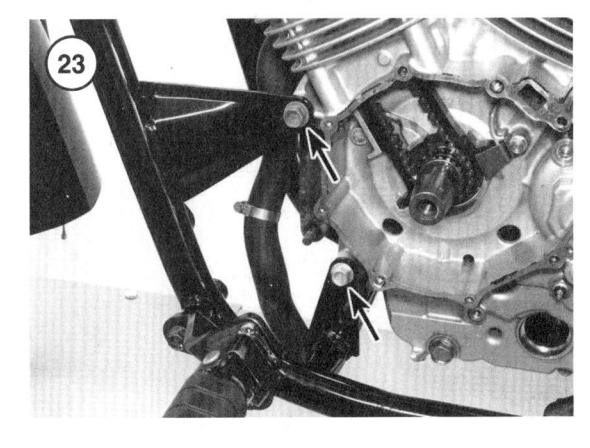

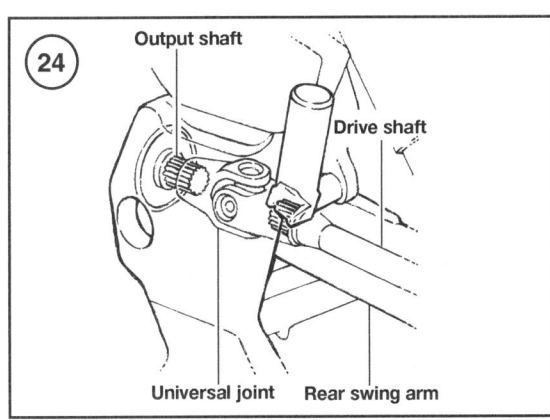

33. Remove the engine from the frame as follows:

> *WARNING*
> *Engine removal requires the aid of helpers to safely remove the engine assembly from the frame.*

   a. Release the boot from the output gearcase on the engine. Then slowly move the jack and engine forward to release the output driven gear shaft from the universal joint in the swing arm **(Figure 24)**. Have an assistant position the cylinders to keep the engine centered.
   b. Lift the engine and remove it from the right side of the frame **(Figure 25)**.
   c. Take the engine to a workbench and support it with wooden blocks to prevent it from falling over.

34. Before removing the jack used to support the engine, measure the jack pad's raised height position so it can be set to the same approximate position when installing the engine in the frame.

Inspection

After engine removal, perform the following:
1. Inspect the frame for cracks or other damage. If found, have the frame inspected by a dealership or frame alignment specialist.
2. Touch up the frame with paint as required.
3. Inspect and replace any worn or damaged coolant hoses and clamps.
4. Inspect the vacuum hoses for hardening, cracks and other damage. On old and hardened hoses, it is common to find small cracks or holes where the hose fits onto the mating nozzle. Replace damaged hoses before reinstalling the engine.
5. Check all engine mounting fasteners for corrosion and thread damage. Clean each fastener in solvent. Replace worn or damaged fasteners before reassembly.
6. Inspect the wiring harness for signs of damage that may have occurred when removing the engine. If any wires were damaged, check the wires for continuity with an ohmmeter. If necessary, repair the damaged wires and retape the harness.
7. Replace the boot installed between the output gearcase and swing arm if damaged.

Installation

1. If the swing arm is mounted in the frame, perform the following:
   a. Remove the universal joint **(Figure 24)** through the front of the swing arm and lubricate the

drive shaft and universal joint splines with Honda Moly 60 paste, or an equivalent.
   b. Reinstall the universal joint onto the drive shaft.
   c. Install the boot onto the swing arm by sliding its larger end onto the groove in the swing arm with the tab marked ENG SIDE and the arrow mark pointing up.
   d. Use the scissor jack to raise the frame so the rear wheel just clears the ground. This will allow the rear wheel to turn when aligning the output driven gear shaft and the universal joint splines.
   e. Shift the transmission into gear so the output driven gear shaft will not turn when meshing it with the universal joint later in this procedure.
2. Lubricate the output driven gear shaft splines (**Figure 24**) with Honda Moly 60 pastes, or an equivalent.
3. Install the engine in the frame as follows:
   a. Position the engine on the right side of the frame (**Figure 25**).
   b. Position the floor jack between the lower rails to support the engine when it is installed in the frame. Raise the jack pad to the height recorded during removal.
   c. Lift the engine and install it through the frame from the right side and place it on the jack pad. If the swing arm is mounted on the motorcycle, mesh the output driven gear shaft with the universal joint (**Figure 24**). If necessary, turn the rear wheel to mesh the mating splines.
4. Position the cables and hoses as noted during *Removal* (this section).

CAUTION
Do not tighten the hanger plate and engine mount fasteners (nuts and bolts) until all of the hanger plates and fasteners are installed. Make sure the fastener threads are clean and dry. Do not oil them.

5. Install the engine brackets, bolts and nuts as follows:
   a. Right rear upper (C, **Figure 18**) and lower (D, **Figure 18**) rear engine hanger plates and bolts.
   b. Lower and upper rear engine mounting bolts from the left side. Install the nuts.
   c. Front engine hanger plate (D, **Figure 17**) and bolts on the right side.
   d. Front engine mounting bolts from the left side (**Figure 23**). Install the collar (B, **Figure 22**) on the bottom mounting bolt. Install the nuts (A, **Figure 22**) onto the bolts.
6. Tighten the fasteners in the following order:

   a. Tighten the front lower engine mounting nut (A, **Figure 22**) to 54 N.m (40 ft.-lb.).
   b. Tighten the front upper engine mounting nut (C, **Figure 17**) to 54 N.m (40 ft.-lb.).
   c. Tighten the rear lower engine mounting nut (A, **Figure 18**) to 54 N.m (40 ft.-lb.).
   d. Tighten the rear upper engine mounting nut (B, **Figure 18**) to 54 N.m (40 ft.-lb.).
   e. Tighten the front engine hanger plate bolts (D, **Figure 17**) to 26 N.m (19 ft.-lb.).
   f. Tighten the right rear lower engine hanger plate bolts (C, **Figure 18**) to 26 N.m (19 ft.-lb.).
   g. Tighten the right rear upper engine hanger plate bolts (D, **Figure 18**) to 26 N.m (19 ft.-lb.).
   h. Tighten the left rear engine hanger plate bolts (B, **Figure 21**, typical) to 26 N.m (19 ft.-lb.).
7. Install the rear brake pedal (B, **Figure 17**) and right footpeg (B, **Figure 15**) mounting brackets. Install and tighten the bolts and nut to 39 N.m (29 ft.-lb.).
8. If the swing arm is installed on the motorcycle, install the boot over the output gearcase. Make sure there are no gaps between the boot and output gearcase.
9. Inspect the air filter and replace if it is close to its replacement interval or if the air filter is noticeably dirty or damaged (Chapter Three).
10. Clean electrical connections and apply dielectric grease before reconnecting.
11. Reverse the removal steps to complete engine installation, plus the following steps.
   a. On 2004-2007 Aero models, clean the starter motor cable end and install it onto the starter motor terminal. Hold the inner nut on the starter motor terminal with a wrench (A, **Figure 13**) and tighten the outer starter cable nut to 10 N.m (89 in.-lb.).
   b. On all other models, clean the starter motor cable end and install it onto the starter motor ground terminal (B, **Figure 14**). Tighten the outer starter cable nut to 10 N.m (89 in.-lb.).
   c. Reconnect the clutch cable (B, **Figure 3**) at the release lever. Then tighten the clutch cable holder bolt (A, **Figure 3**).
   d. Adjust the clutch (Chapter Three).

NOTE
Before installing the shift arm pinch bolt, inspect the bolt and replace if bent or if there is any thread damage. If thread damage is present, chase the shift arm threads with an M6 x 1.00 tap or thread chaser before installing the new bolt.

   e. Install the shift arm by aligning its punch mark with the punch mark on the shift shaft (B, **Figure 12**). Install the pinch bolt (A) and tighten to 12 N.m (106 in.-lb.).

ENGINE LOWER END

12. Refill the engine with coolant as described in Chapter Three. Check all of the coolant hoses for leaks.
13. If the oil filter was removed, install a new oil filter (Chapter Three).
14. Fill the engine with oil as described in Chapter Three.
15. Reconnect the negative battery cable at the battery as described in Chapter Ten.
16. Remove the jack from underneath the frame. Roll the motorcycle outside. Before starting the engine, refer to *Restarting the Engine* in this chapter.

RESTARTING THE ENGINE

After installing the engine in the frame, check the following before restarting the engine.
1. Make sure there is no oil or coolant on the tires.
2. Make sure the throttle works properly.
3. If necessary, fill the fuel tank with fresh fuel.
4. Connect a voltmeter to the battery leads so battery voltage can be monitored to make sure the charging system is operating correctly once the engine is running. If not, check for loose or damaged alternator connectors or battery terminals. Refer to *Charging Voltage Test* in *Charging System* in Chapter Ten.
5. If the engine was rebuilt, perform the following:
   a. On fuel injected models, disconnect the fuel pump connector as described in *Engine Compression Test* (Chapter Three).
   b. Remove the spark plugs (Chapter Three) and ground each plug with a grounding tool as described in *Ignition Grounding Tool* (Chapter One).
   c. Turn the ignition switch on and operate the starter motor for several seconds to build oil pressure in the engine. The oil pressure indicator on the speedometer unit should turn off after a few seconds. Turn the ignition switch off.
   d. Remove the grounding tools, reinstall the spark plugs (Chapter Three) and connect the spark plug caps.
   e. On fuel injected models, reconnect the fuel pump connector (Chapter Three).
6. Review *Starting the Engine* (Chapter Two). Note the proper indicator operation and check them after turning the ignition switch on and when the engine is running.
7A. Start the engine and allow it to run at idle speed while monitoring the oil pressure indicator, high coolant temperature indicator and the voltmeter that was installed previously.
7B. If the engine will not start, refer to *Engine Will Not Start* in Chapter Two.
8. With the engine running at idle speed, note the following:
   a. If new clutch plates were installed and not soaked in oil, the clutch may squeal until the plates become saturated with oil.
   b. Listen for any hissing noises, which may indicate a disconnected or damaged vacuum hose.
   c. Note that there will be noticeable smoking from the exhaust pipes at the cylinder heads when the engine is first started from the grease installed on the exhaust pipe gaskets. The grease will soon burn off. If the smoking continues or there is the smell of exhaust around the engine, check for a loose or damaged exhaust pipe gasket(s).
   d. Check for any odors indicating fuel, oil or coolant leaks. Steam indicates coolant leaking onto a hot engine part. Coolant and fuel odors may not become evident until after the engine warms up.
9. Operate all controls and adjust as needed.
10. Shift the transmission into gear to check clutch and transmission operation.
11. With the engine idling in gear, lower the sidestand. The engine should turn off. If not, check the sidestand switch as described in Chapter Three. Turn the ignition switch off.
12. Use a flashlight and carefully check the engine and hoses for leaks. Also check the oil drain bolt, oil filter and coolant drain bolt for leaks.
13. Disconnect the voltmeter and install the seat (Chapter Seventeen).
14. Make sure all of the lights work properly.
15. Check the front and rear brakes to make sure the brake lever and brake pedal operate normally.
16. Slowly test ride the motorcycle to ensure all systems are operating correctly.
17. If the engine top-end was rebuilt, perform a compression check (Chapter Three). Record the results for future reference.
18. Refer to *Engine Break-In* in this chapter.

ENGINE BREAK-IN

CAUTION
Because oil consumption during break-in may be higher than normal, check the engine oil level frequently during beak-in.

If the rings were replaced, new pistons installed, the cylinders rebored or honed or major lower end work performed, break in the engine just as though it were new. The performance and service life of the engine depends greatly on a careful and sensible break-in for the initial 300 miles. During this period, avoid full-throttle starts and hard acceleration.

Replace the engine oil and oil filter after completing the first 600 miles (1000 km). This ensures that all of the particles produced during break-in are removed from the engine.

CRANKCASE

The crankcase must be disassembled to service the crankshaft, oil pump, transmission and output gear housing.

Special Tool

Shaft holder A (Honda part No. 07923-6890101 [A, **Figure 26**]) and a holder handle (Honda part No. 07PAB-0010400 [B, **Figure 26**]), or their equivalents are required to hold the output driven gear shaft when turning the output drive gear shaft bolt. Before ordering the shaft holder, check with a dealership on whether the handle must be ordered separately.

Disassembly

As components are removed, keep each part/assembly separated from the other components. Keep seals and O-rings oriented with their respective parts to help with inspection, identification of new parts and reassembly.

NOTE
The right and left side of the engine relates to the engine as it sits in the frame, not as it may sit on the workbench.

1. Remove the engine from the frame (this chapter).
2. Remove all engine assemblies as described in this chapter and other related chapters.

WARNING
Even with all of the engine assemblies removed from the engine, the crankcase is still heavy and awkward to handle.

CAUTION
Do not move or lift the crankcase assembly by grabbing the cylinder studs. Bent or damaged cylinder studs may cause oil leaks or prevent correct tightening of the cylinder head fasteners.

3. Remove the bolts (A, **Figure 27**) and the bearing plate (B).

NOTE
It will be necessary to hold the engine securely when loosening the output drive gear bolt in Step 4.

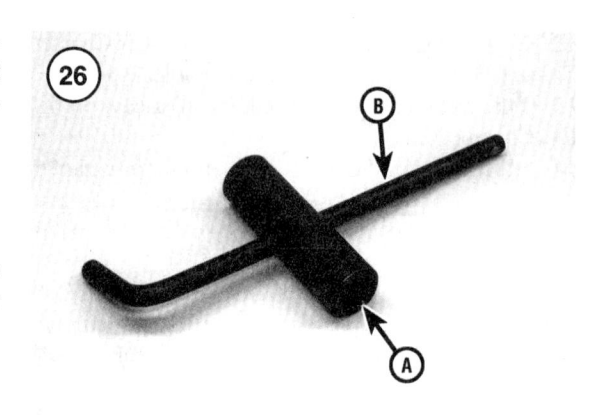

4. Hold the output drive gear with shaft holder A and its handle (A, **Figure 28**) or their equivalents. Then, loosen and remove the output drive gear bolt (B) and washer.

NOTE
To ensure that the crankcase bolts are correctly located during assembly, make an outline of the case halves on a piece of cardboard. Punch holes in the cardboard at the same locations as the bolts. Place the bolts in their respective holes (**Figure 29**).

ENGINE LOWER END

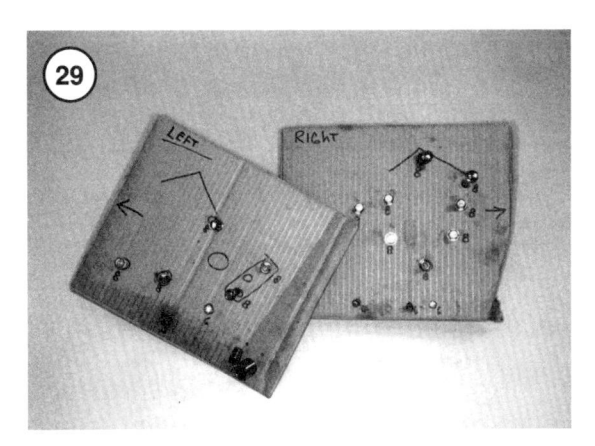

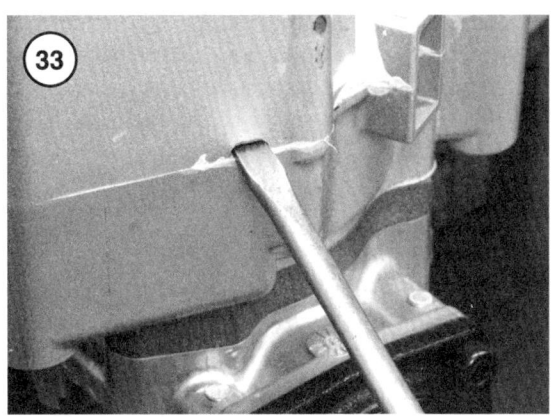

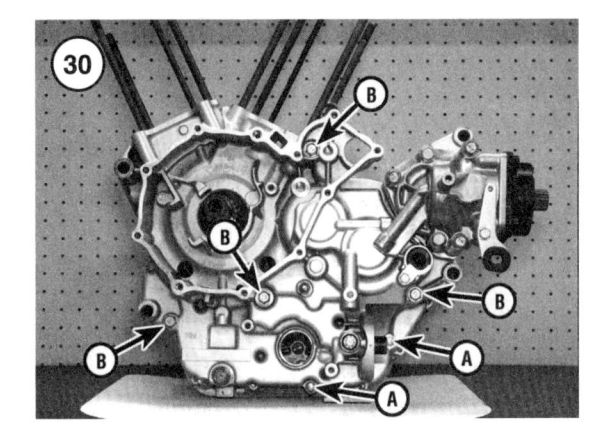

5. Loosen and remove the left case half mounting bolts in several steps and in a crossing pattern in the following order:
   a. 6-mm bolts (A, **Figure 30**).
   b. 8-mm bolts (B, **Figure 30**).
6. Loosen and remove the right case half mounting bolts in several steps and in a crossing pattern in the following order:
   a. 6-mm bolts (A, **Figure 31**).
   b. 8-mm bolts (B, **Figure 31**).
   c. Washer (C, **Figure 31**).
7. Support the engine with the right case half facing up. Turn and align the shift drum cam plate with the crankcase as shown in **Figure 32**.
8. Remove the right case half as follows:

> *CAUTION*
> *Never pry between the case halves. Doing so may result in oil leaks, requiring replacement of the case halves.*

> *NOTE*
> *Sealer is used to seal the case halves and there are no press fits between the shafts and the right case half bearings. If the right case half is tight and will not separate, check for a missed mounting bolt. Rusted dowel pins can also bind the case halves and make separation difficult.*

   a. Locate the *pry* points around the mating surfaces of the engine cases and carefully pry the right case half upward with a screwdriver (**Figure 33**) to break the case seal and separate the case halves. Do *not* pry between the gasket surfaces.
   b. When the right case half is free of the dowel pins and the gap around the case halves is even, carefully lift and remove it from the left case half. If necessary, wiggle or walk the right

case half up and off the shafts. If the mainshaft moved and is binding against its right case half bearing, have an assistant tap on the end of the mainshaft while removing the right case half. Do not allow the right case half or mainshaft to bind. If necessary, reseat the right crankcase half and start again.

c. Slowly raise and remove the right case half.
d. Locate the washers installed on the end of the output drive gear shaft (A, **Figure 34**) and the countershaft (B). Reinstall if necessary.
e. Remove the two dowel pins (C, **Figure 34**) if they are not stuck.

CAUTION
Lift the crankshaft straight out of its main journal bearing to prevent from damaging the bearings and the crankshaft.

9. Lift out the crankshaft (D, **Figure 34**) and place in a plastic bag to prevent contamination.
10. Remove the oil pump and oil pressure relief valve as follows:
    a. Note the O-ring installed on the pipe (A, **Figure 35**).
    b. Remove the oil pump mounting bolts (B, **Figure 35**) and the oil pump (C) with the oil pipe attached.
    c. Remove the two O-rings and collars (A, **Figure 36**).
    d. Remove the dowel pin (B, **Figure 36**).
    e. Store the oil pump and pressure relief valve in a plastic bag to prevent contamination. Refer to *Oil Pump* in this chapter to service the oil pipe and pressure relief valve.

NOTE
If shifting problems were occurring, inspect the transmission assembly before removing it. Look for severe wear or damaged parts. Spin the mainshaft and turn the shift drum by hand to shift the transmission. Check the movement and operation of each shift fork and sliding gear. Look for hard shifting and incomplete gear dog engagement. Check also for seized gears and bushings.

11. Remove the transmission assembly from the left case half as follows:
    a. Remove the shift fork shaft (A, **Figure 37**).
    b. Pivot the shift forks away from the shift drum and remove the shift drum (B, **Figure 37**).

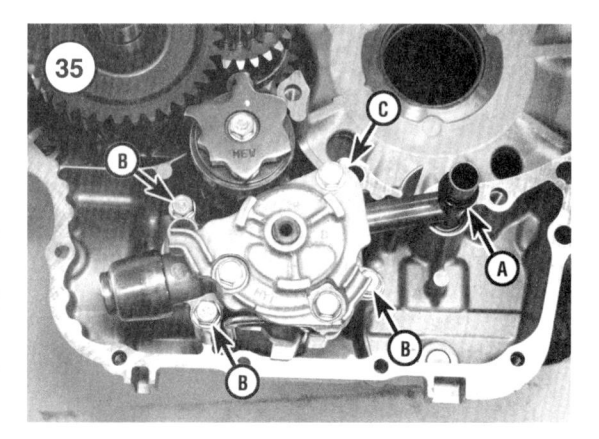

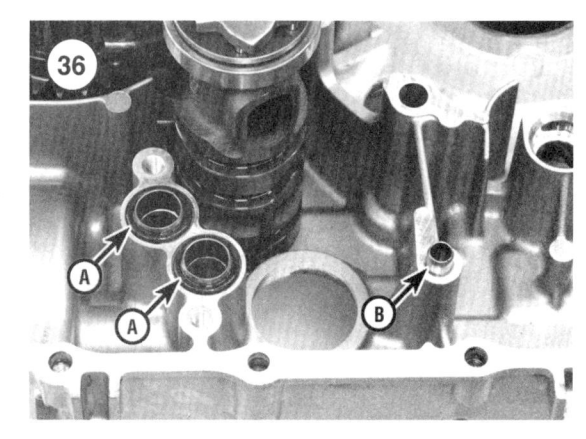

ENGINE LOWER END

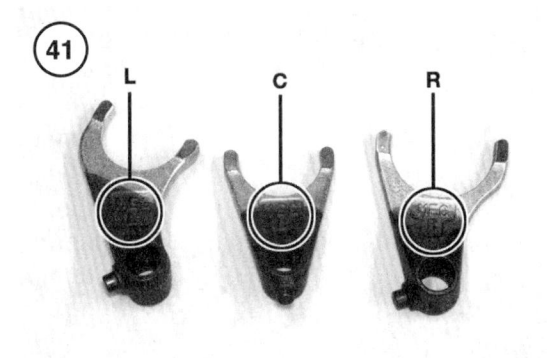

c. Remove the shift forks **(Figure 38)**.

NOTE
Gears on both ends of the countershaft and on the left side of the mainshaft are not secured with snap rings and can slide off when removing the shafts.

d. Lift and remove the mainshaft (A, **Figure 39**) and countershaft (B) assemblies at the same time **(Figure 40)**.

12. Remove the output gear assembly as described in this chapter.
13. Inspect the case halves, crankshaft, connecting rods, oil pump and output gear as described in this chapter.
14. Service the transmission as described in Chapter Seven.
15. Clean and inspect the case halves as described under *Inspection* in this section.

Assembly

CAUTION
Do not move or lift the crankcase assembly by grabbing the cylinder studs. Bent or damaged cylinder studs may cause oil leaks or prevent the correct tightening of the cylinder head fasteners.

1. Install the output gear assembly as described in this chapter.
2. Lubricate the transmission bearings with engine oil.
3. Install the transmission shafts as follows:
    a. Apply grease onto the thrust washer next to countershaft second gear to help prevent the washer from falling off the shaft during installation.
    b. Mesh the two shafts together **(Figure 40)** and install them into the left crankcase **(Figure 39)**. Make sure the washer did not fall off the countershaft.
4. Install the shift forks, shift drum and shift shaft as follows:
    a. Each shift fork can be identified by its letter mark **(Figure 41)**—L (left shift fork), C (center shift fork) and R (right shift fork). Install the shift forks with these marks facing up (toward right case half).
    b. Install the L shift fork into the countershaft fifth gear groove **(Figure 42)**.
    c. Install the C shift fork into the mainshaft fourth gear groove **(Figure 43)**.

d. Install the R shift fork into the countershaft third gear groove **(Figure 44)**.
e. Pivot the shift forks so they do not contact the shift drum, then install the shift drum (A, **Figure 45**).
f. Mesh each shift fork pin with its mating shift drum groove (B, **Figure 45**).
g. Lubricate the shift fork shaft with engine oil and slide it through each shift fork **(Figure 46)**. When properly installed, the shaft will bottom solidly against the left case half.

NOTE
It is difficult to identify the different gear positions when turning the shift drum without the stopper arm installed on the engine. This step shows whether the shift forks can move through their complete operational range.

h. Spin the transmission shafts and turn the shift drum by hand to check transmission operation. Check that each fork travels through its operating groove in the shift drum and bottoms against both ends of the shift drum **(Figure 47)**. Observe the shift forks as the transmission is shifted into the different gears.

ENGINE LOWER END

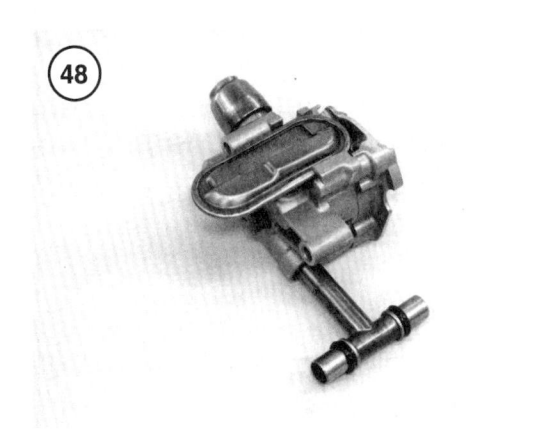

5. Install the oil pump (**Figure 48**) as follows:
   a. If a new oil pump is being installed or the existing oil pump was cleaned in solvent, the oil pump must be primed. Pour fresh engine oil into one of the openings in the oil pump. Rotate the pump shaft several times by hand to make sure the rotors are coated with oil.
   b. Install the seals, O-ring, oil pipe and oil pressure relief valve (if removed) onto the oil pump as described under *Oil Pump* in this chapter.
   c. Lubricate two new O-rings with engine oil. Install the collars and O-rings (A, **Figure 49**).
   d. Install the dowel pin (B, **Figure 49**).
   e. Install the oil pump (A, **Figure 50**) over the dowel pin and collars, while inserting the oil pipe (B) into the crankcase.
   f. Install the oil pump mounting bolts (C, **Figure 50**) and tighten securely. Turn the oil pump shaft by hand to make sure there is no roughness or binding.
   g. Make sure the O-ring (D, **Figure 50**) is installed on the oil pipe.
6. Lubricate the two crankshaft main journals and two main journal bearings (C, **Figure 39**) with molybdenum disulfide oil.

CAUTION
Install the crankshaft carefully to prevent from damaging the main journal bearings in the crankcase and the bearing journals on the crankshaft.

7. Install the crankshaft with the right connecting rod (A, **Figure 51**) facing forward and the left connecting rod (B) facing rearward.
8. Make sure the washers are installed on the end of the output drive gear shaft (C, **Figure 51**) and the countershaft (D).
9. Turn the shift drum so that the cam plate's fifth gear detent aligns with the shift fork shaft as shown in **Figure 52**. This approximately positions the cam plate detents so they will align with the cutouts in the

right case half. Keep a 10-mm socket mounted onto an extension and ratchet close by to turn and align the shift drum if necessary when installing the right case half.

10. Clean the crankcase half mating surfaces with an aerosol electrical contact cleaner. Allow the cleaner to evaporate before applying gasket sealant.

NOTE
Use one of the following semi-drying liquid gasket sealers: HondaBond 4, ThreeBond 1104 or Yamabond 4. Many sealants have a shelf life of one year, starting when a new tube is first opened. For best results, date the tube to prevent from using old sealant.

11. Apply a light coat of gasket sealant to the right and left crankcase half mating surfaces as shown in **Figure 53**. Observe the sealant manufacturer's instructions. Do not get any on the bearings or in the oil passageways.

12. Clean the two dowel pins (E, **Figure 51**), and install them into the left crankcase half.

13. Make sure the connecting rods are positioned properly (**Figure 51**).

14. Install the right crankcase half onto the left crankcase half, making sure the shift drum cam plate aligns with the right crankcase (**Figure 54**). Make sure there are no gaps between the crankcase halves.

CAUTION
*Throughout the tightening process, occasionally turn the crankshaft and countershaft. If there is any binding, **stop**. Remove the right case half and find the trouble. Usually it is an incorrectly installed gear or an incorrectly installed dowel pin.*

15. Install the right case half 8-mm (A, **Figure 55**), the 6-mm (B) mounting bolts and washer (C). Following a crossing pattern, tighten the 8-mm bolts in two steps to 23 N.m (17 ft.-lb.). Tighten the 6-mm bolts securely.

16. Install the left case half 8-mm (A, **Figure 56**) and 6-mm (B) mounting bolts. Following a crossing pattern, tighten the 8-mm bolts in two steps to 23 N.m (17 ft.-lb.). Tighten the 6-mm bolts securely.

17. Turn the crankshaft and both transmission shafts. If there is binding, separate the cases to determine the cause.

18. Check the transmission for proper shifting as follows:
   a. Install the stopper arm assembly (A, **Figure 57**) as described in *External Shift Mechanism* in Chapter Six.

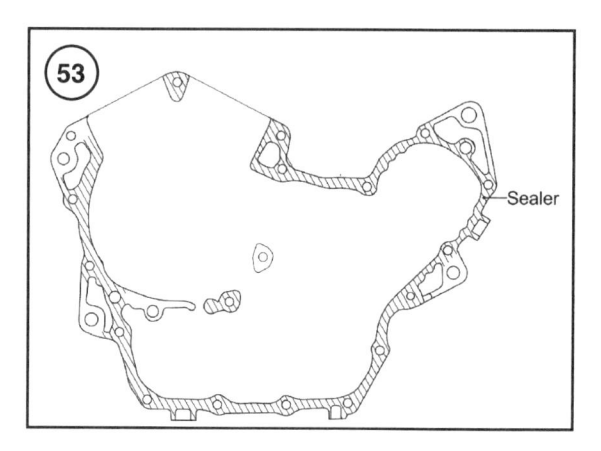

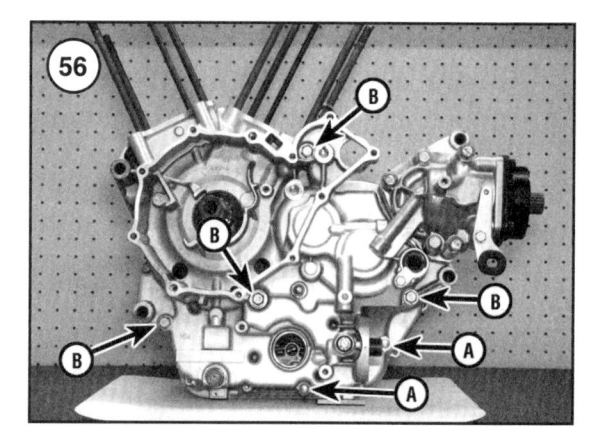

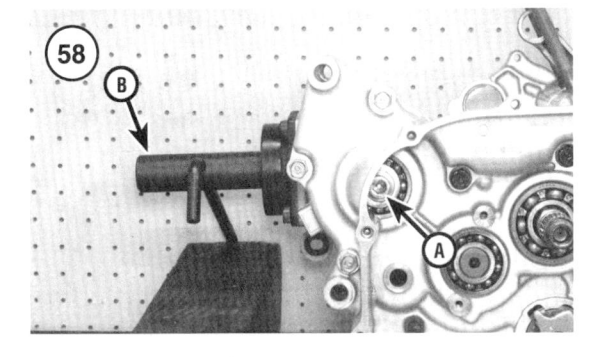

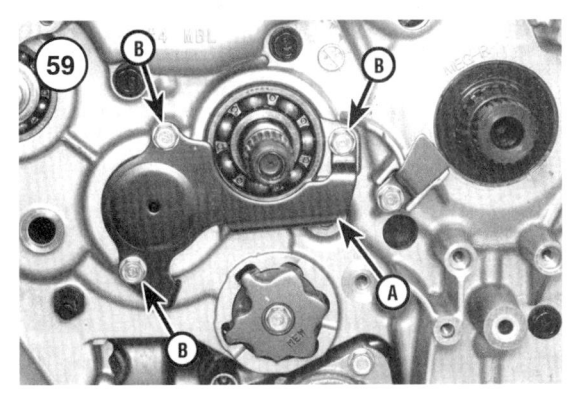

ENGINE LOWER END 149

gage properly, disassemble the crankcase and inspect the transmission for proper assembly or damaged parts.

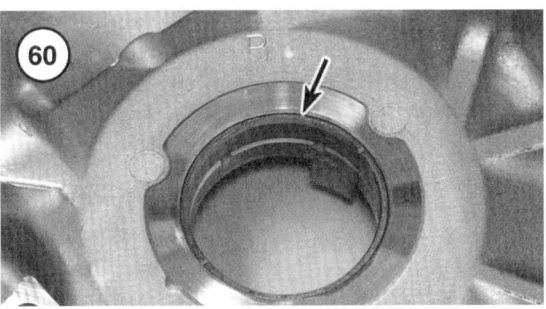

NOTE
It will be necessary to hold the engine securely when tightening the output drive gear bolt.

19. Lubricate the output driveshaft gear bolt threads with engine oil. Then install the bolt (A, **Figure 58**) with its washer and finger tighten. Hold the output drive gear with shaft holder A and its handle (B). Tighten the output driveshaft gear bolt (A, **Figure 58**) to 49 N.m (36 ft.-lb.).
20. Recheck the crankcase bolt torque as described in this section.
21. Apply a medium-strength threadlock onto the bearing plate mounting bolt threads. Install the bearing plate (A, **Figure 59**) and tighten the bolts (B) securely.
22. Install the assemblies that were removed from the engine during *Removal* (this section).
23. Reinstall the engine into the frame as described in *Installation* (this section).

b. Turn the mainshaft and then turn the shift drum to align the raised ramp on the cam plate (B) with the stopper arm roller (C). This shifts the transmission into neutral. The mainshaft and countershaft should turn freely of one another.
c. Turn the mainshaft while turning the shift drum *counterclockwise*. Stop when the stopper arm seats between the ramps on the cam plate. The transmission is in first gear. The mainshaft and countershaft should be meshed together.
d. Turn the shift drum *clockwise* past the neutral position and place the stopper arm between the ramps, one at a time, to check the remaining gears for proper engagement. The mainshaft and countershaft should mesh (turn together) whenever the transmission is in gear.
e. Remove the stopper arm when the function test is completed. If the transmission did not en-

Inspection

CAUTION
When cleaning the case halves, work carefully to prevent gasket residue from entering the oil passage holes.

1. Remove sealer residue from the gasket surfaces with solvent and a scraper or a razor blade mounted in a holder. Sealer often runs into the threaded holes when the cases are assembled. Remove sealer residue from the threaded holes with a small, stiff brush. A suitable-size gun cleaning brush clamped in a pair of locking pliers works well for cleaning threaded holes.

CAUTION
Do not damage the main journal bearings **(Figure 60)** *when cleaning and servicing the case halves. The bearing surfaces are easily damaged.*

2. Initially clean the case halves with solvent. Then check all gasket residue has been removed the all gasket surfaces. Do not forget to clean the cylinder base and the left and right crankcase cover surfaces.

3. Check all threaded holes for damage or debris buildup. Clean and repair threads with a thread chaser that will not remove aluminum material from the hole. Lubricate the tool with kerosene or tap fluid before use.

4. When the gasket surfaces and the outer case half surfaces are clean, reclean the cases in solvent.

NOTE
The left and right case halves can be replaced separately.

5. Inspect the crankcases for fractures around all mounting and bearing bosses, stiffening ribs and threaded holes. Check the water pump mounting bore **(Figure 61)** in the left case half for scoring and heat damage. If damage is noted, have a dealership inspect the case halves. Replace the case if necessary.

6. When all major work has been completed to the case halves, flush each bearing with clean solvent.

7. Soak each case half in a tub filled with hot, soapy water. Then remove and clean with clear water.

WARNING
When drying a bearing with compressed air, do not allow the inner bearing race to spin. The air can spin the bearing at excessive speed, possibly damaging the bearing.

8. Dry the crankcase halves and bearings with compressed air.

NOTE
*Raised surfaces like those identified in A, **Figure 62** are oil passages. However, not all oil passages can be identified this way.*

9. Flush and dry each oil passage with compressed air. Then inspect the passages with a flashlight. **Figure 63** shows the mainshaft and countershaft oil guide plates installed in the left case halves. Make sure the oil holes are clear. Also check the oil jet passage hole (B, **Figure 63**) in the left case half. An oil jet is mounted in this hole and supplies oil to the output shaft assembly. Service the oil jet as described in *Output Gearcase* (this chapter).

10. Turn each bearing inner race by hand. If there is any catching or roughness, the bearing may not be clean. Reclean the bearing and recheck.

11. Lightly oil the transmission bearings with new engine oil before inspecting their condition. A dry bearing will exhibit more sound and looseness than a properly-lubricated bearing.

12. Inspect the bearings for roughness, pitting, galling and play. Replace any bearing that is not in good condition. Always replace the opposite bearing at the same time. Refer to *Transmission and Output Drive Gear Bearings* (this chapter).

13. Determine the shift drum journal bore inside diameter and the shift drum-to-shift drum journal clearance as described in *Shift Drum Inspection* (Chapter Seven).

14. Retighten or replace damaged cylinder studs. Refer to *Cylinder Stud* (Chapter Four).

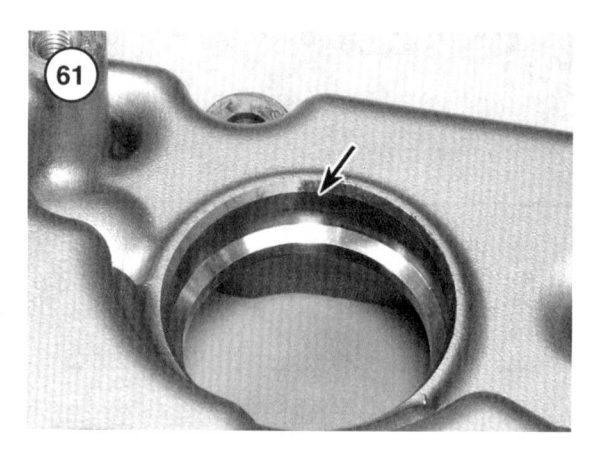

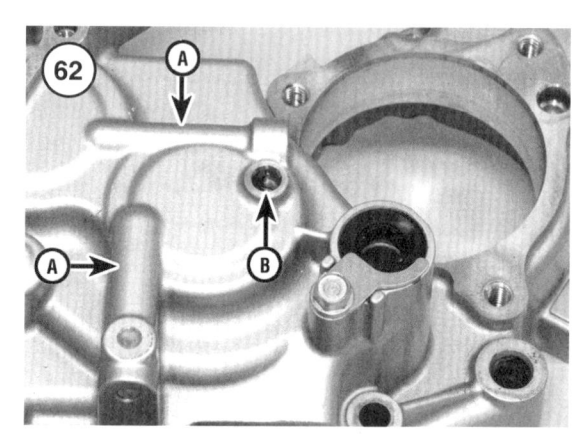

ENGINE LOWER END

15. Install a new washer on the engine oil drain bolt and tighten to 29 N.m (21 ft.-lb.).
16. Replace the shift shaft oil seal as described in *Shift Shaft Oil Seal Replacement* in *External Shift Mechanism* in Chapter Six.

NOTE
The left and right case halves can be replaced separately.

17. If replacing one or both crankcase halves, refer to *Main Journal Bearings and Crankshaft Main Journal Oil Clearance* in this chapter to select and install new main journal bearings.
18. Refer to Chapter Ten to service the oil pressure switch and/or the neutral switch.

TRANSMISSION AND OUTPUT DRIVE GEAR BEARINGS

This section services the transmission shaft bearings installed in the crankcase halves and the output drive gear bearing installed in the right case half.

NOTE
*Refer to **Main Journal Bearings and Crankshaft Main Journal Oil Clearance** in this chapter to inspect and replace the crankshaft main journal bearings (Figure 60).*

Replacement

1. When replacing crankcase bearings, note the following:
   a. Identify and record the size code of each bearing before it is removed from the crankcase. This will eliminate confusion when installing the bearings. Otherwise, record the bearing size code after removing it.
   b. Record the orientation of each bearing in its bore. Note if the size code faces toward the inside or outside of the crankcase.
   c. Heat the crankcase area around the bearing or bearing bore to approximately 80° C (176° F) before removing and installing the bearing. Refer to *Service Methods* in Chapter One for additional information on bearing service.
   d. Remove bearings that are only accessible from one side with a blind bearing puller (**Figure 64**). The puller is fitted through the bearing, then expanded to grip the back-side of the bearing.
   e. Refer to *Main Journal Bearings and Crankshaft Main Journal Oil Clearance* in this chapter to inspect and service the main journal bearings.
2. Identify the *left* case half bearings as follows:
   a. Countershaft bearing (A, **Figure 65**).
   b. Mainshaft bearing (B, **Figure 65**).

NOTE
*When replacing the transmission bearings in the left case half, make sure to clean and inspect the oil guide plates (**Figure 62**) installed behind the bearings. Install the oil guide plates with their nozzle facing up toward the bearings.*

3. Identify the *right* case half bearings as follows:
   a. Countershaft bearing (A, **Figure 66**).
   b. Mainshaft bearing (B, **Figure 66**).
   c. Output drive gear bearing (C, **Figure 66**).

MAIN JOURNAL BEARINGS AND CRANKSHAFT MAIN JOURNAL OIL CLEARANCE

Split-type main journal bearings are installed in both case halves and can be replaced if worn or damaged or if new bearings must be installed with a new crankshaft. The operating clearance between the main journal bearing inside diameter and the crankshaft main journal outside diameter determines the crankshaft main journal oil clearance.

This section inspects the main journal bearings and determines the crankshaft main journal oil clearance. If the clearance is out of specification, steps are provided to determine what parts to replace and how to replace the main journal bearings. New bearings must also be selected and installed when replacing one or both crankcase halves and/or the crankshaft.

Inspection

Refer to **Table 2** for new and service limit specifications.

1. Carefully clean the main journal bearings (**Figure 67**).
2. Inspect the bearing surfaces for color change (indicating wear), cracks, grooves, flaking and other damage.

NOTE
Make sure the gauge contact points are clean before using them to measure the bearings.

3. Using a bore gauge or telescoping gauge, measure the main journal bearing inside diameter on the side of the bearing between the bearing groove and the outside of the crankcase (**Figure 68**). Measure the bearing at 90° to the crankcase index mark (A, **Figure 67**). Record the measurement (B, **Figure 67**) and note the following:
    a. If the measurement is within specification, continue with the procedure.
    b. If the measurement is too large, continue the inspection procedure to determine the crankshaft main journal condition and record the sizes. Then select and install new bearings as described in *Bearing Selection* in this section.
4. Clean the crankshaft main journals (A, **Figure 69**) and measure the crankshaft main journal outside diameter. Record the measurement and note the following:
    a. If the measurement is within specification, continue with the procedure.
    b. If the measurement is out of specification, replace the crankshaft. Then select and install new bearings as described in *Bearing Selection* (this section).
5. Subtract the main jounal bearing inside diameter measurement from the crankshaft main journal outside diameter measurement to determine the crankshaft main journal oil clearance. Note the following:
    a. If the oil clearance is within specification and the bearings do not show any type of damage, bearing replacement is not required.
    b. If the oil clearance is too large or if the bearings are damaged, select and install new bearings as described in *Bearing Selection* (this section).

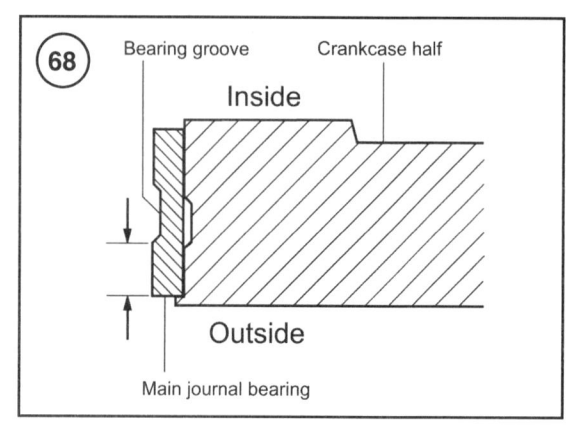

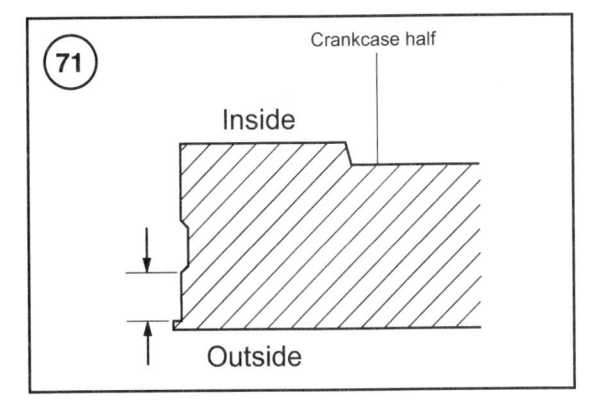

ENGINE LOWER END

Procedure

1. Position one case half in the press bed with its outside surface facing up (A, **Figure 70**).
2. Position the 57-mm driver onto the bearing (B, **Figure 70**). The driver must be able to pass through the crankcase without contacting the crankcase bore.
3. Press the main journal bearing out through the inside of the crankcase.
4. Measure the crankcase bearing support inside diameter on the side of the crankcase between the crankcase groove and the outside of the crankcase (**Figure 71**). Measure the bearing support at 90° to the crankcase index mark (A, **Figure 67**). This is the crankcase bearing support inside diameter. Record the measurement.
5. Noting the crankcase bearing support inside diameter and those measurements taken in *Inspection* (this section), there are four separate guidelines for selecting new main journal bearings:
    a. The crankshaft and one or both crankcase halves are being replaced (**Table 3**).
    b. Only the crankcase is being replaced (**Table 4**).
    c. Only the crankshaft is being replaced (**Table 5**).
    d. Only the main journal bearings are being replaced (**Table 6**).

NOTE
*Using the information recorded in this section, refer to **Tables 3-6** and cross-reference the crankcase and crankshaft codes and/or the actual recorded measurements to select the new main journal bearing sizes. Refer to the procedure for examples of each replacement guideline.*

6. New bearings are selected by referring to the measurements previously recorded and/or by cross-referencing crankcase and crankshaft codes. Identify the codes by noting the following:
    a. The letter A or B has been stamped next to the bearing on the inside of the crankcase (**Figure 72**) as a code for the bearing support inside diameter.

Bearing Selection

1. Two separate measurements recorded in *Inspection* (this section) are required to select the new main journal bearings:
    a. Main journal bearing inside diameter.
    b. Crankshaft main journal outside diameter.
2. In addition to these measurements, crankcase code letters and crankshaft code numbers may be required, depending on the parts being replaced. These are described in *Procedure* (this section).

Tools

1. A press is required to remove and install the bearings.
2. A 57-mm driver (Honda part No. 070MF-MEG0100) or an equivalent is required to remove the bearings.
3. A metal installer set (Honda part No. 070MF-MEG0200) or its equivalent is required to install the new bearings. The set includes two holders and a cap.

NOTE
*The tools described here are shown in **Procedure** (this section).*

73 Main journal bearings / Color code

Oversize E (Yellow)
Oversize F (Pink)
Oversize G (Red)
A (Blue)
B (Black)
C (Brown)
D (Green)

Thick ↕ Thin

74

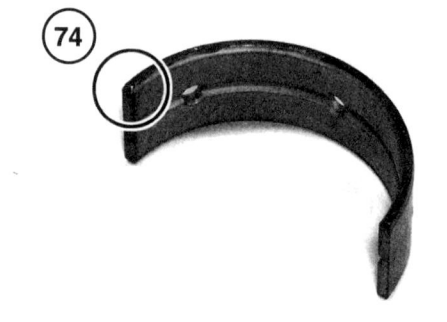

75 Pin / Bearing / Holder / Align / Bearing / Pin Holder / Pin

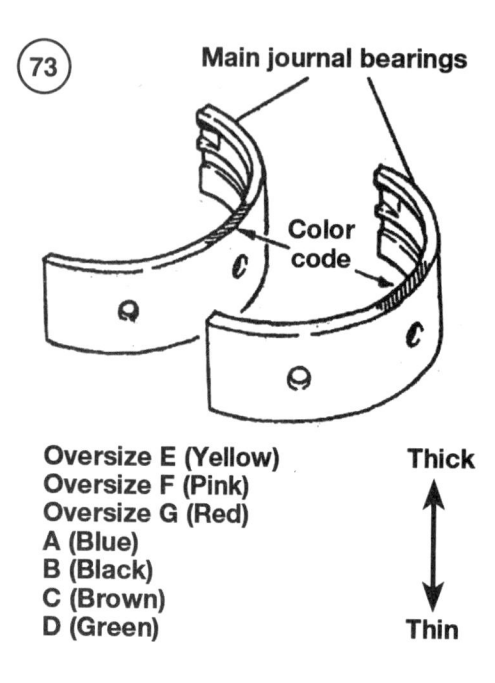

b. The number 1, 2 or 3 has been marked on the crankshaft weights (B, **Figure 69**) as a code for the crankshaft main journal outside diameters. Match the left and right crankshaft sides and code marks with their mating left and right crankcase halves.

NOTE
*The bearing thicknesses are identified by letters and color (**Figure 73**).*

7A. If the crankshaft and one or both crankcase halves are being replaced, perform the following:
  a. In **Table 3**, cross-reference the bearing support inside diameter code on the new crankcase with the main journal outside diameter code on the new crankshaft.
  b. For example, if the bearing support inside diameter code is B and the main journal outside diameter code is 3, the new bearing is B (black).

7B. If one or both crankcase halves are being replaced, perform the following:
  a. In **Table 4**, cross-reference the crankcase bearing support inside diameter code found on the new crankcase with the main journal outside diameter measurement recorded in this section.
  b. For example, if the crankcase bearing support inside diameter code is A and the main journal outside diameter is 52.994-53.000 mm, the new bearing is C (brown).

7C. If only the crankshaft is being replaced, perform the following:
  a. In **Table 5**, cross-reference the main journal bearing inside diameter recorded in this section with the crankshaft main journal outside diameter code on the new crankshaft.
  b. For example, if the main journal bearing inside diameter is 58.010-58.016 mm and the crankshaft main journal outside diameter code is 1, the new bearing is D (green).

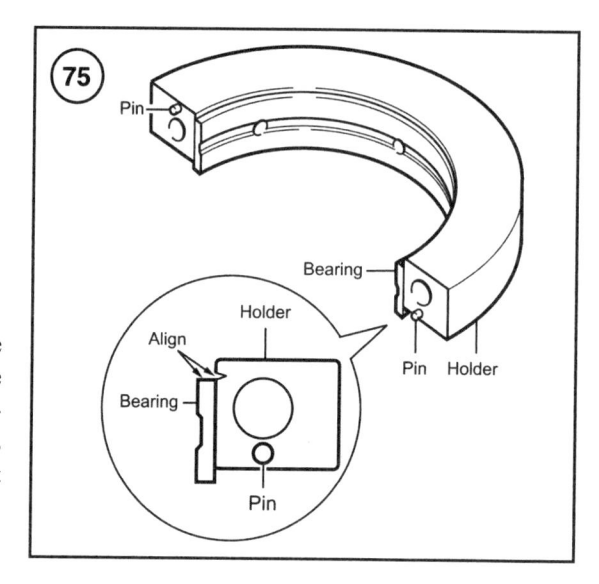

7D. If only replacing the main journal bearings, perform the following:
  a. In **Table 6**, cross-reference the crankcase bearing support inside diameter and the main journal outside diameter recorded in this section.
  b. For example, if the bearing support inside diameter is 58.010-58.016 mm and the main journal outside diameter is 52.994-53.000 mm, the new bearing is D (green).

NOTE
Continue the procedure to install the new bearings.

8. Clean and then lubricate the new bearings with engine oil before installing them.
9. Position a new bearing half into one of the metal installer holders by aligning the bearing's raised

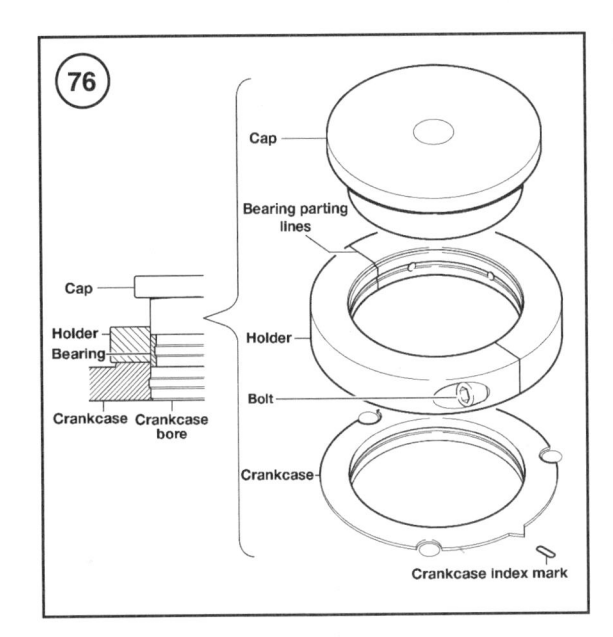

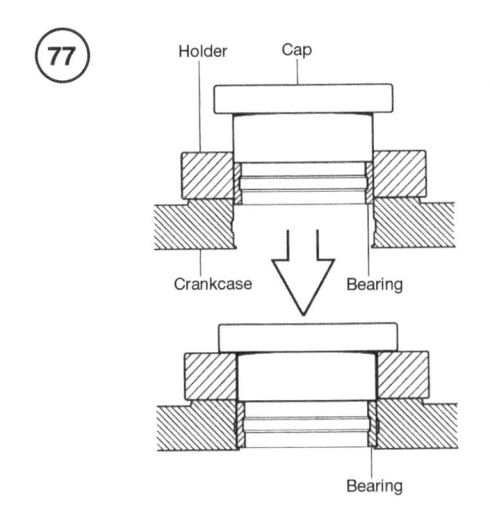

ENGINE LOWER END

install the two bolts **(Figure 76)**. Tighten the metal installer bolts in a crossing pattern and in several steps to 23 N.m (17 ft.-lb.).

10. Position the crankcase half in the press bed with its inside surface facing up.

11. Position the metal installer so the bearing seats into the crankcase half. Then, align bearing parting lines with the crankcase index mark. See **Figure 76**.

12. Center the metal installer cap onto the bearings as shown in **Figure 77**, while making sure the bearings' parting lines remain aligned with the crankcase index mark as described in Step 11. Then press the bearings into the crankcase until the metal installer cap bottoms against the metal installer holder as shown in **Figure 77**.

13. Remove the metal installer assembly and check that the bearing parting lines (C, **Figure 67**) align with the crankcase index mark (A) and the bearing is fully seated.

CAUTION
An incorrect crankshaft main journal oil clearance can cause severe engine damage.

14. Recheck the crankshaft main journal oil clearance as described in this section. If the clearance measurement is incorrect, repeat this procedure to determine the correct clearance and install new bearings.

CRANKSHAFT

Removal/Installation

Remove and install the crankshaft as described under *Crankcase* in this chapter.

Inspection

1. Clean the crankshaft and connecting rods thoroughly with clean solvent. Clean the crankshaft oil passageways with compressed air. Dry the crankshaft with compressed air and lubricate all bearing surfaces with a light coat of engine oil.

2. Inspect each crankshaft main journal (A, **Figure 78**) for scratches, ridges, scoring, nicks or heat discoloration. Very small nicks and scratches may be removed with crocus cloth. Anything more serious should be referred to a dealership for inspection.

3. To determine main journal wear, perform *Inspection* in *Main Journal Bearings and Crankshaft Main Journal Oil Clearance* in this chapter.

4. Check the drive sprocket (B, **Figure 78**) teeth for cracks and other damage. If damage is noted, inspect the cam chains and cam sprockets (Chapter Four) for damage.

side edge **(Figure 74)** with the groove in the holder **(Figure 75)**. Repeat for the other bearing half. Then align the bearing halves and assemble the metal installer holders by aligning their pins and holes and

5. Inspect the crankshaft splines, flywheel taper and Woodruff key groove for damage.

6. Measure crankshaft runout with the crankshaft mounted on V-blocks or a truing stand as shown in **Figure 79**. Rotate the crankshaft two full turns and measure runout at each main journal. If the runout exceeds the service limit in **Table 1**, replace the crankshaft.

7. If replacing the crankshaft, refer to *Main Journal Bearings and Crankshaft Main Journal Oil Clearance* in this chapter to select and install new main journal bearings.

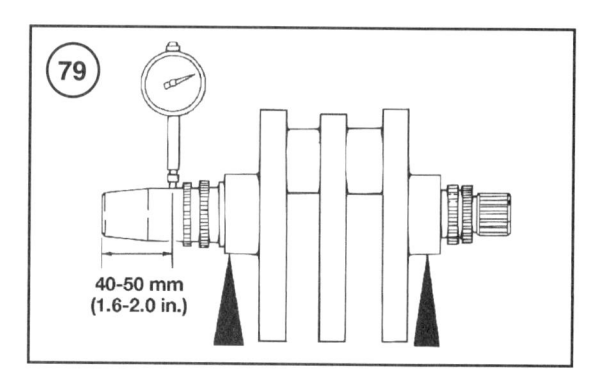

CONNECTING RODS

Connecting Rod Side Clearance

Measure the connecting rod side clearance with a feeler gauge between the connecting rod and crankshaft machined surfaces (**Figure 80**). Compare to the connecting rod side clearance specifications in **Table 2**. Measure each connecting rod. If the measurement is out of specification, replace the connecting rod as described in this chapter. Recheck the clearance with the new rod.

Removal/Installation

1. Identify the connecting rods, bearings and caps so they can be reinstalled in their original mounting positions and facing in their original directions. Use the following to identify the front and rear connecting rods:
   a. The front connecting rod is mounted next to the right crank wheel.
   b. Each connecting rod is equipped with an oil jet (A, **Figure 81**). The oil jets are directional and the connecting rods must be reinstalled with the oil jets facing in their original direction.
   c. Letter and number marks on the connecting rods and caps (B, **Figure 81**) are used for bearing and connecting rod replacement.

2. Remove the crankshaft as described under *Crankcase* in this chapter.

3. Remove the nuts securing the connecting rod caps and remove the caps (**Figure 82**).

4. Carefully remove the connecting rod from the crankshaft. Mark the rod, bearing and cap (**Figure 83**) to show its correct cylinder and crankpin position for reassembly.

5. Remove and label each bearing insert (**Figure 84**) as upper or lower.

6. Clean these parts and the crankshaft in solvent and dry with compressed air.

7. Inspect the connecting rods and bearings as described in this section.

8. If new bearing inserts are being installed, check the connecting rod bearing clearance as described in this section.

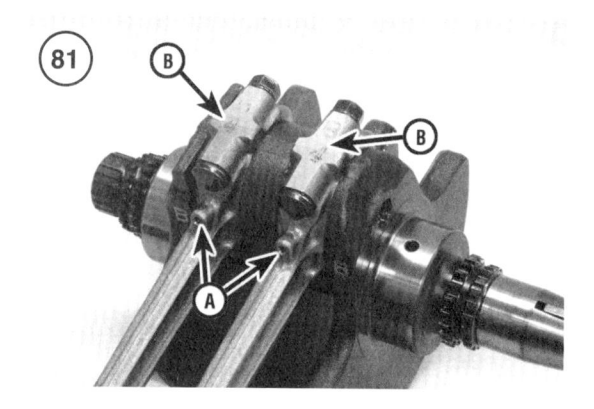

9. Wipe off any oil from the bearing inserts, connecting rod and cap contact surfaces. There must be no

ENGINE LOWER END

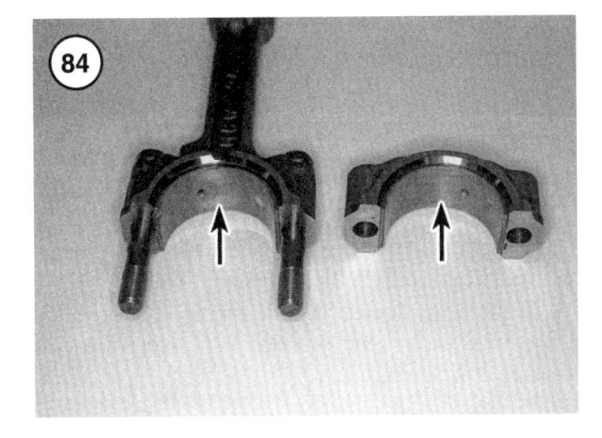

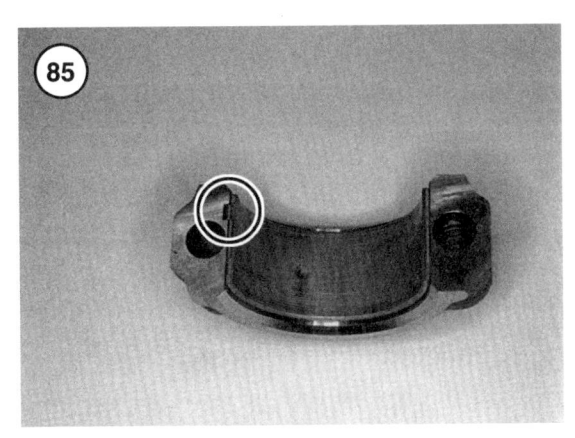

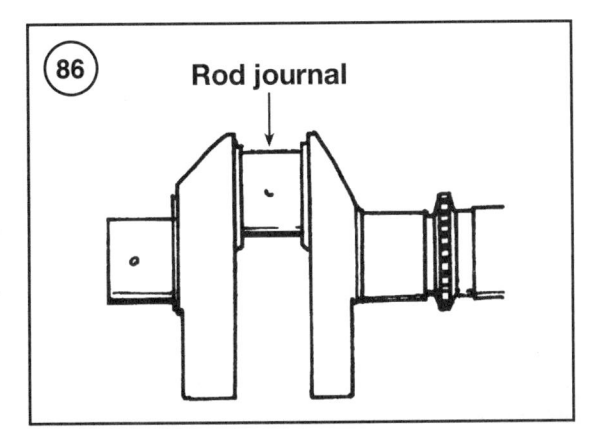

lint or debris on the contact surfaces when installing the inserts.

> *CAUTION*
> *If reusing the original bearing inserts, install them in the original mounting positions noted during removal. Otherwise, engine damage may occur.*

10. Install the bearing inserts into each connecting rod and cap **(Figure 84)** by aligning the raised tab on the insert with the notch in the rod or cap and then snapping them into place **(Figure 85)**.
11. Apply molybdenum disulfide grease to the bearing inserts and rod journal **(Figure 86)** on the crankshaft.
12. Install the connecting rod onto the crankshaft so that it is facing in its original position, as noted during removal.
13. Match the code number on the end of the cap with the mark on the rod (B, **Figure 81**) and install the cap.

> *NOTE*
> *The fine threads used on the connecting rod studs and cap nuts are easily damaged. Start the nuts carefully by hand.*

14. Lubricate the bearing cap nut threads and seating surfaces with engine oil. Install the cap nuts **(Figure 82)** and tighten the connecting rod bearing cap nuts in several steps to 33 N.m (24 ft.-lb.).
15. Rotate the connecting rod several times to check that there is no binding or roughness.
16. Repeat the installation procedure for the other connecting rod.

Connecting Rod Inspection

1. Remove and identify the connecting rods from the crankshaft as described in this section.
2. Clean the connecting rods and inserts in solvent and dry with compressed air.
3. Carefully inspect each rod journal **(Figure 86)** on the crankshaft for scratches, ridges, scoring and other damage.
4. Inspect each bearing insert **(Figure 84)** for evidence of wear, abrasion and scoring. They are reusable if in good condition and the connecting rod bearing clearance is within specification.
5. Measure the crankshaft rod journal outside diameter **(Figure 86)** with a micrometer and check for out-of-roundness and taper. Compare results with specifications **(Table 7)** and replace crankshaft if necessary.
6. With the bearing inserts removed, check each connecting rod big end for signs of seizure and other damage. The insert mating surface on the big end

must be smooth with no burrs or other surface roughness. Replace the connecting rod if there is any damage.

7. Check each connecting rod small end for signs of excessive heat (blue coloration), seizure and other damage.
8. Measure the inside diameter of the small end of the connecting rod with an inside micrometer or small hole gauge. Replace the connecting rod if the small end inside diameter exceeds the service limit (**Table 2**).
9. If the connecting rods, bearing inserts and crankshaft rod journals do not show any type of visible damage, check the connecting rod bearing clearance as described in this section.

Connecting Rod Bearing Clearance

Clearance measurement

1. Clean any oil from the bearing insert and crankpin surfaces. These surfaces must be clean and dry for the results to be accurate.

NOTE
Do not rotate the connecting rod on the crankshaft while the Plastigage strips are in place.

2. Place a strip of Plastigage over each rod bearing journal parallel to the crankshaft as shown in **Figure 87**. Do not place the Plastigage material over an oil hole in the crankshaft.

NOTE
Be sure the bearing inserts are installed in their original mounting positions.

3. Install the bearing inserts into each connecting rod and cap. Make sure they are locked in place correctly (**Figure 84**).
4. Install the connecting rod onto the crankshaft so that it is facing in its original position as described in *Removal/Installation* in this section.
5. Match the code number on the end of the cap with the mark on the rod (C, **Figure 81**) and install the cap.
6. Lubricate the bearing cap nut threads and seating surfaces with engine oil. Install the cap nuts (**Figure 82**) and tighten the connecting rod bearing cap nuts in several steps to 33 N.m (24 ft.-lb.).
7. Remove the rod cap nuts and rod cap.
8. Measure the width of the flattened Plastigage (**Figure 87**) following the product manufacturer's instructions to determine the connecting rod bearing clearance. Measure both ends of the Plastigage strip and compare results to the specifications (**Table 2**).

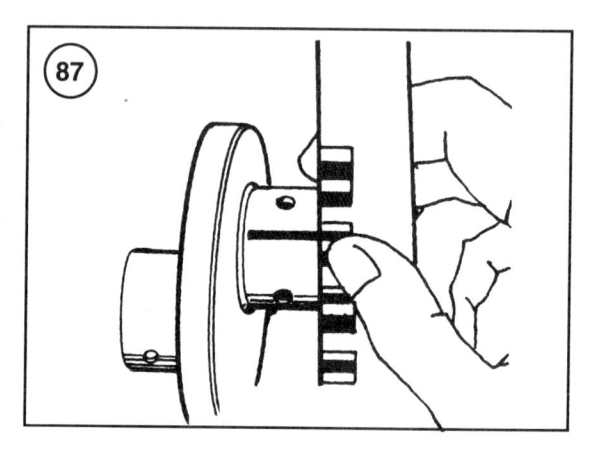

Note the following:
  a. A difference of 0.025 mm (0.001 in.) or more indicates a tapered rod journal (**Figure 86**). Confirm the measurement using a micrometer.
  b. If the connecting rod bearing clearance exceeds the service limit (**Table 2**), select new bearings (this section).

9. Remove all of the Plastigage material from the crankshaft journals and connecting rod caps.
10. If the bearing clearance is greater than specified (**Table 2**), follow the procedure to select the new bearings (this section).

Selection

NOTE
If a code on either part is undecipherable, refer selection to a dealership.

1. The code number stamped on the side of each connecting rod and cap (A, **Figure 88**) identifies the connecting rod inside diameter. Half the number is stamped on the rod and the other half is stamped on the cap. Record the connecting rod inside diameter code number (3 or 4) on the rod and cap (A, **Figure 88**).
2. The code letter stamped on each crankshaft web (B, **Figure 88**) identifies the crankshaft rod journal outside diameter. Record the crankshaft rod journal outside diameter code letter (A or B) on the crankshaft web (B, **Figure 88**).
3. Measure the crankshaft rod journal outside diameter (**Figure 86**) with a micrometer and compare it with either the A or B crankshaft rod journal outside diameter code letter specification in **Table 7** (vertical column).
4a. If the outside diameter is within specification, the new bearing can be selected by color code. Continue the procedure.
4b. If the outside diameter is too small, the crankshaft is worn and should be referred to a dealership for further inspection.

ENGINE LOWER END

88

89

A (green)
B (yellow)
C (pink)

Thick ↕ Thin

Color code

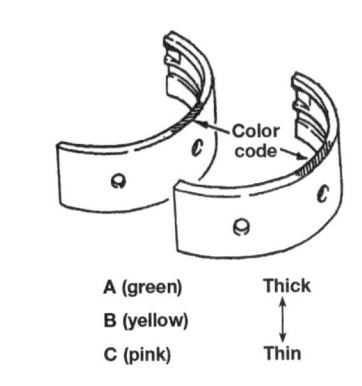

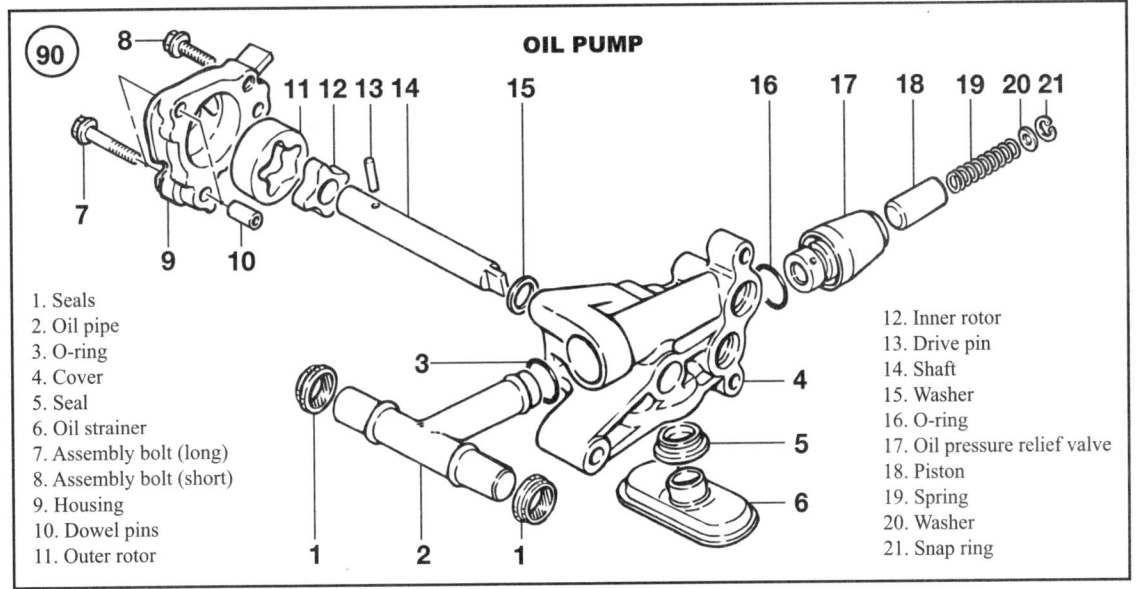

90 OIL PUMP

1. Seals
2. Oil pipe
3. O-ring
4. Cover
5. Seal
6. Oil strainer
7. Assembly bolt (long)
8. Assembly bolt (short)
9. Housing
10. Dowel pins
11. Outer rotor
12. Inner rotor
13. Drive pin
14. Shaft
15. Washer
16. O-ring
17. Oil pressure relief valve
18. Piston
19. Spring
20. Washer
21. Snap ring

5. Select new bearings by cross-referencing the crankshaft rod journal outside diameter code letter (B, **Figure 88**) in the vertical column of **Table 7** with the connecting rod inside diameter code number (A, **Figure 88**) in the horizontal column. Where the two columns intersect, the new bearing insert color is indicated. For example, if the crankshaft rod journal outside diameter code letter is B and the connecting rod inside diameter code number is 4, the new bearing size is A (green). **Figure 89** identifies the different bearing colors with their code letters and thicknesses.

6. After installing the new bearing inserts, recheck the bearing clearance (this section).

Connecting Rod and Crankshaft Selection

The front and rear connecting rods are matched to the crankshaft according to the weight of the individual connecting rods. A code letter stamped on the side of each connecting rod cap (C, **Figure 78**) identifies the connecting rod weight. When replacing a connecting rod, replace it with the same weight code found on the original rod (C, **Figure 78**). If the same weight code is unavailable, perform the following to select replacement connecting rods:

1. Record the connecting rod weight code letter (A, B or C) on each rod cap (C, **Figure 78**).
2. Select a new connecting rod by cross-referencing the connecting rod weight code letters (C, **Figure 78**) in the vertical and horizontal columns of **Table 8**. Where the two columns intersect with a + mark, a match is made.
3. **Table 9** lists the weight of each connecting rod.

OIL PUMP

Removal/Installation

Remove and install the oil pump as described under *Crankcase* in this chapter.

Disassembly

Refer to **Figure 90**.

1. Pull and remove the oil pipe (A, **Figure 91**), seals (B)

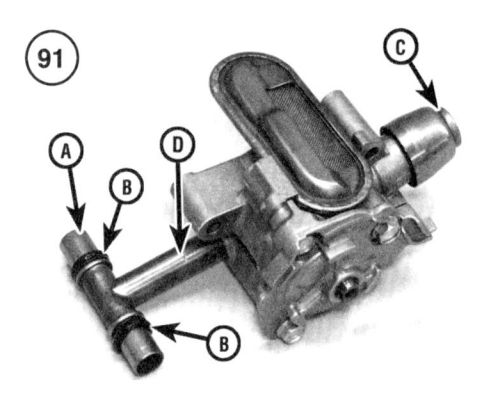

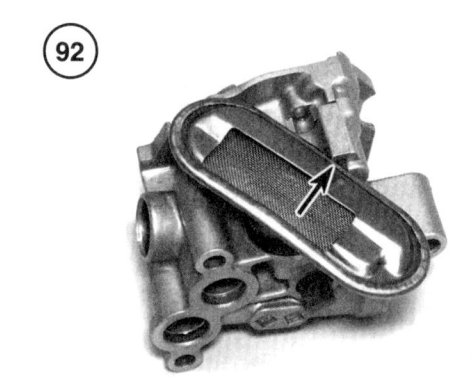

and O-ring. Discard the seals and O-ring.
2. Pull and remove the pressure relief valve (C, **Figure 91**) from the oil pump.
3. Turn the oil strainer until it clears the boss (**Figure 92**) on the oil pump as much as possible. Then tilt and remove the stainer (A, **Figure 93**).
4. Remove and discard the seal (B, **Figure 93**).
5. Hold the pump and turn the pump shaft by hand. The shaft and rotors should turn without any roughness or binding.
6. Note the following before disassembling the oil pump:
   a. Different length assembly bolts are used to secure the oil pump. Identify the bolts for reassembly.
   b. The outer rotor may have a punch mark to help identify its installation position in the pump. Record whether the mark is facing up or down so the rotor can be installed facing in its original position. If there is no mark, identify one side of the rotor for installation.
7. Remove the three mounting bolts (**Figure 94**) and disassemble the oil pump assembly.

Inspection

When measuring the oil pump components in this section, compare the actual measurements to the specifications in **Table 10**. If any measurement is out of specification, or if any component is damaged, replace the oil pump assembly. Replacement parts are not available to rebuild the oil pump.
1. Clean and dry all parts (**Figure 95**).
2. Inspect the cover and housing for cracks and other damage.
3. Check the rotors and bore (**Figure 96**) for deep scratches and wear.
4. Inspect the oil strainer screen (**Figure 97**) for broken areas. Replace if the screen is damaged or if it cannot be thoroughly cleaned.
5. Inspect the shaft, drive pin and washer for cracks, scoring and other damage.

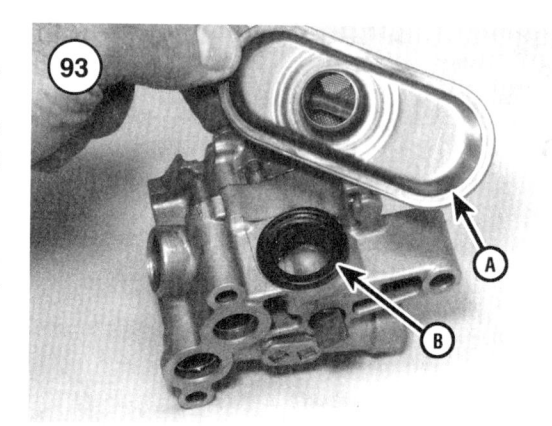

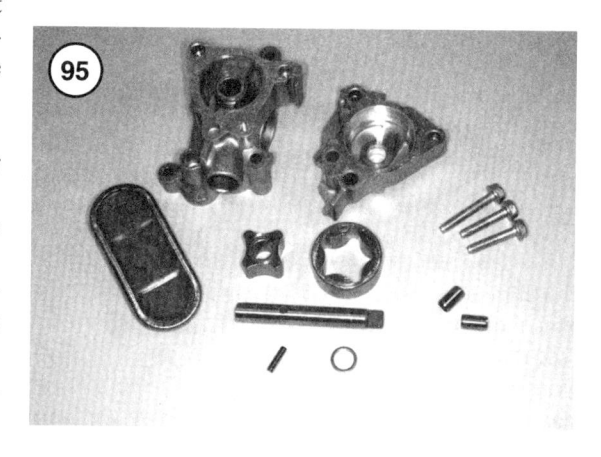

ENGINE LOWER END

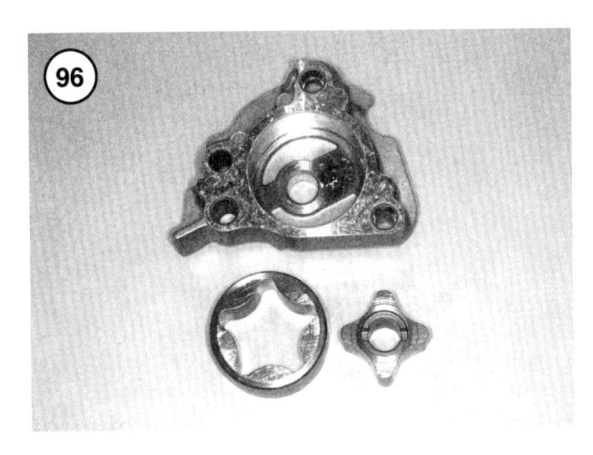

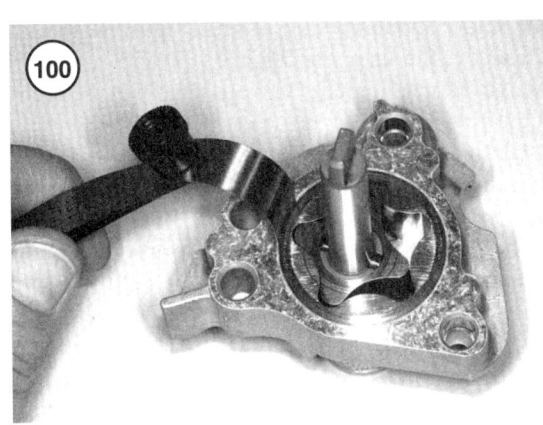

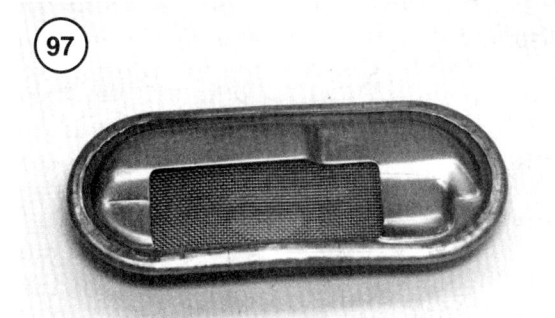

6. Inspect the oil pipe for damage.
7. Install the outer rotor into the pump housing with its punch mark (or ID mark) facing in its original position (up or down).
8. Install the inner rotor into the pump housing with its pin groove facing out.
9. Place a straightedge across the pump housing. Measure the axial clearance between the pump housing and rotors with a flat feeler gauge (**Figure 98**).
10. Install the pin into the shaft and install the shaft and pin into the inner rotor.
11. Measure the tip clearance between the inner and outer rotors with a flat feeler gauge (**Figure 99**).
12. Measure the side clearance between the outer rotor and housing bore with a flat feeler gauge (**Figure 100**).
13. Inspect the oil pressure relief valve as described in this section.

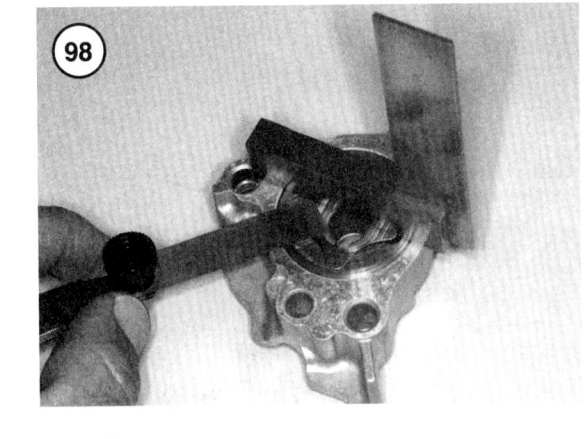

Oil Pressure Relief Valve Inspection

If any part is damaged, replace the valve assembly. Replacement parts are not available to rebuild the oil pressure relief valve.

> *CAUTION*
> *Because the snap ring is not available, only disassemble the valve when troubleshooting a problem with the lubrication system. Removing and then reinstalling the snap ring may weaken it and possibly cause it to fail when the engine is under operation. During reassembly, install a new oil pressure relief valve. The expense is small compared to possibly having to service the engine a second time.*

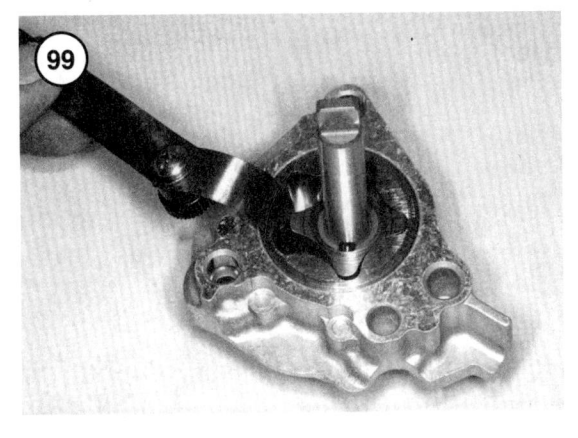

1. Remove and discard the O-ring **(Figure 101)**.
2. Remove the snap ring **(Figure 102)** and disassemble the oil pressure relief valve assembly in the order shown in **Figure 90**.
3. Clean and dry all parts.
4. Inspect the valve bore and piston outside diameter for scratches or wear.
5. Inspect the spring for cracks, distortion or other damage. The gaps between the spring coils must be uniform.
6. Make sure the holes in the relief valve are not clogged.
7. Install the piston, spring, washer and snap ring. Make sure the snap ring seats in the groove completely **(Figure 102)**.
8. Lubricate a new O-ring with engine oil and install it into the valve body groove **(Figure 101)**.
9. Store the oil pressure relief valve in a plastic bag until reassembly.

Assembly

1. Lubricate the rotors, shaft and washer with engine oil, then place the parts on a clean, lint-free cloth until reassembly.
2. Install the outer rotor (A, **Figure 103**) into the pump housing with its punch mark (or identification mark) facing in its original mounting direction.
3. Install the inner rotor (B, **Figure 103**) into the pump housing with its pin groove facing out.
4. Install the drive pin (A, **Figure 104**) into the shaft, then install the shaft (B, **Figure 104**) and pin (A) into the inner rotor (B, **Figure 103**).
5. Install the washer (C, **Figure 104**) over the shaft and seat it against the inner rotor.
6. Install the two dowel pins (D, **Figure 104**) into the housing.
7. Lubricate the shaft with engine oil.
8. Install the cover over the shaft and against the pump housing.

NOTE
The threads on the mounting bolts and in the oil pump cover must be clean and dry.

9. Install the oil pump assembly bolts **(Figure 94)** and tighten to 13 N.m (115 in.-lb.).
10. Turn the shaft and make sure the shaft and rotors turn freely with no binding or roughness.
11. Lubricate a new seal with engine oil and install it into the oil pump (B, **Figure 93**).
12. Align the oil strainer with the pump boss **(Figure 92)** and begin installing it into the seal at an angle. Then turn the oil strainer (A, **Figure 105**) and align it with the raised groove (B) on the oil pump. Because the sides of the strainer are offset, the strainer will

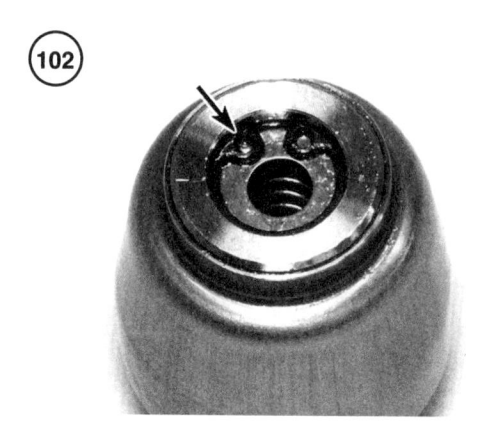

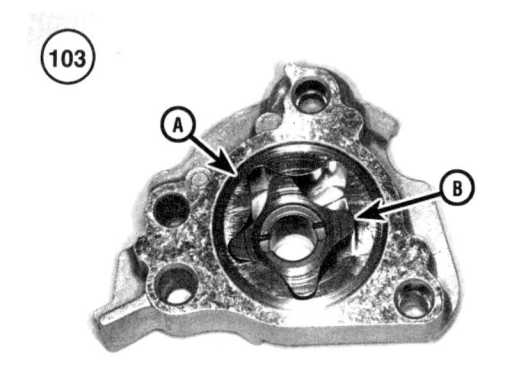

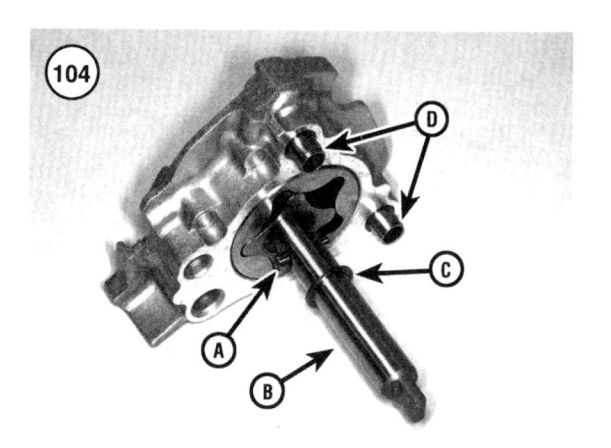

ENGINE LOWER END

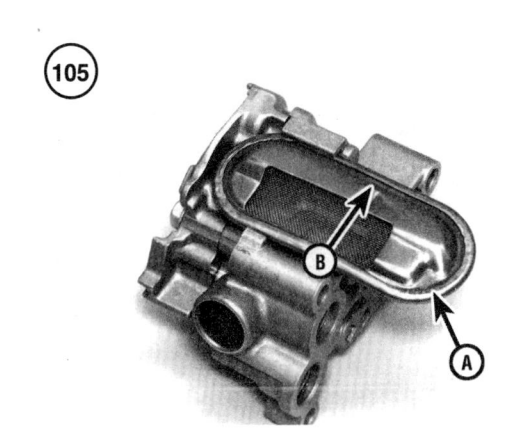

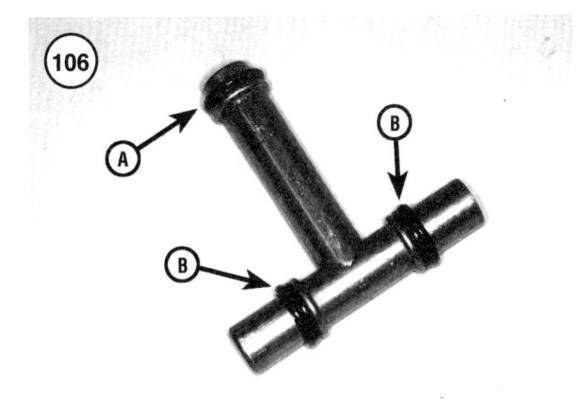

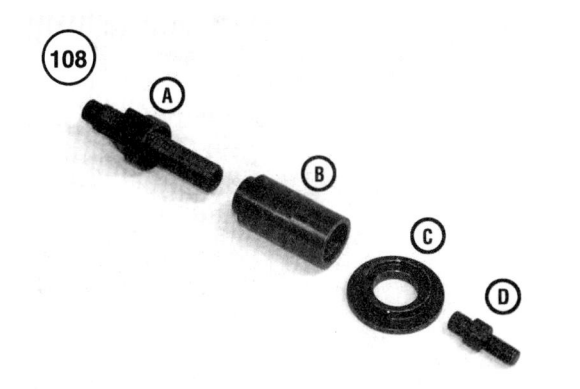

only fit one way against the groove.

NOTE
Because the oil strainer enters the seal at an angle, check the seal to make sure it is seated squarely in the oil pump after installing the oil strainer.

13. Lubricate the oil pressure relief valve O-ring with engine oil **(Figure 101)**, then turn and install the valve (C, **Figure 91**) into the oil pump.
14. Lubricate the new oil pipe O-ring and seals with engine oil. Install the O-ring (A, **Figure 106**) onto the long arm of the pipe. Install the two seals (B, **Figure 106**) with their larger end facing out.
15. Insert the long arm of the oil pipe (D, **Figure 91**) into the oil pump.
16. Install the oil pump as described under *Crankcase* in this chapter.

OUTPUT GEARCASE

This section describes removal and installation of the output gearcase.

Tools

A snap ring (A, **Figure 107**) secures the damper cam (B) and damper spring (C) onto the output drive gear. Because these parts are held under strong tension, special tools are required to compress the damper spring when removing and installing the snap ring. The snap ring, damper cam and damper spring must be removed before the output gearcase can be removed from the left crankcase. The following tools or their equivalents are required:
1. Assembly bolt and nut (Honda part No. 07965-1660200): A, **Figure 108**.
2. Assembly collar (Honda part No. 07965-166030A or 07965-1660302): B, **Figure 108**.
3. Compressor seat (Honda part No. 07967-9690200): C, **Figure 108**.
4. Threaded adaptor (Honda part No. 07965-KA3000): D, **Figure 108**.

Removal

1. Separate the crankcase halves and remove the crankshaft and transmission as described under *Crankcase* in this chapter.

2. Remove the thrust washer (A, **Figure 109**) and output gear (B).
3. Remove the bushing (A, **Figure 110**).
4. Perform the following to compress the damper spring and remove the snap ring **(Figure 111)** from the groove in the output drive gear:

WARNING
Safety goggles must be worn when compressing the damper spring and removing the snap ring.

 a. Install the threaded adaptor (A, **Figure 112**) into the output drive gear until it bottoms.
 b. Place the compressor seat onto the damper cam ramps with its shoulder side facing up (B, **Figure 112**).
 c. Install the assembly collar (A, **Figure 113**) over the end of the output drive gear and center it onto the compressor seat.
 d. Install the assembly bolt (B, **Figure 113**) onto the threaded adaptor until it bottoms.
 e. Hold the assembly bolt (B, **Figure 113**) and turn the nut (C), to compress the damper spring. Make sure the compressor seats remains centered on the damper cam ramps.
 f. Continue to compress the damper spring until the snap ring **(Figure 114)** is accessible and

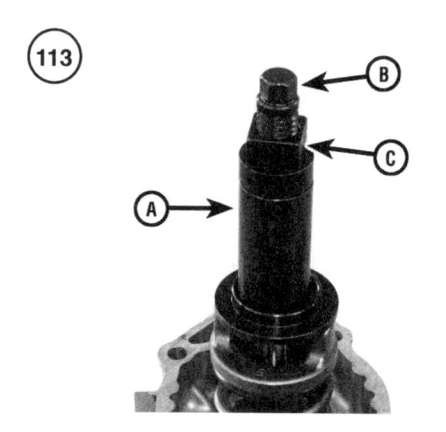

ENGINE LOWER END

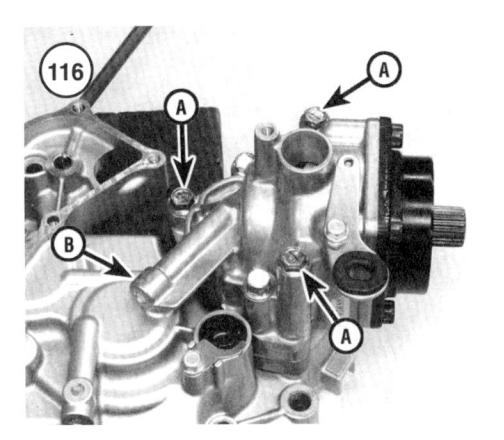

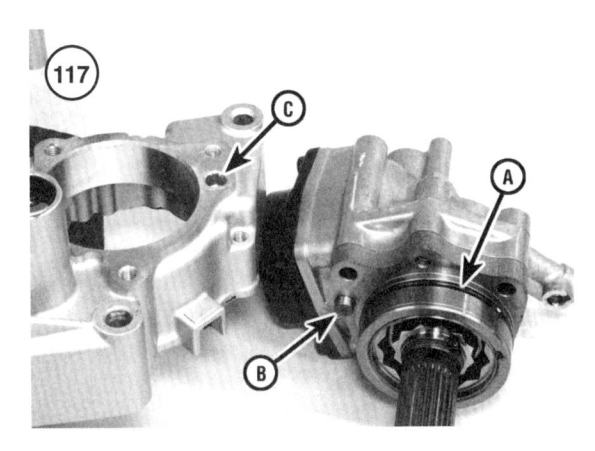

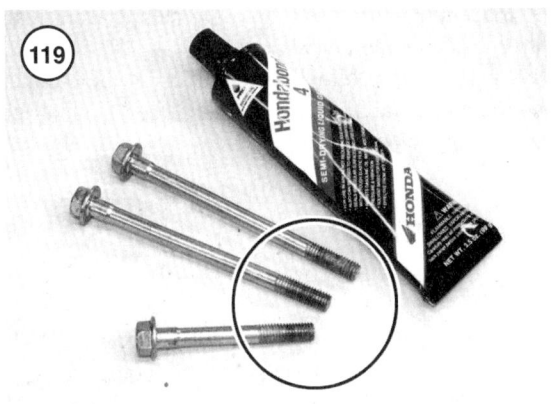

remove it from the output drive gear groove with snap ring pliers.

g. When the snap ring is free, slowly turn the nut (B, **Figure 113**) to release all tension from the spring. Then, remove the tools and the snap ring. Discard the snap ring.

5. Remove the damper cam (A, **Figure 115**) and damper spring (B).
6. Remove the output gearcase mounting bolts (A, **Figure 116**) and the gearcase (B). Discard the O-ring (A, **Figure 117**)
7. Remove the oil jet **(Figure 118)** and discard the two O-rings.
8. Inspect the output gearcase components (this section).

Installation

1. Make sure the crankcase and gearcase mating surfaces are clean.
2. Lubricate two new O-rings with engine oil and install them in the oil jet grooves. Then install the oil jet into the left crankcase **(Figure 118)**.
3. Lubricate a new O-ring with engine oil and install it into the gearcase groove (A, **Figure 117**).
4. Install the gearcase by aligning its dowel pin (B, **Figure 117**) with the hole in the crankcase (C, **Figure 117**) and with the oil jet.
5. Apply HondaBond No. 4 (or an equivalent sealer) to the threads on the gearcase mounting bolts **(Figure 119)**.
6. Install the output gearcase mounting bolts (A, **Figure 116**) and tighten to 31 N.m (23 ft.-lb.).
7. Install the damper spring over the output drive gear with the spring's narrow end (B, **Figure 115**) facing down and seat it onto the inner locknut.
8. Install the damper cam (A, **Figure 115**) by inserting its shoulder into the top of the damper spring. The ramps on the damper cam must face up.

9. Place a new snap ring onto the damper cam with its flat side facing up **(Figure 120)**.
10. Perform the following to compress the damper spring and install the snap ring **(Figure 111)** into the groove in the output drive gear:

> *WARNING*
> *Safety goggles must be worn when compressing the damper spring and installing the snap ring.*

   a. Install the threaded adaptor (A, **Figure 112**) into the output drive gear until it bottoms.
   b. Place the compressor seat onto the damper cam ramps with its shoulder side facing up (B, **Figure 112**).
   c. Install the assembly collar (A, **Figure 113**) over the end of the output drive gear and center it onto the compressor seat.
   d. Install the assembly bolt (B, **Figure 113**) onto the threaded adaptor until it bottoms.
   e. Hold the assembly bolt (B, **Figure 113**) and turn the nut (C), to compress the damper spring. Make sure the compressor seats remains centered on the damper cam ramps.
   f. Continue to compress the damper spring until the snap ring groove in the output drive gear is accessible. Then install the snap ring into the output drive gear groove with snap ring pliers. Make sure the snap ring is fully seated in the groove **(Figure 114)**.
   g. When the snap ring is fully installed in the groove, slowly turn the nut to release all tension from the spring. Then remove the tools.
   h. Recheck the snap ring **(Figure 111)**.

11. Lubricate the output drive gear shaft end and the bushing with engine oil and install the bushing (A, **Figure 110**).
12. Lubricate the output gear bore and gear dog holes and the damper cam ramps with engine oil.
13. Install the output gear (B, **Figure 109**) by aligning its detents (B, **Figure 110**) with the ramps (C) on the damper cam.
14. Install the thrust washer (A, **Figure 109**).
15. Install the transmission and crankshaft. Then, assemble the crankcase (this chapter).

Inspection

When measuring the components in this section, compare the actual measurements to the specifications in **Table 11**. Replace parts that are out of specification or damaged as described in this section. Refer to *Output Gearcase Overhaul* in this chapter to service the output gearcase assembly.

1. Clean and dry the damper cam, output gear, bushing and damper spring.
2. Inspect the ramps (A, **Figure 121**) on the damper cam and the gear dog holes (B) in the output gear for excessive wear, scoring and other damage. The mating surfaces must be smooth.
3. Inspect the output gear teeth (C, **Figure 121**) for cracks and other damage. If damaged, check the final drive gear mounted on the countershaft for the same conditions.
4. Inspect the output gear bore (D, **Figure 121**) for cracks, scoring and other damage.
5. Measure the output gear inside diameter (D, **Figure 121**).

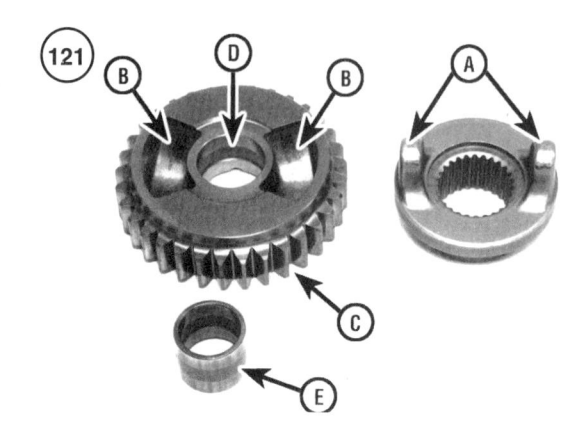

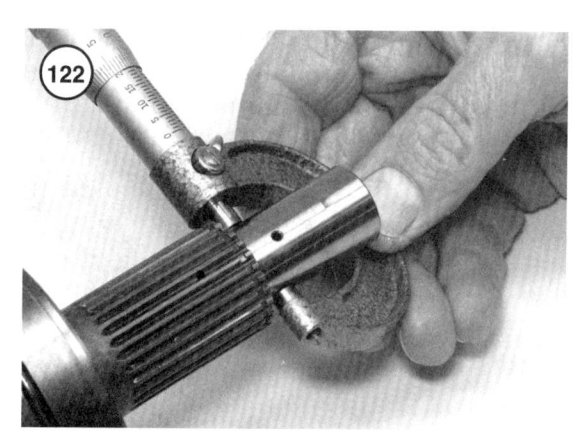

ENGINE LOWER END

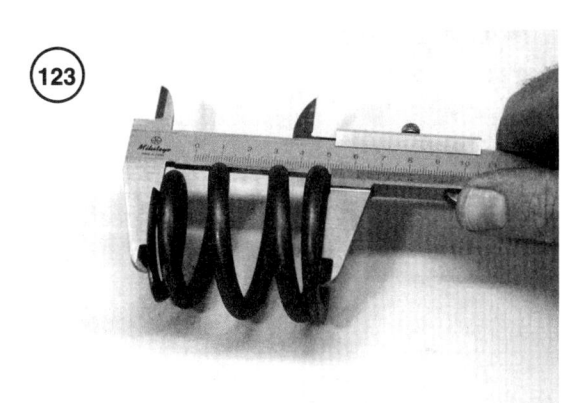

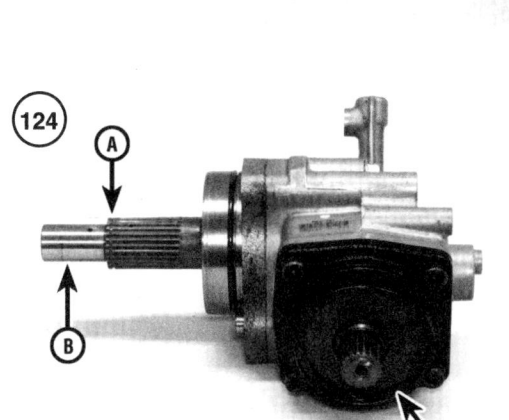

123

124

125

6. Measure the output gear bushing (E, **Figure 121**) inside and outside diameters.
7. Use the output gear inside diameter and the output gear bushing outside diameter to determine the output gear-to-bushing clearance.
8. Measure the output drive gear shaft outside diameter at the bushing operating position (**Figure 122**).
9. Use the output gear bushing inside diameter and the output gear driveshaft outside diameter to determine the output gear bushing-to-shaft clearance.
10. Inspect the damper spring for cracks and other damage.
11. Measure the damper spring free length (**Figure 123**).
12. Inspect the snap ring groove (A, **Figure 124**) in the output drive gear for cracks and other damage. If the groove is damaged, replace the output drive gear as described in this chapter.
13. Turn the output drive gear (B, **Figure 124**). Both the drive gear and driven gears should turn smoothly with no binding or roughness. If there is noticeable roughness or noise, disassemble the gearcase and inspect both gears and their bearings for damage as described in this chapter.
14. Inspect the output gearcase seal (A, **Figure 125**). If the seal is leaking, replace it as described in this chapter.

OUTPUT GEARCASE SEAL REPLACEMENT

The output gearcase seal can be replaced without disassembling the gearcase.

Tools

1. A seal removal tool is required to pry the seal out of the housing.
2. Drill bit and drill. Select a drill bit that is large enough to accept the end of the seal removal tool.
3. The seal uses a metal backing plate and will take more effort to drill through than a typical neoprene or rubber seal. Mount a drill stop onto the drill bit to prevent the drill from moving too far into the housing once it breaks through the seal.

Procedure

1. Remove the rear swing arm (Chapter Fourteen). Thoroughly clean the swing arm boot of oil that leaked through the output gearcase seal.
2. Place a drain pan underneath the output gearcase.
3. Clean the seal and the area around the seal to prevent dirt from entering the output gearcase.
4. If the output gearcase is removed from the engine, mount the gearcase in a holding fixture as described in *Output Gearcase Overhaul* in this chapter.
5. Remove the snap ring (B, **Figure 125**). Replace the snap ring if weak or damaged.

NOTE
If the engine is installed in the frame, determine the best position to drill the hole in the seal that will allow full movement of the seal removal tool when prying the seal out of the housing.

6. Carefully drill a small hole in the oil seal, making sure to drill only through the oil seal. Place a drill stop on the drill bit, if available.

168   **CHAPTER FIVE**

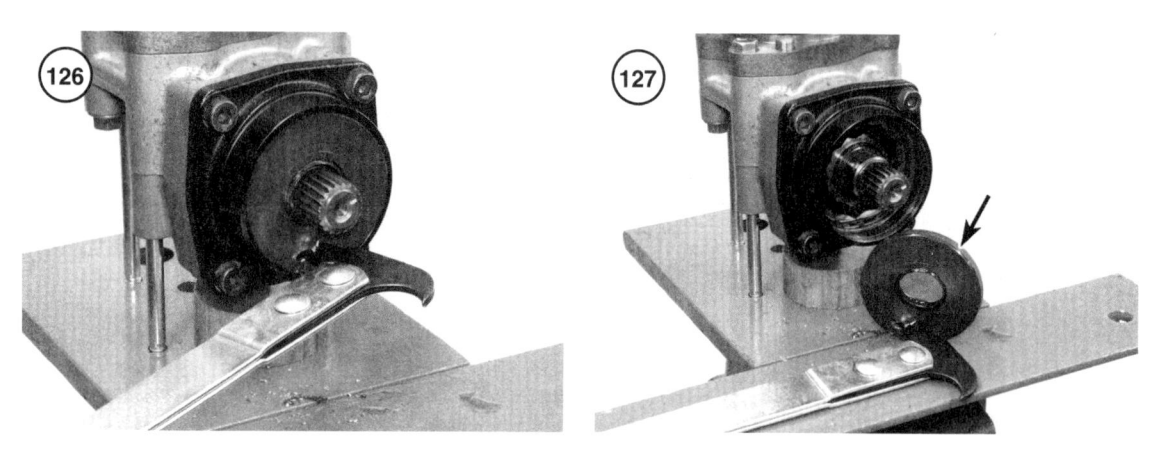

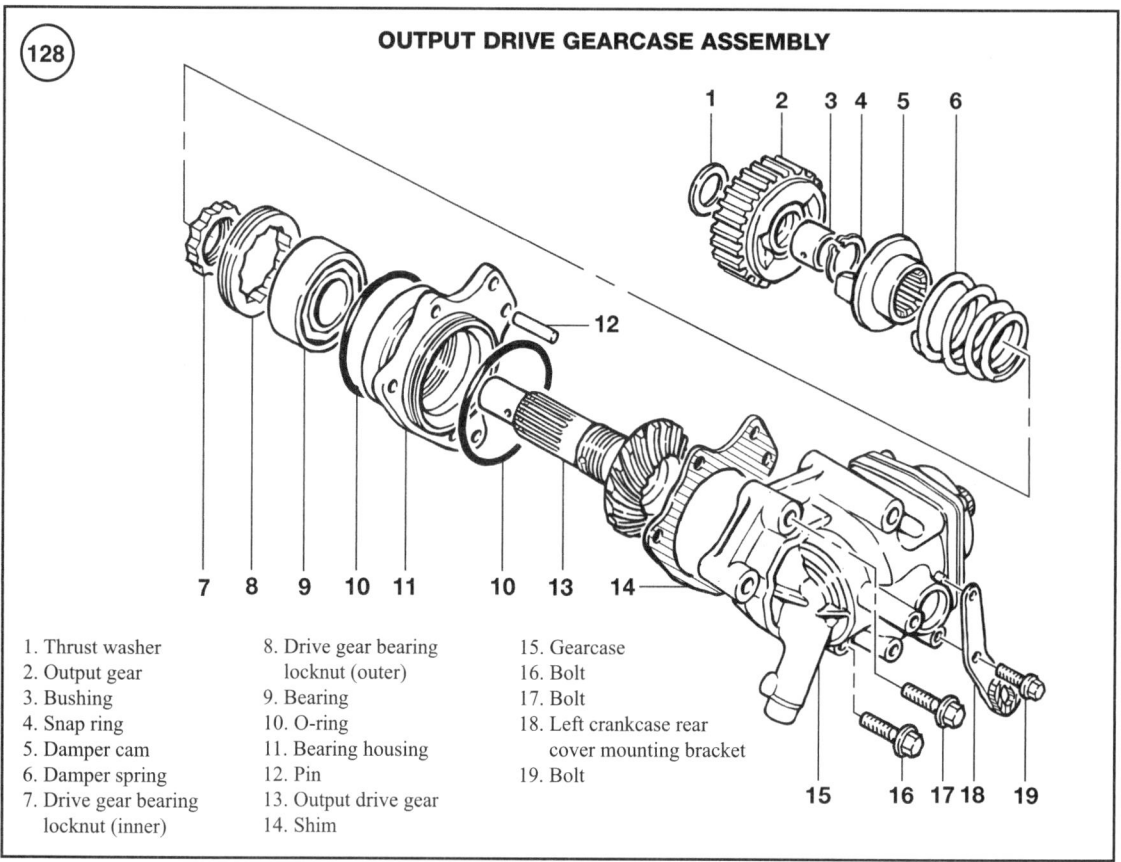

OUTPUT DRIVE GEARCASE ASSEMBLY

1. Thrust washer
2. Output gear
3. Bushing
4. Snap ring
5. Damper cam
6. Damper spring
7. Drive gear bearing locknut (inner)
8. Drive gear bearing locknut (outer)
9. Bearing
10. O-ring
11. Bearing housing
12. Pin
13. Output drive gear
14. Shim
15. Gearcase
16. Bolt
17. Bolt
18. Left crankcase rear cover mounting bracket
19. Bolt

CAUTION
When removing the seal, keep the seal removal tool level so that its tip does not angle downward and possible contact the seal surface inside the gearcase.

7. Insert the tip of a seal removal tool into the hole (**Figure 126**) and carefully pry the oil seal out of the gearcase. See **Figure 127**.
8. Clean the seal bore. Clean the driven gear splines. Check the shaft for any visible wear or damage where it operates against the seal.
9. Lubricate the seal lips with grease if it was not previously lubricated by the manufacturer.

NOTE
Before installing the new seal, check the splines on the end of the driven gear for burrs and other conditions that could damage the new seal.

10. Install the new seal over the driven gear with its flat side facing out (A, **Figure 125**) and center it in the gearcase. Turn the seal slightly while installing it to prevent the splines from cutting the seal lip. Then drive the new seal into the gearcase with a suitable driver placed on the outer perimeter of the seal.

ENGINE LOWER END

129 OUTPUT DRIVEN GEAR ASSEMBLY

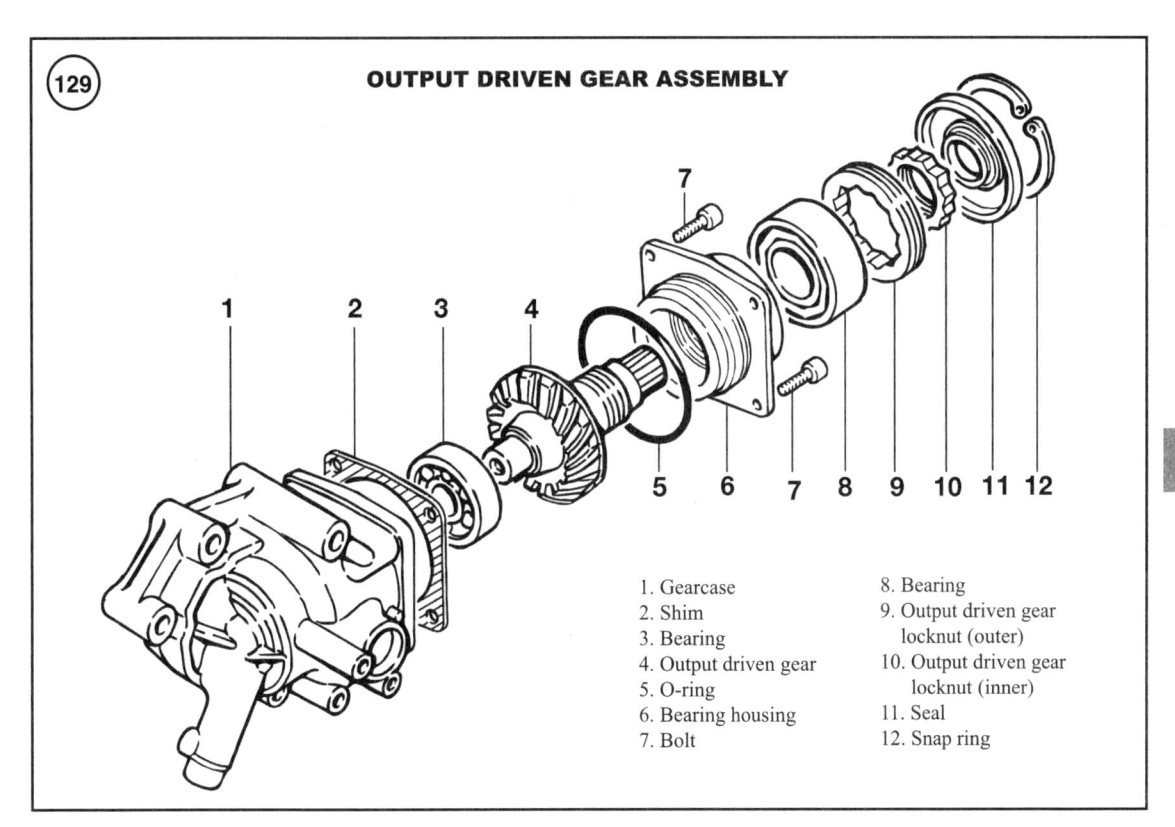

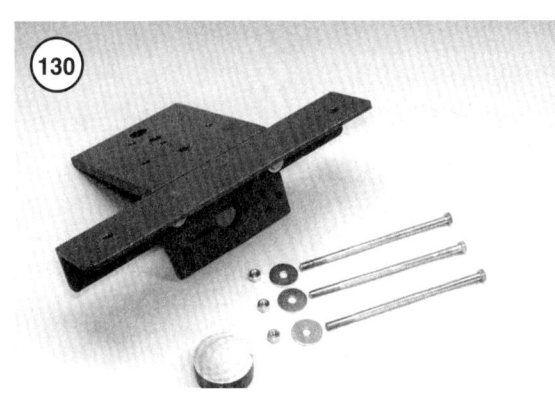

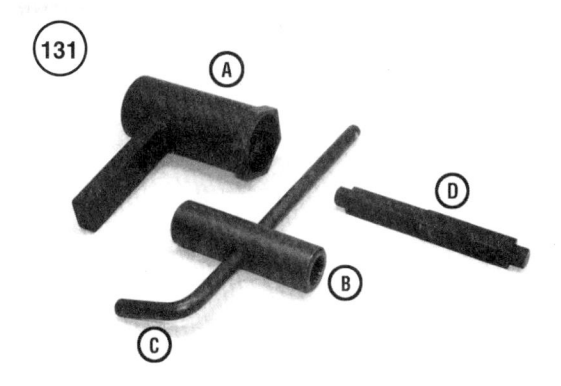

1. Gearcase
2. Shim
3. Bearing
4. Output driven gear
5. O-ring
6. Bearing housing
7. Bolt
8. Bearing
9. Output driven gear locknut (outer)
10. Output driven gear locknut (inner)
11. Seal
12. Snap ring

130

131

Drive the seal into the gearcase until it bottoms and the snap ring groove is accessible.

11. Install the snap ring (B, **Figure 125**) with its flat side facing out. Make sure the snap ring seats in the groove completely.

12. Install the rear swing arm (Chapter Fourteen).

OUTPUT GEARCASE OVERHAUL

This section covers rebuilding the output gearcase assembly (**Figure 129**). If it is only necessary to replace the output shaft seal, refer to the seal replacement procedure (this chapter).

Tools and Locknuts

1. The output gearcase must be held securely when loosening and tightening the four locknuts. If a large vise is available, the gearcase can be held in the vise with the use of soft jaws. Otherwise, a holding fixture can be made by bolting or welding together two pieces of angle plate (**Figure 130**). A sturdy vise is required to support the holding fixture. The holding fixture is shown in the following procedures.

2. Locknut wrench (Honda part No. 07916-MB00002 [A, **Figure 131**]). This tool, or an equivalent, is required to loosen and tighten the inner and outer locknuts.

3. Shaft holder A (Honda part No. 07PAB-0010100 [B, **Figure 131**]) and holder handle (Honda part No. 07PAB-0010400 [C, **Figure 131**]). These tools, or

their equivalents, are used to hold the drive and driven gears. In the text, both tools will be referred to as shaft holder A.
4. Differential inspection tool (Honda part No. 07KMK-HC50101 [D, **Figure 131**]). This tool, or its equivalent, is inserted into the shaft holder and used to hold the driven gear.
5. Hydraulic press with suitable bearing removers and drivers are required to the remove the shafts and bearings.
6. Tools for checking backlash and shimming the gearcase. Refer to *Output Drive and Driven Gear Measurements* in this chapter.

CAUTION
Work carefully when unstaking the locknuts. Avoid contacting the housing and shafts with the grinding wheel as contact can damage the threads and the oil seal surface on the driven gear shaft. If available, slide a plastic sleeve over the gear shafts to protect them.

7. The four locknuts are staked in place. Before loosening the locknuts, carefully grind the staked area on the locknut with a small grinding wheel to weaken the staked area and help prevent shaft and housing thread damage. Do not grind completely through the staked area as this may allow the grinding wheel to contact and damage the shaft or housing. Before using a grinding tool, pack the area above bearings with a paper towel to protect the bearings from contamination (**Figure 132**, typical).
8. Refer to *Bearings* under *Service Methods* in Chapter One for general bearing removal and installation information.
9. When tightening the inner and outer locknuts, mount the torque wrench onto the locknut wrench at a right angle (**Figure 133**). If the torque wrench is mounted so it lengthens the torque wrench, the torque applied to the locknut will be incorrect. Refer to **Torque Adapters** in Chapter One for more information.

Disassembly

This section describes complete disassembly of the gearcase. Do not remove the bearings unless bearing replacement is required.
1. Remove the bolt (A, **Figure 134**) and the left crankcase rear cover mounting bracket (B).
2. Secure the gearcase in a vise or mount it on a holding fixture with the output drive gear facing up (**Figure 135**).
3. Unstake the output drive gear (**Figure 136**) and output driven gear (**Figure 137**) locknuts as described under *Tools and Locknuts* in this section.

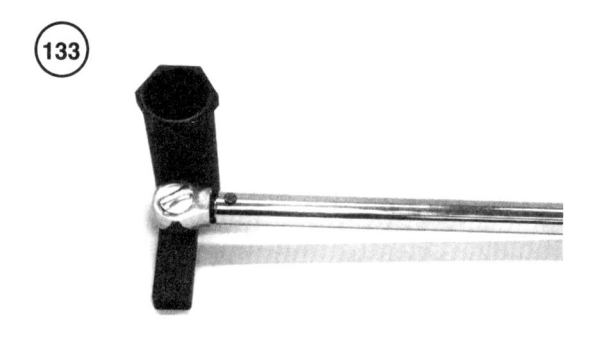

ENGINE LOWER END 171

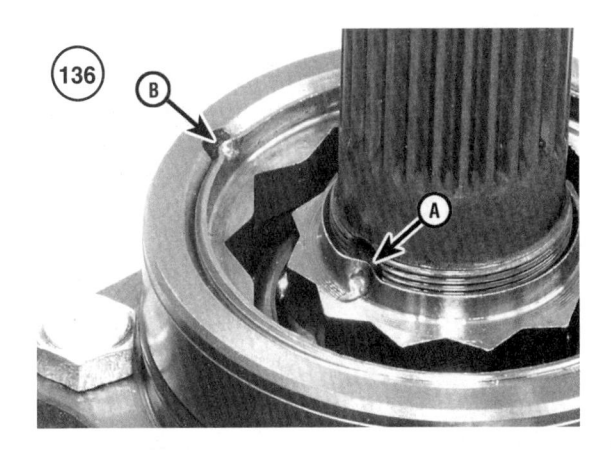

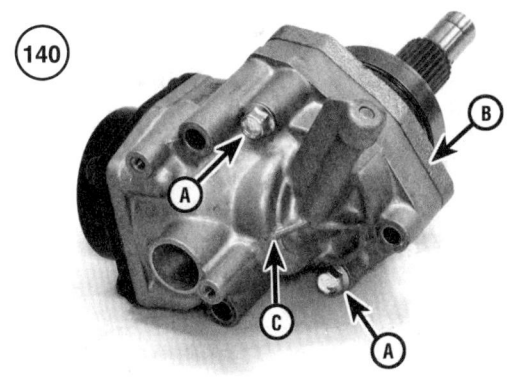

136

137

138

139

140

141

4. Hold the driven gear with shaft holder A (A, **Figure 138**) and loosen the drive gear inner locknut (A, **Figure 136**) with the locknut wrench (B) and a breaker bar. Remove the tools.

5. Turn the locknut wrench over and loosen the drive gear outer locknut (B, **Figure 136**) with the locknut wrench and a breaker bar.

6. Remove the snap ring and seal as described under *Output Gearcase Seal Replacement* in this chapter.

7. Loosen the driven gear inner locknut (A, **Figure 137**) as follows:
   a. Hold inner locknut with the locknut wrench (A, **Figure 139**).
   b. Install shaft holder A (B, **Figure 131**) without the handle (C) through the locknut wrench and onto the driven gear splines. Then install the differential inspection tool (B, **Figure 139**) into the opposite end of shaft holder A. Hold the differential inspection tool with a wrench and loosen the inner locknut with the locknut wrench and a breaker bar (A, **Figure 139**).
   c. Remove the tools from the gearcase.

8. With the gearcase still secured in the vise or on the holder, loosen the driven gear outer locknut (B, **Figure 137**) with the locknut wrench and breaker bar.

9. Remove the four gear locknuts and discard them.

10. Remove the two bolts (A, **Figure 140**) and remove the drive gear bearing housing (B) from the gearcase (C).

11. Remove the shim (A, **Figure 141**), dowel pin (B)

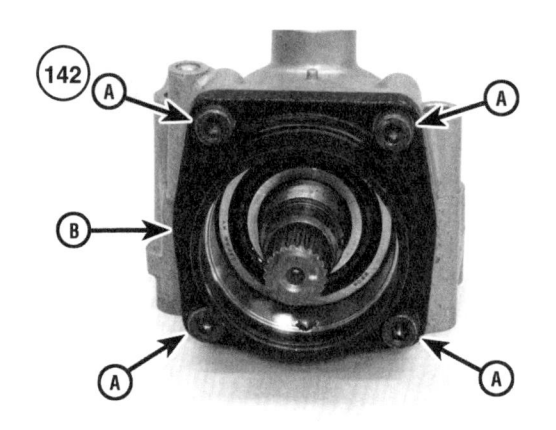

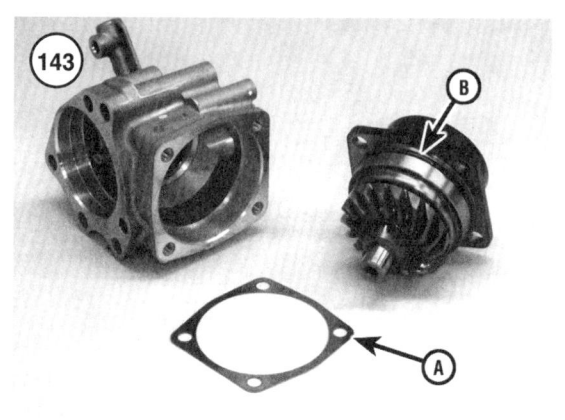

and O-ring (C). Discard the O-ring.

12. Remove the bolts (A, **Figure 142**) and remove the driven gear bearing housing (B) from the gearcase.

13. Remove the shim (A, **Figure 143**) and O-ring (B). Discard the O-ring.

> *NOTE*
> *A hydraulic press is required to remove the shafts and bearings in the following steps. Make sure to catch the gears and bearings once they are free to prevent them from hitting the floor.*

14. Press the driven gear **(Figure 144)** out of the bearing.

15. Press the driven gear bearing out of the bearing housing **(Figure 145)**.

16. Press the drive gear **(Figure 146)** out of the bearing.

17. Press the drive gear bearing out of the bearing housing **(Figure 147)**.

18. Remove the driven gear gearcase bearing with a 17-mm collet and blind bearing removal tool (A, **Figure 148**). Bolt the gearcase onto a wooden block (B) to help support it when removing the bearing.

19. Discard all bearings and O-rings.

ENGINE LOWER END

following:
  a. Damaged gear teeth (A, **Figure 151**).
  b. Scored or damaged bearing surface (B, **Figure 151**).
  c. Damaged threads (C, **Figure 151**). Check visually and then by threading a new inner locknut onto the threads.
  d. Damaged oil seal surface (D, **Figure 151**).
  e. Damaged splines (E, **Figure 151**).
4. If either shaft is damaged, both shafts must be replaced as a set and the gearcase reshimmed as described in *Output Drive and Driven Gear Measurements* (this chapter).
5. Inspect the threads in both bearing housings for damage. Check visually and then by threading a new outer locknut onto the threads.
6. Inspect the gearcase housing for damage.

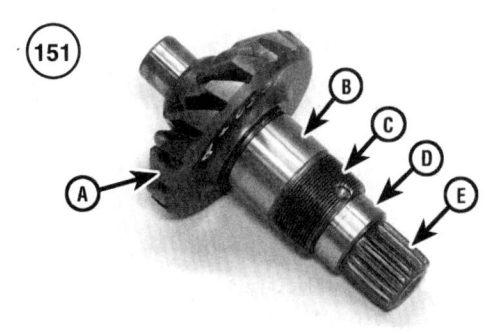

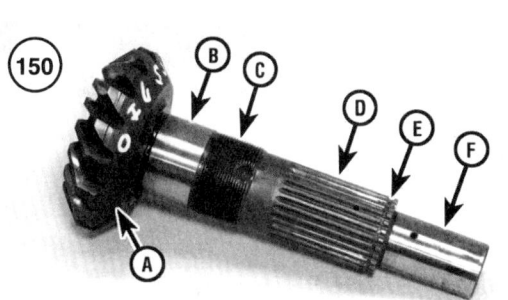

Cleaning and Inspection

1. Clean and dry all components. Flush the gearcase oil passage **(Figure 149)** with compressed air.
2. Inspect the output drive gear **(Figure 150)** for the following:
  a. Damaged gear teeth (A, **Figure 150**).
  b. Scored or damaged bearing surface (B, **Figure 150**).
  c. Damaged threads (C, **Figure 150**). Check visually and then by threading a new outer locknut onto the threads.
  d. Damaged splines (D, **Figure 150**). Check the snap ring groove for cracks and damage (E, **Figure 150**).
  e. Measure the output drive gear shaft outside diameter at the bushing operating position (F, **Figure 150**) as described in *Output Gearcase Inspection* (this chapter).
3. Inspect the output driven gear **(Figure 151)** for the

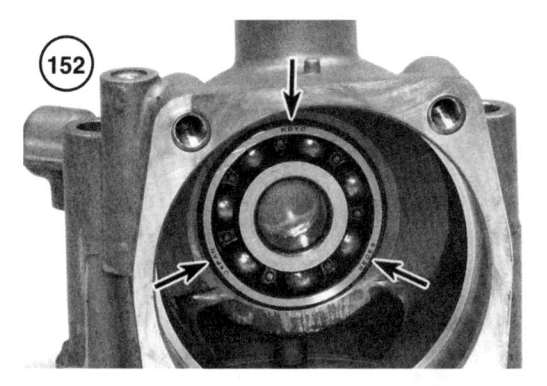

Assembly

NOTE
The gearcase housing is difficult to support when installing the driven gear gearcase bearing. Before installing the bearing, heat the housing and freeze the driven gear gearcase bearing as described in Chapter One.

1. Press a new driven gear gearcase bearing into the gearcase with its manufacturer's marks facing up **(Figure 152)**. Make sure the bearing bottoms in its bore.

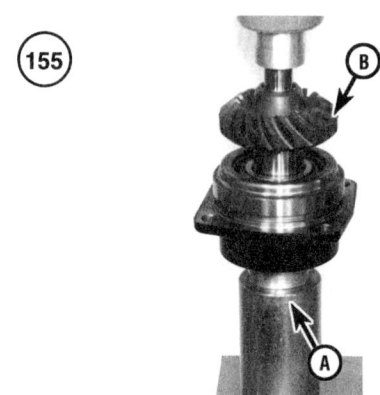

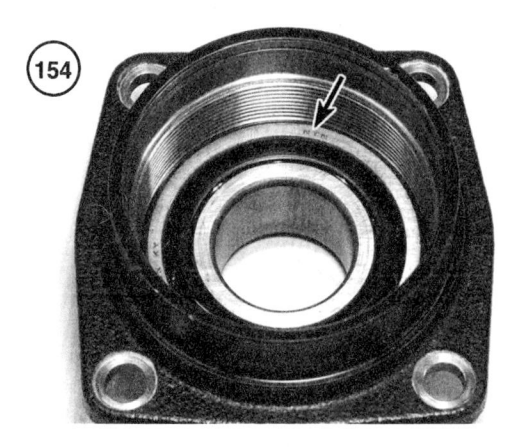

2. Press a new driven gear bearing into its bearing housing (**Figure 153**) with its marks facing up. Make sure the bearing (**Figure 154**) bottoms in its bore.

3. Press the output driven gear into its bearing as follows:
   a. Support the driven gear bearing inner race with a driver (A, **Figure 155**).
   b. Press the output driven gear (B, **Figure 155**) into the bearing until it bottoms.
   c. Turn the gear to make sure it turns smoothly.

4. Press a new drive gear bearing into its bearing housing (**Figure 156**) with its marks facing up. Make sure the bearing bottoms in its bore (**Figure 157**).

5. Press the output drive gear into its bearing as follows:
   a. Support the drive gear bearing inner race with a driver (A, **Figure 158**).
   b. Place a shouldered pilot driver (**Figure 159**) into the top of the gear. See B, **Figure 158**.
   c. Press the output driven gear (C, **Figure 158**) into the bearing until it bottoms.
   d. Turn the gear to make sure it turns smoothly.

NOTE
*When tightening the inner and outer locknuts (**Figure 160**), mount the*

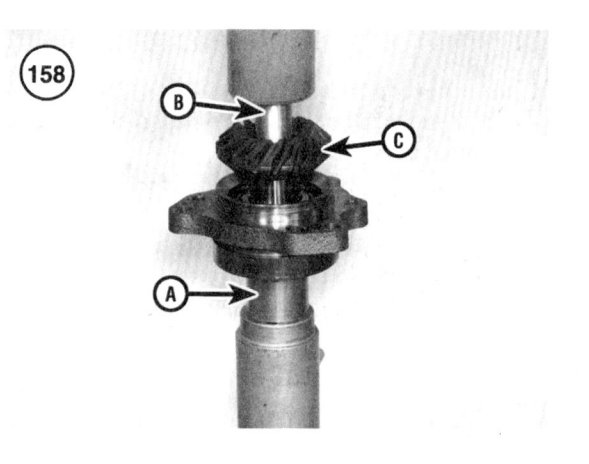

ENGINE LOWER END

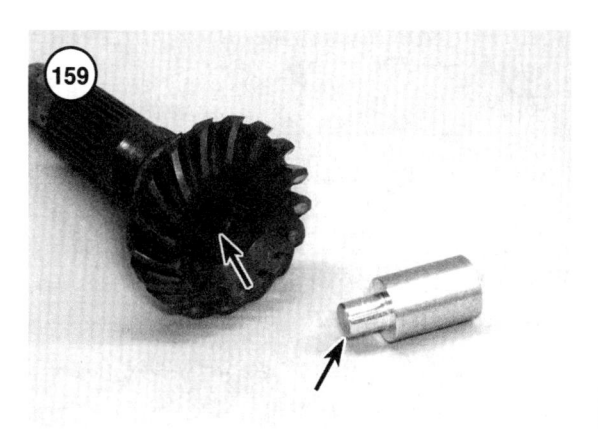

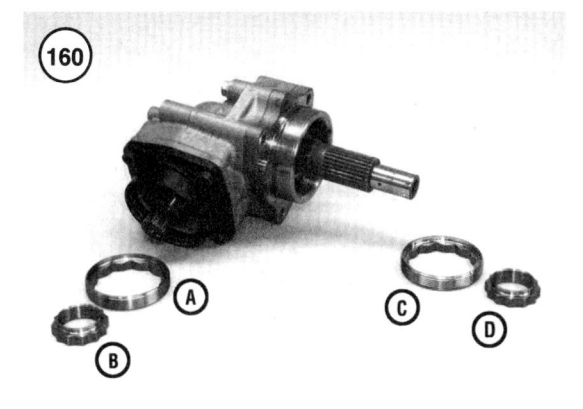

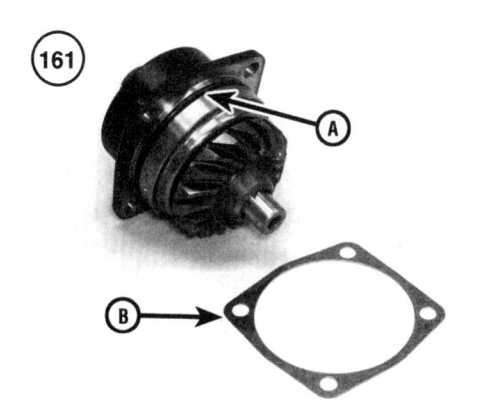

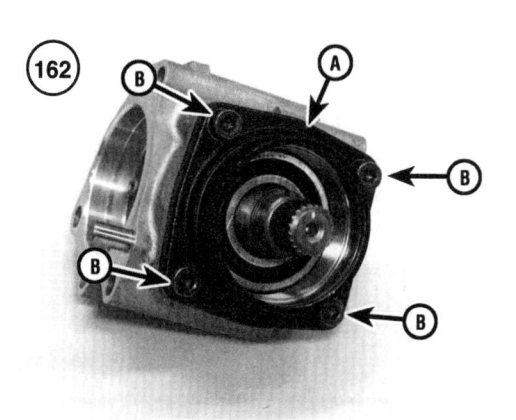

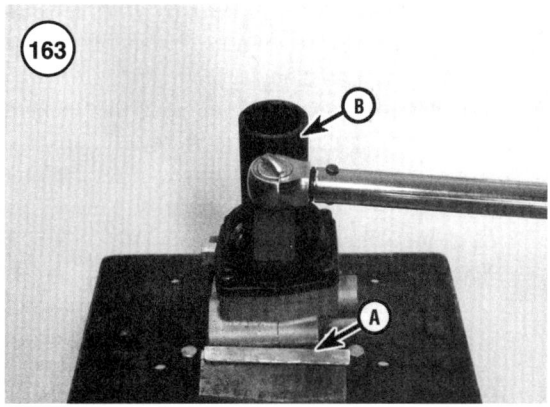

*torque wrench onto the locknut wrench at a right angle. If the locknut wrench is mounted so it lengthens the torque wrench, the torque applied to the locknut will be incorrect (too high). Refer to **Torque Adapters** in Chapter One for more information.*

6. Install the output driven gear bearing housing and tighten the locknuts as follows:
   a. Lubricate a new O-ring with engine oil and install it into the bearing housing groove (A, **Figure 161**).
   b. Install the shim (B, **Figure 161**) over the bearing housing shoulder.

NOTE
*If the gearcase, drive and driven gears, bearing holders or bearings have been replaced, install a 0.40 mm (0.016 in.) shim for reference when measuring the backlash and checking the tooth contact pattern as described in **Output Drive and Driven Gear Measurements** in this chapter.*

   c. Install the output driven gear bearing housing (A, **Figure 162**) and shim into the gearcase.
   d. Lubricate the bearing housing Allen bolt threads and seating surfaces with engine oil and install them (B, **Figure 162**) finger-tight.
   e. Secure the gearcase onto the holding fixture or in a vise with soft jaws (A, **Figure 163**).
   f. Following a crossing pattern, tighten the output driven gear bearing housing Allen bolts in two or three steps to 31 N.m (23 ft.-lb.).

NOTE
*Do not stake the inner and outer locknuts until after performing the **Output Drive and Driven Gear Measurements** in this chapter.*

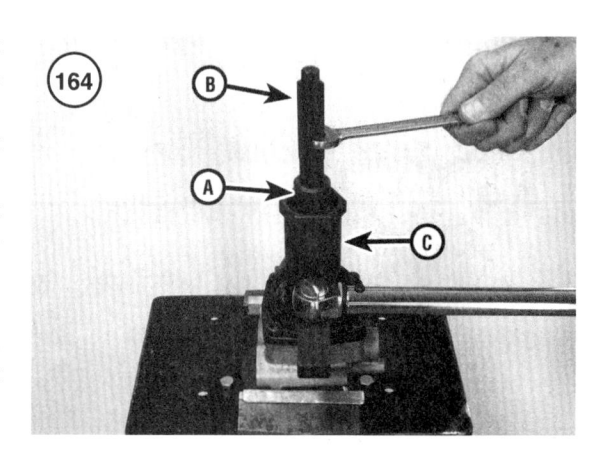

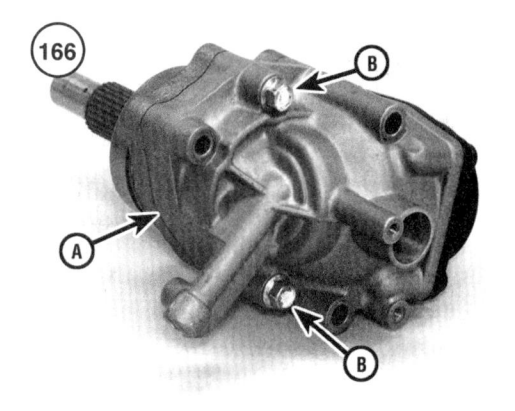

g. Lubricate the threads of a new outer locknut (A, **Figure 160**) with engine oil and install the locknut with its shoulder facing out.
h. Tighten the outer locknut with the locknut wrench (B, **Figure 163**) to 98 N.m (72 ft.-lb.).
i. Lubricate the threads of a new inner locknut (B, **Figure 160**) with engine oil and install the locknut with its shoulder facing out.
j. Secure the driven shaft with shaft holder A (A, **Figure 164**) and differential inspection tool (B). Tighten the inner locknut with the locknut wrench (C) to 74 N.m (55 in.-lb.). Remove the tools.

NOTE
*Do not install the gearcase oil seal or snap ring until after performing the **Output Drive and Driven Gear Measurements** in this chapter.*

7. Install the output drive gear bearing housing and tighten the locknuts as follows:
    a. Install the dowel pin (A, **Figure 165**) into the housing.
    b. Lubricate a new O-ring with engine oil and install it into the bearing housing groove (B, **Figure 165**).
    c. Install the shim (C, **Figure 165**) over the bearing housing shoulder.

NOTE
*If the gearcase, drive and driven gears, bearing holders or bearings have been replaced, install a 0.50 mm (0.020 in.) shim for reference when measuring the backlash and checking the tooth contact pattern as described in **Output Drive and Driven Gear Measurements** in this chapter.*

d. Install the bearing housing and shim (A, **Figure 166**) into the gearcase by aligning them with the dowel pin.
e. Lubricate the bearing housing bolt threads and seating surfaces with engine oil and install the bolts (B, **Figure 166**) and finger-tighten them.
f. Secure the gearcase on a holding fixture or in a vise with soft jaws. Tighten the output drive gear bearing housing bolts in two or three steps to 31 N.m (23 ft.-lb.).

NOTE
*Do not stake the inner and outer locknuts until after performing the **Output Drive and Driven Gear Measurements** in this chapter.*

ENGINE LOWER END

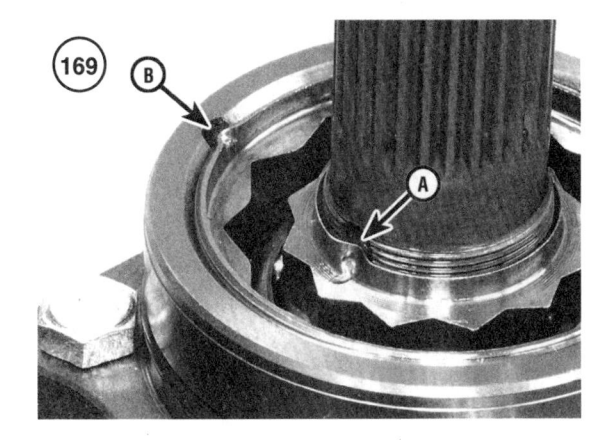

g. Lubricate the threads of a new outer locknut (C, **Figure 160**) with engine oil and install the locknut with its shoulder facing out.

h. Tighten the output drive gear outer locknut with the locknut wrench **(Figure 167)** to 98 N.m (72 ft.-lb.).

i. Lubricate the threads of a new inner locknut (D, **Figure 160**) with engine oil and install the locknut with its shoulder facing out.

j. Secure the driven shaft with the shaft holder as shown in A, **Figure 168**. Then tighten the inner locknut with the locknut wrench (B, **Figure 168**) to 74 N.m (54 in.-lb.).

8. Perform the *Output Drive and Driven Gear Measurements* in this chapter.

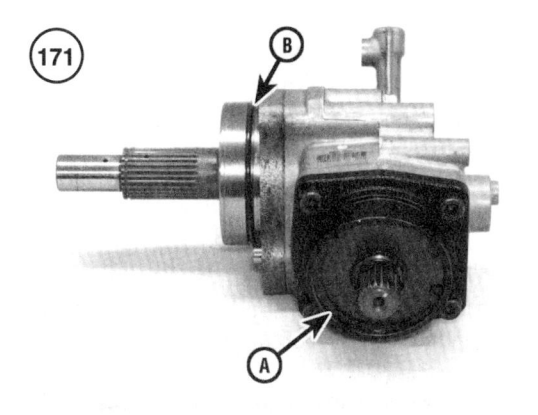

9. Stake the drive gear locknuts as follows:
   a. Stake the inner locknut into the notch in the drive gear shaft (A, **Figure 169**).
   b. Stake the outer locknut into the notch in the bearing housing (B, **Figure 169**).

10. Stake the driven gear locknuts as follows:
    a. Stake the inner locknut into the notch in the driven gear shaft (A, **Figure 170**).
    b. Stake the outer locknut into the notch in the bearing housing (B, **Figure 170**).

11. Install a new gearcase seal and snap ring (A, **Figure 171**) as described in *Output Gearcase Seal Replacement* in this chapter.

12. Lubricate a new O-ring with engine oil and install into the output gearcase groove (B, **Figure 171**).

13. Install the left crankcase rear cover mounting bracket by aligning the hole in the bracket with the pin on the gearcase (A, **Figure 172**) and tighten the bolt (B) securely.

OUTPUT DRIVE AND DRIVEN GEAR MEASUREMENTS

Whenever the output gearcase, drive and driven gears, bearing holders or bearings have been replaced, check the output drive gear backlash and the gear tooth contact pattern as described in this section.

Output Drive Gear Backlash Measurement

This procedure checks the output drive gear backlash to determine gear wear and if the gears are running true. Measuring backlash is also necessary after a general overhaul of the output gearcase.

1. Remove the output gearcase as described in this chapter.
2. Mount the output gearcase on a holder or in a vise with soft jaws.
3. Lock the driven gear shaft with shaft holder A (A, **Figure 173**).
4. Measure backlash with a dial indicator mounted on a magnetic stand. Position the indicator so its stem is parallel to the output drive gear shaft and its tip contacts the side of the shaft (**Figure 174**).
5. Rotate the output drive gear shaft (B, **Figure 173**) back and forth to measure the backlash. Refer to **Table 11** for the specified backlash. Record the reading.
6. Remove the dial indicator, then rotate the driven shaft and take two additional backlash readings 120° from the original measuring point.
   a. If the difference between any two readings exceeds 0.10 mm (0.004 in.), the shafts are running out of true. This can be caused by damaged bearings, bearing housings or the gearcase is damaged.
   b. If the backlash measurement is being performed after reassembling the gearcase, the bearings may not have been installed correctly.
   c. If the backlash reading is out of specification, but the shafts are running true, continue the procedure.
   d. If the backlash reading indicates that the shafts are running out of true, disassemble the output gearcase and inspect the parts for damage.
7. To correct backlash, perform the following:
   a. If backlash is too small, replace the drive gear shim (C, **Figure 165**) with a thicker one.
   b. If backlash to too large, replace the drive gear shim (C, **Figure 165**) with a thinner one.
   c. Refer to **Table 12** for the output drive gear shim thicknesses.
   d. Changing the shim thickness 0.10 mm (0.004 in.) changes the backlash approximately 0.06-0.07 mm (0.002-0.003 in.).
   e. Disassemble and reassemble the output gearcase as described in *Output Gearcase Overhaul* in this chapter.
8. When the backlash reading is correct, perform the *Gear Tooth Contact Pattern Check* (this section).

Gear Tooth Contact Pattern Check

Refer to *Output Gearcase Overhaul* in this chapter when disassembling and reassembling the output gearcase assembly in this section.

1. Remove the output drive gear bearing housing and shim.
2. Using a brush, apply Prussian blue or an equivalent non-drying gear marking compound to both sides of the driven gear teeth.
3. Reinstall the output drive gear bearing housing and shim.
4. Rotate the drive gear shaft to turn the gears in their normal operating direction so a pattern becomes evident on the gear teeth.
5. Examine the contact pattern on the drive side of the ring gear teeth as follows:
   a. Refer to **Figure 175** to identify the parts of the gear teeth.
   b. The desired gear tooth contact pattern (**Figure 176**) shows the pattern positioned approximately in the center of each tooth and slightly toward the toe or inside of the gear tooth.
   c. If the contact pattern is low, install a thicker output driven gear shim (**Figure 177**).
   d. If the pinion contact pattern is high, install a thinner output driven gear shim (**Figure 177**).

ENGINE LOWER END

175

Toe (inside of gear)

Coast side (contacts during engine braking)

Drive side (contacts during engine acceleration)

Heel (outside of gear)

176

DESIRED TOOTH CONTACT PATTERN

Heel — Toe — Heel
Face — Face
Flank — Flank

LOW TOOTH CONTACT PATTERN

Drive side — Coast side
Flank — Flank

HIGH TOOTH CONTACT PATTERN

Drive side — Coast side
Face — Face

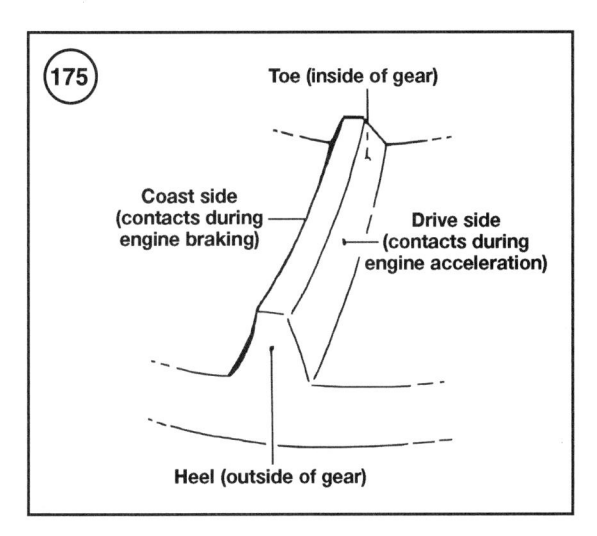

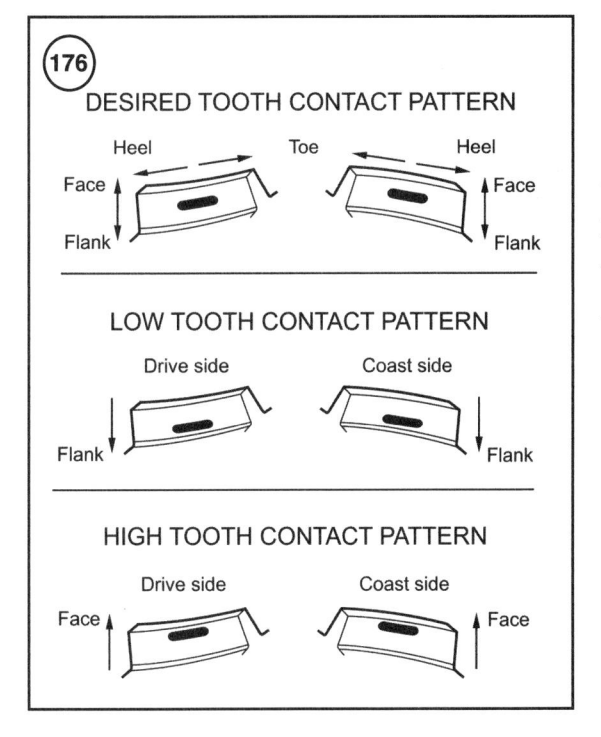

177

e. Changing shim thickness 0.10 mm (0.004 in.) moves the contact pattern approximately 1.5-2.0 mm (0.06-0.08 in.). Refer to **Table 13** for output driven gear shim sizes.

f. The output driven gear must be removed to replace the shim.

6. Reassemble the gearcase as described in this chapter. After obtaining a satisfactory gear tooth contact pattern, check the backlash as described under *Output Drive Gear Backlash Measurement* in this section.

7. Stake the locknuts and complete gearcase assembly (this chapter).

Table 1 GENERAL ENGINE SPECIFICATIONS

Engine dry weight	
Aero models	
2004-2007	72.3 kg (159.4 lbs.)
2008-2009	71.5 kg (157.6 lbs.)
2011-2013	71.0 kg (156.5 lbs.)
Spirit models	
2007-2009	72.3 kg (159.4 lbs.)
2010-2013	70.8 kg (156.1 lbs.)
Phantom models	70.8 kg (156.1 lbs.)
Lubrication system	Wet sump, forced pressure
Oil pump type	Trochoid

Table 2 ENGINE LOWER END SPECIFICATIONS

	New mm (in.)	Service limit mm (in.)
Crankshaft main journal oil clearance	0.020-0.038 (0.0008-0.0015)	0.07 (0.003)
Crankshaft main journal outside diameter	52.982-53.000 (2.0859-2.0866)	52.976 (2.0857)
Crankshaft rod journal outside diameter (1)	--	--
Crankshaft runout	--	0.03 (0.001)
Connecting rod bearing clearance	0.028-0.052 (0.0011-0.0020)	0.07 (0.003)
Connecting rod side clearance	0.05-0.20 (0.002-0.008)	0.30 (0.012)
Connecting rod small end inside diameter	18.016-18.034 (0.7093-0.7100)	18.07 (0.711)
Main journal bearing inside diameter (2)	58.010-58.022 (2.2839-2.2843)	58.070 (2.2862)

1. The rod journal outside diameter measurements depend on the crankshaft rod journal outside diameter codes listed in Table 7.
2. This measurement is made with the main journal bearing installed in the crankcase.

Table 3 BEARING SELECTION: CRANKSHAFT AND CRANKCASE REPLACEMENT

	Crankshaft Main Journal Outside Diameter Code		
	1	2	3
Bearing support inside diameter code	52.994-53.000 mm (2.0864-2.0866 in.)	52.988-52.994 mm (2.0861-2.0864 in.)	52.982-52.988 mm (2.0859-2.0861 in.)
A: 58.016-58.022 mm (2.2841-2.2843 in.)	C (Brown)	B (Black)	A (Blue)
B: 58.010-58.016 mm (2.2839-2.2841 in.)	D (Green)	C (Brown)	B (Black)

Table 4 BEARING SELECTION: CRANKCASE REPLACEMENT ONLY

	Main Journal Outside Diameter			
Crankcase bearing support inside diameter code	52.994-53.000 mm (2.0864-2.0866 in.)	52.988-52.994 mm (2.0861-2.0864 in.)	52.982-52.988 mm (2.0859-2.0861) in.	52.976-52.982 mm (2.0857-2.0859 in.)
A: 58.016-58.022 mm (2.2841-2.2843 in.)	C (Brown)	B (Black)	A (Blue)	A (Blue)
B: 58.010-58.016 mm (2.2839-2.2841 in.)	D (Green)	C (Brown)	B (Black)	A (Blue)

ENGINE LOWER END

Table 5 BEARING SELECTION: CRANKSHAFT REPLACEMENT ONLY

	Crankshaft Main Journal Outside Diameter Code		
Main journal bearing inside diameter	1= 52.994-53.000 mm (2.0864-2.0866 in.)	2= 52.988-52.994 mm (2.0861-2.0864 in.)	3= 52.982-52.988 mm (2.0859-2.0861 in.)
58.010-58.016 mm (2.2839-2.2841 in.)	D (Green)	C (Brown)	B (Black)
58.016-58.022 mm (2.2841-2.2843 in.)	C (Brown)	B (Black)	A (Blue)
58.022-58.034 mm (2.2843-2.2848 in.)	B (Black)	A (Blue)	A (Blue)
58.034-58.046 mm (2.2848-2.2853 in.)	A (Blue)	O.S. G (Red)	O.S. G (Red)
58.046-58.058 mm (2.2853-2.2857 in.)	O.S. G (Red)	O.S. F (Pink)	O.S. F (Pink)
58.058-58.070 mm (2.2857-2.2862 in.)	O.S. F (Pink)	O.S. E (Yellow)	O.S. E (Yellow)

Table 6 BEARING SELECTION: MAIN JOURNAL BEARING REPLACEMENT ONLY

	Main Journal Outside Diameter			
Crankcase bearing support inside diameter code	52.994-53.000 mm (2.0864-2.0866 in.)	52.988-52.994 mm (2.0861-2.0864 in.)	52.982-52.988 mm (2.0859-2.0861) in.	52.976-52.982 mm (2.0857-2.0859 in.)
58.010-58.016 mm (2.2839-2.2841 in.)	D (Green)	C (Brown)	B (Black)	A (Blue)
58.016-58.022 mm (2.2841-2.2843 in.)	C (Brown)	B (Black)	A (Blue)	A (Blue)
58.022-58.034 mm (2.2843-2.2848 in.)	B (Black)	A (Blue)	A (Blue)	O.S. G (Red)
58.034-58.046 mm (2.2848-2.2853 in.)	A (Blue)	O.S. G (Red)	O.S. G (Red)	O.S. F (Pink)
58.046-58.058 mm (2.2853-2.2857 in.)	O.S. G (Red)	O.S. F (Pink)	O.S. F (Pink)	O.S. E (Yellow)
58.058-58.070 mm (2.2857-2.2862 in.)	O.S. F (Pink)	O.S. E (Yellow)	O.S. E (Yellow)	O.S. E (Yellow)

Table 7 CONNECTING ROD BEARING SELECTION

Crankshaft rod journal outside diameter code	Connecting rod inside diameter code	
	3	4
	43.000-43.008 mm (1.6929-1.6932 in.)	43.008-43.016 mm (1.6932-1.6935 in.)
A 39.982-39.990 mm (1.5741-1.5744 in.)	C (pink)	B (yellow)
B 39.974-39.982 (1.5738-1.5741)	B (yellow)	A (green)

Table 8 CONNECTING ROD WEIGHT CODE SELECTION

Front weight code	Rear weight code		
	A	B	C
A	--	+	+
B	+	+	+
C	+	+	--
-- No match.			
+ Possible match.			

Table 9 CONNECTING ROD WEIGHT

Connecting rod weight code	Weight
A	398-403 g (14.0-14.2 oz.)
B	403-408 g (14.2-14.4 oz.)
C	408-413 g (14.4-14.6 oz.)

Table 10 OIL PUMP SPECIFICATIONS

	New mm (in.)	Service limit mm (in.)
Axial clearance	0.15-0.21 (0.006-0.008)	0.35 (0.014)
Side clearance	0.02-0.08 (0.0008-0.003)	0.10 (0.004)
Tip clearance	0.15 (0.006)	0.20 (0.008)

Table 11 OUTPUT GEARCASE SPECIFICATIONS

	New mm (in.)	Service limit mm (in.)
Backlash difference between measurements	--	0.10 (0.004)
Output drive gear backlash	0.08-0.23 (0.003-0.009)	0.40 (0.016)
Output drive gear shaft outside diameter	19.979-20.000 (0.7866-0.7874)	19.97 (0.786)
Output gear bushing		
Outside diameter	23.959-23.980 (0.9433-0.9441)	23.70 (0.933)
Inside diameter	20.020-20.041 (0.7882-0.7890)	20.06 (0.790)
Output gear bushing-to-shaft clearance	0.020-0.042 (0.0008-0.0017)	0.08 (0.003)
Output gear damper spring free length	62.3 (2.45)	59 (2.3)
Output gear inside diameter	24.000-24.021 (0.9449-0.9457)	24.04 (0.946)
Output gear-to-bushing clearance	0.020-0.062 (0.0008-0.0024)	0.082 (0.0032)

Table 12 OUTPUT DRIVE GEAR SHIMS

0.30 mm (0.012 in.)
0.35 mm (0.014 in.)
0.40 mm (0.016 in.)
0.45 mm (0.018 in.)
0.50 mm (0.020 in.) Standard shim
0.55 mm (0.022 in.)
0.60 mm (0.024 in.)
0.65 mm (0.026 in.)
0.70 mm (0.028 in.)
0.75 mm (0.030 in.)

ENGINE LOWER END

Table 13 OUTPUT DRIVEN GEAR SHIMS

0.20 mm (0.008 in.)
0.25 mm (0.010 in.)
0.30 mm (0.012 in.)
0.35 mm (0.014 in.)
0.40 mm (0.016 in.) Standard shim
0.45 mm (0.018 in.)
0.50 mm (0.020 in.)
0.55 mm (0.022 in.)
0.60 mm (0.024 in.)

Table 14 ENGINE BOTTOM END TORQUE SPECIFICATIONS

	N.m	in.-lb.	ft.-lb.
Connecting rod bearing cap nuts (1)	33	--	24
Crankcase bolts			
6-mm	--	Refer to text	--
8-mm	23	--	17
Engine mounting fasteners			
Engine hanger plate mounting bolts	26	--	19
Engine mounting nuts	54	--	40
Engine oil drain bolt	29	--	21
Metal installer set (2)	23	--	17
Oil pump assembly bolts	13	115	--
Starter cable terminal nut			
2004-2007 Aero (1)	9.8	87	--
All other models	10	89	--
Output drive gear bearing housing bolt (1)	31	--	23
Output drive gear bearing locknut			
Inner (1)	74	--	55
Outer (1)	98	--	72
Output drive gear shaft bolt (1)	49	--	36
Output driven gear bearing housing Allen bolt (1)	31	--	23
Output driven gear bearing locknut			
Inner (1)	74	--	55
Outer (1)	98	--	72
Output gear case mounting bolts (1)	31	--	23
Right brake pedal bracket mounting bolt and nut	39	--	29
Right footpeg mounting bracket bolt and nut	39	--	29
Shift arm pinch bolt	12	106	--

1. Refer to text for additional information.
2. This tool is required to install the main journal bearings. The specified torque is required to assemble the tool. Refer to the text for additional information.

NOTES

CHAPTER SIX

CLUTCH AND EXTERNAL SHIFT MECHANISM

This chapter covers procedures for the clutch cable, right crankcase cover, clutch release lever, clutch, primary drive gear and external shift mechanism.

Clutch specifications are located in **Table 1**. **Table 1** and **Table 2** are located at the end of this chapter.

CLUTCH CABLE REPLACEMENT

1. Remove the fuel tank (Chapter Eight or Chapter Nine).
2. Hold the new cable up to the motorcycle and compare it with the old cable. Make sure the length of the cable and both cable ends are correct.
3. Lubricate the new clutch cable as described in Chapter Three.
4. Loosen the clutch cable adjuster locknut (A, **Figure 1**) and adjuster (B) at the handlebar.
5. Loosen the clutch cable adjuster nuts (A, **Figure 2**) and disconnect the cable from the release arm (B).
6. Tie a piece of heavy string to the lower end of the old cable. Cut the string to a length that is longer than the new clutch cable.
7. Tie the lower end of the string to a frame or engine component.

NOTE
It may be necessary to detach cable clamps or guides when replacing the cable.

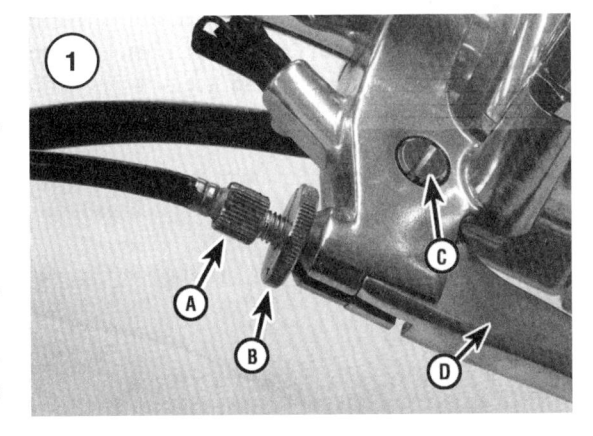

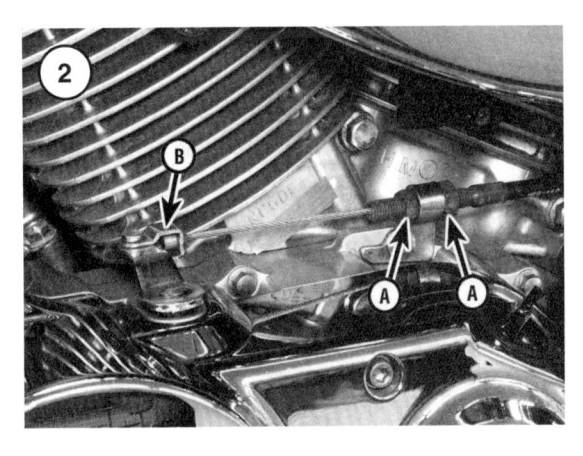

8. Remove the old clutch cable by pulling it from the top (upper cable end). Continue until the cable is removed from the frame, leaving the attached piece of string in its mounting position.
9. Untie the string from the old cable and discard the old cable.
10. Tie the string onto the bottom end of the new clutch cable.
11. Slowly pull the string and cable to install the cable along the path of the original clutch cable. Continue until the new cable is correctly routed beside the engine and through the frame. Untie and remove the string.
12. Visually check the entire length of the clutch cable. Make sure there are no kinks or sharp bends. Reroute the cable if necessary.
13. Lubricate the clutch hand lever bore and pivot bolt before attaching the cable. Note the following:
   a. Remove the nut, clutch pivot bolt (C, **Figure 1**) and lever.
   b. Clean and dry the pivot bolt and clutch lever bore. Inspect the operating areas (**Figure 3**) for excessive wear or damage.
   c. Clean the recess in the clutch perch of all old grease
   d. Lubricate the pivot bolt with grease and reinstall the lever, pivot bolt and nut. Tighten the pivot bolt to 1 N.m (8.9 in.-lb.). Then hold the pivot bolt and tighten the nut to 6 N.m (53 in.-lb.). Operate the clutch lever to make sure there is no binding.
14. Connect the upper cable end to the clutch lever.
15. Reattach the lower end of the clutch cable as shown in **Figure 2**.
16. Adjust the clutch cable as described in Chapter Three.

RIGHT CRANKCASE COVER

Removal

NOTE
The clutch and right crankcase covers can be removed with the stock exhaust system mounted on the engine. The following procedure shows the covers with the exhaust system removed for clarity.

NOTE
If the right crankcase cover is being removed to troubleshoot a clutch or other engine-related problem, drain the oil into an open, clean container so that it can be examined for debris and small, broken parts.

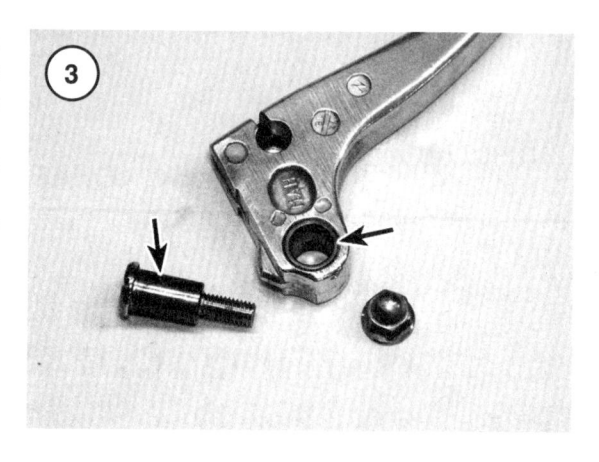

1. Drain the engine oil (Chapter Three).
2. Remove the bolts (A, **Figure 4**) and the clutch cover (B).
3. Clean the right crankcase cover and the area around the cover to prevent dirt from entering the engine.
4. Loosen the clutch cable adjuster locknut (A, **Figure 1**) and adjuster (B) at the handlebar.

NOTE
Different length bolts are used to retain the right crankcase cover. Note and record the length and location of the bolts during removal.

5. Loosen the clutch cable adjuster nuts (A, **Figure 2**) and disconnect the cable from the release arm (B).
6. Remove the bolts securing the crankcase cover (**Figure 5**) to the engine. If necessary, lightly tap the cover to loosen it from the engine. Do not pry the cover off. If the cover is difficult to remove, thread a small knock puller (**Figure 6**) into one of the threaded holes in the cover. Then, operate the puller to break the cover loose. A knock puller can be assembled using a long 6-mm bolt, fender washers and a large socket.
7. Remove the dowel pins (**Figure 7**).
8. Note the pushrod (A, **Figure 8**) installed in the bearing.

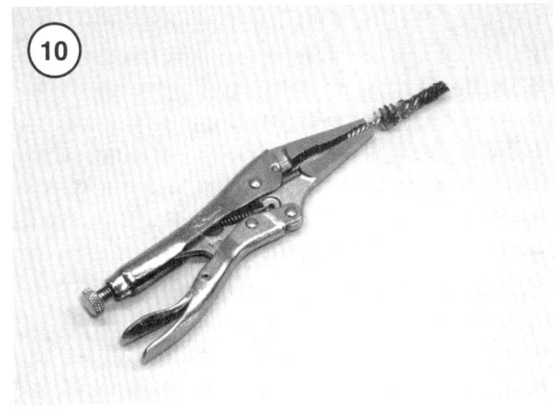

CLUTCH AND EXTERNAL SHIFT MECHANISM

9. Service the clutch release lever as described in this chapter.

Installation

NOTE
When cleaning the crankcase gasket surfaces and threaded holes, cover the clutch and other components with plastic to prevent cleaning material and debris from entering the engine.

1. Remove all sealer residue from the crankcase and cover surfaces. Do not damage the seal surfaces or leaks will occur. Also remove the CKP sensor grommets (A, **Figure 9**) and clean the grommets and their mounting area on the crankcase.
2. Flush the crankcase threaded bolt holes of all oil and sealer residue with an aerosol electrical contact cleaner. If necessary, remove stubborn gasket residue from the threaded holes with a stiff brush. A suitable size rifle cleaning brush mounted in a pair of locking pliers works well for this **(Figure 10)**. Then dry the bolt holes with compressed air.
3. Remove all sealer residue from the cover mounting bolts. Then clean and dry the bolts.

4. Make sure the pushrod (A, **Figure 8**) is in place in the cover.

NOTE
The gasket surfaces, threaded bolt holes and bolts must be clean and dry before applying the gasket sealer.

5. Apply HondaBond 4, Yamabond No. 4 or ThreeBond 1104 to the crankcase cover gasket surface (A, **Figure 11**). Make sure to apply sealer to the CKP sensor cover's grommet seating area (B, **Figure 11**).
6. Apply sealer to the grommets (A, **Figure 9**). Then make sure the CKP sensor wiring harness is properly routed so that it will not interfere with the cover (B, **Figure 9**) and install the grommets (A) firmly into the crankcase.
7. Install the two dowel pins **(Figure 7)**.
8. Install the right crankcase cover, making sure the cover seats flush against the crankcase and grommets. Then install the mounting bolts and tighten in a crossing pattern and in several steps.

NOTE
Allow the gasket sealer to set before filling the engine with oil and starting the engine. Refer to the sealer manufacturer's recommendations.

9. Refill the engine with the recommended type and quantity of oil as described in Chapter Three.
10. Reattach the lower end of the clutch cable (B, **Figure 2**).
11. Install the clutch cover (B, **Figure 4**) and tighten the mounting bolts (A) to 10 N.m (89 in.-lb.).
12. Adjust the clutch (Chapter Three).
13. After starting the engine, check the cover for oil leaks.

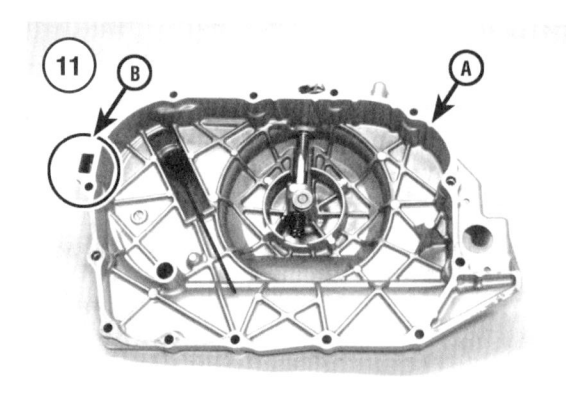

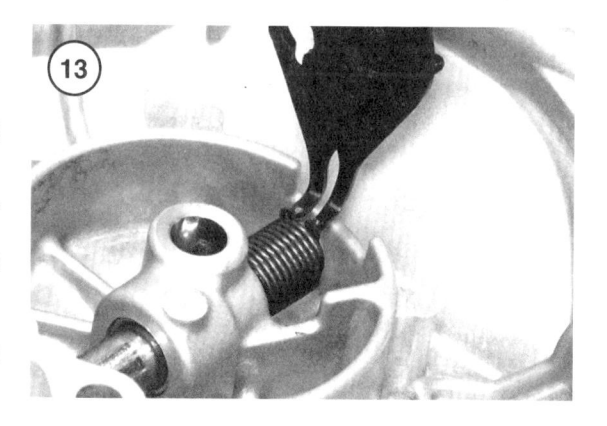

CLUTCH RELEASE LEVER

The clutch release lever is mounted in the right crankcase cover. The assembly consists of the clutch release lever, pushrod and return spring. The clutch cable and clutch lever at the handlebar are part of the system and are covered under *Clutch Cable* in this chapter.

Clutch disengagement is accomplished via the clutch release lever assembly. The clutch cable is attached between the clutch lever at the handlebar and the clutch release lever at the engine. Operating the clutch lever causes the release lever to rotate. This forces the pushrod against the pressure plate, thereby compressing the clutch springs and releasing the clutch plates where they can rotate freely. This system requires routine adjustment (Chapter Three) to compensate for cable stretch and friction plate wear.

Removal/Inspection/Installation

Refer to **Figure 12**.
1. Remove the right crankcase cover as described in this chapter.
2. Remove the pushrod (A, **Figure 8**).
3. Remove the snap ring **(Figure 13)**, return spring (B, **Figure 8**) and slide the clutch release lever from the cover.
4. Remove and discard the seal **(Figure 14)**.
5. Remove any burrs or roughness from the release lever and pushrod operating areas. These areas must be smooth.

CLUTCH AND EXTERNAL SHIFT MECHANISM

6. Reinstall the release lever and turn it by hand. If there is any binding or roughness, inspect the release lever and cover bore bushings for damage.
7. If the seal was leaking, inspect the seal operating area at the top of the release lever. If wear grooves are visible, replace the lever.
8. Lubricate the lips of a new seal with grease. Install the seal with its closed side facing out.
9. Install the release lever. Hook the lower spring end into the groove in the lever (**Figure 15**). Hook the upper spring end against the cover boss as shown in C, **Figure 8**.
10. Install the snap ring into the lever groove (D, **Figure 8**). Make sure it seats in the groove completely.
11. Turn the release lever so the flat surface on the lever is visible through the pushrod hole in the cover. Then lubricate the pushrod with oil and install it in the hole (A, **Figure 8**).
12. Reinstall the right crankcase cover as described in this chapter.

CLUTCH

The clutch is a multi-plate type that operates immersed in the engine oil supply. The clutch assembly consists of a clutch housing, pressure plate and clutch hub (**Figure 16**). A set of drive and driven

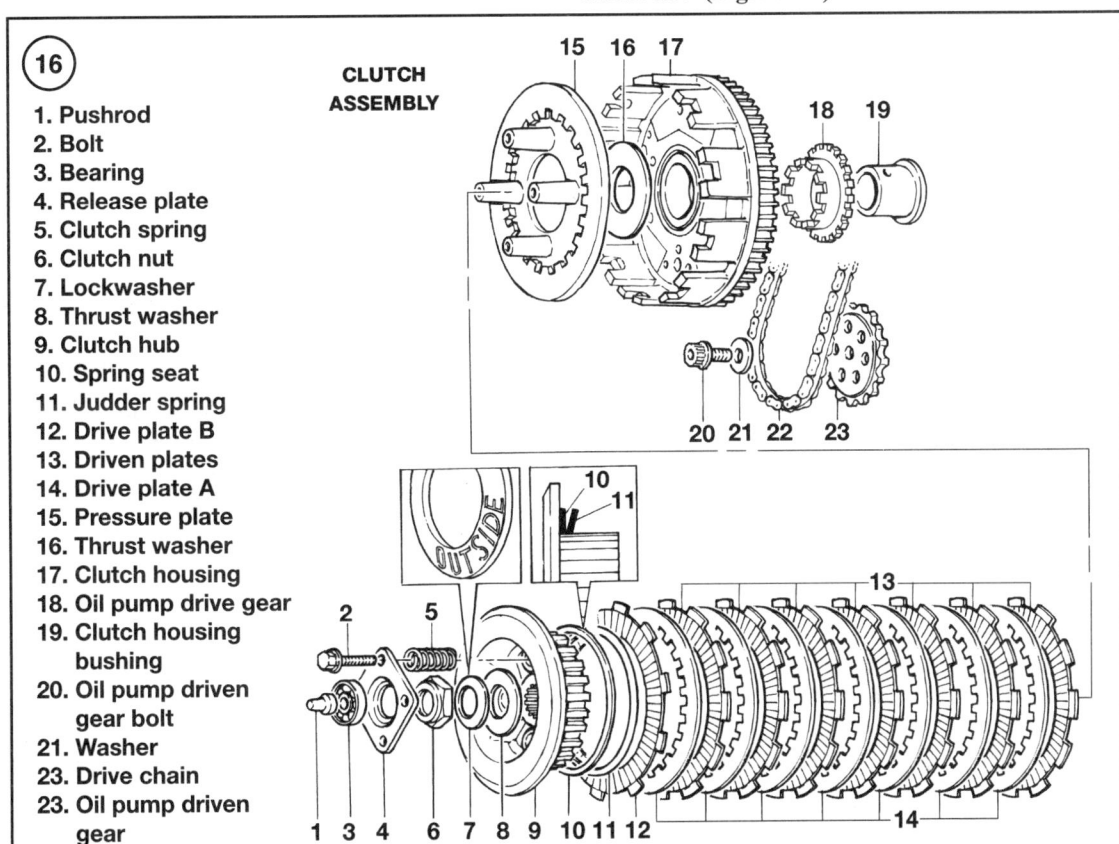

CLUTCH ASSEMBLY

1. Pushrod
2. Bolt
3. Bearing
4. Release plate
5. Clutch spring
6. Clutch nut
7. Lockwasher
8. Thrust washer
9. Clutch hub
10. Spring seat
11. Judder spring
12. Drive plate B
13. Driven plates
14. Drive plate A
15. Pressure plate
16. Thrust washer
17. Clutch housing
18. Oil pump drive gear
19. Clutch housing bushing
20. Oil pump driven gear bolt
21. Washer
23. Drive chain
23. Oil pump driven gear

clutch plates are alternately locked to the two parts. The gear-driven clutch housing is mounted on the transmission mainshaft. The housing receives power from the primary drive gear mounted on the crankshaft. The housing then transfers the power via the drive plates to the driven clutch plates locked to the clutch hub. The clutch hub is splined to the mainshaft and powers the transmission. The clutch plates are engaged by springs and disengaged by a cable-actuated release lever assembly.

Component Identification

Refer to **Figure 16**.

Some clutch parts have two or more common names, which can cause confusion. The following lists the terms used in the manual and often used alternatives:
1. Drive plate—Clutch disc, clutch plate, friction disc, friction plate and outer plate.
2. Driven plate—Aluminum plate, clutch disc, clutch plate, inner plate and steel plate.
3. Clutch plates—When clutch plates are used in the text, it refers to both the drive and driven plates as an assembly.
4. Clutch hub—Clutch boss, clutch center and inner hub.
5. Clutch housing—Clutch basket, clutch outer, outer clutch hub and primary driven gear basket.

Tools

A clutch holder and collar set or its equivalent is required to hold the clutch when removing and tightening the clutch nut. The tool consists of a holder plate with eight slots and a set of holder collars and nuts. The slots in the holder plate are marked with the numbers 4, 5 or 6. These numbers correspond to the number of springs used in the clutch assembly. Before using the tool, set the holder collars to the No. 6 holder slot position. The tools include:
   a. Honda holder plate (part No. 07HGB-001010B [**Figure 17**]).
   b. Honda holder collars (part No. 07HGB-001020B [**Figure 17**]).

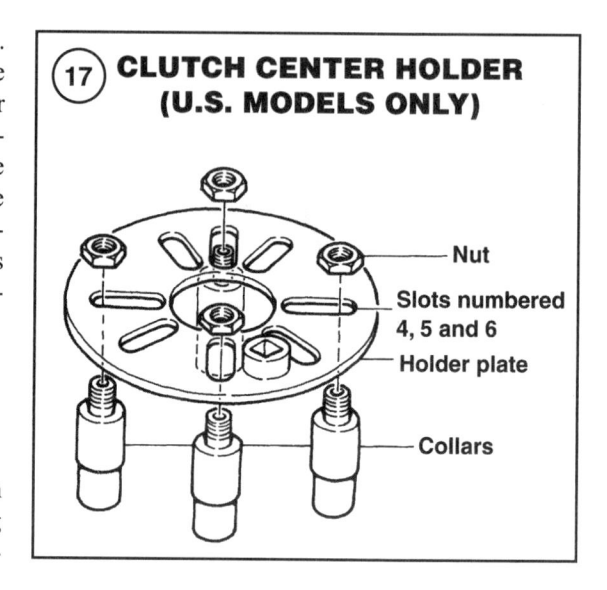

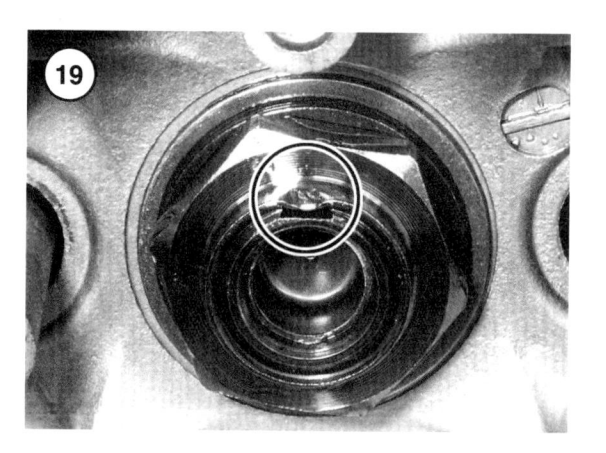

Removal/Disassembly

Refer to **Figure 16**.
1. Remove the right crankcase cover as described in this chapter.
2. If removing the oil pump driven sprocket, loosen the sprocket bolt (A, **Figure 18**) before removing the clutch.
3. Using a crisscross pattern, gradually and evenly loosen the clutch spring bolts (B, **Figure 18**).
4. Remove the release plate and bearing (C, **Figure 18**) and clutch springs.
5. Using a hand grinder with a small grinding stone, carefully grind the staked portion of the clutch nut (**Figure 19**) to *weaken* it. Do not grind through the nut or the mainshaft will be damaged.
6. Hold the clutch with the holder plate (**Figure 20**). Then hold the holder plate with a 1/2 in. drive break-

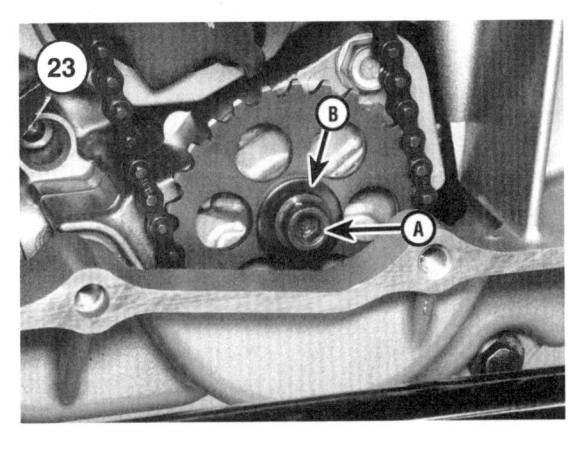

CLUTCH AND EXTERNAL SHIFT MECHANISM

er bar and loosen the clutch nut. Remove the tool.
7. Remove the clutch nut and discard it.
8. Remove the lockwasher and thrust washer.

NOTE
*To remove the clutch plate assembly without disturbing their alignment, install one or two clutch springs, flat washers and clutch spring bolts as shown in A, **Figure 21**.*

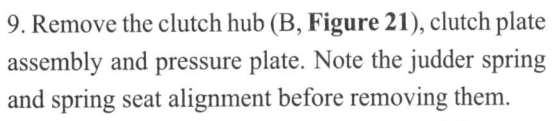

9. Remove the clutch hub (B, **Figure 21**), clutch plate assembly and pressure plate. Note the judder spring and spring seat alignment before removing them.
10. Remove the thrust washer (A, **Figure 22**).
11. Remove the clutch housing (B, **Figure 22**).
12. Remove the oil pump driven sprocket bolt (A, **Figure 23**) and washer (B).
13. Remove the drive sprocket (A, **Figure 24**), driven sprockets (B) and chain (C) as a set.
14. Remove the clutch housing bushing (**Figure 25**).
15. Inspect all parts as described in this section.

Assembly/Installation

Refer to **Figure 16**.

> **NOTE**
> *If removed, install the external shift mechanism and primary drive gear before installing the clutch.*

1. Lubricate all clutch parts and the mainshaft with engine oil before reassembly. Do not lubricate the mainshaft or clutch nut threads.
2. Install the clutch housing bushing **(Figure 25)** onto the mainshaft.
3. Clean the oil pump shaft threads **(Figure 26)** and oil pump driven sprocket bolt threads of all threadlock residue and then spray with contact cleaner and allow to dry. The shaft and bolt threads must be clean and dry.
4. Assemble the oil pump drive and driven sprockets and chain as follows:
    a. Position the drive sprocket with its bosses facing up (A, **Figure 27**).
    b. Position the driven sprocket (B, **Figure 27**) with its IN mark or circle marks facing down. This side will face the engine when the sprocket is installed. If there is no IN mark or circle marks on the sprocket, position the sprocket with its flat side facing up. The flat side will face away from the engine when the sprocket is installed.
    c. Connect both sprockets with the drive chain (C, **Figure 27**).
5. Install the drive sprocket, driven sprocket and chain as shown in **Figure 24**.

> **NOTE**
> *The oil pump driven sprocket bolt will be installed and tightened after the clutch housing is installed.*

6. Assemble the drive plates, driven plates, clutch hub and pressure plate as follows:

> **NOTE**
> *Lubricate the clutch plates with clean engine oil prior to assembly. If installing new drive plates, soak them in engine oil for approximately ten minutes.*

   a. Install drive plate B **(Figure 28)** onto the clutch hub. The inside diameter of drive plate B is larger than the inside diameter of drive plate A **(Figure 29)**.
   b. Install the spring seat and judder spring as noted during removal.

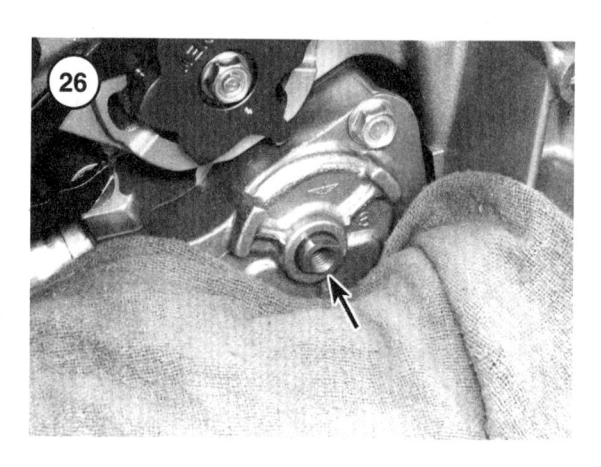

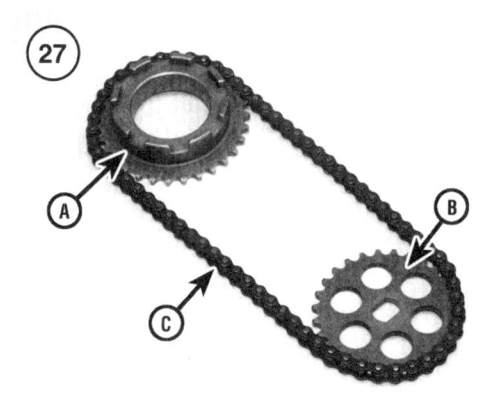

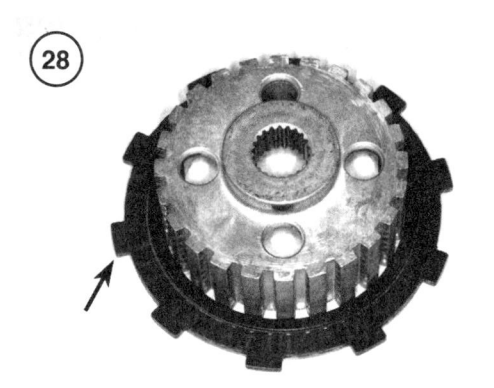

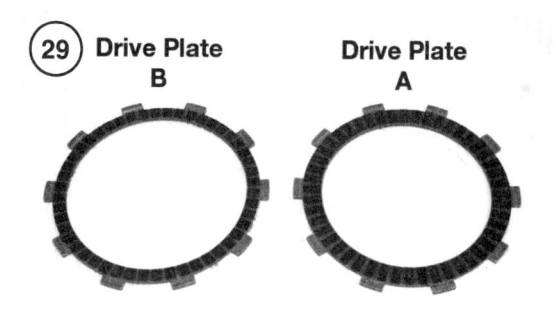

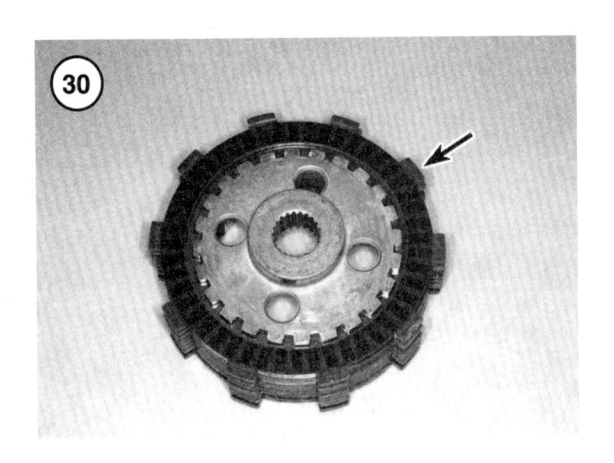

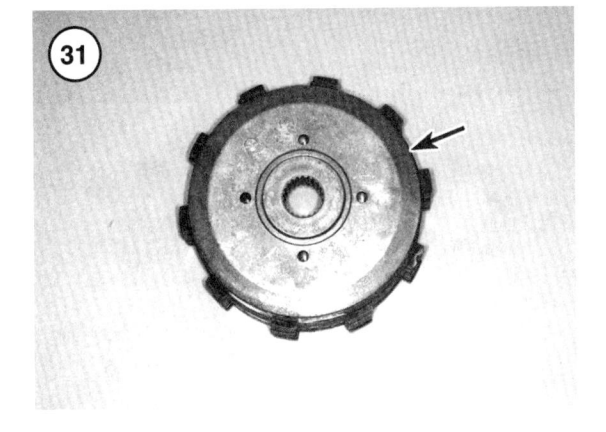

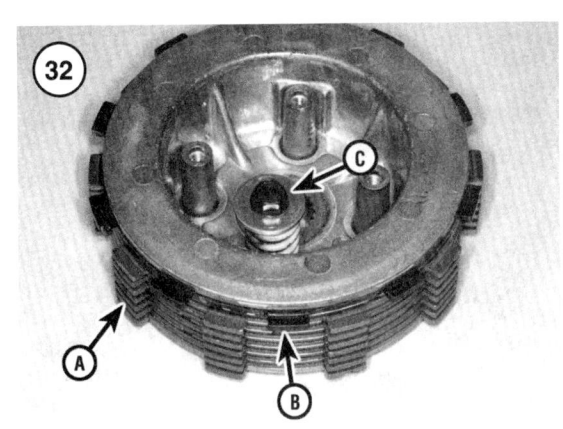

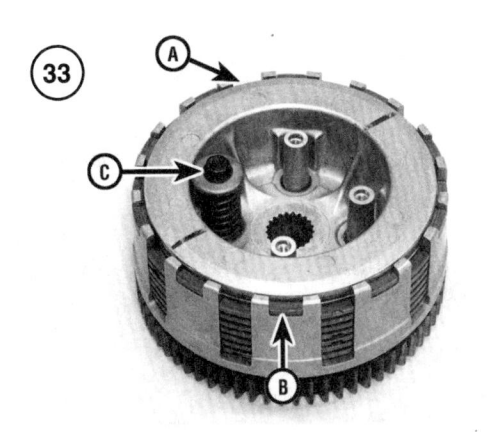

CLUTCH AND EXTERNAL SHIFT MECHANISM

NOTE
The driven plates are stamped during manufacturing and have one flat side and one chamfered side. Install all of the driven plates with the flat side facing in the same direction (either in or out).

c. Install a driven plate next to drive plate B.
d. Install a drive plate A. Continue to install a driven plate, then a drive plate, alternating them until all are installed. The last plate installed is a drive plate (**Figure 30**).
e. Install the pressure plate (**Figure 31**) and seat it against the final drive plate. Make sure the splines on the drive plate align with the clutch hub splines.
f. Align all of the drive plate A tabs as shown in A, **Figure 32**.
g. Turn and offset the tabs on drive plate B as shown in B, **Figure 32**.
h. Install a clutch spring, flat washer and clutch spring bolt (C, **Figure 32**) to keep the assembly together during installation. Do not tighten the bolt.
i. Install the clutch hub assembly (A, **Figure 33**) into the clutch housing to align the plates. Make sure the tabs on drive plate B fit into the shallow grooves in the clutch housing as shown in B, **Figure 33**.
j. When all of the drive plates are properly installed and aligned in the clutch housing, tighten the bolt (C, **Figure 33**) to hold the plates in position. Then remove the clutch hub assembly (**Figure 34**) from the clutch housing and set aside until final assembly.

7. Align the grooves (A, **Figure 35**) in the clutch housing with the bosses (B) on the oil pump drive sprocket and install the clutch housing (B, **Figure 22**).
8. Apply a medium strength threadlock onto the

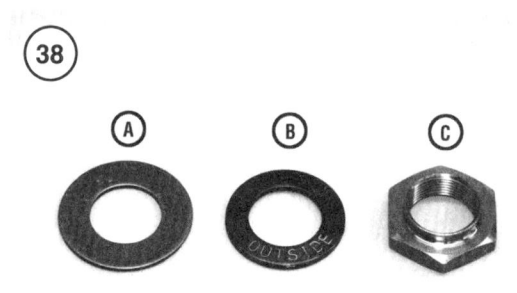

oil pump driven sprocket bolt threads. Install the washer (B, **Figure 23**) and bolt (A) and tighten to 15 N.m (11 ft.-lb.).

9. Install the thrust washer (A, **Figure 22**).
10. Install the clutch hub assembly (A, **Figure 36**) into the clutch housing, making sure the tabs on drive plate B fit into the shallow grooves in the clutch housing **(Figure 37)**. It may be necessary to turn the mainshaft to align the clutch hub and mainshaft splines.

NOTE
*If it is difficult to install the clutch assembly into the clutch housing, install a second clutch spring, washer and bolt (B, **Figure 36**) to square the assembly and help it to align and fit into the clutch housing.*

11. Install the thrust washer (A, **Figure 38**), lockwasher (B) and clutch nut (C) as follows:
 a. Install the thrust washer (A, **Figure 39**) and set it against the clutch hub.
 b. Install the lockwasher with its OUTSIDE mark facing out (B, **Figure 39**).
 c. Lubricate the clutch nut threads and its seating surface with engine oil, then install it with its shoulder side facing out (A, **Figure 40**). Tighten the locknut finger-tight.

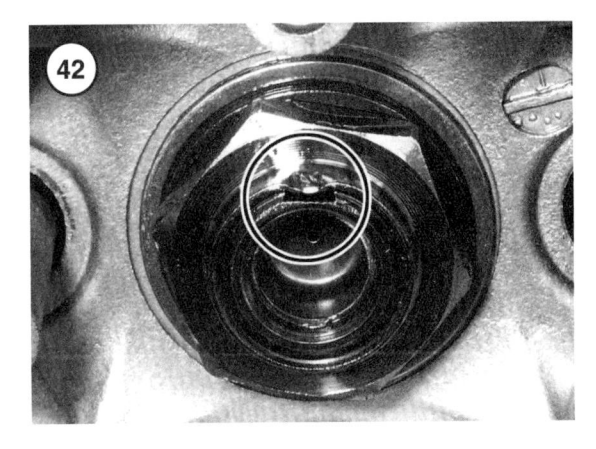

CLUTCH AND EXTERNAL SHIFT MECHANISM

15. Install the clutch springs and postion the release plate (A, **Figure 43**) over the springs with bearing side facing out. Install the bolts (B, **Figure 43**).

16. Following a crossing pattern, tighten the clutch spring bolts (B, **Figure 43**) in several steps until secure. Then tighten the bolts to 12 N.m (106 in.-lb.).

NOTE
If merely loosened and not removed during dissassembly, make sure the oil pump driven sprocket mounting bolt has been tightened at the time (this section).

17. Install the pushrod and right crankcase cover as described in this chapter.

18. Shift the transmission into NEUTRAL and start the engine. After the engine warms up, pull the clutch in and shift the transmission into first gear. Note the following:
   a. If the clutch makes a loud grinding and spinning noise immediately after the engine is started and then stops, either the engine oil level is low or the new friction plates were not lubricated with oil.
   b. If the motorcycle jumps forwards and stalls, or creeps with the transmission in gear and the clutch pulled in, recheck the clutch adjustment. If the clutch will not adjust properly, either the clutch cable or the friction plates are excessively worn. Replace them.
   c. If the clutch adjustment is okay but the clutch is not working correctly, the clutch may have been assembled incorrectly or there is a broken part in the clutch. Disassemble the clutch as described in this chapter and inspect the parts.

12. Remove the bolt(s), washer(s) and clutch spring(s) (B, **Figure 40**) installed previously.

13. With the same tool arrangement used during *Removal/Disassembly*, tighten the clutch nut (**Figure 41**) to 128 N.m (94 ft.-lb.).

CAUTION
*Stake the locknut into the groove in the mainshaft. Do **not** stake the locknut against any other part of the mainshaft*

14. Use a punch and stake a portion of the clutch nut shoulder into the groove in the mainshaft (**Figure 42**).

Inspection

Always replace drive plates, driven plates or clutch springs as a set if individual components do not meet specifications (**Table 1**). If parts show other signs of wear or damage, replace them, regardless of their specifications. Individual parts that operate together or against each other must be inspected for the same wear and damage. When the damage on one part is more apparent than on the other part, replace both parts to prevent premature wear to the new part.

1. Clean and dry all parts.
2. Inspect the clutch springs for cracks and blue discoloration (heat damage).

3. Measure the free length of each clutch spring **(Figure 44)**.
4. Inspect each drive plate **(Figure 45)** as follows:
   a. The friction material on the drive plates are bonded to an aluminum plate for warp resistance and durability. Inspect the friction material for excessive or uneven wear, cracks and other damage.
   b. The tabs on the drive plates operate along the grooves in the clutch housing. Inspect the tabs for rough spots, notches or other damage. The tabs must slide smoothly in the clutch housing grooves; otherwise, clutch drag will result.
   c. Measure the thickness of each drive plate **(Figure 46)** at different locations around the plates. Note that the thickness specification in **Table 1** for drive plates A (quantity 7) and drive plate B (quantity 1) are different. Drive plate B also has a larger inside diameter than drive plate A **(Figure 45)**.
5. Inspect each driven plate **(Figure 47)** as follows:
a. Inspect the driven plates for cracks, damage or color change. Overheated driven plates will have a blue discoloration.
b. Check the driven plates for an oil glaze buildup. Remove by lightly sanding both sides of each plate with 400 grit sandpaper placed on a surface plate or a flat piece of glass.
c. The driven plate's inner teeth mesh with the clutch hub splines. Inspect the teeth for rough spots or other damage. The teeth must slide smoothly on the splines; otherwise, clutch drag will result.
d. Place each driven plate on a flat surface, such as a piece of glass, and check for warp at several places with a feeler gauge **(Figure 47)**. If any plate is warped more than specified, replace the entire set of driven plates. Do not replace only one or two plates, as clutch operation will be unsatisfactory.
6. Inspect the spring seat and judder spring for roughness and other damage. Lay them on a flat surface and check for warpage.
7. Check the clutch housing (A, **Figure 48**) as follows:

NOTE
Filing the clutch housing slots is only a temporary fix as removing metal from the sides of the slots provides more room for the plates to move around and start wearing new grooves.

   a. Inspect the clutch housing slots for notches, grooves or other damage. Repair minor damage with a file. If damage is excessive, replace the clutch housing. The slots must be smooth so the drive plates can move freely when the clutch is released.

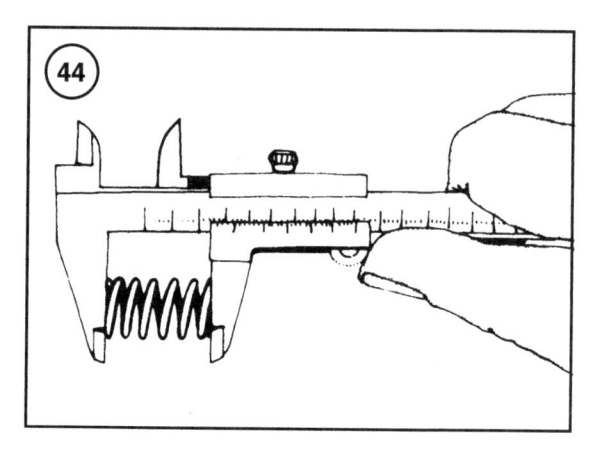

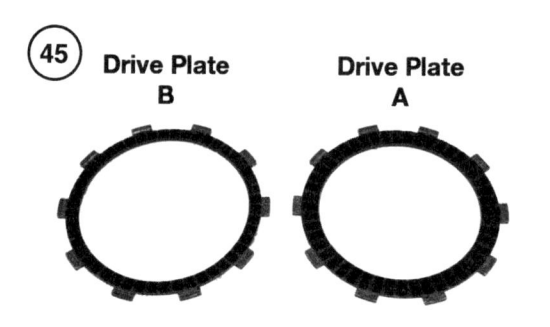

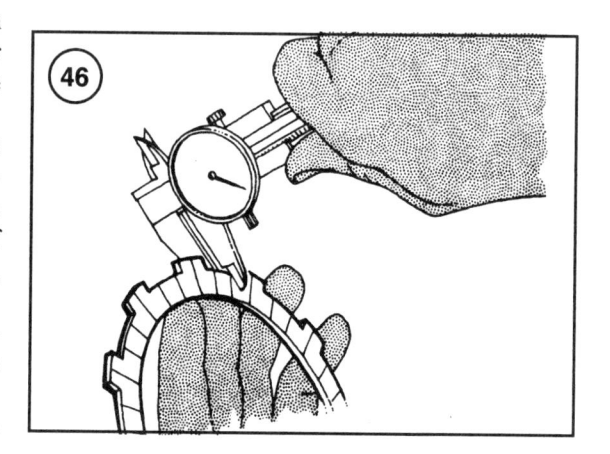

CLUTCH AND EXTERNAL SHIFT MECHANISM

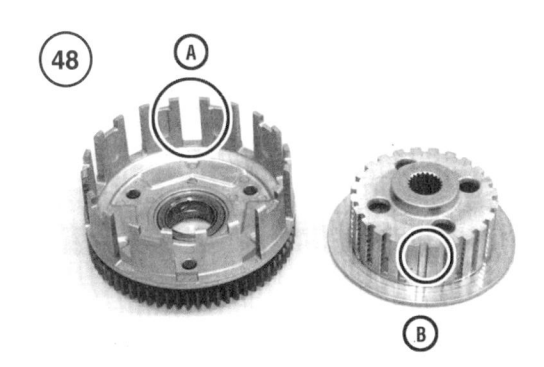

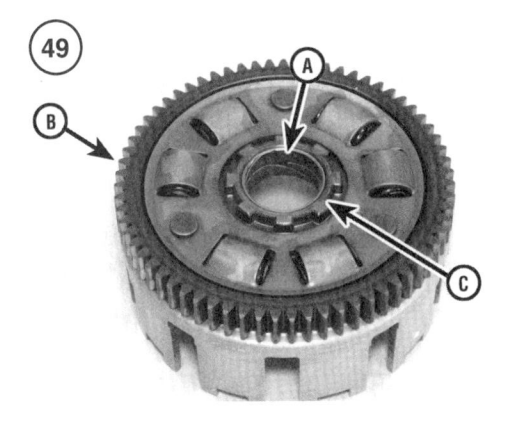

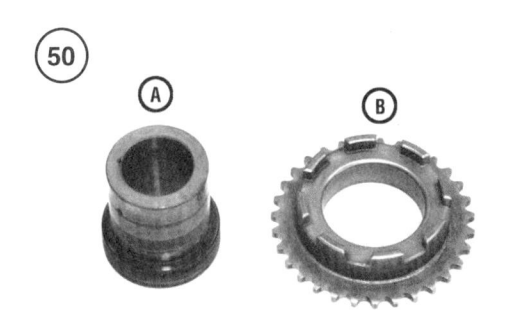

b. Check the clutch housing bore (A, **Figure 49**) for scoring, cracks, pitting or other damage.

c. Measure the clutch housing bore inside diameter.

d. Check the primary driven gear (B, **Figure 49**) for excessive wear, pitting, chipped gear teeth or other damage.

e. Hold the clutch housing and try to turn the primary driven gear (B, **Figure 49**). Replace the clutch housing if there is any free play.

f. Check the grooves (C, **Figure 49**) in which the bosses on the oil pump drive sprocket operate. Replace the clutch housing if these grooves are cracked, enlarged or otherwise damaged.

8. Check the clutch housing bushing (A, **Figure 50**) as follows:

a. Check the bushing for scoring, cracks and other damage.

b. Measure the clutch housing bushing inside diameter.

c. Measure the clutch housing bushing outside diameter.

9. Subtract the clutch housing bushing outside diameter from the clutch housing bore inside diameter to determine the clutch housing-to-clutch housing bushing clearance.

10. Check the oil pump drive sprocket (B, **Figure 50**) as follows:

a. Check the sprocket teeth for cracks and other damage.

b. Check the sprocket bore for scoring, cracks and other damage.

c. Check the sprocket bosses for cracks and other damage.

d. Measure the sprocket inside diameter.

11. Subtract the oil pump drive sprocket outside diameter from the clutch housing bore inside diameter to determine the oil pump drive sprocket-to-clutch housing bushing clearance.

12. Measure the mainshaft outside diameter at the clutch housing bushing operating area **(Figure 51)**. If out of specification, disassemble the crankcase (Chapter Five) and replace the mainshaft (Chapter Seven). If the measurement is within specification, continue the procedure.

13. Subtract the clutch housing bushing inside diameter from the mainshaft outside diameter to determine the clutch housing bushing-to-mainshaft clearance.

14. Check the oil pump driven sprocket (B, **Figure 27**) for cracks and other damage.

15. Inspect the links on the oil pump drive chain. If any are worn or damaged, or there are any cracks along the chain, replace the chain and both sprockets.

16. Check the clutch hub as follows:
    a. Inspect the outer splines (B, **Figure 48**) for rough spots, grooves or other damage. Repair minor damage with a file or oil stone. If the damage is excessive, replace the clutch hub. The splines must smooth so the driven plates can move freely when the clutch is released.
    b. Check the hub's clutch plate surface for cracks and other damage.
17. Check the pressure plate as follows:
    a. Inspect for damaged spring towers.
    b. Inspect the plate surface area for cracks, grooves and other damage.
18. Inspect the release plate bearing (C, **Figure 43**). Turn the bearing inner race and check for any roughness, catching or binding. Replace the bearing if damage is noted. The outer bearing race should fit in the plate bore without any play.
19. Check the pushrod for damage.

PRIMARY DRIVE GEAR

The primary drive gear is mounted on the crankshaft and positioned behind the CKP sensor rotor.

Tools

A small gear tooth holding tool is required to hold the primary gears when loosening and tightening the primary drive gear mounting nut and the clutch housing locknut. Use one of the following:
1. Gear holder, 2.5 (Honda part No. 07724-0010100 or 07724-001A100 [A, **Figure 52**]), or its equivalent.
2. Make a tool by cutting a section of gear teeth (B, **Figure 52**) from a discarded gear.

> *NOTE*
> *The section of gear shown in B, **Figure 52** was cut from a discarded transmission gear using a Dremel and cut-off wheel.*

Removal

1. Remove the right crankcase cover as described in this chapter.
2. Remove the CKP sensor mounting bolts (A, **Figure 53**), then remove the grommets (B, **Figure 53**) from the crankcase.
3. If the clutch was removed, temporarily install the clutch housing bushing, oil pump drive sprocket and clutch housing (this chapter).
4. Place a gear holding tool in mesh with the primary drive and driven gears (A, **Figure 54**).

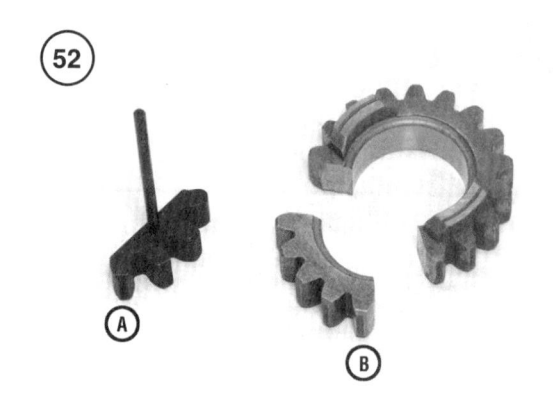

> *CAUTION*
> *Do not hold the gears with metal washers or screwdrivers. This could chip or break a gear tooth.*

5. Loosen the primary drive gear mounting bolt (B, **Figure 54**). Remove the tool from between the gears.
6. Remove the clutch housing as described in this chapter.
7. Remove the primary drive gear bolt and washer

CLUTCH AND EXTERNAL SHIFT MECHANISM

(B, **Figure 54**), CKP sensor rotor (A, **Figure 55**) and primary drive gear (A, **Figure 56**).

Installation

1. Install the primary drive gear assembly by aligning the wide groove in the gear with the wide spline on the crankshaft (B, **Figure 56**) and with its OUT mark facing out (C).
2. Install the CKP sensor rotor by aligning the wide groove in the rotor with the wide spline on the crankshaft (B, **Figure 55**).
3. Lubricate the primary drive gear bolt threads, washer and seating surfaces with engine oil.
4. Install the bolt and washer (A, **Figure 57**) and tighten hand-tight.
5. Temporarily install the clutch housing bushing, oil pump drive sprocket and clutch housing (B, **Figure 57**) as described in this chapter.
6. Lock the primary drive and primary driven gears with the same tool used during removal (C, **Figure 57**).
7. Tighten the primary drive gear mounting bolt to 88 N.m (65 ft.-lb.).
8. Remove the gear holding tool (C, **Figure 57**).
9. Install the CKP sensor:
   a. Clean the threads on the CKP sensor bolts and mounting holes of any oil and threadlock residue.
   b. Apply a medium-strength threadlock onto the CKP sensor bolt threads.
   c. Install the CKP sensor and tighten the mounting bolts (A, **Figure 53**) securely.
   d. Install the CKP sensor grommets and reposition the wiring harness as described under *Right Crankcase Cover* in this chapter.
10. Install the clutch (this chapter), if removed.
11. Install the right crankcase cover as described in this chapter.

Inspection

1. Clean and dry all parts.
2. Inspect the primary drive gear (A, **Figure 58**) for broken or chipped teeth and worn or damaged splines. If the teeth are damaged, check the teeth on the primary driven gear (clutch housing) for the same conditions.
3. Inspect the CKP sensor (B, **Figure 58**) for broken or chipped pickup teeth and worn or damaged splines.

EXTERNAL SHIFT MECHANISM

The external shift mechanism consists of the shift pedal and linkage, shift shaft, stopper arm assembly and cam plate assembly. These parts can be removed with the engine mounted in the frame. Access to the shift drum and shift forks requires removing the engine and splitting the crankcase (Chapter Five).

Shift Linkage Adjustment

The shift pedal is connected to the shift arm with an adjustable linkage rod **(Figure 59)**. Turning the linkage rod will raise or lower the shift pedal.
1. Remove the left crankcase rear cover (Chapter Seventeen).
2. Loosen the locknut **(Figure 60)** at each end of the shift linkage rod.
3. Turn the linkage rod **(Figure 59)** to raise or lower the shift pedal. Then hold the linkage rod with a pair of locking pliers and tighten both locknuts.
4. Recheck the pedal position.
5. Install the left crankcase rear cover (Chapter Seventeen).

Shift Pedal and Linkage

Removal/installation

1. Remove the left crankcase rear cover (Chapter Seventeen).

> **CAUTION**
> *Before removing the shift pedal and linkage assembly, note the routing position of the sidestand switch wiring harness in relation to the shift rod (Figure 59) so the assembly can be correctly installed without damaging the wiring harness.*

> **NOTE**
> *If the shift arm is tight, check the splines for bending or other damage.*

2. Remove the pinch bolt (A, **Figure 61**) and slide the shift arm off the shift shaft.
3. Remove the shift pedal pivot bolt **(Figure 62)**, washer and shift pedal and linkage assembly.
4. Inspect and lubricate the assembly as described in this section.
5. Installation is the reverse of removal. Note the following:
   a. Lubricate the pivot bolt shoulder with waterproof grease.
   b. Tighten the shift pedal pivot bolt **(Figure 62)** to 39 N.m (29 ft.-lb.).

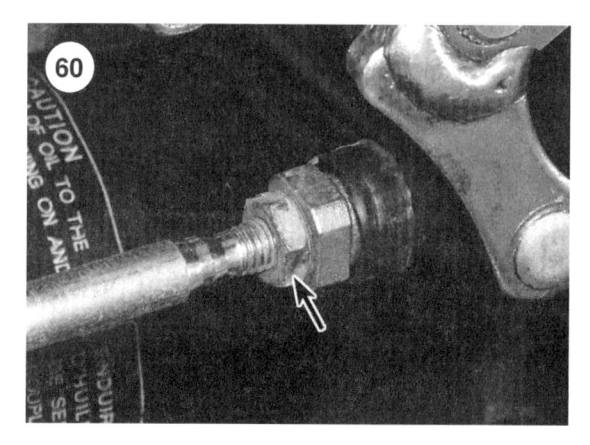

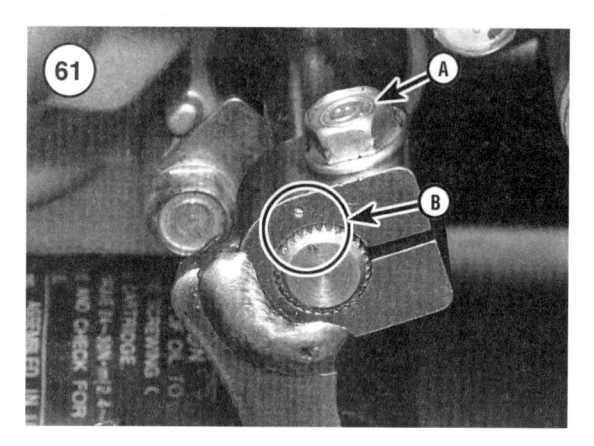

CLUTCH AND EXTERNAL SHIFT MECHANISM

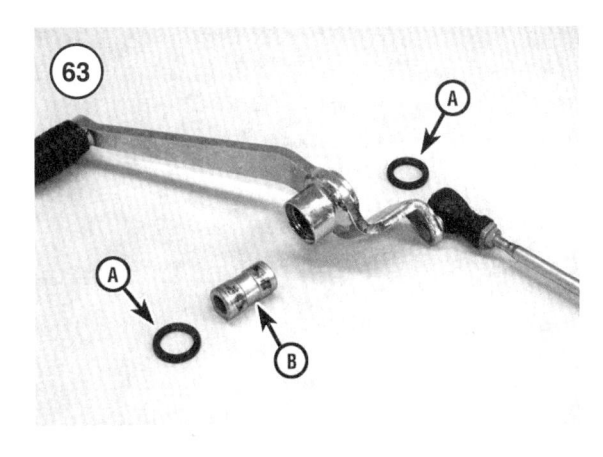

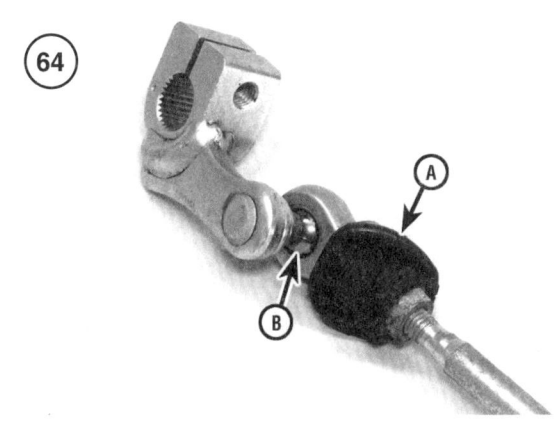

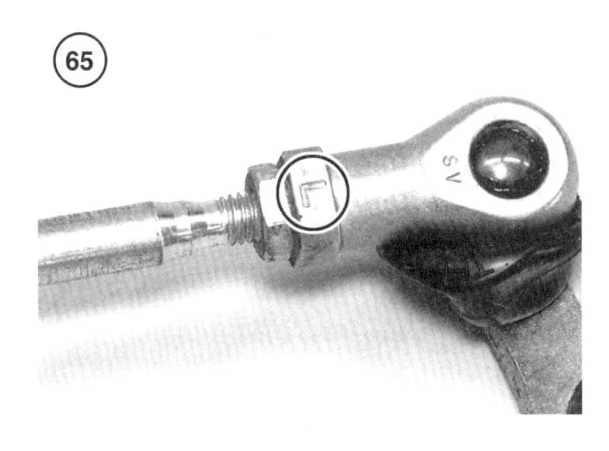

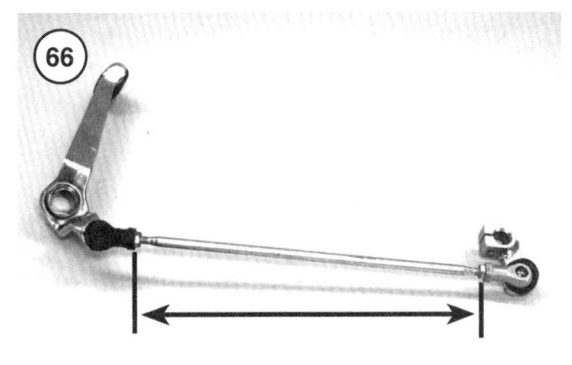

c. Install the shift arm by aligning its index mark with the index mark on the shift shaft (B, **Figure 61**).
d. Tighten the shift arm pinch bolt (A, **Figure 61**) to 12 N.m (106 in.-lb.).
e. Check the shift pedal position and operation.

Inspection and lubrication

1. Remove the seals (A, **Figure 63**) and collar (B) from the shift pedal.
2. Clean and dry all pivot and bore surfaces.
3. Replace the seals (A, **Figure 63**) if leaking or damaged.
4. Inspect the shift rod joint rubber boots (A, **Figure 64**) for cracks, deterioration and other damage. The boots can be replaced separately.
5. Inspect the pivot joints (B, **Figure 64**) for any binding or roughness and replace if necessary.

> *NOTE*
> *The rear pivot joint uses left hand threads and is identified by its L mark (Figure 65).*

6. To service the shift linkage assembly:
   a. Measure the distance between the locknuts (**Figure 66**) and record it so the shift rod can be reassembled to its original length.
   b. Loosen the locknuts and remove the pivot joints and rubber boots.
   c. Replace worn or damaged parts.
   d. Reinstall the rubber boots and pivot joints on the shift rod.
   e. Adjust the shift rod to the length recorded during disassembly and tighten the locknuts securely.

7. Lubricate the collar (B, **Figure 63**) and the collar bore in the shift pedal with waterproof grease. Install the collar into the shift pedal and then install the two seals.
8. If the shift linkage assembly was disassembled, perform the *Shift Linkage Adjustment* in this section.

Shift Mechanism

Removal

1. Remove the left crankcase rear cover (Chapter Seventeen).
2. Remove the right crankcase cover and clutch as described in this chapter.

> *CAUTION*
> *Before removing the shift pedal and linkage assembly, note the routing position of the sidestand switch wiring harness*

202   **CHAPTER SIX**

in relation to the shift rod (**Figure 59**) so the assembly can be correctly installed without damaging the wiring harness.

NOTE
If the shift arm is tight, check the splines for bending or other damage.

3. Remove the pinch bolt (A, **Figure 61**) and slide the shift arm off the shift shaft.

NOTE
*If troubleshooting a shifting problem, inspect the external shift mechanism before removing it. Refer to **Gearshift Linkage** in Chapter Two.*

NOTE
*If the stopper arm is not going to be removed, lift it with a screwdriver (A, **Figure 67**) when removing the shift pawl/shift shaft (B).*

4. Lift the shift pawl (B, **Figure 67**) and remove the shift shaft from the crankcase.
5. Remove the bolt (A, **Figure 68**) and washer, stopper arm (B), bushing and return spring (C).

NOTE
*If it is necessary to remove the cam plate (D, **Figure 68**), refer to **Shift Drum Inspection** in **Internal Shift Mechanism** in Chapter Seven.*

6. If the shift shaft oil seal is leaking, replace it as described in this section.

Installation

1. Install the stopper arm assembly (**Figure 69**) as follows:
   a. Assemble the stopper arm (**Figure 70**).
   b. Install the stopper arm as shown (B, **Figure 68**). Finger-tighten the stopper arm pivot bolt. Make sure the spring (C, **Figure 68**) is aligned around the bolt and against the crankcase.
   c. Pry the stopper arm up with a screwdriver (A, **Figure 67**), then release it. When properly installed, the stopper arm will move and return under spring tension. If the stopper arm will not move, the spring is pinched against the pivot bolt. Loosen the bolt and center the spring on the bolt's shoulder. Tighten the bolt (A, **Figure 68**) securely.
2. Install the shift shaft as follows:
   a. Clean the shift shaft oil seal with a rag, then lubricate the seal lips with grease.

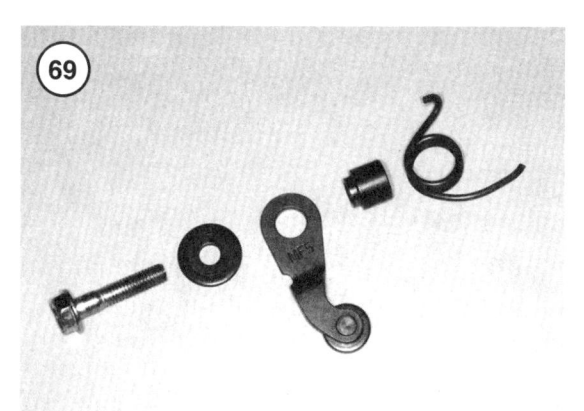

CLUTCH AND EXTERNAL SHIFT MECHANISM

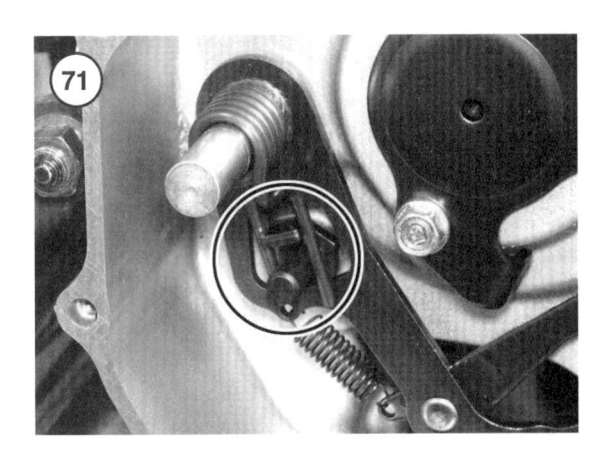

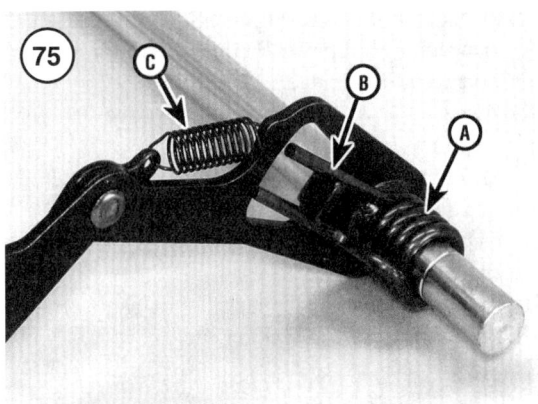

b. Slide the shaft slowly through the engine and seal, then engage the return spring with the spring pin **(Figure 71)** while raising the stopper arm (A, **Figure 67**) so the shift pawl (B, **Figure 67**) can engage shift drum.

3. Install the shift arm by aligning its index mark with the index mark on the shift shaft (B, **Figure 61**).
4. Tighten shift arm pinch bolt (A, **Figure 61**) to 12 N.m (106 in.-lb.).
5. Support the motorcycle with the rear wheel off the ground and check the shifting as follows:
    a. Mount a plate across the crankcase to hold the shift shaft in position **(Figure 72)**.
    b. Slowly turn the rear wheel and shift the transmission into first gear, then shift to neutral and the remaining forward gears.

NOTE
Figure 73 shows the cam plate in neutral.

   c. If the shift shaft moves and then locks in place, the return spring **(Figure 71)** may not be centered on the spring pin.
   d. If the transmission over-shifts, check for an incorrectly assembled stopper arm assembly.
   e. If the transmission does not shift properly, check for an incorrectly installed shift shaft return spring. Then check the shift lever assembly.

6. Install the right crankcase cover and clutch assembly (this chapter).
7. Install the left crankcase rear cover (Chapter Seventeen).

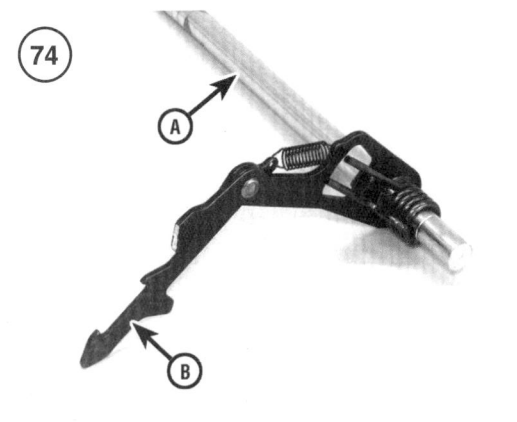

Inspection

Worn or damaged shift linkage components will cause missed shifts and wear to the transmission gears, shift forks and shift drum. Replace parts that show excessive wear or damage.

1. Clean and dry the parts.
2. Inspect the shift shaft assembly as follows:
    a. Inspect the splines for damage.

b. Inspect the shaft (A, **Figure 74**) straightness.

c. Inspect the shift pawl (B, **Figure 74**) for excessive wear or damage.

d. Inspect the return spring (A, **Figure 75**) for wear and fatigue cracks.

e. Make sure the return spring arms are centered across the shift shaft arm (B, **Figure 75**).

f. Inspect the tension spring (C, **Figure 75**) for damage.

3. Check for a loose or damaged shift shaft return spring pin **(Figure 71)**. Tighten the pin to 23 N.m (17 ft.-lb.).

4. Check the stopper arm **(Figure 69)** assembly for:

a. Weak or damaged spring. Check spring for cracks.

b. Bent, cracked or damaged stopper arm. Check roller for flat spots.

c. Damaged stopper arm pivot bolt.

Shift Shaft Oil Seal Replacement

The oil seal can be replaced with the engine installed in the frame.

1. Remove the shift shaft as described under *Shift Mechanism* in this section.

2. On 2006 and later models, remove the bolt (A, **Figure 76**) and oil seal stopper plate (B).

3. Carefully pry the oil seal out of the crankcase **(Figure 77)**. Do not let the end of the pry tool contact the crankcase surface. Discard the seal.

4. Clean the crankcase bore and check for cracks and other damage.

5. Apply grease onto the lip of the new seal and install the seal with its flat side facing out (C, **Figure 76**). Install the seal until it bottoms in its bore.

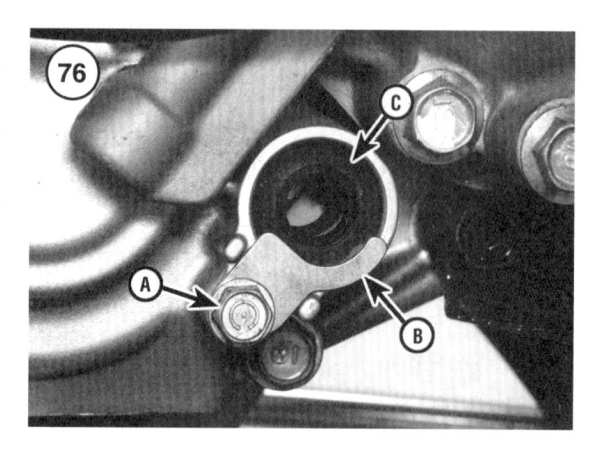

6. On 2006 and later models, install the stopper plate and tighten its mounting bolt to 13 N.m (115 in.-lb.).

7. Reverse Step 1.

CLUTCH AND EXTERNAL SHIFT MECHANISM

Table 1 CLUTCH SPECIFICATIONS

	New mm (in.)	Service limit mm (in.)
Clutch housing bushing		
Inside diameter	21.991-22.016 (0.8658-0.8668)	22.03 (0.867)
Outside diameter	31.959-31.975 (1.2582-1.2589)	31.92 (1.257)
Clutch housing bushing-to-mainshaft clearance	0.011-0.049 (0.0004-0.0019)	0.08 (0.003)
Clutch housing bore inside diameter	32.000-32.025 (1.2598-1.2608)	32.09 (1.263)
Clutch housing-to-clutch housing bushing clearance	0.025-0.066 (0.0010-0.0026)	0.18 (0.007)
Clutch spring free length	45.3 (1.78)	43.9 (1.73)
Drive plate thickness		
Plate A	2.62-2.78 (0.103-0.109)	2.3 (0.09)
Plate B	2.92-3.08 (0.115-0.121)	2.6 (0.10)
Driven clutch plate warpage	--	0.30 (0.012)
Mainshaft outside diameter at clutch housing bushing	21.967-21.980 (0.8648-0.8654)	21.95 (0.864)
Oil pump drive sprocket inside diameter	32.025-32.145 (1.2608-1.2655)	32.16 (1.266)
Oil pump drive sprocket-to-clutch housing bushing clearance	0.050-0.186 (0.0020-0.0073)	0.23 (0.009)

Table 2 TORQUE SPECIFICATIONS

	N.m	in.-lb.	ft.-lb.
CKP sensor mounting bolt (1)	--		
Clutch cover mounting Allen bolt			
2004-2009 Aero models	9.8	87	--
All other models	10	88	--
Clutch housing locknut (2, 3)			
2004-2009 Areo models	127	--	94
All other models	128	--	94
Clutch lever pivot bolt nut	6	53	--
Clutch lever pivot bolt	1	8.8	--
Clutch Lifter plate/clutch spring bolt	12	106	--
Oil pump driven sprocket bolt (1)	15	--	11
Primary drive gear mounting bolt (2)	88	--	65
Shift arm pinch bolt	12	106	--
Shift pedal pivot bolt	39	--	29
Shift shaft return spring pin	23	--	17
Shift shaft oil seal stopper plate mounting bolt			
2006-2013	13	115	--

1. Apply a medium strength threadlock onto bolt threads.
2. Lubricate threads and flange surface with engine oil.
3. Install a new locknut and stake in place.

Notes

CHAPTER SEVEN

TRANSMISSION AND INTERNAL SHIFT MECHANISM

This chapter describes disassembly and reassembly of the transmission shafts and internal shift mechanism. Remove the engine and separate the crankcase halves to service these components as described in Chapter Five.

Table 1 lists transmission gear ratios. Service specifications are listed in **Tables 2-5**. **Tables 1-5** are at the end of the chapter.

TRANSMISSION

Operation

The engine is equipped with a 5-speed constant-mesh transmission. The gears on the mainshaft (A, **Figure 1**) are meshed with the gears on the countershaft (B). Each pair of meshed gears represents one gear ratio. For each pair of gears, one of the gears is splined to its shaft, while the other gear freewheels on its shaft.

Next to each freewheeling gear is a gear that is splined to the shaft. Each splined gear can slide on the shaft and lock onto the freewheeling gear, making that gear ratio active. Any time the transmission is in gear, one pair of meshed gears are locked to their shafts, and that gear ratio is selected. All other meshed gears are freewheeling, making those ratios inoperative.

To engage and disengage the various gear ratios, the splined gears are moved by shift forks. The shift forks are guided by grooves in the shift drum, which is operated by a shift pedal and linkage assembly. As the transmission is upshifted and downshifted, the shift drum rotates and guides the forks to engage and disengage pairs of gears on the transmission shafts.

Removal/Installation

Refer to *Crankcase* in Chapter Five.

Service

1. Clean and dry the mainshaft and countershaft assemblies before disassembly.
2. As a shaft is disassembled, store the individual parts in a divided container, or make an identification mark on each part to indicate orientation. Use marking pens, such as those made by Speedry, to identify gears and other metal parts. These pens can be purchased in different colors at tool and bearing supply stores.
3. Install *new* snap rings during reassembly. The snap rings will fatigue and distort when they are removed. Do not reuse them, although they may appear to be in good condition.
4. To install new snap rings without distorting them, use the following installation technique:
   a. Open the new snap ring with a pair of snap ring pliers while holding the back of the snap ring with a pair of pliers **(Figure 2)**.
   b. Slide the snap ring down the shaft and seat it into its correct groove.
   c. This technique can also be used to remove the snap rings from a shaft once they are free from their grooves.

208

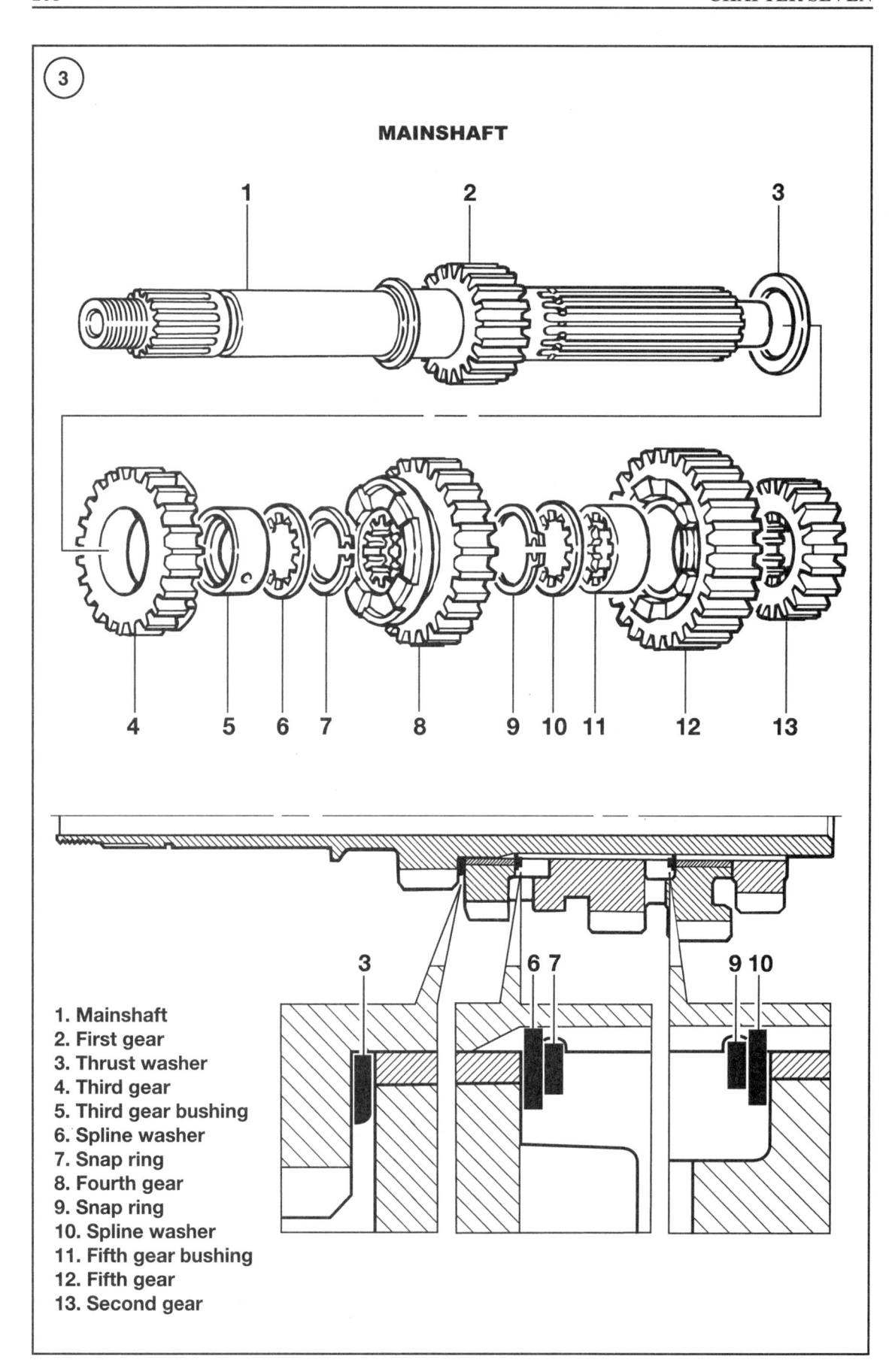

CHAPTER SEVEN

③ MAINSHAFT

1. Mainshaft
2. First gear
3. Thrust washer
4. Third gear
5. Third gear bushing
6. Spline washer
7. Snap ring
8. Fourth gear
9. Snap ring
10. Spline washer
11. Fifth gear bushing
12. Fifth gear
13. Second gear

TRANSMISSION AND INTERNAL SHIFT MECHANISM

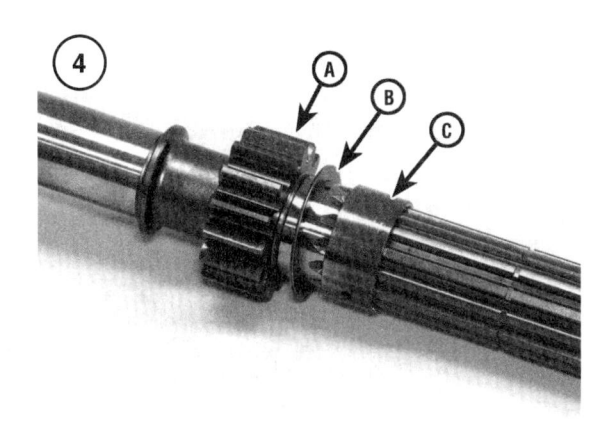

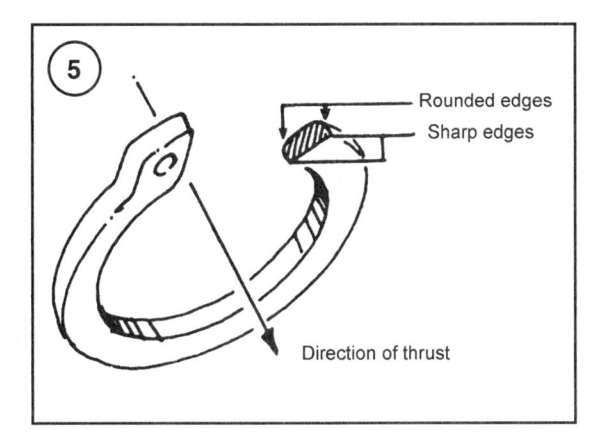

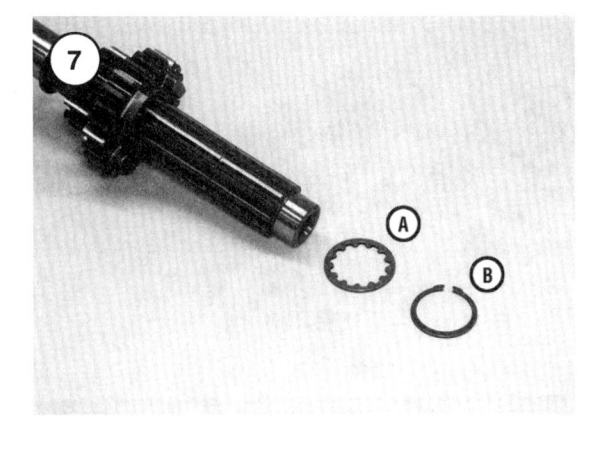

Mainshaft

Refer to **Figure 3**.

Disassembly

1. Remove second gear.
2. Remove fifth gear and its bushing.
3. Remove the spline washer and snap ring.
4. Remove fourth gear.
5. Remove the snap ring and spline washer.
6. Remove third gear and its bushing.
7. Remove the thrust washer.

NOTE
First gear is an integral part of the mainshaft.

8. Inspect the mainshaft assembly as described under *Transmission Inspection* in this chapter.

Assembly

Before beginning assembly, have two *new* snap rings on hand. Throughout the procedure, the orientation of parts is made in relationship to first gear (A, **Figure 4**), which is part of the mainshaft.

CAUTION
*The snap rings and washers used on the transmission shafts are stamped types. One edge is rounded, while the other is sharp (**Figure 5**). The side with the sharp edge, referred to as the flat side, must be installed so the flat side always faces away from the part producing the thrust. The sharp edge prevents the snap ring from rolling out of its groove when thrust is applied.*

1. Clean and dry all parts before assembly. Lubricate all parts with engine oil.
2. Install the thrust washer (B, **Figure 4**) with its flat side facing toward first gear.
3. Install the third gear bushing (C, **Figure 4**) and seat it against the thrust washer.
4. Install third gear so the gear dogs (**Figure 6**) face *away* from first gear.
5. Install the spline washer (A, **Figure 7**) and *new* snap ring (B) onto the shaft. Note the following:
   a. The flat side of both parts must face *away* from first gear.

CAUTION
*Install the snap ring so its ends align with a groove in the splines (**Figure 8** and **Figure 9**).*

   b. The snap ring must seat in the groove in the shaft.

210 **CHAPTER SEVEN**

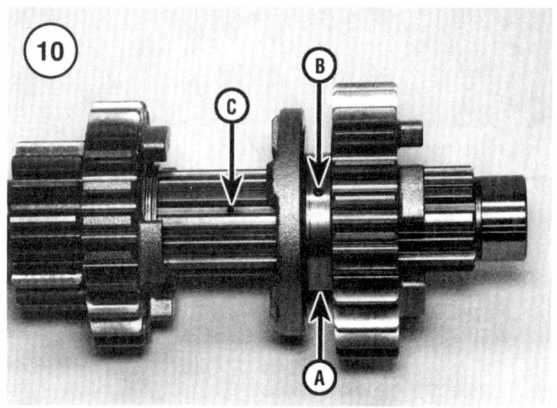

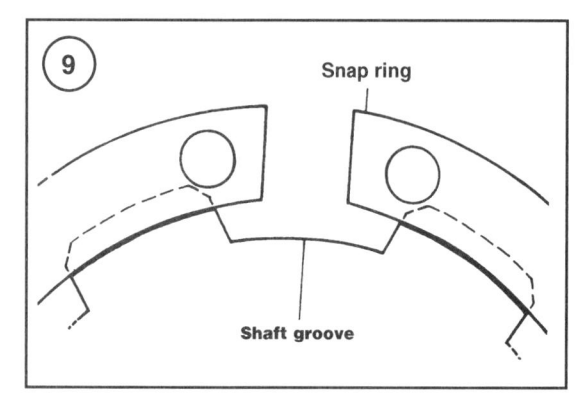

6. Install fourth gear (A, **Figure 10**), so the shift fork groove faces *toward* first gear. Align the oil hole in the gear (B) with the oil hole in the shaft (C).

CAUTION
Install the snap ring so its ends align with a groove in the splines (**Figure 9**).

7. Install a *new* snap ring (A, **Figure 11**) and spline washer (B) onto the shaft. The flat sides of both parts must face *toward* first gear. The snap ring must seat in the groove in the shaft.
8. Install the fifth gear spline bushing and seat it against the spline washer. Align the oil hole in the bushing (A, **Figure 12**) with the oil hole in the shaft (B).

9. Install fifth gear (**Figure 13**), so the gear dogs face *toward* first gear.
10. Install second gear (**Figure 14**) and seat it against fifth gear. Both sides of second gear are symmetrical and can be installed either way. If the gear was marked before removal, install it facing in its original position.
11. Refer to **Figure 15** for the correct placement of the mainshaft gears.
12. Wrap a heavy rubber band around the end of the shaft to prevent parts from sliding off the shaft. Wrap and store the assembly until it is ready for installation into the crankcase.

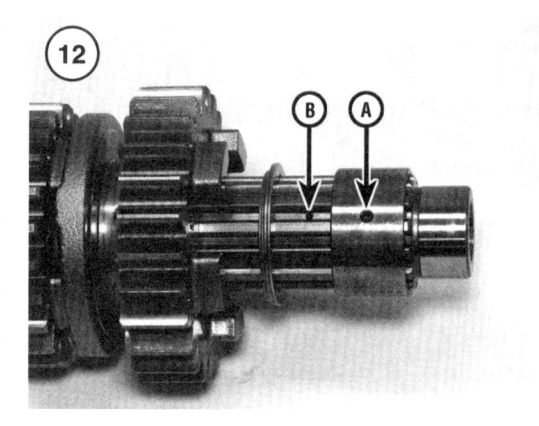

TRANSMISSION AND INTERNAL SHIFT MECHANISM

Countershaft

Refer to **Figure 16**.

Disassembly

1. Remove the thrust washer and the final drive gear.
2. Remove first gear and its bushing.
3. Remove the spline washer and snap ring.
4. Remove third gear.
5. Remove the snap ring and splined washer.
6. Remove fourth gear and its bushing.
7. Remove lockwasher No. 1 and lockwasher No. 2.
8. Remove fifth gear.
9. Remove the thrust washer, second gear, bushing and thrust washer.

COUNTERSHAFT

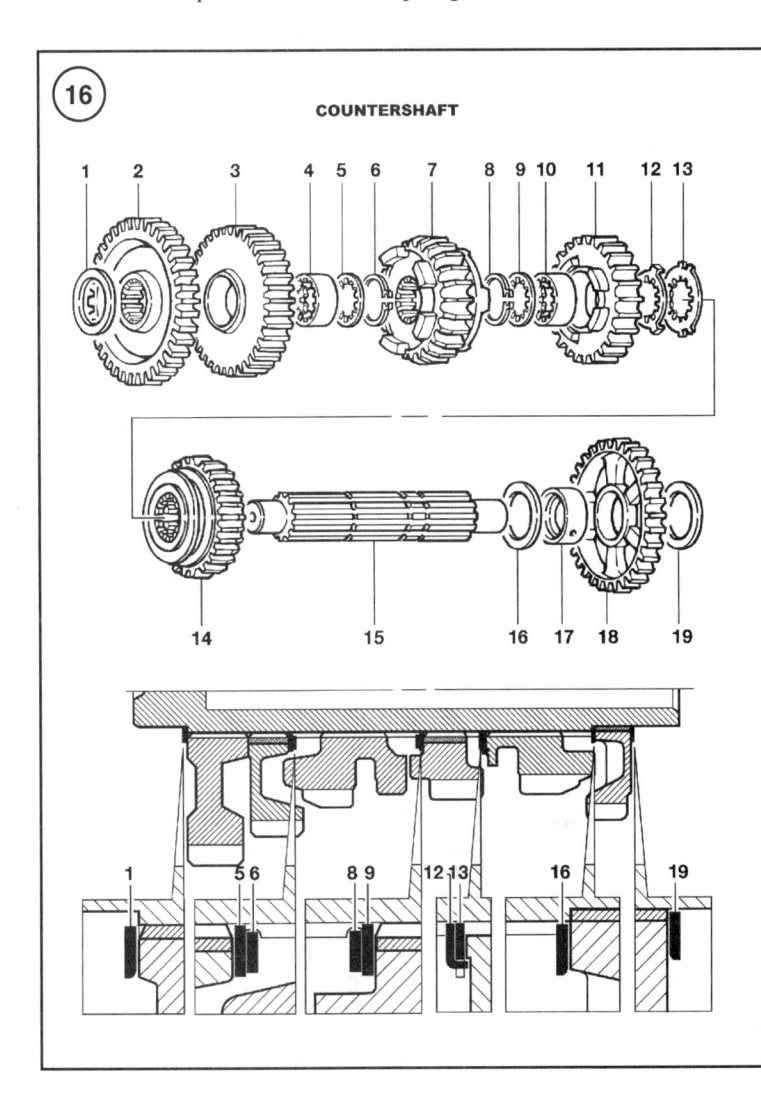

1. Thrust washer
2. Final drive gear
3. First gear
4. First gear bushing
5. Spline washer
6. Snap ring
7. Third gear
8. Snap ring
9. Spline washer
10. Fourth gear bushing
11. Fourth gear
12. Lockwasher No. 2
13. Lockwasher No. 1
14. Fifth gear
15. Countershaft
16. Thrust washer
17. Second gear bushing
18. Second gear
19. Thrust washer

CHAPTER SEVEN

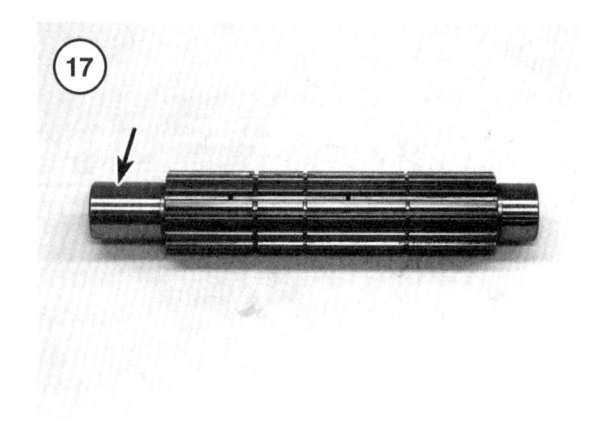

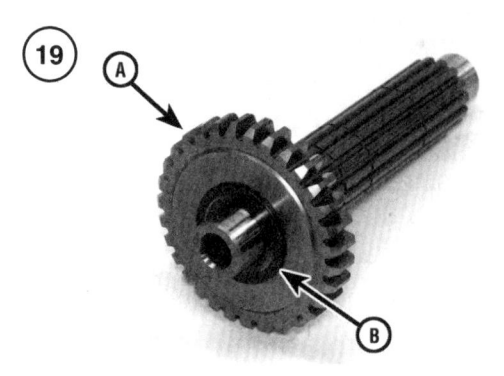

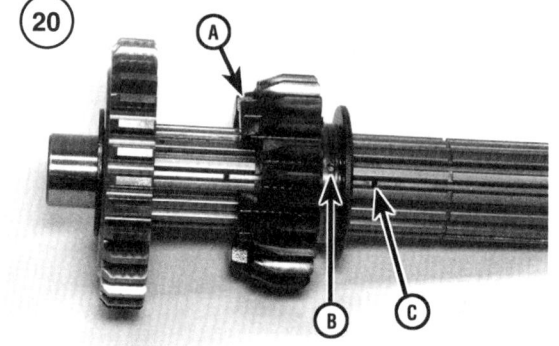

Assembly

Before beginning assembly, have two *new* snap rings on hand. Throughout the procedure, the orientation of many parts is made in relationship to the countershaft's second gear end **(Figure 17)**.
1. Clean and dry all parts before assembly. Lubricate all parts with engine oil.
2. Refer to **Figure 18** and perform the following:
   a. Install the thrust washer (A, **Figure 18**) and seat it against the shaft shoulder. The washer's flat side must face toward the shaft's shoulder.
   b. Install the second gear bushing (B, **Figure 18**) and seat it against the thrust washer.
   c. Install second gear (C, **Figure 18**) with its closed side facing out (A, **Figure 19**).
   d. Install the thrust washer (D, **Figure 18**) and seat it against second gear (B, **Figure 19**). The washer's flat side must face away from second gear.
3. Install fifth gear so the gear dogs (A, **Figure 20**) face *toward* second gear. Align the oil hole in the gear (B) with the oil hole in the counter shaft (C).
4. Install and lock lockwasher No. 1 (A, **Figure 21**) and lockwasher No. 2 (B) as follows:

TRANSMISSION AND INTERNAL SHIFT MECHANISM

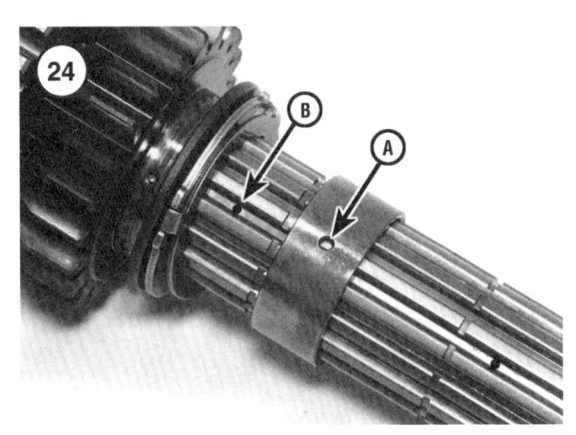

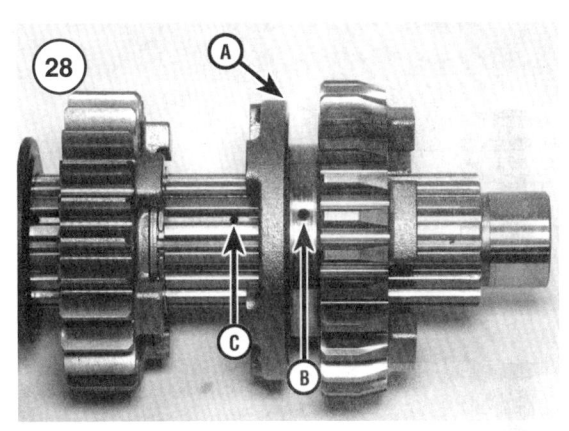

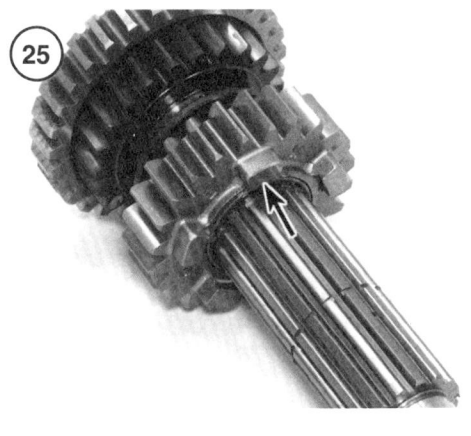

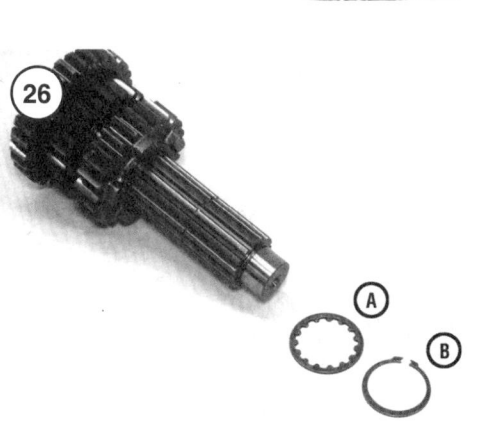

a. Install lockwasher No. 1 (A, **Figure 22**). Rotate the lockwasher in either direction so the tangs on the lockwasher engage the raised grooves in the countershaft and the lockwasher cannot slide off.
b. Install lockwasher No. 2 (B, **Figure 22**) by aligning its bent tabs (C) with the slots (D) in lockwasher No. 1.
c. Lockwasher No. 2 must engage and seat flush against lockwasher No. 1 **(Figure 23)**.

5. Install the fourth gear bushing by aligning its oil hole (A, **Figure 24**) with the oil hole in the shaft (B).
6. Install fourth gear **(Figure 25)** so the gear dogs face *away* from second gear.

CAUTION
Install the snap ring so its ends align with a groove in the splines (Figure 27).

7. Install the spline washer (A, **Figure 26**) and a *new* snap ring (B) onto the shaft. The flat sides of both parts must face *away* from second gear.
8. Install third gear so its slider groove (A, **Figure 28**) faces *toward* second gear. Align the oil hole in the gear (B) with the oil hole in the shaft (C).

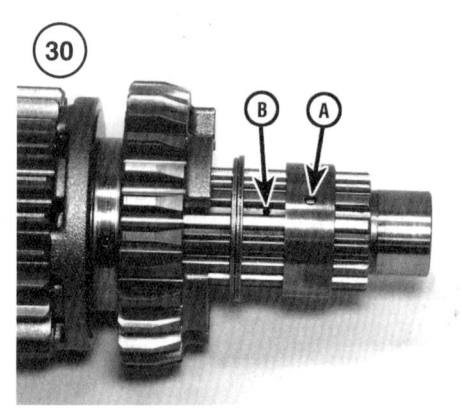

CAUTION
Install the snap ring so its ends align with a groove in the splines.

9. Install a new snap ring (A, **Figure 29**) and spline washer (B) onto the shaft. The flat sides of both parts must face toward second gear. The snap ring must seat in the groove in the shaft.
10. Install the first gear bushing (**Figure 30**) and seat it against the spline washer. Align the oil hole in the bushing (A, **Figure 30**) with the oil hole in the shaft (B).
11. Install first gear so its flat side (**Figure 31**) faces away from second gear.
12. Install the final drive gear, so the side with the larger shoulder (A, **Figure 32**) faces away from second gear.
13. Install the thrust washer (B, **Figure 32**) and seat against the final drive gear. The flat side of the washer must face *away* from the second gear.
14. Refer to **Figure 33** for the correct placement of the countershaft gears.
15. Wrap a heavy rubber band around both ends of the shaft to prevent parts from sliding off the shaft. Wrap and store the assembly until it is ready for installation into the crankcase.

TRANSMISSION INSPECTION

When measuring the transmission components in this section, compare the actual measurements to the specifications in **Table 2** and **Table 3**. Replace parts that are worn or damaged.

NOTE
Maintain the alignment of the transmission components when cleaning and inspecting the parts in this section.

1. Inspect the mainshaft (**Figure 34**) and countershaft (**Figure 35**) for:
   a. Worn or damaged splines (A, **Figure 34** and A, **Figure 35**)

TRANSMISSION AND INTERNAL SHIFT MECHANISM

Figure 34

Figure 35

Figure 36 — Gear dog hole, Gear dog

Figure 37 — GEAR INSIDE DIAMETER

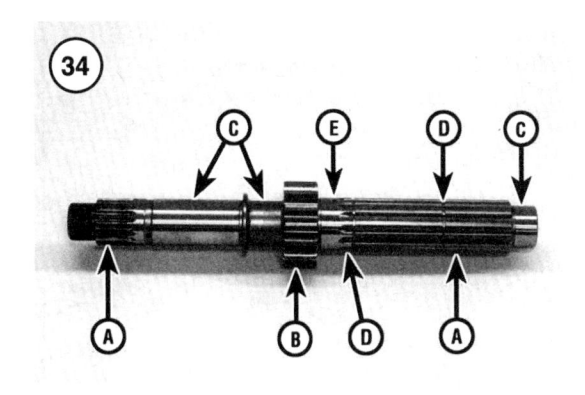

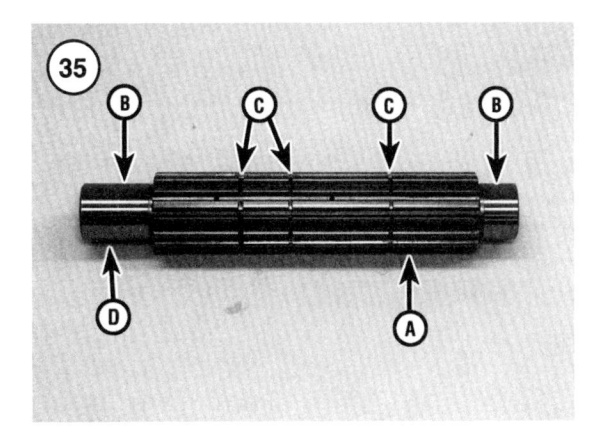

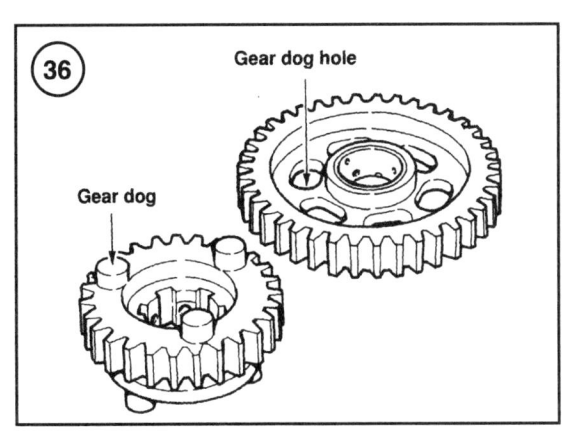

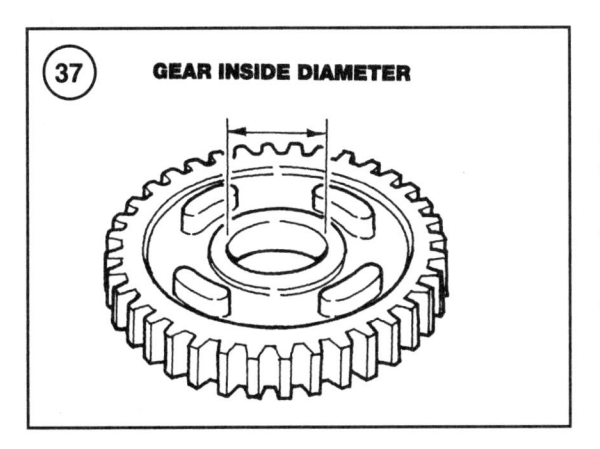

    b. Missing, broken or chipped mainshaft first gear teeth (B, **Figure 34**).
    c. Worn or damaged bearing surfaces (C, **Figure 34** and B, **Figure 35**).
    d. Cracked or rounded-off snap ring grooves (D, **Figure 34** and C, **Figure 35**).

2. Measure the mainshaft outside diameter at its third gear operating position (E, **Figure 34**).
3. Measure the countershaft outside diameter at the second gear operating position (D, **Figure 35**).
4. Check each gear for excessive wear, burrs, pitting, or chipped or missing teeth. Check the splines on sliding gears and the bore on stationary gears for excessive wear or damage.
5. To check stationary gears for wear, install them and their bushing on their correct shaft and in their original operating position. If necessary, use the old snap rings to secure them in place. Then spin the gear by hand. The gear should turn smoothly. A rough turning gear indicates heat damage. Check for a dark blue color or galling on the operating surfaces. Rocking indicates excessive wear, either to the gear, bushing or shaft.
6. To check the sliding gears, install them on their correct shaft and in their original operating position. The gear should slide back and forth without any binding or excessive play.
7. Check the gear dogs and dog engagement slots (**Figure 36**) on the gears for excessive wear, rounding, cracks or other damage. Any wear on the dogs and mating recesses should be uniform. If the dogs are not worn evenly, the remaining dogs will be overstressed and possibly fail.
8. Check engaging gears by installing both gears on their respective shafts and in their original operating position, then twist the gears together to engage the dogs. Check for positive engagement in both directions. If damage is evident, also inspect the condition of the shift forks, as described in this chapter.

NOTE
The side of the gear dogs that carries the engine load will wear and eventually become rounded. The unloaded side of the dogs will remain unworn. Rounded dogs will cause the transmission to jump out of gear.

9. Check for worn or damaged shift fork grooves. Check the gear groove and its mating shift fork.
10. Measure the mainshaft third and fifth gear inside diameters. See **Figure 37**.
11. Measure the countershaft first, second and fourth gear inside diameters. See **Figure 37**.
12. Check the bushings for:
    a. Severely worn or damaged bearing surface.
    b. Worn or damaged splines.
    c. Cracked or scored gear bore.

13. Measure the mainshaft third and fifth gear bushing outside diameters. Measure also the third gear bushing inside diameter (**Figure 38**).
14. Measure the countershaft first, second and fourth gear bushing outside diameters. Measure also the second gear bushing inside diameter (**Figure 38**).

> *NOTE*
> *Replace defective gears and their mating gear at the same time, though they may not show equal wear or damage.*

15. Using the measurements recorded in the previous steps, determine the bushing-to-shaft and gear-to-bushing clearances specified in Table 2 (mainshaft) and Table 3 (countershaft). Replace worn parts to correct any clearance not within specification.
16. Inspect the spline washers. The teeth in the washer should be uniform, and the washers should not be loose on the shaft.
17. Inspect the thrust washers. The washers should be smooth and show no signs of wear or heat damage (bluing).

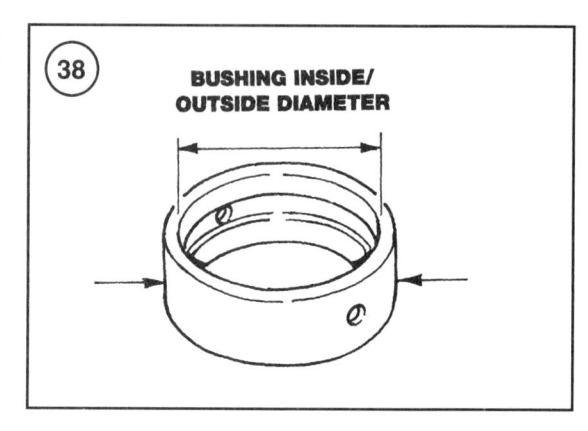

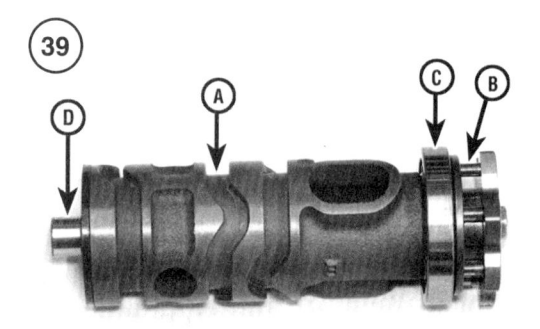

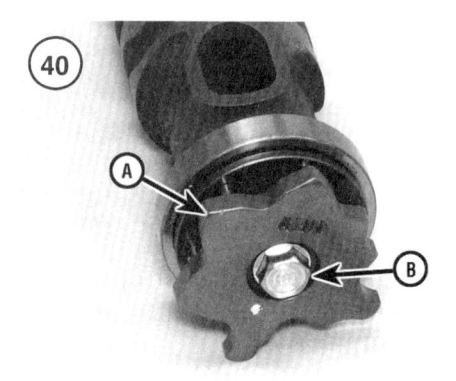

INTERNAL SHIFT MECHANISM

As the transmission is upshifted and downshifted, the shift drum and fork assembly engages and disengages pairs of gears on the transmission shafts. Gear shifting is controlled by the shift forks, which are guided by cam grooves in the shift drum.

It is important that the shift drum grooves, shift forks and mating gear grooves be in good condition. Too much wear between the parts will cause unreliable and poor engagement of the gears. This can lead to premature wear of the gear dogs and other parts.

Shift Drum

Inspection and Overhaul

1. Clean and dry the shift drum.
2. Check the shift drum (**Figure 39**) for wear and damage as follows:
    a. The shift drum grooves (A, **Figure 39**) should be a uniform width. Worn grooves can prevent complete gear engagement, which can cause rough shifting and allow the transmission to disengage.
    b. Check for damaged pins (B, **Figure 39**).
    c. Spin the ball bearing (C, **Figure 39**) by hand. Replace the bearing if there is any excessive noise or the bearing turns roughly.
    d. Check the left side journal (D, **Figure 39**). The journal surface must not be worn or show overheating discoloration due to lack of lubrication. Then measure the shift drum journal outside diameter. Replace the shift drum if the measurement is equal to or less than the service limit in **Table 4**.
    e. The cam plate (A, **Figure 40**) should be uniform in appearance. Check the ramp surfaces for uneven wear and damage.
    f. If necessary, continue the procedure to service the shift drum assembly.
3. Overhaul the shift drum as follows:

> *NOTE*
> *The shift drum pins can be replaced with the engine installed in the frame. Remove the clutch and shift shaft*

TRANSMISSION AND INTERNAL SHIFT MECHANISM

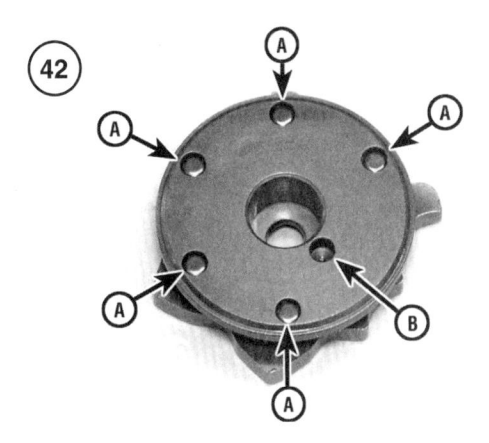

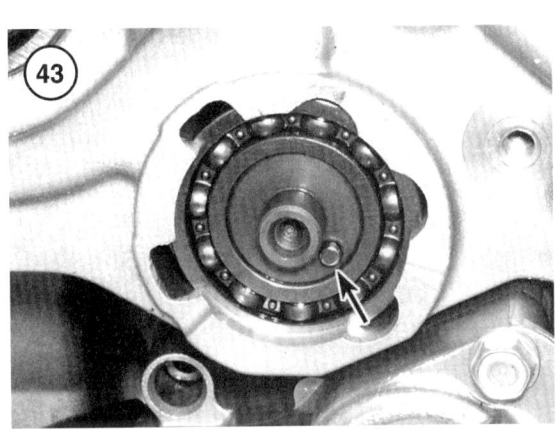

assemblies as described in Chapter Six. Place shop cloths under the shift drum to prevent the small pins from falling into the crankcase.

a. If the shift drum is removed from the engine, secure the shift drum with a holder and remove the bolt (B, **Figure 40**). If the shift drum is installed in the engine, turn the shift drum (A, **Figure 41**) counterclockwise until it stops and then remove the bolt (B, **Figure 41**).
b. Remove the shift drum cam plate and pins (A, **Figure 42**), dowel pin (**Figure 43**) and bearing (if shift drum is removed from engine).
c. Replace damaged parts.
d. Remove all threadlock residue from the bolt and shift drum threads.
e. Install the five pins into the cam plate holes (A, **Figure 42**).
f. Install the bearing onto the shift drum (if removed from engine).
g. Install the dowel pin (**Figure 43**) into the shift drum hole.
h. Install the cam plate by aligning is hole (B, **Figure 42**) with the dowel pin (**Figure 43**).
i. Apply a medium strength threadlock onto the cam plate mounting bolt threads. Install the bolt and tighten to 12 N.m (106 in.-lb.).

4. Measure the shift drum journal bore inside diameter in the left crankcase (**Figure 44**). If the bore is too large, replace the left crankcase. If the bore inside diameter is within specification, subtract the shift drum outside diameter (D, **Figure 39**) from the bore inside diameter to determine the shift drum-to-shift drum journal clearance. If the clearance is too large, determine whether the shift drum, left crankcase or both parts must be replaced to bring the clearance within specification.

Shift Fork and Shaft

Inspection

Table 4 lists new and service limit specifications for the shift forks and shift fork shaft. Replace the shift forks and shaft if out of specification or if they show damage as described in this section.

1. Inspect each shift fork (**Figure 45**) for signs of wear or damage. Examine the shift forks where they contact the slider gear (A, **Figure 45**). These surfaces must be smooth with no signs of excessive wear, bending, cracks, heat discoloration or other damage.
2. Check each shift fork for arc-shaped wear or burn marks. These marks indicate a bent shift fork.
3. The guide pin (B, **Figure 45**) should be symmetrical and not flat on the sides.

4. Check the shift fork shafts for bending or other damage. Install each shift fork on its shaft and slide it back and forth. Each shift fork must slide smoothly with no binding or tight spots. If any fork binds, check the shaft for bending.

5. Measure the thickness of each shift fork claw (A, **Figure 45**).

6. Measure the inside diameter (C, **Figure 45**) of each shift fork.

7. Slide each shift fork along the shaft and check for any binding or roughness.

8. Inspect the shift fork shaft for wear and damage. Measure the shaft diameter.

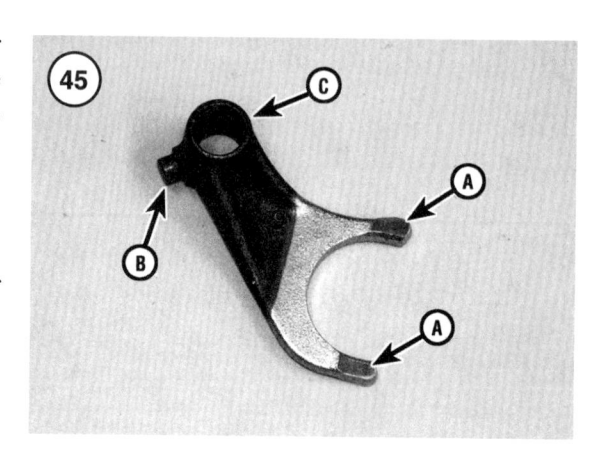

Table 1 TRANSMISSION SPECIFICATIONS

Transmission type	5-speed, constant mesh
Shift pattern	1-N-2-3-4-5
Primary reduction ratio	1.763 (67/38)
Secondary reduction ratio	
Carbureted models	0.891 (33/37)
Fuel injected models	0.821 (32/39)
Third reduction ratio (output drive reduction)	1.059 (18/17)
Final reduction ratio	3.091 (34/11)
Gear ratios	
First gear	2.400 (36/15)
Second gear	1.550 (31/20)
Third gear	1.174 (27/23)
Fourth gear	0.960 (24/25)
Fifth gear	0.852 (23/27)

Table 2 MAINSHAFT SERVICE SPECIFICATIONS

	New mm (in.)	Service limit mm (in.)
Bushing inside diameter		
Third gear	25.000-25.021 (0.9843-0.9851)	25.04 (0.986)
Bushing outside diameter		
Third and fifth gear	27.959-27.980 (1.1007-1.1016)	27.94 (1.100)
Bushing-to-shaft clearance		
Third gear	0.020-0.062 (0.0008-0.0024)	0.10 (0.004)
Gear inside diameter		
Third and fifth gear	28.000-28.021 (1.1024-1.1032)	28.04 (1.104)
Gear-to-bushing clearance		
Third and fifth gear	0.020-0.062 (0.0008-0.0024)	0.10 (0.004)
Mainshaft outside diameter		
Third gear position	24.959-24.980 (0.9826-0.9835)	24.94 (0.982)

TRANSMISSION AND INTERNAL SHIFT MECHANISM

Table 3 COUNTERSHAFT SERVICE SPECIFICATIONS

	New mm (in.)	Service limit mm (in.)
Bushing inside diameter		
Second gear	20.000-20.021 (0.7874-0.7882)	20.04 (0.789)
Bushing outside diameter		
First and fourth gear	30.950-30.975 (1.2185-1.2195)	30.93 (1.218)
Second gear	23.959-23.980 (0.9433-0.9441)	23.94 (0.943)
Bushing-to-shaft clearance		
Second gear	0.007-0.041 (0.0003-0.0016)	0.07 (0.003)
Gear inside diameter		
First and fourth gear	31.000-31.025 (1.2205-1.2215)	31.05 (1.222)
Second gear	24.000-24.021 (0.9449-0.9457)	24.04 (0.946)
Gear-to-bushing clearance		
First and fourth gear	0.025-0.075 (0.0010-0.0030)	0.11 (0.004)
Second gear	0.020-0.062 (0.0008-0.0024)	0.10 (0.004)
Countershaft outside diameter		
Second gear position	19.980-19.993 (0.7866-0.7871)	19.96 (0.786)

Table 4 SHIFT FORK AND SHIFT SHAFT SERVICE SPECIFICATIONS

	New mm (in.)	Service limit mm (in.)
Shift drum journal bore inside diameter	12.000-12.018 (0.4724-0.4731)	12.05 (0.474)
Shift drum outside diameter (@left journal)	11.966-11.984 (0.4711-0.4718)	11.94 (0.470)
Shift drum-to-shift drum journal clearance	0.016-0.052 (0.0006-0.0020)	0.09 (0.0035)
Shift fork claw thickness	5.93-6.00 (0.233-0.236)	5.6 (0.22)
Shift fork inside diameter	13.000-13.018 (0.5118-0.5125)	13.03 (0.513)
Shift fork shaft outside diameter	12.966-12.984 (0.5105-0.5112)	12.90 (0.508)

Table 5 SHIFT DRUM TORQUE SPECIFICATIONS

	N.m	in.-lb.
Cam plate mounting bolt*	12	106

*See text for additional information.

Notes

CHAPTER EIGHT

CARBURETOR AND EMISSION CONTROL SYSTEMS

This chapter covers the carburetor and emission control systems used on 2004-2009 Aero and 2007-2009 Spirit models.

Refer to Chapter Three for air filter service, throttle cable adjustment and lubrication.

Before working on the fuel system, refer to *Safety* in Chapter One.

Fuel system specifications are listed in **Table 1** and **Table 2** at the end of the chapter.

FUEL HOSE IDENTIFICATION

The fuel system uses a number of fuel and vacuum hoses. To allow easier reassembly, develop a system to identify the hoses before disconnecting them. Make tags with strips of masking tape and a fine point permanent-marking pen. There are also a number of reusable aftermarket hose identification kits available from automotive and aftermarket parts suppliers. A typical kit is described in Chapter Five.

FUEL TANK

Draining the Fuel Tank

The fuel tank can be drained while installed on the motorcycle.

1. Disconnect the negative battery cable (Chapter Ten).
2. Turn off the fuel valve.
3. Open the fuel hose clamp and slide it down the hose. Then disconnect the fuel hose (A, **Figure 1**) at the fuel valve. Connect a length of hose onto the fuel valve and insert the other end into a fuel storage can.
4. Disconnect the vacuum hose (B, **Figure 1**) at the fuel valve and connect a vacuum pump onto the fuel valve vacuum hose fitting. Operate the vacuum pump to apply a vacuum at the fuel valve.
5. Turn the fuel valve to its reserve position to drain the fuel tank.
6. Turn off the fuel valve and disconnect the vacuum pump.
7. Reconnect the vacuum hose (B, **Figure 1**).
8. Reconnect the fuel hose (A, **Figure 1**). Leave a 3-5 mm (1/8-3/16 in.) gap between the end of the

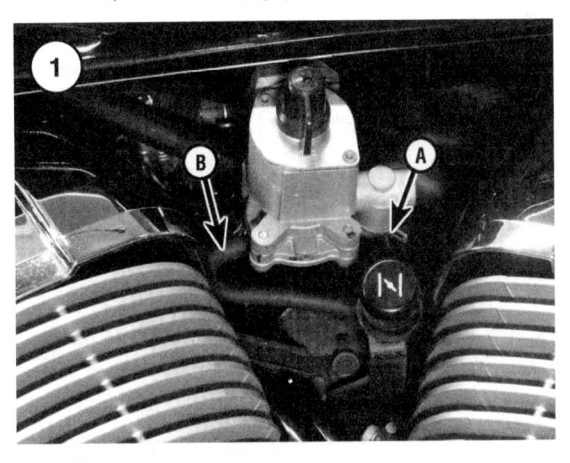

hose and the edge of the fuel valve (**Figure 2**). This gap provides room to insert a pry tool when removing the fuel hose. Secure the fuel hose with its clamp. Position the clamp arms so they do not contact other hoses routed behind the fuel valve.

Removal/Installation

1. Remove the seat (Chapter Seventeen).
2. Disconnect the negative battery cable (Chapter Ten).
3. Remove the speedometer housing (Chapter Ten).
4. Turn off the fuel valve.
5. If necessary, drain the fuel tank as described in this section. Handling the fuel tank will be easier during removal and installation if it is empty.
6. Remove the fuel tank mounting bolt (**Figure 3**) and washer. Note the collar installed inside the rubber damper.
7. Open the fuel hose clamp and slide it down the hose. Then disconnect the hose (A, **Figure 1**) at the fuel valve.
8. Disconnect the vacuum hose (B, **Figure 1**) at the fuel valve.
9. Lift the rear of the tank and disconnect the breather hose (49-state models) or No. 1 (California models) hose at tank fitting (**Figure 4**).

CAUTION
When lifting the tank, make sure the speedometer assembly wiring harness routed at the front of the tank is not pinched or damaged.

10. Lift the rear of the fuel tank slightly and slide it back and off the frame.
11. Check the hoses disconnected at the fuel tank for cracks, soft spots and other damage. Replace if necessary.
12. Installation is the reverse of removal. Note the following:
    a. Make sure a rubber damper is installed on each side of the frame and at the rear of the fuel tank. Replace any rubber damper that is deteriorated or damaged.
    b. Route the speedometer wiring harness and install the speedometer as described in Chapter Ten.
    c. Tighten the fuel tank mounting bolt (**Figure 3**) to 27 N.m (20 ft.-lb.).
    d. Refill the fuel tank if previously drained.
    e. Check for fuel leaks.

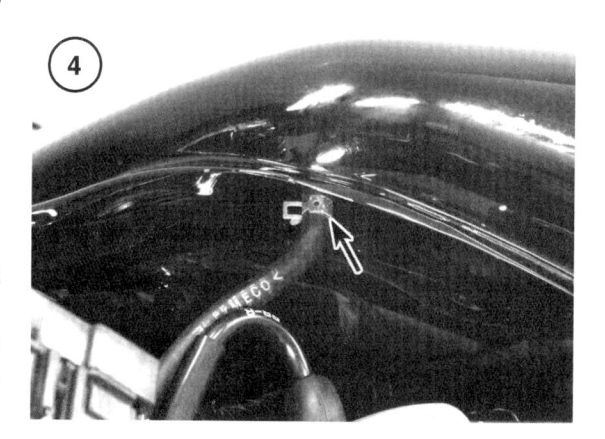

FUEL VALVE

Troubleshooting

Fuel valve operation is controlled by vacuum, which is provided by a hose connected between the intake manifold and fuel valve. Vacuum is present when the engine is being started and when the engine is running. If there is a fuel supply problem, test the fuel valve as follows:

1. Make sure the vacuum hose (B, **Figure 1**) is connected to the fuel valve. If not, reconnect the hose and attempt to start the engine. If the vacuum hose is con-

CARBURETOR AND EMISSION CONTROL SYSTEMS

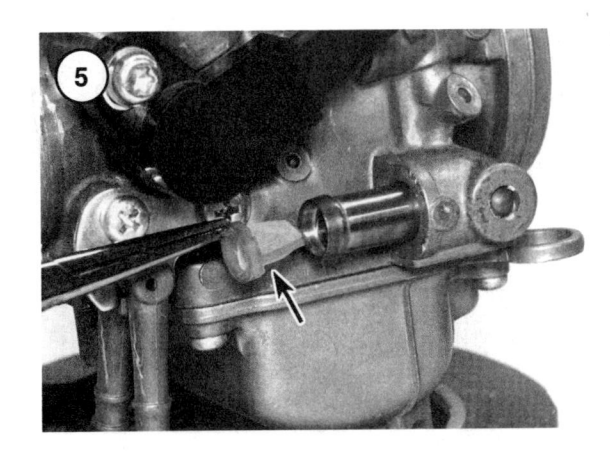

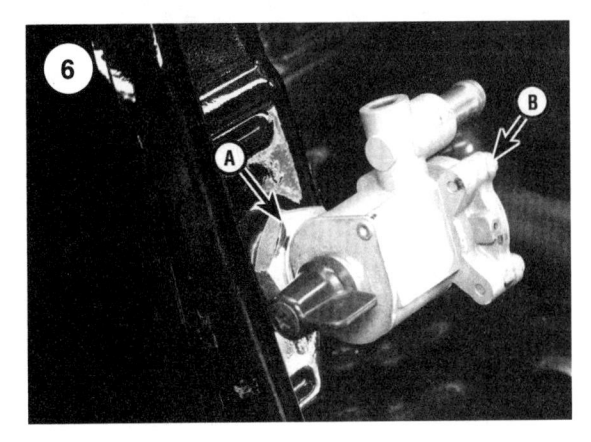

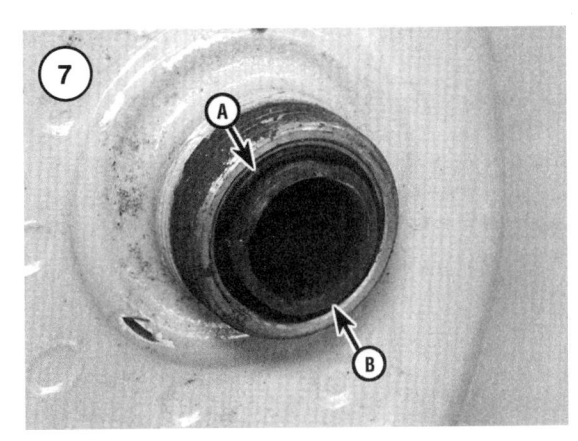

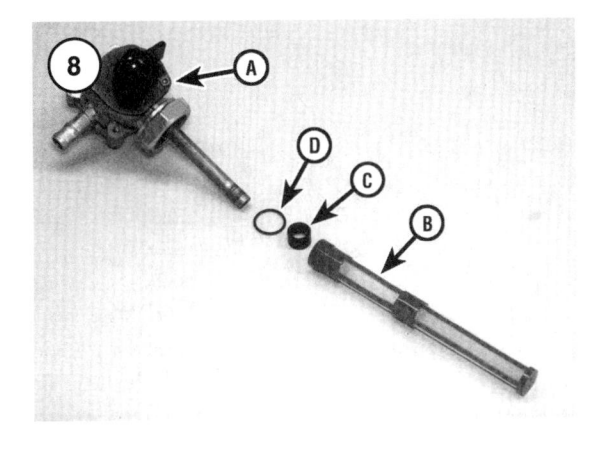

nected, disconnect it at the fuel valve and check it and all connections leading toward the intake manifold for cracks and other damage. If the vacuum hose is okay, do not reconnect it and continue the procedure.

2. Open the fuel hose clamp and slide it down the hose. Then disconnect the hose (A, **Figure 1**) at the fuel valve. Connect a length of hose onto the fuel valve and insert the other end into a fuel storage can.
3. Connect a vacuum pump onto the vacuum hose fitting on the fuel valve.
4. Turn the fuel valve to its reserve position.
5. Operate the vacuum pump to apply a vacuum to the fuel valve. Fuel should begin to flow out the fuel hose and continue as long as a vacuum is applied. If fuel flows in the reserve position, repeat the test with the fuel valve in its on position. Note the following:
   a. If fuel flows when the vacuum pump is applying vacuum, but does not flow when the vacuum hose is connected to the fuel valve, check for a plugged or damaged vacuum hose.
   b. If fuel does not flow with either vacuum source, remove the fuel valve vacuum diaphragm as described in this section. Inspect the diaphragm for damage and the internal fuel valve port for clogging.

NOTE
*There is also a fuel strainer screen mounted inside the carburetor fuel hose fitting (**Figure 5**).*

   c. If the vacuum diaphragm appears in good condition, the fuel strainer screen attached to the fuel valve may be clogged. Remove and inspect the fuel strainer screen as described in this section.
6. Reverse the steps required to disconnect the vacuum pump and reconnect the hoses.

Removal/Installation

1. Drain and remove the fuel tank as described in this section.
2. Place the fuel tank on a padded surface to prevent scratches.
3. Loosen the mounting nut (A, **Figure 6**) and remove the fuel valve (B) assembly.
4. Remove the O-ring (A, **Figure 7**) and fuel strainer (B) from the fuel tank if they did not come off with the fuel valve.
5. If the fuel strainer remains attached onto the fuel valve, (A, **Figure 8** typical) remove the strainer (B), guide (C) and O-ring (D).
6. Replace the O-ring if cracked or if the fuel valve previously leaked at its mounting nut.
7. Clean the fuel strainer and then check the screen

for damage. Replace the fuel strainer if the screen cannot be cleaned or is torn.

8. Installation is the reverse of removal. Note the following:

   a. Install the O-ring over the fuel valve pickup tube and seat against the fuel valve. Then install the guide over the tube and the fuel strainer.
   b. Align the fuel valve so its knob faces out and tighten the mounting nut (A, **Figure 6**) to 34 N.m (25 ft.-lb.).
   c. Partially fill the tank with fuel and check for fuel leaks.
   d. If the fuel valve does not leak, install the fuel tank as described in this section.

Diaphragm Replacement

The diaphragm assembly (A, **Figure 9**) can be replaced with the fuel valve (B) mounted on the fuel tank. However, the fuel tank must be removed to ensure the diaphragm plate and cover are properly centered on the fuel valve.

1. Drain and remove the fuel tank as described in this section.
2. Scribe an alignment mark across the fuel valve, diaphragm plate and diaphragm cover so the parts can be reinstalled facing in their original direction or used as a reference to align the new parts.
3. Remove the screws (A, **Figure 10**), diaphragm cover (B), spring and diaphragm plate.
4. Inspect the diaphragm for tearing, deterioration and other damage. Replace the diaphragm assembly if necessary.
5. Clean the spring and diaphragm cover and check for damage.
6. Assemble the diaphragm plate, spring and cover (**Figure 11**) while using two of the mounting screws for alignment. Compress the parts together, then check that the diaphragm is centered within its cover (**Figure 12**). If the diaphragm is off-center, reassemble the parts. An off-center diaphragm can cause a fuel leak or fuel starvation.
7. Install the diaphragm assembly onto the fuel valve by aligning the pins on the diaphragm plate with the holes in the fuel valve while also aligning the marks made during dissassembly. Install the screws and tighten securely in a crossing pattern.
8. Install the fuel tank as described in this section and check for fuel leaks. Before riding the motorcycle, verify that the fuel valve is operational by checking fuel flow with a vacuum pump as described under *Fuel Tank* in this section.

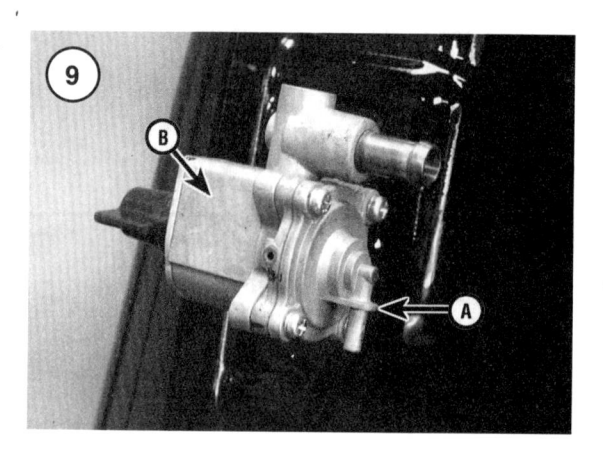

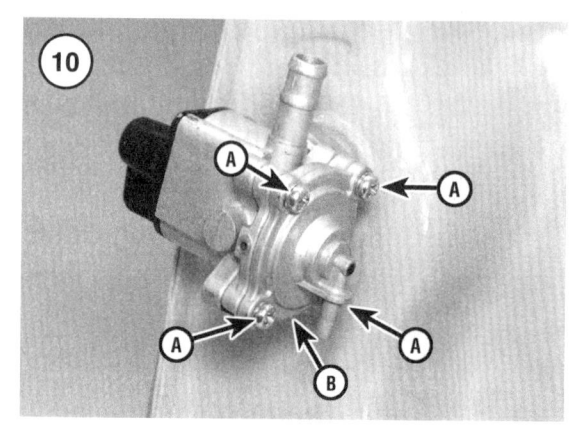

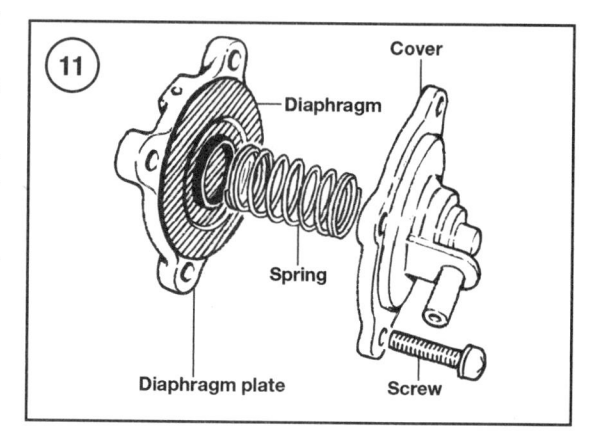

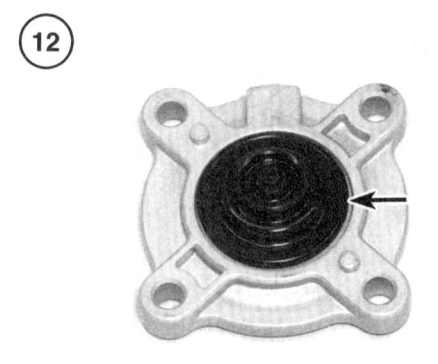

CARBURETOR AND EMISSION CONTROL SYSTEMS

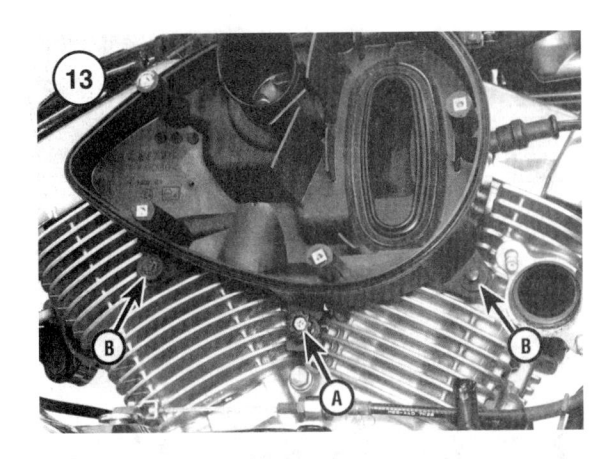

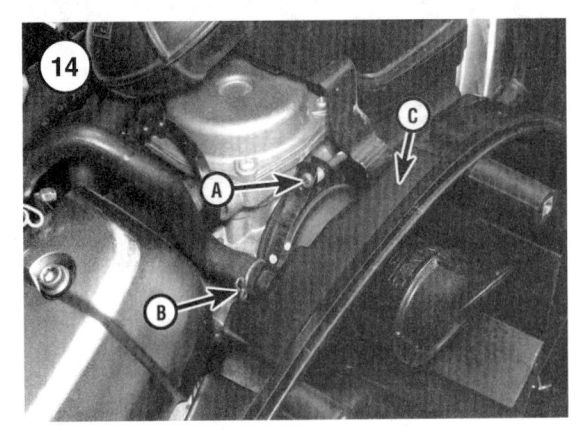

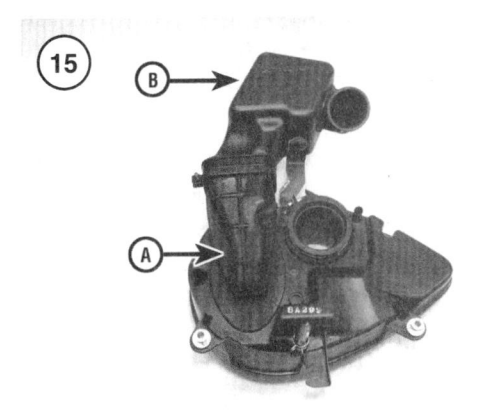

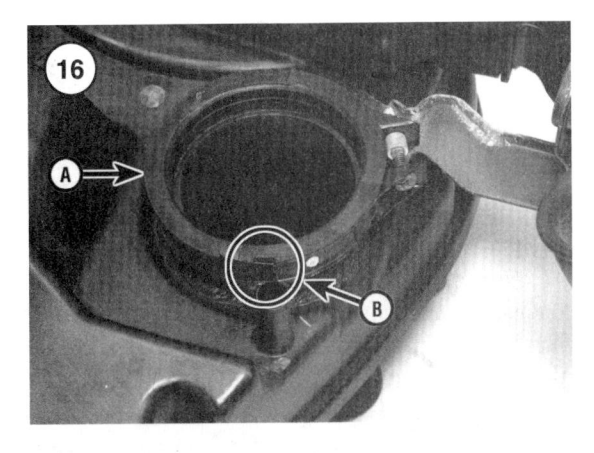

AIR FILTER HOUSING

Removal/Installation

1. Remove the fuel tank as described in this chapter.
2. If necessary, remove the air filter as described in Chapter Three. The housing can be removed with the air filter cover installed.
3. Push the idle speed screw knob out of the grommet (A, **Figure 13**) at the bottom of the air filter housing.
4. Remove the air filter housing mounting bolts (B, **Figure 13**).
5. Loosen the air filter housing hose clamp at the carburetor (A, **Figure 14**).
6. Disconnect the crankcase breather hose (B, **Figure 14**) from the backside of the air filter housing. Then remove the air filter housing (C, **Figure 14**).
7. Inspect the inside of the air filter housing and the carburetor for dirt and other debris. These areas must be clean. If dirt is noticed inside the air filter housing or carburetor, either the filter is worn or damaged or there is a problem with the air filter housing.

NOTE
The air filter housing components identified in this section can be replaced separately. To seal rubber joints, use a weatherstrip adhesive that can be used on rubber parts and resists gasoline.

8. Make sure the connecting tube (A, **Figure 15**) is sealed and secured to the air filter housing. Check the tube for cracks and other damage. Tighten the hose clamp to the specification in **Table 2**.
9. Make sure the air filter chamber (B, **Figure 15**) is secured to the air filter housing with the clamp and bracket. Tighten the air cleaner chamber bracket mounting screw to the specification in **Table 2**.
10. Check the intake boot (A, **Figure 16**) for any cracks, splitting or other damage.
11. Make sure the intake boot (A, **Figure 16**) is sealed to the air filter housing.
12. Check the intake boot clamp for weakness or damage. If removed, position the tab on the clamp into the notch in the boot (B, **Figure 16**).
13. Make sure the air filter seating surface inside the air filter housing is in good condition.
14. Replace the air filter cover O-ring if missing or damaged.
15. Installation is the reverse of removal. Tighten the air filter housing mounting bolts (B, **Figure 13**) securely.

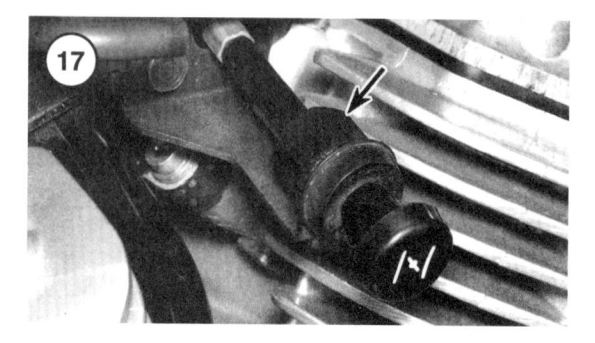

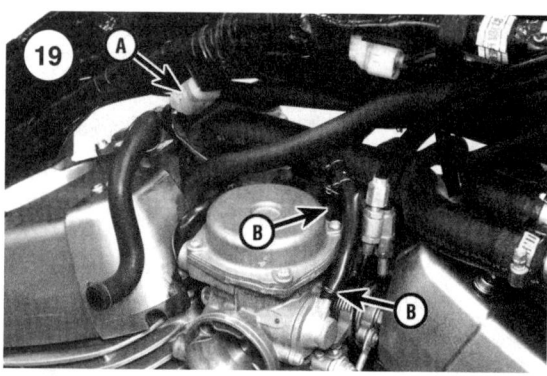

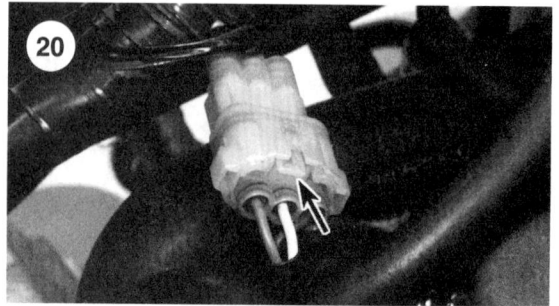

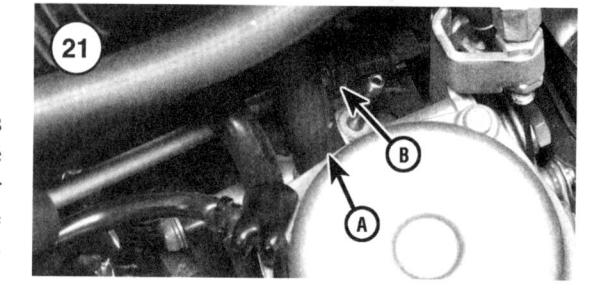

CARBURETOR

Removal

Carburetor vacuum and vent hose connections and routing differ between model years and where the motorcycle was originally sold (49-state or California). Refer to *Fuel Hose Identification* at the beginning of this chapter for information on identifying components.

1. Disconnect the battery negative cable (Chapter Ten).
2. Remove the fuel tank as described in this chapter.
3. Remove the air filter housing as described in this chapter.
4. Loosen the nut (**Figure 17**) and disconnect the choke cable from its mounting bracket on the left side of the engine. The carburetor is removed with the choke cable attached to it.
5. Install a length of hose onto the float bowl drain nozzle (A, **Figure 18**) and put the other end of the hose into a clean plastic container. Open the drain screw (B, **Figure 18**) and drain the float bowl. Tighten the drain screw and pour the fuel back into the fuel tank or into a fuel storage can.

NOTE
C, Figure 18 identifies the air vent hose guide.

6. On all models except 2007 and later California models, remove the air vent hose from the guide (C, **Figure 18**) on the carburetor.
7. Disconnect the TP sensor connector (A, **Figure 19**) by lifting the center locking arm identified in **Figure 20**.
8. Disconnect the two vacuum hoses from the carburetor (B, **Figure 19**).
9. On California models, disconnect the EVAP purge control valve hose (A, **Figure 21**).
10. Loosen the outer carburetor clamp screw (B, **Figure 21**) and remove the carburetor from the intake boot.
11. Loosen the throttle cable locknuts (**Figure 22**) and disconnect the pull and return cables at the carburetor.
12. Disconnect the air vent hose at the carburetor (**Figure 23**).
13. On California models, disconnect the EVAP purge control valve vacuum hose at the carburetor (A, **Figure 24**).
14. Identify the two coolant hoses (B, **Figure 24**) at the carburetor. One hose is connected to the intake manifold and the other hose is connected to the radiator. Then clamp the two coolant hoses to prevent coolant leakage and disconnect them.

CARBURETOR AND EMISSION CONTROL SYSTEMS

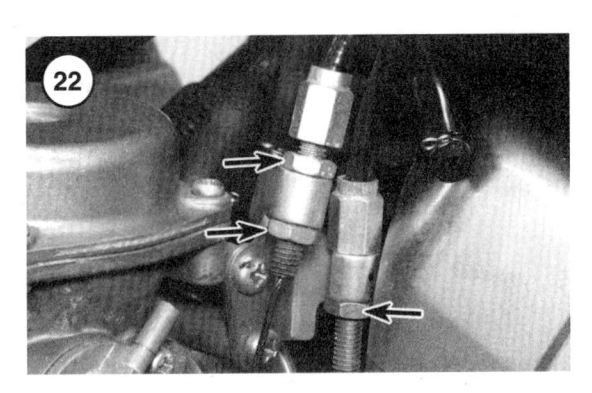

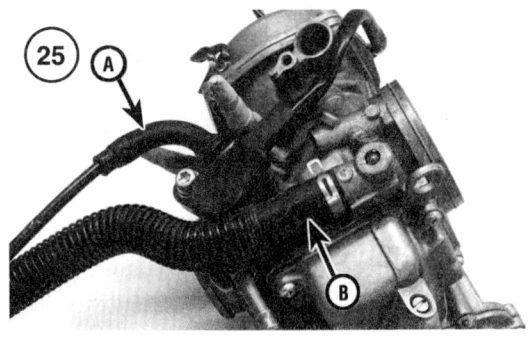

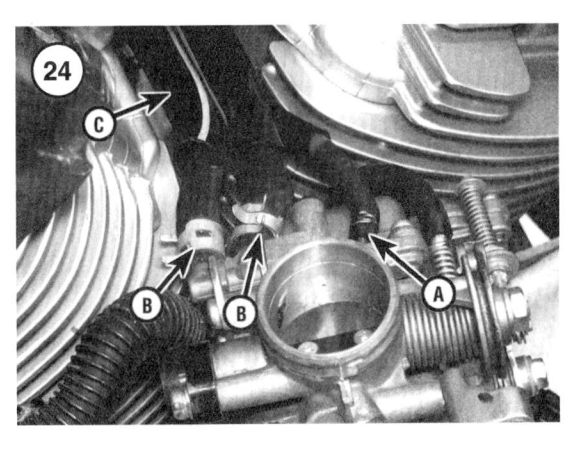

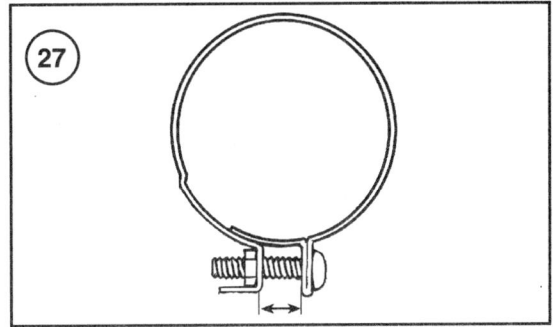

15. Remove the carburetor with the choke cable (A, **Figure 25**) and fuel hose (B) attached.

Installation

NOTE
Install the carburetor with the fuel hose (B, Figure 25) and choke cable (A) attached.

1. Reconnect the two coolant hoses at the carburetor (B, **Figure 24**). The hose with the white stripe (C, **Figure 24**) is connected to the intake manifold. Position the clamps so their arms do not contact and damage the opposite hose. Make sure that the clamps are tight and the hoses are secured in place.

2. On California models, reconnect the EVAP purge control valve vacuum hose at the carburetor (A, **Figure 24**).

3. Reconnect the air vent hose at the carburetor (**Figure 23**).

4. Reconnect the return (A, **Figure 26**) and pull (B) throttle cables onto the throttle drum and cable brackets. Do not tighten the cable locknuts at this time.

NOTE
Route the fuel hose and choke cable between the cylinders when installing the carburetor.

5. Install the carburetor onto the intake boot by aligning the lug on the carburetor with the groove in the intake boot. On 2004-2009 Aero models, tighten the clamp (B, **Figure 21**) so the distance between the clamp ends (**Figure 27**) is 13.5-15.5 mm (0.53-0.61 in.). On 2007-2009 Spirit models, tighten the clamp securely.

CHAPTER EIGHT

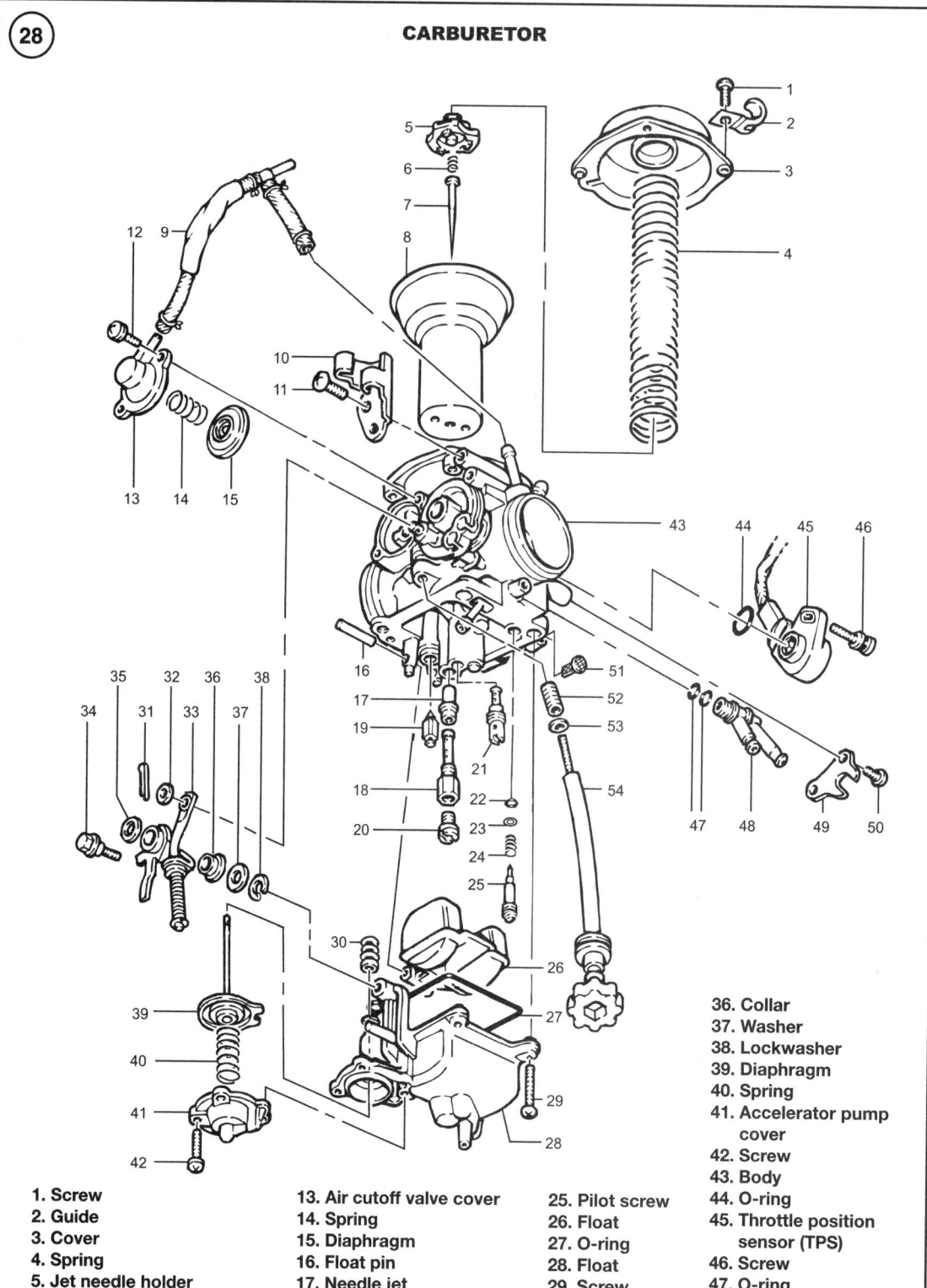

CARBURETOR

1. Screw
2. Guide
3. Cover
4. Spring
5. Jet needle holder
6. Spring
7. Jet needle
8. Vacuum piston assembly
9. Hose
10. Throttle cable holder
11. Screw
12. Screw
13. Air cutoff valve cover
14. Spring
15. Diaphragm
16. Float pin
17. Needle jet
18. Needle jet holder
19. Float valve
20. Main jet
21. Pilot jet
22. O-ring
23. Washer
24. Spring
25. Pilot screw
26. Float
27. O-ring
28. Float
29. Screw
30. Boot
31. Cotter pin
32. Washer
33. Accelerator pump rod
34. Bolt
35. Washer
36. Collar
37. Washer
38. Lockwasher
39. Diaphragm
40. Spring
41. Accelerator pump cover
42. Screw
43. Body
44. O-ring
45. Throttle position sensor (TPS)
46. Screw
47. O-ring
48. Carburetor heater
49. Plate
50. Screw
51. Fuel filter
52. Spring
53. Washer
54. Idle speed screw

CARBURETOR AND EMISSION CONTROL SYSTEMS

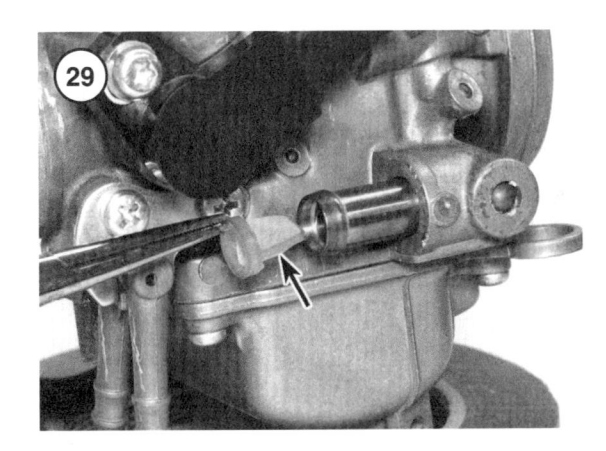

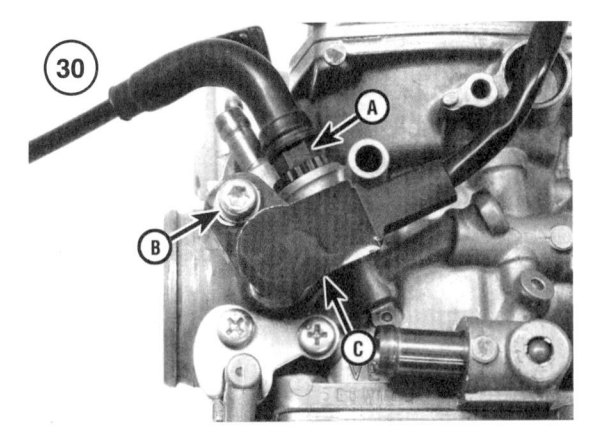

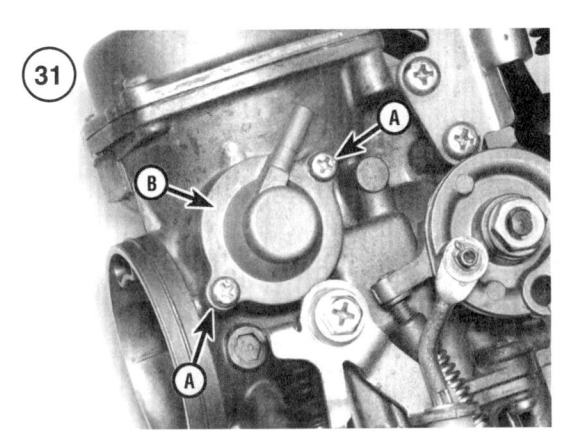

6. On California models, reconnect the EVAP purge control valve hose (A, **Figure 21**).
7. Reconnect the two vacuum hoses from the carburetor (B, **Figure 19**).
8. Reconnect the TP sensor connector (A, **Figure 19**).
9. On all models except 2007 and later California models, install the air vent hose through the guide identified in C, **Figure 18**.
10. Reinstall the choke cable onto its mounting bracket and secure with the nut **(Figure 17)**.
11. Adjust the throttle cables (Chapter Three).
12. Adjust the choke cable (Chapter Three).
13. Install the air filter housing as described in this chapter.
14. Reconnect the battery negative lead (Chapter Ten).
15. Install the fuel tank as described in this chapter.
16. Turn the fuel valve on and start the engine to check for fuel leaks.
17. Confirm the throttle cable operation is correct with the fuel tank mounted. Refer to *Throttle Cable Adjustment* in Chapter Three.

Disassembly

The carburetor does not have to be completely disassembled to service some of the components. Disassemble the carburetor only as far as necessary to inspect/clean/replace the damaged part. During disassembly, keep all parts identified and organized. Refer to **Figure 28**.

1. Disconnect and remove the fuel hose (B, **Figure 25**) and its wire cage.
2. Remove the fuel filter **(Figure 29)** from the nozzle in the carburetor.
3. Slide the cap off the choke cable nut. Then loosen the choke cable nut (A, **Figure 30**) and remove the choke valve from the carburetor.

NOTE
Do not remove the TP sensor unless replacement is required or it is necessary to overhaul and soak the carburetor assembly.

4. Remove the Torx screw (B, **Figure 30**) and the TP sensor (C). Replace the O-ring in the TP sensor if flattened or damaged.
5. Remove the air cutoff valve assembly as follows:
   a. Remove the screws (A, **Figure 31**) from the cover (B). The cover is under strong spring pressure. Keep pressure on the cover as the screws are removed.
   b. Remove the spring and diaphragm **(Figure 32)**.

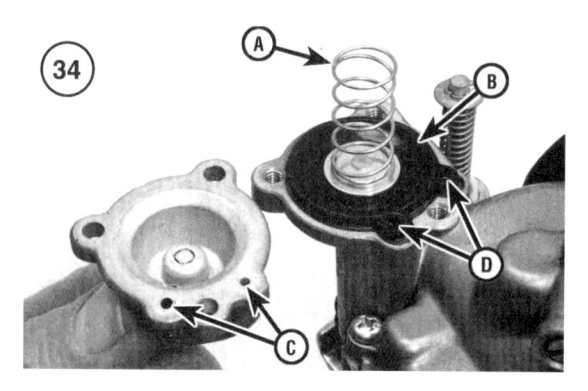

6. Remove the accelerator pump assembly as follows:
   a. Remove the screws (A, **Figure 33**) from the cover (B). The cover is under spring pressure. Keep pressure on the cover as the screws are removed.
   b. Remove the spring (A, **Figure 34**).
   c. Carefully remove the diaphragm (B, **Figure 34**) with its attached rod.
   d. Remove the boot **(Figure 35)**.
7. Remove the screws (A, **Figure 36**), bracket (B) and carburetor heater (C). Discard the O-rings.
8. Remove the diaphragm cover, vacuum piston and jet needle as follows:
   a. Remove the diaphragm cover (A, **Figure 37**) and clamp (B). The cover is under slight pressure. Hold the cover in place as the screws are removed, then lift off the cover and remove the spring.

CAUTION
Do not lift or hold the vacuum piston by the diaphragm. Do not damage the jet needle.

   b. From the intake side, push up on the vacuum piston and remove it from the carburetor **(Figure 38)**.
   c. Push the jet needle holder **(Figure 39)** in with a Phillips screwdriver or socket and turn it counterclockwise to release it.

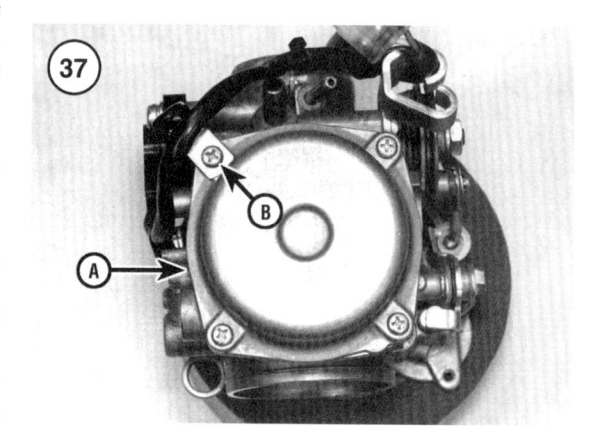

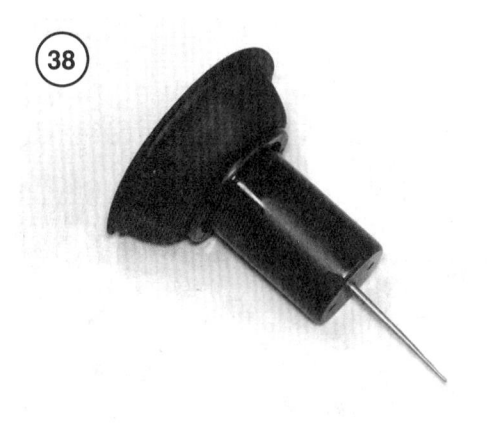

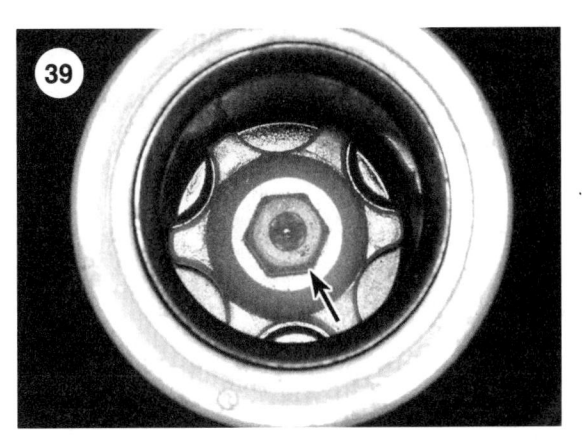

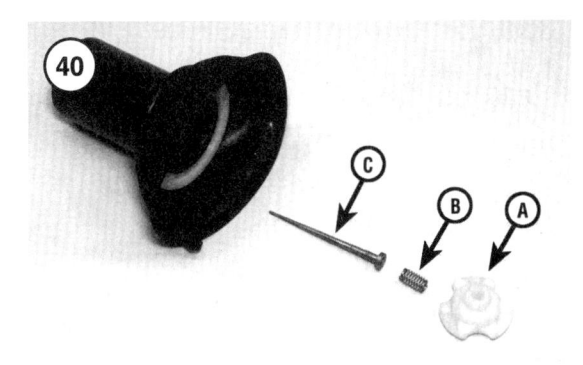

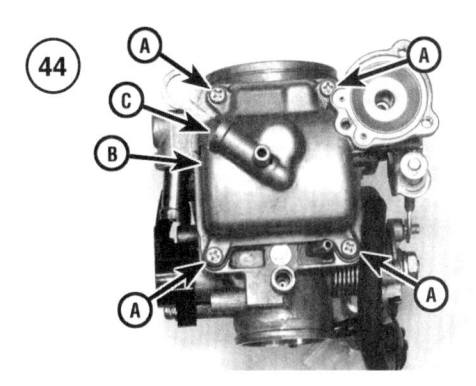

CARBURETOR AND EMISSION CONTROL SYSTEMS

d. Remove the jet needle holder (A, **Figure 40**), spring (B) and jet needle (C).

CAUTION
The pilot screw tip is easily damaged. Do not overtighten the pilot screw when setting it. If the pilot screw tip breaks off, its removal from the pilot screw bore may be impossible.

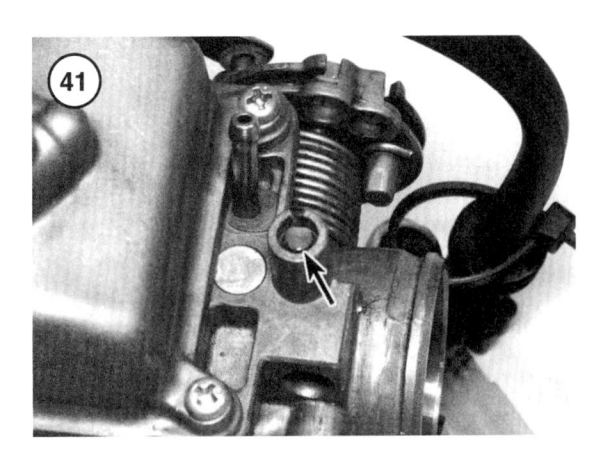

NOTE
The pilot screw requires a D-shaped tool to turn and remove it. Suitable tools are described in this chapter.

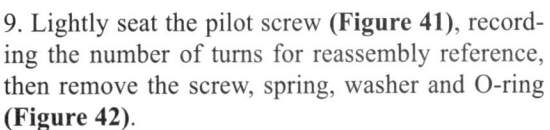

9. Lightly seat the pilot screw **(Figure 41)**, recording the number of turns for reassembly reference, then remove the screw, spring, washer and O-ring **(Figure 42)**.

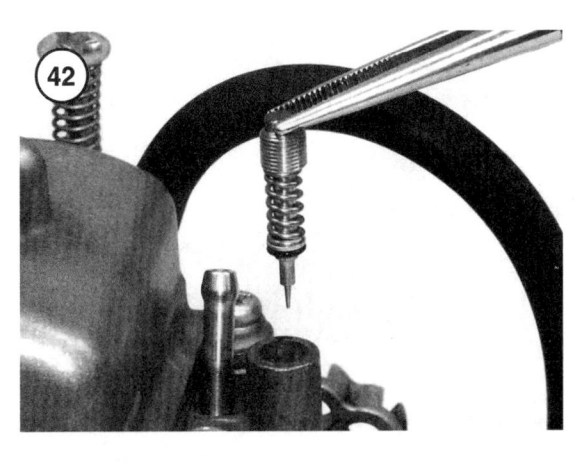

10. Remove the float bowl as follows:

NOTE
*The accelerator pump rod (A, **Figure 43**) is attached to the throttle drum with a cotter pin and washer.*

a. Remove the cotter pin and washer (B, **Figure 43**) securing the accelerator pump rod to the throttle drum.

b. Remove the screws (A, **Figure 44**) and the float bowl (B).

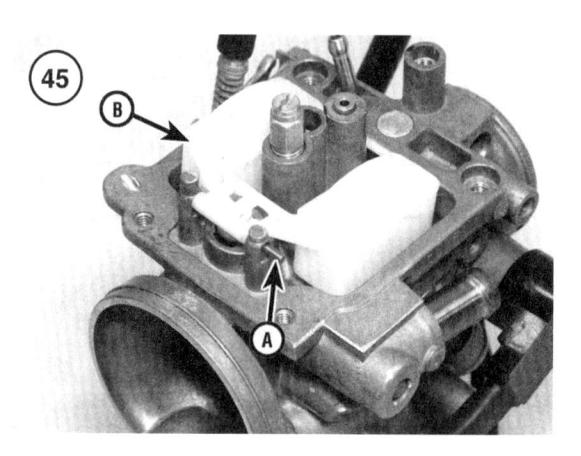

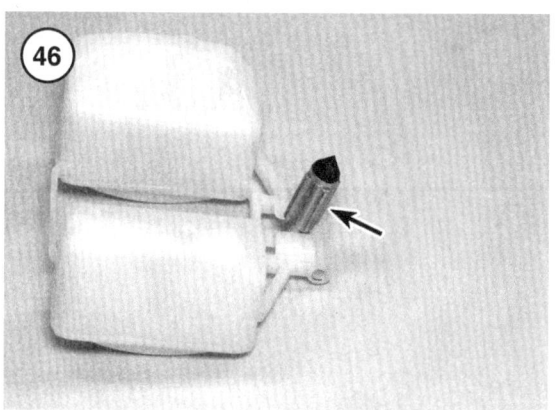

c. If leaking or damaged, remove the O-ring from the float bowl.
d. Remove the drain screw (C, **Figure 44**) and its O-ring from the float bowl.

11. Remove the float assembly as follows:
    a. Remove the float pin (A, **Figure 45**) and float (B).
    b. Slide the float valve **(Figure 46)** off the float arm.

12. Remove the pilot jet (A, **Figure 47**).

13. Remove the main jet (B, **Figure 47**) and needle jet holder (C) or remove the needle jet holder with the main jet attached.

14. Working from the top side of the carburetor, carefully push the needle jet **(Figure 48)** out through the bottom side.

CAUTION
Do not remove the throttle valve or throttle shaft assembly from the carburetor. Replacement parts are not available.

15. Clean and inspect all parts as described in this section.

Assembly

Refer to **Table 2** for fastener specifications. If no specification is given, tighten the fasteners securely.

1. Install the needle jet **(Figure 48)** through the bottom side of the carburetor so its curved end will seat against the needle jet holder. See **Figure 49**.
2. Install the needle jet holder (C, **Figure 47**) and tighten.
3. If removed, hold the needle jet holder (C, **Figure 47**), and then install and tighten the main jet (B).
4. Install and tighten the pilot jet (A, **Figure 47**).
5. Install the float assembly as follows:

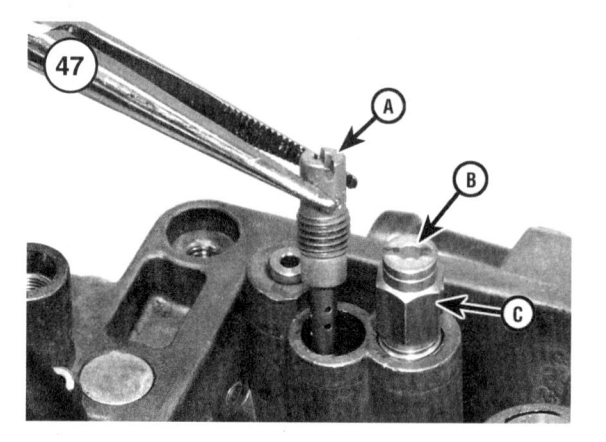

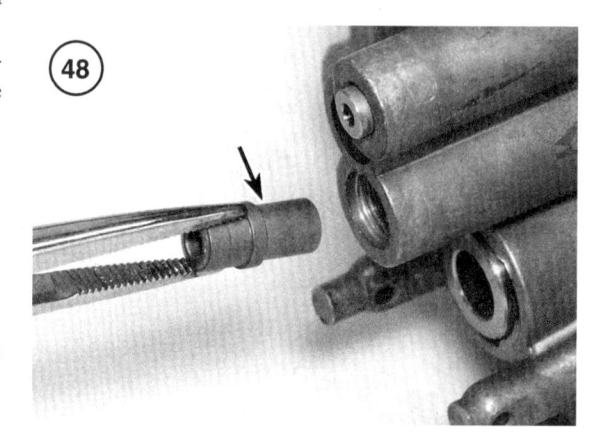

CARBURETOR AND EMISSION CONTROL SYSTEMS

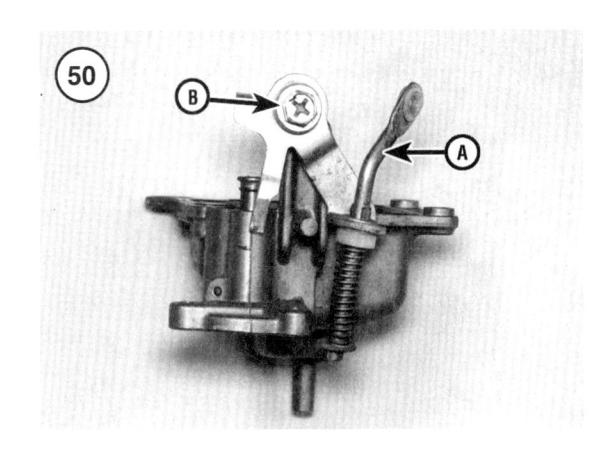

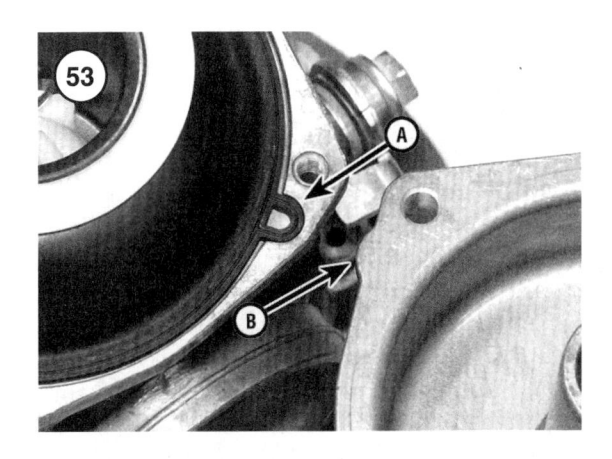

a. Hook the float valve onto the float as shown in **Figure 46**.
b. Install the float valve into its seat, then install the float pin (A, **Figure 45**) through the pedestals and float (B, **Figure 45**).
c. Measure the float height as described in this chapter.

6. Install the float bowl (B, **Figure 44**) as follows:

NOTE
If the accelerator pump rod (A, Figure 50) was removed from the float bowl, attach it to the float bowl before installing the float bowl. Tighten the bolt (B Figure 50) securely, making sure the rod pivots smoothly.

a. Install the drain screw (C, **Figure 44**) and a new O-ring and tighten.
b. If necessary, install a new O-ring **(Figure 51)** into the float bowl groove.
c. Install the float bowl (B, **Figure 44**) and tighten the screws (A).
d. Secure the accelerator pump rod (A, **Figure 43**) to the throttle drum with the washer and a new cotter pin (B). Bend the cotter pin arms over to lock it.

7. Install the spring, washer and O-ring onto the pilot screw **(Figure 52)**.
8. Install the pilot screw **(Figure 42)** and lightly seat it, then back the pilot screw out the number of turns recorded during removal. If the number of turns is not known, or if installing a new pilot screw, set it to the initial setting listed in **Table 1**. Adjust the idle screw (this chapter) after reassembling and installing the carburetor onto the motorcycle.
9. Install the jet needle, vacuum piston and cover as follows:

a. Install the jet needle (C, **Figure 40**) into the vacuum piston.
b. Install the jet needle holder (A, **Figure 40**) and spring (B) into the vacuum piston, then compress and turn the holder 90° clockwise with a screwdriver until it clicks and locks in place (**Figure 39**). Hold the vacuum piston and press on the jet needle. It should be under spring tension.
c. Position the carburetor upright and install the vacuum piston by inserting the jet needle into the needle jet and while aligning the tab on the diaphragm with the air hole on the carburetor (A, **Figure 53**).

NOTE
The rod helps to hold the edge of the diaphragm in the groove when installing the cover and compressing the spring. If the rod is not used, the diaphragm will pop out of the groove when the vacuum piston drops to the bottom of the bore.

d. Lift the bottom of the vacuum piston slightly and support it with a small rod (A, **Figure 54**) to help seat the edge of diaphragm (B, **Figure 54**) into the groove in the carburetor.
e. Install the spring over the shoulder in the cover and compress it (**Figure 55**) to reduce its length when installing it.
f. Install the spring and cover, making sure the edge of the diaphragm remains seated in the groove. The raised section on the cover (B, **Figure 53**) must align with the tab on the diaphragm (A, **Figure 53**). Hold the cover (A, **Figure 37**) in place. Then install the clamp (B, **Figure 37**) and screws (A). Tighten the screws.
g. Lift the bottom of the vacuum piston and release it. The vacuum piston should move and return under slight resistance. If there is any binding or roughness, remove the cover and check the spring and diaphragm.

10. Lightly coat two new O-rings with engine oil and install into the carburetor heater grooves (**Figure 56**). Then install the carburetor heater (C, **Figure 36**), with the bracket (B) and two screws (A). Tighten the screws.

11. Install the accelerator pump assembly as follows:
    a. Position the boot underneath the accelerator pump rod as shown in **Figure 35**.
    b. Slide the accelerator pump shaft through its bore and the boot until the end of the shaft contacts the accelerator pump rod. Make sure the bottom end of the boot remains seated into the bore funnel.
    c. Seat the diaphragm into the bowl groove as shown in B, **Figure 34**.
    d. Install the spring (A, **Figure 34**) onto the center of the diaphragm.
    e. Align the two passage holes in the cover (C, **Figure 34**) with the two holes in the bowl (D) and install the cover, making sure the diaphragm remains seated at its edge.
    f. Compress the cover (B, **Figure 33**), then install and tighten the screws (A, **Figure 33**).

12. Install the air cutoff valve as follows:
    a. Seat the diaphragm (**Figure 32**) into its groove with its shaft seating into the hole in the carburetor.
    b. Install the spring over the cover shoulder, then center the spring onto the diaphragm and compress the cover (B, **Figure 31**), making sure the diaphragm remains seated at its edge.
    c. Install the screws (A, **Figure 31**) and washers and tighten them.

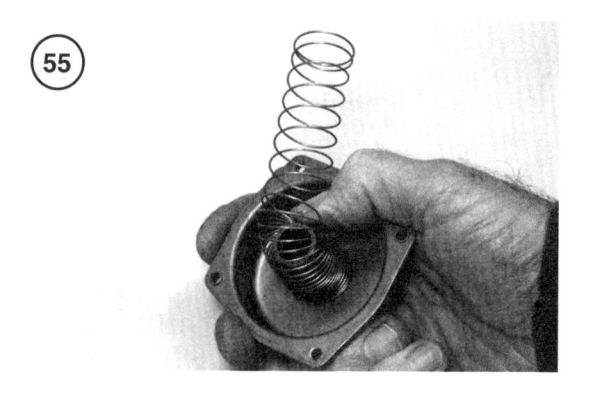

13. Install and adjust the TP sensor (Chapter Ten).

14. If removed, install the spring (A, **Figure 57**) and choke valve (B) onto the end of the choke cable. Then insert the choke valve into the carburetor and tighten the choke cable nut (A, **Figure 30**). Reposition the cap over the nut. Operate the choke knob, making sure the choke valve opens and closes without any binding.

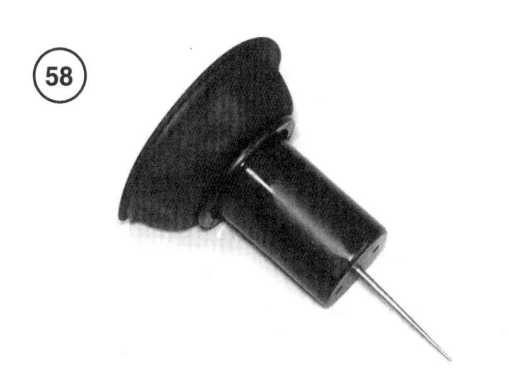

CARBURETOR AND EMISSION CONTROL SYSTEMS

1. Clean the carburetor:
   a. Use an aerosol carburetor cleaner with a plastic tube to clean fuel and air passages.
   b. Used compressed air to clean all passages, orifices and vents in the carburetor body.
   c. Do not clean the jets or seats with drill bits. These items can scratch the surfaces and alter flow rates, or cause leaks.
   d. Clean rubber and plastic parts with a clean towel. If passages in the carburetor or carburetor jets are plugged cannot be opened, have the parts cleaned by a dealership with an ultrasonic cleaner.
   e. After cleaning the carburetor, clean it again with soapy water and then rinse with clear water and dry thoroughly with compressed air. Make sure all passages are clean and dry.
2. Inspect the main jet assembly and pilot jet. Check that all holes are clean and undamaged.
3. Inspect the pilot screw and choke valve:
   a. Inspect the screw and plunger tips for dents and wear.
   b. The spring coils should be evenly spaced and not crushed or spread apart.
4. Inspect the diaphragm and vacuum piston assembly (**Figure 58**). If either part is damaged, replace the assembly. Note the following:
   a. Inspect the vacuum piston for wear and scratches. Install the vacuum piston into the carburetor and check for smooth operation. The vacuum piston should move up and down freely.
   b. Inspect the diaphragm for cracks, tears and holes. The diaphragm must be undamaged in order to isolate the pressure differences that are above and below the diaphragm. A leaking diaphragm will prevent the vacuum piston from reaching/maintaining its normal level, for any off idle throttle position. Engine performance will be noticeably diminished.
5. Inspect the cover and the jet needle assembly. Note the following:
   a. The cover must be undamaged in order to maintain low pressure in the upper chamber of the carburetor. A cracked or loose cover will affect engine performance similarly to a damaged diaphragm.
   b. The jet needle must be smooth and evenly tapered. If it is stepped, dented, worn or bent, replace the needle.
   c. The spring coils must be uniform and not damaged.
6. Inspect the float and float valve assembly. Note the following:
   a. Inspect the tip of the float valve (A, **Figure 59**) and replace if the rubber part is not smooth.

15. Install the fuel filter (**Figure 29**) into the carburetor fuel hose fitting.
16. Install the fuel hose and its wire band (A, **Figure 25**).

Cleaning and Inspection

CAUTION
Because the carburetor body cannot be completely disassembled, it is not recommended to soak the carburetor in a carburetor cleaner unless the cleaner specifically will not damage plastic or rubber parts that may be installed on the throttle shaft. Follow the product manufacturer's instructions when using a cleaner.

b. Lightly press on the spring-loaded pin (**Figure 60**) in the float valve. The pin should easily move in and out of the valve. If there is any roughness or binding or the pin sticks in place, replace the float valve.
c. Inspect the float valve seat (B, **Figure 59**) for steps and other damage. If the tapered seat is not smooth and if fuel is leaking past the seat (even with a new float valve), replace the carburetor assembly. The float valve seat is not replaceable.
d. Submerge the float in water and check for leaks. Replace the float if there is fuel or water in the float.
e. Check that the float pin is smooth and straight.

7. Inspect the float bowl. Note the following:
   a. Removal all residue from the interior of the float bowl.
   b. Make sure all fuel and air passages are clear.
   c. Replace the float bowl and drain screw O-rings if leaking or damaged.

8. Inspect the air cutoff valve assembly (**Figure 61**). Note the following:
   a. Check the diaphragm for cuts, tears and age deterioration. Hold the diaphragm up to a light to check for pin holes.
   b. Check the diaphragm shaft for burrs and other damage. Check the shaft operating hole in the carburetor for debris and damage. These surfaces must be smooth.
   c. The small air hole and passage in the diaphragm chamber must be clear.
   d. The spring must be in good condition to apply pressure against the diaphragm.

9. Inspect the accelerator pump assembly (**Figure 62**). Note the following:
   a. Check the diaphragm for cuts, tears and age deterioration. Hold the diaphragm up to a light to check for pin holes.
   b. Check the diaphragm shaft for burrs and other damage. Check the shaft operating hole in the float bowl for debris and damage.
   c. The small air holes and passages in the cover and diaphragm chamber must be clear.
   d. The spring must be in good condition to apply pressure against the diaphragm.
   e. Replace the boot if damaged.

10. Inspect the throttle valve assembly. Note the following:
    a. The spring (A, **Figure 63**) must be clean and in good condition.
    b. The throttle valve plate (B, **Figure 63**) must fully open and close. Make sure the plate is tightly secured to the shaft.
    c. The shaft must not be loose or bind.

11. Clean the fuel filter (**Figure 29**) and inspect for

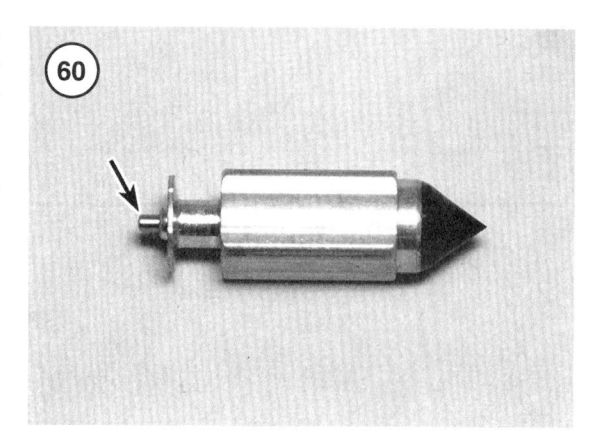

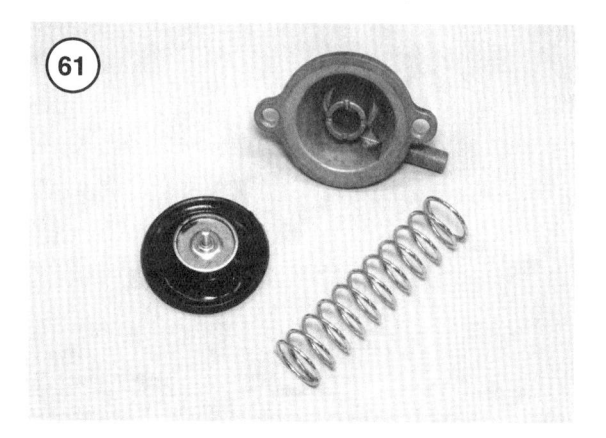

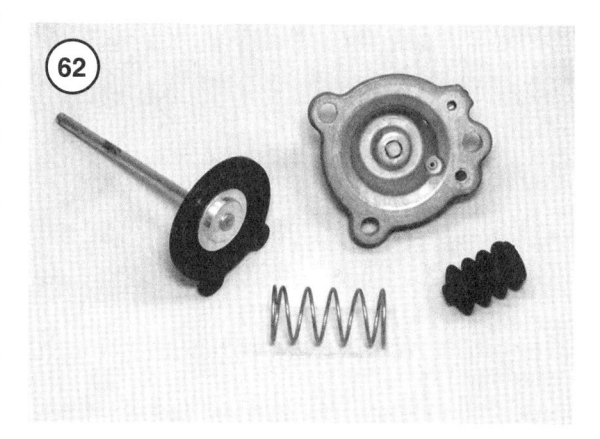

CARBURETOR AND EMISSION CONTROL SYSTEMS

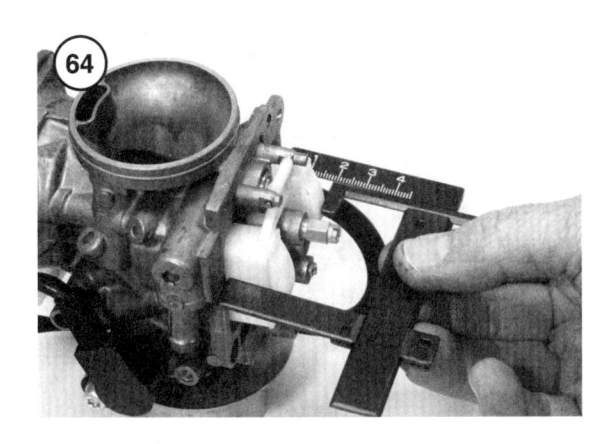

damage. Replace if the screen is plugged or damaged.

12. Check the fuel hose for cracks, splitting and other damage and replace if necessary. Replace weak or damaged hose clamps. Install the protective spring cage over the fuel hose, if removed.

Float Height Measurement

Check the float height whenever the carburetor has been disassembled, when the carburetor is overflowing or when troubleshooting a rich air/fuel mixture.

1. Remove the carburetor as described in this section.
2. Remove the float bowl as described under *Disassembly* as described in this section.
3. Position the carburetor so the float hangs freely and the float valve is open. Tilt the carburetor until the float valve closes and the tab on the float lightly touches the spring-loaded pin in the valve. The float tab must not compress the pin.
4. Measure the distance from the carburetor gasket surface to the highest point on the float **(Figure 64)**. Refer to **Table 1** for the required float height.
5. If the float height is incorrect, replace the float as described under in this section. The float is not adjustable. Remeasure the float height with the new float.
6. Install the float bowl and carburetor as described in this section.

INTAKE MANIFOLD

Removal/Installation

1. Drain the cooling system (Chapter Three).
2. Remove the carburetor as (this chapter).
3. Loosen the clamp and remove the intake boot **(Figure 65)**.
4. With the intake boot opening covered, clean the area around the intake manifold with compressed air.

NOTE
Compare the vacuum and water hose routing on and around the intake manifold shown in these images with the motorcycle being worked on. Note any differences so the parts can be assembled correctly. The intake manifold shown in these images is used on a 2008 California VT750C model.

5. Remove the bolts and the choke cable mounting bracket **(Figure 66)**.
6. Disconnect the water hose at the cylinder water pipe (A, **Figure 67**). It is easier to remove the intake

manifold with the water hose attached to the manifold.

NOTE
The Allen wrench must fit the Allen bolts fully. Otherwise, the wrench could strip the Allen bolt recesses and damage the bolts so they are difficult to remove. Make sure the Allen bolt recesses are clean and the Allen wrench flats are straight and not rounded. Grind the end of the Allen wrench or use a new Allen wrench if necessary.

7. Remove the Allen bolts securing the intake manifold base to the cylinder heads and remove the manifold (B, **Figure 67**).
8. Plug or tape over both cylinder head openings to prevent dirt from entering the engine.
9. Remove and discard the O-rings (**Figure 68**).
10. Check the intake manifold for coolant leaks and other damage.
11. Inspect the water hoses for cracks or damage and replace if necessary. Inspect and replace weak or damaged hose clamps.
12. Check the intake boot for hardness, cracks and other damage and replace if necessary. Replace the hose clamp if damaged.
13. Installation is the reverse of removal. Note the following:
   a. Remove all tape or plugs from the cylinder head intake ports when assembling and installing the parts in this section.
   b. Install a new O-ring (**Figure 68**) into the groove in each intake manifold base groove.
   c. Tighten the intake manifold mounting bolts securely in a crossing pattern.
   d. Tighten the choke cable mounting bracket bolts securely.
   e. Install the carburetor intake boot with its CARB mark (**Figure 65**) facing out while aligning the slot in the intake boot (A, **Figure 69**) with the raised tab (B, **Figure 69**) on the intake manifold.
   f. On VT750C models, tighten the intake boot hose clamp so the distance between the clamp ends (**Figure 70**) is 13.5-15.5 mm (0.53-0.61 in.). On VT750C2 models, tighten the clamp securely.
   g. Install the carburetor as described in this chapter.
   h. Refill and bleed the cooling system (Chapter Three). Check for coolant leaks.

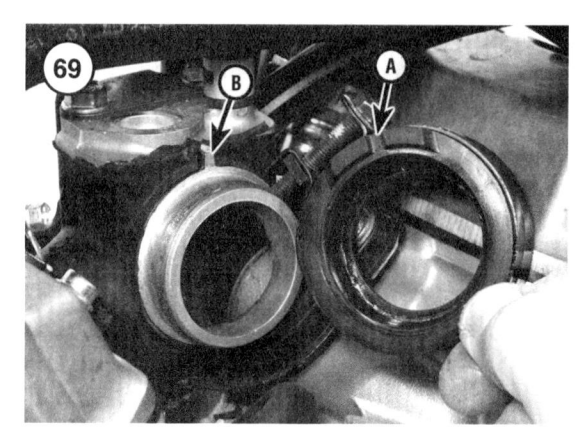

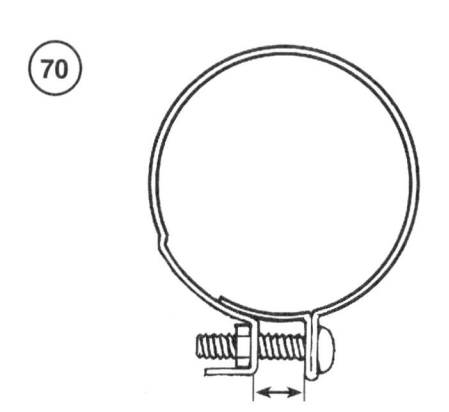

PILOT SCREW ADJUSTMENT (IDLE DROP PROCEDURE)

The carburetor uses a pilot screw (**Figure 71**) for adjustment. The screw is also referred to as a fuel adjustment screw. Turning the pilot screw clockwise leans the air/fuel mixture while counterclockwise richens the mixture. The pilot screw is preset by the manufacturer. Adjustment is not necessary except when the pilot screw is removed, replaced or when operating the motorcycle at altitudes above 6500 ft. (2000 m).

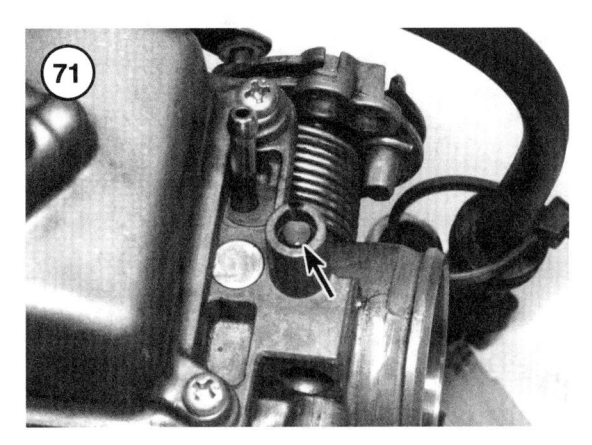

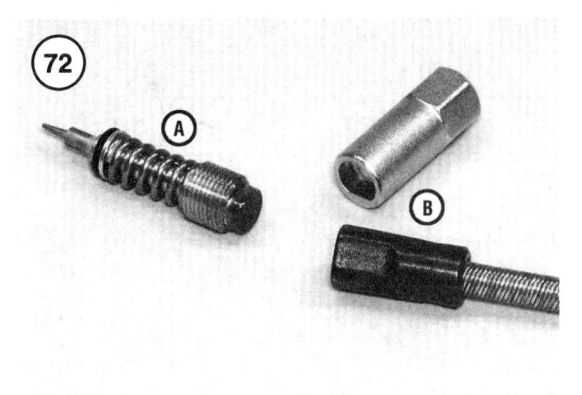

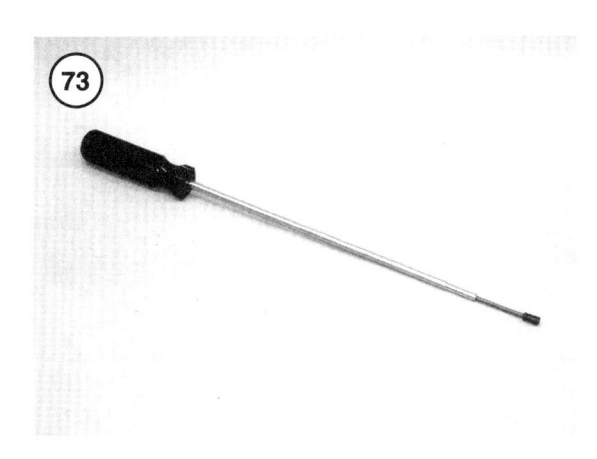

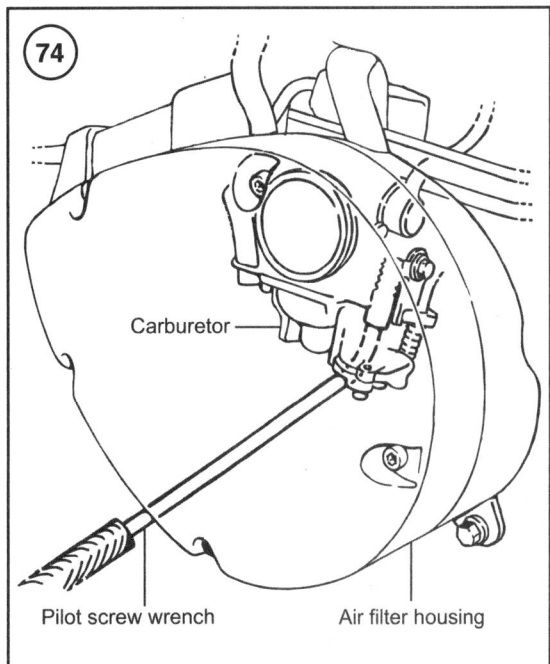

CARBURETOR AND EMISSION CONTROL SYSTEMS

the end of the wrench at the correct angle to contact the pilot screw.
2. Vacuum pump with a gauge.
3. Tachometer that can read rpm changes of 50 rpm or less.

Procedure

Before adjusting the carburetor, read the procedure through to understand the tools and steps required.
1. Replace the air filter if dirty (Chapter Three).

CAUTION
The pilot screw tip is small and easily damaged. Do not overtighten the pilot screw when seating it. If the pilot screw tip breaks off, its removal from the pilot screw bore may be impossible.

NOTE
Figure 71 *shows the pilot screw position with the carburetor removed for clarity.*

2. Working from the right side, mount the tool onto the pilot screw (**Figure 74**). Turn the pilot screw clockwise until it lightly seats, then back the screw out the number of turns listed under pilot screw initial opening in **Table 1**. This is the initial setting.
3. Start the engine and ride it approximately 10 minutes to warm it up
4. Remove the fuel tank as described in this chapter.

Tools

The following tools are required to adjust the pilot screw:
1. The pilot screw uses a D-shaped head (A, **Figure 72**) and requires a D-shaped driver head tool (B) for adjustment:
   a. Pilot screw wrench, D type (Honda part No. 07MMA-MT3010B).
   b. Pilot screw elbow guide (Honda part No. 07PMA-MZ2011A). The pilot screw wrench (**Figure 73**) slides into this tool, which bends

5. Perform the following:
   a. Disconnect the vacuum hose at the PAIR valve control valve. See **Figure 75** (2004-2007 Aero) or A, **Figure 76** (2008-2009 Aero and Spirit).
   b. Plug the vacuum hose to prevent air from entering.
   c. Connect a vacuum pump to the PAIR control valve vacuum hose fitting and apply more than 485 mm Hg (19.10 in. Hg) of vacuum to the valve. This amount of vacuum must be maintained during the adjustment procedure.
   d. Support the vacuum pump so that it hangs below where the fuel tank is originally mounted.

6. Reinstall the fuel tank as described in this chapter or connect an auxiliary fuel tank to the fuel tank fitting to supply fuel to the engine. If an auxiliary fuel tank is used, plug the vacuum hose originally connected to the tank's fuel valve.

7. Start the engine and turn the idle speed screw (**Figure 77**) to set the engine idle speed to 1100-1300 rpm.

8. Turn the pilot screw in or out to obtain the highest engine idle speed.

9. Turn the idle speed screw to reset the engine idle speed to 800-1000 rpm.

10. Slowly open the throttle two or three times (less than 1/4 throttle) and release it.

11. When the engine idle speed is constant, turn the pilot screw in until the engine speed drops 50 rpm.

12. Turn the pilot screw counterclockwise the number of turns listed under pilot screw final opening in Table 1. This is the final pilot screw adjustment.

13. Remove the fuel tank as described in this chapter or remove the auxiliary fuel tank.

14. Remove the vacuum pump and reconnect the vacuum hose at the PAIR control valve.

15. Reinstall the fuel tank as described in this chapter.

16. Start and run the engine at idle speed. Then turn the idle speed screw to reset the engine idle speed to 1100-1300 rpm.

17. Open the throttle and check throttle response. If the engine rpm does not increase smoothly, repeat these steps.

18. Turn the engine off and remove the tachometer.

HIGH ALTITUDE ADJUSTMENT

CAUTION
Always adjust the carburetor for the elevation that it is operated in. Operating the motorcycle at altitudes lower than 1500 m (5000 ft.) with the carburetor adjusted for high altitude may cause the engine to idle roughly and stall. Overheating may also cause engine damage.

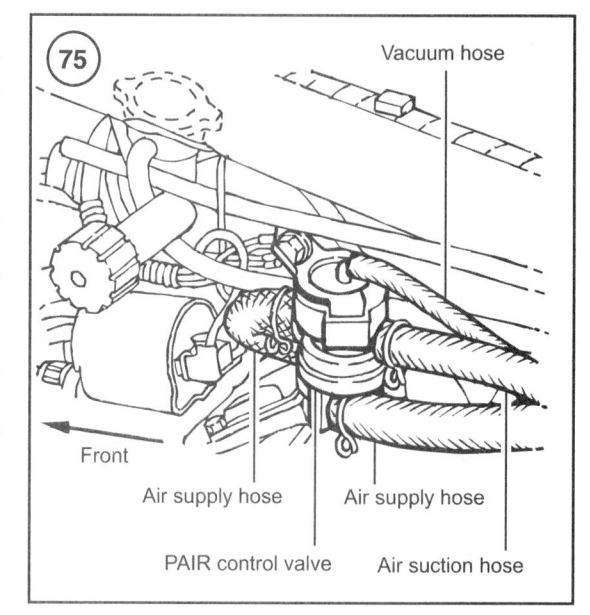

If the motorcycle is ridden for a sustained period at high elevation above 2000 m (6500 ft.), readjust the carburetor to improve engine performance and decrease emissions. Otherwise, the standard jetting will be too rich. This will cause hard starting and spark plug fouling, reduce engine performance and increase fuel consumption.

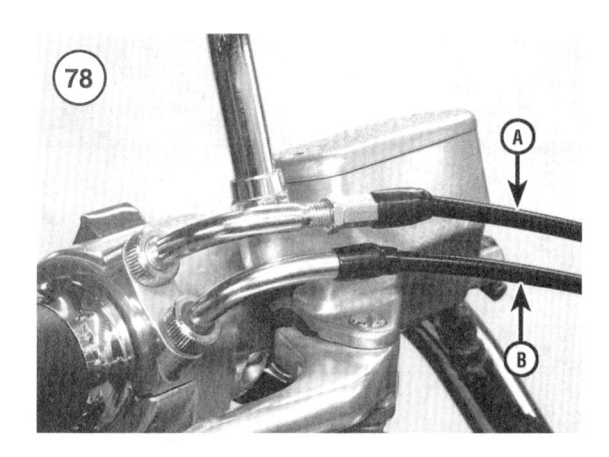

CARBURETOR AND EMISSION CONTROL SYSTEMS

NOTE
If backfiring or popping occurs after closing the throttle during engine braking when the main jet was replaced and the pilot screw adjusted, install the high altitude PAIR control valve (Honda part No. 18650-MEG-801).

4. With the motorcycle at an altitude above 2000 m (6500 ft), start the engine and warm to normal operating temperature. Adjust the idle speed to 800-1000 rpm with the idle speed screw **(Figure 77)**.
5. When the motorcycle is returned to elevations below 2000 m (6500 ft.), perform the following:
   a. Remove the carburetor and float bowl as described in this chapter.
   b. Replace the main jet with the original main jet specified in **Table 1**. Reinstall the float bowl.
   c. Turn the pilot screw counterclockwise to its original preset position.
   d. Reinstall the original PAIR control valve (B, **Figure 76**) if it was replaced with the high altitude valve.
   e. Reinstall the carburetor as described in this chapter.
6. With the motorcycle at a lower altitude, start the engine and warm to normal operating temperature. Reset the engine idle speed (Chapter Three).

THROTTLE CABLE REPLACEMENT

The throttle uses two cables. Always replace both cables at the same time.
1. Remove the fuel tank as described in this chapter.
2. Remove the air filter housing as described in this chapter.
3. Note how the cables are routed.
4. At the carburetor, disconnect the cables as described in *Removal* under *Carburetor* in this chapter.
5. At the handlebar, disconnect the cables as described in *Removal/Installation* under *Handlebar* in Chapter Thirteen.
6. Note the original throttle cable routing from the throttle drum to the carburetor and remove the throttle cables.
7. Lubricate the new throttle cables as described in Chapter Three.
8. Clean the throttle assembly and handlebar.
9. Install the new throttle cables by routing them along their original path.
10. Identify the throttle cables as follows:
    a. Pull cable: A, **Figure 78** and A, **Figure 79**.
    b. Return cable: B, **Figure 78** and B, **Figure 79**.
11. At the handlebar, reconnect the cables **(Figure 78)** as described in *Removal/Installation* under

NOTE
If a dealership performs this adjustment they place a Vehicle Emission Control Information Update label on the frame between the battery and rear fender (2004-2007 Aero and Spirit) or on the left side of the swing arm (2008-2009 Aero). When working on an unfamiliar motorcycle, check for this label before making the adjustment.

NOTE
*Refer to **Pilot Screw Adjustment** in this chapter for tools required to turn the D-shaped pilot screw.*

1. Perform the following:
   a. Remove the carburetor and float bowl as described in this chapter.
   b. Replace the main jet with the high altitude main jet specified in **Table 1**.
   c. Install the float bowl and carburetor.
2. Start the engine and warm to normal operating temperature (approximately 10 minutes), then turn the engine off.
3. Turn the pilot screw **(Figure 74)** clockwise to the high altitude position specified in **Table 1**.

Handlebar in Chapter Thirteen.

12. At the carburetor, reconnect the cables (**Figure 79**) as described in *Installation* under *Carburetor* in this chapter.
13. Adjust the throttle cables as described in Chapter Three.
14. Install the air filter housing and fuel tank as described in this chapter.

> *WARNING*
> *Do not ride the motorcycle until the throttle cables are properly routed and adjusted and the throttle snaps back after releasing it.*

15. Start the engine and run at idle speed with the transmission in neutral. Turn the handlebar from side to side without operating the throttle. The idle speed must remain constant with no increase in idle speed. If the idle speed increases when turning the handlebar, the throttle cable routing and/or adjustment is incorrect. Reroute and/or readjust the throttle cables as required.

CHOKE CABLE REPLACEMENT

1. Disconnect the choke cable from the left side of the motorcycle and partially remove the carburetor as described under *Carburetor* in this chapter. It is not necessary to disconnect the two coolant hoses (A, **Figure 80**) at the carburetor.
2. Slide the rubber cap off the choke cable nut. Then loosen the choke cable nut (B, **Figure 80**) and remove the choke valve from the carburetor.
3. Compress the spring (A, **Figure 81**) and remove the choke valve (B) and spring from the end of the cable.
4. Replace the choke valve if damaged.
5. Install the spring (A, **Figure 81**) and choke valve (B) onto the end of the choke cable. Then insert the choke valve into the carburetor and tighten the choke cable nut (B, **Figure 80**) securely. Reposition the cap over the nut. Operate the choke knob, making sure the choke valve opens and closes without any binding.
6. Install the carburetor and secure the choke cable to the left side of the motorcycle (this chapter).

CRANKCASE BREATHER SYSTEM

The engine is equipped with a closed crankcase breather system. The system draws blow-by gasses from the crankcase and recirculates them into the combustion chamber to be burned.

Liquid residues collect in the air filter housing breather drain tube. These must be emptied at periodic intervals. Refer to *Crankcase Breather Inspection* in Chapter Three for service intervals and procedures.

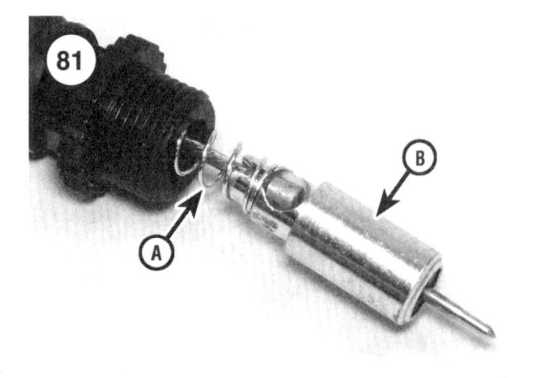

PULSE SECONDARY AIR SUPPLY SYSTEM

All models are equipped with a pulse secondary air supply system that lowers emissions output by introducing filtered secondary air into the exhaust ports. The introduction of air raises the exhaust temperature, which consumes some of the unburned fuel in the exhaust.

The system uses the momentary pressure variance created by the exhaust gas pulses to introduce air into the exhaust ports. During deceleration the PAIR control valve shuts off the air flow to the exhaust. This prevents exhaust backfire due to the rich mixture conditions on deceleration. The PAIR check valves prevents the reverse flow of air back through the PAIR control valve.

The system consists of a PAIR control valve, PAIR check valves, sub-air filters and the vacuum and outlet hoses. See **Figure 82** (2004-2007 Aero) or **Figure 83** (2008-2009 Aero and 2007-2009 Spirit).

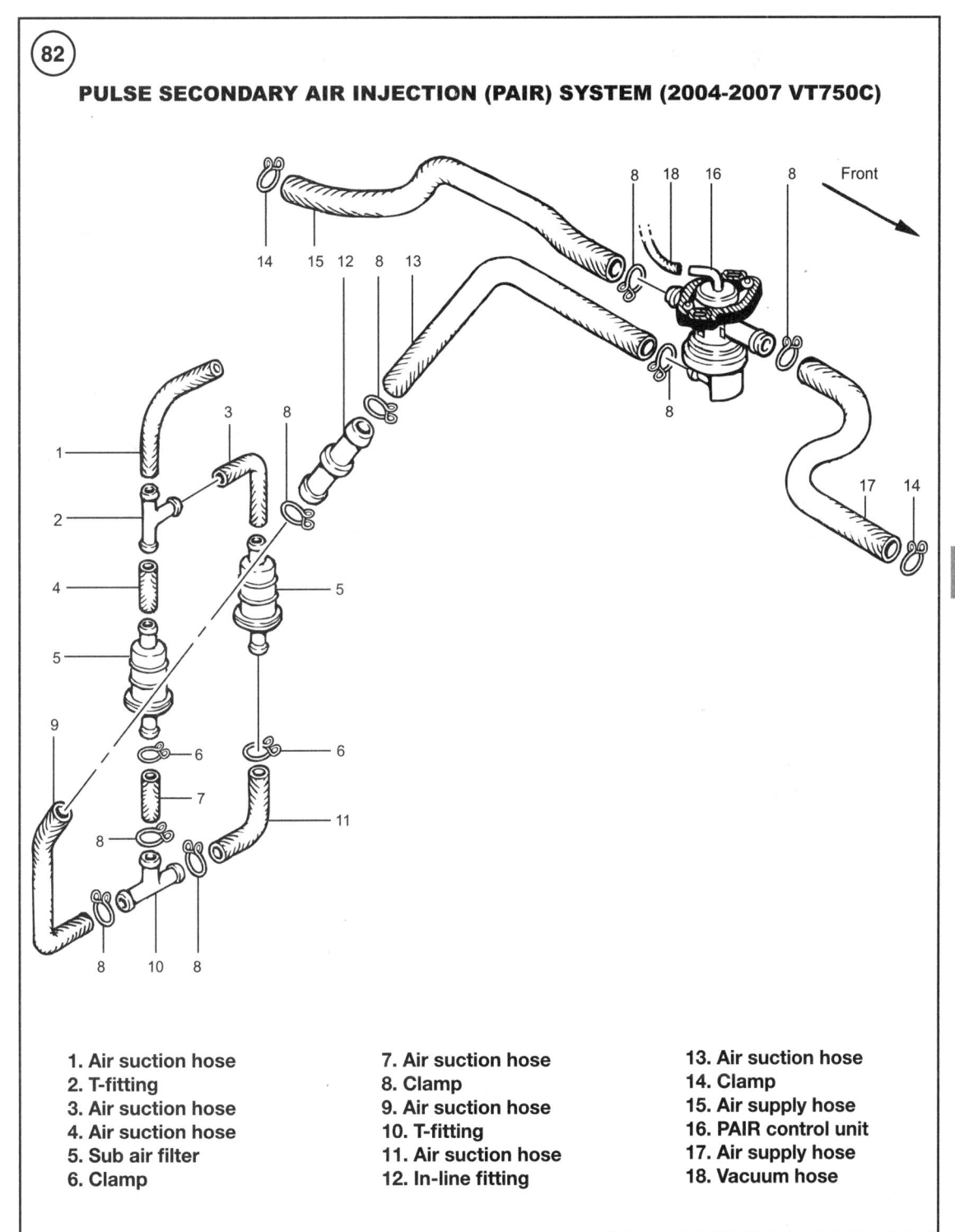

CARBURETOR AND EMISSION CONTROL SYSTEMS

82

PULSE SECONDARY AIR INJECTION (PAIR) SYSTEM (2004-2007 VT750C)

1. Air suction hose
2. T-fitting
3. Air suction hose
4. Air suction hose
5. Sub air filter
6. Clamp
7. Air suction hose
8. Clamp
9. Air suction hose
10. T-fitting
11. Air suction hose
12. In-line fitting
13. Air suction hose
14. Clamp
15. Air supply hose
16. PAIR control unit
17. Air supply hose
18. Vacuum hose

Inspection

Refer to **Figure 82** or **83**.

1. Start and warm the engine up to normal operating temperature, then turn it off.
2. Disconnect the secondary air supply hoses at the PAIR control valve and check that the hoses and the hose connections on the valve are clean and free of all carbon particles. If carbon is found, remove and inspect the PAIR check valves as described in this section.
3. Reinstall the PAIR check valves (if removed) and reconnect their hoses.
4. Remove the fuel tank as described in this chapter.

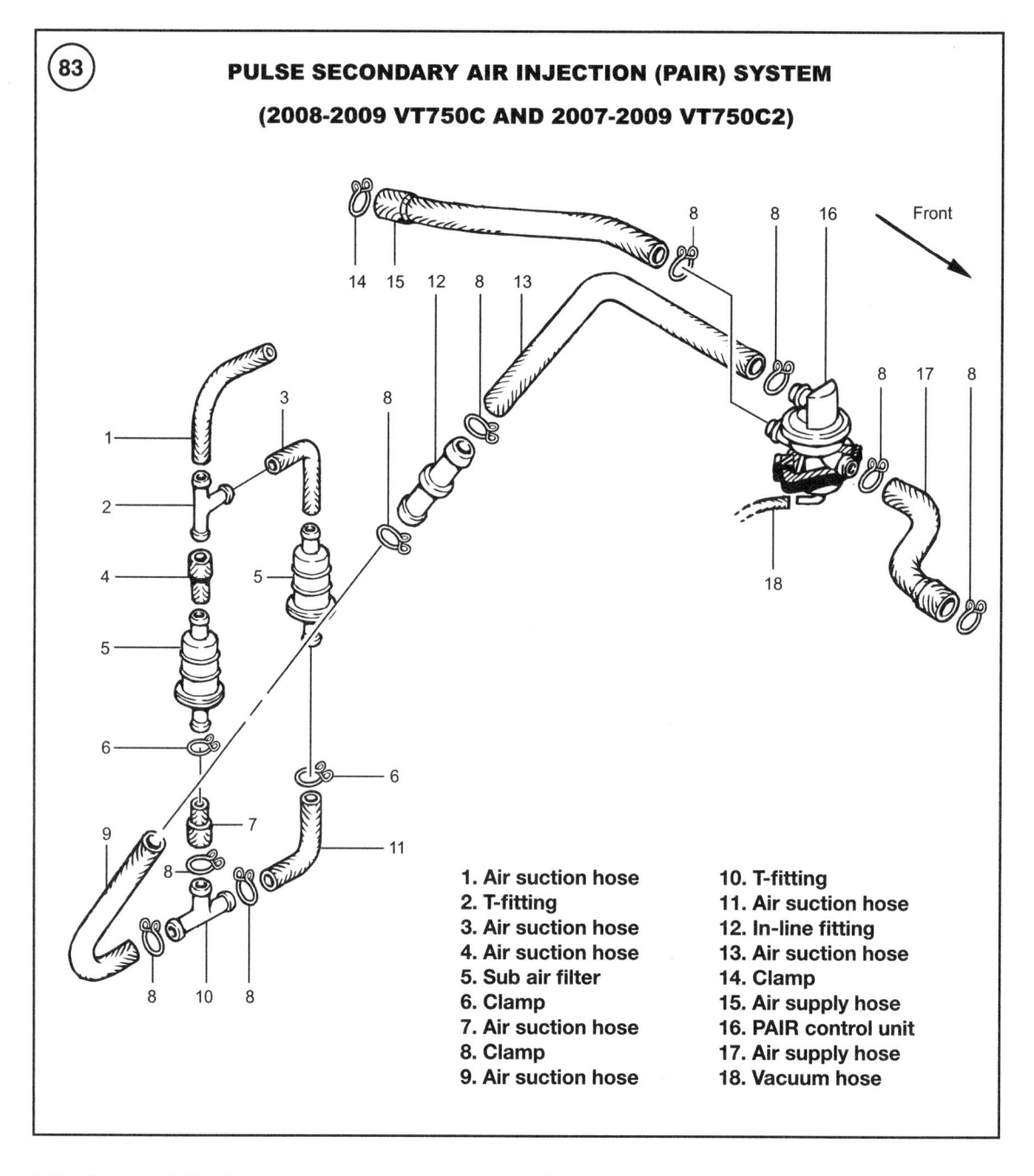

PULSE SECONDARY AIR INJECTION (PAIR) SYSTEM
(2008-2009 VT750C AND 2007-2009 VT750C2)

1. Air suction hose
2. T-fitting
3. Air suction hose
4. Air suction hose
5. Sub air filter
6. Clamp
7. Air suction hose
8. Clamp
9. Air suction hose
10. T-fitting
11. Air suction hose
12. In-line fitting
13. Air suction hose
14. Clamp
15. Air supply hose
16. PAIR control unit
17. Air supply hose
18. Vacuum hose

5. Perform the following:
   a. Disconnect the PAIR control valve vacuum hose and plug the end of the hose.
   b. Connect a vacuum pump to the PAIR control valve vacuum hose fitting.
   c. Support the vacuum pump so that it hangs below where the fuel tank is originally mounted.

6. Reinstall the fuel tank (this chapter) or connect an auxiliary fuel tank to the fuel tank fitting to supply fuel to the engine. If an auxiliary fuel tank is used, plug the vacuum hose originally connected to the tank's fuel valve.

7. Start the engine and slightly open the throttle. Check that air is being drawn into the air supply hose. If not, check for a clogged or damaged air supply hose.

8. With the engine running, apply 485 mm Hg (19.10 in. Hg) of vacuum to the PAIR control valve with the vacuum pump. If checking a model tuned for high altitude, apply 425 mm Hg (16.7 in.Hg) of vacuum. With vacuum applied, check that the air supply hose stops drawing air. Then check that the vacuum reading on the gauge does not bleed off.

9. If air is drawn in or if the specified vacuum is not maintained, the PAIR control valve is defective and must be replaced.

CARBURETOR AND EMISSION CONTROL SYSTEMS

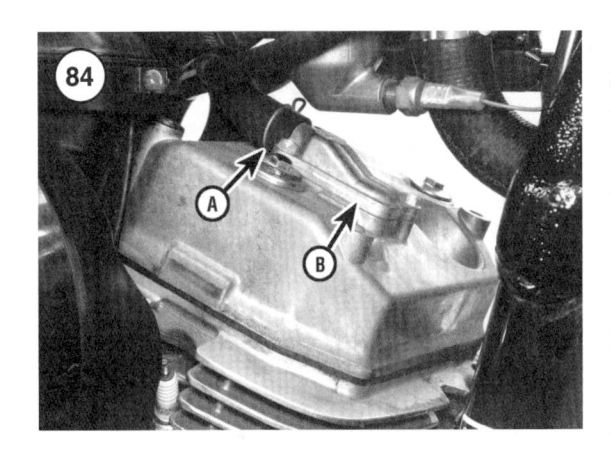

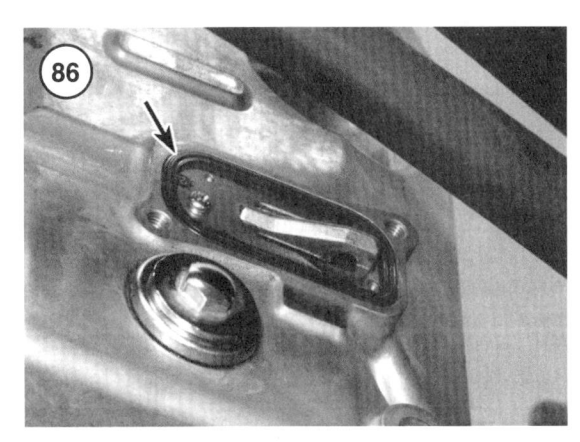

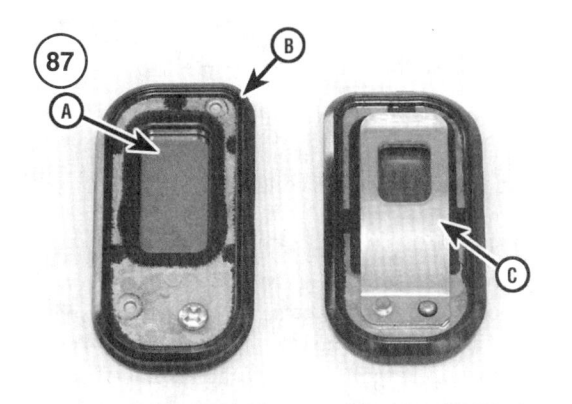

10. If backfiring occurs on deceleration and the tests just performed were all correct, the air cutoff valve installed on the carburetor may be defective. Refer to *Carburetor Disassembly* in this chapter.
11. Disconnect the vacuum pump and reconnect the vacuum hose at the PAIR control valve.
12. Install all parts previously removed.

PAIR Control Valve
Removal/Installation

Refer to **Figure 75** and **Figure 82** (2004-2007 Aero) or B, **Figure 76** and **Figure 83** (2008-2009 Aero and 2007-2009 Spirit).
1. Remove the fuel tank as described in this chapter.
2. Label and then disconnect the hoses at the PAIR control valve.
3. Remove the bolt and the PAIR control valve.
4. Reverse the removal steps to install the PAIR control valve. Tighten the mounting bolt securely.

PAIR Check Valves
Removal/Inspection/Installation

1. Remove the fuel tank as described in this chapter.
2. To remove the front check valve, remove the left and right front outer cylinder covers (Chapter Four).
3. Disconnect the air supply hose from the PAIR check valve cover. See A, **Figure 84** (front) and A, **Figure 85** (rear).
4. Remove the bolts and cover. See B, **Figure 84** (front) and B, **Figure 85** (rear).
5. Remove the PAIR check valve (**Figure 86**) from the cylinder head cover.

NOTE
Do not disassemble the check valves. Do not bend the stopper or remove the screws to remove and turn the reed plate over.

6. Inspect each PAIR check valve assembly (**Figure 87**) for fatigue, damage and carbon deposits. The reed plate (A) must set flush against its seat. Inspect the rubber seat (B) on the check valve body for cracks, flat spots, deterioration and other damage. Make sure the reed plate (C) is secured tightly and not damaged. If damaged or wear is noted, or if the mounting screw is loose, replace the check valve assembly.
7. Clean the check valve mounting area in the cylinder head cover with a rag.
8. Install the check valve into the cylinder head cover as shown in **Figure 86**.
9. Install the PAIR check valve cover with the hose fitting facing as shown in B, **Figure 84** (front) or B,

EVAPORATIVE EMISSION CONTROL SYSTEM (2004-2007 VT750C)

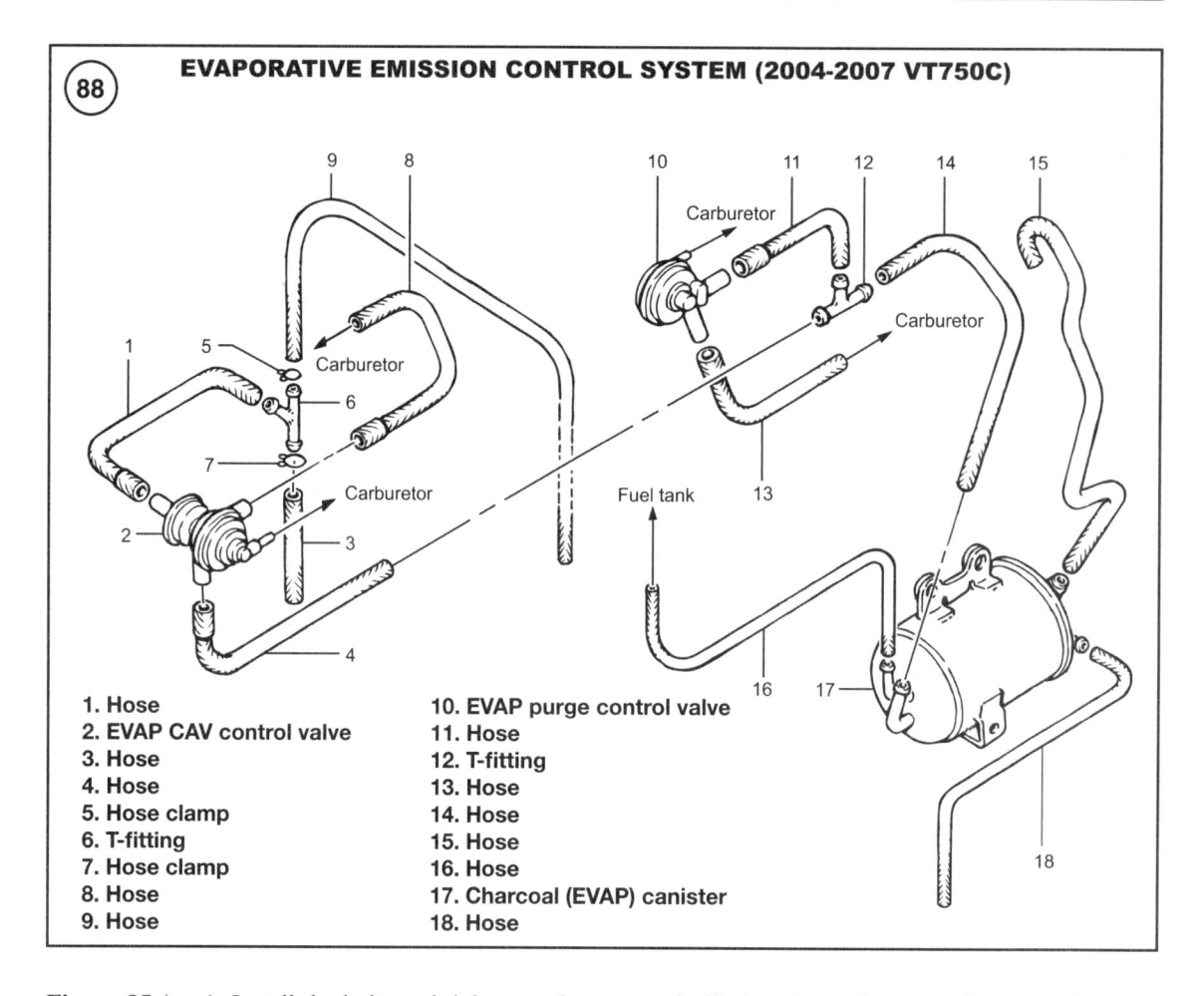

1. Hose
2. EVAP CAV control valve
3. Hose
4. Hose
5. Hose clamp
6. T-fitting
7. Hose clamp
8. Hose
9. Hose
10. EVAP purge control valve
11. Hose
12. T-fitting
13. Hose
14. Hose
15. Hose
16. Hose
17. Charcoal (EVAP) canister
18. Hose

Figure 85 (rear). Install the bolts and tighten to the specification in **Table 2**.
10. Connect the air supply hoses to the front and rear check valve covers.
11. Install the left and right front outer covers (Chapter Four).
12. Install the fuel tank (this chapter).

EVAPORATIVE EMISSION CONTROL SYSTEM (CALIFORNIA MODELS)

Refer to **Figure 88** or **89**

The evaporative emission control (EVAP) system captures fuel system vapors and stores them in the EVAP canister so they cannot be released into the atmosphere. When the engine is started, the stored vapors are drawn from the canister. They pass through the EVAP purge control valve, flow into the carburetor and then into the engine where they are burned. At the same time, the EVAP CAV control valve opens so air is drawn into the carburetor. On 2007-2009 Aero and Spirit models, a fuel cutoff solenoid valve, which is controlled by the ICM, was added to stop fuel flow to the carburetor when the rev limiter is operated or when the engine stop switch is turned off when the engine is running. See **Figure 88** (2004-2007 Aero) and **Figure 89** (2008-2009 Aero and 2007-2009 Spirit).

Make sure all hoses are correctly routed, properly attached to the different components and all hose clamps are tight. Check all hoses for deterioration, and replace them as necessary.

There are many vacuum hoses used on this system. Without clear identifying marks, reconnecting the hoses can be difficult. Label each hose as it is removed.

EVAP Canister
Removal/Installation

Refer to **Figure 88** or **89**

1. Support the motorcycle on a workstand.
2. Remove the bolt and collar (A, **Figure 90**) and lower the canister (B).
3. Label and then disconnect the hoses from the canister. See **Figure 88** or **Figure 89**.
4. Inspect the hoses for cuts, damage or soft spots. Replace any damaged hoses.
5. Installation is the reverse of these steps. Tighten the mounting bolt securely.

CARBURETOR AND EMISSION CONTROL SYSTEMS

89 EVAPORATIVE EMISSION CONTROL SYSTEM
(2008-2009 VT750C and 2007-2009 VT750C2)

1. Hose
2. Hose
3. Fuel cutoff solenoid valve
4. Hose
5. Hose
6. EVAP CAV control valve
7. Housing
8. EVAP CAV control valve sub-air filter
9. Cover
10. Hose
11. T-fitting
12. Hose
13. Hose
14. T-fitting
15. Hose
16. Hose
17. EVAP purge control valve
18. Hose
19. Hose clamp
20. Hose
21. Hose
22. Hose fitting
23. Charcoal (EVAP) canister
24. Hose

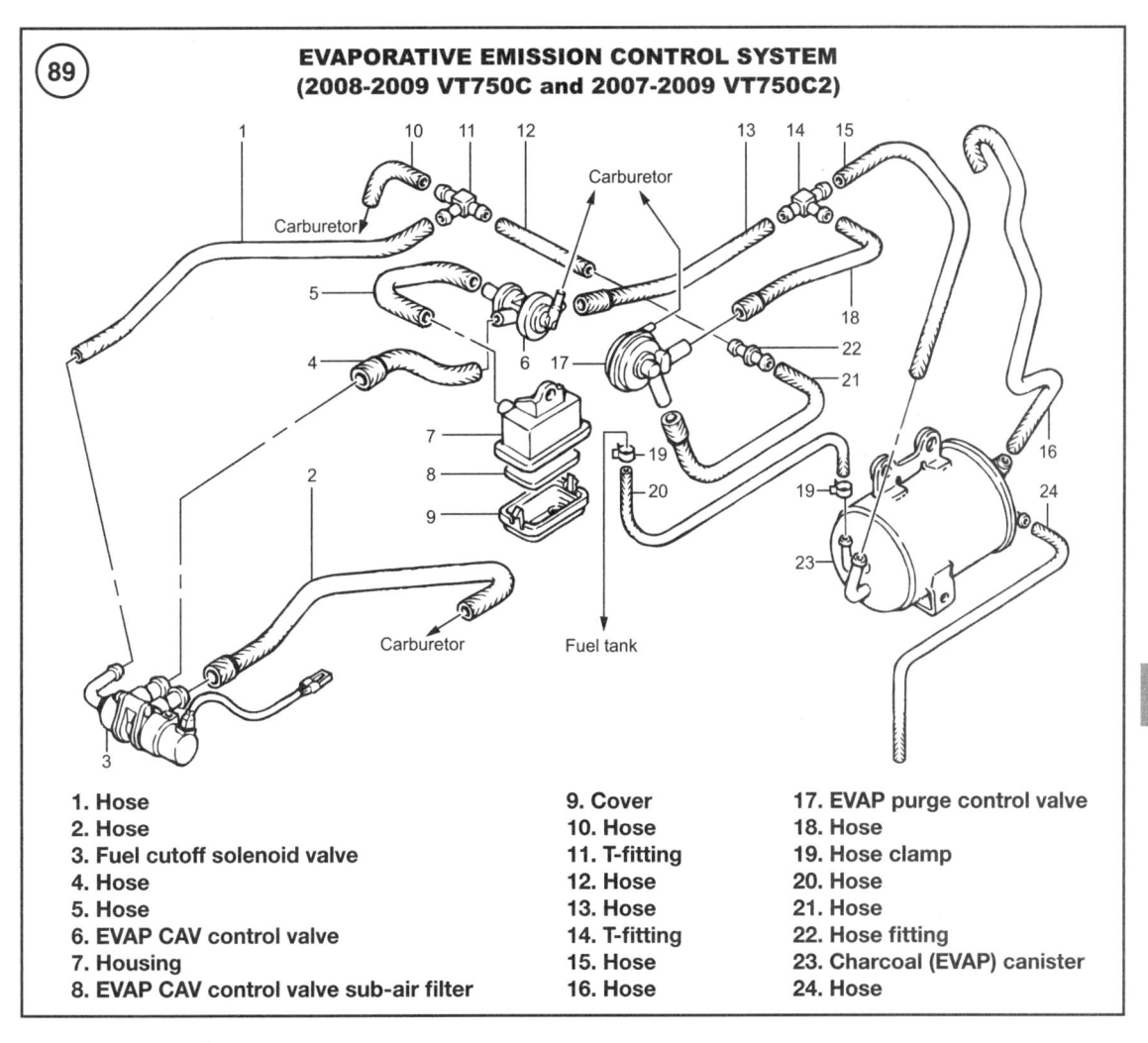

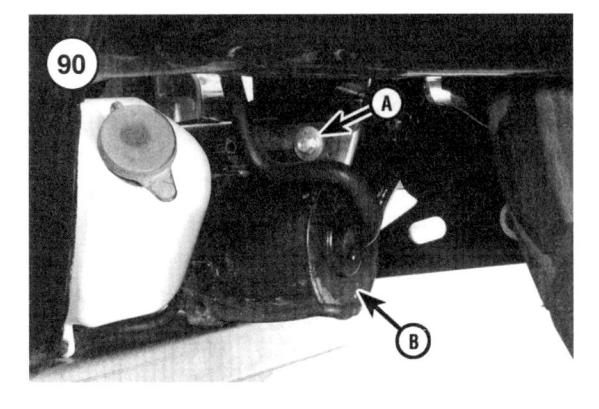

Evaporative Emission Carburetor Air Vent (EVAP CAV) Control Valve

If the engine is difficult to restart when hot, test the EVAP CAV control valve as described in this section.

Removal/installation

1. Remove the fuel tank as described in this chapter.

2. Label and disconnect the hoses from the EVAP CAV control valve (A, **Figure 91**).

3. Remove the EVAP CAV control valve from its mounting bracket.

4. Reverse the removal steps to install the EVAP CAV control valve. Make sure the EVAP CAV control valve is secure in its mounting bracket

Testing

Refer to **Figure 92**.

A hand-operated vacuum pump (with gauge) and pressure pump are required.

1. Remove the EVAP CAV control valve as described in this section.
2. Connect a vacuum pump to hose fitting C and apply 500 mm Hg (19.7 in. Hg) of vacuum. The vacuum should hold. If the vacuum does not hold, replace the EVAP CAV control valve.
3. Disconnect the vacuum pump.
4. Connect the vacuum pump to hose fitting A and apply vacuum to the EVAP CAV control valve. The vacuum should hold. If the vacuum does not hold, replace the EVAP CAV control valve.
5. Disconnect the vacuum pump.

CAUTION
Use only a hand-operated pressure pump. Using air from a high-pressure source may damage the EVAP CAV control valve.

6. Connect the vacuum pump to hose fitting C and a pressure pump to hose fitting A.
7. Apply vacuum to hose fitting C, then pump air through hose fitting A. Air must flow through the valve and exit through hose fitting B. Release the vacuum from the valve.
8. Plug hose fitting B.
9. Apply vacuum to the hose fitting C, then pump air through hose fitting A. If the air pressure does not hold, replace the EVAP CAV control valve.
10. Disconnect the vacuum and pressure pumps.
11. Install the EVAP CAV control valve as described in this section.

EVAP CAV Control Valve Sub-Air Filter (2008-2009 Aero and 2007-2009 Spirit Models)

Removal/Cleaning/Installation

The sub-air filter (B, **Figure 91**) for the EVAP CAV control valve is mounted on the EVAP CAV control valve mounting bracket.

1. Remove the fuel tank as described in this chapter.
2. Remove the bolt and filter housing.
3. Disconnect the hose from the filter housing.
4. Remove the bottom cover and filter.
5. If dirty, remove and clean the sub-air filter with soapy water and rinse with clear water. Replace the filter if deteriorated or damaged.
6. Reverse the removal steps to install the sub-ar filter. Tighten the filter housing bolt securely.

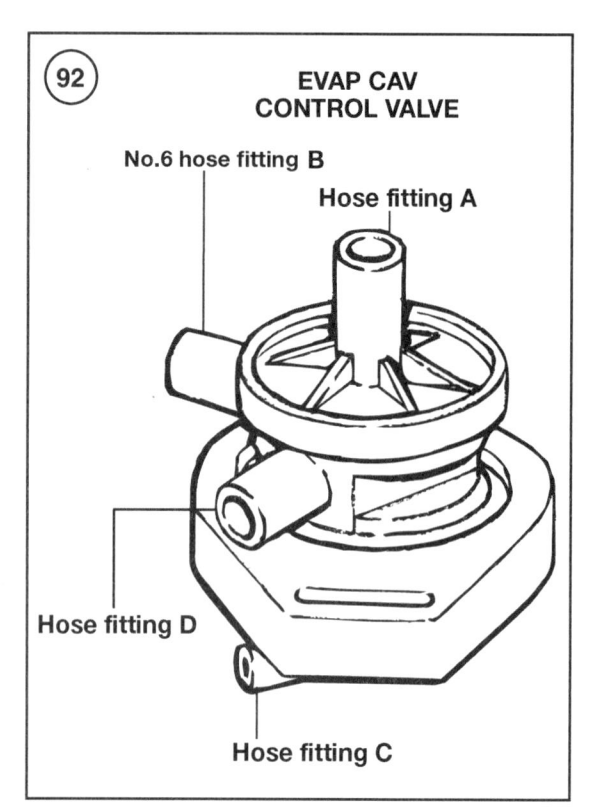

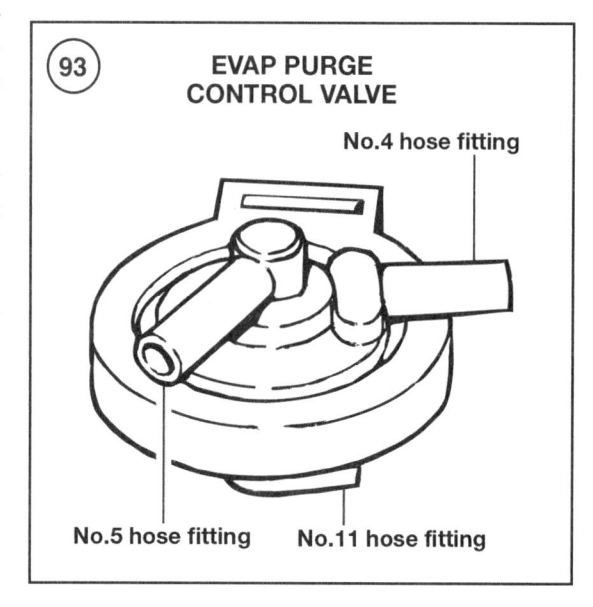

Evaporative Emission (EVAP) Purge Control Valve

If the engine is difficult to restart when hot, test the EVAP purge control valve as described in this section.

Removal/installation

1. Remove the fuel tank as described in this chapter.

CARBURETOR AND EMISSION CONTROL SYSTEMS

and apply 50 mm Hg (2.0 in. Hg) of vacuum. The vacuum should hold. If the vacuum does not hold, replace the EVAP purge control valve.

3. Disconnect the vacuum pump.

4. Connect the vacuum pump to the No. 11 hose fitting and apply 250 mm Hg (9.8 in. Hg) of vacuum. The vacuum should hold. If the vacuum does not hold, replace the EVAP purge control valve. If continuing, leave the vacuum pump connected to the No. 11 hose fitting and perform Step 5.

CAUTION
Use only a hand-operated pressure pump. Using air from a high-pressure source may damage the EVAP purge control valve.

5. Connect a pressure pump to the No.4 hose fitting and apply 25 mm (1.0 in.) HG of vacuum, then pump air through the No. 11 hose fitting. Air should flow through the No. 5 hose fitting. If air did not flow through the No. 5 hose fitting, replace the EVAP purge control valve.

6. Disconnect the vacuum and pressure pumps.

7. Install the EVAP purge control valve as described in this section.

Evaporative Emission (EVAP) Fuel Cutoff Solenoid Valve (2008-2009 Aero and 2007-2009 Spirit Models)

Removal/installation

1. Remove the fuel tank as described in this chapter.
2. Remove the steering side covers (Chapter Seventeen).
3. Open the clamp (A, **Figure 94**) securing the wiring harness to the frame. Then disconnect the fuel cutoff solenoid valve 2-pin white connector.
4. Label and disconnect the hoses at the fuel cutoff solenoid valve (B, **Figure 94**).
5. Remove the fuel cutoff solenoid valve from its mounting bracket.
6. Reverse these steps to install the fuel cutoff solenoid valve.

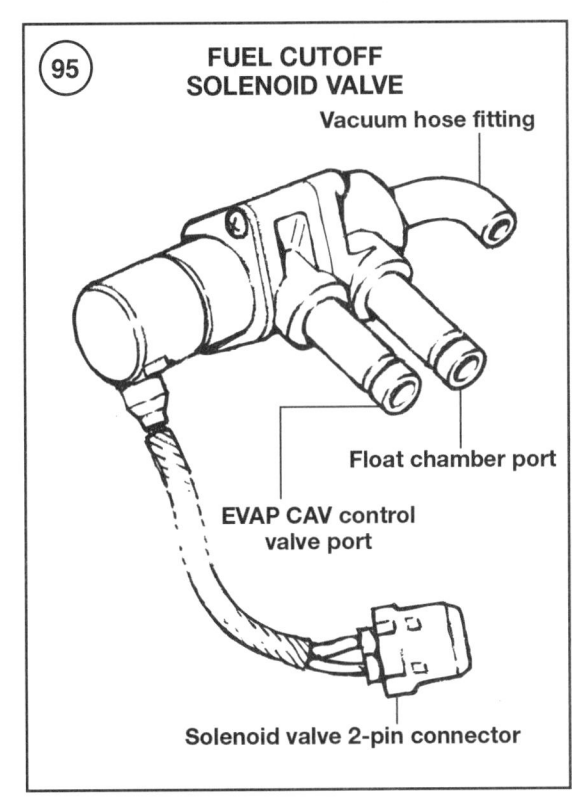

2. Label and disconnect the hoses from the EVAP purge control valve (C, **Figure 91**).

3. Remove the EVAP purge control valve off its mounting bracket.

4. Reverse the removal steps to install the EVAP purge control valve.

Testing

Refer to **Figure 93**.

A hand-operated vacuum pump (with gauge) and pressure pump are required.

1. Remove the EVAP purge control valve as described in this section.
2. Connect a vacuum pump to the No. 5 hose fitting

Testing

Refer to **Figure 95**.

A hand-operated vacuum pump (with gauge) and pressure pump are required.

1. Remove the fuel cutoff solenoid valve as described in this section.
2. Connect a vacuum pump to the vacuum hose fitting and apply 250 mm Hg (9.8 in. Hg) of vacuum.

The vacuum should hold. If the vacuum does not hold, replace the fuel cutoff solenoid valve.

3. Disconnect the vacuum pump.

CAUTION
Use only a hand-operated pressure pump durning testing. Using air from a high-pressure source may damage the fuel cutoff solenoid valve.

4. Connect a pressure pump to the float chamber port and pump air into the valve. Air must flow through the valve and exit through the EVAP CAV control valve port. If air did not exit through the EVAP CAV control valve port, replace the fuel cutoff solenoid valve.

5. Disconnect the pressure pump.

6. Connect a pressure pump to the EVAP CAV control valve port and pump air into the valve. Air must flow through the valve and exit through the float chamber port. If air did not exit through the float chamber port, replace the fuel cutoff solenoid valve.

7. Remove the pressure pump.

8. Perform the following test:
   a. Connect a vacuum pump to the EVAP CAV control valve port.
   b. Connect a 12-volt battery to the 2-pin fuel cutoff solenoid valve electrical connector. Connect the positive battery lead to the black terminal and the negative battery lead to the black/green terminal.
   c. Apply 250 mm Hg (9.8 in. Hg) of vacuum. The vacuum should hold. If the vacuum does not hold, replace the fuel cutoff solenoid valve.
   d. Disconnect the battery test leads and the vacuum pump.

9. Perform the following test:
   a. Connect the pressure pump to the vacuum hose fitting.
   b. Connect a 12-volt battery to the fuel 2-pin cutoff solenoid valve electrical connector. Connect the positive battery lead to the black terminal and the negative battery lead to the black/green terminal.
   c. Pump air through the vacuum port. Air should flow through the valve and exit through the float chamber port. If air did not exit through the float chamber port, replace the fuel cutoff solenoid valve.
   d. Disconnect the battery test leads and the pressure pump.

10. Install the fuel cutoff solenoid valve as described in this section.

Table 1 CARBURETOR AND FUEL TANK SPECIFICATIONS

Throttle bore	34 mm (1.3 in.)
Identification number	
Aero	
2004-2007	
49-state and Canada	VE5BA
California	VE5BB
2008-2009	
49-state and Canada	VE5EA
California	VE5EV
Spirit	
49-state and Canada	VE5EA
California	VE5EB
Idle speed	1100 - 1300 rpm
Idle drop procedure	Refer to text
Pilot screw initial opening	
Aero	
2004-2007	2 3/4 turns out
2008-2009	
49-state and Canada	2 turns out
California	2 1/8 turns out
Spirit	
49-state and Canada	2 turns out
California	2 1/8 turns out
Pilot screw final opening	
Aero	
2004-2007	1/2 turn out
2008-2009	1/4 turn out
Spirit	1/4 turn out
Main jet	
Aero	
2004-2007	
Standard	125
High altitude	122
2008-2009	
Standard	122
High altitude	120
Spirit	
Standard	122
High altitude	120
Slow jet	50
Pilot screw high altitude opening	
Aero	
2004-2007	7/8 turn clockwise from preset position
2008-2009	3/4 turn clockwise from preset position
Spirit	3/4 turn clockwise from preset position
Float height	18.5 mm (0.73 in.)
Fuel tank capacity	
Total	14 L (3.7 gal.)
Reserve	3.3 L (0.87 gal.)

Table 2 FUEL SYSTEM TORQUE SPECIFICATIONS

	N.m	in.-lb.	ft.-lb.
Fuel tank mounting bolt	27	--	20
Fuel valve mounting nut	34	--	25
PAIR check valve cover mounting bolt			
2004-2009 Aero models	6.9	61	--
2007-2009 Spirit models	7.0	62	--
Air cleaner cover Allen bolt			
2004-2009 Aero models	2.0	18	--
2007-2009 Spirit models	1.5	13	--
Air cleaner chamber bracket mounting screw			
2004-2009 Aero models	1.0	8.9	--
2007-2009 Spirit models	1.1	10	--
Air cleaner connecting tube hose clamp screw			
2004-2009 Aero models	1.0	8.9	--
2007-2009 Spirit models	0.7	6.2	--

Table 2 FUEL SYSTEM TORQUE SPECIFICATIONS (continued)

	N.m	in.-lb.	ft.-lb.
2007-2009 Spirit models			
Vacuum chamber cover screw	2.1	19	--
TP sensor Torx screw	3.4	30	--
Carburetor heater set plate screw	3.4	30	--
Float chamber screw	2.1	19	--
Accelerator pump cover screw	2.1	19	--
Air cut-off valve cover screw	2.1	19	--
Accelerator pump link mounting bolt	3.4	30	--
Choke valve nut	2.3	20	--
Float bowl drain screw	1.5	13	--
Slow jet	1.8	16	--
Needle jet holder	2.3	20	--
Main jet	2.1	19	--

CHAPTER NINE

FUEL INJECTION AND EMISSION CONTROL SYSTEMS

The chapter covers the fuel injection and emission control systems used on models so equipped.

Refer to Chapter Three for air filter service, throttle cable adjustment and lubrication.

Before working on the fuel system, refer to *Safety* in Chapter One.

Fuel system specifications are listed in **Tables 1-5** at the end of the chapter.

FUEL SYSTEM PRECAUTIONS

WARNING
Fuel will spill and fuel vapors will be present when servicing and troubleshooting the fuel system as described in this chapter. Because gasoline is extremely flammable, perform the procedure away from all open flames, including appliance pilot lights and sparks. Do not smoke or allow someone who is smoking in the work area as an explosion and fire may occur. Always work in a well-ventilated area. Wipe up spills immediately. Keep a fire extinguisher nearby.

WARNING
*The fuel system is pressurized. Always wear eye protection whenever working on the fuel system, especially when depressurizing the system. Refer to **Depressurizing the Fuel System** (this chapter) for more information.*

1. Turn the ignition switch off before disconnecting any connectors in the fuel or engine management systems. ECM damage may occur if electrical components are disconnected/connected when the ignition switch is turned on.
2. Spring clamps are used to secure many of the hoses in the fuel system. Before disconnecting the hoses, note the position of the extended arms on the clamps so the clamps can be reinstalled facing in their original direction. Otherwise, the arms on the clamps may contact another hose or wiring harness and damage the part. These clamps often leave imprints in the hoses that can be used to help realign the clamps.
3. Certain fasteners on the throttle body are pre-set by the manufacturer and must not be loosened or removed. Refer to **Throttle Body** (this chapter) for additional information.

DEPRESSURIZING THE FUEL SYSTEM

The fuel system is under pressure at all times, even when the engine is not operating. Before disconnecting the fuel feed hose (A, **Figure 1**) located between the throttle body and the fuel pump, depressurize the fuel system as follows:

1. Read *Fuel System Precautions* in this chapter.
2. Remove the seat (Chapter Seventeen).
3. With the ignition switch turned off, disconnect the fuel pump connector (B, **Figure 1**).
4. Start the engine and run at idle speed until it stalls.
5. Turn the ignition switch off.
6. Disconnect the negative battery cable at the battery (Chapter Ten).
7. Remove the connector boot or the clips and the connector holder located over the top of the fuel pump, if used.
8. Wipe off the fuel feed hose connector (B, **Figure 1**) with a damp rag to prevent dirt from contaminating the fuel pump and the open hose end when the connector is disconnected.
9. Place a shop rag over the fuel feed hose connector.

CAUTION
The fuel feed hose is expensive. Handle the hose and its connector ends carefully during all service work.

10. Disconnect the fuel feed hose connector (A, **Figure 1**) from the fuel pump fuel pipe as follows:

NOTE
If the connector is stuck, continue to squeeze the retainer tabs while pulling and pushing the connector. Repeat until the connector breaks free and slides off the fuel pipe.

  a. Hold the fuel feed hose connector and squeeze the retainer tabs **(Figure 2)** to release the connector from the fuel pipe. Then pull the connector off the fuel pipe.
  b. Remove the retainer (A, **Figure 3**) and the rubber guide (B) from the fuel pipe. Discard the retainer. Replace the rubber guide if cracked or damaged.
  c. Cover the fuel feed hose connector and fuel pipe with plastic bags to prevent contamination.

11. Connect the fuel feed hose connector onto the fuel pipe as follows:
  a. Install a new retainer into the connector by aligning the pawls on the retainer with the grooves in the connector **(Figure 4)**.
  b. Position the rubber guide (B, **Figure 3**) over the fuel pipe.

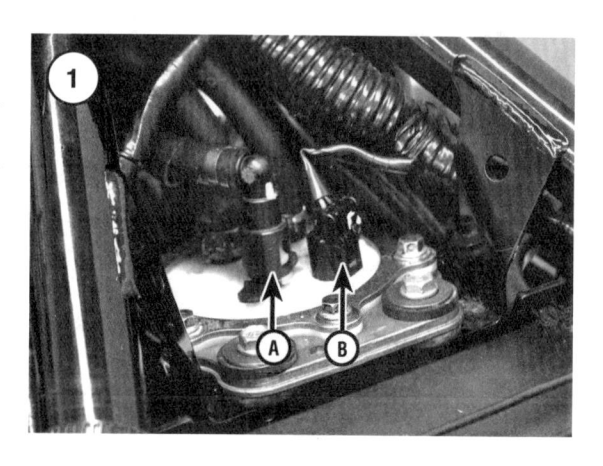

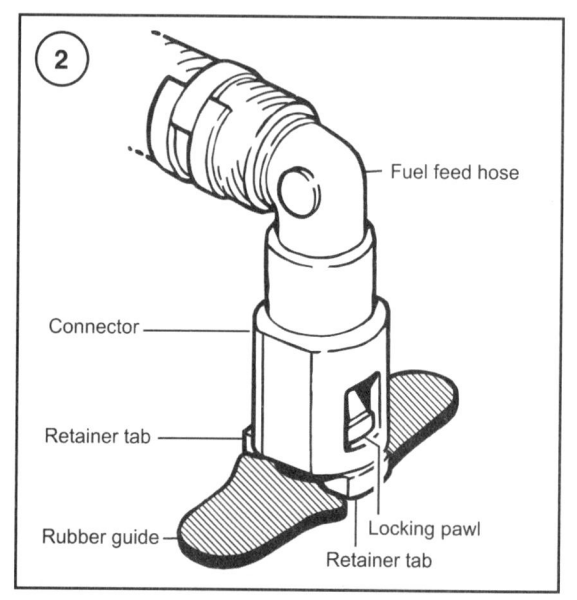

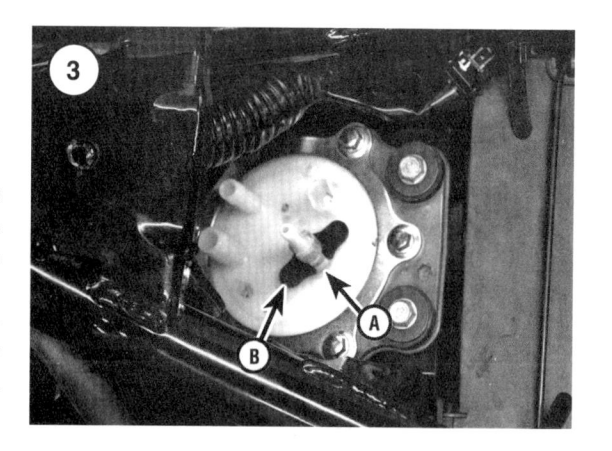

NOTE
*If it is difficult to install and lock the connector, apply a small amount of engine oil onto the end of the fuel pipe. Also make sure the retainer tabs in the connector are properly aligned with the rubber guide (**Figure 5**).*

FUEL INJECTION AND EMISSION CONTROL SYSTEMS

4

Retainers
Fuel feed hose
Connector
Locking pawl
Locking pawl
Retainer tabs

5

Fuel feed hose
Connector
Locking pawl
Fuel pipe
Align
Notch
Rubber guide

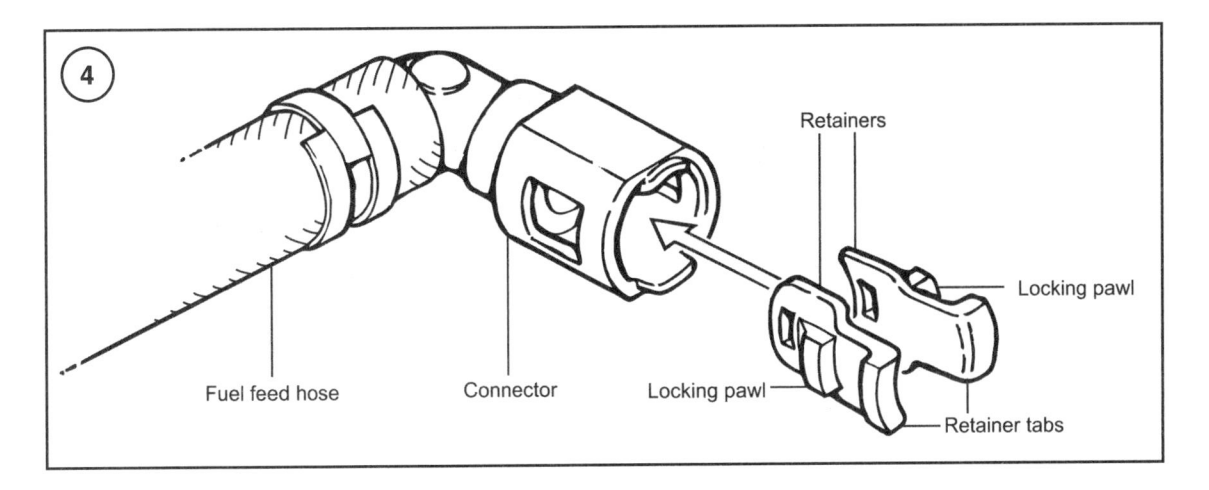

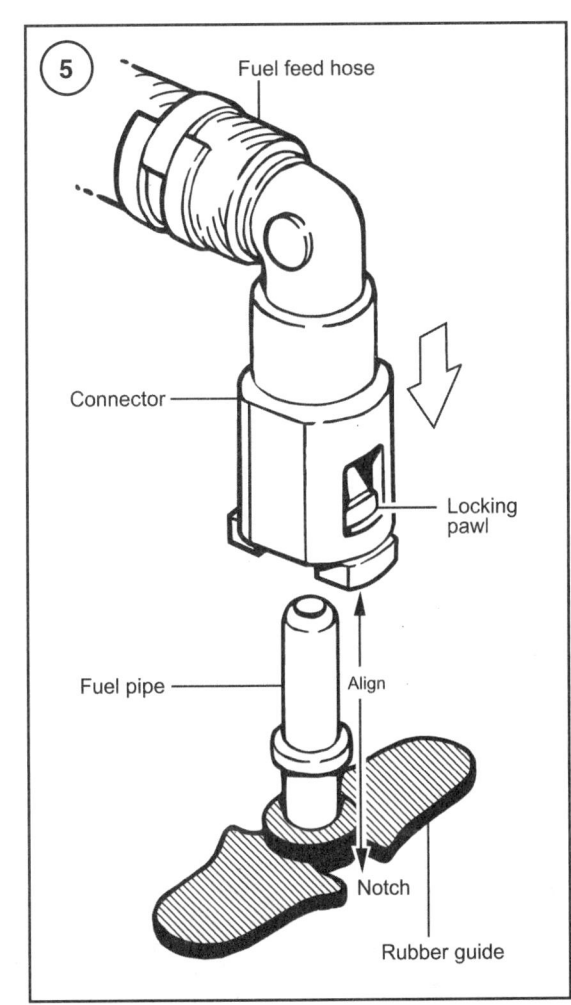

c. Install the connector by aligning the tabs on the retainer with the grooves in the rubber guide **(Figure 5)**. Then push the connector down until both retainer pawls click into the notches and lock the connector in place.

d. Pull on the connector gently to make sure it is locked in place.

12. Reconnect the fuel pump connector (B, **Figure 1**).
13. Install the connector boot or the connector holder, if used.
14. Reconnect the negative battery cable at the battery (Chapter Ten).
15. Turn the engine stop switch to run.
16. Turn the ignition switch on, but do not start the engine. Listen for the fuel pump. It should run for two seconds (pressurizing the fuel system) and then stop. Turn the ignition switch off. Check for leaks.

WARNING
Do not start and run the engine if the fuel feed hose or its connectors are leaking. Doing so may cause the motorcycle to catch on fire. If there is a leak, remove the fuel feed hose and check the hose and connectors for damage.

17. Repressurize the system two or three more times while checking the fuel feed hose and its connector for fuel leakage.
18. Reinstall the seat (Chapter Ten).

FUEL TANK

Removal/Installation

1. Read *Fuel System Precautions* in this chapter.
2. Remove the seat (Chapter Seventeen).
3. Disconnect the negative battery cable at the battery (Chapter Ten).
4. Remove the speedometer housing (Chapter Ten).

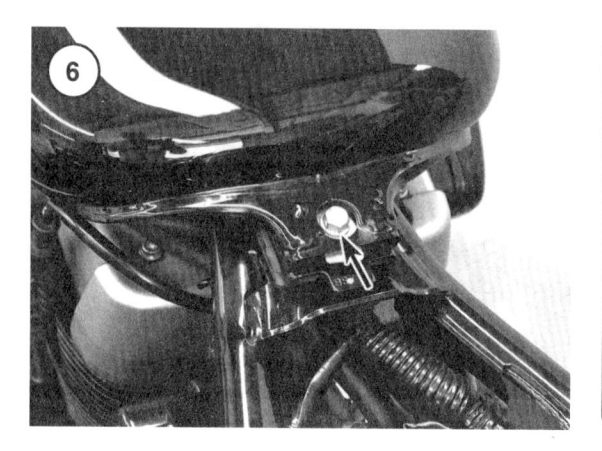

5. Remove the bolt **(Figure 6)** securing the fuel tank to the frame. Then remove the washer (A, **Figure 7**) and collar (B).

> *NOTE*
> *It is helpful to raise and support the fuel tank with a wooden block when disconnecting the hoses.*

> *NOTE*
> *Before disconnecting the fuel hose and fuel return hose, note their routing from the fuel tank to the fuel pump.*

6. Block off the fuel hose (A, **Figure 8**) and fuel vapor return hose (B) with clamps. Make sure the hose clamps do not cut or damage the hoses.
7. Disconnect the fuel reserve sensor connectors (C, **Figure 8**) at the fuel tank.
8. Disconnect the breather hose **(Figure 9)** at the fuel tank.
9. Disconnect the fuel hose (A, **Figure 10**) and fuel vapor return hose (B) at the fuel pump.
10. Remove the fuel tank with the fuel and fuel vapor return hoses attached to the tank.
11. Check all of the fuel hoses for cracks, deterioration, soft sport and other damage and replace if necessary.
12. Reverse the removal steps to install the fuel tank. Note the following:
    a. Replace the fuel tank dampers mounted on the side of the frame if missing or damaged.
    b. Tighten the fuel tank mounting bolt to 27 N.m (20 ft.-lb.).
    c. Check the hoses at the fuel tank and fuel pump for leaks.

FUEL PRESSURE TEST

The fuel pressure at the injectors must be kept constant as a rise or drop in fuel pressure can greatly affect engine operation. Check the fuel pressure if

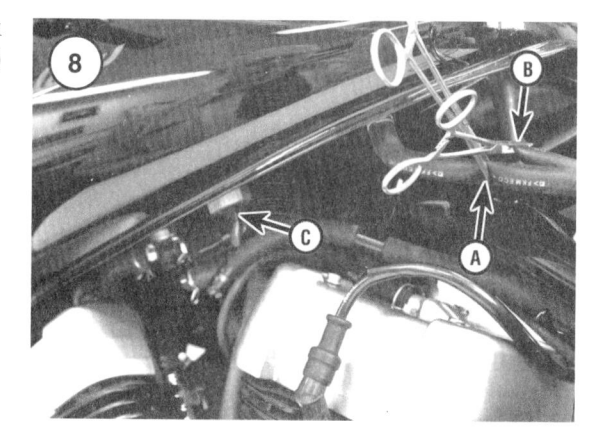

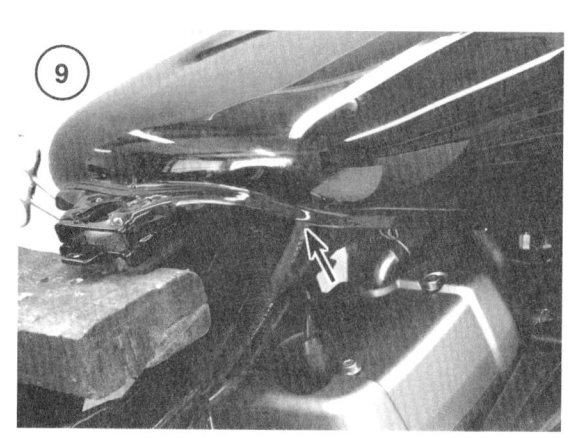

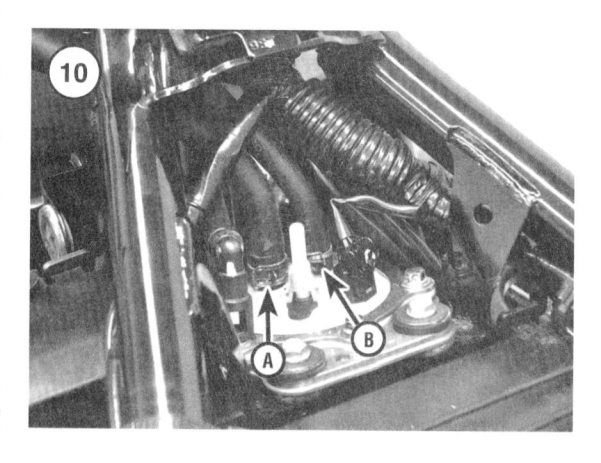

FUEL INJECTION AND EMISSION CONTROL SYSTEMS

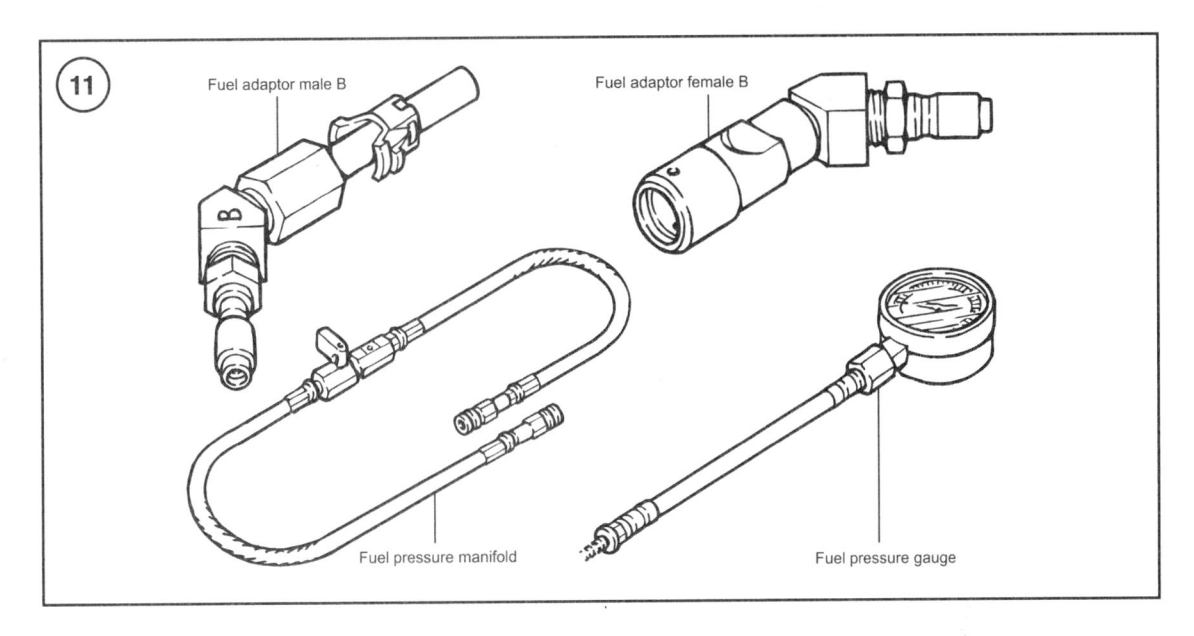

11 Fuel adaptor male B — Fuel adaptor female B — Fuel pressure manifold — Fuel pressure gauge

12 Fuel pressure gauge — Fuel adaptor male B — Fuel adaptor female B — Fuel pressure manifold

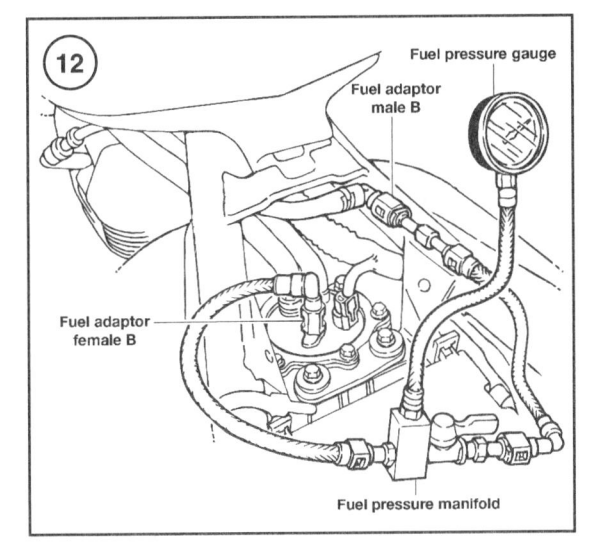

symptoms indicate that improper fuel discharge or flow through the injectors may be occurring. The fuel supply system is not part of the engine management system controlled by the ECM. Refer to *Fuel System (Fuel Injected Models)* in Chapter Two for fuel system troubleshooting.

Tools

Refer to **Figure 11**.

A fuel pressure gauge and adaptor are required to check the fuel pressure. OEM part numbers are provided for test equipment. Aftermarket fuel pressure gauges may be used provided adaptors can be fabricated or improvised from other sources.

1. Fuel pressure gauge: Honda part No. 07406-004000B.
2. Fuel pressure manifold: Honda part No. 07AMJ-HW3A100.
3. Fuel adapter male B: Honda part No. 07AAJ-S6MA200.
4. Fuel adapter female B: Honda part No. 07AAJ-S6MA400.

Procedure

1. Depressurize the fuel system (this chapter).

   NOTE
   After depressurizing the fuel system, the negative battery cable, the fuel feed hose and the fuel pump electrical connector are all disconnected.

2. Connect the fuel pressure testing tools (this section) between the fuel feed hose open end and the fuel pipe on the fuel pump (**Figure 12**).
3. Reconnect the fuel pump connector (B, **Figure 1**).
4. Reconnect the negative battery cable at the battery (Chapter Ten).

   WARNING
   Turn the engine off immediately if there is a fuel leak.

5. Start the engine and read the fuel pressure gauge with the engine running at idle speed. The standard fuel pressure reading is 333-353 kPa (48-51 psi).
6. Turn the engine off.
7. If the fuel pressure reading is lower than specified (**Table 1**), check for the following:
   a. Leaking fuel line.
   b. Pinched or clogged fuel feed hose.
   c. Pinched or clogged breather hose.

d. Faulty fuel pump.

e. Clogged fuel filter (installed in the fuel pump assembly).

8. If the fuel pressure reading is higher than specified (**Table 1**), replace the fuel pump assembly and retest.

9. Depressurize the fuel system as described in *Depressurizing the Fuel System* in this chapter. With the fuel pressure testing tools installed, disconnect the fuel adapter female B at the fuel pump (**Figure 12**).

10. When the fuel system is depressurized, remove the fuel pressure testing tools.

11. Complete the appropriate assembly steps in *Depressurizing the Fuel System* in this chapter.

FUEL FLOW TEST

NOTE
The battery must be fully-charged when performing this test.

1. Depressurize the fuel system (this chapter).

NOTE
After depressurizing the fuel system, the negative battery cable, the fuel feed hose and the fuel pump electrical connector are all disconnected.

2. Remove the fuel cut-off relay from the relay box as described in this chapter. Then connect a jumper wire between the black/white and brown connector block terminals (**Figure 13**) in the relay box.

3A. If a separate fuel feed hose is available, connect it onto the fuel feed hose fitting on the fuel pump (**Figure 14**). Place the open end of the hose into a plastic graduated beaker.

3B. If the fuel pressure testing tools (this chapter) are available, perform the following:

a. Assemble and connect the fuel pressure gauge to the fuel pipe at the fuel pump (**Figure 12**).

b. Insert the other end of the fuel pressure gauge into a plastic graduated beaker (**Figure 14**).

4. Reconnect the fuel pump connector (B, **Figure 1**).

5. Reconnect the negative battery cable at the battery (Chapter Ten).

6. Turn the engine stop switch to its run position.

WARNING
Turn the engine off immediately if there is a fuel leak.

7. Turn the ignition switch on for ten seconds, then turn it off.

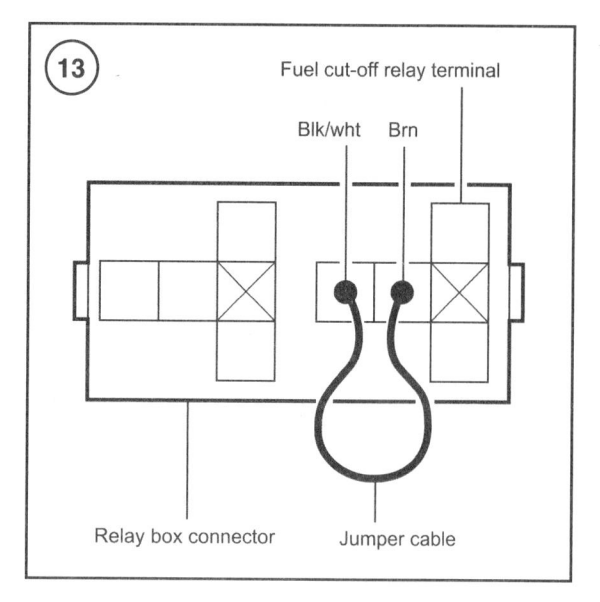

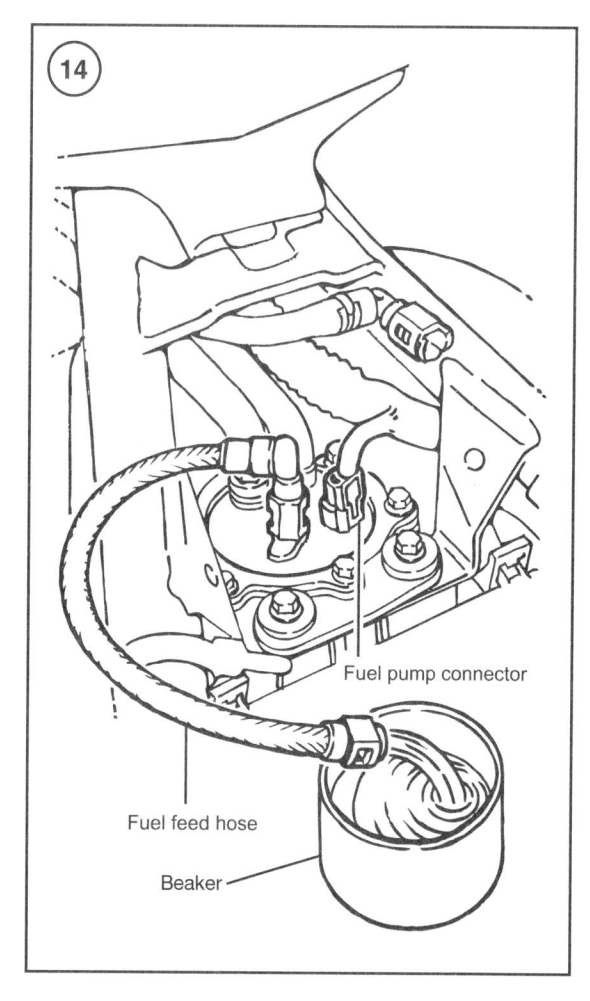

8. Measure the amount of fuel in the container and compare to the fuel pump flow specification in **Table 3**. Pour the measured fuel into an approved gasoline storage container.

FUEL INJECTION AND EMISSION CONTROL SYSTEMS

15

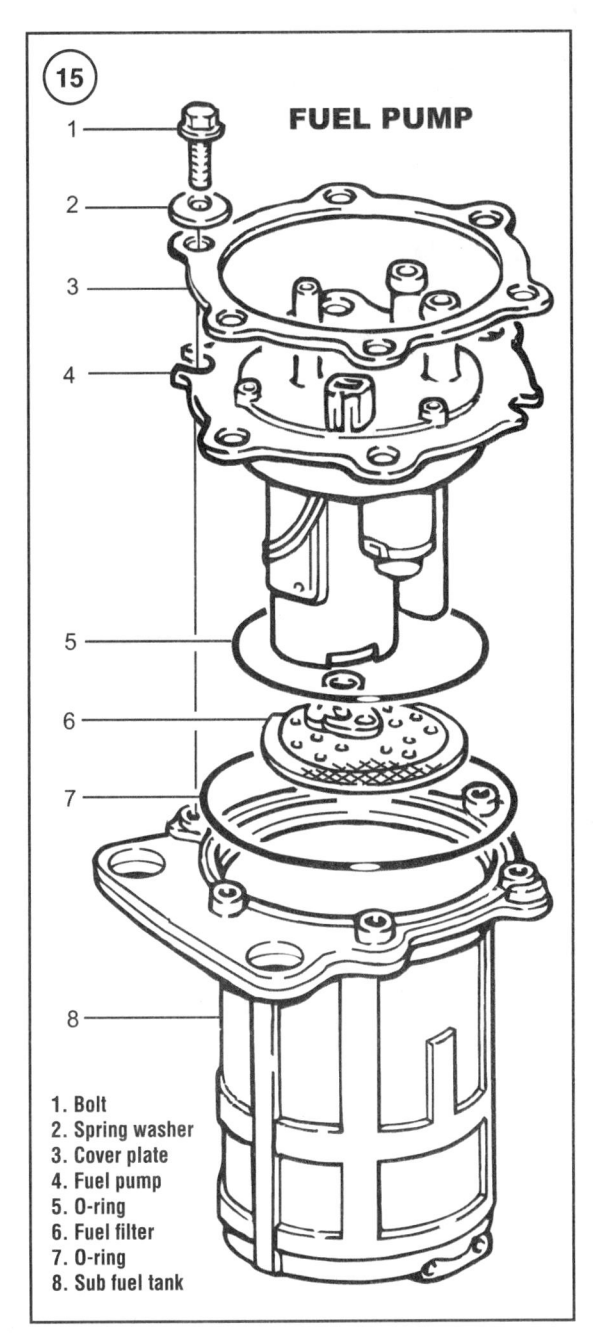

FUEL PUMP

1. Bolt
2. Spring washer
3. Cover plate
4. Fuel pump
5. O-ring
6. Fuel filter
7. O-ring
8. Sub fuel tank

16

9. If the fuel flow is less than specified, check the following:
   a. Clogged fuel tank breather hose.
   b. Faulty fuel pump.
   c. Clogged fuel filter (installed in the fuel pump assembly).
   d. Clogged fuel feed hose.
10. Remove the jumper wire and reinstall the fuel cut-off relay as described in this chapter.
11. Remove the fuel feed hose or the fuel pressure gauge assembly.
12. Complete assembly by performing the appropriate steps in *Depressurizing the Fuel System* in this chapter.

FUEL PUMP/SUB FUEL TANK ASSEMBLY

The fuel pump is mounted behind the engine and installed in a sub fuel tank assembly. A replaceable fuel filter is mounted below the fuel pump in the sub fuel tank.
Refer to **Figure 15**.

Fuel Pump Voltage Check

1. Turn the ignition switch on and check that noise can be heard from the fuel pump for a few seconds and then stops, indicating that the fuel pump is running properly. Turn the ignition switch off and note the following:
   a. If the fuel pump ran for a few seconds, voltage is being supplied to the fuel pump and the pump's wiring harness circuit is normal.
   b. If the fuel pump did not make noise, continue with Step 2.
2. Remove the seat (Chapter Seventeen).
3. Remove the connector boot or the clips and the connector holder located over the top of the fuel pump, if used.
4. Disconnect the fuel pump connector (A, **Figure 16**).
5. Connect a voltmeter between the wire harness connector brown (+) and green (-) terminals. Turn the ignition switch on. The voltmeter should read battery voltage for a few seconds. Turn the ignition switch off.
6A. If there is battery voltage for a few seconds, replace the fuel pump as described in this section.
6B. A problem with one or more components will prevent the fuel pump from operating. If there is no battery voltage, check the following components in the order listed:
   a. Starter solenoid/bank angle sensor 10 amp fuse (Chapter Ten).
   b. Meter 10 amp fuse (Chapter Ten).
   c. Main 30 amp fuse (Chapter Ten).

d. FI 15 amp fuse (Chapter Ten).
e. Open circuit in fuel pump brown and/or green wire(s).
f. Fuel cut-off relay (this chapter).
g. Engine stop relay (this chapter).
h. Engine stop switch (Chapter Ten).
i. Bank angle sensor (this chapter).
j. ECM (this chapter).

7. Reconnect the fuel pump connector (A, **Figure 16**).
8. Install the connector boot or the clips and the connector holder located over the top of the fuel pump, if used.
9. Install the seat (Chapter Seventeen).

Removal/Installation

1. Depressurize the fuel system as described in *Depressurizing the Fuel System* in this chapter.

NOTE
After depressurizing the fuel system the negative battery cable, the fuel feed hose and the fuel pump electrical connector are all disconnected.

2. Remove the fuel tank as described in this chapter.
3. Disconnect the fuel hose (B, **Figure 16**) and the fuel return hose (C) at the fuel pump if they were not disconnected at the fuel tank.
4. Remove the mounting bolts (A, **Figure 17**) and collars and remove the fuel pump/sub-fuel tank assembly (B).
5. Installation is the reverse of removal. Note the following:
   a. Install the fuel pump/sub fuel tank assembly by inserting the tab on the bottom of the sub fuel tank into the grommet mounted on the frame.
   b. Install the collars and mounting bolts (A, **Figure 17**) and tighten securely.
   c. Complete the appropriate assembly steps in *Depressurizing the Fuel System* in this chapter. After completing assembly, turn the ignition switch on to allow the fuel system to pressurize and check for leaks. Do this two or three times. If there are no leaks, start the engine and check for leaks again.

Disassembly/Reassembly and Fuel Filter Replacement

Refer to **Figure 15**.
1. Before disassembly, plug all of the hose openings and clean the outside of the sub fuel tank to prevent dirt from entering the tank.

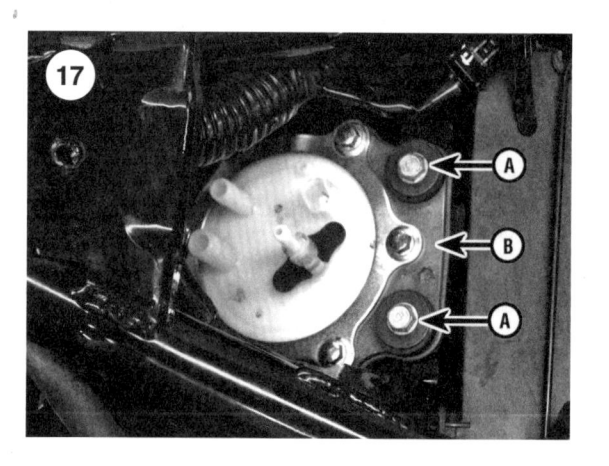

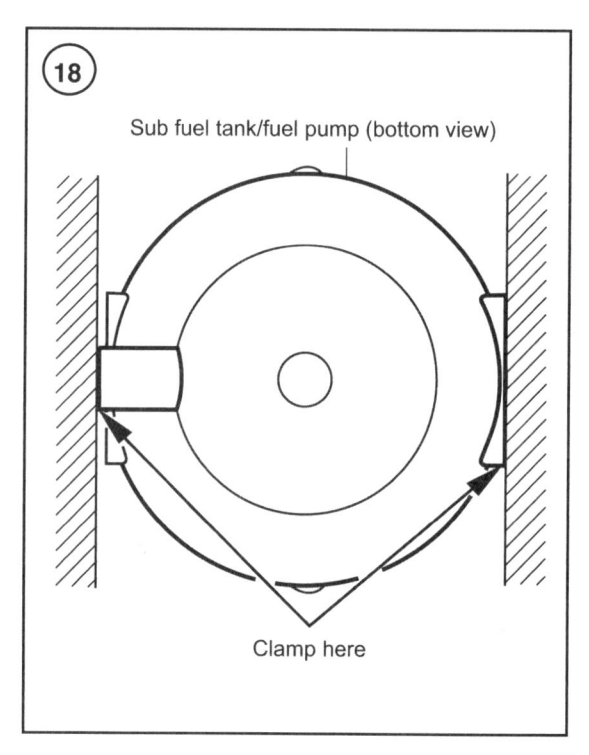

Sub fuel tank/fuel pump (bottom view)

Clamp here

CAUTION
Do not overtighten the sub fuel tank when securing it in a vise; otherwise, the tank may crack.

2. Secure the bottom of the sub fuel tank in a vise with soft jaws at the points shown in **Figure 18**.
3. Loosen the assembly bolts in the numerical order shown in **Figure 19**.
4. Remove the assembly bolts, spring washers and cover plate (A, **Figure 19**).

CAUTION
Carefully remove the fuel pump to prevent from damaging the wires on the side of the pump.

FUEL INJECTION AND EMISSION CONTROL SYSTEMS

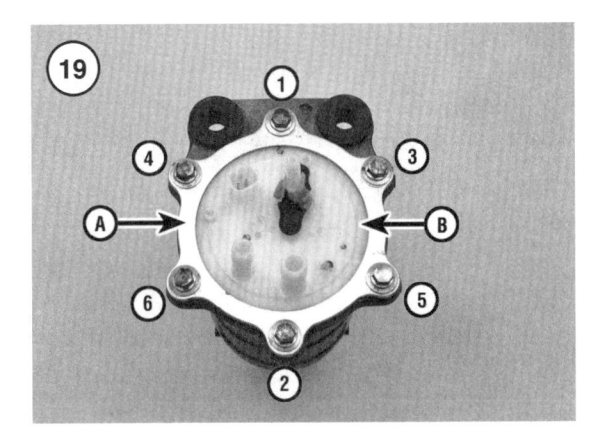

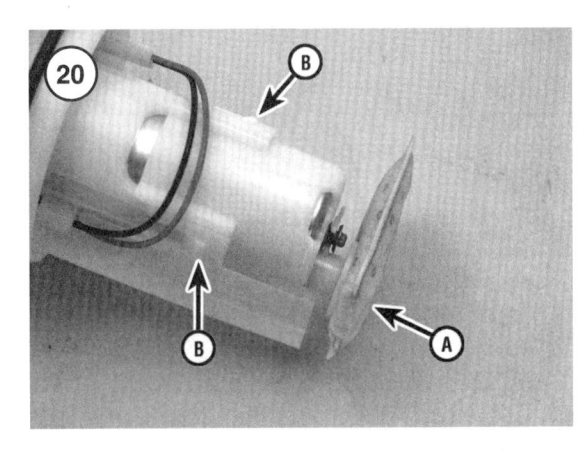

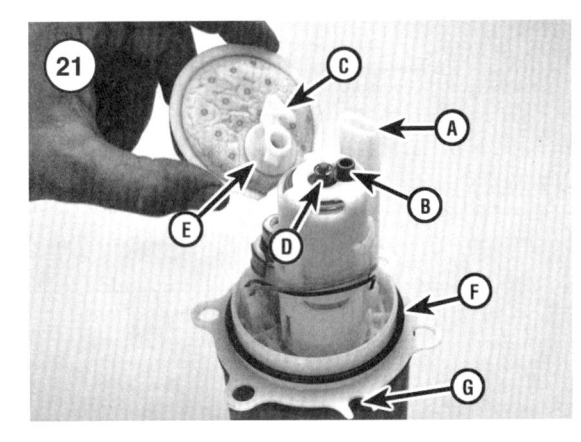

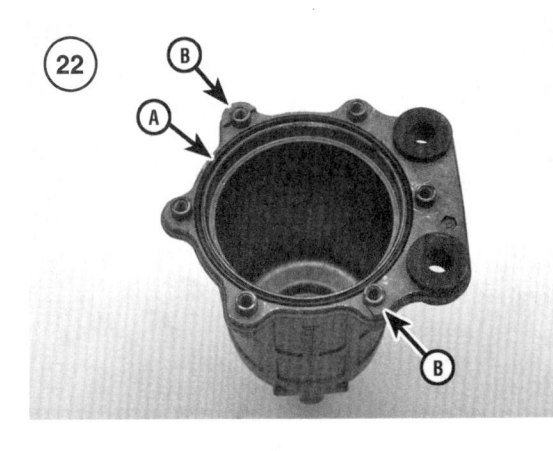

NOTE
The two O-rings and fuel filter are only available as a set.

5. Remove the fuel pump (B, **Figure 19**) from the sub fuel tank.
6. Empty the fuel in the sub fuel tank into a fuel storage can.
7. Remove and discard the two O-rings.
8. Check the exterior of the fuel pump for dirt and debris. Carefully wipe the pump with a clean rag if necessary. Do not clean the fuel pump with throttle body cleaner.
9. Inspect the fuel filter (A, **Figure 20**) for dirt and other contamination. If necessary, replace the fuel filter.
10. Replace the fuel filter as follows:

NOTE
*While the fuel filter is removed from the fuel pump, handle the pump carefully to prevent dirt and other contamination from entering the feed pipe (A, **Figure 21**) and suction port (B).*

   a. Turn the fuel filter clockwise to disconnect its hook (C, **Figure 21**) from the boss (D) on the fuel pump.
   b. Install the fuel filter by aligning the hole in the filter (E, **Figure 21**) with the suction port (B) and push the filter firmly onto the pump.
   c. Turn the fuel filter counterclockwise to engage the hook (C, **Figure 21**) on the filter with the boss (D) on the fuel pump.

11. Make sure the three fuel pump locking tabs (B, **Figure 20**) are firmly locked in place.
12. Lubricate a new O-ring with silicone grease and install it onto the shoulder of the fuel pump (F. **Figure 21**).
13. Lubricate a new O-ring with silicone grease and install it onto the groove on the sub fuel tank (A, **Figure 22**).
14. Install the fuel pump into the sub fuel tank by aligning the two mounting notches (G, **Figure 21**) in the fuel pump with the two bosses (B, **Figure 22**) on the sub fuel tank.
15. Install the cover plate (A, **Figure 19**) with its chamfered edges facing up.
16. Install the spring washers with their tapered end facing up.
17. Install the fuel pump assembly bolts. Following the sequence shown in Figure 19. Tighten the bolts to 8.8 N.m (78 in.-lb.).

AIR FILTER HOUSING

Removal/Installation

1. Remove the fuel tank as described in this chapter.
2. If necessary, remove the air filter as described in Chapter Three. The housing can be removed with the air filter cover installed.
3. Remove the air filter housing mounting bolts (**Figure 23**).
4. Loosen the air filter housing hose clamp at the throttle body (A, **Figure 24**).
5. Disconnect the crankcase breather hose (B, **Figure 24**) from the backside of the air filter housing.
6. Pull the air filter housing outward and disconnect the PAIR air suction hose (**Figure 25**) at the air filter housing and remove the air filter housing.
7. Inspect the inside of the air filter housing and the throttle body for dirt and other debris. These areas must be clean. If dirt is noticed inside the air filter housing or throttle body, either the air filter is worn or damaged or there is a problem with the air filter housing.

NOTE
The air filter housing components identified in the following steps can be replaced separately. To seal rubber joints, use a weatherstrip adhesive that can be used on rubber parts and resists gasoline.

8. Make sure the connecting tube (A, **Figure 26**) is sealed and secured to the air filter housing. Check the tube for cracks and other damage.
9. Make sure the air filter chamber (B, **Figure 26**) is secured to the air filter housing with the clamp and bracket. Make sure the clamp screw is tight.
10. Check the intake boot (A, **Figure 27**) for any cracks, splitting or other damage.
11. Make sure the intake boot (A, **Figure 27**) is sealed to the air filter housing.

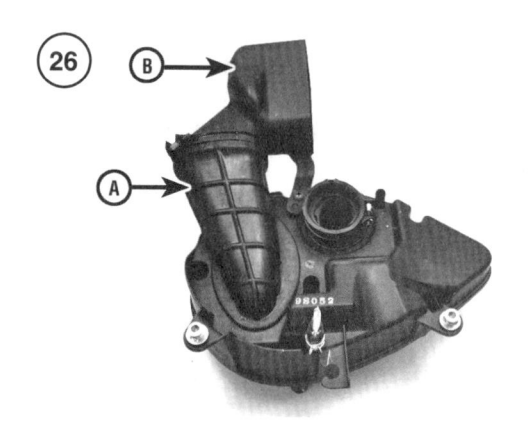

FUEL INJECTION AND EMISSION CONTROL SYSTEMS

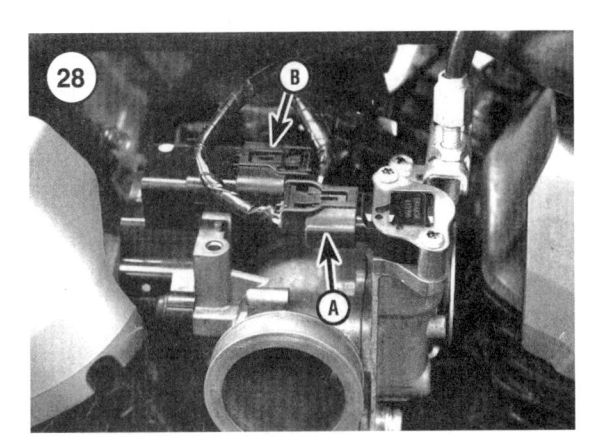

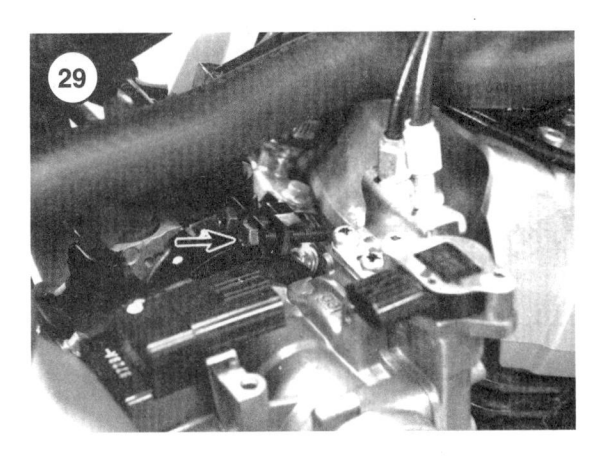

12. Check the intake boot clamp for weakness or damage. If removed, position the tab on the clamp into the notch in the boot (B, **Figure 27**).
13. Make sure the air filter seating surface inside the air filter housing is in good condition.
14. Replace the air filter cover O-ring if missing or damaged.
15. Installation is the reverse of removal. Note the following:
   a. Tighten the air filter housing mounting bolts securely.
   b. Tighten the air filter housing intake boot clamp screw to 1 N-m (8.9 in-lbs).

THROTTLE BODY

CAUTION
After disconnecting the throttle cables, do not turn the throttle drum and then release it. Doing so may alter the idle speed operation and/or damage its mechanism.

Removal

1. Read the information under *Fuel System Precautions* in this chapter.
2. Remove the fuel tank as described in this chapter.
3. Remove the air filter housing as described in this chapter.
4. Disconnect the IACV connector (A, **Figure 28**).
5. Disconnect the sensor unit connector (B, **Figure 28**).
6. Loosen the outer intake boot hose clamp **(Figure 29)**.
7. Remove the throttle body from the intake boot.
8. Loosen the throttle cable locknuts and disconnect the pull (A, **Figure 30**) and return (B) throttle cables from the throttle drum.
9. Plug the intake boot openings to prevent dirt from entering into the engine.

Installation

1. If necessary, lubricate the throttle cables as described in Chapter Three. Clean any excessive lubricant from the cable ends.
2. Reconnect the pull (A, **Figure 30**) and return (B) throttle cables onto the throttle drum. Secure each cable to the cable mounting bracket as shown in Figure 30. Note that the pull (A, **Figure 30**) and return (B) lower cable ends are different. The pull cable (A, **Figure 30**) is equipped with an adjuster (two locknuts). The return cable (B) is not equipped with an adjuster (one locknut).

3. Install the throttle body into the intake boot by aligning the tab on the throttle body **(Figure 31)** with the slot in the boot (A, **Figure 32**). Tighten the clamp screw until the distance between the clamp arms **(Figure 33)** is 6.5-8.5 mm (0.26-0.33 in.).
4. Check the throttle cable alignment from the throttle body to the throttle housing to make sure the cables are not twisted or binding.
5. Reconnect the sensor unit connector (B, **Figure 28**).
6. Reconnect the IACV connector (A, **Figure 28**).
7. Adjust the throttle cables (Chapter Three).
8. Install the air filter housing as described in this chapter.

Disassembly/Reassembly

Only certain components can be replaced on the throttle body. Note the following:
1. The throttle body is pre-set by the manufacturer. Do not disassemble or adjust the throttle body in any way.
2. Do not loosen or tighten the white painted screws (A, **Figure 34**) and nut (B) on the throttle body. Doing so may cause throttle and idle valve synchronization failure.
3. The throttle body is equipped with an IACV and a sensor unit. Service these items as described in this chapter.
4. If loose, tighten the screws (C, **Figure 34**) that secure the throttle cable guide onto the throttle body to 3.4 N.m (30 in.-lb.).

INTAKE MANIFOLD

This section removes the intake manifold with the fuel injectors installed in the manifold. If it is necessary to service just the fuel injectors, refer to *Fuel Injectors. Injector Cap and Fuel Feed Hose* (this chapter).

Removal

1. Depressurize the fuel system as described in *Depressurizing the Fuel System* in this chapter.
2. Disconnect the fuel feed hose from the injector cap as described in *Fuel Injectors and Injector Cap* in this chapter.
3. Remove the throttle body as described in this chapter.
4. Loosen the hose clamp (B, **Figure 32**) and remove the intake boot (C) from the intake manifold.
5. Disconnect the No. 1 cylinder (rear) fuel injector connector (A, **Figure 35**).
6. Disconnect the No. 2 cylinder (front) fuel injector connector (B, **Figure 35**).
7. Disconnect the EVAP purge control solenoid valve hose **(Figure 36)** at the intake manifold.

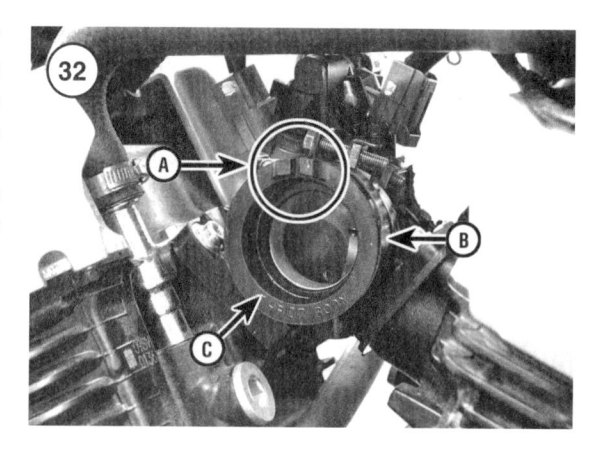

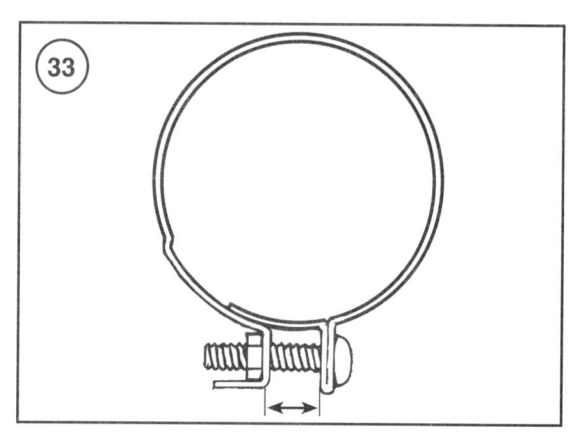

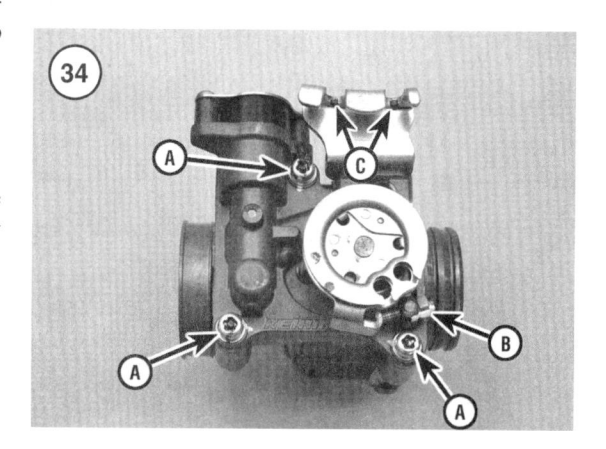

FUEL INJECTION AND EMISSION CONTROL SYSTEMS

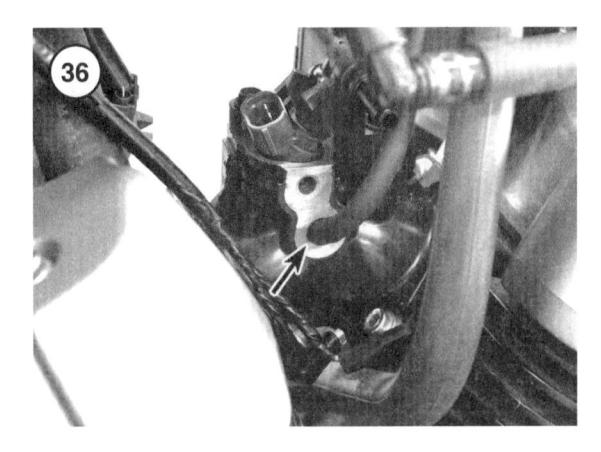

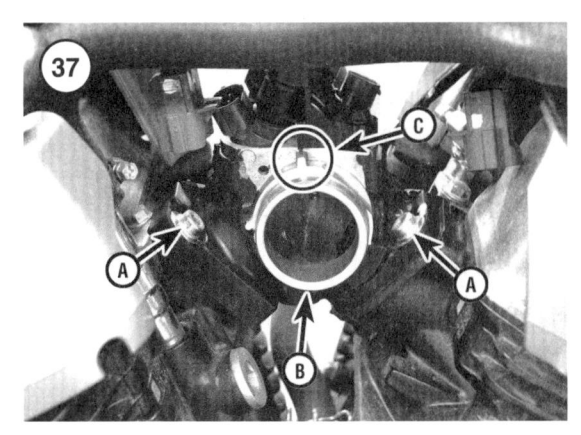

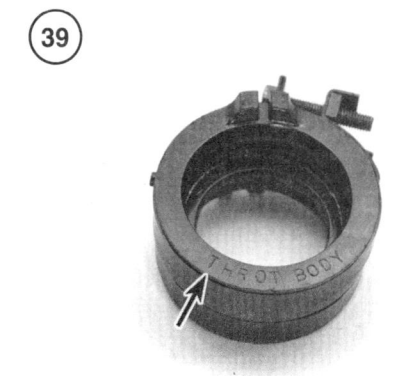

8. Remove the bolts (A, **Figure 37** and **Figure 38**) and the intake manifold (B, **Figure 37**), fuel injectors and injector cap. Discard the O-rings installed in the intake manifold.
9. Plug each cylinder head opening to prevent dirt and small objects from falling into the engine.

Installation

1. If removed, install the fuel injectors into the intake manifold as described in this chapter.
2. Install two new O-rings into the intake manifold grooves. Make sure the O-rings are fully seated in the grooves.
3. Remove the plugs from the cylinder head openings.
4. Install the intake manifold between the cylinder heads and install the mounting bolts (A, **Figure 37** and **Figure 38**). Tighten the bolts securely in a crossing pattern.
5. Connect the EVAP purge control solenoid valve hose **(Figure 36)** onto the hose nozzle on the intake manifold.
6. Reconnect the connectors onto the fuel injectors in their original positions. Note the following:
    a. The No. 1 cylinder fuel injector (rear) connector (A, **Figure 35**) uses black/white and pink/yellow wires.
    b. The No. 2 cylinder fuel injector (front) connector (B, **Figure 35**) uses black/white and pink/blue wires.
    c. When reconnecting the connectors, align the groove on the connector with the tab in the fuel injector cap.
7. Install the intake boot with its THROT BODY mark **(Figure 39)** facing out (toward the throttle body) while aligning its slot (A, **Figure 32**) with the raised tab (C, **Figure 37**) on the intake manifold. Tighten the clamp screw until the distance between the clamp arms **(Figure 33)** is 13.5-15.5 mm (0.53-0.61 in.).
8. Reconnect the fuel feed hose onto the injector cap (this chapter).
9. Install the throttle body (this chapter).
10. Reconnect the fuel feed hose onto the fuel pump as described in *Depressurizing the Fuel System* in this chapter.

Inspection

1. Remove the fuel injectors from the manifold (this chapter).
2. Inspect the intake manifold as follows:
    a. Inspect the manifold-to-cylinder head mating surfaces for cracks, warpage and other damage.

b. Inspect the manifold-to-intake boot mating surface for cracks and other damage.
c. Inspect the fuel injector bores for cracks, scoring and other damage.

3. Install the fuel injectors as described in *Fuel Injectors and Injector Cap* in this chapter.

FUEL INJECTORS, INJECTOR CAP AND FUEL FEED HOSE

Fuel Injector Operation Check

The fuel injectors can be checked before removing them from the intake manifold.
1. Start the engine and allow to idle.
2. Use a mechanic's stethoscope and listen for a clicking sound at each fuel injector. Place the end of the stethoscope rod against the injector directly underneath its connector (A, **Figure 40**).
3. If an injector is quiet, replace it (this section).
4. Look and feel around the fuel injectors where they enter the intake manifold. Check for any signs of wetness indicating a leak.

Removal

1. Depressurize the fuel system (this chapter).
2. Use compressed air to clean the fuel feed hose (B, **Figure 40**) and at the base of the fuel injectors to prevent dirt and other debris from entering the intake manifold.

> *CAUTION*
> *The fuel feed hose is expensive. Handle the hose and its connector ends carefully during all service work.*

3. Disconnect the fuel feed hose connector (B, **Figure 40**) from the fuel pipe as follows:
   a. Release the rubber guide from the retainer (**Figure 41**).

> *NOTE*
> *If the connector is stuck, continue to squeeze the retainer tabs while pulling and pushing the connector. Repeat until the connector breaks free and slides off the fuel pipe.*

   b. Hold the fuel feed hose connector and squeeze the retainer tabs (**Figure 41**) to release the connector from the fuel pipe, then pull the connector off the fuel pipe.
   c. Cover the connector and fuel pipe with plastic bags to prevent contamination.

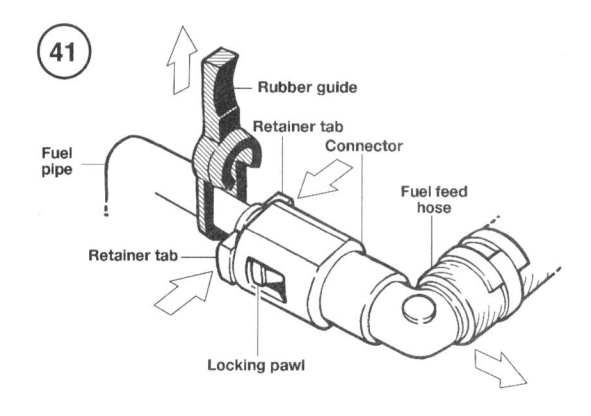

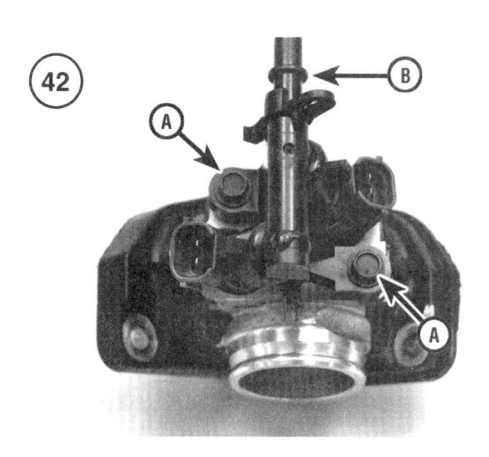

4. Disconnect the No. 1 cylinder (rear) fuel injector connector (A, **Figure 35**).
5. Disconnect the No. 2 cylinder (front) fuel injector connector (B, **Figure 35**).

> *NOTE*
> *Figure 42 shows the injector cap/intake manifold removed for clarity.*

6. Remove the bolts (A, **Figure 42**) and the injector cap (B). The fuel injectors (**Figure 43**) may remain in the injector cap. If necessary, remove them from the intake manifold.

FUEL INJECTION AND EMISSION CONTROL SYSTEMS

43

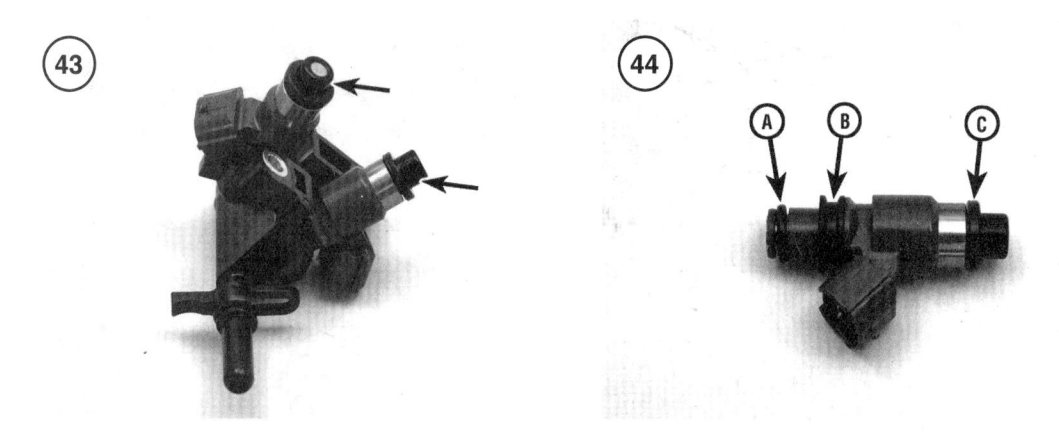

44

45

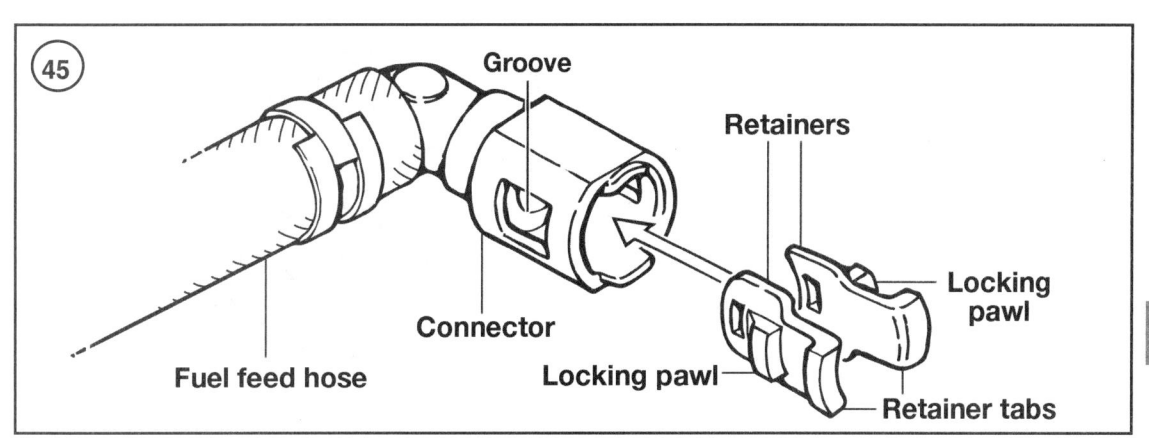

Groove
Retainers
Locking pawl
Connector
Fuel feed hose
Locking pawl
Retainer tabs

46

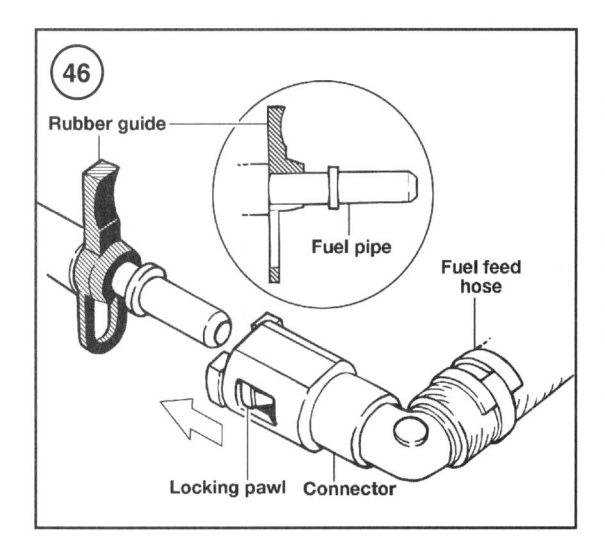

Rubber guide
Fuel pipe
Fuel feed hose
Locking pawl Connector

7. Remove the O-ring (A, **Figure 44**), cushion ring (B) and seal ring (C) from each fuel injector and discard them.
8. If necessary, remove the fuel feed hose.

Installation

1. Lubricate the new O-ring, cushion ring and seal ring with engine oil.

2. Carefully install the O-rings (A, **Figure 44**), cushion rings (B) and seal rings (C) onto the fuel injectors. Make sure they seat squarely on the fuel injectors.
3. Carefully install the fuel injectors (**Figure 43**) into the intake manifold, making sure not to damage the seal rings as they pass through the manifold.
4. Install the injector cap (B, **Figure 42**) over the fuel injectors, making sure not to damage the cushion ring and O-ring. Install the injector cap mounting bolts (A, **Figure 42**) and tighten to 5.1 N.m (45 in.-lb.).
5. Reconnect the connectors onto the fuel injectors in their original positions. Note the following:
   a. The No. 1 cylinder fuel injector (rear) connector (A, **Figure 35**) uses black/white and pink/yellow wires.
   b. The No. 2 cylinder fuel injector (front) connector (B, **Figure 35**) uses black/white and pink/blue wires.
   c. When reconnecting the connectors, align the groove on the connector with the tab in the fuel injector cap.
6. Connect the fuel feed hose connector onto the fuel pipe as follows:
   a. Install a new retainer into the connector by aligning the pawls on the retainer with the grooves in the connector (**Figure 45**).

b. Install the rubber guide and seat it against the fuel pipe shoulder as shown in **Figure 46**.

NOTE
If it is difficult to install and lock the connector, apply a small amount of engine oil onto the end of the fuel pipe.

c. Install the connector over the fuel pipe, then push it until both retainer pawls click and lock in place **(Figure 46)**.
d. Pull on the connector to make sure it is locked in place.

7. Reconnect the fuel feed hose onto the fuel pump as described in *Depressurizing the Fuel System* in this chapter. When turning the ignition switch on, check both ends of the fuel feed hose for leakage

Inspection

1. Visually inspect the fuel injectors for damage. Check for cracks on the sides of the injectors.
2. Inspect the spray nozzle for clogging or other damage.
3. Use an ohmmeter and measure resistance across the two fuel injector terminals. The specification is 11-13 ohms.
4. Inspect the fuel feed hose for cracks, deterioration, soft spots and other damage. Replace the feed hose if necessary.

SENSOR UNIT

The sensor unit is mounted on the throttle body **(Figure 47)** and contains the IAT, MAP and TP sensors. If any one sensor is damaged, the sensor unit must be replaced. It is not rebuildable.

Removal/Installation

1. Remove the throttle body as described in this chapter.
2. Remove the Torx screws (A, **Figure 48**) and the sensor unit (B).
3. Remove and discard the O-ring installed between the throttle body and sensor unit.
4. Install a new O-ring into the throttle body.
5. Install the sensor unit by aligning the slots in the TP sensor with the throttle valve shaft.
6. Hold the sensor unit in place and install the Torx screws. Tighten the sensor unit mounting screws to 3.4 N.m (30 in.-lb.).
7. Perform the *Throttle Valve Reset Adjustment* in this section.

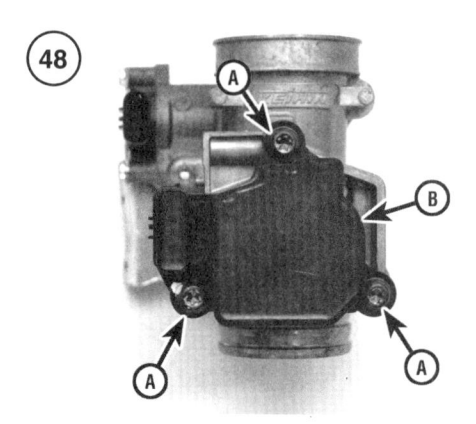

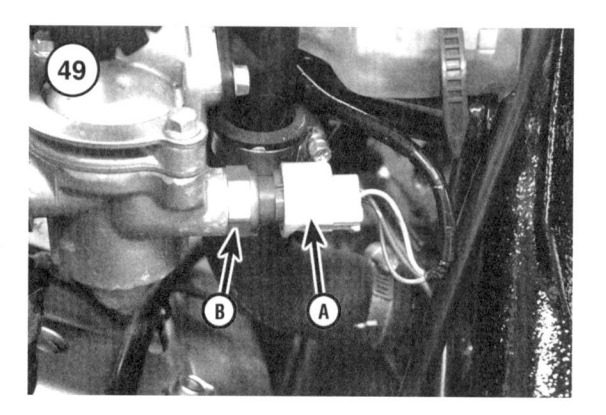

Throttle Valve Reset Adjustment

Whenever the sensor unit is removed from the throttle body, this adjustment must be performed to reset the throttle valve to its fully closed position.
1. Remove either the right (non-ABS) or left (ABS) side cover (Chapter Seventeen).
2. Clear the DTC(s) as described in *Erasing DTC(s)* in this chapter. Turn the engine off.
3. Reinstall the SCS connector or short the DLC terminals again as described in *Erasing DTC(s)* in this chapter.
4. Disconnect the ECT sensor connector **(Figure 49)** at the thermostat housing. Then short the ECT wir-

FUEL INJECTION AND EMISSION CONTROL SYSTEMS

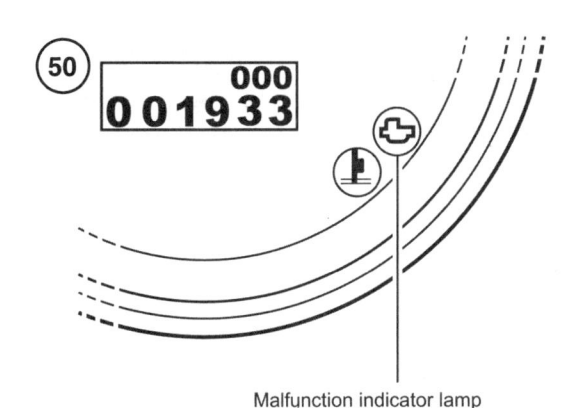

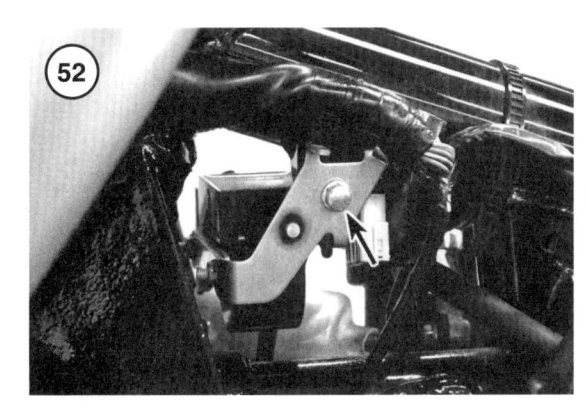

ing harness connector pink/white and green/orange wires with a jumper wire.

5. Turn the engine stop switch to run.
6. Turn the ignition switch on while observing the MIL **(Figure 50)**. It should be blinking (MIL on for 0.1 seconds and then off for 1.2 seconds, and repeats). Within 10 seconds disconnect the jumper wire from the ECT connector. Observe the MIL and note the following:
    a. If the MIL then begins to blink in shorter intervals (0.3 seconds), the throttle valve is fully closed and successfully reset.
    b. If the MIL stays on, the throttle valve is not closed. Repeat this procedure.

7. Turn the ignition switch off.
8. Remove the jumper wire and reconnect the ECT sensor connector **(Figure 49)**.
9. Remove the SCS connector and reinstall the dummy connector as described in *Erasing DTC(s)* in this chapter.
10. Reinstall either the right (non-ABS) or left (ABS) side cover (Chapter Seventeen).

BANK ANGLE SENSOR

The bank angle sensor is designed to turn the engine and fuel pump off when the motorcycle falls on its side. If this happens, raise and support the motorcycle on its sidestand. Turn the ignition off and then turn it back on. The engine will not restart until these steps are performed.

A faulty bank angle sensor can prevent the engine from starting, even when the motorcycle has not fallen on its side. Before testing the bank angle sensor, check its connectors for loose, corroded or damaged pins. Also make sure the connector is firmly plugged into the wiring harness.

Testing/Replacement

1. Support the motorcycle on a workstand so the seat is level.
2. Remove the fuel tank as described in this chapter.
3. Remove the steering covers (Chapter Seventeen).
4. Measure and record battery voltage as described in Chapter Ten.
5. Locate the bank angle sensor connector **(Figure 51)**.
6. Turn the ignition switch on.
7. Back probe the connector, and check the voltage by performing the following:
    a. Connect the voltmeter positive test probe to the white, power-supply terminal and connect the negative test probe to the red terminal. The measured voltage should equal the battery voltage recorded in Step 4.
    b. Connect the voltmeter positive test probe to the green terminal and connect the negative test probe to the red terminal. The measured voltage should equal 0-1 volts.
8. If these readings are not obtained, check the voltage supply from the engine stop/starter switch to the bank angle sensor and the wiring from the engine stop relay to the bank angle sensor. If the wiring is good, the bank angle sensor is faulty.
9. Turn the ignition switch off.
10. Remove the bolt and the bank angle sensor and its mounting bracket **(Figure 52)**. Keep the sensor connected to the wiring harness.

11. Locate the position of the engine stop relay as described in *Engine Stop Relay* in this chapter. Do not remove the relay.

12. Position the bank angle sensor so it is sitting in its normal operating position. The top, flat part of the sensor must be positioned horizontally as shown in **Figure 53**.

13. Back probe the bank angle sensor white (+) and red (-) terminals. Turn the ignition switch on and listen to the engine stop relay. It should click audibly as the contact closes. Battery voltage should be present.

14. Turn the ignition switch off.

15. Back probe the bank angle sensor green (+) and red (-) terminals. Position the bank angle sensor (**Figure 53**) so it forms a 42.5° or greater angle with the ground. Turn the ignition switch on and listen to the engine stop relay. It should click audibly as the contacts open. The voltmeter should read zero volts.

16. Turn the ignition switch off and disconnect the voltmeter.

17. Replace the bank angle sensor if it failed any part of the test.

18. Reverse the removal steps to install the bank angle sensor (**Figure 53**). Note the following:
   a. Make sure its top, flat upper surface is positioned horizontally.
   b. Tighten the mounting bolt securely.

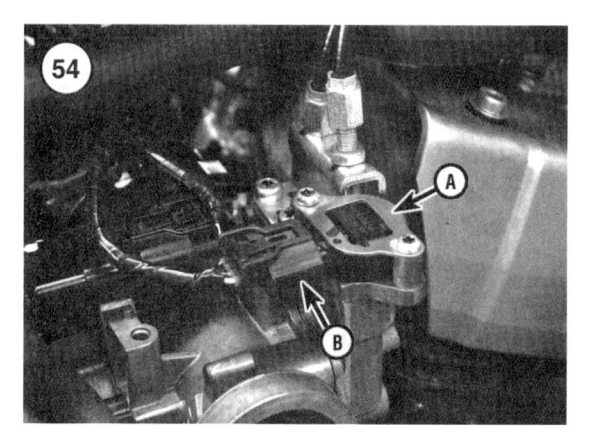

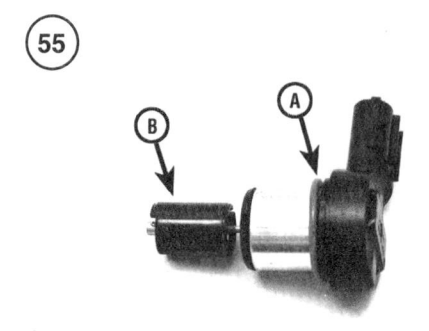

IDLE AIR CONTROL VALVE (IACV)

Inspection/Replacement

1. Remove the air filter housing as described in this chapter.
2. Inspect the IACV (A, **Figure 54**) as follows:

   NOTE
   The IACV can also be checked in the same way once it is removed from the throttle body and connected to its wiring harness.

   a. While leaning next to the IACV, turn the ignition switch on.
   b. The IACV should click or beep audibly when the ignition switch is turned on.
   c. Turn the ignition switch off.
   d. Replace the IACV if it failed this test.

3. Clean the IACV and the area around the valve to prevent dirt from falling into the IACV bore in the throttle body.
4. Disconnect the IACV connector (B, **Figure 54**).
5. Remove the Torx screws, set plate and the IACV (A, **Figure 54**).
6. Install a new O-ring (A, **Figure 55**) onto the IACV.
7. Turn the slide valve (B, **Figure 55**) clockwise until lightly seated.
8. Install the IACV by aligning the slot in the side of the valve (**Figure 56**) with the guide pin in the throttle body bore.
9. Install the set plate by aligning its groove with the tab on the top of the IACV (**Figure 57**). Install the set plate mounting screws and tighten to 2.1 N.m (19 in.-lb.).
10. Reconnect the IACV connector (B, **Figure 54**).
11. Install the air filter housing as described in this chapter.

FUEL INJECTION AND EMISSION CONTROL SYSTEMS

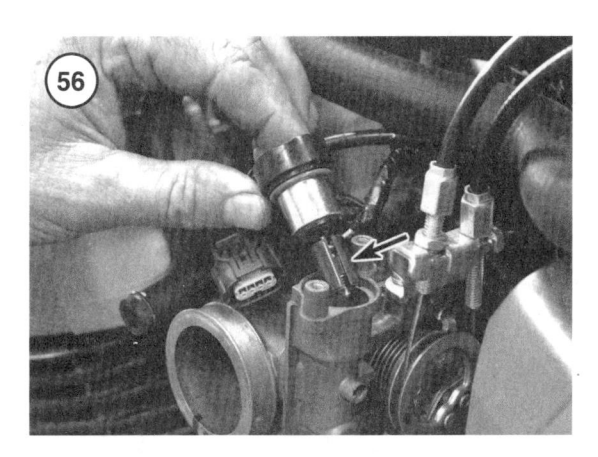

CRANKSHAFT POSITION (CKP) SENSOR

Refer to Chapter Ten for CKP sensor testing and replacement procedures.

ENGINE COOLANT TEMPERATURE (ECT) SENSOR

Refer to *Coolant Temperature Indicator and Engine Coolant Temperature (ECT) Sensor* in Chapter Ten.

ENGINE STOP RELAY

On non-ABS models, the engine stop relay is mounted in the relay box located behind the left side cover. On ABS models, the engine stop relay is mounted inside the fuse box.

Testing/Replacement

1. Remove the left side cover (Chapter Seventeen).

NOTE
Refer to the wiring diagram at the end of this manual to identify the wires colors plugged into the engine stop relay.

2A. On non-ABS models, perform the following:
    a. Remove the relay box **(Figure 58)** from its frame mount.
    b. Pull the rubber cover (A, **Figure 59**) away from the relay box. Then release the brown locking tabs (B) on both sides of the relay box and remove the brown relay connector from the box.
    c. Remove the engine stop relay from the connector **(Figure 60)**.

2B. On ABS models, open the fuse box cover and remove the engine stop relay from the fuse box as described in *Fuses (ABS Models)* in Chapter Ten.

3. Check for continuity across terminals 1 and 2 **(Figure 61)**; there should be no continuity.
4. Connect a 12-volt battery across terminals 3 and 4 and check for continuity across terminals 1 and 2 **(Figure 61)**; there should be continuity.
5. Replace the engine stop relay if it failed any part of this test.
6. Reverse the removal steps to install the engine stop relay.

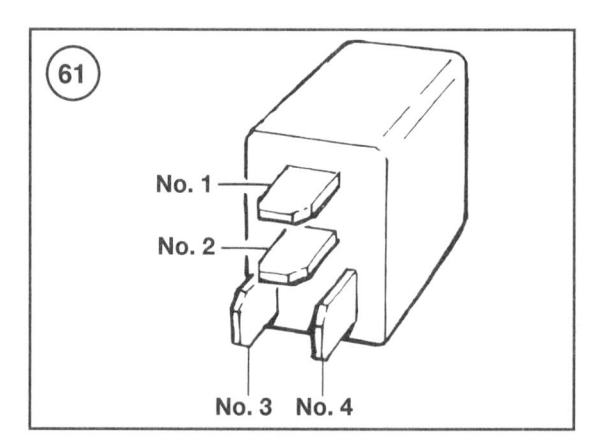

FUEL CUT-OFF RELAY

On non-ABS models, the fuel cut-off relay is mounted in the relay box located behind the left side cover. On ABS models, the fuel cut-off relay is mounted inside the fuse box.

Testing/Replacement

1. Remove the left side cover (Chapter Seventeen).
2A. On non-ABS models, perform the following:

NOTE
Refer to the wiring diagram at the end of this manual to identify the wires colors plugged into the fuel cut-off relay.

 a. Remove the relay box **(Figure 58)** from its frame mount.
 b. Pull the rubber cover (A, **Figure 59**) away from the relay box. Then release the brown locking tabs (B) on both sides of the relay box and remove the brown relay connector from the box.
 c. Remove the fuel cut-off relay from the connector **(Figure 60)**.

2B. On ABS models, open the fuse box cover and remove the fuel-cut off relay from the fuse box as described in *Fuses (ABS Models)* in Chapter Ten.
3. Check for continuity across terminals 1 and 2 **(Figure 61)**; there should be no continuity.
4. Connect a 12-volt battery across terminals 3 and 4 and check for continuity across terminals 1 and 2 **(Figure 61)**; there should be continuity.
5. Replace the fuel cut-off relay if it failed any part of this test.
6. Reverse the removal steps to install the fuel cut-off relay.

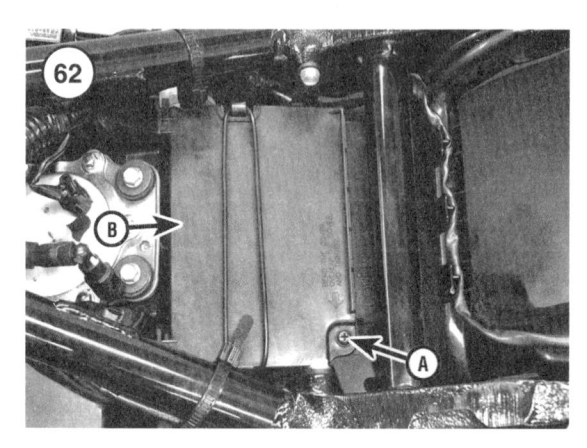

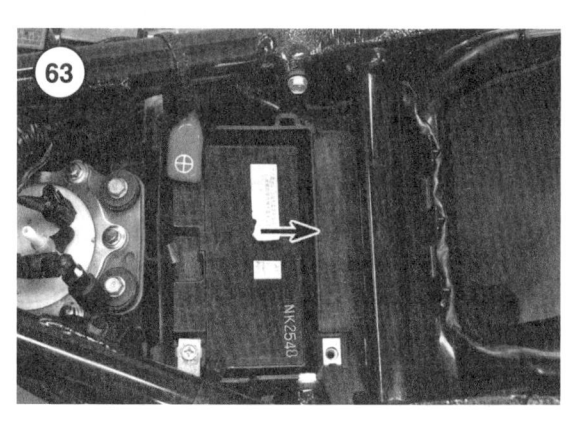

ENGINE CONTROL MODULE (ECM)

No testing procedure is available. If all other ignition components and systems have been tested, replace the ECM and recheck the engine operation. Faulty wiring and connections cause many electrical problems. Make sure to check all wires and connections before presuming the ECM is faulty. Because electrical components are not returnable, if possible, install a known good ECM for testing and check operation before purchasing a new unit.

Removal/Installation

The ECM is mounted underneath the seat and behind the battery.
1. Turn the ignition switch off.
2. Remove the seat (Chapter Seventeen).
3. Remove the screw (A, **Figure 62**), then slide the battery cover (B) rearward and remove it.
4. Open the ECM cover **(Figure 63)**.

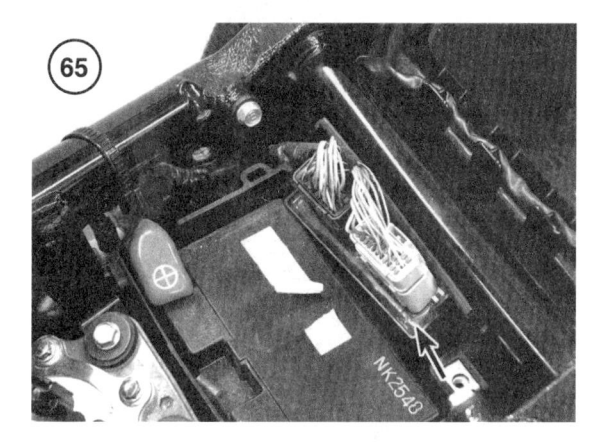

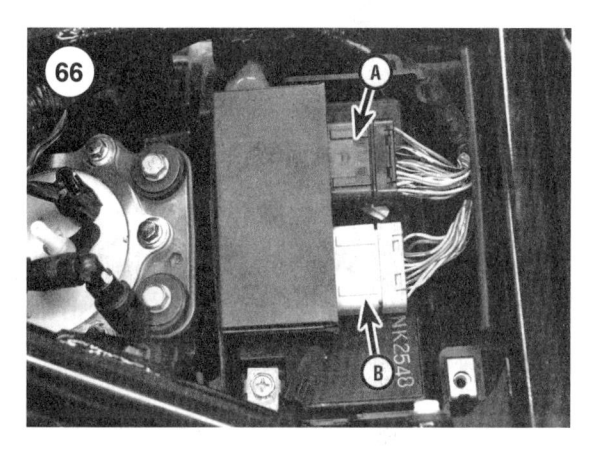

FUEL INJECTION AND EMISSION CONTROL SYSTEMS

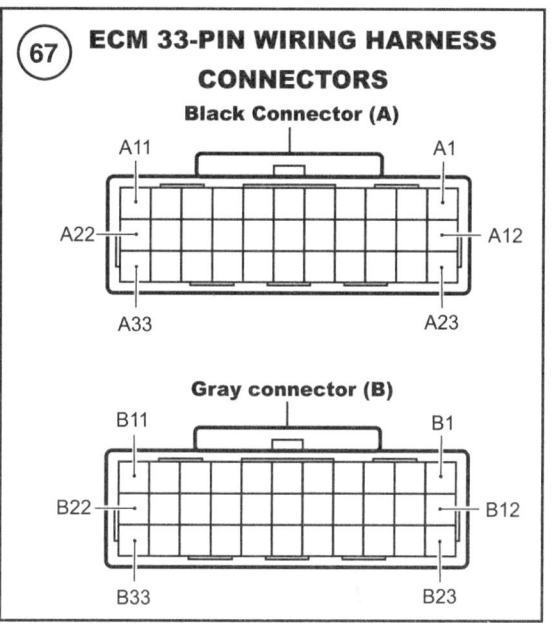

ECM Circuit Test

If the engine does not start and the MIL does not blink, perform the tests in this section. Note the following:

1. Before making the following tests, check for a blown FI fuse (15 amp) as described in Chapter Ten.
2. Remove the ECM and disconnect the ECM connectors as described in this section.
3. Check the black and gray 33-pin connectors for looseness, corrosion inside the connectors and pin damage. Disconnecting and reconnecting the connectors a few times may clean the connector terminals and repair the problem if it was caused by corrosion.
4. Refer to **Figure 67** for a diagram of the black (A) and gray (B) ECM 33-pin wiring harness side connectors. The connectors are identified by color (black or gray) during the following tests.
5. When substituting a known good ECM during the test procedure, refer the service to a dealership. Most dealerships will not accept the return of electrical components.

ECM power and ground circuit test

1. Turn the ignition switch on and the engine stop switch to run.
2. Measure voltage between the ECM black connector A4 terminal (+) and ground (-). Note the following:
   a. If there is voltage, continue the procedure.
   b. If there is no voltage, perform the *Engine Stop Relay Test 1* in this section.

5. Use a screwdriver (**Figure 64**) to release the tab securing the ECM in place, then remove the ECM with its connectors. See **Figure 65**.

CAUTION
Once the ECM connectors are removed, the pins in the ECM unit are exposed. Handle the assembly carefully to prevent from damaging them.

6. Disconnect the black (A, **Figure 66**) and gray (B) 33-pin connectors from the ECM.
7. Installation is the reverse of these steps.

3. Turn the ignition switch off. Check for continuity between the A23 terminal in the black ECM wiring harness connector and ground. Then, check for continuity between the B4 terminal in the gray ECM wiring harness connector and ground. There should be continuity in each test. Note the following:
   a. If there was continuity in both tests, replace the ECM and retest.
   b. If there was no continuity in one or both tests, check for an open circuit in the A23 green/pink ground wire and/or the B4 green ground wire.

Engine stop relay test 1

1. Turn the ignition switch off.
2. Remove the engine stop relay (this chapter).
3. Turn the ignition switch on and the engine stop switch to run.
4. Measure voltage across the engine stop switch relay terminals inside the connector. Connect the positive test lead to the black wire terminal and the negative test led across the red/blue wire terminal **(Figure 68)**. There should be battery voltage. Note the following:
   a. If there is battery voltage, perform the *Engine Stop Relay Test 2* in this section.
   b. If there is no battery voltage, test the bank angle sensor as described in this chapter.
5. Turn the ignition switch off.
6. Reinstall the engine stop relay as described in this chapter.

Engine stop relay test 2

1. Turn the ignition switch off.
2. Remove the engine stop relay as described in this chapter.
3. Connect a jumper wire across the black/white and red/white terminals inside the engine stop relay connector **(Figure 68)**.
4. Turn the ignition switch on and the engine stop switch to run.
5. Measure voltage between the A4 terminal (+) in the black ECM wiring harness connector and ground (-) **(Figure 67)**. Note the following:
   a. If there is battery voltage, test the engine stop relay as described in this chapter. If the relay is good, test the engine stop switch as described in Chapter Ten.
   b. If there is no battery voltage, check for a blown FI fuse (15 amp) as described in Chapter Ten. If the fuse is good, check for an open circuit in the red/white and black/white engine stop relay wires.
6. Turn the ignition switch off and reinstall all parts.

68 ENGINE STOP RELAY CONNECTOR TERMINALS
Blk/wht   Red/wht   Blk

Red/blu

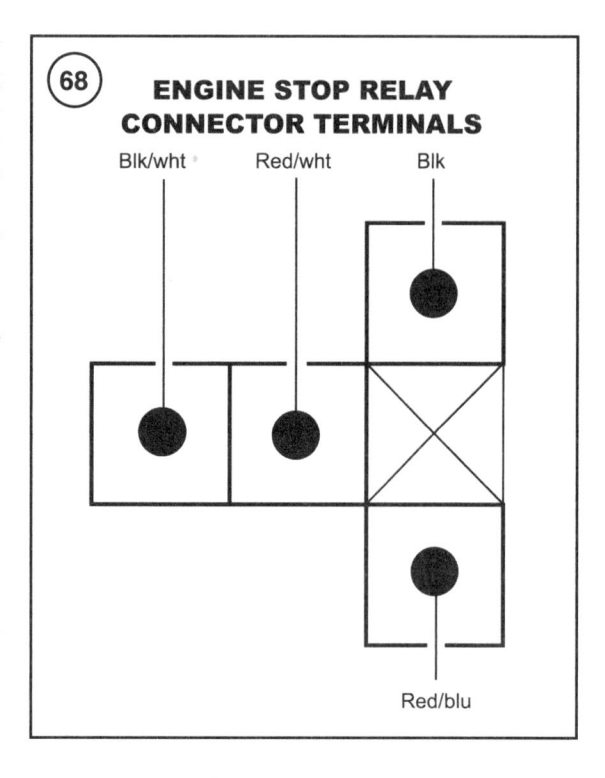

69

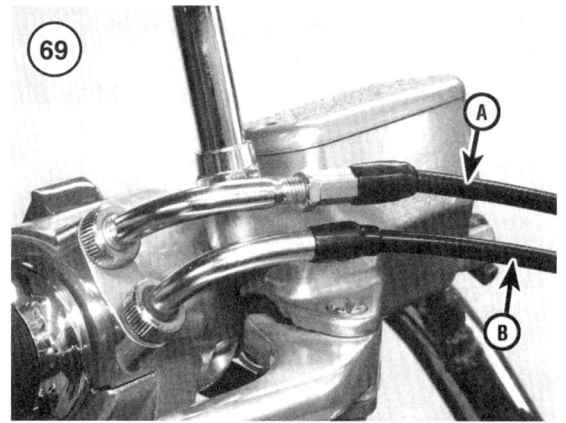

THROTTLE CABLE REPLACEMENT

The throttle uses two cables. Always replace both cables at the same time.
1. Remove the fuel tank as described in this chapter.
2. Remove the air filter housing as described in this chapter.
3. Note how the cables are routed. Make a sketch or take pictures as needed.
4. At the throttle body, disconnect the cables as described in *Removal* under *Throttle Body* in this chapter.
5. At the handlebar, disconnect the cables as described in *Removal/Installation* under *Handlebar* in Chapter Thirteen.
6. Remove the throttle cables.
7. Lubricate the new throttle cables as described in Chapter Three.

FUEL INJECTION AND EMISSION CONTROL SYSTEMS

13. Adjust the throttle cables as described in Chapter Three.
14. Install the air filter housing and fuel tank as described in this chapter.

WARNING
Do not ride the motorcycle until the throttle cables are properly routed and adjusted and the throttle snaps back after releasing it.

15. Start the engine and run at idle speed with the transmission in neutral. Turn the handlebar from side to side without operating the throttle. The idle speed must remain constant with no increase in idle speed. If the idle speed increases when turning the handlebar, the throttle cable routing and/or adjustment is incorrect. Reroute and/or readjust the throttle cables as required.

EMISSION CONTROL SYSTEM LABELS

The Vehicle Emission Control Information label is attached to the left frame down tube.

PULSE SECONDARY AIR SUPPLY SYSTEM

The pulse secondary air supply system lowers emissions output by introducing secondary air into the exhaust gases in the exhaust port. This function is performed by the Pulse Secondary Air Injection (PAIR) control valve. The introduction of air raises the exhaust temperature, which consumes some of the unburned fuel in the exhaust and changes most of the hydrocarbons and carbon monoxide into carbon dioxide and water vapor. The PAIR control solenoid valve is part of the fuel injection system and controlled by the ECM. PAIR check valves installed in the cylinder head covers prevent a reverse flow of air though the system.

No adjustments are provided for or required by the pulse secondary air supply system. However, inspect the system at the intervals listed in Chapter Three.

System Inspection

1. Start the engine and warm up to normal operating temperature. Turn the engine off.
2. Remove the air filter (Chapter Three).
3. Visually check the secondary intake port in the air filter housing (**Figure 71**). The port should be clear. If there are traces of carbon on or around the port, inspect the PAIR check valves as described in this section.
4. Install the air filter (Chapter Three).
5. Disconnect the air supply hoses (A and B, **Figure 72**) at the cylinder head covers.

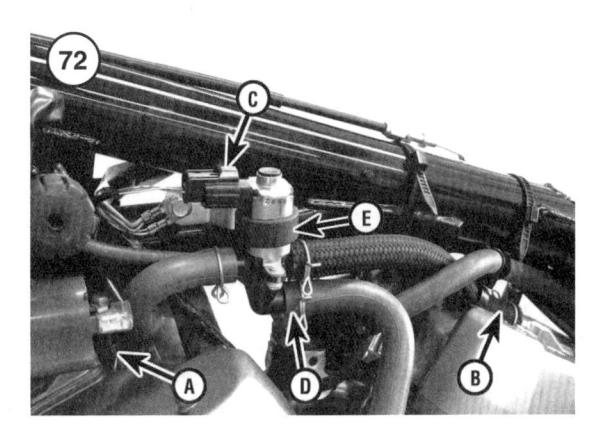

8. Clean the throttle assembly and handlebar.
9. Install the new throttle cables by routing them along their original path, as noted during removal.
10. Identify the throttle cables as follows:
    a. Pull cable: A, **Figure 69** and A, **Figure 70**.
    b. Return cable: B, **Figure 69** and B, **Figure 70**.
11. At the handlebar, reconnect the cables (**Figure 69**) as described in *Removal/Installation* under *Handlebar* in Chapter Thirteen.
12. At the throttle body, reconnect the cables (**Figure 70**) as described in *Installation* under *throttle body* in this chapter.

6. Start the engine and open the throttle slightly while holding a finger over the end of the front air supply hose (A, **Figure 72**). A vacuum should be felt, indicating air is being sucked through the hose. Repeat for the rear cylinder air supply hose (B, **Figure 72**). If there is no vacuum present in the hoses, check the hoses for obstruction or damage. If the hoses are clear, check the PAIR control solenoid valve as described in this section
7. Reconnect the air supply hoses.

PAIR Control Solenoid Valve

Removal/installation

1. Remove the fuel tank as described in this chapter.
2. Disconnect the connector (C, **Figure 72**) at the PAIR control solenoid valve.
3. Disconnect the air supply hoses (A and B, **Figure 72**).
4. Disconnect the air suction hose (D, **Figure 72**).
5. Remove the PAIR control solenoid valve (E, **Figure 72**).
6. Check for plugged or damaged hoses.
7. Installation is the reverse of these steps.

Testing

1. Remove the PAIR control solenoid valve as described in this section.
2. Connect an air pump to the air suction hose port (D, **Figure 72**). Operate the air pump and check that air flows through both air support hose ports (A and B, **Figure 72**).
3. Connect a 12-volt battery to the 2-pin PAIR control valve connector terminals (C, **Figure 72**). Operate the air pump and check that no air flows through the air supply hose ports (A and B, **Figure 72**).
4. Disconnect the battery and air pump from the PAIR control solenoid valve.
5. Measure resistance between the two PAIR control valve terminals (C, **Figure 72**). The measured resistance should read 23-27 ohms at 20° C (68° F).
6. Replace the PAIR control solenoid valve if it failed any part of this test.

PAIR Check Valves

Removal/Inspection/Installation

Refer to *PAIR Check Valves Removal/Inspection/Installation* in Chapter Eight. Tighten the PAIR check valve cover (**Figure 73**) bolts to 7 N.m (62 in.-lb.).

EVAPORATIVE EMISSION CONTROL SYSTEM (CALIFORNIA MODELS ONLY)

An evaporative emission control system (EVAP) is installed on all models sold in California.

Fuel vapor from the fuel tank is routed into an EVAP canister, where it is stored when the engine is not running. When the engine is running, these vapors are drawn into the EVAP purge control solenoid valve and flow through the throttle body and into the engine to be burned. Make sure all hose clamps are tight. Check all hoses from deterioration and replace as necessary.

Inspect the EVAP control system at the intervals specified in Chapter Three.

EVAP Canister

Removal/Installation

Refer to **Figure 74**.
1. Support the motorcycle on a workstand.
2. Remove the bolt and collar, then lower the canister.
3. Label and disconnect the hoses from the canister.
4. Inspect the hoses for cuts, damage or soft spots. Replace any damaged hoses.
5. Installation is the reverse of the removal steps.

EVAP Purge Control Solenoid Valve

Removal/installation

Refer to **Figure 74**.
1. Remove the rear wheel (Chapter Twelve).
2. Remove the rear fender (Chapter Seventeen).
3. Remove the battery (Chapter Ten).
4. Remove the starter relay switch (Chapter Ten).
5. Remove the rear ignition coil (Chapter Ten).
6. Remove the ECM as described in this chapter.

FUEL INJECTION AND EMISSION CONTROL SYSTEMS

74 EVAPORATIVE EMISSION CONTROL SYSTEM (EVAP) (CALIFORNIA MODELS ONLY)

- Evap purge control solenoid valve
- Evap purge control solenoid valve hose (to throttle body)
- Connector
- Hose port B
- Hose port A
- Evap canister hose (to fuel tank)
- Evap canister hose
- Bolt
- Evap canister
- Evap canister drain hose
- Evap canister air vent hose

75 Malfunction indicator lamp

2. Connect an air pump to hose port A. Operate the air pump and check that air flows through hose port B.
3. Connect a 12-volt battery to the two terminals on the EVAP purge control solenoid valve. Operate the air pump and check that air does not flow through hose port B.
4. Disconnect the battery and air pump from the EVAP purge control solenoid valve.
5. Measure resistance between the two EVAP purge control solenoid valve terminals. The measured resistance should read 30-34 ohms at 20° C (68° F).
6. Replace the EVAP purge control solenoid valve if it failed any part of this test.

MALFUNCTION INDICATOR LAMP (MIL)

Refer to **Figure 75**.

The fuel injection system is equipped with self-diagnostic capability. Under normal operating conditions, when the ignition switch is turned on and the engine stop switch is in the run position, the malfunction indicator lamp (MIL) lights for a few seconds and then turns off. This check informs the rider that the MIL light is operational. If the MIL light stays on or comes on at any time when the engine is running, a fault has occurred in the FI system. The engine control module (ECM) stores a diagnostic trouble code (DTC) in the system's memory. Under most conditions, the motorcycle can still run when the MIL is illuminated. A DTC can be set from a variety of causes: ignition system, fuel system, secondary air injection system, or a combination of these systems and conditions. Start fuel injection troubleshooting by retrieving the DTCs and following the information listed in the specified troubleshooting procedure in *DTC Troubleshooting* in this chapter.

Intermittent Problems

An intermittent problem means that a system that had a problem is now working correctly. When troubleshooting an intermittent problem where the MIL may be turning on and then off, try to determine the DTC as described in this section. Then check the connectors in the affected system for contamination or loose terminals.

Driveability Problems When the MIL Does Not Come On

If there is a driveability problem that is not intermittent and the MIL did not come on, refer to *Fuel System* in Chapter Two.

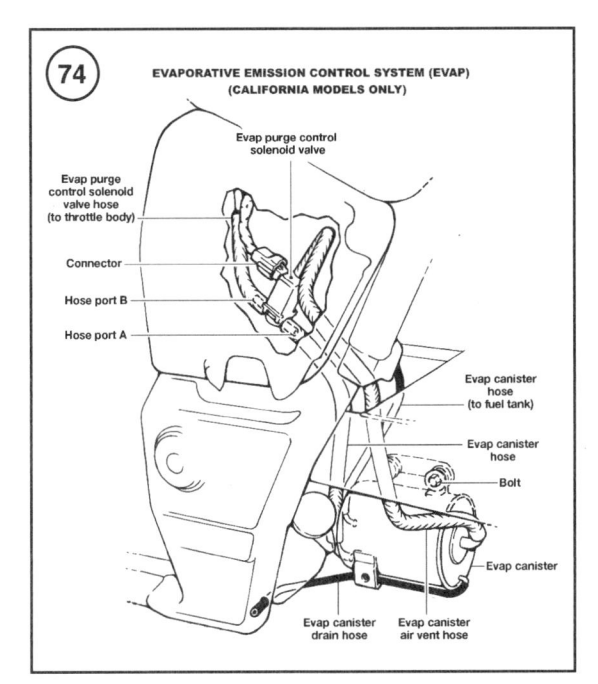

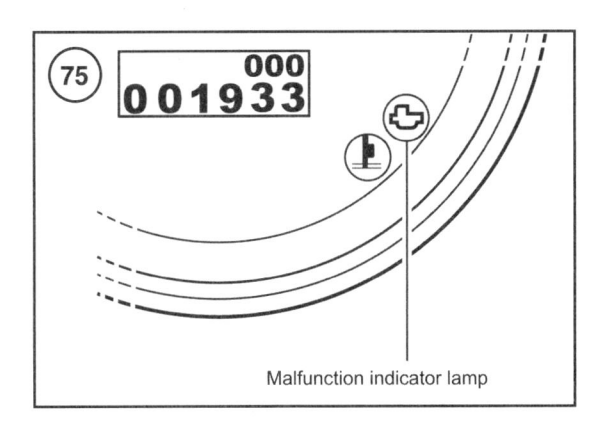

7. Remove the tools from the battery box. Then remove the screws and the tool box cover.
8. Remove the battery box mounting bolts. The release the tab on the bottom of the battery box from its mounting stay and remove the battery box.
9. Disconnect the connector at the EVAP purge control solenoid valve.
10. Label and then disconnect the hoses at the EVAP purge control solenoid valve.
11. Remove the mounting bolts and the EVAP purge control solenoid valve.
12. Inspect the hoses for cuts, damage or soft spots. Replace any damaged hoses.
13. Installation is the reverse of these removal steps.

Testing

Refer to **Figure 74**.
1. Remove the EVAP purge control solenoid valve as described in this section.

Tools

DTCs can be retrieved by one of two methods:
1. Shorting the data link connector (DLC) leads with the Service Check Short (SCS) connector (Honda part No. 070PZ-ZY30100) or a jumper wire and then reading the number of flashes displayed by the MIL.
2. Using the Honda Diagnostic System (HDS) pocket tester.

Main codes can be read by using the SCS (**Figure 76**) or shorting the DLC. The main code indicates the faulty component. Further testing can be done using the HDS. The HDS also reads a sub-code that identifies the component's operating symptom. Refer to *Reading DTCs* in this section.

Diagnostic Trouble Codes (DTC)

Diagnostic trouble codes (DTC) consists of a numbered main code and a numbered sub-code, each separated by a hyphen. The first number set identifies the component. The second number set identifies the component's operating symptom. For example, the DTC 1-1 indicates a MAP sensor low voltage circuit problem. DTC 1-2 indicates a MAP sensor high voltage circuit problem. Main codes and sub-codes can be read using the HDS and are listed in **Table 4**.

Note the following before retrieving DTCs:
1. The DTC set in the ECU memory will remain in memory until the problem is repaired and the DTC is erased. Turning the ignition switch off during or after retrieving the DTC does not erase it. However, to view the DTC again after turning the ignition switch off then on, the retrieval procedure must be repeated. See *Reading DTCs* in this section.
2. The ECU can store more than one DTC. The system displays the DTCs, starting with the lower number first. For example, DTC 7-1 would be displayed before DTC 9-1.
3. Always write down the DTC number(s).
4. After troubleshooting and servicing the fuel injection system, erase the DTC to ensure the problem has been successfully repaired.

Fail-Safe Operation

When a DTC is set, the motorcycle can either continue to run in a fail-safe mode or will stop (or cannot restart once the ignition switch is turned off). Whether or not the motorcycle can continue to run will depend on the affected fuel injection component.

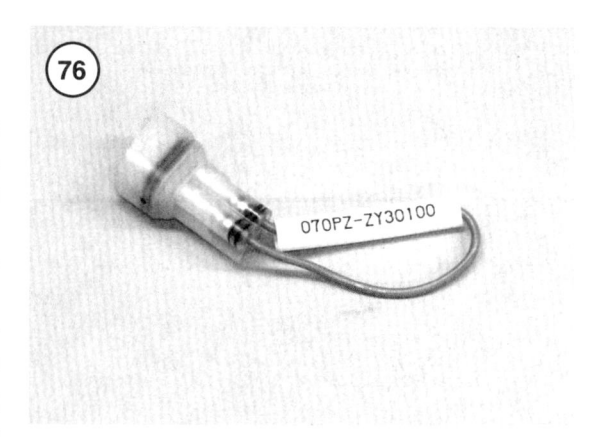

76

Self-Diagnostic Check (MIL Lamp Check)

This is a standard check to make prior to starting the engine. The diagnostic system indicates a normal condition or an operating problem each time the ignition key is turned on.
1. Support the motorcycle on its sidestand.
2. Turn the ignition switch on position and the engine stop switch to run.
3. The MIL (**Figure 75**) should light for a few seconds and then turn off. Note the following:
   a. If the MIL did not turn on, there is a problem within the MIL lighting circuit. Refer to *MIL Lamp Circuit Test* in this section
   b. If the MIL turned off after a few seconds, there are no codes stored in the ECM.

NOTE
If the engine will not start, operate the starter motor for at least 10 seconds to trigger codes that cause a no-start condition. If the MIL now blinks, a code has been set.

   c. If the MIL stayed on, a DTC has been set in the ECM. Perform the *Reading DTCs* procedure in this section.
4. Turn the ignition switch off.

Reading DTCs

Using the HDS pocket tester

The HDS pocket tester reads the DTC main code and sub-code.

The HDS pocket tester also reads current data, freeze data and other ECM information. Current data is the system operating information recorded as the test is being made. Freeze data is the system operating information recorded when the malfunction was detected
1. Turn the ignition switch off.

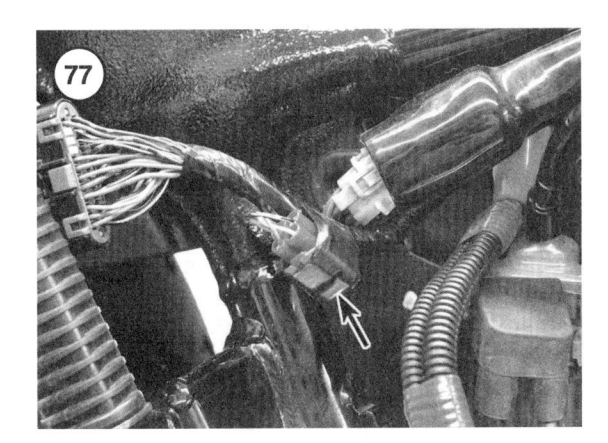

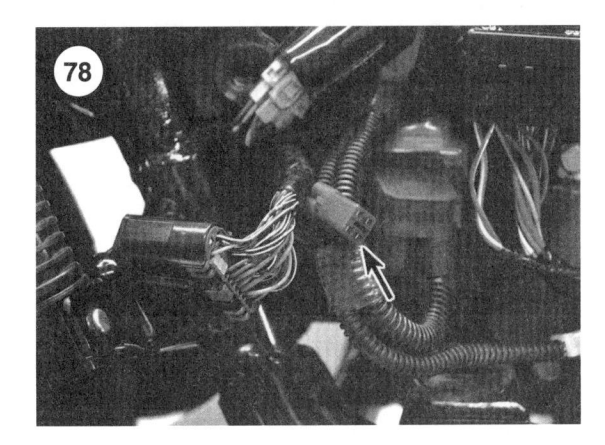

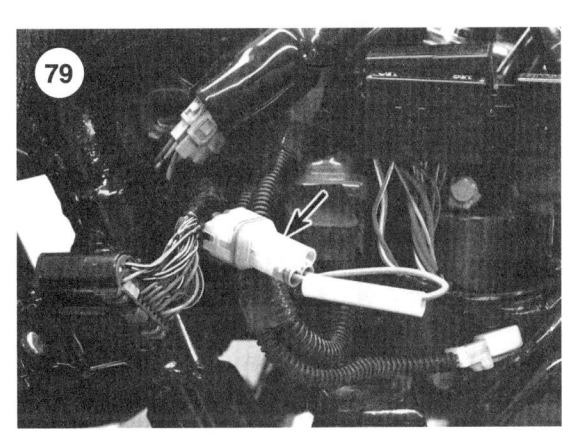

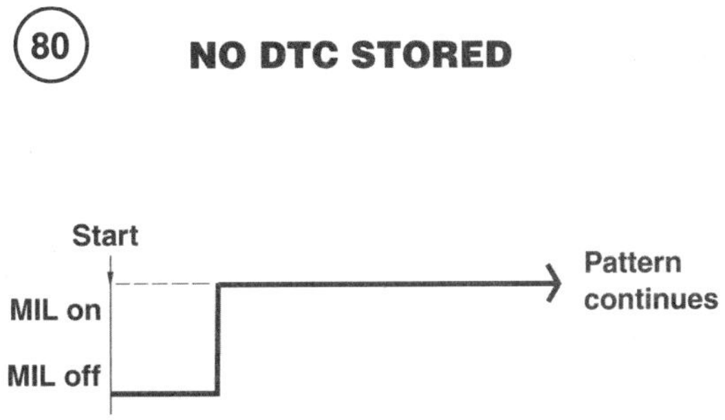

FUEL INJECTION AND EMISSION CONTROL SYSTEMS

2. Remove the right (non-ABS) or left (ABS) side cover (Chapter Seventeen).
3. Remove the red connector cover from the DLC. **Figure 77** shows the DLC connector used on non-ABS models. On ABS models, the DLC connector is located on the left side of the motorcycle in front of the rear ignition coil.
4. Connect the HDS pocket tester to the DLC (**Figure 78**) following the information listed in the HDS owner's manual.
5. Turn the ignition switch on.
6. After retrieving the DTC and freeze data, refer to **Table 4** to identify the DTC, symptoms and possible causes, then refer to the appropriate troubleshooting procedure under *DTC Troubleshooting* in this chapter.
7. After repairing the problem, erase the DTC(s) as described under *Erasing DTCs* in this section.
8. Refer to the HDS pocket tester owner's manual for additional operating information.

Shorting the DLC connector

Diagnostic trouble codes (DTCs) are retrieved from the ECM by triggering a series of timed flashes across the MIL (**Figure 75**). The number of flashes displayed by the MIL indicator indicates the stored DTC (**Table 4**).
1. Turn the ignition switch off.
2. Remove the right (non-ABS) or left (ABS) side cover (Chapter Seventeen).
3. Remove the red connector cover from the DLC. **Figure 77** shows the DLC connector used on non-ABS models. On ABS models, the DLC connector is located on the left side of the motorcycle in front of the rear ignition coil.
4. Short the DLC connector with the Honda SCS connector (**Figure 79**) or connect a jumper wire across the green and brown DLC terminals.
5. Turn the ignition switch on and the engine stop switch to run. Observe the MIL and note the following:
   a. If the ECM has no stored DTCs, the MIL will illuminate when the ignition switch is turned on.

NOTE
Figure 80 shows a graphic representation of observing the MIL indicator when there are no codes stored in memory.

NOTE
If the engine will not start, the engine must be turned over to generate a DTC from memory. Turn the ignition switch on and the engine stop switch to run. Operate the starter motor for more than

10 seconds. Check the MIL to see if it blinks. If so, continue with the procedure.

b. If the MIL starts blinking, DTCs are stored in the ECM. Continue with the procedure.

6. Determine the self-diagnostic failure code(s) as follows:

NOTE
Figure 81 shows a graphic representation of observing the MIL indicator when reading DTC 13-1.

a. The system indicates codes with a series of long (1.3 second) and short (0.5 second) blinks. Each long blink equals 10. Each short blink equals 1. For example, a 1.3 second blink (1.3 second × 10 = 10) followed by three 0.5 second blinks (0.5 second × 3 = 3) indicates a failure code of 13-1 (10 + 3).

NOTE
Figure 82 shows a graphic representation of retrieving two DTCs: code 7-1 and code 33-1.

b. When more than one failure code occurs, the system will display the codes from lowest to highest. A short gap separates individual codes.

7. After retrieving the DTC, refer to Table 4 to identify the DTC, symptoms and possible causes, then refer to the appropriate troubleshooting procedure under *DTC Troubleshooting* in this chapter.

8. After repairing the problem, erase the DTC(s) as described in *Erasing DTCs* in this section.

Erasing DTCs

After DTC has been retrieved and the system repaired, erase the DTC(s) from memory as follows. If the motorcycle was repaired at a dealership, the DTC(s) likely will have been erased at the dealership.

Using the HDS pocket tester

1. Before connecting the HDS to the electrical system, turn the engine stop switch to run. Then, turn the ignition switch on. The MIL light should operate for two seconds and then turn off. The fuel pump should also operate (able to hear it running). If these conditions did not occur as described, the HDS pocket tester will not receive power. If so, perform the *MIL Lamp Circuit Test* in this section.
2. Turn the ignition switch off.
3. Remove the right (non-ABS) or left (ABS) side cover (Chapter Seventeen).
4. Remove the red connector cover (**Figure 77**) from the DLC. **Figure 77** shows the DLC connector used on non-ABS models. On ABS models, the DLC connector is located on the left side of the motorcycle in front of the rear ignition coil.
5. Connect the HDS pocket tester to the DLC (**Figure 78**).
6. Erase the DTC(s) with the HDS pocket tester following the manufacturer's instructions.
7. Disconnect the HDS pocket tester.
8. Install the red connector cover on to the DLC connector.

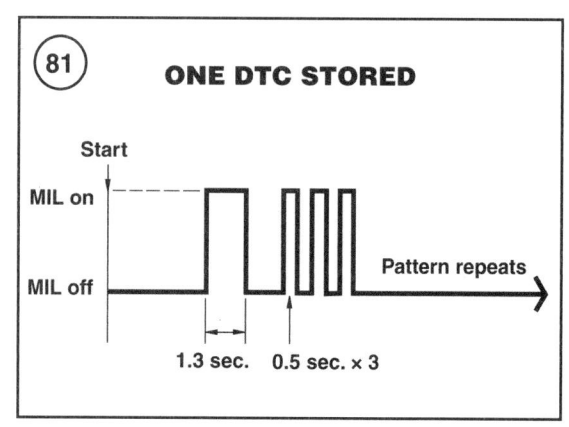

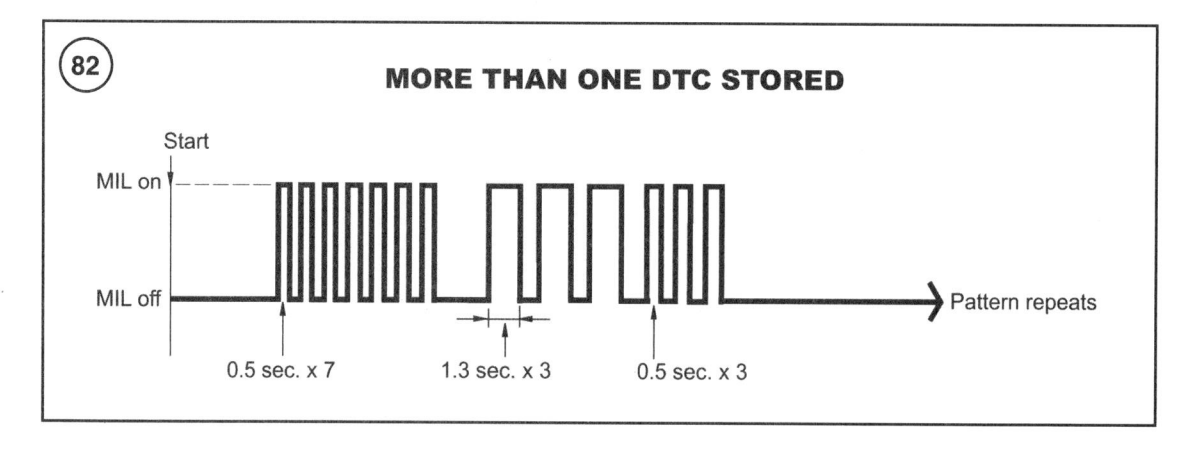

81 ONE DTC STORED

82 MORE THAN ONE DTC STORED

FUEL INJECTION AND EMISSION CONTROL SYSTEMS

83

ECM 33-PIN WIRING HARNESS CONNECTORS

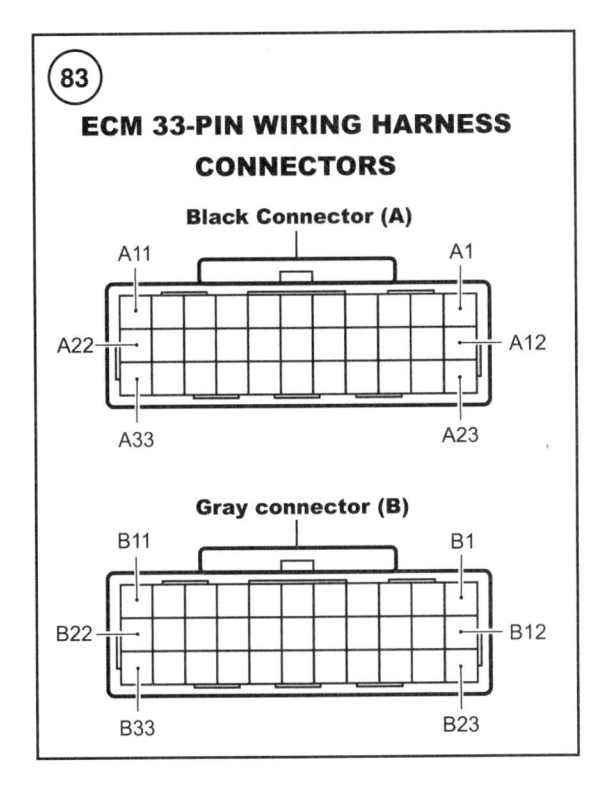

Black Connector (A)
A11, A1, A22, A12, A33, A23

Gray connector (B)
B11, B1, B22, B12, B33, B23

9. Install the left (ABS) or right (non-ABS) side cover (Chapter Seventeen).
10. Perform the *Self-Diagnostic Check (MIL Lamp Check)* in this section to confirm the DTC(s) were successfully cleared from memory.

Shorting the DLC connector

NOTE
Read the procedure throughly. Then, perform the procedure.

1. Turn the ignition switch off.
2. Remove the right (non-ABS) or left (ABS) side cover (Chapter Seventeen).
3. Remove the red connector cover from the DLC. **Figure 77** shows the connector used on non-ABS models. On ABS models, the connector is located on the left side of the motorcycle in front of the rear ignition coil.
4. Short the DLC connector with the Honda SCS connector **(Figure 79)** or connect a jumper wire across the green and brown DLC terminals.
5. With the engine stop switch in its RUN position, turn the ignition switch on and disconnect the SCS connector or jumper wire from the DLC.

NOTE
The DLC connector must be shorted when the MIL is illuminated. If not, the MIL will not blink.

6. The MIL will come on for approximately 5 seconds. While the light is on, short the DLC once again with SCS connector or the jumper wire to erase the memory. If the diagnostic memory was properly erased, the MIL will turn off, and then start blinking.
7. Turn the ignition switch off and remove the SCS connector or jumper wire from the DLC.
8. Perform the *Self-Diagnostic Check (MIL Lamp Check)* in this section to confirm that the DTC(s) was successfully cleared from memory.

MIL Lamp Circuit Test

If the MIL does not light when the ignition switch is turned on and with the engine stop switch set to run, perform the following:

1. Support the motorcycle on its sidestand and turn the ignition switch on. Check that the speedometer and the other indicator lights work correctly.
2A. If the speedometer and the other indicator lights do not function correctly. Check the speedometer power circuit as described under *Speedometer/VS Sensor Power/Ground Circuit Test* in Chapter Ten.
2B. If the speedometer and the other indicator lights function correctly, continue the procedure.
3. Turn the ignition switch off.
4. Disconnect the black 33-pin ECM wiring harness connector as described in *Engine Control Module (ECM)* in this chapter.
5. Connect a jumper wire between the A20 terminal **(Figure 83)** in the black ECM wiring harness connector and ground. Turn the ignition switch on and set the engine stop switch to run. The MIL should turn on. Note the following:
   a. If the MIL came on, the ECM is faulty. Replace the ECM as described in this chapter and retest.
   b. If the MIL did not come on, check the white/blue wire between the ECM and speedometer for damage. If the white/blue wire is good, replace the speedometer as described in Chapter Ten.
6. Connect the black 33-pin ECM connector (this chapter).

DTC TROUBLESHOOTING

To troubleshoot the fuel injection system, perform the *Self-Diagnostic Check (MIL Lamp Check)* as described in this chapter and retrieve any DTCs. Find the DTC(s) in Table 4 and then turn to the appropriate procedure in this section to troubleshoot the system.

Before troubleshooting, note the following:

1. Refer to the wiring diagrams at the end of this manual to identify the connectors and their wire colors. Refer to the appropriate section in this chapter and in Chapter Ten to locate the individual components. Refer to **Table 1** for component abbreviations.

2. Turn the ignition switch off before disconnecting and reconnecting connectors.

3. Do not disconnect or reconnect electrical connectors when the ignition switch is on. A voltage spike may damage the ECM.

4. The terms open circuit and short circuit are used in the troubleshooting procedures. A short circuit occurs when a wire incorrectly contacts a ground or another wire causing an unwanted current path or circuit. This can be caused from worn insulation. Most shorts will burn a fuse or open some other type of circuit protector. An open circuit is an accidental break or opening in a wire, electrical component or connector that prevents a complete current path. A blown bulb is one example of an open circuit.

5. Make sure the electrical connectors are secure and free of corrosion before testing.

6. Before troubleshooting, check the connectors identified in the procedure for corrosion, loose or damaged terminals. Then check the wiring harness for damage such as frayed wiring, breaks or excessive heat.

CAUTION
Do not force a meter test lead into a connector as this may damage the connector and cause an open circuit.

7. When testing at the ECM harness side connectors, always insert the test probe into the connector terminal. Do not back-probe into the connector as this may damage the wire or connector.

8. To check for an intermittent problem, carefully move the wiring harness and/or connector(s) by hand with the meter connected to the circuit. Then check for loose or contaminated connectors and terminals.

9. If the affected system has a vacuum function, make sure the hose(s) are attached securely, are in good condition and that there are no leaks.

10. If a DTC refers to a particular component, refer to the tests in this chapter or Chapter Ten to determine if further testing is possible.

11. When a test refers to battery voltage, measure and use the battery's actual voltage reading as the specified voltage reading.

12. Do not perform tests with a battery charger attached to the battery or circuit. Test and charge the battery as described in Chapter Ten.

13. All resistance and voltage readings are specified at a test temperature of 20 degrees C (68 degrees F).

14. Before replacing the ECM, take the motorcycle to a dealership for further testing. Most parts suppliers will not accept the return of electrical components. Have the dealership confirm that the ECM is faulty before purchasing a replacement.

15. After troubleshooting, clear any DTC and perform self-diagnosis as described in *Malfunction Indicator Lamp (MIL)* in this section to assure the problem has been corrected.

16. If the specified tests fail to locate the problem, refer troubleshooting and repair to a dealership.

17. The troubleshooting procedures use the HDS tester. If this tester is not available, use a digital multimeter to perform the resistance and voltage tests described in the procedures.

18. Refer to **Figure 83** to identify the black 33-pin and gray 33-pin ECM wiring harness connector terminal numbers.

19. After troubleshooting, reverse the removal steps to reinstall all previously removed parts.

DTC 1-1: MAP Sensor Low Voltage Test

1. Turn the ignition switch off.
2. Connect the HDS pocket tester to the DLC connector as described under *Reading DTCs* in this section.
3. Turn the ignition switch on and set the engine stop switch to run.
4. Read the MAP sensor voltage with the HDS pocket tester. Note the following:
   a. If the test indicates 0 volts, continue the procedure.
   b. If the test does not indicate 0 volts, the problem is intermittent. Check the connectors for contamination or damage.
5. Disconnect the sensor unit electrical connector as described under *Sensor Unit* in this chapter.
6. Turn the ignition switch on and measure voltage between the sensor unit yellow/red (+) and green/orange (-) wiring harness terminals with a digital voltmeter. The specified voltage is 4.75-5.25 volts. Turn the ignition switch off. Note the following:
   a. If the voltage is correct, continue with Step 8.
   b. If voltage is incorrect, continue the procedure.
7. Disconnect the black ECM 33-pin connector. Check for continuity in the yellow/red wire between the sensor unit wiring harness connector and the black ECM 33-pin wiring harness connector terminal A9 in (**Figure 83**) with an ohmmeter. Note the following:
   a. If there is continuity, replace the ECM with a known good unit and retest.
   b. If there is no continuity, check for loose connectors or an open yellow/red wire circuit.
8. Reconnect the black ECM 33-pin connector (if disconnected). Check for continuity in the light green/

FUEL INJECTION AND EMISSION CONTROL SYSTEMS

yellow wire between the sensor unit wiring harness connector and ground with an ohmmeter. Note the following:
    a. If there is continuity, check for a short in the light green/yellow wire circuit.
    b. If there is no continuity, continue the procedure.
9. Replace the sensor unit as described in *Sensor Unit* in this chapter.
10. Erase the DTC as described under *Erasing DTCs* in this chapter.
11. Use the HDS pocket tester to read the DTC:
    a. If the HDS pocket tester reads DTC 1-1, replace the ECM with a known good unit and retest.
    b. If the HDS pocket tester does not read DTC 1-1, replace the sensor unit and retest.

DTC 1-2: Map Sensor High Voltage Test

1. Turn the ignition switch off.
2. Connect the HDS pocket tester to the DLC connector as described under *Reading DTCs* in this section.
3. Turn the ignition switch on and the engine stop switch to run.
4. Read the map sensor voltage with the HDS pocket tester and note the following:
    a. If the test indicates approximately 5 volts, continue the procedure.
    b. If the test does not indicate approximately 5 volts, the problem is intermittent. Check the connectors for contamination or damage.
5. Disconnect the sensor unit connector as described in *Sensor Unit* in this chapter.
6. Connect a jumper wire between the sensor unit green/orange and light green/yellow wiring harness connector terminals. Turn the ignition switch on and set the engine stop switch to run. Then, read the MAP sensor voltage with the HDS pocket tester:
    a. If the voltage is 0 volts, replace the sensor unit and retest.
    b. If the voltage is not 0 volts, continue the procedure.
7. Turn the ignition switch off and disconnect the jumper wire.
8. Turn the ignition switch on and measure voltage between the sensor unit yellow/red (+) and green/orange (-) wiring harness side terminals with a digital voltmeter. The specified voltage is 4.75-5.25 volts. Turn the ignition switch off. Note the following:
    a. If the voltage is correct, continue the procedure.
    b. If voltage is incorrect, check the yellow/red and green/orange wires for an open circuit.
9. Disconnect the gray ECM 33-pin connector. Check for continuity in the light green/yellow wire between the sensor unit wire harness connector and terminal B9 **(Figure 83)** the gray ECM 33-pin wiring harness connector with an ohmmeter. Note the following:
    a. If there is continuity, replace the ECM with a new unit and retest.
    b. If there is no continuity, check for loose connectors or an open circuit in the light green/yellow wire.

DTC 7-1: ECT Sensor Low Voltage Test

1. Turn the ignition switch off.
2. Connect the HDS pocket tester to the DLC connector as described under *Reading DTCs* in this section.
3. Turn the ignition switch on and set the engine stop switch to run.
4. Read the ECT sensor voltage with the HDS pocket tester. Note the following:
    a. If the test indicates 0 volts, continue the procedure.
    b. If the test does not indicate 0 volts, the problem is intermittent. Check the connectors for contamination or damage.
5. Turn the ignition switch off.
6. Disconnect the ECT sensor connector **(Figure 49)** at the thermostat housing.
7. Turn the ignition switch on and set the engine stop switch to run. Read the ECT sensor voltage with the HDS pocket tester. Note the following:
    a. If the test does not indicate 0 volts, continue the procedure.
    b. If the test indicates 0 volts, continue with Step 9.
8. Measure resistance across the ECT sensor pink/white (+) and green/orange (-) terminals. The correct resistance reading is 2.3-2.6 K ohms. Note the following:
    a. If the resistance reading is correct, replace the ECM and retest.
    b. If the resistance reading is incorrect, the ECT sensor is damaged. Replace the ECT sensor (Chapter Ten) and retest.
9. Turn the ignition switch off and check for continuity between the ECT sensor pink/white wiring harness connector terminal and ground:
    a. If there is continuity, repair the short in the pink/white wire.
    b. If there is no continuity, replace the ECM and retest.

DTC 7-2: ECT Sensor High Voltage Test

1. Turn the ignition switch off.
2. Connect the HDS pocket tester to the DLC connector as described under *Reading DTCs* n this section.

3. Turn the ignition switch on and set the engine stop switch to run.
4. Read the ECT sensor voltage with the HDS pocket tester and note the following:
   a. If the test indicates approximately 5 volts, continue with the procedure.
   b. If the test does not indicate approximately 5 volts, the problem is intermittent. Check the connectors for contamination or damage.
5. Turn the ignition switch off.
6. Disconnect the ECT sensor electrical connector (**Figure 49**).
7. Connect a jumper wire between the ECT sensor pink/white and green/orange wiring harness connector terminals. Turn the ignition switch on and set the engine stop switch to run. Read the ECT sensor voltage with the HDS pocket tester:
   a. If 0 volts is indicated, replace the ECT sensor and retest.
   b. If 0 volts is not indicated, continue with the procedure.
8. Turn the ignition switch off and disconnect the jumper wire. Then, disconnect the black and gray ECM 33-pin connectors.
9. Check for continuity in the green/orange wire between the ECT sensor wiring harness connector and terminal A18 (**Figure 83**) in the black ECM 33-pin wiring harness connector with an ohmmeter. Then check for continuity in the pink/white wire between the ECT sensor wiring harness connector and terminal A13 (**Figure 83**) in the gray ECM 33-pin wiring harness connector with an ohmmeter.
Note the following:
   a. If there is continuity, replace the ECM and retest.
   b. If there is no continuity, check for loose connectors or an open green/orange and/or pink/white wire circuit(s).

DTC 8-1: TP Sensor Low Voltage Test

1. Turn the ignition switch off.
2. Connect the HDS pocket tester to the DLC connector as described under *Reading DTCs* in this section.
3. Turn the ignition switch on and set the engine stop switch to run.
4. Read the TP sensor voltage with the HDS pocket tester and note the following:
   a. If the test indicates 0 volts, continue the procedure.
   b. If the test does not indicate 0 volts, the problem is intermittent. Check the sensor unit connector for contamination or damage.
5. Turn the ignition switch off.
6. Disconnect the sensor unit connector as described in this chapter.
7. Turn the ignition switch on and set the engine stop switch to run. Measure voltage between the sensor unit yellow/red (+) and green/orange (-) wiring harness terminals with a digital voltmeter. The specified voltage is 4.75-5.25 volts. Turn the ignition switch off. Note the following:
   a. If the voltage is incorrect, continue the procedure.
   b. If voltage is correct, continue with Step 9.
8. Disconnect the black ECM 33-pin connector. Check for continuity in the yellow/red wire between the sensor unit wiring harness connector and in terminal A9 (**Figure 83**) the black ECM 33-pin wiring harness connector with an ohmmeter. Note the following:
   a. If there is continuity, replace the ECM and retest.
   b. If there is no continuity, check for loose connectors or an open circuit in the yellow/red wire.
9. Disconnect the gray ECM 33-pin connector. Check for continuity in the red/yellow wire between the sensor unit wiring harness connector and terminal B31 (**Figure 83**) in the gray ECM 33-pin wiring harness connector, with an ohmmeter. Note the following:
   a. If there is continuity, continue the procedure.
   b. If there is no continuity, check for loose connectors or an open circuit in the red/yellow wire.
10. Reconnect the gray ECM 33-pin connector. Check for continuity in the red/yellow wire between the sensor unit wiring harness connector and ground with an ohmmeter. Note the following:
    a. If there is continuity, check for a short in the red/yellow wire.
    b. If there is no continuity, continue the procedure.
11. Replace the sensor unit as described in this chapter.
12. Erase the DTCs as described under *Erasing DTCs* in this chapter.
13. Use the HDS pocket tester to read the DTC:
    a. If the HDS pocket tester reads DTC 8-1, replace the ECM and retest.
    b. If the HDS pocket tester does not read DTC 8-1, the original sensor unit was faulty.

DTC 8-2: TP Sensor High Voltage Test

1. Turn the ignition switch off.
2. Connect the HDS pocket tester to the DLC connector as described under *Reading DTCs* in this section.
3. Turn the ignition switch on and set the engine stop switch to run.
4. Read the TP sensor voltage with the HDS pocket tester and note the following:
   a. If the test indicates approximately 5 volts, continue the procedure.

FUEL INJECTION AND EMISSION CONTROL SYSTEMS

(84)

b. If the test does not indicate approximately 5 volts, the problem is intermittent. Check for loose or corroded connectors.
5. Turn the ignition switch off.
6. Disconnect the sensor unit connector as described in this chapter.
7. Turn the ignition switch on and set the engine stop switch to run. Measure voltage between the sensor unit yellow/red (+) and green/orange (-) wiring harness terminals with a digital voltmeter. The specified voltage is 4.75-5.25 volts. Turn the ignition switch off. Note the following:
   a. If the voltage is correct, continue the procedure.
   b. If voltage is incorrect, check for an open circuit in the yellow/red and green/orange wires.
8. Turn the ignition switch off.
9. Remove the throttle body as described in this chapter.
10. Measure resistance at the sensor unit connector on the throttle body between the red/yellow and green/orange wire terminals **(Figure 84)**. The correct reading is 0.5-1.5 K ohms. Note the following:
   a. If the resistance reading is correct, replace the ECM and retest.
   b. If the resistance reading is incorrect, replace the sensor unit and retest.

DTC 9-1: IAT Sensor Low Voltage Test

1. Turn the ignition switch off.
2. Connect the HDS pocket tester to the DLC connector.
3. Turn the ignition switch on and set the engine stop switch to run.
4. Read the IAT sensor voltage with the HDS pocket tester and note the following:
   a. If the test indicates approximately 0 volts, continue the procedure.
   b. If the test does not indicate approximately 0 volts, the problem is intermittent. Check the connectors for contamination or damage.

5. Turn the ignition switch off.
6. Disconnect the sensor unit connector as described in this chapter.
7. Turn the ignition switch on and set the engine stop switch to run. Read the IAT sensor voltage with the HDS pocket tester:
   a. If the test indicates approximately 0 volts, continue the procedure.
   b. If the test does not indicate approximately 0 volts, replace the sensor unit and retest.
8. Turn the ignition switch off and check for continuity between the sensor unit gray/blue wiring harness connector terminal and ground:
   a. If there is continuity, repair the short in the gray/blue wire.
   b. If there is no continuity replace the ECM and retest.

DTC 9-2: IAT Sensor High Voltage Test

1. Turn the ignition switch off.
2. Connect the HDS pocket tester to the DLC connector as described under *Reading DTCs* in this section.
3. Turn the ignition switch on and set the engine stop switch to run.
4. Read the IAT sensor voltage with the HDS pocket tester and note the following:
   a. If the test indicates approximately 5 volts, continue the procedure.
   b. If the test does not indicate approximately 5 volts, the problem is intermittent. Check the connectors for contamination or damage.
5. Turn the ignition switch off.
6. Disconnect the sensor unit connector as described in this chapter.
7. Connect a jumper wire between the sensor unit green/orange and gray/blue wiring harness connector terminals. Turn the ignition switch on and set the engine stop switch to run. Read the IAT sensor voltage with the HDS pocket tester:
   a. If approximately 0 volts is indicated, the sensor unit is faulty. Replace the sensor unit and retest.
   b. If approximately 0 volts is not indicated, continue with Step 8.
8. Turn the ignition switch off and disconnect the jumper wire.
9. Disconnect the black and gray ECM 33-pin connectors.
10. Check for continuity in the green/orange wire between the sensor unit wiring harness connector and terminal A18 in **(Figure 83)** the black ECM 33-pin harness side connector with an ohmmeter. Then check for continuity in the gray/blue wire between the sensor unit wiring harness connector and termi-

nal B29 (**Figure 83**) in the gray ECM 33-pin harness side connector with an ohmmeter.
Note the following:
   a. If there is continuity, replace the ECM and retest.
   b. If there is no continuity, check for loose connectors or an open circuit in the green/orange and/or gray/blue wire(s).

DTC11-1: VS Sensor

1. Support the motorcycle on a stand with the rear wheel off the ground.
2. Connect the HDS pocket tester to the DLC connector as described under *Reading DTCs* in this section.
3. Start the engine and shift the transmission into gear.
4. Read the DTC with the HDS pocket tester and note whether the vehicle speed is accurately reported on the tester:
   a. Yes. Continue the procedure.
   b. No. Continue with Step 9.
5. Erase the DTC as described under *Erasing DTCs* in this Chapter.
6. Test ride the motorcycle. Then stop and turn the engine off.
7. Turn the ignition switch on and set the engine stop switch to run.
8. Use the HDS pocket tester to read the DTC. Note the following:
   a. If the HDS pocket tester reads DTC 11-1, replace the ECM and retest.
   b. If the HDS pocket tester does not read DTC 11-1, the problem is either intermittent or the ECM connectors are loose or corroded.
9. Remove the HDS pocket tester.
10. Test ride the motorcycle and note the speedometer operation. Note the following:
    a. If the speedometer does not operate correctly, inspect the speedometer circuit as described in Chapter Ten.
    b. If the speedometer operates correctly, continue the procedure.
11. Turn the ignition switch off.
12. Disconnect the VS sensor connector as described in Chapter Ten. Turn the ignition switch on and set the engine stop switch to run. Check for battery voltage between the VS sensor brown (+) and green/black (-) wiring harness terminals. Note the following:
    a. If there is a battery voltage, continue the procedure.
    b. If battery voltage is not present, check for an open circuit in the green/black wire. Then, check for an open or short circuit in the brown wire.
13. Turn the ignition switch off.
14. Disconnect the gray ECM 33-pin connector (this chapter).
15. Check for continuity in the pink/green wire between the VS sensor wiring harness connector and terminal B28 (**Figure 83**) in the gray ECM 33-pin wiring harness connector with an ohmmeter. Note the following:
    a. If there is continuity, continue the procedure.
    b. If there is no continuity, check for a break in the pink/green wire.
16. Reconnect the gray ECM 33-pin connector.
17. Check for continuity in the pink/green wire between the VS sensor wiring harness connector and ground. Note the following:
    a. If there is continuity, check for a short in the pink/green wire.
    b. If there is no continuity, replace the VS sensor and retest.

DTC 12-1: No. 1 (Rear) Fuel Injector

1. Erase the DTC as described under *Erasing DTCs* in this chapter.
2. Turn the ignition switch off.
3. Connect the HDS pocket tester to the DLC connector as described under *Reading DTCs* in this section.
4. Start the engine and allow to idle. Use the HDS pocket tester to read the DTC:
   a. If the HDS pocket tester reads DTC 12-1, continue the procedure.
   b. If the HDS pocket tester does not read DTC 12-1, the problem is intermittent. Check for contaminated or damaged connectors.
5. Turn the ignition switch off.
6. Disconnect the No. 1 fuel injector connector. Turn the ignition switch on and set the engine stop switch to run. Measure the battery voltage between the fuel injector connector black/white wire terminal and ground. Note the following:
   a. If there is battery voltage, continue the procedure.
   b. If there is no battery voltage, check the black/white wire for an open circuit.
7. Turn the ignition switch off.
8. Disconnect the black ECM 33-pin connector. Check for continuity in the pink/yellow wire between the No. 1 fuel injector wiring harness connector and terminal A17 (**Figure 83**) in the black ECM 33-pin wiring harness connector with an ohmmeter. Note the following:
   a. If there is continuity, continue the procedure.
   b. If there is no continuity, check for a break in the pink/yellow wire.
9. Reconnect the black ECM 33-pin connector.

FUEL INJECTION AND EMISSION CONTROL SYSTEMS

85

10. Check for continuity in the pink/yellow wire between the No. 1 fuel injector connector and ground. Note the following:
    a. If there is continuity, check for a short in the pink/yellow wire.
    b. If there is no continuity, continue the procedure.
11. At the No. 1 fuel injector, measure the resistance between the two fuel injector terminals. Specified resistance is 11-13 ohms.
    a. If the resistance is within specification, replace the ECM with a known good unit and retest.
    b. If the resistance is not within specification, replace the fuel injector and retest.

DTC 13-1: No. 2 (Front) Fuel Injector

1. Erase the DTCs as described under *Erasing DTCs* in this chapter.
2. Turn the ignition switch off.
3. Connect the HDS pocket tester to the DLC connector as described under *Reading DTCs* in this Chapter.
4. Start the engine and allow to idle. Use the HDS pocket tester to read the DTCs:
    a. If the HDS pocket tester reads DTC 13-1, continue the procedure.
    b. If the HDS pocket tester does not read DTC 13-1, the problem is intermittent. Check for contaminated or damaged connectors.
5. Turn the ignition switch off.
6. Disconnect the No. 2 fuel injector connector. Turn the ignition switch on and the engine stop switch to run. Measure the battery voltage between the fuel injector connector black/white wire terminal and ground. Note the following:
    a. If there is battery voltage, continue the procedure.
    b. If there is no battery voltage, check the black/white wire for an open circuit.
7. Turn the ignition switch off.

8. Disconnect the black ECM 33-pin connector. Check for continuity in the pink/blue wire between the No. 2 fuel injector wiring harness connector and terminal A6 (**Figure 83**) in the black ECM 33-pin wiring harness connector with an ohmmeter. Note the following:
    a. If there is continuity, continue the procedure.
    b. If there is no continuity, check for a break in the pink/blue wire.
9. Reconnect the black ECM 33-pin connector.
10. Check for continuity in the pink/blue wire between the No. 2 fuel injector connector and ground. Note the following:
    a. If there is continuity, check for a short in the pink/blue wire.
    b. If there is no continuity, continue the procedure.
11. At the No. 2 fuel injector, measure the resistance between the two fuel injector terminals. Specified resistance is 11-13 ohms.
    a. If the resistance is within specification, replace the ECM with a known good unit and retest.
    b. If the resistance is not within specification, replace the fuel injector and retest.

DTC 29-1: IACV

1. Erase the DTC as described under *Erasing DTCs* in this chapter.
2. Start the engine and recheck the DTC. Note the following:
    a. If the DTC 29-1 is still indicated, continue the procedure.
    b. If DTC 29-1 is not indicated, the failure is intermittent. Check the IACV connector for loose or contaminated terminals.
3. Turn the ignition switch off.
4. Disconnect the IACV connector. Check for continuity separately between each wire in the IACV wiring harness connector (yellow/green, black/blue, black and black/yellow) and ground. Note the following:
    a. If there is no continuity in any wire, continue the procedure.
    b. If there is continuity in one or more wires, check the wire(s) for a short circuit.
5. Disconnect the black ECM 33-pin connector.
6. Check for continuity between the IACV wiring harness connector and the black ECM 33-pin wiring harness connector as follows:
    a. Yellow/green wire to terminal A19.
    b. Black/blue/ wire to terminal A27.
    c. Black to wire terminal A16.
    d. Black/yellow wire to terminal A29.
    e. If there is continuity, continue the procedure.

f. If there is no continuity in one or more wires, check the wire(s) for an open circuit.

7. Measure resistance across the black/yellow to yellow/green and black/blue to black wires in the IACV **(Figure 85)**. The correct resistance is 99-121 ohms at 25°C (77°F)

　a. If the resistance is correct for both tests, replace the ECM and retest.

　b. If the resistance is incorrect for one or both tests, the IACV is damaged. Replace the IACV and retest.

DTC 33-2: EEPROM

1. Connect the HDS pocket tester to the DLC connector as described under *Reading DTCs* in this chapter.
2. Erase the DTC as described under *Erasing DTCs* in this chapter.
3. Turn the ignition switch on and set the engine stop switch to run.
4. Use the HDS pocket tester to read the DTC:

　a. If DTC 33-2 is indicated, replace the ECM and retest.

　b. If DTC 33-2 is not indicated, the problem is intermittent. Check the ECM connectors for loose or corroded terminals.

Table 1 FUEL INJECTION TECHNICAL ABBREVIATIONS

CKP sensor	Crankshaft position sensor
DLC	Data link connector
DTC	Diagnostic trouble code
ECM	Engine control module
ECT sensor	Engine coolant temperature sensor
EVAP	Evaporative emission
IACV	Idle air control valve
IAT sensor	Intake air temperature sensor
MAP sensor	Manifold absolute pressure sensor
MIL	Malfunction indicator lamp
PAIR	Pulse secondary air injection system
PGM-FI	Programmed fuel injection
SCS connector	Service check short connector
TP sensor	Throttle position sensor
VS sensor	Vehicle speed sensor

Table 2 FUEL INJECTION SYSTEM GENERAL SPECIFICATIONS

Engine idle speed	1100-1300 rpm
Fuel tank capacity	
Aero	
Total	14.5 L (3.8 gal.)
Reserve	3.5 L (0.92 gal.)
Spirit and Phantom	
Total	14 L (3.7 gal.)
Reserve	3.3 L (0.87 gal.)
Fuel injection system type	Programmed fuel injection (PGM-FI)
Throttle body identification number	
Aero and Spirit	GQB3A
Phantom	GQ9KA
Throttle bore	34 mm (1.3 in.)
Throttle grip freeplay	2-6mm (1/16"-1/4")

Table 3 FUEL INJECTION SYSTEM TEST SPECIFICATIONS (1)

Item	Specification
ECT sensor resistance	2.3-2.6 K ohms
EVAP purge control solenoid valve resistance	30-34 ohms
Fuel injector resistance	11-13 K ohms
Fuel pump full flow[2]	
Minimum rate for 10 seconds	50 cc (1.7 oz.)
Fuel pressure at idle speed	333-353 kPa (48-51 psi)
IACV resistance	99-121 ohms
PAIR control solenoid valve resistance	23-27 ohms

1. All resistance and voltage readings taken at 20 degrees C (68 degrees F).
2. Battery must be fully charged when performing test.

FUEL INJECTION AND EMISSION CONTROL SYSTEMS

Table 4 DIAGNOSTIC TROUBLE CODES (DTC)

DTC*	Symptoms	Cause(s)
1-1 (1)	Engine runs normally	Low voltage in MAP sensor circuit (less than 0.2V). Loose or poor contacts on MAP sensor. Open or short circuit in MAP sensor wire. Damaged MAP sensor.
1-2 (2)	Engine runs normally	High voltage in MAP sensor circuit (more than 3.9V). Loose or poor contacts in MAP sensor or its connector. Open or short circuit in MAP sensor wire. Damaged MAP sensor.
7-1 (7)	Hard start at low temperature	Low voltage in ECT sensor circuit (less than 0.08V). Loose or poor contacts in ECT sensor or its connector. Open or short circuit in ECT sensor wire. Damaged ETC sensor.
7-2 (7)	Hard start at low temperature	High voltage in ECT sensor circuit (more than 4.93V). Loose or poor contacts in ECT sensor or its connector. Open or short circuit in ECT sensor wire. Damaged ETC sensor.
8-1 (8)	Poor engine response when operating the throttle quickly	Low voltage in TP sensor circuit (less than 0.3V). Loose or poor contacts in TP sensor or its connector. Open or short circuit in TP sensor wire. Damaged TP sensor.
8-2 (8)	Poor engine response when operating the throttle quickly	High voltage in TP sensor circuit (more than 4.93V). Loose or poor contacts on TP sensor. Open or short circuit in TP sensor wire. Damaged TP sensor.
9-1 (9)	Engine runs normally	Low voltage in IAT sensor circuit (less than 0.08V). Open or short circuit in IAT sensor wire. Damaged IAT sensor.
9-2 (9)	Engine runs normally	High voltage in IAT sensor circuit (more than 4.93V). Loose or poor contacts on IAT sensor or its connector. Open or short circuit in IAT sensor wire. Damaged IAT sensor.
11-1 (11)	Engine runs normally	No signal at VS sensor. Loose or poor contacts in VS sensor or its connector. Damaged VS sensor.
12-1 (12)	Engine does not start	Loose or poor contacts in No. 1 fuel injector or its connector. Open or short circuit in No. 1 fuel injector wire. Damaged No. 1 fuel injector.
13-1 (13)	Engine does not start	Loose or poor contacts in No. 2 fuel injector or its connector. Open or short circuit in No. 2 fuel injector wire. Damaged No. 2 fuel injector.
29-1 (29)	Engine is hard to start, idles roughly or stalls	Loose or poor contacts in IACV or its connector. Damaged IACV or circuit.
33-2 (0)	Engine runs normally	ECM EEPROM failure.

*Each DTC consists of a main code and a sub-code, each separated by a hyphen. For example, the code 1-1 indicates a MAP sensor low voltage circuit problem. Code 1-2 indicates a MAP sensor high voltage circuit problem. The sub-code is not displayed by the MIL. The sub-code can only be read when the DTC is read with the Honda HDS pocket tester, which is only available to Honda dealerships.

Table 5 FUEL INJECTION SYSTEM TORQUE SPECIFICATIONS

	N.m	in.-lb.	ft.-lb.
Air filter housing intake boot clamp screw	1.0	8.9	--
ECT sensor	24.5	--	18
Fuel pump assembly bolts	8.8	78	--
Fuel tank mounting bolt	27	--	20
IACV set plate Torx screw	2.1	19	--
Injector cap mounting bolts	5.1	45	--
O2 sensor	44	--	32
PAIR check valve cover bolt	7	62	--
Sensor unit Torx screw	3.4	30	--
Throttle cable guide screw	3.4	30	--
Throttle position sensor (TPS) mounting screws	3.4	30	--

CHAPTER TEN

ELECTRICAL SYSTEM

This chapter covers procedures for the electrical system. Specifications are in **Tables 1-10** at the end of this chapter.

ELECTRICAL COMPONENT REPLACEMENT

Most motorcycle dealerships and parts suppliers will not accept the return of any electrical part. If you cannot determine the exact cause of any electrical system malfunction, have a dealership retest that specific system to verify your test results. If you purchase a new electrical component(s), install it, and then find that the system still does not work properly, you will probably not be able to return the unit for a refund.

Consider any test result carefully before replacing a component that tests only *slightly* out of specification, especially resistance. A number of variables can affect test results dramatically. These include the testing meter's internal circuitry, ambient temperatures and conditions under which the motorcycle has been operated. All instructions and specifications have been checked for accuracy; however, successful test results depend largely upon individual accuracy.

ELECTRICAL CONNECTORS

Corrosion-causing moisture can enter electrical connectors and cause poor electrical connections leading to component failure. Before reconnecting electrical connectors, pack them with a dielectric grease compound. Do not use a substitute that may interfere with the current flow within the electrical connector. Do not use silicone sealant.

BATTERY

A sealed, maintenance-free battery is installed on all models. The battery electrolyte level cannot be serviced. When replacing the battery, use a sealed type; do not install a non-sealed battery. Never attempt to remove the sealing cap from the top of the battery. The battery does not require periodic electrolyte inspection or refilling. See Table 1 for battery specifications.

To prevent accidental shorts that could blow a fuse when working on the electrical system, always disconnect the negative battery cable from the battery.

Safety Precautions

WARNING
Although the battery is a sealed type, protect your eyes, skin and clothing; electrolyte is corrosive and can cause severe burns and permanent injury. The battery case may be cracked and leaking electrolyte. If electrolyte gets into your eyes, flush your eyes thoroughly with clean, running water and get immediate medical attention. Always wear safety goggles when servicing the battery.

WARNING
While batteries are being charged, highly explosive hydrogen gas forms in each cell. Some of this gas escapes through a vent opening and may form an explosive atmosphere in and around the battery. This condition can persist for several hours. Sparks, an open flame or a lighted cigarette can ignite the gas, causing an internal battery explosion and possible serious personal injury.

Take the following precautions:
1. Do not disconnect live circuits at the battery. A spark usually occurs when a live circuit is broken.
2. Do not smoke or permit any open flame near any battery being charged or which has been recently charged.
3. Take care when connecting or disconnecting a battery charger. Be sure the power switch is off before making or breaking connections. Poor connections are a common cause of electrical arcs, which cause explosions.
4. Keep children and pets away from the charging equipment and battery.
5. If only the negative battery terminal is being disconnected, insulate the cable or battery terminal so it cannot accidentally reconnect the battery circuit.
6. Be sure the battery cables are connected to their proper terminals. Connecting the battery backward reverses the polarity and damages components in the electrical system. When installing a replacement battery, make sure the negative and positive battery terminals are in the same positions as the original battery.

Removal/Installation

NOTE
Recycle the old battery. Most motorcycle dealerships accept old batteries in trade when purchasing a new one. Never place an old battery in the trash.

Carbureted models

1. Read *Safety Precautions* in this section.
2. Turn the ignition switch off.
3. Remove the seat (Chapter Seventeen).
4. Remove the ICM as described in this chapter.
5. Remove the screw (A, **Figure 1**). Then, disconnect the battery box cover from the hooks (B, **Figure 1**) at the rear of the cover and remove the cover.
6. Disconnect the negative battery lead (A, **Figure 2**) first. Then, disconnect the positive lead (B, **Figure 2**).
7. Thread a long 6-mm bolt into each battery terminal (**Figure 3**) and use them to lift the battery out of the battery box. After removing the battery, remove the bolts from the battery terminals.
8. After servicing the battery, install it by reversing these removal steps while noting the following:
   a. Always connect the positive cable (B, **Figure 2**) first, then the negative cable (A, **Figure 2**).
   b. Coat the battery leads with dielectric grease or petroleum jelly.

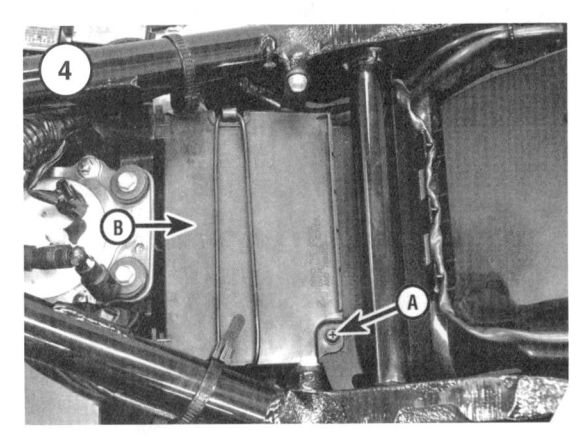

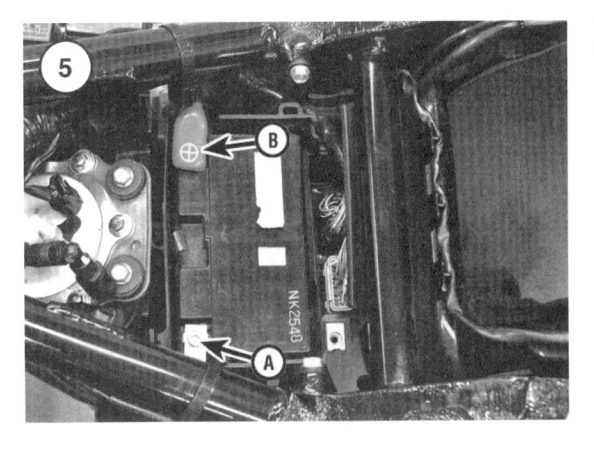

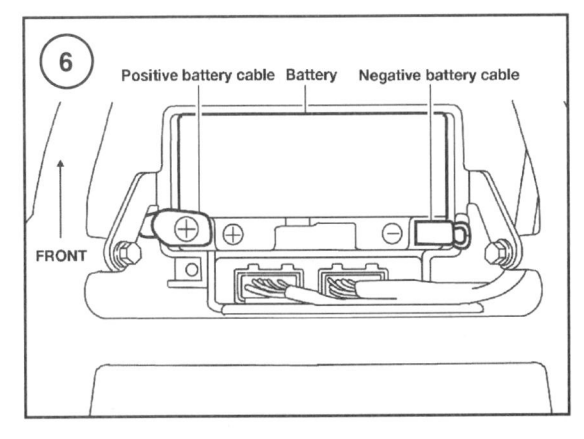

ELECTRICAL SYSTEM

Fuel injected models

1. Remove the seat (Chapter Seventeen).
2. Remove the screw (A, **Figure 4**), then slide the battery cover (B, **Figure 4**) rearward and remove it.
3A. On non-ABS models, disconnect the negative battery lead (A, **Figure 5**) first. Then disconnect the positive lead (B, **Figure 5**).
3B. On ABS models, disconnect the negative battery lead first. Then disconnect the positive lead. Thread a long 6-mm bolt into each battery terminal (**Figure 3**) and use them to lift the battery out of the battery box. After removing the battery, remove the bolts from the battery terminals.
4. After servicing the battery, install it by reversing these removal steps while noting the following:
   a. If necessary, remove the left and right side covers (Chapter Seventeen) to provide additional room when routing and connecting the battery cables.

   NOTE
   *Make sure to install the battery into the battery box with its terminals facing in the correct position. See **Figure 5** (non-ABS models) or Figure 6 (ABS models).*

   b. On non-ABS models, connect the positive cable (B, **Figure 5**) first, then the negative cable (A).
   c. On ABS models, connect the positive cable first, then the negative cable (**Figure 6**).
   d. Coat the battery leads with dielectric grease or petroleum jelly.

Cleaning/Inspection

Once a sealed battery has been filled with electrolyte and the sealing cap installed, the battery electrolyte level cannot be serviced. *Never* remove the sealing cap from the top of the battery (**Figure 7**) as this could damage the cap or battery and cause a

leak. The battery does not require periodic electrolyte inspection or refilling.
1. Read *Safety Precautions* in this section.
2. Remove the battery from the motorcycle as described in this section. Do not clean the battery while it is mounted in the motorcycle.
3. Clean the battery case **(Figure 7)** with a solution of warm water and baking soda. Rinse thoroughly with clean water.
4. Inspect the physical condition of the battery. Look for bulges or cracks in the case, leaking electrolyte or corrosion buildup.
5. Check the battery terminal bolts and nuts for corrosion and damage. Clean parts with a solution of baking soda and water and rinse thoroughly. Replace if damaged.
6. Check the battery cable clamps for corrosion and damage. If corrosion is minor, clean the battery cable clamps with a stiff brush. Replace excessively worn or damaged cables.

Voltage Test

Static

Use a digital voltmeter to test the battery while it is mounted on the motorcycle. See Table 1 for battery voltage readings.
1. Remove the battery cover as described under *Removal/Installation* in this section.

NOTE
To prevent false test readings, do not test the battery if the battery terminals are corroded. Remove and clean the battery and terminals as described in this chapter, then test the battery.

2. Connect a digital voltmeter between the battery positive (+) and negative (-) terminals.
   a. If the battery voltage is 13.0-13.2, the battery is fully-charged.
   b. If the battery voltage is below 12.3 volts, the battery is undercharged and requires charging.
3. If the battery is undercharged, recharge it as described in this section. Then test the charging system as described under *Charging System* in this chapter.

Starting

This procedure tests the battery's capacity when starting the motorcycle.
1. Read *Safety Precautions* in this section.
2. Remove the battery cover as described under *Removal/Installation* in this section.

NOTE
To prevent false test readings, do not test the battery if the battery terminals are corroded. Remove and clean the battery and terminals as described in this chapter, then install and test the battery.

3. Connect a digital voltmeter between the battery positive (+) and negative (-) leads.
4. Turn the ignition switch on and set the engine stop switch to run. Push the start button while reading the voltmeter. If the voltage drops below 9.5 volts, recharge the battery as described in this section and then repeat the test. If the voltage still drops below 9.5 volts, replace the battery.

Load Testing

Low load test

1. Remove the battery cover as described under *Removal/Installation* in this section.
2. Connect a digital voltmeter between the battery positive (+) and negative (-) leads.
3. Turn the ignition switch on while making sure the headlight is on.
4. The voltmeter should read a minimum of 11.5 volts. If the voltage reading is lower, charge the battery as described in this section.
5. Turn the ignition switch off and disconnect the voltmeter.

High load test

This test requires a battery load tester and checks the battery's performance with a current draw or load applied and is the best indication of battery condition. When using a load tester, follow the equipment manufacturer's instructions.

Charging

WARNING
During the charging process, highly explosive hydrogen gas is released from the battery. Charge the battery only in a well-ventilated area away from any open flames (including pilot lights on home gas appliances). Do not allow any smoking in the area. Never check the charge of the battery by connecting screwdriver blades or other metal objects between the terminals; the resulting spark can ignite the hydrogen gas.

ELECTRICAL SYSTEM

Refer to *Safety Precautions* in this section. Refer to *New Battery Setup* in this section if the battery is new.

To recharge a maintenance-free battery, use an automatic battery charger with variable voltage and amperage outputs. Excessive voltage and amperage from an unregulated charger can damage the battery and shorten service life.

The battery should only self-discharge approximately one percent of its given capacity each day. If a battery not in use, without any loads connected, loses its charge within one week after charging, the battery is defective.

1. Remove the battery as described in this section.
2. Measure the battery voltage as described under *Voltage Test* (this section). Locate the voltage reading in **Table 2** to determine the battery state of charge.
3. Clean the battery terminals and case.
4. Connect the positive (+) charger lead to the positive battery terminal and the negative (–) charger lead to the negative battery terminal.

CAUTION
When using an adjustable battery charger, follow the charger manufacturer's instructions. Do not use a larger output battery charger or increase the charge rate on an adjustable battery charger to reduce charging time. Doing so can cause permanent battery damage.

NOTE
If the voltage reading is low, internal resistance in the battery may prevent it from recovering when following normal charging attempts. When a battery's state of charge is 25 percent or less, it is necessary to increase the charging voltage of the battery by applying a low current rate to allow the battery to recover. This will require an adjustable battery charger with a separate amp and volt meter or a battery charger that can do this automatically. Automatic battery chargers that can diagnose and recover deep-discharged batteries can also be used without overcharging or overheating the battery.

5. Charge the battery following the manufacturer's instructions. Set the charger at 12 volts and switch it on. If using an automatic battery charger, follow the charger manufacturer's instructions. Otherwise, charge the battery at a slow charge rate of 1/10 its given capacity. To determine the current output in amps, divide the battery amp hour capacity by 10. See Charging Current in **Table 1**.
6. After the battery has been charged for 4-5 hours or within the time determined by the automatic battery charger, turn the charger off, disconnect the leads and allow the battery to set for a minimum of 30 minutes. Then check the battery with a digital voltmeter and compare to the voltage specifications in **Table 2**.

Battery Storage

When the motorcycle is ridden infrequently or put in storage for an extended amount of time, the battery must be periodically charged to ensure it will be capable of working correctly when returned to service. Use an automatic battery charger.

1. Remove the battery as described in this chapter.
2. Clean the battery and terminals with a solution of baking soda and water.
3. Inspect the battery case for any cracks, leaks or bulging. Replace the battery if the case is leaking or damaged.
4. Clean the battery box in the motorcycle.
5. Charge the battery to 100 percent. Store the battery in a cool dry place. Continue to charge the battery once a month when stored in temperatures below 16° C (61°F) and every two weeks when stored in temperatures above 16° C (61°F).

New Battery Setup

Read *Safety Precautions* in this section.

When ordering a new battery from a mail order company, it will be necessary to fill and charge the battery. Follow the battery manufacturer's instructions while observing the following guidelines when activating a new battery:

CAUTION
A new battery must be fully-charged before installation. Failure to do so reduces the life of the battery. Using a new battery without an initial charge causes permanent battery damage. That is, the battery will never be able to hold more than an 80 percent charge. Charging a new battery after it has been used will not bring its charge to 100 percent. When purchasing a new battery, verify its charge status. If necessary, have the initial or booster charge performed before accepting the battery.

1. Use the electrolyte that comes with the battery. Do not use electrolyte from a common container.
2. Fill the battery with all of the electrolyte included with the battery kit.
3. Allow the battery to sit for one hour. This allows

the plates to absorb the electrolyte for optimum performance.
4. Loosely install the sealing cap over the battery filling holes.
5. Charge the battery following the manufacturer's instructions.

CAUTION
Never remove the sealing cap or add additional electrolyte to the battery.

6. When the battery is fully charged, press the sealing cap **(Figure 7)** firmly to seal each of the battery fill holes. Make sure the cap seats flush into the battery.

CHARGING SYSTEM

The charging system supplies power to operate the engine and electrical system components and keeps the battery charged. The charging system consists of the battery, alternator and a voltage regulator/rectifier. A 30-amp fuse protects the circuit. Refer to the appropriate wiring diagram at the end of this manual.

Alternating current generated by the alternator is rectified to direct current. The voltage regulator maintains constant voltage to the battery and electrical loads despite variations in engine speed and load.

Troubleshooting

Because the charging system is not equipped with an indicator system (light or gauge), slow cranking may be the first indicator of a charging system problem.
1. A fully charged battery is required to accurately test the charging system. If the battery is damaged or worn out, the charging system may not be at fault.
2. Check all of the connections to make sure they are tight and free of corrosion. Use the correct wiring diagram at the end of this manual to identify and locate the appropriate connectors.
3. Perform the *Current Drain Test* (this section).
   a. If the current drain is incorrect, continue the procedure
   b. If the current drain is correct, skip to Step 5.
4. Disconnect the regulator/rectifier connector and repeat the *Current Drain Test* (this section).
   a. If the current drain is acceptable, the regulator/rectifier is faulty. Replace the regulator/rectifier as described in this section and retest.
   b. If the current drain is high, the problem is probably caused by a short in the wiring or the ignition switch is faulty. Check for a short circuit in the charging system by disconnecting the connectors one at a time while repeating the current draw test (this section).

NOTE
Reconnect the connector before disconnecting another connector.

   c. If the current drain returns to normal when a connector is disconnected, the circuit is shorting to ground.
   d. If a short circuit cannot be located, test the ignition switch (this chapter).
5. Check the stator coil resistance as described in *Left Crankcase Cover and Stator Coil* in this chapter. If the charge coil resistance is incorrect, the charge coil is damaged and should be replaced. If the resistance is correct, continue the procedure.
6. Perform the *Charging Voltage Test* in this section. If the voltage reading is incorrect, continue with the procedure. If the voltage reading is correct, the battery is damaged. Replace the battery and retest.
7. Perform the *Wiring Harness Test* in this section. If all of the tests are correct, the regulator/rectifier is damaged and must be replaced. If one or all of the tests are incorrect, check for an open circuit in the related circuit wire. Then, check for loose or contaminated connector terminals and for a short circuit in the wiring harness.
8. Once a repair has been made, repeat the *Charging Voltage Test* in this section to confirm the charging system is working correctly.

Current Drain Test

NOTE
When installing electrical accessories, do not wire them into a live circuit where they stay on all the time. Refer to the part manufacturers instructions.

A short circuit will increase current draw and drain the battery. Perform this test before troubleshooting the charging system or before performing the charging voltage test to determine if the current drain is normal or excessive. If the battery discharges because of a short, the charging system may not be at fault.
1. Turn the ignition switch off.
2. Disconnect the negative battery cable as described in *Battery* in this chapter.

CAUTION
Before connecting the ammeter into the circuit, set the meter to its highest amperage scale. This prevents a large current flow from damaging the meter or blowing the meter's fuse.

3. Connect an ammeter between the negative battery cable and the negative battery terminal as shown in

ELECTRICAL SYSTEM

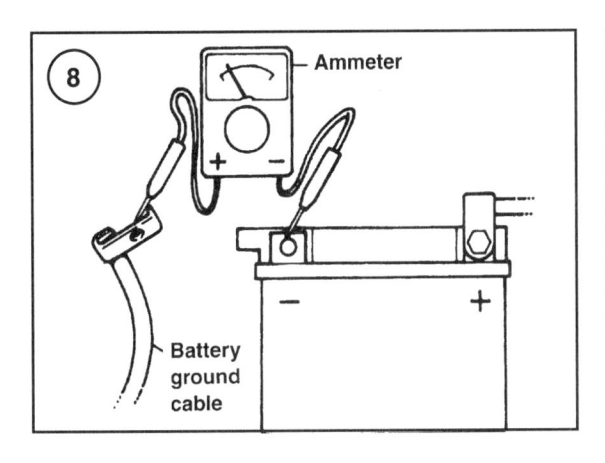

Figure 8. Do *not* turn the ignition switch on once this connection is made.

4. Switch the ammeter to its lowest scale and note the reading. The maximum current drain rate is 1.0 mA or less. A current drain rate that exceeds 1.0 mA must be found and repaired.
5. If the current drain rate is excessive, consider the following probable causes:
    a. Damaged battery.
    b. Faulty voltage regulator/rectifier.
    c. Short circuit in the system.
    d. Loose, dirty or faulty electrical connectors.
    e. Aftermarket electrical accessories incorrectly added to the electrical system.
6. To find the short circuit that is causing the excessive current drain, refer to the wiring diagrams at the end of this book. Then disconnect different electrical connectors one by one while monitoring the ammeter. When the current drain rate returns to an acceptable level, the faulty circuit is indicated. Test the circuit further to find the problem.
7. Disconnect the ammeter.
8. Reconnect the negative battery cable.

Charging Voltage Test

This procedure tests charging system operation. It does not measure maximum charging system output.

To obtain accurate test results, the battery must be fully charged (13.0-13.2 volts).

1. Start and run the engine until it reaches normal operating temperature, then turn the engine off.
2. Remove the battery box cover as described in *Battery* in this chapter.
3. On carbureted models, reconnect the ICM connector.
4. Connect a digital voltmeter to the battery terminals (positive-to-positive and negative-to-negative). To prevent a short, make sure the voltmeter leads attach firmly to the battery terminals. Record the voltage reading.

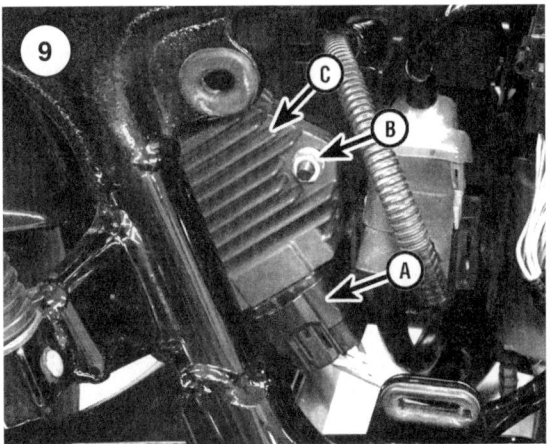

CAUTION
Do not disconnect either battery cable when making this test. Doing so may damage the voltmeter or electrical accessories.

5. Start the engine and allow it to idle. Turn the headlight to HI beam. Gradually increase engine speed to 5000 rpm and read the voltage indicated on the voltmeter. The voltmeter should show a reading greater than the measured battery voltage recorded in Step 4 and less than 15.5 volts.

NOTE
If the battery is often discharged, but the charging voltage tested normal during Step 5, the battery may be damaged. Perform a battery load-test to accurately test the battery.

6. If the voltage reading is incorrect, perform the *Wiring Harness Test* in this section, while noting the following:
    a. If the charging voltage is too low, check for an open or short circuit in the charging system wiring harness, an open or short in the alternator or high resistance in the red/white wire between the starter relay switch and the regulator/rectifier.
    b. If the charging voltage is too high, check for a poor regulator/rectifier ground, damaged regulator/rectifier or a damaged battery.

Wiring Harness Test

This procedure tests the integrity of the wires and connectors attached to the regulator/rectifier.

Use the appropriate wiring diagram at the end of this manual to identify the connectors and wire colors called out in this test.

1. Turn the ignition switch off.

2A. On carbureted models, perform the following:
   a. Remove the right side cover (Chapter Seventeen).
   b. Disconnect the regulator/rectifier connector (A, **Figure 9**).
2B. On fuel injected models, perform the following:
   a. Remove the left side cover (Chapter Seventeen).
   b. This regulator rectifier is equipped with two connectors. Disconnect the white 2-pin connector (A, **Figure 10**) with the red and green wires.
3. Check for loose or corroded connector terminals.

NOTE

Perform all of the tests on the wiring harness connector side, not on the regulator/rectifier connector side.

4. Check the battery charge line as follows:
   a. On carbureted models, connect a voltmeter between the red/white wire (+) and a good engine ground (-).
   b. On fuel injected models, connect a voltmeter between the red wire (+) and a good engine ground (-).
   c. The voltmeter should read battery voltage at all times (ignition switch on or off).
   d. If there is no voltage, check the red/white (carbureted models) or red (fuel injected models) wire for an open circuit.
   e. Disconnect the voltmeter leads.
5. Check the ground circuit as follows:
   a. Switch an ohmmeter to R x 1.
   b. Connect the ohmmeter between the green wire in the connector and a good engine ground.
   c. The ohmmeter should read continuity.
   d. If there is no continuity, check the green wire for an open circuit.
6. Check the charge coil circuit as described under *Left Crankcase Cover and Stator Coil* in this chapter.
7. Reconnect the voltage regulator/retifier connector and reinstall the corresponding side cover (Chapter Seventeen).

Voltage Regulator/Rectifier Removal/Installation

Carbureted models

1. Turn the ignition switch off.
2. Remove the right side cover (Chapter Seventeen).
3. Disconnect the regulator/rectifier connector (A, **Figure 9**).
4. Remove the nuts (B, **Figure 9**), regulator/rectifier (C) and plate.
5. Installation is the reverse of removal. Tighten the mounting nuts securely.

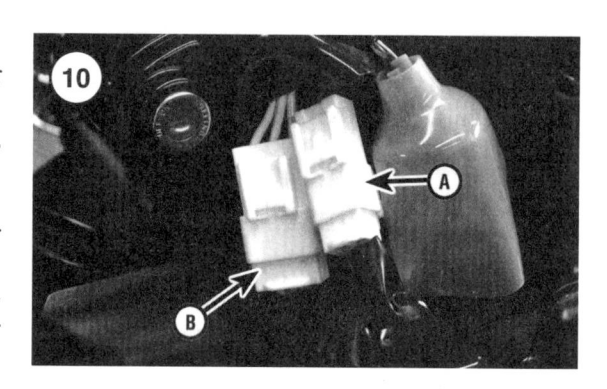

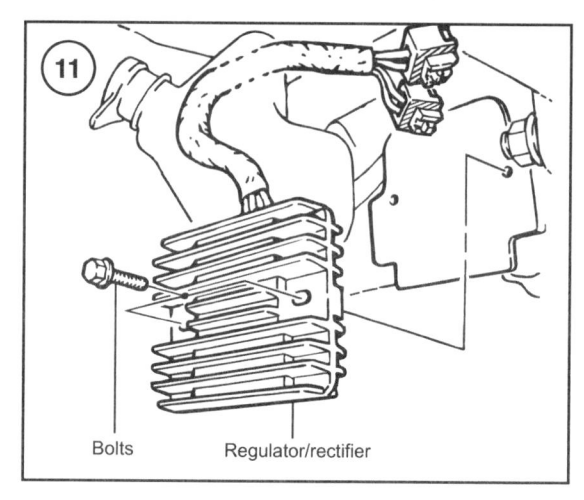

Fuel injected models

1. Turn the ignition switch off.
2. Remove the left side cover (Chapter Seventeen).
3. Remove the left crankcase rear cover (Chapter Seventeen).
4. Disconnect the regulator/rectifier white 2-pin (A, **Figure 10**) and white 3-pin (B) connectors.
5. Disconnect the plastic guides securing the regulator/rectifier wiring harness in place.
6. Remove the bolts and the regulator/rectifier (**Figure 11**).
7. Installation is the reverse of removal. Tighten the mounting bolts securely.

LEFT CRANKCASE COVER AND STATOR COIL

The stator coil is mounted inside the left crankcase cover.

Left Crankcase Cover Removal/Installation

1. Drain the engine oil (Chapter Three).

ELECTRICAL SYSTEM

2. Remove the following as described in Chapter Seventeen:
   a. Seat (carbureted models).
   b. Left side cover.
   c. Left crankcase rear cover.

3A. On carbureted models, disconnect the alternator connector located inside the wiring harness boot **(Figure 12)**.

3B. On fuel injected models, disconnect the white 3-pin alternator connector (B, **Figure 10**).

NOTE
Note the wiring harness routing on the left side of the engine before removing the left crankcase cover.

4. Release the wiring harnesses from the clamps. See **Figure 13** (carbureted models) or **Figure 14** (fuel injected models).

NOTE
Some engine oil will drain out when the left crankcase cover is removed.

5. Place a clean drain pan underneath the left crankcase cover.

NOTE
It is not necessary to remove the alternator cover when removing the left crankcase cover.

NOTE
*To ensure that the left crankcase cover bolts are installed correctly during assembly, make an outline of the left crankcase cover on a piece of cardboard. Punch holes in the cardboard at the same locations as the bolts. Place the bolts in their respective holes **(Figure 15)** along with any related clamps*

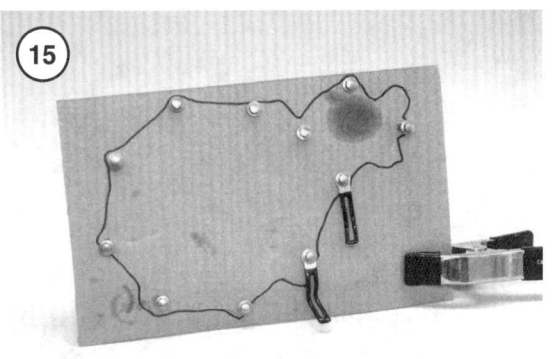

6. Remove the bolts securing the left crankcase cover **(Figure 16)** to the engine, noting the position of the

wiring harness clamps and remove the cover. If necessary, lightly tap the cover to loosen it from the engine. If the cover is tight, mount a small knock puller into the cover's threaded hole and operate the puller to loosen the cover from the engine. Do not pry the cover off.
7. Remove the dowel pins (**Figure 17**).
8. If necessary, service the stator coil as described in this section.
9. Do not clean the cover or stator coil in solvent. Wipe the coil and cover with a clean rag.
10. Installation is the reverse of removal. Note the following:

NOTE
Because a liquid sealer is used on the left crankcase cover, clean the parts and mating surfaces prevent an oil leak.

a. Carefully remove all sealer from the cover and crankcase mating surfaces. Block off the crankcase opening to prevent the sealer from entering the crankcase.
b. Spray the crankcase bolt holes with an aerosol cleaner to remove all oil and sealer residue. If necessary, use a stiff brush to loosen the sealer from the threads.
c. Clean the cover mounting bolts to remove all oil and sealer residue. The cardboard holder used to hold the bolts can also be used to hold the bolts when cleaning and drying them (**Figure 18**).
d. Make sure the starter drive gears are properly installed. Refer to *Flywheel, Starter Clutch and Starter Drive Gears* in this chapter.
e. Make sure the grommet (A, **Figure 19**) on the stator coil wiring harness is positioned firmly into the cover notch.
f. Because the magnetic force against the cover can cause it to twist during installation, install a few alignment studs into the cover crankcase threads (**Figure 20**). These keep the cover in proper alignment and help prevent the sealer from smearing if the magnetic force pulls the cover out of alignment. The studs can be made by cutting the heads off of 6-mm bolts. Select bolts that are longer than the cover's original mounting bolts. A screwdriver slot can also be cut into the top of the bolts with a hacksaw to help remove the studs.
g. Apply a light coat of gasket sealer onto the left crankcase cover gasket surface (B, **Figure 19**). Use HondaBond 4, ThreeBond 1104 Yamabond, or an equivalent gasket sealer. Also apply sealer against the grommet.
h. Install the two dowel pins (**Figure 17**) and the left crankcase cover (**Figure 16**). Make sure there are no gaps between the cover and engine.

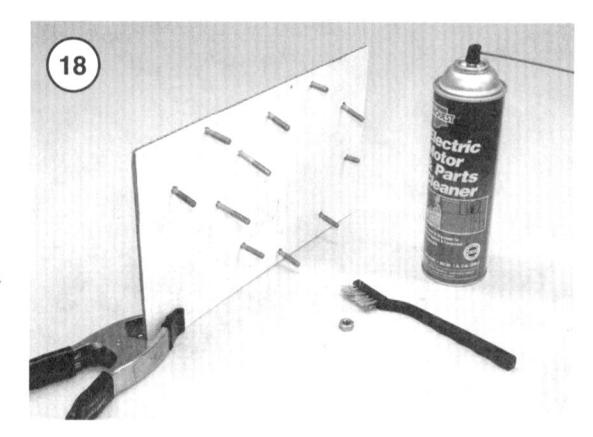

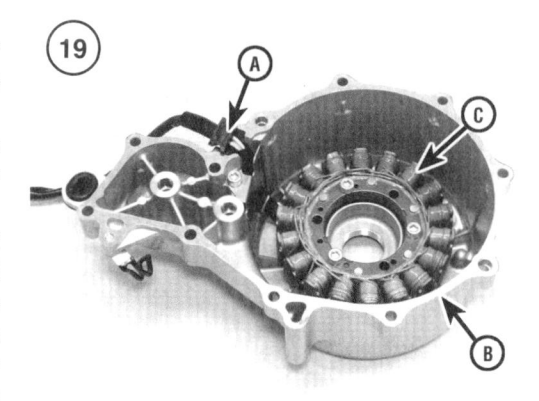

ELECTRICAL SYSTEM

301

a. Remove the seat (Chapter Seventeen).
b. Disconnect the alternator connector located inside the wiring harness boot **(Figure 12)**.

1B. On fuel injected models, perform the following:
  a. Remove the left side cover (Chapter Seventeen).
  b. Disconnect the white 3-pin alternator connector (B, **Figure 10**).

2. Measure the resistance between each combination of yellow wires on the stator coil side of the connector. Refer to **Table 3** for the specified stator coil resistance.
3. Replace the stator coil assembly if any resistance reading is incorrect.
4. Check continuity from each yellow stator wire to a good ground on the motorcycle. If the cover is removed, check for ground between each stator wire and the cover. Replace the stator coil if any yellow terminal has continuity to ground, indicating a short within the stator coil winding.
5. If the stator coil (C, **Figure 19**) fails either of these tests, replace it as described in this section.
6. Make sure the electrical connector is secure and corrosion free.

Stator Coil
Removal/Installation

1. Remove the left crankcase cover as described in this section.
2. Note the stator coil wire harness routing before removing the coil.
3. Remove the bolt (A, **Figure 21**) and the wire harness guide plate (B).
4. Remove the stator coil mounting bolts (C, **Figure 21**) and the stator coil (D).
5. Clean and dry the left crankcase cover. Clean the mounting bolt holes of all threadlock residue.
6. If reusing the stator coil, check the screw **(Figure 22)** and the wiring harness guide on the coil for looseness.
7. Installation is the revere of removal. Note the following:
  a. Apply a medium strength threadlock onto all the stator coil and wire harness guide plate mounting bolts (A and C, **Figure 21**)
  b. Tighten the bolts to 12 N.m (106 in.-lb).

i. Install a medium-stength thread lock to the rear most cover bolt (B, **Figure 16**) and install it.
j. Remove any aligment studs (**Figure 20**) from the crankcase.
k. Use the cardboard template made during disassembly to identify the cover bolts and clamps and install them.
l. Following a crossing pattern, tighten the bolts securely in two or three steps.

NOTE
Allow the gasket sealer to set before adding engine oil to the crankcase.

m. Make sure the electrical connectors are free of corrosion. Check the wiring harness routing.
n. Refill the engine with oil (Chapter Three).
o. Check the cover for oil leaks.
p. If the alternator cover was removed, tighten the Allen bolts to 10 N.m (89 in.-lb.).

Stator Coil Resistance Test

The stator coil (C, **Figure 16**) is mounted inside the left crankcase cover. The stator coil can be tested while the left crankcase cover is mounted on the engine.
1A. On carbureted models, perform the following:

FLYWHEEL, STARTER CLUTCH AND STARTER DRIVE GEARS

The flywheel (alternator rotor) is mounted on the left end of the crankshaft. The starter clutch is mounted on the back of the flywheel. The starter drive gears can be removed without removing the flywheel.

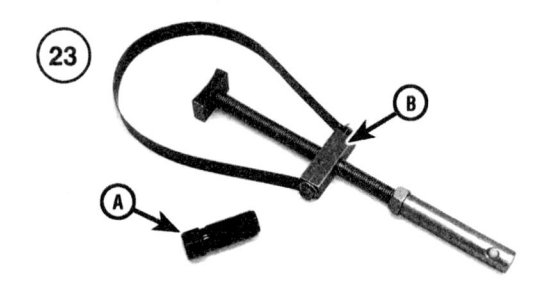

Tools

> **CAUTION**
> Do not try to remove the flywheel without the correct puller. Doing so may damage the flywheel and crankshaft.

The following tools, or their equivalents, are required to remove the flywheel (alternator rotor):
1. Flywheel puller with M22 x 1.5 right-hand threads (Motion Pro part No. 08-0074 [A, **Figure 23**] or Honda part No. 07733-002001 or 07933-3290001 [US only]).
2. Strap type flywheel holder (B, **Figure 23**, typical).

Removal/Installation

1. Remove the left crankcase cover as described in this chapter.
2. Remove the reduction gear shaft (A, **Figure 24**) and gear (B).
3. Remove the idle gear shaft (C, **Figure 24**) and gear (D).

> *NOTE*
> *The flywheel mounting bolt uses left hand threads.*

4. Hold the flywheel with the holding tool (A, **Figure 25**) and turn the flywheel mounting bolt (B, **Figure 25**) clockwise to loosen it. Then remove the flywheel bolt and washer.
5. Screw the flywheel puller **(Figure 26)** into the flywheel by hand.

> *CAUTION*
> *Do not force the puller. Excessive force may damage the flywheel threads. If necessary, have a dealership remove the flywheel.*

6. Hold the flywheel with the flywheel holder and gradually tighten the flywheel puller **(Figure 26)** until the flywheel pops off the crankshaft taper. Remove the flywheel while also holding onto the starter driven gear installed on the back of the flywheel.
7. Remove the holder and puller from the flywheel.

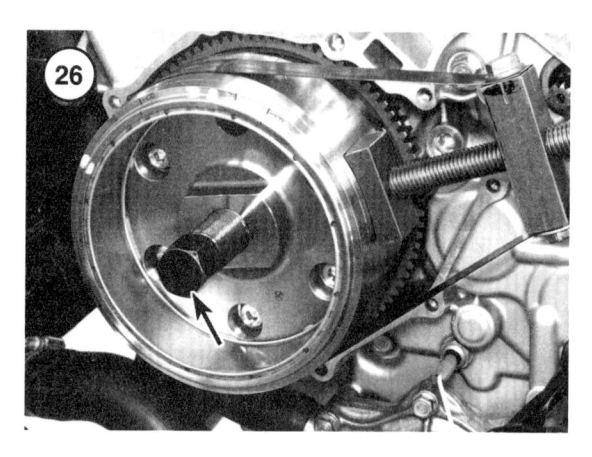

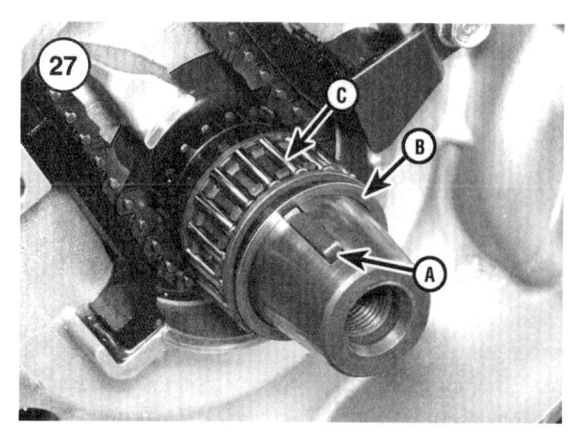

ELECTRICAL SYSTEM

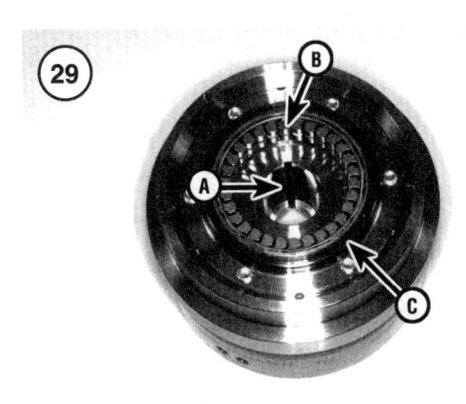

8. Remove the Woodruff key (A, **Figure 27**) from the crankshaft groove.
9. On Aero models starting with engine No. RC50E-2234066 and on all other models, remove the washer (B, **Figure 27**).
10. Remove the needle bearing (C, **Figure 27**).
11. Remove the starter driven gear **(Figure 28)** from the starter clutch by turning it counter clockwise.
12. Inspect and service the components (this section).

Installation

1. Lubricate the starter driven gear shoulder and the starter clutch with engine oil. Then install the starter driven gear **(Figure 28)** into the starter clutch by turning it counterclockwise.
2. Lubricate the needle bearing with engine oil and install it onto the crankshaft (C, **Figure 27**).
3. On Aero models starting with engine No. RC50E-2234066 and all other models, install the washer (B, **Figure 27**).
4. Install the Woodruff key (A, **Figure 27**) into the crankshaft keyway.
5. Degrease the crankshaft outer taper and the flywheel inner taper with an aerosol parts cleaner. Allow both tapers to dry before installing the flywheel.
6. Align the flywheel keyway with the Woodruff key and install the flywheel. Then visually check that the Woodruff key is installed in the keyway.

NOTE
The flywheel mounting bolt uses left hand threads.

7. Lubricate the flywheel mounting bolt threads and washer with engine oil and install the bolt counterclockwise until it is finger-tight.
8. Hold the flywheel with the flywheel holder (A, **Figure 25**) and tighten the flywheel mounting bolt (B, **Figure 25**) to 128 N.m (94 ft.-lb.). Remove the flywheel holder.
9. Lubricate the reduction gear and idle gear shafts and the bores in both gears and crankcase with engine oil.

NOTE
The idle gear shaft is longer than the reduction gear shaft.

10. Install the idle gear (D, **Figure 24**) and its shaft (C).
11. Install the reduction gear (B, **Figure 24**) with its OUT mark (E) facing out and by meshing it with the teeth on the idle gear and starter. Then install the reduction gear shaft (A, **Figure 24**).
12. Install the left crankcase cover as described in this chapter.

Inspection

WARNING
Replace a cracked or chipped flywheel. A damaged flywheel can fly apart at high engine speeds.

1. Clean the flywheel/starter clutch assembly and the starter gears in solvent and dry with compressed air.
2. Check the flywheel for cracks or breaks.
3. Check the flywheel tapered bore and the crankshaft taper for pitting and other damage.
4. Inspect the flywheel keyway (A, **Figure 29**) and Woodruff key (A, **Figure 27**) for damage.
5. Inspect the starter clutch assembly as follows:
   a. Inspect the one-way clutch roller cage (B, **Figure 29**) for overheating, pitting or flaking. If damaged, replace the starter clutch as described in this section.
   b. Inspect the starter reduction gear for damaged gear teeth (A, **Figure 30**). Then inspect the needle bearing (B) and starter clutch (C) operating surfaces for pitting, cracks and other damage.
   c. Measure the starter driven gear inside (B, **Figure 30**) and outside (C) diameters and compare to the specifications in **Table 4**. Replace the gear if any measurement is out of specification.

d. Inspect the needle bearing for damage. Check the cage for cracks or areas where the needles can fall out. Check the needles for flat spots, pitting and other damage.

e. If there is no visible damage, continue the procedure to check the starter clutch operation.

6. Install the starter driven gear (**Figure 28**) into the starter clutch. Hold the flywheel and try to turn the gear clockwise and then counterclockwise. The gear should only turn *counterclockwise* (**Figure 31**). If the gear turns clockwise, replace the starter clutch as described in this section.

7. Inspect the idle gear (A, **Figure 32**), reduction gear (B) and both shafts for:

   a. Broken or chipped gear teeth.
   b. Worn or scored gear bores.
   c. Pitted or damaged shaft surfaces.

NOTE
If the gears or shafts are damaged, inspect the mating bores in the left crankcase cover and left crankcase half for damage.

8. Inspect the flywheel mounting bolt and washer for damage. Replace only with original equipment parts.

9. On Aero models starting with engine No. RC50E-2234066 and all other models, inspect the washer for cracks and other damage.

Starter Clutch
Disassembly/Assembly

The starter clutch (**Figure 33**) can be inspected while assembled and installed on the flywheel. Do not remove the starter clutch unless replacement is necessary.

1. Inspect the starter clutch as described in this section.

2. Secure the flywheel with the flywheel holder (A, **Figure 34**) used to remove the flywheel. Then remove the mounting bolts (B) securing the starter clutch assembly to the flywheel. Remove the starter clutch housing (C, **Figure 29**) from the flywheel.

NOTE
If the one-way clutch was going to be reused but the center spring band slipped off the one-way clutch, most of the small parts that make up this assembly will probably fall off. This will require replacement of the one-way clutch.

3. Remove the one-way clutch (B, **Figure 29**) from the starter clutch housing and discard it.

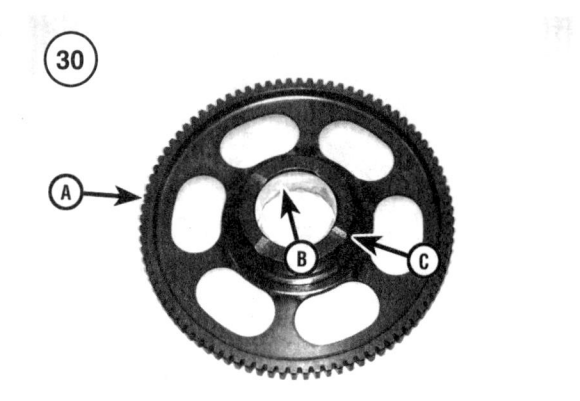

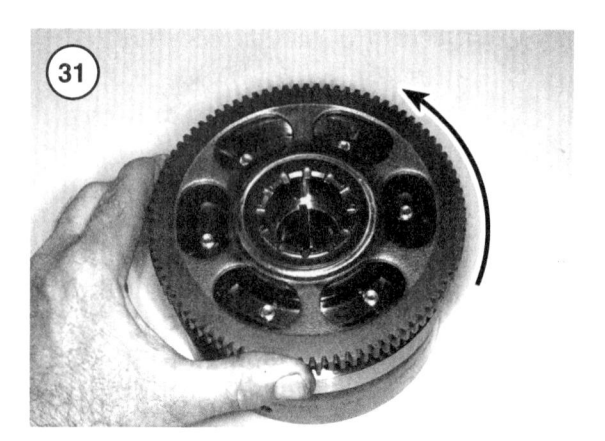

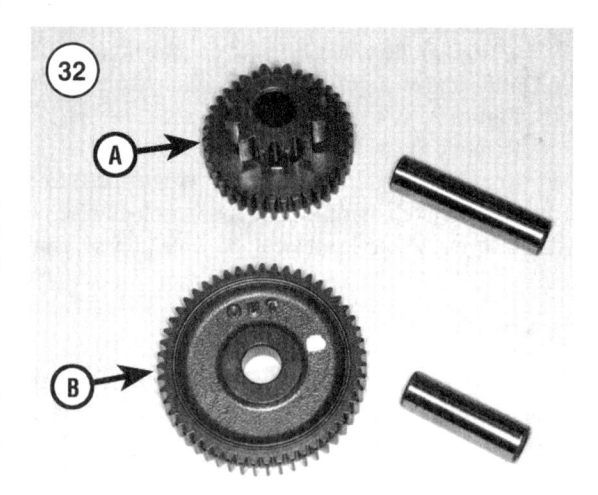

4. Clean and dry all parts. Remove all thread sealer residue from the mounting bolts and starter clutch housing threads.

5. Measure the starter clutch housing (C, **Figure 29**) inside diameter and compare to the specifications in **Table 4**. Replace the starter clutch housing and the one-way clutch if the inside diameter is too large.

6. Install the new one-way clutch (B, **Figure 29**) into the starter clutch housing in the direction shown in **Figure 33**.

ELECTRICAL SYSTEM

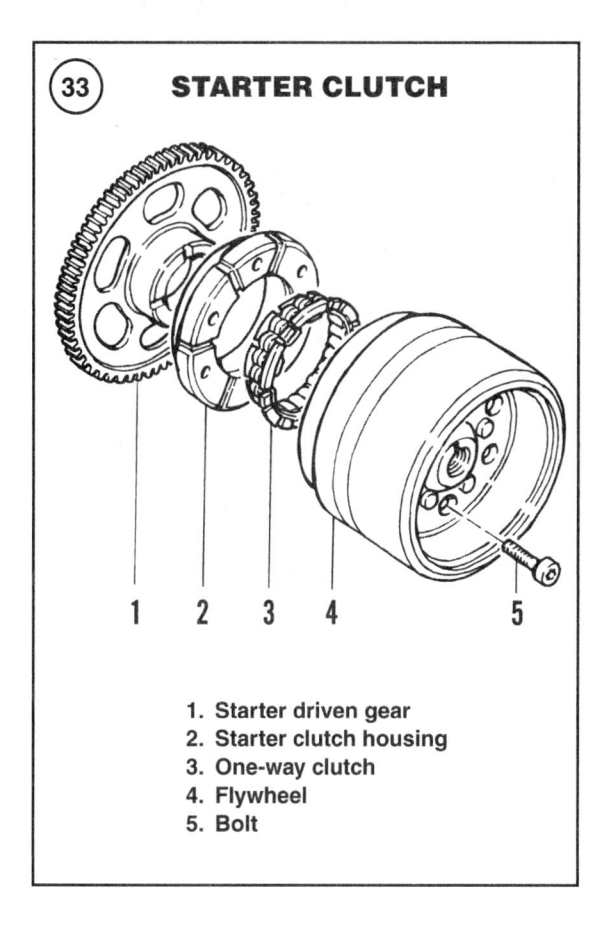

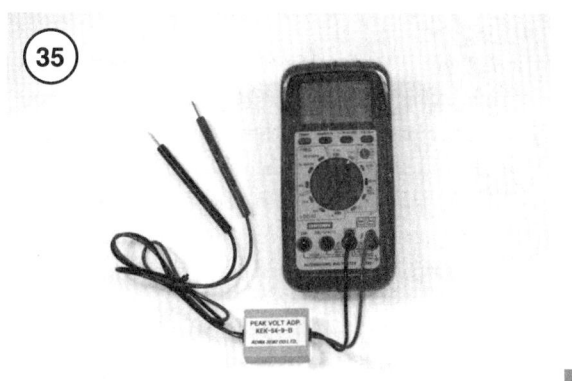

33 STARTER CLUTCH

1. Starter driven gear
2. Starter clutch housing
3. One-way clutch
4. Flywheel
5. Bolt

34

35

7. Install the starter clutch housing onto the flywheel.

8. Apply a medium strength threadlock onto the threads of each starter clutch mounting bolts (B, **Figure 34**) and tighten to 30 N.m (22 ft.-lb.).

9. Insert the starter driven gear **(Figure 28)** into the starter clutch. Hold the flywheel and try to turn the gear clockwise and then counterclockwise. The gear should only turn *counterclockwise* **(Figure 31)**. If the gear turns clockwise, the one-way clutch was installed incorrectly or is damaged.

IGNITION SYSTEM TESTING

WARNING
High voltage is present during ignition system operation. Do not touch ignition components, wires or test leads while cranking or running the engine.

Peak Voltage Tests and Equipment

Peak voltage tests check the voltage output of the ignition coils and pulse generator at normal cranking speed. These tests make it possible to accurately test the voltage output under operating conditions.

The peak voltage specifications listed in **Table 5** are minimum values. If the measured voltage meets or exceeds the specification, the test results are satisfactory. In some cases, the voltage may greatly exceed the minimum specification.

Tools

A peak voltage tester is required to measure peak voltage. Use one of the following testers or an equivalent. Refer to the equipment manufacturer's instructions when using these tools.

NOTE
The Kowa Seiki tool is shown used in the following procedures.

1. Peak voltage adapter (Kowa Seiki part No. KEK-54-9B). This tool must be used in combination with a digital multimeter **(Figure 35)** with a minimum impedance of 10M ohms/DCV. A meter with a lower impedance will not display accurate measurements. The peak voltage adapter plugs directly into the multimeter and the peak voltage readings are read directly off the meter.

2. Ignition Mate peak voltage tester (Honda part No. MTP07-0286 [**Figure 36**]).

Preliminary Tests

Before testing the ignition system, perform the following tests:
1. Make sure the battery is fully charged and in good condition. A weak battery will result in a slow engine cranking speed and incorrect peak voltage readings.
2. Perform the *Spark Test* in Chapter Two. If a crisp, blue spark is noted, the ignition system is working correctly. Test each spark plug and note the following:
   a. If there is no spark available at all spark plugs, check for a disconnected or contaminated connector or a damaged ignition switch or engine stop switch. Test each switch (this chapter).
   b. If the spark test shows there is no spark at one coil group (front or rear cylinder), switch the ignition coils and repeat the spark test. If the inoperative cylinder now has spark, the original ignition coil is defective. Replace it and retest. However, if the inoperative cylinder still does not have spark, check the ignition coil wires for an open circuit.
   c. Also check for a fouled or damaged spark plug, loose spark plugs caps or water in the spark plugs caps.
3. If the problem has not been found and the spark plugs, plug caps and all electrical system connectors are in good working order, the problem is probably due to a defective switch or ignition system component. Perform the peak voltage tests in this section to locate the damaged component.

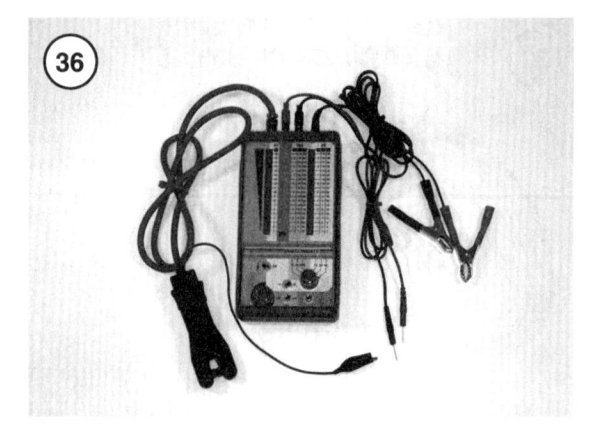

Ignition Coil Peak Voltage Test

Refer to **Figure 37** for test results.
1. Remove the seats (Chapter Seventeen).

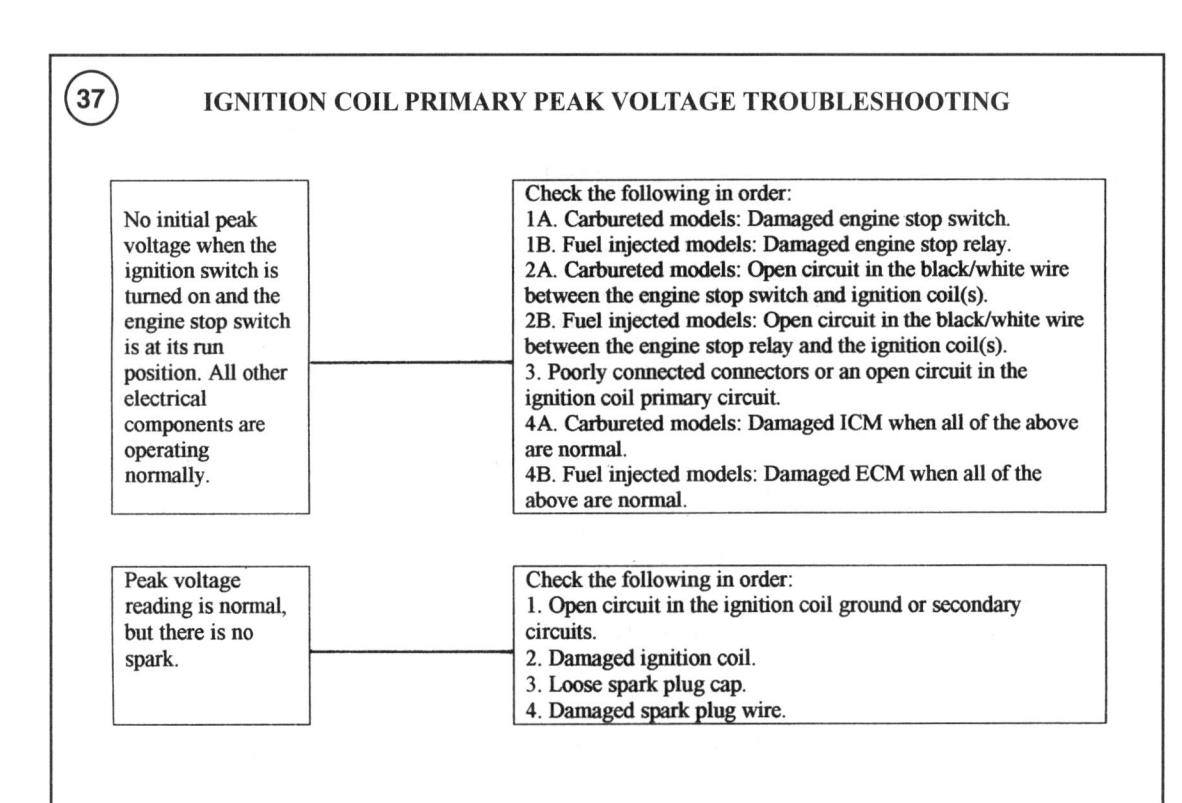

---

37 IGNITION COIL PRIMARY PEAK VOLTAGE TROUBLESHOOTING

No initial peak voltage when the ignition switch is turned on and the engine stop switch is at its run position. All other electrical components are operating normally.	Check the following in order: 1A. Carbureted models: Damaged engine stop switch. 1B. Fuel injected models: Damaged engine stop relay. 2A. Carbureted models: Open circuit in the black/white wire between the engine stop switch and ignition coil(s). 2B. Fuel injected models: Open circuit in the black/white wire between the engine stop relay and the ignition coil(s). 3. Poorly connected connectors or an open circuit in the ignition coil primary circuit. 4A. Carbureted models: Damaged ICM when all of the above are normal. 4B. Fuel injected models: Damaged ECM when all of the above are normal.
Peak voltage reading is normal, but there is no spark.	Check the following in order: 1. Open circuit in the ignition coil ground or secondary circuits. 2. Damaged ignition coil. 3. Loose spark plug cap. 4. Damaged spark plug wire.

ELECTRICAL SYSTEM

Initial voltage is normal, but drops 2-4 volts when engine is cranked.	Check the following in order:
	1. Incorrect peak voltage adapter connections.
	2. Cranking speed is too low, probably due to a weak battery. Monitor the battery voltage during the test and if necessary, test the battery as described in this chapter.
	3A. Carbureted models: No battery voltage at the black wire at the ICM connector. Check also for a loose or contaminated ICM connector.
	3B. Fuel injected models: No battery voltage between the black/white wire (+) and vehicle ground (-) at the ECM connectors. Check also for a loose or contaminated ECM connector(s).
	4A. Carbureted models: Open circuit in the green wire in the ICM connector. Check also for a loose wire connection or connector.
	4B. Fuel injected models: Open circuit in the green wire in the gray ECM 33-pin connector. Check also for a loose wire connection or connector.
	5A. Carbureted models: Poorly connected connectors or an open circuit in the yellow/blue or blue/yellow wires between the ignition coils and the ICM.
	5B. Fuel injected models: Poorly connected connectors or an open circuit in the yellow/blue or blue/yellow wires between the ignition coils and the ECM.
	6. Carbureted models: Short circuit in ignition coil primary circuit.
	7. Fuel injected models: Damaged clutch switch or open circuit in the green/white wire between the clutch switch and the gray ECM 33-pin connector.
	8. Damaged neutral switch.
	9. Damaged sidestand switch.
	10. Poorly connected connectors or an open circuit in the following:
	   a. Neutral switch circuit light green wire.
	   b. Sidestand switch green/white wire.
	11. Damaged CKP sensor. Check peak voltage at the CKP sensor as described in this chapter.
	12A. Carbureted models: Damaged ICM when all of the above are normal.
	12B. Fuel injected models: Damaged ECM when all of the above are normal.

Initial battery voltage is normal, but there is no peak voltage reading when engine is cranked.	Check the following in order: 1. Incorrect peak voltage adapter connections. 2. Damaged peak voltage adapter or test unit. 3. Damaged CKP sensor. Check peak voltage at the CKP sensor as described in this chapter. 4A. Carbureted models: Damaged ICM when all of the above are normal. 4B. Fuel injected models: Damaged ECM when all of the above are normal.
Initial battery voltage is normal, but peak voltage reading is lower than the minimum.	Check the following in order: 1. Meter impedance is too low. 2. Cranking speed is too low, probably due to a weak battery. Monitor the battery voltage during the test and if necessary, test the battery as described in this chapter. 3. The test sampling and measured pulse were not synchronizing. If measured voltage is over the minimum voltage at least once, the system is normal. 4A. Carbureted models: Damaged ICM when all of the above are normal. 4B. Fuel injected models: Damaged ECM when all of the above are normal.

2. On fuel injected models, perform the following:
   a. Turn the ignition switch off.
   b. Disconnect the fuel pump connector **(Figure 38)**.
3. Check engine compression as described in Chapter Three. If the compression is low in one or both cylinders, the following test results will be inaccurate.
4. Check all of the ignition component electrical connectors and wiring harnesses. Make sure the connectors are clean and properly connected.
5. Disconnect each spark plug cap. Then connect a new spark plug to each plug cap and ground the plug against the cylinder head **(Figure 39)**. Do not remove the spark plugs installed in the cylinder heads. These must remain in the cylinder heads.
6. Assemble the peak voltage adapter and multimeter as shown in **Figure 35**.

NOTE
*Refer to **Ignition Coils** in this chapter to access and identify the ignition coils.*

NOTE
Do not disconnect the ignition coil primary connectors when connecting the test leads. Back probe the connector terminals to test the ignition coil.

7. Locate the ignition coil to be checked and connect the peak voltage test leads as follows:
   a. At the front cylinder ignition coil, connect the positive test lead to the blue/yellow terminal and the negative test lead to ground **(Figure 40)**.
   b. At the rear cylinder ignition coil, connect the positive test lead to the yellow/blue ignition coil terminal and the negative test lead to ground **(Figure 40)**.
8. Shift the transmission into neutral.
9. Turn the ignition switch on and set the engine stop switch to run.
10. The meter should read battery voltage. Note the following:
    a. If there is no battery voltage or the voltage reading is low, refer to the test results in **Figure 37**. Perform the steps in order to find the problem.
    b. If the battery voltage reading is correct, continue the procedure.

WARNING
High voltage is present during ignition system operation. Do not touch spark plugs, ignition components, connectors or test leads while cranking the engine.

11. Press the starter button while reading the meter.
12. Release the starter button, then connect the test lead to the other ignition coil primary and repeat the test.
13. Turn the ignition switch off and interpret the test results as follows:

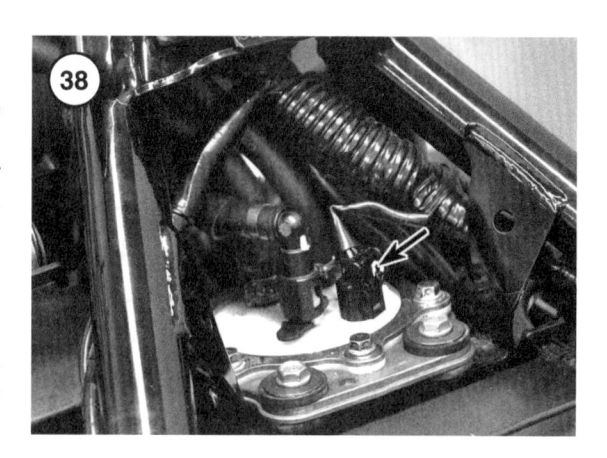

NOTE
*All peak voltage specifications in the text and **Table 5** are **minimum** voltages. As long as the measured voltage meets or exceeds the specification, consider the test results satisfactory. On some components, the voltage may greatly exceed the minimum specification.*

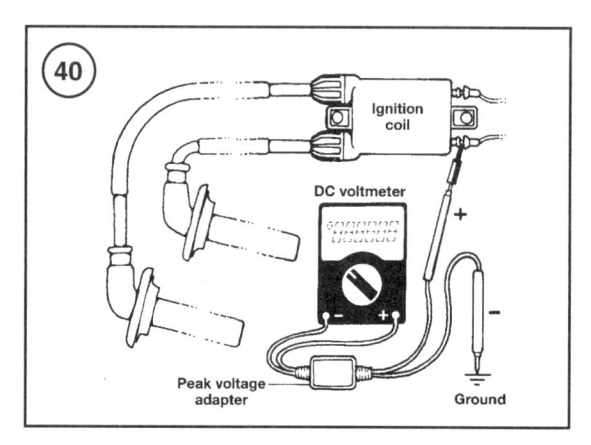

ELECTRICAL SYSTEM

41

CRANKSHAFT POSITION SENSOR (CKP) PEAK VOLTAGE TROUBLESHOOTING

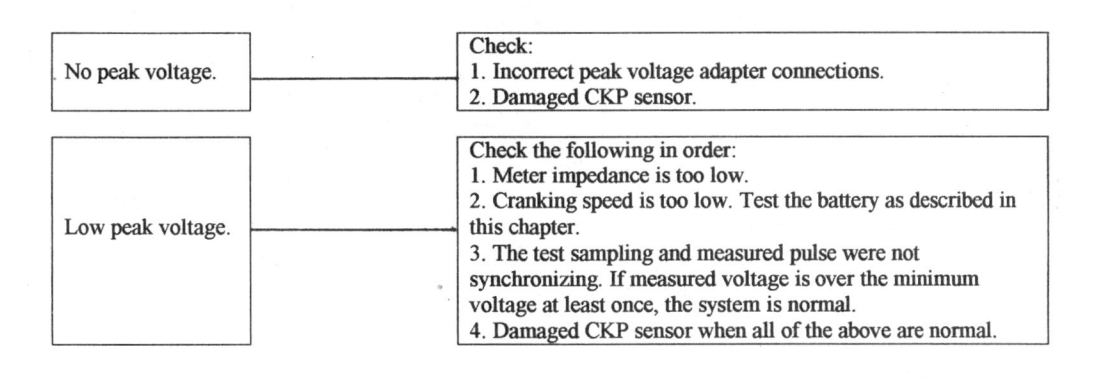

No peak voltage.	Check: 1. Incorrect peak voltage adapter connections. 2. Damaged CKP sensor.
Low peak voltage.	Check the following in order: 1. Meter impedance is too low. 2. Cranking speed is too low. Test the battery as described in this chapter. 3. The test sampling and measured pulse were not synchronizing. If measured voltage is over the minimum voltage at least once, the system is normal. 4. Damaged CKP sensor when all of the above are normal.

a. The minimum ignition coil primary peak voltage reading is 100 volts minimum.
b. The individual peak voltage reading recorded for each ignition coil can vary as long as the voltage readings are higher than the specified minimum value.
c. If the peak voltage reading for one or both ignition coils is less than 100 volts, refer to the test results in **Figure 37** and perform the steps in order to find the problem.

14. Disconnect the test leads.
15. Remove the spark plugs from the plug caps, then reconnect the plug caps onto the spark plugs installed in the cylinder head.
16. Reconnect the fuel pump connector (**Figure 38**) on fuel injected models.
17. Replace the seat (Chapter Seventeen).

CKP Sensor Peak Voltage Test

Refer to **Figure 41** for test results.
1. Support the motorcycle on a workstand so the sidestand can be raised during this test.
2. Remove the seat (Chapter Seventeen).
3. Check engine compression as described in Chapter Three. If the compression is low in one or both cylinders, the following test results will be inaccurate.
4. Check all of the ignition component electrical connectors and wiring harnesses. Make sure the connectors are clean and properly connected.
5. Assemble the peak voltage adapter and multimeter as shown in Figure 35.
6. Turn the ignition switch off.
7A. On carbureted models, perform the following:
   a. Disconnect the 22-pin ignition control module (ICM) connector as described in this chapter.
   b. Connect the peak voltage tester positive test lead to the white/yellow connector terminal and the negative test lead to the yellow connector terminal in the 22-pin connector (**Figure 42**).
7B. On fuel injected models, perform the following:
   a. Remove the engine control module (ECM) and disconnect the gray 33-pin connector as described in Chapter Nine.

43 ECM 33-PIN WIRING HARNESS CONNECTORS

Black Connector (A)
A11, A1, A22, A12, A33, A23

Gray connector (B)
B11, B1, B22, B12, B33, B23

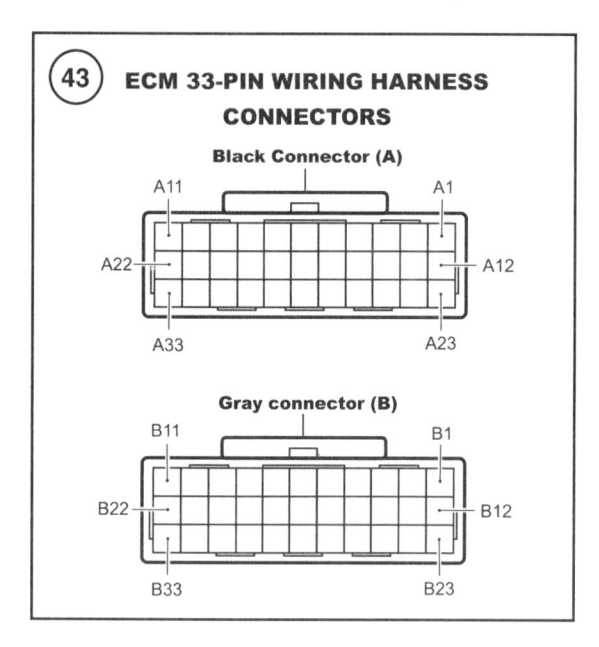

b. Connect the peak voltage tester positive test lead to the yellow wire terminal (**Figure 43**) in the gray ECM 33-pin wiring harness connector and the negative test lead to ground.

8. Shift the transmission into neutral.
9. Raise the sidestand.
10. Turn the ignition switch on and set the engine stop switch to run.

WARNING
High voltage is present during ignition system operation. Do not touch spark plugs, ignition components, connectors or test leads while cranking the engine.

NOTE
*All peak voltage specifications in the text and **Table 5** are **minimum** voltages. If the measured voltage meets or exceeds the specification, consider the test results satisfactory. On some components, the voltage may greatly exceed the minimum specification.*

11. Press the starter button while reading the meter. The meter should indicate a minimum peak voltage reading of 0.7 volts DC. If the reading is less than this, continue the procedure.
12. Measure the peak voltage at the CKP sensor connector:
   a. Turn the ignition switch off.
   b. Remove the steering side covers (Chapter Seventeen).

NOTE
Refer to the appropriate wiring diagram at the end of this manual to iden-

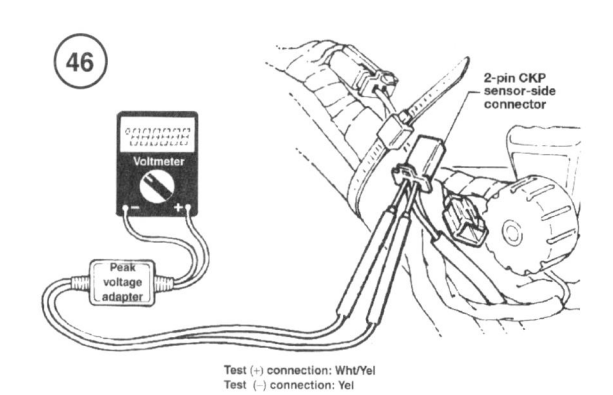

tify the CKP sensor connector and its wire colors.

c. Disconnect the CKP sensor connector located in the connector pouch in front of the thermostat housing. See **Figure 44** (carbureted models) or **Figure 45** (fuel injected models).
d. Connect the peak voltage tester test leads to the two terminals in the CKP sensor connector (**Figure 46**). Do not connect the test leads to the wire harness connector terminals.
e. Turn the ignition switch on and set the engine stop switch to run.

ELECTRICAL SYSTEM

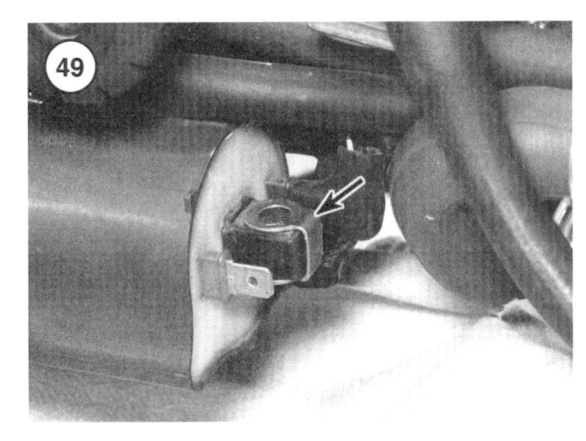

f. Press the starter button while reading the meter. The meter should indicate a minimum peak voltage reading of 0.7 volts DC.

g. On carbureted models, if the reading is now correct, check the white/yellow and yellow wires between the CKP sensor and the ICM connector for an open or short circuit.

h. On fuel injected models, if the reading is now correct, check the white/yellow wire between the CKP sensor and terminal A32 (**Figure 43**) in the black ECM 33-pin connector, and the yellow wire between the CKP sensor and terminal B22 (**Figure 43**) in the gray ECM 33-pin connector for an open or short circuit.

i. Also check the connectors for loose terminals or contamination. If the reading is still incorrect, refer to the test results in **Figure 41** and continue troubleshooting.

13. Install the seat and the steering side covers (Chapter Seventeen).

IGNITION COILS

Removal/Installation

Front ignition coil

Refer to **Figure 47** (carbureted models) or **Figure 48** (fuel injected models).

1. Turn the ignition switch off.
2. Remove the fuel tank (Chapter Eight or Chapter Nine).
3. Remove the steering side covers (Chapter Seventeen).
4. Disconnect the spark plug caps at the spark plugs. Note the secondary wire routing before removing them.
5. Identify and then disconnect the two primary wires from the coil.
6. Remove the bolts, ground wire terminal and spacers. The spacers are U-shaped and fit around the ignition coil mounting hole bosses (**Figure 49**).
7. Installation is the reverse of removal. Tighten the mounting bolts securely.

Rear ignition coil

1A. On non-ABS models, remove the right side cover (Chapter Seventeen).
1B. On ABS models, remove the left and right side covers (Chapter Seventeen).
2. Disconnect the negative battery cable as described in this chapter.
3A. On carbureted models, perform the following:
   a. Disconnect the voltage regulator connector (A, **Figure 50**).

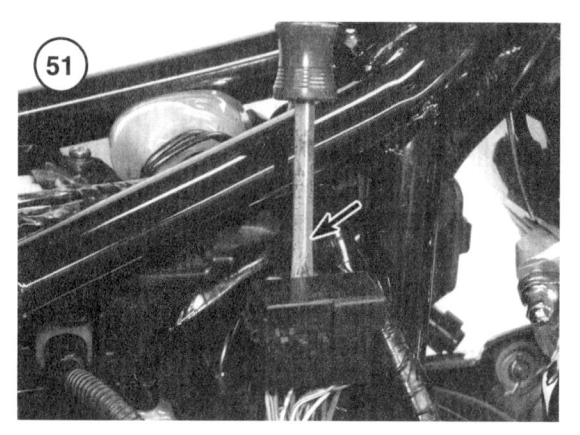

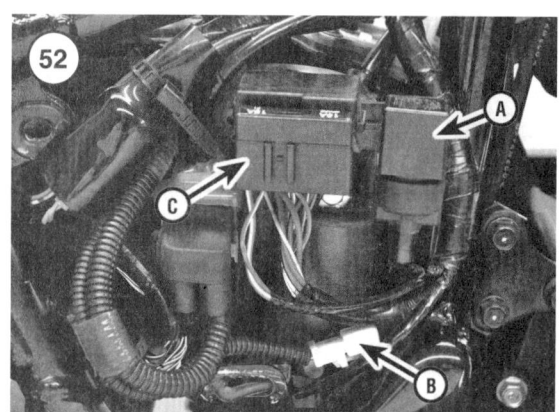

b. On Aero models, remove the fuse box (B, Figure 50) by releasing is mounting tabs with a wide-blade screwdriver **(Figure 51)**.

c. On Spirit models, remove the fuse box/turn signal relay mounting plate from the battery box by releasing the tabs on the mounting plate.

3B. On non-ABS fuel injected models, perform the following:

   a. On Phantom models, remove the turn signal relay (A, **Figure 52**).

   b. Disconnect the engine stop relay connector (B, **Figure 52**).

   c. Remove the fuse box (C, **Figure 52**) by releasing its mounting tabs with a wide-blade screwdriver **(Figure 51)**.

3C. On ABS models, remove the fuse box by releasing its mounting tabs with a screwdriver.

NOTE
Note the secondary wire routing behind the rear cylinder head around the frame before removing them.

4. Release the clamps securing the secondary wires. Then disconnect the spark plug caps at the spark plugs.

5. Identify and then disconnect the two primary wires from the coil. See **Figure 53** (carbureted models) or **Figure 54** (fuel injected models).

6. Remove the bolts, spacers and ignition coil. The spacers are U-shaped and fit around the ignition coil mounting hole bosses **(Figure 55)**.

7. Inspect the ignition coils for cracks and other damage.

8. The spark plug caps and secondary wires can be replaced as described in this section.

9. Installation is the reverse of these steps. Note the following:

   a. Make sure the mounting bolts are secure.

   b. Verify the fuse box is mounted securely.

   c. Make sure the secondary wires are routed along their orginal path as noted (this section).

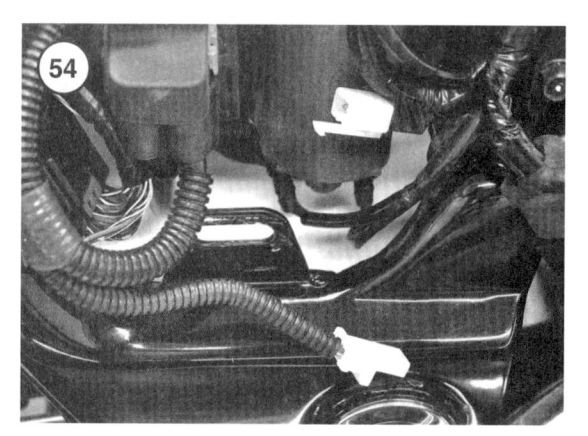

ELECTRICAL SYSTEM

wire so the new cap can be reinstalled correctly.

b. Hold the secondary wire and twist the spark plug cap to break its seal and loosen it. Do not pull the cap as this may damage the secondary wire. Continue to unscrew the cap until it is free. Check the end of the secondary wire for any rust or corrosion and clean with a small file or sandpaper. Hold the secondary wire and turn the spark plug cap until its screw threads into the end of the wire and the cap bottoms.

NOTE
All four secondary wires have different part numbers. Match and replace one secondary wire at a time until they are all replaced.

2. To replace the secondary wire, unscrew the cap (A, **Figure 57**) and pull the secondary wire (B) out of the end of the ignition coil. Check the ignition coil terminal for any rust or corrosion and clean with a small file or sandpaper. Insert the secondary wire into the ignition coil, then install and tighten the cap.

CKP SENSOR

Removal/Installation

1. Remove the steering side covers (Chapter Seventeen).
2. Remove the clutch (Chapter Six).
3. Disconnect the CKP sensor connector located in the connector pouch in front of the thermostat housing. See **Figure 44** (carbureted models) or Figure 45 (fuel injected models).
4. Remove the CKP sensor mounting bolts (A, **Figure 58**), then remove the grommets (B) from the crankcase.
5. Remove the wiring harness from its routing path and remove the CKP sensor.
6. Clean the threads on the CKP sensor bolts and mating threaded holes of any oil and threadlock residue.
7. Apply a medium strength threadlock onto the CKP sensor bolt threads.
8. Install the CKP sensor and tighten the mounting bolts (A, **Figure 58**) to 12 N.m (106 N.m.).
9. Install the clutch as described in Chapter Six.
10. Install the CKP sensor grommets and reposition the wiring harness as described under *Right Crankcase Cover* in Chapter Six.

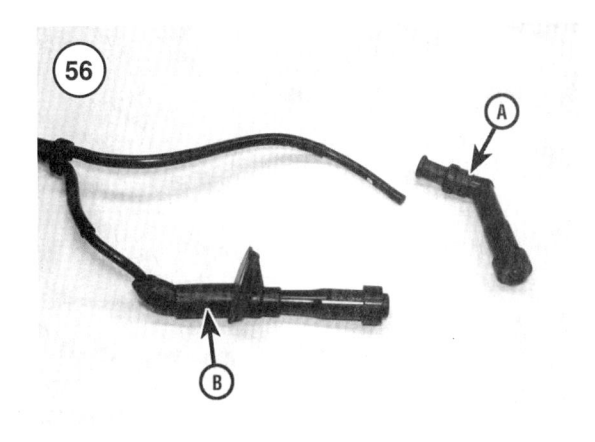

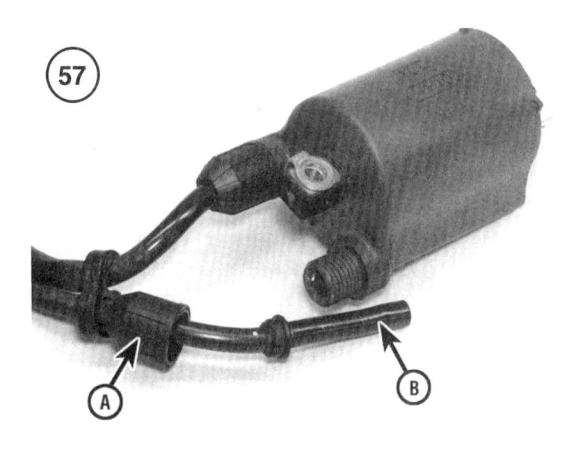

Spark Plug Cap and Secondary Wire Replacement

The two spark plug caps on each ignition coil are different. The cap without the cylinder plug can be replaced separately (A, **Figure 56**). The cap with the cylinder plug is permanently attached to the secondary wire (B, **Figure 56**) and must be replaced with the wire.

1. To replace the spark plug cap without the cylinder plug (A, **Figure 56**), perform the following:
   a. Before removing the spark plug cap, note the angled position of the cap on the secondary

IGNITION CONTROL MODULE (ICM) (CARBURETED MODELS)

Testing

No testing procedure is available. If all other ignition components and systems have been tested, replace the ICM with a known good unit and recheck the ignition system operation. Faulty wiring and connections cause many electrical problems. Make sure to check all wires and connections before presuming the ICM is faulty. Because electrical components are not returnable, if possible, install a known good ICM for testing and check operation before purchasing a new unit.

Removal/Installation

The ICM is mounted on top of the battery box.
1. Remove the seat (Chapter Seventeen).
2. Remove the ICM (**Figure 59**) from the battery box cover.
3. Disconnect the 22-pin connector (**Figure 60**) and remove the ICM.
4. Installation is the reverse of these steps.

ENGINE CONTROL MODULE (ECM) (FUEL INJECTED MODELS)

Refer to Chapter Nine.

IGNITION TIMING

Refer to Chapter Three.

THROTTLE POSITION (TP) SENSOR (CARBURETED MODELS)

A TP sensor is installed on the carburetor to provide the ICM with an electronic signal that coincides with the throttle valve position. This varying signal is analyzed by the ICM, along with the engine speed signal from the stator coil. The ICM then adjusts the ignition timing for the immediate engine load. The TP sensor unit must be accurately adjusted so the signal represents the actual throttle position.

CAUTION
Do not loosen the TP sensor screw, except to adjust or replace the sensor. If the screw is loosened, the TP sensor must be readjusted as described in this section. Failing to adjust the TP sensor unit will reduce engine performance.

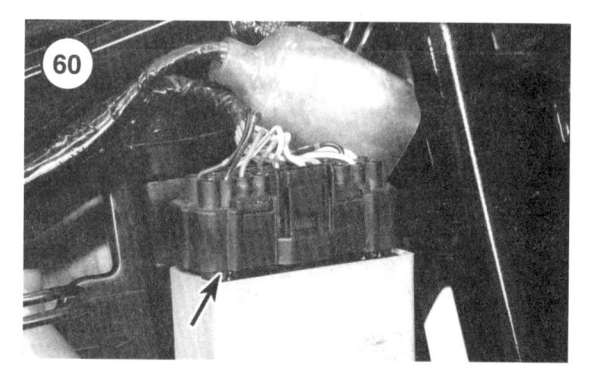

Testing

1. Remove the seats (Chapter Seventeen).
2. Remove the ICM (**Figure 59**) from the battery box cover and disconnect the 22-pin connector (**Figure 60**).
3. Measure resistance between the following wire terminals on the ICM wiring harness connector (**Figure 61**):
    a. 2004-2007 Aero and 2007-2009 Spirit models: Yellow/red and blue/green.
    b. 2008-2009 Aero: Blue and black/red.
    c. The correct reading is 4000-6000 ohms.
4. Connect the ohmmeter between the following terminals in the ICM wiring harness connector (**Figure 61**):

ELECTRICAL SYSTEM

62

63

64

Throttle shaft
Align
O-ring
Throttle position sensor

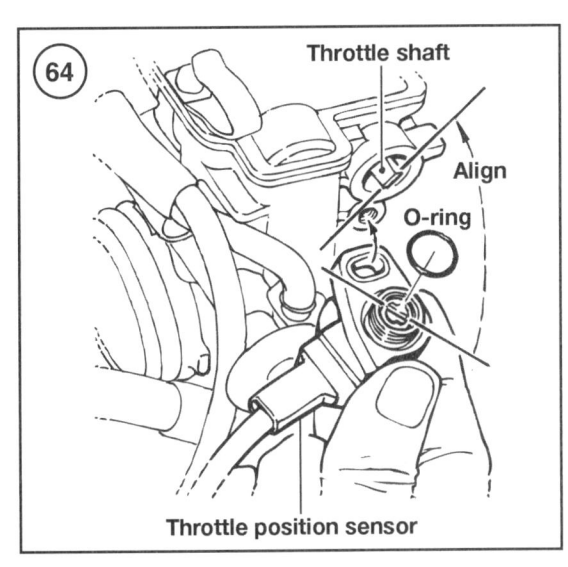

  a. 2004-2007 Aero models and 2007-2009 Spirit models: Red/Yellow and blue/green wires.
  b. 2008-2009 Aero models: Yellow/red and black/red wires.
  c. Continue the procedure.
5. Note the following while operating the throttle grip:
  a. When opening the throttle grip from its fully closed to full open position, the resistance should increase.

  b. When closing the throttle grip from its fully open to fully closed position, the resistance should decrease.
6. If either test result was incorrect, continue the procedure. If the test results were correct, skip to Step 10.
7. Remove the air filter housing (Chapter Eight).
8. Disconnect the TP sensor 3-pin connector **(Figure 62)**.
9. Repeat both resistance tests at the TP sensor side terminals. Note the following:
  a. On all carbureted models, check for 4,000-6,000 ohms resistance between the blue and black wire terminals in the 3-pin TPS-side connector.
  b. On all carbureted models, check for resistance variances between the yellow and black wire terminals in the 3-pin TPS-side connector as the throttle grip is operated. Resistance should increase as the throttle is opened, and decrease as it is closed.
  c. If both test results are incorrect, replace the TP sensor as described in this section.
  d. If one or both test results are correct, check the wiring harness between the TP sensor connector and the ICM 22-pin connector for an open or short circuit. Then check for loose, corroded or damaged terminals in both connectors. After inspecting these items, repeat the resistance tests.
10. Reconnect the ICM 22-pin connector **(Figure 60)**.
11. Turn the ignition switch on and set the engine stop switch to run.
12. Measure input voltage between the following terminals on the TP sensor wiring harness side terminals:
  a. 2004-2007 Aero models and 2007-2009 Spirit models: Yellow/red (+) and blue/green (-) wires.
  b. 2008-2009 Aero models: Blue (+) and black/red (-) wires.
  c. The correct reading is 5 volts.
  d. If the reading is correct, continue the procedure.
  e. If the reading is incorrect or there was no reading, check the wiring harness between the TP sensor connector and the ICM 22-pin connector for an open or short circuit. Then check for loose, corroded or damaged terminals in both connectors.
13. Installation is the reverse of removal. Make sure the connectors are fastened securly.

Replacement/Adjustment

1. Remove the carburetor (Chapter Eight).
2. Remove the Torx screw (A, **Figure 63**) and the TP

sensor (B). Note the O-ring installed on the TP sensor and replace if flattened or damaged.
3. Install the O-ring onto the TP sensor (**Figure 64**).
4. Install the TP sensor by aligning the groove in the TP sensor shaft with the shoulder on the throttle shaft (**Figure 64**).
5. Apply a medium strength threadlock onto the Torx screw threads and install the screw (A, **Figure 63**) finger-tight.

CAUTION
Do not insert the ohmmeter test leads too far into the TP sensor connector. Doing so may damage the waterproof material in the connector. If necessary, insert thin electrical conductors into the TP sensor connector, then attach the meter leads to the conductors.

6. Before adjusting the TP sensor, determine the actual TP sensor coil resistance as follows:
    a. Connect the ohmmeter between the blue and black wire terminals (**Figure 65**) in the TP sensor-side connector.
    b. The ohmmeter should read 4000-6000 ohms. Record the actual reading.
7. Determine the TP sensor idle speed resistance and adjust the TP sensor as follows:
    a. Calculate the TP sensor idle speed resistance by multiplying the actual measured TP sensor coil resistance by 0.09 and 0.11. For example, if the measured TP sensor coil resistance is 5500 ohms, the required variable coil resistance is 495-605 ohms at idle speed (5500 x 0.09 = 495; 5500 x 0.11 = 605 ohms).
    b. Connect the ohmmeter to the yellow and black wire connector terminals (**Figure 65**) in the TP sensor-side connector.
    c. Loosen the screw (A, **Figure 63**) and turn the TP sensor (B, **Figure 63**) until the required reading is achieved. Tighten the screw securely and recheck the resistance measurement.
8. Install the carburetor (Chapter Eight).

STARTER SYSTEM TROUBLESHOOTING

The starting system consists of the battery, starter, starter relay switch, start button, starter mechanism and related wiring.

When the ignition is turned on and the start button is pushed, current is transmitted from the battery to the starter relay switch. When the relay is activated, it activates the starter solenoid that mechanically engages the starter with the engine.

A starting system problem may be an electrical or mechanical problem. The troubleshooting procedure (Chapter Two) lists general test steps to help isolate starting problems.

1. If troubleshooting a starting system problem, check the following before proceeding with more in-depth testing:
    a. Make sure the battery is fully charged and has passed a battery load test as described in this chapter.
    b. Make sure the battery cables are the proper size and length. Replace damaged or undersized cables.
    c. Make sure all electrical connections are clean and tight. High resistance caused from dirty or loose connections can affect voltage and current levels.
    d. Make sure the wiring harness is in good condition, with no worn or frayed insulation or lose harness sockets.
    e. Make sure the fuel tank is filled with an adequate supply of fresh gasoline.
    f. Make sure the spark plugs are in good condition and properly gapped.
    g. Make sure the ignition system is working correctly.
2. If the starter does not turn over, perform these quick tests to isolate the problem:
    a. Turn the ignition switch on and shift the transmission into neutral. The headlight should come on. If not, check the main fuse and appropriate subfuse. See *Fuses* in this chapter. If the fuses are okay, test the battery as described in this chapter.
    b. If the headlight came on, push the starter button to start the engine. The solenoid should click. If not, the problem is in the wiring to the solenoid, ignition switch or the solenoid is faulty.
    c. If the solenoid did click but the starter did not turn the engine over, the problem may be due to excessive voltage drop in the starter circuit or the starter is damaged. This could be due to worn brushes or a shorted commutator. The problem can also be in the starter drive system or engine.

ELECTRICAL SYSTEM

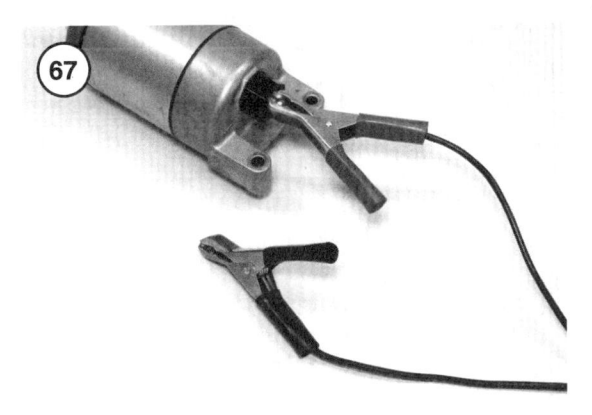

4. If the problem is traced to the starter circuit, refer to the troubleshooting procedure (this section) that best matches the starting problem symptom listed.
5. To inspect the starter drive gears, refer to *Flywheel, Starter Clutch and Starter Drive Gears* in this chapter.

Symptom-Based Tests

CAUTION
Never operate the starter for more than 5 seconds at a time. Allow the starter to cool 10 seconds before reusing it. Failing to allow the starter to cool after continuous starting attempts can damage the starter.

The following symptom related sections are:
1. Starter spins slowly.
2. Starter relay switch clicks but engine does not turn over.
3. Starter operates but engine does not turn over.
4. Starter does not spin.
5. Starter spins with the transmission in neutral but does not turn with the transmission in gear with the clutch lever pulled in and the sidestand up.

Starter spins slowly

If the starter operates but does not turn the engine over at normal speed, check the following:

1. Test the battery as described in this chapter.
2. Check for the following:
   a. Loose or corroded battery terminals.
   b. Loose or corroded battery ground cable.
   c. Loose starter cable.
3. If the battery is fully charged and passes a load test, and the cables are in good condition, the starter may be faulty. Remove, disassemble and bench test the starter as described in this chapter.

Starter relay switch clicks but engine does not turn over

1. Test the battery as described in this chapter.
2. Make sure all connections are clean and tight.
3. Damaged starter gears.
4. Crankshaft cannot turn over because of mechanical failure.

Starter operates, but engine does not turn over

1. If the starter was just overhauled, it may have been assembled incorrectly.
2. Check for a damaged starter clutch as described in this chapter.
3. Check for damaged starter gears as described in this chapter.

Starter does not spin

1. Check for a blown main or subfuse as described in this chapter. If the fuses are okay, continue the procedure.
2. Check the starter cable for an open circuit or dirty or loose-fitting terminals. Repair any dirty, loose fitting or damaged connectors or wiring.
3. Disconnect the starter relay connector **(Figure 66)** and check for dirty or loose-fitting terminals. Clean and repair as required. Reconnect the connector and continue the procedure.
4. Check the starter relay switch as follows.
   a. Turn the ignition switch on.
   b. Push the starter button while listening for a click at the starter relay.
5. Turn the ignition switch off and note the following:
   a. If the starter relay clicks, continue the procedure.
   b. If there was no click, skip to Step 7.

CAUTION
Because of the large amount of current that will flow from the battery to the starter, use a large diameter cable when making the connection. To avoid damaging the starter, do not leave the battery connected for more than 5 seconds.

6. Remove the starter from the motorcycle as described this chapter. Using an auxiliary battery, apply battery voltage directly to the starter **(Figure 67)**. The starter should turn when battery voltage is applied directly to the starter. Note the following:
   a. If the starter did not turn, disassemble and inspect the starter as described in this chapter. Test the starter components and replace worn or damaged parts as required.
   b. If the starter turned, check for loose or damaged starter cables. If the cables are okay, remove and test the starter relay switch as described in this chapter. Replace the starter relay switch if necessary.
   c. Reinstall the starter as described in this chapter.
7. Check the starter relay switch ground line for continuity as described under *Starter Relay Switch Testing* in this chapter. There should be continuity.
   a. If there is continuity, continue the procedure.
   b. If there is no continuity, check for a loose or damaged connector or an open circuit in the wiring harness.
   c. If these items are okay, test the following items as described in this chapter: sidestand switch, neutral switch, clutch switch and diode.
   d. Reconnect the starter relay switch electrical connector.
8. Check the starter relay for voltage as described under *Starter Relay Switch Testing* (this chapter). There should be voltage when the ignition switch is on and the starter button is pushed.
   a. If there is battery voltage, continue the procedure.
   b. If there is no battery voltage, check for a blown main or subfuse.
   c. If the fuses are good, check for an open circuit in the wiring harness or for dirty or loose-fitting terminals.
   d. If the wiring and connectors are in good condition, check for a faulty ignition and/or starter switch as described in this chapter.
9. Perform the starter relay switch operational test as described under *Starter Relay Switch Testing* in this chapter.
   a. If the starter relay switch is normal, check for dirty or loose-fitting connector terminals.
   b. If the starter relay switch is faulty, replace it and retest.

Starter works with the transmission in neutral but does not turn with the transmission in gear with the clutch lever pulled in and the sidestand up

1. Test the clutch switch as described in this chapter.
   a. If the clutch switch is good, continue the procedure.
   b. If the clutch switch is defective, replace the switch and retest.
2. Test the sidestand switch as described in this chapter.
   a. If the sidestand switch is good, perform Step 3.
   b. If the sidestand switch is defective, replace the switch and retest.
3. Check for an open circuit in the wiring harness. Check for loose or damaged electrical connectors.

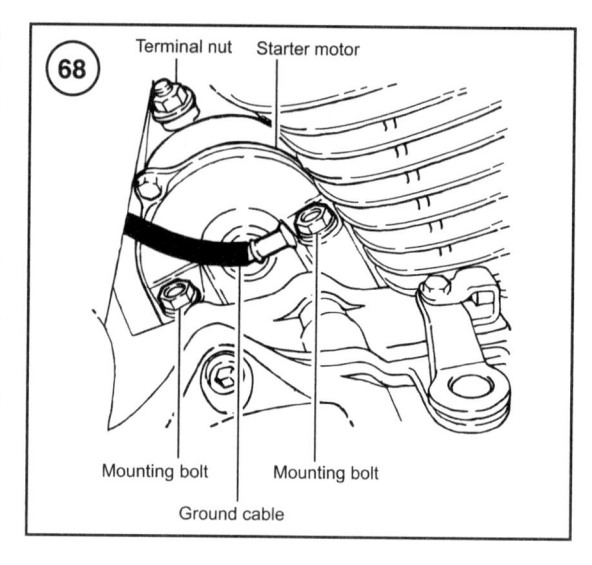

WARNING
Before riding the motorcycle, make sure the sidestand switch is working properly. Riding the motorcycle with the sidestand down can cause loss of control.

STARTER (2004-2007 AERO MODELS)

CAUTION
Do not operate the starter for more than 5 seconds at a time. Wait approximately 10 seconds between starting attempts.

Removal/Installation

1. Disconnect the negative battery cable at the battery as described in this chapter.

NOTE
The insulator cannot be purchased separately. If this part is damaged, either a new starter must be purchased, or scavenge the part from a discarded starter.

2. Disconnect the starter cable by holding the inner nut with a wrench and removing the starter cable nut **(Figure 68)** to disconnect the cable. Holding the in-

ELECTRICAL SYSTEM

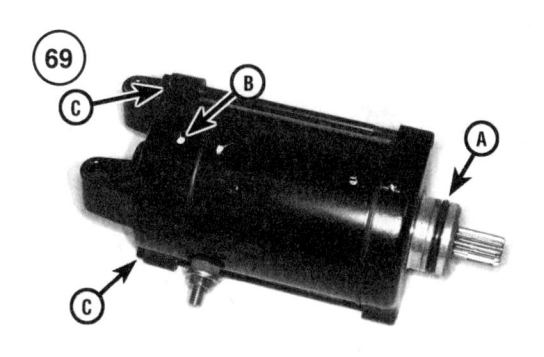

ner nut prevents the terminal bolt from turning and damaging the insulator installed on the inside of the starter.

3. Remove the mounting bolts and ground cable **(Figure 68)**.
4. Pull the starter toward the right side to disconnect it from the starter drive mechanism. Then remove the starter.
5. Install by reversing these removal steps, plus the following:
   a. Lubricate the starter O-ring (A, **Figure 69**) with engine oil.
   b. Remove all corrosion from the starter cables.
   c. Tighten the starter mounting bolts securely.
   d. Hold the inner nut and tighten the starter cable nut to 9.8 N.m (87 in.-lb.).
   e. Fit the rubber boot securely over the starter cable. Replace the boot if damaged.
   f. Start the engine to make sure the starter works correctly.

Disassembly

Refer to **Figure 70** for this procedure.

1. Find the alignment marks across the armature housing and both end covers. If necessary, scribe or paint the alignment marks (B, **Figure 69**) to identify them.
2. Remove the assembly bolts (C, **Figure 69**).

NOTE
The number of shims used in each starter varies. The shims and washers must be reinstalled in their correct order and number. Failing to install the correct number of shims and washers may increase armature end play and cause the starter to draw excessive current. Record the thickness and alignment of each shim and washer removed during disassembly.

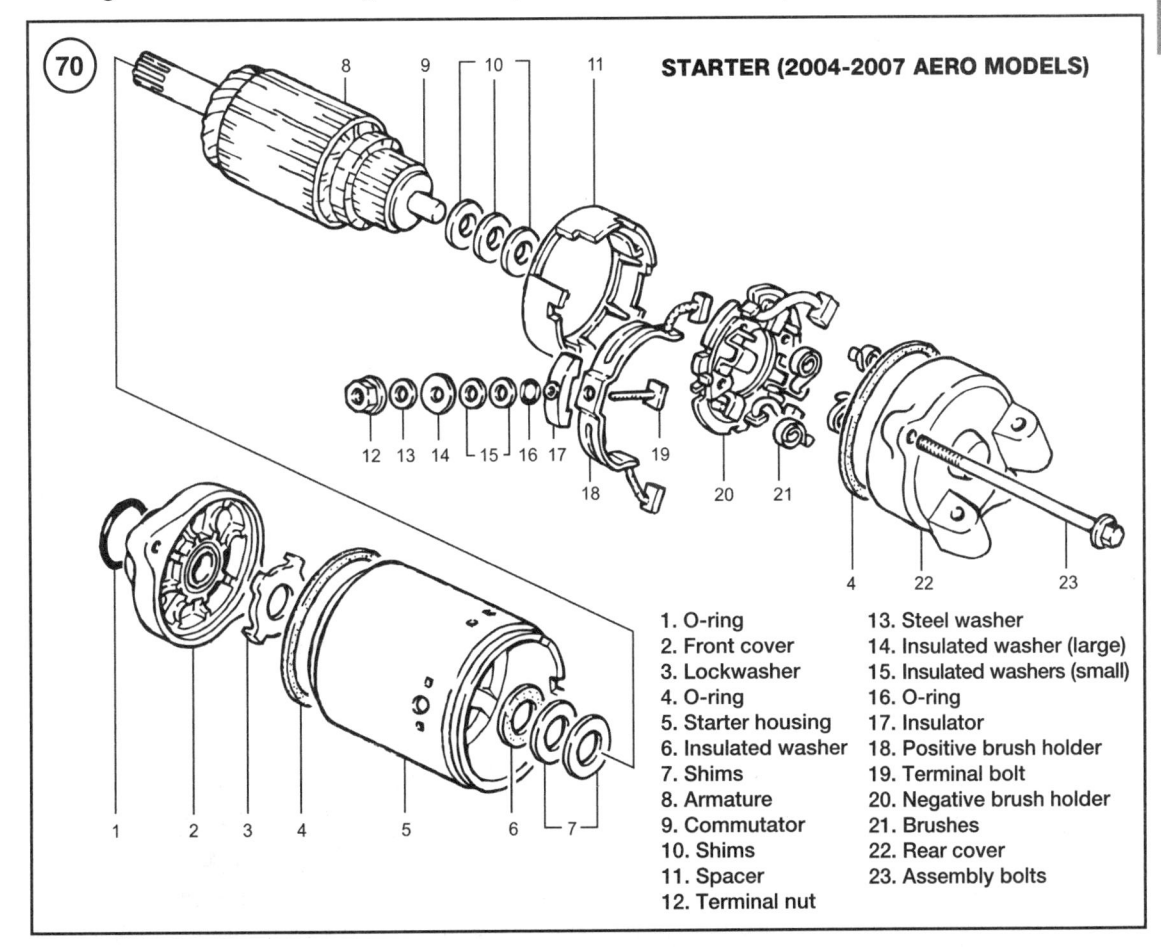

STARTER (2004-2007 AERO MODELS)

1. O-ring
2. Front cover
3. Lockwasher
4. O-ring
5. Starter housing
6. Insulated washer
7. Shims
8. Armature
9. Commutator
10. Shims
11. Spacer
12. Terminal nut
13. Steel washer
14. Insulated washer (large)
15. Insulated washers (small)
16. O-ring
17. Insulator
18. Positive brush holder
19. Terminal bolt
20. Negative brush holder
21. Brushes
22. Rear cover
23. Assembly bolts

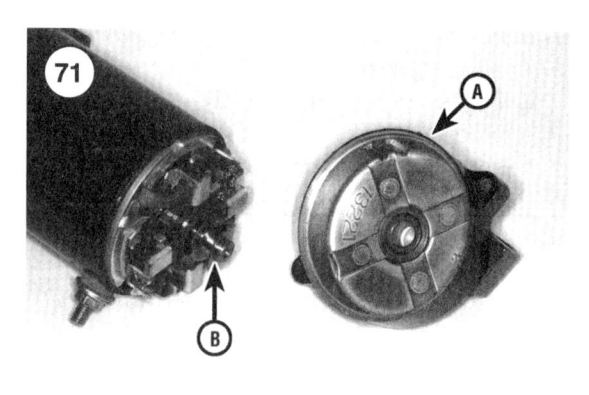

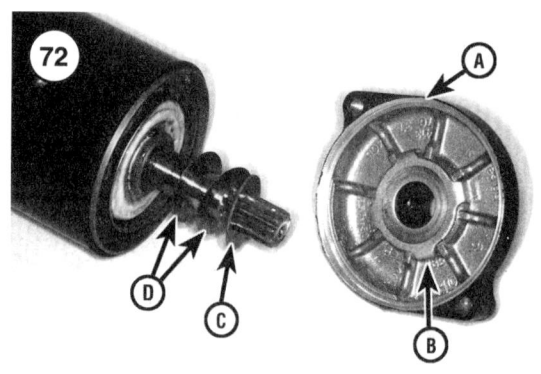

NOTE
If disassembling the starter just to check brush condition, remove only the rear cover. The brushes can be inspected and the cover reinstalled if further disassembly is not required. When doing so, locate and reinstall the shims onto the armature shaft.

3. Remove the rear cover (A, **Figure 71**) and shims (B).
4. Remove the front cover (A, **Figure 72**) and the lockwasher (B).

NOTE
Do not remove the seal from the front cover. It is not available as a replacement part.

5. Remove the insulated washer (C, **Figure 72**) and shim (D).
6. Remove the armature from the housing.
7. Before removing the brush holder, test the brushes and terminal bolt as follows:

NOTE
The positive brushes have insulation sleeves covering the wires.

  a. Check for continuity between the starter terminal and each positive brush **(Figure 73)**. There should be continuity. If there is no continuity, replace the positive brush holder during reassembly.
  b. Check for continuity between the cable terminal and starter housing **(Figure 74)**. There should be no continuity. If there is continuity, check for damaged, missing or improperly installed insulators. Compare the alignment of the insulated washers with **Figure 70** when removing them.
  c. Check for continuity between the positive and negative brushes **(Figure 75)**. There should be no continuity. If there is continuity, check the positive brush wires for damaged insula-

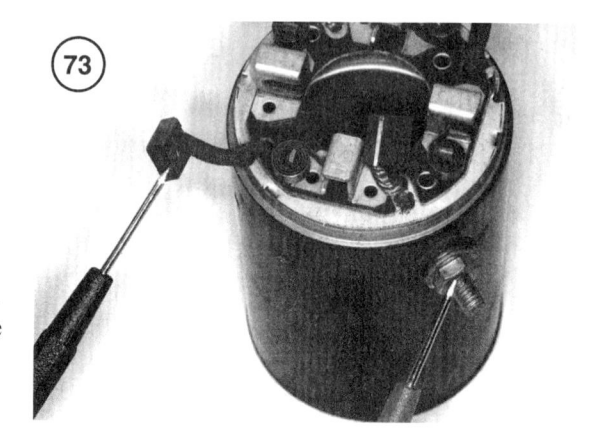

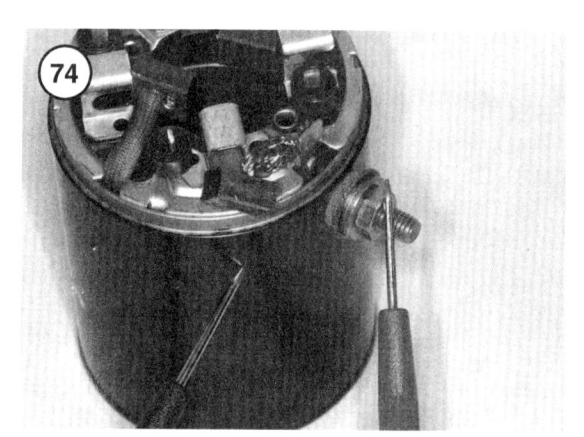

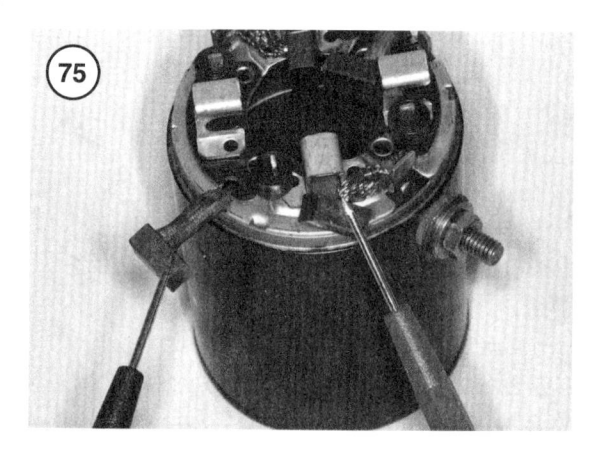

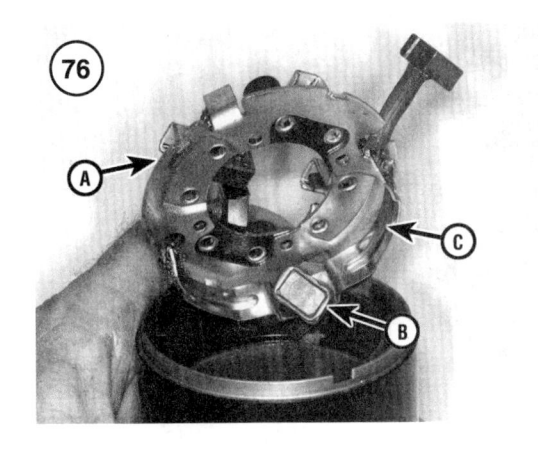

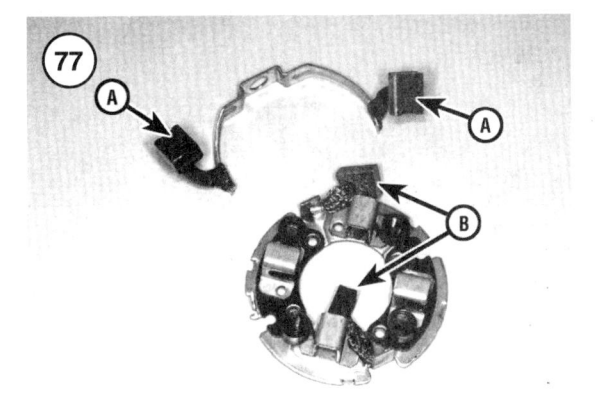

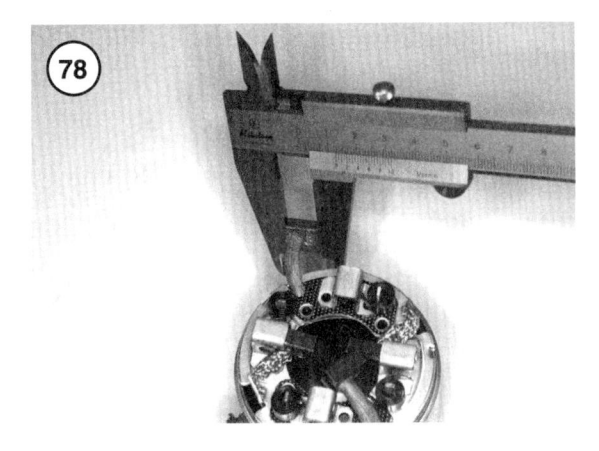

ELECTRICAL SYSTEM

Inspection

If any starter component (other than O-rings and brush sets) are severely worn or damaged, the starter must be replaced as an assembly. Individual replacement parts are not available.

NOTE
Before purchasing a new starter, try to find a replacement starter through a motorcycle wrecking yard. If you cannot locate an identical starter, look for a starter that is similar in design. The internal part needed may be identical or similar.

1. The internal parts in a used starter are often contaminated with carbon and copper dust released from the brushes and commutator. Because a starter can be damaged from improper cleaning, note the following:
   a. Clean all parts (except the armature, starter housing and insulated washers in solvent. Use a rag lightly dampened with solvent to wipe off the armature, insulated washers and the starter housing (inside and outside).
   b. Use only fine-grade sandpaper to clean the brushes. Do not use emery cloth as its fibers may insulate the brushes.
   c. Use only crocus cloth to clean the commutator. Do not use emery cloth or sandpaper. Any abrasive material left on or embedded in the commutator may cause excessive brush wear. Do not leave any debris on or between the commutator bars.
2. Replace the starter housing O-rings if damaged.
3. Inspect the bushing in the front cover for wear or damage.
4. Inspect the seal and needle bearing in the rear cover for damage. Do not remove the seal to check the bearing.

NOTE
The bushing, seal and bearing used in the end covers are not available separately.

5. Check the lockwasher, shims and insulated washers for damage.
6. Inspect the brushes (A and B, **Figure 77**) as follows:
   a. Inspect each brush for cracks and other damage.
   b. Inspect the insulation sleeves on the positive brushes (A, **Figure 77**) for tearing and other damage.
   c. Check each brush where it is fixed to its holder (A or B, **Figure 77**).
   d. Measure the length of each brush (**Figure 78**). If the length of any one brush is out of speci-

tion sleeves. The insulation sleeves must be installed through the negative brush holder so that the positive brush wires cannot short out.

8. Remove the terminal nut and remove the steel washer, insulated washers and O-ring. If the O-ring is recessed inside the starter housing, remove it after removing the positive brush holder.
9. Remove the negative brush holder (A, **Figure 76**), terminal bolt (B) and positive brush holder (C).
10. Remove the insulator installed between the positive brush holder and the starter housing.

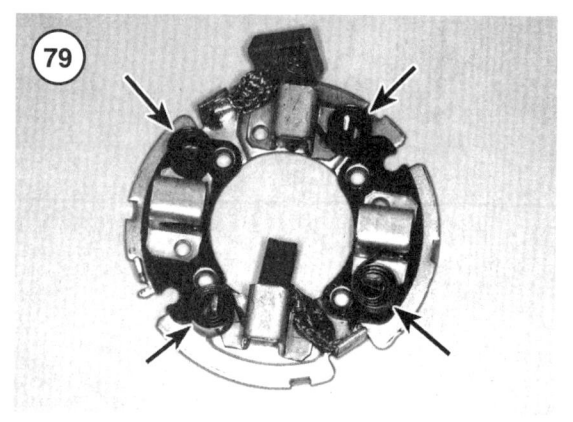

fication (**Table 6**), replace both brush holders (**Figure 77**) as a set. Replacement brushes are permanently fixed to the holders. Soldering is not required.

7. Inspect the brush springs (**Figure 79**) for weakness or damage. Even though a spring tension measurement is not available, compare spring tension using a spring scale as follows:
   a. Assemble the negative brush holder, brushes and commutator as described under *Assembly*. See **Figure 80**.
   b. Support the starter in a vise with soft jaws.
   c. Hook a spring scale to the exposed part of the spring as shown in **Figure 81**.
   d. Pull the spring scale and record the spring tension measurement the moment the spring lifts off the brush.
   e. Repeat for each spring. If there is any noticeable difference in tension measurements, replace the negative brush holder and springs as a set.

8. Inspect the armature (A, **Figure 82**) as follows:
   a. Inspect both shafts for scoring and other damage.
   b. Inspect the windings for obvious damage.
   c. To check the armature for a short circuit, have it tested on a growler. Refer this service to a dealership or an automotive electrical repair shop.

9. Inspect the commutator (B, **Figure 82**) as follows:
   a. Inspect the commutator bars for visual damage.
   b. Clean the commutator surface (this section).
   c. The mica must be below the surface of the copper bars. On a worn commutator the mica and copper bars may be worn to the same level (**Figure 83**).

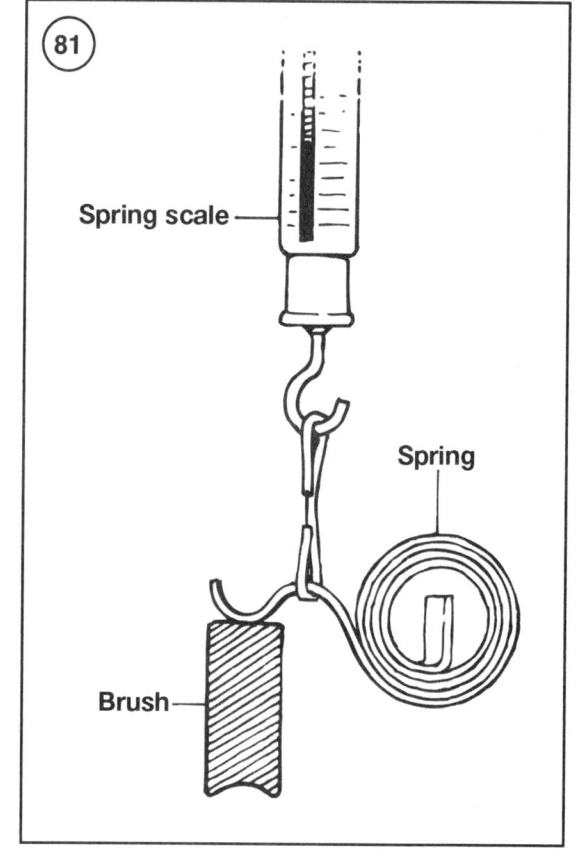

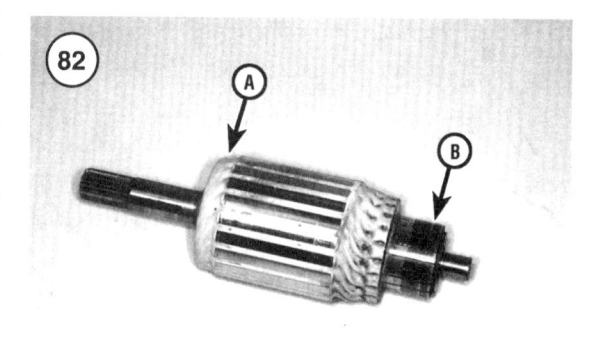

ELECTRICAL SYSTEM

83 Good / Worn

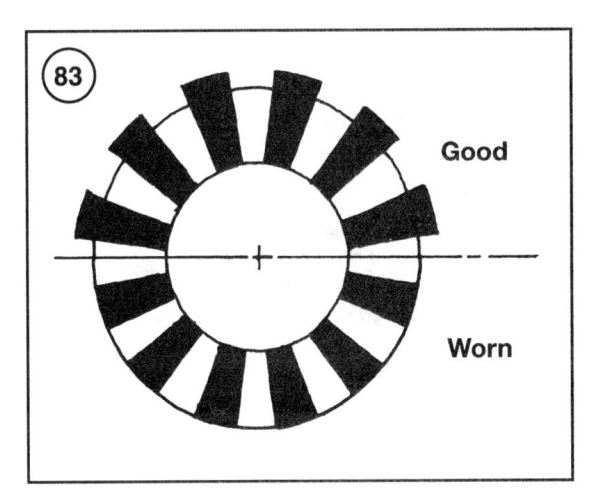

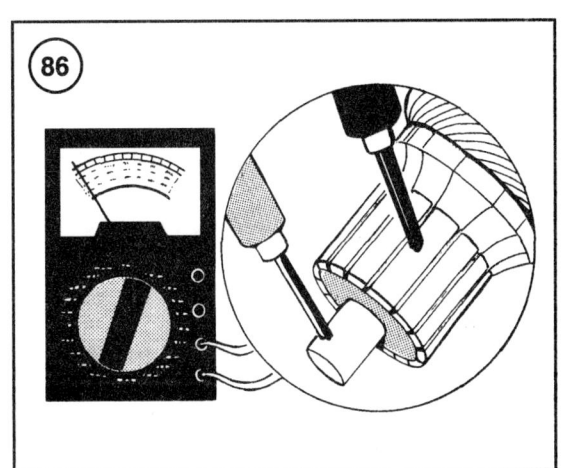

84 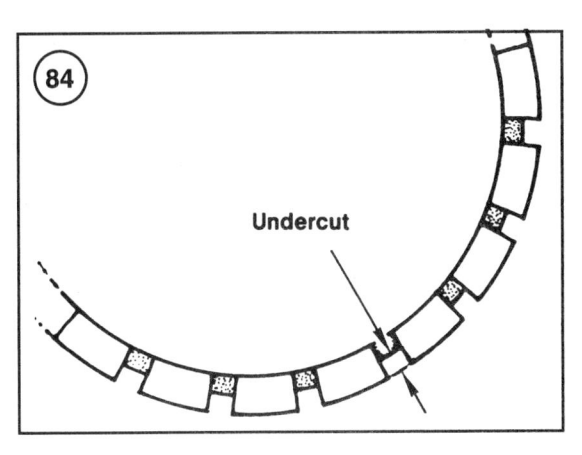 Undercut

85

86

87 A, B, C

g. Check for continuity between the armature shaft and each commutator bar **(Figure 86)**. There should be no continuity. If there is continuity, replace the starter.

h. Check for continuity between the armature coil core and each commutator bar. There should be no continuity. If there is continuity, replace the starter.

10. Inspect the starter housing for cracks or other damage. Then inspect for loose, chipped or damaged magnets.

Assembly

1. Assemble the positive (A, **Figure 77**) and negative (B) brush holders as follows:

    a. Install the insulated brush wires through the two notches in the negative brush holder as shown in A, **Figure 87**. Make sure the insulation sleeves on the wires contact the negative brush holder.

    b. Install the terminal bolt through the brush holder, then install the insulator (B, **Figure 87**) and O-ring (C).

2. Install the terminal bolt through the hole in the

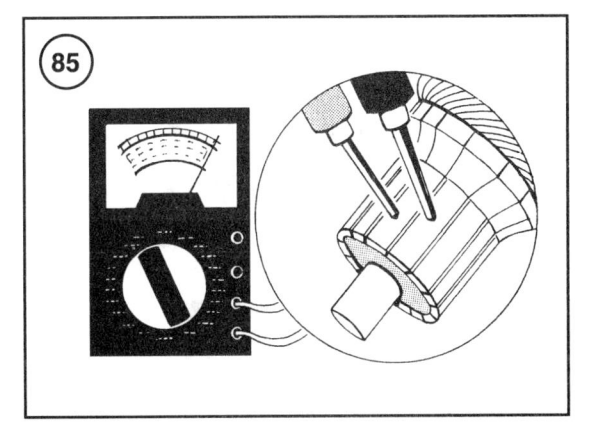

    d. If the mica level is too high or if its shape is too narrow or V-shaped, undercut the mica with a hacksaw blade **(Figure 84)**.

    e. Inspect the commutator copper bars for discoloration. If a pair of bars are discolored, grounded armature coils are indicated.

    f. Check for continuity across all adjacent pairs of commutator bars **(Figure 85)**. There should be continuity across all pairs of bars. If an open circuit exists between a pair of bars, replace the starter.

starter housing (A, **Figure 88**) while aligning the tab on the negative brush holder with the notch in the starter housing (B). Align the insulator with the notch in the spacer.

NOTE
*Reinstall all parts in the order described (**Figure 70**). This is essential to insulate the positive brushes from the starter housing.*

3. Install the two small insulators, large insulator, steel washer and terminal nut. Tighten the nut to secure the terminal bolt to the starter housing.
4. Perform the continuity tests (this section) to check the positive brushes and terminal bolt for proper installation.
5. Install the brushes into their holders as follows:
    a. Cut a plastic wire tie into four separate pieces, each approximately 20-mm long.
    b. Install the plastic tie pieces between the brush holders and spring **(Figure 89)**. This will allow the commutator to pass under the brushes with no tension placed against the brushes.
    c. Install the brushes into their holders **(Figure 90)**.

CAUTION
During installation, magnetic force will pull the armature against the coils inside the starter housing. Hold the armature tightly when installing it to prevent from damaging the coils or brushes.

6. Install the armature into the starter housing. Then remove the plastic ties **(Figure 91)** to release the brush springs and allow them to push the brushes against the commutator. Check that each brush seats squarely against the commutator **(Figure 80)**.
7. Install the shims (B, **Figure 71**) onto the armature shaft in the original order noted during dissassembly.
8. Install the O-ring onto the commutator side of the starter housing.
9. Apply a thin coat of grease onto the armature shaft.
10. Align the groove in the rear cover (A, **Figure 92**) with the raised tab on the negative brush holder (B) and install the rear cover.
11. Install the O-ring onto the front side of the starter housing.
12. Lubricate the front cover oil seal lips and bearing with grease.
13. Install the front cover as follows:
    a. Install the steel shims (D, **Figure 72**) onto the armature shaft. The number of shims on the starter may differ from the number of shims shown.

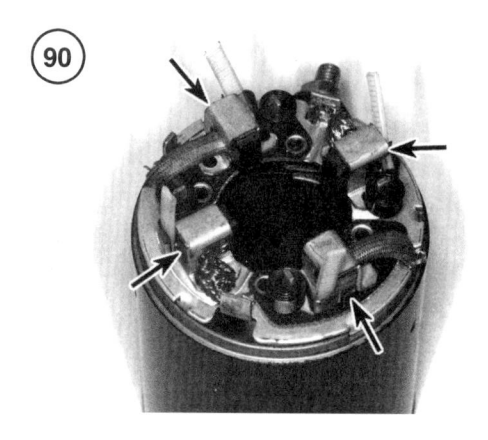

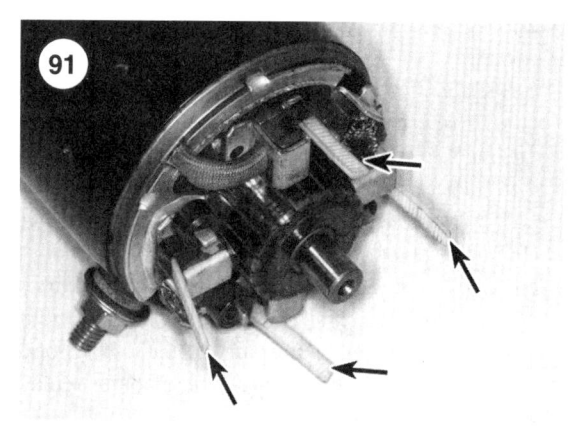

ELECTRICAL SYSTEM

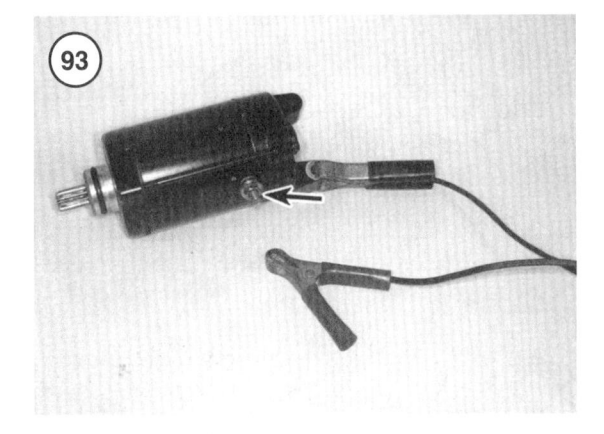

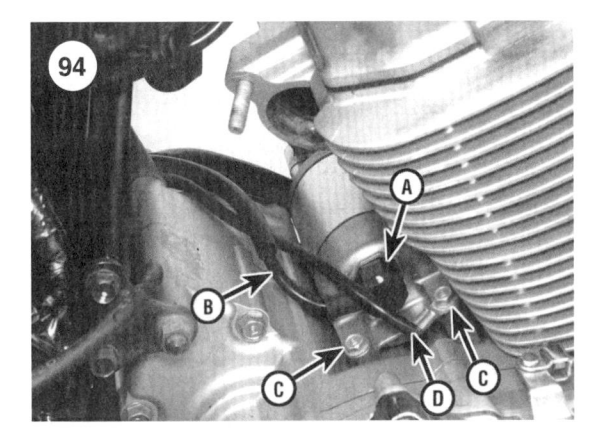

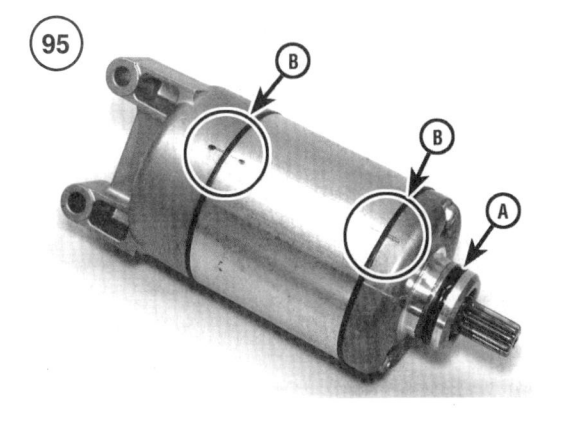

b. Install the insulator (C, **Figure 72**) and seat it against the shims.

c. Install the lockwasher (B, **Figure 72**) onto the front cover.

d. Align the front cover tabs with the lockwasher tabs and install the front cover (A, **Figure 72**). Then, check that the index marks (B, **Figure 69**) on the starter case and both covers align.

NOTE
If one or both assembly bolts will not pass through the starter, the end covers and/or negative brush holder are installed incorrectly.

14. Install the assembly bolts (C, **Figure 69**) and tighten securely.

15. Lubricate the O-ring with grease and install it into the front cover groove.

16. Hold the starter and turn the armature shaft by hand. The armature should turn with some resistance, but should not bind or lockup. If the armature does not turn properly, disassemble the starter and check the shim, insulated washer and lockwasher alignment.

17. Use an auxiliary battery and apply battery voltage directly to the starter **(Figure 93)**. The starter should turn when battery voltage is directly applied. If the starter does not turn, disassemble and inspect the starter as described in this section.

STARTER
(2008-2009 AND 2011-2013 AERO MODELS, 2010-2013 SPIRIT MODELS AND ALL PHANTOM MODELS)

Removal/Installation

1. Disconnect the negative battery cable at the battery as described in this chapter.

NOTE
Figure 94 *shows the rear exhaust pipe removed from the engine. The starter can be removed with the rear exhaust pipe installed on the engine.*

2. Remove the starter terminal boot (A, **Figure 94**) Then, remove the nut and disconnect the starter cable (B, **Figure 94**).

3. Remove the starter motor mounting bolts (C, **Figure 94**) and disconnect the ground cable (D) at the starter motor.

4. Pull the starter toward the right side to disconnect it from the starter drive mechanism. Then remove the starter.

5. Install by reversing these removal steps, plus the following:

STARTER (2008-2009 AND 2011-2013 AERO MODELS, 2010-2013 SPIRIT MODELS AND ALL PHANTOM MODELS)

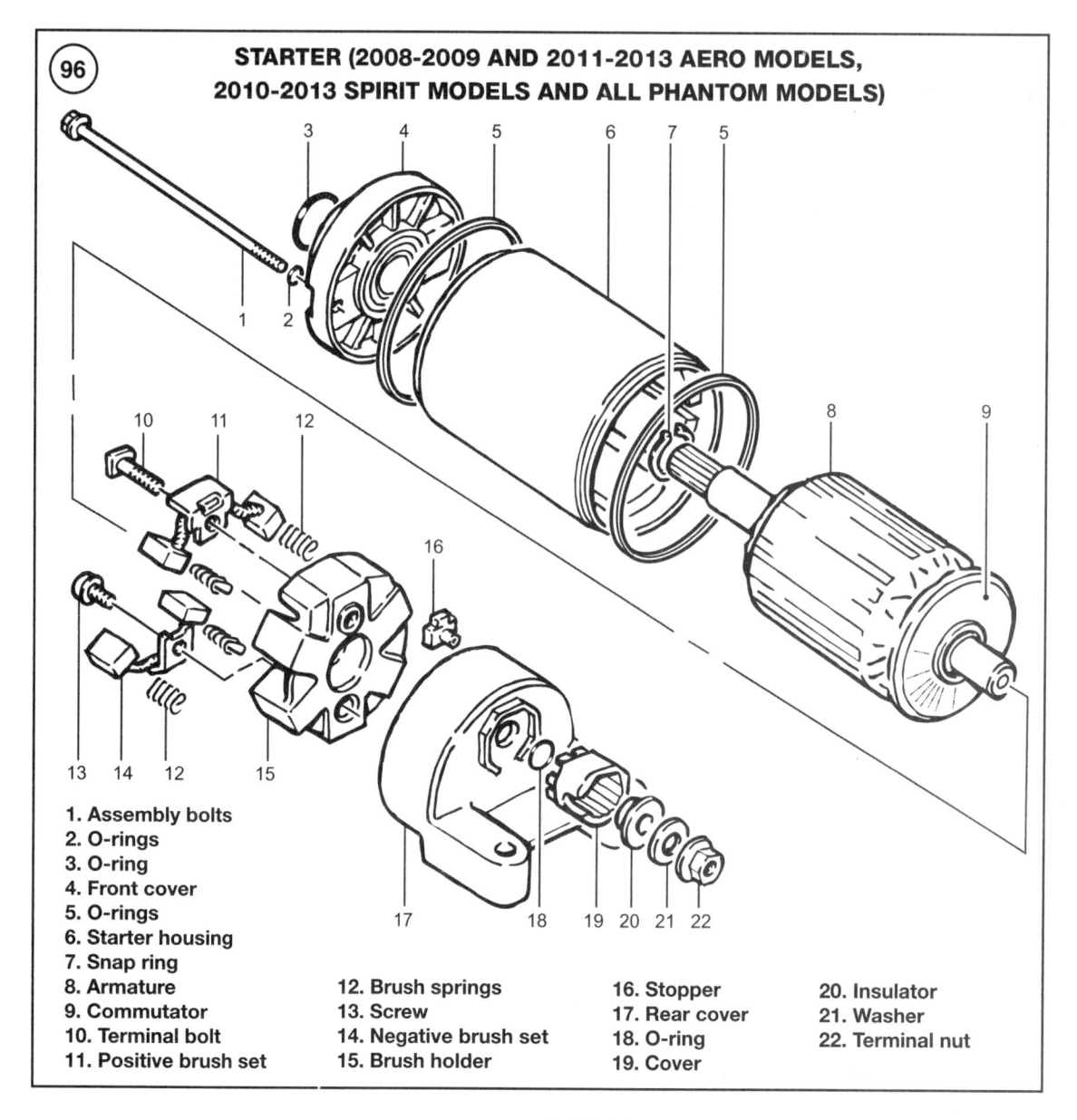

1. Assembly bolts
2. O-rings
3. O-ring
4. Front cover
5. O-rings
6. Starter housing
7. Snap ring
8. Armature
9. Commutator
10. Terminal bolt
11. Positive brush set
12. Brush springs
13. Screw
14. Negative brush set
15. Brush holder
16. Stopper
17. Rear cover
18. O-ring
19. Cover
20. Insulator
21. Washer
22. Terminal nut

a. Lubricate the starter O-ring (A, **Figure 95**) with grease.
b. Remove all corrosion from the starter cable.
c. Tighten the starter mounting bolts securely.
d. Tighten the starter cable nut to 10 N.m (89 in.-lb.).
e. Fit the boot securely over the starter terminal. Replace the boot if it is damaged or will not remain closed.
f. Operate the starter to make sure it works correctly.

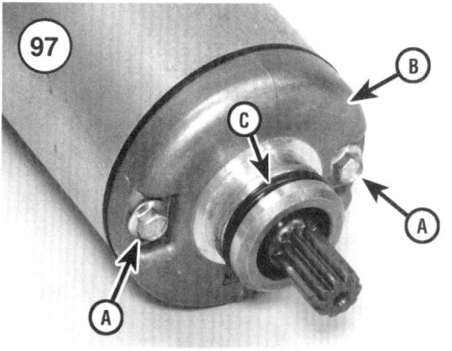

Disassembly

Refer to **Figure 96**.
1. Find the alignment marks (B, **Figure 95**) across the armature housing and both end covers. If necessary, scribe or paint the marks to identify them.
2. Remove the starter assembly bolts and O-rings (A, **Figure 97**). Then, remove the front cover (B) and its large O-ring (C).

ELECTRICAL SYSTEM

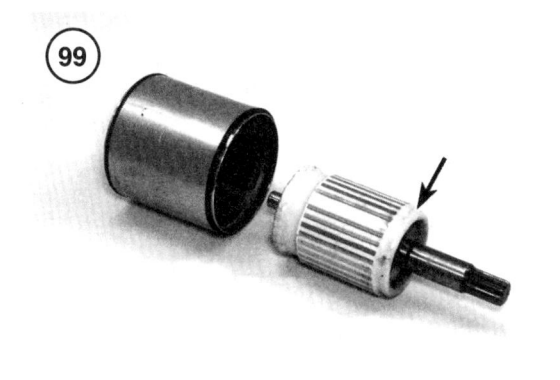

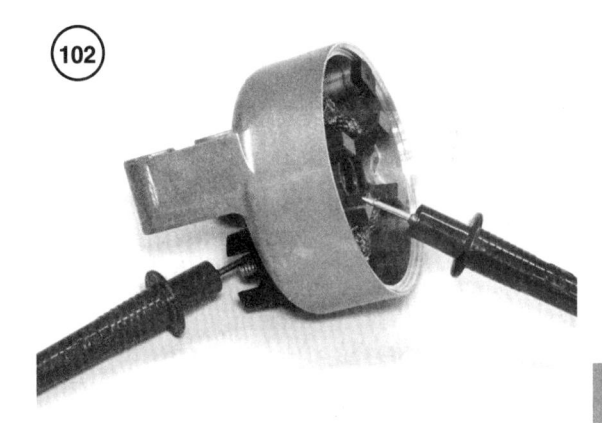

3. Remove the rear cover and brush assembly (**Figure 98**).
4. Hold the housing and remove the armature (**Figure 99**).

NOTE
Do not remove the seal from the front cover. It is not available as a replacement part.

5. Before removing the brush holder, test the positive (A, **Figure 100**) and negative (B) brushes and terminal bolt as follows:

a. Check for continuity between the positive and negative brushes (**Figure 101**). There should be no continuity. If there is continuity, check the brush holder for damage.
b. Check for continuity between the starter terminal and each positive brush (**Figure 102**). There should be continuity. If there is no continuity, replace the positive brush holder during reassembly.
c. Check for continuity between the positive brushes and the rear cover (**Figure 103**). There should be no continuity. If there is continuity, check the brush holder for damage.

d. Check for continuity between the negative brushes and the rear cover. There should be continuity. If there is no continuity, check for corrosion on the negative brush mounting screw (C, **Figure 100**),on the negative brush mounting tab and in the threaded hole in the rear cover.

e. Check for continuity between the cable terminal and starter housing. There should be no continuity. If there is continuity, check for a damaged or improperly installed O-ring and insulator. Also check for a damaged brush holder.

6. Remove the screw (A, **Figure 104**), the negative brush assembly (B) and the springs (A, **Figure 105**).
7. Remove the terminal nut (A, **Figure 106**), steel washer (B), insulator (C) and cover (D).
8. Remove the brush holder (B, **Figure 105**).
9. Remove the positive brush assembly **(Figure 107)** and springs from the brush holder.

Inspection

The armature, starter housing and end covers are not available separately.

1. The internal parts in a used starter are often contaminated with carbon and copper dust released from the brushes and commutator. Because a starter can be damaged from improper cleaning, note the following:
   a. Clean all parts (except the armature, starter housing and insulated washers in solvent. Use a rag lightly dampened with solvent to wipe off the armature and the starter housing (inside and outside).
   b. Use only fine-grade sandpaper to clean the brushes. Do not use emery cloth as its fibers may insulate the brushes.
   c. Use only crocus cloth to clean the commutator. Do not use emery cloth or sandpaper. Any abrasive material left on or embedded in the commutator may cause excessive brush wear. Do not leave any debris on or between the commutator bars.
2. Replace the starter housing O-rings if damaged.
3. Inspect the bushing (A, **Figure 108**) in the rear cover for wear or damage.
4. Inspect the bearing (B, **Figure 108**) and seal in the front cover for damage.

NOTE
The bushing, bearing and seals used in the end covers are not available separately.

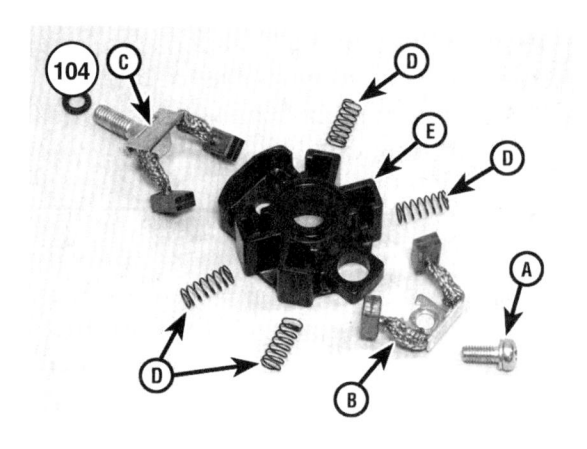

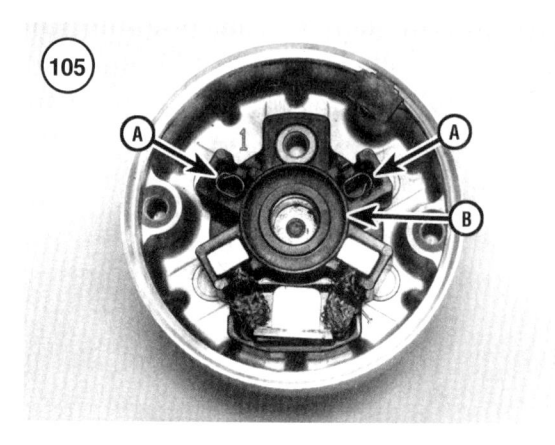

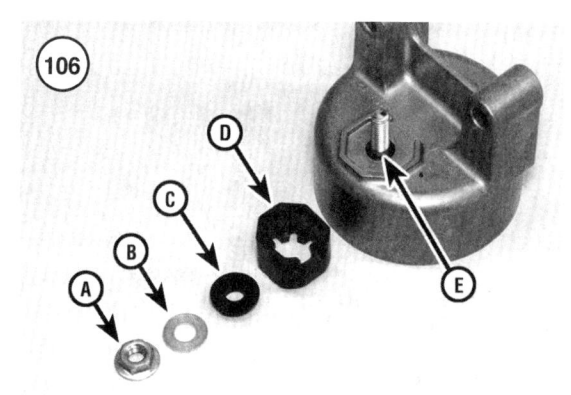

ELECTRICAL SYSTEM

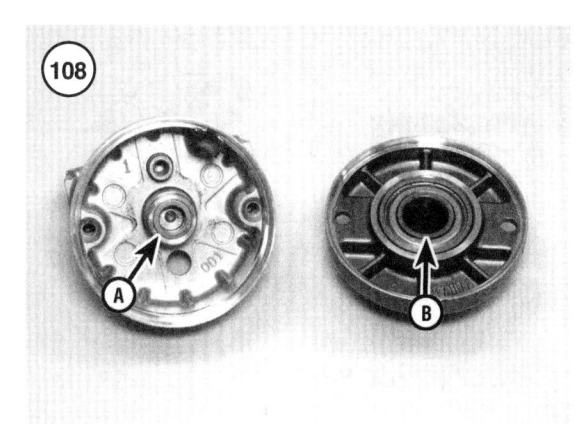

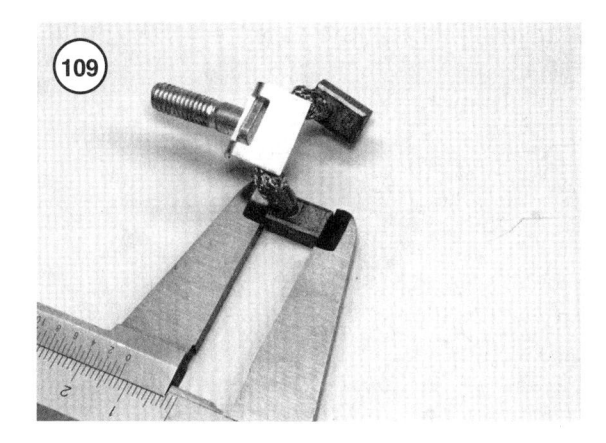

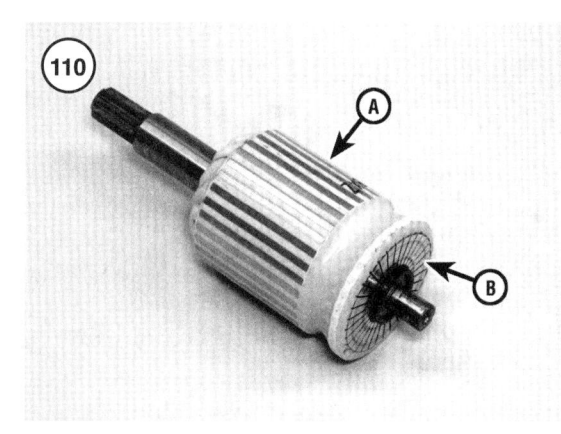

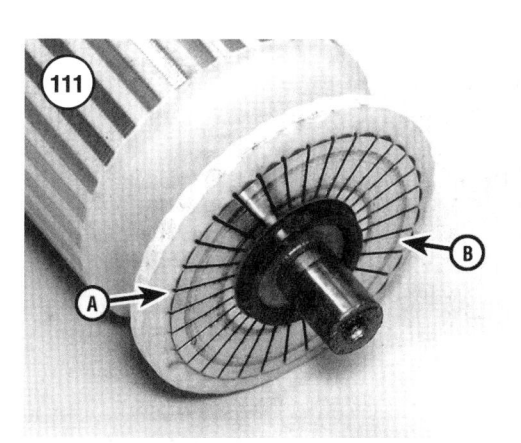

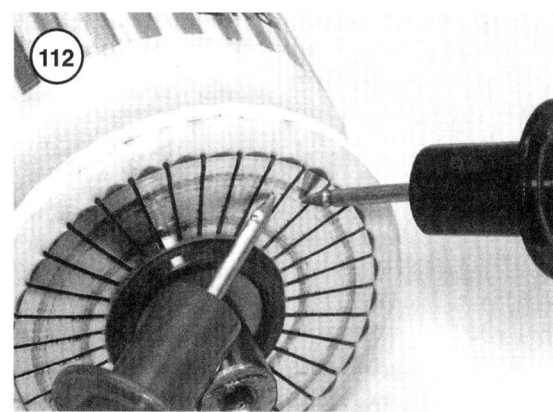

5. Inspect the brushes (B and C, **Figure 104**) as follows:
    a. Inspect each brush for cracks and other damage.
    b. Measure the length of each brush **(Figure 109)**. If the length of any one brush is out of specification **(Table 6)**, replace the positive and negative brushes as a set.
6. Inspect the brush springs (D, **Figure 104**) for weakness or damage. Replace all four brush springs as a set.
7. Inspect the brush holder (E, **Figure 104**) for cracks and other damage.
8. Inspect the armature (A, **Figure 110**) as follows:
    a. Inspect both shafts for scoring and other damage.
    b. Make sure the armature snap ring is installed in the shaft groove.
    c. Inspect the windings for obvious damage.
    d. To check the armature for a short circuit, have it tested on a growler. Refer this service to a dealership or an automotive electrical repair shop.
9. Inspect the commutator (B, **Figure 110**) as follows:
    a. Inspect the commutator bars for visual damage.
    b. Clean the commutator surface (this section).
    c. The mica levels (A, **Figure 111**) must be below the surface of the copper bars. On a worn commutator the mica and copper bars may be worn to the same level.
    d. If the mica level is too high or if its shape is too narrow or V-shaped, undercut the mica with a hacksaw blade. Grind the hacksaw blade to fit the mica groove.
    e. Inspect the commutator copper bars (B, **Figure 111**) for discoloration. If a pair of bars are discolored, grounded armature coils are indicated.
    f. Check for continuity across all adjacent pairs of commutator bars **(Figure 112)**. There should be continuity across all pairs of bars. If an open circuit exists between a pair of bars, replace the starter.

g. Check for continuity between the armature shaft and each commutator bar **(Figure 113)**. There should be no continuity. If there is continuity, replace the starter.

10. Inspect the starter housing for cracks or other damage. Then inspect for loose, chipped or damaged magnets.

Assembly

1. Install the positive brush springs and positive brush assembly into the brush holder **(Figure 107)**.
2. Install the brush holder (B, **Figure 105**) by aligning the mounting screw hole with the screw threads in the end cover.
3. Slide the O-ring (E, **Figure 106**) over the terminal bolt and center it in the bolt hole.
4. Install the cover (D, **Figure 106**) so that the open side faces in the direction shown in **Figure 114**.
5. Install the insulator (C, **Figure 106**), steel washer (B) and terminal nut (A).Tighten the terminal nut securely.
6. Install the negative brush springs (A, **Figure 105**) and the negative brush assembly (B, **Figure 104**).
7. Install the starter brush holder screw (A, **Figure 104**) and tighten to 3.7 N.m (33 in.-lb.).
8. Perform the continuity tests (this section) to check the brushes and terminal bolt for proper installation.
9. Install the armature into the starter housing so the commutator side (A, **Figure 115**) is on the same side as the notch (B) in the housing.
10. Install the two O-rings (C, **Figure 115**) into the housing shoulders.
11. Install the rear cover by inserting the shoulder on the plastic tab (A, **Figure 116**) into the notch in the housing (B). Check that the rear cover and housing alignment marks (B, **Figure 95**) align.
12. Install the front cover (B, **Figure 97**) by aligning the marks on the cover with the marks on the housing (B, **Figure 95**).
13. Install the starter assembly bolts and O-rings (A, **Figure 97**) and tighten to 5 N.m (44 in.-lb.).
14. Hold the starter and turn the armature shaft by hand. The armature should turn with some resistance, but should not bind or lockup. If the armature does not turn properly, disassemble the starter and check the shim, insulated washer and lockwasher alignment.
15. Use an auxiliary battery and apply battery voltage directly to the starter **(Figure 117)**. The starter should turn when battery voltage is directly applied. If the starter does not turn, disassemble and inspect it as described in this section.

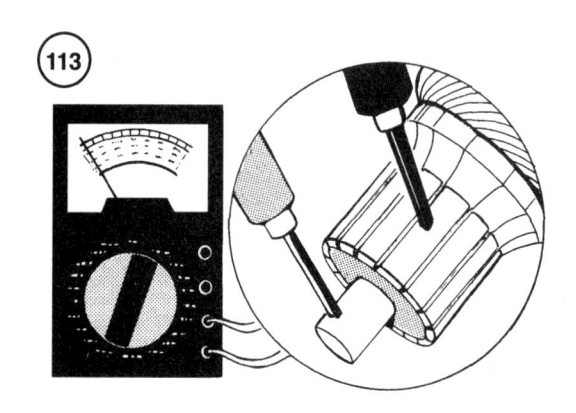

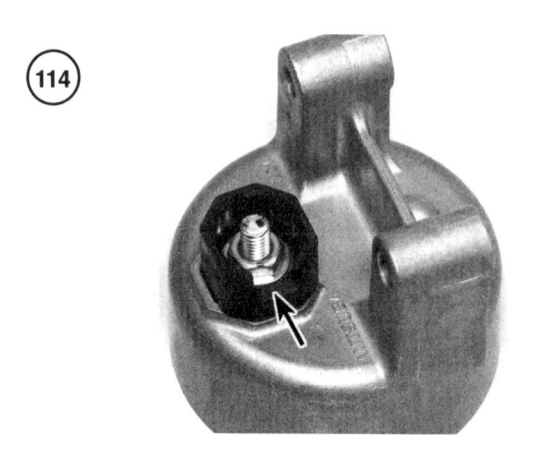

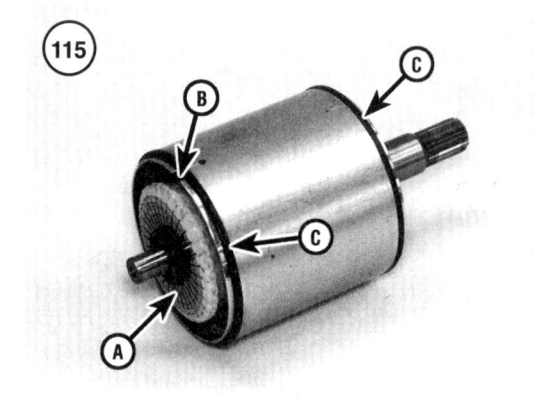

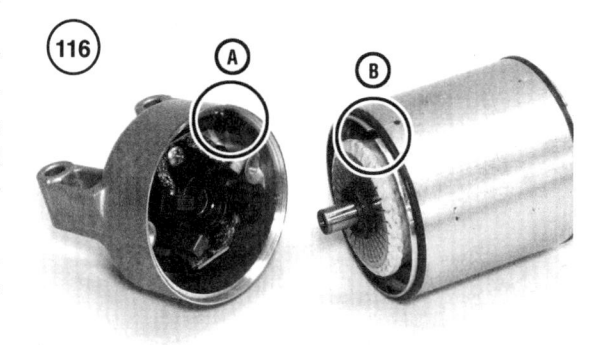

ELECTRICAL SYSTEM

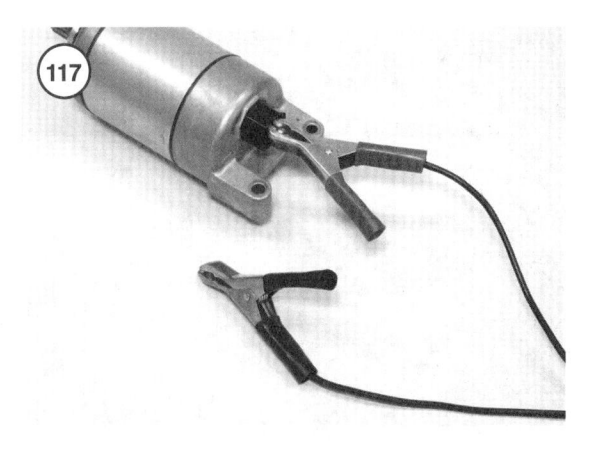

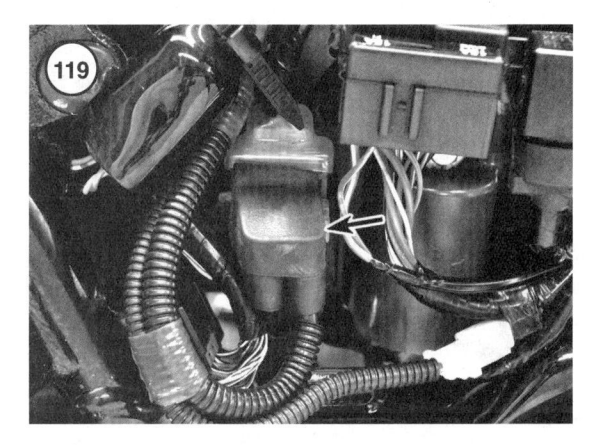

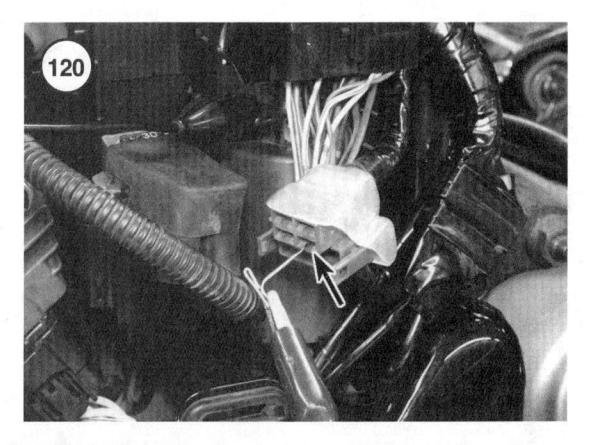

STARTER RELAY SWTICH

The starter relay switch is mounted behind the right side cover on non-ABS models; see **Figure 118** (carbureted models) or **Figure 119** (fuel injected models). The starter relay switch is mounted behind the left side cover on ABS models.

Starter Relay Switch

Testing

1. Refer to *Starter System Troubleshooting* in this chapter to test the starting circuit. If the problem has been isolated to the starter relay switch, perform the following test.
2A. On non-ABS models, remove the right side cover (Chapter Seventeen).
2B. On ABS models, remove the left side cover (Chapter Seventeen).
3. Shift the transmission into neutral.
4. Turn the ignition switch on and the engine stop switch to run and press the starter button. The starter relay should click. Note the following:
   a. If the starter relay clicked, the starter relay switch is okay.
   b. If the starter relay didn't click, continue the procedure.

NOTE
Use the wire colors in the connector to identify the terminals in the starter relay switch.

5. Disconnect the 4-pin connector at the starter relay switch (**Figure 118** or **Figure 119**). Clean or repair any dirty, loose fitting or damaged terminals in the connector or at the starter relay switch. If the terminals are in good condition, leave the connector disconnected and continue the procedure..

NOTE
There should also be continuity when the clutch is disengaged (clutch lever pulled in) and the sidestand is locked in its up position.

NOTE
Normally the ohmmeter will read 0 ohms when making a ground test. However, because of the diode placed in the circuit, it is normal for the ohmmeter to show a slight resistance reading when the transmission is shifted into neutral.

6. Ground line connection test: Shift the transmission into neutral. Check for continuity between the green/

red wire terminal in the starter relay switch connector (**Figure 120**, typical) and ground. There should be continuity or a slight resistance reading. Note the following:
   a. If there is continuity, continue the procedure.
   b. If there is no continuity, repair the open circuit in the green/red wire.
7. Starter relay switch voltage check: Reconnect the starter relay 4-pin connector. Turn the ignition switch on and measure voltage between the starter relay switch yellow/red wire (at the 4-pin connector [**Figure 121**, typical]) and ground when pressing the starter button. There should be battery voltage.
   a. If there is battery voltage, continue the procedure.
   b. If there is no battery voltage, repair the open circuit in the yellow/red wire.
8. Bench test the starter relay switch as follows:
   a. Remove the starter relay switch as described in this section. Clean the switch electrical contacts.
   b. Switch an ohmmeter to the R x 1 scale and connect its test leads across the two large leads on the starter relay switch (**Figure 122**, typical). There should be no continuity.
   c. If there is continuity, replace the starter relay switch.
   d. If there is no continuity, leave the ohmmeter connected to the switch and continue the procedure.
   e. Connect the positive lead from a fully-charged 12 volt battery to the starter relay switch yellow/red wire terminal and the negative battery lead to the green/red wire terminal (**Figure 122**, typical). There should be continuity.
   f. If there is no continuity, replace the starter relay switch.
   g. If there is continuity, the starter relay switch is operational. Reinstall the starter relay switch and check the wires and cables in the starting circuit.
9. Install the left (ABS models) or right (non-ABS models) side cover (Chapter Seventeen).

Removal/Installation

1. Remove the left (ABS models) or right (non-ABS models) side cover (Chapter Seventeen).
2. Disconnect the negative battery cable as described in this chapter
3. On carbureted models, remove the fuse box from its mounting position as described under *Fuses* in this chapter.
4. Label the connectors and cables before disconnecting them from the starter relay switch.
5. Disconnect the starter relay switch 4-pin connec-

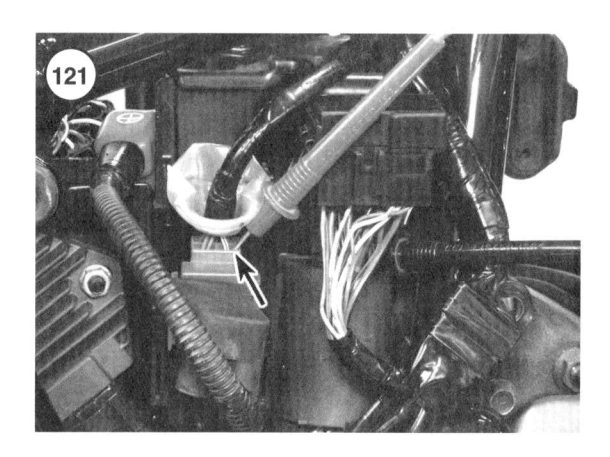

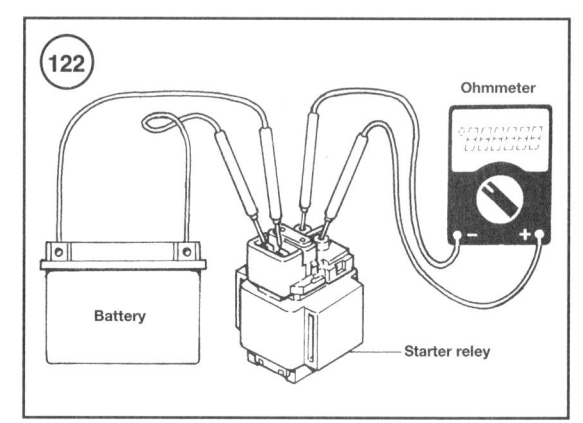

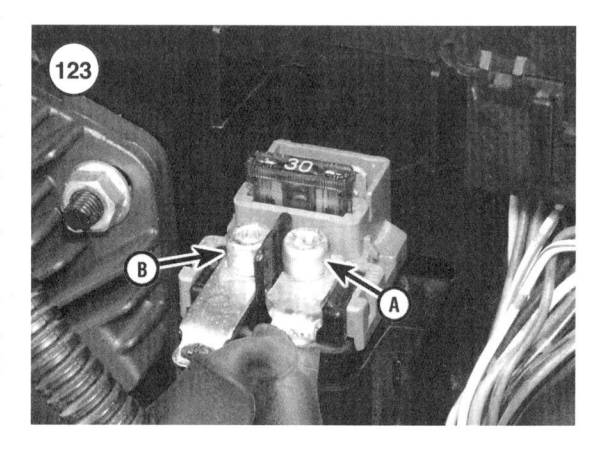

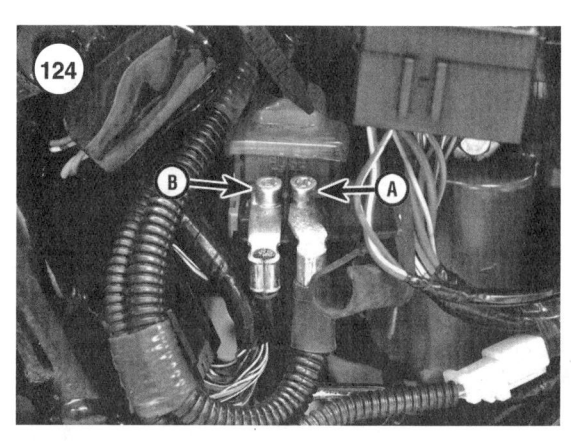

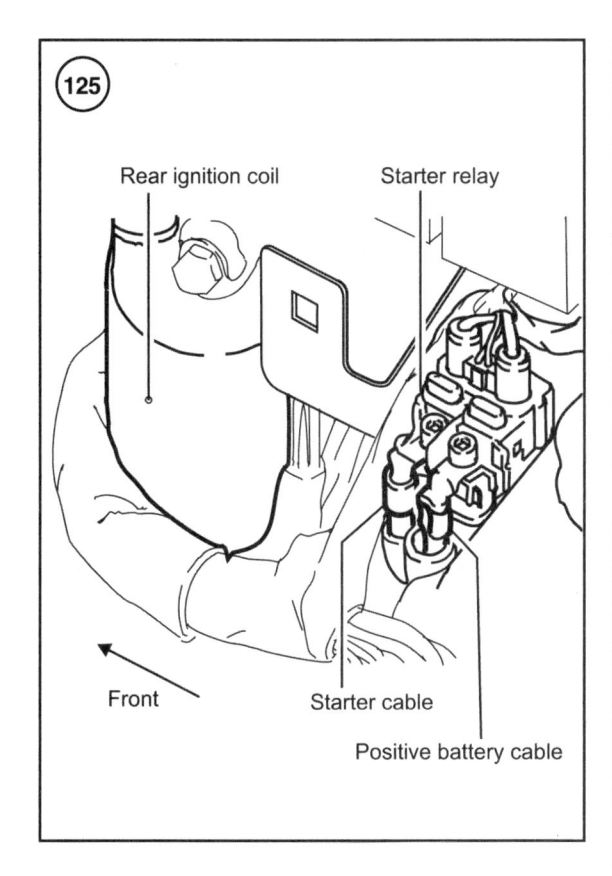

ELECTRICAL SYSTEM

125

Rear ignition coil
Starter relay
Front
Starter cable
Positive battery cable

126

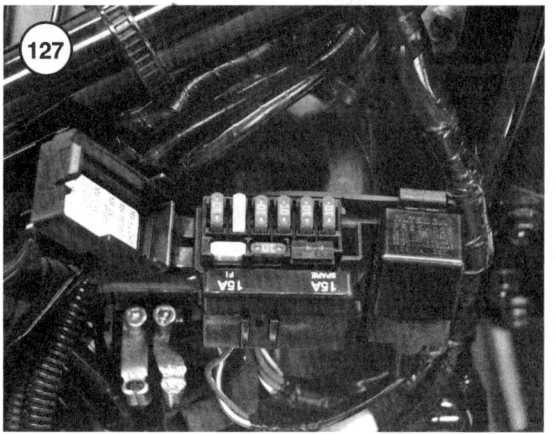

127

tor at the switch. See **Figure 118** (carbureted models) or **Figure 119** (fuel injected models).

6A. On carbureted models, disconnect the positive battery cable (A, **Figure 123**) and the starter cable (B) at the starter relay switch.

6B. On fuel injected models without ABS, disconnect the positive battery cable (A, **Figure 124**) and the starter cable (B) at the starter relay switch.

6C. On ABS models, disconnect the positive battery cable and the starter cable at the starter relay switch **(Figure 125)**.

7. Remove the starter relay switch from the frame.

8. Installation is the reverse of removal. Note the following:
   a. Clean the battery and starter cable leads before connecting them to the relay.
   b. Tighten the cable mounting bolts securely.

CLUTCH DIODE

The clutch diode is part of the starter circuit and is wired between the clutch switch and neutral switch. The diode prevents the flow of current from the neutral switch back through the clutch switch.

Suspect a faulty clutch diode if the neutral light comes on when the transmission is in gear and the clutch is disengaged. Also, look for a dirty or loose clutch diode connection if the starter does not operate when the transmission is in neutral.

Testing/Replacement

1A. On non-ABS models, remove the right side cover (Chapter Seventeen).

1B. On ABS models, remove the left side cover (Chapter Seventeen)

2. Open the fuse box cover and remove the diode from the fuse box. See **Figure 126** (carbureted models), **Figure 127** (fuel injected models without ABS) or **Figure 128** (ABS models).

3. Set an ohmmeter to the R x 1 scale.

4. Connect an ohmmeter test lead to the A terminal **(Figure 129)**. Touch the opposite ohmmeter test lead to the B, and then to the C terminals. Reverse the first test lead attached to the A terminal and check continuity in the opposite direction at the B, and then the C terminals. Each pair of connections should have continuity in one direction and no continuity when the test leads are reversed.

5. Replace the diode if it fails any part of this test.

6. Install the diode by aligning the raised tab on the diode with the slot in the fuse box.

128 **FUSE BOX (ABS MODELS)**

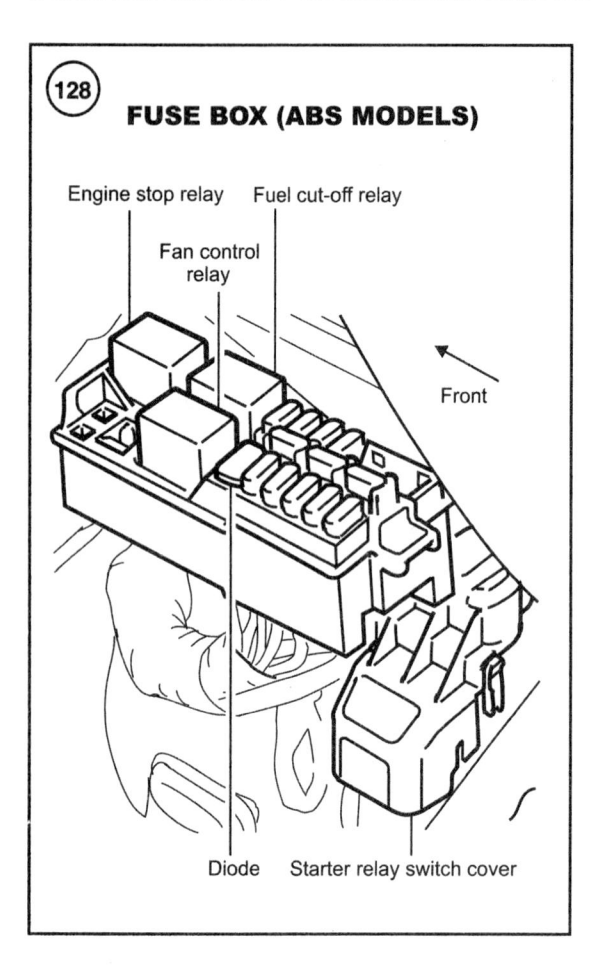

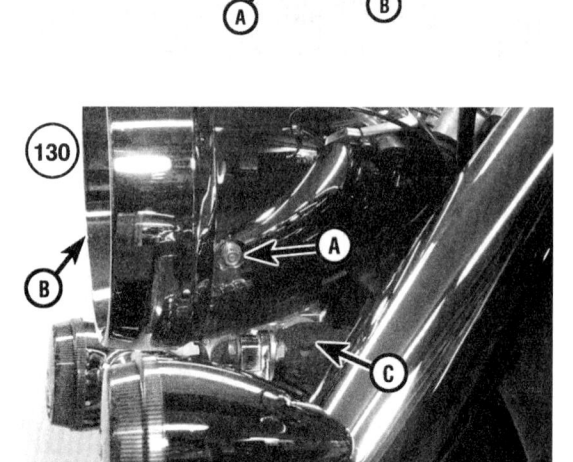

LIGHTING SYSTEM

Refer to **Table 7** for bulb specifications. Always use the correct wattage of bulb. Using the wrong size bulb gives a dim light or causes the bulb to burn out prematurely.

Always turn the ignition switch off before servicing the lighting components.

NOTE
Handle the wiring harnesses carefully when removing lighting components in this section. It is easy to strip the wires when sliding them past guides and other components, which would expose bare wire to frame components. This could cause a short circuit.

Headlight Unit Removal/Installation (Bulb Replacement)

WARNING
If the headlight just burned out or it was just turned off it will be hot! Do not touch the bulb until it cools off.

CAUTION
All models use a quartz-halogen bulb. Because traces of oil on the glass will reduce the life of the bulb, do not touch the bulb glass. Clean any oil or other chemicals from the bulb glass with an alcohol-moistened cloth.

1. Place a towel on the front fender.
2A. On Aero models, remove the two bolts (A, **Figure 130**) and the headlight (B) from the housing. Remove the collars if they are loose in the headlight housing.
2B. On Spirit and Phantom models, perform the following:
   a. On Phantom models, loosen or remove the front turn signal light bolt.
   b. Remove the two bolts (A, **Figure 131**) and the headlight (B) from the housing.
3. Disconnect the electrical connector (A, **Figure 132**) at the bulb and remove the headlight unit.
4. Remove the dust cover (B, **Figure 132**) from around the bulb.
5. Unhook the bulb retainer (A, **Figure 133**) and remove the bulb (B).
6. Install the bulb and headlight unit by reversing

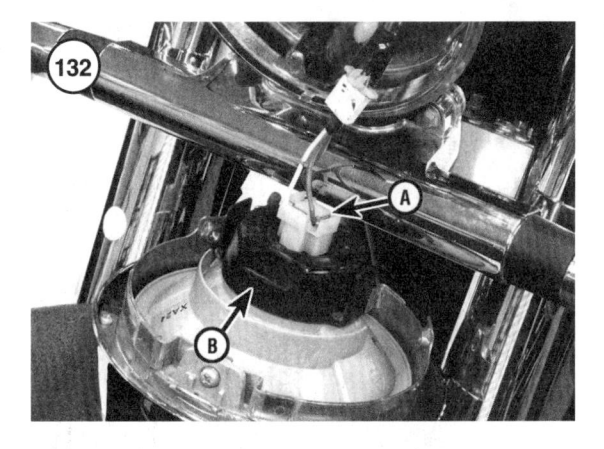

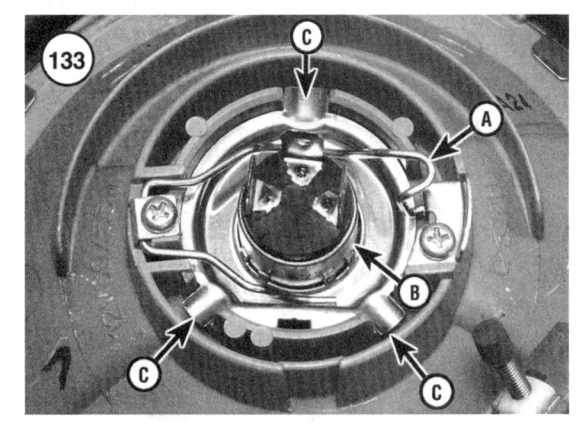

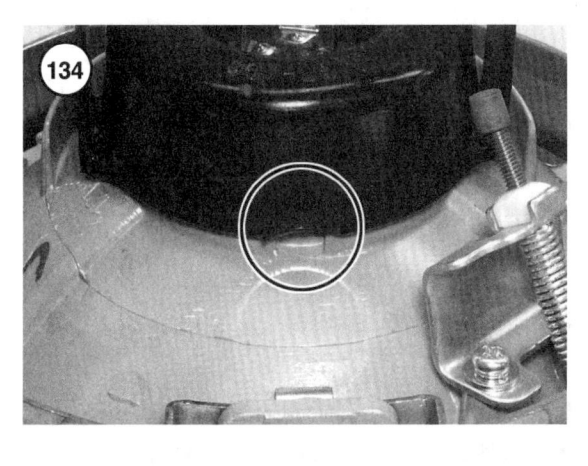

ELECTRICAL SYSTEM

these removal steps, while noting the following:
  a. Align the tabs on the bulb with the notches in the bulb holder (C, **Figure 133**) and install the bulb (B).
  b. Install the dust cover completely with its "TOP" mark at the top of the headlight unit. Then check that the vent on the bottom of the dust cover aligns with the notch in the headlight unit **(Figure 134)**.
  c. Hook the tab at the top of the headlight unit **(Figure 135)** into the retainer at the top of the headlight housing.
  d. Then pivot the headlight unit into the housing and install the two bolts.
  e. On Aero models, tighten the bolts to 3.9 Nm (35 in-lbs.).
  f. On Spirit models and Phantom models, tighten the bolts to 4.1 Nm (36 in-lb.).
  g. Turn the ignition switch on and check the headlight operation. If necessary, perform the *Headlight Adjustment* in this section.

Headlight Adjustment

Adjust the headlight as follows or according to local regulations if they differ from the following:
1. Check tire inflation pressure (Chapter Three).
2. Park the motorcycle on a level surface 7.6 m (25 ft.) from a wall.
3. Draw a horizontal line on the wall the same height as the center of the headlight **(Figure 136)**.
4. Have an assistant (with the same approximate weight as the primary rider) sit on the seat.
5. Turn the ignition switch on and the light switch to HIGH beam. Turn the handlebars so they point straight ahead and the beam is centered with the horizontal mark on the wall.
6. Check the headlight beam alignment. The broad, flat pattern of light (main beam of light) must be centered on the horizontal light with an equal area of light above and below the line **(Figure 136)**.

136 HEADLIGHT ADJUSTMENT

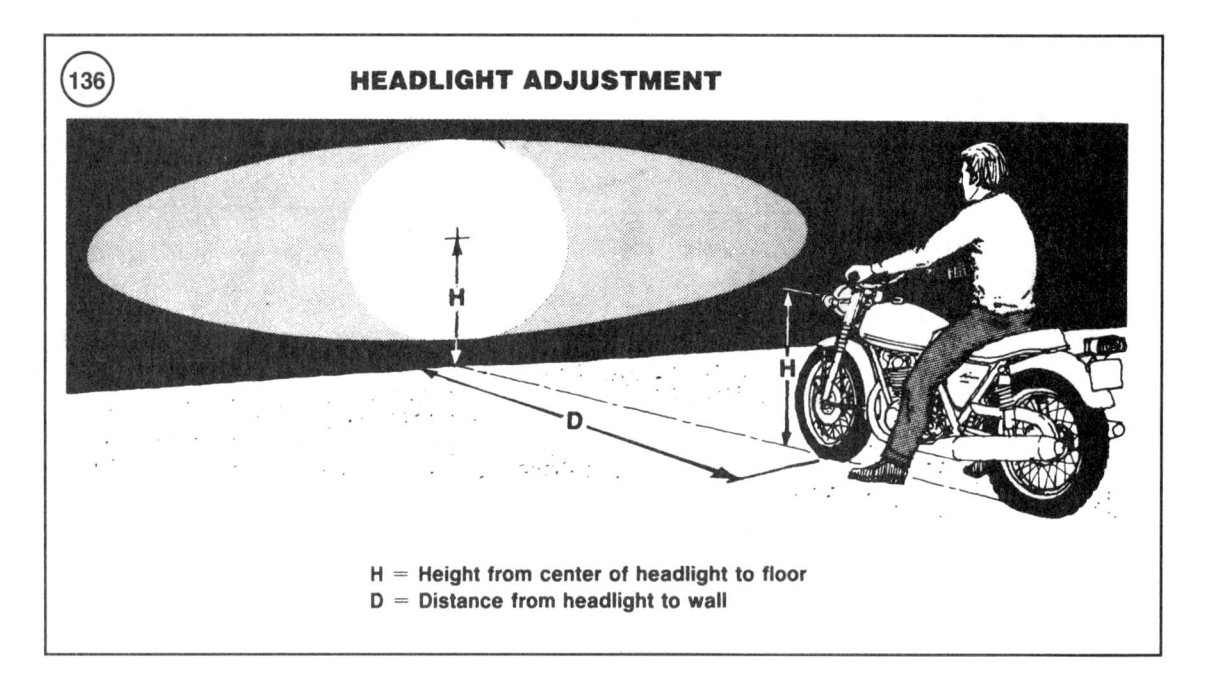

H = Height from center of headlight to floor
D = Distance from headlight to wall

7. Check the headlight beam lateral alignment. With the front wheel pointed straight ahead, there should be an equal area of light to the left and right of center.
8A. On Aero models, if the beam is incorrect, adjust it as follows:
   a. To adjust the headlight vertically, loosen the bolt/nut (C, **Figure 130**) below the headlight housing on the left side and reposition the headlight unit. Tighten the bolt/nut to 12 N.m (106 in.-lb.).
   b. To adjust the headlight horizontally, turn the screw on the right side of the headlight housing (**Figure 137**).
8B. On Spirit models, if the beam is incorrect, adjust it as follows:
   a. To adjust the headlight vertically, turn the left adjusting screw (**Figure 138**).
   b. To adjust the headlight horizontally, turn the right adjusting screw (**Figure 138**).
8C. On Phantom models, if the beam is incorrect, adjust it as follows:
   a. To adjust the headlight vertically, turn the right adjusting screw.
   b. To adjust the headlight horizontally, turn the left adjusting screw.

Headlight Housing Removal/Installation

1. Remove the headlight unit as described in this section.
2. Disconnect the connectors mounted inside the headlight housing.

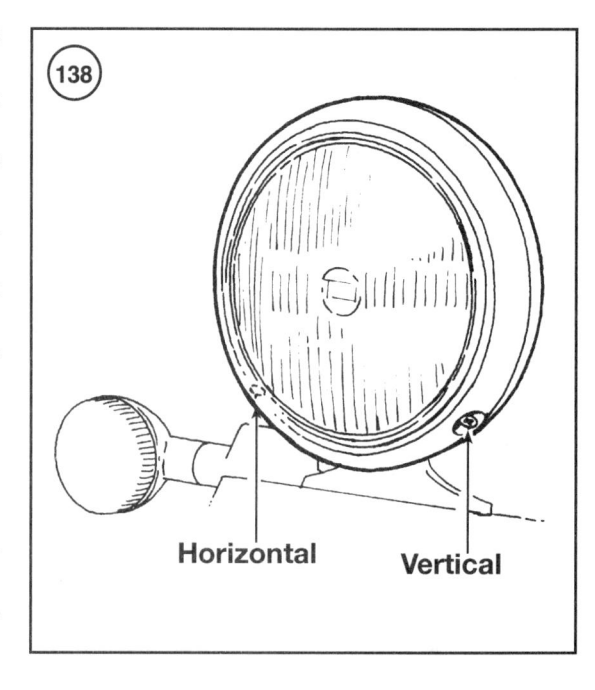

ELECTRICAL SYSTEM

c. Check the headlight adjustment as described in this chapter.

Turn Signal Bulb Replacement

1. Remove the screws, lens and gasket.
2. Replace the gasket if damaged.
3. Push the bulb in and turn it counterclockwise to remove it (**Figure 140**, typical).
4. Installation is the reverse of removal. Note the following:
    a. Push the bulb in and turn it clockwise to secure it in the housing.
    b. Install the lens and tighten the screw to Nm (8.9 in-lb.) on Aero models. Tighten the screw securely on all other models, but do not overtighten or the lens may be damaged.

Front Turn Signal Assembly Removal/Installation

Aero Models

1. Note the wiring harness routing from the turn signal to the headlight housing.
2. Remove the headlight unit (this chapter) and disconnect the turn signal connectors located inside the headlight housing. See **Figure 141**, typical.
3. Release the wiring harness from the clamp and pull the harness out of the headlight housing.
4. Remove the bolts, washers and collars securing the turn signal cover assembly to the mounting bracket and remove the turn signal cover assembly.
5. To remove the turn signal from the cover assembly, remove the screws securing the mounting bracket to the cover assembly. Then remove the Allen bolt securing the mounting bracket to the turn signal.
6. Installation is the reverse of these steps, plus the following:
    a. Install the turn signal onto the mounting bracket by aligning the tab on the turn signal with the slot in the mounting bracket.
    b. Tighten the Allen bolt securing the mounting bracket to the turn signal to 5 Nm (45 in-lb.).
    c. Tighten all remaining fasteners securely.
    d. Route the wiring harness correctly and secure it with the clamp.
    e. Reconnect the turn signal connectors. The left turn signal wiring harness connector is orange. The right turn signal wiring harness connector is light blue.
    f. Turn the ignition switch on and check the operation of both front turn signals and the headlight.

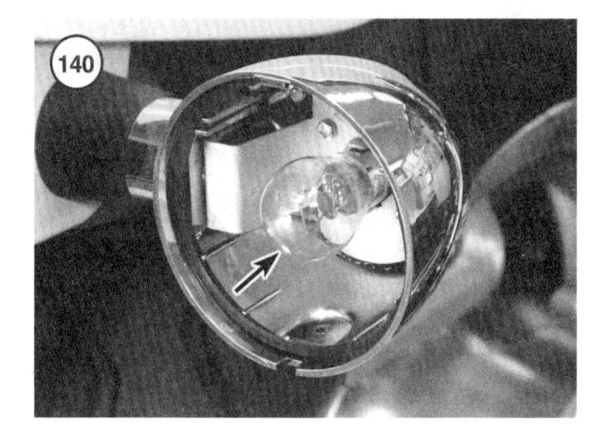

3. Note how the wire harness clamps are installed and routed inside the headlight housing.
4. Remove the nuts and bolts (**Figure 139**, typical) securing the headlight housing to the mounting bracket and remove the headlight housing.
5. Installation is the reverse of removal. Note the following:
    a. On Aero models, tighten the headlight housing mounting nuts to 12 N.m (106 in.-lb.). On all other models, tighten the nuts securely.
    b. Turn the ignition switch on and check the operation of all switches and indicators.

Spirit and Phantom Models

1. Note the wiring harness routing from the turn signal to the headlight housing.
2. Remove the headlight unit (this chapter) and disconnect the turn signal connectors located inside the headlight housing. See **Figure 141**, typical.
3. Release the wiring harness from the clamp and pull the harness out of the headlight housing.
4. Remove the bolt and collar and remove the turn signal assembly from the fork tube.
5. Installation is the reverse of these steps, plus the following:
    a. Install the turn signal by aligning the pin on the inside of the turn signal clamp with the hole in the mounting bracket on the lower fork bridge.
    b. Tighten all mounting fasteners securely.
    c. Route the wiring harness correctly and secure it with the clamp.
    d. Reconnect the turn signal connectors. The left turn signal wiring harness connector is orange. The right turn signal wiring harness connector is light blue.
    e. Turn the ignition switch on and check the operation of both front turn signals and the headlight.

Rear Turn Signal Assembly
Removal/Installation

Aero Models

1. Remove the rear fender (Chapter Seventeen).
2. Remove the turn signal wiring harness from the clamps on the rear fender.
3. Remove the Allen bolt and the rear turn signal assembly from the grab rail.
4. Installation is the reverse of removal, plus the following:
    a. Install the turn signal by aligning the tab on the turn signal with the slot in the grab rail.
    b. Install the Allen bolt securing the turn signal assembly to the grab rail. Tighten the Allen bolt to the specification in **Table 10**.
    c. Turn the ignition switch on and check the operation of both rear turn signal lights.

Spirit and Phantom Models

1. Remove the rear frame/rear fender A (Chapter Seventeen).
2. Carefully remove the turn signal wiring harnesses from the clamps on the rear frame.
3. Remove the bolt securing the turn signal to the rear frame and remove the turn signal assembly.

4. Installation is the reverse of removal, plus the following:
    a. Install the turn signal by aligning the shoulder on the turn signal with the hole in the rear frame.
    b. Tighten the turn signal assembly mounting bolt securely.
    c. Turn the ignition switch on and check the operation of both rear turn signal lights.

Tail/Brake Light
Bulb Replacement

WARNING
Do not ride the motorcycle until the taillight and brake light operate properly.

Aero Models

1. Remove the screws, lens **(Figure 142)** and gasket.
2. Replace the gasket if damaged.
3. Push the bulb in and turn it counterclockwise to remove it.
4. Install the new bulb and lens by reversing these steps. Note the following:
    a. Tighten the lens screws securely, but do not overtighten the screws or the lens may crack.
    b. Turn the ignition switch on and check the taillight and brake light operation.

Spirit and Phantom Models

1. Remove the lens screws. Then push the lens (A, **Figure 143**) down to release its upper mounting tabs from the housing and remove the lens and gasket.
2. Replace the gasket if damaged.
3. Push the bulb in and turn it counterclockwise to remove it.
4. Install the new bulb and lens by reversing these

ELECTRICAL SYSTEM

following:
  a. Tighten the nuts securing the tail/brake light housing to the specification in **Table 10**.
  b. Turn the ignition switch on and check the taillight and brake light operation.

Spirit and Phantom Models

1. Remove the rear frame/rear fender A (Chapter Seventeen).
2. Carefully remove the tail/brake light wiring harness from the clamps on the rear frame.
3. Disconnect the license light connector and remove its wiring harness from the rear fender A.
4. Remove the nuts and collars securing the tail/brake light housing to the rear fender and remove the housing.
5. Installation is the reverse of these steps. Note the following:
  a. Tighten the nuts securing the tail/brake light housing to the specification in **Table 10**.
  b. Turn the ignition switch on and check the taillight and brake light operation.

License Plate Light Bulb Replacement

1. Remove the screws, lens and gasket. See **Figure 144** (Aero) or B, **Figure 143** (Spirit and Phantom).
2. Replace the gasket if damaged.
3. Pull the bulb **(Figure 145)** straight out to remove it from its socket.
4. Install the new bulb and lens by reversing these steps. Note the following:
  a. Tighten the lens screws, but do not overtighten the screws or the lens may crack.
  b. Turn the ignition switch on and check the license plate light operation.

License Plate Light Housing Removal/Installation

Aero Models

1. Working inside the rear fender, remove the nuts, collars and rubber washer securing the license plate housing to the rear fender.
2. Partially remove the license plate housing, then disconnect the license plate connector and remove the housing.
3. To remove the license plate light housing from the plate housing:
  a. Remove the license plate from the reflector bracket.
  b. Remove the license plate light bulb as described in this section.

steps. Note the following:
  a. Tighten the lens screws securely, but do not overtighten the screws or the lens may crack.
  b. Turn the ignition switch on and check the tail-light and brake light operation.

Tail/Brake Light Housing Replacement

Aero Models

1. Remove the rear fender (Chapter Seventeen).
2. Remove the license plate light (this section).
3. Release the wiring harness from the clamps on the inside of the rear fender.
4. Remove the nuts and collars securing the tail/brake light housing to the rear fender and remove the housing.
5. Installation is the reverse of these steps. Note the

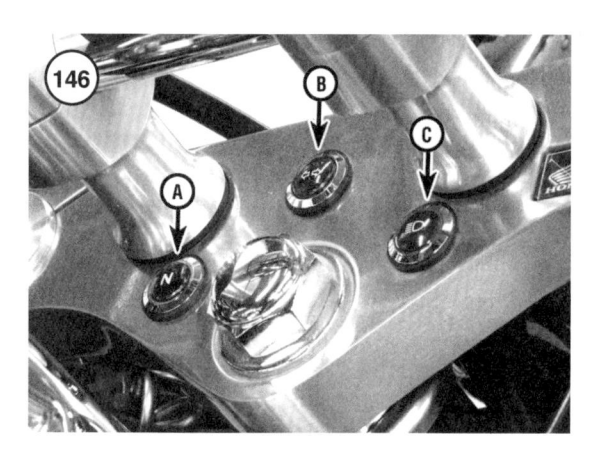

c. Unbolt and remove the reflector bracket from the license light bracket.
d. Remove the bolts securing the license plate light bracket to its mounting bracket.
e. Remove the nuts and remove the license plate light housing.

4. Installation is the reverse of removal. Note the following:
   a. Tighten the fasteners securely.
   b. Turn the ignition switch on and check the license light operation.

2007-2009 Spirit Models

1. Remove the rear frame/rear fender A (Chapter Seventeen).
2. Disconnect the 2-pin license plate light connector from rear fender A.
3. Remove the nuts, collars, clamp and license plate light.
4. Installation is the reverse of removal. Note the following:
   a. Tighten the nuts securely.
   b. Turn the ignition switch on and check the license light operation.

2010-2013 Spirit Models and all Phantom Models

The license plate light housing is integral with the rear fender assembly.

UPPER FORK BRIDGE INDICATOR LIGHTS (2008-2009 AND 2011-2013 AERO MODELS, 2012-2013 SPIRIT AND PHANTOM MODELS)

The following indicator lights are located in the upper fork bridge:
   a. 2008-2009 Aero: Neutral indicator (A, **Figure 146**), Turn signal indicator (B) and high beam indicator (C).

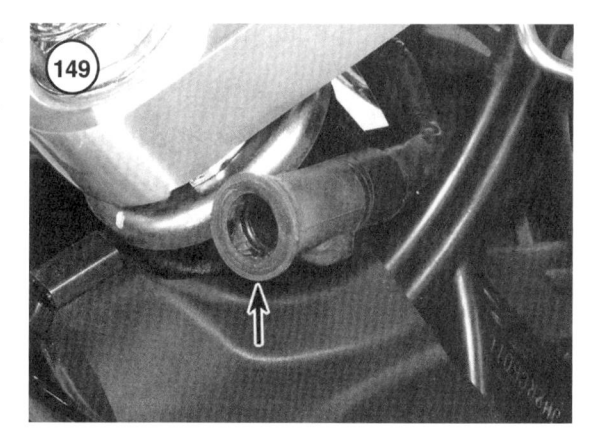

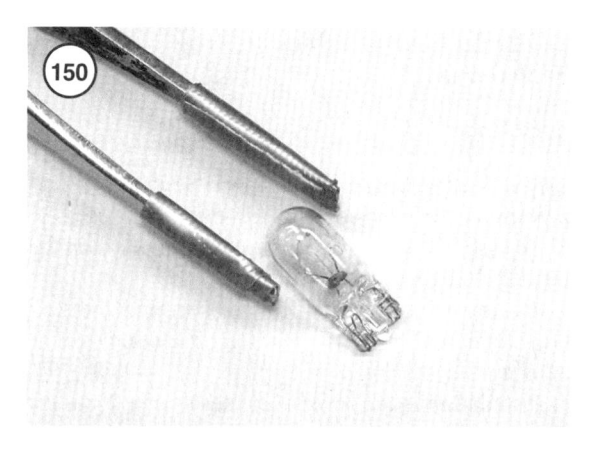

ELECTRICAL SYSTEM

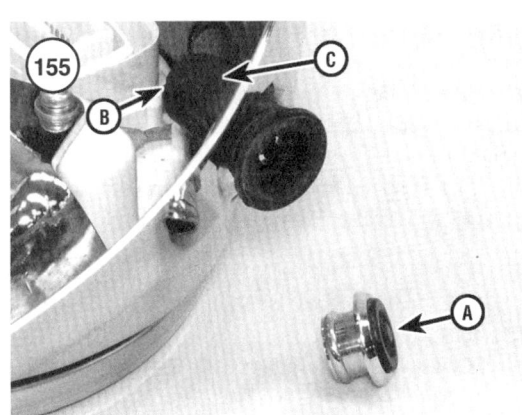

b. 2011-2013 Aero and Phantom: Fuel reserve indicator (A, **Figure 147**), turn signal indicator (B) and high beam indicator (C).
c. 2012-2013 Spirit: Fuel reserve indicator and high beam indicator.

Replacement

1. Turn the ignition switch off.
2. Carefully pry the lens out of the bulb holder **(Figure 148)**.
3. Twist and remove the bulb holder out of the upper fork bridge **(Figure 149)**.
4. Use padded tweezers to remove the bulb from the bulb holder **(Figure 150)**.
5. Installation is the reverse of removal. Note the following:
    a. Make sure the lens and bulb holder are securely installed in the fork bridge.
    b. Turn the ignition switch on and check the indicator operation.

SPEEDOMETER

The speedometer is mounted on the fuel tank and consists of the speedometer and reset switch. LED's provide illumination for the speedometer.

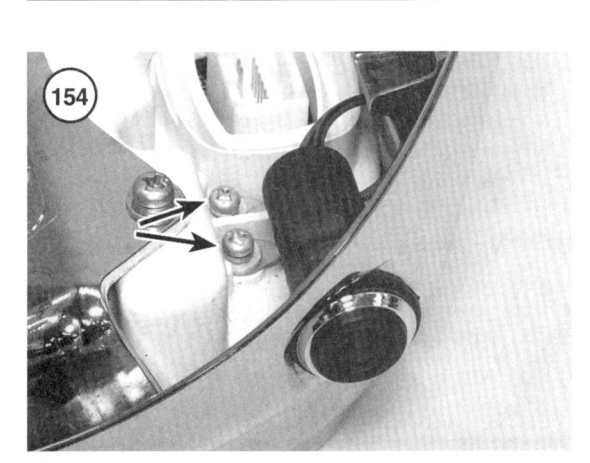

Speedometer Housing Removal/Installation

1. Turn the ignition switch off.
2. Remove the mounting bolts and lift the speedometer housing off the fuel tank. See **Figure 151** (Aero and Spirit) or **Figure 152** (Phantom).
3. Turn the speedometer housing over. Slide the dust cover away from the connector and disconnect the connector (A, **Figure 153**).
4. Replace the damper (B, **Figure 153**) if missing or damaged.
5. Inspect the speedometer wiring harness for damage.

6. Reconnect the speedometer connector (A, **Figure 153**).
7. Slide the dust cover over the connector. Make sure the dust cover completely covers the connector to protect it from dust and water.
8. Install the speedometer by inserting its slot (C, **Figure 153**) over the damper (B).

CAUTION
After installing the speedometer, make sure the wiring harness is properly routed and not pinched between the speedometer and fuel tank.

9. Install the speedometer housing mounting bolts and tighten to 10 N.m (89 in.-lb.).
10. Turn the ignition switch on and check the speedometer indicator lights.

Reset Switch Testing/Replacement

1. Remove the speedometer housing as described in this section.
2. Remove the reset switch mounting screws (A, **Figure 154**).
3. Remove the reset switch button (B, **Figure 154**) from the switch. See A, **Figure 155**.
4. Remove the reset switch from inside the housing (B, **Figure 155**).
5. Test the reset switch as follows:
   a. Connect an ohmmeter across the switch wires **(Figure 156)**.
   b. The ohmmeter should read infinity when the switch button is free.
   c. The ohmmeter should read continuity when the switch button is pushed.
   d. Replace the reset switch if it fails either test.
6. Installation is the reverse of removal. Install the reset switch with its alignment boss (C, **Figure 155**) facing down (toward the fuel tank).

Speedometer Removal/Installation

1. Remove the speedometer housing as described in this section.
2. Remove the reset switch mounting screws (A, **Figure 154**).
3. Remove the screws (A, **Figure 157**) and clamp (B) securing the speedometer to the housing and remove the speedometer.
4. Replace the O-ring **(Figure 158)** if leaking or damaged.
5. Installation is the reverse of removal. Tighten the mounting screws securely.

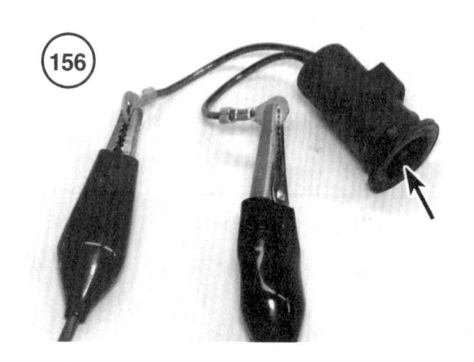

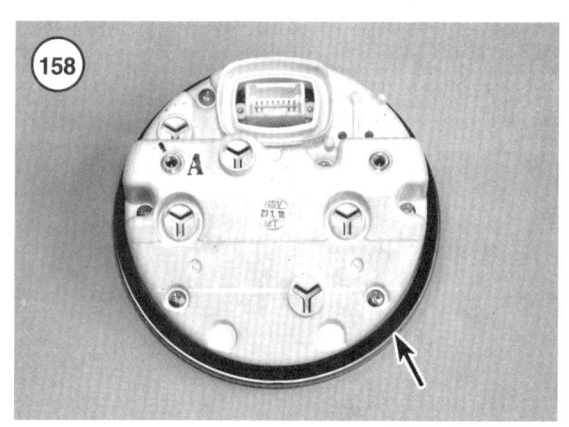

Power/Ground Circuit Test

NOTE
Refer to the appropriate wiring diagram at the end of the manual to identify the electrical connectors referred to in this procedure.

Refer to **Figures 159-161**.
If none of the indicators on the speedometer work correctly, perform the following:
1. Check for a blown taillight/meter fuse as described in this chapter. If the fuse is okay, continue with Step 2.
2. Remove the speedometer housing as described in this section.

ELECTRICAL SYSTEM

159
SPEEDOMETER WIRING HARNESS CONNECTOR (NON-ABS AERO MODELS)

2004-2009 MODELS

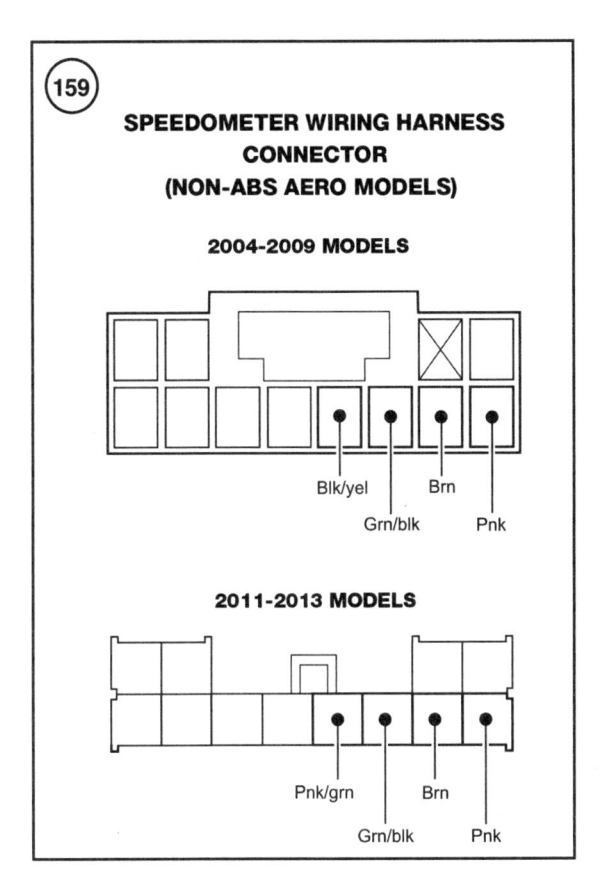

- Blk/yel
- Grn/blk
- Brn
- Pnk

2011-2013 MODELS

- Pnk/grn
- Grn/blk
- Brn
- Pnk

160
SPEEDOMETER WIRING HARNESS CONNECTOR (NON-ABS SPIRIT AND PHANTOM MODELS)

2007-2009 MODELS

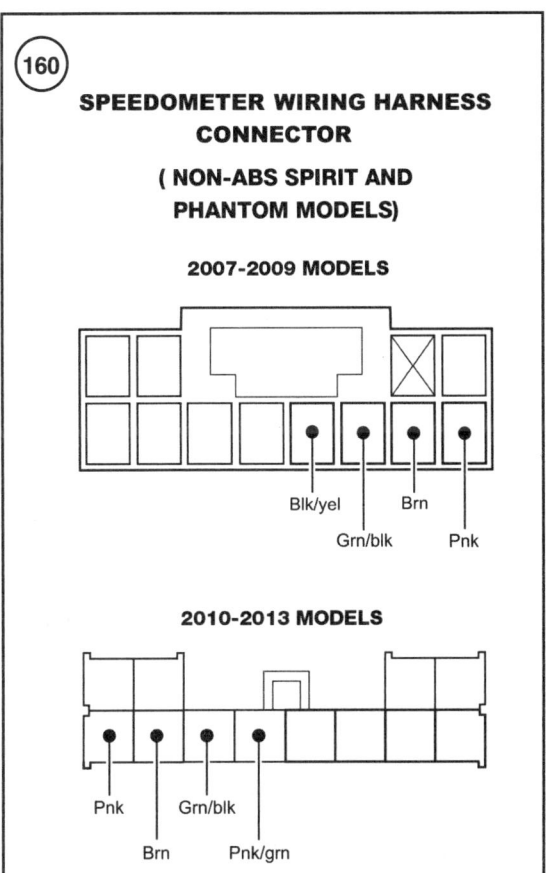

- Blk/yel
- Grn/blk
- Brn
- Pnk

2010-2013 MODELS

- Pnk
- Brn
- Grn/blk
- Pnk/grn

161
SPEEDOMETER WIRING HARNESS CONNECTOR (ABS MODELS)

2011-2013 AERO MODELS

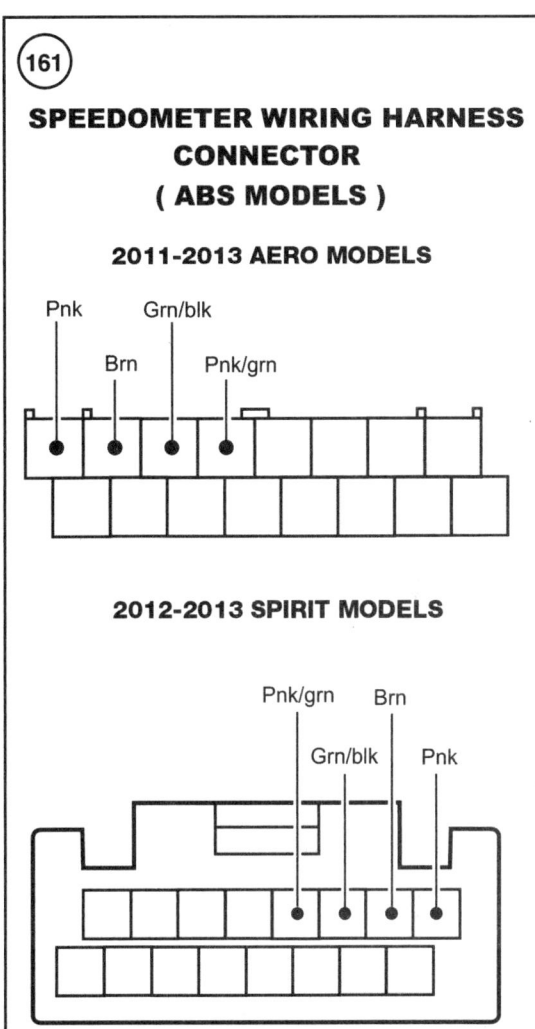

- Pnk
- Brn
- Grn/blk
- Pnk/grn

2012-2013 SPIRIT MODELS

- Pnk/grn
- Grn/blk
- Brn
- Pnk

3. To test the power line circuit, turn the ignition switch on and measure voltage between the brown wire terminal (+) in the speedometer wiring harness connector and ground (-). There should be battery voltage.

   a. If there is battery voltage, skip to Step 5.

   b. If there is no battery voltage, and the fuse is okay, check the brown wire for an open circuit.

4. To test the ground line circuit, check for resistance between the green/black wire terminal in the speedometer wiring harness connector and ground. If there is no continuity, check the green/black wire for an open circuit.

NOTE
Check voltage if the odometer/trip meter does not work.

5. Measure voltage between the pink wire terminal (+) in the speedometer wiring harness connector and ground (-). There should be battery voltage at all times (ignition switch on and off). If there is no battery voltage, perform the following:
   a. Check for a blown odometer fuse as described in this chapter.
   b. Check for an open circuit in the pink wire between the speedometer 7-pin connector and the fuse box.
   c. Check for an open circuit in the red wire between the fuse box and battery.
6. Reinstall the speedometer housing (this section).

Speedometer Test

Refer to **Figures 159-161**.

If the speedometer does not operate, perform the following:

NOTE
Refer to the appropriate wiring diagram at the end of the manual to identify the electrical connectors referred to in this procedure.

1A. If none of the indicators on the speedometer work correctly, perform the *Power/Ground Circuit Test* (this section).
1B. If the indicators work correctly, continue the procedure.
2. Remove the speedometer housing as described in this chapter.
3. Support the motorcycle with the rear wheel off the ground.
4. Shift the transmission into neutral.
5. Turn the ignition switch on and slowly turn the rear wheel while measuring voltage between following terminals in the speedometer wiring harness connector.
   a. 2004-2009 Aero models and 2007-2009 Spirit models: Black/yellow (+) and green/black (-).
   b. All other models: Pink/green (+) and green/black (-).
6. The voltmeter should read 0-5 volts (intermittently)
7A. If the voltage reading is correct, replace the speedometer as described in this section.
7B. If the voltage reading is incorrect, perform the following:
   a. Check the green/black wire for an open circuit.
   b. Check the black/yellow (2004-2009 Aero models and 2007-2009 Spirit models) or pink/green (all other models) wire for an open circuit or a short.
   c. If the wires are in good condition, test the VS sensor as described in this chapter.
8. Lower the motorcycle so both wheels are on the ground and the motorcycle is supported by the sidestand.
9. Install the speedometer housing (this section).

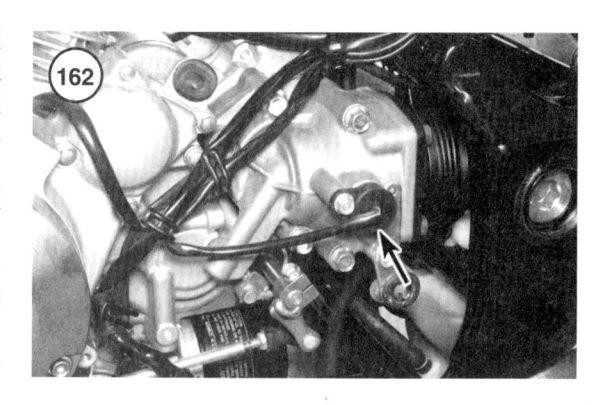

VEHICLE SPEED SENSOR (VS SENSOR)

Removal/Installation

1A. On 2004-2009 Aero models and 2007-2009 Spirit models, remove the seat (Chapter Seventeen).
1B. On all other models, remove the left side cover (Chapter Seventeen).
2. Remove the left crankcase rear cover (Chapter Seventeen).
3. Trace the VS sensor wiring harness from the sensor (**Figure 162**, typical) to its 3-pin connector and disconnect the connector.
4. Clean the area around the VS sensor to prevent dirt from entering the engine.
5. Unbolt and remove the VS sensor and its O-ring (**Figure 163**) from the crankcase. Discard the O-ring.
6. Installation is the reverse of removal. Note the following:
   a. Lubricate a new O-ring with engine oil and install it onto the VS sensor.
   b. Tighten the VS sensor mounting bolt to 9.8 N.m (87 in.-lb.).

ELECTRICAL SYSTEM

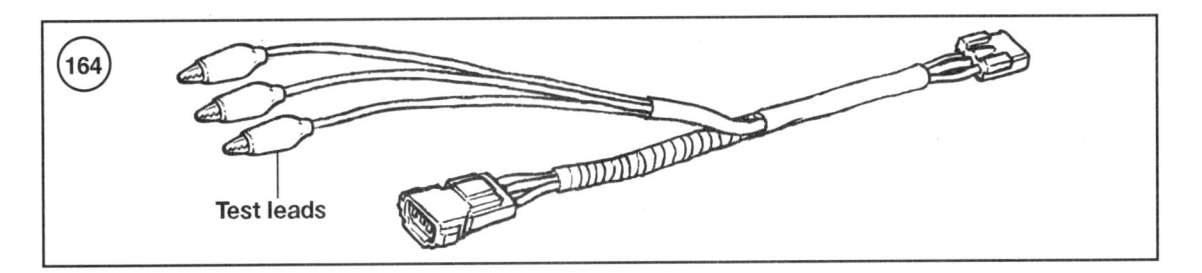

164

Test leads

165

166

Testing

On 2008 and later models, the inspection adapter (Honda part No. 07GMJ-ML80100 [**Figure 164**]), or its equivalent, is required for this test.

1A. On 2004-2009 Aero models and 2007-2009 Spirit models, remove the seat (Chapter Seventeen).
1B. On all other models, remove the left side cover (Chapter Seventeen).
2. Disconnect the 3-pin VS sensor connector (this section). Check both connector halves for dirty, loose or damaged terminals. Note the following:
   a. On 2004-2007 Aero models, reconnect the VS sensor connectors.
   b. On all other models, leave the VS sensor connectors disconnected.
3. Measure voltage between the brown (+) and green/black (-) VS sensor wiring harness connector terminals. On all models except 2004-2007 Aero, measure the voltage at the wiring harness side connector. There should be battery voltage. Note the following:
   a. If there is battery voltage, continue the procedure.
   b. If there is no battery voltage, check the brown and green/black wires for an open circuit.

4A. On 2004-2007 Aero models, reconnect the VS sensor connectors if they were disconnected.
4B. On all other models, connect the inspection adapter (**Figure 164**) between the VS sensor and wiring harness connectors.

NOTE
When using the inspection adapter, the clip colors called out in the procedure correspond to the clip colors on the adapter.

5. Support the motorcycle with its rear wheel off the ground and shift the transmission into neutral. Then turn the ignition switch on and slowly turn the rear wheel while measuring voltage.
6A. On 2004-2007 Aero models, measure voltage between the black/yellow (+) and green/black (-) wire connector terminals.
6B. On all other models, measure voltage between the red (+) and white (-) clips.
7. The voltmeter should read 0-5 volts (intermittently). If the voltage reading is incorrect, replace the VS sensor.
8. If used, remove the inspection adapter and reconnect the VS sensor and wiring harness connectors.
9. Installation is the reverse of the removal steps.

COOLANT TEMPERATURE INDICATOR AND ENGINE COOLANT TEMPERATURE (ECT) SENSOR

The ECT sensor threads into the thermostat housing and controls current flow to the coolant temperature indicator according to coolant temperature.

When the coolant temperature is below 108° C (226° F), the sensor is open and no current can flow to the indicator and the indicator is off. When the coolant temperature increases to 112-118 ° C (234-244° F), the sensor closes and current flows to the indicator and turns it on, indicating an overheating condition.

CAUTION
The ECT sensor can be damaged if dropped. Handle the sensor carefully during service and testing.

Removal/Installation

1. Remove the fuel tank (Chapter Eight or Chapter Nine).
2. Remove the air filter housing (Chapter Eight or Chapter Nine).
3. Remove the steering covers (Chapter Seventeen).
4. Drain the cooling system (Chapter Three).
5. Disconnect the ECT sensor electrical connector and remove the sensor and washer (if used). See **Figure 165** (carbureted models) or **Figure 166** (fuel injected models).
6. Installation is the reverse of removal. Note the following:
   a. On carbureted models, clean the thermostat housing threads and the ECT sensor threads (if reusing it) of all sealant residue. Allow the threads to dry. Then apply a sealer onto the ECT sensor threads and tighten to 7.8 N.m (69 in.-lb.) on Aero models or 7 N.m (62 in.-lb.) on Spirit models.
   b. On fuel injected models, install the ECT sensor with a new washer and tighten to 24.5 N.m (18 ft.-lb.).
   c. Fill and bleed the cooling system (Chapter Three).

Resistance Test

Test the ECT sensor to ensure proper operation or when troubleshooting the cooling system.

NOTE
Read the procedure through first to know the procedures and steps involved.

1. Remove the ECT sensor as described in this section.
2. Place the ECT sensor in a pan filled with a 50:50 mixture of coolant (water/antifreeze). Support the ECT sensor so that its sensor tip, and not its threads, is covered by the coolant. Make sure that the sensor tip is at least 40 mm (1.57 in.) away from the bottom of the pan.

NOTE
A thermometer capable of reading temperatures in excess of 120° C (248°F) is required.

3. Place a shop thermometer in the pan. Use a thermometer that is rated higher than the test temperature (**Table 8**).
4A. On carbureted models, connect an ohmmeter between the sensor terminal and its threads. Heat the coolant and check the sensor operation at the temperatures specified in **Table 8**. Note the following:

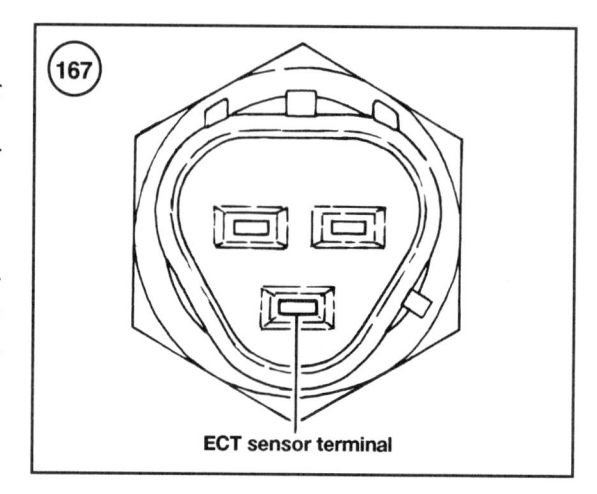

   a. Maintain the coolant at the temperatures specified in **Table 8** for three minutes before determining the sensor's operating condition.
   b. Replace the ECT sensor it if failed to operate as described.

4B. On fuel injected models, heat the coolant and check resistance between the ECT terminal identified in **Figure 167** and the threads (ground) on the ECT sensor. Note the following:

   a. Maintain the coolant at the temperatures specified in **Table 8** for three minutes before determining the actual resistance readings.
   b. Replace the ECT sensor if one or more resistance readings are incorrect.

Circuit Test

The coolant temperature indicator lights, but the engine coolant temperature is low

1. Disconnect the ECT sensor connector at the sensor as described under *Removal/Installation* in this section.
2. Turn the ignition switch on and check coolant temperature indicator on the speedometer:
   a. If the indicator came on, check the green/blue wire between the ECT sensor and the speedometer for a short circuit. If the green/blue wire is okay, replace the speedometer as described in this chapter.
   b. If the indicator did not come on, test the ECT sensor as described in this section.

The coolant temperature indicator does not light when the engine temperature is too high

1. Shift the transmission into neutral and turn the ignition switch on. The neutral and oil pressure indicators should come on. Note the following:

ELECTRICAL SYSTEM

2. Disconnect the electrical connector (A, **Figure 168**) at the fan motor switch.
3. Remove the fan motor switch (B, **Figure 168**) and O-ring.
4. Install a new O-ring onto the fan motor switch.
5. Install the fan motor switch and tighten to 18 N.m (13 ft.-lb.).
6. Fill and bleed the cooling system (Chapter Three).
7. Check for leaks.

System Test

Fan motor switch opening and closing temperatures are listed in **Table 8**. However, to isolate the fan motor switch as the problem, perform the following procedure that best describes the fan motor operation.

Fan motor does not stop

1. Turn the ignition switch off.
2. Disconnect the fan motor switch connector (A, **Figure 168**), then turn the ignition switch on and note the operation of the fan motor:
    a. If the fan motor did not start running, replace the fan motor switch as described in this section.
    b. If the fan motor is running, check for a short circuit in the black wire between the fan motor switch and fan motor.
3. Reconnect the fan motor switch connector (A, **Figure 168**).

Fan motor does not start

1. Check for a blown fan motor fuse as described in this chapter. If the fuse is okay, continue the procedure.
2. Check that the ground terminal mounted on the fan is clean. Check the bolt for tightness. If necessary, remove the bolt and remove any paint or corrosion from the attachment area, then reinstall the bolt and tighten securely.
3. Disconnect the connector at the fan motor switch (A, **Figure 168**).
4. Connect a jumper wire between the fan motor switch connector and ground. Then turn the ignition switch on. The fan motor should run.
    a. If the fan motor ran, continue the procedure.
    b. If the fan motor did not run, skip to Step 6.
5. Check the connector at the fan motor switch for a dirty or loose fitting terminal. If the connector is okay, replace the fan motor switch and retest.
6. Remove the steering covers (Chapter Seventeen).
7. Disconnect the 2-pin fan motor switch connector

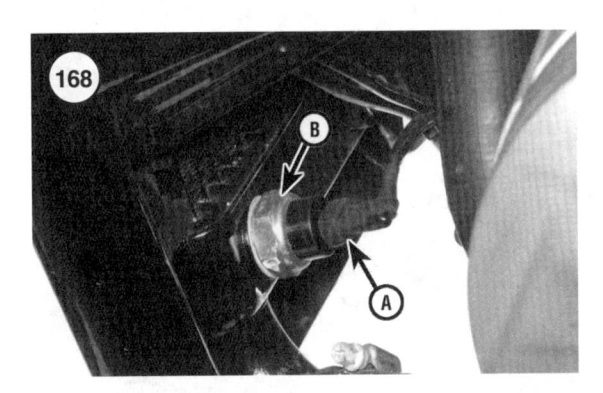

    a. If both indicators did not come on, perform the *Power/Ground Line Test* under *Speedometer* in this chapter.
    b. If both indicators came on, continue the procedure.
2. Disconnect the ECT sensor connector at the sensor as described under *Removal/Installation* in this section.
3. Connect a jumper wire between the ECT sensor wiring harness connector and a good engine ground. Turn the ignition switch on and note the following:
    a. If the indicator came on, test the ECT sensor as described in this section.
    b. If the indicator did not come on, check the green/blue wire between the ECT sensor and the speedometer for a short circuit. If the green/blue wire is okay, replace the speedometer as described in this chapter.
4. Remove the jumper wire and reconnect the ECT sensor.

FAN MOTOR SWITCH (CARBURETED MODELS)

The fan motor switch is mounted on the bottom of the radiator and controls the radiator fan according to engine coolant temperature.

Replacement

1. Drain the cooling system (Chapter Three).

located in the wiring harness bundle in front of the thermostat housing **(Figure 169)**.

8. Turn the ignition switch on and measure voltage between black/blue (+) and green (-) wires in the harness side of the 2-pin connector. There should be battery voltage.

   a. If there is battery voltage, the fan motor is damaged. Replace the fan motor (Chapter Eleven).
   b. If there is no battery voltage, check for an open circuit in the green and black/blue wires. If the wires are okay, continue the procedure.

9. Check for the following conditions:

   a. Dirty or damaged wiring between the ignition switch and fuse box.
   b. Damaged ignition switch. Test the ignition switch as described in this chapter.

10. Reconnect the fan motor switch connector (A, **Figure 169**).

FAN CONTROL RELAY (FUEL INJECTED MODELS)

The fan control relay is mounted in the relay box (non-ABS models) or in the fuse box (ABS models) located behind the left side cover.

Testing/Replacement

This section tests and services the fan control relay. To inspect the fan control relay circuit, refer to *System Inspection* in this section for the procedure that best matches the operating condition.

1. Remove the left side cover (Chapter Seventeen).
2A. On non-ABS models, perform the following:

   a. Remove the relay box **(Figure 170)** from its frame mount.
   b. Pull the rubber cover (A, **Figure 171**) away from the relay box. Then release the blue locking tabs (B) on both sides of the relay box and remove the blue relay connector from the box.

   NOTE
   Refer to the wiring diagram at the end of this manual to identify the wire colors plugged into the fan control relay.

   c. Remove the fan control relay from the connector.

2B. On ABS models, open the fuse box cover and remove the fan control relay from the fuse box as described in *Fuses (ABS Models)* in this chapter.

3. Check for continuity across terminals 1 and 2 **(Figure 172)**; there should be no continuity.
4. Connect a 12-volt battery across terminals 3 and 4 and check continuity across terminals 1 and 2 **(Figure 172)**; there should be continuity.
5. Replace the fan control relay if it failed any part of this test.
6. Installation is the reverse of removal.

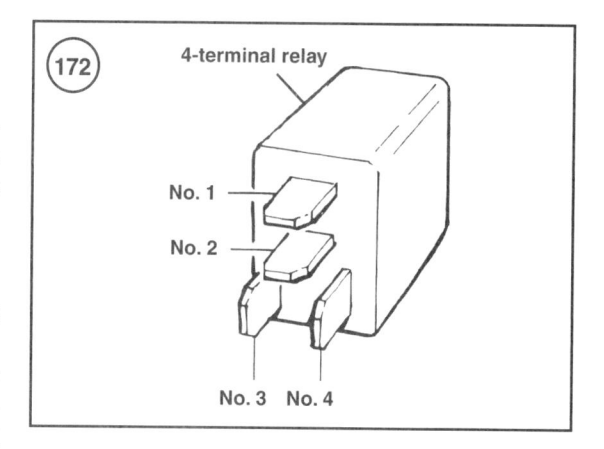

System Inspection

Fan motor does not stop

1. Remove the fan control relay as described in this section.
2. Turn the ignition switch on and note the following:

   a. If the fan motor did not run, replace the fan control relay.
   b. If the fan motor ran, check for a short circuit in the fan control relay wires.

3. Install the fan control relay.

ELECTRICAL SYSTEM

173

FAN CONTROL RELAY WIRING HARNESS CONNECTOR

Blk/blu   Blu/org

174

175

The coolant temperature indicator comes on but the fan motor does not start

1. Check for a blown fan motor fuse as described in this chapter. If the fuse is okay.
2. Check that the ground terminal mounted on the fan is clean. Check the bolt for tightness. If necessary, remove the bolt and remove any paint or corrosion from the attachment area, then reinstall the bolt and tighten securely.
3. Remove the fan control relay as described in this section.
4. Connect a jumper wire across the black/blue and blue/orange fan control relay connector terminals **(Figure 173)**. Then turn the ignition switch on and note the following:
   a. If the fan motor did not run, continue the procedure.
   b. If the fan motor ran, replace the fan control relay.
5. Remove the steering covers (Chapter Seventeen).
6. Disconnect the 2-pin fan motor switch connector located in the connector pouch in front of the thermostat housing **(Figure 174)**.
7. Turn the ignition switch on and measure voltage between the black/blue (+) terminal in the wire harness side of the 2-pin connector and ground (-). There should be battery voltage.
   a. If there is battery voltage, the fan motor is damaged. Replace the fan motor (Chapter Eleven).
   b. If there is no battery voltage, check for an open circuit in the black/blue wire and the green fan motor connector wire.
8. Installation is the reverse of these steps.

OIL PRESSURE SWITCH AND OIL PRESSURE INDICATOR

Oil Pressure Switch
Replacement

1. Support the motorcycle on a workstand so the seat is level.
2. Remove the left crankcase rear cover (Chapter Seventeen).
3. Slide the rubber cover (A, **Figure 175**) off the oil pressure switch.
4. Clean the switch and the area around the switch of all debris.
5. Remove the screw (B, **Figure 175**) and disconnect the wire at the oil pressure switch.
6. Loosen and remove the oil pressure switch (C, **Figure 175**).
7. Clean the oil pressure switch and crankcase threads of all sealer and oil residue.

8. Apply an RTV sealer to the oil pressure switch threads. Do not apply sealer within 3-4 mm (0.1-0.2 in.) from the end of the switch threads. Refer to **Figure 176**.

CAUTION
Do not overtighten the switch to correct an oil leak as this may strip the crankcase threads. If oil leaks from the switch after installing it, remove the switch and reclean the threads. Reseal and reinstall the switch.

9. Install the oil pressure switch and tighten to 12 N.m (106 in.-lb.).
10. Reconnect the wire onto the switch and tighten the screw to the specification in **Table 10**. Then, slide the rubber cover over the switch.

NOTE
The oil pressure indicator should go out within 1-2 seconds after starting the engine. If it stays on, shut off the engine immediately and locate the problem. Do not run the engine with the oil pressure indicator on.

11. Follow the sealer manufacturer's recommendations for drying time, then start the engine and check for leaks.

Troubleshooting

When the ignition switch is turned on, the oil pressure indicator comes on and will remain on until the engine is started. When the engine is started, the oil pressure rises and the oil pressure indicator turns off (usually within 1-2 seconds). If the indicator fails to operate as specified, perform the test (this section) that best matches the indicator's operating condition.

Refer to *Engine Lubrication* in Chapter Two for additional troubleshooting information.

NOTE
Make sure the engine oil level (Chapter Three) is correct before performing any of these tests.

Oil pressure indicator does not come on when ignition switch is turned on

1. Shift the transmission into neutral and turn the ignition switch on. The neutral and coolant temperature indicators should come on. Note the following:

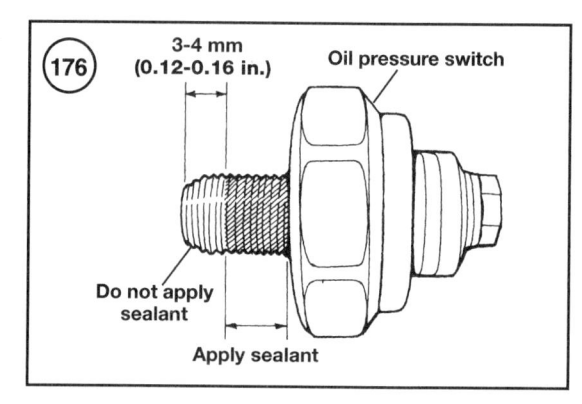

    a. If both indicators did not come on, perform the *Power/Ground Line Test* under *Speedometer* in this chapter.
    b. If both indicators came on, continue the procedure.

2. Slide the rubber cover (A, **Figure 175**) off the oil pressure switch. Then, remove the screw (B, **Figure 175**) and disconnect the wire at the oil pressure switch.
3. Ground the oil pressure switch wire with a jumper wire.
4. Turn the ignition switch on. The oil pressure indicator should come on.

    a. If the indicator came on, replace the oil pressure switch (this section) and retest.
    b. If the indicator did not come on, check the blue/red wire between the oil pressure switch and speedometer for an open circuit or dirty or damaged connector terminals. If the wire and connectors are okay, replace the speedometer (this chapter).

5. Installation is the reverse of removal. Note the following:

    a. Remove the ground wire.
    b. Connect the wire and tighten the screw to the specification in **Table 10**.

Oil pressure indicator stays on when engine is running

1. Turn the engine off and check the engine oil level (Chapter Three).
2. Support the motorcycle on its sidestand.
3. Slide the rubber cover (A, **Figure 175**) off the oil pressure switch. Then remove the screw (B, **Figure 175**) and disconnect the wire at the oil pressure switch.
4. Check for continuity between the oil pressure switch wire and ground. There should be no continuity.

    a. If there is no continuity, check the oil pressure as described in Chapter Two. If the oil pressure is normal, replace the oil pressure switch.

ELECTRICAL SYSTEM

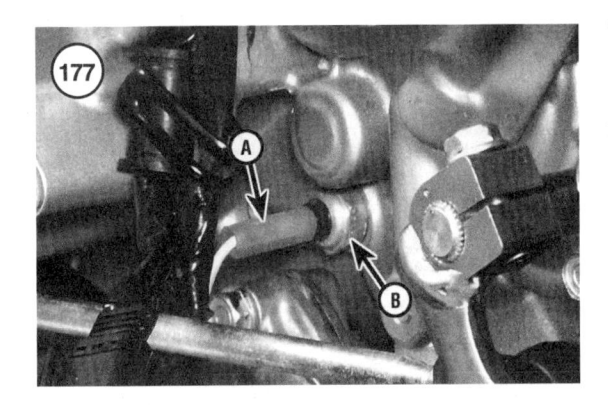

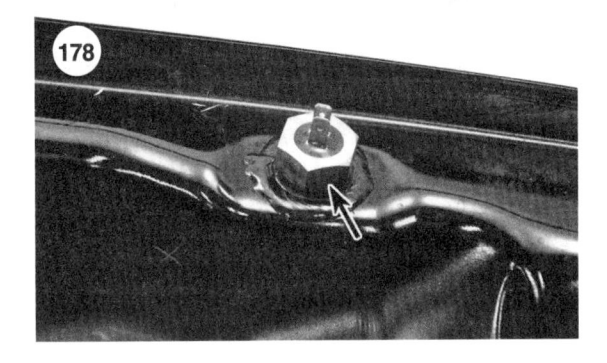

b. If there is continuity, check the blue/red wire between the oil pressure switch and speedometer for a short circuit.

CAUTION
Do not ride the motorcycle until the problem is corrected. Low oil pressure will damage the engine.

5. Installation is the reverse of removal. Tighten the screw to the specification in **Table 10**.

NEUTRAL SWITCH

Replacement

1. Support the motorcycle so it is upright.
2. Remove the left crankcase rear cover (Chapter Seventeen).
3. Disconnect the wire (A, **Figure 177**) at the neutral switch.
4. Remove the neutral switch and sealing washer (B, **Figure 177**).
5. Install the neutral switch (B, **Figure 177**) with a new sealing washer and tighten to 12 N.m (106 in.-lb.). Reconnect the wire at the neutral switch.
6. Turn the ignition switch on and shift the transmission into neutral. The neutral indicator light should come on.
7. Installation is the reverse of removal.

Testing

1. Shift the transmission into neutral and turn the ignition switch on. The neutral indicator should come on.
   a. If the neutral indicator came on, the system is normal.
   b. If the neutral indicator did not come on, continue the procedure.
2. Disconnect the wire at the neutral switch as described under *Replacement* in this section.
3. Check for continuity between the terminal on the neutral switch and ground. There should be continuity with the transmission in neutral and no continuity with the transmission in any gear (except neutral).
   a. Replace the neutral switch (this section) if it failed either test.
   b. If the switch is good, check for an open circuit in the light green wire.
4. Reconnect the wire at the neutral switch.

FUEL RESERVE INDICATOR AND FUEL RESERVE SENSOR (FUEL INJECTED MODELS)

The fuel reserve indicator should light for a few seconds when the ignition switch is turned on and then turn off. This is a lamp check that indicates that the indicator is working properly. The fuel reserve indicator will turn on and remain on when there is approximately 3.5L/0.92 gal. (Aero models) or 3.3L/0.87 gal. (Spirit and Phantom models) of fuel remaining in the fuel tank.

Removal/Installation

1. Remove the fuel tank (Chapter Nine).
2. Drain the fuel into a fuel storage can.
3. Remove the fuel reserve sensor and O-ring (**Figure 178**). Discard the O-ring.
4. Install a new O-ring onto the fuel reserve sensor and tighten to 23 N.m (17 ft.-lb.).
5. Install the fuel tank (Chapter Nine).
6. Partially fill the fuel tank, then check the sensor for a fuel leak.

Circuit Test

Refer to the circuit test that best matches the fuel reserve indicator's operating condition.

Fuel reserve indicator stays on when there is an adequate amount of fuel in the fuel tank

1. Turn the ignition switch off.
2. Disconnect the fuel reserve sensor connectors at the fuel tank **(Figure 179)**.
3. Check for continuity between the black/light green wire terminal in the harness-side connector and ground. Note the following:
   a. If there is no continuity, replace the fuel reserve sensor as described in this section.
   b. If there is continuity, check the black/light green wire for a short circuit.

The fuel reserve indicator does not come on when the fuel tank is empty

1. Check for a blown fuel reserve indicator bulb (this chapter). If the bulb is okay, continue the procedure.
2. Disconnect the fuel reserve sensor connectors at the fuel tank **(Figure 179)**.
3. Connect a jumper wire between the fuel reserve sensor black/light green wire terminal and the green wire terminal in the harness side connectors. Turn the ignition switch and check the fuel reserve indicator. Note the following:
   a. If the indicator turned on, replace the fuel reserve sensor (this section).
   b. If the indicator did not turn on, continue the procedure.
   c. Turn the ignition switch off.
4. Reconnect the fuel reserve sensor connectors **(Figure 179)** at the fuel tank.
5. Remove the headlight unit as described in this chapter.
6. Disconnect the white 4-pin fuel reserve/high beam indicator connector located inside the headlight housing. Refer to the wiring diagram at the end of this manual to identify the connector wire colors.
7. Turn the ignition switch on and measure voltage between the brown (+) and black/light green (-) wires in the sensor side connector (male connector). Note the following:
   a. If there is no battery voltage, check for an open circuit in the brown and black/light green wires.
   b. If there is battery voltage, check for an open circuit in the light green/red and brown wires on 2011-2013 Aero models or in the light green/red and black/brown wires on 2010-2013 Spirit and Phantom models located between the fuel reserve indicator light and the white 4-pin fuel reserve/high beam indicator connector.
   c. If the wires are okay, either the fuel reserve indicator bulb is blown or not making contact with its connector terminals.
   d. Repeat the test procedure to isolate the problem.

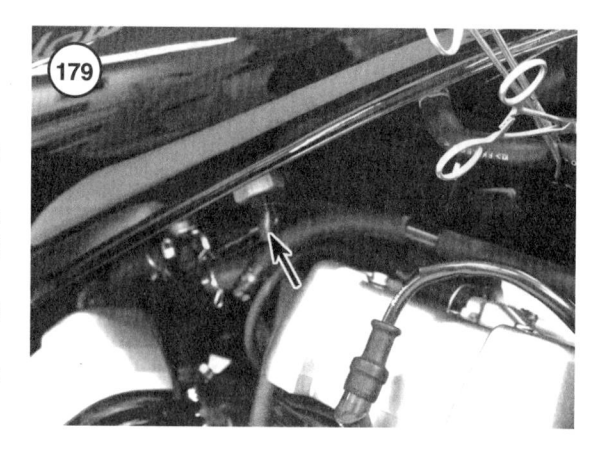

SIDESTAND SWITCH

The sidestand switch is part of the ignition cut-off system. This system is designed to prevent the motorcycle from being ridden when the sidestand is down. When the sidestand is down, the engine will only start when the transmission is in neutral. When the sidestand is up, the engine can be started in neutral, or in gear when the clutch lever is pulled in. If the engine is started with the transmission in neutral and the sidestand down, the engine cuts off if the transmission is shifted into gear before the sidestand is raised.

Refer to Chapter Seventeen to service the sidestand assembly.

Replacement

1. Support the motorcycle on a workstand so the sidestand can be raised and lowered by hand.
2. On carbureted models models, remove the seat (Chapter Seventeen).
3. Remove the left side cover (Chapter Seventeen).
4. Remove the left crankcase rear cover (Chapter Seventeen).

NOTE
Note the sidestand switch wiring harness routing before disconnecting and removing the switch.

5. Trace the wiring harness from the sidestand switch (A, **Figure 180**) to the main wiring harness and disconnect the 2-pin sidestand switch connector (B).
6. Remove the bolt (C, **Figure 180**) and sidestand switch (A). Discard the bolt.

ELECTRICAL SYSTEM

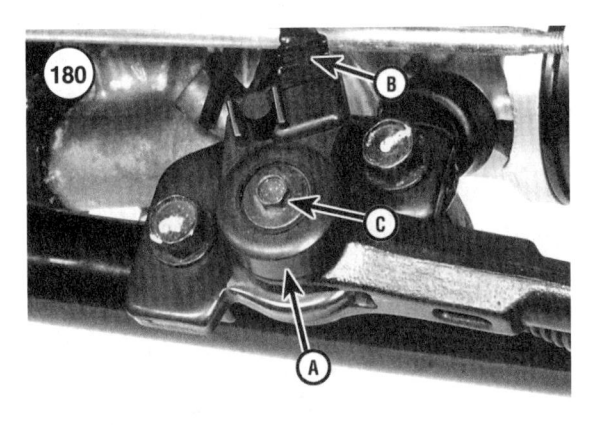

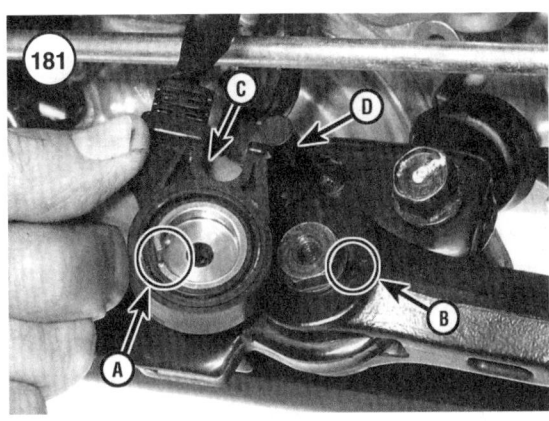

7. Clean and dry the threads in the sidestand pivot bolt hole.
8. Install the sidestand switch by inserting the pin (A, **Figure 181**) on the switch into the hole (B) in the sidestand and by aligning the groove (C) in the switch with the mounting bracket pin (D).
9. Install the washer and plate. Align the tab on the plate with the groove in the switch and the groove on the plate with the return spring pin.

NOTE
The sidestand switch is secured with an ALOC bolt, which has a threadlock preapplied to the bolt threads. If a new ALOC bolt is not available, remove the threadlock residue from the original bolt. Then, apply a medium strength threadlock onto the bolt threads before installing it.

10. Install a new sidestand switch ALOC mounting bolt (B, **Figure 180**) and tighten to 10 N.m (89 in.-lb.).
11. Route the sidestand switch wiring harness along its original path and reconnect its connector.
12. Test the sidestand switch as described in this section.
13. Install the parts previously removed.

WARNING
Do not ride the motorcycle until the sidestand switch operates correctly. Riding the motorcycle with the sidestand down will cause the rider to loose control when the sidestand contacts the ground.

14. Perform the *Sidestand and Ignition Cut-off Switch Test* in Chapter Three.

Testing

A problem in the sidestand switch circuit can prevent the engine from starting or can cause the engine to cut-out.

1. Support the motorcycle on a workstand so the sidestand can be raised and lowered by hand.
2. Disconnect the sidestand connector as described in this section.

WARNING
Do not ride the motorcycle until the sidestand switch operates correctly. Riding the motorcycle with the sidestand down will cause the rider to loose control when the sidestand contacts the ground.

NOTE
Perform the test on the switch side of the connector, not on the wire harness side.

3. Test the sidestand switch as follows:
   a. Check for continuity between the 2-pin connector green/white and green wire terminals.
   b. There should be continuity with the sidestand up.
   c. There should be no continuity with the sidestand down.
   d. Replace the sidestand switch if it failed any part of this test.
4. Reconnect the sidestand connector (B, **Figure 180**).

CLUTCH SWITCH

The clutch switch is mounted inside the clutch lever housing.

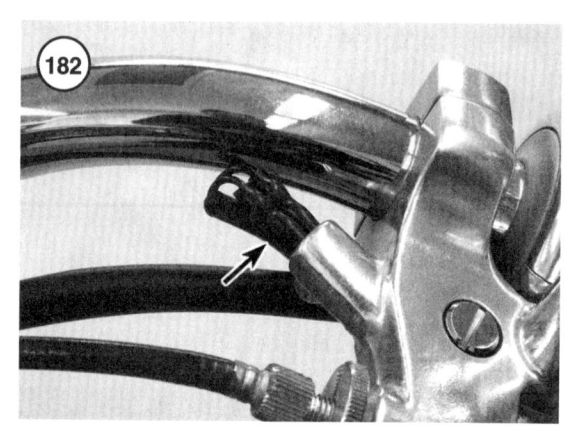

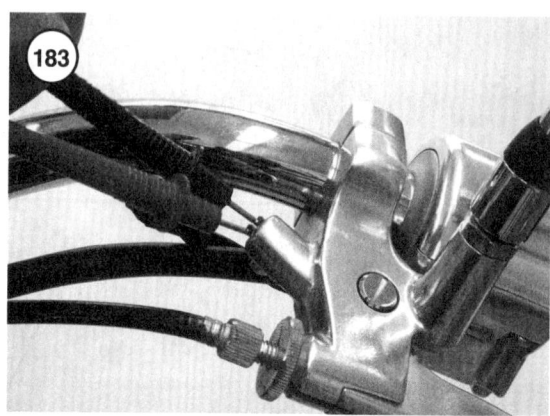

Testing/Replacement

1. Disconnect the two electrical connectors at the clutch switch **(Figure 182)**.
2. Connect ohmmeter leads across the two clutch switch terminals **(Figure 183)**. There should be continuity with the clutch lever applied and no continuity with the clutch lever released. Replace the switch if faulty.
3. Replace the clutch switch as follows:
    a. Disconnect the clutch cable from the clutch lever at the handlebar (Chapter Three).
    b. Remove the nut, pivot bolt and clutch lever.
    c. Gently push the clutch switch out of the housing.
    d. Install the clutch switch by aligning the tab on the switch with the notch in the housing **(Figure 184)**. Push the switch into the housing until it bottoms.
4. Clean the clutch lever and pivot bolt. Lightly grease the pivot bolt and install it through the perch and clutch lever. Tighten the pivot bolt to 1 Nm (8.9 in-lb.), Then, hold the pivot bolt and tighten the nut to the specification in **Table 10**. Check that the clutch lever pivots smoothly.
5. Reconnect the clutch cable and adjust the clutch (Chapter Three).
6. Reconnect the electrical connectors **(Figure 182)** at the clutch switch.

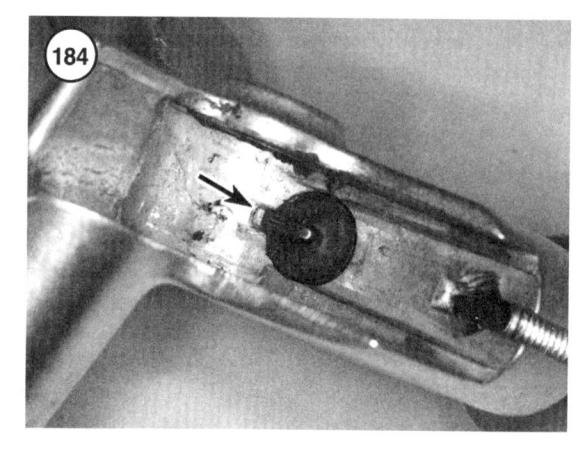

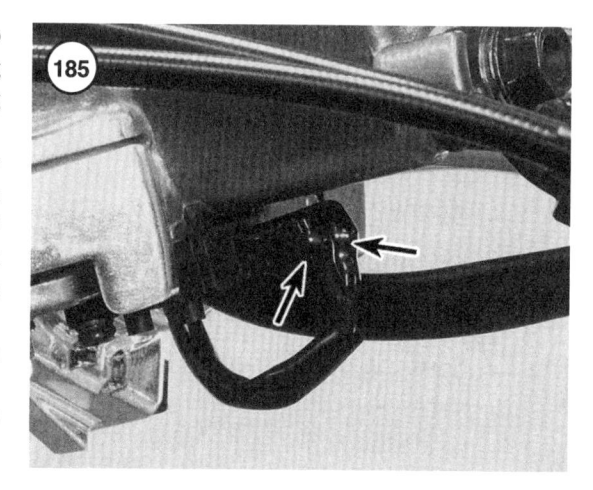

FRONT BRAKE LIGHT SWITCH

The front brake light switch is mounted on the bottom of the front master cylinder.

Testing/Replacement

1. Disconnect the two electrical connectors **(Figure 185)** from the switch terminals.
2. Check for continuity between the switch terminals (A, **Figure 186**). There should be continuity with the brake lever applied and no continuity with the brake lever released. Replace the switch if faulty (this section).
3. Replace the switch by removing the screw (B, **Figure 186**) and switch (C).
4. Installation is the reverse of removal. Note the following:
    a. Make sure both connectors are plugged tightly into the switch. Then position the connector covers so they fully enclose the switch and connector terminals.

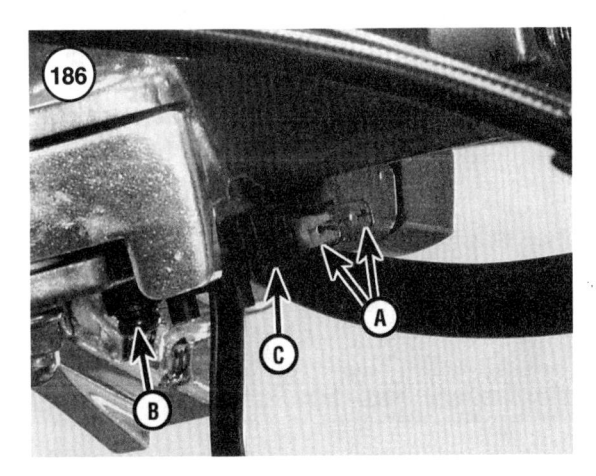

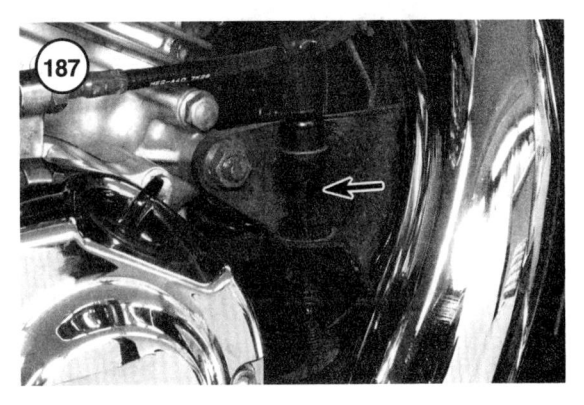

ELECTRICAL SYSTEM

4. To remove the switch (**Figure 187**):
   a. Disconnect the spring and remove the switch and spring.
   b. Note the rear brake light switch wiring harness routing and remove it.
5. Installation is the reverse of removal.

WARNING
Do not ride the motorcycle until the brake light works correctly. Always check brake light operation by applying the front and rear brakes with the ignition switch turned on before riding the motorcycle.

6. Adjust the rear brake light switch (Chapter Three).

IGNITION SWITCH

The ignition switch is mounted on the left side of the motorcycle.

Testing/Replacement

1. On carbureted models, remove the seat (Chapter Seventeen).
2A. On non-ABS models, remove the left side cover.
2B. On ABS models, remove the left crankcase rear cover (Chapter Seventeen).

NOTE
Refer to the wiring diagrams at the end of this manual to identify the ignition switch wiring harness colors.

3. Trace the wiring from the ignition switch to its harness connectors and disconnect the connectors.
4. Test the ignition switch as described under *Switch Continuity Test* in this chapter. Refer to the wiring diagram at the end of this manual for the ignition switch continuity diagram. Replace the switch if faulty.
5. To replace the ignition switch, perform the following:
   a. Note the ignition switch wiring harness routing. Remove any clamps securing the wiring harness in place.
   b. Remove the screws (A, **Figure 188**) and the cover (B).

NOTE
The ignition switch is mounted onto a collar using break-off bolts. Remove these bolts (A, Figure 189) when replacing the ignition switch.

WARNING
Do not ride the motorcycle until the brake light works correctly. Always check brake light operation by applying the front and rear brakes with the ignition switch turned on before riding the motorcycle.

   b. Turn the ignition switch on and operate the front brake lever and check the brake light operation.

REAR BRAKE LIGHT SWITCH

The rear brake light switch is mounted on the rear brake pedal assembly.

Testing/Replacement

1. Remove the steering covers (Chapter Seventeen).
2. Trace the wiring harness from the rear brake light switch (**Figure 187**) to the main wiring harness located in front of the thermostat housing and disconnect the 2-pin rear brake light switch connector.
3. Check for continuity between the switch terminals. There should be no continuity with the brake pedal released and continuity with the brake pedal applied. Replace the switch if faulty.

c. Mark the center of one of the break-off bolts (A, **Figure 189**) with a sharp pencil, then center punch an indention into center of the bolt. Carefully drill through the bolt head with a drill bit until it breaks off of the bolt shank. Repeat for the other bolt.

d. Remove the ignition switch (B, **Figure 189**), switch base (C) and collar (D). The collar is mounted behind the ignition switch mounting bracket.

e. Remove the remainder of the threaded bolt shanks from the collar threads and discard them.

f. Install the collar through the back of the ignition switch mounting bracket.

g. Install the base and the ignition switch over the shoulders on the collars.

h. Install new break-off mounting bolts and hand-tighten the bolts. Then install the key into the ignition switch and turn it to make sure it turns freely.

i. Tighten the bolt heads (approximately 12 N.m [106 in.-lb.]) until they break off.

NOTE
*If it is only necessary to remove the ignition switch from its mounting position on the frame without having to replace it, remove the two mounting bracket bolts (**Figure 190**).*

6. To remove the ignition switch without replacing it, remove the two ignition switch mounting bracket bolts (**Figure 190**), then set the ignition switch aside.

7. Installation is the reverse of the removal steps. Note the following:
   a. Tighten the ignition switch mounting bracket bolts (**Figure 190**) securely.
   b. On 2004-2009 Aero models, tighten the ignition switch cover screw to 2.0 Nm (18 in.-lb.). On all Spirit models and all Phantom models,. Tighten the ignition cover screw to 1.0 Nm (8.9 in.-lb.). On all 2011-2013 Aero models, tighten the ignition cover screw securely.
   c. If installing a new ignition switch, record the new key number in the *Quick Reference Data* section at the front of this manual.
   d. Check the switch for proper operation.

HANDLEBAR SWITCH

The left handlebar switch housing (**Figure 191**) includes the headlight dimmer switch, turn signal switch and horn button.

The right handlebar switch housing (**Figure 192**) includes the engine stop switch and the starter switch.

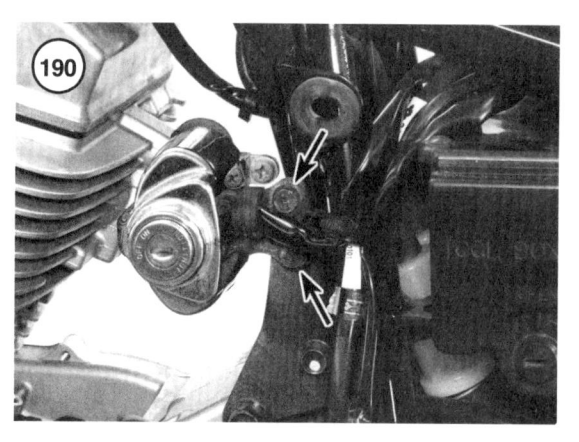

Testing/Replacement

1. Remove the headlight lens as described in this chapter.

2. Trace the switch wiring harness from the switch assembly to the connectors in the headlight housing and disconnect them. Refer to the appropriate wiring diagram at the end of this manual to identify the connectors and wire colors for each switch.

3. Test the switch as described under *Switch Continuity Test* in this chapter. Note the following:

ELECTRICAL SYSTEM

ate wiring diagram at the end of this manual. The horizontal line indicates which terminals should show continuity when the horn button is pushed. Continuing with the example, in the push position there should be continuity between both terminals. When the switch is in the free position, there should be no continuity between the terminals.

1. Refer to the appropriate switch procedure in this chapter to access the switch connectors. Some switches do not use a continuity diagram for testing. Instead, follow the componet test procedure in the appropriate section of this chapter.
2. Check the subfuse as described under *Fuses* in this chapter.
3. Check the battery as described under *Battery* in this chapter. Charge the battery to the correct state of charge, if required.

CAUTION
Do not attempt to start the engine with the battery disconnected.

4. Disconnect the negative battery cable at the battery if the switch connectors are not disconnected from the circuit.
5. When separating two connectors, unlock and pull on the connector housings and not the wires.
6. After locating a defective circuit, check the connectors to make sure they are clean and properly connected. Check all wires going into a connector to make sure each wire is properly positioned and the wire ends are not loose.
7. Before disconnecting two connectors, check them for any locking tabs or arms that must be pushed or opened. If two connectors are difficult to separate, do not force them as damage may occur.
8. When reconnecting electrical connector halves, push them together until they click or snap into place.
9. If the switch is operating erratically, the contacts may be oily, dirty or corroded. Disassemble the switch housing as described in this section to access the switch contacts. Clean the contacts as required.
10. If a switch or button does not perform properly, replace the switch assembly as described in its appropriate section. The individual switches cannot be replaced separately.

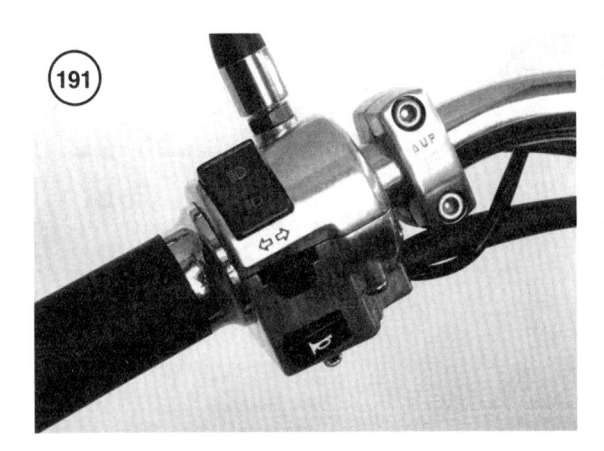

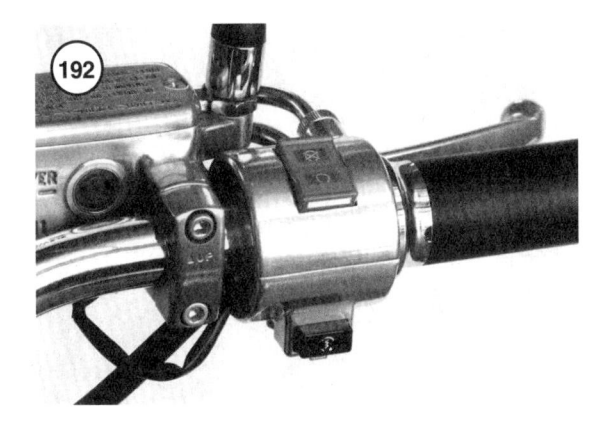

a. If the continuity test indicates a faulty switch, continue the procedure to replace the switch assembly.
b. If the switch is okay, reconnect the connectors and install the headlight lens.

4. Note how the switch wiring harness is routed from the switch to the headlight housing. Then carefully pull the wiring harness and connectors from the headlight housing.
5. Remove the left (**Figure 191**) and right (**Figure 192**) side handlebar switches from the handlebar as described in *Handlebar* in Chapter Thirteen.

WARNING
Do not ride the motorcycle until each switch works properly.

6. Installation is the reverse of removal. Check each switch function for proper operation.

SWITCH CONTINUITY TEST

Test the switches for continuity using an ohmmeter (see Chapter One) or a self-powered test light at the switch connector by operating the switch in each of its operating positions. Compare the results with the switch operation diagram. For example, refer to the horn switch continuity diagram on the appropri-

TURN SIGNAL RELAY

Testing/Replacement

1. If only one bulb or individual side does not work, check for a blown bulb or a disconnected turn signal connector. If the turn signals do not work, test the

turn signal relay as described in this section.

2A. On Aero models, remove the headlight lens as described in this chapter. Disconnect and remove the turn signal relay from inside the headlight housing (**Figure 193**, typical).

2B. On Spirit models without ABS and all Phantom models, remove the right side cover (Chapter Seventeen). Disconnect the turn signal relay from its connector (**Figure 194**).

2C. On Spirit models with ABS, remove the fuel tank (Chapter Nine). Disconnect the turn signal relay from its connector (**Figure 195**).

3. Check for loose, bent or corroded turn signal relay terminals. Then check the socket terminals in the connector for corrosion or damage.

4. Connect a jumper wire between the white/green and gray terminals in the turn signal relay wiring harness side connector. Turn the ignition switch on and operate the turn signal switch. The turn signals should light and stay on. Turn the turn signal off and the ignition switch off. Disconnect the jumper wire.
   a. If the light did not come on, check for an open circuit in the white/green and gray turn signal wires.
   b. If the light came on, either the turn signal relay connector is dirty or damaged or the turn signal relay is damaged. Check and clean the connector first and retest. If the turn signals still do not work, replace the turn signal relay.

5. Installation is the reverse of removal. Install the turn signal relay, turn the ignition switch on and check the turn signal operation.

HORN

The horn is an important safety device and must be kept in good working order.

Testing

1. Disconnect the electrical connectors (A, **Figure 196**) from the horn.
2. Connect a 12-volt battery across the horn terminals. The horn must sound loudly. If not, replace the horn.

Removal/Installation

NOTE
If adding an aftermarket horn, a separate relay may be required. Follow the manufacturer's instructions for horn and relay installation.

1. Disconnect the electrical connectors from the horn (A, **Figure 196**).

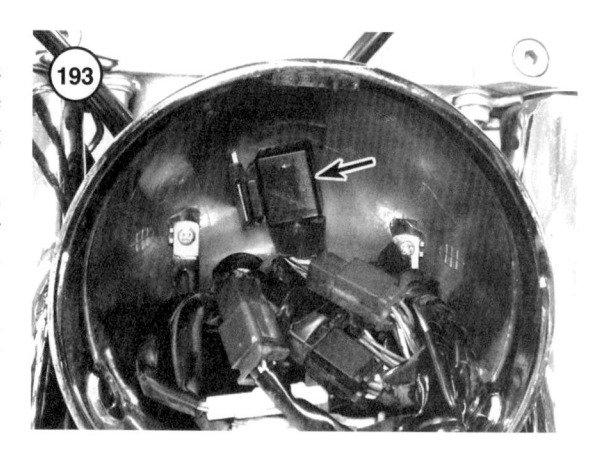

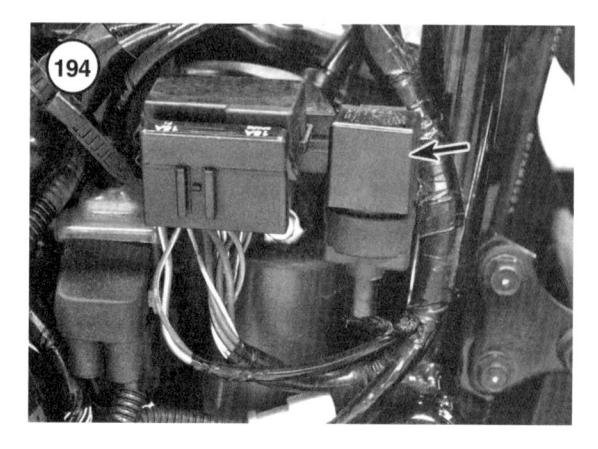

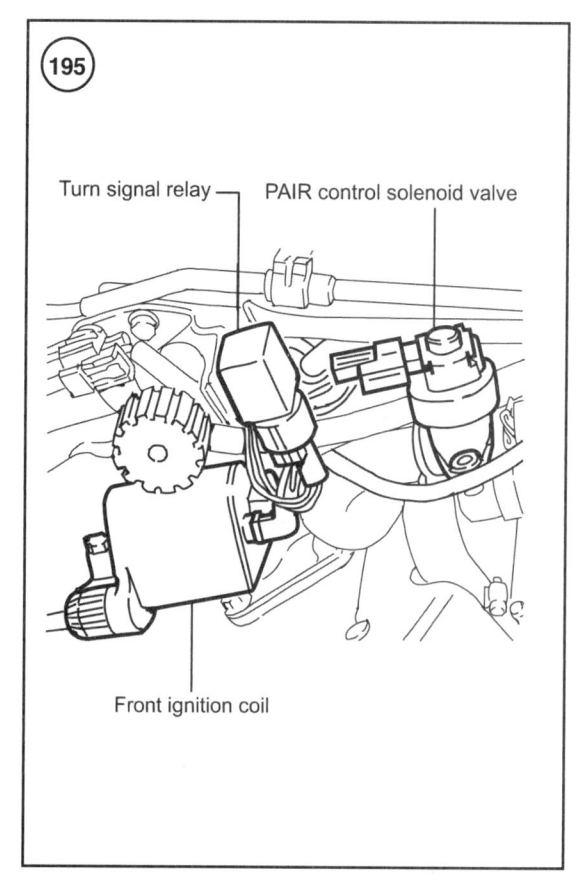

ELECTRICAL SYSTEM

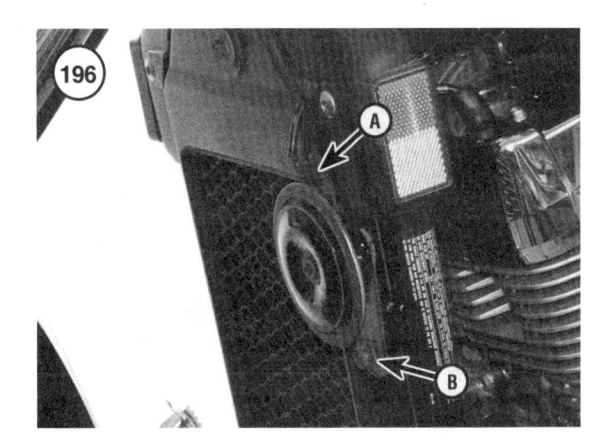

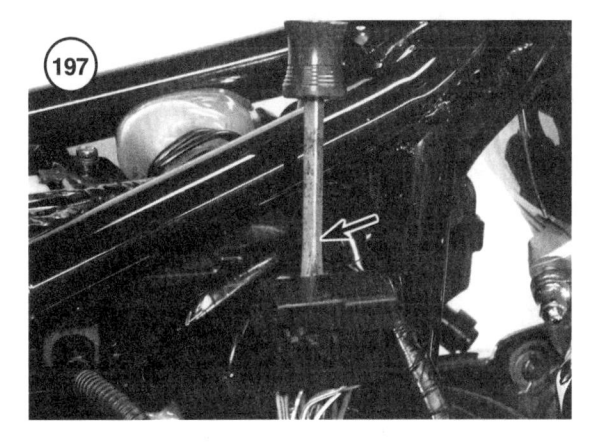

2. Remove the bolt (B, **Figure 196**) and the horn assembly.
3. Install by reversing these removal steps. Note the following:
    a. Align the horn bracket with the shoulder on the frame bracket.
    b. Tighten the horn mounting bolt to 21 N.m (15 ft.-lb.).
    c. Make sure the electrical connections are secure and corrosion-free.
    d. Check the horn operation. If the horn does not work properly, test the horn as described in this section.

WARNING
Do not ride the motorcycle until the horn works properly.

FUSE BOX

Removal/Installation

The fuse box can be removed from its mounting position to access components installed behind it.
1. Remove the seat (Chapter Seventeen).
2A. On non-ABS models, remove the right side cover (Chapter Seventeen).

2B. On ABS models, remove the left side cover (Chapter Seventeen).
3. Insert a wide-blade screwdriver behind the fuse box and pry the lock forward (**Figure 197**, typical) or disconnect any tabs. Then slide the fuse box off of its mounting position.

NOTE
Because the fuse box and its lock are plastic, debris and wear can make it difficult to slide the fuse box off its mounting bracket on the battery box.

4. Installation is the reverse of these steps, plus the following:
    a. Apply ArmorAll or a similar plastic protectant to the lock components to help with future removal.
    b. When reinstalling the fuse box, make sure the fuse box wiring harness is not twisted.
    c. Slide the fuse box along the guide on the battery box until it locks in place.

FUSES

CAUTION
If replacing a fuse, make sure the ignition switch is turned off. This lessens the chance of a short circuit.

CAUTION
Never substitute any metal object for a fuse. Never use a higher amperage fuse than specified. An overload could cause a fire and the complete loss of the motorcycle.

Whenever a fuse blows, determine the cause before replacing the fuse. Usually, the trouble is a short circuit in the wiring caused by worn-through insulation or a short to ground from a disconnected or damaged wire. Refer **Table 9** for fuse ratings.

Main Fuse

The 30 amp main fuse is mounted in a fuse holder located on the starter relay switch.
1. Turn the ignition switch off.
2A. On non-ABS models, perform the following:
    a. Remove the right side cover (Chapter Seventeen).
    b. Disconnect the electrical connector from the starter relay switch.
    c. Remove the main fuse (**Figure 198**) and inspect it. Replace the fuse if blown (**Figure 199**).

d. Reconnect the starter relay switch connector.
e. Reinstall the right side cover (Chapter Seventeen).

2B. On ABS models, perform the following:
   a. Remove the left side cover (Chapter Seventeen).
   b. Remove the cover **(Figure 200)** from the top of the starter relay switch.
   c. Remove the main fuse **(Figure 200)** and inspect it. Replace the fuse if blown **(Figure 199)**.
   d. Install the cover onto the starter relay switch.
   e. Reinstall the left side cover (Chapter Seventeen).

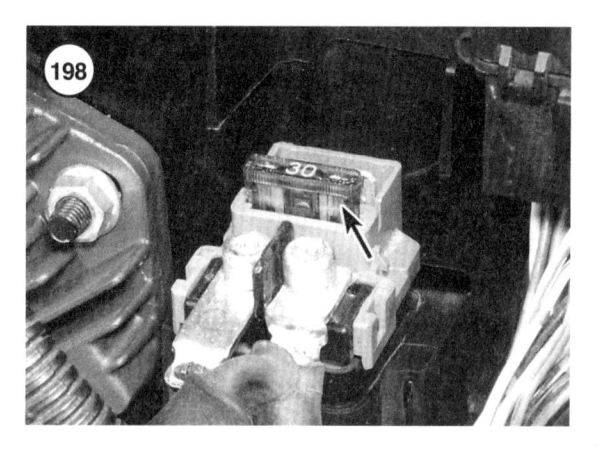

Fuel Injection (FI) Fuse
(Fuel Injected Models)

1. Turn the ignition switch off.
2A. On non-ABS models, perform the following:
   a. Remove the right side cover (Chapter Seventeen).
   b. Open the fuel box cover (A, **Figure 201**) located beside the main fuse box.
   c. Remove the FI fuse and inspect it. Replace the fuse if blown **(Figure 199)**.
   d. Close and secure the fuse box cover.
   e. Reinstall the right side cover (Chapter Seventeen).
2B. On ABS models, perform the following:
   a. Remove the left side cover (Chapter Seventeen).
   b. Remove the cover **(Figure 200)** from the top of the starter relay switch.
   c. Remove the FI fuse **(Figure 200)** and inspect it. Replace the fuse if blown **(Figure 199)**.
   d. Install the cover onto the starter relay switch.
   e. Reinstall the left side cover (Chapter Seventeen).

Fuse Box

To identify an individual fuse and its amperage, refer to the printed information on the fuse box cover (B, **Figure 201**, typical) and **Table 9**. The individual fuses are also identified on the wiring diagrams at the end of the manual.

Non-ABS models

1. Turn the ignition switch off.
2. Remove the right side cover (Chapter Seventeen).
3. Open the fuse box cover (B, **Figure 201**). Use the label on the fuse box cover to identify the fuses. If necessary, refer to the appropriate wiring diagram at the end of this manual to identify the fuse and its wiring color(s)
4. Remove and inspect the fuse (C, **Figure 201**). Replace the fuse if blown **(Figure 199)**.
5. Close and secure the fuse box cover.
6. Install the right side cover.

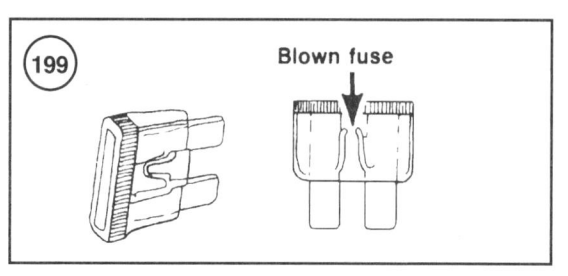

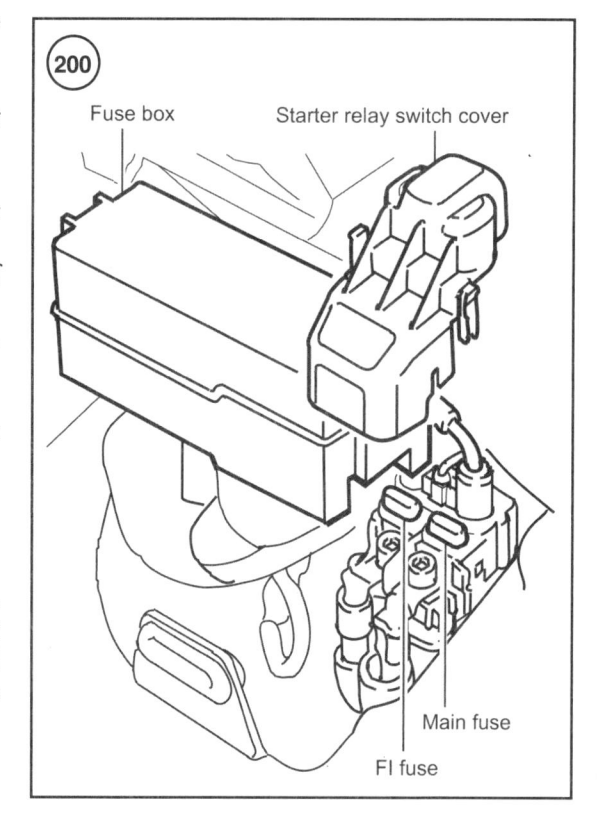

ELECTRICAL SYSTEM

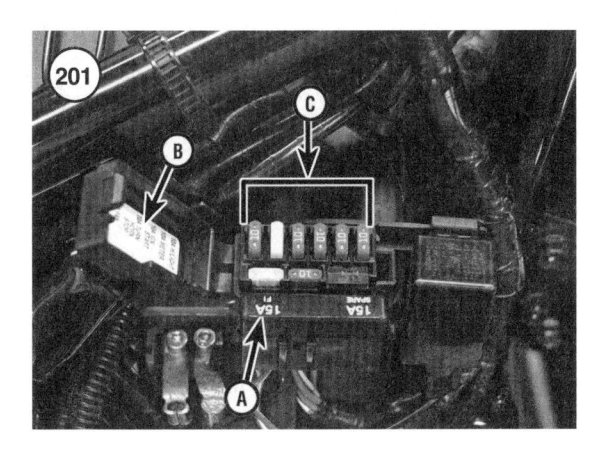

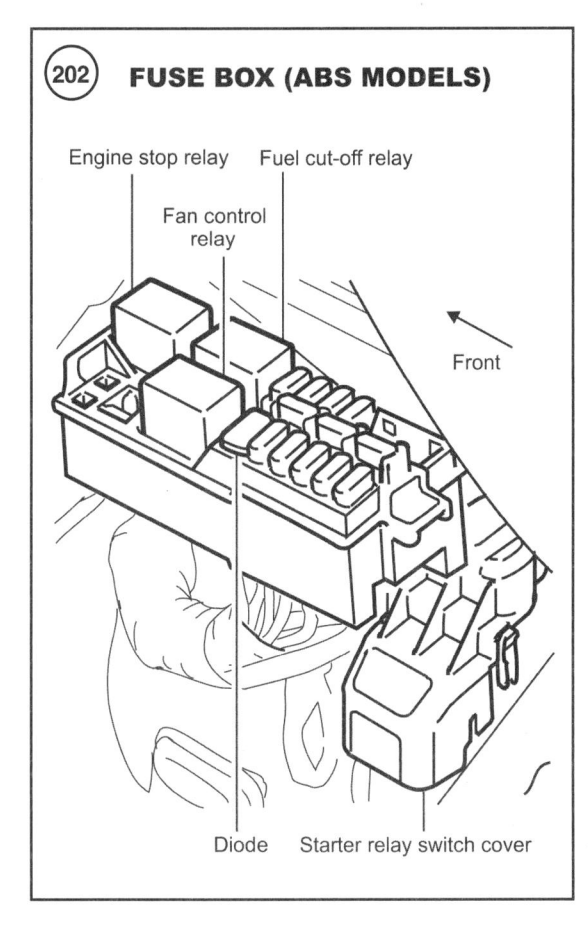

ABS models

1. Turn the ignition switch off.
2. Remove the left side cover (Chapter Seventeen).
3. Open the fuse box cover **(Figure 202)**. Use the label on the fuse box cover to identify the fuses. If necessary, refer to the appropriate wiring diagram at the end of this manual to identify the fuse and its wiring color(s)
4. Remove and inspect the fuse. Replace the fuse if blown **(Figure 199)**.
5. Close and secure the fuse box cover (B, **Figure 201**).
6. Install the left side cover (Chapter Seventeen).

FUSE BOX RELAYS (ABS MODELS)

The following relays are mounted inside the fuse box **(Figure 202)**:
   a. Engine stop relay.
   b. Fan control relay.
   c. Fuel cut-off relay

Replacement

1. Remove the left side cover (Chapter Seventeen).
2. Open the fuse box cover.
3. Remove and replace the damaged relay.
4. Close and secure the fuse box cover.
5. Install the left side cover (Chapter Seventeen).

WIRING DIAGRAMS

Color wiring diagrams for all models are located at the end of this manual.

Table 1 BATTERY SPECIFICATIONS

Type	Maintenance-free (sealed)*
Capacity	
Carbureted models	12 volts, 10 amp hour or 11 amp hour
Fuel injected models	12 volts, 11.2 amp hour
Current draw (parasitic drain)	1.0 mA maximum
Voltage at 20 degrees C (68 degrees F)	
Fully-charged	13.0-13.2 volts
Needs charging	Below 12.4 volts
Charging current	
Normal	1.1 amps x 5-10 hours
Quick	5.5 amps x 1 hour

* A maintenance-free battery is installed on all models described in this manual. Because this type of battery requires a high-voltage charging system, do not install a standard type battery.

Table 2 MAINTENANCE-FREE BATTERY CHARGING TIMES

Voltage reading	State of charge	Approximate charging time
11.5 volts (1)	0%	--
11.9 volts	25%	13-20 hours
12.3 volts	50%	5-11 hours
12.7 volts	75%	3-6 hours
13.0 volts	100% (2)	--

1. Voltage readings of 11.5 volts or less require a different charging procedure and equipment. Refer to text for information.
2. A fully charged battery should read 12.8 volts or higher after the battery has been removed from the charger for 1 to 2 hours.

Table 3 ALTERNATOR AND CHARGING SYSTEM SPECIFICATIONS*

Alternator	
Type	Triple phase
Charging system output	
Carbureted models	350 watts @ 5000 rpm
Fuel injected models	390 watts @ 5000 rpm
Charging voltage test (regulated voltage)	Refer to text
Stator coil resistance*	0.1-1.0 ohms

*Test must be made at an ambient temperature of 20° C (68° F). Do not test when the engine or component is hot.

Table 4 STARTER CLUTCH SPECIFICATIONS

	New mm (in.)	Service limit mm (in.)
Starter clutch housing inside diameter	74.414-74.440 (2.9297-2.9307)	74.46 (2.931)
Starter driven gear		
Inside diameter	37.000-37.025 (1.4567-1.4577)	37.10 (1.461)
Outside diameter	57.749-57.768 (2.2736-2.2743)	57.73 (2.273)

Table 5 IGNITION SYSTEM SPECIFICATIONS*

Ignition pulse generator/CKP sensor peak voltage	0.7 volts minimum
Ignition coil primary peak voltage	100 volts minimum
Throttle position sensor	
Carbureted models	
Input voltage	5 volts
Resistance	4000-6000 ohms

*Tests must be made at an ambient temperature of 20° C (68° F). Do not test when the engine or component is hot.

ELECTRICAL SYSTEM

Table 6 STARTING SYSTEM SPECIFICATIONS

Starter motor brush length	
New	12.5 mm (0.49 in.)
Service limit	6.5 mm (0.26 in.)

Table 7 BULB SPECIFICATIONS

Item	Specification (12 volt)
Brake/taillight	21/5W
Front turn signal/running light	
Aero models	
2004-2009	21/5W
2011-2013	21W
Spirit models	21/5W
Phantom models	21/5W
Headlight	60/55W
Indicators	
Aero models	
ABS indicator	
2011-2013	LED
Coolant temperature indicator	LED
Fuel reserve	
2011-2013	3.4W
High beam indicator	
2004-2007	LED
2008-2009 and 2011-2013	3.4W
MIL indicator	
2011-2013	LED
Neutral indicator	
2004-2007	LED
2008-2009	3.4W
2011-2013	LED
Oil pressure indicator	LED
Turn signal indicator	
2004-2007	LED
2008-2009 and 2011-2013	3.4W
Spirit models	
ABS indicator	
2010-2013	LED
Coolant temperature indicator	LED
High beam indicator	
2007-2009	LED
2010-2013	3.4W
MIL	
2010-2013	LED
Neutral indicator	LED
Oil pressure indicator	LED
Turn signal indicator	LED
Phantom models	
Coolant temperature indicator	LED
Fuel reserve indicator	3.4W
High beam indicator	3.4W
MIL	LED
Neutral indicator	LED
Oil pressure indicator	LED
Turn signal indicator	3.4W
Instrument panel	LED
License light	5W
Rear turn signal light	21W

Table 8 SENSOR TEST SPECIFICATIONS

ECT sensor	
Carbureted models	
Starts to open (OFF)	108° C (226° F) minimum
Starts to close (ON)	112-118° C (234-244° F)
Fuel injected models	
50° C (122° F)	6.8-7.4 K ohms
80° C (176° F)	
2010-2013 Spirit models	2.1-2.6 K ohms
2011-2013 Aero models	2.1-2.7 K ohms
120° C (248° F)	
2010-2013 Spirit models	0.6-0.7 K ohms
2011-2013 Aero models	0.6-0.8 K ohms
Fan motor switch	
Carbureted models	
Aero	
2004-2009	
Starts to open (OFF)	93-97° C (199-207° F)
Starts to close (ON)	98-102° C (208-216° F)
Spirit	
Starts to open (OFF)	94-98° C (201-208° F)
Starts to close (ON)	103-107° C (217-225° F)
VS sensor voltage	0-5 volts intermittently

Table 9 FUSE SPECIFICATIONS

Type	Specification
Main fuse	30A
Subfuses	
Aero models	
2004-2009	
Fan	10A
Headlight	10A
Ignition/starter	10A
Meter/taillight/license light/position light	10A
Odometer	
2004-2007	5A
2008-2009	10A
Turn/horn/stop	10A
2011-2013	
ABS equipped	
Main fuse	10A
Motor	30A
Solenoid	30A
Fan	20A
Fuel injection	
Non-ABS equipped	15A
ABS equipped	20A
Headlight	10A
Meter/taillight/license light/position light	10A
Odometer	10A
Solenoid/bank angle sensor	10A
Turn/horn/stop	10A
Spirit models	
2007-2009	
Fan	20A
Headlight	10A
Ignition/solenoid	10A
Meter/taillight/license light/position light	10A
Odometer	10A
Turn/horn/stop	10A
2010-2013	
ABS equipped	
Main fuse	10A
Motor	30A
Solenoid	30A
Fan	20A
Fuel injection	
Non-ABS equipped	15A

ELECTRICAL SYSTEM

Table 9 FUSE SPECIFICATIONS (continued)

Type	Specification
ABS equipped	20A
Headlight	10A
Meter/taillight/license light/position light	10A
Odometer	10A
Solenoid/bank angle sensor	10A
Turn/horn/stop	10A
Phantom models	
Fan	20A
Fuel injection	15A
Headlight	10A
Meter/taillight/license light/ position light	10A
Odometer	10A
Solenoid/bank angle sensor	10A
Turn/horn/stop	10A

Table 10 ELECTRICAL SYSTEM TORQUE SPECIFICATIONS

	N.m	in.-lb.	ft.-lb.
Alternator cover mounting Allen bolts	10	89	--
Clutch pivot bolt	1.0	8.9	--
Clutch pivot nut			
2004-2009 Aero models	5.9	52	--
All other models	6.0	53	--
ECT sensor			
Carbureted models			
Aero models (1)	7.8	69	--
Spirit models (1)	7	62	--
Fuel injected models	24.5	--	18
Fan motor switch			
Carbureted models	18	--	13
Flywheel mounting bolt 2, 3			
2004-2009	127	--	93.7
All other models	128	--	94.4
Fuel reserve sensor			
Fuel injected models	23	--	17
Headlight housing mounting nuts			
Aero models	12	106	--
Headlight vertical beam adjust bolt/nut			
Aero models	12	106	--
Headlight mounting bolts			
2004-2009 Aero models	3.9	35	--
All other models	4.1	36	--
Horn mounting bolt	21	--	15
Ignition switch cover screw			
2004-2009 Areo models	2.0	18	--
All Spirit models and Phantom models	1.0	8.9	--
Ignition switch mounting bolt	12	106	--
Neutral switch	12	106	--
Oil pressure switch (1)	12	106	--
Oil pressure switch wire connector screw			
2004-2009 Aero models	2.0	18	--
All other models	1.9	17	--
Sidestand switch mounting bolt (4)			
2004-2009 Aero models	9.8	87	--
All other models	10	89	--
Speedometer housing mounting bolts	10	89	
2004-2009 Aero models	9.8	87	--
All other models	10	89	--
Starter assembly bolts			
2008-2013	4.9	44	--
Starter brush (negative) holder screw			
2008-2013	3.7	33	--
	(continued)		

Table 10 ELECTRICAL SYSTEM TORQUE SPECIFICATIONS (continue)

Starter cable terminal nut (outer)			
2004-2007 Aero models	9.8	87	--
All other models	10	89	--
Starter one-way clutch outer Allen bolt			
2004-2009 Aero models	29	--	21
All other models	30	--	22
Stator mounting bolt (5)	12	106	--
Stator wiring harness guide plate Allen bolt (5)	12	106	--
Tail/brake light mounting nuts			
Aero models			
2004-2009	5.9	52	--
2011-2013	6.3	56	--
Spirit and Phantom models	6.3	56	--
Turn signal lens screw			
Aero models	1.0	8.9	--
Turn signal mounting Allen bolt			
Aero models			
Front	5.1	45	--
Rear			
2004-2007	5.1	45	--
2008-2013	6.7	59	--
VS sensor mounting bolt	9.8	87	--

1. Apply sealer to switch threads.
2. Left-hand threads.
3. Lubricate threads and flange surfaces with engine oil.
4. Install new ALOC bolt.
5. Apply medium strength threadlock to threads.

CHAPTER ELEVEN

COOLING SYSTEM

This chapter describes repair and replacement of cooling system components.

Drain and flush the cooling system at the intervals specified in Chapter Three.

Table 1 and **Table 2** are located at the end of the chapter.

WARNING
*Never remove the radiator cap (**Figure 1**), coolant drain plug, or disconnect any coolant hose while the engine and radiator are hot. Scalding fluid and steam may be blown out under pressure and cause serious injury.*

CAUTION
Do not reuse the old coolant as it deteriorates with use. Do not operate the cooling system with only distilled water (even if freezing temperatures are not expected); the antifreeze inhibits internal engine corrosion and provides lubrication of moving parts in the water pump.

COOLING SYSTEM INSPECTION

Inspection

1. If steam is observed at the muffler after the engine has sufficiently warmed up, a head gasket might be damaged. If enough coolant leaks into a cylinder(s), the cylinders could hydrolock. This would prevent the engine from being turned over. Coolant may also be present in the engine oil. If the oil visible in the oil level inspection window is foamy or milky-looking, there is coolant in the oil. If so, correct the problem before returning the motorcycle to service. Performing a leak-down test as described in Chapter Two can help identify a blown head gasket and/or warped cylinder head.

2. Refer to Chapter Three, *Cooling System* to check the coolant level.

3. Check the radiator for clogged or damaged fins.

4. Check the radiator for loose or missing mounting bolts.

5. Check all coolant hoses for cracks or damage. With the engine cold, squeeze the hoses by hand. If a hose collapses easily, it is damaged and must be replaced. Make sure the hose clamps are tight. See *Hoses* in this section.

6. Make sure the siphon hose is connected to the filler neck (next to the radiator cap) and is not clogged or damaged.

7. To check the cooling system for leaks, pressure test it as described in this section.

Hoses

After removing any cooling system component, inspect the adjoining hose(s) to determine if replacement is necessary. Hoses deteriorate with age and should be inspected carefully for conditions that may cause them to fail. Loss of coolant will cause the engine to overheat, and spray from a leaking hose can injure the rider. A collapsed hose prevents coolant circulation and will cause overheating. Observe the following when servicing hoses:

1. Make sure the cooling system is cool before removing any coolant hose or component.

2. Use original equipment replacement hoses; they are formed to a specific shape and dimension for a correct fit.

3. Loosen the hose clamps on the hose that is to be replaced. Slide the clamps back off the component fittings.

4. Before disconnecting a formed hose, look for a paint mark on the end of the hose. This mark usually

aligns with a raised boss on the connecting part to ensure the hose is properly installed.

> *CAUTION*
> *Do not use excessive force when attempting to remove a stubborn hose. Also, use caution when attempting to loosen hoses with hose pliers. The aluminum radiator and water pump hose joints are easily damaged.*

5. Twist the hose to release it from the joint. If the hose is difficult to break loose, insert a small screwdriver between the hose and joint and spray WD-40 or a similar lubricant into the opening and carefully twist the hose to break it loose.
6. Examine the fittings for cracks or other damage. Repair or replace as necessary. If the fitting is good, use a wire brush and clean off any hose residue that may have transferred to the fitting. Wipe clean with a cloth.
7. Inspect the hose clamps for rust, corrosion and damage. Replace if necessary.

> *NOTE*
> *Remove all lubricant residue from the hose and hose fitting before reinstalling the hose.*

8. If a hose is difficult to install on the joint, soak the end in hot water to make it more pliable. Do not use any lubricant when installing hoses.
9. Formed hoses must be properly installed. Align any paint marks with the raised boss on the connecting part noted during removal.
10. With the hose correctly installed, position and tighten the clamp securely. Position the clamp head so it is accessible for future removal and does not contact other parts.

Pressure Test

This test simulates the integrity of the cooling system under engine running conditions by placing pressure on the hoses, gaskets and seals. Perform this test whenever troubleshooting the cooling system. The test is performed when the engine is cold. A hand pump tester is used to pressurize the system.

> *WARNING*
> *Never remove the radiator cap (Figure 1), coolant drain plug, or disconnect any coolant hose while the engine and radiator are hot. Scalding fluid and steam may be blown out under pressure and cause serious injury.*

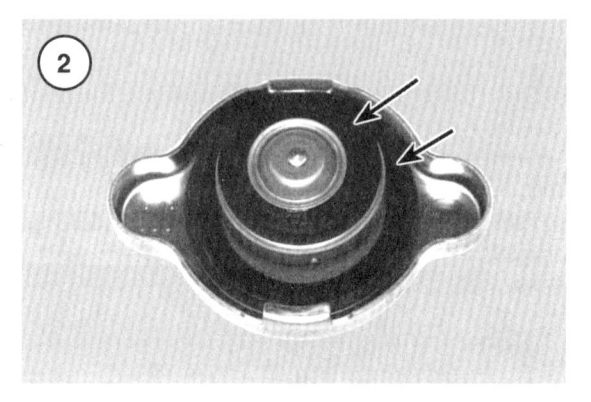

1. Remove the fuel tank (Chapter Eight or Chapter Nine).
2. With the engine cold, remove the radiator cap **(Figure 1)**.
3. Add coolant to the radiator to bring the level up to the filler neck.
4. Check the rubber washers on the radiator cap **(Figure 2)**. Replace the cap if the washers show signs of deterioration, cracking or other damage. If the radiator cap is good, continue the procedure.

> *CAUTION*
> *Do not exceed 137 kPa (20 psi) or the cooling system components may be damaged.*

5. Lubricate the rubber washer on the bottom of the radiator cap with coolant and install it on a cooling system pressure tester **(Figure 3)**. Apply 108-137 kPa (16-20 psi) and check for a pressure drop. Replace the cap if it cannot hold this pressure for six seconds.

> *NOTE*
> *If the test pressure drops rapidly, but there are no visible coolant leaks, coolant may be leaking into one of the cylinder heads. Perform a leak down test as described in Chapter Two.*

COOLING SYSTEM

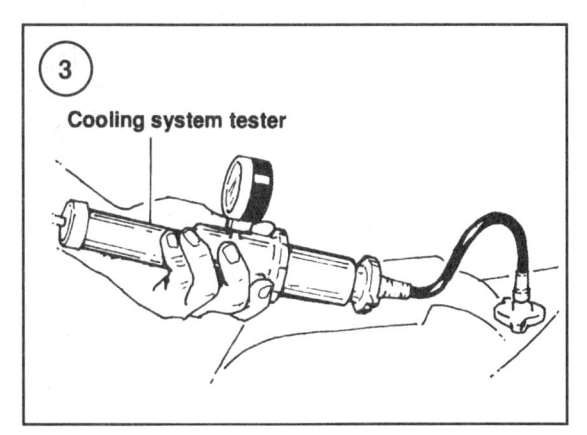

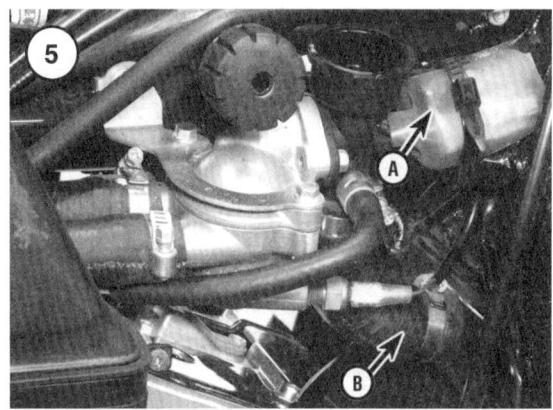

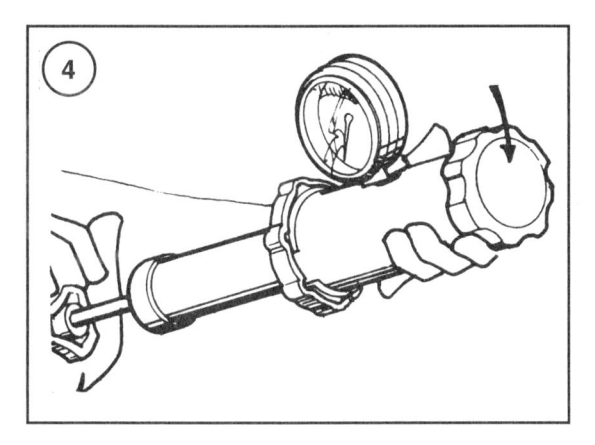

6. Mount the pressure tester onto the thermostat housing filler neck (**Figure 4**) and pressure test the cooling system to 108-137 kPa (16-20 psi). If the system cannot hold this pressure for six seconds, check for a coolant leak:
   a. Radiator cap. If the radiator cap passed the pressure test, but is now leaking, inspect the filler neck and cap mounting flange for damage.
   b. Leaking or damaged coolant hoses.
   c. Damaged or deteriorated O-rings installed in coolant hose connectors.
   d. Damaged water pump mechanical seal.
   e. Water pump leakage.
   f. Loose coolant drain bolt.
   g. Warped cylinder head or cylinder mating surfaces.
7. Check all cooling system hoses for damage or deterioration. Replace any questionable hose. Make sure all hose clamps are tight.
8. Remove the tester and install the radiator cap.
9. Install the fuel tank (Chapter Eight or Chapter Nine).

RADIATOR

Removal/Installation

1. Remove the fuel tank (Chapter Eight or Chapter Nine).
2. Remove the steering covers (Chapter Seventeen).
3. Drain the cooling system (Chapter Three).
4A. On carbureted models, disconnect the fan motor switch connector located in the connector pouch on the right side of the motorcycle (A, **Figure 5**).
4B. On fuel injected models, disconnect the fan motor connector located in the connector pouch on the right side of the motorcycle (A, **Figure 6**).

NOTE
If it is difficult to disconnect the upper radiator hose, wait until after removing the upper radiator mounting bolt so the radiator is more maneuverable.

5. Disconnect the upper radiator hose at the radiator. See B, **Figure 5** (carbureted models) or B, **Figure 6** (fuel injected models).

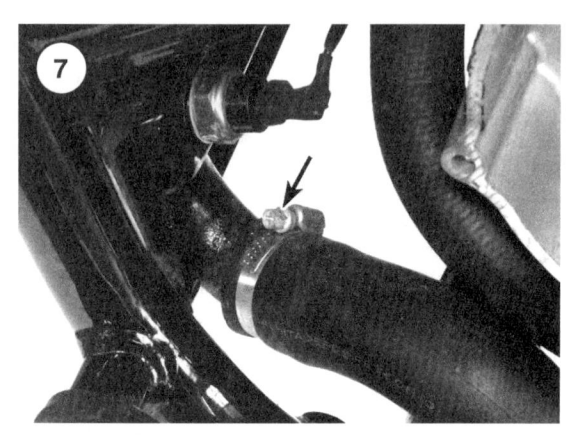

6. Disconnect the lower radiator hose at the radiator. See **Figure 7** (carbureted models) or **Figure 8** (fuel injected models).
7. Release the wiring harnesses from the radiator grill on the right side of the radiator.
8. Remove the upper radiator mounting bolt and washer **(Figure 9)**.
9. Pivot the radiator forward and release the fan motor wiring harness from the clamp on the left engine mount (**Figure 10**, typical).
10. Lift the radiator to disconnect its lower rubber dampers from the mounting bracket **(Figure 11)**, then remove the radiator with the front grill and cooling fan.
11. Installation is the reverse of removal. Note the following:
   a. Remove the cooling fan mounting nut and retighten it with a threadlock as described in *Cooling Fan* in this chapter. A loose mounting nut may allow the cooling fan to run off its shaft and damage the radiator.
   b. Tighten the upper radiator mounting bolt **(Figure 9)** securely.
   c. Check the radiator hoses for damage that may have occurred during radiator removal.
   d. Refill and bleed the cooling system (Chapter Three).
   e. After starting the engine, check the coolant hoses for leaks.

Inspection

1. Flush off the exterior of the radiator with a garden hose on low pressure. Spray the front and back sides to remove all debris. Carefully use a whisk broom or stiff paint brush to remove any stubborn dirt.

> *CAUTION*
> *Do not press too hard or the cooling fins and tubes may be damaged.*

2. Carefully straighten out any bent cooling fins with

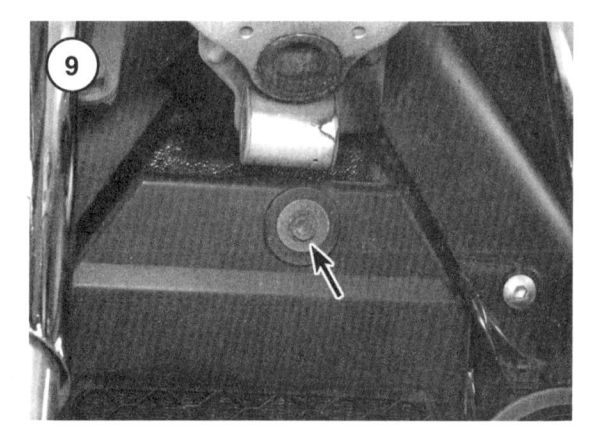

COOLING SYSTEM

connect the ground terminal at the bottom of the radiator (D, **Figure 12**).
6. Remove the fan mounting bolts and the fan shroud (E, **Figure 12**).
7. Remove the cooling fan mounting nut and the cooling fan. Remove all threadlock residue from the nut and shaft threads.
8. Make an alignment mark across the fan motor and the shroud for proper alignment. Then, remove the bolts securing the fan motor to the shroud and remove the fan motor.
9. Installation is the reverse of the removal steps. Note the following:
   a. Install the fan motor onto the shroud by using the alignment marks made prior to disassembly. Tighten the fan motor mounting bolts to the torque specification in **Table 2**.
   b. Install the cooling fan onto the fan motor shaft by aligning the flat surfaces. Apply a medium strength threadlock onto the shaft threads. Install and tighten the cooling fan mounting nut to the torque specification in **Table 2**.
   c. Tighten the fan motor shroud mounting bolts to the torque specification in **Table 2**. On carbureted models, make sure to secure the ground wire with the lower mounting bolt (D, **Figure 12**).
   d. Check the wire harness routing.

Testing

Carbureted models

To test the fan motor switch, refer to *Fan Motor Switch (Carbureted Models)* in Chapter Ten.

Fuel injected models

To test the fan control relay, refer to *Fan Control Relay (Fuel Injected Models)* in Chapter Ten.

COOLANT RESERVE TANK

Removal/Installation

1. Remove the left crankcase rear cover (Chapter Seventeen).
2. Note the breather hose (A, **Figure 13**) routing on the coolant reserve tank so it can be returned to its original position.
3. Disconnect the siphon hose (B, **Figure 13**) from the bottom of the coolant reserve tank and drain the coolant from the tank.
4. Remove the mounting bolt (C, **Figure 13**) and the coolant reserve tank.

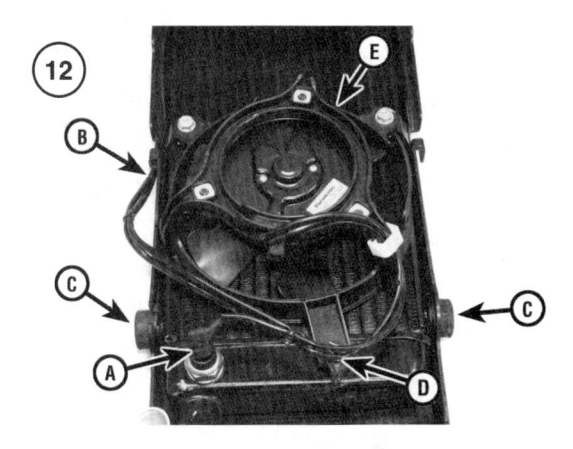

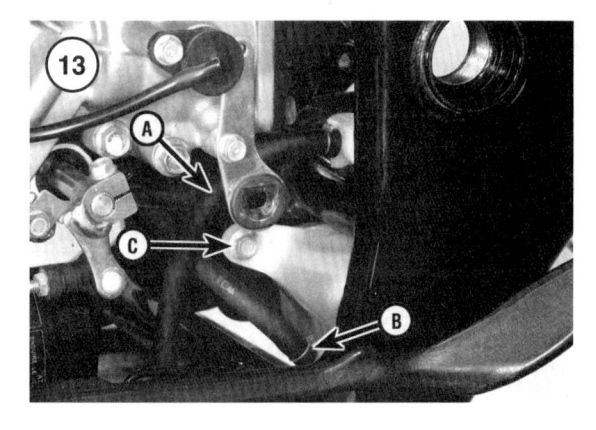

a broad-tipped screwdriver or putty knife.
3. Check for cracks or leakage (usually a moss-green colored residue) at the filler neck, the inlet and outlet hose fittings and the upper and lower tank seams.
4. If paint has been worn off in any area of the radiator, repaint with a quality black spray paint. This will help to prolong the radiator life by cutting down on oxidation from the outside. Do not apply too much paint to the cooling fin area as this will cut down on the cooling capabilities of the radiator.
5. Replace the lower mounting bracket rubber dampers (**Figure 11**) if damaged.
6. Inspect the rubber washers (**Figure 2**) on the radiator cap. Replace the cap if they are hardened or starting to deteriorate.

COOLING FAN

Removal/Installation

1. Remove the radiator as described in this chapter.
2. On carbureted models, disconnect the fan motor switch connector (A, **Figure 12**).
3. Remove the wiring harness from the clamps on the radiator grill (B, **Figure 12**).
4. Remove the rubber dampers (C, **Figure 12**) and the grill.
5. On carbureted models, remove the bolt and dis-

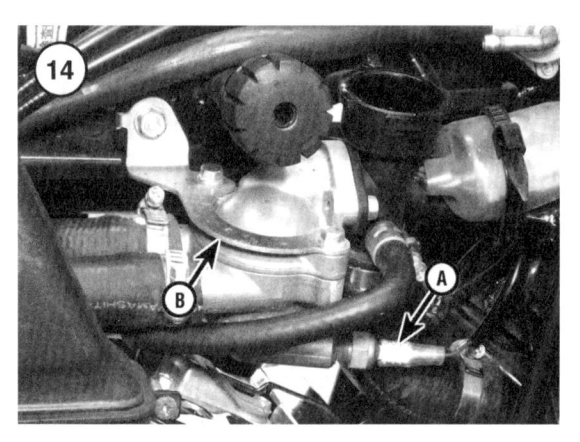

5. Flush the tank with clean water. Check the tank for cracks or other damage.
6. Replace the breather and/or siphon hose(s) if leaking or damaged.
7. Install the coolant reserve tank by reversing these steps. Note the following:
   a. Tighten the coolant reserve tank mounting bolt securely.
   b. Fill the coolant reserve tank (Chapter Three).

THERMOSTAT

The thermostat is a temperature-sensitive valve used to control the flow of coolant into the radiator. When the engine is cold, the thermostat is closed and coolant bypasses the radiator. This condition helps the engine to warm up quickly. When the engine reaches operating temperature, the thermostat opens and coolant flows between the engine and radiator.

Thermostat Check

A stuck thermostat will cause the engine to warm up slowly (when stuck open) or can cause overheating (stuck partially or fully closed). Check by starting the engine (when cold) and allow to warm to normal operating temperature. During this time, carefully touch the top radiator hose. If the hose becomes hot quickly, the thermostat is probably stuck open. This condition will cause the engine to run colder for a longer period. If the hose gradually warms and then becomes hot, the thermostat is probably opening correctly. However, if the upper hose and radiator do not feel hot after the engine has run long enough to warm to normal operating temperature, the thermostat is probably stuck closed and is blocking coolant flow through the radiator. This condition will cause the engine to overheat.

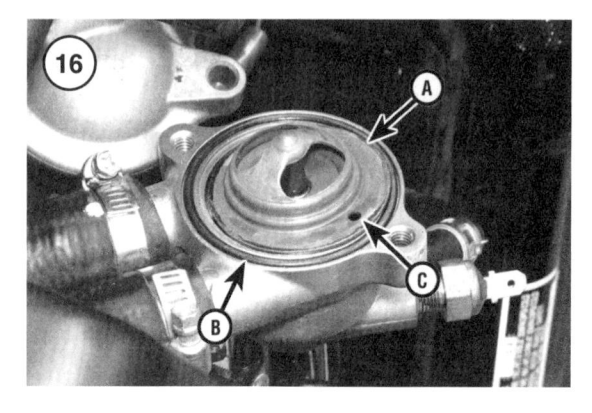

Removal/Installation

The thermostat can be removed without having to remove the thermostat housing or disconnect any coolant hoses.
1. Remove the fuel tank (Chapter Eight or Chapter Nine).
2. Remove the air filter housing (Chapter Eight or Chapter Nine).
3. Remove the steering covers (Chapter Seventeen).
4. Drain the engine coolant (Chapter Three).
5. Place a rag underneath the thermostat to catch any residue coolant spilled from the thermostat housing.

NOTE
Make sure the front cylinder head spark plugs and spark plug caps are installed to prevent coolant from entering the cylinder block.

6. Disconnect the ECT sensor electrical connector. See A, **Figure 14** (carbureted models) or A, **Figure 15** (fuel injected models).
7. Remove the bolts securing the cover ring to the thermostat cover and the bolt securing the cover ring to the frame. Then remove the cover ring and cover. See B, **Figure 14** (carbureted models) or B, Figure 15 (fuel injected models).
8. Remove the thermostat (A, **Figure 16**).

COOLING SYSTEM

a. Install the thermostat by aligning its support arm (A, **Figure 18**) with the housing groove (B). The vent hole on the thermostat flange must face up (C, **Figure 16**).
b. Install a new O-ring (B, **Figure 16**) into the housing groove.
c. Tighten the thermostat cover ring bolts to 10 N.m (89 in.-lb.).
d. Tighten the cover ring to frame mounting bolt securely.
e. Fill and bleed the cooling system (Chapter Three). Check for coolant leaks.

Testing

Test the thermostat to ensure proper operation or when troubleshooting the cooling system. Replace the thermostat if it remains open at normal room temperature or stays closed after the specified temperature is reached during the test procedure.

Support the thermostat and a thermometer (rated higher than the test temperature) in a pan of water **(Figure 19)**. The thermostat and thermometer must not touch the sides or bottom of the pan or a false reading will result. Gradually heat the water and continue to gently stir the water until it reaches 80-84 degrees C (176-183 degrees F). At this temperature, the thermostat valve should start to open. At 95 degrees C (203 degrees F), the minimum valve lift should be 8 mm (0.32 in.).

NOTE
Valve operation is sometimes sluggish; it may take 3-5 minutes for the valve to operate properly.

If the valve fails to operate at the listed temperatures, or if the valve lift is below minimum at the specified temperature, replace the thermostat. Always replace the thermostat with one of the same temperature rating.

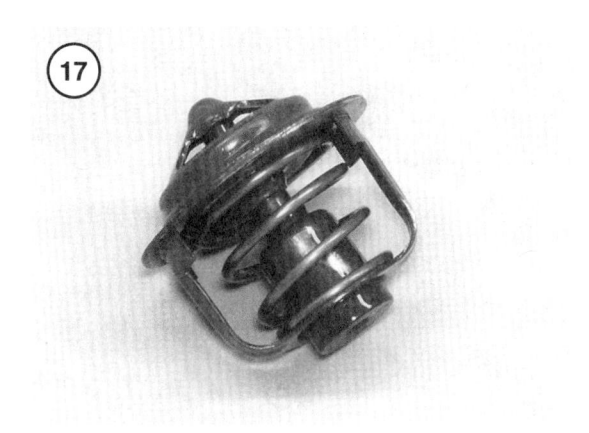

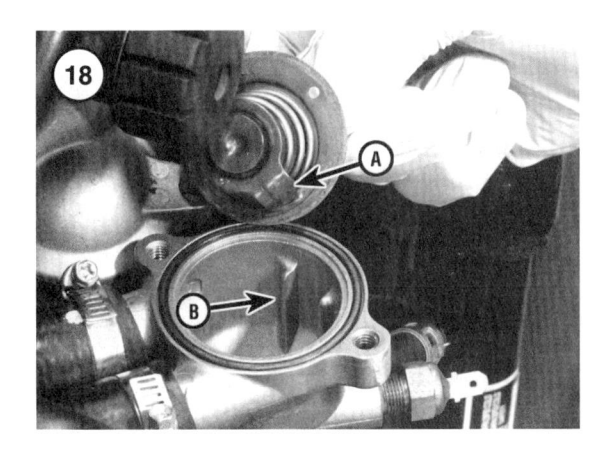

9. Remove and discard the O-ring (B, **Figure 16**).
10. Rinse the thermostat with clean water.
11. Inspect the thermostat **(Figure 17)** for damage. Make sure the spring has not sagged or broken.
12. Inspect the thermostat valve and valve seat for any gaps, indicating a stuck thermostat.
13. If necessary, test the thermostat as described in this section.
14. Clean the thermostat housing, O-ring groove and all mating surfaces.
15. Installation is the reverse of removal. Note the following:

THERMOSTAT HOUSING

The thermostat housing contains the thermostat, filler neck and serves as a hose manifold. The ECT sensor is mounted on the thermostat housing.

Removal/Installation

1. Remove the fuel tank (Chapter Eight or Chapter Nine).
2. Remove the air filter housing (Chapter Eight or Chapter Nine).
3. Remove the steering covers (Chapter Seventeen).
4. Drain the engine coolant (Chapter Three).

5. Disconnect the ECT sensor electrical connector. See A, **Figure 14** (carbureted models) or A, **Figure 15** (fuel injected models).
6. Remove the mounting bolt securing the thermostat housing cover ring to the frame.
7. Note the hose routing at the thermostat housing.
8. Disconnect the coolant hoses at the thermostat housing and remove the housing.
9. Installation is the reverse of removal. Note the following:
   a. Tighten the cover ring to frame mounting bolt securely.
   b. Make sure the coolant hoses are routed correctly.
   c. Fill and bleed the cooling system (Chapter Three). Check for coolant leaks.

Radiator Filler Neck
Removal/Installation

1. Remove the bolts securing the radiator filler neck to the thermostat cover. Remove and discard the O-ring.
2. Clean the radiator filler neck and thermostat cover mating surfaces.
3. Installation is the reverse of these steps. Note the following:
   a. Install a new O-ring
   b. Tighten the radiator filler neck mounting bolts to 10 N.m (89 in.-lb.).

Engine Coolant Temperature (ECT) Sensor

Refer to *Coolant Temperature Indicator and Engine Coolant Temperature (ECT) Sensor* (Chapter Ten) to test and service the sensor.

WATER PUMP

The water pump is mounted on the bottom, left side of the engine and can be removed with the engine installed in the frame.

The water pump is sold as a complete unit only. If any component is damaged, the entire water pump assembly must be replaced. The water pump O-rings, mounting and assembly bolts and washers can be replaced separately.

Weep Hole Check

NOTE
Figure 20 shows the water pump removed for clarity.

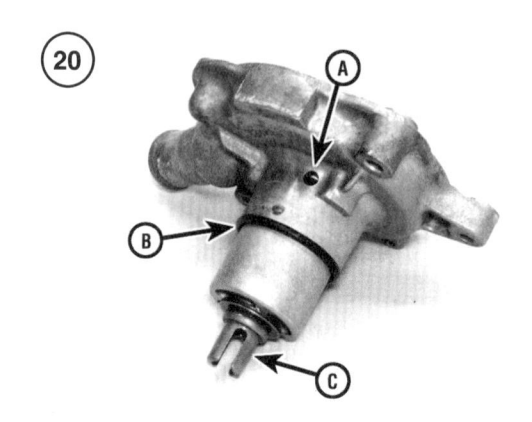

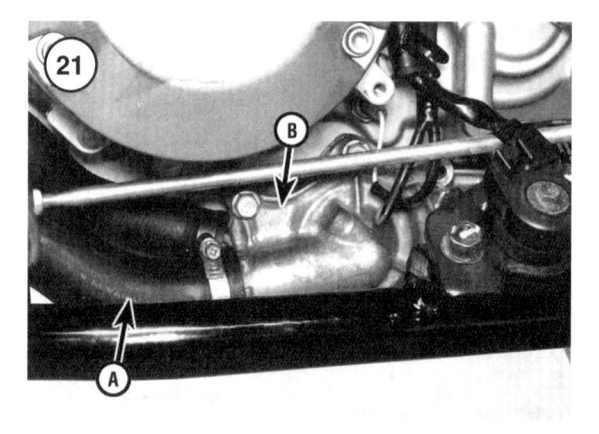

An inspection or weep hole (A, **Figure 20**) is built into the bottom of the water pump. When coolant leaks from the hole, the mechanical seal in the water pump is damaged and must be replaced. Note the following at the inspection hole:
1. Check for signs of coolant or coolant stains on the bottom of the water pump. If there is coolant in this area, check the condition of the two hoses and hose clamps mounted on the water pump. Check the hose clamps for tightness.
2. Clean up any spilled coolant so that it does not contact the rear tire.

Removal

1. Remove the fuel tank (Chapter Eight or Chapter Nine).
2. Remove the left crankcase rear cover (Chapter Seventeen).
3. Drain the engine oil (Chapter Three).
4. Drain the engine coolant (Chapter Three).
5. Disconnect the outer hose at the water pump cover (A, **Figure 21**).
6. Remove the water pump cover (B, **Figure 21**) as follows:
   a. **Figure 22** shows the bolt and washer alignment. The two short bolts are assembly bolts.

COOLING SYSTEM

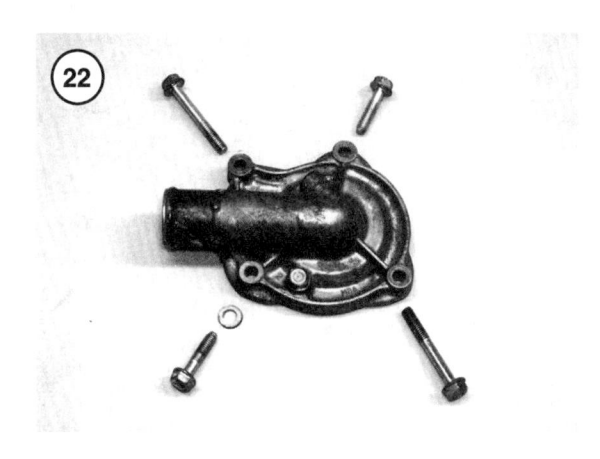

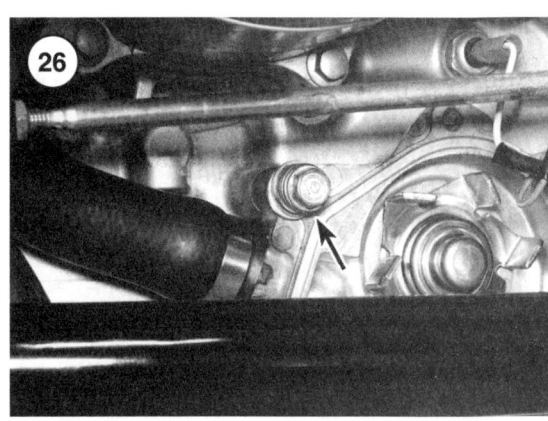

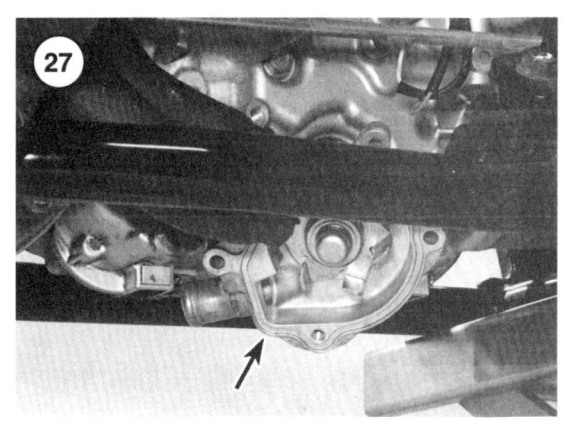

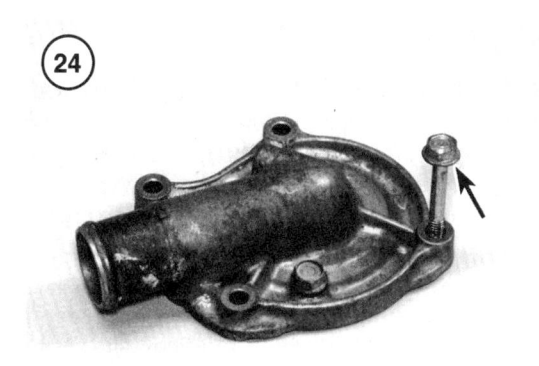

The two long bolts mount the water pump onto the engine. Loosen all of the bolts.

b. Remove the upper assembly bolt and the mounting bolt.

c. Remove the front lower assembly bolt and its washer.

d. Pivot the water pump cover down (**Figure 23**), then remove the cover with the rear lower mounting bolt. The rear lower mounting bolt must be removed with the cover (**Figure 24**).

7. Remove the O-ring from the groove in the pump housing (A, **Figure 25**) and discard it.

NOTE
*If it is difficult to disconnect the hose because the pump housing is loose, install a mounting bolt (**Figure 26**) with some spacer washers to help hold the pump housing in place. Then, disconnect the hose.*

8. Disconnect the rear hose (B, **Figure 25**) at the water pump housing.
9. Slide the water pump housing (**Figure 27**) out and then tilt it downward to remove it from the engine.
10. Remove the O-ring (B, **Figure 20**) from the shoulder on the pump housing and discard it.
11. Inspect the water pump (this section).

Installation

1. Make sure the hose clamps are installed over the inner and outer two hoses.

NOTE
The inner hose is connected to the hose nozzle on the front cylinder. The outer hose is connected to the radiator (and the bypass hose on fuel injected models).

2. Clean the water pump opening in the left case half.
3. Lubricate a new O-ring with engine oil and seat it next to the water pump housing shoulder (B, **Figure 20**).
4. Align the water pump with its hose nozzle facing forward (**Figure 27**). Then, install the water pump into the engine. The water pump will have to be maneuvered so its shaft can slip into the engine opening. Do not force it. The fit is tight, but once the proper angle is obtained, the pump shaft will slip into the hole and the pump can be tilted up and squared with the engine and oil pump shaft.
5. Turn the impeller to align the notch (C, **Figure 20**) on the water pump shaft with the shoulder (**Figure 28**) on the oil pump shaft. When the engagement is made, the water pump impeller can be turned a few degrees either way but should not turn past this point.

CAUTION
When the inner coolant hose is installed and the pump is aligned with the crankcase, turn the impeller to make sure its shaft is still engaged with oil pump shaft. If not, the shafts will be damaged when the mounting bolts are installed.

6. Pivot the hose nozzle on the front of the water pump down and connect the inner hose onto the nozzle. Slide the hose in place until it bottoms against the shoulder on the water pump housing. Then pivot the pump housing up and align its front upper mounting hole with the crankcase threads.

NOTE
Because the engine oil was drained, thread the engine oil drain bolt in and out of the crankcase to make sure it does not interfere with the inner hose clamp.

7. Position the inner hose clamp (B, **Figure 25**) and tighten securely. Make sure the clamp does not interfere with the engine oil drain bolt.
8. Lubricate a new O-ring (A, **Figure 25**) with grease and install it into the water pump housing groove.
9. Insert the rear lower mounting bolt into the cover hole shown in **Figure 24**. This bolt cannot be installed after the cover is in place. Then install the cover by tilting it upward while installing the mounting bolt into the hole in the pump housing (**Figure 23**). When the bolt is in the hole, pivot the cover up and install the remaining bolts, making sure the O-ring is not pinched between the cover and housing. Refer to **Figure 22** to identify the bolt and washer positions. Install a new sealing washer on the bolt shown in **Figure 22**.

NOTE
*To access the upper mounting bolts with a torque wrench, remove the shift arm as described in **Shift Pedal and Linkage Removal/Installation** in **External Shift Mechanism** in Chapter Six. A 10-mm torque adaptor (**Figure 29**) will be required to access the lower two bolts with a torque wrench.*

10. Tighten the water pump assembly and mounting bolts evenly until the pump cover is positioned flush against the pump housing. Then tighten the bolts in a crossing pattern to 13 N.m (115 in.-lb.).
11. Slide the outer hose onto the pump cover until it

bottoms against the cover (A, **Figure 21**). Position the hose clamp and tighten securely.

12. Refill the cooling system (Chapter Three) and check for leaks.
13. Reinstall the engine oil drain bolt and refill the engine with oil (Chapter Three).
14. Start the engine and bleed the cooling system (Chapter Three). Check for coolant leaks.
15. Install the left crankcase rear cover (Chapter Seventeen).
16. Install the fuel tank (Chapter Eight or Chapter Nine).

Inspection

1. Replace the water pump if there is engine oil in the pump. This indicates that the seal mounted over the pump shaft is damaged.
2. Check the impeller blades **(Figure 30)** for corrosion or damage. If the corrosion buildup on the blades is minor, clean the blades. If the corrosion is severe or if the blades are cracked or broken, replace the water pump assembly.
3. Turn the impeller shaft and check the pump bearing for excessive noise or roughness. If the bearing operation is rough or abnormal, replace the water pump assembly.

Table 1 COOLING SYSTEM SPECIFICATIONS

Coolant	
Standard concentration	50% mixture coolant and purified water
Type	Honda HP coolant or an equivalent*
Coolant capacity	
Radiator and engine	1.58 L (1.67 U.S. qt.)
Reserve tank	0.38 L (0.40 qt.)
Cooling system test pressure	108-137 kPa (16-20 psi)
Radiator cap test pressure	108-137 kPa (16-20 psi)
Thermostat	
Begins to open	80-84° C (176-183° F)
Fully open	95° C (203° F)
Valve lift (minimum)	8.0 mm (0.32 in.)

* Coolant must not contain silicate inhibitors as they can cause premature wear to the water pump seals.

Table 2 COOLING SYSTEM TORQUE SPECIFICATIONS

	N.m	in.-lb.
Coolant drain bolt	13	115
Cooling fan mounting nut*		
Aero models		
2004-2009	2.9	26
2011-2013	2.7	24
Spirit and Phantom models	2.7	24
Fan motor mounting bolts		
Aero		
2004-2009	4.9	43
2011-2013	5.1	45
Spirit and Phantom models	5.1	45
Fan motor shroud mounting bolts		
Aero		
2004-2009	8.8	78
All other models	8.4	74
Radiator filler neck mounting bolts		
2004-2009 Aero models	9.8	87
All other models	10	89
Thermostat ring/cover bolts		
2004-2009 Aero models	9.8	87
All other models	10	89
Water pump assembly bolts	13	115
Water pump mounting bolts	13	115

*See text for additional information.

CHAPTER TWELVE

WHEELS AND TIRES

This chapter describes repair and maintenance for the front and rear wheels, hubs and tires. Routine maintenance procedures for these components are found in Chapter Three.

Specifications are in **Tables 1-4** at the end of this chapter.

MOTORCYCLE LIFT

WARNING
Regardless of the type of jack or stand used to lift the motorcycle, make sure the motorcycle is properly supported before walking away from it.

Many procedures in this chapter require lifting either the front or rear wheel off the ground. Because the motorcycle is not equipped with a centerstand, a separate jack or chain hoist will be required. A center jack (K&L part No. MC450) is used in this chapter by placing it under the motorcycle to lift either the front or rear wheel. When using a center jack **(Figure 1)** or scissors jack, have an assistant sit on the motorcycle and center it upright. Place a block of wood across the jack and position the jack underneath the front or rear part of the frame, depending on which wheel will be raised. Operate the jack and lift the motorcycle until the front or rear wheel just clears the ground. When using a chain hoist, cover or remove the fuel tank (Chapter Eight or Chapter Nine) and the steering covers (Chapter Seventeen), then install the chain around the motorcycle's steering neck. Slowly operate the hoist, making sure the motorcycle remains centered.

FRONT WHEEL

Removal

1. Support the motorcycle securely with the front wheel off the ground.

NOTE
Do not operate the front brake lever while the front wheel/brake disc is removed from the motorcycle. Insert a spacer block between the pads until the front wheel/brake disc is reinstalled. This will prevent the caliper pistons from extending if the lever is operated.

2. Push the brake caliper in toward the brake disc to spread the brake pads. This makes it easier to install the brake disc between the pads during installation.

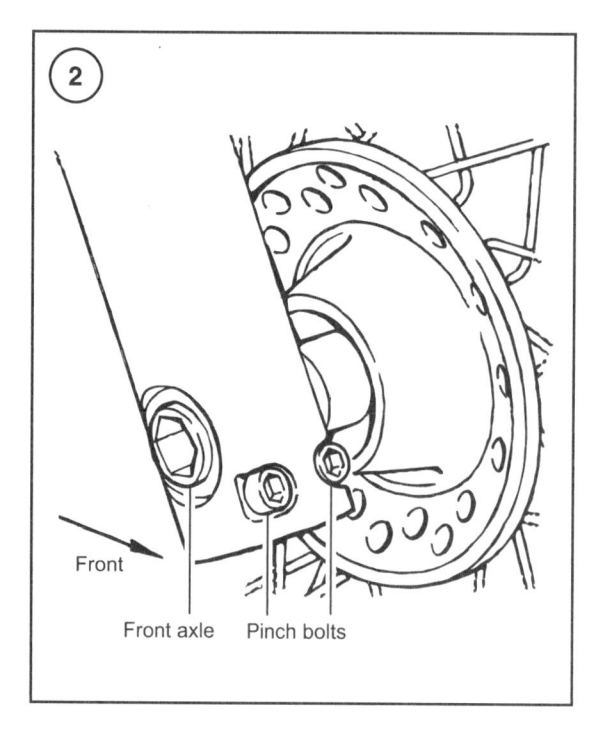

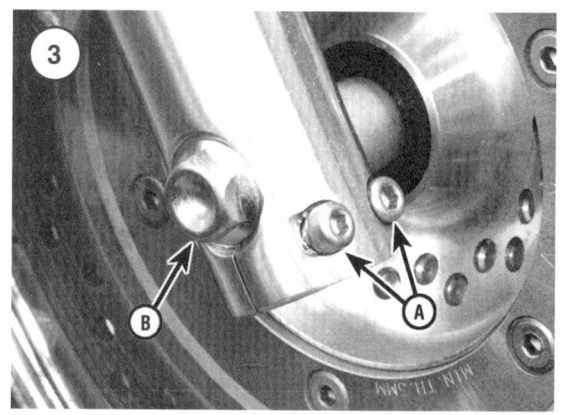

3A. On 2004-2007 Aero models, perform the following:
   a. Loosen the axle pinch bolts (**Figure 2**).
   b. Remove the axle (**Figure 2**) and the front wheel.
3B. On all other models, perform the following:
   a. Loosen the right side axle pinch bolts (A, **Figure 3**).
   b. Loosen and remove the axle bolt (B, **Figure 3**).
   c. Loosen the left side axle pinch bolts (A, **Figure 4**).
   d. Remove the axle (B, **Figure 4**) and the front wheel.
4. Remove the left (**Figure 5**) and right (**Figure 6**) axle spacers.
5. Inspect the front wheel and axle as described in this section.

Installation

1. Clean the front axle, spacers and axle bolt (if used).
2. Check the axle bearing surfaces on both fork tubes and the axle for burrs and nicks. Smooth with a file.
3. On 2004-2007 Aero models, clean the axle threads in the left fork slider.
4. Apply a light coat of grease to the axle and both spacers. Do not lubricate the axle threads. These threads must be free of oil and grease when the axle bolt is tightened.
5. Install the left (**Figure 5**) and right (**Figure 6**) axle spacers. Install the spacer with the shoulder on the

WHEELS AND TIRES

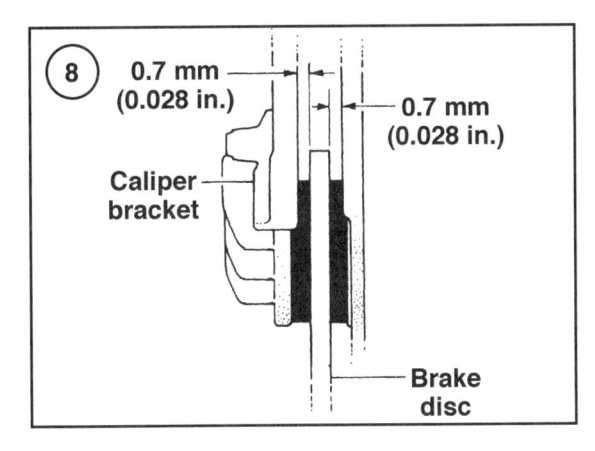

brake disc side of the wheel and with the shoulder facing out.

CAUTION
The front axle and pinch bolt tightening sequence correctly seats the front axle so both sliders are positioned parallel with each other. Fork misalignment can cause premature fork seal and bushing wear, increases the wear against the slider, reduces fork performance and may cause steering problems.

6A. On 2004-2007 Aero models, perform the following:
  a. Remove the spacer block from between the pads in the front caliper.
  b. Center the front wheel between the sliders while positioning the brake disc between the brake pads.
  c. Install the front axle (**Figure 2**) from the right side and tighten to 74 N.m (54 ft.-lb.).
  d. Apply the front brake lever several times to seat the pads against the brake disc.
  e. Lower the motorcycle so the front wheel is on the ground. Then apply the front brake and pump the forks several times to help seat the front axle and align the sliders.
  f. Tighten the axle pinch bolts (**Figure 2**) to 22 N.m (16 ft.-lb.).
6B. On all other models, perform the following:
  a. Remove the spacer block from between the pads in the front caliper.
  b. Center the front wheel between the sliders while positioning the brake disc between the brake pads.
  c. Install the front axle (B, **Figure 4**) from the left side and align the index groove on the axle with the slider's axle bore edge as shown in **Figure 7**. Then tighten the left axle pinch bolts (A, **Figure 4**) to 22 N.m (16 ft.-lb.).
  d. Install the axle bolt (B, **Figure 3**) and tighten to 59 N.m (44 ft.-lb.).
  e. Tighten the right axle pinch bolts (A, **Figure 3**) to 22 N.m (16 ft.-lb.).
  f. Apply the front brake lever several times to seat the brake pads against the brake disc.
  g. Spin the front wheel. The wheel should turn freely and without any brake drag.
  h. Remove the motorcycle from the stand so the front wheel is on the ground. Apply the front and rear brakes, then compress and release the front forks several times.

WARNING
Determine if there is adequate brake disc to caliper clearance. Failure to provide adequate clearance may cause brake disc damage and reduced braking efficiency. Both conditions can cause brake failure.

WARNING
If the correct clearance cannot be obtained, check the brake disc for loose mounting bolts, excessive runout or damage (Chapter Fifteen). Do not ride the motorcycle until the brake disc clearance is correct.

  i. Check that the brake disc is centered between the caliper bracket and caliper (not the pads) as shown in **Figure 8**. If the clearance is incorrect, loosen the left axle pinch bolts (A, **Figure 4**) and move the left slider inward or outward until the clearance is correct, then tighten the pinch bolts to 22 N.m (16 ft.-lb.). Turn the front wheel and apply the front and rear brakes several times, then recheck the clearance.
7. Apply the front brake several times to make sure proper brake pressure is felt at the brake lever.
8. On ABS models, perform the *Air Gap Inspection* for the front wheel as described in *Wheel Speed Sensors* in Chapter Sixteen.

Inspection

1. Inspect the seals (A, **Figure 9**) for wear, hardness, cracks or other damage. If necessary, replace the seals as described under *Front and Rear Hubs* in this chapter.
2. Inspect the bearings on both sides of the wheel as follows:
    a. Turn each bearing inner race (B, **Figure 9**) by hand and check for smooth, quiet operation.
    b. Try to push the bearing in and out to check for axial play **(Figure 10)**. Slight play is normal. Try to push the bearing up and down to check for radial play **(Figure 10)**. Any radial play should be difficult to feel. If play is easily felt, the bearing is worn out. Always replace bearings as a set. Refer to *Front and Rear Hubs* in this chapter.
3. Check the axle for straightness with a set of V-blocks and dial indicator. Refer to **Table 2** for maximum axle runout. Actual runout will be one-half of the gauge reading. If the special tools are not available, roll the axle on a flat surface and check for any up and down movement. Do not straighten a bent axle.
4. Check the brake disc bolts for tightness. To service the brake disc or pulser rings, refer to *Brake Discs and Pulser Rings* in Chapter Fifteen.
5. Refer to *Wheel Service* in this chapter to inspect the spokes and wheel runout.

REAR WHEEL AND DRIVEN FLANGE

Rear Wheel Removal

> *NOTE*
> *On models with deep rear fenders, the rear of the motorcycle must be raised considerably to provide clearance when removing and installing the rear wheel. Before beginning this procedure, make sure the lift can support the motorcycle at the required height. An alternative is to lift the motorcycle with a hoist or remove the rear fender as described in Chapter Seventeen.*

1. Support the motorcycle on its sidestand. Remove the license plate holder to provide additional clearance when removing the wheel.
2. Remove the exhaust system (Chapter Seventeen).
3. Remove the rear axle nut **(Figure 11)**.
4. Support the motorcycle so the rear wheel is off the ground.
5A. On non-ABS models, perform the following:

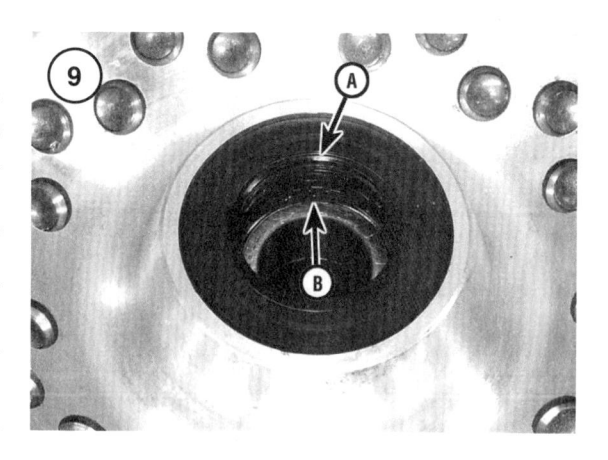

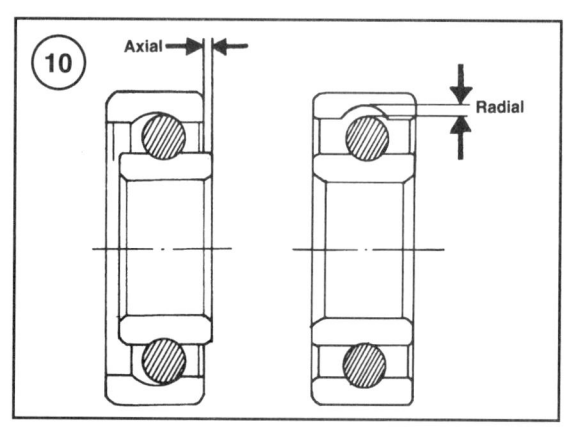

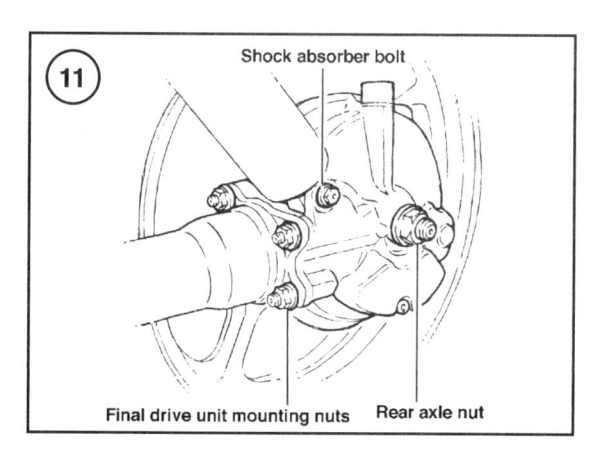

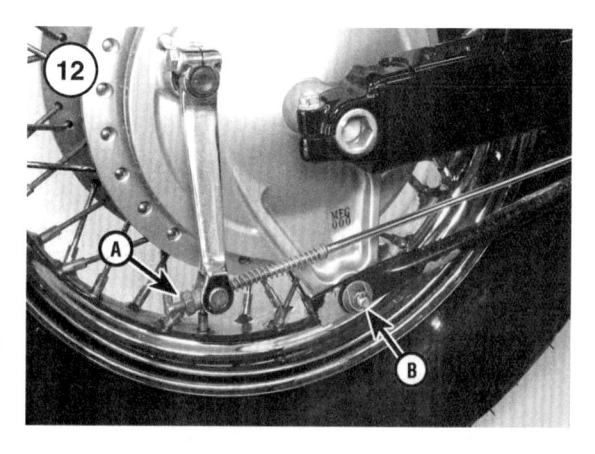

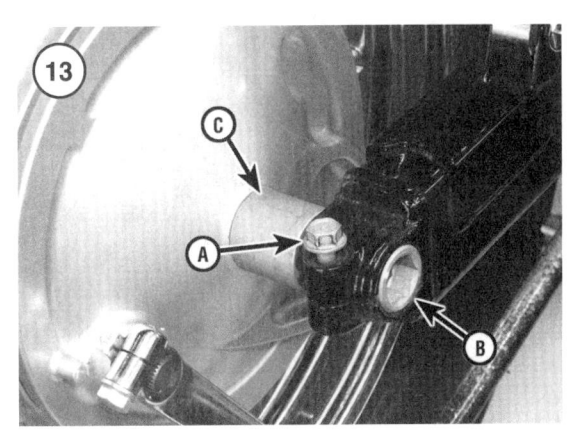

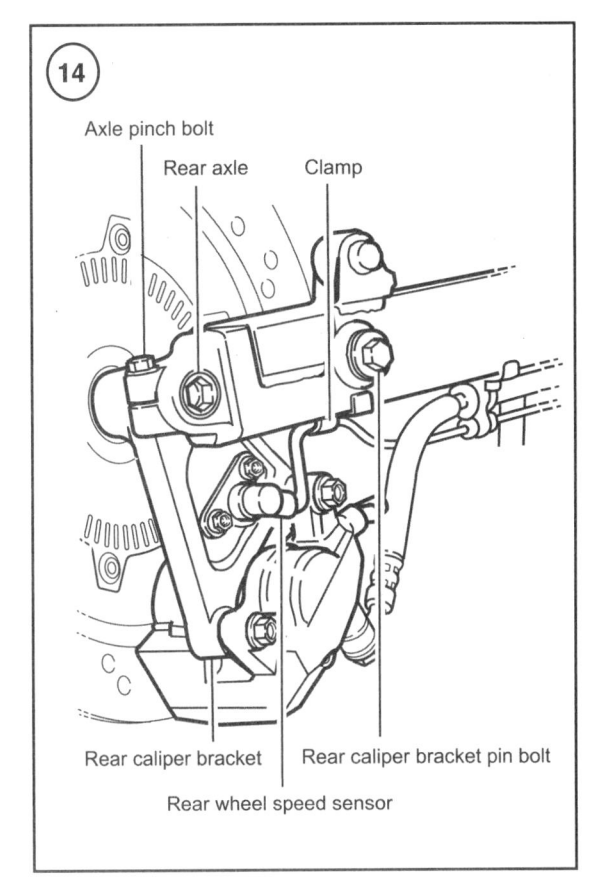

WHEELS AND TIRES

13

14
- Axle pinch bolt
- Rear axle
- Clamp
- Rear caliper bracket
- Rear caliper bracket pin bolt
- Rear wheel speed sensor

15

16

a. Remove the brake rod adjusting nut, collar and spring (A, **Figure 12**).
b. Remove the brake stopper arm cotter pin, nut, washer, rubber washer and bolt (B, **Figure 12**).
c. Loosen the rear axle pinch bolt (A, **Figure 13**).
d. Remove the rear axle (B, **Figure 13**) and spacer (C).

5B. On ABS models, refer to **Figure 14** and perform the following:

a. Remove the rear caliper bracket pin bolt.
b. Remove the bolt and clamp securing the rear wheel speed sensor wiring harness to the swing arm.
c. Loosen the axle pinch bolt.
d. Remove the rear axle and thrust washer. The thrust washer is installed between the caliper bracket and swing arm.
e. Lower the rear brake caliper and bracket away from the brake disc. Support the weight of the rear caliper and bracket to prevent it from damaging the brake hose and rear wheel speed sensor wiring harness.

NOTE
*When removing the rear wheel, the driven flange (**Figure 15**) must remain in the wheel. If the driven flange remains attached to the final drive ring gear, there will not be enough clearance to remove the wheel. If there is a problem, support the rear wheel with a jack, then carefully pry the driven flange back into the rear wheel.*

6. Slide the rear wheel toward the right side to free the driven flange (mounted on the rear wheel) from the final drive ring gear and lower the wheel.

7. On non-ABS models, remove the rear brake panel **(Figure 16)**.

WARNING
Do not use compressed air to blow out the brake drum or brake shoes as the brake dust may contain asbestos. Wipe these parts with a damp cloth to remove brake dust and then spray with a brake cleaner and allow to dry.

8. Remove the rear wheel from inside the swing arm.
9. On ABS models, remove the spacer from the right side of the wheel.
10. Remove the collar (A, **Figure 17**) from the ring gear.
11. Service the driven flange as described in this section.
12. If necessary, service the driven flange dampers as described in this chapter.
13. Inspect the rear wheel as described in this section.

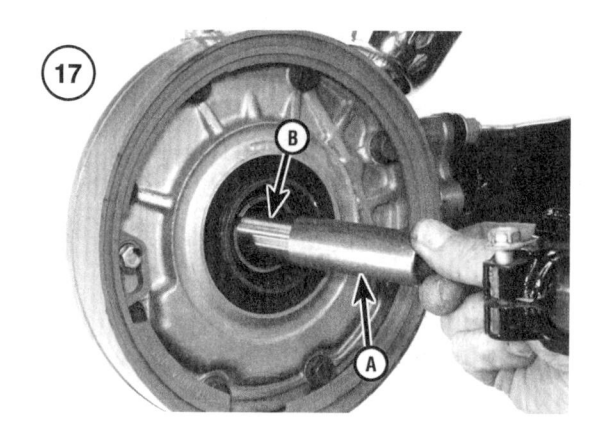

Driven Flange
Removal/Inspection/Lubrication/Installation

The procedures in this section should be performed whenever the rear wheel is removed from the motorcycle. For most riders, this will occur when replacing the rear tire. Each time the rear wheel is removed, note how much lubricant remains on the driven flange and ring gear splines. If the splines have started to dry or appear dry, it will be necessary to remove the rear wheel between tire changes to lube the splines.

CAUTION
Severe ring gear and driven flange spline wear will occur if the splines are not routinely lubricated.

1. Lift and remove the driven flange (**Figure 15**) from the rear wheel.
2. Remove the thrust washer (A, **Figure 18**) installed between the driven flange and the rear hub. Clean the thrust washer and replace it there is any surface wear or heat damage (blue color) caused by a lack of lubrication.

NOTE
The O-ring installed on the rear hub (B, Figure 18) is thin and should be replaced when it has stretched. After cleaning this O-ring, fit it into the groove in the rear hub. If the O-ring is a loose fit, replace it.

3. Remove the O-rings installed in the rear hub (B, **Figure 18**) and driven flange (A, **Figure 19**) grooves. Clean the O-rings and replace if cracked, flattened or otherwise worn or damaged.
4. Clean the rear hub surface where the driven flange is installed and check for any roughness or other damage. Lack of lubrication will score and damage the hub surface.
5. Clean the driven flange assembly and inspect it as follows:
   a. Inspect the splines (B, **Figure 19**) for severe wear (sharpness), cracks and other damage. If damage is noted, also inspect the final drive ring gear splines for damage. Lack of lubrication on the splines will cause excessive spline wear and permanent damage to both parts.
   b. Inspect the pins (A, **Figure 20**) on the driven flange for severe wear and damage. Do not loosen the nuts in order to remove the pins. If a pin is damaged, replace the driven flange assembly.
   c. Inspect the machined bore surface (B, **Figure 20**) for scoring, and heat damage. Lack of lubrication will damage the bore surface.
   d. Do not attempt to repair the driven flange or remove the pins. If damage is noted, replace the flange.

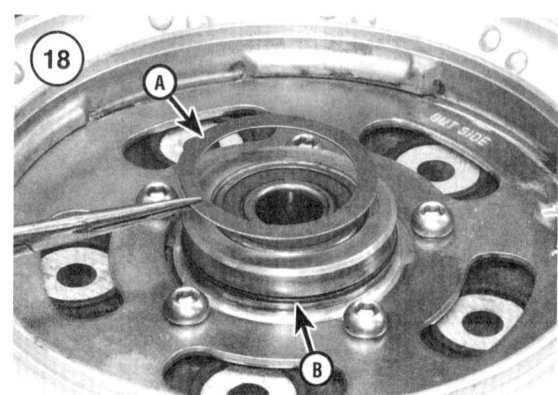

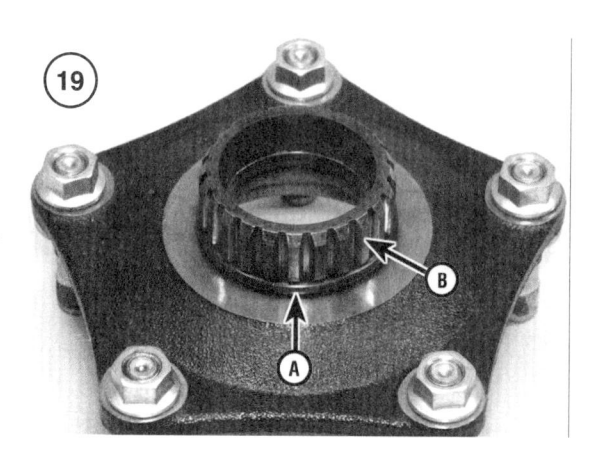

WHEELS AND TIRES

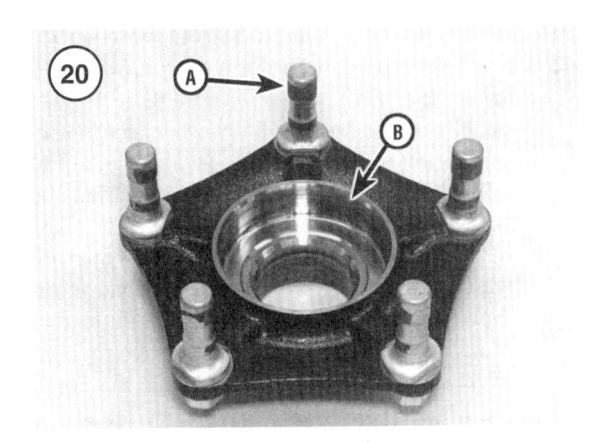

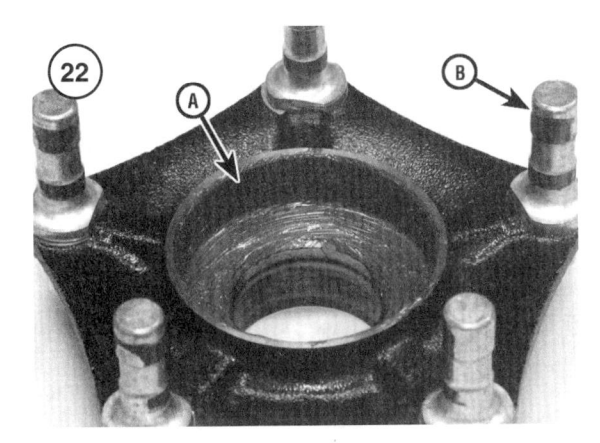

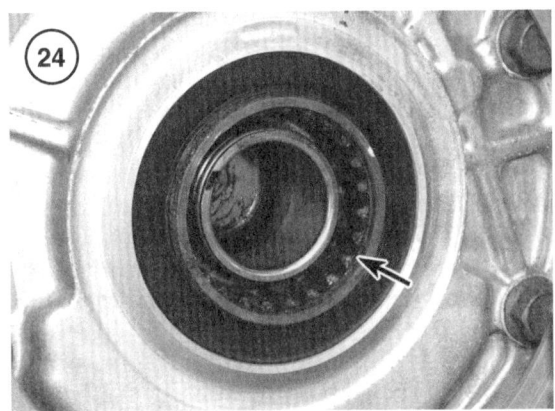

6. Insert a cloth into the ring gear splines and remove as much of the old grease as possible. Using a small wooden dowel inside the cloth helps to remove the grease from between the splines.

NOTE
Use Pro Honda Moly 60 Paste or an equivalent molybdenum disulfide paste that contains more than 40% molybdenum disulfide when lubricating the driven flange in this section. Use a small acid brush to apply the grease.

7. Lubricate the top and sides of the hub where the driven flange operates (A, **Figure 21**). Then lubricate the O-ring (B, **Figure 21**) and install it into the hub groove. Lubricate both sides of the thrust washer and install it on top of the hub (C, **Figure 21**).
8. Lubricate the driven flange bore (A, **Figure 22**). Do **not** lubricate the pins (B) installed on the driven flange or the rubber dampers installed inside the hub.

NOTE
If new rubber dampers were installed into the hub, it may be necessary to tap the driven flange into the rear hub.

9. Install the driven flange into the rear hub, making sure the thrust washer (C, **Figure 21**) is installed between the flange and hub.
10. Lubricate the driven flange splines (A, **Figure 23**). Then lubricate the O-ring (B, **Figure 23**) and install it into the groove. Replace the O-ring if it is a loose fit.

Rear Wheel Installation

1. Clean the rear axle, spacer and axle nut.
2. Check the axle bearing surfaces for burrs and nicks. Smooth with a file.
3. Service, lubricate and install the driven flange into the rear wheel as described in this section.

4. Lubricate the final drive ring gear splines (**Figure 24**) with Pro Honda Moly 60 Paste or an equivalent molybdenum disulfide paste that contains more than 40% molybdenum disulfide.

5. Install the machined end of the collar (B, **Figure 17**) into the final drive. Push the collar into the final drive until it bottoms.

6. Apply a light coat of grease to the axle and inside the spacer. Do not lubricate the axle threads. These threads must be free of oil and grease when the axle nut is tightened.

7. On non-ABS models, install the rear brake panel (**Figure 16**) into the brake drum.

8. On ABS models, install the spacer into the right side of the wheel.

9. Shift the transmission into first gear. This will prevent the ring gear from turning when meshing the driven flange and ring gear splines.

10. Position the rear wheel inside the swing arm. Then lift the rear wheel and move it toward the left side and mesh the driven flange and ring gear splines.

NOTE
Due to the weight of the rear wheel, it is helpful to raise and position the rear wheel with a jack.

11A. On non-ABS models, install the spacer (C, **Figure 13**) and the rear axle (B). Reclean the exposed axle threads of all grease.

11B. On ABS models, refer to **Figure 14** and perform the following:
   a. Make sure the spacer is still installed in the right side of the hub.
   b. Install the rear brake caliper and bracket by centering the pads between the brake disc.
   c. Position the thrust washer between the caliper bracket and swing arm, the install the rear axle from the right side.
   d. Install the rear caliper bracket pin bolt and tighten to 69 N.m (51 ft.-lb.).
   e. Install the clamp securing the rear wheel speed sensor wiring harness to the swing arm. Install the bolt and tighten securely. Make sure the wiring harness is not twisted.

12. Remove the jack from underneath the rear wheel (if used).

13. If the final drive unit was previously removed, perform the following:
   a. Tighten the final drive housing mounting nuts (**Figure 11**) in a crossing pattern and in several steps to 64 N.m (47 ft.-lb.).
   b. Tighten the lower left shock absorber mounting bolt (**Figure 11**) to 23 N.m (17 ft.-lb.) on 2004-2009 Aero models and 22 N.m (16 ft.-lb.) on all other models.

14. Install the axle nut (**Figure 11**). Then hold the axle and tighten the axle nut to 88 N.m (65 ft.-lb.).

15. On non-ABS models, perform the following:
   a. Secure the brake stopper arm to the rear brake panel with the bolt, rubber washer, steel washer and nut (B, **Figure 12**). Tighten the nut to 22 N.m (16 ft.-lb.). Install a new cotter pin and bend its arms over to lock it.
   b. Install the collar into the brake arm, then install the spring onto the brake rod and insert the brake rod through the collar. Push the rear brake pedal down to move the brake rod forward so it can be installed through the collar (A, **Figure 12**). Install the adjusting nut.
   c. Adjust the rear brake pedal free play (Chapter Three).

16. Remove the jack from underneath the vehicle so both wheels are on the ground. Sit on the seat, apply the rear brake and compress the rear suspension several times to seat the axle.

17. Tighten the rear axle pinch bolt (A, **Figure 13**) to 27 N.m (20 ft.-lb.).

18. Support the motorcycle with the jack so the rear wheel is off the ground. Rotate the rear wheel to make sure it turns freely.

19. On ABS models, apply the front brake lever and rear brake pedal until the rear brake pads are seated against the brake disc. Then rotate the rear wheel to make sure it turns freely without any excessive brake drag.

20. Install the exhaust system (Chapter Seventeen).

WARNING
Do not ride the motorcycle until you are sure the front and rear brakes are operating properly.

Inspection

1. Inspect the driven flange and its rubber dampers as described in this chapter.

2. Clean and inspect the rear brake drum and brake shoes (Chapter Fifteen).

3. Inspect the wheel bearings:
   a. Turn each bearing inner race (**Figure 25**) by hand and check for smooth, quiet operation.
   b. Try to push the bearing in and out to check for axial play (**Figure 10**). Slight play is normal. Try to push the bearing up and down to check for radial play (**Figure 10**). Any radial play should be difficult to feel. If play is easily felt, the bearing is worn out. Always replace bearings as a set. Refer to *Front and Rear Hubs* in this chapter.

4. Check the axle for straightness with a set of V-blocks and dial indicator. Refer to **Table 2** for maximum axle runout. Actual runout will be one-

WHEELS AND TIRES

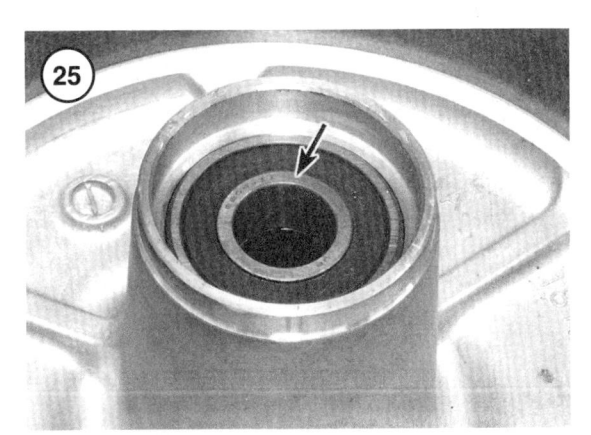

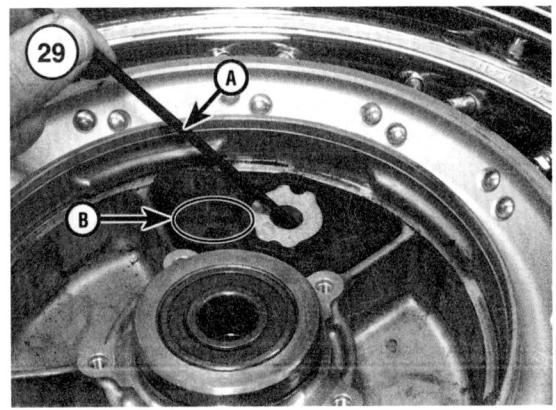

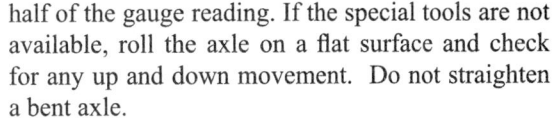

half of the gauge reading. If the special tools are not available, roll the axle on a flat surface and check for any up and down movement. Do not straighten a bent axle.

5. Refer to *Driven Flange Dampers* to service the dampers installed in the rear hub.

6. Refer to *Wheel Service* in this chapter to inspect the spokes and wheel runout.

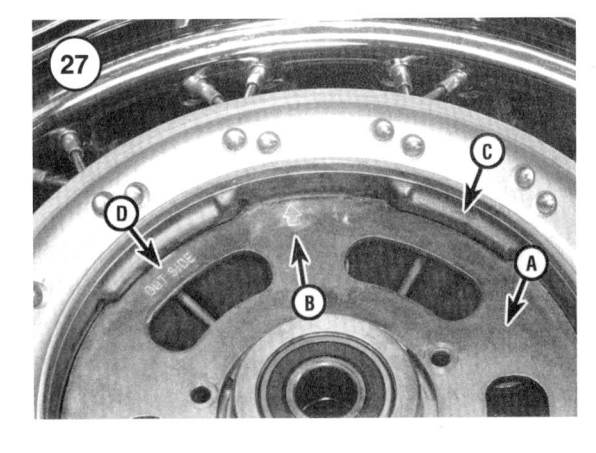

DRIVEN FLANGE DAMPERS

The 5-pin driven flange **(Figure 14)** connects the rear wheel to the final drive. Wedge-shaped rubber dampers with aluminum inserts installed in the rear hub absorb some of the shock that results from torque changes during acceleration and braking.

Removal/Inspection/Installation

1. Remove the bolts **(Figure 26)** and turn the damper holder plate (A, **Figure 27**) to align its arrow mark (B) between any two projection tabs (C) on the hub, then remove the damper holder plate. Discard the bolts.

2. Inspect the damper holder plate for cracks, warpage or other damage. Replace the plate if necessary.

NOTE
The rubber dampers should not slide out of the hub easily. If they do, they are severely worn and should be replaced. This difference will be noticed when installing new dampers.

3. Remove the rubber dampers **(Figure 28)** from the hub. If the dampers are tight, pry them out with a thin metal rod as shown in A, **Figure 29**.

4. Hold a rubber damper and try to move the insert. If there is any play, the rubber damper is probably worn or damaged. Check the rubber damper in the area where the insert is installed for excessive wear and damage. Then check the rubber damper body for cracks, deterioration and other damage. Repeat this

check for each damper.

5. Check the insert bore for uneven wear, cracks and other damage. Uneven wear is distinguished by a shoulder or step worn inside the bore. If this type of wear is noted, replace the insert. Repeat this check for each insert.

NOTE
While the rubber dampers and inserts can be replaced separately, it is best to replace all of the rubber dampers and inserts as a set when any severe wear or damage is noted. Play in this area can cause the driven flange to move slightly and result with noticeable backlash and a clunking sound on acceleration. This will cause wear to the driven flange and ring gear splines.

6. When replacing the rubber dampers and inserts, the inserts must be installed inside the dampers. When doing so, do not lubricate the inserts to ease installation. Instead, start the insert at a slight angle while carefully prying up the opposite end to make room for the insert. When the insert is fully installed, check that the edge of the rubber damper that runs along the insert bore overlaps the insert fully. If not, carefully pry the rubber damper edge up with a small screwdriver.
7. Inspect the hub and damper guides (A, **Figure 30**) for cracks and other damage.
8. Clean the threaded holes in the hub (B, **Figure 30**) and check for thread damage.
9. Install the rubber dampers with their OUTSIDE mark (B, **Figure 29**) facing out.
10. Install the damper holder plate as follows:
    a. Install the damper holder plate (A, **Figure 29**) with its OUTSIDE mark (D) facing out.
    b. Align the damper holder plate arrow (B, **Figure 27**) between any two projection tabs (C) on the hub and install the plate onto the hub. Make sure the plate is sitting flush in the hub.
    c. Turn the damper holder plate to align the bolt holes in the plate with the holes in the hub.
    d. Install 5 **new** damper holder plate bolts (**Figure 26**) and tighten to 20 N.m (15 ft.-lb.).

NOTE
Threadlock is preapplied to the new damper holder plate bolts, which the manufacturer calls ALOC bolts. If reusing the original bolts, remove the threadlock residue from the bolt threads, then spray the bolts with an electrical contact cleaner and allow to dry. During installation, apply a medium strength threadlock to the bolt threads.

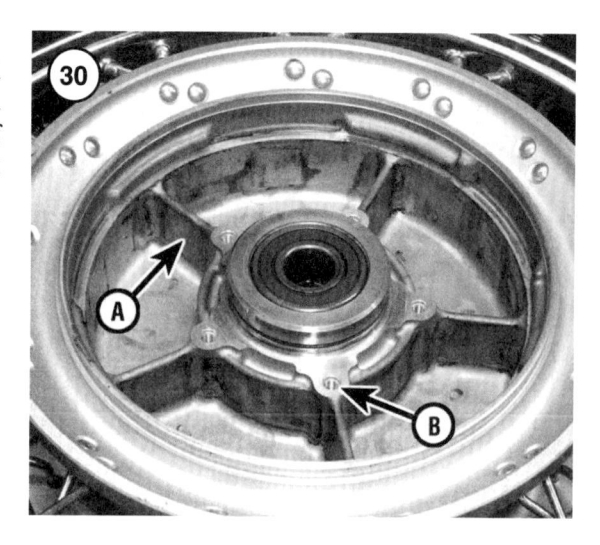

FRONT AND REAR HUBS

Each hub contains two wheel bearings and a distance collar. Seals are also installed in the front hub. Refer to Chapter Fifteen to service the brake discs.

Procedures for servicing the front and rear hubs are essentially the same. Where differences occur, they will be described in the procedure.

Refer to *Service Methods* in Chapter One for typical bearing service procedures and information.

Wheel Bearing Inspection

Initially inspect the bearings with the wheels installed on the motorcycle where leverage can be applied to the bearings to detect wear. In addition, the wheels can be spun to listen for roughness in the bearings. Use the following procedure to check the bearings while the wheels are installed. If the wheels must be removed for further bearing inspection, refer to *Front Wheel* or *Rear Wheel* n this chapter.

1. Support the motorcycle with the wheel off the ground. The axle nut must be tight.
2. Grasp the wheel with both hands, 180° apart. Rock the wheel up and down, and side to side, to check for radial and axial bearing play (**Figure 10**). Have an assistant apply the brake while the test is repeated. If the bearings are severely worn, play will be detected even though the wheel is locked.
3. Spin the wheel and listen for bearing noise. A grinding or catching noise indicates worn bearings.
4. If damage is evident, replace the bearings as a set. Always install new hub seals.

WHEELS AND TIRES

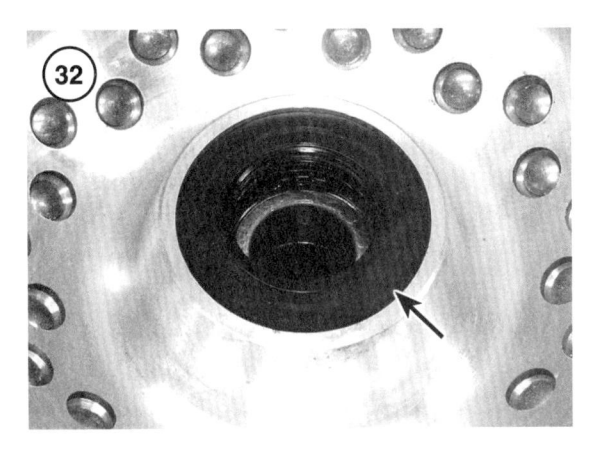

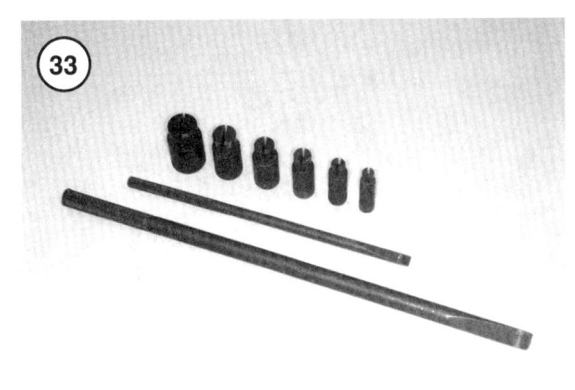

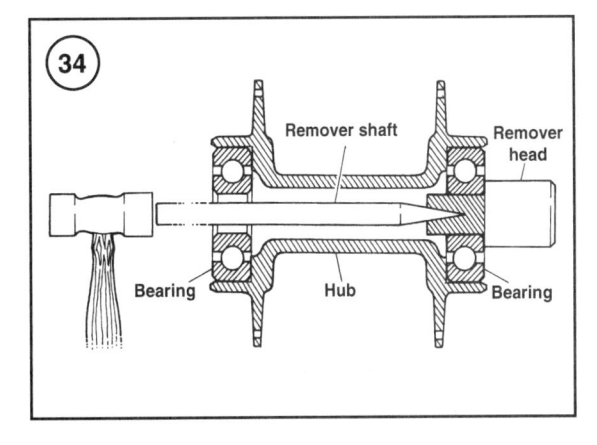

Front Wheel Bearing Seal Replacement

Seals protect the bearings from dirt and moisture contamination. Always install new seals when replacing bearings.

CAUTION
In the following procedure, do not allow the wheel to rest on the brake disc. Support the wheel on wooden blocks.

1. Pry the seals out of the hub with a seal puller, tire iron or wide-blade screwdriver **(Figure 31)**. Place a shop cloth under the tool to protect the hub from damage.

NOTE
If necessary, replace the bearings before installing the seals.

2. Clean the seal bore.
3. Inspect unshielded bearings for proper lubrication. If necessary, clean and repack the bearings while installed in the hub.
4. Pack grease into the lip of the new seal.
5. Place the seal in the bore with the closed side of the seal facing out. The seal must be square in the bore

CAUTION
Make sure the edge of the seal driver fits the perimeter of the seal. If the seal driver's outside diameter is significantly smaller than that of the seal, the driver will damage the seal.

6. Use a seal driver or socket to install the seal in the bore. Install the seal until it is flush with the top of the hub bore surface **(Figure 32)**.

Wheel Bearing Tools

The wheel bearings are installed with a press fit and can be removed with or without special tools.

1. Remover sets **(Figure 33)** use a remover head (split collet) that can be wedged against the inner bearing race. A 20-mm remover head is required for this procedure. The bearing can then be driven from the hub using a driver rod **(Figure 34)**. The Motion Pro set shown in **Figure 33** includes 10, 12, 15, 17, 20 and 25-mm remover heads and two driver rods. The remover heads and driver rods are also available separately.

2. Removing the wheel bearings with common shop tools requires a propane torch, drift and hammer.

Wheel Bearing Removal

This section describes removal of the wheel bearings from the front and rear hubs. If the bearings are intact, one of the removal methods described in this section may be used. To remove a bearing where the inner race assembly has fallen out, refer to Step 4.

CAUTION
In the following procedure, do not allow the wheel to rest on its brake disc. Support the wheel with wooden blocks placed on the tire.

1. On the front wheel, remove the seals s described in this section.
2. Examine the wheel bearings for excessive damage, especially the inner race. If the inner race of one bearing is damaged, remove the other bearing first. If both bearings are damaged, select the bearing with the least amount of damage and remove it first. On severely damaged bearings, the inner race can pop out, leaving the outer race in the hub.

WARNING
Wear safety glasses when removing the bearings.

CAUTION
When using a propane torch to heat the hub, work in a well-ventilated area away from combustible materials. Wear eye protection and insulated gloves.

3A. Remove the wheel bearings with a remover set **(Figure 33)** as follows:
   a. Select the correct size remover head tool and insert it into one of the hub bearings **(Figure 35)**.
   b. From the opposite side of the hub, insert the driver into the slot in the backside of the remover head. Position the hub with the remover head tool resting against a solid surface and strike the driver to wedge it firmly in the remover head **(Figure 34)**.
   c. Position the hub so the remover head is free to move and the driver can be struck again.
   d. Strike the driver **(Figure 36)** to force the bearing **(Figure 37)** from the hub. Then release the driver from the remover head and remove the first bearing and distance collar. If the bearing will not move, heat the hub area around the bearing with a propane torch as described in this section.
   e. Repeat the procedure to remove the opposite bearing.
3B. Remove the wheel bearings with a hammer, drift and propane torch as follows:
   a. Clean all lubricants from the hub.
   b. Heat the hub around the bearing to be removed. Work the torch in a circular motion around the hub, taking care not to hold the torch in one particular area. Turn the wheel over and remove the bearing as described in this section.

NOTE
Do not damage the distance collar when removing the bearing. If there is not enough room to tilt the distance collar away from the bearing, grind a clearance groove in the drift to allow it to contact the bearing while clearing the distance collar.

WHEELS AND TIRES

evenly with a propane torch. Drive out the outer race with a drift and hammer. It may be necessary to grind a clearance tip on the end of the drift, to avoid damaging the hub bore. Check before heating the hub. Remove the race evenly by applying force at different points around the race. Do not allow the race to bind in its bore. After removing the race, inspect the hub mounting bore for cracks or other damage.

Inspection

1. Clean and dry the interior of the hub.
2. Check the hub bearing bore for cracks or other damage. If a bearing fits loosely in the hub bore (no longer a press fit), replace the hub.
3. Inspect the distance collar for corrosion and damage. Clean the bore of all corrosion and other debris. Check the ends for cracks or other damage. Do not try to repair the distance collar by cutting or grinding its end surfaces as this will shorten the distance collar. Replace the distance collar if one or both ends are damaged.

NOTE
The distance collar operates against both wheel bearing inner races to prevent them from moving inward when the axle is tightened. If a distance collar is too short, or if it is not installed, the inner bearing races will move inward and bind on the axle when the axle nut is tightened. This can damage the bearings and the bearing bores in the hub.

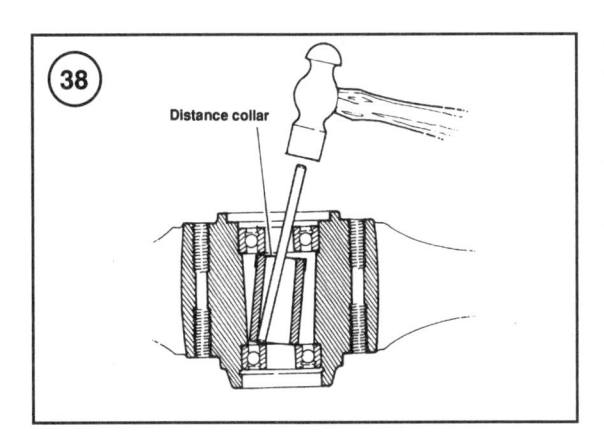

c. Tilt the distance collar away from one side of the bearing with a long driver **(Figure 38)**.

CAUTION
The bearing must be removed evenly to prevent it from binding into and damaging the hub bearing bore. Reheat the hub as required.

d. Tap around the inner bearing race to remove the bearing. Make several passes until the bearing is removed evenly from the hub. Do not allow the bearing to bind in the bore.
e. Remove the distance collar from the hub.
f. Turn the hub over and heat the opposite side.
g. Drive out the opposite bearing using a large socket or bearing driver placed on the bearing's outer race.
h. Inspect the distance collar for burrs created during removal. Remove burrs with a file.

4. On severely damaged bearings, the inner race can break apart, leaving the outer race pressed in the hub. Removal is difficult because only a small part of the race is accessible above the hub's shoulder, leaving little material to drive against. To remove a bearing's outer race under these conditions, first heat the hub

Wheel Bearing Installation

1. Before installing the new bearings and seals, note the following:
   a. Install both bearings with their closed side facing out. If a bearing is sealed on both sides, install the bearing with its manufacturer's marks facing out. If a shield is installed on one side of the bearing, the shield faces out.
   b. Apply waterproof grease to bearings that are not lubricated by the manufacturer or that are not sealed on both sides. Work the grease into the cavities between the balls and races.
   c. Always support the bottom side of the hub, near the bore, when installing bearings.
2. Heat the hub around the bearing bore with a propane torch.
3. Place the first bearing squarely against the bore opening with its closed side facing out.
4. Place a driver or socket over the bearing **(Figure 39)**. The driver should seat against the bearing's outer

race. Drive the bearing into the hub until it bottoms.
5. Turn the hub over and install the distance collar.
6. Position the opposite bearing squarely against the bore opening and drive the bearing partway into the bearing bore. Make sure the distance collar is centered in the hub. If not, install the axle through the hub to align the distance collar with the bearing. Then remove the axle and continue installing the bearing until it bottoms.
7. Insert the axle though the hub and turn it by hand. If the axle does not go in, the distance collar is not aligned correctly with one of the bearings. Check for any roughness or binding, indicating bearing damage.
8. On the front wheel, install the seals as described in this section.

WHEEL SERVICE

Inspection

Inspect the wheels regularly for axial (side-to-side) and radial (up-and-down) runout, even spoke tension and visible rim damage. When a wheel has a noticeable wobble, it is out of true. This is usually caused by loose spokes, but it can be caused by a damaged hub or rim.

Truing a wheel corrects the axial and radial runout to bring the wheel back into specification. The condition of the individual wheel components will affect the ability to successfully true the wheel. Note the following:
1. Do not attempt to true a wheel with bent or damaged spokes. Doing so places an excessive amount of tension on the spokes, hub and rim. Overtightening the spoke may damage the spoke nipple hole in the hub or rim. It can also cause the spokes to be drawn through the rim and possibly puncture the tube. Inspect for and replace damaged spokes.
2. When truing the wheels the nipples must turn freely on the spoke. However, corroded and rusted spoke threads are common and difficult to adjust. Spray a penetrating liquid onto the nipple and allow sufficient time for it to penetrate before trying to turn the nipples. Turn the spoke wrench in both directions and continue to apply penetrating liquid. If the spoke wrench rounds off the nipple, it will be necessary to remove the tire from the rim and cut the spoke(s) out of the wheel.
3. Minor rim runout can be corrected by truing the wheel. However, do not attempt to correct rim damage by overtightening the spokes. Inspect the rims for cracks, flat spots or dents. Check the spoke holes for cracks or elongation. Replace damaged rims and hubs.

Tightening Loose Spokes

This section describes steps for checking and tightening loose spokes without affecting the wheel runout. When many spokes are loose and the wheel is running out of true, refer to *Wheel Truing Procedure* in this section. If using a spoke torque wrench, refer to Table 4 for spoke torque specifications.
1. Support the wheel so that it can turn freely.
2. Spokes can be checked for looseness by one of three ways:
   a. Use a spoke torque wrench to tighten the spokes to the proper specification (**Table 4**).
   b. Hand check by grasping and squeezing two spokes where they cross. Loose spokes can be flexed by hand. Tight spokes feel stiff with little noticeable movement. Tighten the spokes until the tension between the different spoke groups feels the same.
   c. Listen to the spoke tone by tapping a spoke. Loose and tight spokes produce different sounds or tones. A tight spoke will ring. A loose spoke has a soft or dull ring. Tap each spoke with a spoke wrench or screwdriver to identify loose spokes.
3. Check the spokes using one of the methods described. If there are loose spokes, spin the wheel and note the following:
   a. If the wheel is running true, continue with Step 4 to tighten the loose spokes.
   b. If the wheel is running out of true, go to *Wheel Truing Procedure* to measure runout and true the wheel.
4. Use a marking pen and divide the rim into four equally spaced sections. Number the sections as shown in **Figure 40**.
5. Start by tightening the loose spokes in Section 1, then in sections 2, 3 and 4. Do not turn each spoke more than 1/4 to 1/2 turn at a time as this will overtighten the spokes and bring the wheel out of true. Work slowly while checking spoke tightness. Continue until all of the spokes are tightened evenly.

> *NOTE*
> *If the spokes are hard to turn, spray penetrating oil into the top of the nipple. Remove excess oil from the rim and tire.*

6. When all of the spokes are tightened evenly, spin the wheel. If there is any noticeable runout, true the wheel as described in the following procedure.

WHEELS AND TIRES

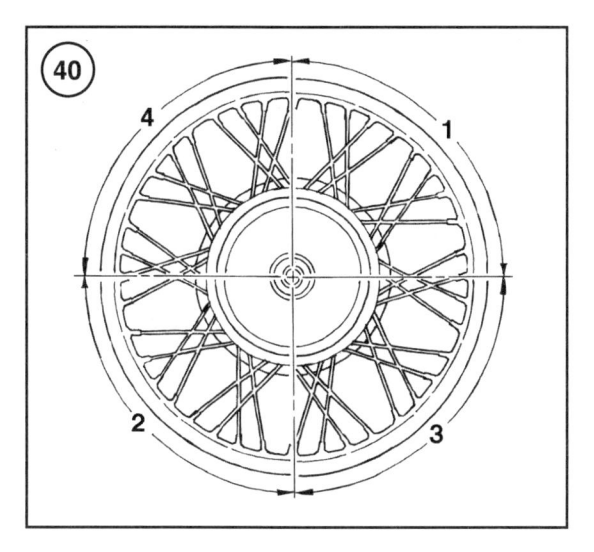

Wheel Truing Procedure

If using a spoke torque wrench, refer to **Table 4** for spoke torque specifications.

Service note

Before checking the runout and truing the wheel, note the following:
1. Make sure the wheel bearings are in good condition.
2. Check each spoke hole on both sides of the hub for cracks.
3. Check runout by mounting a pointer against the fork or swing arm and slowly rotating the wheel. A truing stand can also be used.
4. Use the correct size spoke wrench. Using the wrong type of tool or incorrect size spoke wrench may round off the spoke nipples, making adjustment difficult.

Procedure

Refer to **Table 2** for specifications.
1. Clean the rim, spokes and nipples.
2. Position a pointer against the rim as shown in **Figure 41**. If the tire is mounted on the rim, position the pointer as shown in **Figure 42**.
3. Spin the wheel slowly and check the axial and radial runout. If the rim is out of adjustment, continue the procedure to true the rim.

> *NOTE*
> *It is normal for the rim to jump at the point where the rim is welded together. Also small cuts and dings in the rim will affect the runout reading, especially when using a dial indicator.*

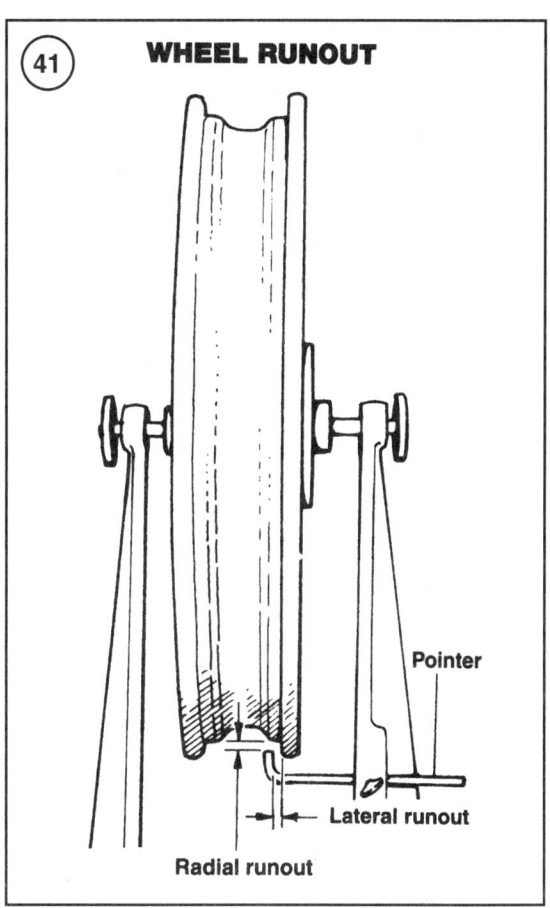

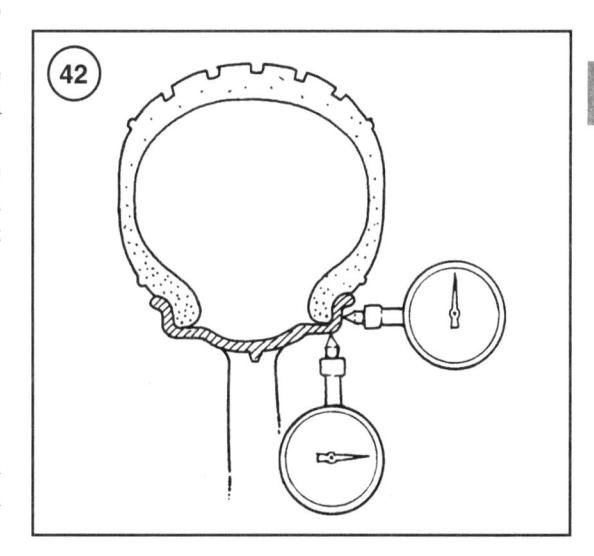

4. Spray penetrating oil into the top of each nipple. Wipe excess oil from the rim and tire.

> *NOTE*
> *If the runout is minimal, the tire can be left on the rim. However, if the runout is excessive, or if the rim must be centered with the hub, remove the tire from the rim.*

CHAPTER TWELVE

43 FRONT HUB-TO-RIM OFFSET MEASUREMENT

Rim
79 mm $- \frac{B}{2}$
(3.11 in.)
Brake disc

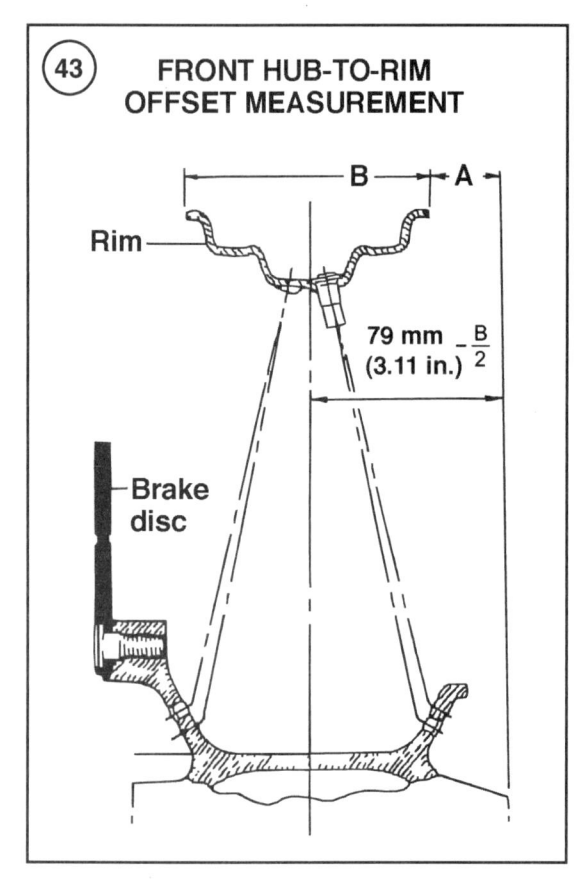

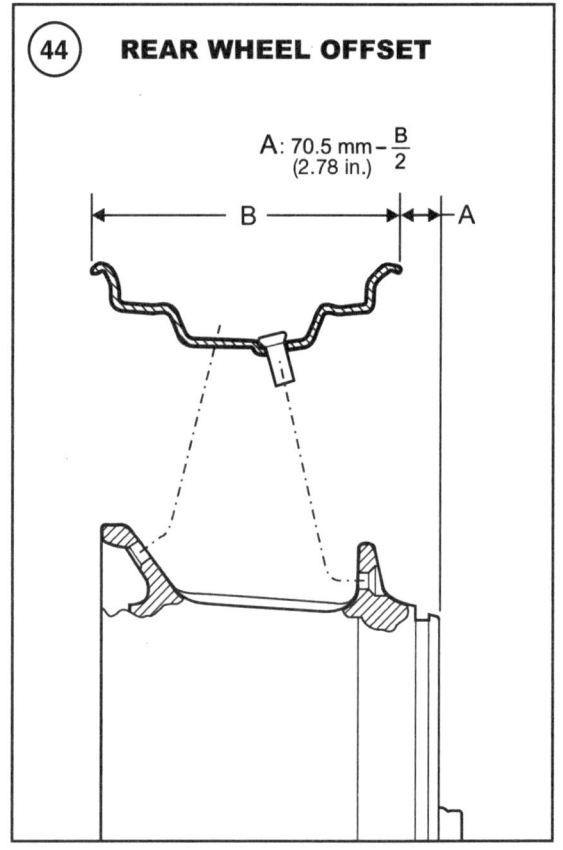

44 REAR WHEEL OFFSET

A: 70.5 mm $- \frac{B}{2}$
(2.78 in.)

5. If there are a large number of loose spokes, or if some or all of the spokes were replaced, check the hub to rim offset as shown in **Figure 43** (front) or **Figure 44** (rear). If necessary, reposition the hub when truing the wheel.

NOTE
Determining the number of spokes to loosen and tighten will depend on how far the runout is out of adjustment. Loosen two or three spokes, then tighten the opposite two or three spokes. If the runout is excessive and affects a greater area along the rim, loosen and tighten a greater number of spokes.

6. Axial runout adjustment: If the side-to-side runout is out of specification, adjust the wheel. For example, to pull the rim to the left side **(Figure 45)**, tighten the spokes on the left side of the hub (at the runout point) and loosen the adjacent spokes on the right side of the hub. Always loosen and tighten the spokes an equal number of turns.

7. Radial runout adjustment: If the up and down runout is out of specification, the hub is not centered in the rim. Draw the high point of the rim toward the centerline of the wheel by tightening the spokes in the area of the high point, and loosening the spokes on

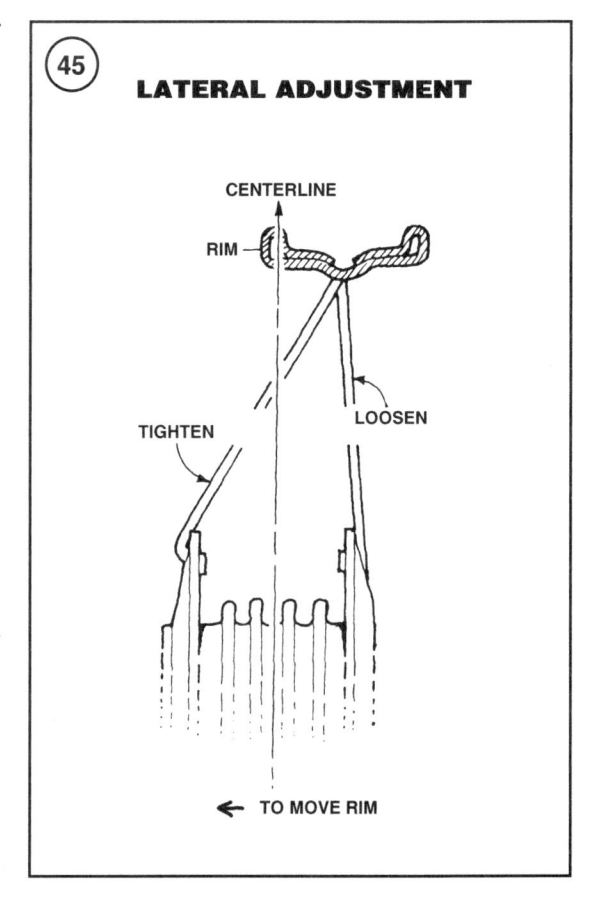

45 LATERAL ADJUSTMENT

CENTERLINE
RIM
TIGHTEN
LOOSEN
← TO MOVE RIM

WHEELS AND TIRES

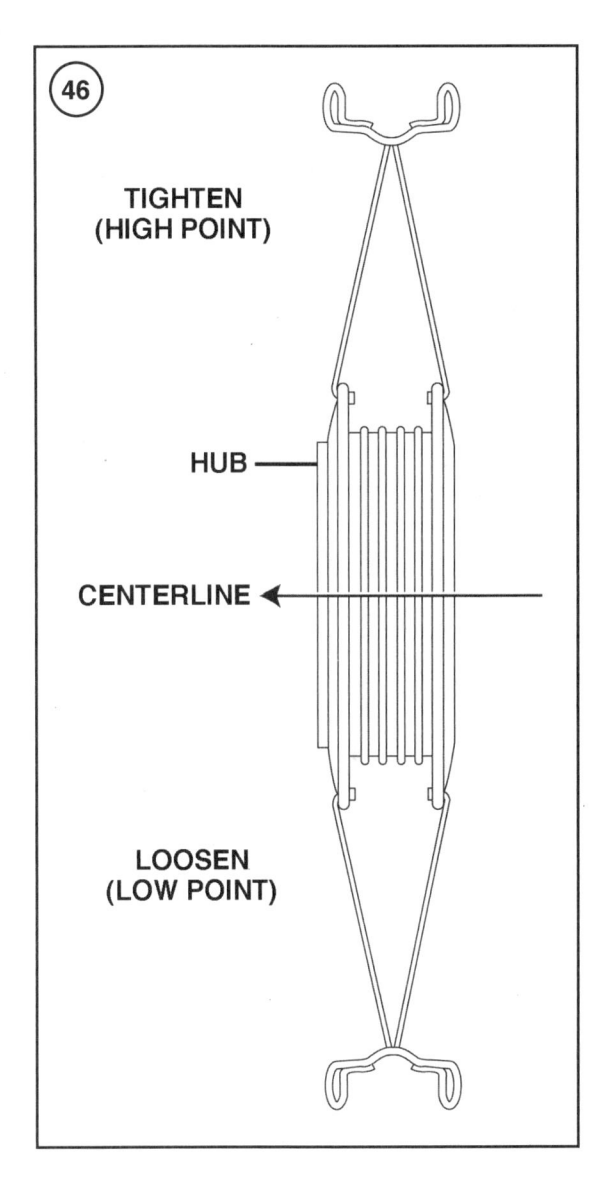

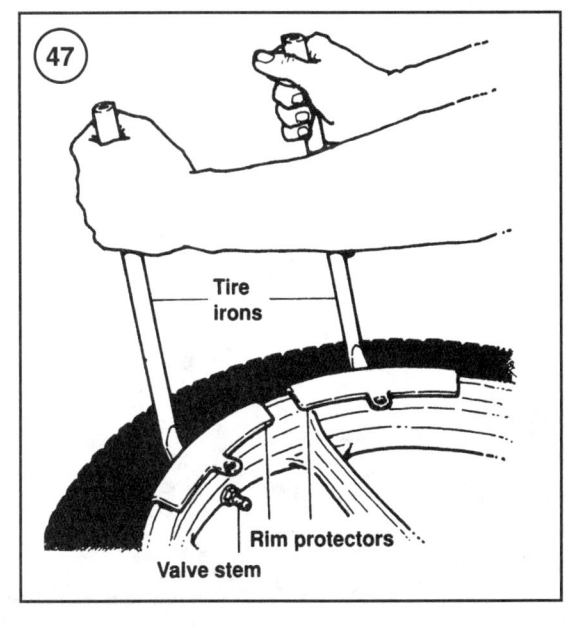

the side opposite the high point (**Figure 46**). Tighten the spokes in equal amounts to prevent distortion.

NOTE
Alternate between checking and adjusting lateral and radial runout. Remember, changing spoke tension on one side of the rim affects the tension on the other side of the rim.

8. After truing the wheel, seat each spoke in the hub by tapping it with a flat nose punch and hammer. Then recheck the spoke tension and wheel runout. Readjust if necessary as described under *Tightening Loose Spokes* in this section.
9. Check the ends of the spokes where they are threaded in the nipples. Grind off any ends that protrude through the nipples to prevent them from puncturing the tube.

TIRE CHANGING

Removal

NOTE
It is easier to change tires when the wheel is mounted on some type of raised platform. A popular item used by many home mechanics is a metal drum. Before placing the wheel on a drum, cover the drum edge with a length of garden hose, split lengthwise and secured in place with plastic ties. When changing the front tire at ground level, support the wheel on two wooden blocks to prevent the brake disc from contacting the floor.

NOTE
Warming the tire will make it softer and more pliable. Place the tire and wheel assembly in the sun or in a completely closed automobile. Place the new tire in the same location.

1. Remove the valve core and deflate the tire.
2. Press the entire bead on both sides of the tire into the center of the rim. If necessary, step on the sidewall, and not the rim, to break the bead. Check that the beads are free on both sides of the rim.
3. Lubricate the beads on both sides of the tire with soapy water.

NOTE
*Use rim protectors (**Figure 47**) or insert scraps of leather between the tire iron and the rim to protect the rim from damage.*

4. Insert the first tire iron under the bead on the opposite side of the valve stem. Force the bead into the center of the rim, then pry the bead over the rim with the tire iron **(Figure 48)**.

> *CAUTION*
> *If it is difficult to pry the bead over the rim with the second tire iron, stop and make sure the bottom bead was broken from the rim. Excessive force will split and tear the tire bead and cause permanent tire damage.*

5. Insert a second tire iron next to the first to hold the bead over the rim **(Figure 49)**. While holding the tire with one tire iron, work around the tire with the second tire iron, prying the tire over the rim and working in small bites of one to two inches at a time. Be careful not to pinch the inner tube with the tire irons.

> *CAUTION*
> *If the tube is being removed to fix a flat, identify the tube's installed position in the tire immediately after removing it to help locate the foreign object in the tire.*

6. When the upper bead is free of the rim, remove the inner tube from the tire **(Figure 50)**.

7. Stand the tire upright and pry the second tire bead **(Figure 51)** over the rim. Then peel the tire off the rim by hand. If necessary, use a second tire iron.

Inspection

1. Inspect the tire for damage. If the tube was leaking air, pump air into it to locate the leak. Then place the tube on top of the tire, facing in its original position, to help locate the object in the tire. Remove the object and check the tire for damage.

> *NOTE*
> *Cracks in the inner tire liner can pinch and damage the tube. If the tube is leaking air, but there are no foreign objects in the tire, spread the tire and check the inner liner for cracks.*

2. Run a rag through the inside of the tire to locate any protruding objects. Do not use bare hands.

> *WARNING*
> *Carefully consider whether a tire should be replaced. If there is any doubt about the condition of the existing tire, replace it with a new one. Do not take a chance on a tire failure at any speed.*

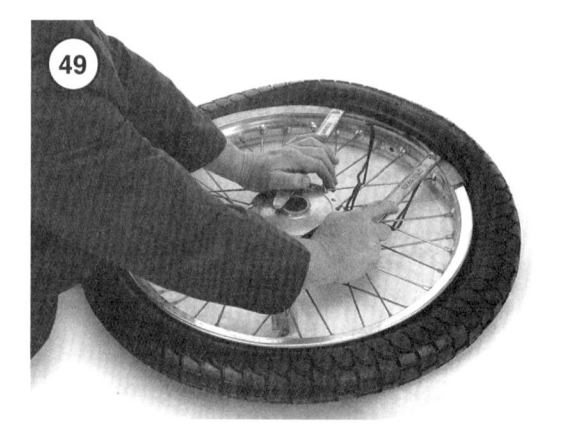

WHEELS AND TIRES

8. Check the valve stem hole in the rim for any cracks, roughness or cuts that could damage the valve stem. Remove any roughness with a file
9. Mount the wheel onto a truing stand and check runout before mounting the tire.
10. If possible, install a new tube. If not, inflate the original tube to make sure it was not punctured during tire removal. However, discard the tube if it has been previously patched, or if it appears balancing liquids were introduced into the tube. Check the inner nut on the valve stem to make sure it is tight. Check the area around the valve stem for cracks and other weak spots.

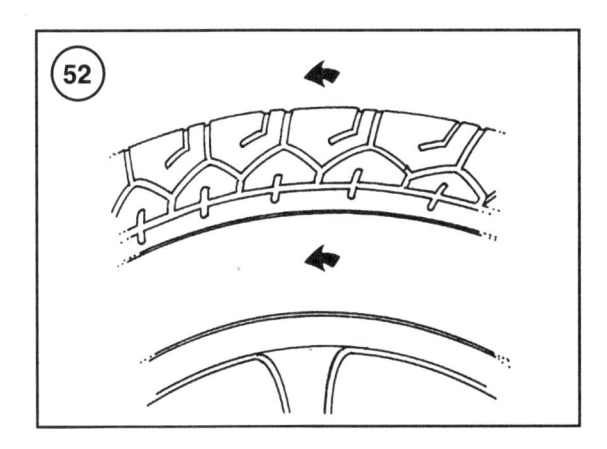

3. If any one of the following is observed, replace the tire with a new one:
    a. A noticeable puncture or split.
    b. A scratch or split on the sidewall or along the inner liner.
    c. Any type of ply separation.
    d. Tread separation or abnormal wear pattern.
    e. Tread depth of less than the minimum value specified in **Table 1** for original equipment tires. The minimum depth on aftermarket tires may vary. Refer to the tire manufacturer's information.
    f. Scratches on either sealing bead.
    g. The cord is cut in any place.
    h. Flat spots in the tread from skidding.
    i. Any abnormality in the inner liner
4. If the tire can be reused, clean and dry the inside of the tire with compressed air.
5. Remove the rim strap from the center of the rim. Replace if damaged.
6. Use a brush to clean dirt, rust and rubber from the inside of the rim.
7. Inspect the spokes for rust and corrosion. Then check for any spoke ends that protrude above the nipple head and into the center of the rim. Grind or file the exposed part of the spoke flush with the nipple.

Installation

NOTE
Installation will be easier if the tire is pliable. This can be achieved by warming the tire in the sun or inside an enclosed automobile.

1. Install the rim band around the rim by aligning the hole in the band with the hole in the rim.
2. When installing the tire on the rim, make sure the correct tire, either front or rear, is installed on the correct wheel. Also, install the tire with the direction arrow facing the normal direction of wheel rotation **(Figure 52)**.

NOTE
*The rear tire uses an angled valve stem (**Figure 53**) that must face toward the right side of the wheel when installed. When installing the rear tire, begin by positioning the wheel with the brake drum side facing up.*

CAUTION
Use a tire lubricant when installing the tire over the rim and when seating the beads. Use a commercial tire lubricant, if available. Plain or soapy water can also be used. Do not use Teflon and WD-40 aerosol spray lubes and other petroleum chemicals as a tire lubricant. These lubricants will stay on the tire beads without drying out and can cause the tire to slip on the rim and damage the valve stem. Some chemicals will also damage the rubber.

NOTE
If installing the rear tube, make sure the valve stem is correctly angled with the hole in the rim.

3. Sprinkle the tube with talcum powder and install it into the tire **(Figure 54)**. The powder minimizes tube chafing and helps the tube distribute itself when inflated.

4. Inflate the tube to shape it against the tire. Then bleed most of the air from the tube. Too much air will make tire installation difficult and too little air will increase the chance of pinching the tube.

5. Most tires are marked with a colored spot near the bead that indicates a lighter point on the tire. Align this spot with the valve stem hole in the rim **(Figure 55)**.

6. Lubricate the lower bead. Then start pushing the lower bead over the rim while inserting the air valve through the hole in the rim **(Figure 56)**. Install the nut onto the valve stem to prevent the stem from sliding back into the tire.

7. Continue to push the lower bead over the rim by hand-fitting it as much as possible. The last part of the bead will be the toughest to install. If necessary, grasp the spokes to steady the wheel and push the front part of the tire toward the inside of the rim with your knees. This may provide additional room at the back of the bead to help with its installation. If it is necessary to use a tire lever, use it carefully to prevent from pinching the tube or tearing the tire bead.

8. When the lower bead is installed over the rim, turn the wheel over and check that the tube is not pinched between the bead and rim. If so, carefully push the tube back into the center of the tire by hand.

9. Turn the wheel back over and lift the upper bead to check the tube. Make sure the tube is positioned evenly around the tire. If necessary, inflate the tube to remove any wrinkles, then bleed most of the air from the tube.

NOTE
Properly aligning the tire weight mark with the valve stem hole helps to reduce the amount of weight required to balance the tire.

10. Turn the tire so the air valve is straight up **(Figure 57)** for the front tire or angled as shown in **Figure 53** for the rear tire. Also, check that the tire weight mark identified in Step 5 aligns with the valve stem hole in the rim **(Figure 55)**.

NOTE
*Do not use excessive force when using the tire irons to install the upper tire bead. Instead, use your knees to push the front part of the tire (the part closest to you) toward the inside of the rim and to keep the lower bead positioned in the **center** of the rim. Forcing the tire irons between the upper bead and rim*

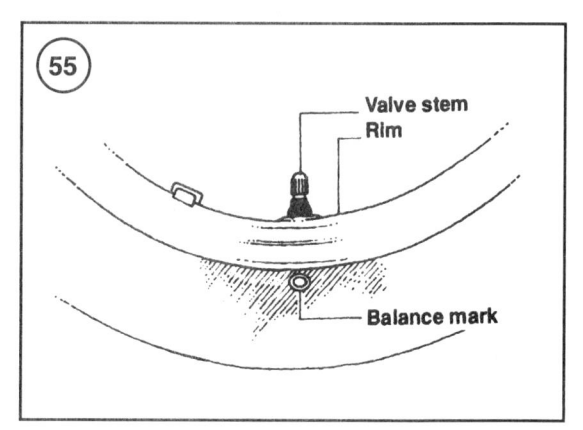

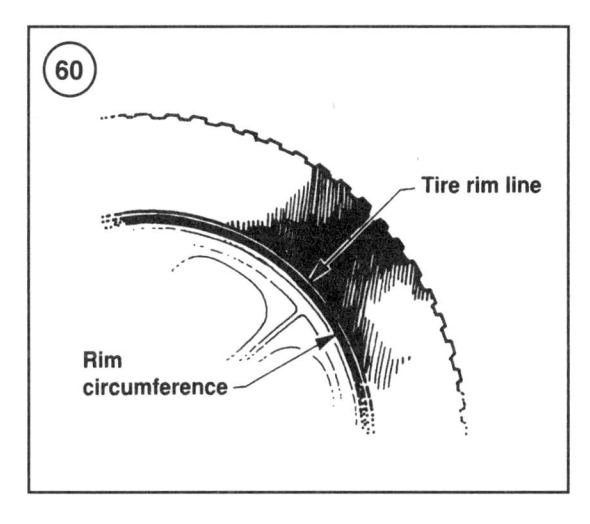

WHEELS AND TIRES

tioned in the center of the rim when installing the upper bead.

12. When both beads are installed over the rim, perform the following:

    a. Check the bead for uniform fit, on both sides of the tire.

    b. Check both sides of the tire for any part of the tube that is pinched between the tire bead and rim. Lift the tire and carefully push the tube back into the tire.

    c. Turn the tire so the air valve is straight up and the tire weight mark **(Figure 55)** aligns with the valve stem hole.

WARNING
Special care must be taken when inflating the tire and seating the tire beads in the next step. Never exceed 300 kPa (43.5 psi) inflation pressure as the tire could burst, causing severe injury. If the tire does not seat at the recommended pressure, do not continue by overinflating the tire. Doing so could cause the tire to burst, and cause severe injury. Deflate the tire and repeat the procedure.

NOTE
The safest way to inflate the tire is to use a clamp-on air chuck and a remote air gauge/inflator. Wear safety glasses and stand as far away from the tire as possible. Never stand directly over a tire while inflating it.

13. Lubricate both beads. Use a clamp-on air chuck and inflate the tire to seat the beads on the rim. Do not exceed 300 kPa (43.5 psi).

14. After inflating the tire, check to see that the beads are fully seated and that the rim lines are the same distance from the rim all the way around the tire **(Figure 60)**. If not, deflate the tire and repeat the procedure.

15. When the beads are correctly seated, deflate the tire (but do not break the tire beads). Then inflate the tire again to help stretch the tube and seat it fully against the tire. Set the tire to the required tire pressure listed in **Table 3**. Tighten the outer valve stem nut **(Figure 57 [front]** or **Figure 53 [rear])** and the valve stem cap.

16. Balance the tire and wheel assembly as described in this chapter.

because the lower bead is not properly positioned can damage the rim, cut the tire bead and pinch the tube.

11. Lubricate the upper tire bead, then start installation opposite the valve stem **(Figure 58)** by hand. If necessary, relubricate the bead. Use the tire irons to pry the remaining section of bead over the rim **(Figure 59)**. Remember, keep the lower bead posi-

WHEEL BALANCE

A wheel that is not balanced is unsafe because it seriously affects the steering and handling of the motorcycle. Depending on the degree of unbalance and the speed of the motorcycle, anything from a mild vibration to a violent shimmy, may occur, which may result in loss of control. An imbalanced wheel also causes abnormal tire wear.

Motorcycle wheels can be checked for balance either statically (single plane balance) or dynamically (dual plane balance). This section describes how to static balance the wheels using a wheel balancing stand. To obtain a higher degree of accuracy, take both wheels to a dealership and have them balanced with a two plane computer dynamic wheel balancer. This machine spins the wheel to accurately detect any imbalance.

Balance weights are used to balance the wheel and are attached to the spokes **(Figure 61)**. Weight kits are available from motorcycle dealerships.

The wheel must be able to rotate freely when checking wheel balance. Because excessively worn or damaged wheel bearings affect the accuracy of this procedure, check the wheel bearings as described in this chapter. Also, confirm that the tire balance mark, a paint mark on the tire, is aligned with the valve stem **(Figure 55)**.

NOTE
Leave the brake disc mounted on the front wheel when checking and adjusting wheel balance.

1. Remove the wheel as described in this chapter.
2. Clean the seals and inspect the wheel bearings as described in this chapter.
3. Clean the tire, rim and spokes. Remove any stones or pebbles stuck in the tire tread.
4A. Mount the front wheel (with brake disc attached) on a balance stand **(Figure 62)**.
4B. Mount the rear wheel on a balance stand **(Figure 62)**.

NOTE
To check the original balance of the wheel, leave the original weights attached to the spokes.

5. Spin the wheel by hand and let it coast to a stop. Mark the tire at its bottom point with chalk.
6. Spin the wheel several more times. If the same spot on the tire stops at the bottom each time, the wheel is out of balance. This is the heaviest part of the tire. When an unbalanced wheel is spun, it always comes to rest with the heaviest spot at the bottom.
7. Attach a test weight to the wheel at the point opposite the heaviest spot and spin the wheel again.
8. Experiment with different weights until the wheel, when spun, comes to rest at a different position each time. When a wheel is correctly balanced, the weight of the tire and wheel assembly is distributed equally around the wheel.

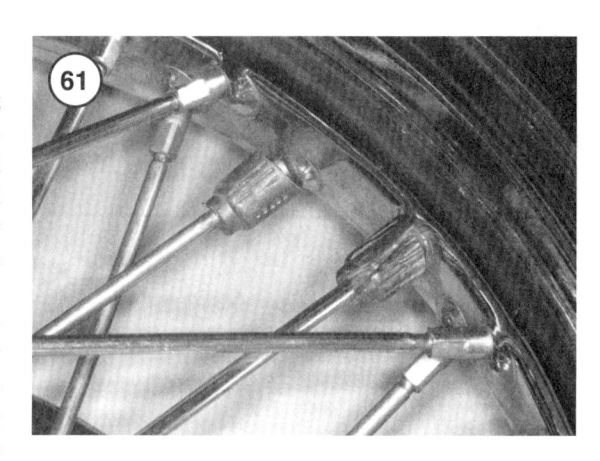

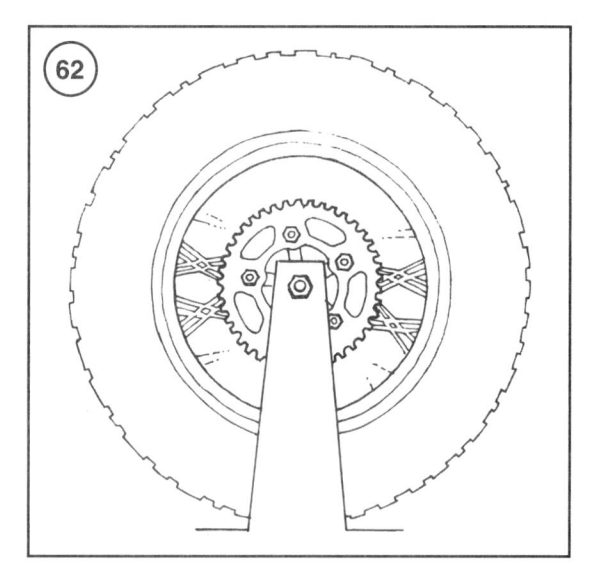

NOTE
Do not exceed 60 grams (2.1 oz.) to the front wheel or 70 grams (2.5 oz.) to the rear wheel. If a wheel requires an excessive amount of weight, make sure the weight mark on the tire aligns with the valve stem.

9. Remove the test weight and install the correct size weight or weights to the rim. Crimp the weight tightly against the spoke and nipple **(Figure 61)**.
10. In the *NOTES* section at the back of this book, record the weight, number and position of the weights on the wheel. Then, if the motorcycle experiences a handling or vibration problem later, first check for any missing balance weights.
11. Install the wheel as described in this chapter.

WHEELS AND TIRES

Table 1 TIRE AND WHEEL SPECIFICATIONS

Tire size	
Front	
Aero, Phantom models	120/90-17 M/C 64S
Spirit models	90/90-21 M/C 54S
Rear	160/80-15 M/C 74S
Tire brands	
Front	
Aero, Phantom models	Bridgestone EXEDRA G701
	Cheng Shin M-6002
	Dunlop D404FG
Spirit models	Bridgestone EXEDRA G701
	Dunlop D404F
Rear	
Aero and Phantom models	Bridgestone EXEDRA G702
	Cheng Shin M-6011R
	Dunlop D404
Spirit models	Bridgestone EXEDRA G702
	Dunlop D404
Minimum tire tread depth	
Front	1.5 mm (0.06 in.)
Rear	2.0 mm (0.08 in.)

Table 2 WHEEL AND AXLE SERVICE SPECIFICATIONS

	Service Limit
Axle runout	0.20 mm (0.008 in.)
Wheel balance weight	
Maximum weight limit	
Front	60 g (2.1 oz.)
Rear	70 g (2.5 oz.)
Wheel runout	
Axial (side-to-side)	2.0 mm (0.08 in.)
Radial (up-and-down)	2.0 mm (0.08 in.)

Table 3 TIRE INFLATION PRESSURE*

	(kPa) psi Front	(kPa) psi Rear
Rider (up to 90 kg [200 lbs] load)	200 (29)	200 (29)
Maximum weight capacity	200 (29)	250 (36)

* The tire inflation pressures listed here are for factory equipped tires. Aftermarket tires may require different inflation pressure. Refer to tire manufacturer's specifications.

Table 4 WHEEL TORQUE SPECIFICATIONS

	N.m	in.-lb.	ft.-lb.
Damper plate holder bolts*	20	--	15
Final drive housing mounting nuts	64	--	47
Front axle			
Aero models			
2004-2007	74	--	55
All other models	59	--	44
Front axle pinch bolt	22	--	16
Spoke			
Aero models			
2004-2009	3.9	35	--
All other models	4.2	37	--
Rear axle nut	88	--	65
Rear axle pinch bolt			
2004-2009 Aero	26	--	19
All other models	27	--	20
Rear brake arm adjuster/stopper nut	22	--	16
Rear brake arm pinch bolt	26	--	19
Rear caliper bracket pin bolt (ABS models)	69	--	51
Rear shock absorber left side lower mounting bolt			
Aero models			
2004-2009	23	--	17
All other models	22	--	16

*ALOC bolt.

CHAPTER THIRTEEN

FRONT SUSPENSION AND STEERING

This chapter describes procedures for the repair and maintenance of the handlebar, front forks and steering components. See Chapter Twelve for front wheel and tire service.

Specifications are listed in **Tables 1-3** at the end of the chapter.

HANDLEBAR

Refer to **Figures 1-4**.

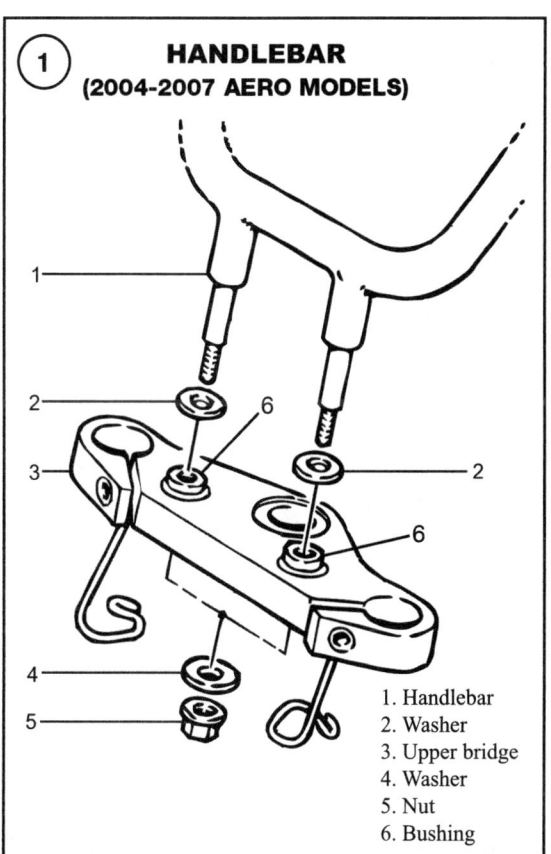

Removal

1. Note the throttle cables, clutch cable and wiring harness routing before removing the handlebar. Make sketches or take photos as needed.
2. Cover the fuel tank with a thick blanket to protect it from scratches and other damage.
3. Remove the mirrors.

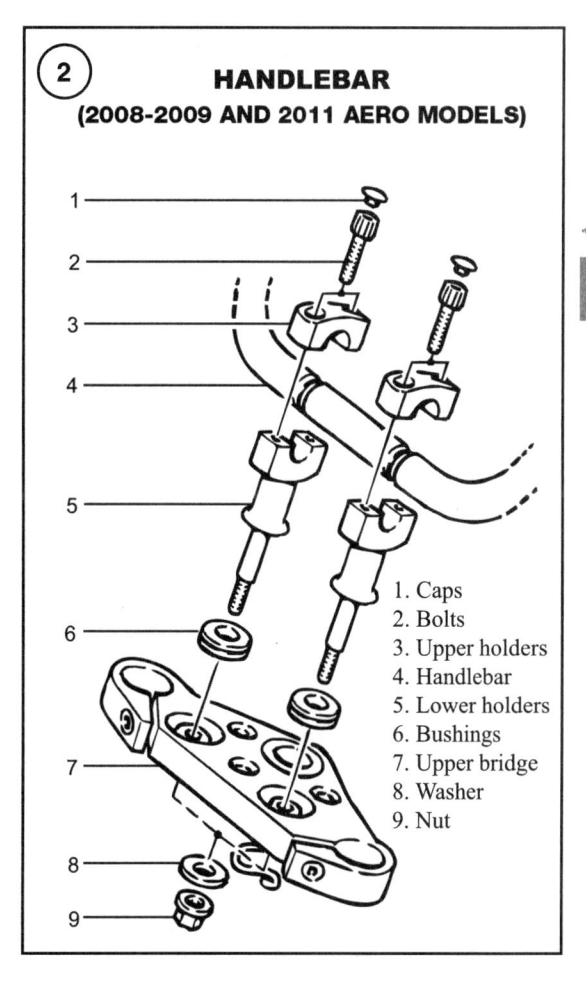

① HANDLEBAR (2004-2007 AERO MODELS)

1. Handlebar
2. Washer
3. Upper bridge
4. Washer
5. Nut
6. Bushing

② HANDLEBAR (2008-2009 AND 2011 AERO MODELS)

1. Caps
2. Bolts
3. Upper holders
4. Handlebar
5. Lower holders
6. Bushings
7. Upper bridge
8. Washer
9. Nut

HANDLEBAR (VT750C2)

1. Bolt
2. Upper holders
3. Handlebar
4. Lower holders
5. Bushings
6. Upper bridge
7. Washer
8. Nut

HANDLEBAR (VT750C2B)

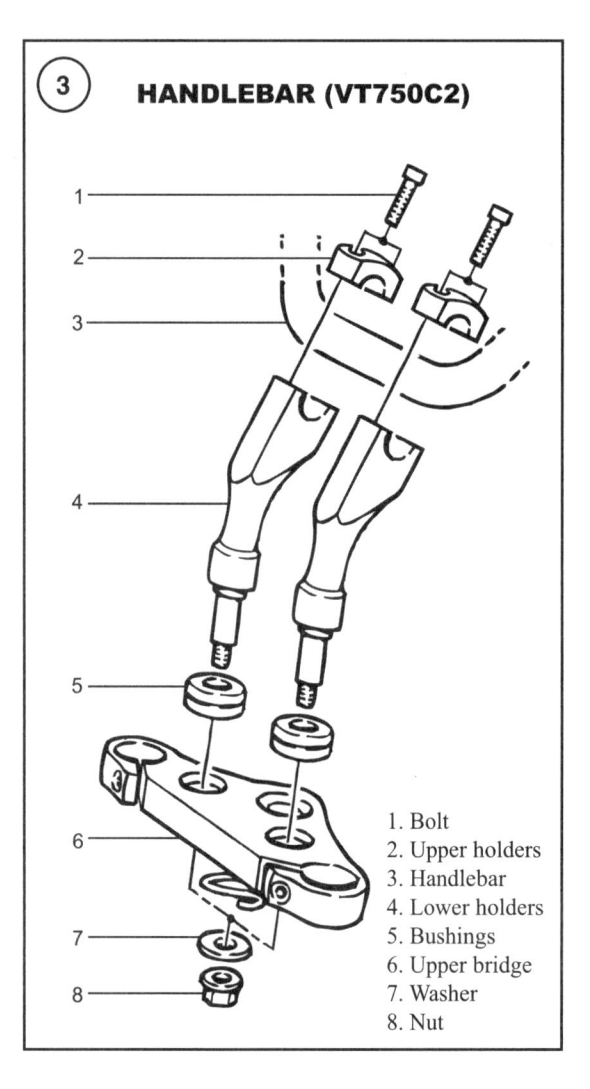

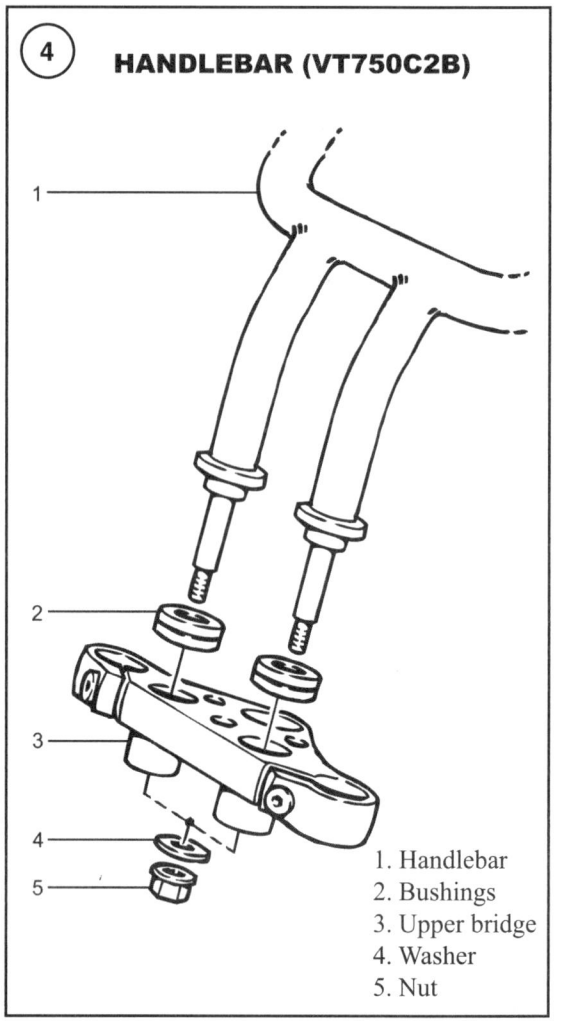

1. Handlebar
2. Bushings
3. Upper bridge
4. Washer
5. Nut

4. Use a screwdriver to pry and release the wiring harness clamp from the pin on each side of the handlebar (if used). See **Figure 5**.

5. Disconnect the clutch switch electrical connectors at the clutch switch (**Figure 6**).

6. Disconnect the clutch cable at the lever, if necessary.

7. Remove the two clutch lever bracket mounting bolts and remove the clutch bracket holder (A, **Figure 7**) and lever bracket.

NOTE
*Before removing the throttle and switch housing screws, check the screw slots (**Figure 8**) for damage. If the screws are damaged, use a No. 2 Phillips bit installed in a hand impact driver to loosen them (**Figure 9**). Coating the end of the bit with valve grinding compounds helps the bit to grip the screw tighter and turn the screw without further damaging the screw grooves.*

FRONT SUSPENSION AND STEERING

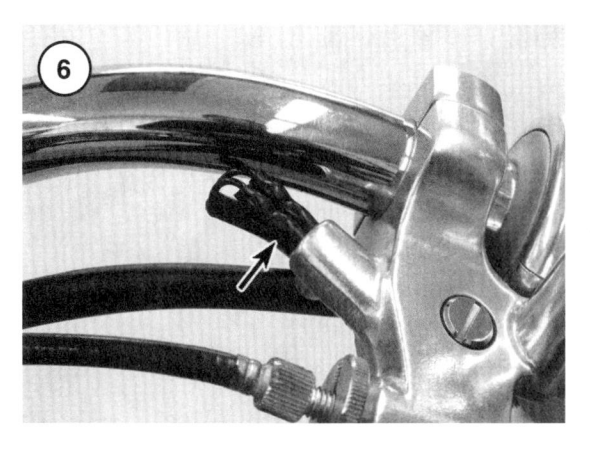

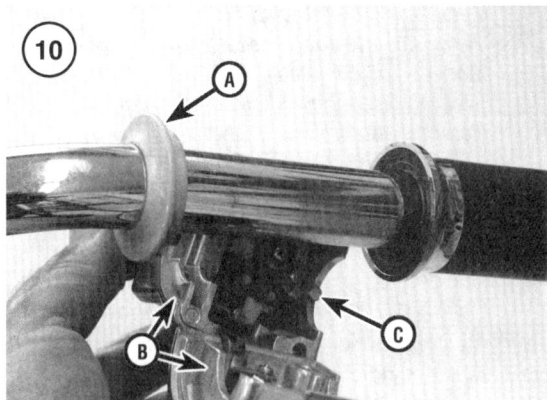

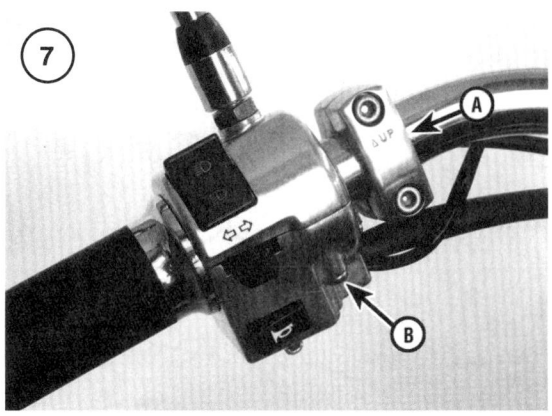

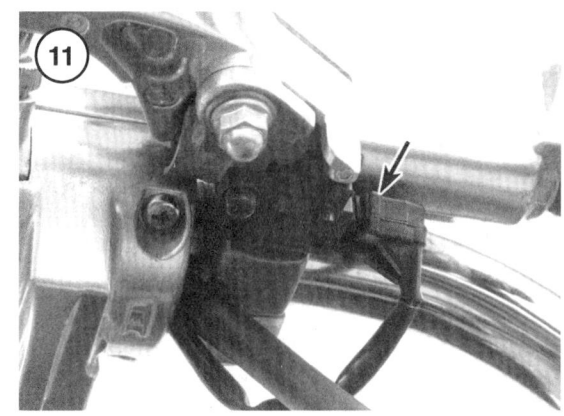

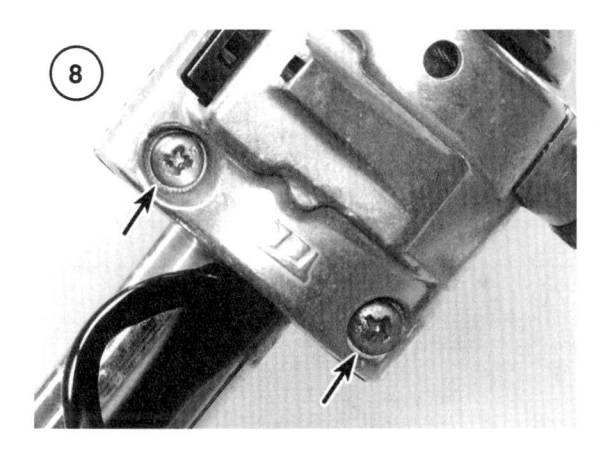

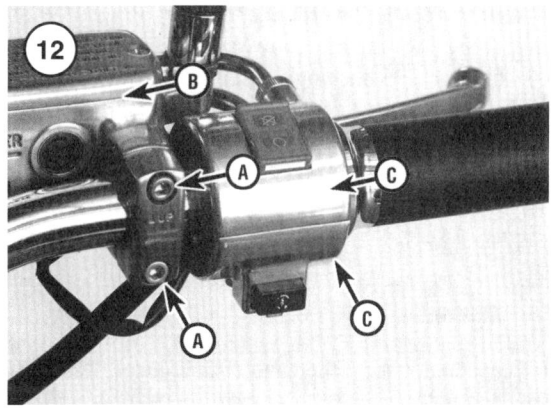

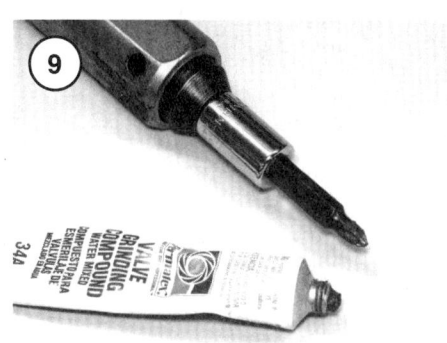

8. Remove the front (B, **Figure 7**) and rear left handlebar switch housing screws. Then remove the end adapter (A, **Figure 10**) and separate the switch housing halves (B) from around the handlebar.
9. Disconnect the front brake light switch connectors at the switch **(Figure 11)**.
10. Then, remove the two master cylinder holder bolts (A, **Figure 12**) and remove the holder and front master cylinder (B, **Figure 12**). Support the master cylinder upright so air does not enter the master cylinder.
11. Remove the two right side handlebar switch housing screws and separate the switch housing halves (C, **Figure 12**) from around the handlebar.

NOTE
If the throttle cables are tight and cannot be disconnected at the throttle sleeve, disconnect them at the carburetor (Chapter Eight) or throttle body (Chapter Nine).

12. Disconnect the throttle cables (A, **Figure 13**) from the throttle sleeve and slide the throttle sleeve off the handlebar.

13A. On 2004-2007 Aero models **(Figure 1)** and on all Phatom models **(Figure 4)**, remove the nuts, washers and handlebar.

13B. On 2008-2009 and 2011-2013 Aero models **(Figure 2)** and all Spirit models **(Figure 3)**, perform the following:
   a. If the lower handlebar holders are going to be removed, loosen the lower handlebar holder mounting nuts while the handlebar is still mounted in place.
   b. Remove the handlebar upper holder bolt caps (if used), bolts and holders. Then, remove the handlebar.
   c. To remove the lower handlebar holders, identify and mark the holders so they can be installed facing in their original direction.
   d. Remove the holder mounting nut from under the upper steering bracket, then remove the washer.
   e. Remove the lower holder and bushing.
   f. Repeat for the other lower handlebar holder.

14. Inspect the bushings installed into the upper bridge (if used) for deterioration and other damage. If necessary, replace the bushings and their collars.

15. Install new bushings with their larger inside diameter end facing toward the top of the bridge **(Figure 14)**.

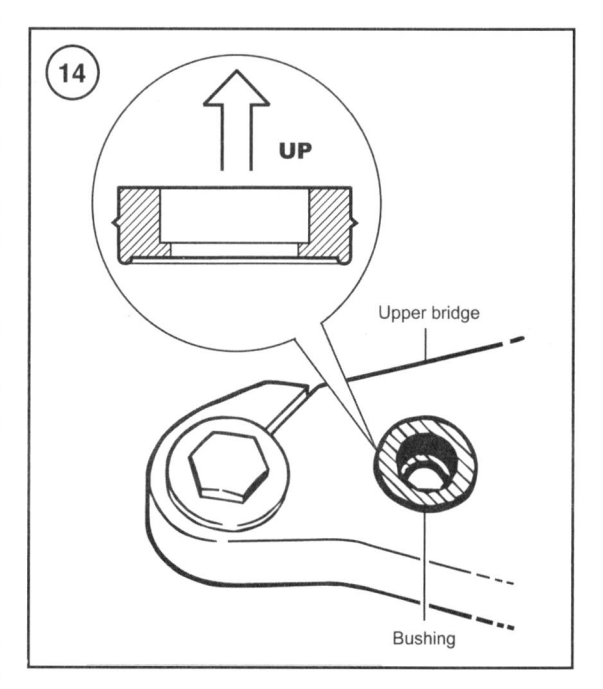

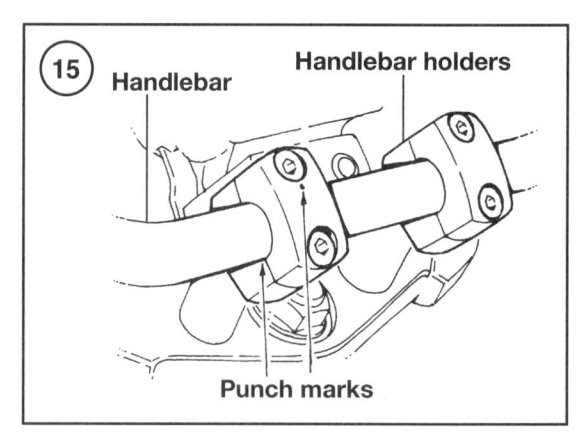

Installation

1. Clean and inspect the handlebar holders, washers, nuts and bolts.

2A. On 2004-2007 Aero models **(Figure 1)**, perform the following:
   a. Install the handlebar, washers and mounting nuts. The upper washers have a smaller inside diameter than the lower washers.
   b. Tighten the mounting nuts to 54 N.m (40 ft.-lb.).

2B. On 2008-2009 and 2011-2013 Aero models **(Figure 2)** and all Spirit models **(Figure 3)**, perform the following:
   a. If removed, install the lower holders, washers and nuts onto the upper bridge. Finger tighten the nuts.
   b. Install the handlebar.
   c. Install the upper holders with their punch mark facing forward **(Figure 15)**.
   d. Install the handlebar holder mounting bolts and tighten finger-tight.

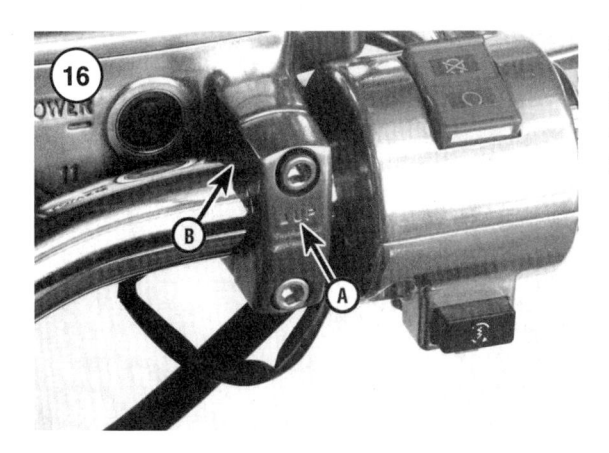

FRONT SUSPENSION AND STEERING 407

side of the handlebar. Then lightly lubricate the inside of the throttle sleeve with a lightweight oil. Lubricate the holes in the throttle sleeve with grease.

4. Install the right side handlebar switch housing as follows:
   a. Reconnect the two throttle cables (A, **Figure 13**) to the throttle sleeve.
   b. Align the switch housing locating pin (B, **Figure 13**) with the hole in the handlebar and close the switch halves (C, **Figure 12**) around the handlebar and throttle sleeve.
   c. Install the long screw into the front housing hole and the short screw into the rear housing hole. Tighten the front, and then the rear screw securely.

5. Install the master cylinder (B, **Figure 12**) as follows:
   a. Clean the handlebar, master cylinder and clamp mating surfaces.
   b. Mount the master cylinder onto the handlebar, then install its clamp and both mounting bolts. Install the clamp with the UP mark facing up (A, **Figure 16**).
   c. Align the master cylinder and clamp mating halves with the punch mark (B, **Figure 16**) on the handlebar. Tighten the upper master cylinder clamp bolt first, then the lower bolt. Tighten the master cylinder clamp bolts to 12 N.m (106 in.-lb.).

6. Reconnect the front brake light switch connectors (**Figure 11**) at the switch.

7. Install the left side handlebar switch housing as follows:
   a. Align the switch housing locating pin (C, **Figure 10**) with the hole in the handlebar and close the switch halves (B) around the handlebar.
   b. Slide the end adapter (A, **Figure 10**) into the switch recess (**Figure 17**).
   c. Install the long screw (B, **Figure 7**) in the front housing hole and the short screw in the rear housing screw. Tighten the front screw, then the rear screw securely.

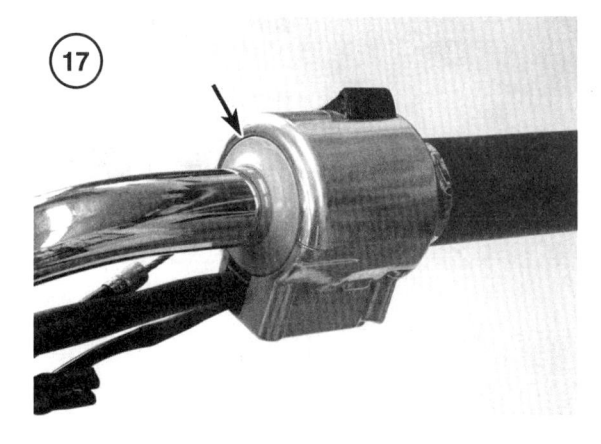

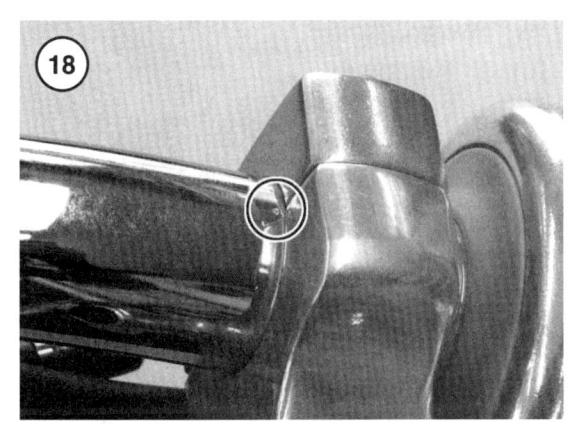

   e. Position the handlebar so the punch mark on the handlebar aligns with the gap between the holders as shown in **Figure 15**.
   f. Tighten the front handlebar holder bolts, then the rear bolts to 23 N.m (17 ft.-lb.).
   g. Install the bolt caps, if used.
   h. Tighten the lower holder nuts to 23 N.m (17 ft.-lb.).

2C. On Phantom models (**Figure 4**), perform the following:
   a. Install the handlebar, washers and nuts.
   b. Tighten the nuts to 23 N.m (17 ft.-lb.).

3. Clean the inside of the throttle sleeve and the right

8. Install the clutch lever bracket as follows:
   a. Clean the handlebar, clutch lever bracket and holder mating surfaces.
   b. Mount the clutch lever bracket onto the handlebar, then install its clamp (A, **Figure 7**) and both mounting bolts. Install the clamp with the UP mark facing up.
   c. Align the end of the clutch lever bracket with the punch mark on the handlebar (**Figure 18**). Tighten the upper holder bolt first, then tighten the lower bolt. Tighten the bolts securely.
   d. Reconnect the electrical connectors at the clutch switch (**Figure 6**).

9. Install, adjust and tighten the mirrors.
10. Adjust the throttle cables (Chapter Three).
11. Adjust the clutch (Chapter Three).
12. If air entered the front master cylinder brake line, bleed the front brake (Chapter Fifteen).

> **WARNING**
> *An improperly installed throttle sleeve assembly may cause the throttle to stick open. Failure to properly assemble and adjust the throttle cables and throttle sleeve could cause a loss of steering control. Do not start or ride the motorcycle until the throttle sleeve is installed correctly and snaps back when released.*

13. After all assemblies are installed, test each one to make sure it operates correctly. Correct any problem at this time.

HANDLEBAR GRIPS AND WEIGHTS

> **NOTE**
> *Only Spirit and Phantom models are equipped with handlebar weights.*

Handlebar Grip Inspection

The handlebar grips must be secured tightly to the handlebar (left side) and to the throttle sleeve (right side). Replace cut or damaged grips as water may enter between the grip and its mounting surface and cause the grip to slip. This could cause a loss of steering control. Replace the handlebar grips as described in the following procedure.

Replacement

1A. When servicing the left hand grip, remove the clutch holder and left handlebar switch as described under *Handlebar* in this chapter.
1B. When servicing the right hand grip, remove the throttle sleeve as described under *Handlebar* in this chapter.
2. Measure the distance from the inside of the right grip to the cable flange on the throttle sleeve (**Figure 19**). This gap must be maintained to prevent the grip from contacting the switch housing.

> **NOTE**
> *If reusing the hand grips, remove them carefully to avoid damaging them.*

3. Insert a thin blade screwdriver between the grip and handlebar or throttle sleeve and spray electrical contact cleaner into the open gap (**Figure 20**). Quickly turn the grip to break the cement bond and slide it off (**Figure 21**).

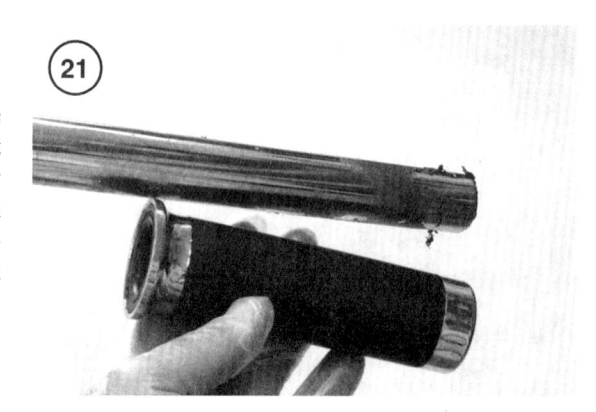

4. If reusing the grips, use an electrical contact cleaner to remove cement residue from inside the grips.

> **NOTE**
> *If the original hand grips are torn or damaged, install new grips.*

5. Remove all sealant residue from the handlebar or throttle sleeve.
6. On Spirit and Phantom models, service the handlebar weights as follows:
   a. Squeeze the lock arms on the end of the handlebar weight (**Figure 22**) and pull the weight assembly from the handlebar. See **Figure 23**.
   b. Inspect the handlebar weight for damage. Replace if necessary.
   c. Slide the handlebar weight into the handlebar with the lock arms facing out (**Figure 23**).
   d. Position the weight so that the lock arms spring

FRONT SUSPENSION AND STEERING

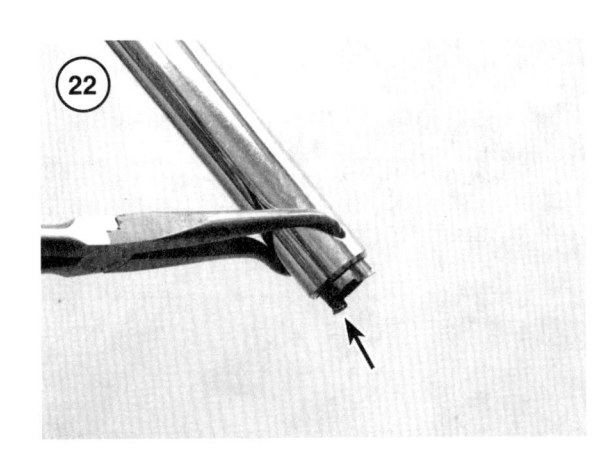

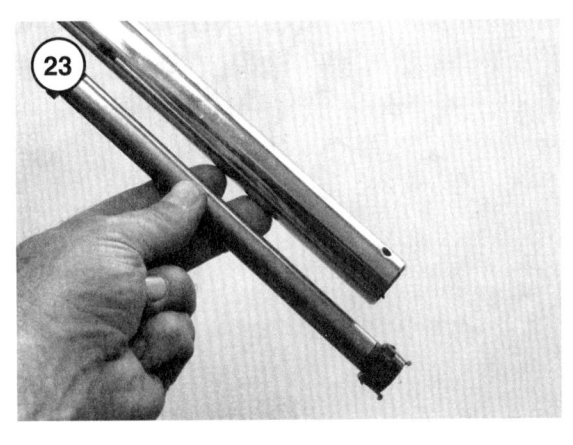

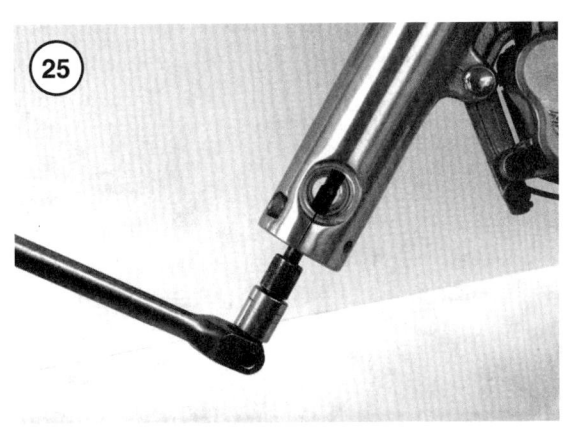

out and lock into the holes in the handlebar.

7. If the end adapter was removed from the handlebar, install it onto the left side of the handlebar as shown in A, **Figure 10**.

8. Install the left handlebar switch **(Figure 24)** before installing the grip. This will position the grip and help prevent it from being installed too far on the handlebar.

NOTE
When using a grip cement in the next step, follow the manufacturer's instructions for application and drying time.

9. Apply Honda Grip Cement, ThreeBond Griplock or an equivalent grip cement onto the left side of the handlebar or onto the outside of the throttle sleeve. Install the grip as follows:
   a. Install the grip with the chrome end cap installed on the grip.
   b. Install the left side grip until it almost contacts the left switch housing. When the grip is positioned correctly, remove the left switch housing and clean excess cement from the end of the grip, handlebar and left switch housing.
   c. Install the right side grip onto the throttle sleeve to the dimension recorded in Step 2. Wipe off all excess cement.

WARNING
Do not ride the motorcycle until the appropriate amount of drying time has elapsed; otherwise, the grip could move or slide off the handlebar or throttle sleeve and cause a loss of control. Refer to the manufacturer's recommended drying time.

WARNING
Loose or damaged hand grips can slide off and cause loss of steering control. Make sure the hand grips are correctly installed and cemented in place before operating the motorcycle.

FRONT FORK

Front Fork Removal

1. Remove the front wheel (Chapter Twelve).
2. If the fork is going to be disassembled, loosen, but do not remove, the Allen bolt in the bottom of each fork tube **(Figure 25)**.

NOTE
Do not remove the brake hose banjo bolt when removing the brake caliper.

3. Remove the bolts (A, **Figure 26**) and the front brake caliper (B). Support the caliper with a piece of stiff wire.

4. Note the routing of any cables or wiring harnesses prior to removing the fork tubes so that they can be installed along their original path. Make a sketch or take photos as needed.

5. Remove the front fender (Chapter Seventeen).

6. Loosen the upper fork tube pinch bolt (A, **Figure 27**).

7. If the fork tube is going to disassembled, loosen, but do not remove, the fork caps (B, **Figure 27**).

8A. If the front turn signals are mounted onto the fork tubes, perform the following:
  a. Remove the bolt, collar and turn signal light from the fork tube **(Figure 28)**.
  b. Support the turn signal assembly with a piece of stiff wire.

8B. On Aero and Phantom models, perform the following:
  a. Remove the top fork bridge as described under *Steering Head and Stem* in this chapter.
  b. Remove the bolts and the upper fork cover (A, **Figure 29**). Locate the upper O-ring installed in the fork cover.

NOTE
The bushing has two different inside diameters. The smaller inside diameter faces up.

  c. Mark the top of the bushing so that it can be installed facing in its original mounting position, then remove it from the fork tube.
  d. Measure the distance from the lower fork bridge to the top of the fork tube.

NOTE
Rust and corrosion built up around the fork tube and bridge clamp surfaces can lock the fork tube in place. Support the fork tube and spray the top area of each clamp with a penetrating oil.

9. While supporting fork tube, loosen the lower fork tube pinch bolts (B, **Figure 29**) and remove the fork tube.

10. Repeat the procedure to remove the other fork tube.

11. If necessary, remove the lower fork cover (if so equipped).

Front Fork Installation

1. Clean the fork tube pinch bolts and fork bridge threads.

2A. On Spirit models, perform the following:
  a. Slide the fork tube through the lower and upper

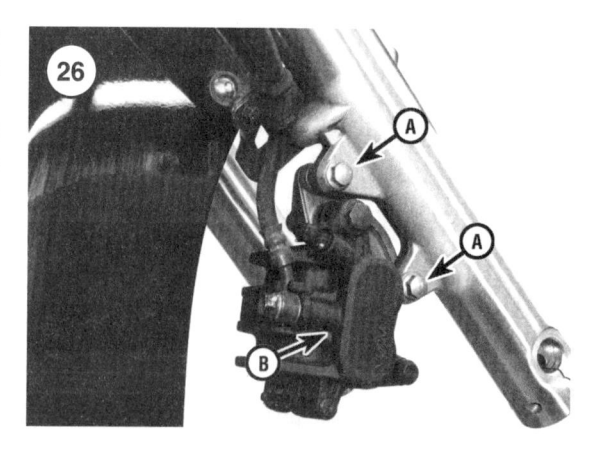

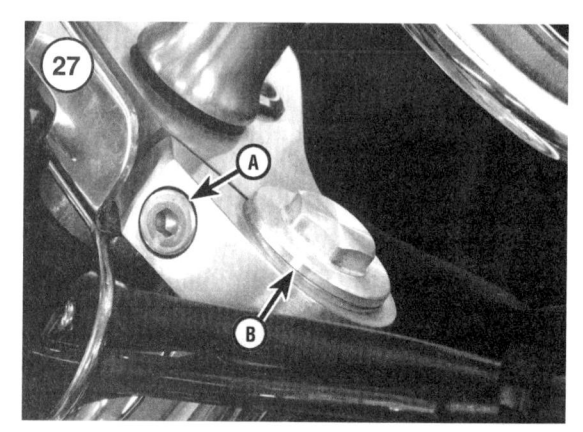

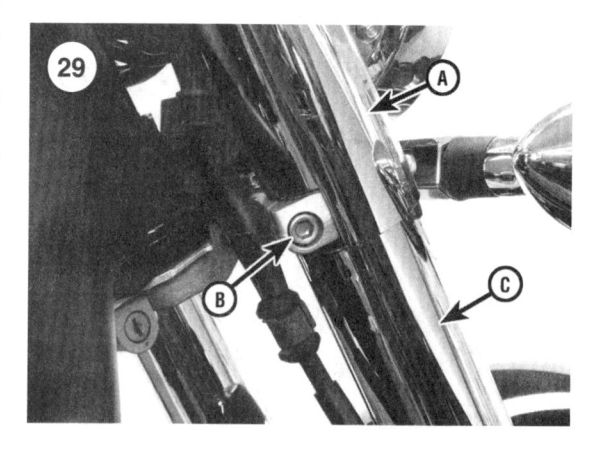

FRONT SUSPENSION AND STEERING

Figure 27) to 22 N.m (16 ft.-lb.) on 2007-2009 Spirit models or to 27 N.m (20 ft-lb.) on 2010-2013 Spirit models.

d. Install the front turn signal assembly **(Figure 28)**. Position the assembly and tighten the mounting bolt securely.

2B. On Aero and Phantom models, perform the following:

a. Install the lower fork cover, if previously removed.

b. Slide the fork tube through the lower fork cover and lower fork bridge. Position the fork tube to the height position recorded during removal and tighten the lower fork tube pinch bolt hand-tight. The bolt will be tightened to its final torque later.

c. Install the lower bushing (A, **Figure 31**) into the upper fork cover **(Figure 32)** with its smaller inside diameter side facing up. This should be the side of the bushing previously identified during removal.

d. Install the upper fork cover (A, **Figure 29**) over the fork tube and install the mounting bolts. Tighten the 8-mm bolt to 26 N.m (20 ft.-lb.) and the 6-mm bolt to 12 N.m (106 in.-lb.).

e. Install the O-ring (B, **Figure 31**) down the fork tube until it is below the upper surface of the upper fork cover **(Figure 33)**.

f. Repeat for the other fork tube.

g. Install the top fork bridge as described under *Steering Head and Stem* in this chapter.

h. Loosen the lower fork tube pinch bolt and position the fork so that the top of the fork tube is flush with the top bridge surface **(Figure 30)**. Tighten the lower fork tube pinch bolt (B, **Figure 29**) to 49 N.m (36 ft.-lb.).

i. Tighten the fork cap (B, **Figure 27**) to 22 N.m (16 ft.-lb.) on 2004-009 Aero models or to 22.1 N.m (16 ft lb.) on 2011-2013 Aero models and all Phantom models.

j. Tighten the upper fork tube pinch bolt (A, **Figure 27**) to 26 N.m (19 ft.-lb.) on 2004-2009 Aero models and 27 N.m (20 ft.-lb.) on 2011-2013 Aero and Phantom models.

NOTE
Make sure any cables or wiring harnesses are routed correctly around the fork tubes. Refer to the notes made prior to removing the fork tubes.

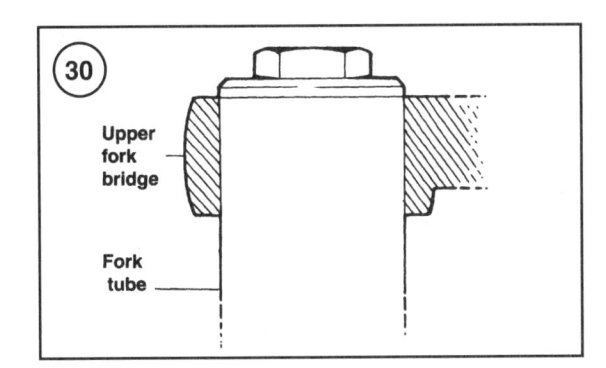

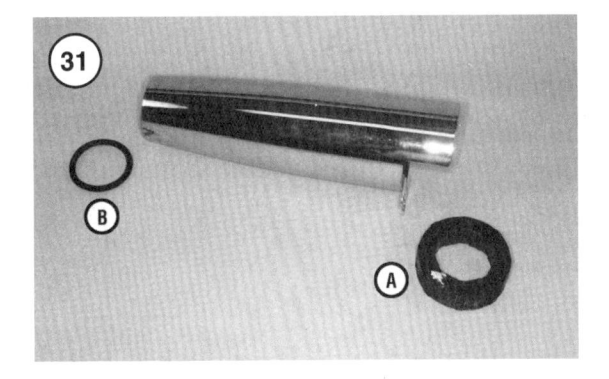

fork bridges. Position the fork tube so that the top is flush with the top bridge surface **(Figure 30)**. Tighten the lower fork tube pinch bolt (B, **Figure 29**) to 49 N.m (36 ft.-lb.).

b. Tighten the fork cap (B, **Figure 27**) to 22.1 N.m (16 ft.-lb.).

c. Tighten the upper fork tube pinch bolt (A,

3. Install the front fender (Chapter Seventeen).

4. Secure the front brake hose to the front fender. Tighten the mounting bolt securely.

5. Install the front brake caliper using two new mounting bolts **Figure 26**. Tighten the mounting bolts to 30 N.m (22 ft.-lb.).

CHAPTER THIRTEEN

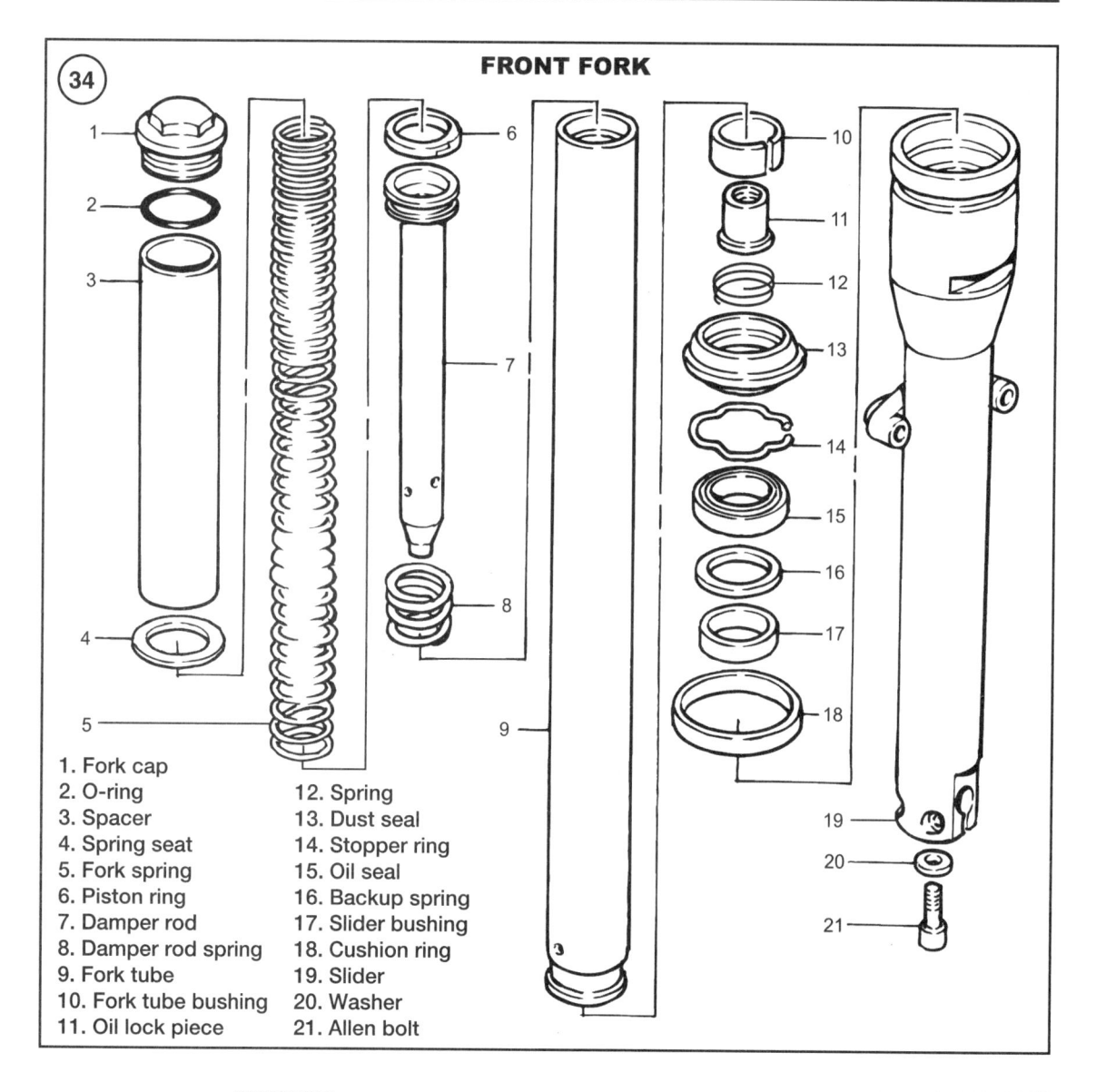

FRONT FORK

34

1. Fork cap
2. O-ring
3. Spacer
4. Spring seat
5. Fork spring
6. Piston ring
7. Damper rod
8. Damper rod spring
9. Fork tube
10. Fork tube bushing
11. Oil lock piece
12. Spring
13. Dust seal
14. Stopper ring
15. Oil seal
16. Backup spring
17. Slider bushing
18. Cushion ring
19. Slider
20. Washer
21. Allen bolt

WARNING
After installing the front wheel, operate the front brake lever to reposition the caliper pistons. If the brake lever feels spongy, bleed the front brake as described in Chapter Fifteen.

6. Install the front wheel (Chapter Twelve).

Disassembly

This section describes complete disassembly of the fork tubes. If only changing the fork oil and/or setting the oil level, follow just the required steps listed in the text.

Refer to **Figure 34**.

1. Remove the fork tube as described in this chapter.
2. Bolt a flat metal plate onto the fork tube and clamp the metal plate in a vise to support the fork tube when loosening and tightening the fork tube Allen bolt **(Figure 35)**.

NOTE
If only changing the fork oil and/or setting the oil level, disregard loosening the fork tube Allen bolt.

FRONT SUSPENSION AND STEERING

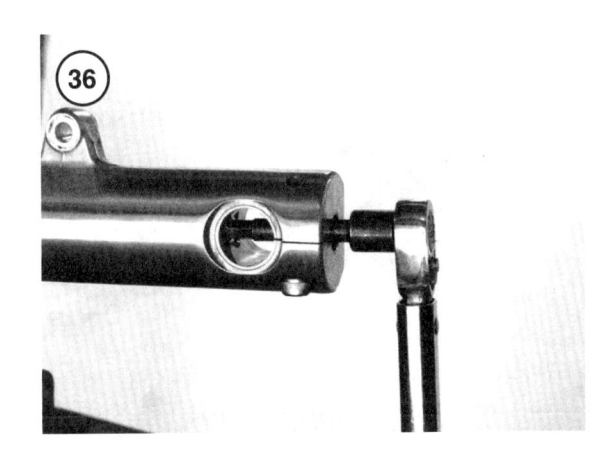

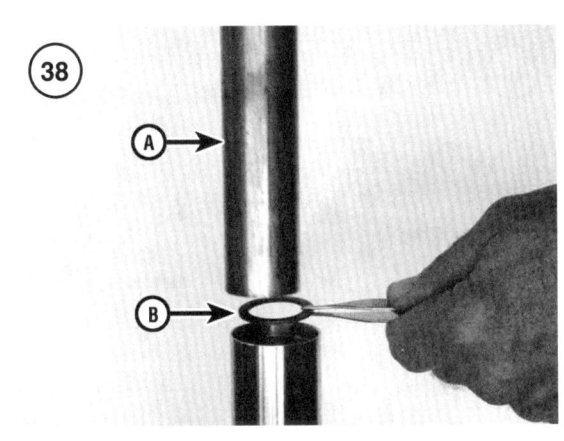

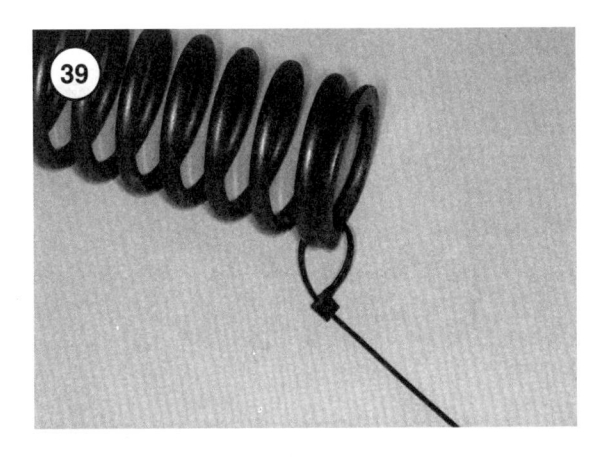

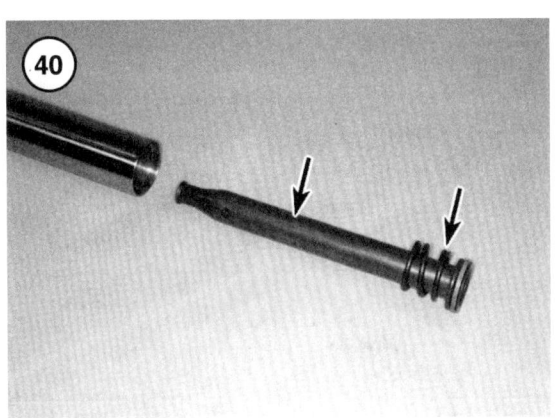

NOTE
Disregard this step if the fork tube Allen bolt was loosened during fork removal.

3. Loosen the fork tube Allen bolt as follows:
   a. Clean the recess in the top of the bolt of all dirt and debris.
   b. Have an assistant compress the fork tube assembly as much as possible and hold it compressed against the damper rod. Then loosen, but do not remove, the fork tube Allen bolt **(Figure 36)**.

WARNING
Be careful when removing the fork cap as the spring is under pressure. Protect your eyes and face accordingly.

4. Slowly unscrew and remove the fork cap **(Figure 37)** and its O-ring.
5. Remove the spacer (A, **Figure 38**), spring seat (B) and fork spring. Place a plastic tie **(Figure 39)** on the top of the fork spring to identify its upper end.
6. Turn the fork tube over a drain pan and pour out the fork oil by operating the fork tube several times.

NOTE
*If only changing the fork oil and/or setting the oil level, refer to the **Fork Oil Adjustment** procedure at the end of this section. If disassembling the fork, continue the procedure.*

7. Remove the previously loosened Allen bolt and washer from the base of the slider. Discard the washer.
8. Turn the fork over and slide out the damper rod and rebound spring **(Figure 40)**.

CAUTION
Do not use excessive force when removing the dust seal.

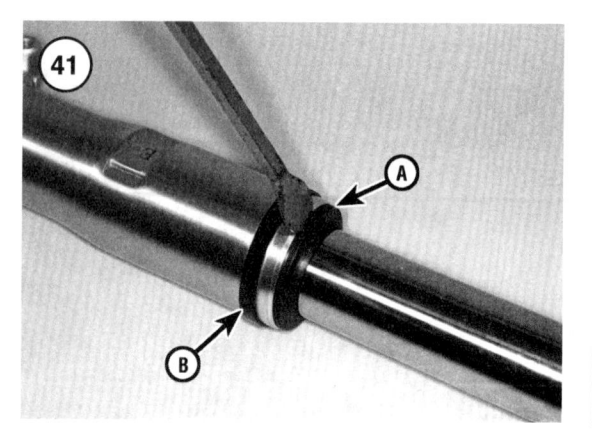

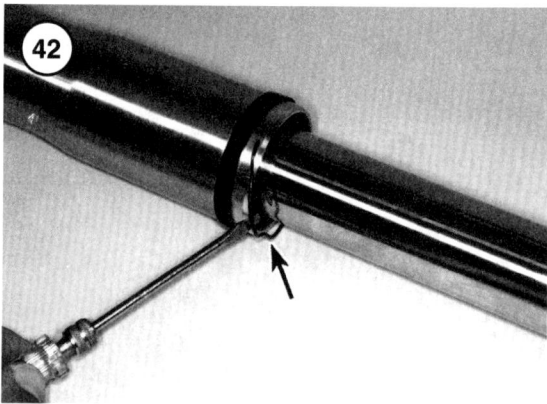

9. Carefully pry the dust seal (A, **Figure 41**) out of the slider with a suitable tool. Move the tool around the seal in small increments. It is easy to scratch and damage the slider at the top of the dust seal bore. When selecting a starting point, choose the side facing into the wheel.

NOTE
*On models so equipped, do not remove the cushion ring (B, **Figure 41**) installed in the top of the slider unless it is going to be replaced.*

10. Slip the tip of a small screwdriver behind the stopper ring and carefully pry the ring out of the slider groove **(Figure 42)** and remove it from the fork tube.

NOTE
A pressed-in bushing in the slider and a bushing on the fork tube keep the slider and fork tube from separating. To remove the fork tube from the slider, use these two parts as a slide hammer.

11. Hold the fork tube and pull hard on the slider, using quick in-and-out strokes **(Figure 43)**. Doing so withdraws the oil seal, backup ring and guide bushing from the slider. See **Figure 44**.
12. Remove the slider and pour any remaining oil in the oil pan.
13. Remove the oil lock piece (A, **Figure 45**) from the slider if it did not come with the other parts. Note the spring **(Figure 46)** installed inside the oil lock piece.
14. Slide off the oil seal (B, **Figure 45**), backup ring (C) and slider bushing (D) from the fork tube. Discard the dust seal and oil seal.

NOTE
*Do not remove the fork tube bushing (E, **Figure 45**) unless it is going to be replaced.*

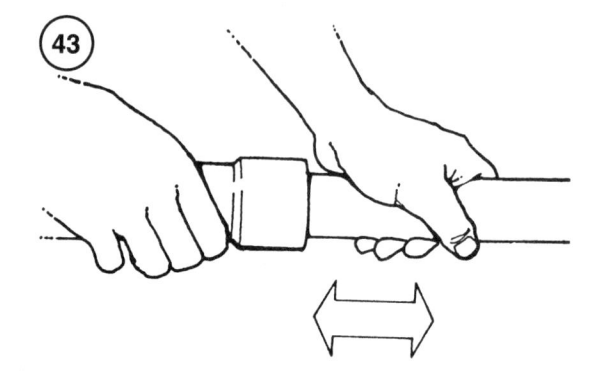

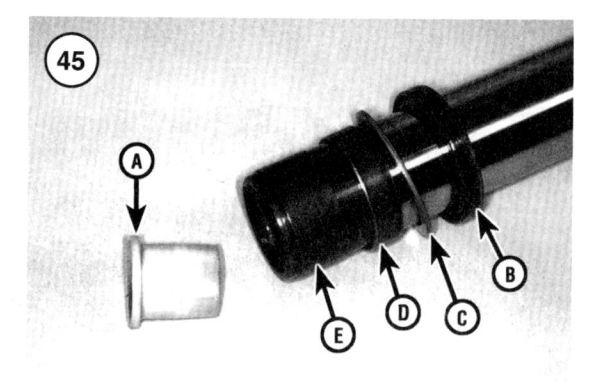

FRONT SUSPENSION AND STEERING

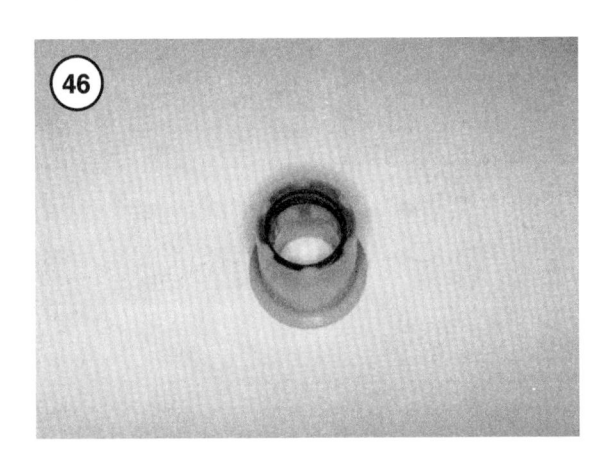

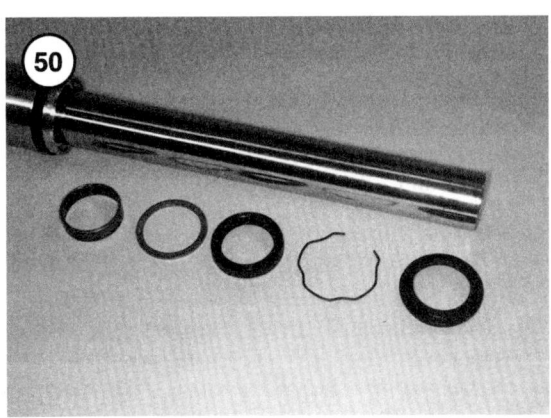

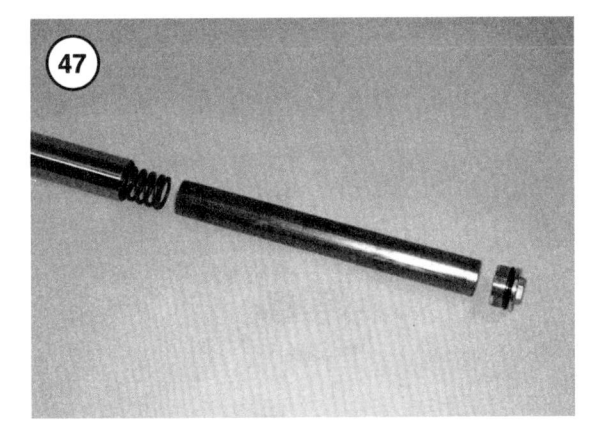

15. Clean and inspect the fork components as described in this section.

Assembly

Refer to **Figure 34** for this procedure.

1. Before assembling the parts, make sure there is no solvent left in the slider or on any part.
2. Lubricate the inside of the slider with fork oil.
3. Install the rebound spring onto the damper rod and slide the damper rod assembly through the fork tube **(Figure 40)**.
4. Temporarily install the fork spring, spacer and fork cap **(Figure 47)** to apply tension against the damper rod.
5. Install the spring inside the oil lock piece **(Figure 46)**, if removed.
6. Install the oil lock piece onto the end of the damper rod **(Figure 48)**.
7. Mount the slider in a vise by attaching a piece of metal to the fender mounting holes.
8. Carefully install the fork tube and the damper rod into the slider **(Figure 49)** until the oil lock piece bottoms against the slider.
9. Install a new washer onto the Allen bolt.
10. Install a medium strength threadlock onto the fork tube Allen bolt threads and thread the Allen bolt into the bottom of the damper rod and tighten until the damper rod starts to turn. Have an assistant compress the fork tube as much as possible and tighten the fork tube Allen bolt **(Figure 36)** to 29 N.m (21ft.-lb.).
11. Remove the fork cap, spacer and fork spring.
12. Using the same piece of metal to hold the fork assembly, position the slider in the vise so the fork tube faces straight up.

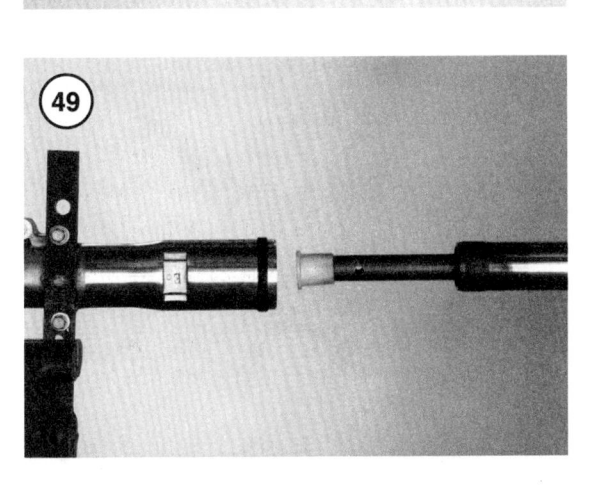

NOTE
Figure 50 *shows the alignment of the bushing and seal assembly.*

13. Install the fork slider bushing and backup ring as follows:
   a. Slide the bushing (A, **Figure 51**) and backup ring (B) down the fork tube. Install the backup ring with its chamfered side facing down and set it on top of the bushing.

   NOTE
   *Motion Pro fork oil seal drivers (**Figure 52**), or their equivalent, can be purchased from aftermarket suppliers. To select a driver, first measure the outside diameter of one fork tube.*

   b. Use a fork oil seal driver (**Figure 52**) to drive the bushing into the fork slider until it bottoms out in the recess in the slider. The knocking sound made by the driver changes when the bushing bottoms out.

   NOTE
   To avoid damaging the fork seal and dust seal when installing them over the top of the fork tube, first place a plastic bag over the fork tube and coat it thoroughly with fork oil.

14. Install a new fork seal as follows:
   a. Lubricate the seal lips with fork oil.
   b. Install the seal (**Figure 53**) over the fork tube with its size code facing up. Slide it down the fork tube and center it into the top of the slider until its outer surface is flush with the slider's outer bore surface.
   c. Drive the oil seal into the slider with the same tool (**Figure 52**) used for the slider bushing and backup ring.
   d. Continue to install the seal until the groove in the slider can be seen above the top surface of the seal.

   NOTE
   If the stopper ring cannot seat completely into the slider groove, the seal is not installed far enough into the slider.

15. Slide the stopper ring (**Figure 54**) over the fork tube and install it into the groove in the slider. Make sure that the stopper ring is completely seated in the slider groove.
16. Slide the dust seal down the fork tube and seat it into the slider (**Figure 55**).
17. Fill the fork with oil and set the oil level as described under *Fork Oil Adjustment* in this section.
18. Install the fork spring (**Figure 56**) with the closer wound coils facing up. If an aftermarket spring is used, install it facing in its original position. If a plastic tie was used to identify the spring end (**Figure 39**), install

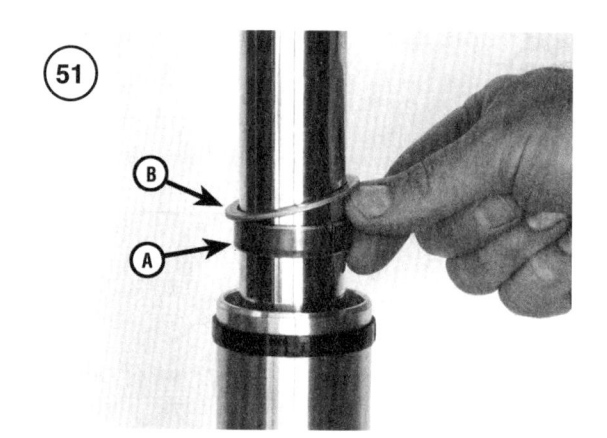

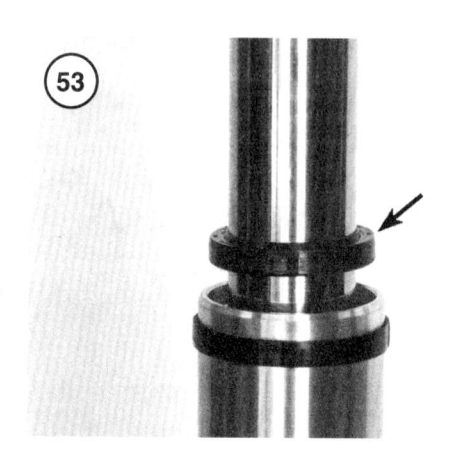

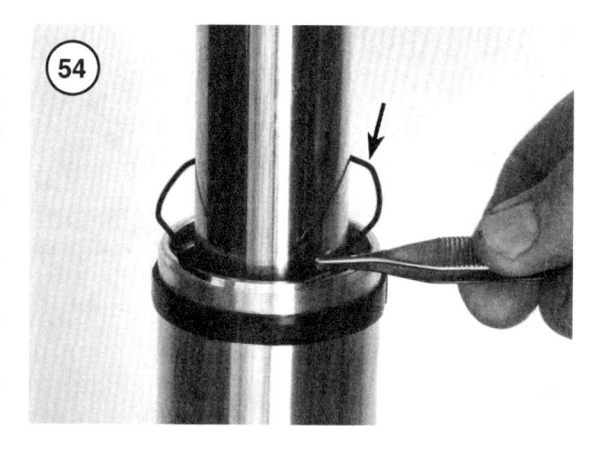

FRONT SUSPENSION AND STEERING

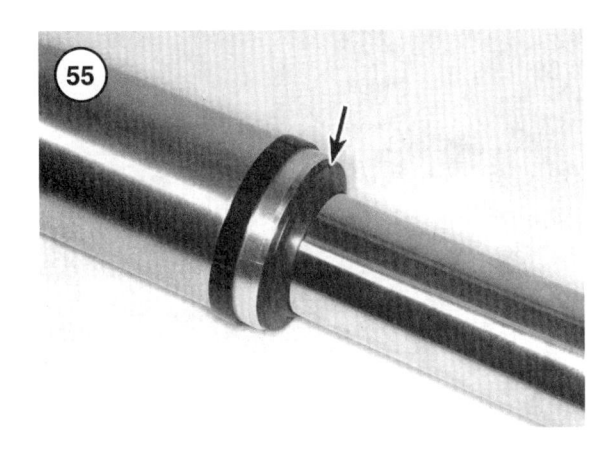

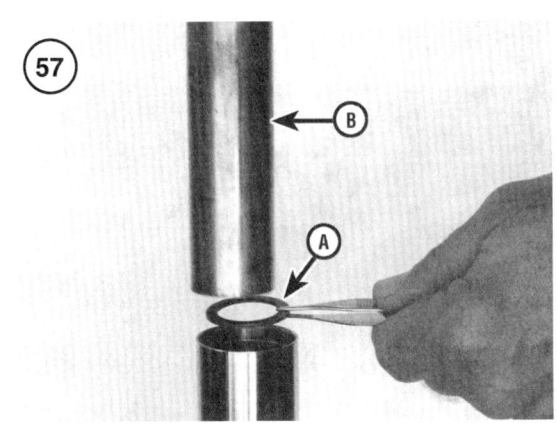

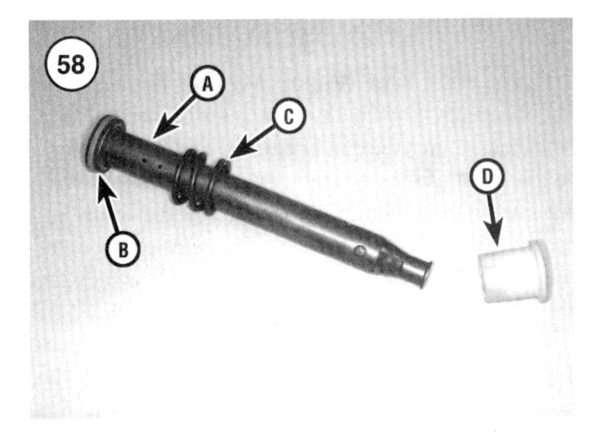

the spring with the plastic tie end facing up. Cut and remove the plastic tie from the fork spring.

19. Install the spring seat (A, **Figure 57**) and spacer (B).

20. Install a new O-ring onto the fork cap, if needed.

NOTE
The fork cap will be tightened completely after the fork tube is installed onto the motorcycle.

21. Lubricate the fork cap O-ring with fork oil. Install the fork cap **(Figure 37)** hand tight at this time.

Fork Inspection
(All Models)

When measuring the fork components, compare the actual measurements to the specifications in **Table 2**. Replace worn or damaged parts in this section.

1. Thoroughly clean all parts in solvent and dry them. Remove all threadlocking residue from the fork damper and Allen bolt threads.
2. Check the fork tube for severe wear or scratches. Check the chrome for flaking or other damage that could damage the oil seal.
3. Check the fork tube for straightness. Place the fork tube on V-blocks and measure runout with a dial indicator. If the runout is excessive, replace the fork tube.
4. Check the slider for dents or exterior damage. Check the stopper ring groove for cracks or damage. Check the oil seal mounting bore for dents or other damage.
5. Inspect the damper rod (A, **Figure 58**) for straightness and damage. Check the threads in the bottom of the damper rod for damage.
6. Inspect the piston ring (B, **Figure 58**) on the end of the damper rod for wear or damage. Replace if necessary.
7. Inspect the rebound spring (C, **Figure 58**) on the damper rod for cracks or other damage.
8. Inspect the oil lock piece (D, **Figure 58**) for wear or damage. Inspect the spring installed inside the oil lock piece for damage.
9. Measure the free length of the fork spring with a tape measure. Replace the spring if it is too short. Replace the left and right side springs as a set if they are unequal in length.

10. Inspect the slider and fork tube bushings (**Figure 59**) for scoring, excessive wear or damage. Check for discoloration and material coating damage. If the coating is worn off so that the base material is showing on approximately 3/4 of the total surface, the bushing is severely worn. Replace both bushings as a set.

11. To replace the fork tube bushing, pry its slot open with a screwdriver (**Figure 60**) and slide it off the fork tube. Clean the groove on the bottom of the fork tube. Then, install the new bushing (**Figure 61**) until it seats fully in the groove.

12. Replace the fork cap O-ring if damaged or leaking.

Fork Oil Adjustment

This section describes steps on filling the fork with oil and setting the oil level.

See **Table 2** for the recommended type of fork oil.

1. Remove the fork spring and drain the fork tube as described under *Disassembly* in this section.
2. Push the fork tube down and bottom against the slider. Support the slider so it cannot tip over.
3. Slowly pour the recommended type of fork oil (**Table 2**) into the fork.

> *NOTE*
> *As oil replaces air during the bleeding procedure, the oil level in the fork drops. Continue to add oil to maintain a high oil level in the fork. When bleeding the fork tube, do not be concerned with maintaining or achieving the proper oil capacity. Setting the oil level determines the actual amount of oil used in each fork tube.*

4. Hold the slider with one hand and slowly extend the fork tube. Repeat until the fork tube moves smoothly with the same amount of tension through the compression and rebound travel strokes. Then stop with the fork tube bottomed out.
5. Set the fork tube aside for approximately five minutes to allow any suspended air bubbles in the oil to surface.
6. Set the oil level (**Figure 62**) as follows:
   a. Make sure the fork tube is bottomed against the slider and placed in a vertical position.
   b. Use an oil level gauge (**Figure 63**) and set the oil level to the specification listed in **Table 2**.
   c. Remove the oil level gauge.
7. Complete fork assembly as described under *Assembly* in this section.

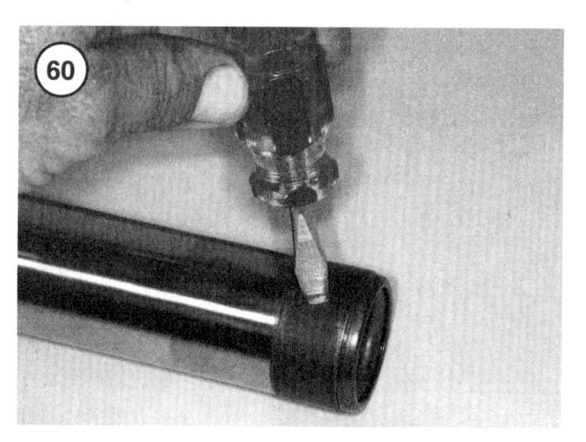

STEERING HEAD AND STEM

The steering head (**Figure 64**) uses retainer-type steel bearings. Each bearing consists of three pieces: inner race, outer race and bearing. The bearings can be lifted out of their operating positions after removing the steering stem. Do not remove the lower inner race (pressed onto the steering stem) or the outer bearing races (pressed into the frame) unless they are to be replaced.

Regular maintenance consists of steering inspection, adjustment and bearing lubrication. When the steering cannot be adjusted correctly, the bearings

FRONT SUSPENSION AND STEERING

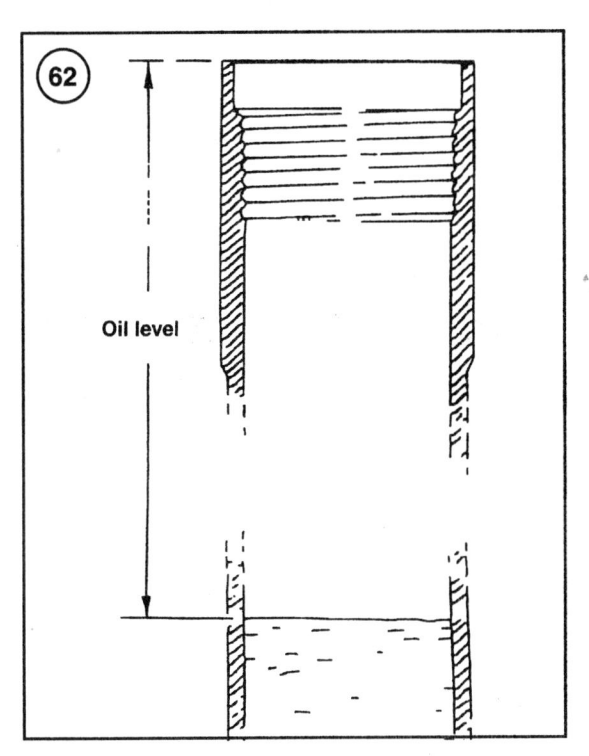

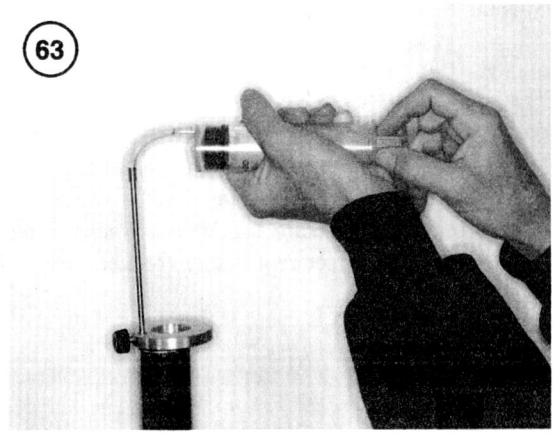

62 Oil level

63

may require replacement. However, to determine bearing condition, the steering assembly must be removed and inspected. Inspect the steering adjustment and check the bearings at the intervals listed (Chapter Three). Adjust the steering and lubricate or replace the bearings as necessary.

This section describes complete service and adjustment procedures for the steering head assembly.

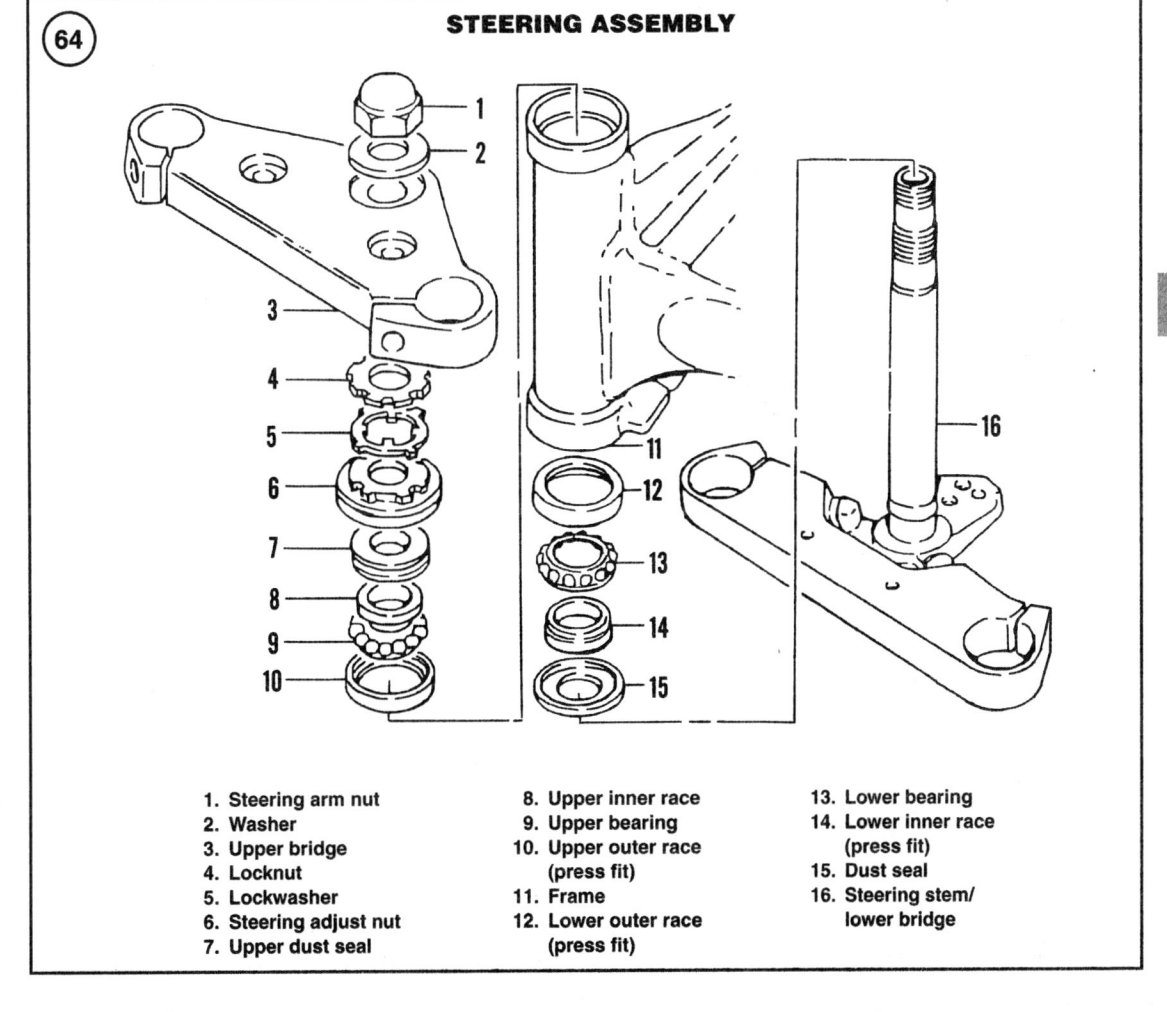

64 STEERING ASSEMBLY

1. Steering arm nut
2. Washer
3. Upper bridge
4. Locknut
5. Lockwasher
6. Steering adjust nut
7. Upper dust seal
8. Upper inner race
9. Upper bearing
10. Upper outer race (press fit)
11. Frame
12. Lower outer race (press fit)
13. Lower bearing
14. Lower inner race (press fit)
15. Dust seal
16. Steering stem/lower bridge

Special Tools

A steering stem socket (Honda part No. 07916-3710100), or its equivalent, and a spring scale are required to adjust the steering stem/bearing. These tools are shown in the appropriate procedure.

Refer to *Steering Head Bearing Race Replacement* and *Steering Stem Bearing Race Replacement* in this chapter for bearing race replacement procedures and special tools.

Troubleshooting

Before removing the steering assembly to troubleshoot a steering complaint, refer to Chapter Two, *Front Steering and Suspension*. Refer to the topic that most identifies the problem and check the items listed as possible causes.

Removal

Refer to **Figure 64**.
1. Note the cable and wiring harness routing around the steering assembly.
2. Remove the handlebar as described in this chapter.
3. Remove the headlight housing (Chapter Ten).
4. On Aero and Phantom models, remove the front turn signal assembly (Chapter Ten).
5. Identify and remove the indicator bulb holders mounted in the upper bridge, if so equipped (Chapter Ten).
6A. On Aero models without ABS and all Phantom models, remove the bolt and brake hose clamp from the lower bridge.
6B. On Aero models with ABS, remove the bolt and the brake hose/pipe clamp.
6C. On Spirit models without ABS, remove the bolt and the brake hose from the lower bridge.
6D. On Spirit models with ABS, perform the following:
   a. Remove the bolt and the brake hose clamp mounted on the left side of the lower bridge.
   b. Remove the brake hose from the clamp on the right side of the upper bridge. If necessary, remove the clamp mounting bolt.

NOTE
At this point there should be no cables, hoses or wiring harnesses interfering with the movement of the steering stem. Check by turning the steering stem. If so, reposition the item so the steering stem can move with no interference.

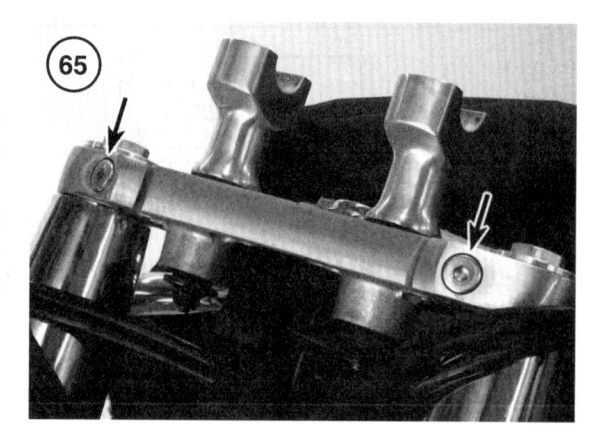

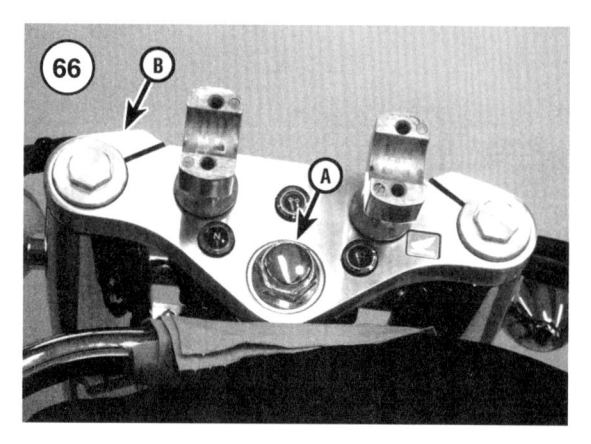

7. Before loosening the steering stem nut, check the steering adjustment as described in *Steering Bearing Preload Inspection (*this chapter).
8. Remove the front wheel (Chapter Twelve).
9. Loosen the upper fork tube pinch bolts **(Figure 65)**.
10. Remove the steering stem nut and washer (A, **Figure 66**).
11. Remove the upper bridge (B, **Figure 66**). See **Figure 67**.
12. Remove the front wheel (Chapter Twelve), front brake caliper (Chapter Fifteen), front fender (Chapter Seventeen) and front fork legs (this chapter).

FRONT SUSPENSION AND STEERING

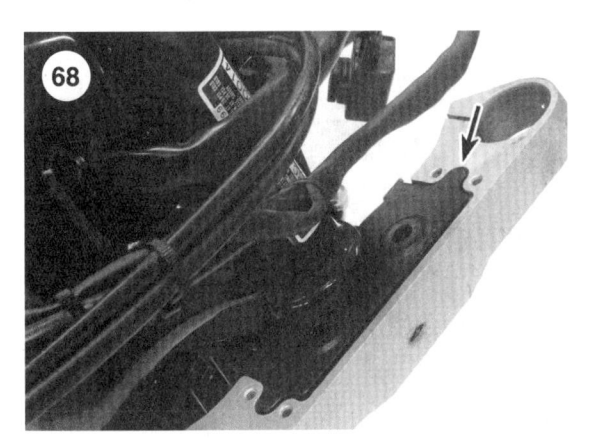

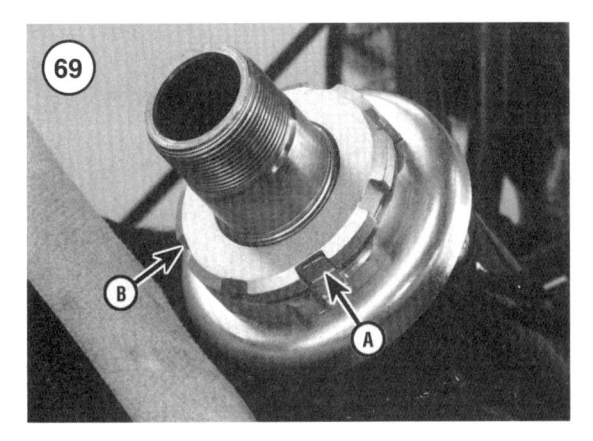

13. On models with chrome fork covers, remove the mounting bolts and the lower fork covers.

14A. On Aero and Phantom models, remove the nuts and bolts securing the headlight and turn signal mounting brackets to the lower bridge. Then remove the cover (**Figure 68**, typical) from the lower bridge.

14B. On Spirit models, remove the nuts and bolts securing the headlight housing mounting brackets to the lower bridge. Then remove the cover (**Figure 68**, typical) from the lower bridge.

15. Pry the lockwasher tabs (A, **Figure 69**) away from the locknut grooves. Then remove the locknut (B) and lockwasher (A). Discard the lockwasher.

NOTE
Before loosening the steering adjust nut, turn the steering stem from lock-to-lock to check the steering adjustment.

16. Loosen the steering adjust nut with one of the following tools **(Figure 70)**:
    a. A steering stem socket (Honda part No. 07916-3710100), or its equivalent.
    b. A fabricated tool made from a piece of pipe or deep socket.
    c. A spanner wrench.

NOTE
Support the weight of the steering stem assembly while removing the steering adjust nut, or the assembly will drop out of the steering head.

17. Support the steering stem and remove the following:
    a. Steering adjust nut **(Figure 71)**.
    b. Dust seal **(Figure 72)**.

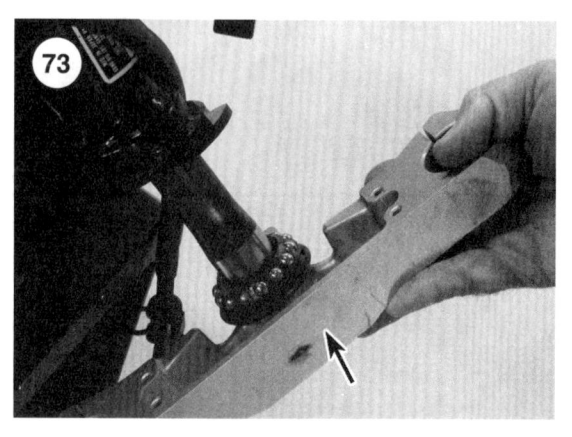

c. Lower the steering stem and remove it and the lower bearing assembly **(Figure 73)** from the frame.
d. Upper inner race and bearing assembly **(Figure 74)**.

NOTE
The upper outer race, lower outer race and lower inner race are installed with a press fit. Only remove these parts when replacing the bearing assembly.

19. Clean and inspect the parts as described in this section.

Steering Stem Assembly and Steering Adjustment

1. Make sure the upper and lower outer bearing races are properly seated in the steering head. Then lubricate each bearing race with grease.
2. Thoroughly lubricate each bearing **(Figure 75)** with grease.
3. Lubricate the upper dust seal (bottom side) with grease and set aside until installation.
4. Lower bearing:
    a. Lubricate the lower outer bearing race and dust seal lip **(Figure 76)** with grease.
    b. Install the lower steering bearing **(Figure 77)** onto the lower inner bearing race.
5. Upper bearing:
    a. Lubricate the upper inner bearing race with grease.
    b. Install the upper inner race into its bearing **(Figure 78)**.
    c. Install the upper bearing and its inner race into the outer race in the steering head **(Figure 74)**.
6. Install the steering stem **(Figure 73)** into the steering head and through the upper bearing race and hold in place. Make sure the lower bearing is centered inside the lower outer race.
7. Install the upper dust seal **(Figure 72)** and seat it

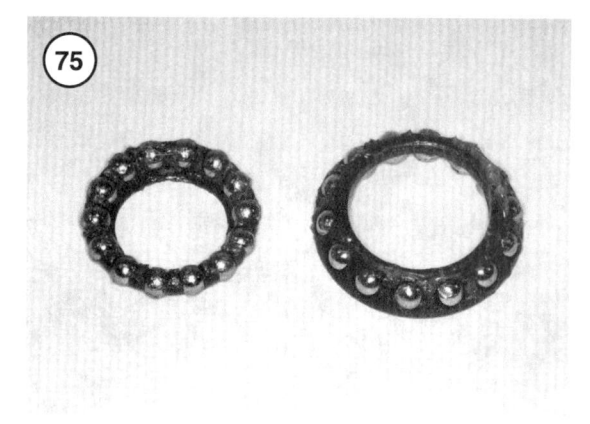

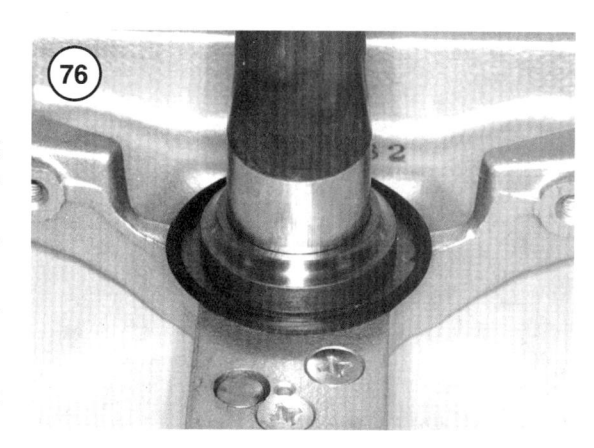

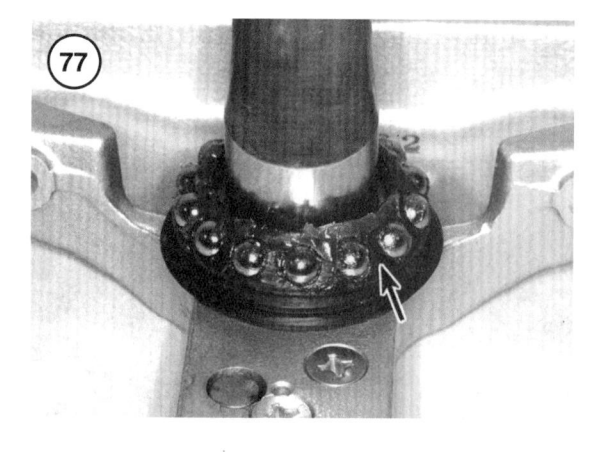

FRONT SUSPENSION AND STEERING

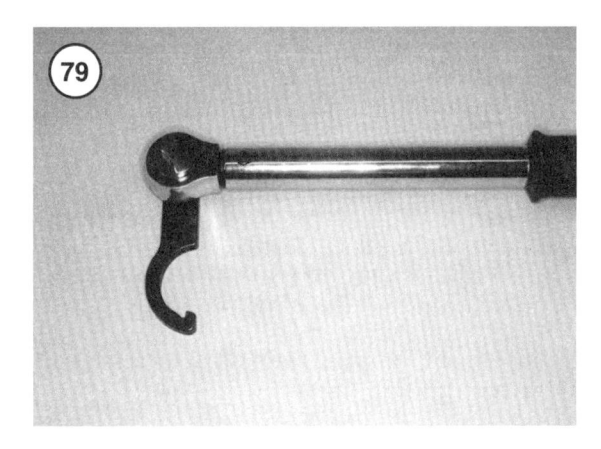

78

79

80

over the bearing assembly.

NOTE
The steering stem, steering stem nut and steering adjust nut threads must be clean for accurate tightening of these fasteners. Dirt, grease or other residue on the threads can affect the steering stem tightening torque and bearing preload adjustment.

8. Lubricate the steering adjust nut threads with oil and install the nut onto the steering stem **(Figure 71)**. Finger-tighten the nut.

9. Tighten the steering adjust nut **(Figure 71)** as follows:

NOTE
*If the special tool is not available, use a spanner wrench and torque wrench **(Figure 79)** to seat the bearings. Refer to **Torque Wrench Adapters** in Chapter One for information.*

 a. Use a steering stem socket or equivalent to seat the bearings in the following steps.
 b. Tighten the steering adjust nut **(Figure 70)** to 25 N.m (18 ft.-lb.).

NOTE
If the steering stem does not pivot smoothly, one or both bearing assemblies may be damaged. Remove the steering stem and inspect the bearings.

NOTE
Do not continue the procedure until the steering stem turns correctly. If there is any excessive play or roughness, recheck the steering adjustment.

 c. Turn the steering stem from lock-to-lock five times to seat the bearings. The steering stem must pivot smoothly. Retighten the steering adjust nut to 25 N.m (18 ft.-lb.).

CAUTION
Never reinstall a used lockwasher, as the tabs may break off, making the lockwasher ineffective.

10. Align the tabs of a *new* lockwasher with the grooves in the steering adjust nut and install the lockwasher **(Figure 80)**. The outer two tabs will be bent into the locknut grooves.

11. Install and tighten the locknut as follows:
 a. Install the locknut (B, **Figure 69**) and tighten finger-tight.
 b. Hold the steering adjust nut (to keep it from turning) and tighten the locknut approximately 1/4 turn (90 degrees) to align its grooves with the outer lockwasher tabs.
 c. Bend the outer lockwasher tabs (A, **Figure 69**) up into the locknut grooves.

12A. On non-ABS Aero and all Phantom models, perform the following:
 a. Install the cover (**Figure 68,** typical) into the lower bridge. Then install the front brake hose bracket by aligning the tabs on the bracket with the cover. Install two new mounting bolts at the rear of the cover and tighten securely.

b. Install the front turn signal and headlight mounting brackets and secure with the nuts and bolts. Tighten all fasteners securely.

12B. On ABS Aero models, perform the following:
  a. Install the cover (**Figure 68,** typical) into the lower bridge.
  b. Position the brake pipe/hose clamp onto the lower cover and secure with a new mounting bolt. Install a second new mounting bolt on the opposite side of the cover. Tighten the bolts securely.

12C. On Spirit models, perform the following:
  a. Install the cover (**Figure 68,** typical) onto the lower bridge. Then install the headlight mounting bracket and the mounting bolts and nuts and tighten finger-tight. Final tightening will take place after the headlight housing is installed.
  b. On non-ABS models, position the brake hose against the lower bridge. Install a new mounting bolt and tighten securely.

13. Install the upper bridge, washer and steering stem nut. Do not tighten the nut.
14. Install the fork covers (if used) and front fork legs described in this chapter. Tighten the pinch bolts temporarily to hold the forks in place. The pinch bolts will be tightened to their final torque later in the procedure.
15. Tighten the steering stem nut to 103 N.m (76 ft.-lb.).
16. Turn the steering stem lock-to-lock. Make sure it moves smoothly. There must be no play or binding. Note the following:
  a. If the steering stem turns correctly, continue the procedure.

NOTE
If the steering adjustment is too loose, the steering will become unstable and cause front wheel wobble. If the steering adjustment is too tight, the bearings will eventually score or notch the races. The steering will then become sluggish as the damaged bearings and races operate against each other. Both conditions will hamper steering performance.

  b. If the steering stem is too loose or tight, remove the steering stem nut, washer and upper bridge. Then readjust the steering adjust nut. Repeat until the steering play feels correct. Damaged bearings and races can also cause tightness.

NOTE
Arriving at the proper steering adjustment usually comes down to the steering effort required to turn the handlebar. The number of attempts required to arrive at the correct steering adjustment (feel) can vary considerably.

17. When the steering adjustment is correct, position the fork tubes and tighten the upper and lower pinch bolts to specifications (this chapter).
18. Install the front fender (Chapter Seventeen) front wheel (Chapter Twelve) and front brake caliper (Chapter Fifteen).
19. Install the headlight housing (Chapter Ten.).
20. On Aero and Phantom models, install the turn signal assembly (Chapter Ten).
21. Install the indicator bulb holders into the upper bridge, if so equpped (Chapter Ten).
22. Install the handlebar (this chapter).

WARNING
Do not ride the motorcycle until the horn, lights, controls and brakes work properly.

NOTE
The steering bearing preload inspection measures the amount of weight required to move the steering stem. This inspection confirms whether the steering adjustment is correct.

23. Perform the *Steering Bearing Preload Inspection* (this chapter).

Inspection

Replace parts that show excessive wear or damage as described in this section.

WARNING
Improper repair of damaged frame and/or steering components can cause loss of steering control. If there is apparent frame, steering stem or fork bridge damage, consult with a dealership or qualified frame shop for professional inspection and possible repair.

1. Clean and dry all parts. Make certain the cleaning solution is compatible with the rubber dust seals.
2. Check the frame for cracks and fractures.
3. Inspect the steering stem nut, locknut, and steering adjust nut for excessive wear or damage.
4. Inspect the upper dust seal for tearing, deterioration or other damage.
5. Check the steering stem (**Figure 81**) for:
  a. Cracked or bent stem.
  b. Damaged lower bridge.
  c. Damaged threads.
6. Check the upper bridge for cracks or other damage. Replace if necessary.
7. Inspect the bearing assemblies as follows:
  a. Inspect the bearing races for severe wear, pit-

FRONT SUSPENSION AND STEERING

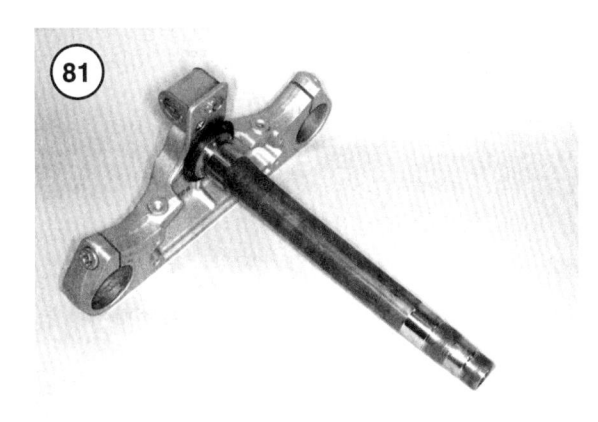

ting, cracks or other damage. To replace the outer bearing races, refer to *Steering Head Bearing Race Replacement* in this chapter. To replace the lower inner bearing race, refer to *Steering Stem Bearing Race Replacement* in this chapter.

b. Inspect the upper and lower bearings **(Figure 75)** for dents, pitting, excessive wear, corrosion, retainer damage or discoloration.

NOTE
*Each bearing assembly consists of the bearing and an inner and outer race **(Figure 64)**. Always replace the bearings in upper and lower sets.*

c. Replace the upper and lower bearing assemblies at the same time.

8. When reusing bearings, clean them thoroughly with a bearing degreaser and dry thoroughly. Repack each bearing with grease.

STEERING BEARING PRELOAD INSPECTION

Proper steering bearing preload is important as it controls bearing play and steering control. If the preload is too loose, excessive play in the steering will allow the wheel to wobble, which is best defined as a slight to severe side-to-side movement or oscillation of the handlebars. A wobble may occur at all vehicle speeds, or start and then stop at certain speeds. In all respects, it is very frustrating condition and can be difficult to troubleshoot. If the preload is too tight, the bearings and races will suffer unnecessary wear and cause stiff and uneven steering, requiring the rider to make a greater steering effort when turning the handlebars. Dry or damaged bearings can cause similar conditions.

Check the steering head for looseness at the intervals specified in Chapter Three or whenever the following symptoms or conditions exist:
1. The handlebars vibrate more than normal.
2. The front fork makes a clicking or clunking noise when the front brake is applied.
3. The steering feels tight or slow.
4. The motorcycle does not steer straight on level road surfaces.

Inspection

When installing the steering stem assembly, the steering bearings are preloaded (bearing placed under pressure) by carefully tightening the steering adjust nut and the steering stem nut. When the bearings are lubricated and correctly preloaded, the bearings should not move out of alignment. To check bearing preload, the manufacturer specifies the use of a spring scale attached to one of the fork tubes. This method measures the amount of weight required to move the steering stem with the front end assembled and the front wheel off the ground. When measuring bearing preload with a spring scale, the steering stem must be free to turn without interference from cables, hoses or wiring harnesses.

A spring scale is required for this procedure.

NOTE
This procedure must be performed with the front forks and front wheel mounted on the motorcycle.

1. Support the motorcycle so that it is sitting level with the front wheel off the ground.
2. Turn the steering stem side-to-side. There should be no interference or drag from a cable, wire harness or the front brake hose when the steering stem is rotated. If there still interference, reposition or remove the affecting part as required.
3. Attach a plastic zip tie onto one of the fork tubes (between the fork bridges). Then attach a spring scale onto the zip tie **(Figure 82)**.
4. Center the wheel. Position the spring scale at a 90° angle with the steering stem **(Figure 83)**. Pull the

spring scale and note the reading on the scale when the steering stem begins to turn. This reading is steering stem bearing preload. See Table 1 for the correct steering stem bearing preload reading.

5. If the preload reading is incorrect, adjust the steering assembly as described under *Steering Stem Assembly and Steering Adjustment* in this chapter. Perform the adjustment with the front forks and front wheel mounted on the motorcycle.

WARNING
Do not ride the motorcycle until the horn, lights, controls and brakes work properly.

STEERING HEAD BEARING RACE REPLACEMENT

The steering head bearing races (**Figure 84** and **Figure 85**) are pressed into the frame's steering head. The bearing races should only be removed when new races will be installed.

A threaded rod and disc tool **(Figure 86)** will be used to install the races. When properly used, this tool exerts even pressure around the race. One disc is sized to fit the outer diameter of the races, while the other disc is larger than the diameter of the steering head. This tool is shown in the following procedure.

NOTE
The following procedure describes simple home shop techniques to remove the bearing races. If removal is difficult, do not chance damaging the frame or the new bearing races. Have the task performed by a dealership or a qualified specialist.

Replace the upper and lower bearing assemblies at the same time.

CAUTION
If binding occurs when removing or installing the bearing races, stop and release tension from the bearing race. Check the tool alignment to make sure the bearing race is moving evenly in its mounting bore. Otherwise, the bearing race may gouge the frame mounting bore and cause permanent damage.

1. Chill the new bearing races in a freezer for a few hours to shrink the outer diameter of the race as much as possible.
2. Insert a drift into the steering head and position it on the edge of the lower race (**Figure 87**). Carefully drive out the race. To prevent binding, make several

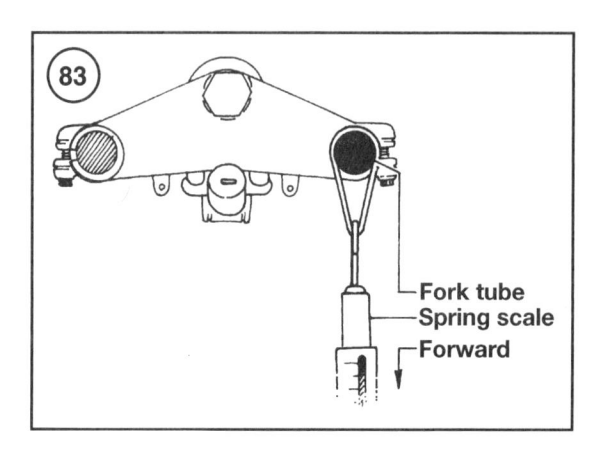

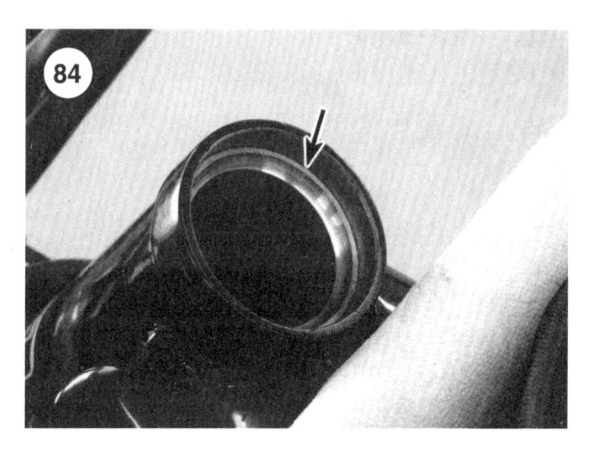

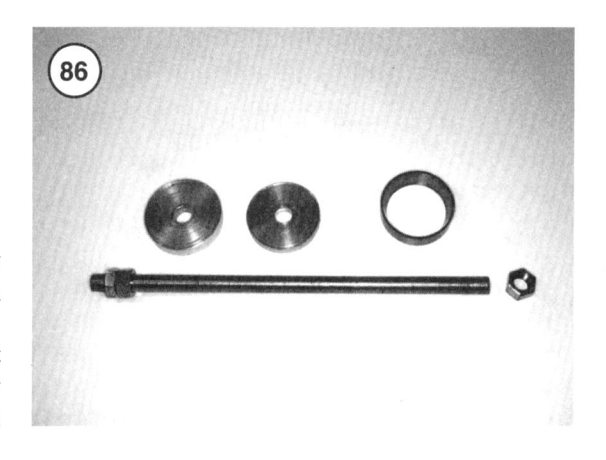

FRONT SUSPENSION AND STEERING

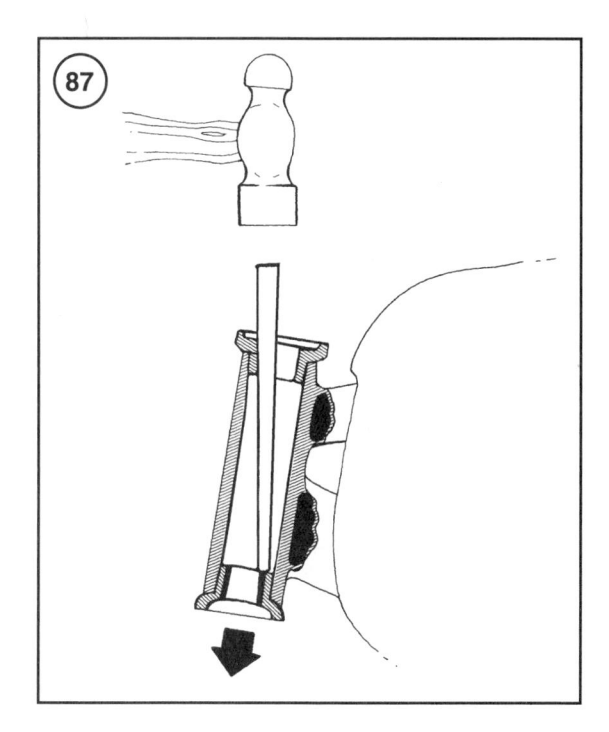

passes around the perimeter of the race. Repeat to remove the upper race.

3. Clean the race bores in the frame and check for damage.
4. To install the upper race, do the following:
   a. Place the new upper race (**Figure 88**) squarely into the mounting bore opening with its bearing side facing out.
   b. Assemble the threaded rod tool as shown in **Figure 89**.

CAUTION
If there is any binding when installing the bearing races in the following steps, stop and release all tension from the bearing race. Check the tool alignment to make sure the bearing race is moving evenly in its mounting bore. Otherwise, the bearing race may gouge the frame mounting bore and cause permanent damage.

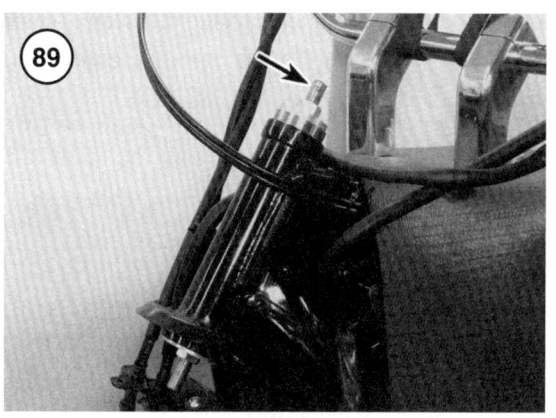

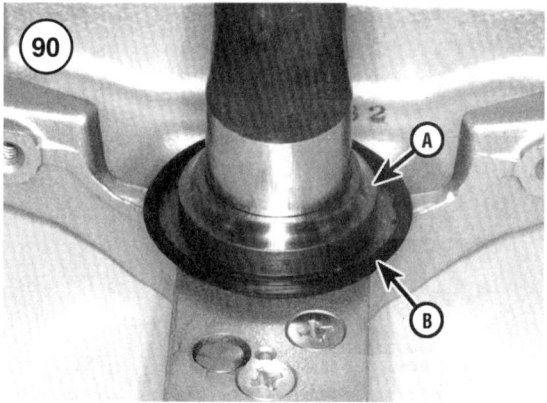

   c. Hold the lower nut and tighten the upper nut to draw the race into the frame tube. Continue until the race bottoms out in its mounting bore. Remove the puller assembly and inspect the bearing race. It must seat fully and squarely in the frame tube (**Figure 84**).

CAUTION
Do not allow the installer shaft to contact the bearing race.

5. Reverse the tool and repeat Step 4 to install the lower race (**Figure 85**). Insert the threaded rod tool carefully through the frame to prevent from scratching the upper bearing race.
6. Lubricate the upper and lower bearing races with grease.

STEERING STEM BEARING RACE REPLACEMENT

The lower inner race (A, **Figure 90**) is a press fit on the steering stem. Replace the lower dust seal (B) when replacing the lower inner race.

1. Thread the steering stem nut onto the steering stem (**Figure 91**) to help protect the steering stem threads when removing the lower inner race.

WARNING
Striking a chisel with a hammer can cause flying chips. Wear safety glasses in Step 2 to prevent eye injury.

2. Remove the lower inner bearing race and dust seal with a chisel as shown in **Figure 91**. To prevent damaging the steering stem, remove the bearing race evenly by applying pressure against the bearing race at different points around the bearing.
3. Discard the lower inner bearing race and dust seal.
4. Clean the steering stem with solvent and dry thoroughly.
5. Inspect the steering stem race surface for cracks or other damage. Replace the steering stem if necessary.
6. Install a new lower dust seal (B, **Figure 90**) over the steering stem.
7. Slide the new lower inner bearing race with the bearing surface facing up onto the steering stem until it stops.
8A. Install the bearing race with a press as follows:
   a. Install the steering stem in a press. Support the bottom of the steering stem with a bearing driver or piece of round metal. Then install a bearing driver (**Figure 92**) over the steering stem and seat it against the inner bearing race inside shoulder. Do not allow the bearing driver to contact the bearing race surface.
   b. Press the lower inner race onto the steering stem until it bottoms.
   c. Remove the steering stem from the press.
8B. If a press is unavailable, install a bearing driver over the steering stem and seat it against the inner bearing race inside shoulder (**Figure 93**). Do not allow the bearing driver to contact the bearing race surface. Carefully drive the race onto the steering stem until it bottoms.
9. Lubricate the bearing race and dust seal (**Figure 92**) with grease.

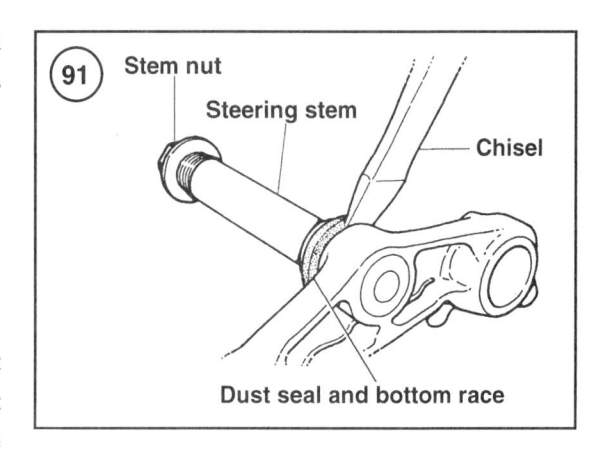

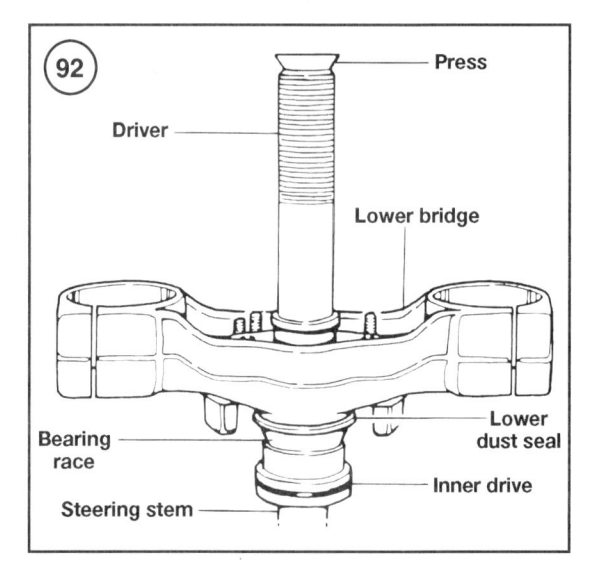

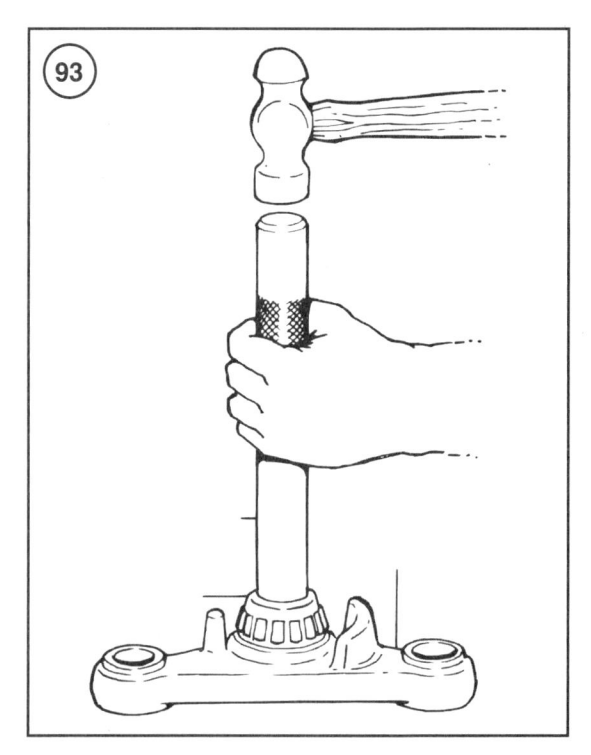

FRONT SUSPENSION AND STEERING

Table 1 STEERING AND FRONT SUSPENSION SPECIFICATIONS

Front axle travel	
Aero and Phantom models	117 mm (4.6 in.)
Spirit models	115 mm (4.5 in.)
Front axle runout limit	0.20 mm (0.008 in.)
Steering	
Caster angle	
Aero, Phantom models	34° 00'
Spirit models	34° 30'
Trail length	
Aero, Phantom models	161 mm (6.3 in.)
Spirit models	158 mm (6.2 in.)
Steering stem bearing preload	0.9-1.3 kg (1.9-2.9 lbs.)

Table 2 FRONT FORK SERVICE SPECIFICATIONS

Fork tube runout limit	0.20 mm (0.008 in.)
Fork oil capacity	
Aero models	
2004	466.5 - 471.5 ml (15.77 - 15.94 oz.)
2005-2009 and 2011-2013	471.5 - 476.5 ml (15.94 - 16.11 oz.)
Spirit models	475.5 - 480.5 ml (16.07 - 16.25 oz.)
Phantom models	471.5 - 476.5 ml (15.94 - 16.11 oz.)
Fork oil level	
Aero models	
2004	105 mm (4.1 in.)
2005-2009 and 2011-2013	100 mm (3.9 in.)
Spirit and Phantom models	100 mm (3.9 in.)
Fork oil type	
2011-2013 Areo models	Honda ULTRA CUSHION OIL or 10 wt. fork oil
All other models	Pro-Honda Suspension Fluid SS-8 or 10 wt. fork oil
Fork spring free length	
Aero, Phantom models	
New	367.8 mm (14.49 in.)
Service limit	360.4 mm (14.19 in.)
Spirit models	
New	371.8 mm (14.64 in.)
Service limit	364.4 mm (14.35 in.)

Table 3 FRONT SUSPENSION AND STEERING TORQUE SPECIFICATIONS

	N.m	in.-lb.	ft.-lb.
Fork cap			
2004-2009 Areo models	22	--	16
All other models	22.1	--	16
Fork tube bottom Allen bolt			
2004-2009 Aero models	29	--	21
All other models	29.5	--	22
Fork cover bolts			
Aero and Phantom models			
6-mm	12	106	--
8-mm	26	--	19
Fork tube pinch bolts			
Upper			
Aero models			
2004-2009	26	--	19
2011-2013	27	--	20
Spirit models (2007-2009 and			
2010-2013 w/o ABS)	22	--	16
Phantom models and 2010-2013 Spirit			
models w/ABS	27	--	20
Lower (all models)	49	--	36
	(continued)		

Table 3 FRONT SUSPENSION AND STEERING TORQUE SPECIFICATIONS (continued)

	N•m	in.-lb.	ft.-lb.
Front brake caliper mounting bolt (2)	30	--	22
Handlebar			
Aero models			
2004-2007			
Mounting nut	54	--	40
2008-2009, 2011-2013			
Upper holder bolt	23	--	17
Lower holder nut	23	--	17
Spirit models			
Upper holder bolt	23	--	17
Lower holder nut	23	--	17
Phantom models			
Mounting nut	23	--	17
Master cylinder clamp bolt	12	106	--
Steering adjust nut (3)	--	--	--
Steering stem nut (3)	103	--	76

1. Apply a medium strength threadlock onto fastener threads.
2. ALOC fastener. Install new fastener during assembly.
3. Refer to text for adjustment procedure.

CHAPTER FOURTEEN

REAR SUSPENSION AND FINAL DRIVE

REAR SUSPENSION AND FINAL DRIVE

This chapter contains service information for the rear suspension, drive shaft and final drive components. Refer to Chapter Twelve for rear wheel and tire service.

Specifications are listed in **Tables 1-5** are at the end of this chapter.

SHOCK ABSORBER

The shocks are sealed units. Do not attempt to replace the shock springs or disassemble the shocks in anyway. Service is limited to shock adjustment and replacing the shock mount dampers installed in each end of the shock absorber.

Adjustment

WARNING
Both shock absorbers must be adjusted to the same preload number or an unstable riding condition may result.

Each shock absorber can be adjusted to any of 5 spring preload settings. The softest setting is No. 1 and the stiffest setting is No. 5. The standard factory setting is No. 2. Adjust the shock absorbers to best suit different load and riding conditions. On some models, a label **(Figure 1)** is attached to the bottom of the shock absorber that identifies the different spring preload positions.

1. If so equipped, remove the tool kit and assemble the spanner wrench and its extension bar.

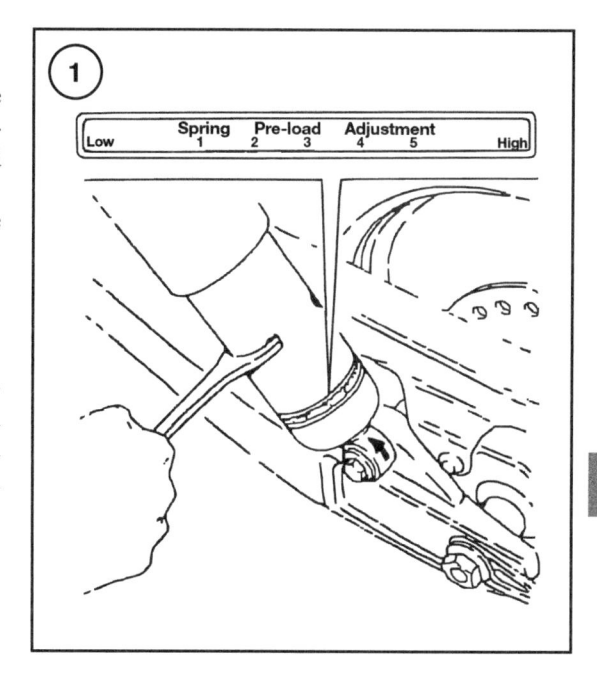

CAUTION
Adjust the shock absorber in single increments. For example, if the shock is in position No. 2 and it is necessary to adjust the spring to position No. 5, turn the adjuster to the No., 3, No. 4 and then to position No. 5. Do not turn the adjuster directly from the No. 2 to the No. 5 position without stopping at the other adjustment numbers or the adjuster may be damaged.

2. Using a spanner wrench, adjust the shock absorber to the desired adjustment position. See **Figure 1** or **Figure 2**.
3. Adjust the other shock to the same setting.

Removal/Installation

Removal and installation of the rear shocks is easier if performed separately. The remaining unit will support the rear of the motorcycle and maintain the correct relationship between the top and bottom mounts.

1. Support the motorcycle so the rear wheel clears the ground.
2. Remove the upper and lower shock mounting bolts **(Figure 3)** and outer washers and remove the shock absorber.
3. Inspect the shock absorber as described in this section.
4. Installation is the reverse of removal. Note the following:
   a. Install chrome bodied shock absorbers with the arrow mark on the lower mounting boss facing forward **(Figure 4)**.
   b. Tighten the upper shock mounting bolts to 26 N.m (19 ft.-lb.).
   c. On 2004-2009 Aero models, tighten the lower left side shock mounting bolt to 23 N.m (17 ft.-lb.).
   d. On all other models, tighten the lower left side shock mounting bolt to 22 N.m (16 ft.-lb.).
   e. Tighten the lower right side shock mounting bolt to 34 N.m (25 ft.-lb.).

Shock Inspection

1. Inspect the shock absorber (A, **Figure 5**) for oil leaks or other damage. Replace the shock absorber if it is leaking.
2. Inspect the upper (B, **Figure 5**) and lower (C) shock dampers for severe wear, age deterioration, hardness or other damage. If necessary, replace the dampers as described in Step 3.
3. To replace the shock dampers, perform the following:

NOTE
Collars are installed in the lower shock dampers and they are different sizes. The collars can be replaced separately.

   a. Assemble a socket, driver and threaded rod with two nuts and install through one of the shock dampers as shown in **Figure 6**. The deep socket must be large and deep enough to accept the damper as it is pressed out.

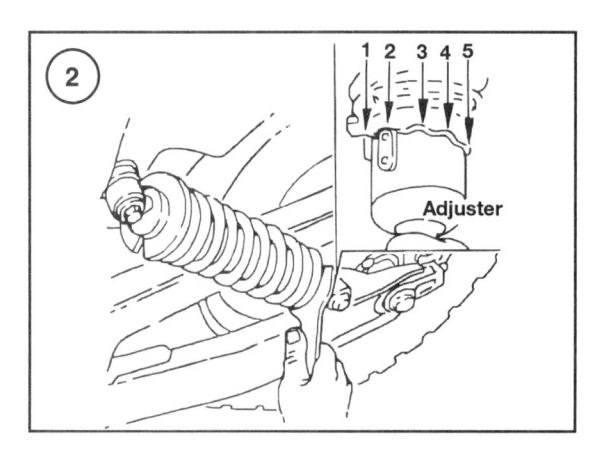

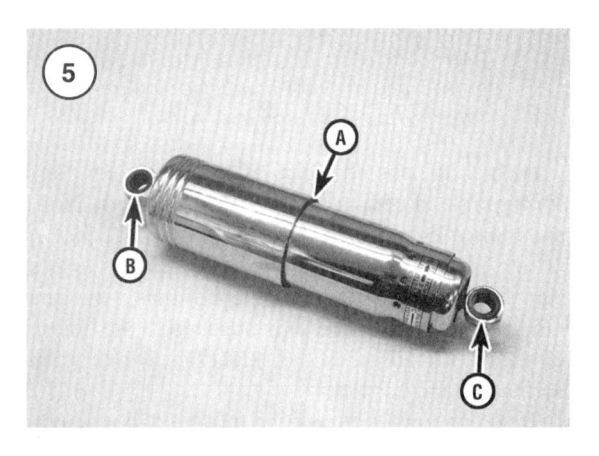

REAR SUSPENSION AND FINAL DRIVE

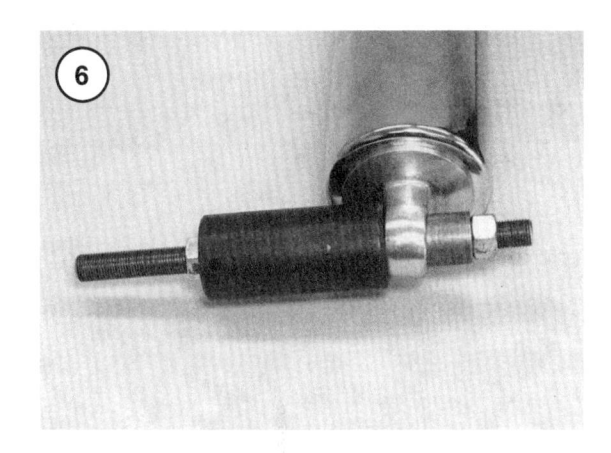

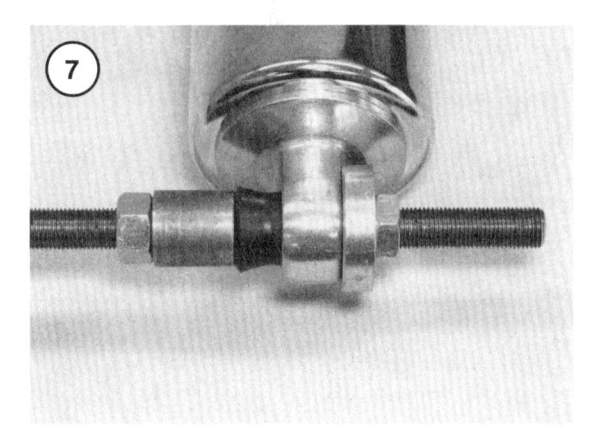

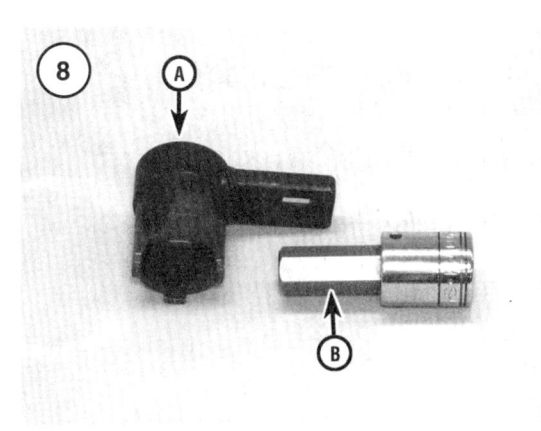

b. Hold the nut placed against the socket and turn the other nut to press the damper out of the shock damper bore.
c. Clean the shock damper bore.
d. Assemble the threaded rod so the damper is placed against one side of the shock damper bore and the driver is placed against the shock damper (**Figure 7**). A thick metal plate can be used in place of the socket used during removal. Hold the nut on the opposite side of the damper and turn the other nut to press the damper into the shock damper bore.
e. Remove the tools and inspect the damper for proper installation.
f. Repeat to replace the other damper.

REAR SWING ARM

Tools

The following tools are required to removal and install the swing arm:
 a. Pivot adjust wrench (Honda part No. 07908-4690003 [A, **Figure 8**]). This wrench is used as a torque adapter when loosening and tightening the right pivot bolt locknut.
 b. 17-mm hex socket (B, **Figure 8**).

Removal

1. Remove the exhaust system (Chapter Seventeen).
2. Remove the left crankcase rear cover (Chapter Seventeen).
3. Remove the rear wheel (Chapter Twelve).
4. Remove the left shock absorber as described in this chapter.
5. Remove the final drive unit and drive shaft as described in this chapter.
6. On ABS models, remove the rear wheel speed sensor and its wiring harness from the swing arm as described in *Wheel Speed Sensors* in Chapter Sixteen.
7. Remove the right shock absorber as described in this chapter.
8. Disconnect the vent hose at the EVAP canister (**Figure 9**).

NOTE
Have an assistant steady the motorcycle when checking for bearing play.

9. Grasp the rear end of the swing arm and try to move it from side to side in a horizontal arc. There must be no noticeable side play. Then grasp the rear of the swing arm and pivot it up and down through its full travel. The swing arm must pivot smoothly. If excessive play or binding is evident and the pivot

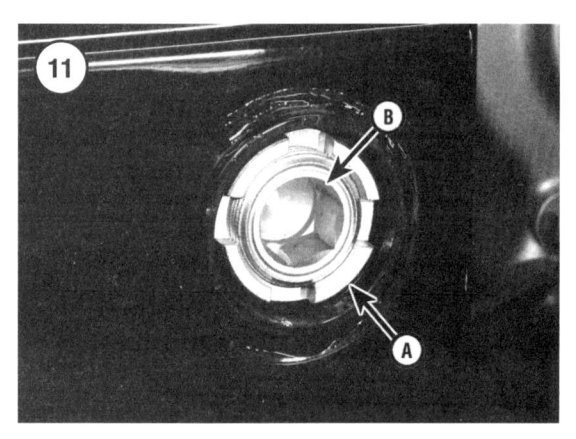

bolts are tightened correctly, inspect the swing arm bearings for severe wear or damage.

10. Remove the left and right side swing arm pivot caps.
11. Use the pivot adjust wrench (A, **Figure 10**) to loosen and remove the right pivot bolt locknut (A, **Figure 11**).
12. Use the 17-mm hex drive socket (B, **Figure 10**) to loosen and remove the right pivot bolt (B, **Figure 11**).
13. Loosen and remove the left pivot bolt (A, **Figure 12**) and swing arm.
14. Remove the universal joint (A, **Figure 13**) and boot (B).

NOTE
Identify the bearings if they are going to be reused.

NOTE
*The seals (**Figure 14**) are an integral part of the bearings. Do not separate them from the bearings.*

15. Remove the left and right side bearings and dust seals (A, **Figure 15**).
16. Clean and inspect the pivot bolts, swing arm and bearings as described in this section.

REAR SUSPENSION AND FINAL DRIVE

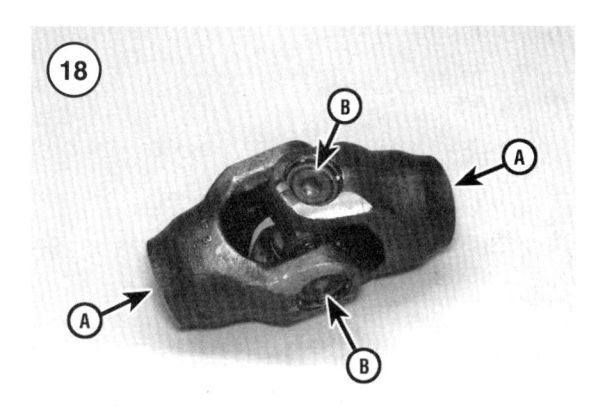

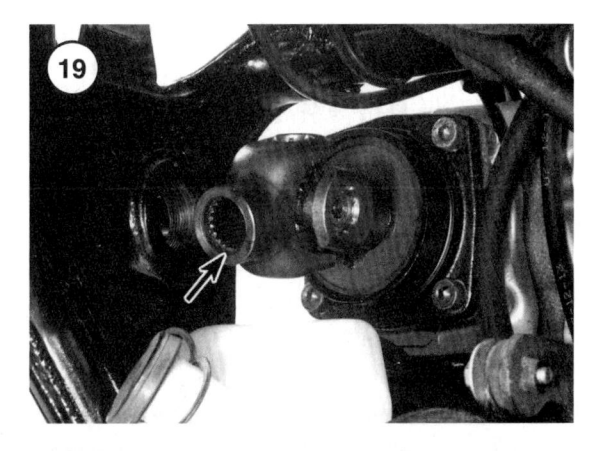

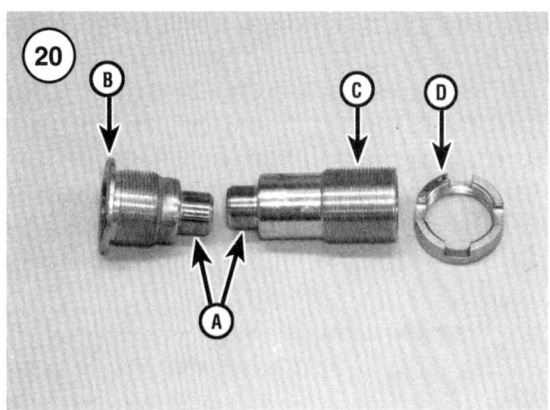

Installation

1. Install the boot by sliding its large outside diameter end onto the groove in the swing arm and with the tab marked ENG SIDE (with the arrow mark) pointing up (**Figure 16**).
2. Lubricate the seal lips, bearings (A, **Figure 15**) and races (B) with Bel-Ray Waterproof Grease (or equivalent).
3. Install the left and right side bearings and dust seals into the swing arm (**Figure 14**).
4. Clean the splines on the output driven gear shaft (**Figure 17**) and lubricate with Pro Honda Moly 60 Paste (or equivalent).
5. Lubricate the splines in both ends of the universal joint (A, **Figure 18**) with Pro Honda Moly 60 Paste (or equivalent).
6. Install the universal joint onto the output driven gear shaft (**Figure 19**).
7. Clean and dry the frame threads. There must be no grease, sand or other debris on the threads.
8. Lubricate the machined end (A, **Figure 20**) on both pivot bolts with Bel-Ray Waterproof Grease (or equivalent). Do not lubricate the threads in the frame or on the pivot bolts.
9. Install the swing arm into the frame and align its bearings with the frame threads.
10. Install the pivot bolts as follows:
    a. Align the left swing arm pivot flange with the frame threads, then thread the left pivot bolt (B, **Figure 20**) into the frame so that its machined end enters the bearing.
    b. Thread the right swing arm pivot bolt (C, **Figure 20**) into the frame so that its machined end enters the bearing.
    c. Hand-tighten each pivot bolt, then pivot the swing arm to make sure the ends on both pivot bolts are properly installed inside the swing arm bearings.
11. Tighten the left swing arm pivot bolt (A, **Figure 12**) to 103 N.m (76 ft.-lb.).

12. Tighten the right swing arm pivot bolt (B, **Figure 11**) as follows:
   a. 2004-2009 Aero and 2007-2009 Spirit: 28 N.m (21 ft.-lb.).
   b. All other models: 20 N.m (15 ft.-lb.).
13. Pivot the swing arm several times to help seat the bearings and to check for roughness and binding.
14. Turn (loosen) the right swing arm pivot bolt counterclockwise 1/4 turn **(Figure 21)**.
15. Retighten the right swing arm pivot bolt (B, **Figure 11**) to its final torque specification as follows:
   a. 2004-2009 Aero and 2007-2009 Spirit: 22 N.m (16 ft.-lb.).
   b. All other models: 15 N.m (11 ft.-lb.).

> *NOTE*
> *Mount the torque wrench onto the Honda pivot adjust wrench at a right angle as shown in A, **Figure 22**. If the pivot adjust wrench (B) is mounted so it lengthens the torque wrench, the torque applied to the locknut will be incorrect (too high). Refer to **Torque Adapters** in Chapter One for more information.*

16. Thread the right pivot bolt locknut (A, **Figure 11**) onto the pivot bolt. Hold the right pivot bolt with a 17-mm hex drive socket (C, **Figure 22**) and tighten the right pivot bolt locknut with the pivot adjust wrench (B) to 103 N.m (76 ft.-lb.).
17. Pivot the swing arm several times. There must be no binding or roughness.
18. Install the left and right side swing arm pivot caps.
19. Install the boot (B, **Figure 12**) over the output gearcase.
20. Reconnect the vent hose at the EVAP canister **(Figure 9)**.
21. Install the right shock absorber as described in this chapter.
22. On ABS models, install the rear wheel speed sensor and its wiring harness as described in *Wheel Speed Sensors* in Chapter Sixteen.
23. Install the final drive gear unit and drive shaft as described in this chapter.
24. Install the left shock absorber as described in this chapter.
25. Install the rear wheel (Chapter Twelve).
26. Install the left crankcase cover (Chapter Seventeen).
27. Install the exhaust system (Chapter Seventeen).

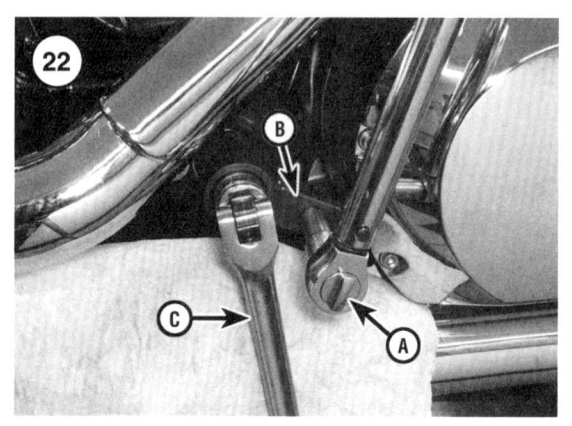

Inspection

Swing arm

1. Clean and dry the parts.
2. Clean the pivot bolt threads in the frame.
3. Inspect the swing arm for cracks and other damage.
4. Inspect each bearing (A, **Figure 15**) and race (B) for severe wear, pitting or other damage. If necessary, replace the bearing races and grease retainer plates (this section).
5. Check that each grease retainer plate (C, **Figure 15**) fits tightly in the swing arm.
6. Inspect the pivot bolts (B and C, **Figure 20**) for severe wear, thread damage or corrosion. Make sure the machined end on each pivot bolt is smooth. Replace if necessary.
7. Replace the right pivot bolt locknut (D, **Figure 20**) if damaged.
8. Replace the boot (B, **Figure 13**) if damaged.
9. If the brake stopper arm is removed from the swing arm, tighten the nut to 22 N.m (16 ft.-lb.).

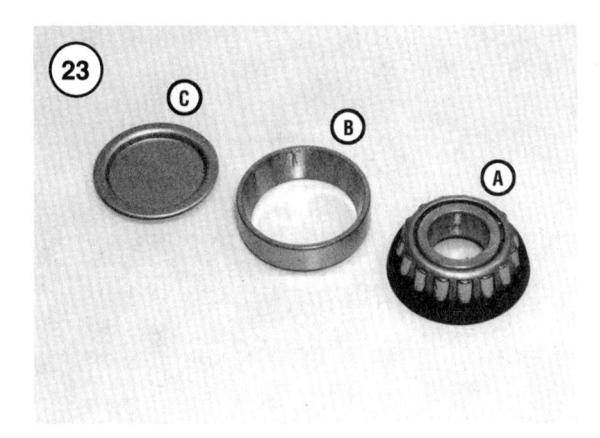

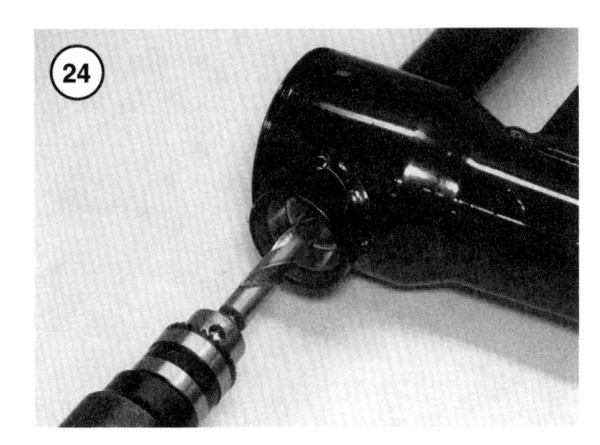

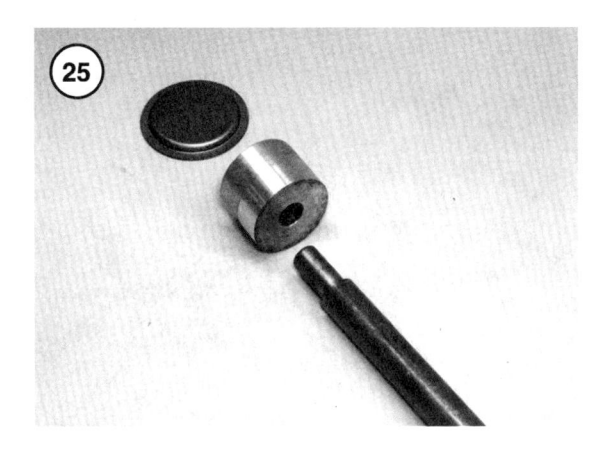

REAR SUSPENSION AND FINAL DRIVE

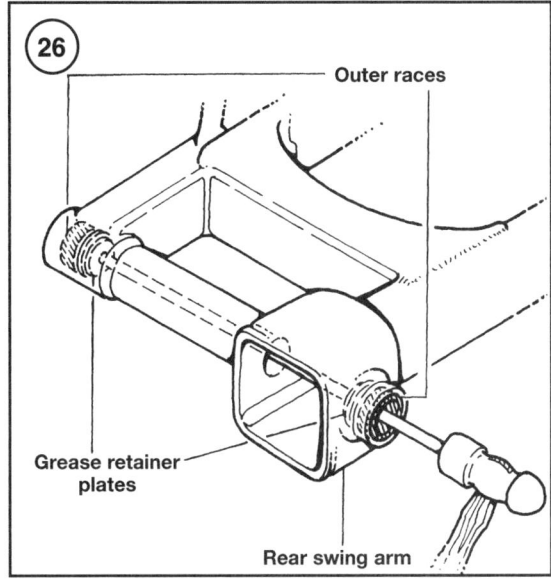

Grease Retainer and Bearing Race Replacement

Replace the left and right side bearings (A, **Figure 23**), races (B) and grease retainer plates (C) at the same time.

1. Drill a suitable size hole through one of the grease retainer plates (**Figure 24**). The hole should be large enough to allow a driver rod to pass through.

NOTE
A two-piece driver that can be used to remove the grease retainer plates can be made using a small bearing driver or piece of aluminum and a driver rod (Figure 25).

2. Insert the driver rod through the drilled hole (**Figure 26**) and drive out the opposite bearing race and grease retainer plate.
3. Repeat Step 2 to remove the opposite bearing race and grease retainer plate.
4. Clean the bearing race seating areas in the swing arm.

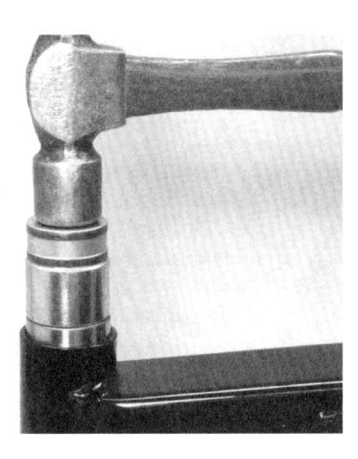

Universal joint

1. Make sure the universal joint pivots smoothly (B, **Figure 18**) with no binding or roughness.
2. Inspect both universal joint spline ends (A, **Figure 18**) for damage. If these splines are damaged, inspect the mating output driven gear and drive shaft splines for damage.
3. The universal joint cannot be rebuilt. Replace if damaged.

5. Using a bearing driver **(Figure 27)**, install a new grease retainer plate (A, **Figure 28**) and bearing race (B) into each side of the swing arm.
6. Lubricate each bearing race with Bel-Ray Waterproof Grease (or equivalent).

FINAL DRIVE UNIT AND DRIVE SHAFT

Removal

1. Drain the final drive oil (Chapter Three), if necessary.
2. Remove the rear wheel (Chapter Twelve).
3. Remove the bolt (A, **Figure 29**) and disconnect the shock absorber at the final drive unit.
4. Remove the nuts (B, **Figure 29**) and then remove the final drive unit (C) with drive shaft attached.
5. Hold the final drive unit, then pull and remove the drive shaft (A, **Figure 30**).
6. Remove the spring (B, **Figure 30**) and stopper ring (C). Discard the stopper ring.
7. Remove the seal (D, **Figure 30**) as follows:

NOTE
The seal is a tight fit and installed over a machined surface on the drive shaft. Do not damage this surface when removing the seal.

 a. Mount a bearing splitter **(Figure 31)** or some type of ring over the seal.
 b. Carefully drive the seal off the shaft, making sure not to damage the drive shaft.
 c. Discard the seal.
8. Inspect and service the final drive unit and drive shaft as described in this chapter.

Installation

Use Pro Honda Moly 60 Paste (or equivalent) when grease is called for in the following steps.
1. Install a new seal (D, **Figure 30**) as follows:
 a. Pack the lips of a new oil seal with grease and install it over the drive shaft (A, **Figure 32**) with its closed side facing up (away from gear end of shaft).
 b. Place a thick washer against the top of the seal (B, **Figure 32**) to protect it.
 c. Drive the new seal onto the drive shaft with a long piece of PVC pipe (C, **Figure 32**) until the seal is fully seated and bottomed on the drive shaft. Remove the washer from the top of the seal. See **Figure 33**.
2. Install a new stopper ring (C, **Figure 30**) into the drive shaft groove. The stopper ring is a loose fit as it is designed to close around the drive shaft groove when

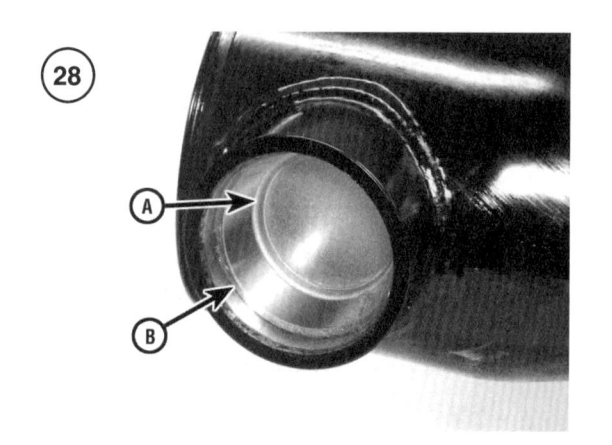

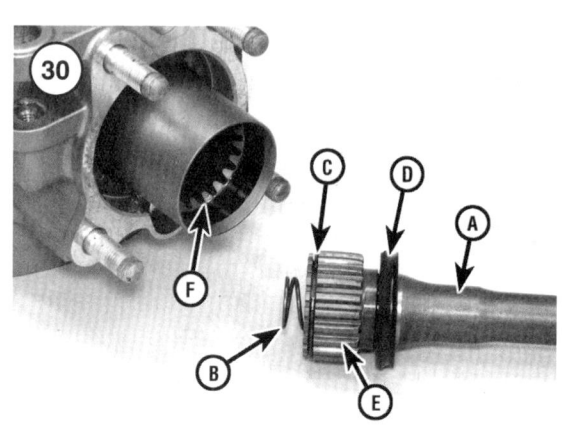

REAR SUSPENSION AND FINAL DRIVE

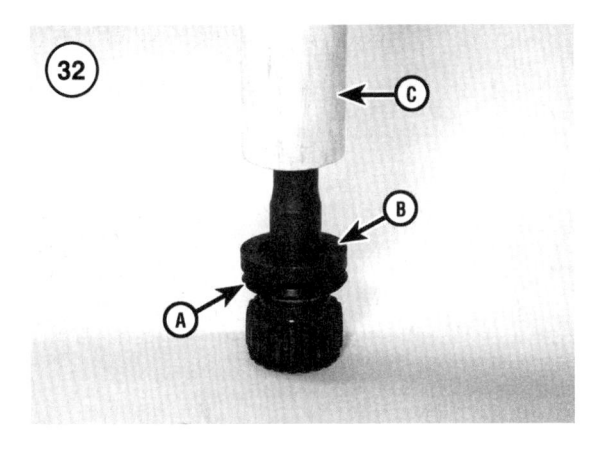

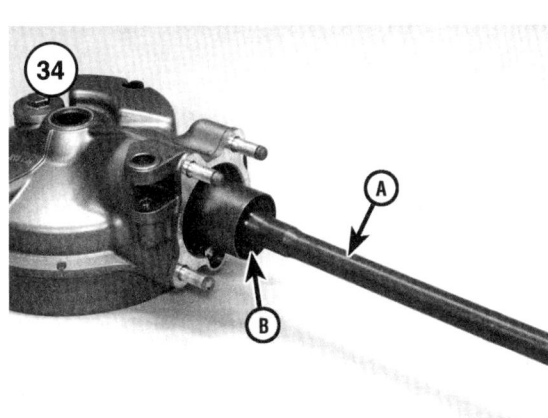

the drive shaft is installed inside the pinion joint.

3. Install the spring (B, **Figure 30**) into the end of the drive shaft.

4. Lubricate the drive shaft (E, **Figure 30**) and pinion joint (F) splines with grease.

5. Align the drive shaft splines with the pinion joint splines and install the drive shaft (A, **Figure 34**) until the stopper ring seats into the pinion joint spline groove. Lightly pull back on drive shaft to make sure stopper ring is properly seated in the groove.

6. If necessary, tap the oil seal (B, **Figure 34**) into the pinion joint.

7. Lubricate the drive shaft splines with grease.

NOTE
*To help turn the ring gear when trying to engage the drive shaft with the universal joint, install the driven flange (**Figure 35**) onto the final drive unit.*

8. Shift the transmission into gear. Insert the drive shaft through the swing arm and then turn the ring gear to help align and engage the drive shaft and universal joint splines. When the drive shaft engages the universal joint, push the final drive unit (C, **Figure 29**) studs through the holes in the swing arm and install the nuts (B, **Figure 29**) finger-tight.

NOTE
*Do not tighten the final drive unit mounting nuts (B, **Figure 29**) until the rear wheel is installed.*

9. Install the rear wheel and tighten the final drive housing mounting nuts as described in *Rear Wheel Installation* in Chapter Twelve.

10. Install the shock absorber onto the final drive unit and tighten the left lower shock absorber mounting bolt (A, **Figure 29**) as follows:
   a. 2004-2009 Aero models: 23 N.m (17 ft.-lb.).
   b. All other models: 22 N.m (16 ft.-lb.).

11. Refill the final drive unit with the correct type and quantity of gear oil (Chapter Three), if the unit was previously drained.

Inspection

Drive shaft

NOTE
To inspect and service the universal joint, remove the swing arm as described in this chapter.

1. Clean and dry the drive shaft and spring.
2. Check the drive shaft splines **(Figure 36)** for severe wear, cracks and other damage.

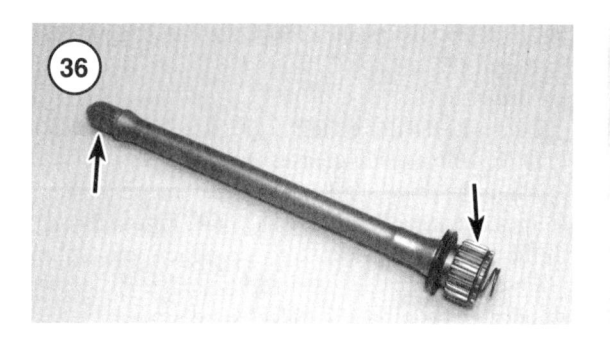

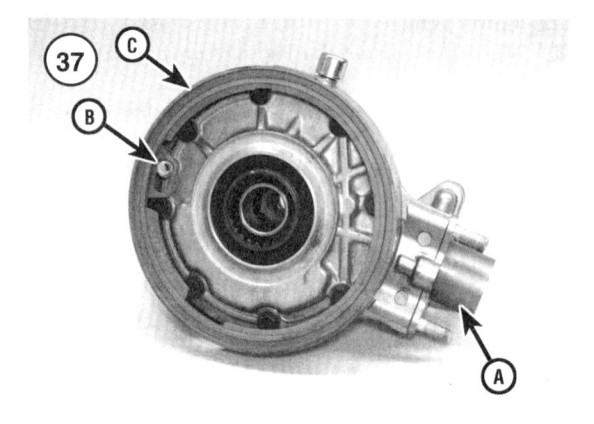

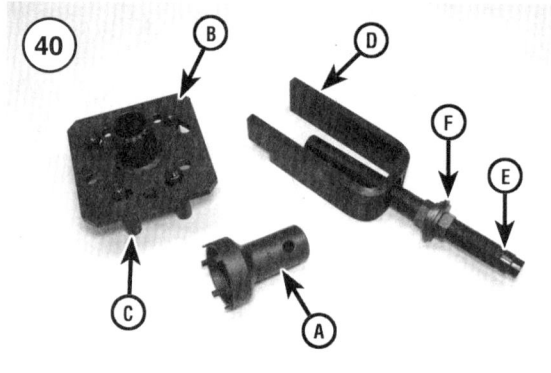

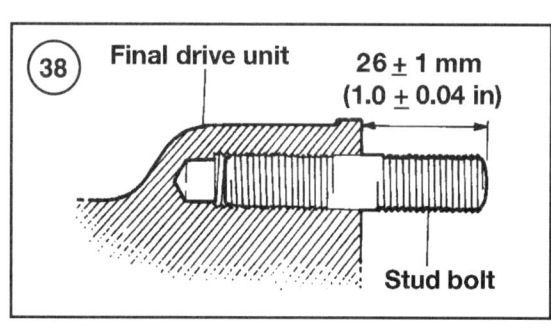

3. Replace the spring (B, **Figure 30**) if the coils are unequally spaced or if there are cracks along the spring coils.

Final drive unit

If additional service or inspection is required, refer to *Final Drive Unit Overhaul* in this chapter.
1. Check for oil leaks at the inner ring gear seal. If the seal is leaking, the ring gear bearing may be worn and allowing the shaft to run out of true.

NOTE
Because of the holes in the pinion joint, oil will pass through these holes and collect in the pinion joint.

2. Check for oil leaks around the outside of the pinion gear seal.
3. Turn the pinion joint (A, **Figure 37**). If the gears turn roughly, first remove the oil fill cap and visually check the ring gear for damage. If necessary, disassemble the unit and check for wear and damage.
4. Check for loose or damaged final drive unit studs. If necessary replace damaged studs as described in Chapter One. Apply a medium strength threadlock onto the stud threads and install to the dimension shown in **Figure 38**.

FINAL DRIVE UNIT OVERHAUL

Tools

Before beginning final drive overhaul, note the following:
1. A holding fixture is recommended for final drive overhaul. A holding fixture can be made by drilling holes in a flat steel plate **(Figure 39)** and using the appropriate metric fasteners.
2. A sturdy vise is required to support the holding fixture/final drive unit during use.
3. A heat gun is required when replacing some of the bearings pressed into the housing. Make sure the heat gun can supply and maintain the heat specified in the text. Monitor temperature with heat sticks or an infrared thermometer.
4. A retainer wrench (A, **Figure 40** [Honda part No. 07910-4630100]) is required to loosen and tighten the pinion retainer.
5. A pinion holder plate (B, **Figure 40** [Honda part No. 07924-ME40010]) and collar set (C, **Figure 40**

REAR SUSPENSION AND FINAL DRIVE

[Honda part No. 07924-ME40020]) is required to hold the pinion joint when loosening and tightening the pinion joint nut.

6. A pinion puller set (puller base, puller shaft and special nut) is required to remove the pinion gear assembly from the housing:
   a. Puller base (D, **Figure 40** [Honda part No. 07HMC-MM8011A]).
   b. Puller shaft (E, **Figure 40** [Honda part No. 07931-ME4010B]).
   c. Special nut (F, **Figure 40** [Honda part No. 07931-HB3020A]).

7. Various bearing removers, drivers and splitters are also required. Many of these tools can be rented from tool rental outlets. A hydraulic press is recommended for bearing replacement.

Service Notes

Before servicing the final drive unit, note the following:

1. Refer to *Final Drive* in Chapter Two to troubleshoot the final drive unit. A new or rough sounding noise from the final drive unit is usually the first indication of a problem with the unit.
2. Ring gear removal also requires removal of the ring gear bearing. If the bearing is in good condition, it can be reused.
3. The pinion gear bearing pressed onto the pinion gear shaft can also be reused if in good condition.
4. When checking bearings, they should turn freely and without any sign of roughness, catching or excessive noise. Always replace questionable bearings.
5. Refer to *Bearings* in Chapter One for bearing removal and installation techniques. Refer to *Interference fit* and *Heating Components* in Chapter One when it is necessary to use heat for the removal and installation of bearings.
6. Use a heat gun when necessary to heat the parts. Do not use a welding torch as this heats the parts unevenly and may cause warpage. When heating parts, monitor heat with heat sticks available from a welding supply store or use an infrared thermometer. The text will list the temperature required to remove and install parts.
7. Inspect the ring gear by supporting the motorcycle with the rear wheel off the ground. Remove the oil fill cap and turn the rear wheel to inspect the gear through the filler hole. If wear or damage is apparent, drain the oil (Chapter Three) and inspect the oil and the magnet on the oil drain bolt for metal fragments.
8. Do not remove and discard used seals until all of the service and measurement procedures have been competed. Install new seals during final assembly.
9. Use HondaBond 4, ThreeBond 1104, Yamabond No. 4 , or an equivalent gasket sealer, to seal the housing cover during assembly.

Ring Gear and Housing Cover

Refer to **Figure 41**.

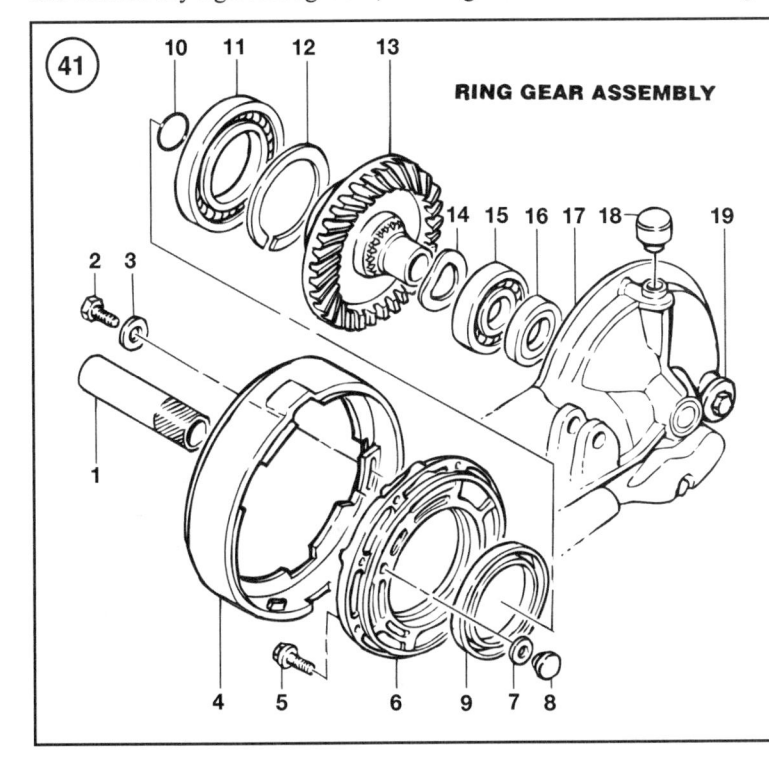

41 RING GEAR ASSEMBLY

1. Distance collar
2. Bolt
3. Washer
4. Dust guard plate
5. Bolts (8-mm and 10-mm)
6. Housing cover
7. Shim
8. Stop pin
9. Oil seal
10. O-ring
11. Inner ring gear bearing
12. Ring gear shim
13. Ring gear
14. Wave washer
15. Outer ring gear bearing
16. Oil seal
17. Final drive unit housing
18. Breather cap
19. Oil fill cap

CHAPTER FOURTEEN

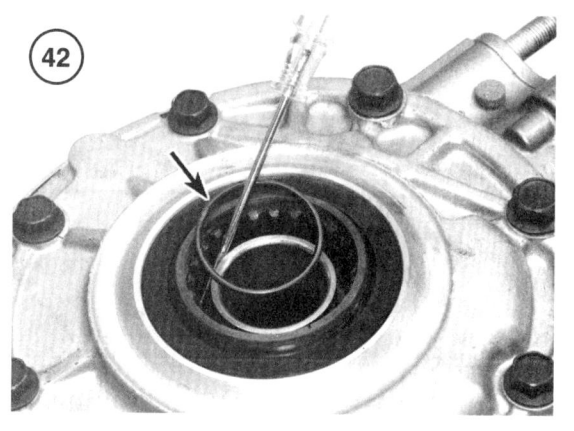

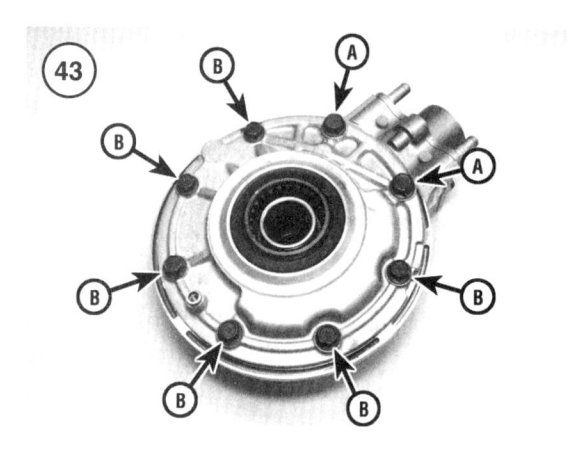

Removal

1. Review *Service Notes* in this section.
2. Remove the distance collar (1, **Figure 41**).
3. Remove the bolt (B, **Figure 37**), washer and dust guard plate (C, **Figure 37**).
4. Perform the backlash measurement described under *Ring and Pinion Gear Measurements* in this section.
5. Remove the O-ring from the groove inside the ring gear **(Figure 42)**.
6. Remove the housing cover 10-mm (A, **Figure 43**) and 8-mm (B) bolts in a crossing pattern.
7. Carefully pry the housing cover off the housing with a wide-blade screwdriver at the two pry points **(Figure 44)**. Note the small wooden stick placed underneath the screwdriver used to prevent damage to the final drive unit housing surface. See **Figure 45**.
8. Remove the wave washer **(Figure 46)** from the ring gear.
9. Support the housing cover in a press with the ring gear facing down **(Figure 47)**. Press the ring gear and bearing out of the housing cover. Make sure to catch the ring gear once it is free from the housing. Remove the ring gear shim if the bearing remained

REAR SUSPENSION AND FINAL DRIVE

in the housing cover.

10A. If the bearing remained on the ring gear (**Figure 48**), perform the following:

    a. Support the ring gear bearing in a press with a bearing splitter (**Figure 49**) and press the ring gear out of the bearing. Make sure to catch the ring gear once it is free from the bearing.

    b. Remove the ring gear shim (A, **Figure 50**).

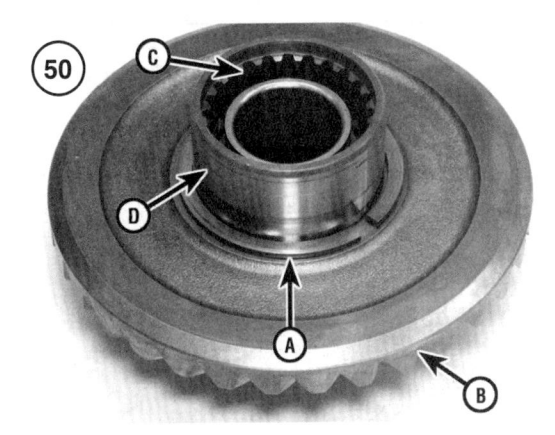

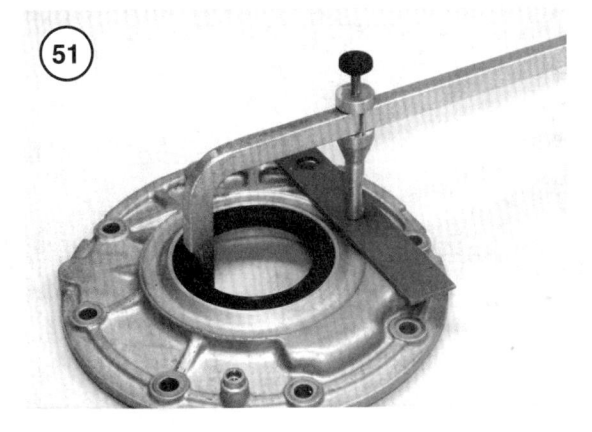

    c. Remove the seal with a seal puller as shown in **Figure 51**. Use caution to prevent from damaging the housing cover or the seal bore. If a seal puller is not available, pad a tire iron with a rag and pry the seal out. When using a tire iron, do not let the tip of the tire iron contact the seal bore surface. Move the tool around the seal, taking small bites, to prevent from damaging the cover. Discard the seal.

10B. If the bearing remained in the housing cover, press the bearing and oil seal out of the housing cover with a press.

11. Perform the *Inspection* in this section.

12. Perform *Ring Gear Shim Replacement* in this section.

Inspection

With the housing cover and ring gear removed from the housing, the ring and pinion gears can be inspected. Replace worn or damaged parts as described in this section.

1. Clean the ring gear in solvent and dry with compressed air.

2. Inspect the ring gear (B, **Figure 50**) for broken, chipped or cracked teeth.

3. Check the ring gear splines (C, **Figure 50**) for cracks, severe wear and other damage. If damage is noted, check the mating splines on the driven flange for damage.

4. Check the oil seal operating area on the ring gear (D, **Figure 50**) for scoring and other damage that could damage the new seal. Carefully smooth any surface roughness with a fine-cut file or 400-600 grade sandpaper.

5. Inspect the ring gear bearing for pitting, galling or cracks. Hold the ring gear and turn the bearing by hand. There should be no roughness, binding or catching.

6. Check the housing cover for an elongated or enlarged bearing bore **(Figure 52)**. Then check the bore for pitting, cracks and other damage.

7. Inspect the outer ring gear bearing (A, **Figure 53**) for pitting, galling, cracks or a loose fit in the bore. Hold the housing and turn the bearings by hand. There should be no roughness, binding or catching. If necessary, replace the bearing and seal as described in *Final Drive Housing Bearing Replacement* in this chapter.

8. Check the pinion gear (B, **Figure 53**) for broken, chipped or worn teeth. Then rotate the pinion shaft and check for any roughness, grinding or catching, indicating a damaged pinion gear bearing. Refer to *Pinion Gear* in this section to service the pinion gear and its bearing assembly.

9. Check for an oil leak at the front of the housing. If necessary, replace the pinion shaft seal as described under *Pinion Gear* in this section.

Ring gear shim replacement

1. If the housing was disassembled to correct the backlash measurement, select the correct size ring gear shim (12, **Figure 41**) determined during *Ring and Pinion Gear, Backlash Measurements* in this section.

2. If the ring gear, pinion gear, ring gear bearing, pinion bearing, housing cover or housing are being replaced, install a 2.00 mm (0.079) thick shim as a starting point. Then repeat the backlash measurement procedure.

3. Install the ring gear and ring gear shim as described under *Installation* in this section.

Ring gear stop pin side clearance check/adjustment

1. Install the inner ring gear bearing, ring gear shim and ring gear into the housing cover as described in *Installation* in this section.

2. Measure the clearance between the ring gear and the stop pin with a feeler gauge **(Figure 54)**. See Table 2 for the recommended clearance. The shim (7, **Figure 41**) installed under the stop pin (8) adjusts the clearance.

CAUTION
Heat the housing cover evenly in Step 3 to prevent warpage. Do not concentrate the heat in one spot or area for any length of time.

3. To adjust the clearance, remove the ring gear from the housing cover. Heat the housing cover to 80° C (176° F) with a heat gun. When the specified tem-

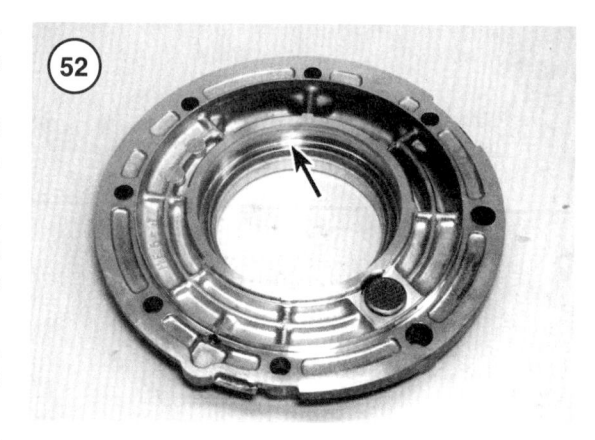

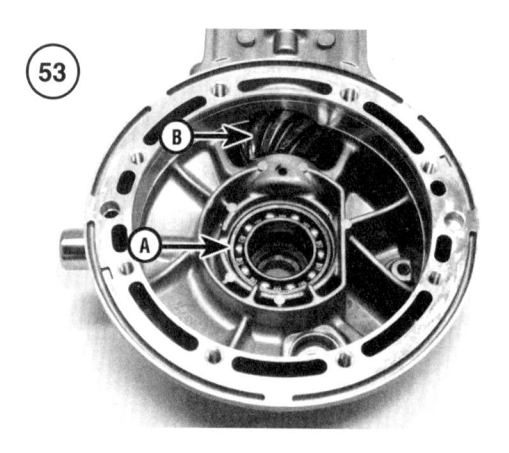

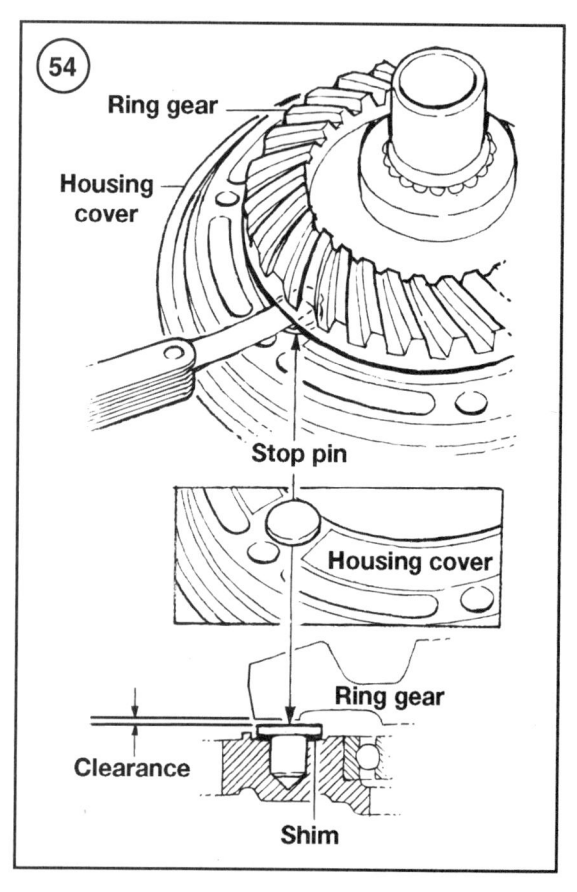

REAR SUSPENSION AND FINAL DRIVE

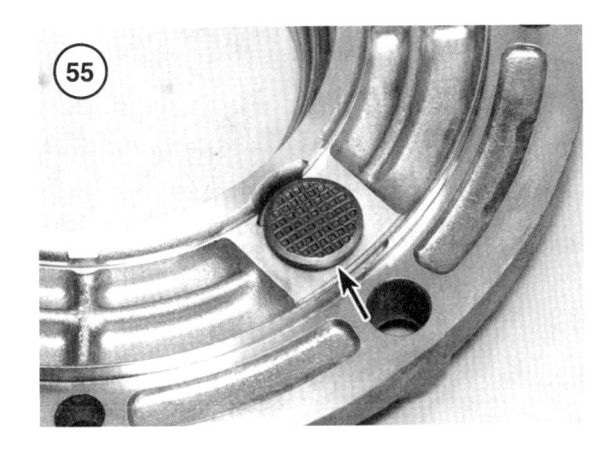

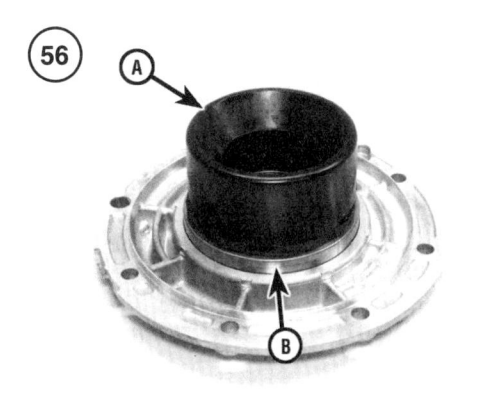

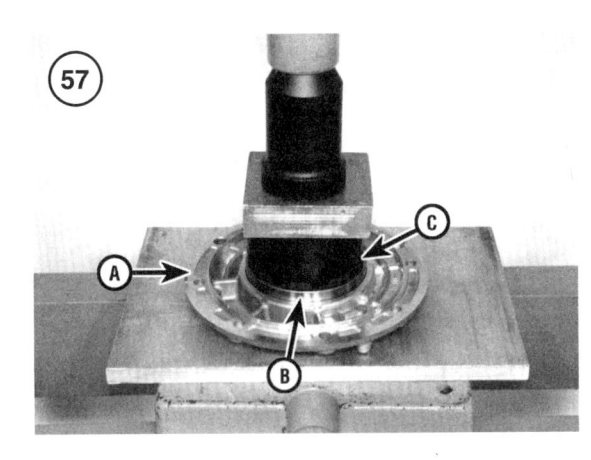

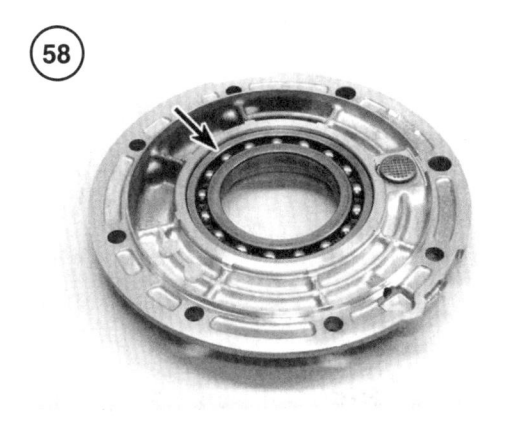

perature is reached, tap the cover to remove the stop pin **(Figure 55)**.

4. Install either a 0.10 mm (0.004 in.) or 0.15 mm (0.006 in.) stop pin shim onto the stop pin to obtain the desired clearance. Reheat the housing cover and drive the stop pin **(Figure 55)** (with the shim) into the housing cover and recheck the clearance after reinstalling the inner ring gear bearing, shim and ring gear. Repeat until the ring gear-to-stop pin clearance is within specifications **(Table 2)**.

Installation

This section covers installation of the ring gear assembly, housing cover and final assembly of the final drive unit. If the unit is being assembled to check gear mesh and will then be disassembled, do not install the new inner ring gear seal or apply sealer to the housing cover and housing mating surfaces.

1. If the pinion gear was removed, reinstall it as described under *Pinion gear* (this section). When the pinion gear is properly installed and the pinion retainer and pinion joint are properly installed and tightened, continue with Step 2.
2. Clean the breather passage as follows:
   a. Twist and pull the breather cap (18, **Figure 41**) from the housing.
   b. Clean the breather passages in the gear case cover and housing with compressed air.
   c. Reinstall the breather cap.
3. Install the inner ring gear bearing into the housing cover as follows:

NOTE
A 3 x 2 in. ABS plumbing fitting (A, Figure 56) is used as a driver to install the bearing (B). The hex corners on the plumbing fitting were filed off so they would not contact the housing cover surface when installing the bearing.

   a. Place the housing cover (A, **Figure 57**) into a press bed with its bearing bore side facing up.
   b. Align the inner ring gear bearing (B, **Figure 57**) and press it into the housing cover bore with a driver (C) placed on the bearing's outer race. Press the bearing until it bottoms in its bore. See **Figure 58**.
4. Install the ring gear shim and ring gear as follows:
   a. Install the ring gear shim **(Figure 59)** onto the ring gear.

NOTE
A short length of ABS plumbing pipe (Figure 60) is used to support the bear-

ing's inner race when pressing the ring gear into the bearing.

b. Support the bearing's inner race with a suitable piece of pipe or driver (A, **Figure 61**) and place the housing cover into the press with its inner side facing up (B).
c. Install the ring gear (with the ring gear shim) into the bearing. Center the ring gear so it sits squarely in the bearing (C, **Figure 61**).
d. Press the ring gear into the bearing until the ring gear shim/gear bottoms against the bearing.
e. Remove the housing cover assembly and turn the ring gear to make sure it turns smoothly and there is no roughness.

5. Perform the *Ring Gear Stop Pin Side Clearance Check/Adjustment* in this section. When the clearance is correct, continue with Step 6.
6. Install the inner ring gear seal as follows:
    a. Lubricate the seal lips with grease.
    b. Position and center the inner ring gear seal into the top of the housing cover with its closed side facing out.

NOTE
The same driver used to install the inner ring bearing is used to install the inner ring gear seal (Figure 62).

c. Install the seal with a large driver **(Figure 63)** that fits the outer circumference of the seal. The driver should clear the lip part of the seal to prevent from damaging it. Install the seal until it rests flush with the top of the housing cover **(Figure 64)**. Make sure the garter spring remains in the seal lip.

NOTE
To help hold the final drive unit housing during final assembly and when tightening the housing cover bolts, bolt a plate onto the front of the housing and mount the plate in a vise (Figure 65).

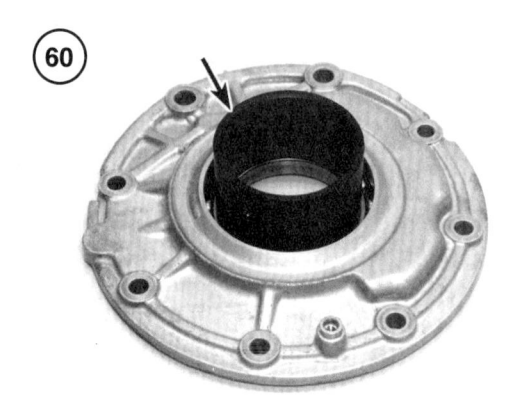

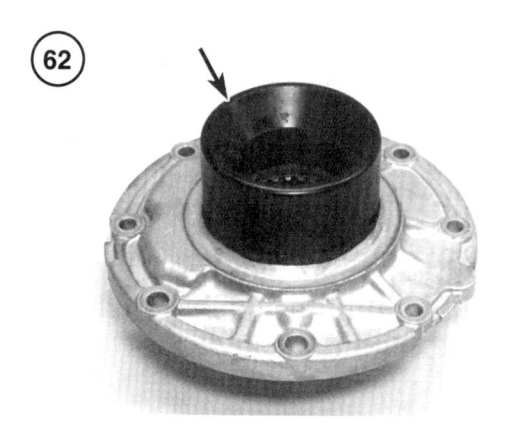

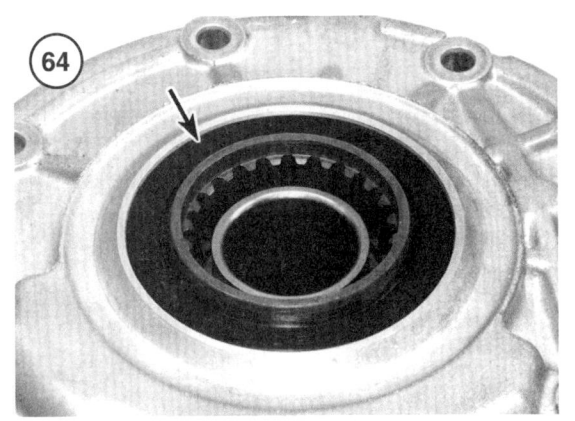

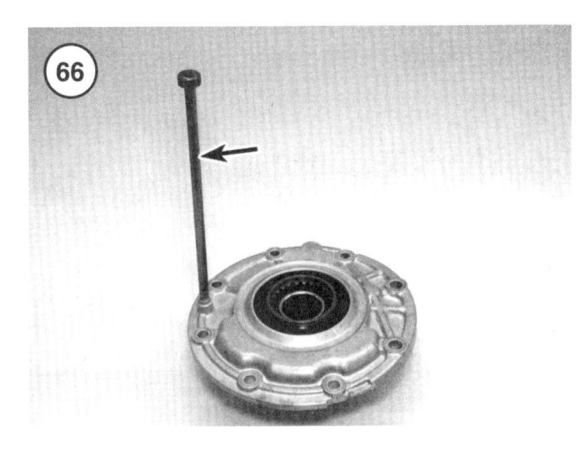

REAR SUSPENSION AND FINAL DRIVE

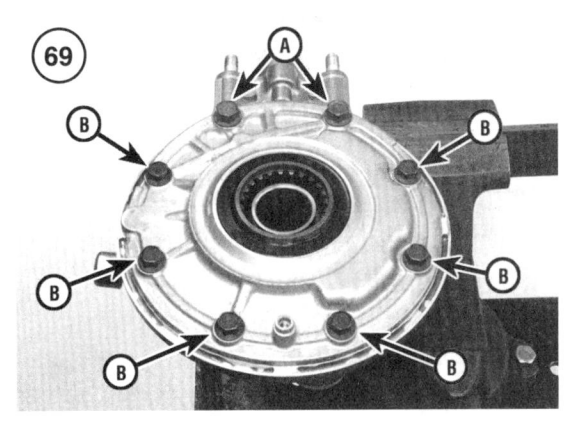

NOTE
*A long 6-mm bolt threaded into the housing cover can be used as a handle when installing the cover (**Figure 66**). Using the bolt helps to prevent your hands from contacting the sealer applied to the housing.*

7. Use electrical contact cleaner to clean the housing cover and housing mating surfaces of all oil residue. Allow the surfaces to dry before applying the sealer.
8. Apply HondaBond No. 4, ThreeBond 1104, Yamabond No. 4, or an equivalent gasket sealer, to the housing cover and housing mating surfaces (A, **Figure 67**). Do not apply sealer into the breather hole (B, **Figure 67**) and into the mating groove in the housing cover.
9. Lubricate the wave washer (**Figure 68**) with gear oil and center against the bearing's inner race.
10. Install the housing cover/ring gear assembly onto the housing by aligning the two 10-mm bolt holes (A, **Figure 69**). It is normal if there is a gap between the housing cover and the housing surfaces.
11. Apply a medium strength threadlock onto the two 10-mm bolt threads.
12. Install the 10-mm (A, **Figure 69**) and 8-mm (B) bolts, but do not tighten them yet.
13. Hand-tighten the housing cover bolts in a cross-

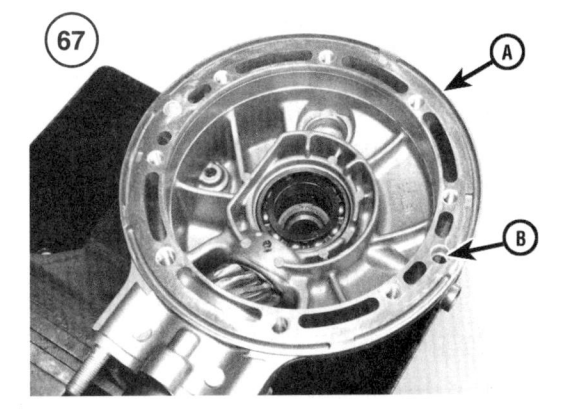

ing pattern and in several steps until the housing cover evenly contacts the housing.

14. Tighten all of the bolts in a crossing pattern and in several steps to 25 N.m (18 ft.-lb.).

15. Tighten the 10-mm bolts to 47 N.m (35 ft.-lb.).

16. Use the holding fixture and support the final drive housing in a vise. Turn the pinion shaft with a beam type torque wrench and a 22-mm socket and measure the final drive gear assembly preload. The correct preload reading is 0.2-0.4 N.m (1.8-3.5 in.-lb.). If the preload reading is incorrect, disassemble the final drive and check the bearings for damage and proper installation.

17. Install the dust guard plate (A, **Figure 70**) by aligning its tabs with the grooves in the housing cover, then turn the plate counterclockwise and align the groove in the plate with the threads in the housing cover. Install the bolt (B, **Figure 70**) and washer and tighten to 10 N.m (89 in.-lb.).

18. Install the final drive unit as described in this chapter.

19. Refill the final drive unit with the correct type and amount of gear oil (Chapter Three).

Pinion Gear

Refer to **Figure 71**.

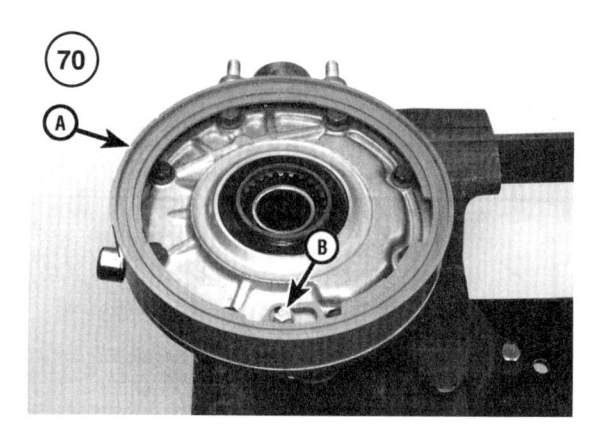

Removal

1. Review *Service* in this section.
2. Review *Tools* in this section to identify the tools used in this procedure.
3. Remove the housing cover and ring gear as described in this section.
4. Remove the pinion joint nut (3, **Figure 71**) as follows:

   a. Bolt the holding fixture across the housing and then secure the holding fixture in a vise as shown in **Figure 72**.

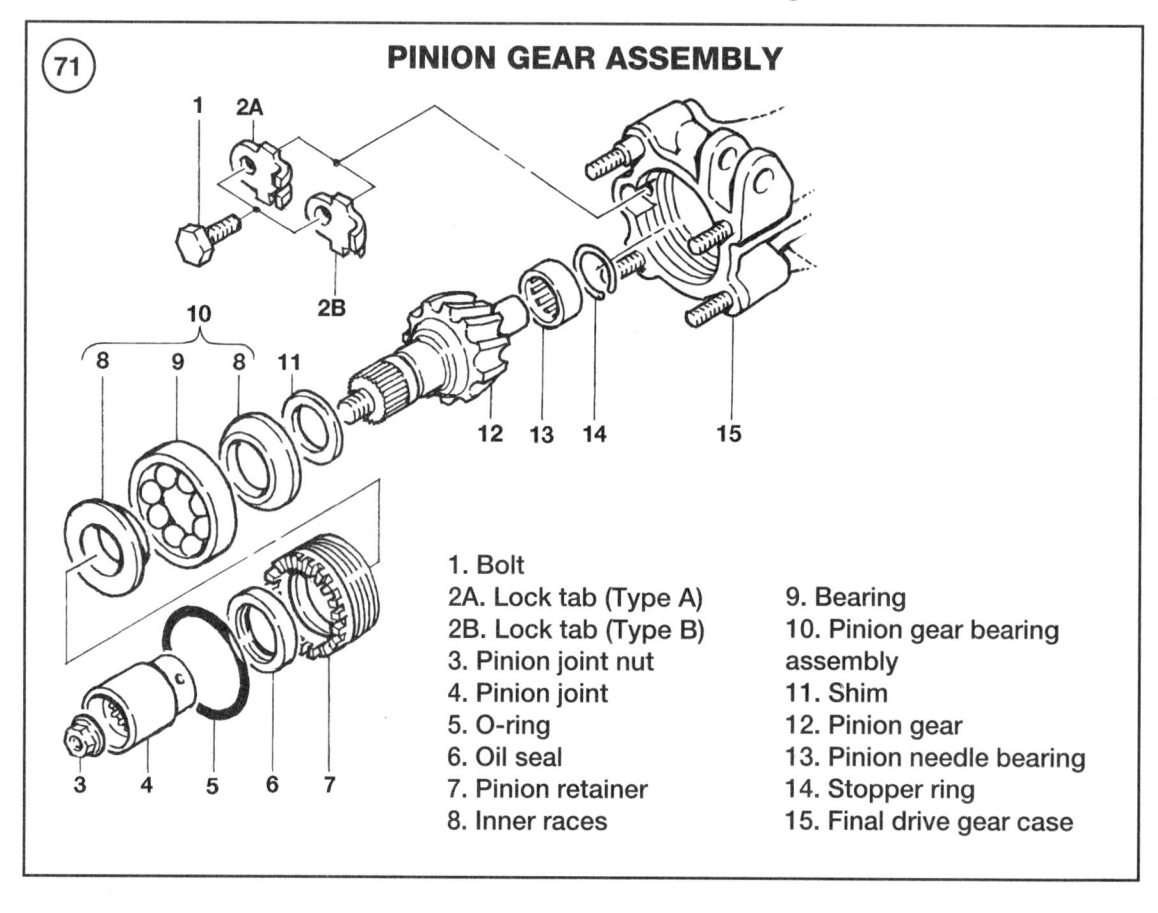

PINION GEAR ASSEMBLY

1. Bolt
2A. Lock tab (Type A)
2B. Lock tab (Type B)
3. Pinion joint nut
4. Pinion joint
5. O-ring
6. Oil seal
7. Pinion retainer
8. Inner races
9. Bearing
10. Pinion gear bearing assembly
11. Shim
12. Pinion gear
13. Pinion needle bearing
14. Stopper ring
15. Final drive gear case

REAR SUSPENSION AND FINAL DRIVE

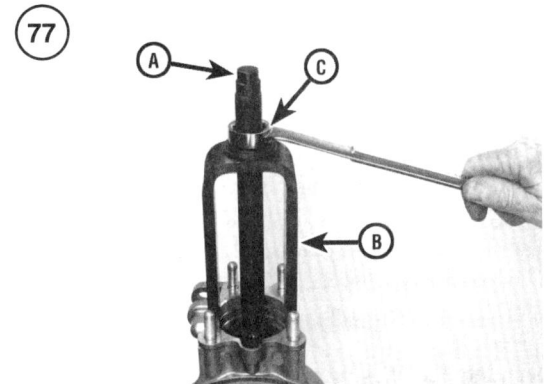

b. Install a 22-mm socket inside the pinion joint and engage it with the pinion joint nut.
c. Install the pinion holder plate (A, **Figure 73**) and collar set C (B) as shown. The pinion holder plate fits inside the pinion joint to prevent it from turning. The collars fit over the studs on the final drive housing and are secured to the pinion holder plate.
d. Loosen the pinion joint nut.
e. Remove the tools from the housing.
f. Remove the pinion joint nut (A, **Figure 74**) and pinion joint (B).

5. Remove the bolt (A, **Figure 75**) and the retainer lock tab (B).

NOTE
Make sure the all of the arms on the retainer wrench grip the pinion retainer fully when loosening the pinion retainer.

6. Loosen and remove the pinion retainer (C, **Figure 75**) with the retainer wrench **(Figure 76),** or its equivalent.
7. Thread the puller shaft (A, **Figure 77**) fully onto the end of the pinion gear shaft. Install the puller base (B, **Figure 77**) over the puller shaft and seat it against the housing surface. Then thread the special

nut (C, **Figure 77**) over the puller shaft and seat it into and against the puller base.

8. Hold the special nut (C, **Figure 77**) and turn the puller shaft (A, **Figure 77**) to pull the pinion gear assembly from the housing. Remove the tools from the pinion gear assembly (**Figure 78**).

Inspection

1. Clean and dry the pinion gear assembly.
2. Check the pinion gear for the following conditions:
    a. Broken, chipped or worn teeth (A, **Figure 79**).
    b. Rotate the pinion gear bearing (B, **Figure 79**) and check for any roughness, grinding or catching, indicating a damaged bearing.
    c. Damaged threads (C, **Figure 79**).
    d. Damaged pinion joint splines (D, **Figure 79**).
    e. Worn or damaged needle bearing shoulder (E, **Figure 79**). If this shoulder is damaged, the pinion gear needle bearing installed inside the housing is also likely damaged.
3. Inspect the pinion gear needle bearing (**Figure 80**). The rollers should be smooth and polished with no flat spots, burrs or other damage. Inspect the bearing cage for cracks or other damage. This bearing is pressed deep into the housing and difficult to inspect. If necessary, remove the pinion bearing from the pinion gear and install the pinion gear into the bearing. Turn the pinion gear to check the bearing. If the bearing is damaged, replace as described in *Final Drive Housing Bearing Replacement* in this chapter.

Disassembly/reassembly

This section services the bearing assembly and pinion gear shim installed on the pinion gear. The bearing assembly consists of three separate parts. During removal, the outer bearing race and bearing are removed at the same time. The inner bearing race is removed separately.

1. Support the bearing cage with a bearing splitter in a press (**Figure 81**).
2. Operate the press to remove the outer bearing race (A, **Figure 82**) and the bearing (B).
3. Support the inner bearing race and press it off the shaft (C, **Figure 82**).
4. Remove the pinion gear shim (D, **Figure 82**).
5. Recheck the bearing to see if it was damaged during removal. If not, the bearing can be reused.
6. Clean and dry all parts. Inspect the parts as described in this section.
7. If only the bearing is being replaced, use the original shim on the pinion shaft. If the final drive housing cover or housing, ring gear, pinion gear, or the

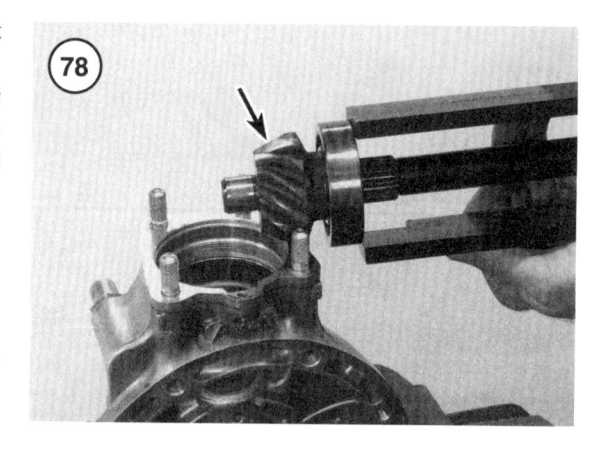

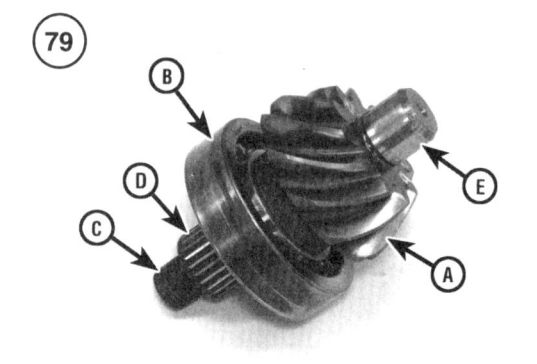

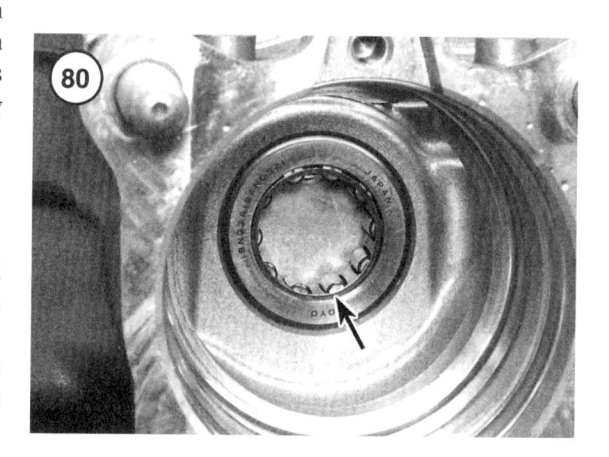

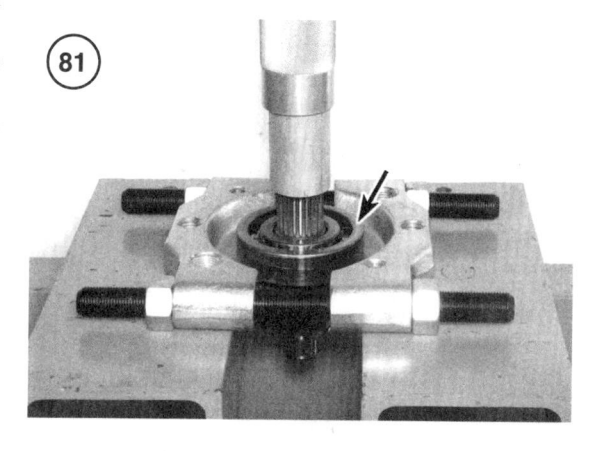

REAR SUSPENSION AND FINAL DRIVE

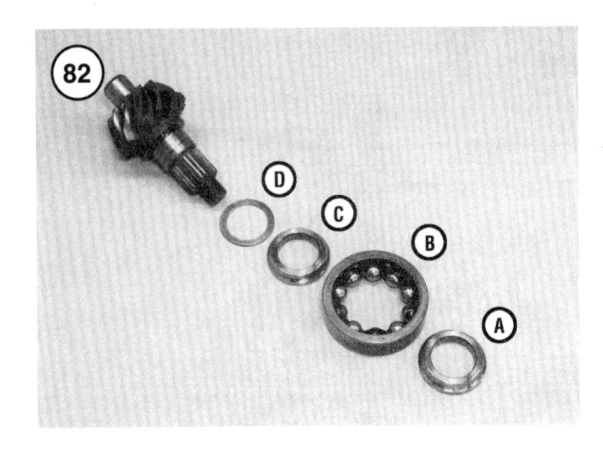

side bearings are being replaced, install a 2.0 mm (0.079 in.) pinion gear shim (D, **Figure 82**) as a starting point for the gear position adjustments.

8. Install the pinion gear shim (D, **Figure 82**).
9. Press the inner bearing race (C, **Figure 82**) onto the shaft until it bottoms against the pinion gear shim.
10. Press the bearing (B, **Figure 82**) on and seat it against the inner bearing race.
11. Press the outer bearing race (A, **Figure 82**) onto the pinion gear shaft until it seats against the bearing.
12. Install the pinion gear as described in this section.
13. Perform the *Gear Mesh Pattern Check* described in this chapter.

Pinion retainer seal and O-ring replacement

Service the oil seal (A, **Figure 83**) and O-ring (B) as follows:

1. Support the pinion retainer with one hand and remove the oil seal with a tire iron or similar wide-blade tool **(Figure 84)**. Discard the oil seal.
2. Remove the O-ring (B, **Figure 83**) and discard it.
3. Clean and dry the pinion retainer. Check the threads and the seal bore for damage.
4. Install a new oil seal as follows:
    a. Lubricate the seal's lip with grease (if not previously lubricated by the manufacturer).
    b. Position the seal into the top of the retainer with its closed side facing out.
    c. Place a driver on top of the seal **(Figure 85)** and install it until it bottoms in the retainer (A, **Figure 83**).
5. Lubricate a new O-ring with grease and install it into the retainer groove (B, **Figure 83**).

Installation

Assemble the pinion gear assembly as described in this section.

1. Clean and dry the final drive gear housing and pinion gear assembly. Make sure the threads on the pinion gear, pinion retainer and inside the housing are clean and dry.
2. Lubricate the pinion gear bearing and the needle bearing in the housing with gear oil.
3. Bolt the holding fixture across the housing and then secure the holding fixture in a vise as shown in **Figure 72**.
4. Install the pinion gear as follows:
    a. Install the pinion gear into the housing by aligning the end of the pinion gear shaft with the needle bearing.

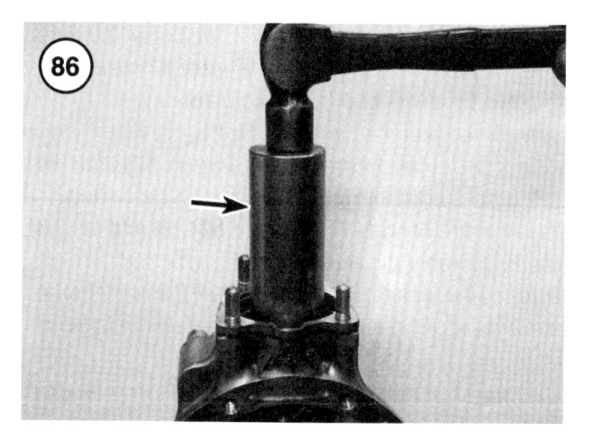

b. Place a bearing driver against the pinion gear bearing's outer race **(Figure 86)**.
c. Drive the pinion gear squarely into the housing.

5. Thread the pinion retainer (C, **Figure 75**) into the housing until it seats against the pinion gear bearing. Use the retainer wrench **(Figure 87)** and tighten the pinion retainer to 108 N.m (80 ft.-lb.).

6. Align the pinion retainer lock tab with the notches on the pinion retainer **(Figure 88)**. Install the pinion retainer lock tab bolt and tighten to 10 N.m (89 in.-lb.).

NOTE
*Two lock tab designs **(Figure 89)** are available from the manufacturer. If the original lock tab will not align properly, use the other lock tab.*

7. Install the pinion joint (4, **Figure 71**) onto the pinion gear shaft.
8. Apply a medium strength threadlock onto the pinion joint nut and install it finger-tight.
9. Secure the pinion joint with the pinion holder plate (A, **Figure 90**) and collar set (B) and tighten the pinion joint nut to 108 N.m (80 ft.-lb.). Remove the tools.

FINAL DRIVE HOUSING BEARING REPLACEMENT

This section services the outer ring gear bearing (A, **Figure 53**) and the pinion gear needle bearing **(Figure 80)**. The inner ring gear bearing **(Figure 58)** is serviced during disassembly and reassembly of the final drive housing.

Outer Ring Gear Bearing and Seal Replacement

The outer ring gear bearing **(Figure 91)** is only accessible from one side of the housing and requires a bridge type bearing puller (K&L part No. 35-2231)

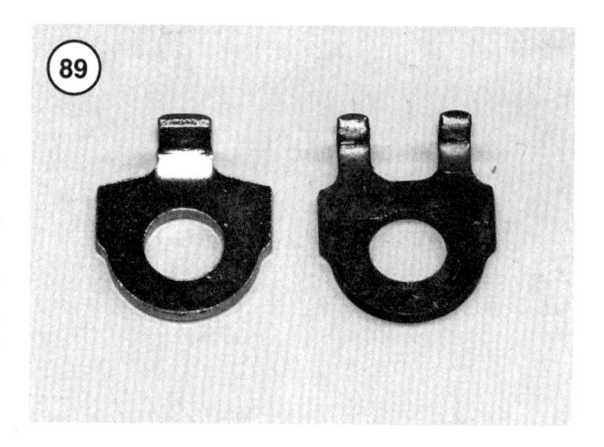

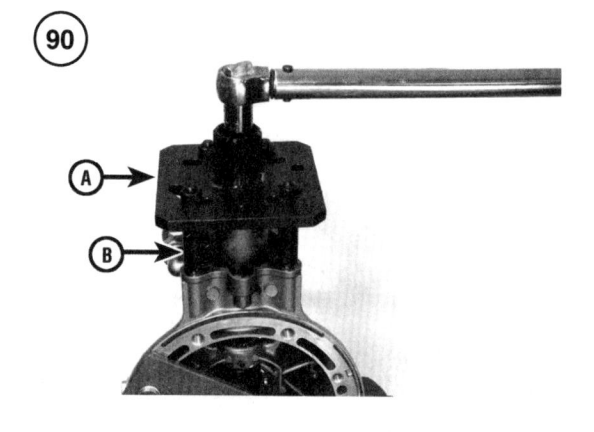

REAR SUSPENSION AND FINAL DRIVE

or a knock puller and a 35 mm collet for removal. A hydraulic press is also required for installation. While this bearing rarely requires replacement, it must be replaced when it is removed to replace a damaged seal **(Figure 92)**.

1. Heat the housing to 80° C (176° F).
2A. Remove the bearing with a bridge type puller as follows:
   a. Use two metal plates (A, **Figure 93**) for support and mount the puller (B, **Figure 93**) onto the housing. Adjust the puller so the arms engage the bearing's inner race. Tension the puller arms and check they are centered and positioned correctly.
   b. Operate the puller and remove the bearing.
2B. Remove the bearing with a knock puller as follows:
   a. Inserting the 35-mm collet through the bearing.
   b. Adjusting the collet so that it locks against the bearing's inner race. Support the housing and operate the puller to remove the bearing.
3. Pry the seal **(Figure 92)** out of the housing with a tire iron or seal removal tool and discard.
4. Clean the housing in clean solvent. Dry with compressed air.
5. Inspect the bearing and seal bores for damage.
6. Drive a new seal **(Figure 92)** into the housing with its open side facing toward the inside of the housing. Make sure the seal bottoms in its housing bore. Apply grease to the seal lips.
7. Place the new bearing in a freezer for approximately two hours.

CAUTION
Heat the housing carefully to prevent from damaging the seal.

8. Reheat the housing to 80° C (176° F).

CAUTION
Check the bearing carefully to make sure it starts and moves squarely into the bore.

9. Support the housing in a press and press the bearing into the housing bore until it bottoms **(Figure 91)**.

Pinion Gear Needle Bearing Replacement

The pinion gear needle bearing **(Figure 80)** is pressed into the housing and equipped with a stopper ring **(Figure 94)** that seats in a groove in the bearing bore. The stopper ring ensures that the pinion gear is positioned at its correct depth and cannot float or move during operation. This would change the ring and pinion gear engagement position.

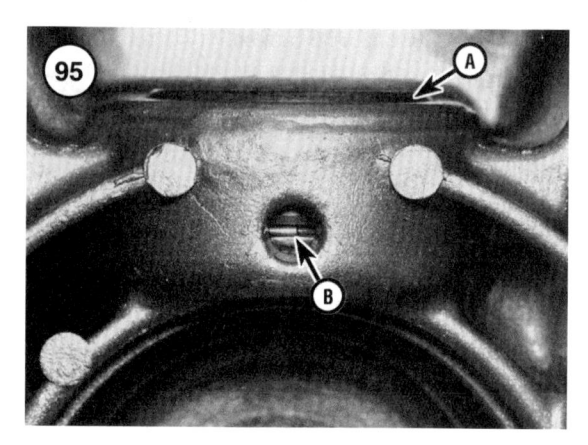

The pinion gear needle bearing (**Figure 80**) is only accessible from one side of the housing (A, **Figure 95**) and requires a knock puller with a 20-mm collet for removal and a bearing driver for installation.

NOTE
*The stopper ring (**Figure 96**) must be removed before the bearing can be removed from the housing.*

1. Remove the stopper ring through the access hole as follows:
   a. Working through the access hole, rotate the stopper ring until its end gap is visible (B, **Figure 95**).
   b. Use a small tool and carefully pry one end of the stopper ring up until it can be grabbed with a pair of needle-nose pliers. Then slowly pull and remove the stopper ring through the access hole (**Figure 96**).
2. Mount the holding fixture across the front of the housing and secure the holding fixture in a vise so the needle bearing is horizontal with the floor (**Figure 97**).
3. Heat the housing to 80° C (176° F).
4. Install a 20-mm bearing collet through the bearing, then expand the collet to grip the back-side of the bearing. Operate the puller and remove the bearing (**Figure 98**) from the housing.
5. Remove the holding fixture and housing from the vise and separate them.
6. Clean and dry the bearing bore. Then inspect the bearing bore for damage.
7. Place a new stopper ring into the groove on the new bearing (**Figure 99**) and place the bearing in a freezer for approximately two hours.
8. Mount the holding fixture (A, **Figure 100**) across the side of the housing and secure the holding fixture in a vise so the bearing bore is facing up.
9. Heat the housing to 80° C (176° F).
10. Remove the needle bearing from the freezer and quickly align it with the housing so the stopper

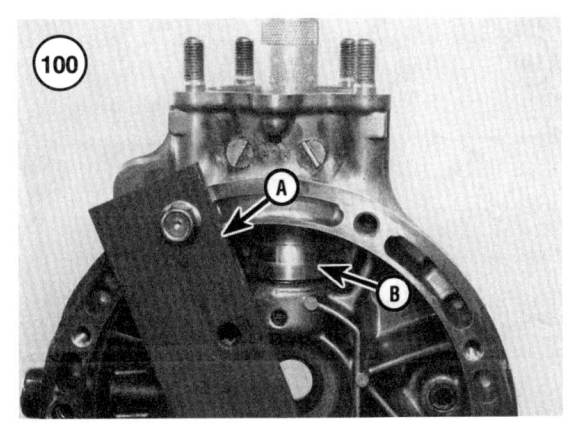

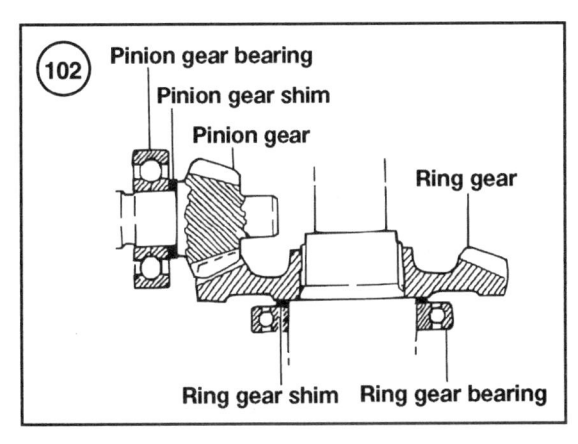

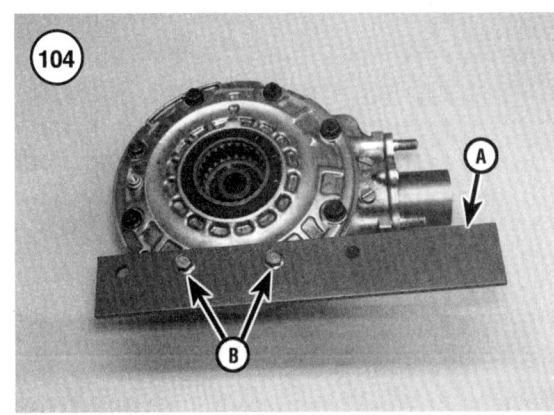

REAR SUSPENSION AND FINAL DRIVE

ring end is facing down (toward housing). Drive the bearing (B, **Figure 100**) squarely into the housing until the stopper ring seats into the housing groove **(Figure 94)**.

11. Check the new bearing for damage.

RING AND PINION GEAR MEASUREMENTS

Whenever the ring and pinion gears **(Figure 101)**, bearing(s), housing or housing cover are replaced, inspect and adjust the ring gear backlash and the gear tooth contact pattern (this section).

Backlash Measurement

This procedure checks the backlash between the ring gear and pinion gear to determine gear wear and if the ring gear is running true. Measuring gear backlash is also necessary after a general overhaul. **Figure 102** shows ring and pinion gear engagement and the position of their adjustment shims.

1. Remove the final drive unit as described in this chapter.

NOTE
There are two methods of locking the pinion gear when measuring backlash.

2A. If using the pinion holder tool, perform the following:

   a. Remove the bolt (A, **Figure 103**), washer and dust guard plate (B).

   b. Remove the two housing cover mounting bolts (C, **Figure 103**).

   c. Bolt the holding fixture (A, **Figure 104**) across the final drive housing using the vacant bolt holes (B, **Figure 104**). Use spacers to position the holding fixture away from the curved ribs on the housing cover.

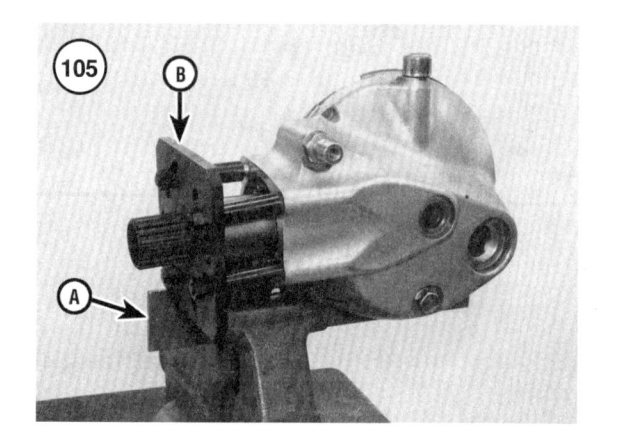

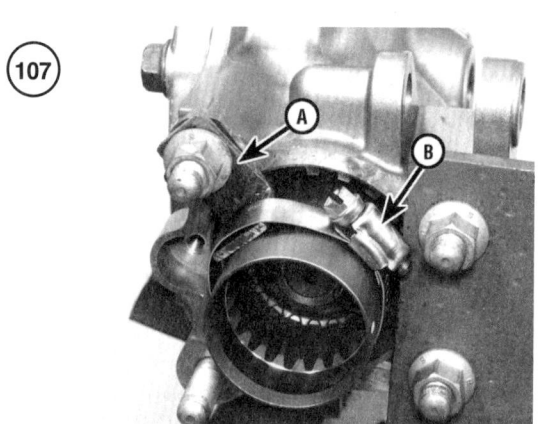

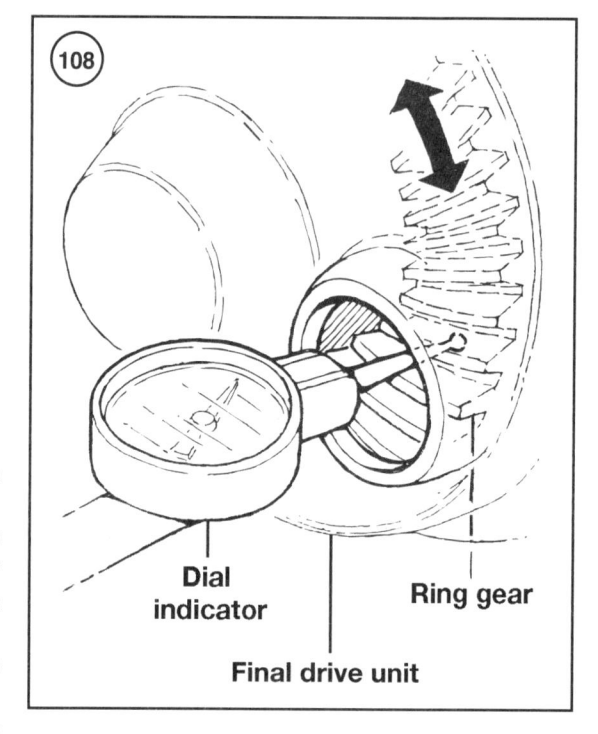

d. Secure the holding fixture (A, **Figure 105**) in a vise.

e. Mount the pinion holder plate and collar set as shown in B, **Figure 105**. The pinion holder plate engages the splines inside the pinion joint to prevent the pinion gear from turning.

2B. To lock the pinion joint/pinion gear without the use of special tools, perform the following:

   a. Bolt the holding fixture across the final drive housing using the vacant bolt holes. Then, mount the holding fixture (A, **Figure 106**) in a vise.

   b. Drill a 10-mm hole through a small angle bracket and mount it onto a final drive stud as shown in A, **Figure 107**. Secure the angle bracket to the pinion joint with a hose clamp (B, **Figure 107**). This arrangement locks the pinion joint in place to prevent the pinion gear from turning.

   c. Support the final drive housing with a small scissor jack (B, **Figure 106**) to help steady the unit when measuring backlash. A dial indicator positioned to contact the housing and held in place by a magnetic stand can also be used to monitor housing movement.

3. Remove the oil fill cap.

4. Measure backlash with a dial indicator mounted on a magnetic stand (C, **Figure 106**). Position the indicator so its stem is parallel to the ring gear shaft and its tip contacts the side of one gear tooth as shown in **Figure 108**.

5. Use a pair of snap ring pliers to move the ring gear back and forth to determine initial final drive gear backlash **(Figure 109)**. Refer to **Table 2** for the specified backlash. Record the reading.

6. Remove the dial test indicator, then rotate the ring gear and take two additional backlash readings 120° from the original measuring point.

   a. If the difference between any two readings exceeds 0.10 mm (0.004 in.), the ring gear is running out of true. This can be caused by a damaged bearing or the bearing bore may be damaged.

   b. If the backlash measurement is being performed after reassembling the final drive unit, the ring

REAR SUSPENSION AND FINAL DRIVE

109

110

111

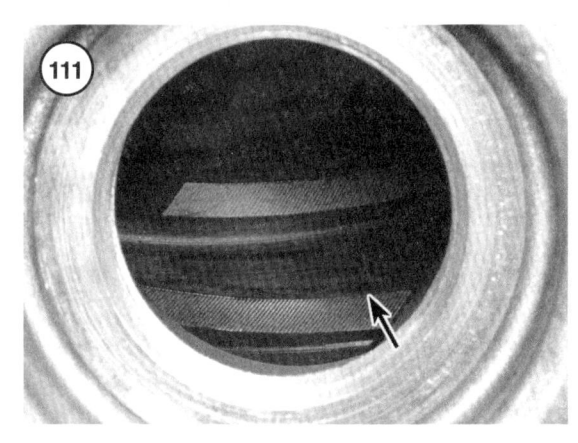

112

Toe (inside of gear)

Coast side (contacts during engine braking)

Drive side (contacts during engine acceleration)

Heel (outside of gear)

gear bearings may not have been installed correctly.
- c. If the backlash reading is out of specification, but the ring gear is running true, continue the procedure.
- d. If the backlash reading indicates that the ring gear is running out of true, remove the ring gear and inspect the parts and housing for damage.

7. To correct backlash, perform the following:
   a. If gear backlash is too small, replace the ring gear shim with a thinner one.
   b. If gear backlash to too large, replace the ring gear shim with a thicker one.
   c. Refer to **Table 3** for ring gear shim sizes.
   d. Remove the ring gear and press off its bearing to install the correct size shim (this chapter).

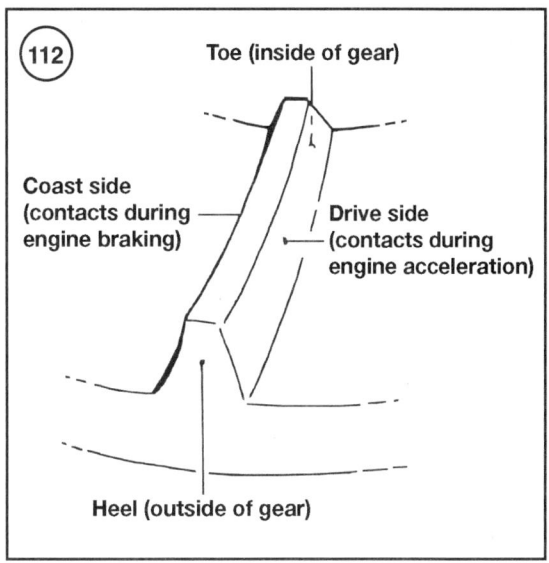

8. Install the oil filler cap.

9. Remove the holding tools or fixture. If removed, tighten the two housing cover 8-mm mounting bolts (C, **Figure 103**) to 25 N.m (18 ft.-lb.).

10. Install the final drive unit (this chapter).

Gear Mesh Pattern Inspection

1. Remove the housing cover, ring gear and wave washer (this chapter).
2. Clean and dry the ring gear and pinion gear teeth.
3. Using a brush, apply Prussian blue, or an equivalent non-drying gear marking compound, to both sides of the pinion gear teeth (**Figure 110**).
4. Install the wave washer, ring gear and housing cover as described in this chapter.
5. Remove the oil fill cap.
6. Rotate the pinion joint several rotations to turn the ring gear in its normal operating direction so a pattern becomes evident on the ring gear teeth (**Figure 111**).
7. Examine the wear pattern on the drive side of the ring gear teeth as follows:
   a. Refer to **Figure 112** to identify the parts of the gear teeth.
   b. The desired gear tooth wear pattern (**Figure 113**) shows the pattern positioned approximately in the center of each tooth and slightly toward the flank side of the tooth.

c. If the pinion contact pattern is low, install a thinner pinion shim **(Figure 113)**.

d. If the pinion contact pattern is high, install a thicker pinion shim **(Figure 113)**.

e. The pinion gear bearing must be removed to replace the shim. Refer to *Final Drive Unit Overhaul* in this chapter.

f. Changing shim thickness 0.1 mm (0.004 in.) moves the contact pattern approximately 1.5-2.0 mm (0.06-0.08 in.). Refer to **Table 4** for pinion gear shim sizes.

8. Reinstall the pinion gear and bearing, if they were removed, as described in this chapter. After obtaining a satisfactory pinion gear contact pattern, check the ring gear backlash as described under *Backlash Measurement* in this section.

9. Remove the housing cover and ring gear assembly. Refer to *Ring Gear and Housing Cover* in this chapter to continue with the final assembly procedure.

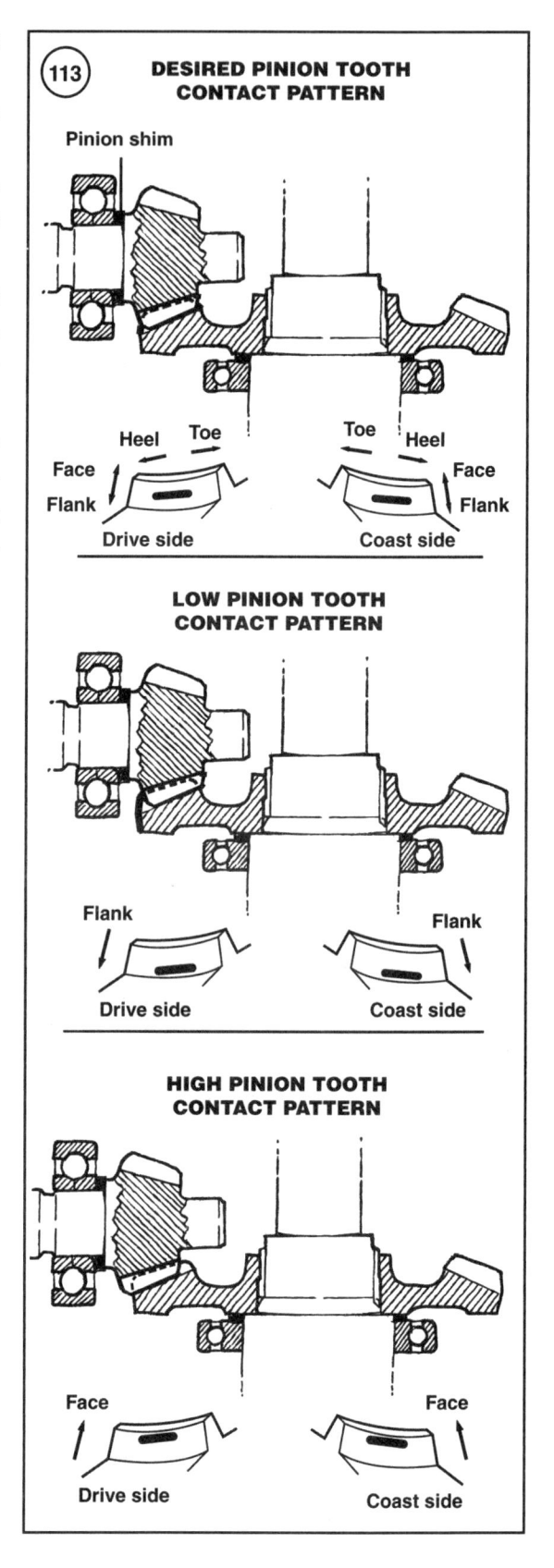

113 DESIRED PINION TOOTH CONTACT PATTERN

LOW PINION TOOTH CONTACT PATTERN

HIGH PINION TOOTH CONTACT PATTERN

REAR SUSPENSION AND FINAL DRIVE

Table 1 REAR SUSPENSION SPECIFICATIONS

Rear axle travel	90 mm (3.5 in.)
Shock absorber standard preload adjuster setting	Second position
Rear axle runout limit	0.2 mm (0.01 in.)

Table 2 FINAL DRIVE UNIT SERVICE SPECIFICATIONS

	New mm (in.)	Service limit mm (in.)
Final drive gear backlash		
Standard	0.05-0.15 (0.002-0.006)	0.30 (0.012)
Maximum difference in backlash measurements	–	0.10 (0.004)
Final drive gear assembly preload	0.2-0.4 N·m (1.8-3.5 in.-lb.)	–
Ring gear-to-stop pin clearance	0.30-0.60 (0.012-0.024)	–

Table 3 RING GEAR SHIM SIZES

Ring gear shim	Thickness mm (in.)
A	1.82 (0.072)
B	1.88 (0.074)
C	1.94 (0.076)
D (standard shim)	2.00 (0.079)
E	2.06 (0.081)
F	2.12 (0.083)
G	2.18 (0.086)
H	2.24 (0.088)
I	2.30 (0.091)

Table 4 PINION GEAR SHIM SIZES

Pinion gear shim	Thickness mm (in.)
A	1.82 (0.072)
B	1.88 (0.074)
C	1.94 (0.076)
D (standard shim)	2.00 (0.079)
E	2.06 (0.081)
F	2.12 (0.083)
G	2.18 (0.086)

Table 5 REAR SUSPENSION AND FINAL DRIVE TORQUE SPECIFICATIONS

	N.m	in.-lb.	ft.-lb.
Brake stopper arm nut			
Non-ABS models	22	--	16
Final drive dust guard plate mounting bolt			
2004-2009 Aero models	9.8	87	--
All other models	10	89	--
Final drive gear case mounting nut	64	--	47
Final drive housing cover mounting bolts			
8-mm	25	--	18
10-mm*	47	--	35
Pinion joint nut*	108	--	80
Pinion retainer	108	--	80
(continued)			

Table 5 REAR SUSPENSION AND FINAL DRIVE TORQUE SPECIFICATIONS (continued)

Pinion retainer lock tab bolt			
2004-2009 Aero models	9.8	87	--
All other models	10	89	--
Rear shock absorber mounting bolt			
Lower			
Left side	--	--	--
2004-2009 Aero models	23	--	17
All other models	22	--	16
Right side	34	--	25
Upper	26	--	19
Swing arm pivot bolt			
Right		Refer to text	
Right locknut	103	--	76
Left	103	--	76

*Refer to text for additional information.

CHAPTER FIFTEEN

BRAKES

This chapter covers the front and rear brake systems. Brake maintenance intervals and routine inspection and adjustment procedures are found in Chapter Three.

Refer to Chapter Sixteen for ABS troubleshooting and component service.

Read *Safety* and *Service Methods* (Chapter One) before servicing the brake system and related components.

Refer to **Tables 1-4** at the end of the chapter for brake specifications.

BRAKE SERVICE

WARNING
Do not ride the motorcycle until the front and rear brakes are operating correctly.

WARNING
Do not use brake fluid labeled DOT 5. This is a silicone-based brake fluid that is not compatible with glycol-based DOT 3, DOT 4 or DOT 5.1. Do not intermix two different types of brake fluid as it can cause brake component damage and lead to brake system failure.

WARNING
Never reuse brake fluid expelled during brake bleeding. Contaminated brake fluid can cause brake failure. Dispose of brake fluid properly.

WARNING
*Whenever working on the brake system, do **not** inhale brake dust. Do **not** use compressed air to blow off brake parts. It may contain asbestos, which can cause lung injury and cancer. Wear a face mask that meets OHSA requirements for trapping asbestos particles, and wash hands and forearms thoroughly after completing the work. Before working on the brake system, spray the components with an aerosol brake cleaner. Secure and dispose of all brake dust and cleaning materials properly.*

CAUTION
Cover all parts that could become contaminated by the accidental spilling of brake fluid. Wash any spilled brake fluid from any surface immediately, as it damages the finish. Use soapy water and rinse completely.

When adding brake fluid, only use DOT 4 brake fluid from a sealed container. However, because DOT 4 brake fluid is glycol-based and draws moisture, purchase brake fluid in small containers and discard any small leftover quantities. Do not store a container of brake fluid with less than 1/4 of the fluid remaining.

The front brake system transmits hydraulic pressure from the master cylinder to the brake caliper. This pressure is transmitted from the caliper to the brake pads, which grip both sides of the brake discs and slows the motorcycle. As the pads wear, the pistons move out of the caliper bores to automatically compensate for wear. As this occurs, the fluid level in the master cylinder reservoir goes down. This must be compensated for by occasionally adding fluid.

The proper operation of the system depends on routine inspection, a supply of clean DOT 4 brake fluid and a clean work environment when any service is performed. Any debris that enters the system or contaminates the pads or brake disc can damage the components and cause poor brake performance.

Perform brake service procedures carefully. Do not use any sharp tools inside the master cylinder, caliper or on the pistons. Damage to these components could cause a loss of hydraulic pressure. If there is any doubt about your ability to correctly and safely service the brake system, have a professional technician perform the task.

Consider the following when servicing the brake system:

1. Do not allow brake fluid to contact any plastic parts or painted surfaces; damage will result.
2. Always keep the master cylinder reservoir and spare cans of brake fluid closed to prevent dust or moisture from entering. This contaminates the brake fluid and can cause brake failure.
3. Clean parts with an aerosol brake parts cleaner. Never use petroleum-based solvents on internal brake system components or any rubber part. They cause seals to swell and distort.
4. Do not allow any grease or oil to contact the brake pads.
5. When cleaning the brake components, wear rubber gloves to keep brake fluid off skin.

NOTE
Removing the reservoir cover does not allow air to enter the hydraulic system unless the fluid level drops so low and exposes the brake fluid passage holes in the master cylinder.

6. If the hydraulic system has been opened, bleed the system to remove air from the system. Refer to *Brake Bleeding* in this chapter.

BRAKE BLEEDING

Bleeding the brakes removes air from the brake system. Air in the brake system increases brake lever or pedal travel while causing it to feel spongy and less responsive. Under extreme braking (heat) conditions, it can cause complete loss of brake pressure.

Read *Brake Service* in this chapter.

Bleeding Tips

Before bleeding the brakes, note the following:

CAUTION
Brake fluid can damage painted and finished surfaces. Use water and immediately wash any surface that becomes contaminated with brake fluid.

1. Clean the bleed valve and the area around the valve of all dirt and debris. Make sure the passageway in the end of the valve is open and clear.
2. Use a box-end wrench to open and close the bleed valve. This prevents damage to the hex-head.
3. Replace the bleed valve if its hex-shoulder is damaged. A damaged bleed valve is difficult to loosen and cannot be tightened fully.
4. Install a box-end wrench on the bleed valve before installing the catch hose. This allows operation of the wrench without having to disconnect the hose.
5. Use a clear catch hose to allow visual inspection of the brake fluid as it leaves the caliper or brake unit. Air bubbles visible in the catch hose indicate that there still may be air trapped in the brake system.
6. Depending on the play of the bleed valve when it is loosened, it is possible to see air exiting through the catch hose even through there is no air in the brake system. A loose or damaged catch hose also causes air leaks. In both cases, air is being introduced into the bleed system at the bleed valve threads and catch hose connection, and not from within the brake system itself. This condition can be misleading and cause excessive brake bleeding when there is no air in the system.
7. Open the bleed valve just enough to allow fluid to pass through the valve and into the catch bottle. The farther the bleed valve is opened, the looser the valve becomes. This allows air to be drawn into the system from around the valve threads.
8. If the system is difficult to bleed, tap the brake line on the master cylinder a few times to remove air bubbles trapped in the hose connection where the brake fluid exits the master cylinder. Also, tap the banjo bolt at the brake caliper.
9. When bleeding the brake system, check the fluid level in the master cylinder frequently to prevent it from running dry, especially when using a vacuum

BRAKES

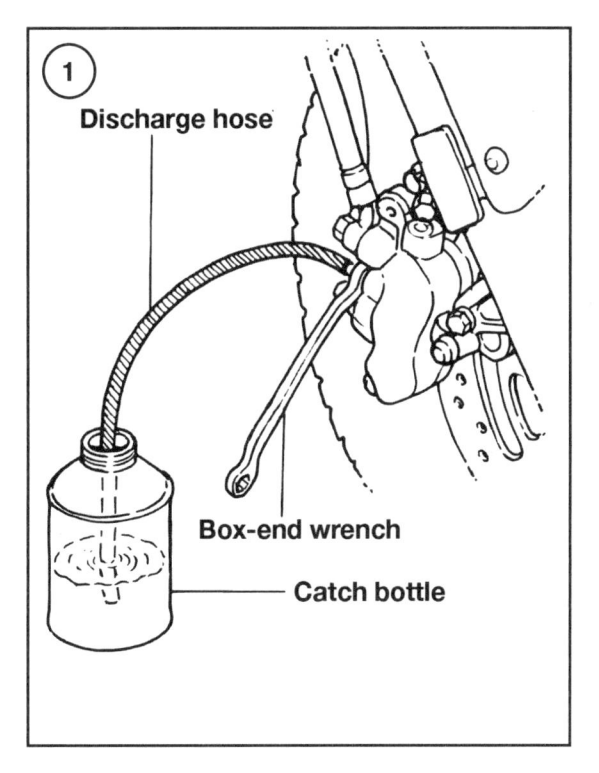

1
Discharge hose
Box-end wrench
Catch bottle

pump. If the fluid level drops too low, air can enter the system and must be bled again.

10. Brake calipers used on ABS models are each equipped with two bleed valves. Bleed brake fluid from the bleed valves in the order specified in the text.

Brake Bleeding Procedure (Non-ABS Models)

Manual bleeding

This procedure describes how to bleed the brake system with an empty bottle, a length of clear hose that fits tightly onto the bleed valve, and a box-end wrench. Two people will be required to perform the procedure. One person can open and close the bleed valve while the other person operates the brake lever. Use the following procedure to bleed the front brake.

1. Read *Bleeding Tips* in this section.
2. Check that the banjo bolts are tight and there are no leaks at the bolts or along the brake hose.
3. Connect the catch hose to the bleed valve on the brake caliper (**Figure 1**). Submerge the other end of the hose into the bottle partially filled with clean DOT 4 brake fluid. This prevents air from being drawn into the catch hose and back into the brake system.
4. Remove the cover, diaphragm plate and diaphragm,
5. Apply the brake lever firmly (do not pump) until it stops and hold in this position. Then open the bleed valve. As air and brake fluid is forced from the system, the lever will travel the full length of operation. When the lever can move no farther, hold the lever down and close the bleed valve. Do not allow the lever to return to its up position when the bleed valve is open. Doing so will allow air to be drawn back into the system.
6. When the bleed valve is closed, release the lever so it returns to its resting position. Check the fluid level in the reservoir and replenish, if necessary.
7. Repeat the bleeding procedure until clear fluid is seen passing from the bleed valve.

NOTE
If small bubbles remain in the system after several bleeding attempts, install the diaphragm, diaphragm plate and reservoir cover and allow the system to stand undisturbed for a few hours. The system will stabilize and the air can be purged as large bubbles.

8. Tighten the bleed valve to the torque specification in **Table 4**. Then operate the lever, hold it in position and check the bleed valve for leaks.

NOTE
If the brake feels firm but there are still air bubbles visible in the brake fluid, air is probably leaking around the bleed valve.

9. The bleeding procedure is completed when the feel of the lever is firm and there are no air bubbles visible on the brake fluid.
10. Check the brake fluid reservoir and fill the reservoir to the upper level, if necessary.
11. Install the diaphragm, diaphragm plate and cover. Install and tighten the cover screws to the specification in **Table 4**. Then wipe the cover edge with a rag to remove any brake fluid that may have seeped past the diaphragm when the screws were tightened. When the cover screws are tight, turn the handlebar from side to side and check for any leakage around the cover.
12. Test ride the motorcycle slowly at first to make sure that the front brake is operating correctly.

Vacuum bleeding

This procedure uses a hand-operated vacuum pump with a hydraulic brake bleeding kit. Use the following procedure to bleed the front brake.

1. Read *Bleeding Tips* in this section.
2. Check that the banjo bolts are tight and there are no leaks at the bolts or along the front brake hose.

CHAPTER FIFTEEN

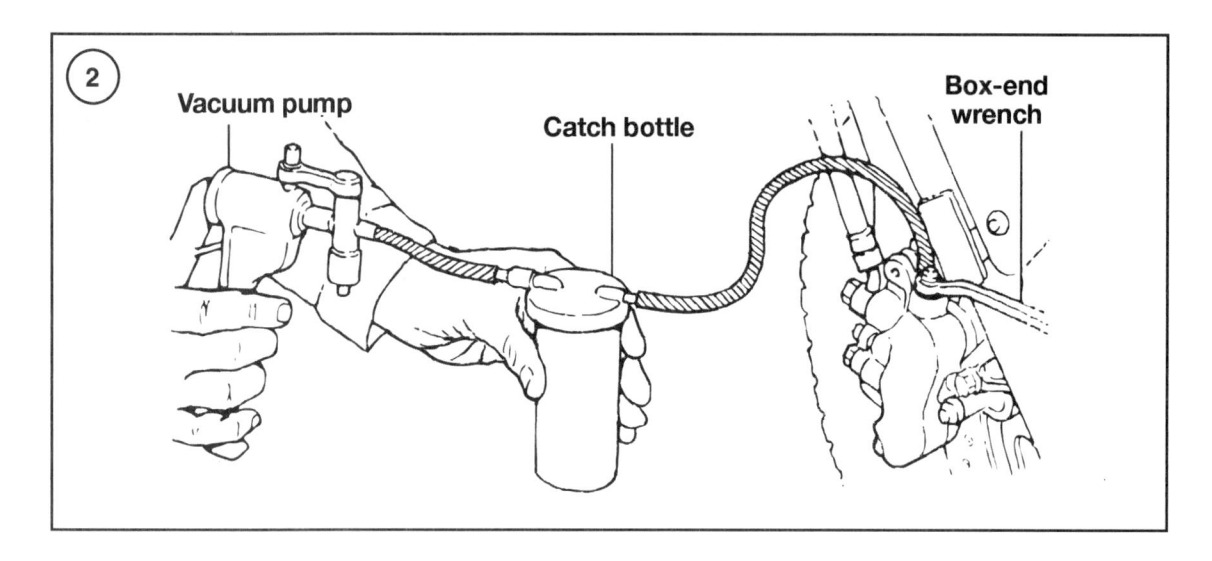

② Vacuum pump — Catch bottle — Box-end wrench

3. Connect the catch hose between the bleed valve and catch bottle (**Figure 2**). Connect the other hose between the catch bottle and vacuum pump. If necessary, refer to the tool manufacturer's instructions for additional information.

4. Secure the vacuum pump to the motorcycle with a length of stiff wire so it will be possible to check and refill the master cylinder reservoir without having to disconnect the catch hose.

5. Remove the cover, diaphragm plate and diaphragm,

6. Pump the handle on the vacuum pump to create a vacuum in the catch hose connected to the bleed valve.

7. Open the bleed valve with a wrench to allow air and brake fluid to be drawn through the master cylinder, brake hoses and lines. Close the bleed valve *before* the brake fluid stops flowing from the system (no more vacuum in line) or the vacuum pump gauge reads zero (if so equipped). Replenish the fluid level in the reservoir.

8. Repeat the bleeding procedure until clear fluid is seen passing from the bleed valve.

NOTE
If small bubbles remain in the system after several bleeding attempts, install the diaphragm, diaphragm plate and reservoir cover and allow the system to stand undisturbed for a few hours. The system will stabilize and the air can be purged as large bubbles.

9. Tighten the bleed valve to the torque specification in **Table 4**. Then, operate the lever, hold it in position and check the bleed valve for leaks.

NOTE
If the brake feels firm but there are still air bubbles visible in the brake fluid, air is probably leaking around the bleed valve.

10. The bleeding procedure is completed when the feel of the lever is firm and there are no air bubbles visible on the brake fluid.

11. Check the brake fluid reservoir and fill the reservoir to the upper level, if necessary.

12. Install the diaphragm, diaphragm plate and cover. Install and tighten the cover screws to the specification in **Table 4**. Then wipe the cover edge with a rag to remove any brake fluid that may have seeped past the diaphragm when the screws were tightened. When the cover screws are tight, turn the handlebar from side to side and check for any leakage around the cover.

13. Test ride the motorcycle slowly at first to make sure that the front brake is operating correctly.

Front Brake Line Bleeding Procedure (ABS Models)

This section bleeds the brake line assembly controlled by the front brake lever.

Manual bleeding

1. Connect the catch hose to the upper bleed valve on the brake caliper (**Figure 3**). Submerge the other end of the hose into the bottle partially filled with DOT 4 brake fluid. This prevents air from being drawn into the catch hose and back into the brake system.

2. Perform the appropriate manual bleeding steps (this section).

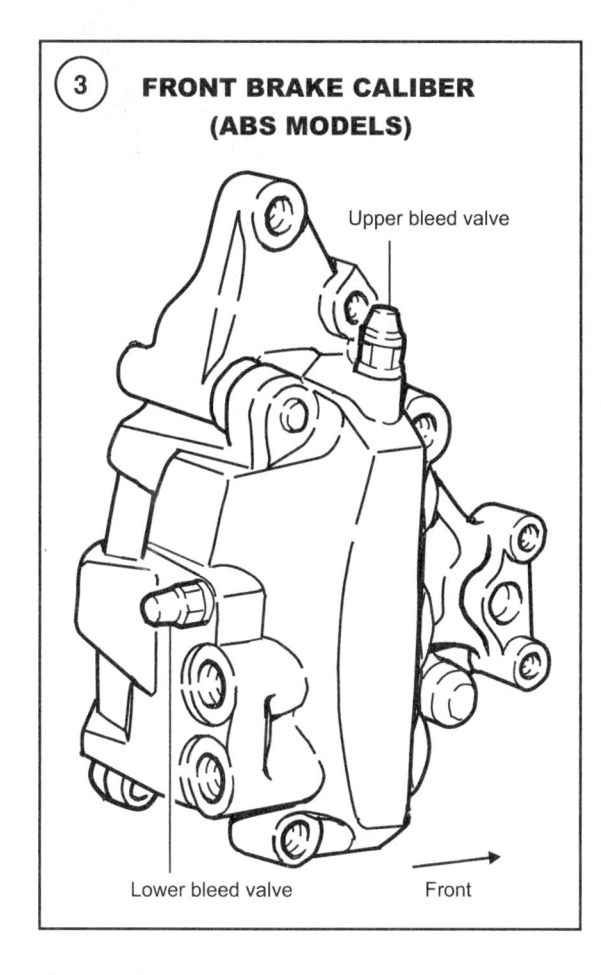

BRAKES

FRONT BRAKE CALIPER (ABS MODELS) — Figure 3
- Upper bleed valve
- Lower bleed valve
- Front

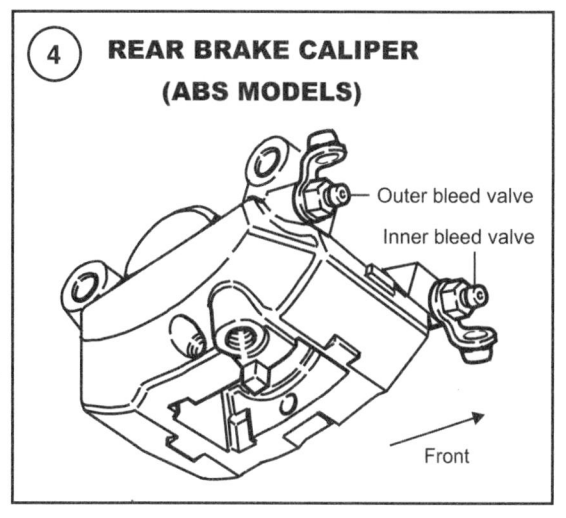

REAR BRAKE CALIPER (ABS MODELS) — Figure 4
- Outer bleed valve
- Inner bleed valve
- Front

repeat the bleeding procedure at each bleed valve several times and in the correct order.

   a. Front brake caliper lower bleed valve **(Figure 3)**.
   b. Rear brake caliper inner bleed valve **(Figure 4)**.
   c. Rear brake caliper outer bleed valve **(Figure 4)**.
2A. Manual bleeding: Perform the appropriate manual bleeding steps (this section).
2B. Vacuum bleeding: Perform the appropriate vacuum bleeding steps (this section).

BRAKE FLUID FLUSHING

When flushing the front brake system, use *only* DOT 4 brake fluid as a flushing fluid. Flushing consists of pulling enough new brake fluid through the system until all of the old fluid is removed, and the fluid exiting the bleed valve appears clean and without any bubbles. To flush the brake system, use one of the bleeding procedures described in *Brake Bleeding* in this chapter.

BRAKE FLUID DRAINING

1. Read the information under *Brake Bleeding* in this chapter.
2. Remove the reservoir cover, diaphragm plate and diaphragm.
3. Connect a brake bleeder tool to the brake caliper as described in this chapter. Operate the bleed tool to remove as much brake fluid from the system as possible.
4. Close the bleed valve and disconnect the brake bleed tool.
5. Service the brake components as described in this chapter.

Vacuum bleeding

1. Connect the catch hose to the upper bleed valve on the brake caliper **(Figure 3)**. Submerge the other end of the hose into the bottle partially filled with DOT 4 brake fluid. This prevents air from being drawn into the catch hose and back into the brake system.
2. Perform the appropriate vacuum bleeding steps (this section).

Rear Brake Line

This section bleeds the brake line assembly controlled by the rear brake pedal.
1. Bleed the rear brake line assembly in the following order:

NOTE
Because of the PCV installed in the brake system, a strong brake pedal resistance may be felt when bleeding at the rear brake caliper. This is normal.

NOTE
Due to the number of brake lines used in the system, it may be necessary to

FRONT BRAKE PADS

The pistons in the front brake caliper are self-adjusting to compensate for brake pad wear. When the brake is applied, hydraulic pressure against the pistons causes the piston seals to stretch and deflect slightly. This allows the pistons to move out where they contact the brake pads and then push them against the brake disc. When the brake is released, pressure against the piston seals is reduced and allows them to retract and return to their original shape. This action draws the pistons away from the brake pads and disengages the brake. As the brake pads wear, the pistons will travel farther through the seals in order to contact the brake pads. The brake fluid level also drops as the pads wear and the pistons move farther outward.

There is no recommended mileage interval for changing the brake pads. Pad wear depends greatly on riding habits and the condition of the brake system.

Refer to *Brakes* in Chapter Three to inspect the brake pad wear.

A more thorough job of pad replacement is accomplished by cleaning the exposed parts of the pistons before they are pushed back into their bores, thus preventing dirt and debris that has collected and hardened on the pistons from damaging the caliper seals. The caliper bracket can also be removed to clean and lubricate the pin bolts and replace the pin boots if damaged.

Removal/Installation

Non-ABS models

1. Read *Brake Service* in this chapter.

> *NOTE*
> *Before repositioning the caliper pistons, visually check the exposed parts of the caliper pistons. If the pistons are contaminated, pitted or have a rough appearance, remove the brake caliper (do not disconnect the brake hose) and clean the pistons **(Figure 5)** with a soft brush and cleaner that will not damage or swell the caliper seals. At the same time, clean and relubricate the caliper and caliper bracket pin bolts and pin boots. Refer to **Front Brake Caliper** in this chapter.*

2. Remove the front master cylinder cover, diaphragm plate and diaphragm. Use a large syringe to remove and discard about 50 percent of the fluid from the reservoir. This prevents the master cylinder from overflowing when the caliper pistons are compressed for reinstallation. Do *not* drain the entire reservoir or air will enter the system. Reinstall the diaphragm, diaphragm plate and cover.

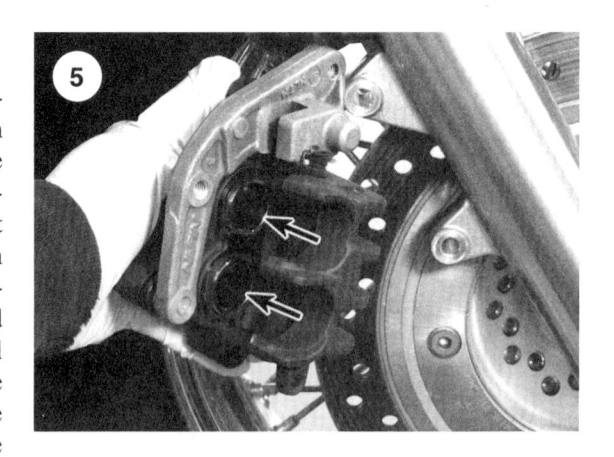

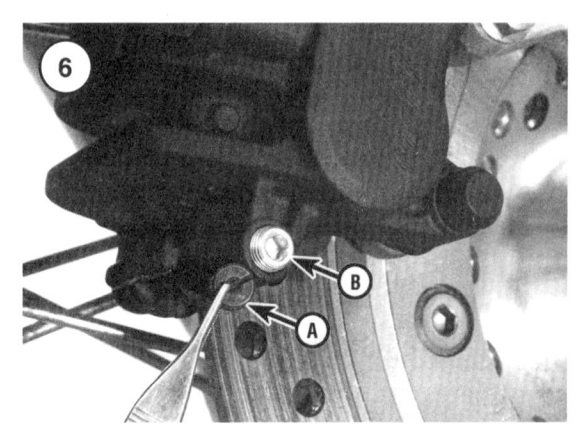

> *CAUTION*
> *Do not allow the master cylinder reservoir to overflow when compressing the pistons Brake fluid damages most surfaces it contacts.*

3. Push against the side of the brake caliper so the brake pads push the caliper pistons into their bores to make room for the new brake pads. If the caliper pistons do not move properly, remove and service the caliper as described in this chapter.
4. Remove the pad pin plug (A, **Figure 6**).
5. Remove the pad pin (B, **Figure 6**) and both brake pads **(Figure 7)**.
6. Remove the pad spring **(Figure 8)** and clean it. Then inspect it (A, **Figure 9**) for cracks and other damage and replace if necessary.
7. Inspect the pad pin (B, **Figure 9**) for excessive wear, corrosion or damage. Remove corrosion and dirt from the pad pin. A dirty or damaged pad pin prevents the brake pads from sliding properly and results in brake drag and overheating of the brake disc.

BRAKES

Wear limit groove

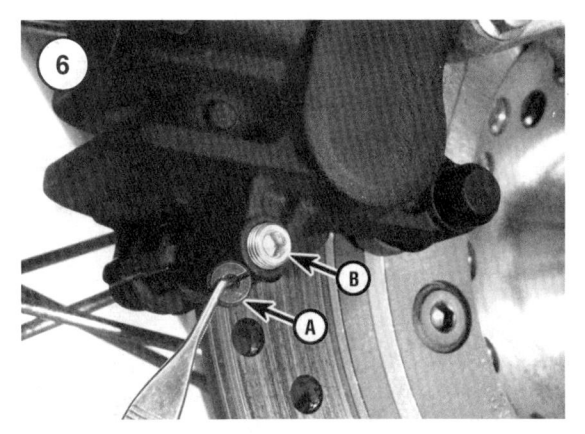

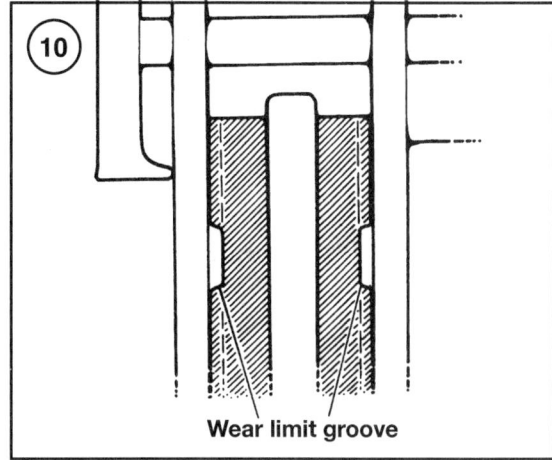

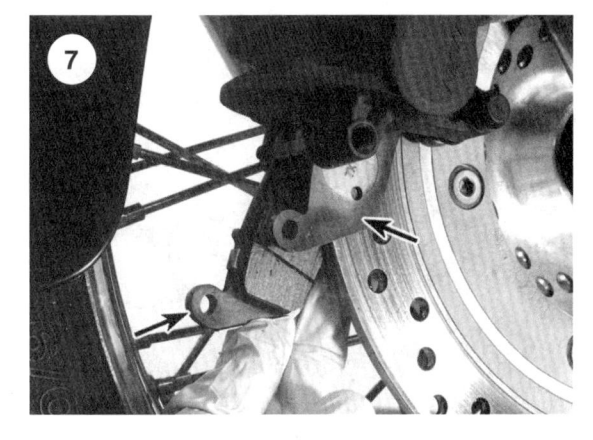

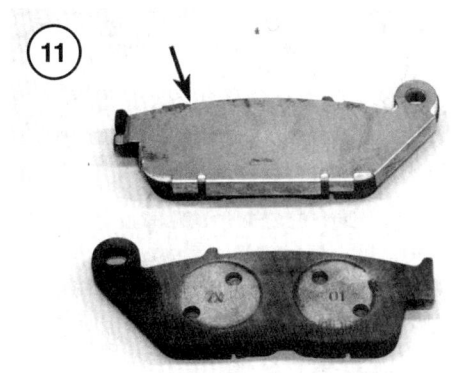

8. Inspect the brake pads (C, **Figure 9**) as follows:
   a. Inspect the friction material for light surface dirt, grease and oil contamination. Remove light contamination with sandpaper. If the contamination has penetrated the surface, replace the brake pads.

   NOTE
   Figure 10 shows the brake pads and the wear limit grooves with the pads installed and seated against the brake disc.

   b. Inspect the brake pads for excessive wear or damage. Replace the brake pads when the friction material is worn to the wear limit groove.
   c. Inspect the brake pads for uneven wear. If one pad has worn more than the other, it may be binding on its pad pin, on the pin bolt or the caliper is not sliding properly.
   d. Inspect the shim **(Figure 11)** on the inner pad for corrosion, looseness and damage.

   NOTE
   If brake fluid is leaking from around the pistons, overhaul the brake caliper as described in this chapter.

9. Slide the caliper in and out of the caliper bracket, checking for excessive drag or to see if it is stuck. If the caliper does not move smoothly or the boots appear damaged, service the pin bolts and pin boots as described in *Front Brake Caliper* in this chapter.

10. Service the brake disc as follows:

NOTE
Cleaning the brake disc is especially important if changing brake pad compounds. Many compounds are not compatible with each other.

a. Use brake cleaner and fine-grade emery cloth to remove road debris and brake pad residue from the brake disc. Clean both sides of the disc.
b. Check the brake disc for wear as described in this chapter.

NOTE
Figure 12 *shows the pad spring installed with the caliper removed for clarity.*

11. Reinstall the pad spring (**Figure 12**), making sure it clamps firmly to the caliper housing.

12. Install the brake pads (**Figure 7**) into the caliper so the friction material on both brake pads faces toward the brake disc while inserting the extended arm on the upper end of each pad against the pad retainer in the caliper bracket (**Figure 13**).

13. Push both brake pads up against the pad spring and install the pad pin (B, **Figure 6**) through the brake caliper and brake pads. Tighten the pad pin to 18 N.m (13 ft.-lb.).

14. Tighten the pad pin plug (A, **Figure 6**) to the follows specifications:
   a. 2004-2009 Aero models: 2.9 N.m (26 in.-lb.).
   b. All other models: 2.5 N.m (22 in.-lb.).

15. Operate the front brake lever to seat the pads against the disc. Then, check the brake fluid level in the reservoir. If necessary, add new DOT 4 brake fluid (Chapter Three).

WARNING
Do not ride the motorcycle until both brakes and the rear brake light work properly.

16. While riding in a safe area, break in the pads gradually following the part manufacturer's instructions. Immediate hard application glazes the new pads and reduces their effectiveness.

ABS models

Refer to **Figure 14** and **Figure 15**.
1. Read *Brake Service* in this chapter.

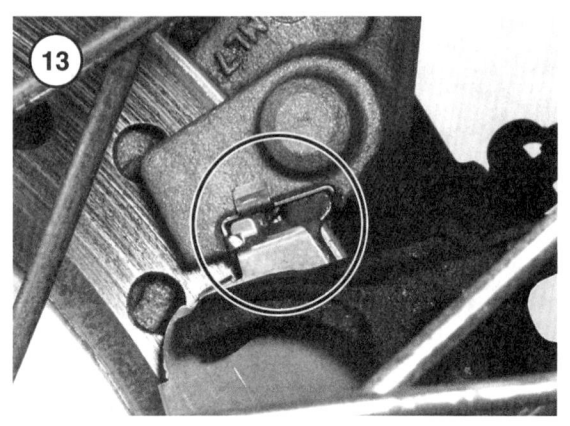

NOTE
*Before repositioning the caliper pistons, visually check the exposed parts of the caliper pistons. If the pistons are contaminated, pitted or have a rough appearance, remove the brake caliper (do not disconnect the brake hose) and clean the pistons with a soft brush and cleaner that will not damage or swell the caliper seals. At the same time, clean and relubricate the caliper and caliper bracket pin bolts and pin boots. Refer to **Front Brake Caliper** in this chapter.*

2. Remove the front master cylinder cover, diaphragm plate and diaphragm. Use a large syringe to remove and discard about 50 percent of the fluid from the reservoir. This prevents the master cylinder from overflowing when the caliper pistons are compressed for reinstallation. Do *not* drain the entire reservoir or air will enter the system. Reinstall the diaphragm, diaphragm plate and cover.

CAUTION
Do not allow the master cylinder reservoir to overflow when compressing the pistons. Brake fluid damages most surfaces it contacts.

BRAKES

FRONT BRAKE CALIPER (ABS MODELS)

1. Banjo bolt
2. Washer
3A. Brake hose
3B. Brake hose
4. Inner brake pad
5. Outer brake pad
6. Pad pin
7. O-ring
8. Housing
9. Clamp
10. Front speedsensor
11. Bolt
12. Bolt
13. Bolt
14. Bleed valve

FRONT BRAKE PADS (ABS MODELS)

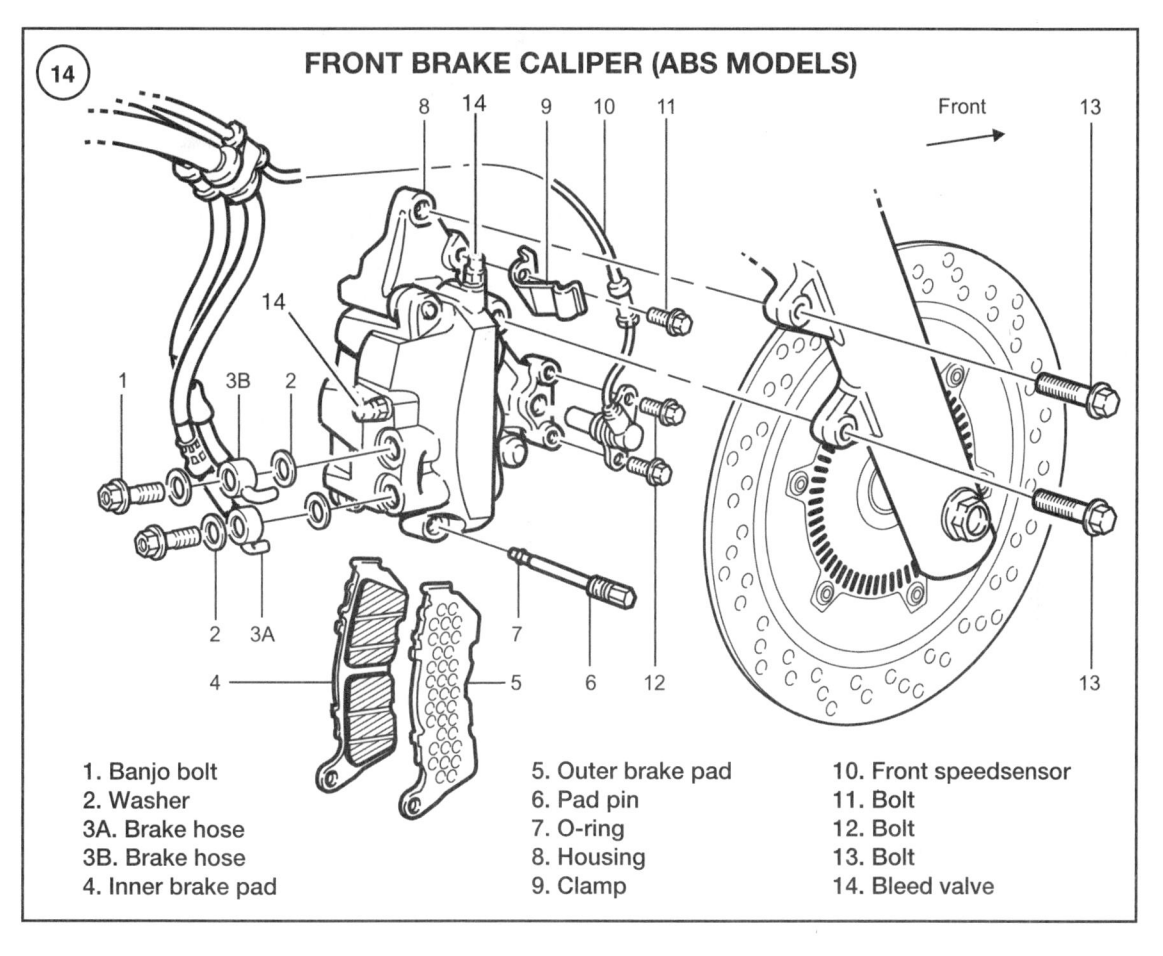

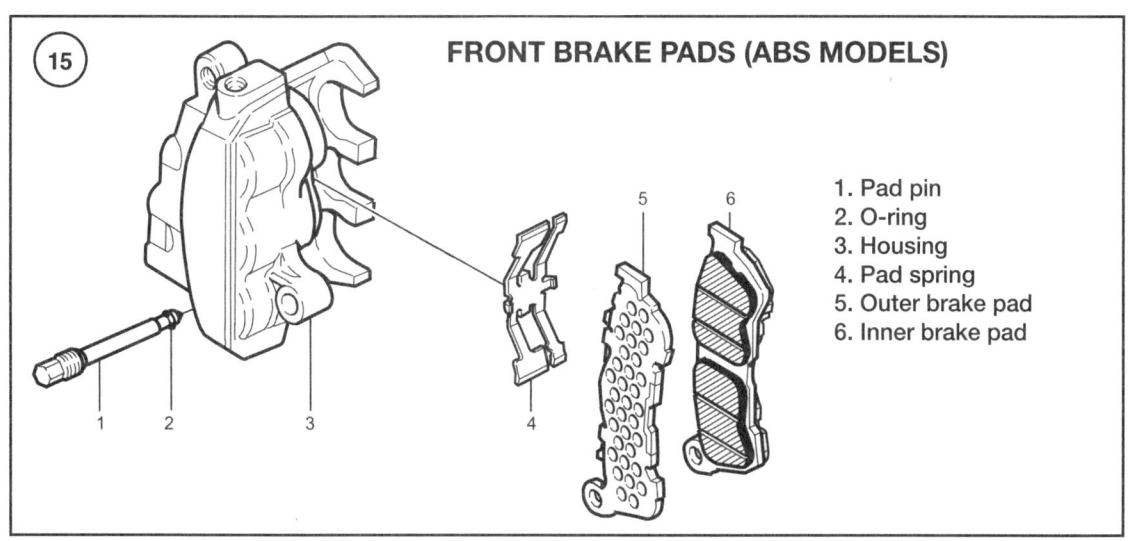

1. Pad pin
2. O-ring
3. Housing
4. Pad spring
5. Outer brake pad
6. Inner brake pad

3. Push against the side of the brake caliper so the brake pads push the caliper pistons into their bores to make room for the new brake pads. If the caliper pistons do not move properly, remove and service the caliper as described in this chapter.

4. Remove the pad pin and both brake pads.

5. Remove the pad spring **(Figure 15)** and clean it. Then inspect the pad spring for cracks and other damage and replace if necessary.

6. Inspect the O-ring on the end of the pad pin and replace if deteriorated or damaged.

7. Inspect the pad pin for excessive wear, corrosion or damage. Remove corrosion and dirt from the pad pin surface. A dirty or damaged pad pin prevents the

brake pads from sliding properly and results in brake drag and overheating of the brake disc.

8. Inspect the brake pads as follows:
   a. Inspect the friction material for light surface dirt, grease and oil contamination. Remove light contamination with sandpaper. If the contamination has penetrated the surface, replace the brake pads.

   NOTE
   Figure 10 *shows the brake pads and the wear limit grooves with the pads installed and seated against the brake disc.*

   b. Inspect the brake pads for excessive wear or damage. Replace the brake pads when the friction material is worn to the wear limit groove.
   c. Inspect the brake pads for uneven wear. If one pad has worn more than the other, it may be binding on its pad pin, on the pin bolt or the caliper is not sliding properly.
   d. Inspect the shim on the inner pad for corrosion, looseness and damage.

   NOTE
   If brake fluid is leaking from around the pistons, overhaul the brake caliper as described in this chapter.

9. Slide the caliper in and out of the caliper bracket, checking for excessive drag or to see if it is stuck. If the caliper does not move smoothly or the boots appear damaged, service the pin bolts and pin boots as described under *Front Brake Caliper* in this chapter.
10. Service the brake disc as follows:
    a. Use brake cleaner and a fine-grade emery cloth to remove road debris and brake pad residue from the brake disc. Clean both sides of the disc.

    NOTE
    Cleaning the brake disc is especially important if changing brake pad compounds. Many compounds are not compatible with each other.

    b. Check the brake disc for wear as described in this chapter.
11. Reinstall the pad spring (**Figure 15**), making sure it clamps firmly to the caliper housing.
12. Lubricate the O-ring on the pad pin with silicone brake grease.
13. Install the inner and outer brake pads into the caliper so the friction material on both brake pads faces toward the brake disc while inserting the extended arm on the upper end of each pad against the pad retainer in the caliper bracket.
14. Push both brake pads up against the pad spring and install the pad pin through the brake caliper and brake pads and tighten to 18 N.m (13 ft.-lb.).
15. Operate the front brake lever to seat the pads against the disc, then check the brake fluid level in the reservoir. If necessary, add new DOT 4 brake fluid. See Chapter Three.

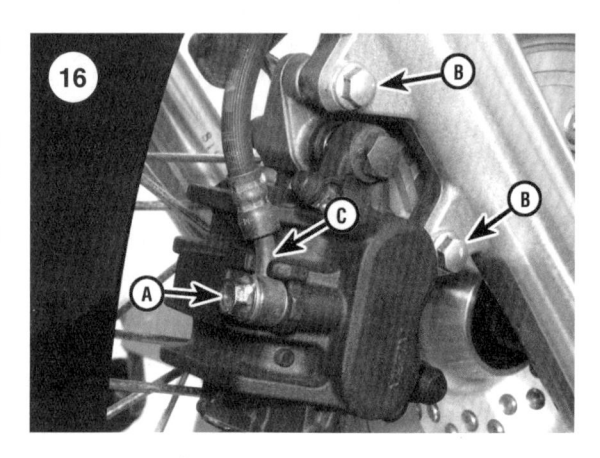

WARNING
Do not ride the motorcycle until both brakes and the rear brake light work properly.

16. While riding in a safe area, break in the pads gradually following the part manufacturer's instructions. Immediate hard application glazes the new pads and reduces their effectiveness.

FRONT BRAKE CALIPER

Read *Brake Service* in this chapter.

Removal/Installation

Non-ABS models

1. Support the motorcycle on its sidestand and turn the front wheel to access the caliper.
2. If the caliper is going to be removed from the motorcycle:
   a. Remove the brake pads as described in this chapter.
   b. Drain the brake fluid as described in this chapter.
   c. Remove the brake hose banjo bolt and washers at the caliper (A, **Figure 16**).
   d. Place the loose end of the brake hose in a plastic bag to prevent brake fluid from leaking onto the wheel or fork.
3. Remove the brake caliper mounting bolts (B, **Figure 16**) and remove the brake caliper.

BRAKES

NOTE
A spacer block prevents the pistons from being forced out of the caliper if the front brake lever is applied while the brake caliper is removed from the brake disc.

4. If the brake hose was not disconnected at the caliper, insert a spacer block between the brake pads and support the caliper with a wire hook.
5. If necessary lubricate and service the pin bolts and boots as described in this section.
6. If necessary, service the brake caliper as described in this chapter.
7. Installation is the reverse of these steps. Note the following:

NOTE
If reusing the original brake caliper mounting bolts, remove all threadlock residue from the bolt threads and reinstall with a medium strength threadlock applied to the bolt threads. The threads on new bolts have threadlock preapplied.

   a. Install the caliper assembly over the brake disc. If the pads are installed in the caliper, be careful not to damage their leading edge. Install two new brake caliper mounting bolts (B, **Figure 16**) and tighten to 30 N.m (22 ft.-lb.).
   b. Place a new sealing washer on each side of the brake hose. Position the hose (C, **Figure 16**) against the stopper on the caliper and tighten the banjo bolt (A, **Figure 16**) to 34 N.m (25 ft.-lb.).
   c. If removed, install the brake pads as described in this chapter.
   d. Bleed the front brake line (this chapter). Tighten the bleed valve to the specification in **Table 4**.
   e. Remove the spacer, then operate the front brake lever to seat the pads against the brake disc.

ABS models

1. Support the motorcycle on its sidestand and turn the front wheel to access the caliper.
2. Remove the front wheel speed sensor (10, **Figure 14**) as described in Chapter Sixteen.
3. If the caliper is going to be removed from the motorcycle:
   a. Remove the brake pads as described in this chapter.
   b. Drain the brake fluid as described in this chapter.

NOTE
Identify and label the individual brake hoses at the caliper before disconnecting them so they can be installed in their original positions.

   c. Remove the brake hose banjo bolts (A, **Figure 16**) and washers at the caliper.
   d. Place the loose end of each brake hose in a plastic bag to prevent brake fluid from leaking onto the wheel or fork.
4. Remove the brake caliper mounting bolts (B, **Figure 16**) and remove the brake caliper.

NOTE
The spacer block prevents the pistons from being forced out of the caliper if the front brake lever and/or the rear brake pedal are applied while the front brake caliper is removed from the brake disc.

5. If the brake hoses were not disconnected at the caliper, insert a spacer block between the brake pads and support the caliper with a wire hook.
6. If necessary lubricate and service the pin bolts and boots as described in this section.
7. If necessary, service the brake caliper as described in this chapter.
8. Installation is the reverse of these steps. Note the following:

NOTE
If reusing the original brake caliper mounting bolts, remove all threadlock residue from the bolt threads and reinstall with a medium strength threadlock applied to the bolt threads. The threads on new bolts have a threadlock preapplied.

   a. Install the caliper assembly over the brake disc. If the pads are installed in the caliper, be careful not to damage their leading edge. Install two new brake caliper mounting bolts (B, **Figure 16**) and tighten to 30 N.m (22 ft.-lb.).
   b. Place a new sealing washer on each side of both brake hoses. Position the stopper arms on the hoses against the caliper in their orginal locations. Refer to the identification marks made on the brake hoses during removal to make sure they are installed in their correct position. Tighten the banjo bolts to 34 N.m (25 ft.-lb.).
   c. If removed, install the brake pads as described in this chapter.
   d. Bleed the front and rear brake lines (this chapter). Tighten the bleed valve to the specification in **Table 4**.

FRONT BRAKE CALIPER (NON_ABS MODELS)

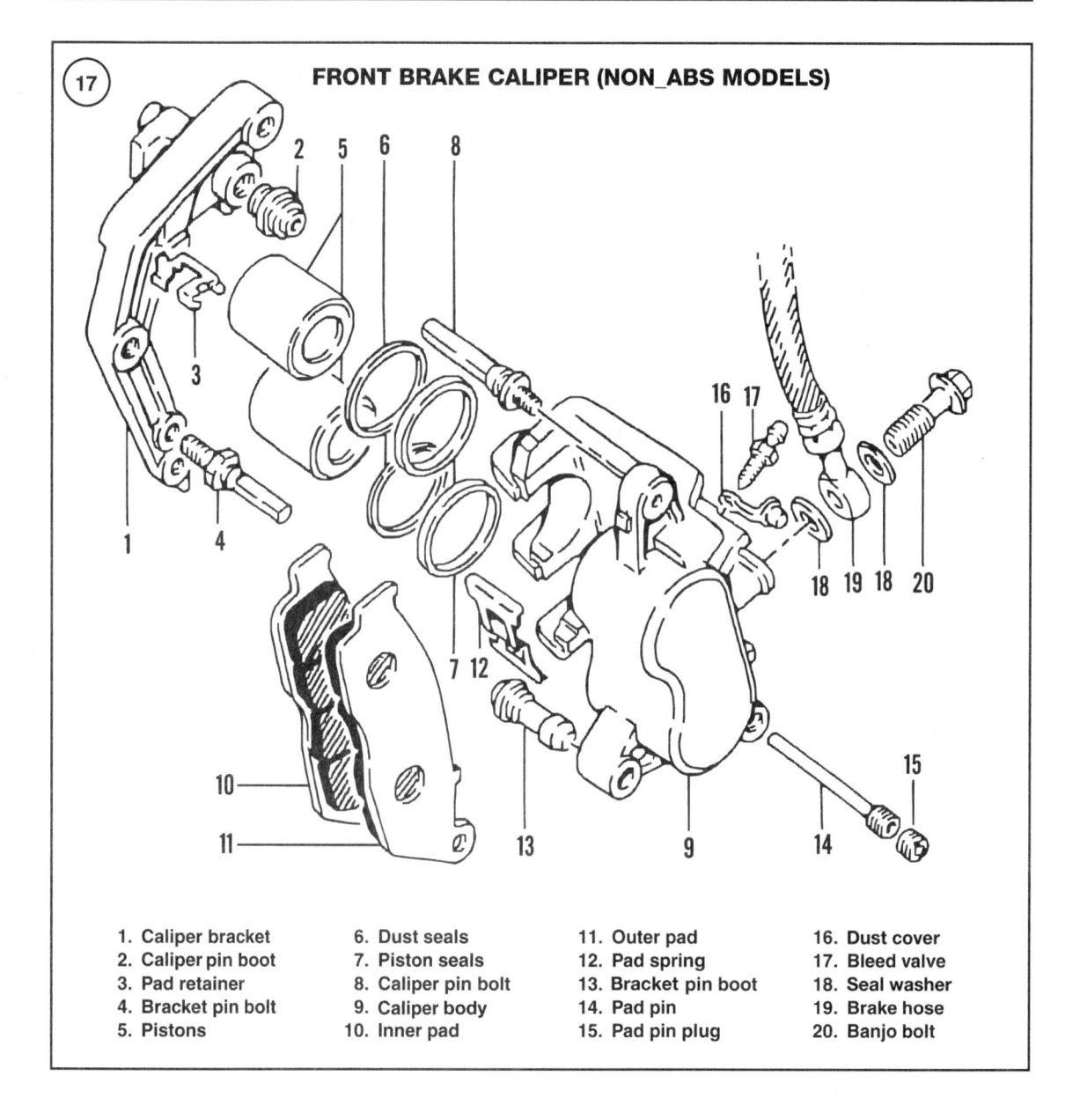

1. Caliper bracket
2. Caliper pin boot
3. Pad retainer
4. Bracket pin bolt
5. Pistons
6. Dust seals
7. Piston seals
8. Caliper pin bolt
9. Caliper body
10. Inner pad
11. Outer pad
12. Pad spring
13. Bracket pin boot
14. Pad pin
15. Pad pin plug
16. Dust cover
17. Bleed valve
18. Seal washer
19. Brake hose
20. Banjo bolt

e. Remove the spacer, then operate the front brake lever to seat the pads against the brake disc.
f. Install the front wheel speed sensor as described in Chapter Sixteen.
g. Measure the front wheel speed sensor air gap as described in Chapter Sixteen.

Caliper Bracket, Pin Bolts and Boots Inspection/Removal/Installation/Lubrication

The brake calipers are a floating design. Pin bolts mounted on the caliper housing and caliper bracket allow the brake caliper to slide or float during piston movement. The pin boots installed over each pin bolt prevent dirt from entering and causing pin bolt wear. A grooved or damaged pin bolt may prevent caliper movement. If a caliper is not free to float, it causes the brake pads to drag on the brake disc. This will cause unnecessary pad wear and may overheat the disc and brake fluid.

The pin bolts and boots can be serviced with the brake caliper mounted on the motorcycle.

Refer to **Figure 17** (non-ABS models) or **Figure 18** (ABS models).

NOTE
*The photographs in this section show the service performed on a non-ABS brake caliper. Procedures required for the ABS brake caliper are the same. Refer to **Figure 18** for parts alignment on the ABS brake caliper.*

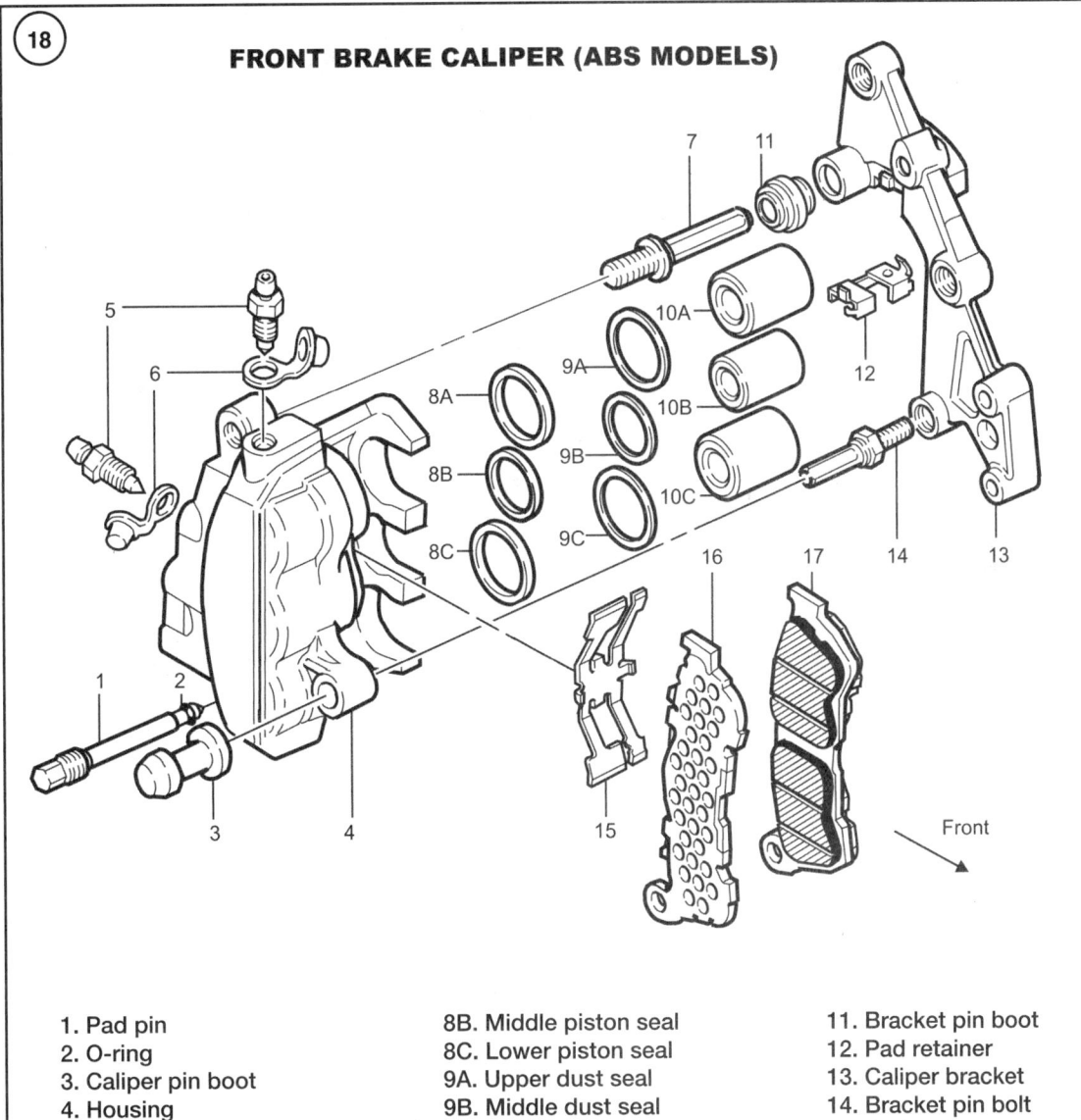

BRAKES

FRONT BRAKE CALIPER (ABS MODELS)

1. Pad pin
2. O-ring
3. Caliper pin boot
4. Housing
5. Bleed valve
6. Cover
7. Caliper pin bolt
8A. Upper piston seal
8B. Middle piston seal
8C. Lower piston seal
9A. Upper dust seal
9B. Middle dust seal
9C. Lower dust seal
10A. Upper piston
10B. Middle piston
10C. Lower piston
11. Bracket pin boot
12. Pad retainer
13. Caliper bracket
14. Bracket pin bolt
15. Pad spring
16. Outer pad
17. Inner pad

1. On ABS models, remove the front wheel speed sensor (Chapter Sixteen).
2. Remove the brake pads as described in this chapter.
3. Remove the brake caliper as described in this section. Do not disconnect the brake hose(s) unless necessary.
4. Slide the caliper bracket (**Figure 19**) out of the caliper.
5. Pinch the bracket pin boot (A, **Figure 20**) on its open side and remove it from the opposite side of the caliper.

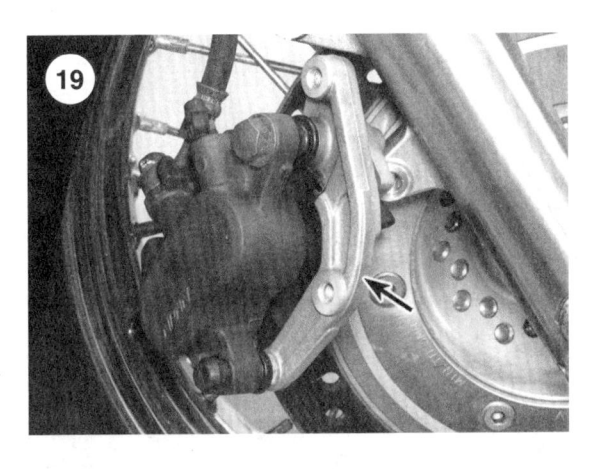

6. Remove the pad retainer (A, **Figure 21**).
7. Remove the caliper pin boot (B, **Figure 21**).
8. Inspect the pin boots and pin bolts as follows:
    a. Inspect the pin boots for age deterioration and other damage.
    b. Inspect the caliper pin bolt (B, **Figure 20**) and bracket pin bolt (C, **Figure 21**) for excessive wear, uneven wear and other damage. Replace damaged pin bolts as described in this section.
9. When reinstalling or replacing a damaged pin bolt, apply a medium strength threadlock onto the bolt threads and tighten to the torque specification in **Table 4**.
10. Inspect the pad retainer (A, **Figure 21**) mounted on the caliper bracket and replace if damaged. Apply HondaBond HT (or an equivalent silicone sealer that will not corrode aluminum) onto the retainer and install it on the caliper bracket.
11. Installation is the reverse of these steps, plus the following:
    a. Partially pack the pin boots with silicone brake grease and install the boots facing in their original direction. (Non-ABS: A, **Figure 20** and B, **Figure 21**).
    b. Lightly lubricate the pin bolt shoulders (B, **Figure 20** and C, **Figure 21**) with silicone brake grease.

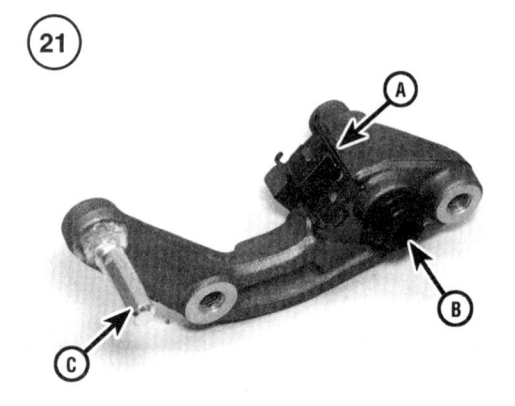

Disassembly

1. Remove the brake pads and brake caliper as described in this chapter.
2. Remove the caliper bracket as described in this section.
3. Remove the pin boot (A, **Figure 20**) from the caliper as described in this section.
4. Close the bleed valve(s) so air cannot escape.

WARNING
Wear eye protection when using compressed air to remove the pistons and keep your fingers away from the pistons.

CAUTION
Do not pry the piston(s) out. This may damage the piston and caliper bore.

NOTE
*On ABS calipers, three different size pistons and seal seats are used (**Figure 18**). Identify the parts during removal to help identify the new parts during assembly.*

5. Cushion the caliper pistons with a shop rag and position the caliper with the piston bores facing down. Be sure to keep hands away from the pistons. Apply compressed air through the brake hose port **(Figure 22)** to pop the pistons out. If only one piston came out, block the bore opening with a piece of thick rubber (old inner tube), wooden block and clamp (**Figure 23**). Position the caliper with the piston facing down and apply compressed air again and remove the remaining piston(s).

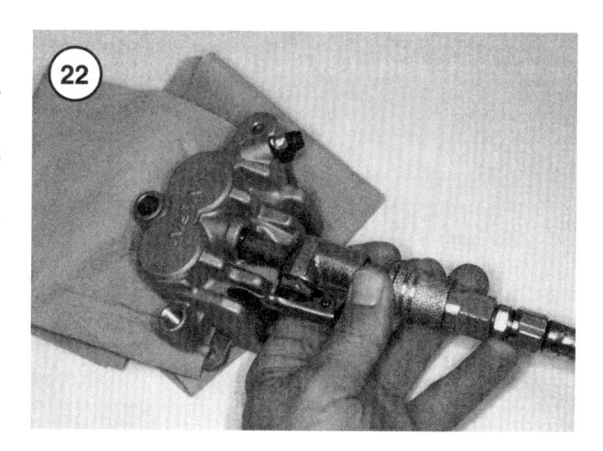

CAUTION
Do not damage the caliper bore grooves when removing the seals.

BRAKES

per. Finger-tighten the bleed valve.
2. Soak the new piston seals and dust seals in fresh brake fluid.
3. Lubricate the pistons with fresh brake fluid.

NOTE
The piston seals are thicker than the dust seals.

NOTE
*On ABS calipers, there are three different size piston and seal sets. The brake caliper bore inside diameter measurements (**Table 1**) can be used to identify the different bore sizes. Make sure to install the parts in their correct position.*

4. Install new piston seals (B, **Figure 24** or **Figure 25**) into the cylinder bore's rear grooves.
5. Install new dust seals (A, **Figure 24** or **Figure 25**) into the cylinder bore's front groove.

NOTE
Check that each seal fits squarely in its groove.

6. Install the pistons into the caliper bores with their open side facing out (**Figure 25**). To prevent the pistons from damaging the seals, turn them into the bore by hand until they bottom.
7. Lubricate and install the pin boot into the caliper as described in this section.
8. If necessary, service the caliper bracket as described in this section.
9. Install the caliper bracket as described in this section.
10. Install the brake caliper and brake pads as described in this chapter.
11. Bleed the front (non-ABS models) or front and rear (ABS models) brake line(s). Tighten the bleed valve to the specification in **Table 4**.

Inspection

Refer to the specifications in **Table 1**. Replace worn or damaged parts as described in this section.

WARNING
Do not get oil or grease onto any of the brake caliper components. These chemicals cause the rubber parts in the brake system to swell, permanently damaging them and leading to possible brake system failure.

1. Clean and dry the caliper assembly as follows:

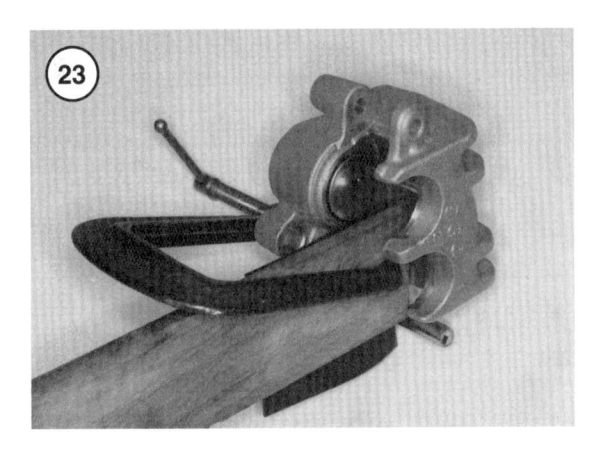

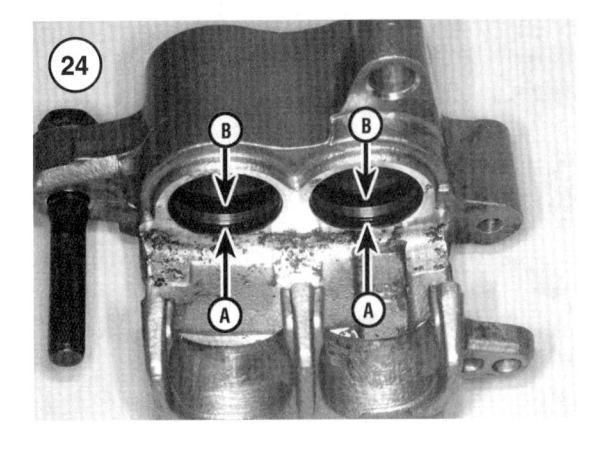

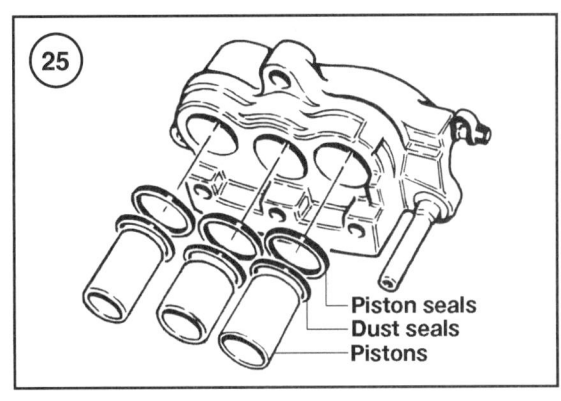

6. Carefully remove the dust seals (A, **Figure 24** or **Figure 25**) and piston seals (B, **Figure 24** or **Figure 25**) from the caliper bore grooves and discard them.
7. Remove the bleed valve(s) and cover(s) from the caliper.
8. Clean and inspect the brake caliper assembly as described in this section.

Assembly

Use new DOT 4 brake fluid when lubricating the parts in the following steps.
1. Install the bleed valve(s) and cover(s) into the cali-

a. Handle the brake components carefully when servicing them.
b. Use only DOT 4 brake fluid or isopropyl alcohol to wash rubber parts in the brake system.
c. Clean the dust and piston seal grooves carefully to prevent from damaging the caliper bore. Use a small pick or brush to clean the grooves. If a hard varnish residue has built up in the grooves, soak the caliper housing in solvent to help soften the residue. Then wash the caliper in soapy water and rinse completely.
d. If alcohol or solvent was used to clean the caliper, blow dry with compressed air.
e. Check the fluid passages to make sure they are clean and dry.
f. After cleaning the parts, place them on a clean lint-free cloth until reassembly.

2. Check each cylinder bore for corrosion, deep scratches and other wear marks. Do not hone the cylinder bores.
3. Measure each caliper cylinder bore inside diameter with a bore gauge or use a telescoping gauge and micrometer.
4. Inspect the pistons for pitting, corrosion, cracks or other damage.
5. Measure each caliper piston outside diameter with a micrometer.
6. Clean the bleed valve with compressed air. Check the valve threads for damage. Replace the cover if missing or damaged.
7. Clean the banjo bolt with compressed air.
8. Inspect and service the caliper bracket, pin boots and pin bolts as described in this section.

FRONT MASTER CYLINDER

Read the information listed under *Brake Service* in this chapter before servicing the front master cylinder.

Removal/Installation

1. Remove the rear view mirror from the master cylinder.

CAUTION
Wash brake fluid off any surface immediately, as it damages the finish. Use soapy water and rinse completely.

2. Cover the fuel tank and front fender to prevent damage from brake fluid contact.
3. Clean the top of the master cylinder of all dirt and debris.
4. Turn the handlebar so that the master cylinder reservoir is level. Remove the cover, diaphragm plate and diaphragm. 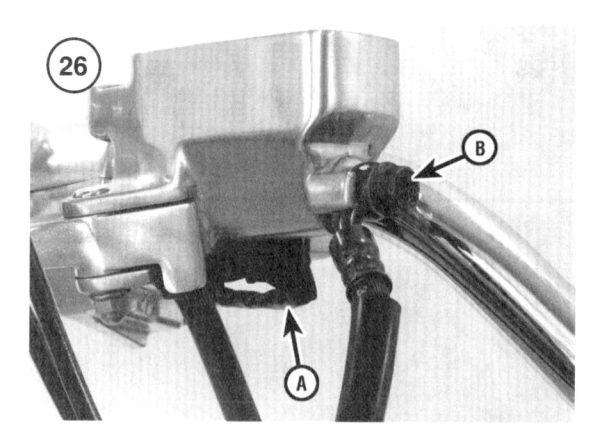 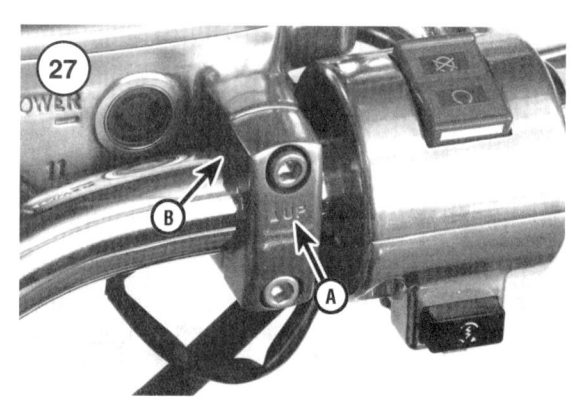
5. Drain the brake system (this chapter). Then, remove any remaining brake fluid from the reservoir with a syringe. Reinstall the parts.
6. Disconnect the brake light switch connectors (A, **Figure 26**) at the switch.
7. Remove the banjo bolt (B, **Figure 26**) and two washers securing the brake hose to the master cylinder. Cover the open end of the hose with a plastic bag to prevent leakage and hose contamination.
8. Remove the bolts and clamp (A, **Figure 27**) securing the master cylinder to the handlebar and remove the master cylinder.
9. If necessary, service the master cylinder as described in this chapter.
10. Clean the handlebar, master cylinder and clamp mating surfaces.
11. Installation is the reverse of removal. Note the following:
    a. Mount the master cylinder onto the handlebar and align the upper master cylinder and clamp mating surfaces with the punch mark on the handlebar (B, **Figure 27**).
    b. Install the clamp with its UP mark (A, **Figure 27**) facing up and secure with the mounting bolts. Tighten the upper, then the lower master cylinder mounting bolt to 12 N.m (106 in.-lb.). Make sure that there is a gap at the bottom of the clamp.

BRAKES

FRONT MASTER CYLINDER

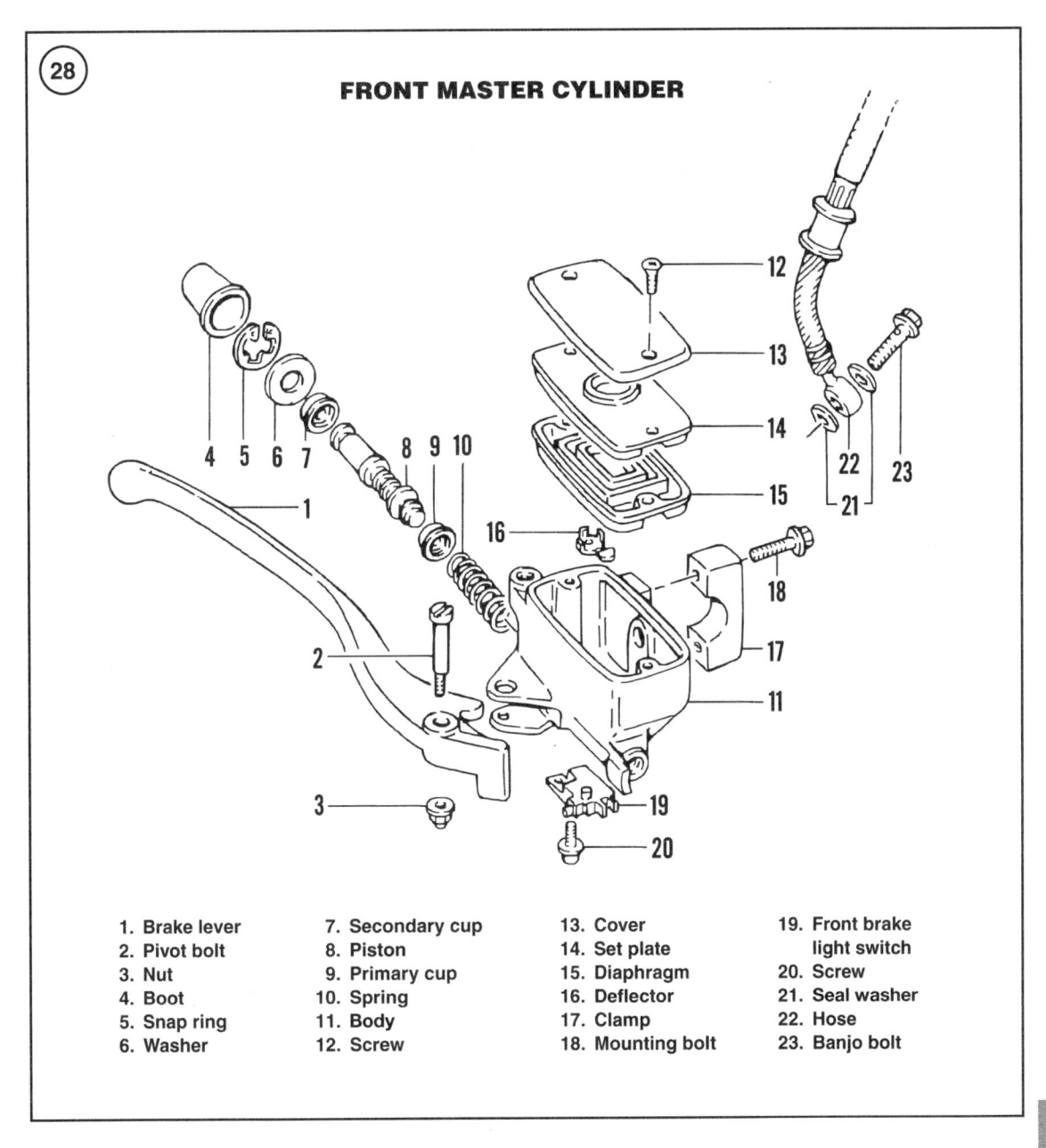

Figure 28

1. Brake lever
2. Pivot bolt
3. Nut
4. Boot
5. Snap ring
6. Washer
7. Secondary cup
8. Piston
9. Primary cup
10. Spring
11. Body
12. Screw
13. Cover
14. Set plate
15. Diaphragm
16. Deflector
17. Clamp
18. Mounting bolt
19. Front brake light switch
20. Screw
21. Seal washer
22. Hose
23. Banjo bolt

c. Install a *new* washer on each side of the brake hose. Secure the brake hose to the master cylinder with the banjo bolt (B, **Figure 26**) and two *new* washers. Position the brake hose arm against the master cylinder bracket and tighten the banjo bolt to 34 N.m (25 ft.-lb.).

d. Reconnect the front brake light switch connectors (A, **Figure 26**) at the switch.

e. On non-ABS models, bleed the front brake as described in this chapter.

f. On ABS models, bleed the front and rear brake lines as described in this chapter.

g. Tighten the master cylinder cover screw to the specification in **Table 4**.

h. Apply and hold the front brake lever. Then check the banjo bolt and the piston bore area in the front of the master cylinder for leaks.

i. Turn the ignition switch on and apply the front brake lever. Make sure the brake light turns on when operating the front brake lever and turns off when the brake lever is released.

Disassembly

Refer to **Figure 28**.

1. Remove the front master cylinder (this chapter).
2. If not already removed, remove the cover, diaphragm plate and diaphragm.

CHAPTER FIFTEEN

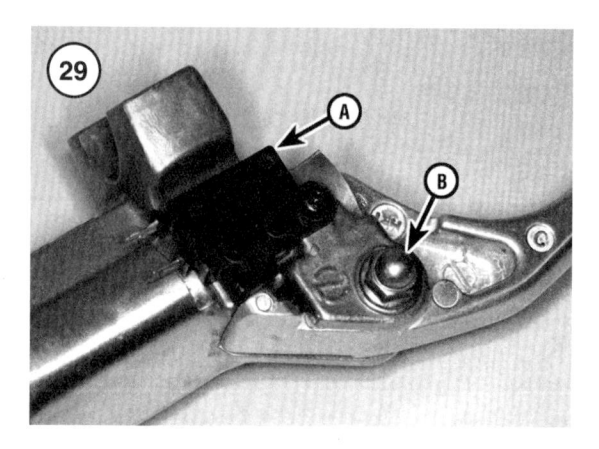

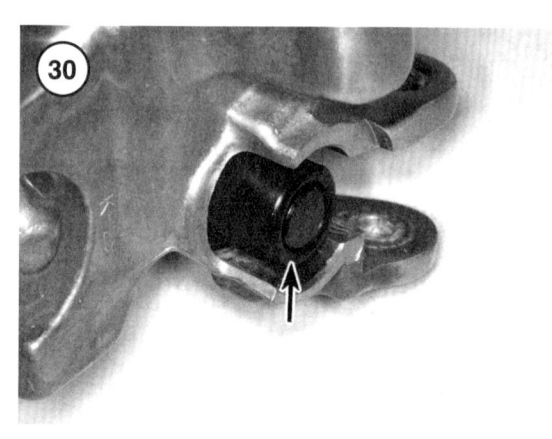

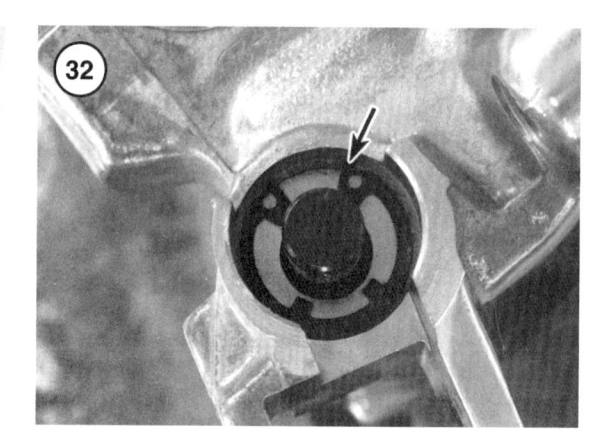

3. Remove the screw and the brake light switch (A, **Figure 29**).
4. Remove the nut (B, **Figure 29**), pivot bolt and front brake lever.
5. Remove the boot **(Figure 30)** from the groove in the end of the piston.

> *NOTE*
> *If brake fluid is leaking from the piston bore, the piston cups are worn or damaged. Replace the piston assembly.*

> *NOTE*
> *To aid in the removal and installation of the master cylinder snap ring, thread a bolt and nut into the brake hose port, and secure the bolt in a vise (**Figure 31**). Tighten the nut against the master cylinder to prevent it from turning.*

6. Compress the piston and remove the snap ring **(Figure 32)** from the groove in the master cylinder.
7. Remove the piston assembly **(Figure 33)** from the master cylinder bore. Do not remove the primary and secondary cups from the piston.
8. Remove the deflector **(Figure 34)** from the reservoir.
9. Clean and inspect the master cylinder assembly as described in this section.

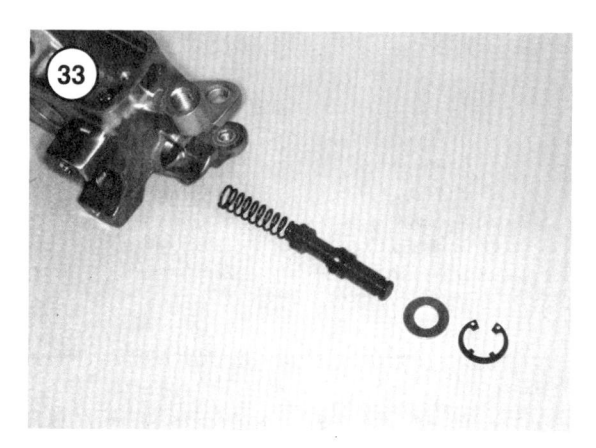

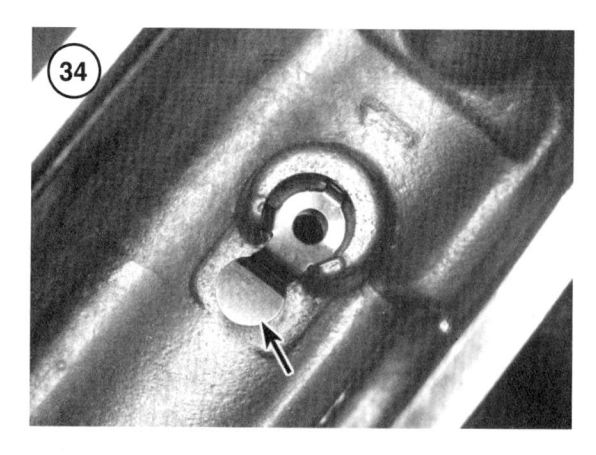

BRAKES

Assembly

1. If installing a new piston assembly, assemble it as described under *Inspection* in this section.
2. Lubricate the piston assembly and cylinder bore with DOT 4 brake fluid. Check that the surfaces are free of dust and other particles.

CAUTION
Do not allow the piston cups to tear or turn inside out when installing the piston into the master cylinder bore. Both cups are larger than the bore.

3. Insert the piston assembly with the spring end first, into the master cylinder bore (**Figure 33**).
4. Install the washer (**Figure 33**) and seat it against the piston.

CAUTION
The snap ring must seat in the master cylinder groove completely. Push and release the piston a few times to make sure it moves smoothly and that the snap ring does not pop out.

5. Secure the master cylinder in a vise as described during disassembly. Compress the piston assembly and install a new snap ring with its flat side facing out, into the bore groove (**Figure 32**).
6. Slide the boot over the piston. Seat the large end against the snap ring and the outer lip into the groove in the end of the piston (**Figure 30**).
7. Install the brake lever assembly as follows:
   a. Lubricate the pivot bolt with silicone brake grease.
   b. Install the brake lever.

NOTE
The piston assembly must operate smoothly when pumping the brake lever. If there is any roughness or a change in operation, the snap ring may have popped out of its groove. Remove the brake lever and check the piston and snap ring.

   c. Install and tighten the brake lever pivot bolt to 1 N.m (8.9 in.-lb.). Pump the brake lever to make sure it moves freely. If there is any binding or roughness, remove the pivot bolt and brake lever and inspect the parts.
   d. Hold the pivot bolt, then install and tighten the brake lever pivot bolt nut to 6 N.m (53 in.-lb.). Check that the brake lever moves freely.

NOTE
The deflector prevents brake fluid from spurting out the top of the reservoir when operating the brake lever during brake bleeding.

8. Seat the deflector (**Figure 34**) firmly into the reservoir.
9. Install the front brake light switch (A, **Figure 29**) and secure with the mounting screw.
10. Install the diaphragm, diaphragm plate and cover. Tighten the cover screws to the specification in **Table 4**.
11. Install the master cylinder as described in this section.

Inspection

When measuring the master cylinder components, compare the results to the specifications in **Table 1**. Replace worn or damaged parts as described in this section.

1. Clean and dry the master cylinder assembly as follows:
   a. Handle the brake components carefully when servicing them.
   b. Use only DOT 4 brake fluid or isopropyl alcohol to wash rubber parts in the brake system. Never allow any petroleum-based cleaner to contact the rubber parts. These chemicals cause the rubber to swell, requiring their replacement.
   c. Clean the master cylinder snap ring groove carefully. Use a small pick or brush to clean the groove. If a hard varnish residue has built up in the groove, soak the master cylinder in solvent to help soften the residue. Then wash in soapy water and rinse completely.
   d. Blow the master cylinder dry with compressed air.
   e. Place cleaned parts on a clean lint-free cloth until reassembly.

WARNING
Do not get any oil or grease onto any of the components. These chemicals cause the rubber parts in the brake system to swell, permanently damaging them and leading to possible brake system failure.

CAUTION
Do not remove the primary and secondary cups from the piston assembly for cleaning or inspection purposes. The cups are not available separately and must be replaced with a new piston and spring as an assembly.

2. Check the piston assembly for the following defects:
   a. Broken, distorted or collapsed piston return spring (A, **Figure 35**).
   b. Worn, cracked, damaged or swollen primary (B, **Figure 35**) and secondary cups (C, **Figure 35**).
   c. Scratched or damaged piston (D, **Figure 35**).
   d. Worn or damaged boot **(Figure 30)**.
   e. If any of these parts are worn or damaged, replace the piston assembly.
3. Measure the piston outside diameter at the two points indicated in **Figure 36**.
4. To assemble a new piston assembly, perform the following:
   a. If replacing the piston, install the new primary and secondary cups onto the new piston. Use the original piston assembly **(Figure 33)** as a reference when installing the new cups onto the new piston.
   b. Before installing the new piston cups, lubricate them with brake fluid.
   c. Clean the new piston in brake fluid.
   d. Install the secondary cup (C, **Figure 35**), then the primary cup (B) onto the piston.
5. Inspect the master cylinder bore. Replace the master cylinder if its bore is corroded or damaged. Do not hone the master cylinder bore to remove scratches or other damage.
6. Measure the master cylinder bore (A, **Figure 37**) with a bore gauge or a telescoping gauge and a micrometer.
7. Inspect the threads in the master cylinder body. If damaged, clean with a suitable size metric tap or replace the master cylinder assembly.
8. Inspect the fluid viewing port (B, **Figure 37**) for cracks or signs of fluid leakage. If damage is noted, replace the master cylinder body.
9. Inspect the hand lever pivot hole (C, **Figure 37**) on the master cylinder body. Check for cracks or elongation. If damaged, replace the master cylinder body.
10. Check for plugged supply and relief ports **(Figure 38)** in the master cylinder. Clean with compressed air.
11. Check the brake lever assembly for the following defects:
   a. Damaged brake lever. Replace the brake lever if cracked or broken. Check the pivot hole for cracks and elongation.
   b. Scored or damaged pivot bolt.

REAR BRAKE PADS (ABS MODELS)

The pistons in the rear brake caliper are self-adjusting to compensate for brake pad wear. When

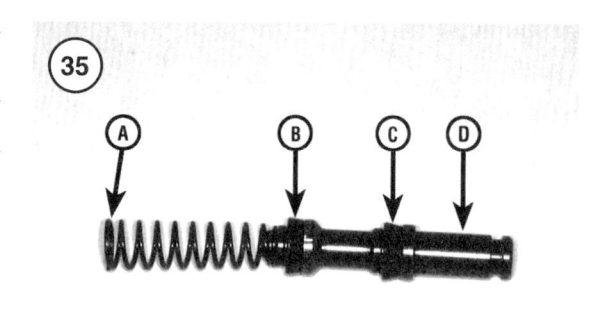

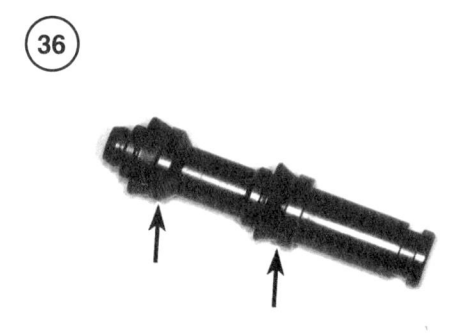

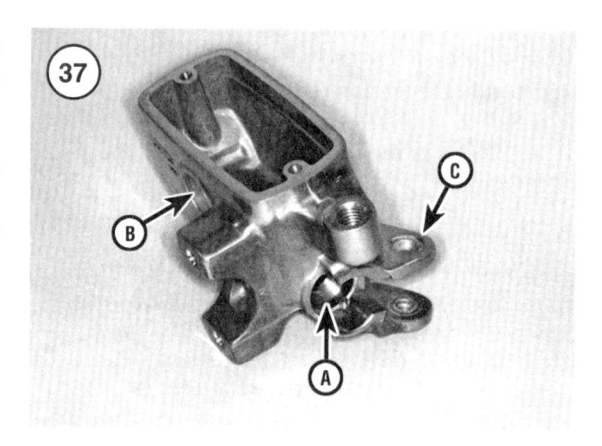

BRAKES

39 REAR BRAKE PADS (ABS MODELS)

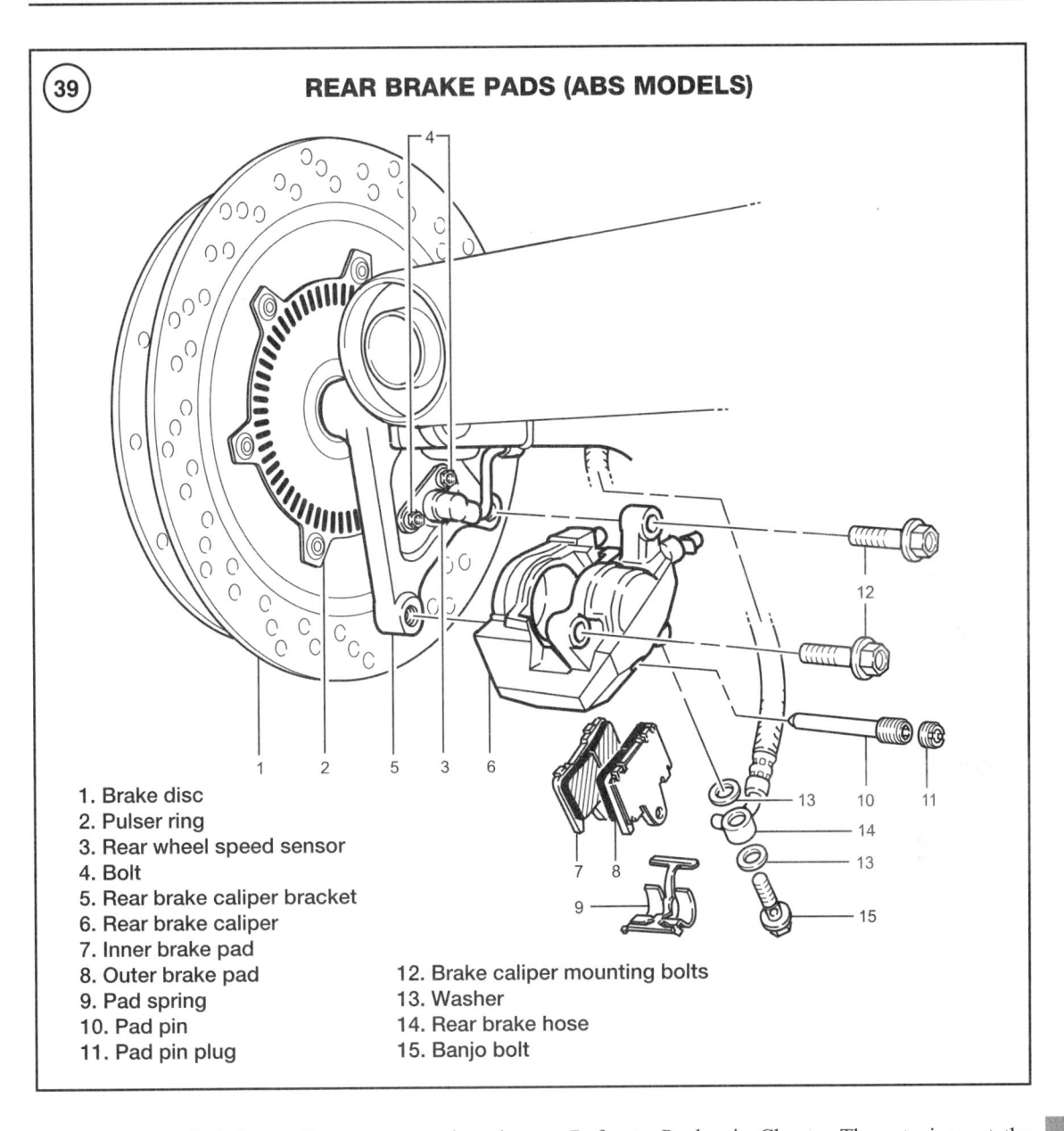

1. Brake disc
2. Pulser ring
3. Rear wheel speed sensor
4. Bolt
5. Rear brake caliper bracket
6. Rear brake caliper
7. Inner brake pad
8. Outer brake pad
9. Pad spring
10. Pad pin
11. Pad pin plug
12. Brake caliper mounting bolts
13. Washer
14. Rear brake hose
15. Banjo bolt

the brake is applied, hydraulic pressure against the pistons causes the piston seals to stretch and deflect slightly. This allows the pistons to move out where they contact the brake pads and then push them against the brake disc. When the brake is released, pressure against the piston seals is reduced and allows them to retract and return to their original shape. This action draws the pistons away from the brake pads and disengages the brake. As the brake pads wear, the pistons will travel farther through the seals in order to contact the brake pads. And as the pads wear and the pistons move farther outward, the brake fluid level drops.

There is no recommended mileage interval for changing the brake pads. Pad wear depends greatly on riding habits and the condition of the brake system.

Refer to *Brakes* in Chapter Three to inspect the brake pad wear.

A more thorough job of pad replacement is accomplished by cleaning the exposed parts of the pistons before they are pushed back into their bores, thus preventing dirt and debris that has hardened on the pistons from damaging the caliper seals.

Removal/Installation

Refer to **Figure 39**.
1. Read *Brake Service* in this chapter.
2. Remove the rear master cylinder cover and diaphragm. Use a large syringe to remove and discard about 50 percent of the fluid from the reservoir. This prevents the master cylinder from overflowing when

the caliper pistons are compressed for reinstallation. Do *not* drain the entire reservoir or air will enter the system. Reinstall the diaphragm and cover.

3. Remove the pad pin plug (A, **Figure 11**).
4. Loosen the pad pin.
5. Remove the rear brake caliper mounting bolts, and lower the brake caliper assembly away from the caliper bracket and brake disc.
6. Remove the pad pin and the pad spring.

CAUTION
Do not allow the master cylinder reservoir to overflow when compressing the pistons. Brake fluid damages most surfaces it contacts.

NOTE
Before repositioning the caliper pistons, visually check the exposed parts of the caliper pistons. If the pistons are contaminated, pitted or have a rough appearance, clean the pistons with a soft brush and cleaner that will not damage or swell the caliper seals.

7. Use a tire iron and pry against the brake pads to push the pistons into their bores to make room for the new pads. If the brake pads will be reused, protect their outer surfaces with a thick shop rag.
8. Remove the brake pads.
9. Clean the pad spring and inspect for cracks and other damage. Replace it if necessary.
10. Inspect the pad pin for excessive wear, corrosion or damage. Remove corrosion and dirt from the pad pin surface. A dirty or damaged pad pin prevents the brake pads from sliding properly and results in brake drag and overheating of the brake disc.
11. Inspect the brake pads as follows:
    a. Inspect the friction material for light surface dirt, grease and oil contamination. Remove light contamination with sandpaper. If the contamination has penetrated the surface, replace the brake pads.
    b. Inspect the brake pads for excessive wear or damage. Replace the brake pads when the friction material is worn to the wear limit groove. **Figure 40** shows the brake pads and wear limit grooves with the pads installed and seated against the brake disc.
    c. Inspect the brake pads for uneven wear. If one pad has worn more than the other, it may be binding on its pad pin or one of the caliper pistons is stuck.

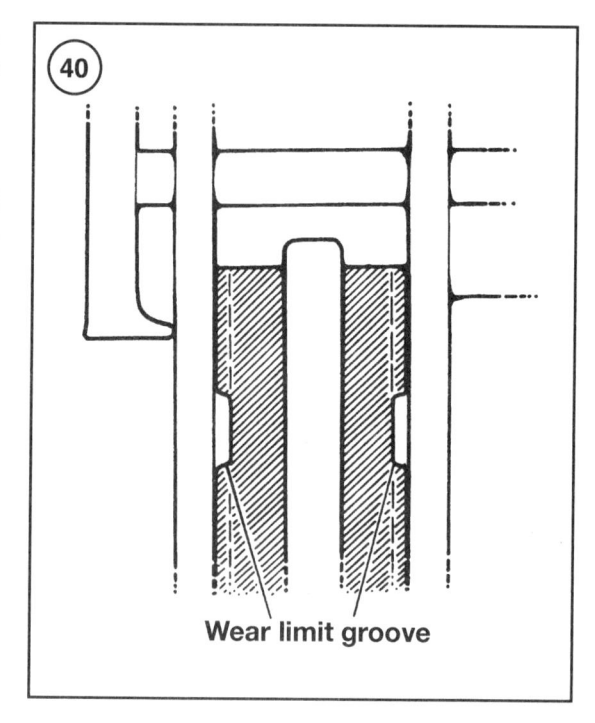

![40 — Wear limit groove]

NOTE
If brake fluid is leaking from around the pistons, overhaul the brake caliper (this chapter).

12. Service the brake disc as follows:
    a. Use brake cleaner and a fine-grade emery cloth to remove road debris and brake pad residue from the brake disc. Clean both sides of the disc.

NOTE
Cleaning the brake disc is especially important if changing brake pad compounds. Many compounds are not compatible with each other.

   b. Check the brake disc for wear as described in this chapter.
13. Install the brake pads into the caliper so the friction material on both brake pads faces toward the brake disc.
14. Install the pad spring into the caliper opening as shown in **Figure 41**.
15. Compress the pad spring lightly and install the pad pin through the brake pads and the pad spring. Tighten the pad pin hand-tight. The pad pin will be tightened to its final torque specification **(Table 4)** after the brake caliper is installed on the motorcycle.
16. Install the brake caliper over the brake disc so that the disc is centered between the pads. Install new brake caliper mounting bolts and tighten to 45 N.m (33 ft.-lb.).

BRAKES

(41) Front ↑

Banjo bolt — Rear brake caliper

Pad pin — Pad spring

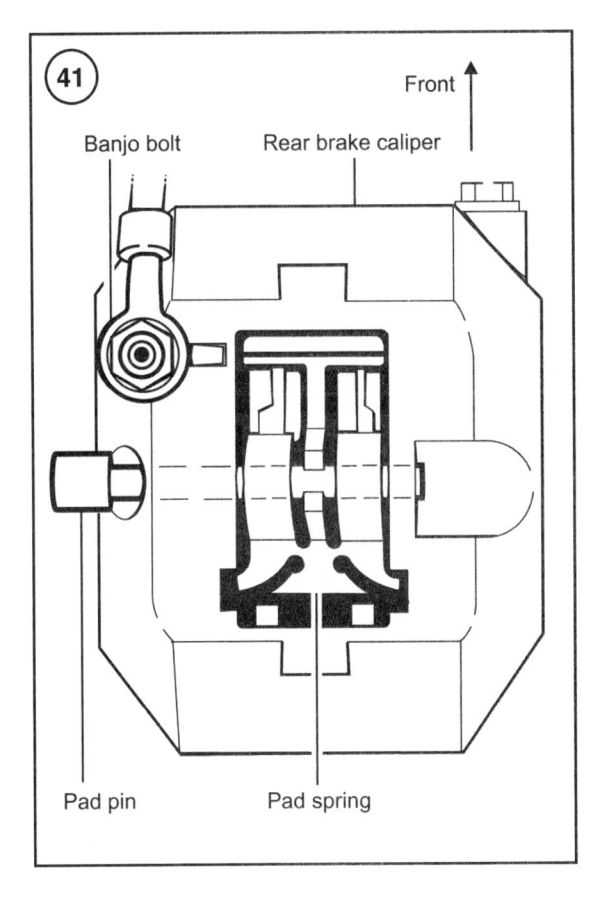

NOTE
If reusing the original brake caliper mounting bolts, remove all threadlock residue from the bolt threads and reinstall with a medium strength threadlock applied to the bolt threads. The threads on new bolts have a threadlock preapplied.

17. Tighten the pad pin (10, **Figure 39**) to 18 N.m (13 ft.-lb.).
18. Install and tighten the pad pin plug (11, **Figure 39**) to 2.5 N.m (22 in.-lb.).
19. Operate the front brake lever and the rear brake pedal to seat the pads against the disc, then check the brake fluid level in the reservoir. If necessary, add new DOT 4 brake fluid. See Chapter Three.

WARNING
Do not ride the motorcycle until both brakes and the rear brake light work properly.

20. While riding in a safe area, break in the pads gradually following the part manufacturer's instructions. Immediate, hard application glazes the new pads and reduces their effectiveness.

REAR BRAKE CALIPER (ABS MODELS)

Read *Brake Service* in this chapter.

Removal/Installation

1. Support the motorcycle on its sidestand.
2. Remove the rear wheel speed sensor (3, **Figure 39**) as described in Chapter Sixteen.

NOTE
When it is necessary to remove the brake caliper from the motorcycle, drain the brake fluid and disconnect the brake hose.

3. If necessary, drain the brake fluid as described in this chapter.
4. If necessary, remove the brake hose banjo bolt and washers at the caliper. Place the brake hose in a plastic bag to prevent brake fluid from leaking onto the wheel.
5. Remove the brake caliper mounting bolts and remove the brake caliper.
6. If the brake hose was not disconnected at the caliper, insert a spacer block between the brake pads and support the caliper with a wire hook.

NOTE
A spacer block prevents the pistons from being forced out of the caliper if the rear brake is applied while the brake caliper is removed from the brake disc.

7. If necessary, service the brake caliper as described in this chapter.
8. Installation is the reverse of these steps. Note the following:

NOTE
If reusing the original brake caliper mounting bolts, remove all threadlock residue from the bolt threads and reinstall with a medium strength threadlock applied to the bolt threads. The threads on new bolts have a threadlock preapplied.

a. Install the caliper assembly over the brake disc. If the pads are installed in the caliper, be careful not to damage their leading edge. Install two new brake caliper mounting bolts (12, **Figure 39**) and tighten to 45 N.m (33 ft.-lb.).
b. Place a new seal washer on each side of the brake hose. Position the stopper arm on the hoses against the caliper and install the banjo

REAR BRAKE CALIPER (ABS MODELS)

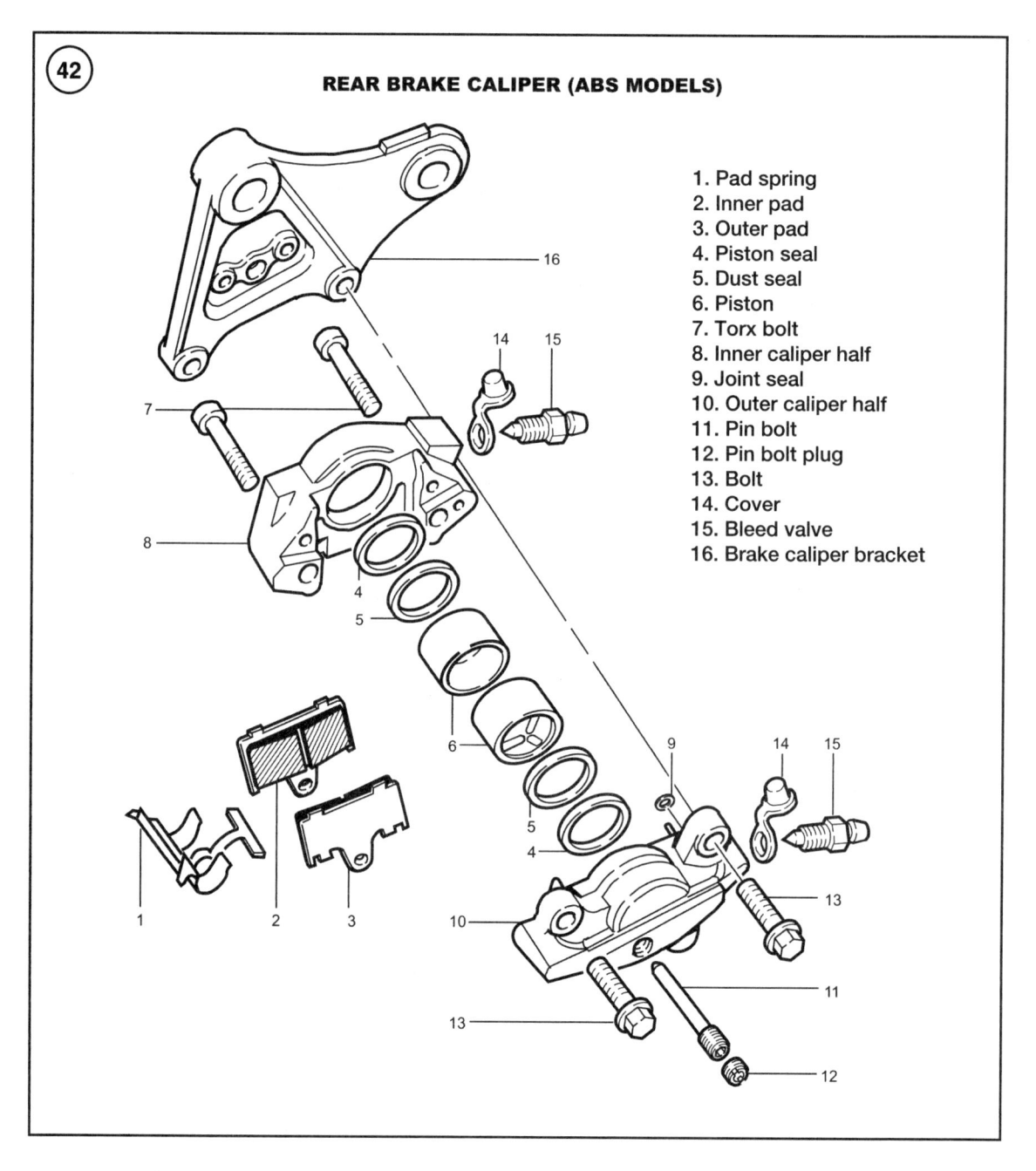

1. Pad spring
2. Inner pad
3. Outer pad
4. Piston seal
5. Dust seal
6. Piston
7. Torx bolt
8. Inner caliper half
9. Joint seal
10. Outer caliper half
11. Pin bolt
12. Pin bolt plug
13. Bolt
14. Cover
15. Bleed valve
16. Brake caliper bracket

bolt. Tighten the banjo bolt to 34 N.m (25 ft.-lb.).

c. If removed, install the brake pads as described in this chapter.
d. Bleed the front and rear brake lines as described in this chapter. Tighten the bleed valve to the specification in **Table 4**.
e. Remove the spacer, then operate the rear brake pedal and front brake lever to seat the pads against the brake disc.
f. Install the rear wheel speed sensor as described in Chapter Sixteen.
g. Measure the rear wheel speed sensor air gap as described in Chapter Sixteen.

Disassembly

Refer to **Figure 42**.

1. Remove the brake pads and brake caliper as described in this chapter.

NOTE
Make sure a new joint seal is available before separating the caliper halves.

2. Support the caliper assembly and remove the two Torx bolts.

3. Separate the caliper halves and remove the joint seal from between the two halves.

BRAKES

WARNING
Wear eye protection when using compressed air to remove the pistons and keep your fingers away from the pistons.

CAUTION
Do not pry the piston(s) out. This may damage the piston and caliper bore.

NOTE
Identify the pistons so they can be reinstalled in their original caliper half.

4A. Remove the piston from the outer caliper half as follows:
   a. Place the outer caliper half on a rubber mat to block off the exposed brake fluid port. The piston must be facing down.
   b. Close the bleed valve so air cannot escape.
   c. Be sure to keep hands away from the piston and apply compressed air through the brake hose port to pop the piston out.

4B. Remove the piston from the inner caliper half (8, **Figure 42**) as follows:
   a. Remove the bleed valve.
   b. Support the inner caliper half on a rubber mat to block off the exposed brake fluid port. The piston must be facing down.
   c. Be sure to keep hands away from the piston and apply compressed air through the bleed valve port to pop the piston out.

CAUTION
Do not damage the caliper bore grooves when removing the seals.

5. Remove the dust seals and piston seals from the caliper bore grooves and discard them.
6. Remove the bleed valve and cover from the outer caliper.
7. Clean and inspect the brake caliper assembly as described in this section.

Assembly

Use new DOT 4 brake fluid when lubricating the parts in the following steps.
1. Install a bleed valve and cover into each brake caliper half and tighten finger-tight.
2. Soak the new piston seals and dust seals in brake fluid.
3. Lubricate one of the pistons with brake fluid.

NOTE
The piston seals are thicker than the dust seals.

4. Install a new piston seal into the cylinder bore's rear groove.
5. Install a new dust seals into the cylinder bore's front groove.

NOTE
Check that each seal fits squarely in its groove.

6. Install the piston into the caliper bore with its open side facing out. To prevent the piston from damaging the seals, turn it into the bore by hand until it bottoms.
7. Repeat the process to install the piston and seals.
8. Lubricate a new joint seal with DOT 4 brake fluid and place into the counterbore in the brake caliper half.
9. Assemble the brake caliper halves together, making sure the joint seal did not fall out or become pinched. Hold the caliper halves together, then install the Torx bolts (7, **Figure 42**) and tighten securely.

Inspection

When measuring the brake caliper components, compare the results to the specifications in **Table 2**. Replace worn or damaged parts as described in this section.

1. Clean and dry the caliper assembly as follows:
   a. Handle the brake components carefully when servicing them.

CAUTION
Do not get oil or grease onto any of the brake caliper components. These chemicals cause the rubber parts in the brake system to swell, permanently damaging them.

   b. Use only DOT 4 brake fluid or isopropyl alcohol to wash rubber parts in the brake system. Never allow any petroleum-based cleaner to contact the rubber parts. These chemicals cause the rubber to swell, requiring their replacement.
   c. Clean the dust and piston seal grooves carefully to prevent from damaging the caliper bore. Use a small pick or brush to clean the grooves. If a hard varnish residue has built up in the grooves, soak the caliper housing in solvent to help soften the residue. Then wash the caliper in soapy water and rinse completely.

d. If alcohol or solvent was used to clean the caliper, blow dry with compressed air.
e. Check the fluid passages to make sure they are clean and dry.
f. After cleaning the parts, place them on a clean lint-free cloth until reassembly.

2. Check each cylinder bore for corrosion, deep scratches and other wear marks. Do not hone the cylinder bores.
3. Measure each caliper cylinder bore inside diameter with a bore gauge or use a telescoping gauge and micrometer.
4. Inspect the pistons for pitting, corrosion, cracks or other damage.
5. Measure each caliper piston outside diameter **(Figure 43)** with a micrometer.
6. Clean the bleed valves with compressed air. Check the valve threads for damage. Replace the dust caps if missing or damaged.
7. Clean the banjo bolt with compressed air.

REAR MASTER CYLINDER (ABS MODELS)

Read *Brake Service* in this chapter.

Removal/Installation

Refer to **Figure 44**.

1. Support the motorcycle on a workstand.

CAUTION
Wipe up any spilled brake fluid immediately, as it damages the finish of most plastic and metal surfaces. Use soapy water and rinse thoroughly.

2. Remove the bolt and the reservoir cover.
3. Drain the rear brake system as described in this chapter.
4. Remove the cotter pin and the clevis pin securing the master cylinder pushrod to the rear brake pedal.
5. Remove the banjo bolt and washers securing the brake hose to the master cylinder.
6. Remove the mounting bolts and the rear master cylinder assembly with the reservoir hose attached.
7. If necessary, service the master cylinder as described in this chapter.
8. Clean the footpeg mounting bracket where the master cylinder is mounted.
9. Installation is the reverse of removal. Note the following:
   a. Install the master cylinder and reservoir into their mounting positions.
   b. Install the rear master cylinder mounting bolts and tighten to 12 N.m (106 in.-lb.).
   c. Secure the brake hose to the master cylinder with the banjo bolt and two *new* seal washers. Install a new washer on each side of the brake hose. Position the stopper on the brake hose against the master cylinder and tighten the banjo bolt to 34 N.m (25 ft.-lb.).
   d. Secure the pushrod onto the rear brake pedal with the clevis pin and a new cotter pin. Bend the cotter pins over to lock it.
   e. Bleed the front and rear brake lines as described in this chapter.
   f. Install the reservoir diaphragm, cover plate and cover. Install and tighten the cover screws to the specification in **Table 4**.
   g. Apply and hold the rear brake pedal. Then check the banjo bolt and the piston bore area in the master cylinder for leaks.
   h. Turn the ignition switch on and apply the rear brake pedal. Make sure the brake light turns on when applying the brake pedal and turns off when the brake pedal is released.

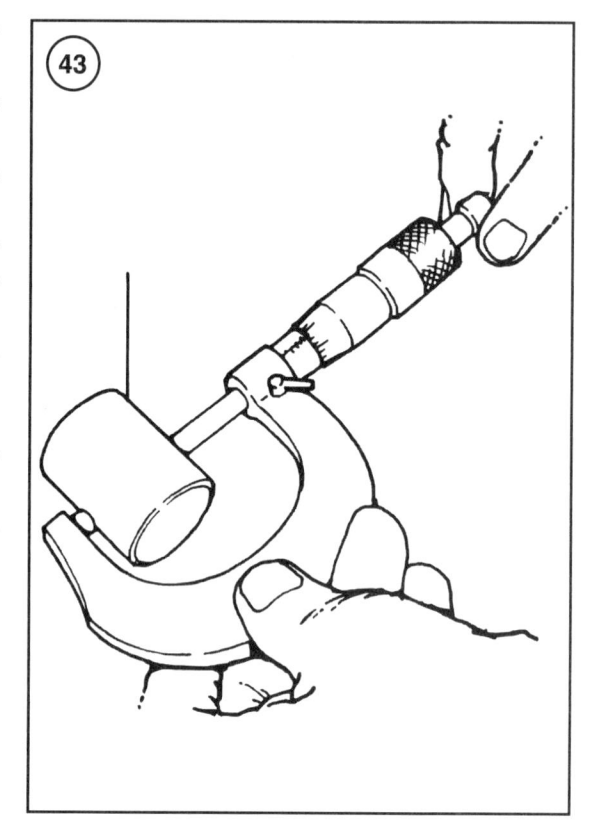

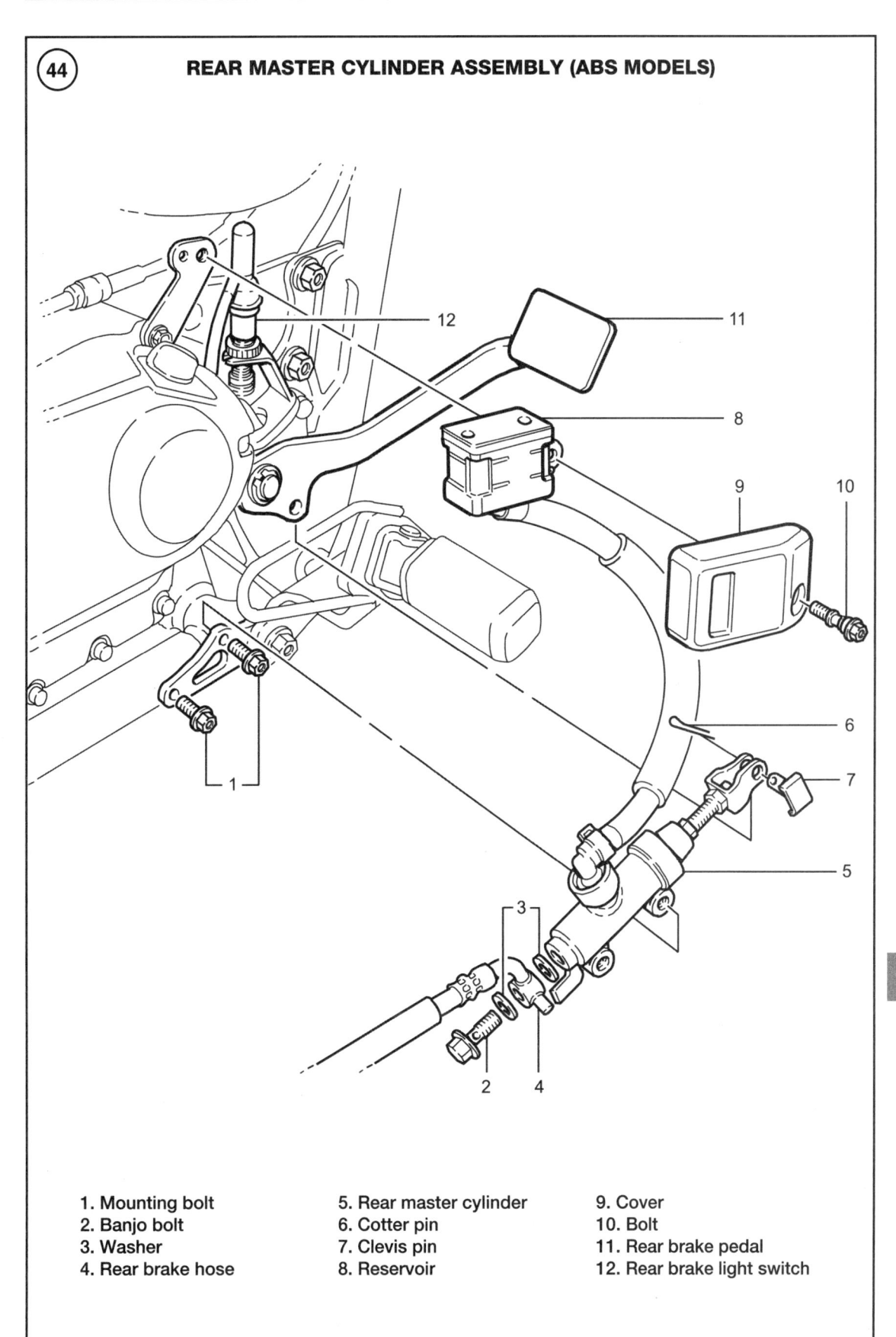

BRAKES

④ REAR MASTER CYLINDER ASSEMBLY (ABS MODELS)

1. Mounting bolt
2. Banjo bolt
3. Washer
4. Rear brake hose
5. Rear master cylinder
6. Cotter pin
7. Clevis pin
8. Reservoir
9. Cover
10. Bolt
11. Rear brake pedal
12. Rear brake light switch

REAR MASTER CYLINDER (ABS MODELS)

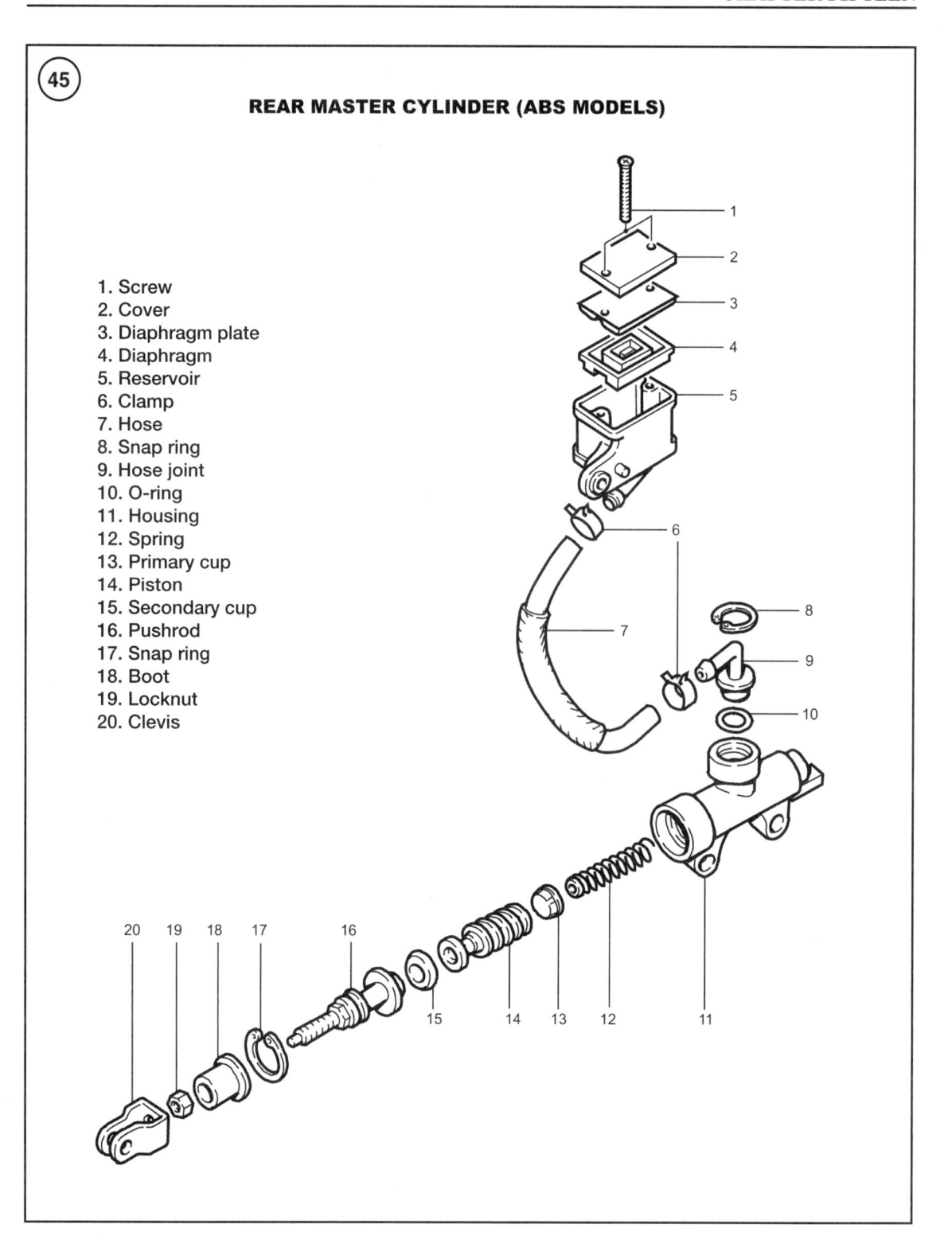

1. Screw
2. Cover
3. Diaphragm plate
4. Diaphragm
5. Reservoir
6. Clamp
7. Hose
8. Snap ring
9. Hose joint
10. O-ring
11. Housing
12. Spring
13. Primary cup
14. Piston
15. Secondary cup
16. Pushrod
17. Snap ring
18. Boot
19. Locknut
20. Clevis

Disassembly

Refer to **Figure 45**.

1. Remove the master cylinder as described in this section.
2. Remove the snap ring and hose joint from the master cylinder.
3. Remove and discard the O-ring.

NOTE
If brake fluid is leaking from the piston bore, the piston cups are worn or damaged. Replace the piston assembly.

BRAKES

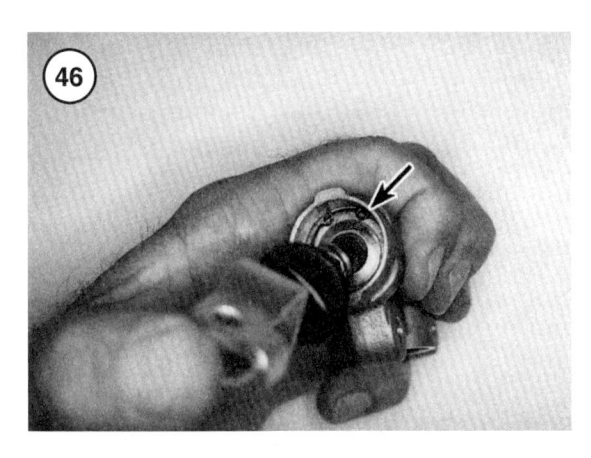

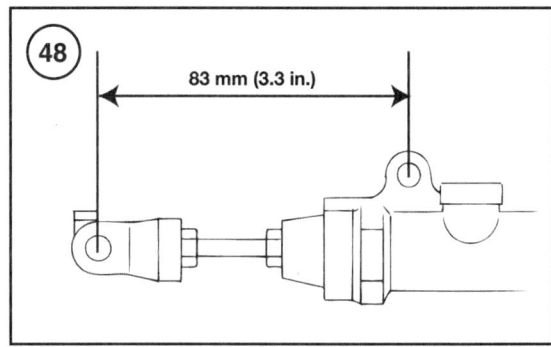

(**Figure 46**) into the master cylinder groove with its flat side facing out. Make sure the snap ring seats in the groove completely. Push and release the pushrod a few times to make sure the piston moves smoothly and the snap ring does not pop out.

5. Slide the boot down the pushrod and seat its large end against the snap ring in the master cylinder bore. Seat the boot's small end into the groove in the pushrod. Push and release the pushrod a few times to make sure the boot's small end stays in the pushrod groove and that it is not twisted or folded incorrectly.

6. Measure the pushrod length from the center of the front master cylinder mounting bolt hole to the center of the clevis hole as shown in **Figure 48**. Refer to **Table 2** for the correct distance. To adjust, loosen the locknut and turn the clevis as required. Hold the clevis and tighten the locknut to 18 N.m (13 ft.-lb.) and then remeasure.

7. Lubricate a new O-ring with DOT 4 brake fluid and install it over the hose joint.

8. Install the hose joint into the master cylinder and secure with the snap ring. Make sure the snap ring seats in the groove completely.

9. Install the master cylinder as described in this section.

4. Pull the rubber boot out of the master cylinder bore. Compress the piston and remove the snap ring (**Figure 46**) with snap ring pliers. Remove the piston assembly from the master cylinder bore (**Figure 47**). Do not remove the cups from the piston.

5. Clean and inspect the master cylinder assembly (this section).

Assembly

1. If installing a new piston assembly, assemble it (this section).
2. Lubricate the piston assembly and cylinder bore with new DOT 4 brake fluid.

> *CAUTION*
> *Do not allow the piston cups to tear or turn inside out when installing them into the master cylinder bore. Both cups are larger than the bore.*

3. Install the piston assembly into the master cylinder (**Figure 47**).
4. Apply silicone brake grease onto the end of the pushrod where it contacts the piston and install the pushrod assembly. Compress the piston with the pushrod so the washer on the pushrod is below the snap ring groove in the master cylinder. Continue to compress the piston and install the new snap ring

Inspection

When measuring the master cylinder components, compare the results to the specifications in **Table 2**. Replace worn or damaged parts as described in this section.

1. Clean and dry the master cylinder assembly as follows:
   a. Handle the brake components carefully when servicing them.

> *WARNING*
> *Never allow any petroleum-based solvents to clean brake components, or allow solvent to contact rubber parts. Petroleum-based chemicals cause the rubber parts to swell, requiring their replacement.*

b. Use only DOT 4 brake fluid or isopropyl alcohol to wash rubber parts in the brake system.
c. Clean the master cylinder snap ring groove carefully. Use a small pick or brush to clean the groove. If a hard varnish residue has built up in the groove, soak the master cylinder in solvent to help soften the residue. Then wash in soapy water and rinse completely.
d. Blow the master cylinder dry with compressed air.
e. Place cleaned parts on a clean lint-free cloth until reassembly.

CAUTION
Do not remove the secondary cup from the piston.

2. Check the piston assembly for:
   a. Broken, distorted or collapsed piston return spring (A, **Figure 49**).
   b. Worn, cracked, damaged or swollen primary (B, **Figure 49**) and secondary (C) cups.
   c. Worn or pitted piston (D, **Figure 49**).

If any of these parts are worn or damaged, replace the piston and seals as an assembly.

3. Measure the piston outside diameter (**Figure 50**) with a micrometer.
4. To assemble a new piston assembly, perform the following:

NOTE
A new piston assembly consists of the piston, primary cup, secondary cup and spring. Because these parts come unassembled, the new primary cup must be installed on the spring and the new secondary cup must be installed onto the piston. Use the original piston and pistons cups as a reference when assembling the new piston assembly.

   a. Soak the new cups in new DOT 4 brake fluid for 15 minutes to soften them and ease installation. Clean the new piston in brake fluid.

CAUTION
*The secondary cup (C, **Figure 49**) can be difficult to install. Do not pry the cup over the piston with any metal tool as this may damage the cup. Carefully stretch the secondary cup by hand to guide it over the piston's shoulder. The cup may turn inside out when installing it, so pay attention to how the cup moves and drops into its groove on the piston.*

   b. Snap the primary cup (B, **Figure 49**) onto the spring. Carefully install the secondary cup (C,

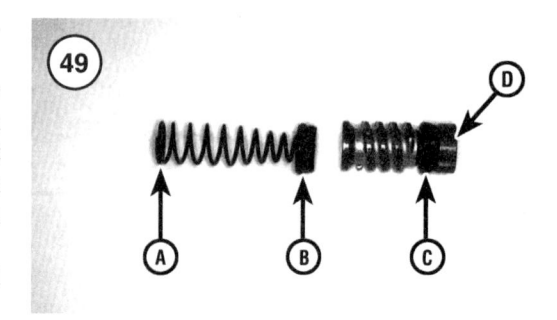

Figure 49) onto the piston. Check that the secondary cup is positioned correctly and did not turn inside out.

5. Inspect the master cylinder bore for corrosion, pitting or excessive wear. Do not hone the master cylinder bore to remove scratches or other damage.
6. Measure the master cylinder bore with a bore gauge or a telescoping gauge and a micrometer.
7. Inspect the master cylinder reservoir diaphragm for tearing, cracks or other damage.

NOTE
A damaged diaphragm will allow moisture to enter the reservoir and contaminate the brake fluid.

BRAKE HOSE AND BRAKE PIPE REPLACEMENT

Check the rubber brake hoses and metal brake pipes at the brake inspection intervals listed in Chapter Three. Replace the brake hoses if they show signs of wear or damage, or if they have bulges or signs of chafing. Replace the brake pipes if they are kinked, cracked or leaking.

To replace a brake hose or brake pipe, perform the following:

1. Drain the brake system as described in this chapter.
2. Use a plastic drop cloth to cover areas that could be damaged by spilled brake fluid.

BRAKES

WARNING
Copper tubing cracks and corrodes easily. Never use this tubing in a hydraulic brake system as it can result in leaks and brake system failure.

b. Blow the new brake pipes out with compressed air before installing them.
c. Wipe the pipe ends and joint nuts to remove any contamination.
d. Do not bend the brake pipes or try to force them into position during installation. This creases the metal and causes it to leak.
e. If there is any chance of the tubing ends becoming contaminated with grease or debris when installing them, cover the ends with a small plastic bag.
f. Install the brake pipes into their original mounting location by following the noted routing.
g. Brake pipes can be damaged from vibration and heat. Install the brake pipes in their original positions while using the original mounting fasteners and heat shields.
h. When a brake pipe was disconnected from both ends, thread both brake pipe joint nuts into their mating joints a few turns only. Do not tighten one nut fully before attempting to install and tighten the other nut. Also make sure there is no stress on the brake pipe.
g. Lubricate the brake pipe joint nuts with DOT 4 brake fluid before installing them.
i. Tighten brake pipe joint nuts to 14 N.m (10 ft.-lb.).

3. When removing a brake hose or brake pipe, note the following:
   a. Snap a photo of the hose or pipe routing or make a sketch on a piece of paper.
   b. Remove any bolts or brackets securing the brake hose or brake pipe to the frame or suspension component.
   c. Before removing the banjo bolts, note how the end of the brake hose is installed or indexed against the part it is threaded into. The hoses must be installed facing in their original position.
4. Replace damaged banjo bolts.
5A. Reverse these steps to install the new brake hoses, while noting the following:
   a. Compare the new and old hoses to make sure they are the same.
   b. Clean the *new* seal washers, banjo bolts and hose ends to remove any contamination.
   c. Referring to the notes made during removal, route the brake hose along its original path.
   d. Install a *new* banjo bolt seal washer **(Figure 51)** on each side of the brake hose.
   e. Tighten the banjo bolts to 34 N.m (25 ft.-lb.).
5B. Reverse these steps to install new brake pipes, while noting the following:
   a. Prefabricated steel brake pipes are available from the manufacturer. These pipes are equipped with joint nuts and preflared ends.

6. After installing new hoses and pipes around the steering and front fork area, turn the handlebars from side to side to make sure the hose or pipe does not rub against any part or pull away from its brake unit.
7. Bleed the brake system as described in this chapter.

WARNING
Do not ride the motorcycle until the front and rear brakes are operating properly.

BRAKE DISCS AND PULSER RINGS

On models with ABS, pulser rings are mounted on the outside of the brake discs.

Inspection

The brake discs **(Figure 52**, typical) can be inspected while installed on the motorcycle. Small marks on the disc are not important, but deep scratches or other marks may reduce braking effectiveness and increase brake pad wear. If these grooves are evident and the brake pads are wearing rapidly, replace the brake disc.

On ABS models, inspect the pulser rings (**Figure 53**) for cracks, pitting and any other damage that would disrupt signal pickup from the wheel speed sensor. Check the pulser ring slots for any iron or similar magnetic debris as this can set a DTC and cause the ABS indicator to blink.

Table 1 and **Table 2** lists new and service limit specifications for brake disc thickness. The minimum (MIN) thickness is stamped on the outside of the disc face (A. **Figure 52**). If the specification stamped on the disc differs from the service limit in **Table 1** or **Table 2**, use the specification on the disc when inspecting it.

When servicing the brake disc, do not have the disc reconditioned (ground) to compensate for warp. The disc is thin and grinding only reduces its thickness, causing it to warp quite rapidly.

1. Support the motorcycle with the wheel off the ground.
2. Measure the disc thickness at several locations around the disc (**Figure 54**). Replace the disc if its thickness at any point is less than the minimum allowable specification stamped on the disc, or if it is less than the service limit in **Table 1** or **Table 2**.
3. Make sure the disc mounting bolts are tight before checking brake disc runout.
4. Turn the wheel to one side. Position a dial indicator stem against the brake disc (**Figure 55**). Zero the dial gauge and slowly turn the wheel and measure runout. Compare the results to the specification in **Table 1** or **Table 2**. If the disc runout is excessive:
   a. Check for loose or missing fasteners.
   b. Remove the wheel and check the wheel bearings for damage (Chapter Twelve).
   c. Check for a damaged hub.
5. Clean the disc of any rust or corrosion, and wipe clean with brake cleaner. Never use an oil-based solvent that may leave an oily residue on the disc.
6. On ABS models, clean the pulser rings of any rust or corrosion, and wipe clean with brake cleaner. Never use an oil-based solvent that may leave an oily residue on the pulser ring.

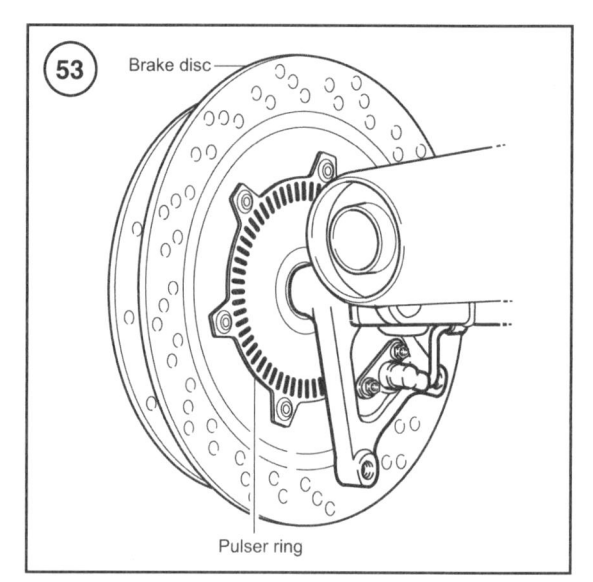

Removal/Installation

1. Remove the wheel (Chapter Twelve).
2. Remove the bolts securing the brake disc to the wheel and remove the disc (B, **Figure 52**). On ABS models, remove the pulser ring before removing the brake disc. Discard the mounting bolts.
3. Perform any necessary service to the hub (wheel bearing or tire replacement) before installing the pulser ring (ABS models) or brake disc.
4. Clean the brake disc threaded holes in the hub.
5. Clean the brake disc mounting surface on the hub.
6. Install the brake disc with the MIN marked side (A, **Figure 52**) facing out.
7. On ABS models, install the pulser ring on the outside of the brake disc (**Figure 53**).

BRAKES

Figure 56: REAR DRUM BRAKE

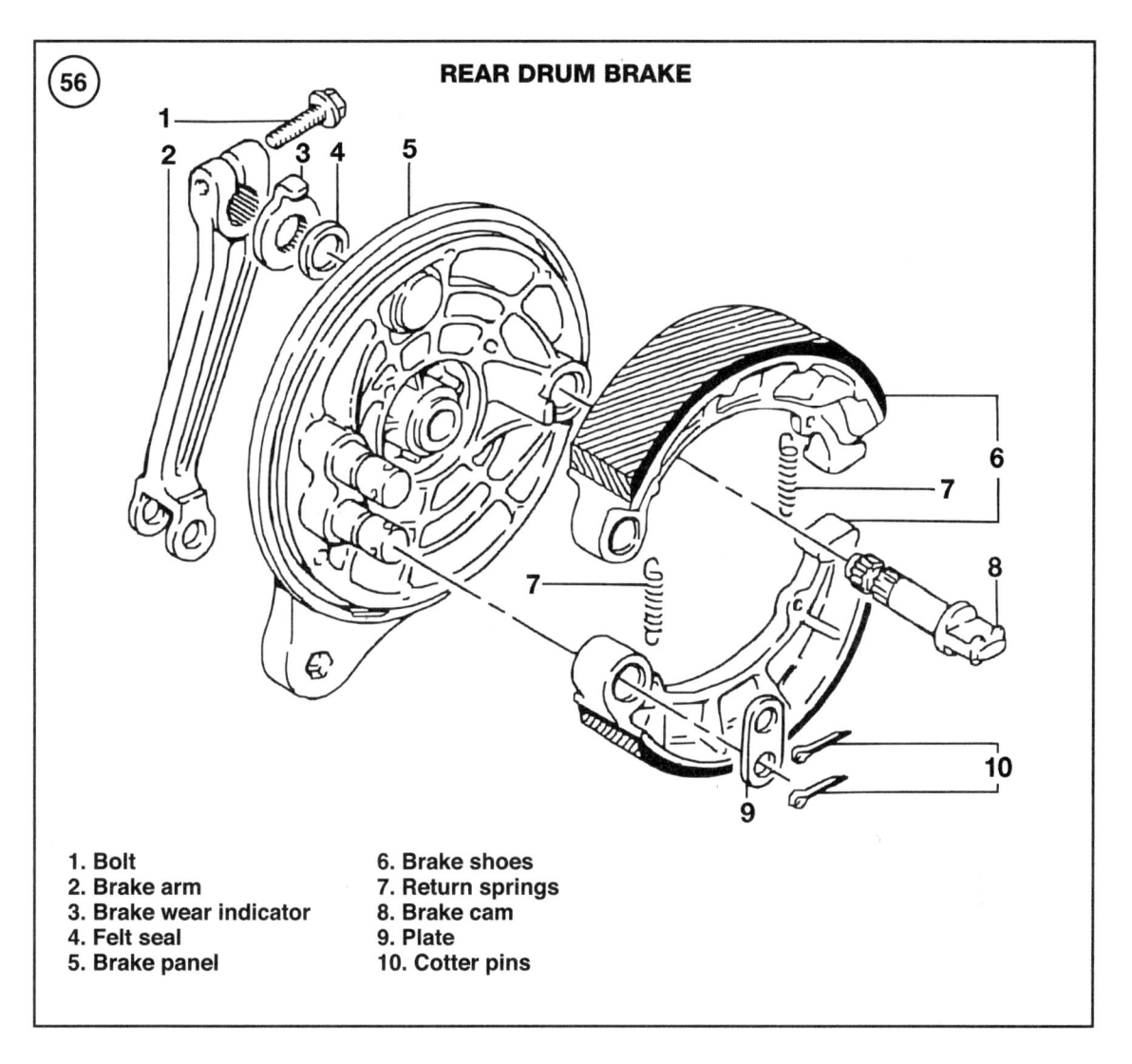

1. Bolt
2. Brake arm
3. Brake wear indicator
4. Felt seal
5. Brake panel
6. Brake shoes
7. Return springs
8. Brake cam
9. Plate
10. Cotter pins

8. Install *new* brake disc mounting bolts and tighten in a crossing pattern and in several steps to 42 N.m (31 ft.-lb.).

WARNING
The disc bolts are made from a harder material than similar bolts used on the motorcycle. When replacing the bolts, use OEM brake disc bolts. Never compromise and use different bolts as they may fail while under use.

9. Clean the disc of any rust or corrosion and spray clean with brake cleaner. Never use an oil-based solvent that may leave an oily residue on the disc.
10. Install the wheel (Chapter Twelve).

REAR DRUM BRAKE

All non-ABS models covered in this manual use a rear drum brake **(Figure 56)**. Activating the foot pedal pulls the brake rods, which in turn rotates the brake cam in the brake drum. This forces the brake shoes out into contact with the drum.

Rear brake pedal free play must be maintained to minimize brake drag and premature brake wear and to maximize braking effectiveness. Refer to *Rear Brake Pedal Free Play* in Chapter Three for complete adjustment procedures.

Brake Shoe Replacement

Refer to **Figure 56** for this procedure.

WARNING
When handling the rear brake assembly, do not inhale brake dust as it may contain asbestos that can cause lung injury and cancer. Wear a disposable face mask and wash hands and forearms thoroughly after completing the work. Use an aerosol brake cleaner to wet down the brake dust on brake components before storing or working on

them. Secure and dispose of all brake dust and cleaning materials properly. Do not use compressed air to blow off brake parts.

1. Wear a dust mask when handling the brake components.
2. Check the brake lining wear with the rear brake panel installed in the brake drum as described in Chapter Three.
3. Remove the rear wheel (Chapter Twelve).
4. Pull the rear brake panel (**Figure 57**) out of the brake drum.

NOTE
When measuring the brake lining thickness, measure the lining thickness only. Do not include the brake shoe thickness.

NOTE
*A brake lining thickness limit is not provided for all models. For these models, use the indicator plate on the brake cam as described in **Rear Brake Shoe Wear Inspection Check** in **Brakes** in Chapter Three.*

5. Measure the brake lining thickness with a caliper (**Figure 58**). Measure at several places along the brake lining. Replace the brake shoes if the lining thickness is worn to the service limit in **Table 3**.
6. Mark the web portion on both shoes so the shoes can be reinstalled in their original position.

NOTE
When handling the brake shoes, place a clean rag over the linings to protect them from oil and grease.

7. Remove the two cotter pins (A, **Figure 59**) and the plate (B).
8. Spread the brake shoes (**Figure 60**) and remove them from the brake panel.
9. Disconnect the return springs (A, **Figure 61**) from the brake shoes.
10. Discard the brake shoes if necessary.
11. Clean and dry the brake panel and springs.
12. Inspect the return springs for cracks, stretched coils or damaged spring ends. Replace both springs as a set.

NOTE
Worn or damaged return springs may not allow the brake pads to fully retract from the drum, resulting in brake drag.

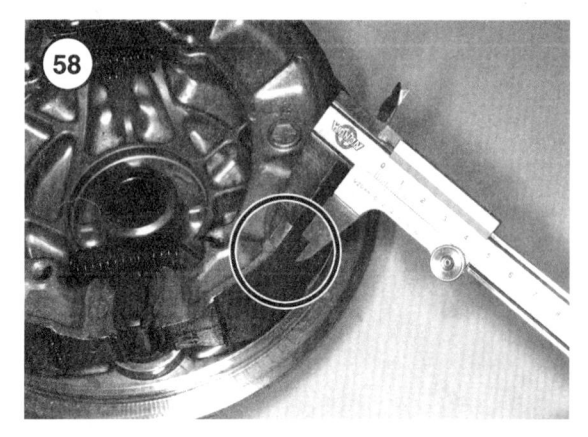

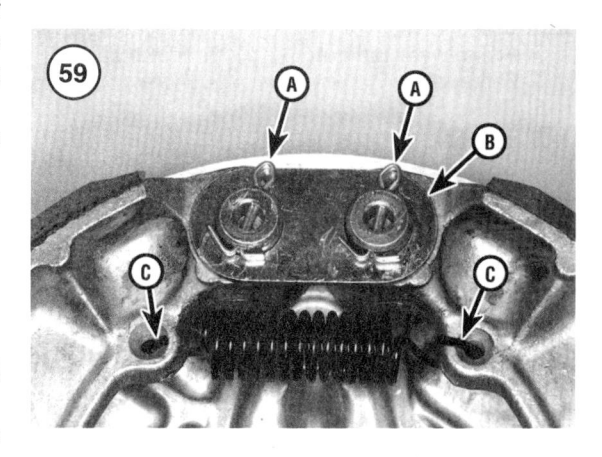

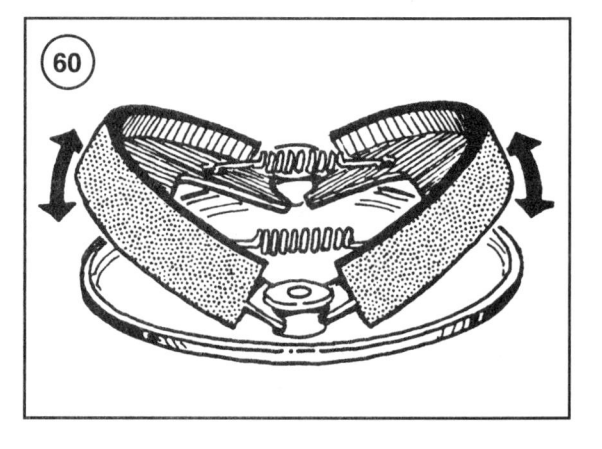

BRAKES

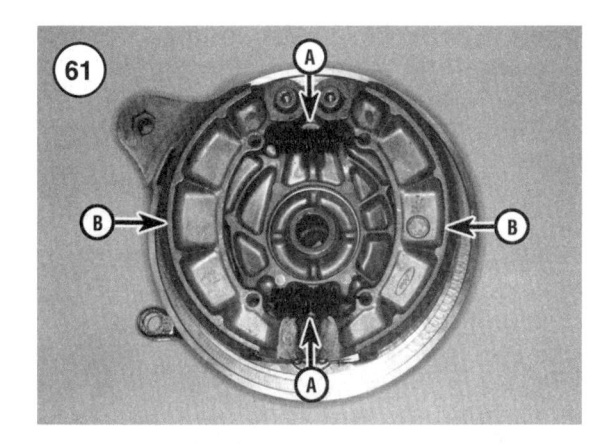

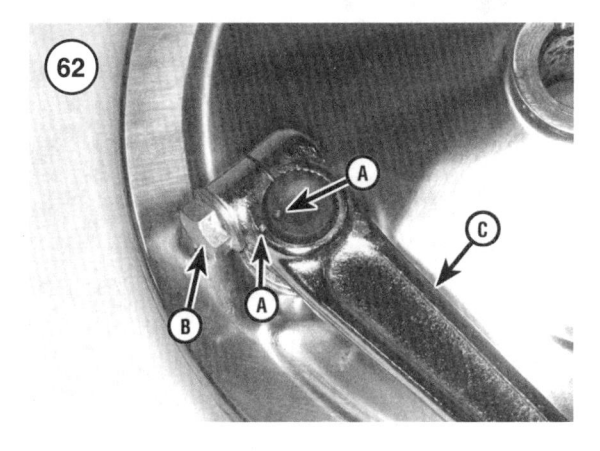

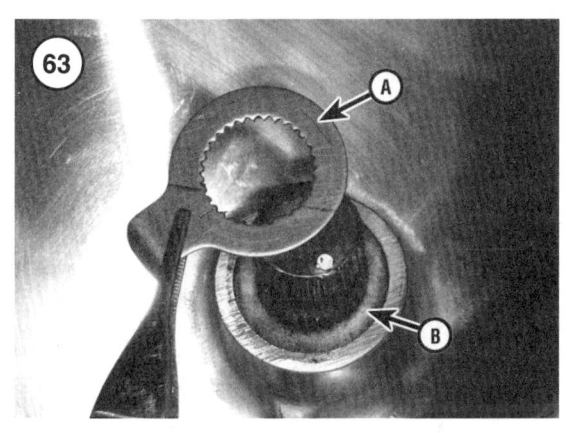

495

13. Lubricate the brake cam and brake panel pivot shafts with a waterproof bearing grease.

CAUTION
To prevent contact with the brake lining and drum surfaces do not use an excessive amount of grease.

14. Install the return springs onto the brake shoes with the open spring ends (C, **Figure 59**) facing away from the brake panel.
15. Spread the brake shoes (one end at a time) and install them (B, **Figure 61**) into the brake panel. Make sure the return springs attach fully to the brake shoes.
16. Wipe excess grease from the end of the pivot shaft and brake cam.
17. Install the plate (B, **Figure 59**) and two new cotter pins. Install the cotter pins (A, **Figure 59**) with their closed side facing out. Bend the cotter pin arms to lock them in place.
18. Operate the brake arm by hand, making sure it moves and returns under spring pressure.
19. Install the brake panel **(Figure 57)** and rear wheel (Chapter Twelve).

Brake Arm
Removal/Inspection/Installation

Refer to **Figure 56** for this procedure.

WARNING
When handling the rear brake assembly, do not inhale brake dust as it may contain asbestos that can cause lung injury and cancer. Wear a disposable face mask and wash hands and forearms thoroughly after completing the work. Use an aerosol brake cleaner to wet down the brake dust on brake components before storing or working on them. Secure and dispose of all brake dust and cleaning materials properly. Do not use compressed air to blow off brake parts.

1. Wear a dust mask when handling the brake components.
2. Remove the brake shoes as described in this section.
3. Note the brake arm and brake cam alignment marks (A, **Figure 62**). Realign these marks during installation. Create alignment marks if there are none present.
4. Remove the rear brake arm pinch bolt (B, **Figure 62**) and brake arm (C).
5. Remove the brake indicator (A, **Figure 63**) and the felt seal (B).
6. Remove the brake cam **(Figure 64)**.

7. Clean all parts in solvent (except the brake shoes and felt seal). The brake shoes can be sprayed with a brake cleaner.
8. Inspect the brake arm for cracks, excessive wear or other damage.
9. Inspect the brake cam for excessive wear or damage.
10. Inspect the splines on the brake arm and brake cam for damage.

WARNING
Damaged splines may allow the brake arm and brake cam to slip and prevent brake application. Replace the parts if there is any excessive spline wear or any spline damage.

11. Inspect the brake panel bore for cracks, wear or elongation. If damaged, replace the brake panel.
12. Replace the brake indicator and felt seal if damaged.
13. Lubricate the brake cam (**Figure 64**) with a waterproof bearing grease and install it into the brake panel. Wipe excess grease off and around the brake cam.
14. Install the felt seal (B, **Figure 63**) into the bore in the brake panel.
15. Install the brake indicator by aligning its wide tooth with the master spline on the brake cam (**Figure 65**).
16. Install the brake arm by aligning its punch mark with the punch mark on the end of the brake cam (A, **Figure 62**).

WARNING
The angle between the brake arm and rear brake rod must not exceed 90° when the brake is applied. Installing the brake indicator and brake arm as described (this section) maintains the correct operational relationship between the brake lever and brake cam. If the brake lever and brake rod angle exceeds 90°, the brake cam could pivot overcenter (turn horizontal) and lock the rear brake and wheel, causing the motorcycle to loose control. Do not reposition the brake lever on the brake cam to compensate for worn brake linings or a worn brake drum.

17. Install the rear brake arm pinch bolt (B, **Figure 62**) and tighten to 26 N.m (19 ft.-lb.). Pivot the brake arm, making sure it moves without any roughness or binding.
18. Install the brake shoes as described in this section.

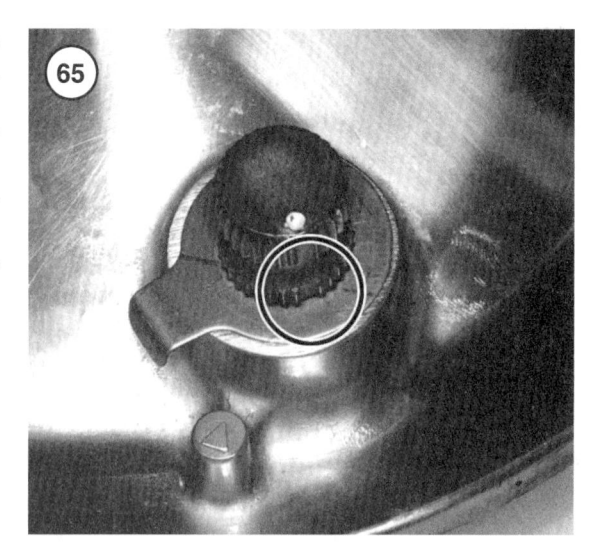

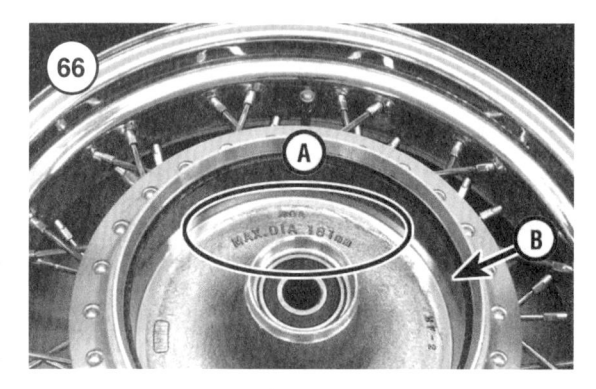

Rear Brake Drum Inspection

Table 3 lists the new and service limit specifications for the brake drum inside diameter. The maximum (MAX) allowable inside diameter is embossed on the hub near the brake drum (A, **Figure 66**). If the specification on the hub differs from the service limit in **Table 3**, use the specification on the hub when inspecting it.

When servicing the brake drum, do not have the drum reconditioned (ground) to compensate for out-of-round or to remove wear grooves.

WARNING
When handling the rear brake assembly, do not inhale brake dust as it may contain asbestos that can cause lung injury and cancer. Wear a disposable face mask and wash hands and forearms thoroughly after completing the work. Use an aerosol brake cleaner to wet down the brake dust on brake components before storing or working on them. Secure and dispose of all brake dust and cleaning materials properly.

BRAKES

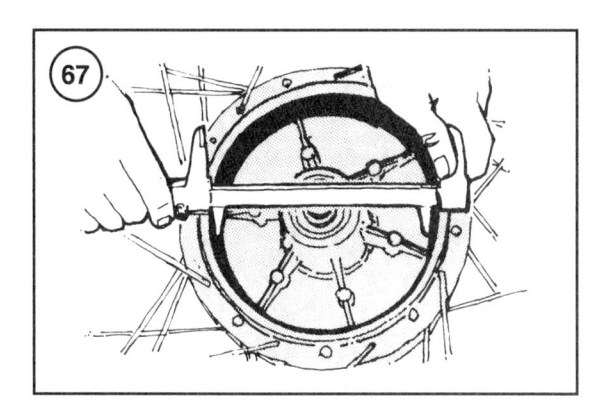

67

Do not use compressed air to blow off brake parts.

1. Wear a dust mask when handling the brake components.
2. Clean the brake drum as follows:
   a. Turn the wheel over and pour any accumulated brake dust into a bag. Tie the bag closed and discard it.
   b. Do not clean the brake drum with compressed air. Instead spray the brake drum with an aerosol brake cleaner and allow to dry.
3. Inspect the brake drum (B, **Figure 66**) for roughness, cracks, distortion and other damage. Service the drum as follows:
   a. Remove light roughness and glaze with a fine-to-medium grade sandpaper.
   b. Replace the rear wheel if the brake drum is cracked or if the drum surface is scored heavily.
4. Measure the brake drum inside diameter with a caliper **(Figure 67)**. Measure at several places around the brake drum to determine any out-of-roundness. Replace the rear hub if the inner diameter exceeds the maximum allowable specification listed on the hub (A, **Figure 66**) or in **Table 3**.

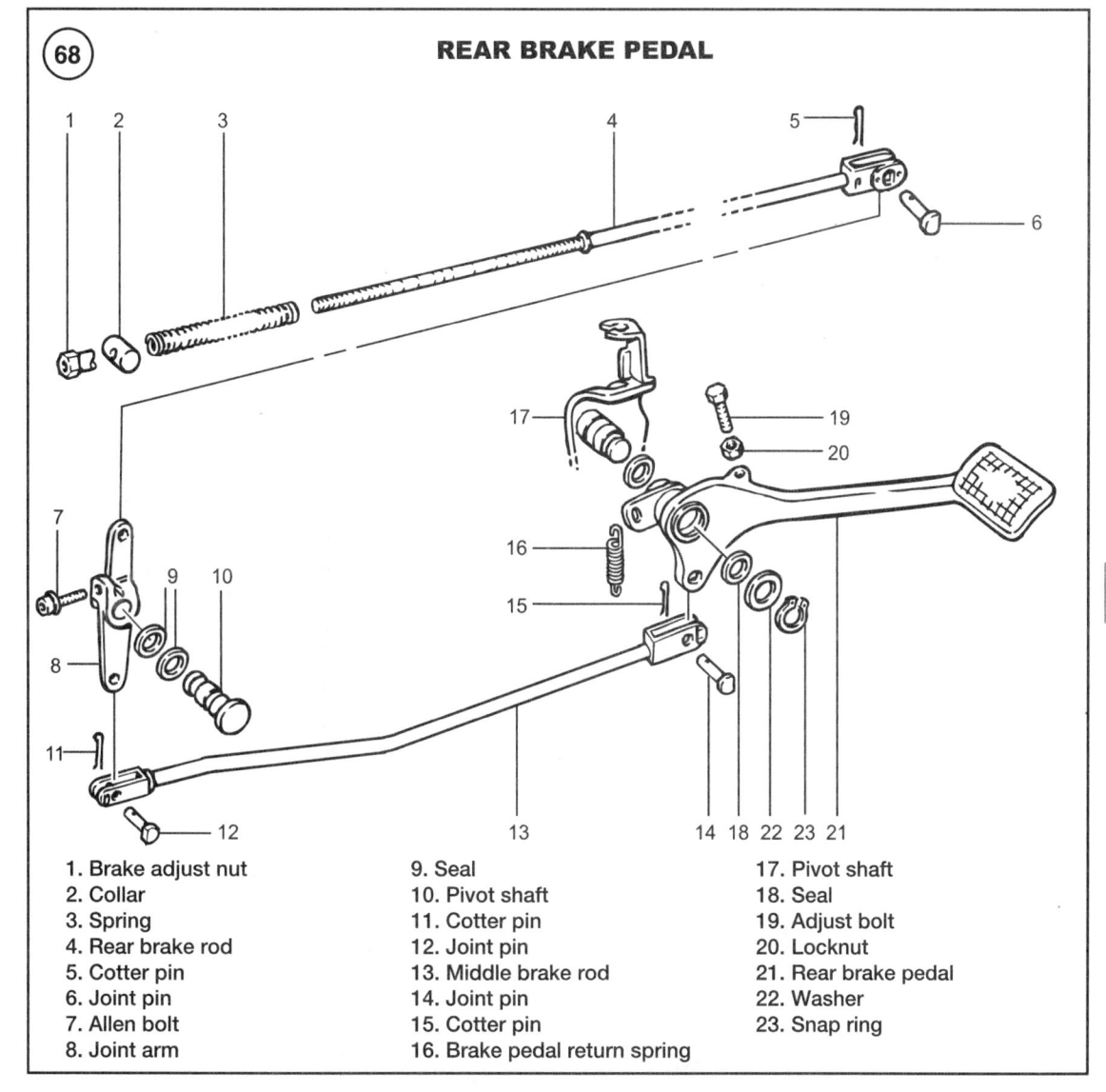

68 REAR BRAKE PEDAL

1. Brake adjust nut
2. Collar
3. Spring
4. Rear brake rod
5. Cotter pin
6. Joint pin
7. Allen bolt
8. Joint arm
9. Seal
10. Pivot shaft
11. Cotter pin
12. Joint pin
13. Middle brake rod
14. Joint pin
15. Cotter pin
16. Brake pedal return spring
17. Pivot shaft
18. Seal
19. Adjust bolt
20. Locknut
21. Rear brake pedal
22. Washer
23. Snap ring

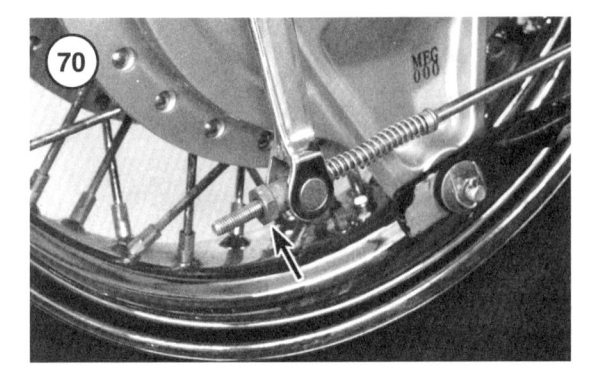

REAR BRAKE PEDAL (DRUM BRAKE MODELS)

Refer to **Figure 68**.

Removal

1. Remove the exhaust system (Chapter Seventeen).
2. Remove the exhaust pipe mounting bracket bolts and bracket (**Figure 69**).

> *NOTE*
> *The rear brake pedal assembly can be removed with the front footpeg mounted on the frame. However, it is easier to remove the exhaust assembly by first removing the footpeg. The footpeg is shown removed in this section for clarity.*

3. Remove the rear brake rod adjusting nut (**Figure 70**), spring and collar.
4. Remove the Allen bolt (**Figure 71**) securing the joint arm to the pivot shaft.
5. Remove the pivot shaft (A, **Figure 72**) and allow the joint arm (**Figure 73**) to pivot down. Note the seals (B, **Figure 72**) installed in the frame.
6. Disconnect the brake lever return spring from its post position on the rear brake pedal (A, **Figure 74**).
7. Remove the snap ring and washer (B, **Figure 74**).
8. Partially remove the brake pedal assembly (C, **Figure 74**), then disconnect the rear brake light switch spring (D) at the pedal and remove the pedal assembly.

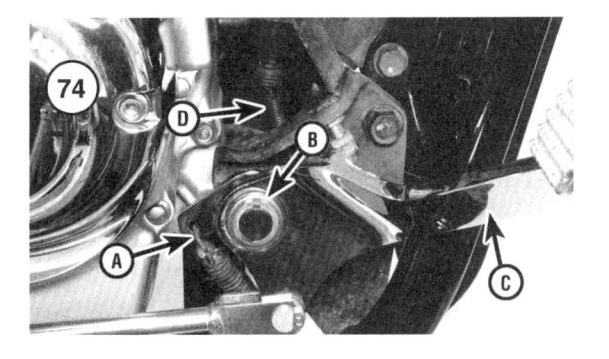

> *NOTE*
> *If it is difficult to disconnect the rear brake light switch spring, remove the switch from its mounting position, then disconnect the spring.*

BRAKES

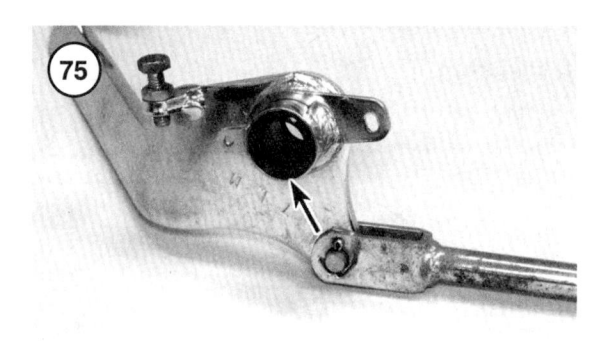

75

9. Inspect the rear brake pedal (this section).

Installation

1. Install the rear brake pedal assembly between the engine and frame.
2. Lubricate the rear brake pedal bore and pivot shaft with grease.
3. Reconnect the rear brake light return spring (D, **Figure 74**) onto the front brake pedal spring hole.

NOTE
Reinstall the rear brake light switch if previously removed.

4. Install the rear brake pedal assembly (C, **Figure 74**) onto its pivot shaft.
5. Install the washer and a *new* snap ring with their flat sides facing out (B, **Figure 74**). Make sure the snap ring seats in the groove completely.
6. Reconnect the brake lever return spring (A, **Figure 74**).
7. Lubricate the pivot shaft and seals with grease and install the pivot shaft (A, **Figure 72**) through the frame and joint arm.
8. Install a new Allen bolt (**Figure 71**), or clean the original bolt and install a medium strength threadlock onto the bolt threads, and tighten securely.
9. Reconnect the brake rod at the brake arm (**Figure 70**).
10. Reinstall the exhaust mounting bracket and tighten the mounting bolts securely.
11. Reinstall the exhaust system (Chapter Seventeen).
12. Perform the following as described in Chapter Three:
　a. Adjust the rear brake.
　b. Adjust the rear brake light switch.
13. Check the rear brake operation.

WARNING
Do not ride the motorcycle until the rear brake, brake pedal and brake light work properly.

Disassembly/Inspection/Lubrication/Reassembly

1. Clean and dry the rear brake pedal assembly, pivot shaft and pivot surfaces.
2. If necessary, refer to **Figure 68** to disassemble the brake pedal assembly. Install new cotter pins during assembly. Bend the cotter pin arms over to lock them.
3. Inspect the frame (B, **Figure 72**) and brake pedal (**Figure 75**) seals and replace if damaged or if the pivot surfaces are contaminated with dirt and other debris.

REAR BRAKE PEDAL (ABS MODELS)

Refer to **Figure 76** and **Figure 77**.

Removal

1. Remove the exhaust system (Chapter Seventeen).
2. Remove the cotter pin and the clevis pin securing the master cylinder pushrod to the rear brake pedal.
3. Disconnect the two springs at the rear brake pedal.
4. Remove the snap ring, washer and the brake pedal.

Lubrication/Installation

1. Lubricate the brake pedal assembly as follows:
　a. Remove the seals.
　b. Clean the brake pedal in solvent and dry thoroughly.
　c. Clean the pivot shaft on the mounting bracket.
　d. Lubricate the pivot shaft with grease.
　e. Lubricate the brake pedal pivot bore with grease.
　f. Lubricate the seal lips with grease and install them into the brake pedal.
2. Slide the brake pedal onto the pivot shaft. Make sure the oil seals remain inside the brake pedal.
3. Install the washer and a new snap ring. Install the snap ring with its flat side facing out. Make sure the snap ring seats in the groove completely.
4. Reconnect the two springs onto the rear brake pedal.
5. Secure the pushrod onto the rear brake pedal with the clevis pin and a new cotter pin. Bend the cotter pins over to lock it.
6. Adjust the rear brake light switch (Chapter Three).
7. Check the rear brake operation.
8. Reinstall the exhaust system (Chapter Seventeen).

WARNING
Do not ride the motorcycle until the rear brake, brake pedal and brake light work properly.

CHAPTER FIFTEEN

REAR BRAKE PEDAL (ABS MODELS)

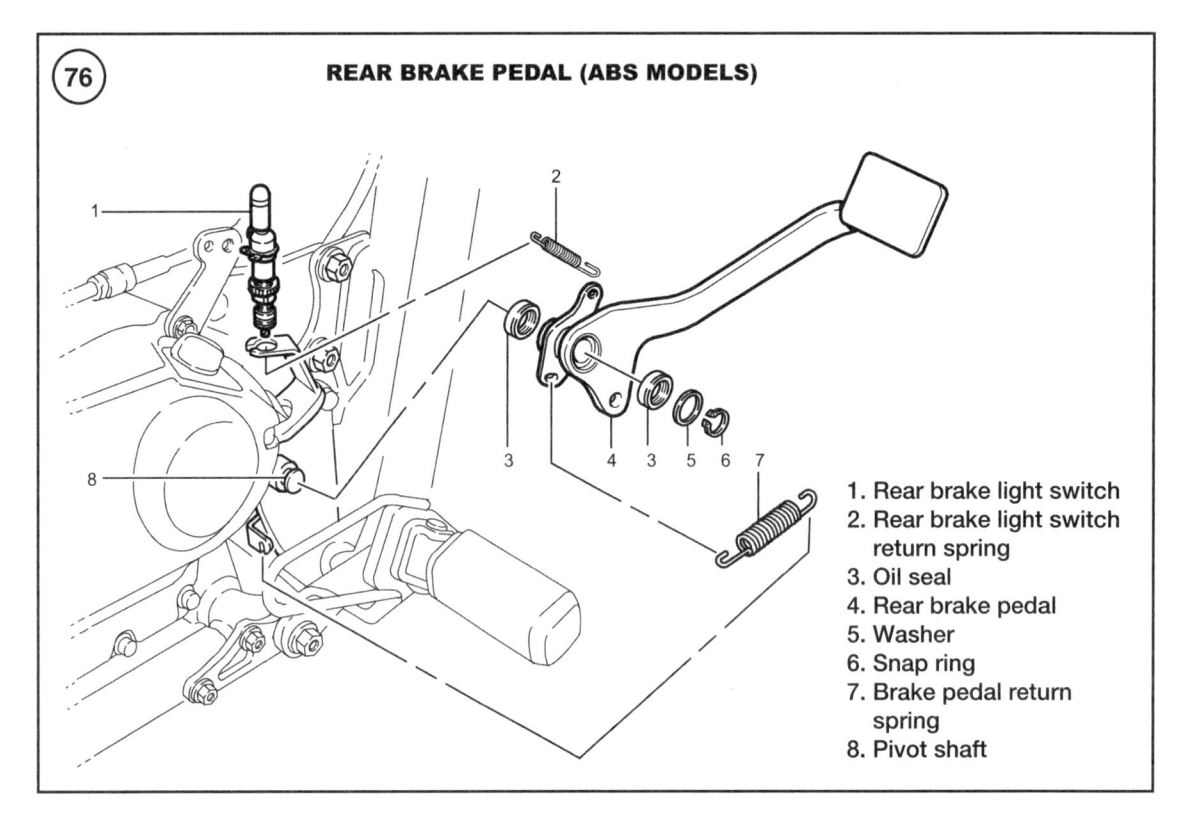

1. Rear brake light switch
2. Rear brake light switch return spring
3. Oil seal
4. Rear brake pedal
5. Washer
6. Snap ring
7. Brake pedal return spring
8. Pivot shaft

REAR BRAKE ASSEMBLY (ABS MODELS)

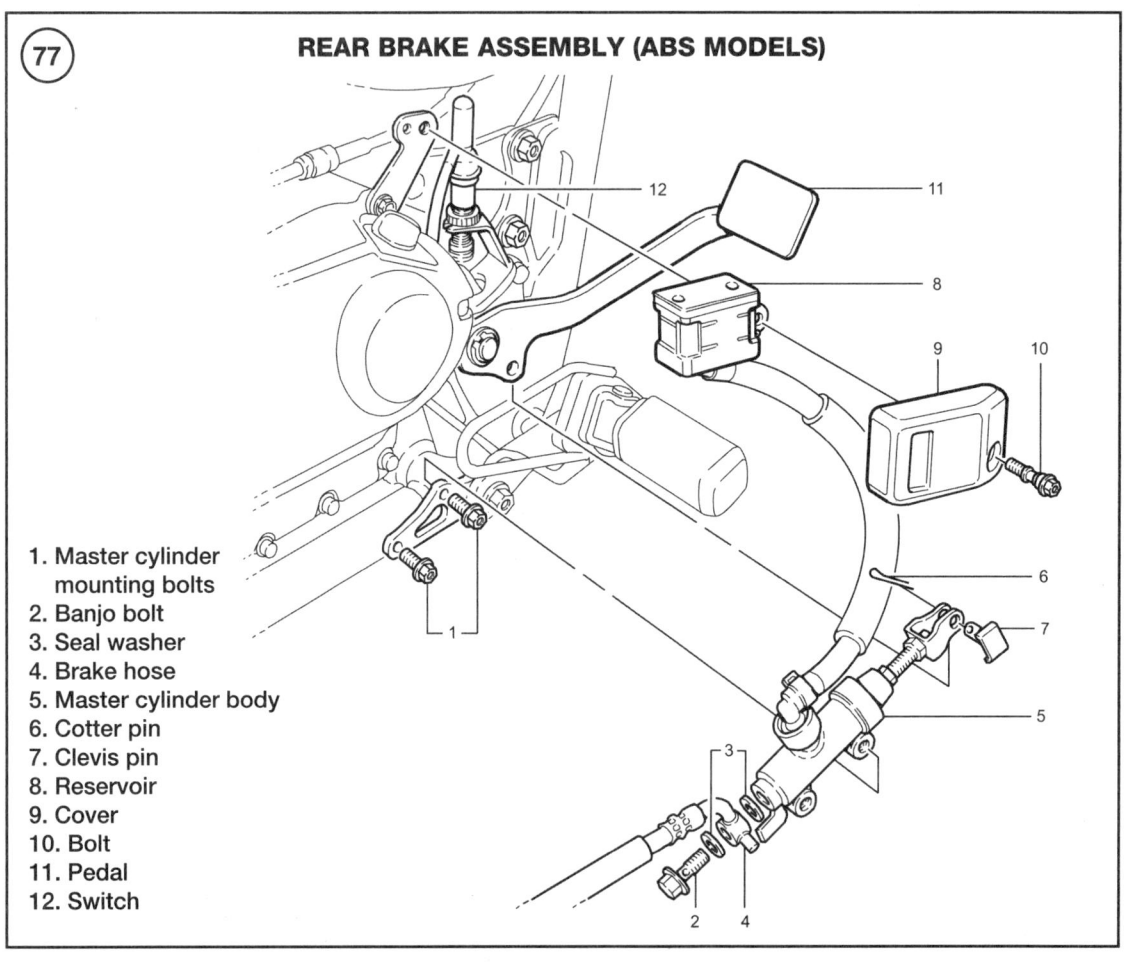

1. Master cylinder mounting bolts
2. Banjo bolt
3. Seal washer
4. Brake hose
5. Master cylinder body
6. Cotter pin
7. Clevis pin
8. Reservoir
9. Cover
10. Bolt
11. Pedal
12. Switch

BRAKES

Table 1 FRONT DISC BRAKE SERVICE SPECIFICATIONS (ALL MODELS)

	New mm (in.)	Service limit mm (in.)
Brake disc runout	--	0.30 (0.012)
Brake disc thickness		
Spirit models (ABS)	4.8-5.2 (0.19-0.20)	4.0 (0.16)
All other models	5.8-6.2 (0.23-0.24)	5.0 (0.20)
Brake caliper cylinder bore inside diameter		
Non-ABS equipped		
Aero and Phantom models	25.400-25.450 (1.0000-1.0020)	25.460 (1.0024)
Spirit models	27.000-27.050 (1.0630-1.0650)	27.060 (1.0654)
ABS equipped		
Upper bore	27.000-27.050 (1.0630-1.0650)	27.060 (1.0654)
Middle bore	22.650-22.700 (0.8917-0.8937)	22.712 (0.8942)
Lower bore	25.400-25.450 (1.0000-1.0020)	25.460 (1.0024)
Brake caliper piston outside diameter		
Non-ABS equipped		
Aero and Phantom models	25.335-25.368 (0.9974-0.9987)	25.320 (0.9968)
Spirit models	26.935-26.968 (1.0604-1.0617)	26.930 (1.0602)
ABS models		
Aero models		
Upper piston	26.935-26.968 (1.0604-1.0617)	26.910 (1.0594)
Middle piston	22.585-22.618 (0.8892-0.8905)	22.560 (0.8882)
Lower piston	25.335-25.368 (0.9974-0.9987)	25.320 (0.9968)
Spirit models		
Upper piston	26.935-26.968 (1.0604-1.0617)	26.930 (1.0602)
Middle piston	22.585-22.618 (0.8892-0.8905)	22.573 (0.8887)
Lower piston	25.318-25.368 (0.9968-0.9987)	25.310 (0.9965)
Master cylinder bore inside diameter	11.000-11.043 (0.4331-0.4348)	11.055 (0.4352)
Master cylinder piston outside diameter	10.957-10.984 (0.4314-0.4324)	10.945 (0.4309)

Table 2 REAR DISC BRAKE SERVICE SPECIFICATIONS (ABS)

	New mm (in.)	Service limit mm (in.)
Brake disc runout	--	0.30 (0.012)
Brake disc thickness	5.8-6.2 (0.23-0.24)	5.0 (0.20)
Brake caliper cylinder bore inside diameter	38.180-38.230 (1.5031-1.5051)	38.240 (1.506)
Brake caliper piston outside diameter	38.098-38.148 (1.4999-1.5019)	38.090 (1.499)
Master cylinder inside diameter	14.000-14.043 (0.5512-0.5529)	14.055 (0.5533)
Master cylinder piston outside diameter	13.957-13.984 (0.5495-0.5506)	13.945 (0.5490)
Master cylinder pushrod adjustment length		
Aero models equipped with ABS	82.0-84.0	(3.23-3.31)
Spirit models equipped with ABS	83.0	(3.28)

Table 3 REAR DRUM BRAKE SERVICE SPECIFICATIONS

	New mm (in.)	Service limit mm (in.)
Brake drum inside diameter	180.0-180.3 (7.09-7.10)	181.0 (7.13)
Brake lining thickness		
Aero models (1)		
2004-2009	4.4-4.7 (0.17-0.19)	2.1 (0.08)
All other models (2)	--	
Brake pedal height	75 (3.0) above top of foot peg	
Brake pedal freeplay	20-30 (0.79-1.18)	--

1. Lining wear can also be determined by the indicator plate mounted on the brake cam.
2. Lining wear is determined by the indicator plate mounted on the brake cam.

Table 4 BRAKE TORQUE SPECIFICATIONS

	N.m	in.-lb.	ft.-lb.
Banjo bolt	34	--	25
Brake lever pivot bolt	1.0	8.9	--
Brake lever pivot bolt nut			
2004-2009 Aero models	5.9	52	--
All other models	6.0	53	--
Brake line flare nuts (ABS) (1)	14	--	10
Front brake caliper bracket pin bolt (2)			
Aero models			
2004-2009	13	115	--
2011-2013	12	106	--
Spirit and Phantom	12	106	--
Front brake caliper mounting bolt (3)	30	--	22
Front brake caliper pin bolt (2)			
Aero models			
2004-2007	23	--	17
2008-2009 and 2011-2013	27	--	20
Spirit and Phantom models	27	--	20
Front brake disc mounting bolt (3)	42	--	31
Front brake caliper bleed valve			
2004-2009 Aero models	5.9	52	--
All other models	5.5	49	--
Front brake caliper pad pin	18	--	13
Front brake caliper pad pin plug			
Aero models			
2004-2009	2.9	26	--
2011-2013	2.5	22	--
Spirit and Phantom models	2.5	22	--
Front brake light switch screw	1.2	11	--
Front master cylinder clamp bolt	12	106	--
Front master cylinder reservoir cap screw			
2004-2009 Aero models	2.0	18	--
All other models	1.5	13	--
Pulser ring bolts			
2011-2013 Aero models	42	--	31
Rear brake arm pinch bolt	26	--	19
Rear brake caliper bleed valve			
All ABS models with rear disc	5.5	49	--
Rear brake caliper pad pin (ABS)	18	--	13
Rear brake caliper pad pin plug (ABS)	2.5	22	--
Rear brake caliper mounting bolt (ABS) (3)	45	--	33
Rear brake caliper stopper pin bolt	69	--	51
Rear brake disc mounting bolt (ABS) (3)	42	--	31
Rear master cylinder mounting bolt	12	106	--
Rear master cylinder pushrod locknut	18	--	13
Rear master cylinder reservoir cap screw			
(ABS) models with rear disc)	1.5	13	--

1. Lubricate brake pipe joint nut threads with DOT 4 brake fluid.
2. Apply a medium strength threadlock onto fastener threads.
3. ALOC fastener. See text for additional information.

CHAPTER SIXTEEN

ANTI-LOCK BRAKE SYSTEM

An optional anti-lock brake system (ABS) is available on some Aero and Spirit VT750 models. ABS prevents wheel lockup during hard braking or when braking on slippery surfaces. During operation, the ABS rapidly pumps the brake(s) and interrupts the flow of hydraulic fluid to the brake caliper(s) of the wheel approaching lockup.

The ABS system includes front and rear wheel speed sensors, front and rear wheel pulser rings, ABS indicator and a combination ABS modulator and ABS control unit (ECU).

NOTE
The ABS control unit (ECU) is permanently mounted on the ABS modulator and neither the ABS modulator nor ECU can be separated, disassembled or serviced. In this chapter both units are referred to as the ABS modulator/ECU.

The ABS control unit monitors the rotational speed of the front and rear wheels. When it determines that a wheel is approaching lockup, the ABS control unit modulates the control piston, which opens and closes the cut-off valve. Hydraulic pressure from the master cylinder to the caliper is momentarily interrupted and then reapplied. The ABS control unit repeats this cycle and rapidly pumps the brake(s) until secure braking is restored.

The front and rear brake systems are also linked on models equipped with ABS. Applying the rear brake pedal applies the rear brake and part of the front brake. Operating the front brake lever applies only the front brake.

The linked brake system (LBS) and ABS are hydraulically independent. If the ABS system is disabled if it fails or shuts down for any reason but the linked brake system will still operate normally if it is in good working order. In addition, problems that occur in the non-ABS part of the brake system can affect the ABS system and cause it to shut down.

This chapter describes troubleshooting and replacement procedures for ABS components. **Table 1** contains ABS system service specifications. **Table 2** provides ABS system troubleshooting DTCs. Replace any part that is damaged. During assembly, install new fasteners when instructed to do so and tighten fasteners to the correct specification listed in **Table 3**.

Before proceeding read *Preventing Brake Fluid Damage* and *Brake Service* in Chapter Fifteen. These sections contain pertinent service information that must be considered when troubleshooting the ABS system.

WARNING
When working on any part of the ABS system, the work area and all tools must be absolutely clean. ABS components can be damaged by even tiny particles of grit that enter the system.

If there is any doubt about your ability to correctly and safely troubleshoot or service the ABS system, refer the job to a dealership.

ABS SERVICE PRECAUTIONS

Before troubleshooting or servicing the ABS, note the following:
1. Handle the ABS components carefully. The ABS modulator/ECU can be damaged if dropped.
2. Turn the ignition switch off before disconnecting or reconnecting ABS harness connectors. If current is flowing when a connector is disconnected, a voltage spike can damage the ECU.
3. While the ECU is constantly monitoring the ABS, it does not recognize problems in other parts of the brake system unless they affect the ABS. For example, worn brake pads and low brake fluid level are not monitored by the ECU. Inspect the brake components at the intervals specified in Chapter Three, or more often when operating under severe riding conditions.

4. Work carefully to prevent from damaging the ABS wiring harness or connectors. Note the routing of the wire harness and the type, number and position of fasteners and clamps used to secure the wiring to the frame and other components.
5. The metal brake lines can be creased and permanently damaged from improper handling. Remove, position and secure the brake lines carefully.
6. The ABS modulator/ECU is not designed to be serviced. Replace the ABS modulator/ECU when faulty.
7. Use OEM fasteners (or equivalents) when replacement is required during service.

ABS INDICATOR OPERATION

When the engine is started, the ABS control unit (ECU) performs self-diagnosis and checks the operating conditions of the ABS components. Self-diagnosis starts when the ignition switch is turned on and ends when the motorcycle speed reaches 10 km/h (6 mph). If the system is operational, the ABS indicator **(Figure 1)** turns off. This system test must be observed each time the motorcycle is ridden.

If a problem is detected, the ABS stores a diagnostic trouble code (DTC) and the ABS indicator light will flash or stay on. A DTC is also set in the ECU memory. When the ABS indicator is flashing or stays on, the ABS function is disabled. However, even when the ABS is disabled, the LBS system (both front and rear brakes) still operates normally. DTCs can be retrieved by performing the DTC retrieval procedure described below.

Self-Diagnosis Test

Perform the following to initiate self-diagnosis.

NOTE
*If the ABS indicator does not turn on when the ignition switch is turned on, perform the **Speedometer Power/Ground Circuit Test** (Chapter Ten).*

1. Turn the ignition switch ON.
2. Check that ABS indicator **(Figure 1)** turns on.
3. Start the engine.
4. Ride the motorcycle until the speed reaches approximately 10 km/h (6 mph).
5. Observe the ABS indicator **(Figure 1)**:
    a. ABS is normal if the ABS indicator turns off.

NOTE
If the ABS indicator turns on or blinks while riding the motorcycle, a malfunction has occurred.

   b. If the ABS indicator remains on or flashes, a malfunction has been detected by the ECU and the ABS system is turned off. Perform the *Pre-Inspection* procedure (this section).

Pre-test Inspection

When the ABS indicator flashes or stays on, make the following general checks before testing the ABS:
1. The ABS indicator **(Figure 1)** can flash if one or more of the following conditions are present:
    a. Tire size is incorrect.
    b. Incorrect tire pressure.
    c. Tire and/or wheel damage.

ANTI-LOCK BRAKE SYSTEM

Figure 2 ABS service check connector / Front / Battery

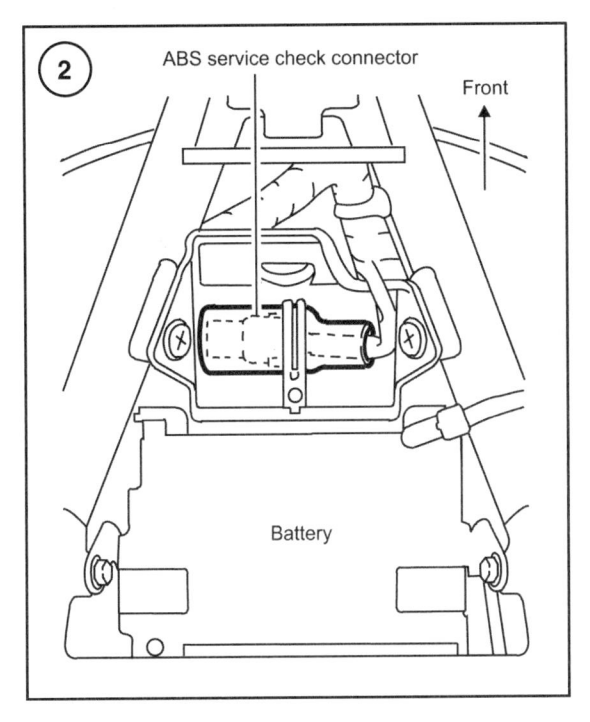

2. The ABS indicator **(Figure 1)** can flash or set a DTC when operating the motorcycle under the following conditions:
   a. Operating the motorcycle on rough and bumpy roads.
   b. Front wheel is not in contact with the ground (wheelie).
   c. Only the front or rear wheel rotates.
   d. When the ABS is operating continuously.
   e. When the ABS modulator/ECU has been interrupted by powerful radio waves.
3. ABS electrical components require a fully-charged battery. When troubleshooting the ABS, make sure the battery is fully charged. When in doubt, test the battery. See Chapter Ten, *Battery*. If the charging system is suspect, test the charging system output. See Chapter Ten, *Charging System*.
4. Check the overall condition of the linked braking system. This includes brake pad wear, tightness of the component fasteners, and brake fluid levels in both master cylinder reservoirs. Check all banjo bolts and metal brake line fittings for tightness. Check for any brake fluid leaks.
5. Inspect the entire ABS wire harness, starting at the ABS modulator/ECU. Check for chaffing and other apparent damage. Particularly check the front and rear wheel speed sensors, wiring harness and connectors.
6. Because electrical components in the ABS operate on low voltage, they are sensitive to any increase in resistance in the circuit. Visually inspect the ABS circuit for any loose or damaged connectors. Then check the voltage drop across the suspect connectors as described in Chapter Two, *Electrical Troubleshooting*. A voltage drop exceeding 0.5 volt indicates excessive resistance and a problem in the circuit.
7. If the ABS indicator flashed or stayed on after a wheel was reinstalled, check the wheel speed sensor and pulser ring for damage. Check the wheel sensor air gap as described under *Wheel Speed Sensor* in this chapter. Check the pulser ring for debris or chipped or damaged teeth.
8. After performing these general checks, retrieve the DTCs from the ECU (this section). Then, clear the DTCs from the ECU (this section) and recheck the system. If the ABS indicator flashes or remains on, retrieve the DTC and troubleshoot/repair the system.

Diagnostic Trouble Codes

Diagnostic trouble codes (DTC) are retrieved from the ECU by triggering a series of timed flashes across the ABS indicator **(Figure 1)**. The number of flashes displayed by the ABS indicator indicates the stored DTC. See **Table 2** for a description of each DTC. Note the following before retrieving DTCs:
1. The DTC set in the ECU memory will remain in memory until the problem is repaired and the DTC is erased. Turning the ignition switch OFF during or after retrieving the DTC does not erase it. However, to view the DTC again after turning the ignition switch OFF and then ON, the retrieval procedure must be repeated (this section).
2. The ECU can store two DTCs and are displayed with the lower number first. For example, if DTCs 12 and 21 are stored, DTC 12 will be displayed first, then DTC 21.
3. Always write down the DTC(s) in the order displayed.
4. After troubleshooting and repairing the ABS, erase the DTC and perform the self-diagnosis. If the ABS indicator does not flash or stay on after completing the self-diagnosis, the problem has been repaired.

Retrieving DTC(s)

NOTE
Do not start the engine during this procedure.

1. Turn the ignition switch off.
2. Remove the seat (Chapter Seventeen).
3. Remove the cover from the ABS service check connector **(Figure 2)**.
4. With the ignition switch turned off, connect a jumper wire between the brown/white and green ter-

minals in the ABS service check connector (**Figure 3**).

5. Turn the ignition switch on and watch the ABS indicator (**Figure 1**). The ABS indicator will turn on for 2 seconds and turn off for 3.6 seconds. If there is a problem code stored in memory it will start flashing the DTC after the 3.6 second interval. If there no problem code stored in memory, the ABS indicator (**Figure 1**) will stay on continuously (**Figure 4**). Note the following:
   a. If a code is flashing, continue the procedure to count the number of flashes.
   b. If there is no code, go to Step 10.

6. Identify the DTC(s) by counting the flashes. For example, refer to **Figure 5** to identify the flash pattern for DTC No. 13.

7. The ECU can store up to two DTCs and will display the codes starting with the lower number first. When there are two codes, they are separated by a 3.6 second pause. Refer to **Figure 6** to identify the flash pattern for DTC No. 11 and DTC No. 21.

8. After retrieving and writing down the DTC(s), refer to Table 2 to identify the effected circuit. Refer to *DTC Troubleshooting* in this section to troubleshoot the DTC.

9. After repairing the problem, erase the trouble code(s) to confirm the problem has been repaired as described in *Erasing DTCs* in this section.

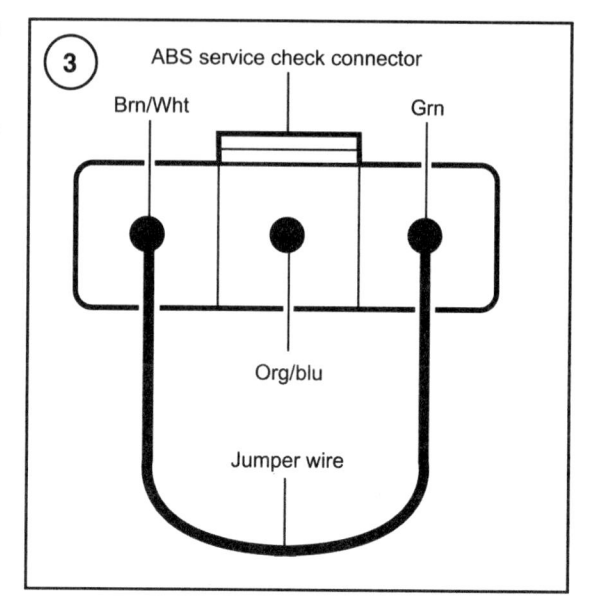

10. Turn the ignition switch off. Remove the jumper wire from the ABS service check connector (**Figure 3**) and install the cover onto the connector (**Figure 2**).

11. Reinstall the seat (Chapter Seventeen).

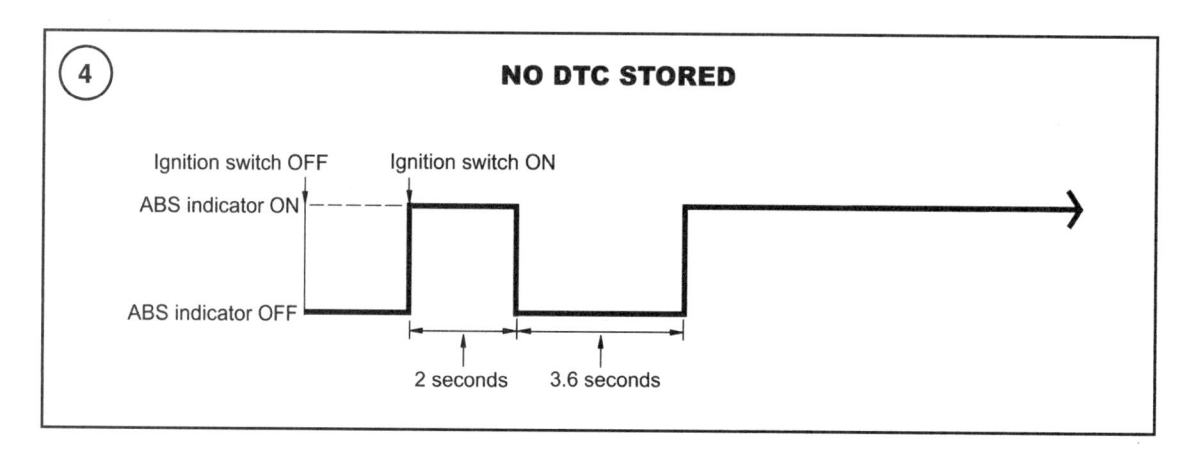

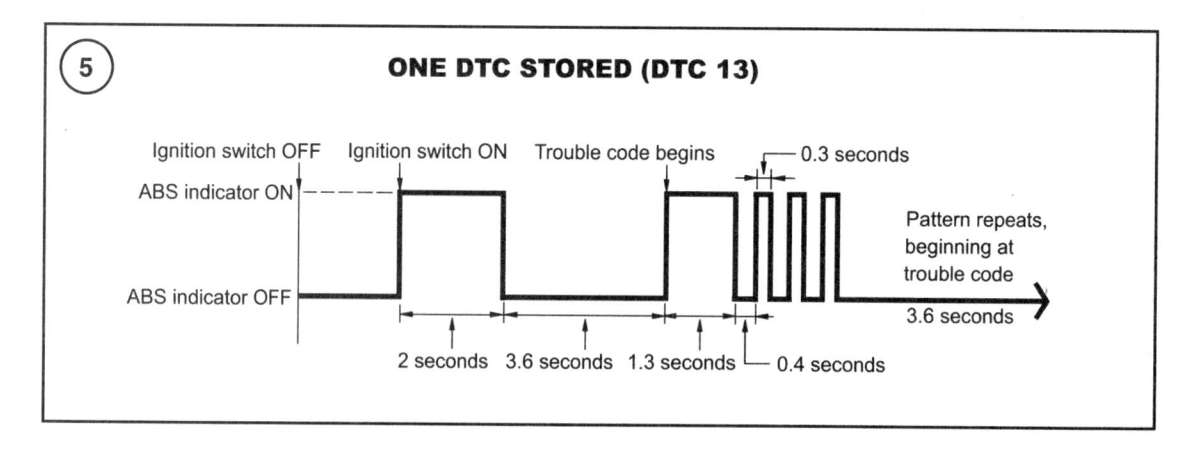

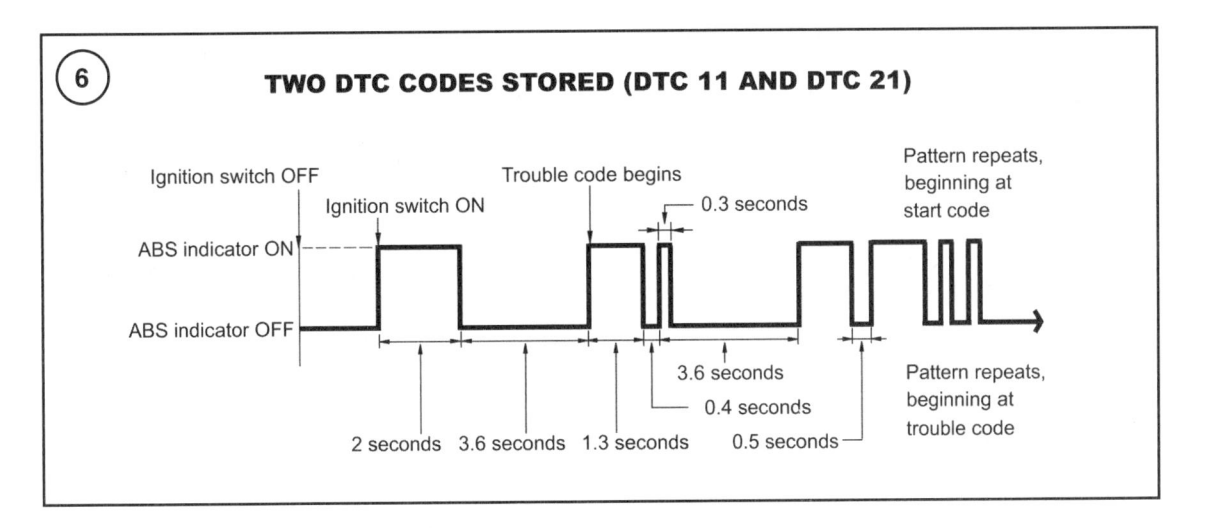

ANTI-LOCK BRAKE SYSTEM

TWO DTC CODES STORED (DTC 11 AND DTC 21)

Figure 6 — Timing diagram showing ABS indicator pattern for two stored DTC codes (DTC 11 and DTC 21): Ignition switch OFF, Ignition switch ON, ABS indicator ON/OFF transitions with intervals of 2 seconds, 3.6 seconds, 1.3 seconds, 0.5 seconds; trouble code begins with 0.3 seconds pulses, 3.6 seconds and 0.4 seconds intervals; pattern repeats beginning at start code and at trouble code.

Erasing DTCs

1. Turn the ignition switch off.
2. Remove the seat (Chapter Seventeen).
3. Remove the cover from the ABS service check connector (**Figure 2**).
4. With the ignition switch turned off, connect a jumper wire between the brown/white and green terminals in the ABS service check connector (**Figure 3**).

NOTE
Read through the following steps to understand the required sequence.

5. Turn the ignition switch to its ON position while at the same time squeezing the front brake lever. The ABS indicator (**Figure 1**) should turn on for 2 seconds and then turn off.
6. Release the front brake lever immediately after the ABS indicator turns off. The ABS indicator should turn on.
7. Apply the front brake lever immediately after the ABS indicator turns on. The ABS indicator should turn off.
8. Release the front brake lever immediately after the ABS indicator turns off.
9. When the codes are completely erased, the ABS indicator will flash 2 times and then turn off and stay off.
10. Turn the ignition switch off. Remove the jumper wire from the ABS service check connector (**Figure 3**) and install the cover onto the connector (**Figure 2**).
11. Reinstall the seat (Chapter Seventeen).

DTC TROUBLESHOOTING

If the *Self-Diagnosis Test* (this chapter) indicates a problem with the ABS, retrieve any DTCs as described in *Diagnostic Trouble Codes* in this chapter. Find the DTC(s) in **Table 2** and refer to the appropriate procedure in this section to troubleshoot the circuit.

NOTE
When diagnosing a problem with the ABS, remember that the problem may not have been caused by a failure with an ABS component. For the ABS to operate properly, the mechanical and hydraulic components of the brake system must be in good working order. Intermittent problems, which are the most difficult to troubleshoot, are often caused by poor electrical connections or damaged wiring. These types of problems can often be found with a thorough visual inspection.

Before troubleshooting, note the following:
1. The electrical components in the ABS require a fully charged battery. When troubleshooting the ABS, make sure the battery is fully charged. When in doubt, test the battery. See *Battery* in Chapter Ten. If the charging system is suspect, test the charging system output. See *Charging System* in Chapter Ten.
2. Make sure the front and rear brake systems are in good condition:
   a. Check the brake fluid level in both reservoirs.
   b. Inspect the brake hoses and banjo fittings for leakage and damage.
   c. Verify that the brakes operate correctly with no brake drag.
   d. Check the wiring harnesses for proper routing and condition. Make sure they are properly secured.
   e. All electrical connectors must be clean and properly connected.

f. Check that the ABS fuses (Chapter Ten) are in good condition.

g. Verify that all of the brake components are properly mounted and that all fasteners are tightened correctly.

3. Make sure both wheels run true. Worn or damaged wheel bearings, damaged tires or wheels can cause the ABS system to malfunction and set a DTC.

4. An incorrect tire size or inflation pressure can cause the ABS to malfunction and set a DTC.

5. Inspect the ABS wire harness, starting at the ECU. Check for chaffing and other apparent damage. Particularly check the front and rear wheel speed sensors, wiring harness and connectors.

6. Because electrical components in the ABS operate on low voltage, they are sensitive to any increase in resistance in the circuit. Visually inspect the ABS circuit for any loose or damaged connectors. Then check the voltage drop across the suspect connectors as described under *Voltage Drop Test* in Chapter Two. A voltage drop exceeding 0.5 volt indicates excessive resistance and a problem in the circuit.

7. If the ABS indicator flashed or stayed on after a wheel was reinstalled, check the wheel speed sensor and pulser rings for damage. Check the wheel sensor air gap as described under *Wheel Speed Sensor* in this chapter. Check the pulser ring for debris or chipped and damaged teeth.

8. After performing these general checks, retrieve the trouble code(s) from the ECU (this Chapter). Then, clear the DTCs from the ECU (this chapter). If the ABS indicator flashes or remains on, retrieve the trouble code and troubleshoot the system.

9. Refer to the wiring diagrams at the end of this manual to identify the connectors and their wire colors. Refer to the appropriate section in this chapter to locate the individual components and their connectors.

10. Turn the ignition switch off before disconnecting and reconnecting connectors.

11. Do not disconnect or reconnect electrical connectors when the ignition switch is on. A voltage spike can damage the ABS modulator/ECU.

12. The terms open circuit and short circuit are used in the troubleshooting procedures. A short circuit occurs when a wire incorrectly contacts a ground or another wire causing an unwanted current path or circuit. This can be caused from worn insulation. Most shorts will burn a fuse or open some other type of circuit protector. An open circuit is a physical break in a wire, electrical component or connector that prevents a complete current path.

13. Before troubleshooting, check the connectors identified in the procedure for corrosion, loose or damaged terminals. Then check the wiring harness for damage such as frayed wiring, breaks or excessive heat.

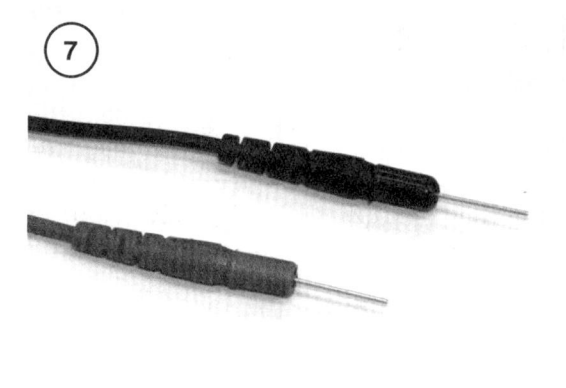

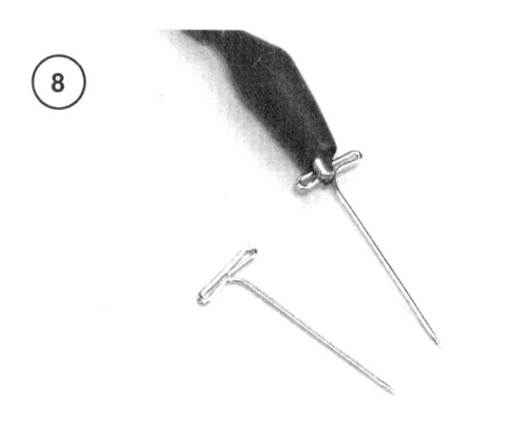

14. When testing at the ABS modulator/ECU harness side connectors, always insert the test probe into the connector terminal. Do not back-probe the connector as this may damage the wire, connector or seals (if used). Note the following:

a. Use test leads equipped with back probe pins **(Figure 7)**. These lead ends are smaller than typical test leads and mount onto standard meter leads. Sharpen the lead ends if blunt.

b. If back probe pins are not available, use T-pins **(Figure 8)** available from fabric and craft stores. The T-shaped head makes an ideal connection point for alligator test leads.

CAUTION
Do not force a test lead into a connector as this may damage the connector and cause an open circuit.

15. To check for an intermittent problem, carefully move the wiring harness and/or connector(s) by hand with the meter connected to the circuit. Then, check for loose or contaminated connectors and terminals.

ANTI-LOCK BRAKE SYSTEM

9 ABS MODULATOR 25-PIN CONNECTOR

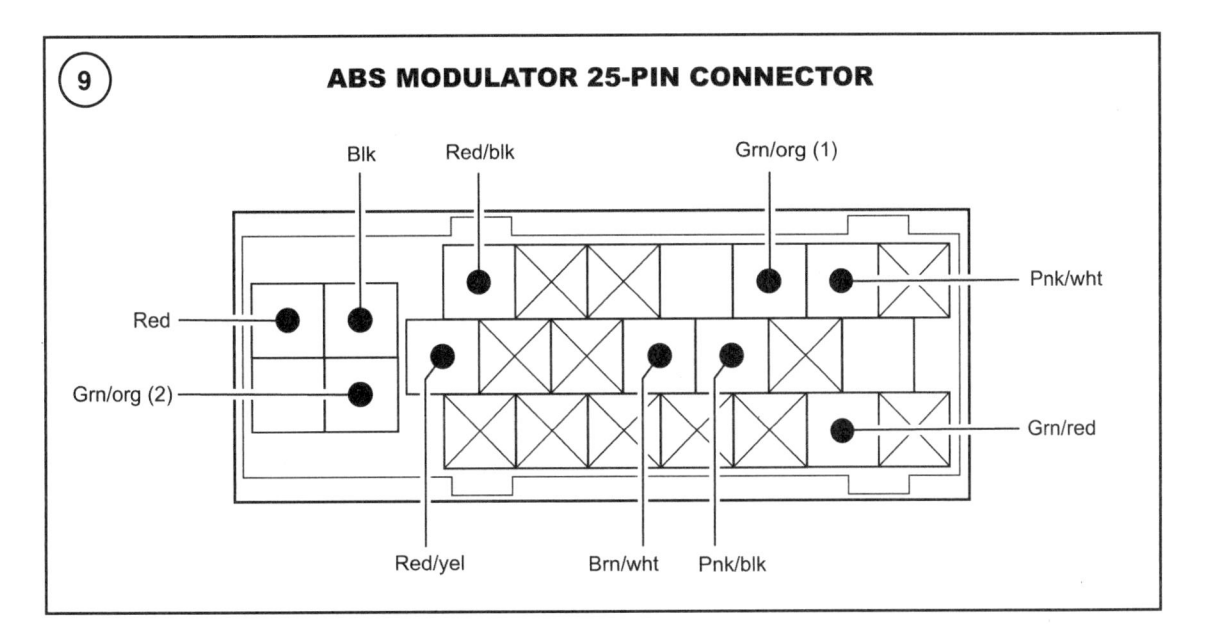

Diagram labels: Blk, Red/blk, Grn/org (1), Pnk/wht, Red, Grn/red, Grn/org (2), Red/yel, Brn/wht, Pnk/blk

16. If a DTC refers to a particular component, refer to the appropriate section in this manual to inspect the component.

17. When a test refers to battery voltage use the battery's actual voltage reading as the specified voltage reading. Refer to *Static Voltage Test* in *Battery* in Chapter Ten.

18. Do not perform tests with a battery charger attached to the battery or circuit. Test and charge the battery as described in Chapter Ten.

19. The last step in all troubleshooting sections is to replace the ABS modulator/ECU with a known good unit. However, before replacing the ABS modulator/ECU, take the motorcycle to a dealership for further testing. Most dealerships will not accept the return of electrical components. Have the dealership confirm that the ABS modulator/ECU is faulty before purchasing a replacement.

20. After troubleshooting and replacing a component, erase any DTC(s) and perform a system self-diagnosis (this chapter) to assure the problem has been corrected.

21. If the specified tests fail to locate the problem, refer troubleshooting and repair to a dealership.

22. After troubleshooting, reverse the removal steps to reinstall all previously removed parts.

23. Refer to the appropriate section in this chapter to access the speed sensors, pulser rings and to disconnect the speed sensor and ABS modulator/ECU connectors.

24. Refer to *Fuses* in Chapter Ten when it is necessary to inspect or replace one of the ABS fuses. These fuses are also identified on the wiring diagrams at the end of this manual.

DTC 11, 12, 21, 41 or 42: Front Wheel Speed Sensor

NOTE
If DTC 41 is recorded, check the front brake calipers for excessive brake drag.

1. Measure the air gap between the front wheel speed sensor and pulser ring as described in this chapter. The correct air gap is 0.4-1.2 mm (0.02-0.05 in.). Note the following:
   a. If the air gap is correct, continue the procedure.
   b. If the air gap is incorrect, there is no adjustment. Check for loose or damaged parts.
2. Perform the following inspections:
   a. Inspect for magnetic debris between the speed sensor and pulser ring.
   b. Inspect the speed sensor tip for chips and other damage.
   c. Check the pulser ring teeth for damage.
   d. Check the pulser ring slots for debris, uneven surfaces and other damage.
   e. If there is no debris or damage, make sure the speed sensor and pulser ring are properly installed.
   f. If a problem was found, clean, repair, tighten or replace the part.
   g. If a problem was not found, continue the procedure.
3. Remove the seat (Chapter Seventeen) and the fuel tank (Chapter Eight or Chapter Nine).
4. Disconnect the green 2-pin speed sensor connector and the 25-pin ABS modulator/ECU connector.
5. Check for continuity between the No. 1 green/orange wire terminal in the ABS connector (**Figure 9**) and ground with an ohmmeter. Then, check for

continuity between the pink/black wire terminal in the ABS connector **(Figure 9)** and ground. Note the following:
  a. If there is no continuity, continue the procedure.
  b. If there is continuity, check for a short in the green/orange wire and the pink/black wire between the speed sensor and the ABS modulator/ECU.

6. Short the pink/black wire and the No. 2 green/orange wire terminals in the 25-pin ABS modulator/ECU connector **(Figure 9)**. Check for continuity between the pink/black wire and green/orange wire terminals in the 2-pin speed sensor connector. Note the following:
a. If there is continuity, continue the procedure.
b. If there is no continuity, check for an open circuit in the wire(s) between the ABS modulator/ECU and speed sensor.

7. At the front speed sensor terminals (sensor side male connector), check for continuity between the blue wire terminal and ground. Then check the continuity between the white wire terminal and ground. Note the following:
  a. If there is no continuity, continue the procedure.
  b. If there is continuity during either test, the front wheel speed sensor is damaged. Replace the speed sensor as described in this chapter.

8. If the problem has not been found, install a new front wheel speed sensor as described in this chapter. Reconnect all ABS connectors. Erase the DTC as described in this chapter and test ride the motorcycle at a speed above 30 km/h (19 mph) and check to see if the ABS indicator flashes **(Figure 1)**. Note the following:
  a. If the ABS indicator does not flash, the original speed sensor was faulty.
  b. If the ABS indicator flashes, replace the ABS modulator/ECU (this chapter).

9. Perform the *Self-Diagnosis Test* (this chapter) to assure the problem has been corrected.

DTC 13, 14, 23 or 43: Rear Wheel Speed Sensor

NOTE
If DTC 43 is recorded, check the rear brake caliper for excessive brake drag.

1. Measure the air gap between the rear wheel speed sensor and pulser ring as described in this chapter. The correct air gap is 0.4-1.2 mm (0.02-0.05 in.). Note the following:
  a. If the air gap is correct, continue the procedure.
  b. If the air gap is incorrect, there is no adjustment. Check for loose or damaged parts.

2. Perform the following inspections:
  a. Inspect for magnetic debris between the speed sensor and the pulser ring.
  b. Inspect the speed sensor tip for chips and other damage.
  c. Check the pulser ring teeth or slots for damage.
  d. Check the pulser ring slots for debris, uneven surfaces and other damage.
  e. If there is no debris or damage, make sure the speed sensor and pulser ring are properly installed.
  f. If a problem was found, clean, repair, tighten or replace the part.
  g. If a problem was not found, continue the procedure.

3. Remove the seat and the left side cover (Chapter Seventeen).

4. Disconnect the green 2-pin speed sensor connector and the 25-pin ABS modulator/ECU connector.

5. Check for continuity between the green/red wire terminal in the ABS connector **(Figure 9)** and ground with an ohmmeter. Then, check for continuity between the pink/white wire terminal in the ABS connector **(Figure 9)** and ground. Note the following:
  a. If there is no continuity, continue the procedure.
  b. If there is continuity, check for a short in the green/red wire and the pink/white wire between the 2-pin speed sensor connector and the 25-pin ABS modulator/ECU connector.

6. Short the pink/white wire and green/red wire terminals in the 25-pin ABS modulator/ECU connector **(Figure 9)**. Check for continuity between the pink/white wire and green/red wire terminals in the 2-pin speed sensor connector. Note the following:
  a. If there is continuity, continue the procedure.
  b. If there is no continuity, check for an open circuit in the wire(s) between the ABS modulator/ECU and the speed sensor.

7. At the rear speed sensor terminals (sensor side male connector), check for continuity between the blue wire terminal and ground and then check for continuity, between the white wire terminal and ground. Note the following:
  a. If there is no continuity, continue the procedure.
  b. If there is continuity during either test, the rear wheel speed sensor is damaged. Replace the speed sensor as described in this chapter.

8. If the problem has not been found, install a new rear wheel speed sensor as described in this chapter. Reconnect all ABS connectors. Erase the DTC(s) as described in this chapter and test ride the motorcycle

ANTI-LOCK BRAKE SYSTEM

at a speed above 30 km/h (19 mph) and check to see if the ABS indicator flashes **(Figure 1)**. Note the following:

    a. If the ABS indicator does not flash, the original speed sensor was faulty.

    b. If the ABS indicator flashes, replace the ABS modulator/ECU (this chapter).

9. Perform the *Self-Diagnosis Test* (this chapter) to assure the problem has been corrected.

DTC 31, 32, 33, 34, 37 or 38: Solenoid Valve

1. Erase the DTC(s) as described in this chapter.
2. Test ride the motorcycle at a speed above 30 km/h (19 mph).
3. If the ABS indicator is flashing, retrieve the DTC(s) as described in this chapter.

    a. If DTC 31, 32, 33, 34, 37 or 38 was retrieved, the ABS modulator/ECU is damaged. Replace the ABS modulator/ECU (this chapter).

    b. If DTC 31, 32, 33, 34, 37 or 38 was not retrieved, a code is not stored in memory and the problem was caused by a temporary failure.

4. Perform the *Self-Diagnosis Test* (this chapter) to assure the problem has been corrected.

DTC 51, 52 or 53: Pump Motor

1. Remove the left side cover (Chapter Seventeen).
2. Open the fuse box and check the ABS motor fuse as described in *Fuses* in Chapter Ten.

    Note the following:

    a. If the fuse is blown, continue the procedure.

    b. If the fuse is not blown, continue with Step 4.

3. Remove the ABS motor fuse from the fuse box (Chapter Ten). Disconnect the 25-pin ABS modulator/ECU connector. Check for continuity between red wire terminal **(Figure 9)** and ground. Note the following:

    a. If there is continuity, there is a short circuit in the red wire between the ABS modulator/ECU and the fuse box.

    b. If there is no continuity, the blown fuse could have been caused by a temporary failure. Install a new ABS motor fuse and recheck.

4. Reinstall the ABS motor fuse if it was removed. Disconnect the 25-pin ABS modulator/ECU connector. Measure the voltage between the red wire terminal **(Figure 9)** and ground. The voltmeter should read battery voltage. Note the following:

    a. If there is no battery voltage, continue the procedure.

    b. If there is battery voltage, continue with Step 6.

5. Disconnect the white 2-pin ABS battery connector attached to the battery's positive terminal. Measure the voltage between the red/green wire terminal on the battery-side connector and ground. Measure voltage at both of the connector's red/green wire terminals. The voltmeter should read battery voltage. Note the following:

    a. If there is battery voltage, check the green/red wire between the 2-pin connector and the fuse box for an open circuit. Then check the red/green wire between the fuse box and the ABS modulator/ECU for an open circuit.

    b. If there is no battery voltage, check for an open circuit in the red/green wire between the battery and the 2-pin connector.

6. If the problem has not been found, reconnect all ABS connectors. Reinstall the ABS motor fuse, if removed. Erase the DTC(s) as described in this chapter and test ride the motorcycle at a speed above 30 km/h (19 mph). Then, check to see if the ABS indicator flashes **(Figure 1)**. Note the following:

    a. If the ABS indicator does not flash, a code is not stored in memory and the blown fuse could have been caused by a temporary failure.

    b. If the ABS indicator flashes a DTC 51, 52 or 53 code, the ABS modulator/ECU is damaged. Replace the ABS modulator/ECU (this chapter).

7. Perform the *Self-Diagnosis Test* (this chapter) to assure the problem has been corrected.

DTC 54: Fail-Safe Relay

1. Remove the left side cover (Chapter Seventeen).
2. Open the fuse box and check the ABS solenoid fuse as described in *Fuses* in Chapter Ten. Note the following:

    a. If the fuse is blown, continue the procedure.

    b. If the fuse is not blown, continue with Step 4.

3. Remove the ABS solenoid fuse from the fuse box (Chapter Ten). Disconnect the 25-pin ABS modulator/ECU connector. Check for continuity between the black wire terminal **(Figure 9)** and ground. Note the following:

    a. If there is continuity, there is a short circuit in the black wire between the ABS modulator/ECU connector and the fuse box.

    b. If there is no continuity, the blown fuse could have been caused by a temporary failure. Install a new ABS solenoid fuse and recheck.

4. Reinstall the ABS solenoid fuse if it was removed. Disconnect the 25-pin ABS modulator/ECU connector. Measure the voltage between the black wire terminal **(Figure 9)** and ground. The voltmeter should read battery voltage. Note the following:

    a. If there is no battery voltage, continue the procedure.

    b. If there is battery voltage, continue with Step 6.

5. Disconnect the 2-pin ABS battery connector attached to the positive battery terminal. Measure the voltage between the red/green wire terminal in the battery-side connector and ground. Measure voltage at both of the connector's red/green wire terminals. The voltmeter should read battery voltage. Note the following:
   a. If there is battery voltage, check the green/red wire between the 2-pin connector and the fuse box for an open circuit. Then check the black wire between the fuse box and the ABS modulator/ECU for an open circuit.
   b. If there is no battery voltage, check for an open circuit in the red/green wire between the battery and the 2-pin connector.
6. If the problem has not been found, reconnect all ABS connectors. Reinstall the ABS solenoid fuse, if removed. Erase the DTC(s) as described in this chapter and test ride the motorcycle at a speed above 30 km/h (19 mph) and check to see if the ABS indicator flashes (Figure 1). Note the following:
   a. If the ABS indicator does not flash, a code is not stored in memory and the blown fuse could have been caused by a temporary failure.
   b. If the ABS indicator flashes DTC 54, the ABS modulator/ECU is damaged. Replace the ABS modulator/ECU (this chapter).
7. Perform the *Self-Diagnosis Test* (this chapter) to assure the problem has been corrected.

DTC 61 or 62: Power Circuit

1. Remove the left side cover.
2. Open the fuse box and check the ABS main fuse as described in *Fuses* in Chapter Ten. Note the following:
   a. If the fuse is blown, continue the procedure.
   b. If the fuse is not blown, continue with Step 4.
3. Remove the ABS main fuse from the fuse box. Disconnect the 25-pin ABS modulator/ECU connector. Check for continuity between the red/yellow wire terminal (Figure 9) and ground. Note the following:
   a. If there is continuity, there is a short circuit in the red/yellow wire between the ABS modulator/ECU and the fuse box.
   b. If there is no continuity, the blown fuse could have been caused by a temporary failure. Install a new ABS main fuse and recheck.
4. Reinstall the ABS main fuse if it was removed. Disconnect the 25-pin ABS modulator/ECU connector. Measure the voltage between the red/yellow wire terminal (Figure 9) and ground. The voltmeter should read battery voltage. Note the following:
   a. If there is battery voltage, continue the procedure.
   b. If there is no battery voltage, check for an open circuit in the red/yellow wire between the ABS modulator/ECU and the fuse box and in the red/black wire between the fuse box and the ignition switch. If both wires are in good condition, test the charging system as described in Chapter Ten.
5. If the problem has not been found, reconnect all ABS connectors. Reinstall the ABS solenoid fuse, if removed. Erase the DTC(s) as described in this chapter and test ride the motorcycle at a speed above 30 km/h (19 mph) and check to see if the ABS indicator flashes (Figure 1). Note the following:
   a. If the ABS indicator does not flash, a DTC is not stored in memory and the blown fuse could have been caused by a temporary failure.
   b. If the ABS indicator flashes DTC 61 or 62, the ABS modulator/ECU is damaged. Replace the ABS modulator/ECU (this chapter).
6. Perform the *Self-Diagnosis Test* (this chapter) to assure the problem has been corrected.

DTC 71: Tire Size and Condition

1. Check the front and rear tire pressure (Chapter Three). If the tire pressure is low, check for a leak or a damaged tire.
2. Check that the correct size tires are installed on the motorcycle. Refer to Chapter Twelve for OEM tire size information.
3. Check for a damaged tire or wheel as described in Chapter Twelve.
4. Erase the DTC(s) as described in this chapter. Test ride the motorcycle at a speed above 30 km/h (19 mph) and check to see if the ABS indicator flashes (Figure 1). Note the following:
   a. If the ABS indicator does not flash, a DTC is not stored in memory. The code could have been set by a temporary failure.
   b. If the ABS indicator flashes DTC 71, the ABS modulator/ECU is damaged. Replace the ABS modulator/ECU.
5. Perform the *Self-Diagnosis Test* (this chapter) to assure the problem has been corrected.

DTC 81: ABS Control Unit and CPU

1. Erase the DTC(s) as described in this chapter. Test ride the motorcycle at a speed above 30 km/h (19 mph) and check to see if the ABS indicator flashes (Figure 1). Note the following:
   a. If the ABS indicator does not flash, a DTC is not stored in memory. The code could have been set by a temporary failure.

ANTI-LOCK BRAKE SYSTEM

b. If the ABS indicator flashes DTC 71, the ABS modulator/ECU is damaged. Replace the ABS modulator/ECU (this chapter).

2. Perform the *Self-Diagnosis Test* (this chapter) to assure the problem has been corrected.

ABS INDICATOR CIRCUIT TROUBLESHOOTING

When the ABS indicator **(Figure 1)** does not turn on when the ignition switch is turned on or does not turn off when there is no DTC set in memory, perform the tests in this section.

NOTE
*Refer to **Self-Diagnosis Test** (this chapter) to review ABS indicator operation.*

ABS Indicator Does Not Turn On When the Ignition Switch is Turned On

If the ABS indicator **(Figure 1)** does not turn on when the ignition switch is turned on, perform the following:

1. Perform the *Speedometer Power/Ground Circuit Test* (Chapter Ten). If a problem was not found, continue the procedure.
2. Disconnect the 25-pin connector at the ABS modulator/ECU as described in *ABS Modulator/ECU* in this chapter.
3. Turn the ignition switch on and check the ABS indicator **(Figure 1)**. Note the following:
   a. If the ABS indicator turned on, the ABS modulator/ECU is damaged. Replace the ABS modulator/ECU (this chapter).
   b. If the ABS indicator did not turn on, continue the procedure.
4. Remove the speedometer (Chapter Ten) but do not disconnect its 16-pin connector. Remove the dust cover from the 16-pin speedometer connector.
5. Check for continuity between the red/black wire in the 16-pin wiring harness side connector and ground. There should be no continuity. Note the following:
   a. If there is continuity, check the red/black wire between the ABS modulator/ECU and the speedometer for a short circuit.
   b. If there is no continuity, the speedometer is damaged. Replace the speedometer (Chapter Ten) and recheck the ABS indicator operation.

ABS Indicator Stays On When There is No DTC

If the ABS indicator stays on and a code cannot be retrieved from memory, perform the following:

1. Check the ABS main fuse as described in Chapter Ten. Note the following:
   a. If the fuse is blown, continue the procedure.
   b. If the fuse is not blown, continue with Step 3.
2. Disconnect the 25-pin ABS modulator/ECU connector as described in this chapter. Check for continuity between the red/yellow wire in the 25-pin wiring harness side connector **(Figure 9)** and ground. There should be no continuity. Note the following:
   a. If there is continuity, check the red/yellow wire between the ABS modulator/ECU and the fuse box for a short circuit.
   b. If there is no continuity, a temporary failure may have caused the problem. Make sure the ABS main fuse is in good condition and reinstall it. Turn the ignition switch on and perform the *Self-Diagnosis Check* in this chapter
3. Reinstall the ABS main fuse if removed. Turn the ignition switch on and measure voltage between the red/yellow wire in the 25-pin wiring harness side connector **(Figure 9)** and ground. There should be battery voltage. Turn the ignition switch off and note the following:
   a. If there is battery voltage, continue the procedure.
   b. If there is no battery voltage, check the red/yellow wire between the ABS modulator/ECU and the fuse box for an open circuit. If red/yellow wire is in good condition, test the charging system as described in Chapter Ten.
4. Check for continuity between brown/white wire in the 25-pin wiring harness side connector **(Figure 9)** and ground. There should be no continuity. Note the following:
   a. If there is continuity, check the brown/white between the ABS modulator/ECU and the ABS service check connector for a short circuit.
   b. If there is no continuity, continue the procedure.
5. Remove the speedometer (Chapter Ten), but do not disconnect its 16-pin connector. Remove the dust cover from the 16-pin speedometer connector.
6. Connect a jumper wire between the red/black wire in the 16-pin speedometer wiring harness connector and ground. Turn the ignition switch on and check the ABS indicator **(Figure 1)**. The ABS indicator should turn off. Remove the jumper wire and note the following:
   a. If the ABS indicator turned off, continue the procedure.
   b. If the ABS indicator did not turn off, the speedometer assembly is damaged. Replace the speedometer assembly (Chapter Ten) and retest.
7. Connect a jumper wire between the red/black wire in the 25-pin wiring harness side connector **(Figure 9)** and ground. Turn the ignition switch on and check

the ABS indicator (**Figure 1**). The ABS indicator should turn off. Remove the jumper wire and note the following:
   a. If the ABS indicator turned off, continue the procedure.
   b. If the ABS indicator did not turn off, check the red/black wire between the ABS modulator/ECU and the speedometer for an open circuit.

8. Check for continuity between the No. 2 green/orange wire in the 25-pin ABS modulator/ECU wiring harness side connector (**Figure 9**) and ground. Note the following:
   a. If there is continuity, the ABS modulator/ECU is damaged. Replace the ABS modulator/ECU (this chapter) and retest.
   b. If there is no continuity, check the green/orange wire between the ABS modulator/ECU and ground for an open circuit.

WHEEL SPEED SENSORS

The wheel speed sensors and pulser rings work as magnetic triggering units to signal the ECU on the speed of the wheels. The wheel speed sensors are permanent magnet-type sensors and are non-adjustable.

The front wheel speed sensor mounts on the right front brake caliper mounting bracket. The rear wheel speed sensor mounts on the rear brake caliper mounting bracket. Each sensor aligns with a pulser ring. The front pulser ring is mounted onto the front wheel hub. The rear pulser ring is mounted on the rear hub.

As the wheel turns, projections on the pulser ring pass across the wheel speed sensor and disturb the magnetic field provided by the speed sensor magnet. This causes the magnetic field to turn off and on and create small voltage signals or pulses at the speed sensor. Because the frequency of the voltage signals varies proportionally to the speed of the pulser ring (wheel), the ECU uses these signals to calculate wheel speed and to determine whether the wheels are about to lock.

Air Gap Inspection

The air gap is a fixed distance between the wheel speed sensor and pulser ring to ensure proper signal pickup from the sensor to the ABS modulator/ECU. The air gap is non-adjustable.

NOTE
An incorrect air gap measurement can set a diagnostic trouble code (DTC).

1. Place the motorcycle on its centerstand.

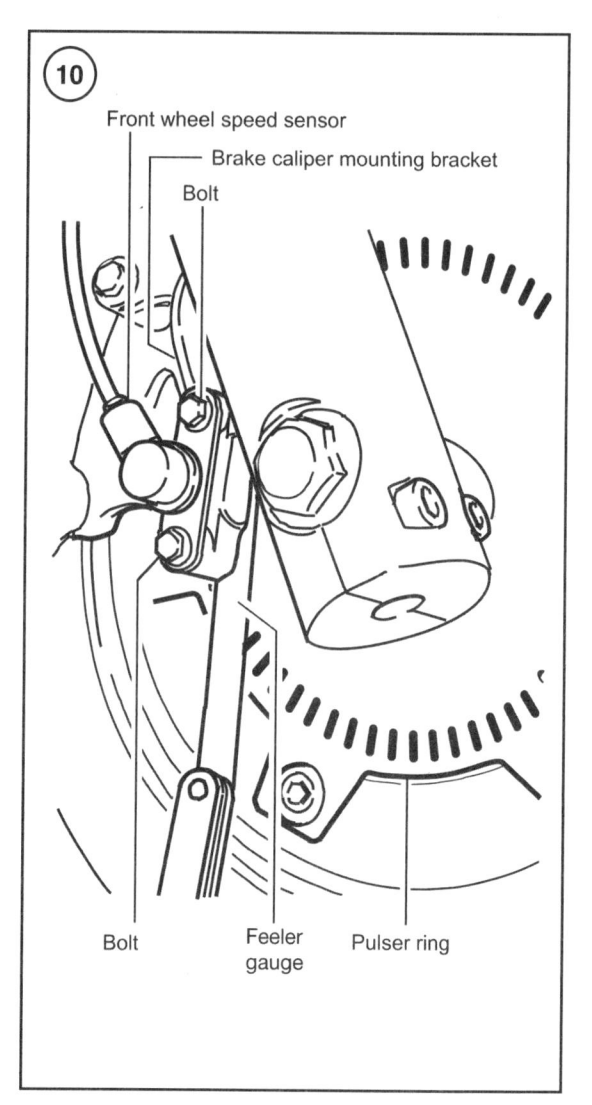

2A. Front wheel—Support the motorcycle with the front wheel off the ground. Refer to *Bike Lift* in Chapter Twelve.

2B. Rear wheel—Support the motorcycle with the rear wheel off the ground. Refer to *Bike Lift* in Chapter Twelve.

3. Spin the wheel slowly by hand. Inspect the pulser ring for any chipped or damaged projections, road tar or other debris that could affect the measurement.

4. Measure the air gap between the wheel sensor and the pulser ring with a non-magnetic feeler gauge. See **Figure 10** (front) or **Figure 11** (rear). Rotate the wheel and measure the air gap all the way around the pulser ring circumference. The air gap measurement for the front and rear wheels is 0.4-1.2 mm (0.02-0.05 in.).

5. The air gap is not adjustable. If the air gap is incorrect, perform the following:
   a. Check the speed sensor for loose or damaged mounting bolts.

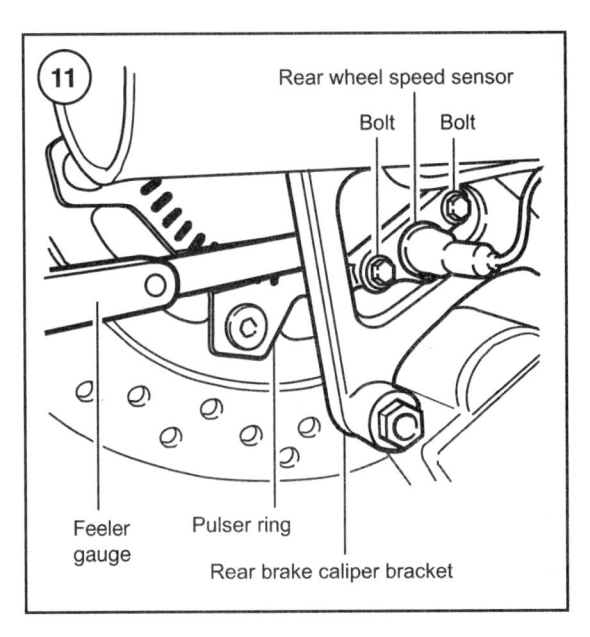

ANTI-LOCK BRAKE SYSTEM

Figure 11 — Rear wheel speed sensor, Bolt, Bolt, Feeler gauge, Pulser ring, Rear brake caliper bracket

Figure 12 — Front wheel speed sensor connector, Front, Front ignition coil

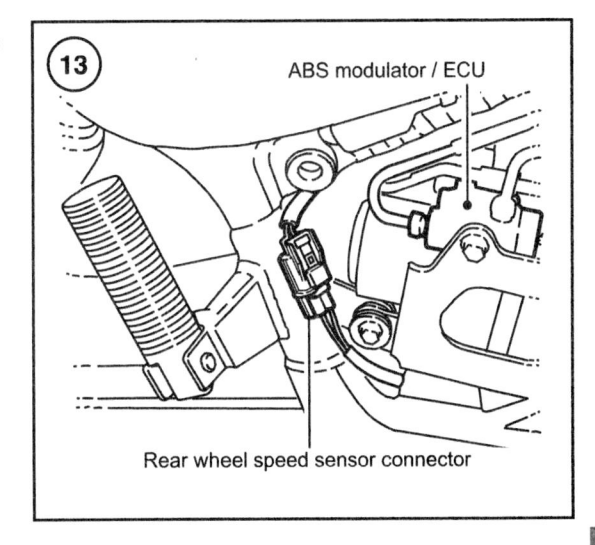

Figure 13 — ABS modulator / ECU, Rear wheel speed sensor connector

b. Check for a damaged speed sensor assembly.
c. Check the front brake caliper mounting bracket for damage.
d. Check the rear brake caliper mounting bracket for damage.
e. Check for loose or missing pulser ring/brake disc mounting bolts.
f. Check for a damaged pulser ring.

WARNING
Do not shim the speed sensor to correct the air gap. An incorrect measurement indicates that the wheel speed sensor, pulser ring or a related component is improperly installed or damaged.

Front Wheel Speed Sensor Removal/Installation

1. Turn the ignition switch off.
2. Remove the fuel tank (Chapter Nine).
3. Note how the speed sensor wire is routed along the fork tube and frame, then release the wiring harness from the clamps that secure it in place.
4. Remove the bolts securing the brake hose and speed sensor wiring harness to the front fender.
5. Disconnect the 2-pin front wheel speed sensor connector (**Figure 12**).
6. Remove the sensor mounting bolts and remove the sensor (**Figure 10**) with its wiring harness attached.
7. Thoroughly clean the speed sensor mounting hole in the caliper bracket of all debris. Also clean the mounting area on the outside of the hole.
8. Thoroughly clean the speed sensor's mounting surface so that it can seat flush against the caliper mounting bracket.
9. Installation is the reverse of these steps, plus the following:
   a. Route the speed sensor wiring harness along the same path noted during removal. Secure the wiring harness with the clamps and tighten the clamp mounting bolts securely. Make sure the speed sensor wiring harness is not twisted.
   b. Measure the speed sensor air gap as described in this section.
   c. Tighten the wheel speed sensor mounting bolts securely.

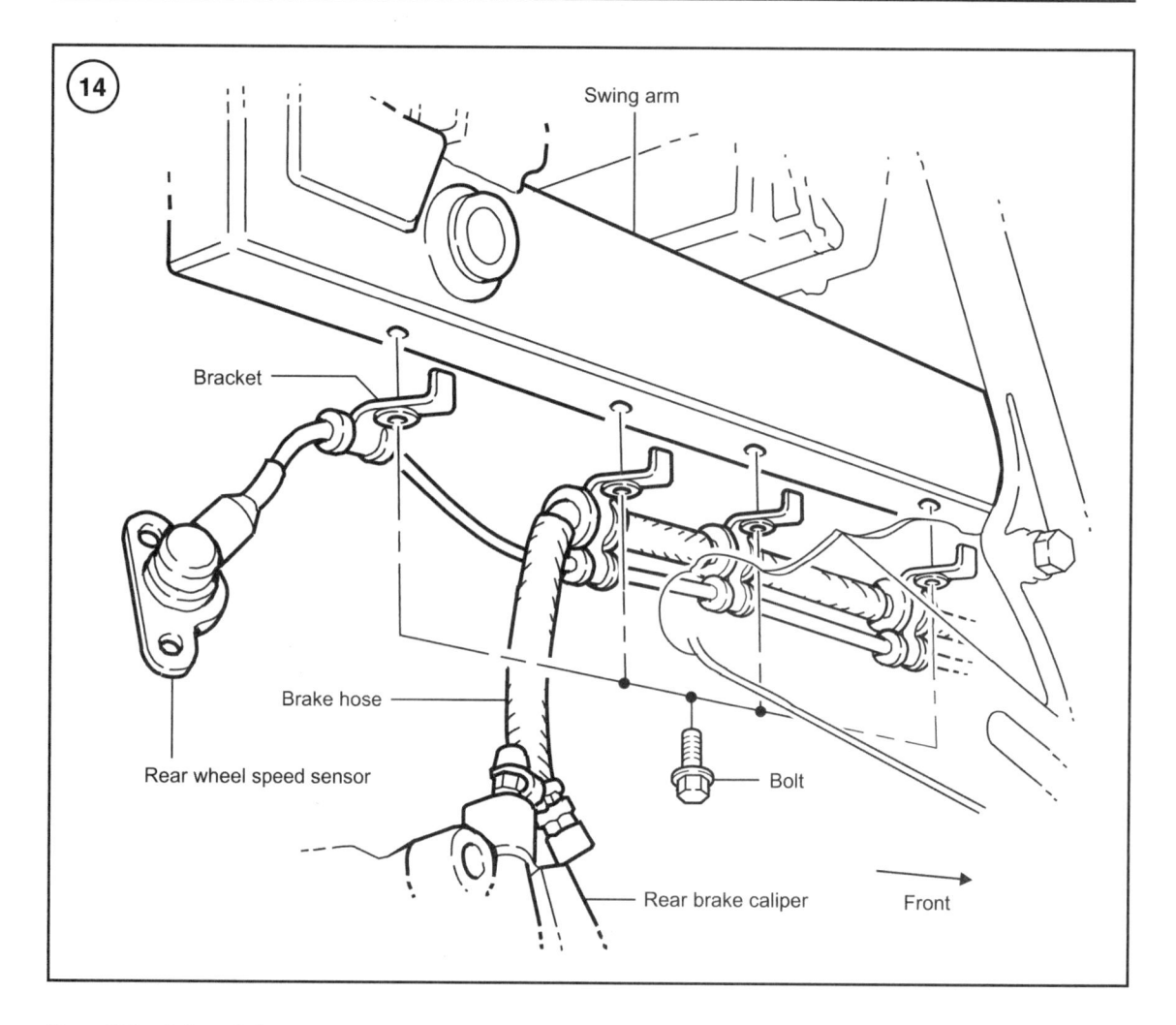

Rear Wheel Speed Sensor Removal/Installation

1. Turn the ignition switch off.
2. Remove the right side cover (Chapter Seventeen).
3. Note how the wheel sensor wiring harness is routed between the rear brake caliper and its connector on the right side of the frame. Release the wiring harness from the clamps that secure it to the frame.
4. Disconnect the 2-pin rear wheel speed sensor connector (**Figure 13**).
5. Remove the rear wheel sensor mounting bolts (**Figure 11**).
6. Remove the bolts securing the speed sensor wiring harness and the rear brake hose to the bottom of the swing arm (**Figure 14**).
7. Remove the rear wheel speed sensor with its attached wiring harness.
8. Thoroughly clean the speed sensor mounting hole in the caliper bracket of all debris. Also clean the mounting area on the outside of the hole.
9. Thoroughly clean the speed sensor's mounting surface so that it can seat flush against the caliper mounting bracket.
10. Installation is the reverse of these steps, plus the following:
   a. Route the speed sensor wiring harness along the same path noted during removal. Secure the wiring harness with the clamps and tighten the clamp mounting bolts at the swing arm securely. Make sure the speed sensor wiring harness is not twisted.
   b. Measure the speed sensor air gap as described in this section.
   c. Tighten the wheel speed sensor mounting bolts securely.

PULSER RINGS

The pulser rings are mounted on the outside of the brake discs. Refer to *Brake Discs and Pulser Rings* in Chapter Fifteen to service the pulser rings

ANTI-LOCK BRAKE SYSTEM

(15)

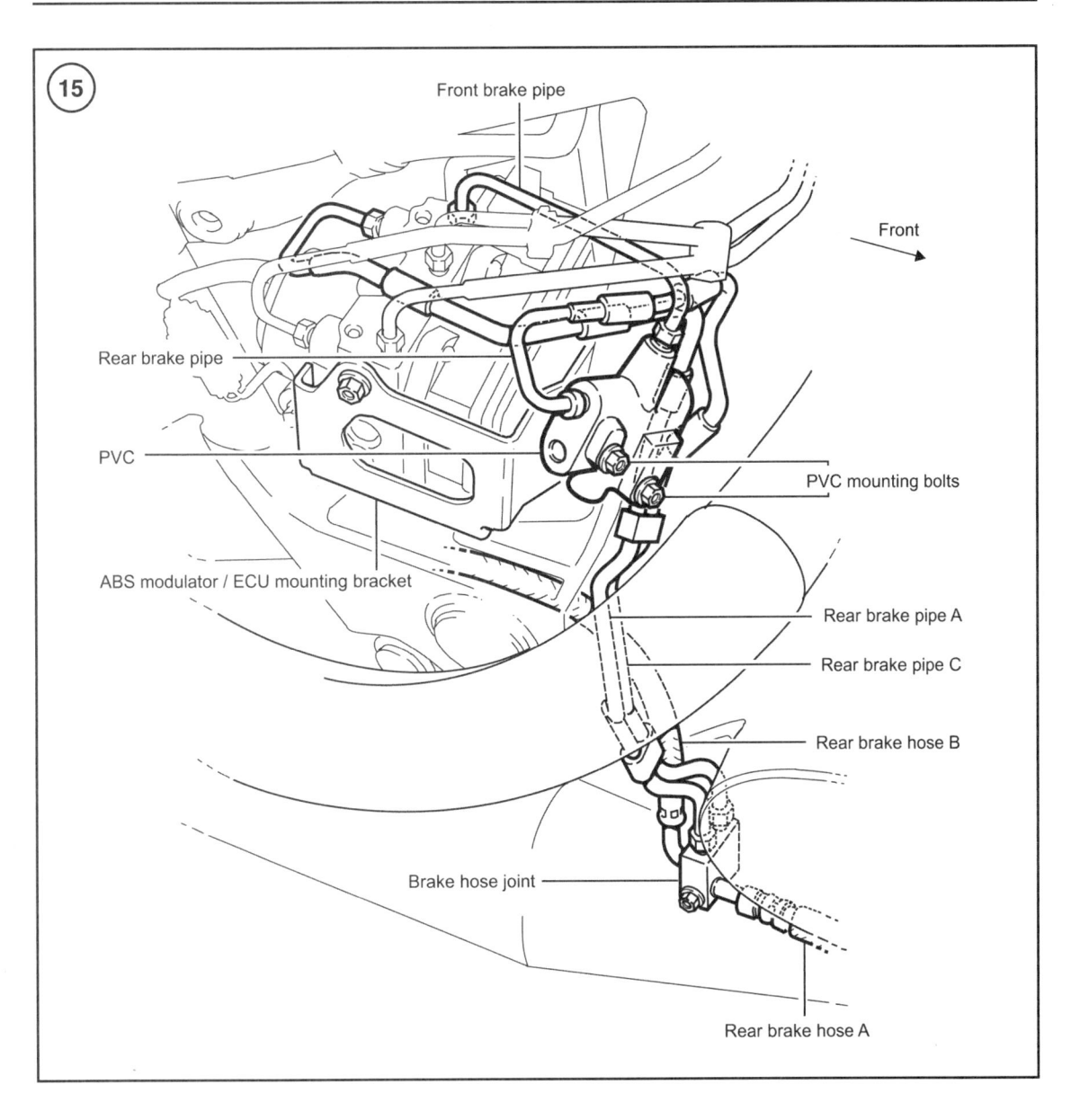

Labels on figure:
- Front brake pipe
- Front
- Rear brake pipe
- PVC
- PVC mounting bolts
- ABS modulator / ECU mounting bracket
- Rear brake pipe A
- Rear brake pipe C
- Rear brake hose B
- Brake hose joint
- Rear brake hose A

PROPORTIONAL CONTROL VALVE (PCV)

Removal/Installation

Refer to **Figure 15**.

1. Remove the right side cover (Chapter Seventeen).
2. Drain the front and rear brake systems (Chapter Fifteen).
3. Identify the two brake pipes to be disconnected at the PCV.
4. Clean the brake lines, ABS modulator/ECU and PCV to prevent contamination of the brake lines and fluid passages.

NOTE
Use a flare-nut wrench to loosen and tighten the brake line nuts. Brake line nuts can be tight and difficult to loosen with a standard open-end wrench as the wrench may round off the flats on the nut and cause permanent damage to the nut. A flare-nut wrench is designed to wrap around the nut to prevent rounding.

5. Loosen the brake line nuts at the PCV. Then disconnect the brake lines from the PCV without bending or creasing the brake lines.
6. Remove the two bolts and the PCV.
7. If the PCV valve will be reinstalled, store it in a clean plastic bag to prevent contamination.
8. Clean the fasteners and check for damage. Replace if necessary.
9. Check the brake lines for creasing, fluid leaks and other damage.

CHAPTER SIXTEEN

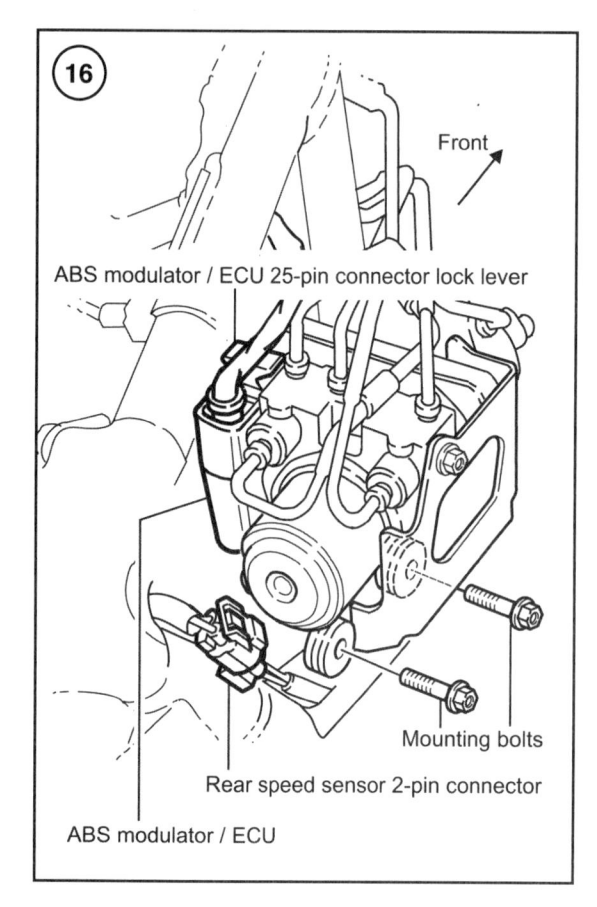

Figure 16

ABS modulator / ECU 25-pin connector lock lever
Front
Mounting bolts
Rear speed sensor 2-pin connector
ABS modulator / ECU

10. Reinstall the PCV and tighten its mounting bolts securely.
11. Wipe the brake lines ends and brake line nut threads with a clean, lint-free rag.

CAUTION
Do not bend the brake lines or try to force them into position during installation. This creases the metal and may cause it to leak.

CAUTION
If a brake line was disconnected from both ends, initially thread both brake line nuts into their mating joints a few turns only. Do not tighten one nut fully before attempting to install and tighten the other nut. Also make sure there is no stress on the brake line.

12. Lubricate the brake joint nut threads with DOT 4 brake fluid. Then thread the brake pipe joint nuts into the PCV and tighten to 14 N.m (10 ft.-lb.).
13. Bleed the front and rear brake system (Chapter Fifteen).
14. Install the right side cover (Chapter Seventeen).

ABS MODULATOR/ECU

The ABS control unit (ECU) is permanently mounted on the ABS modulator and neither the ABS modulator nor ECU can be separated, disassembled or serviced. In this chapter both units are referred to as the ABS modulator/ECU.

ABS Modulator/ECU Electrical Connector Disconnect/Reconnect

When it is necessary to disconnect the ABS modulator/ECU electrical connector during ABS troubleshooting, refer to **Figure 16** and perform the following without disconnecting any brake lines:
1. Support the motorcycle on its sidestand.
2. Remove the right side cover (Chapter Seventeen).
3. Remove the two ABS modulator/ECU mounting bolts.

CAUTION
Do not force the ABS modulator/ECU when pulling it outward. Move and handle the ABS modulator/ECU carefully to prevent damaging the brake lines.

4. Carefully pull the ABS modulator/ECU outward until the electrical connector is accessible. Then pull the lock lever on the connector upward and disconnect the connector.
5. Reverse these steps, plus the following:
   a. Make sure the connector halves are clean before reconnecting them. Then reconnect the connectors and secure with the connector lock lever.
   b. Tighten the ABS modulator/ECU mounting bolts securely.

Removal/Installation

1. Remove the right side cover (Chapter Seventeen).
2. Drain the front and rear brake systems (Chapter Fifteen).
3. Clean the brake lines, ABS modulator/ECU and PCV to prevent contamination of the brake lines and fluid passages.
4. Use tape or a permanent marking pen to identify all of the brake lines at the ABS modulator/ECU and PCV (**Figure 15**).

NOTE
Use a flare-nut wrench to loosen and tighten the brake line nuts. Brake line nuts can be tight and difficult to loosen with a standard open-end wrench as the wrench may round off the flats on the nut and cause permanent damage to the nut. A flare-nut wrench is de-

ANTI-LOCK BRAKE SYSTEM

ABS MODULATOR / ECU

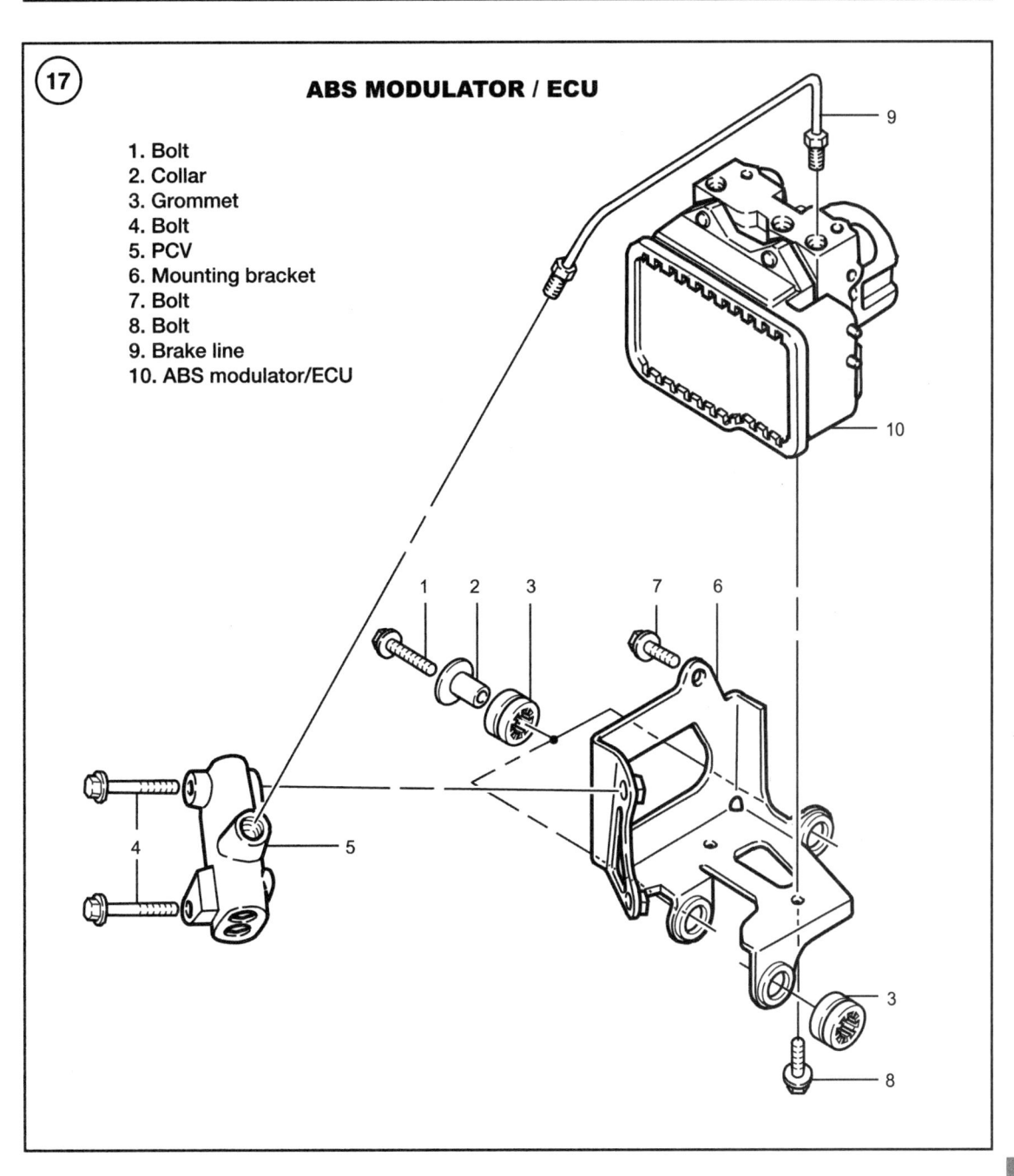

1. Bolt
2. Collar
3. Grommet
4. Bolt
5. PCV
6. Mounting bracket
7. Bolt
8. Bolt
9. Brake line
10. ABS modulator/ECU

signed to wrap around the nut to prevent rounding.

NOTE
Do not remove the brake line connecting the PCV to the ABS modulator/ECU. This brake line can be removed after removing the ABS modulator/ECU and PCV or left in place if the PCV is not going to be removed.

5. Loosen the brake line nuts at the ABS modulator/ECU and PCV (**Figure 15**). Then disconnect the brake lines without bending or creasing the brake lines.

6. Remove the two ABS modulator/ECU mounting bolts (**Figure 16**).

7. Carefully pull the ABS modulator/ECU outward until its electrical connector is accessible. Then pull the lock lever (**Figure 16**) on the connector upward and disconnect the connector.

8. If it is necessary to separate the ABS modulator/ECU, PCV and mounting bracket, perform the following (**Figure 17**):

a. Loosen the brake line nuts and remove the brake line connecting the ABS modulator/ECU to the PCV.

b. Remove the PCV mounting bolts and the PCV.

c. Remove the bolts securing the mounting bracket to the ABS modulator/ECU.

9. Inspect the dampers installed in the mounting bracket and replace if damaged.

10. If the ABS modulator/ECU is damaged, do not attempt to disassemble or service it. Discard it and install a new ABS modulator/ECU.

11. Clean the fasteners and check for damage. Replace if necessary.

12 Check the brake lines for creasing, fluid leaks and other damage.

13. Wipe the brake lines ends and brake line nut threads with a clean rag.

CAUTION
Do not bend the brake lines or try to force them into position during installation. This creases the metal and may cause it to leak.

CAUTION
If a brake line was disconnected from both ends, initially thread both brake line nuts into their mating joints a few turns only. Do not tighten one nut fully before attempting to install and tighten the other nut. Also, make sure there is no stress on the brake line.

14. If the ABS modulator/ECU and PCV were separated, perform the following:

a. Install the mounting bracket onto the ABS modulator/ECU and finger-tighten the mounting bolts.

b. Install the PCV onto the mounting bracket and tighten its mounting bolts finger-tight.

c. Lubricate the brake pipe joint nut threads with DOT 4 brake fluid. Then thread the brake pipe joint nuts into the PCV and ABS modulator/ECU. Make sure the brake pipe is positioned freely and without any stress. Then tighten the nuts to 14 N.m (10 ft.-lb.).

d. Tighten the ABS modulator/ECU mounting bolts and the PCV mounting bolts securely.

15. Install the ABS modulator/ECU partway into the frame. Make sure the connector halves are clean before reconnecting them. Then reconnect the connectors and secure with the connector lock lever (**Figure 16**).

NOTE
*Refer to disassembly notes when connecting the brake lines onto the ABS modulator/ECU and PCV (**Figure 15**).*

16. Lubricate the brake pipe (**Figure 15**) joint nut threads with DOT 4 brake fluid. Then thread the brake pipe joint nuts into the PCV and ABS modulator/ECU. Make sure the brake pipes are positioned freely and without any stress. When all of the brake pipe nuts are threaded into the ABS modulator/ECU and PCV, tighten the nuts to 14 N.m (10 ft.-lb.).

17. Make sure the collars are installed into the grommets. Then install the ABS modulator/ECU mounting bolts (**Figure 16**) and tighten securely.

18. Bleed the front and rear brake system (Chapter Fifteen).

19. Install the right side cover (Chapter Seventeen).

ANTI-LOCK BRAKE SYSTEM

Table 1 ABS WHEEL SPEED SENSOR AIR GAP

Front and rear wheels	0.4-1.2 mm (0.01-0.05 in.)

Table 2 ABS DIAGNOSTIC TROUBLE CODES

DTC	Parts/System	Possible faulty parts/system
11(1)	Front wheel speed sensor	Front wheel speed sensor, wiring and connectors.
12(2)	Front wheel speed sensor	Front wheel speed sensor, wiring and connectors. Intermittent/temporary failure. Noise interruption.
13(1)	Rear wheel speed sensor	Rear wheel speed sensor, wiring and connectors.
14(2)	Rear wheel speed sensor	Rear wheel speed sensor, wiring and connectors. Intermittent/temporary failure. Noise interruption.
21(2)	Front wheel speed sensor pulse	Pulser ring or wheel speed sensor.
23(2)	Rear wheel speed sensor pulse	Pulser ring or wheel speed sensor.
31(1)	Solenoid valve damage	ABS modulator/internal solenoid valve.
32(1)	Solenoid valve damage	ABS modulator/internal solenoid valve.
33(1)	Solenoid valve damage	ABS modulator/internal solenoid valve.
34(1)	Solenoid valve damage	ABS modulator/internal solenoid valve.
37(1)	Solenoid valve damage	ABS modulator/internal solenoid valve.
38(2)	Solenoid valve damage	ABS modulator/internal solenoid valve.
41(2)	Front wheel interruption	Riding condition where front wheel leaves contact with road (wheelie). Front brake drag.
42(2)	Front wheel interruption	Wheel speed sensor or wiring.
43(2) with	Rear wheel interruption	Riding condition where rear wheel leave contact road. Wheel speed sensor or wiring. Rear brake drag.
51(1)	ABS modulator	Motor failure.
52(1)	ABS modulator	Motor stuck in off position.
53(1)	ABS modulator	Motor stuck in on position.
54(1)	Failure-safe relay circuit	ABS modulator.
61(1)	Low power supply voltage	ABS modulator
62(1)	High power supply voltage	ABS modulator
71(2)	Incorrect tire size	Incorrect tire size.
81(1)	CPU malfunction	ABS modulator.

1. This code can be detected during the self-diagnosis check and during motorcycle operation.
2. This code is only detected during motorcycle operation.

Table 3: BRAKE SYSTEM TORQUE SPECIFICATIONS

	N.m	ft.-lb.
Brake line flare nuts*	14	10
Pulser ring bolt		
2011-2013 Aero models	42	31

*Lubricate brake pipe joint nut threads with DOT 4 brake fluid.

Notes

CHAPTER SEVENTEEN

BODY AND EXHAUST SYSTEM

Table 1 is at the end of the chapter.

SEAT

WARNING
Make sure the seat is correctly installed and locked in place before riding the motorcycle.

Removal/Installation

Aero

1. Remove the front (A, **Figure 1**) and rear (B) seat mounting bolts. Push the seat rearward and remove both seats.
2. To separate the front and rear seats, remove the two assembly bolts **(Figure 2)**.
3. Installation is the reverse of these steps. Note the following:

   a. If removed, tighten the two assembly bolts **(Figure 2)** securely.
   b. Install the front seat by inserting the hook on the seat pan under the lip on the front of the fuel tank, and then push the seat forward.
   c. Tighten the front seat mounting bolt to 26 N.m (19 ft.-lb.).
   d. Install a *new* rear seat mounting bolt and tighten to 12 N.m (106 in.-lb.).

   NOTE
   If reusing the original rear seat mounting bolt, remove all threadlock residue from the bolt threads and reinstall with a medium strength threadlock applied to the bolt threads. The threads on a new bolt have threadlock preapplied.

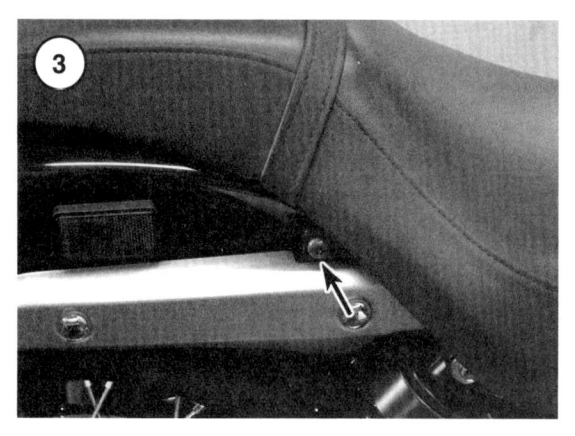

Spirit and Phantom models

1. Remove the front mounting bolt (**Figure 3**) and the rear mounting bolt and washer (**Figure 4**). Push the seat rearward and remove it.
2. Install the front seat by inserting the hook on the seat pan under the lip on the front of the fuel tank, and then push the seat forward.
3. Tighten the front seat mounting bolt to 26 N.m (19 ft.-lb.).
4. Tighten the rear seat mounting bolt securely.

SIDE COVERS

Removal/Installation

1. Carefully pull the three side cover bosses (A, **Figure 5**, typical) out of the frame dampers and remove the side cover (**B**).
2. Replace any missing or damaged frame dampers.
3. Align the bosses with the grommets and push the side cover firmly into place.

LEFT CRANKCASE REAR COVER

Removal/Installation

1. Support the motorcycle on its sidestand or on a workstand.
2. Remove the clip (A, **Figure 6**) and washer (B) from inside the cover.
3. Remove the mounting bolt (A, **Figure 7**).
4. Pull the cover (B, **Figure 7**) outward to release its two bosses from the grommets and remove the cover.
5. Replace missing or damaged grommets (A, **Figure 8**).
6. If necessary, remove the left crankcase rear cover mounting bracket (B, **Figure 8**).

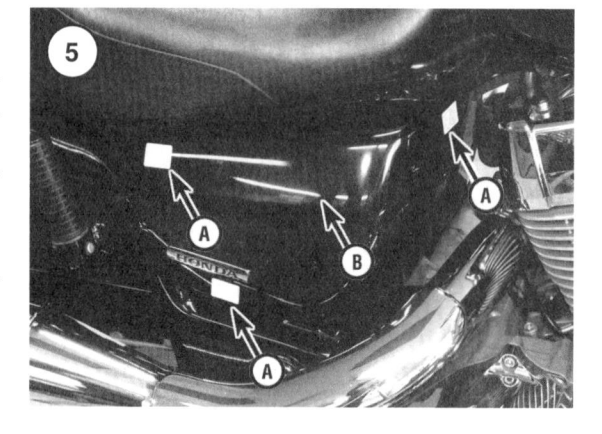

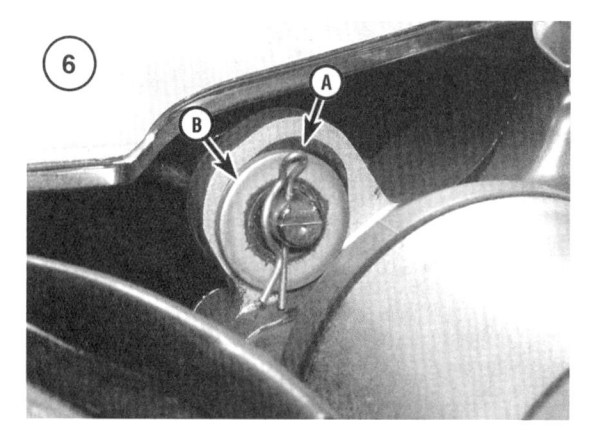

BODY AND EXHAUST SYSTEM

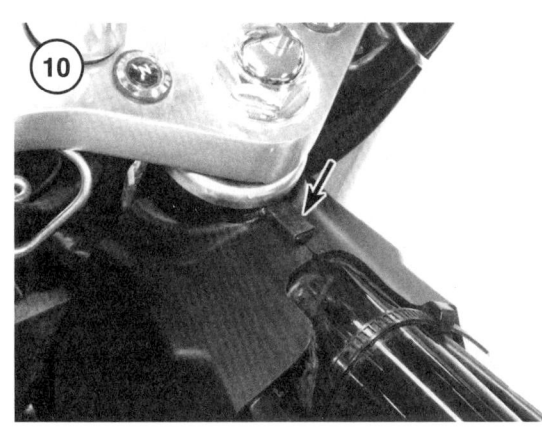

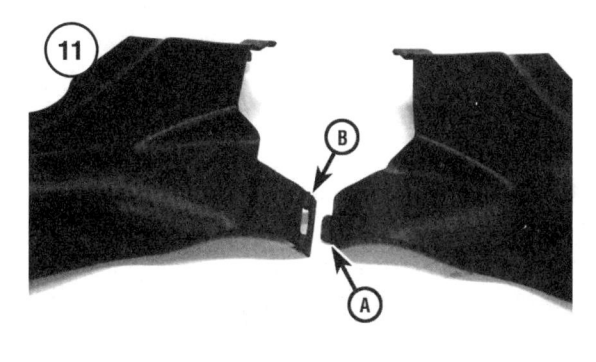

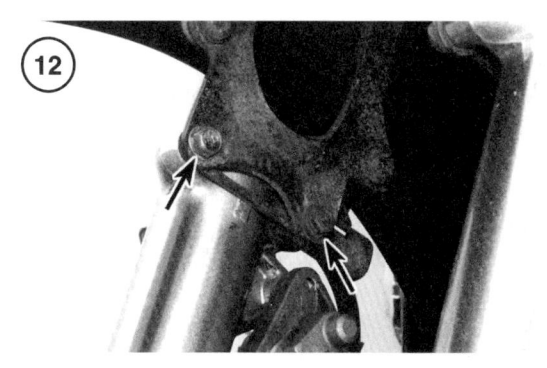

7. Installation is the reverse of removal, plus the following:
   a. If removed, install the left crankcase rear cover mounting bracket (B, **Figure 8**) by aligning the hole in the bracket with the pin on the gearcase. Install the bolt and tighten securely.
   b. Push the cover into place so the two bosses fully engage the grommets.
   c. Make sure the clip (A, **Figure 6**) fits through the upper boss completely and that the washer (B) is locked in place.
   d. Tighten the mounting bolt (A, **Figure 7**) to 10 N.m (89 in.-lb.).

STEERING COVERS

Removal/Installation

1. Remove the speedometer (Chapter Ten).
2. Remove the bolt from each steering cover **(Figure 9)**.
3. Remove the trim clip **(Figure 10)** connecting the steering covers by sliding it rearward.
4. Remove the steering covers by releasing the tab (A, **Figure 11**) on the left cover from the slot (B) in the right cover.
5. Install by reversing the removal steps. Note the following:
   a. Check the wire harness and cable routing after installing the steering covers.
   b. Turn the handlebars to check for interference.
   c. Tighten the steering cover mounting bolts securely.

FRONT FENDER

Removal/Installation

Aero

1. Support the motorcycle on a workstand.
2. Remove the front wheel (Chapter Twelve).
3. While an assistant holds the front fender in place, remove the front fender mounting bolts **(Figure 12)**.

CAUTION
To prevent from damaging the brake hose (Figure 13) when rotating the sliders, do not rotate the right slider more than necessary.

4. Rotate the sliders so their fender mounting bosses face away from the fender, then lower and remove the fender.

5. If necessary, identify the fender brace (**Figure 14**) so that it can be reinstalled facing in its original direction. Then remove the bolts, collars and grommets securing the fender brace to the front fender and remove the brace.

6. Installation is the reverse of these steps, plus the following:
   a. If the fender brace was removed, apply a medium strength threadlock onto the assembly bolts. Then, install and tighten the bolts securely.
   b. Tighten the front fender mounting bolts securely.
   c. Check the brake hose for twisting and damage.

Spirit models

1. Support the motorcycle on a workstand.
2. While an assistant holds the front fender in place, remove the nuts and bolts securing the front fender to the fork sliders. Then remove the front fender and the fender brace.
3. Installation is the reverse of these steps. Tighten the front fender mounting bolts securely.

Phantom

1. Support the motorcycle on a workstand.
2. While an assistant holds the front fender (A, **Figure 15**) in place, remove the bolts (B) securing the front fender to the fender brace (C). Then remove the front fender.
3. Remove the bolts securing the fender brace (C, **Figure 15**) to the sliders and remove the brace.
4. Installation is the reverse of these steps, plus the following:
   a. Install the fender brace with its *Fr* mark facing forward. Tighten the fender brace bolts securely.
   b. Tighten the front fender mounting bolts securely.

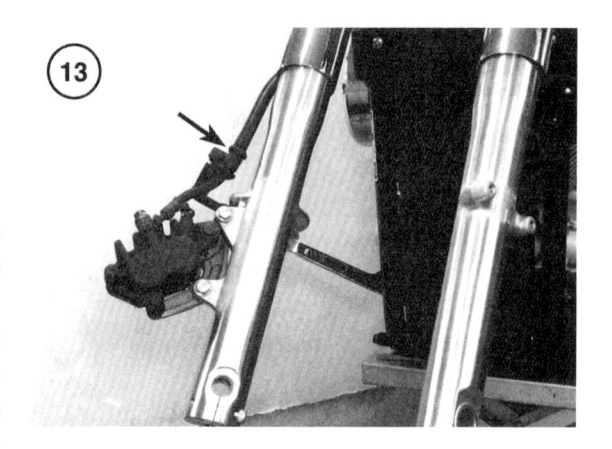

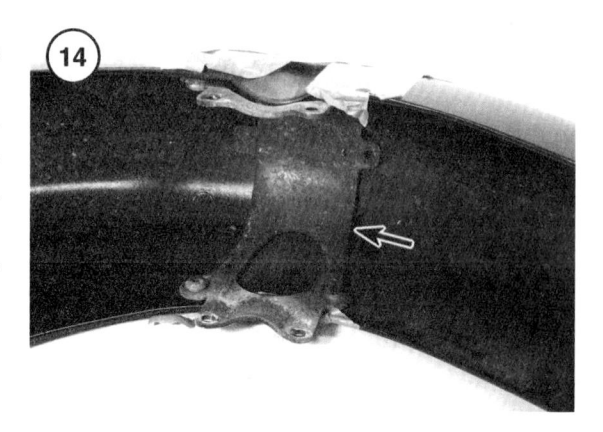

REAR FENDER

Removal/Installation

1. Support the motorcycle on a workstand.
2. Remove the seat and both side covers as described in this chapter.
3A. On 2004-2009 models, disconnect the taillight and brake light electrical connectors located in the connector pouch underneath the seat (**Figure 16**).
3B. On 2011-on models, disconnect the taillight and brake light electrical connectors (**Figure 17**) located

BODY AND EXHAUST SYSTEM

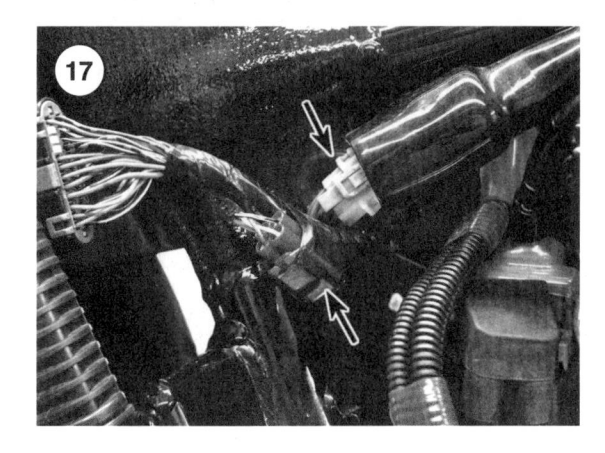

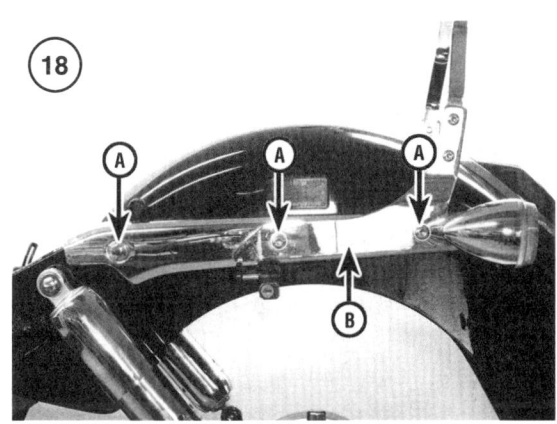

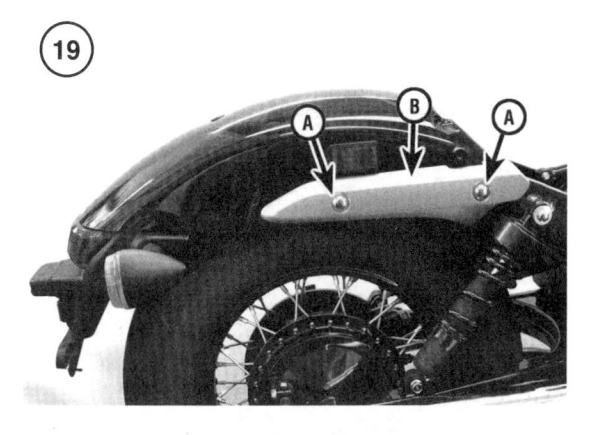

in the connector pouch above the starter relay.

NOTE
Position the fender wiring harness connector ends so they will not catch on the frame when removing the fender.

4. If equipped with an aftermarket passenger backrest, remove it before removing the rear fender.

NOTE
The rear fender is heavy and difficult to remove by one person. To prevent from scratching and damaging the rear fender, have one or more assistants help with its removal.

NOTE
Note the wiring harness routing before removing the grab rails and rear fender.

NOTE
On 2008-2009 and 2011-2013 Aero models, remove the clamp securing the right turn signal wiring harness to the frame.

5A. On Aero models, remove the bolts and washers (A, **Figure 18**) securing the grab rails (B) to the fender and frame. Remove both grab rails and the rear fender.

5B. On Spirit and Phantom models, remove the bolts and washers (A, **Figure 19**) securing the grab rails (B) to the fender and frame. Remove both grab rails and the rear fender.

6. Installation is the reverse of removal, plus the following:
   a. On Aero models, the two front rear fender mounting bolts are longer than the rear mounting bolt (each side).
   b. On 2008-2009 and 2011-2013 Aero models install the clamp securing the right turn signal wiring harness to the frame.
   c. Tighten the rear fender mounting bolts to 64 N.m (47 ft.-lb.).
   d. After reconnecting the brake light and taillight connectors, turn the ignition switch on and check the operation of the brake light and taillights.

Rear Frame Removal/Installation (Aero Models)

Refer to **Figure 20**.
1. Remove the rear fender (this chapter).

Figure 20 REAR FRAME (AERO)
Labels: Rear fender, Rubber grommets, Rubber grommets, Screw, Clamp, Boss, Rear frame, Rubber grommet

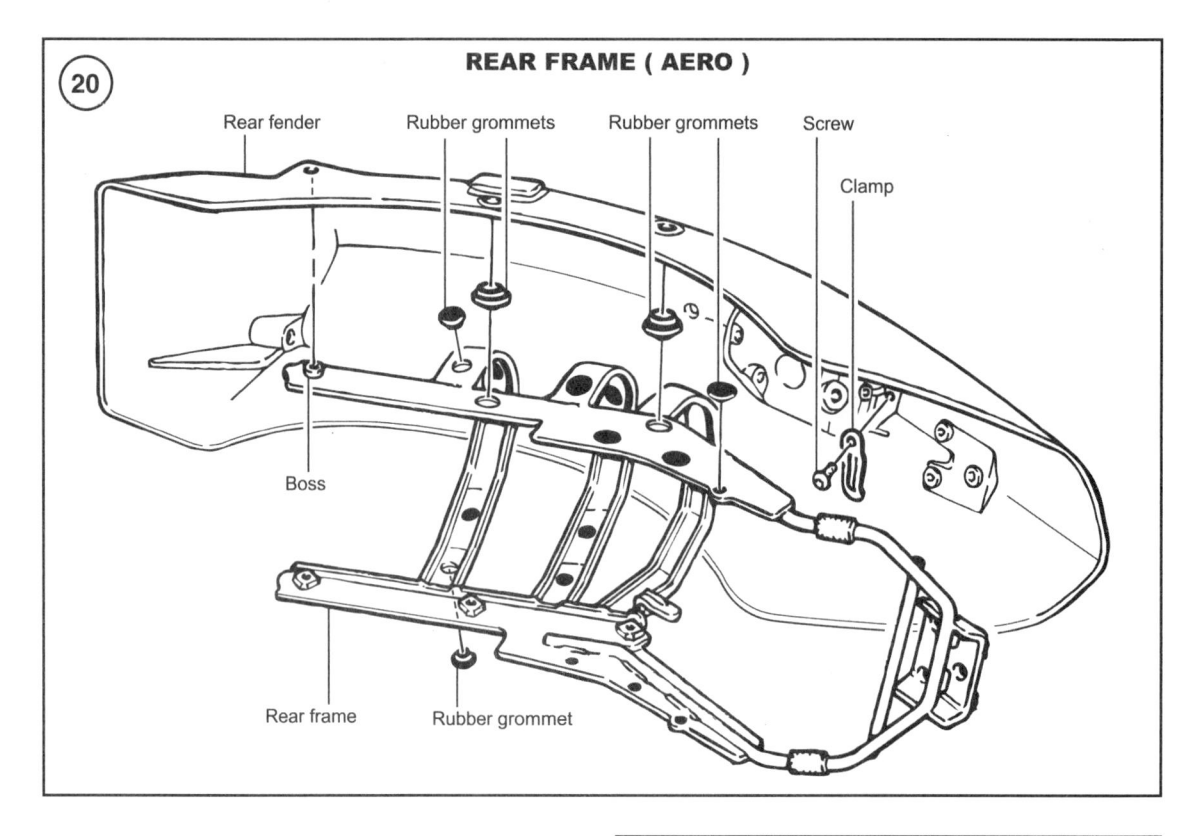

2. Place the rear fender on a blanket to prevent paint damage.
3. Remove the tail/brake light housing (Chapter Ten).
4. Remove the license light housing (Chapter Ten).
5. Remove the screw securing the wiring harness clamp to the rear fender.
6. Carefully release the rear frame bosses from the holes in the rear fender, then remove the rear frame and its rubber grommets from inside the rear fender.
7. Inspect the rubber grommets for cracks, deterioration and other damage and replace if necessary.
8. Install the rubber grommets onto the rear frame.
9. Install the rear frame by inserting its bosses into the holes in the rear fender.
10. Reverse the removal steps to install the rear frame. Note the following:
    a Tighten the clamp screw and any remaining fasteners securely.
    b. Make sure the wiring harness is secured by the clamp.

Rear Frame/Rear Fender A Removal/Installation (Spirit and Phantom Models)

Refer to **Figure 21**.
1. Remove the rear fender (this chapter).
2. Place the rear fender on a blanket to prevent paint damage.

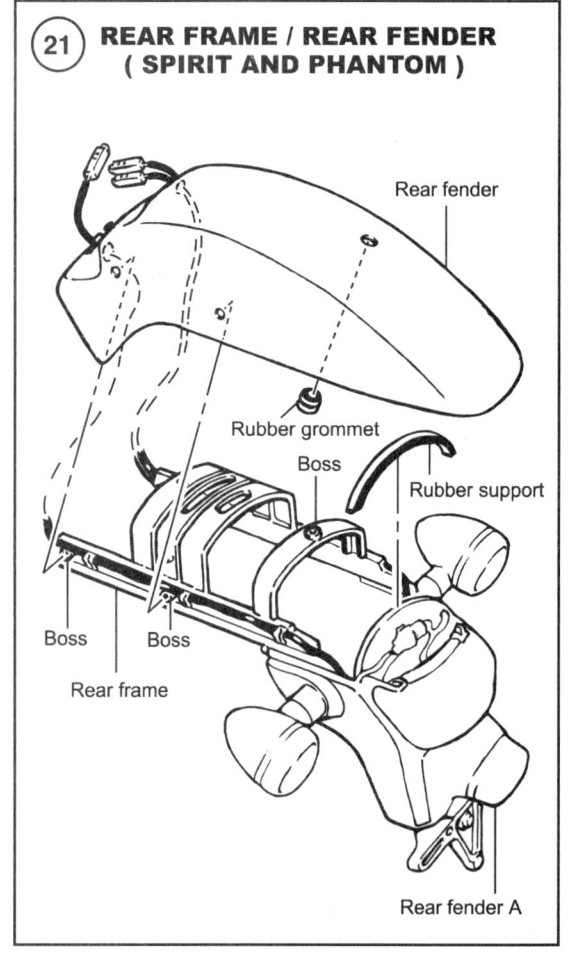

Figure 21 REAR FRAME / REAR FENDER (SPIRIT AND PHANTOM)
Labels: Rear fender, Rubber grommet, Boss, Rubber support, Boss, Boss, Rear frame, Rear fender A

BODY AND EXHAUST SYSTEM

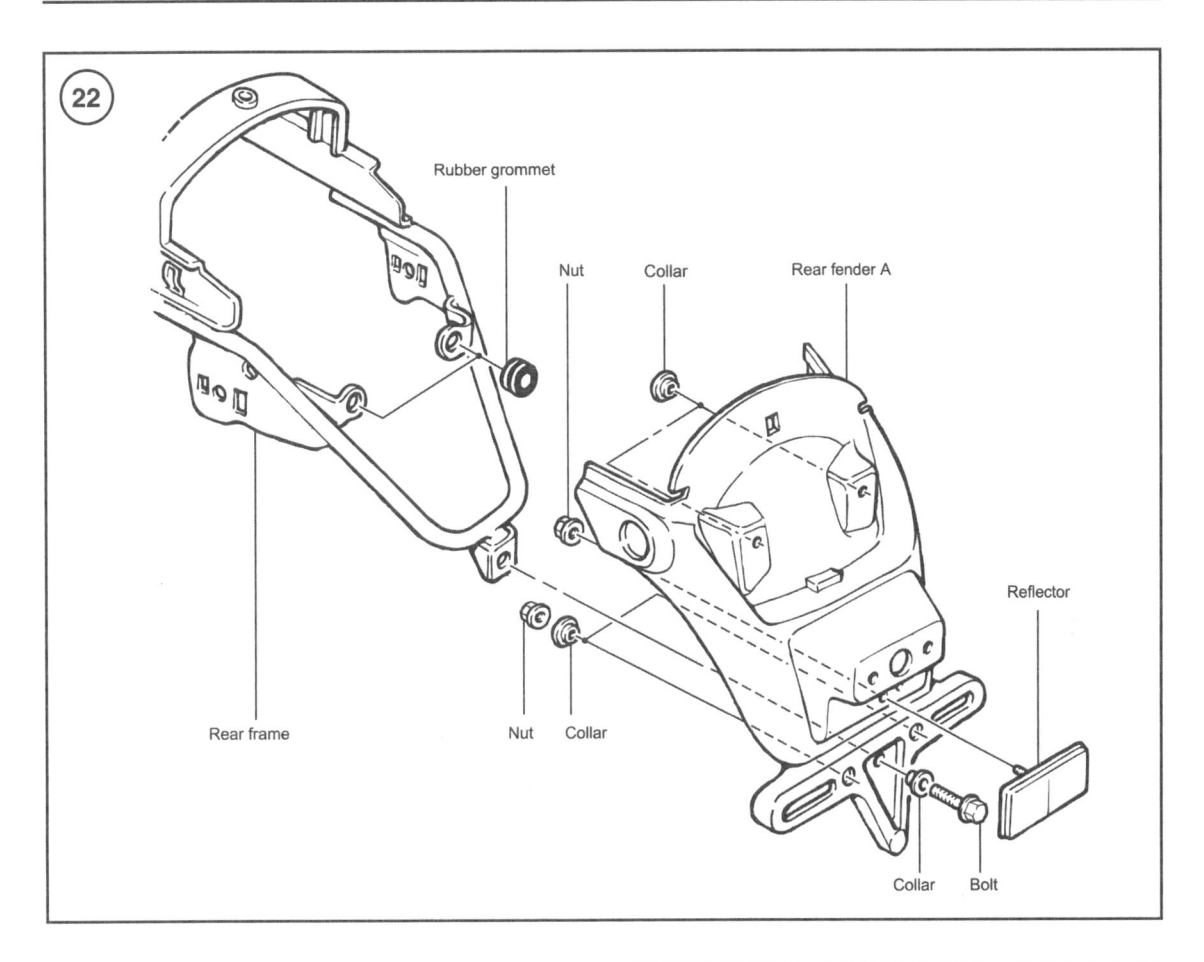

22

Rubber grommet, Nut, Collar, Rear fender A, Reflector, Rear frame, Nut, Collar, Collar, Bolt

3. Carefully release the rear frame bosses from the holes in the rear fender, then remove the rear frame and rear fender A from inside the rear fender.

4. If it is necessary to remove rear fender A from the rear frame, refer to **Figure 22** and perform the following:

   a. Remove the rear turn signal lights (Chapter Ten).
   b. Remove the tail/brake light housing (Chapter Ten).
   c. Remove the license light housing (Chapter Ten).

5. Remove the nuts, bolts and collars securing rear fender A to the rear frame.

6. If necessary, remove the nut and remove the reflector from rear fender A.

7. Inspect the rubber grommets for cracks, deterioration and other damage and replace if necessary.

8. Installation is the reverse of these steps. Tighten all remaining fasteners securely.

23

SIDESTAND

Sidestand Spring Replacement

1. Partially lower the sidestand until the spring coils begin to separate.

2. Lock a thin metal plate (pennies work well) into a pair of locking pliers. Then force the metal plate between two of the spring coils. Repeat by installing several metal plates into the spring. See **Figure 23**.

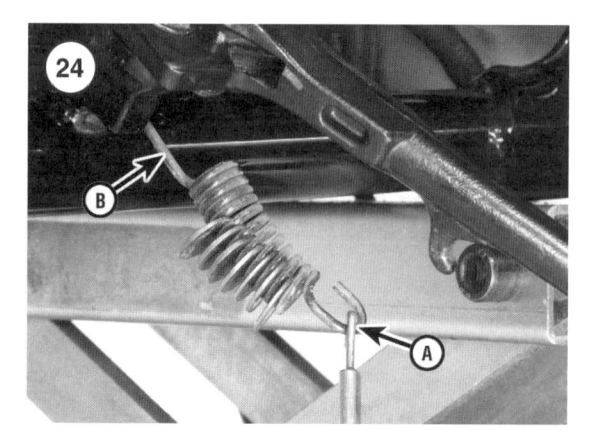

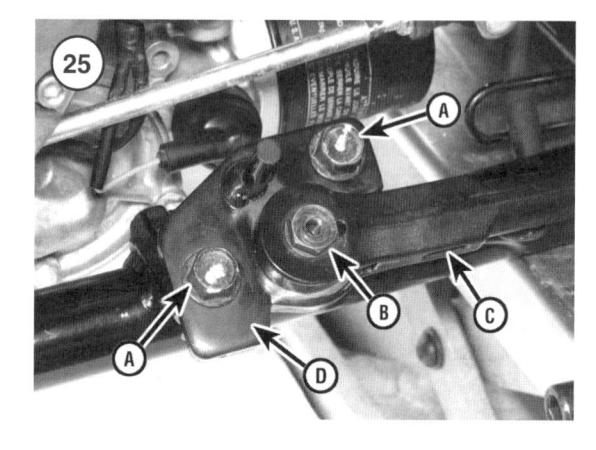

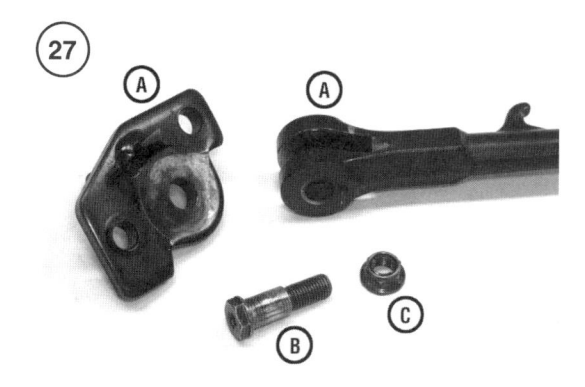

3. When the spring is loose enough, disconnect and remove it (A, **Figure 24**).
4. Installation is the reverse of removal steps. Note the following:
   a. Install the spring with its longer arm (B, **Figure 24**) connected at the top post.
   b. Remove the metal plates from the spring
   c. Raise and lower the sidestand several times. Check that the sidestand locks in both positions and the spring remains firmly attached to the frame and sidestand posts.

WARNING
Do not ride the motorcycle until the sidestand switch operates correctly. Riding the motorcycle with the sidestand down could cause a loss of control.

   d. Test the sidestand switch (Chapter Ten).

Sidestand
Removal/Installation

NOTE
*To replace just the sidestand switch, refer to **Sidestand Switch** in Chapter Ten.*

1. Support the motorcycle on a workstand.
2. Remove the sidestand switch as described in Chapter Ten. Do not disconnect the sidestand switch connector unless necessary.
3A. To remove the sidestand without removing the spring or the pivot bolt, perform the following:
   a. Remove the two sidestand bracket mounting bolts (A, **Figure 25**).
   b. Remove the sidestand assembly (**Figure 26**).
3B. To remove and disassemble the sidestand assembly, perform the following:
   a. Remove the sidestand spring as described in this section.
   b. Hold the pivot bolt (B, **Figure 25**) and remove the pivot bolt locknut at the bottom of the sidestand assembly.
   c. Remove the pivot bolt (B, **Figure 25**) and the sidestand (C).
   d. If necessary, remove the two sidestand bracket mounting bolts (A, **Figure 25**) and remove the bracket (D).
4. Clean and dry all parts (except the sidestand switch).

NOTE
A lack of lubrication can cause severe wear to the sidestand, bracket and pivot bolt mating surfaces. This will in-

BODY AND EXHAUST SYSTEM

crease the clearance between the parts and can allow the spring to fall off its mounting posts.

5. Inspect the sidestand and bracket mating surfaces (A, **Figure 27**) for deep scoring and other damage. Replace damaged parts if necessary. Lubricate the mating surfaces with grease.
6. Inspect the pivot bolt (B, **Figure 27**) shoulder for deep scoring, cracks and other damage. Replace if necessary.
7. Inspect the threads on the pivot bolt and sidestand for damage.
8. Replace the locknut (C, **Figure 27**) if it turns easily on the pivot bolt shaft. This is a U-nut design and must be replaced with an original part.
9A. If the sidestand was removed without disassembly, install the sidestand mounting bracket (D, **Figure 25**) and tighten the bolts (A) to 49 N.m (36 ft.-lb.).
9B. If the sidestand was disassembled, perform the following:
   a. Install the sidestand mounting bracket (D, **Figure 25**) and tighten the bolts (A) to 49 N.m (36 ft.-lb.).
   b. Lubricate the pivot bolt shoulder (B, **Figure 27**) with waterproof grease.
   c. Lightly lubricate the sidestand and mounting bracket mating surfaces (A, **Figure 27**) with grease.
   d. Install the sidestand and then install the sidestand pivot bolt. Tighten the sidestand pivot bolt to the torque specification in **Table 1**.
   e. Apply a medium strength threadlock onto the sidestand pivot bolt locknut. Then hold the sidestand pivot bolt and tighten the locknut to 30 N.m (22 ft.-lb.).
   f. Install the sidestand spring as described in this section.
   g. Operate the sidestand by hand, making sure it pivots smoothly. If there is any binding, remove and inspect the parts for damage.
10. Install the sidestand switch as described in Chapter Ten.
11. Operate the sidestand several times. Check that the sidestand locks in both positions and the spring remains firmly attached to the frame and sidestand posts.

WARNING
Do not ride the motorcycle until the sidestand switch operates correctly. Riding the motorcycle with the sidestand down could cause a loss of control.

12. Test the sidestand switch (Chapter Ten).

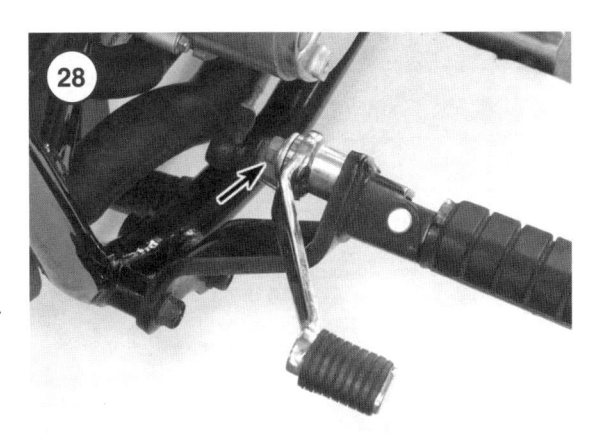

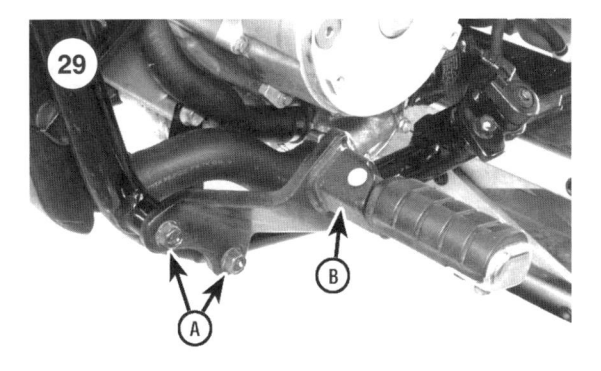

FOOTPEGS

Rider Footpeg
Removal/Installation

Left side

1. Support the motorcycle on a workstand.
2. Remove the shift pedal pivot bolt **(Figure 28)** and washer and remove the shift pedal from the left footpeg.

NOTE
*Notice the collar and 2 seals installed inside the shift pedal. To service the shift pedal assembly, refer to **Shift Pedal and Linkage** in **External Shift Mechanism** in Chapter Six.*

3. Remove the bolts (A, **Figure 29**) and the left footpeg mounting bracket (B).
4. Installation is the reverse of removal. Note the following:
   a. Tighten the left footpeg mounting bracket bolts (A, **Figure 29**) to 39 N.m (29 ft.-lb.).
   b. Lubricate the shift pedal pivot bolt shoulder with waterproof grease.
   c. Tighten the shift pedal pivot bolt **(Figure 28)** to 39 N.m (29 ft.-lb.).

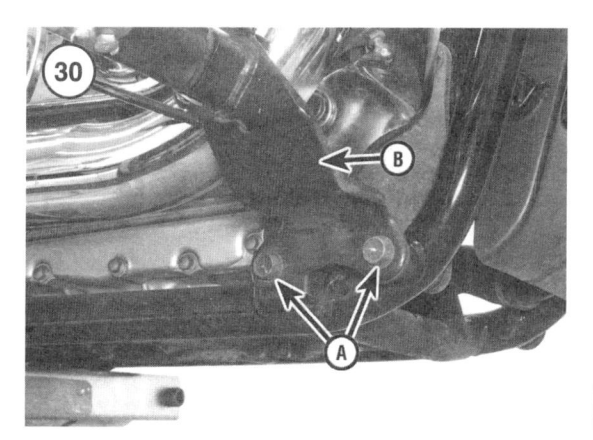

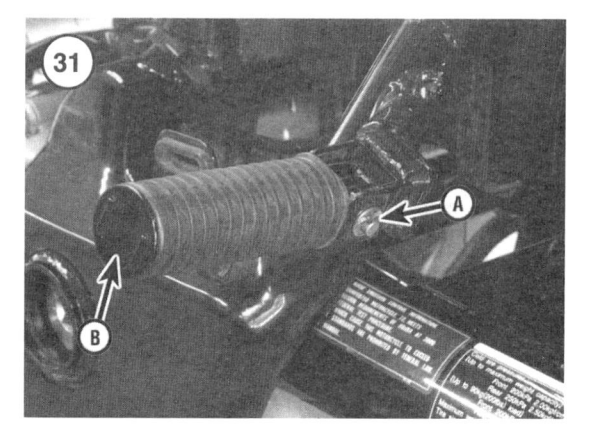

Right side

1. Support the motorcycle on its sidestand.
2. Remove the bolts (A, **Figure 30**) and nut and the right footpeg mounting bracket (B).
3. Installation is the reverse of these steps. Tighten the right footpeg mounting bracket nut and bolts to 39 N.m (29 ft.-lb.).

Disassembly/reassembly

Refer to **Figure 31** (typical) to service the footpeg assembly. During assembly, install a new cotter pin and bend its arms over to lock it in place.

Passenger Footpegs
Removal/Installation

1. Remove the cotter pin (A, **Figure 31**), washer, clevis pin and the footpeg (B). Note the washer installed against the footpeg rubber as it may slide off.
2. Inspect the clevis pin and washer and replace if damaged.
3. Reverse to install, plus the following:
   a. Install a new cotter pin and bend its arms over to lock it in place.
   b. Raise and lower the footpeg, making sure it locks in both positions.

EXHAUST SYSTEM

Removal

The exhaust system is removed as an assembly.
1. Remove the right rider footpeg assembly as described in this chapter.
2. Remove the two exhaust pipe joint nuts at the front (**Figure 32**) and rear (**Figure 33**) cylinder heads.
3. Remove the muffler mounting nuts, bolts (**Figure 35**) and the exhaust system.
4. Use a small screwdriver to carefully pry the gasket

BODY AND EXHAUST SYSTEM

(A, **Figure 36**) from each exhaust port.

5. If necessary, remove the joint collar (**Figure 37**) from each exhaust pipe.

6. If necessary, remove the two collars and grommets (A, **Figure 38**) from the exhaust pipe mounting bracket (B). Replace the grommets if cracked or damaged.

Installation

1. If an exhaust stud is loose, install it so its length from the cylinder head gasket surface to the end of the stud (**Figure 39**) is 40.00-42.00 mm (1.57-1.65 in.). Refer to *Stud Removal/Installation* in *Service Methods* in Chapter One.

2. If removed, install the grommets and collars (A, **Figure 38**) into the exhaust pipe mounting bracket. Make sure the bracket bolts (C, **Figure 38**) are tight.

3. If removed, install the joint collars onto the exhaust pipes (**Figure 37**).

4. Install a new gasket in each exhaust port (A, **Figure 36**). If necessary, apply a small amount of grease onto the gasket to hold it in place. The grease will burn off after the engine is started.

NOTE
If you are installing the exhaust assembly without assistance, use a jack to support and raise the exhaust system.

5. Lift the exhaust pipe assembly and install the two exhaust pipes onto their respective cylinder heads. Make sure the gaskets remain seated against the cylinder head. Then position the front cylinder joint collar so that its open ends (A, **Figure 40**) are facing toward the side of the exhaust pipe where they will not be visible.

6. Slide the front exhaust pipe flange (B, **Figure 40**) over the studs and seat against the joint collar. Then install the exhaust pipe joint nuts (**Figure 33**) finger-tight.

7. Repeat the process for the rear exhaust pipe joint

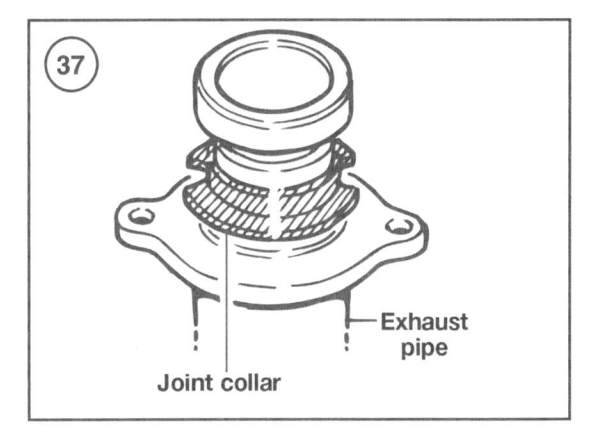

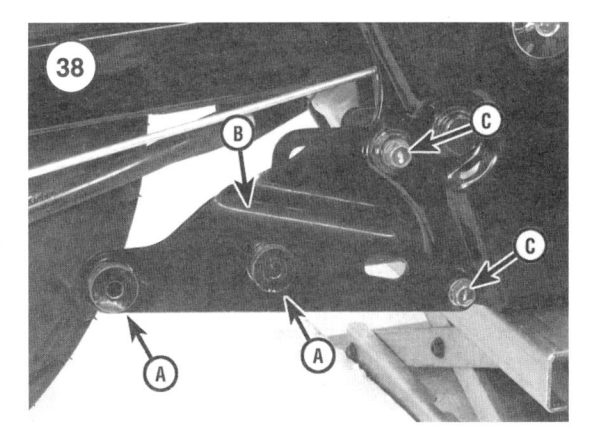

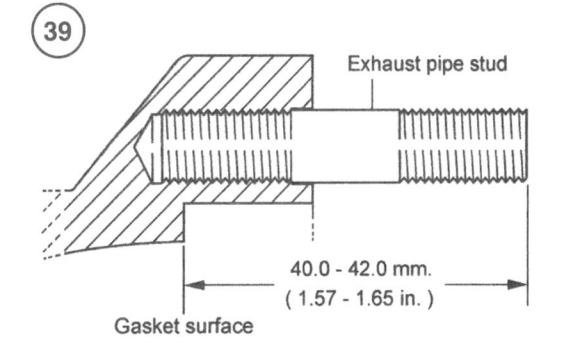

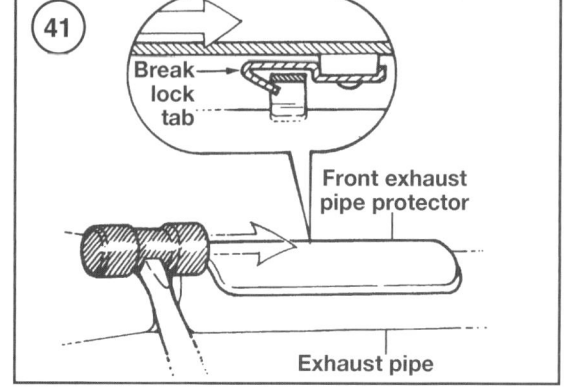

collar and flange.
8. Install the muffler mounting bolts and nuts finger-tight.
9. Tighten the exhaust pipe fasteners in the following order:
    a. Tighten the exhaust pipe joint nuts to 25 N.m (18 ft.-lb.).
    b. On 2004-2007 Aero models, tighten the muffler mounting nuts to 26 N.m (19 ft.-lb.).
    c. On 2008-2009 Aero models, tighten the muffler mounting nuts to 44 N.m (32 ft.-lb.).
    d. On 2011-2013 Aero models, tighten the muffler mounting nuts securely.
    e. On Spirit and Phantom models, tighten the muffler mounting nuts to 44 N.m (32 ft.-lb.).
10. Start the engine and check for exhaust leaks.

NOTE
If grease was applied to the gaskets, allow the engine to run long enough for the grease to burn off before suspecting an exhaust leak.

Muffler Mounting Bracket Removal/Installation

1. Remove the exhaust system as described in this section.
2. Remove the bolts (C, **Figure 38**), and the muffler mounting bracket (B).
3. Installation is the reverse of removal. Tighten the muffler mounting bracket bolts to the specification listed in **Table 1**.

Exhaust Pipe Disassembly/Assembly

2004-2007 Aero models

The front and rear exhaust pipes are permanently connected to a single muffler.

2008-2009 Aero models and all Spirit and Phantom models

1. Remove the muffler support mounting bolts and remove the muffler support from both mufflers.

NOTE
If the pipe clamp bolt is rusted, spray it with WD-40 or a similar chemical penetrant.

2. Loosen the pipe clamp bolt securing the front exhaust pipe/muffler assembly to the rear exhaust pipe/muffler assembly.
3. Twist the two assemblies and separate them.
4. Replace the gasket if leaking or damaged.
5. Install the gasket onto the front exhaust pipe connecting shoulder.
6. Slide the rear exhaust pipe over the gasket.
7. Align the muffler support with both mufflers. Then install and tighten the muffler support mounting bolts to the specification listed in **Table 1**.
8. Tighten the pipe clamp bolt securely.

Exhaust Pipe Protectors Removal/Installation

Protectors (**Figure 41**) are installed on the exhaust pipe and muffler. Note the following when removing and installing the projectors:

NOTE
Do not remove a protector unless it is going to be replaced. During removal, lock tabs on the reverse side of the protector are broken and the protector cannot be reused.

1. On 2004-2007 Aero models, both protectors can be replaced with the exhaust system mounted on the motorcycle.
2. On 2008-2009 and 2011-2013 Aero models and all Spirit and Phantom models, note the following:

BODY AND EXHAUST SYSTEM

a. The front exhaust pipe protector cannot be replaced.

b. The rear exhaust pipe protector can be replaced with the exhaust system mounted on the motorcycle.

3. Drive the protector with a plastic hammer until its lock tab breaks (**Figure 41**) and frees the protector from the exhaust pipe.

4. Discard the protector.

5. Position the new exhaust pipe protector over the exhaust pipe, then align its holder with the flange retainer tabs on the pipe and push in place.

Table 1 BODY AND EXHAUST SYSTEM TORQUE SPECIFICATIONS

	N.m	in.-lb.	ft.-lb.
Exhaust pipe joint nuts	25	--	18
Left crankcase rear cover Allen mounting bolt			
2004-2009 Aero models	9.8	87	--
All other models	10	89	--
Left footpeg mounting bracket bolts	39	--	29
Muffler bracket bolts			
Aero models			
2004-2007	44	--	32
2008-2009	34	--	25
2011-2013 (frameside)	44	--	32
Spirit models			
2007-2009	34	--	25
2012-2013	27	--	20
Phantom models	27	--	20
Muffler bracket nut			
2011-2013 Aero models (muffler side)	27	--	20
Muffler support mounting nut			
Aero models			
2008-2009	27	--	20
2011-2013	44	--	32
Spirit models			
2007-2009	27	--	20
2011-2013	44	--	32
Phantom models	44	--	32
Muffler mounting nuts			
Aero models			
2004-2007	26	--	14
2008-2009	44	--	32
All Spirit and Phantom models	44	--	32
Rear fender/grab rail mounting bolts	64	--	47
Right footpeg mounting bracket bolts and nut	39	--	29
Seat mounting bolts			
Aero models			
Front	26	--	19
Rear*	12	106	--
Spirit and Phantom models	26	--	19
Shift pedal pivot bolt	39	--	29
Sidestand mounting bracket bolts	49	--	36
Sidestand pivot bolt			
Aero models			
2004-2009	9.8	87	--
2011-2013	9	80	--
Spirit and Phantom models	9	80	--
Sidestand pivot bolt locknut			
2004-2009 Aero models	9.8	87	--
All other models	10	89	--
Tool box screw	2.0	18	--

*ALOC fastener. See text for additional information.

INDEX

A

Air filter, 58
Air filter housing, 225, 262
Alternator and charging system specifications, 362
Anti-lock brake system, 503
    ABS
        diagnostic trouble codes, 521
        indicator circuit troubleshooting, 513
        indicator operation, 504
        modulator/ECU, 518
        wheel speed sensor air gap, 521
        service precautions, 503
    Brake system torque specifications, 521
    DTC troubleshooting, 507
    Proportional Control Valve (PCV), 517
    Pulser rings, 516
    Wheel speed sensors, 514

B

Bank angle sensor, 269
Battery, 78, 291
Battery specifications, 362
Bearing selection
    crankcase replacement only, 180
    crankshaft and crankcase replacement, 180
    crankshaft replacement only, 181
    main journal bearing replacement only, 181
Body and exhaust system, 523
    Exhaust system, 532
    Footpegs, 531
    Front fender, 525
    Left crankcase rear cover, 524
    Rear fender, 526
    Seat, 523
    Side covers, 524
    Sidestand, 529
    Steering covers, 525
    torque specifications, 535
Brakes, 461
Brakes, 461
    Brake
        bleeding, 462
        discs and pulser rings, 491
        fluid draining, 465
        fluid flushing, 465
        hose and brake pipe replacement, 490
        service, 461
        system, 53, 81
        system torque specifications, 502, 521
    Front brake
        caliper, 470
        pads, 466
    Front disc brake service specifications, 501
    Front master cylinder, 476
    Rear brake
        caliper (ABS models), 483
        pads (ABS models), 480
        pedal
            ABS models, 499
            drum brake models, 498
    Rear disc brake service specifications (ABS models), 501
    Rear drum brake, 493
        service specifications, 502
    Rear master cylinder (ABS models), 486
Bulb specifications, 363

INDEX

C

Cam chain tensioner and cam chain, 106
Camshafts, 96
Carburetor and emission control systems, 221
    Air filter housing, 225
    Carburetor and fuel tank specifications, 251
    Carburetor, 226
    Choke cable replacement, 242
    Crankcase breather system, 242
    Evaporative emission control system
        (California models), 246
    Fuel
        hose identification, 221
        system torque specifications, 251
        tank, 221
        valve, 222
    High altitude adjustment, 240
    Intake manifold, 237
    Pilot screw adjustment, 238
    Pulse secondary air supply system, 242
    Throttle cable replacement, 241
Charging system, 296
Choke cable
    inspection and adjustment
        (carbureted models), 72
    replacement, 242
Clutch and external shift mechanism, 185
    Clutch, 45, 189
        and external shift mechanism, 185
        cable and clutch lever, 70
        cable replacement, 185
        diode, 333
        release lever, 188
        specifications, 205
        switch, 353
    External shift mechanism, 200
    Primary drive gear, 198
    Right crankcase cover, 186
    Torque specifications, 205
Connecting rods, 156
    bearing selection, 181
    weight, 182
    weight code selection, 181
Coolant capacity, 90
Coolant reserve tank, 371
Coolant temperature indicator and Engine Coolant
    Temperature (ECT) sensor, 345
Cooling system, 367
    Coolant reserve tank, 371
    Cooling fan, 371
    Cooling system
        inspection, 367
        specifications, 378
        torque specifications, 378
    Radiator, 369
    Thermostat housing, 373
    Thermostat, 372
    Water pump, 374
Countershaft service specifications, 219
Crankcase, 142

Crankcase breather
    inspection, 59
    system, 242
Left crankcase
    cover and stator coil, 298
    rear cover, 524
Right crankcase cover, 186
Crankshaft, 155
Crankshaft Position (CKP) sensor, 313
Cylinder, 119
Cylinder head, 107
    and valve service specifications, 130
    covers, 94
Cylinder leakdown test, 45
Cylinder studs, 129

D

Depressurizing the fuel system, 254
Diagnostic trouble codes, 289
Driven flange dampers, 387
DTC troubleshooting, 281, 507

E

Electrical system, 291
    Alternator and charging system
        specifications, 362
    Battery, 291
        Maintenance free battery charging times, 362
        specifications, 362
    Brake light switch
        Front, 354
        Rear, 355
    Bulb specifications, 363
    Charging system, 296
    Clutch
        diode, 333
        switch, 353
    Coolant temperature indicator and Engine Coolant
        Temperature (ECT) sensor, 345
    Crankshaft Position (CKP) sensor, 313
    Electrical component replacement, 291
    Electrical connectors, 291
    Electrical system
        fundamentals, 18
        testing, 47
        torque specifications, 365
    Fan
        control relay (fuel injected models), 348
        motor switch (carbureted models), 437
    Flywheel, starter clutch and starter
        drive gears, 301
    Fuel reserve indicator and fuel reserve sensor (fuel
        injected models), 351
    Fuse box, 359
    Fuse box relays (ABS models), 361
    Fuses, 359
        specifications, 364
    Handlebar switch, 356
    Horn, 358

Ignition coils, 311
Ignition Control Module (ICM) (carbureted models), 314
Ignition switch, 355
Ignition system
   specifications, 362
   testing, 305
Left crankcase cover and stator coil, 298
Lighting system, 334
Neutral switch, 351
Oil pressure switch and oil pressure indicator, 349
Sensor test specifications, 364
Sidestand switch, 352
Speedometer, 241
Starter
   2004-2007 Aero models, 318
   2008-2009 and 2011-2013 Aero models, 2010-2013 Spirit models and all Phantom models, 325
Starter clutch specifications, 362
Starter relay switch, 331
Starter system
   troubleshooting, 316
   specifications, 363
Switch continuity test, 357
Throttle Position (TP) sensor (carbureted models), 314
Turn signal relay, 357
Upper fork bridge indicator lights (2008-2009 and 2011-2013 Aero models, 2012-2013 Spirit and Phantom models), 340
Vehicle Speed (VS) sensor, 344
Electrical testing, 47
Emission control system labels, 275
Engine, 42, 133
   compression test, 60
   Engine Control Module (ECM), 272
   lubrication, 44
   oil
      and filter, 73
      capacity, 90
      pressure check, 75
   rotation, 57
   stop relay, 271
   will not start, 34
Engine lower end, 133
   Bearing selection
      connecting rod, 181
      crankcase replacement only, 180
      crankshaft and crankcase replacement, 180
      crankshaft replacement only, 181
      main journal bearing replacement only, 181
   Connecting rods, 156
      weight, 182
      weight code selection, 181
   Crankcase, 142
   Crankshaft, 155
   Engine, 133
      break-in, 141
   Main journal bearings and crankshaft main journal oil clearance, 152

Oil pump, 159
   specifications, 182
Output drive and driven gear measurements, 177
Output drive gear shims, 182
Output driven gear shims, 183
Output gearcase, 163
   overhaul, 169
   seal replacement, 167
   specifications, 182
Restarting the engine, 141
Servicing the engine in the frame, 133
specifications, 180
torque specifications, 183
Transmission and output drive gear bearings, 151
Engine top end, 93
   Cam chain tensioner and cam chain, 106
   Camshafts, 96
   Cylinder, 119
   Cylinder head, 107
      and valve service specifications, 130
      covers, 94
   Cylinder studs, 129
   General engine specifications, 130
   Outer cylinder covers, 93
   Piston and piston rings, 123
   Piston, rings and bore specifications, 131
   Servicing the engine in the frame, 93
   torque specifications, 132
   Valves and valve components, 111
Evaporative emission control system (California models), 78, 246, 276
Exhaust system, 532
External shift mechanism, 200

F

Fan
   control relay (fuel injected models), 348
   motor switch (carbureted models), 437
Fasteners, 4
   Fastener inspection, 88
Final drive, 52
   housing bearing replacement, 452
   oil, 78
   oil capacity, 90
   unit and drive shaft, 438
   unit overhaul, 440
   unit service specifications, 459
Flywheel, starter clutch and starter drive gears, 301
Footpegs, 531
Front and rear hubs, 388
Front brake
   caliper, 470
   disc brake service specifications, 501
   light switch, 354
   pads, 466
Front fender, 525
Front fork, 409
   oil change, 87
   service specifications, 429
Front suspension and steering, 52, 403

INDEX

Front fork, 409
   service specifications, 429
Handlebar, 403
   grips and weights, 408
specifications, 429
Steering
   bearing preload inspection, 425
   head and stem, 418
   head bearing race replacement, 426
   stem bearing race replacement, 427
torque specifications, 429
Front suspension check, 80
Front wheel, 379
Fuel injection and emission control systems, 253
   Air filter housing, 262
   Bank angle sensor, 269
   Depressurizing the fuel system, 254
   Diagnostic trouble codes, 289
   DTC troubleshooting, 281
   Emission control system labels, 275
   Engine Control Module (ECM), 272
   Engine stop relay, 271
   Evaporative emission control system (California models), 276
   Fuel, 57
      cut-off relay, 272
      filter replacement (fuel injected models), 68
      flow test, 258
      hose identification, 221
      pressure test, 256
      pump/sub fuel tank assembly, 259
      reserve indicator and fuel reserve sensor (fuel injected models), 351
      system
         carbureted models, 40
         fuel injected models, 41
         hose inspection, 68
         precautions, 253
      torque specifications, 251
      tank, 221, 255
      valve, 222
   Fuel injection system
      general specifications, 288
      technical abbreviations, 288
      test specifications, 288
      torque specifications, 290
   Fuel injectors, injector cap and fuel feed hose, 266
   Idle Air Control Valve (IACV), 270
   Intake manifold, 264
   Malfunction indicator lamp (MIL), 277
   Pulse secondary air supply system, 275
   Sensor unit, 268
   Throttle body, 263
   Throttle cable replacement, 274
Fuse box, 359
Fuse box relays (ABS models), 361
Fuses, 359
   specifications, 364

G

Gearshift linkage, 46
General engine specifications, 130, 180
General information, 1
   Electrical system fundamentals, 18
   Fasteners, 4
   Manual organization, 1
   Measuring tools, 14
   Safety, 1
   Serial numbers and information labels, 3
   Service methods, 19
   Shop supplies, 6
   Storage, 24
   Tools, 9
   Warnings, cautions and notes, 1

H

Handlebar, 403
   grips and weights, 408
   switch, 356
Headlight aim, 87
High altitude adjustment, 240
Horn, 358

I

Idle Air Control Valve (IACV), 270
Idle speed, 67
Ignition coils, 311
Ignition Control Module (ICM) (carbureted models), 314
Ignition switch, 355
Ignition system
   specifications, 362
   testing, 305
Ignition timing, 64
Intake manifold, 237, 264
Internal shift mechanism, 216

L

Lighting system, 334
Lubrication, maintenance and tune-up, 57
   Air filter, 58
   Battery, 78
   Brake system, 81
   Choke cable inspection and adjustment (carbureted models), 72
   Clutch cable and clutch lever, 70
   Capacities
      Coolant capacity, 90
      Engine oil capacity, 90
      Final drive oil capacity, 90
   Cooling system, 75
   Crankcase breather inspection, 59
   Engine
      compression test, 60
      oil and filter, 73
      oil pressure check, 75
      rotation, 57

Evaporative emission control system
(California models), 78
Fastener inspection, 88
Final drive oil, 78
Front fork oil change, 87
Fuel, 57
　filter replacement (fuel injected models), 68
　system hose inspection, 68
Headlight aim, 87
Idle speed, 67
Ignition timing, 64
Maintenance and lubrication schedule, 88
Maintenance torque specifications, 91
Pulse secondary air supply system, 78
Recommended lubricants and fuel, 90
Sidestand and ignition cut-off switch test, 87
Spark plugs, 61
Steering bearings, 80
Sub-air filters (carbureted models), 58
Suspension check
　Front, 80
　Rear, 81
Throttle cables, 68
Tire inflation pressure and tread depth, 91
Tires and wheels, 78
Tune-up, 57
　specifications, 89
Valve clearance, 65

M

Main journal bearings and crankshaft main journal oil clearance, 152
Mainshaft service specifications, 218
Maintenance and lubrication schedule, 88
Maintenance free battery charging times, 362
Maintenance torque specifications, 91
Malfunction indicator lamp (MIL), 277
Manual organization, 1
Master cylinder
　Front, 476
　Rear (ABS models), 486
Measuring tools, 14
Motorcycle lift, 379

N

Neutral switch, 351

O

Oil pressure switch and oil pressure indicator, 349
Oil pump, 159
　specifications, 182
Outer cylinder covers, 93
Output drive
　and driven gear measurements, 177
　gear shims, 182
Output driven gear shims, 183
Output gearcase, 51, 163
　overhaul, 169

seal replacement, 167
specifications, 182

P

Pilot screw adjustment, 238
Pinion gear shim sizes, 459
Piston and piston rings, 123
Piston, rings and bore specifications, 131
Poor engine performance, 37
Primary drive gear, 198
Proportional Control Valve (PCV), 517
Pulse secondary air supply system, 78, 242, 275
Pulser rings, 516

R

Radiator, 369
Rear brake
　caliper (ABS models), 483
　disc brake service specifications (ABS models), 501
　light switch, 355
　pads (ABS models), 480
　pedal
　　ABS models, 499
　　drum brake models, 498
Rear drum brake, 493
　service specifications, 502
Rear fender, 526
Rear suspension and final drive, 431
　Final drive
　　housing bearing replacement, 452
　　unit and drive shaft, 438
　　unit overhaul, 440
　　unit service specifications, 459
　　torque specifications, 459
　Pinion gear shim sizes, 459
　Rear suspension
　　check, 81
　　specifications, 459
　　torque specifications, 459
　Rear swing arm, 433
　Ring and pinion gear measurements, 455
　Ring gear shim sizes, 459
　Shock absorber, 431
Rear swing arm, 433
Rear wheel and driven flange, 382
Recommended lubricants and fuel, 90
Restarting the engine, 141
Ring and pinion gear measurements, 455
Ring gear shim sizes, 459

S

Safety, 1
Seat, 523
Sensor test specifications, 364
Serial numbers and information labels, 3
Service methods, 19
Servicing the engine in the frame, 93, 133
Shift drum torque specifications, 219

INDEX

Shift fork and shift shaft service specifications, 219
Shock absorber, 431
Shop supplies, 6
Side covers, 524
Sidestand, 529
    and ignition cut-off switch test, 87
    switch, 352
Spark plugs, 61
Specifications
    ABS diagnostic trouble codes, 521
    ABS modulator/ECU, 518 ABS wheel speed
        sensor air gap, 521
        Maintenance free battery charging times, 362
    Bearing selection
        connecting rod, 181
        crankcase replacement only, 180
        crankshaft and crankcase replacement, 180
        crankshaft replacement only, 181
        main journal bearing replacement only, 181
    Bulb specifications, 363
    Capacities
        Coolant capacity, 90
        Engine oil capacity, 90
        Final drive oil capacity, 90
    Connecting rod
        weight, 182
        weight code selection, 181
    Conversion formulas, 26
    Diagnostic trouble codes, 289
    Maintenance and lubrication schedule, 88
    Metric tap and drill sizes, 28
    Metric, inch and fractional equivalents, 29
    Motorcycle dimensions, 25
    Motorcycle weight specifications, 26
    Output drive gear shims, 182
    Output driven gear shims, 183
    Pinion gear shim sizes, 459
    Recommended lubricants and fuel, 90
    Ring gear shim sizes, 459
    Technical abbreviations, 27
    Tire inflation
        pressure, 401
        pressure and tread depth, 91
Specifications, general systems
    Alternator and charging system specifications, 362
    Brakes
        Front disc brake service specifications, 501
        Rear
            disc brake service specifications
                (ABS models), 501
            drum brake service specifications, 502
    Battery specifications, 362
    Carburetor and fuel tank specifications, 251
    Cooling system specifications, 378
    Countershaft service specifications, 219
    Cylinder head and valve service specifications, 130
    Clutch specifications, 205
    Engine lower end specifications, 180
    Final drive unit service specifications, 459
    Front fork service specifications, 429
    Fuel injection system
        general specifications, 288
        test specifications, 288
        technical abbreviations, 288
    Fuse specifications, 364
    General engine specifications, 130, 180
    Ignition system specifications, 362
    Mainshaft service specifications, 218
    Oil pump specifications, 182
    Output gearcase specifications, 182
    Piston, rings and bore specifications, 131
    Rear suspension specifications, 459
    Sensor test specifications, 364
    Shift fork and shift shaft service specifications, 219
    Starter clutch specifications, 362
    Starting system specifications, 363
    Steering and front suspension specifications, 429
    Tire and wheel specifications, 401
    Transmission specifications, 218
    Tune-up specifications, 89
    Wheel and axle service specifications, 401
Specifications, torque
    Body and exhaust system torque specifications, 535
    Brake system torque specifications, 521
    Brake torque specifications, 502
    Clutch and external shift mechanism torque
        specifications, 205
    Cooling system torque specifications, 378
    Electrical system torque specifications, 365
    Engine
        bottom end torque specifications, 183
        top end torque specifications, 132
    Front suspension and steering torque
        specifications, 429
    Fuel injection system torque specifications, 290
    Fuel system torque specifications, 251
    General torque recommendations, 29
    Maintenance torque specifications, 91
    Rear suspension and final drive torque
        specifications, 459
    Shift drum torque specifications, 219
    Wheel torque specifications, 402
Speedometer, 241
Starter
    2004-2007 Aero models, 318
    2008-2009 and 2011-2013 Aero models, 2010-2013
        Spirit models and all Phantom models, 325
    clutch specifications, 362
    relay switch, 331
    system
        specifications, 363
        troubleshooting, 316
Starting the engine, 31
Steering
    and front suspension specifications, 429
    bearing preload inspection, 425
    bearings, 80
    covers, 525
    head and stem, 418
    head bearing race replacement, 426
    stem bearing race replacement, 427
Storage, 24

INDEX

Sub-air filters (carbureted models), 58
Switch continuity test, 357

T

Thermostat, 372
Thermostat housing, 373
Throttle body, 263
Throttle cable replacement, 241, 274
Throttle cables, 68
Throttle Position (TP) sensor (carbureted models), 314
Tire
    and wheel specifications, 401
    changing, 395
    inflation pressure and tread depth, 91
    inflation pressure, 401
Tires and wheels, 78, 379
Tools, 9
Transmission and internal shift mechanism, 207
    Countershaft service specifications, 219
    Internal shift mechanism, 216
    Mainshaft service specifications, 218
    Shift drum torque specifications, 219
    Shift fork and shift shaft service specifications, 219
    Transmission, 47, 207
        inspection, 214
        specifications, 218
    Transmission and output drive gear bearings, 151
Troubleshooting, 31
    Brake system, 53
    Clutch, 45
    Cylinder leakdown test, 45
    Electrical testing, 47
    Engine lubrication, 44
    Engine will not start, 34
    Engine, 42
    Final drive, 52
    Front suspension and steering, 52
    Fuel system
        carbureted models, 40
        fuel injected models, 41
    Gearshift linkage, 46
    Output gearcase, 51

Poor engine performance, 37
Starting the engine, 31
Transmission, 47
Tune-up, 57
    specifications, 89
Turn signal relay, 357

U

Upper fork bridge indicator lights (2008-2009 and 2011-2013 Aero models, 2012-2013 Spirit and Phantom models), 340

V

Valve clearance, 65
Valves and valve components, 111
Vehicle Speed (VS) sensor, 344

W

Warnings, cautions and notes, 1
Water pump, 374
Wheels and tires, 78, 379
    Driven flange dampers, 387
    Front and rear hubs, 388
    Front wheel, 379
    Motorcycle lift, 379
    Rear wheel and driven flange, 382
    specifications, 401
    Tire
        changing, 395
        inflation pressure, 401
    Wheel
        and axle service specifications, 401
        balance, 400
        service, 392
        speed sensors, 514
        torque specifications, 402
Wiring diagrams, 537

WIRING DIAGRAMS

WIRING DIAGRAMS

2004-2007 HONDA AERO

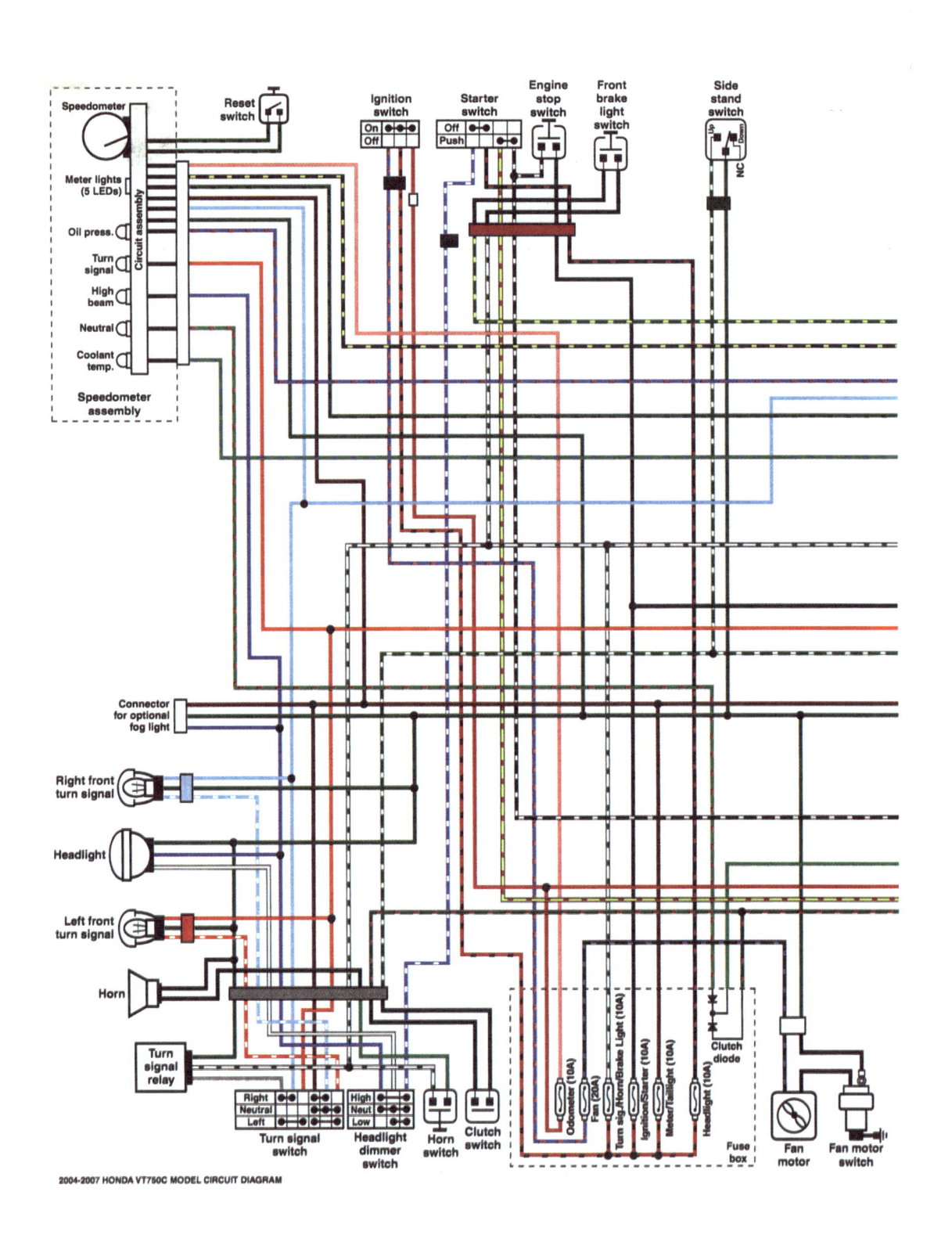

2004-2007 HONDA VT750C MODEL CIRCUIT DIAGRAM

WIRING DIAGRAMS

545

2004-2007 HONDA VT750C MODEL CIRCUIT DIAGRAM

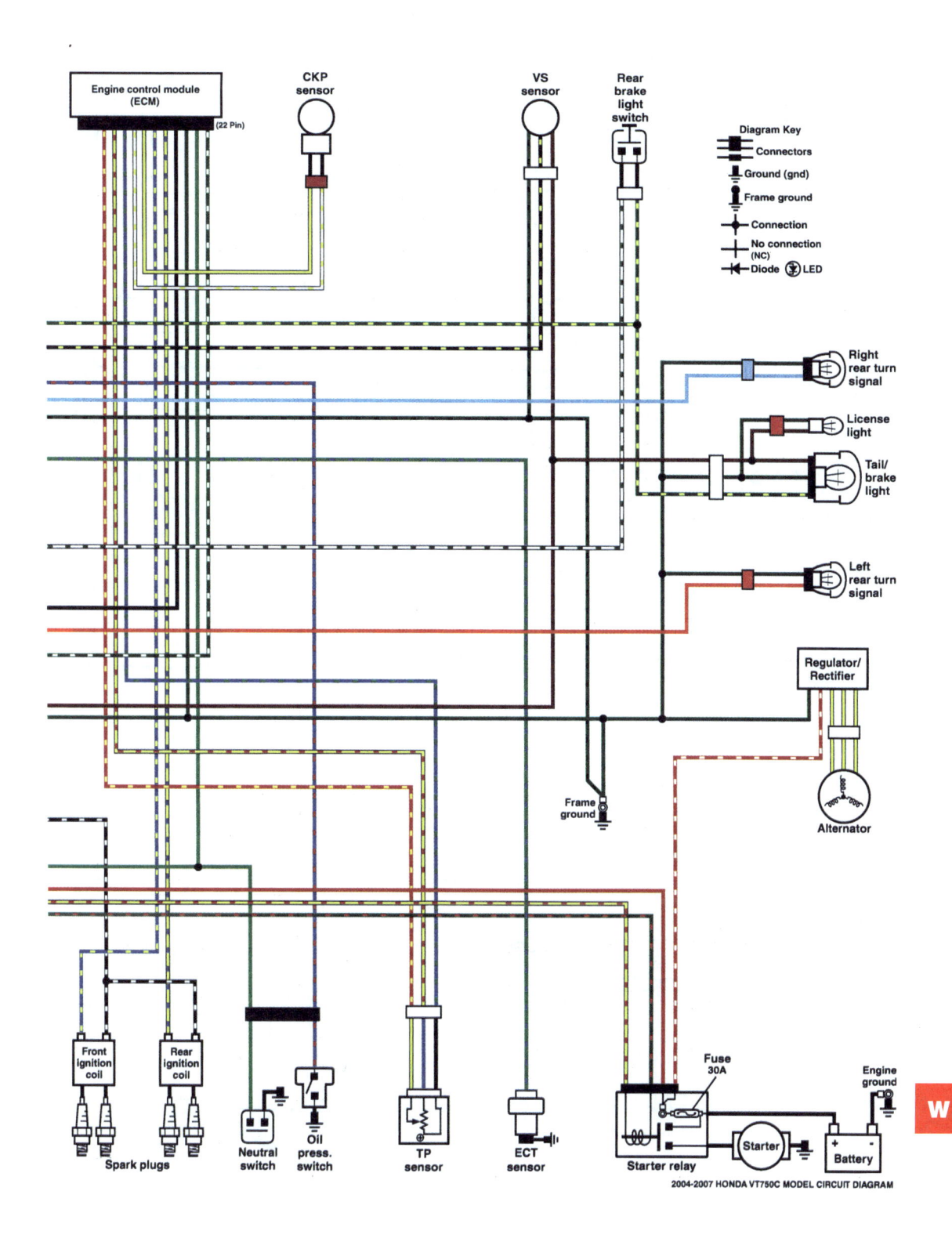

WIRING DIAGRAMS

2008-2009 HONDA AERO

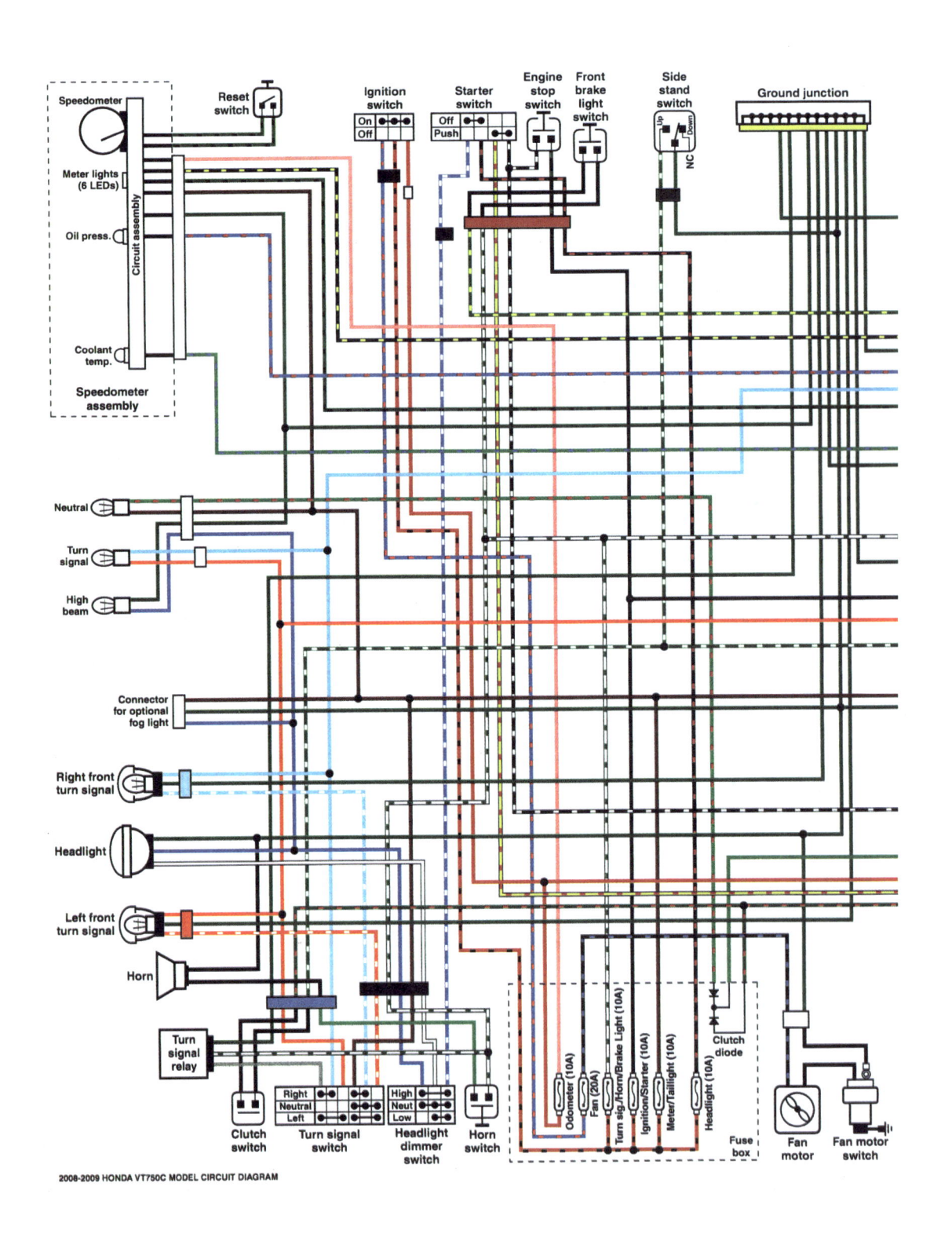

2008-2009 HONDA VT750C MODEL CIRCUIT DIAGRAM

WIRING DIAGRAMS

547

2008-2009 HONDA VT750C MODEL CIRCUIT DIAGRAM

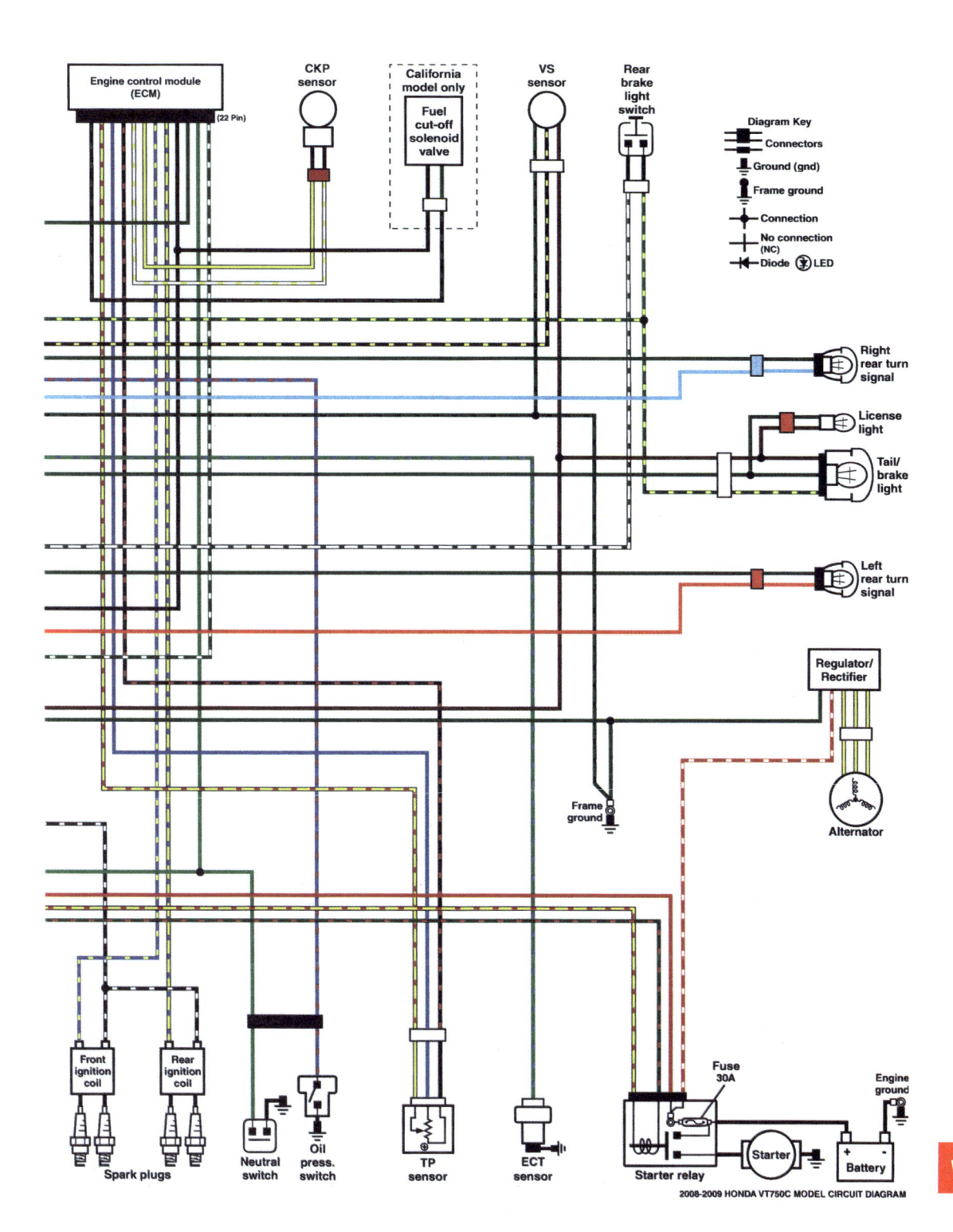

WIRING DIAGRAMS

2011 HONDA AERO

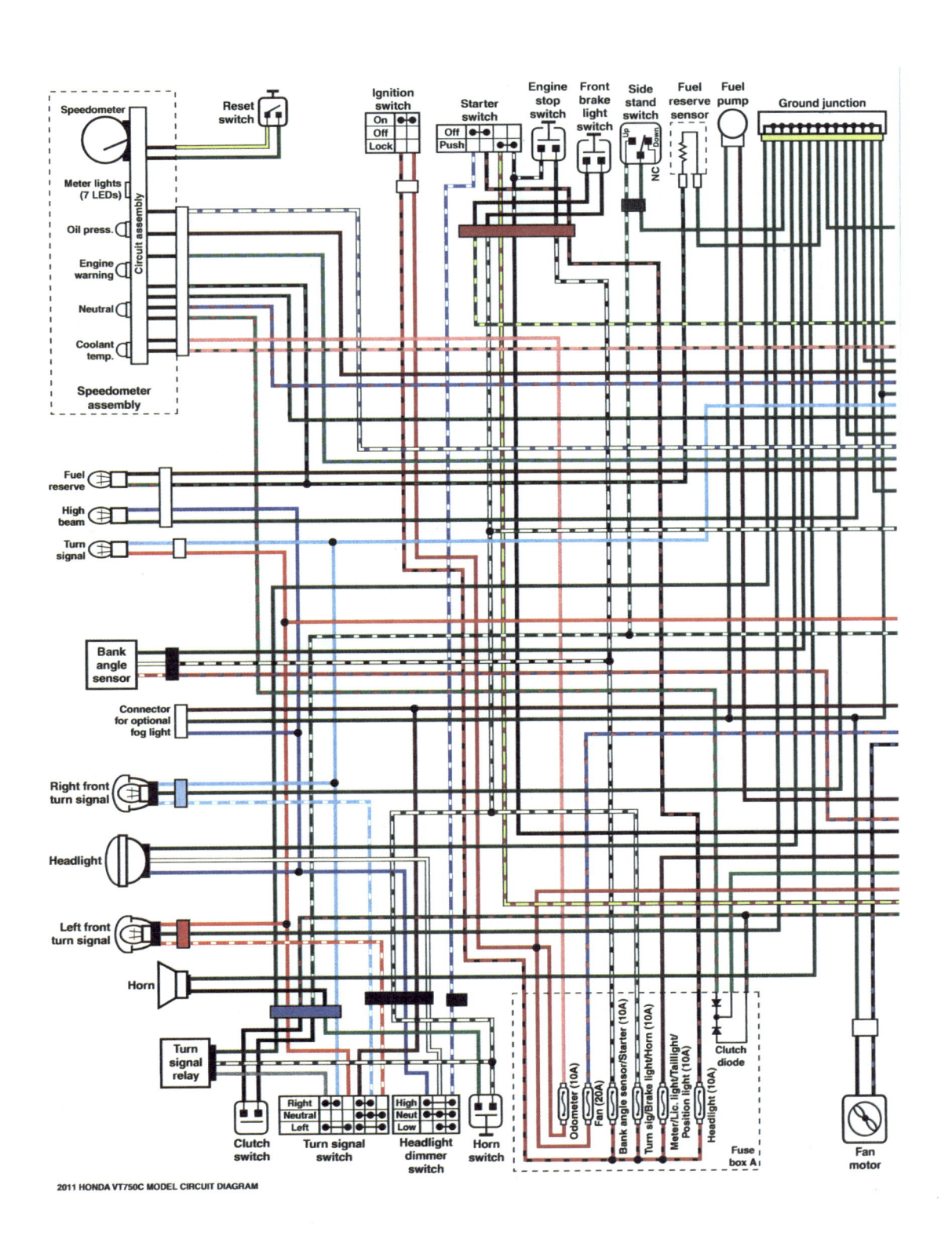

2011 HONDA VT750C MODEL CIRCUIT DIAGRAM

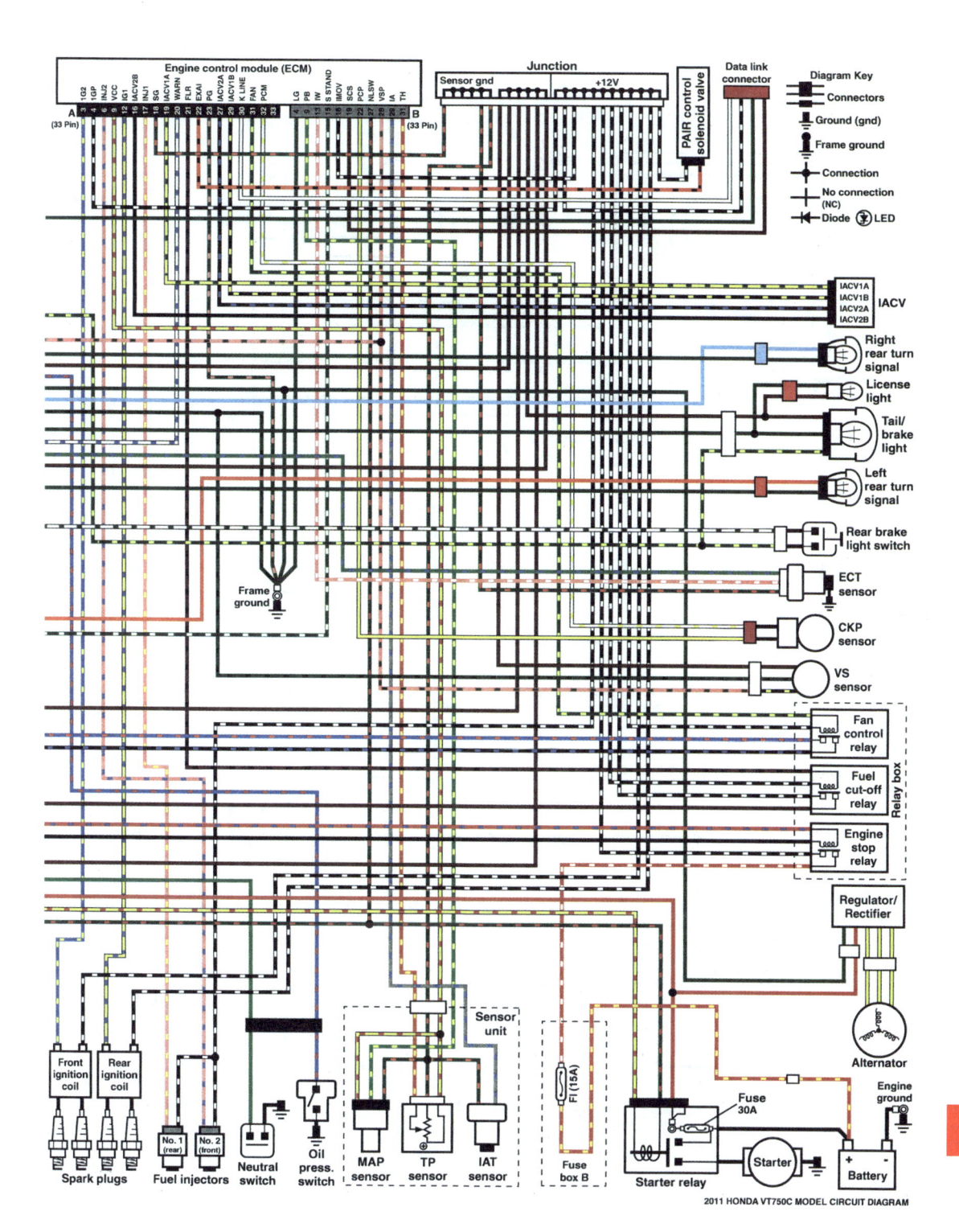

WIRING DIAGRAMS

2011 HONDA VT750C MODEL CIRCUIT DIAGRAM

WIRING DIAGRAMS

2007-2009 HONDA SPIRIT 49-STATES AND CANADA MODELS

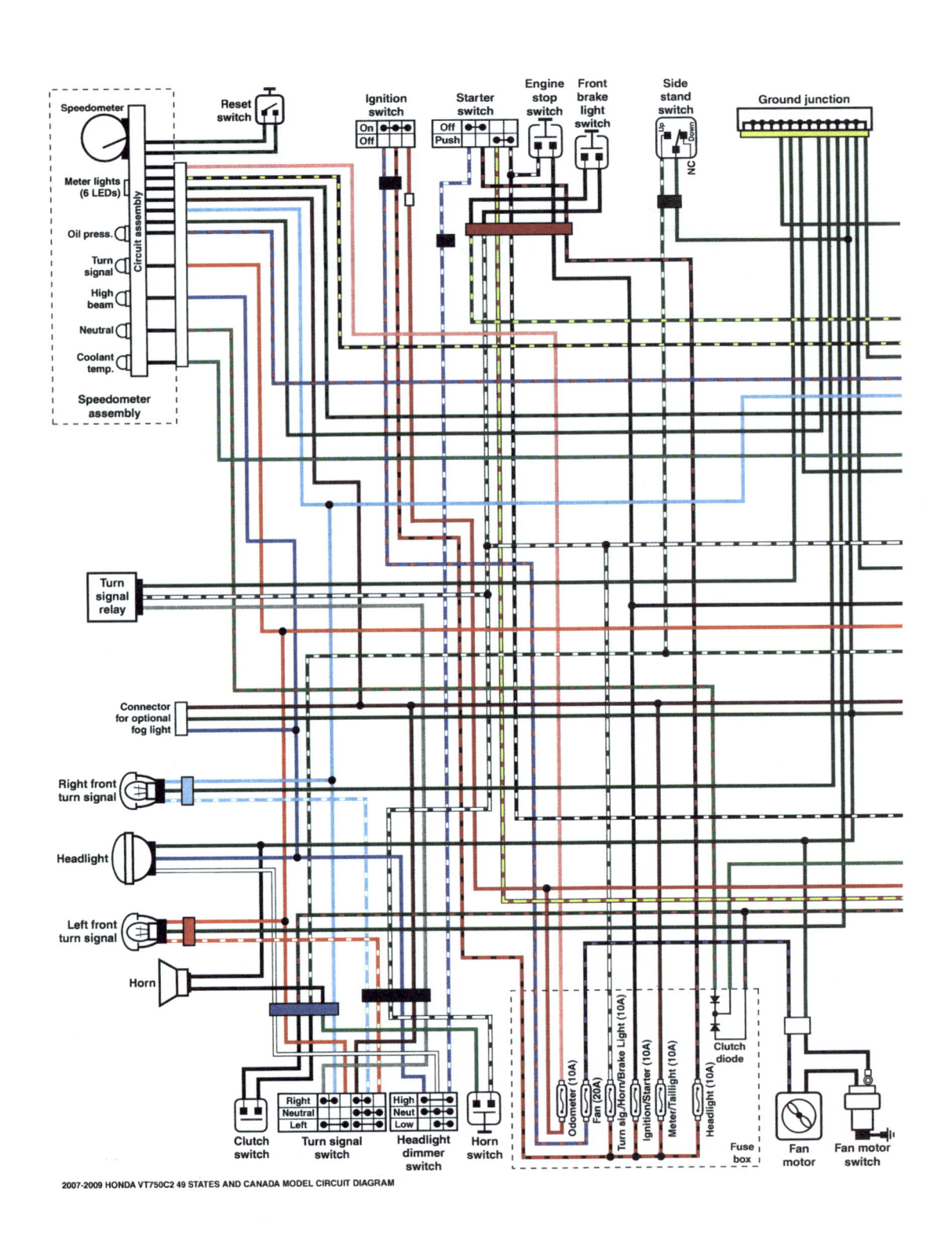

2007-2009 HONDA VT750C2 49 STATES AND CANADA MODEL CIRCUIT DIAGRAM

WIRING DIAGRAMS

WIRING DIAGRAMS

2007-2009 HONDA SPIRIT CALIFORNIA

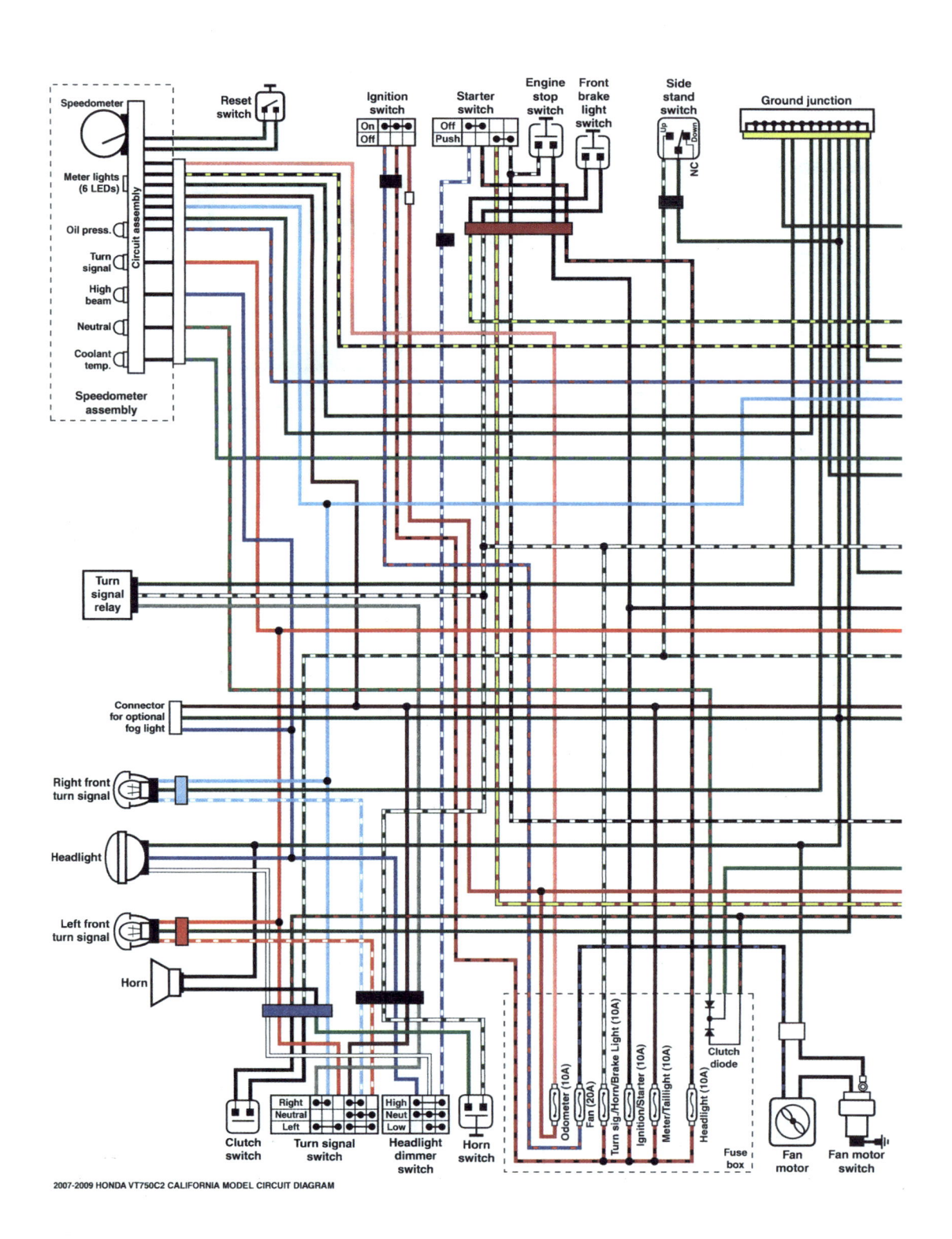

2007-2009 HONDA VT750C2 CALIFORNIA MODEL CIRCUIT DIAGRAM

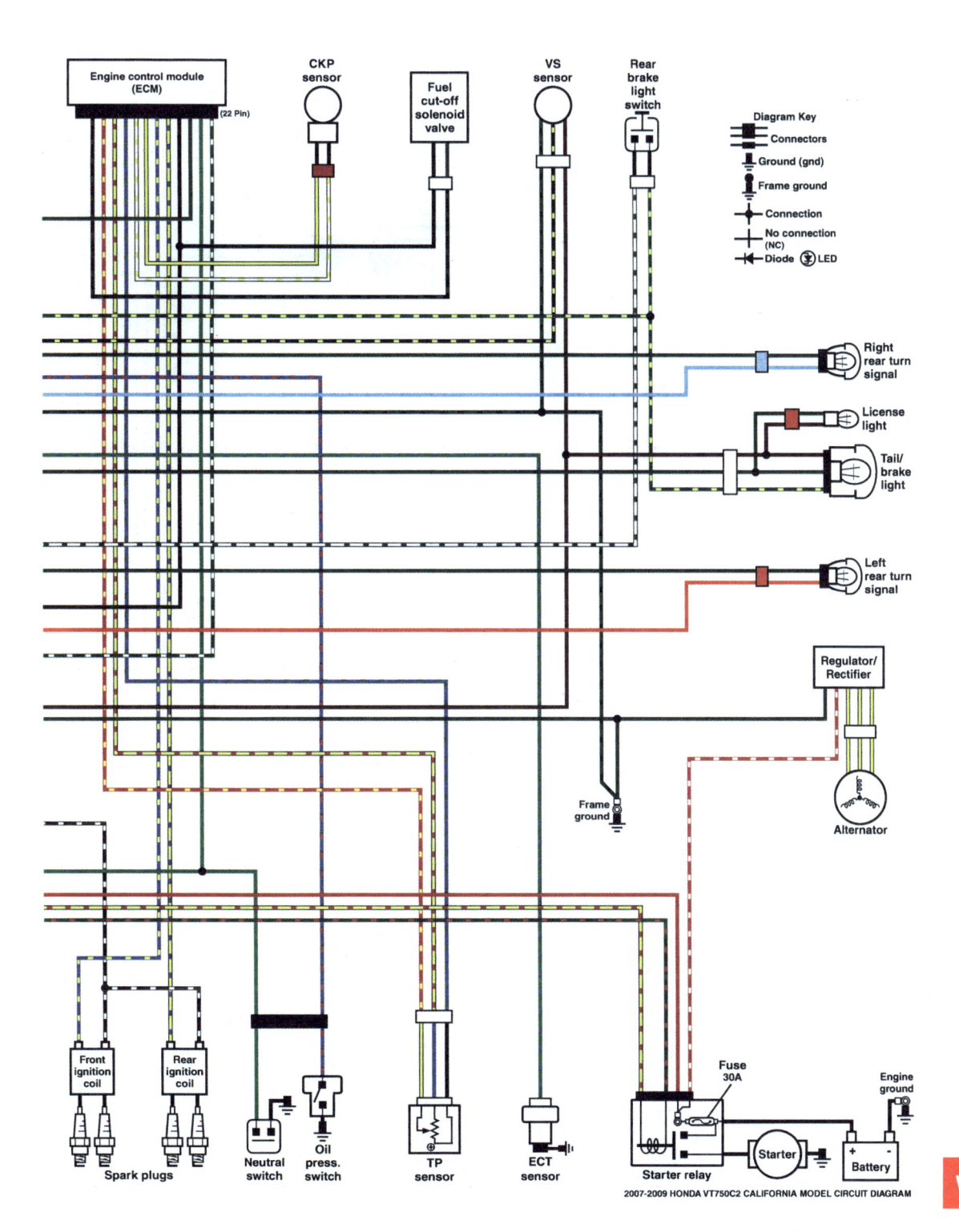

WIRING DIAGRAMS

2007-2009 HONDA VT750C2 CALIFORNIA MODEL CIRCUIT DIAGRAM

WIRING DIAGRAMS

2010-2011 HONDA PHANTOM

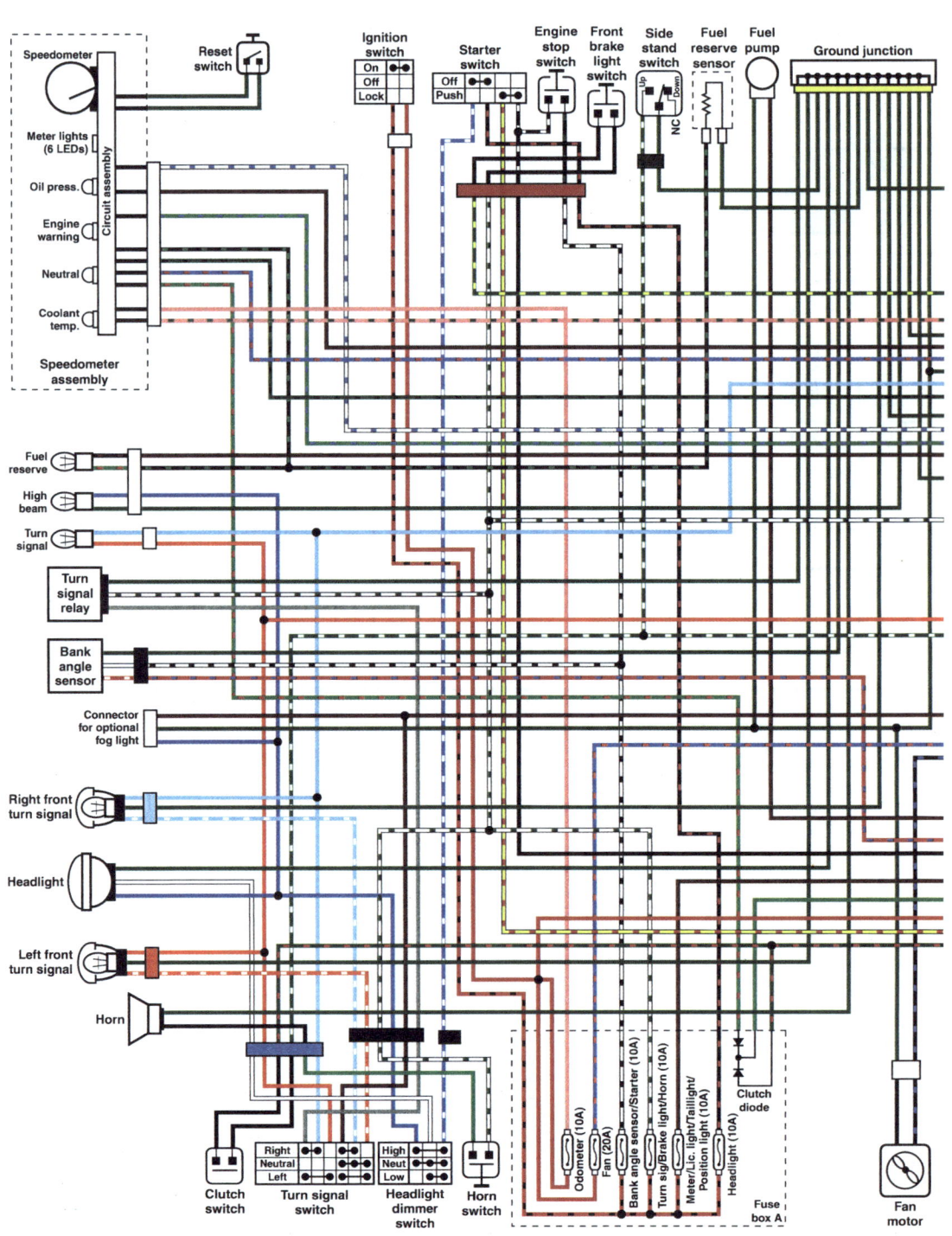

2010-2011 HONDA VT750C2B MODEL CIRCUIT DIAGRAM

WIRING DIAGRAMS

2010-2011 HONDA VT750C2B MODEL CIRCUIT DIAGRAM

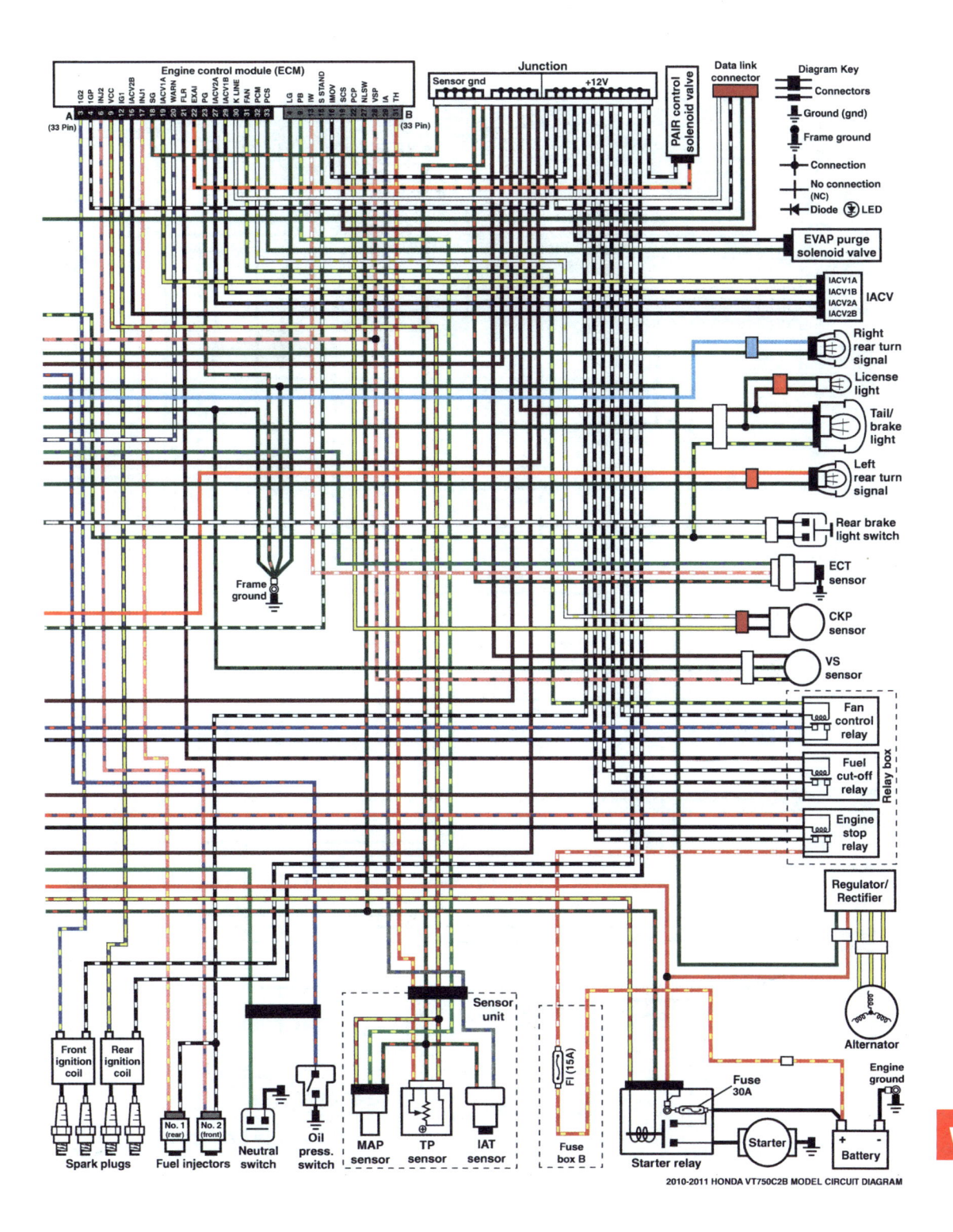

WIRING DIAGRAMS

2011-2013 HONDA AERO NON-ABS

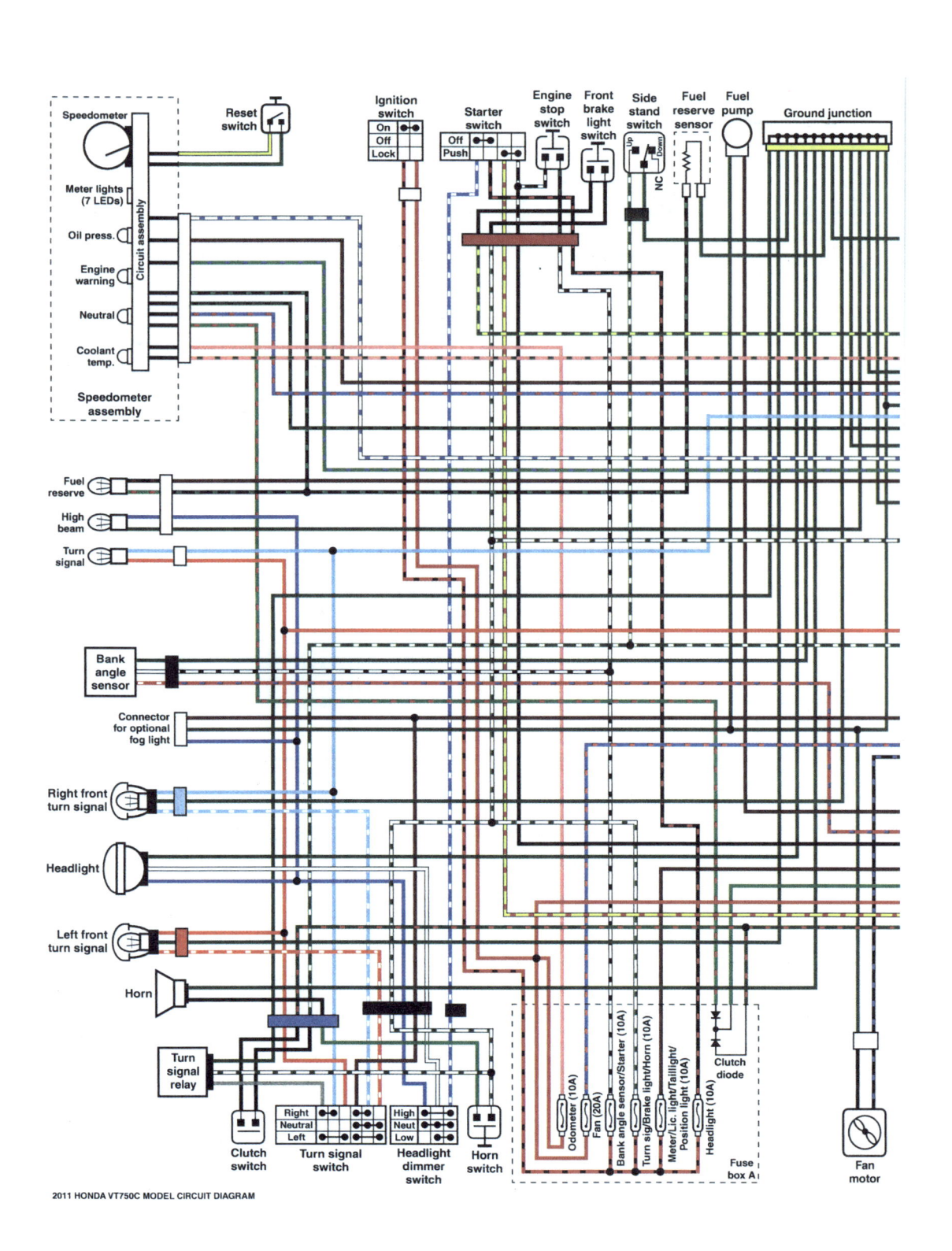

2011 HONDA VT750C MODEL CIRCUIT DIAGRAM

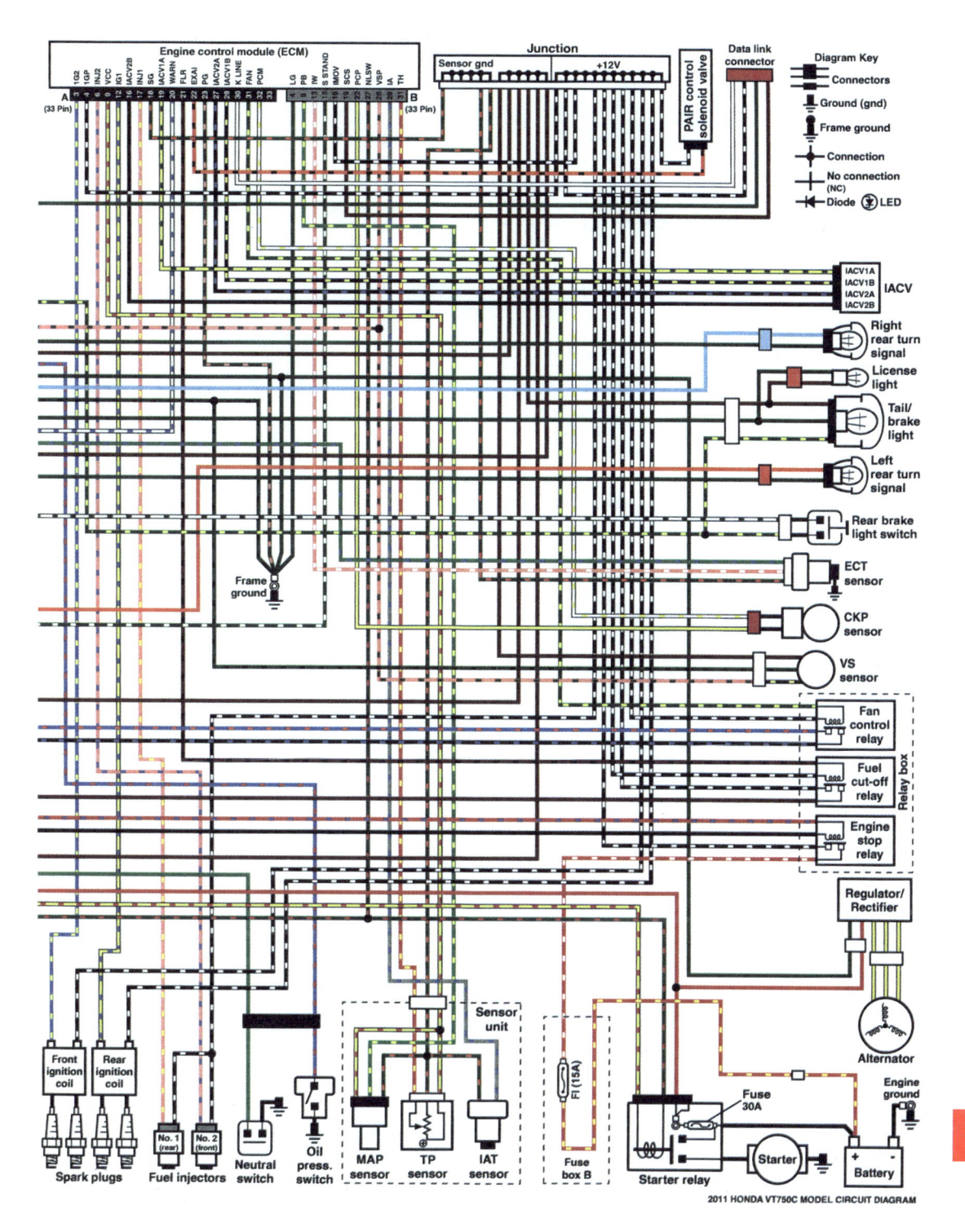

WIRING DIAGRAMS

2012-2013 HONDA AERO ABS

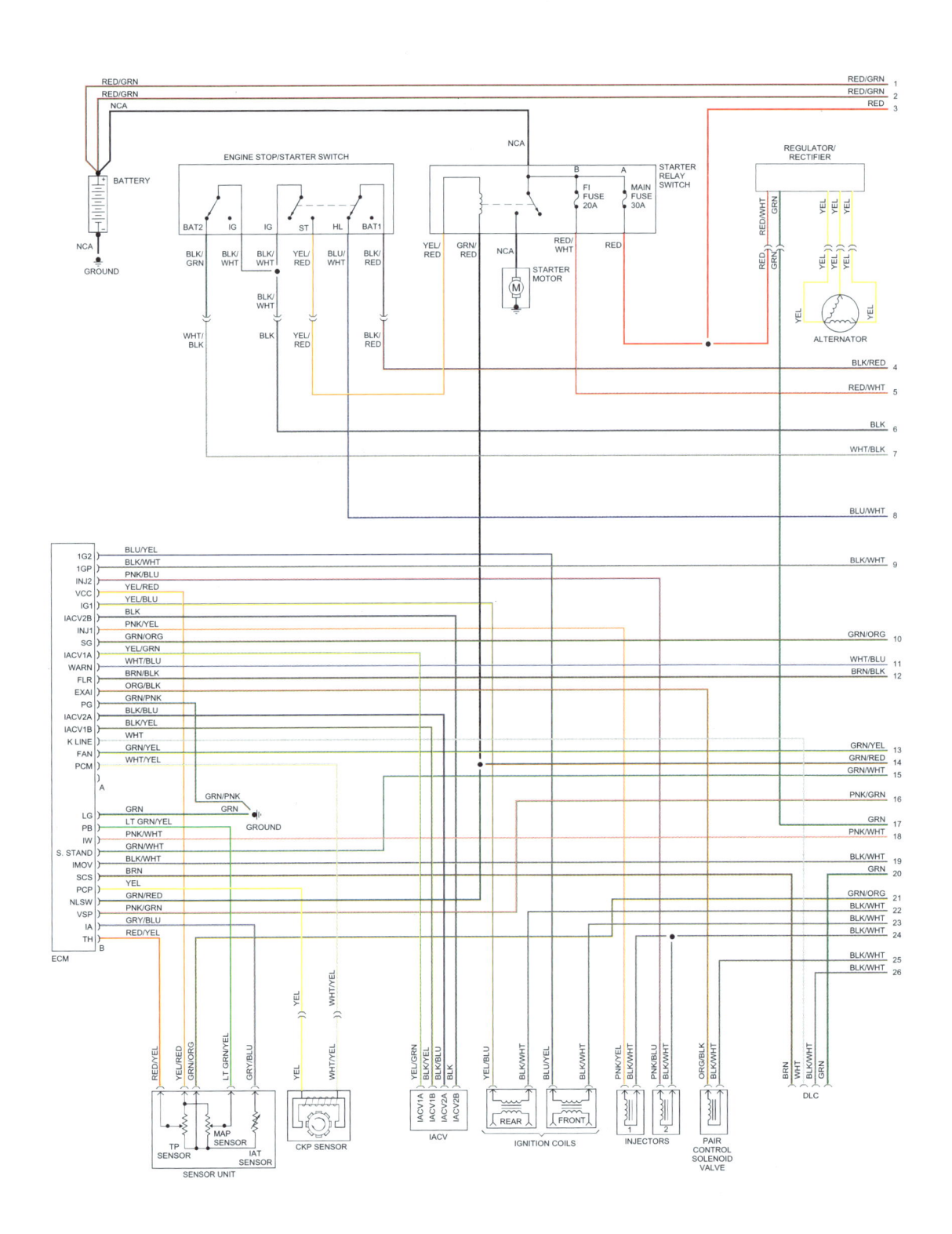

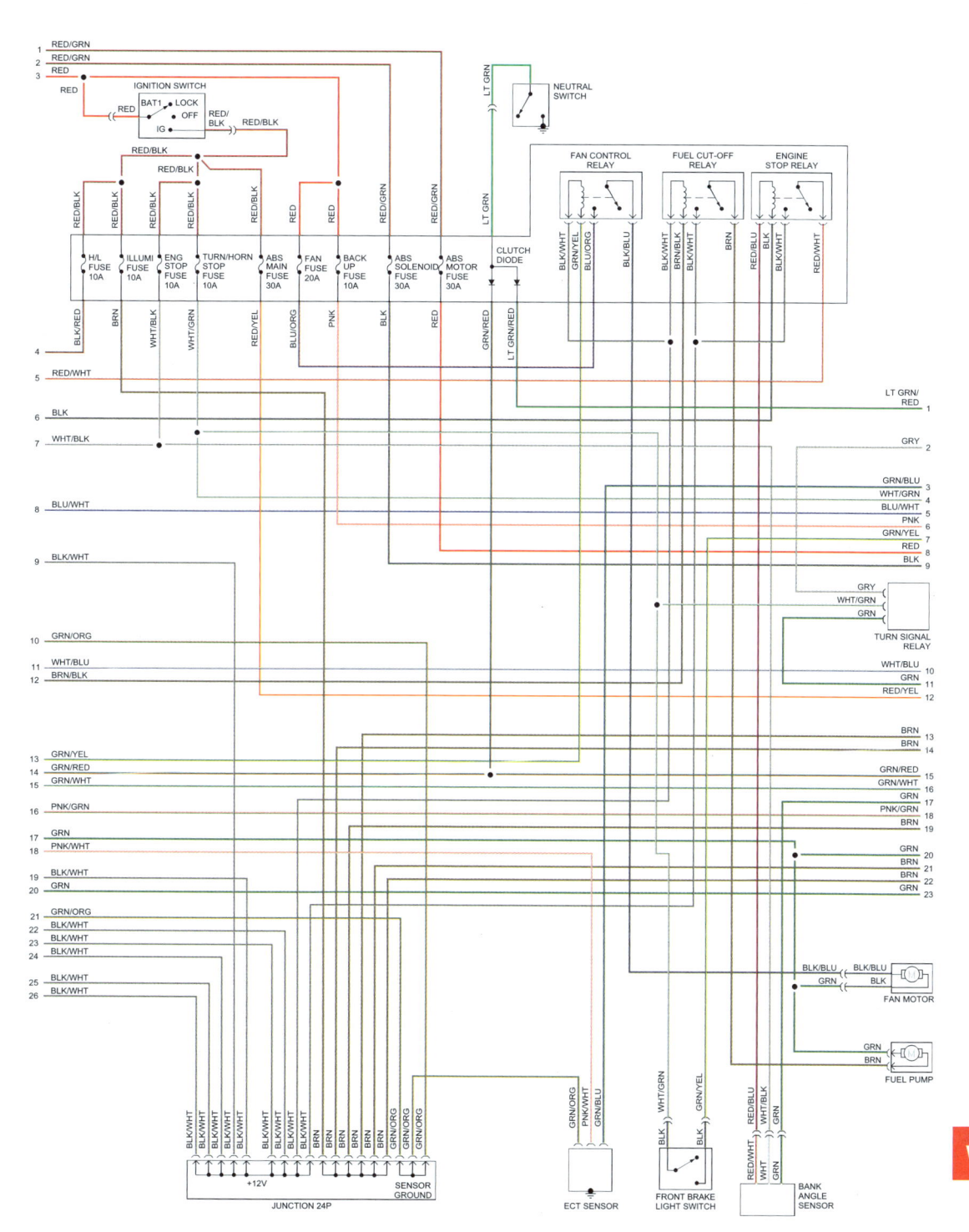

WIRING DIAGRAMS

WIRING DIAGRAMS

2012-2013 HONDA AERO ABS (continued)

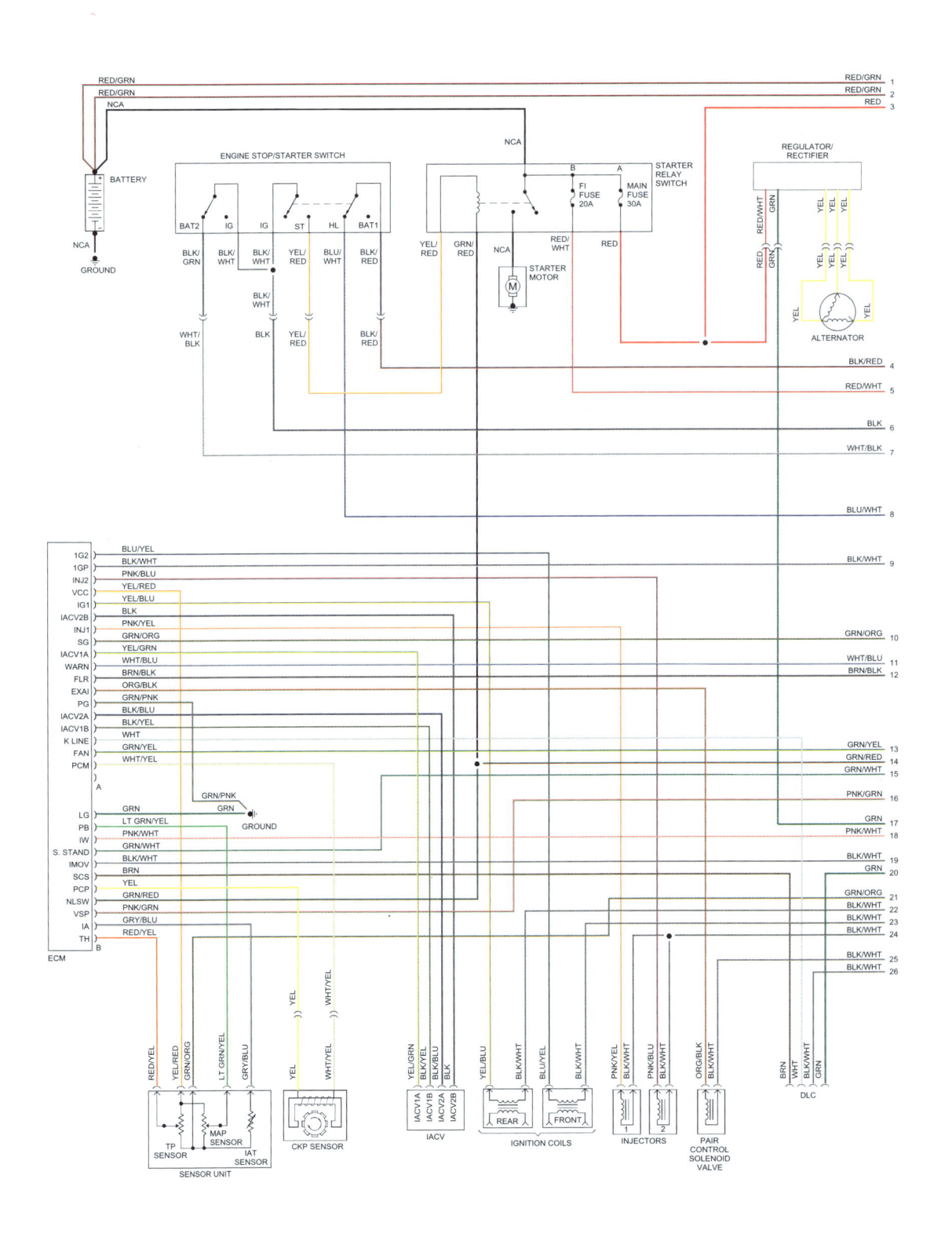

WIRING DIAGRAMS

2010-2013 HONDA SPIRIT NON-ABS

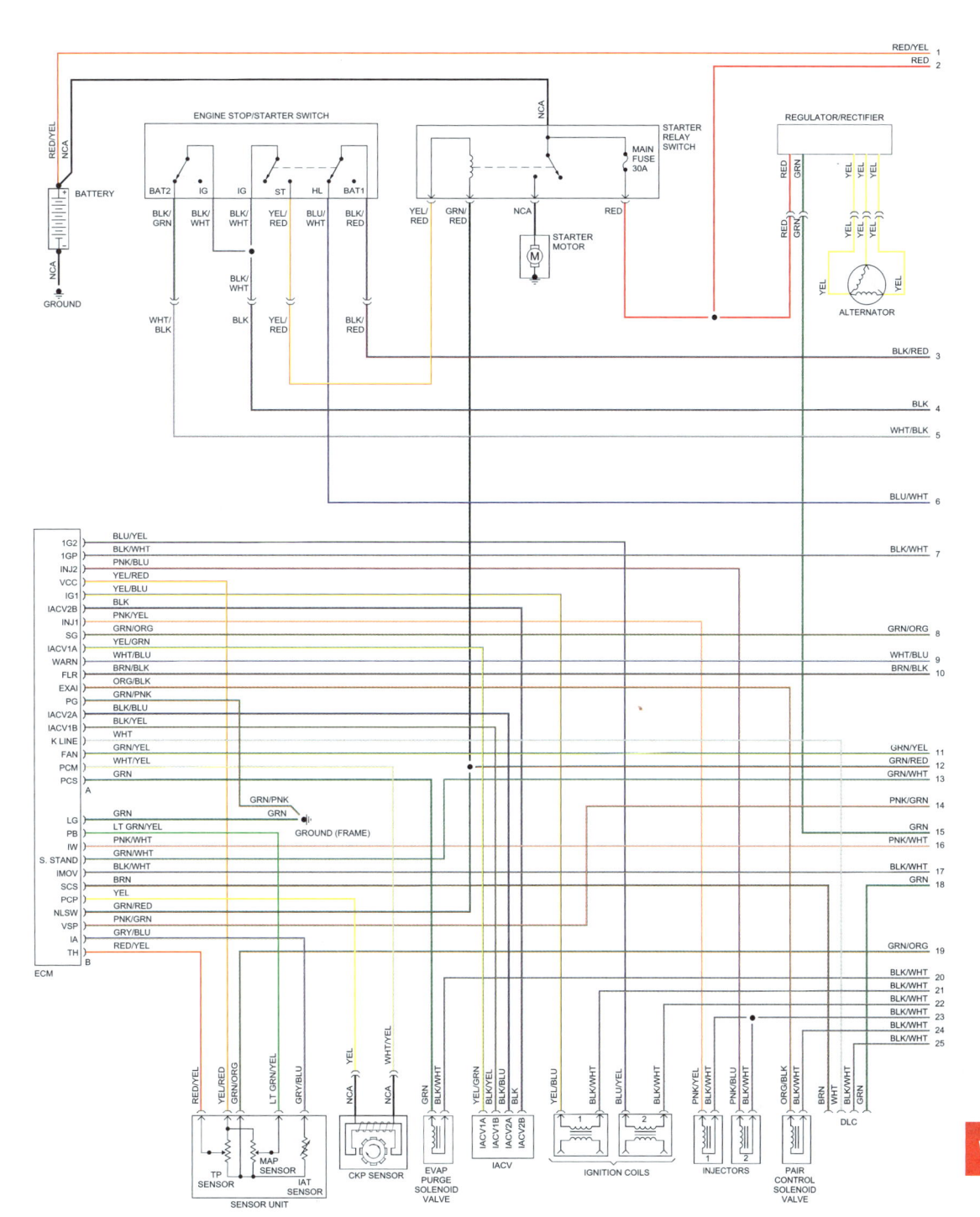

WIRING DIAGRAMS

2010-2013 HONDA SPIRIT NON-ABS (continued)

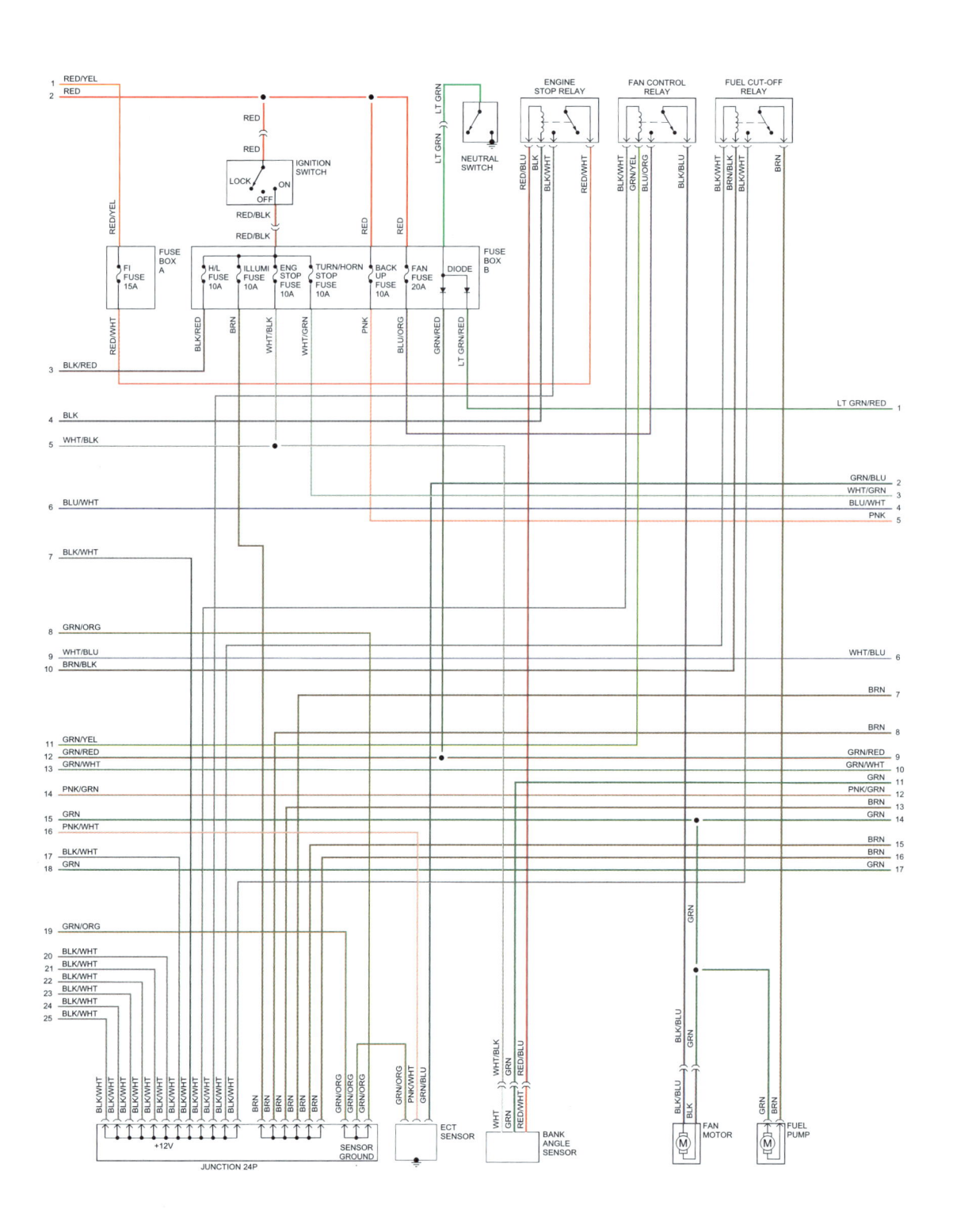

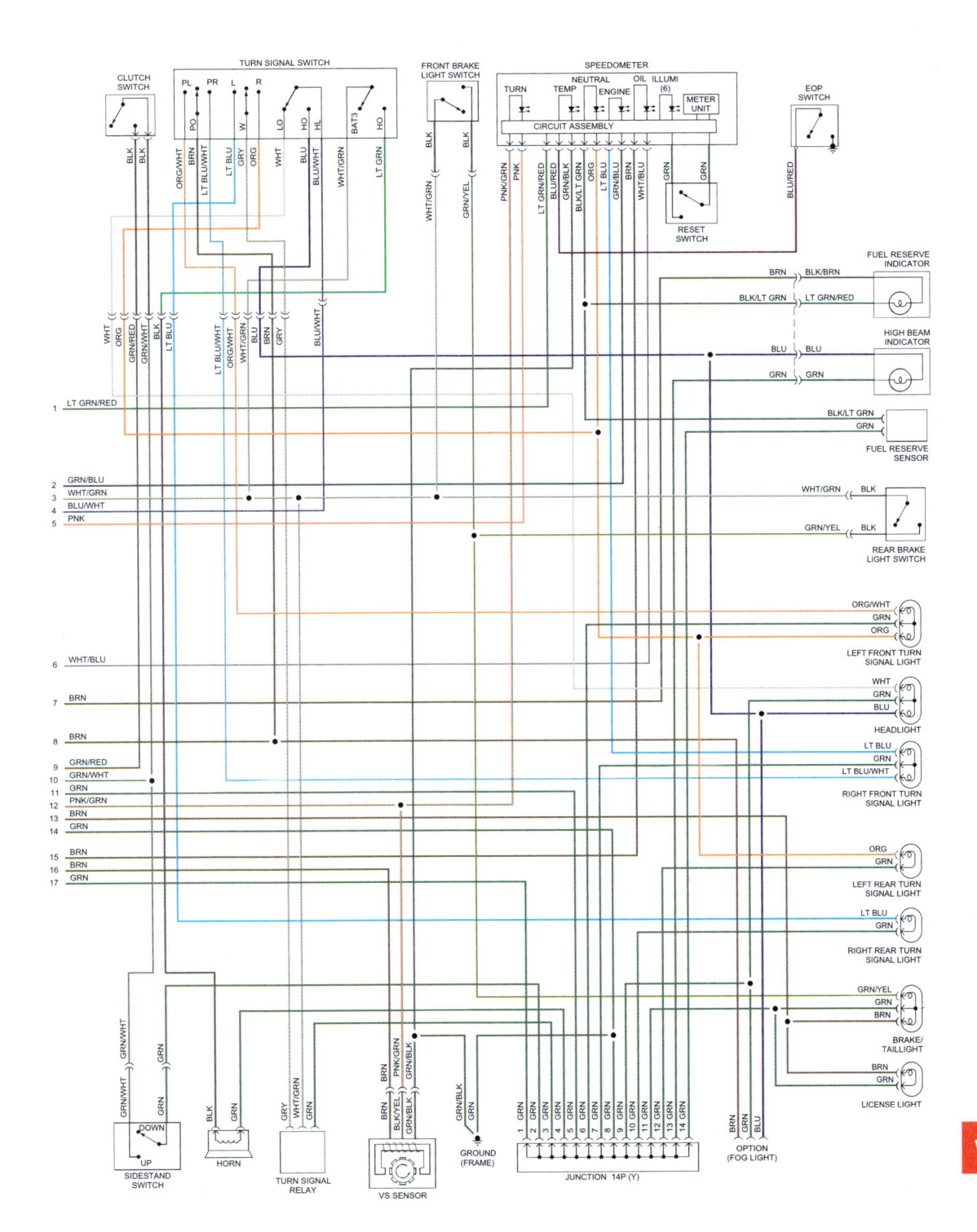

WIRING DIAGRAMS

563

WIRING DIAGRAMS

2013 HONDA SPIRIT ABS

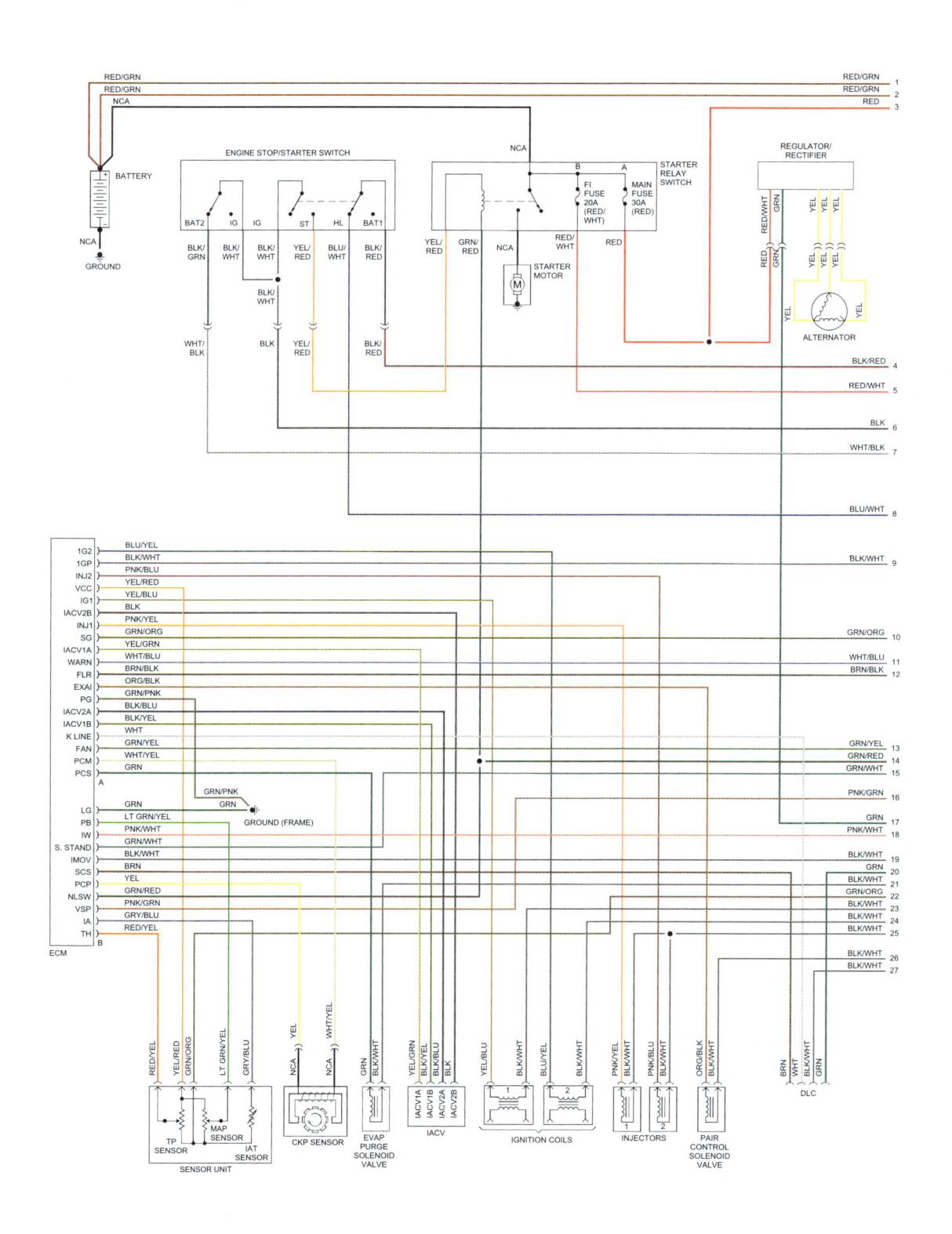

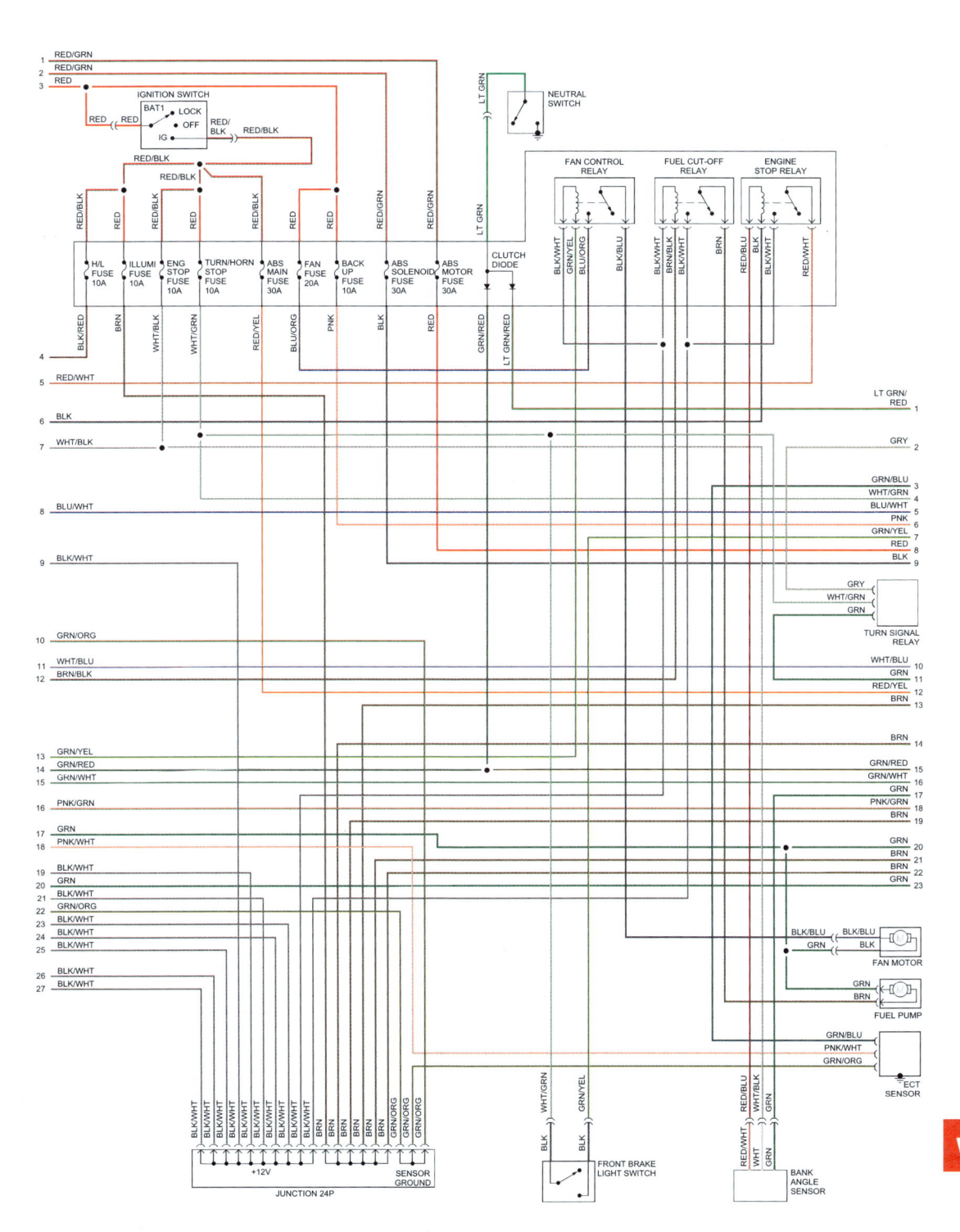

WIRING DIAGRAMS

WIRING DIAGRAMS

2013 HONDA SPIRIT ABS (continued)

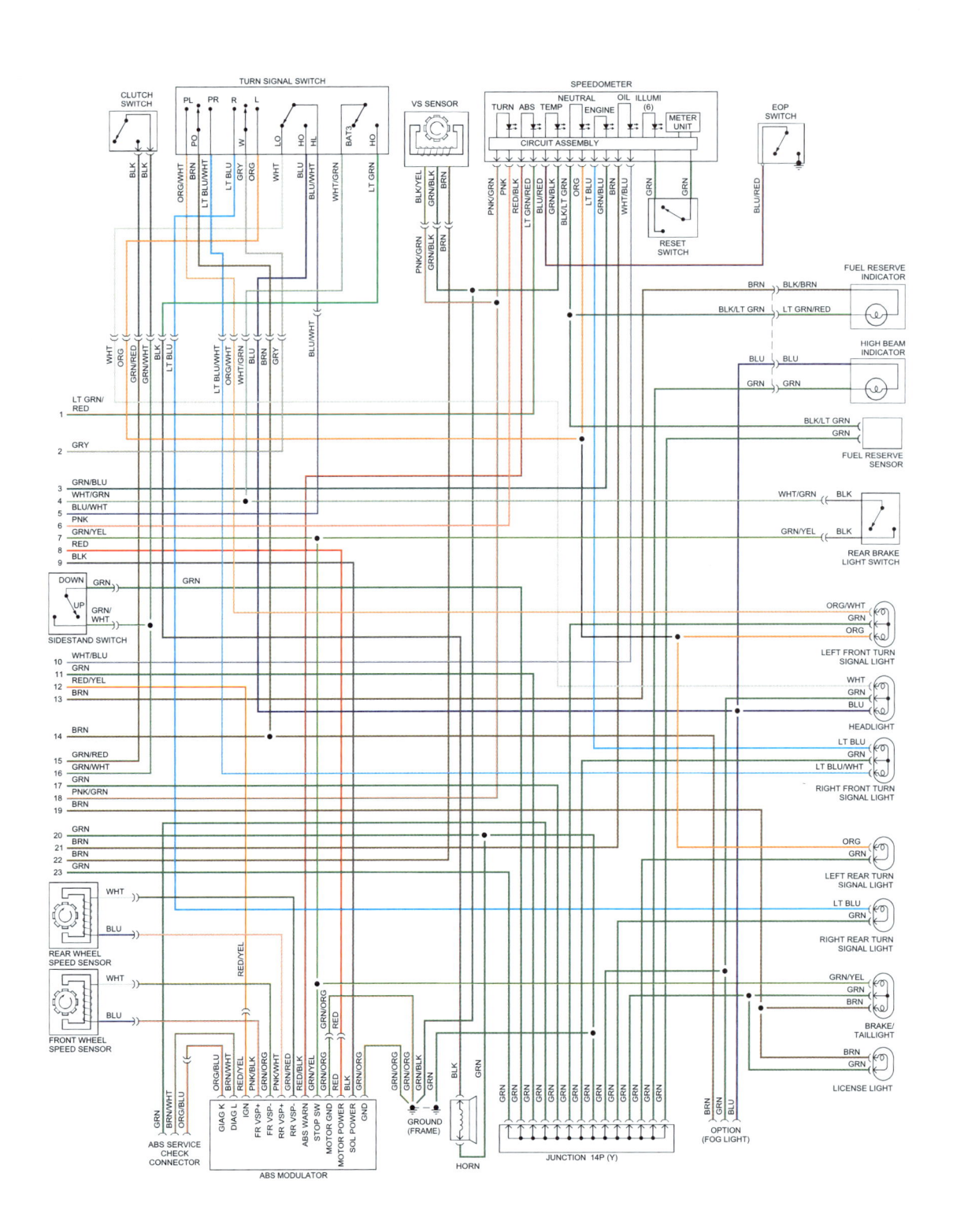

WIRING DIAGRAMS

2010-2013 HONDA PHANTOM

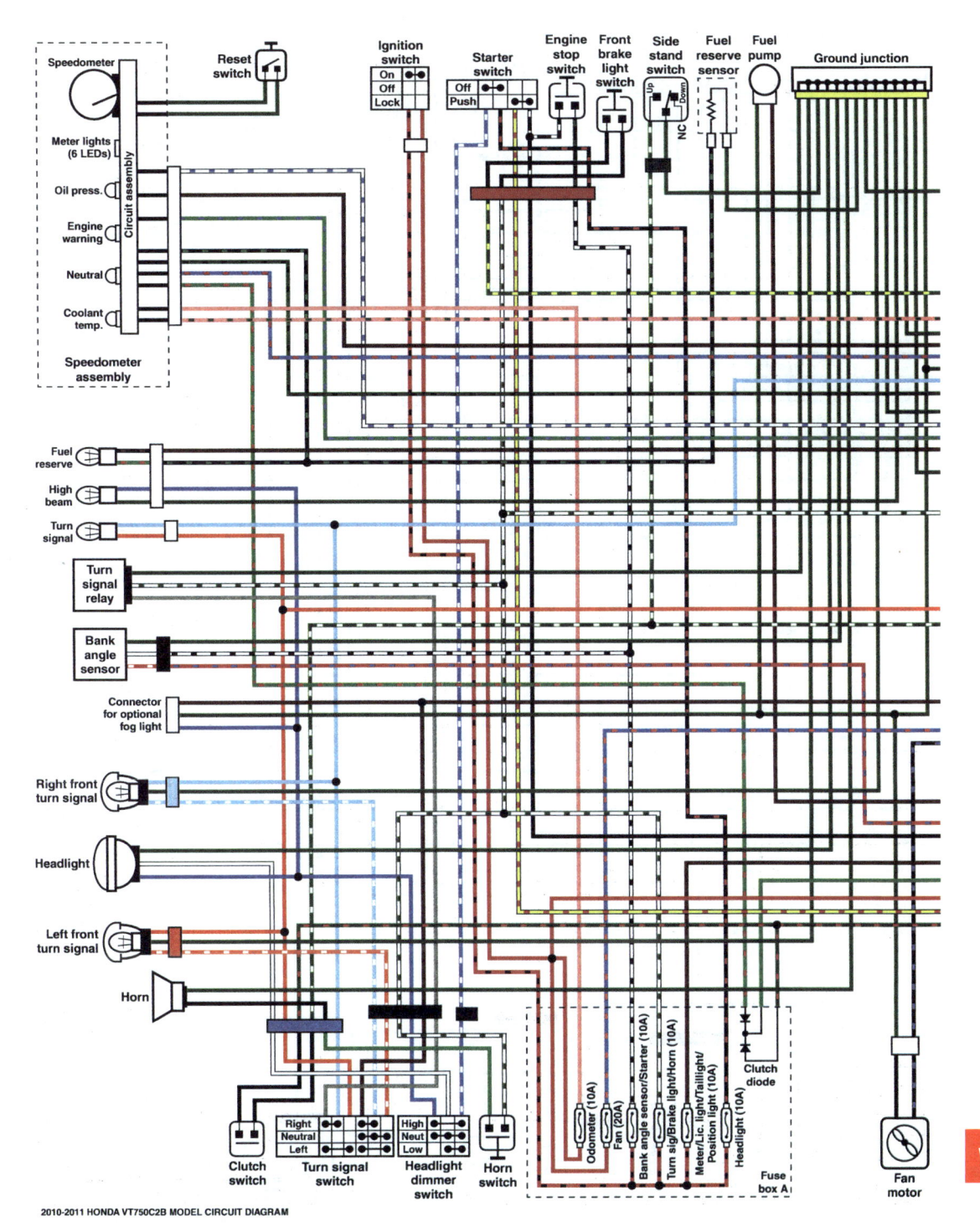

2010-2011 HONDA VT750C2B MODEL CIRCUIT DIAGRAM

WIRING DIAGRAMS

2010-2013 HONDA PHANTOM (continued)

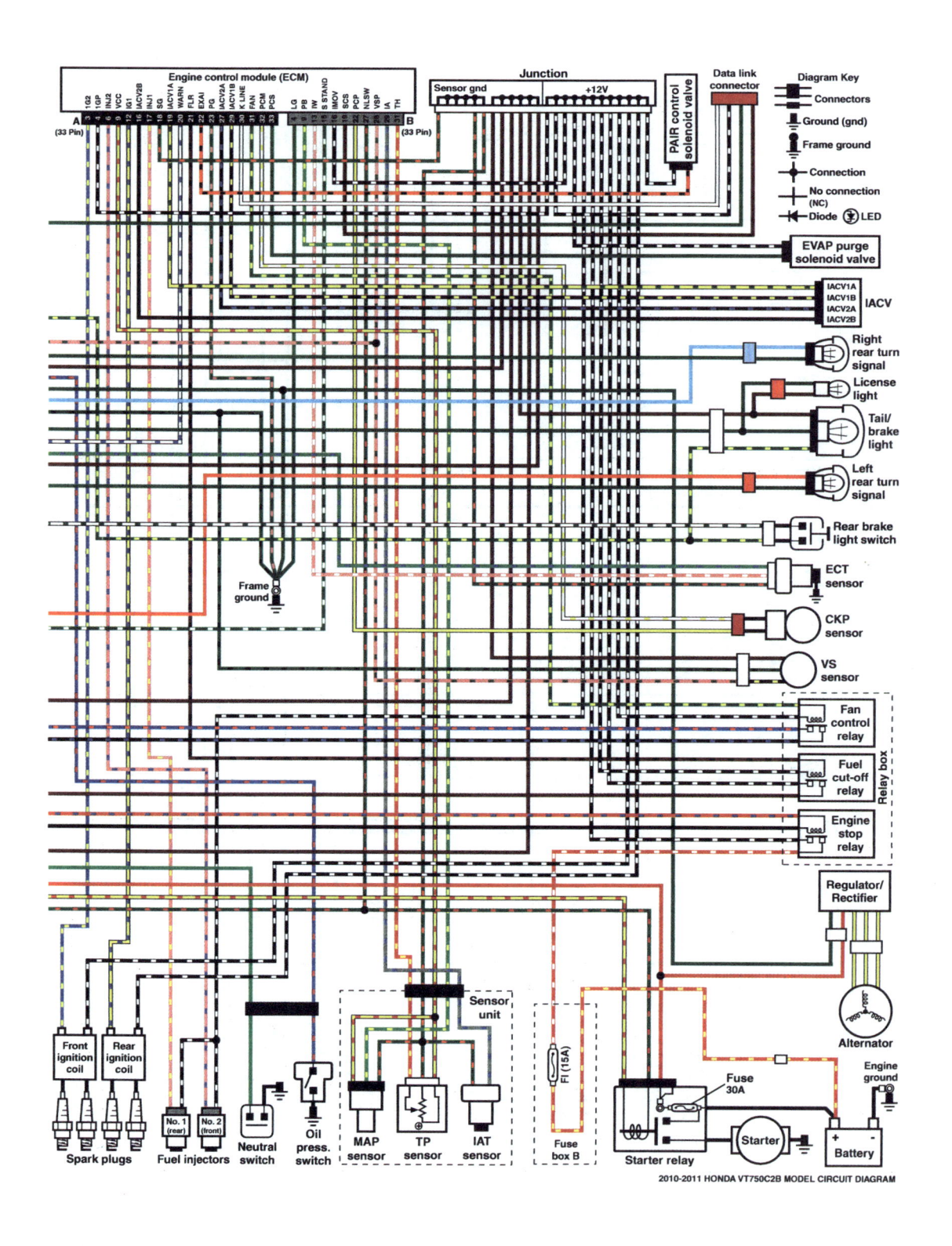

NOTES

NOTES

NOTES

NOTES

NOTES

MAINTENANCE LOG

Date	Miles	Type of Service
8-29-16	1888	LOF NAPA 101000 - 10w30 Synth.

MAINTENANCE LOG

Date	Miles	Type of Service

Check out *clymer.com* for our full line of powersport repair manuals.

BMW
M308	500 & 600cc Twins, 55-69
M502-3	BMW R50/5-R100GS PD, 70-96
M500-3	BMW K-Series, 85-97
M501-3	K1200RS, GT & LT, 98-10
M503-3	R850, R1100, R1150 & R1200C, 93-05
M309	F650, 1994-2000

HARLEY-DAVIDSON
M419	Sportsters, 59-85
M429-5	XL/XLH Sportster, 86-03
M427-4	XL Sportster, 04-13
M418	Panheads, 48-65
M420	Shovelheads, 66-84
M421-3	FLS/FXS Evolution, 84-99
M423-2	FLS/FXS Twin Cam, 00-05
M250	FLS/FXS/FXC Softail, 06-09
M422-3	FLH/FLT/FXR Evolution, 84-98
M430-4	FLH/FLT Twin Cam, 99-05
M252	FLH/FLT, 06-09
M426	VRSC Series, 02-07
M424-2	FXD Evolution, 91-98
M425-3	FXD Twin Cam, 99-05
M254	Dyna Series, 06-11

HONDA
ATVs
M316	Odyssey FL250, 77-84
M311	ATC, TRX & Fourtrax 70-125, 70-87
M433	Fourtrax 90, 93-00
M326	ATC185 & 200, 80-86
M347	ATC200X & Fourtrax 200SX, 86-88
M455	ATC250 & Fourtrax 200/250, 84-87
M342	ATC250R, 81-84
M348	TRX250R/Fourtrax 250R & ATC250R, 85-89
M456-4	TRX250X 87-92; TRX300EX 93-06
M446-3	TRX250 Recon & Recon ES, 97-07
M215-2	TTRX250EX Sportrax and TRX250X, 01-12
M346-3	TRX300/Fourtrax 300 & TRX300FW/Fourtrax 4x4, 88-00
M200-2	TRX350 Rancher, 00-06
M459-3	TRX400 Foreman 95-03
M454-5	TRX400EX Fourtrax & Sportrax 99-13
M201	TRX450R & TRX450ER, 04-09
M205	TRX450 Foreman, 98-04
M210	TRX500 Rubicon, 01-04
M206	TRX500 Foreman, 05-11

Singles
M310-13	50-110cc OHC Singles, 65-99
M315	100-350cc OHC, 69-82
M317	125-250cc Elsinore, 73-80
M442	CR60-125R Pro-Link, 81-88
M431-2	CR80R, 89-95, CR125R, 89-91
M435	CR80R & CR80RB, 96-02
M457-2	CR125R, 92-97; CR250R, 92-96
M464	CR125R, 1998-2002
M443	CR250R-500R Pro-Link, 81-87
M432-3	CR250R, 88-91 & CR500R, 88-01
M437	CR250R, 97-01
M352	CRF250R, CRF250X, CRF450R & CRF450X, 02-05
M319-3	XR50R, CRF50F, XR70R & CRF70F, 97-09
M312-14	XL/XR75-100, 75-91
M222	XR80R, CRF80F, XR100R, & CRF100F, 92-09
M318-4	XL/XR/TLR 125-200, 79-03
M328-4	XL/XR250, 78-00; XL/XR350R 83-85; XR200R, 84-85; XR250L, 91-96
M320-2	XR400R, 96-04
M221	XR600R, 91-07; XR650L, 93-07
M339-8	XL/XR 500-600, 79-90
M225	XR650R, 00-07

Twins
M321	125-200cc Twins, 65-78
M322	250-350cc Twins, 64-74
M323	250-360cc Twins, 74-77
M324-5	Twinstar, Rebel 250 & Nighthawk 250, 78-03
M334	400-450cc Twins, 78-87
M333	450 & 500cc Twins, 65-76
M335	CX & GL500/650, 78-83
M344	VT500, 83-88
M313	VT700 & 750, 83-87
M314-3	VT750 Shadow Chain Drive, 98-06
M440	VT1100C Shadow, 85-96
M460-4	VT1100 Series, 95-07
M230	VTX1800 Series, 02-08
M231	VTX1300 Series, 03-09

Fours
M332	CB350-550, SOHC, 71-78
M345	CB550 & 650, 83-85
M336	CB650, 79-82
M341	CB750 SOHC, 69-78
M337	CB750 DOHC, 79-82
M436	CB750 Nighthawk, 91-93 & 95-99
M325	CB900, 1000 & 1100, 80-83
M439	600 Hurricane, 87-90
M441-2	CBR600F2 & F3, 91-98
M445-2	CBR600F4, 99-06
M220	CBR600RR, 03-06
M434-2	CBR900RR Fireblade, 93-99
M329	500cc V-Fours, 84-86
M349	700-1000cc Interceptor, 83-85
M458-2	VFR700F-750F, 86-97
M438	VFR800FI Interceptor, 98-00
M327	700-1100cc V-Fours, 82-88
M508	ST1100/Pan European, 90-02
M340	GL1000 & 1100, 75-83
M504	GL1200, 84-87

Sixes
M505	GL1500 Gold Wing, 88-92
M506-2	GL1500 Gold Wing, 93-00
M507-3	GL1800 Gold Wing, 01-10
M462-2	GL1500C Valkyrie, 97-03

KAWASAKI
ATVs
M465-3	Bayou KLF220 & KLF250, 88-10
M466-4	Bayou KLF300, 86-04
M467	Bayou KLF400, 93-99
M470	Lakota KEF300, 95-99
M385-2	Mojave KSF250, 87-04

Singles
M350-9	80-350cc Rotary Valve, 66-01
M444-2	KX60, 83-02; KX80 83-90
M448-2	KX80, 91-00; KX85, 01-10 & KX100, 89-09
M351	KDX200, 83-88
M447-3	KX125 & KX250, 82-91; KX500, 83-04
M472-2	KX125, 92-00
M473-2	KX250, 92-00
M474-3	KLR650, 87-07
M240-2	KLR650, 08-12

Twins
M355	KZ400, KZ/Z440, EN450 & EN500, 74-95
M241	Ninja 250R (EX250), 88-12
M360-3	EX500, GPZ500S, & Ninja 500R, 87-02
M356-5	Vulcan 700 & 750, 85-06
M354-3	Vulcan 800, 95-05
M246	Vulcan 900, 06-12
M357-2	Vulcan 1500, 87-99
M471-3	Vulcan 1500 Series, 96-08
M245	Vulcan 1600 Series, 03-08

Fours
M449	KZ500/550 & ZX550, 79-85
M450	KZ, Z & ZX750, 80-85
M358	KZ650, 77-83
M359-3	Z & KZ 900-1000cc, 73-81
M451-3	KZ, ZX & ZN 1000 & 1100cc, 81-02
M452-3	ZX500 & Ninja ZX600, 85-97
M468-2	Ninja ZX-6, 90-04
M469	Ninja ZX-7, ZX7R & ZX7RR, 91-98
M453-3	Ninja ZX900, ZX1000 & ZX1100, 84-01
M409-2	Concours, 86-06

POLARIS
ATVs
M496	3-, 4- and 6-Wheel Models w/250-425cc Engines, 85-95
M362-2	Magnum & Big Boss, 96-99
M363	Scrambler 500 4X4, 97-00
M365-5	Sportsman/Xplorer, 96-13
M366	Sportsman 600/700/800 Twins, 02-10
M367	Predator 500, 03-07

SUZUKI
ATVs
M381	ALT/LT 125 & 185, 83-87
M475	LT230 & LT250, 85-90
M380-2	LT250R Quad Racer, 85-92
M483-2	LT-4WD, LT-F4WDX & LT-F250, 87-98
M270-2	LT-Z400, 03-08
M343-2	LT-F500F Quadrunner, 98-02

Singles
M369	125-400cc, 64-81
M371	RM50-400 Twin Shock, 75-81
M379	RM125-500 Single Shock, 81-88
M386	RM80-250, 89-95
M400	RM125, 96-00
M401	RM250, 96-02
M476	DR250-350, 90-94
M477-4	DR-Z400E, S & SM, 00-12
M272	DR650, 96-11
M384-5	LS650 Savage/S40, 86-12

Twins
M372	GS400-450 Chain Drive, 77-87
M484-3	GS500E Twins, 89-02
M361	SV650, 1999-2002
M481-6	VS700-800 Intruder/S50, 85-09
M261-2	1500 Intruder/C90, 98-09
M260-3	Volusia/Boulevard C50, 01-11
M482-3	VS1400 Intruder/S83, 87-07

Triple
M368	GT380, 550 & 750, 72-77

Fours
M373	GS550, 77-86
M364	GS650, 81-83
M370	GS750, 77-82
M376	GS850-1100 Shaft Drive, 79-84
M378	GS1100 Chain Drive, 80-81
M383-3	Katana 600, 88-96 GSX-R750-1100, 86-87
M331	GSX-R600, 97-00
M264	GSX-R600, 01-05
M478-2	GSX-R750, 88-92; GSX750F Katana, 89-96
M485	GSX-R750, 96-99
M377	GSX-R1000, 01-04
M266	GSX-R1000, 05-06
M265	GSX1300R Hayabusa, 99-07
M338	Bandit 600, 95-00
M353	GSF1200 Bandit, 96-03

YAMAHA
ATVs
M499-2	YFM80 Moto-4, Badger & Raptor, 85-08
M394	YTM200, 225 & YFM200, 83-86
M488-5	Blaster, 88-05
M489-2	Timberwolf, 89-00
M487-5	Warrior, 87-04
M486-6	Banshee, 87-06
M490-3	Moto-4 & Big Bear, 87-04
M493	Kodiak, 93-98
M287-2	YFZ450, 04-13
M285-2	Grizzly 660, 02-08
M280-2	Raptor 660R, 01-05
M290	Raptor 700R, 06-09
M291	Rhino 700, 2008-2012

Singles
M492-2	PW50 & 80 Y-Zinger & BW80 Big Wheel 80, 81-02
M410	80-175 Piston Port, 68-76
M415	250-400 Piston Port, 68-76
M412	DT & MX Series, 77-83
M414	IT125-490, 76-86
M393	YZ50-80 Monoshock, 78-90
M413	YZ100-490 Monoshock, 76-84
M390	YZ125-250, 85-87 YZ490, 85-90
M391	YZ125-250, 88-93 & WR250Z, 91-93
M497-2	YZ125, 94-01
M498	YZ250, 94-98; WR250Z, 94-97
M406	YZ250F & WR250F, 01-03
M491-2	YZ400F, 98-99 & 426F, 00-02; WR400F, 98-00 & 426F, 00-01
M417	XT125-250, 80-84
M480-3	XT350, 85-00; TT350, 86-87
M405	XT/TT 500, 76-81
M416	XT/TT 600, 83-89

Twins
M403	650cc Twins, 70-82
M395-10	XV535-1100 Virago, 81-03
M495-7	V-Star 650, 98-11
M284	V-Star 950, 09-12
M281-4	V-Star 1100, 99-09
M283	V-Star 1300, 07-10
M282-2	Road Star, 99-07

Triple
M404	XS750 & XS850, 77-81

Fours
M387	XJ550, XJ600 & FJ600, 81-92
M494	XJ600 Seca II/Diversion, 92-98
M388	YX600 Radian & FZ600, 86-90
M396	FZR600, 89-93
M392	FZ700-750 & Fazer, 85-87
M411	XS1100, 78-81
M461	YZF-R6, 99-04
M398	YZF-R1, 98-03
M399	FZ1, 01-05
M397	FJ1100 & 1200, 84-93
M375-2	V-Max, 85-07
M374-2	Royal Star, 96-10

VINTAGE MOTORCYCLES
Clymer® Collection Series
M330	Vintage British Street Bikes, BSA 500–650cc Unit Twins; Norton 750 & 850cc Commandos; Triumph 500-750cc Twins
M300	Vintage Dirt Bikes, V. 1 Bultaco, 125-370cc Singles; Montesa, 123-360cc Singles; Ossa, 125-250cc Singles
M305	Vintage Japanese Street Bikes Honda, 250 & 305cc Twins; Kawasaki, 250-750cc Triples; Kawasaki, 900 & 1000cc Fours